D0906582

SOMETHING ABOUT THE AUTHOR®

Something about
the Author *was named
an "Outstanding
Reference Source,"*
*the highest honor given
by the American
Library Association
Reference and Adult
Services Division.*

ISSN 0276-816X

SOMETHING ABOUT THE AUTHOR®

**Facts and Pictures about Authors
and Illustrators of Books for Young People**

volume 179

THOMSON

GALE

Detroit • New York • San Francisco • New Haven, Conn. • Waterville, Maine • London

Something about the Author, Volume 179

Project Editor
Lisa Kumar

Editorial
Dana Ferguson, Amy Elisabeth Fuller, Michelle Kazensky, Kathy Meek, Jennifer Mossman, Joseph Palmisano, Mary Ruby, Robert James Russell, Amanda D. Sams, Marie Toft

Permissions
Beth Beaufore, Barb McNeil, Tracie Richardson

Imaging and Multimedia
Leitha Etheridge-Sims, Lezlie Light

Composition and Electronic Capture
Tracey L. Matthews

Manufacturing
Drew Kalasky

Product Manager
Peg Knight

LIBRARY OF CONGRESS CATALOG CARD NUMBER 62-52046

ISBN-13: 978-0-7876-8803-5
ISBN-10: 0-7876-8803-7
ISSN 0276-816X

This title is also available as an e-book.
ISBN-13: 978-1-4144-2943-4, ISBN-10: 1-4144-2943-6
Contact your Gale Group sales representative for ordering information.

Printed in the United States of America
10 9 8 7 6 5 4 3 2 1

Contents

Authors in Forthcoming Volumes vii

Introduction ix

SATA Product Advisory Board xi

Illustrations Index 203

Author Index 233

A

Anderson, Peggy Perry 1953- 1

Apostolou, Christine Hale
  See Hale, Christy 85

Argueta, Jorge 3

B

Baker, Keith 1953- 5

Barbera, Joe 1911-2006
  Obituary Notice 8

Barbera, Joseph Roland
  See Barbera, Joe 8

Bodanis, David 9

Bradley, Kimberly Brubaker 1967- 12

Brown, Calef 17

Buck, Nola
  See Godwin, Laura 76

Burke, Jim 1973- 19

C

Cann, Helen 1969- 21

Catanese, P.W. 1961- 24

Christie, Ann Philippa
  See Pearce, Philippa 169

Church, Caroline Jayne 25

Cooney, Caroline B. 1947- 27

Corbman, Marjorie 1987- 33

Cruise, Robin 1951- 34

Cyrus, Kurt 1954- 35

D

Davenier, Christine 1961- 38

De la Cruz, Melissa 1971- 41

Delessert, Étienne 1941- 43

E

Ellis, Sarah 1952- 51

Elvgren, Jennifer Riesmeyer 57

F

Falconer, Ian 1959- 58

Firth, Barbara 60

Friedman, Laurie 1964- 63

Frost, Elizabeth
  See Frost-Knappman, Elizabeth 64

Frost-Knappman, Elizabeth 1943- 64

G

Gay, Marie-Louise 1952- 67

Godwin, Laura 1956- 76

Gootman, Marilyn E. 1944- 78

H

Hafner, Marylin 1925- 80

Hale, Christy 1955- 85

Harper, Charise
  See Harper, Charise Mericle 90

Harper, Charise Mericle 90

Harvey, Roland 1945- 92

Hemphill, Helen 1955- 95

Himelblau, Linda (?)-2005 96

Hindley, Judy 1940- 97

Holt, Kimberly Willis 1960- 101

Hort, Lenny 105

J

Jaffe, Michele 1970- 108

Jaffe, Michele Sharon
    See Jaffe, Michele 108

Juan, Ana 1961- 110

K

Kantner, Seth 1965- 112

Katz, Bobbi 1933- 114

Kelley, True 1946- 117

Kelley, True Adelaide
    See Kelley, True 117

Kuijer, Guus 1942- 124

L

Lachtman, Ofelia Dumas 1919- 126

Lerner, Aaron 1920-2007
    Obituary Notice 129

Lerner, Aaron Bunsen
    See Lerner, Aaron 129

Lloyd-Jones, Sally 1960- 129

Long, Sylvia 1948- 133

M

Malkin, Nina 1959(?)- 137

Manuel, Lynn 1948- 138

Marino, Peter 1960- 140

Masson, Sophie 1959- . . . .

McCall Smith, Alexander 1948- 141

McCall Smith, Alexander Alasdair
    See McCall Smith, Alexander 147

McDonnell, Patrick 1956- 152

Monthei, Betty 155

Montijo, Rhode 155

Morris, Jennifer E. 1969- 156

Mortensen, Denise Dowling 157

Mozelle, Shirley 158

O

Orozco, José-Luis 1948- 159

P

Parr, Todd 1962- 161

Payne, C.F. 1956- 166

Payne, Chris Fox
    See Payne, C.F. 166

Pearce, Philippa 1920-2006
    Obituary Notice 169

R

Ray, Delia 1963- 171

Reynolds, Peter H. 1961- 173

Reynolds, Susan 177

Russon, Penni 1974- 178

S

Sanders, Betty Jane
    See Monthei, Betty 155

Shore, Diane Z. 180

Shore, Diane ZuHone
    See Shore, Diane Z. 180

Slater, Dashka 1963- 181

Smith, Lane 1959- 181

Stemple, Jason 188

Stephenson, Lynda 1941- 188

Stohner, Anu 1952- 190

Sullivan, Sarah G. 1953- 191

Symes, Ruth Louise 1962- 193

T

Trueit, Trudi
    See Trueit, Trudi Strain 195

Trueit, Trudi Strain 1963- 195

V

Van Stockum, Hilda 1908-2006
    Obituary Notice 196

Vizzini, Ned 1981- 196

W

Winter, Jonah 1962- 198

Y

Yourgrau, Barry 201

Authors in Forthcoming Volumes

Below are some of the authors and illustrators that will be featured in upcoming volumes of *SATA*. These include new entries on the swiftly rising stars of the field, as well as completely revised and updated entries (indicated with *) on some of the most notable and best-loved creators of books for children.

*Cynthia D. Chin-Lee ▌ Chin-Lee is an award-winning author of children's picture books that focus on diverse locales, from Mongolia to the Chinese laundry owned by the author's grandparents. Her 2005 title *Amelia to Zora: Twenty-six Women Who Changed the World* profiles female athletes, politicians, and artists, among others, and reflects Chin-Lee's cross-cultural interests. In 2006, the author released a companion volume, *Akira to Zoltán: Twenty-six Men Who Changed the World*.

J.M. DeMatteis ▌ A Brooklyn-born comic book writer and musician, DeMatteis's *Brooklyn Dreams* was named one of 2003's ten best graphic novels by the American Library Association. Although he began his career as a music critic, DeMatteis soon shifted his focus to writing comic books and he has since contributed to numerous successful comic series, including *Spider-Man, Batman,* and *Justice League International*, as well as creating works such as *Moonshadow* and *Abadazad* in the graphic novel genre. Although his work has great appeal for adult and teen readers, DeMatteis turned his attention to younger readers in 2005 with the publication of the children's comic *Stardust Kid*.

D. Dina Friedman ▌ Friedman knew she wanted to be a writer from a young age. The children's author grew up in New York City, the setting for her 2006 young adult novel *Playing Dad's Song*. Friedman explores themes of identity in her books for middle-grade readers, with a special focus on protagonists who struggle to define themselves and their Jewish faith. The award-winning *Playing Dad's Song* takes place after September 11, 2001, and features a young man coming to terms with his father's death in the terrorist attacks, with help from a Holocaust survivor.

*M. Sarah Klise ▌ Klise, an illustrator and designer of children's books, works in collaboration with her sister Kate Klise to create picture books and a series of middle-grade novels that includes *Regarding the Fountain: A Tale*, and *Regarding the Bathrooms: A Privy to the Past*. The sisters rely on the telephone, the postal service, and email to produce their books, with Kate developing the story and Sarah contributing the pictures. Their novels *Letters from Camp*, published in 1999, and 2001's *Trial by Journal* are narrated in a collage of letters, notes, and graphic art by protagonists who must, like the Klise sisters, rely on long-distance communication to stay in touch.

Lenore Look ▌ Look draws upon her experiences growing up as a Chinese American to incorporate ideas of individuality and tradition into her books for young readers. Her first picture book, 1999's *Love as Strong as Ginger*, draws on the memories of Look's grandmother, who worked in a Seattle factory and communicated the value of hard work to her granddaughter. Look's "Ruby Lu" chapter books, including *Ruby Lu, Brave and True* and *Ruby Lu, Empress of Everything*, narrate the adventures of feisty eight-year-old Ruby and her Chinese-American family.

William Nicholson ▌ A multi-award winning screenwriter and playwright, British-born Nicholson has also made a name for himself as a children's book author. In addition to writing or co-writing screenplays for the films *Shadowlands* (based on his play of the same name), *Nell*, and *Gladiator*, Nicholson is the author of the "Wind on Fire" fantasy series for young adults. Featuring twins who must save their people from slavery in a dystopian society, *The Wind Singer*, the first book in the trilogy, received the United Kingdom's Smarties Prize Gold Award in 2000.

*W. Nikola-Lisa ▌ Nikola-Lisa has been widely praised for his use of multiculturalism as a theme throughout his children's picture books. A professor of education as well as an author, Nikola-Lisa's titles include 2002's *Summer Sun Risin'*, *Setting the Turkeys Free*, illustrated by Ken Wilson-Max, and the award-winning *Bein' with You This Way*, which features drawings by Michael Bryant. In the latter work, Nikola-Lisa strives to teach children about the shared aspects of the human experience, despite physical differences.

*Patricia Polacco ▌ The author and illustrator of more than thirty children's picture books, Polacco did not begin her career in publishing until she was forty-one. She incorporates childhood memories and elements from her diverse background into her books, including the award-winning *The Keeping Quilt* and 1994's *My Rotten Redheaded Older Brother*. Polacco, who is of Irish, Russian, and Ukrainian descent, spent part of her childhood on her grandmother's farm in rural Michigan, and draws on her recollections of country life and ethnic traditions in her critically-praised work.

Jan Reynolds ▌ A photojournalist, mountaineer, and a former member of the U.S. World Cup biathlon team Reynolds is also the author and photographer of a number of photo essays for young readers. Through her "Vanishing Cultures" series, Reynolds uses a storybook format to teach children about endangered cultures, including those in the Himalayas, Mongolia, and the Amazon basin. First published in the early 1990s, the series was re-issued in the twenty-first century due to its multi-cultural focus.

Ahmet Zappa ▌ A musician, actor, and children's book writer and illustrator, Zappa is the son of legendary rocker Frank Zappa. His childhood pastime of watching monster movies with his father inspired his 2006 self-illustrated picture book *The Monstrous Memoirs of a Mighty McFearless*, which depicts the adventures of a pair of monster-fighting siblings who must use their specialized knowledge and wits after their father, a "monsterminator," is captured.

Introduction

Something about the Author (*SATA*) is an ongoing reference series that examines the lives and works of authors and illustrators of books for children. *SATA* includes not only well-known writers and artists but also less prominent individuals whose works are just coming to be recognized. This series is often the only readily available information source on emerging authors and illustrators. You'll find *SATA* informative and entertaining, whether you are a student, a librarian, an English teacher, a parent, or simply an adult who enjoys children's literature.

What's Inside *SATA*

SATA provides detailed information about authors and illustrators who span the full time range of children's literature, from early figures like John Newbery and L. Frank Baum to contemporary figures like Judy Blume and Richard Peck. Authors in the series represent primarily English-speaking countries, particularly the United States, Canada, and the United Kingdom. Also included, however, are authors from around the world whose works are available in English translation. The writings represented in *SATA* include those created intentionally for children and young adults as well as those written for a general audience and known to interest younger readers. These writings cover the entire spectrum of children's literature, including picture books, humor, folk and fairy tales, animal stories, mystery and adventure, science fiction and fantasy, historical fiction, poetry and nonsense verse, drama, biography, and nonfiction. Obituaries are also included in *SATA* and are intended not only as death notices but also as concise overviews of people's lives and work. Additionally, each edition features newly revised and updated entries for a selection of *SATA* listees who remain of interest to today's readers and who have been active enough to require extensive revisions of their earlier biographies.

Autobiography Feature

Beginning with Volume 103, many volumes of *SATA* feature one or more specially commissioned autobiographical essays. These unique essays, averaging about ten thousand words in length and illustrated with an abundance of personal photos, present an entertaining and informative first-person perspective on the lives and careers of prominent authors and illustrators profiled in *SATA*.

Two Convenient Indexes

In response to suggestions from librarians, *SATA* indexes no longer appear in every volume but are included in alternate (odd-numbered) volumes of the series, beginning with Volume 57.

SATA continues to include two indexes that cumulate with each alternate volume: the Illustrations Index, arranged by the name of the illustrator, gives the number of the volume and page where the illustrator's work appears in the current volume as well as all preceding volumes in the series; the Author Index gives the number of the volume in which a person's biographical sketch, autobiographical essay, or obituary appears in the current volume as well as all preceding volumes in the series.

These indexes also include references to authors and illustrators who appear in *Gale's Yesterday's Authors of Books for Children, Children's Literature Review,* and *Something about the Author Autobiography Series.*

Easy-to-Use Entry Format

Whether you're already familiar with the *SATA* series or just getting acquainted, you will want to be aware of the kind of information that an entry provides. In every *SATA* entry the editors attempt to give as complete a picture of the person's life and work as possible. A typical entry in *SATA* includes the following clearly labeled information sections:

PERSONAL: date and place of birth and death, parents' names and occupations, name of spouse, date of marriage, names of children, educational institutions attended, degrees received, religious and political affiliations, hobbies and other interests.

ADDRESSES: complete home, office, electronic mail, and agent addresses, whenever available.

CAREER: name of employer, position, and dates for each career post; art exhibitions; military service; memberships and offices held in professional and civic organizations.

MEMBER: professional, civic, and other association memberships and any official posts held.

AWARDS, HONORS: literary and professional awards received.

WRITINGS: title-by-title chronological bibliography of books written and/or illustrated, listed by genre when known; lists of other notable publications, such as plays, screenplays, and periodical contributions.

ADAPTATIONS: a list of films, television programs, plays, CD-ROMs, recordings, and other media presentations that have been adapted from the author's work.

WORK IN PROGRESS: description of projects in progress.

SIDELIGHTS: a biographical portrait of the author or illustrator's development, either directly from the biographee—and often written specifically for the *SATA* entry—or gathered from diaries, letters, interviews, or other published sources.

BIOGRAPHICAL AND CRITICAL SOURCES: cites sources quoted in "Sidelights" along with references for further reading.

EXTENSIVE ILLUSTRATIONS: photographs, movie stills, book illustrations, and other interesting visual materials supplement the text.

How a *SATA* Entry Is Compiled

SATA editors examine a wide variety of published sources to gather information for an entry. Biographical and bibliographic sources are consulted, as are book reviews, feature articles, published interviews, and material sometimes obtained from the biographee's family, publishers, agent, or other associates. Whenever possible, the author or illustrator is sent a copy of the entry to check for accuracy and completeness.

Entries that have not been verified by the biographees or their representatives are marked with an asterisk (*).

Contact the Editor

We encourage our readers to examine the entire *SATA* series. Please write and tell us if we can make *SATA* even more helpful to you. Give your comments and suggestions to the editor:

Editor
Something about the Author
The Gale Group
27500 Drake Rd.
Farmington Hills MI 48331-3535

Toll-free: 800-877-GALE
Fax: 248-699-8070

Something about the Author Product Advisory Board

The editors of *Something about the Author* are dedicated to maintaining a high standard of excellence by publishing comprehensive, accurate, and highly readable entries on a wide array of writers for children and young adults. In addition to the quality of the content, the editors take pride in the graphic design of the series, which is intended to be orderly yet inviting, allowing readers to utilize the pages of *SATA* easily and with efficiency. Despite the longevity of the *SATA* print series, and the success of its format, we are mindful that the vitality of a literary reference product is dependent on its ability to serve its users over time. As literature, and attitudes about literature, constantly evolve, so do the reference needs of students, teachers, scholars, journalists, researchers, and book club members. To be certain that we continue to keep pace with the expectations of our customers, the editors of *SATA* listen carefully to their comments regarding the value, utility, and quality of the series. Librarians, who have firsthand knowledge of the needs of library users, are a valuable resource for us. The *Something about the Author* Product Advisory Board, made up of school, public, and academic librarians, is a forum to promote focused feedback about *SATA* on a regular basis. The nine-member advisory board includes the following individuals, whom the editors wish to thank for sharing their expertise:

Eva M. Davis
Youth Department Manager,
Ann Arbor District Library,
Ann Arbor, Michigan

Joan B. Eisenberg
Lower School Librarian,
Milton Academy,
Milton, Massachusetts

Francisca Goldsmith
Teen Services Librarian,
Berkeley Public Library,
Berkeley, California

Susan Dove Lempke
Children's Services Supervisor,
Niles Public Library District,
Niles, Illinois

Robyn Lupa
Head of Children's Services,
Jefferson County Public Library,
Lakewood, Colorado

Victor L. Schill
Assistant Branch Librarian/Children's Librarian,
Harris County Public Library/Fairbanks Branch,
Houston, Texas

Caryn Sipos
Community Librarian,
Three Creeks Community Library,
Vancouver, Washington

Steven Weiner
Director,
Maynard Public Library,
Maynard, Massachusetts

SOMETHING ABOUT THE AUTHOR

ANDERSON, Peggy Perry 1953-

Personal

Born December 2, 1953, in Tulsa, OK; daughter of Albert (a commercial artist) and Mary (a nurse) Perry; married Kurt Anderson (in sales), August 6, 1977; children: Brandon, Ariel, Haley. *Education:* Attended Oklahoma Christian College, 1972-74; Tulsa University, B.F.A. (commercial art), 1976. *Religion:* Church of Christ. *Hobbies and other interests:* Writing music, painting, playing the guitar, gardening, volunteering at a therapy ranch, horseback riding, mentoring elementary-school students.

Addresses

Home and office—Owasso, OK. *E-mail*—authorillustrator@cox.net.

Career

Mobley Art and Design, graphic artist, 1976-91; elementary-school art teacher, 1998-2004; writer and illustrator; motivational speaker at elementary schools.

Member

Society of Children's Book Writers and Illustrators.

Awards, Honors

Governor's State of Excellence Award, 1989; Oklahoma Book Award finalist, 2005, for *We Go in a Circle,* 2007, for *Chuck's Truck.*

Peggy Perry Anderson (Photograph courtesy of Peggy Perry Anderson.)

Writings

SELF-ILLUSTRATED

Time for Bed, the Babysitter Said, Houghton Mifflin (Boston, MA), 1987.

Wendle, What Have You Done?, Houghton Mifflin (Boston, MA), 1994.

To the Tub, Houghton Mifflin (Boston, MA), 1996.

Out to Lunch, Houghton Mifflin (Boston, MA), 1998.

Let's Clean Up!, Houghton Mifflin (Boston, MA), 2002.

We Go in a Circle, Houghton Mifflin (Boston, MA), 2002.

Chuck's Truck, Houghton Mifflin (Boston, MA), 2006.

Joe on the Go, Houghton Mifflin (Boston, MA), 2007.

Chuck's Band, Houghton Mifflin (Boston, MA), 2008.

ILLUSTRATOR

Virginia Poulet, *Blue Bug Goes to the Library,* Children's Press, 1979.

Virginia Poulet, *Blue Bug's Book of Colors,* Children's Press, 1981.

Virginia Poulet, *Blue Bug Goes to School,* Children's Press, 1985.

The Ugly Little Duck, Children's Press, 1986.

Virginia Poulet, *Blue Bug Goes to Paris,* Children's Press, 1986.

Virginia Poulet, *Blue Bug's Christmas,* Children's Press, 1987.

Virginia Poulet, *Blue Bug Goes to Mexico,* Children's Press, 1990.

Bessie Holland Heck, *Danger on the Homestead,* Dinosaur Press (Tulsa, OK), 1991.

Bessie Holland Heck, *Taming the Homestead,* Dinosaur Press (Tulsa, OK), 1994.

Sidelights

An elementary-school art teacher in her native Oklahoma, Peggy Perry Anderson is also the author and illustrator of several picture books, including titles that feature an unsinkable frog named Joe. Introduced to readers while avoiding bath time in *To the Tub,* Joe the frog is also out of his depth while dining with his parents at a fancy restaurant in *Out to Lunch.* Joe tackles a messy room in *Let's Clean Up!,* while in *Joe on the Go* the young frog feels pushed into the background during a family party until a loving wheelchair-bound grandmother turns her attention his way. In *Booklist,* Hazel Rochman cited Anderson's "bright, boisterous" ink-and-watercolor art, noting that *Joe on the Go* is "true to the small child's viewpoint of a world of powerful grown-ups." In her *School Library Journal* review of *Let's Clean Up!,* Sharon R. Pearce described Joe the frog as "joyful and innocently mischievous," while fellow *School Library Journal* contributor Maura Bresnahan wrote that *Joe on the Go* is enlivened by Anderson's engaging rhyming text. According to a *Kirkus Reviews* writer, the author/illustrator's "expressive" line drawings and use of vivid colors in *Joe on the Go* aid the comprehension of beginning readers by providing "visual narratives" to supplement the entertaining story.

In Anderson's self-illustrated picture book *We Go in a Circle* she introduces a dedicated race horse who loses his purpose after he receives a crippling leg injury. Although his leg eventually heals, the horse knows there

Anderson makes light work of a predicament all children encounter in her self-illustrated picture book Let's Clean Up! (Houghton Mifflin, 2002. Illustration © 2002 by Peggy Perry Anderson. Reproduced by permission.)

is no spot for him back at the track. After he is moved to a place where the strange saddles confuse him, the horse learns that he will now work at a therapy ranch, where he can help handicapped youngsters struggling with physical disabilities. Anderson's "simple text and watercolor illustrations convey the pride of all involved," noted Doris Losey in *School Library Journal,* citing the unusual topic in *We Go in a Circle.*

Praised as "a near-perfect marriage of text and illustration" by a *Kirkus Reviews* writer, Anderson's picture book *Chuck's Truck* finds a farmer joined on a trip to town by the farm's resident duck. Then a chicken jumps aboard the truck, followed by a pair of dogs, a horse, and ultimately all the animals living on the man's farm. It surprises no one when the old blue truck breaks down, and Chuck is overjoyed when his old vehicle is replaced by a shiny new one! Using what Susan E. Murray described in *School Library Journal* as "vibrant and energetic" hues in portraying the story's animal characters, Anderson pairs her crayon-resist artwork with a humorous rhyming story that the *Kirkus Reviews* critic suggested would appeal to beginning readers. "Both the pithy rhyming text and the bold, expressive animals are sure to tickle preschoolers' funny bones," predicted Joanna Rudge Long in a review of *Chuck's Truck* for *Horn Book.*

An illustrator for several books by other authors, Anderson once told *SATA* that she has been drawing ever since she "could hold a crayon. It just seemed natural that one day I would be an artist," she explained. "I loved to read and that led me to an interest in illustration. I enjoy creating characters and making them come alive with action. I try to entertain when I make up stories and, of course, my greatest reward is watching children laugh and enjoy the books I've done.

"If I could share something I've learned from becoming a writer and illustrator it would be DON'T GIVE UP! Lots of rejection slips and lots of changes in the stories made me learn patience. Last, but not least, PRACTICE, PRACTICE, PRACTICE! It really is worth the effort when a goal is reached or a dream comes true!"

Biographical and Critical Sources

PERIODICALS

Booklist, June 1, 1998, Annie Ayers, review of *Out to Lunch,* p. 1775; March 1, 2002, Gillian Engberg, review of *Let's Clean Up!,* p. 1138; March 15, 2007, Hazel Rochman, review of *Joe on the Go,* p. 50.

Horn Book, May-June, 2006, Joanna Rudge Long, review of *Chuck's Truck,* p. 288.

Kirkus Reviews, February 1, 2002, review of *Let's Clean Up!,* p. 176; April 1, 2006, review of *Chuck's Truck,* p. 341; March 1, 2007, review of *Joe on the Go,* p. 215.

Publishers Weekly, July 29, 1996, review of *To the Tub,* p. 87; March 30, 1998, review of *Out to Lunch,* p. 81.

School Library Journal, April, 1994, Mary Ann Bursk, review of *Wendle, What Have You Done?* p. 95; April, 1998, Lisa Smith, review of *Out to Lunch,* p. 91; April, 2002, Sharon R. Pearce, review of *Let's Clean Up!,* p. 100; October, 2004, Doris Losey, review of *We Go in a Circle,* p. 108; May, 2006, Susan E. Murray, review of *Chuck's Truck,* p. 84; March, 2007, Maura Bresnahan, review of *Joe on the Go,* p. 150.

*   *   *

APOSTOLOU, Christine Hale
See HALE, Christy

*   *   *

ARGUETA, Jorge

Personal

Born in El Salvador; immigrated to United States, 1980; partner of Teresa Kennett (a poet); children: Luna.

Addresses

Home—San Francisco, CA. *E-mail*—tetl2002@yahoo.com.

Jorge Argueta (Photograph courtesy of Teresa Kennett.)

Career

Poet, lecturer, and activist. Worked variously as a gardener and in a coffeehouse.

Awards, Honors

Américas Award, 2001, and *Skipping Stones* Honor Award and Independent Publishers Book Award, all for *A Movie in My Pillow/Una película en mi almohada;* named San Francisco Library laureate, 2002; Américas Award commended designation, 2003, for *Xochitl and the Flowers/Xóchitl, la niña de las flores;* NAPA Gold Medal, 2006, for *Moony Luna/Luna, Lunita Lunera;* Americas Award commended designation, 2007, and *Lion and the Unicorn* honor, both for *Talking with Mother Earth: Poems/Hablando con Madre Tierra* and *The Fiesta of the Tortillas/La fiesta de las tortillas;* three-time winner of San Francisco Biannual Poetry Award.

Writings

FOR CHILDREN

A Movie in My Pillow/Una película en mi almohada (bilingual), illustrated by Elizabeth Gómez, Children's Book Press (San Francisco, CA), 2001.

El Zipitio, illustrated by Gloria Calderón, Groundwood Books (Toronto, Ontario, Canada), 2003, translated by Elisa Amado as *Zipitio,* 2003.

Los arboles estan colgando del cielo, illustrated by Rafael Yockteng, Groundwood Books (Toronto, Ontario, Canada), 2003, translated by Elisa Amado as *Trees Are Hanging from the Sky,* 2003.

Xochitl and the Flowers/Xóchitl, la niña de las flores (bilingual), illustrated by Carl Angel, Children's Book Press (San Francisco, CA), 2003.

(Translator) Rigoberto González, *Soledad Sigh-Sighs/ Soledad suspiros* (bilingual), illustrated by Rosa Ibarra, Children's Book Press (San Francisco, CA), 2003.

Moony Luna/Luna, Lunita Lunera (bilingual), illustrated by Elizabeth Gómez, Children's Book Press (San Francisco, CA), 2005.

(Translator) Rigoberto González, *Antonio's Card/La tarjeta de Antonio* (bilingual), illustrated by Cecilia Concepción Alvarez, Children's Book Press (San Francisco, CA), 2005.

The Best Match, Hampton, 2005.

The Fiesta of the Tortillas/La fiesta de las tortillas (bilingual), illustrated by María Jesus Alvarez, Alfaguara (Miami, FL), 2006.

The Little Hen in the City/La gallinita en la ciudad (bilingual), illustrated by Mima Castro, Alfaguara (Miami, FL), 2006.

Talking with Mother Earth: Poems/Hablando con Madre Tierra: poemas (bilingual), illustrated by Lucia Angela Pérez, Groundwood Books (Toronto, Ontario, Canada), 2006.

Alfredito Flies Home/Alfredito regresa volando a su casa, illustrated by Luis Garay, Groundwood Books (Toronto, Ontario, Canada), 2007.

POETRY; FOR ADULTS

Love Street (poems), translated by Margot Pepper, Tiki Bob Publishing (San Francisco, CA), 1991.

Corazon del barrio, 1994.

Also author of poetry chapbooks, including *Poemas desnudos/Naked Poems,* Luna's Press; (with Teresa Kennett) *Pintando sombras/Painting Shadows,* Luna's Press; *Las frutas del centro y otros sabores/ Fruit from the Center, and Other Flavors,* Canterbury Press; *Letania de amor y odio/Litany of Love and Hate,* Luna's Press; *De aqui alla/From Here to There,* Luna's Press; *La ciudad proxima al veraño/City Next to Summer,* Luna's Press; *El poeta enamorado/Poet in Love* (audio recording); *Del ocaso a la alborada/From Sundown to Dawn,* and *La puerta del diablo/The Devil's Gate,* Poet's Press.

Sidelights

Jorge Argueta is a native of El Salvador and a Pipil Nahua Indian who immigrated to the United States as a teenager. An award-winning poet, he is also the author of several critically acclaimed bilingual picture books,

including *A Movie in My Pillow/Una película en mi almohada* and *Xochitl and the Flowers/Xóchitl, la niña de las flores.* "There is a piece of El Salvador in everything I write," Argueta told an interviewer in *Críticas,* adding that his works "are not only my own stories but also the story of thousands of Salvadoran children who left their country during the civil war of the '80s." Although Argueta's poetry for adult readers reflects the hardships of his early life in El Salvador and as an immigrant in America, his work for young readers shares his memories of the feelings and experiences of encountering an unfamiliar culture and belonging to two countries.

A Movie in My Pillow/Una película en mi almohada, Argueta's first book for children, contains twenty-one poems written in both English and Spanish that recall his experiences growing up in both El Salvador and his adopted city of San Francisco, California. "The lines capture the pleasures and difficulties of living in each country," observed *School Library Journal* contributor Nina Lindsay, and Annie Ayres noted in *Booklist* that Agueta's volume "will add multicultural depth and historical authenticity to any poetry collection."

Based on a Latin-American folktale, *Zipitio* concerns an odd, lonely gnome with a pot belly and backward feet who falls in love with the local teenaged girls living near his home. When Rufina, a haunting beauty, first meets Zipitio along the riverbank, she is terrified and runs away. To comfort the young woman, Rufina's mother explains that the strange creature can be dismissed by tricking him. When Rufina meets Zipitio a second time, she asks him to prove his love by catching an ocean wave in a basket. According to *Resource Links* critic Ann Ketcheson, "Zipitio is more comical than frightening and we actually sympathize with him at the end when he leaves on his impossible assignment." In *School Library Journal,* Ann Welton described Argueta's tale as "well told and . . . a solid example of a female right of passage."

A youngster learns the value of community support in *Xochitl and the Flowers/Xóchitl, la niña de las flores.* After her family relocates from El Salvador to San Francisco, young Xochitl struggles to adjust to an urban environment. Meanwhile, her parents attempt to recreate the family's flower business, but are opposed by a quarrelsome apartment manager. When Xochitl's neighbors learn of the family's difficulties, they rally around the fledgling business. The author "infuses his work with Salvadoran culture, writing of life in poetic language," noted Julie Kline in *Booklist,* while a critic in *Kirkus Reviews* remarked that Argueta's "bilingual story embodies the belief that positive action can overcome the negatives of circumstance."

Inspired by the author's own daughter, Luna, *Moony Luna/Luna, Lunita Lunera* finds a five year old anxiously awaiting her first day of kindergarten. When Luna's mother reads her a story about a monster who

Argueta's picture book **Zipitio** *features folk-art styled illustrations by Gloria Calderón.* (Groundwood Books, 2003. Illustration © 2003 by Gloria Calderón. Reproduced by permission.)

attends school, the girl's imagination runs wild, and she believes that a real monster lurks somewhere in her classroom. "The Spanish text . . . has a pleasing poetic structure and a comforting rhythm that will reassure young listeners," noted *Booklist* contributor Stella T. Clark.

Talking with Mother Earth: Poems/Hablando con Madre Tierra: Poemas, a collection of verse about Argueta's connection to nature, "stands out for its beauty and depth of expression," observed *School Library Journal* reviewer Maria Otero-Boisvert. Narrowing its focus to El Salvador, Argueta's *The Fiesta of the Tortillas/La fiesta de las tortillas* concerns an eatery visited by a supernatural being. *The Little Hen in the City/La gallinita en la ciudad* details a young girl's efforts to save a guinea hen, which she believes embodies the spirit of her grandfather. In both titles, noted *El Paso Times* contributor Rigoberto González, "a young protagonist is beginning to make important connections between self, family and the cultural imagination they [all] inhabit."

Biographical and Critical Sources

PERIODICALS

Booklist, October 1, 2001, Annie Ayres, review of *A Movie in My Pillow/Una película en mi almohada,* p. 31;

December 1, 2003, Julie Kline, review of *Xochitl and the Flowers/Xóchitl, la niña de las flores,* p. 683; April 1, 2005, Stella T. Clark, review of *Moony Luna/Luna, Lunita Lunera,* p. 1364.

Childhood Education, fall, 2004, Bev Gitter, review of *Zipitio,* p. 46; winter, 2004, Paula Quintana, review of *Xochitl and the Flowers/Xóchitl, la niña de las flores,* p. 107.

Críticas, July 1, 2004, "Argueta's True Stories."

El Paso Times, May 28, 2006, Rigoberto González, "Not Your Average Children's Books: Argueta's New Stories Will Have Kids Thinking."

Instructor, November-December, 2001, Paul Janeczko, "Poetry Workshop: My Grandma's Stories," p. 36.

Kirkus Reviews, October 1, 2003, review of *Zipitio,* p. 1220; July 1, 2003, review of *Xochitl and the Flowers/ Xóchitl, la niña de las flores,* p. 906; March 15, 2005, review of *Moony Luna/Luna, Lunita Lunera,* p. 347.

Publishers Weekly, March 24, 2003, review of *Trees Are Hanging from the Sky,* p. 75.

Resource Links, October, 2003, Ann Ketcheson, review of *Trees Are Hanging from the Sky,* p. 2; February, 2004, Ann Ketcheson, review of *Zipitio,* p. 8.

School Library Journal, May, 2001, Nina Lindsay, review of *A Movie in My Pillow/Una película en mi almohada,* p. 139; November, 2003, Ann Welton, review of *Zipitio,* p. 122; December, 2003, Ann Welton, review of *Xochitl and the Flowers/Xóchitl, la niña de las flores,* p. 142; April, 2003, Gay Lynn Van Vleck, review of *Trees Are Hanging from the Sky,* p. 114; May, 2005, Ann Welton, review of *Moony Luna/Luna, Lunita Lunera,* p. 118; July, 2005, Coop Renner, review of *Xochitl and the Flowers/Xóchitl, la niña de las flores,* p. 43; October, 2006, Maria Otero-Boisvert, *Talking with Mother Earth: Poems/Hablando con Madre Tierra: Poemas,* p. 144.

ONLINE

Children's Book Press Web site, http://www. childrensbookpress.org/ (May 10, 2007), "Jorge Argueta."

Groundwood Books Web site, http://www. groundwoodbooks.com/ (May 10, 2007), "Jorge Argueta."

Jorge Argueta Home Page, http://www.jorgeargueta.com (May 10, 2007).

PaperTigers Web site, http://www.papertigers.org/ (February, 2004), Kathryn Olney, interview with Argueta.

* * *

BAKER, Keith 1953-

Personal

Born 1953, in OR. *Education:* Eastern Oregon State University, degree; attended Art College Center of Design.

Addresses

Home—Seattle, WA. *E-mail*—keith@keithbakerbooks. com.

Career

Author and illustrator. Taught elementary school for seven years.

Awards, Honors

Parents' Choice Awards for illustration, for *The Dove's Letter* and *Who Is the Beast?*; Golden Kite Award, for *Big Fat Hen*; UNICEF/Ezra Jack Keats International Bronze Award, for excellence in children's book illustration.

Writings

SELF-ILLUSTRATED

The Dove's Letter, Harcourt (San Diego, CA), 1988.
The Magic Fan, Harcourt (San Diego, CA), 1989.
Who Is the Beast?, Harcourt (San Diego, CA), 1990, board-book edition, Red Wagon Books (San Diego, CA), 2003.
Hide and Snake, Harcourt (San Diego, CA), 1991, board-book edition, Red Wagon Books (San Diego, CA), 1999.
Big Fat Hen, Harcourt (San Diego, CA), 1994.
Cat Tricks, Harcourt (San Diego, CA), 1997.
Sometimes, Harcourt (San Diego, CA), 1999.
Quack and Count, Harcourt (San Diego, CA), 1999, board-book edition, Red Wagon Books (San Diego, CA), 2003.

Little Green, Harcourt (San Diego, CA), 2001.
Meet Mr. and Mrs. Green, Harcourt (San Diego, CA), 2002, board-book edition, Red Wagon Books (San Diego, CA), 2005.
More Mr. and Mrs. Green, Harcourt (San Diego, CA), 2004.
Lucky Days with Mr. and Mrs. Green, Harcourt (Orlando, FL), 2005.
On the Go with Mr. and Mrs. Green, Harcourt (Orlando, FL), 2006.
Hickory Dickory Dock, Harcourt (Orlando, FL), 2007.

Author's work has been translated into Spanish.

ILLUSTRATOR

Kathi Appelt, *Elephants Aloft,* Harcourt (San Diego, CA), 1993.
Alex Moran, *Six Silly Foxes,* Green Light Readers/ Harcourt (San Diego, CA), 2000.

Sidelights

Keith Baker is the author and illustrator of several highly regarded children's books. A former elementary school teacher, Baker published his debut title, *The Dove's Letter,* in 1988. The work, which concerns a dove's efforts to find the rightful owner of a mysterious letter it discovers in the forest, earned Baker a Parents' Choice award for illustration. He earned another Parents' Choice honor for *Who Is the Beast?,* a tale about the wonders of nature. In this work, the animals of the

Keith Baker weaves barnyard themes into his simple concept book Big Fat Hen, *a toddler-sized volume featuring the author's detailed art.* (Red Wagon, 1997. Illustration © 1994 by Keith Baker. Reproduced by permission.)

jungle flee from a powerful tiger until the friendly creature points out the many characteristics that the creatures all share, including whiskers, paws, and tails. "Graced with a compelling beauty," wrote a *Publishers Weekly* contributor, "this gifted author/illustrator's imaginative story presents a timeless message to young readers."

In *Hide and Snake* a brightly striped reptile slithers its way through balls of yarn, a stack of presents, and a collection of hats as readers attempt to trace its movements. Baker's "acrylic designs, variety of lush hues and sly wit provide a feast for the eyes," noted a critic in *Publishers Weekly.* Based on the nursery rhyme "One, Two, Buckle My Shoe," *Big Fat Hen* is a counting book featuring a stately hen and her newly hatched chicks. "Children who want to skip the counting altogether can just enjoy the singsong text," observed Ilene Cooper in *Booklist,* while a *Publishers Weekly* reviewer praised Baker's acrylic illustrations, especially his depiction of the hen and her barnyard mates as a grouping with "the sparkle of a cluster of gems."

A feline's amazing abilities are the subject of *Cat Tricks.* The tall, narrow book employs an unusual format: alternating pages are half-width, and turning the book completely transforms the image. "The ingenious visual tricks match the cat's activities," noted Susan Dove Lempke in a review of *Cat Tricks* for *Booklist.* In *Quack and Count* a set of playful ducklings helps youngsters learn about addition. According to a critic in *Publishers Weekly,* Baker's book introduces young readers to math concepts "in such an unobtrusive, organic and merry way that they may not even notice how much they're learning." A hummingbird captures the attention of an aspiring artist in *Little Green.* Here Baker's "rhyming text captures the bird's exciting energy," according to *Booklist* critic Helen Rosenberg. The author/illustrator's cut-paper collages "glow with a lovely translucence that captures the feel of a sunlit garden and the evanescence of the hummingbird's mesmerizing movements," a *Publishers Weekly* reviewer maintained.

Baker introduces a pair of lively, fun-loving alligators in *Meet Mr. and Mrs. Green.* In the work, which has also sparked several sequels, Mrs. Green helps alleviate her husband's worries over a camping trip and encourages his efforts to eat one hundred pancakes at one sitting. "There is a nice undertone of acceptance and love between the two characters," observed *School Library Journal* reviewer Martha Topol, and a critic in *Kirkus Reviews* remarked that children will enjoy "the bright and snappy, simply drawn cartoon scenes." The entertaining duo returns in *More Mr. and Mrs. Green.* According to *School Library Journal* contributor Gloria Koster, in this volume "Baker's palette features many bright colors, but the vibrant, green alligators take center stage on every page." In *Lucky Days with Mr. and Mrs. Green* the pair locate some missing pearls, win a swimming pool full of jellybeans, and take first place at a talent show, while the three episodes in *On the Go*

A pair of thick-skinned but kind-hearted crocodiles set out on three entertaining adventures in Baker's chapter book **More Mr. and Mrs. Green.** (Harcourt, 2005. Illustration © 2004 by Keith Baker. Reproduced by permission.)

with *Mr. and Mrs. Green* focus on magic tricks, cookies, and wacky inventions. "The effervescent personalities of the all-alligator cast come through clearly," remarked a *Kirkus Reviews* contributor of *Lucky Days with Mr. and Mrs. Green,* and *Horn Book* reviewer Betty Carter called *On the Go with Mr. and Mrs. Green* "an enjoyable mix of humor and sophisticated tone that recognizes the complexity of children's thinking."

Biographical and Critical Sources

PERIODICALS

Booklist, December 15, 1993, Elizabeth Bush, review of *Elephants Aloft,* p. 762; April 1, 1994, review of *Big Fat Hen,* p. 1453; December 15, 1997, Susan Dove Lempke, review of *Cat Tricks,* p. 701; October 15, 1999, Shelley Townsend-Hudson, review of *Quack and Count,* p. 448; October 1, 1999, Kathy Broderick and Gilbert Taylor, review of *Sometimes,* p. 364; April 15, 2001, Helen Rosenburg, review of *Little Green,* p. 1563; May 1, 2006, Hazel Rochman, review of *On the Go with Mr. and Mrs. Green,* p. 88.

Bulletin of the Center for Children's Books, April, 2001, review of *Little Green,* p. 297; March, 2004, Timnah Card, review of *More Mr. and Mrs. Green,* p. 258; April, 2005, Timnah Card, review of *Lucky Days with Mr. and Mrs. Green,* p. 326.

Emergency Librarian, November, 1991, review of *Hide and Snake,* p. 49; May, 1994, review of *Big Fat Hen,* p. 44.

Horn Book, Betty Carter, review of *On the Go with Mr. and Mrs. Green,* p. 434.

Kirkus Reviews, September 1, 2002, review of *Meet Mr. and Mrs. Green,* p. 1302; January 15, 2004, review of *More Mr. and Mrs. Green,* p. 79; February 1, 2005, review of *Lucky Days with Mr. and Mrs. Green,* p. 173.

New York Times Book Review, November 10, 1991, Joanne Oppenheim, review of *Hide and Snake,* p. 32; July 17, 1994, review of *Big Fat Hen,* p. 18.

Publishers Weekly, October 12, 1990, review of *Who Is the Beast?,* p. 62; September 6, 1991, review of *Hide and Snake,* p. 103; February 8, 1993, review of *The Dove's Letter,* p. 88; February 24, 1997, review of *The Magic Fan,* p. 93; February 28, 1994, review of *Big Fat Hen,* p. 85; July 28, 1997, review of *Cat Tricks,* p. 74; August 2, 1999, review of *Quack and Count,* p. 82; March 15, 1999, review of *Sometimes,* p. 61; February 12, 2001, review of *Little Green,* p. 210; review of *Meet Mr. and Mrs. Green,* p. 71.

Reading Teacher, October, 1991, review of *Who Is the Beast?,* p. 131; November, 1994, review of *Elephants Aloft,* p. 240.

School Library Journal, May, 1999, Sharon R. Pearce, review of *Sometimes,* p. 85; April, 2001, Judith Constantinides, review of *Little Green,* p. 98; November, 2002, Martha Topol, review of *Meet Mr. and Mrs. Green,* p. 111; March, 2004, Gloria Koster, review of *More Mr. and Mrs. Green,* p. 152; June, 2006, Maura Bresnahan, review of *On the Go with Mr. and Mrs. Green,* p. 106.

ONLINE

Keith Baker Home Page, http://www.keithbakerbooks.com (May 10, 2007).*

* * *

BARBERA, Joe 1911-2006
(Joseph Roland Barbera)

OBITUARY NOTICE— See index for *SATA* sketch: Born March 24, 1911, in New York, NY; died December 18, 2006, in Los Angeles, CA. Animator, producer, director, and author. Along with longtime partner William Hanna, Barbera was an Academy Award-and Emmy Award-winning producer and director of television cartoons ranging from *The Flintstones* and *Tom and Jerry* to *The Smurfs* and *The Powerpuff Girls.* Originally contemplating a career in banking, he graduated from the American Institute of Banking and also attended the Pratt Institute. The financial world did not maintain its appeal for him, however, and after two years as a bank clerk Barbera left to explore play writing, drawing, and amateur boxing. His life would change forever when *Collier's* magazine accepted one of his cartoons. Encouraged by this, he unsuccessfully tried to obtain work at Walt Disney Studios. Instead, Van Beuren Studios hired him

in 1932. After the studio went bankrupt due to the Great Depression, Barbera worked for Terrytoons before being hired by Metro-Goldwyn-Mayer (MGM) in 1937. It was here that he met Hanna, and the two found they complemented each other's skills well: Hanna was talented in characterization and comic timing, while Barbera had the artistic talent and was a good gag writer. They initially collaborated on an animated adaptation of the *Katzenjammer Kids* comic strip before creating their own film short, *Puss Gets the Boot,* in 1940. Earning them their first Academy Award nomination,*Puss Gets the Boot* features Jasper the cat and Jinx the mouse, characters who would later be rewritten as Tom and Jerry. Hanna and Barbera would continue to produce *Tom and Jerry* cartoons into the mid-1950s, earning seven Academy awards and six more Academy Award nominations. The team was put in charge of MGM's animation department in 1955, but it proved to be a short run: Two years later, the division was closed. The two animators decided to concentrate on their already established H-B Enterprises, which they founded to produce animated commercials. Renamed Hanna-Barbera Productions, the studio was the first company to produce prime-time television cartoon series. Beginning with 1957's *The Ruff & Reddy Show,* Barbera and Hanna went on to create such favorites as *The Huckleberry Hound Show, The Flintstones, The Jetsons,* and *Scooby-Doo.* By the 1960s and 1970s, Hanna-Barbera cartoons were omnipresent on American television, and shows such as *The Flintstones* regularly made the top-rated listings and were popular among both children and adults. Keeping up with the times, they continued their success through the 1980s and 1990s with such shows as *Space Ghost, The Super-Powers Team, The Smurfs,* and *The Powerpuff Girls.* Also praised for their full-length movie adaptation of E.B. White's classic children's book, *Charlotte's Web* (1973), which won an Annie award, the team operated independently until 1990. Purchased by Turner Broadcasting, Hanna-Barbera was later incorporated into the Warner Brothers media conglomerate. In his later years, Barbera primarily worked as an executive producer, though he still sometimes wrote cartoons. One of his last contributions, a 2005 "Tom and Jerry" cartoon titled *The KarateGuard,* was his last cartoon featuring the cat and mouse and the first he had written since 1960. Frequently credited with making television cartoons a mainstay of American entertainment, Barbera inspired many animators to follow in his footsteps. Among his other awards are seven Emmys, a Golden Globe Award, the Humanitas Prize, and the Governor's Award from the National Academy of Television Arts and Sciences. Barbera recorded his story in his autobiography, *My Life in 'Toons: From Flatbush to Bedrock in under a Century* (1994).

OBITUARIES AND OTHER SOURCES:

BOOKS

Barbera, Joe, and Alan Axelrod, *My Life in 'Toons: From Flatbush to Bedrock in under a Century,* Turner (Atlanta, GA), 1994.

PERIODICALS

Chicago Tribune, December 19, 2006, section 2, p. 10.
New York Times, December 19, 2006, p. C15; December 22, 2006, p. A2.
Times (London, England), December 20, 2006, p. 58.
Washington Post, December 19, 2006, p. B7.

*   *   *

BARBERA, Joseph Roland
See BARBERA, Joe

*   *   *

BODANIS, David

Personal

Born in Chicago, IL; married (divorced); children: two. *Education:* University of Chicago, B.S. (mathematics).

Addresses

Home—London, England. *Agent*—Lavin Agency, 222 3rd St., Ste. 1130, Cambridge, MA 02142. *E-mail*—d. bodanis@virgin.net.

Career

Science writer, consultant, and teacher. International Herald Tribune, Paris, France, reporter, beginning 1977; freelance writer, beginning 1982; St. Antony's College, Oxford, Oxford, England, senior associate member, beginning 1990, and instructor in intellectual history, 1991-97; business consultant, beginning mid-1990s. Talent Foundation, London, England, strategy director. Speaker at major corporations and other organizations on global trends in science and research.

Writings

The Body Book: A Fantastic Voyage to the World Within, Little, Brown (Boston, MA), 1984.
The Secret House: Twenty-four Hours in the Strange and Unexpected World in Which We Spend Our Nights and Days, Simon & Schuster (New York, NY), 1986.
Web of Words: The Ideas behind Politics, Macmillan (Basingstoke, Hampshire, England), 1988.
The Secret Garden: Dawn to Dusk in the Astonishing Hidden World of the Garden, Simon & Schuster (New York, NY), 1992.
The Secret Family: Twenty-four Hours inside the Mysterious World of Our Minds and Bodies, Simon & Schuster (New York, NY), 1997.
(With others; and presenter) *The Secret Family* (television documentary), Discovery Channel/CBC, 1997.

E=mc2: A Biography of the World's Most Famous Equation, Berkley Books (New York, NY), 2001.
Electric Universe: The Shocking True Story of Electricity, Crown (New York, NY), 2005.
Passionate Minds: The Great Love Affair of the Enlightenment, Featuring the Scientist Emilie du Chatelet, the Poet Voltaire, Swordfights, Bookburnings, Assorted Kings, Crown (New York, NY), 2006, published as *Passionate Minds: The Great Enlightenment Love Affair,* Little, Brown (London, England), 2006.

Contributor of reviews, essays, and articles to London *Guardian,* London *Times, Reader's Digest, New Scientist, Times Literary Supplement, Smithsonian,* and London *Observer.*

Adaptations

E=mc2: A Biography of the World's Most Famous Equation was adapted as the television program *Einstein's Big Idea,* Public Broadcasting Service, 2005; it was also adapted as an audiobook.

Sidelights

An academic, mathematician, and author, David Bodanis specializes in writing books that explain the remarkable science behind everyday life. He has written about the human mind and body, the working of nature to be observed in a household garden, the science involved in Albert Einstein's famous equation E=mc2, the story behind the discovery and development of electricity, and even the love affair of an Enlightenment philosopher and his female-scientist contemporary. As a reviewer for *Publishers Weekly* noted, "those who don't generally read science will find that Bodanis is a first-rate popularizer." A writer for the *Economist* found that "his breezy, often poetic prose makes even the most complex subjects seem accessible to non-specialist readers."

Bodanis was born in Chicago, Illinois. "I grew up the last in a big family—five big sisters," he explained to Michael Alec Rose in an interview for *BookPage* online. After graduating from the University of Chicago with a degree in mathematics, he moved to Europe, and worked in Paris as a reporter for the *International Herald Tribune.* Eventually setting down roots in London, England, in 1990 Bodanis was named a senior associate member of St. Antony's College, Oxford. As an advisor to corporations and other organizations, Bodanis now helps groups predict future trends in technology by envisioning the business world of tomorrow.

Bodanis debuted as an author with *The Body Book: A Fantastic Voyage to the World Within,* which S.E. Gunstream described in *Choice* as "an imaginative description of the physiological processes involved in certain emotions, activities, and states commonly experienced." Carol Krucoff, reviewing the work in the *Washington Post Book World,* claimed that "Bodanis packs the book with remarkable physical trivia," while Carla La Croix wrote in *Library Journal* that the author "writes in a clear, lively, nontechnical style" that "includes cultural and historical references."

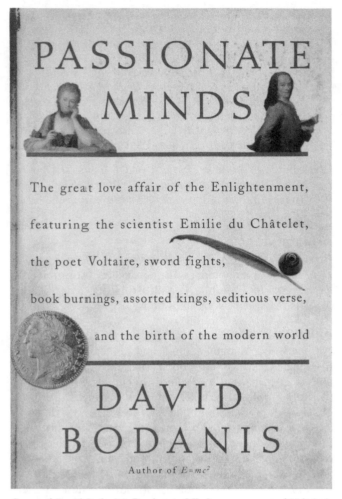

PASSIONATE MINDS

The great love affair of the Enlightenment,

featuring the scientist Emilie du Châtelet,

the poet Voltaire, sword fights,

book burnings, assorted kings, seditious verse,

and the birth of the modern world

DAVID BODANIS

Author of *E=mc²*

Cover of David Bodanis's Passionate Minds, *an account of Voltaire's romance with female scientist Emilie du Chatelet.* (Crown, 2006. Reproduced by permission of Crown Publishers, a division of Random House, Inc.)

The book responsible for launching Bodanis's career as a science writer is *The Secret House: Twenty-four Hours in the Strange and Unexpected World in Which We Spend Our Nights and Days.* Using microphotography, the book focuses on the "hidden world" within the typical home, a world that includes dust mites, water vapor, and the vibrations in the very floorboards upon which we walk. As *Appraisal* reviewer Lavinia C. Demos explained, in the book "Bodanis has highlighted a world that escapes observation," while a *People* contributor dubbed *The Secret House* "a bug-eyed look at the squiggly, squirmy life-forms that go unseen in the ordinary home."

Again employing photomicrographics, *The Secret Garden: Dawn to Dusk in the Astonishing Hidden World of the Garden* focuses on the family garden. David W. Kramer, writing in *Science Books and Films,* noted of the work that Bodanis "skillfully infuses the facts with a dynamic tension that adds excitement to the interactions among plants, soil, fungi, insects, and people," his focus ranging from flowerpots to lawns.

In *The Secret Family: Twenty-four Hours inside the Mysterious Worlds of Our Minds and Bodies* Bodanis

follows a typical family of five throughout the course of a normal day, from breakfast to late at night. He focuses on the silent interactions between family members on a hormonal level, on conversational styles and what they mean, and on the body language Westernized people unconsciously use to express themselves. Along the way, he details such things as the microscopic contents of the foods the family eats and the activities of the dust mites that live on their skin. A.M. Daniels, writing in the *Times Literary Supplement,* described the book as a "cheerful, discursive and highly amusing account of a typical middle-class American family's Saturday." In her *Booklist* review, Donna Seaman called *The Secret Family* "readable, informative, and lively," and Mark L. Shelton wrote in the *Library Journal* that "this is the sort of book that turns grade schoolers into science lovers." Reflecting Shelton's assessment, a *Kirkus Reviews* contributor deemed *The Secret Family* as "the perfect gift for a science-minded teenager."

In his book *E=mc2: A Biography of the World's Most Famous Equation,* Bodanis tells the story of the famous equation "in the manner of a conventional biography," according to *Spectator* critic Steve King, "with chapters on the equation's 'ancestors, childhood, adolescence and adulthood.'" Bodanis patiently explains each part of Einstein's famous equation, beginning with "E" for energy, then moving on to the equal sign, the "m" that stands for "mass," and so on. In this manner, he explains the contributions of earlier scientists to Einstein's formulation of the equation. Energy, for example, leads back to Michael Faraday, the eighteenth-century scientist who first realized that electricity and magnetism are the same force. A reviewer for *Astronomy* wrote that, in his book, Bodanis "brings to life a mathematical formula that enjoys a ubiquitous presence in our daily lives," and *School Library Journal* critic Barbara A. Genco described *E=mc2* as "engaging, accessible, and filled with vividly drawn characters."

In *Electric Universe: The Shocking True Story of Electricity* Bodanis traces the history of how electricity was discovered and developed into the essential force of modern technology. Beginning with the early-nineteenth-century scientists who experimented with electricity, Bodanis tells the stories of such famous figures as Thomas Edison, Alexander Graham Bell, and Guglielmo Marconi, as well as of lesser-known but also important figures like Heinrich Herz and Alan Turing. Praising the book as a "superb popular science tale," Edna Boardman wrote in *Kliatt* that the author mixes scientific fact "with intriguing biographical sketches of the major historic personalities who figured in [electricity's] . . . discovery and development." The many inventions dependent on electricity, and how these inventions have changed the world, are also detailed, as are the ways electricity is used in the human body's nervous system. A reviewer for *Science News* concluded of *Electric Universe* that "Bodanis has written a science book that will appeal to people who usually don't like reading about science," and an *Economist* contributor

Cover of Bodanis's Electric Universe, *which follows man's discovery and gradual understanding of how electricity works.* (Crown, 2005. Reproduced by permission of Crown Publishers, a division of Random House, Inc.)

maintained that the author's "breezy, often poetic prose makes even the most complex subjects seem accessible to non-specialist readers." Gilbert Taylor, in his review of the book for *Booklist,* dubbed *Electric Universe* a "hip history of electricity."

Speaking to Rose about the satisfaction he gains from writing about science for a general readership, Bodanis explained in his *BookPage* online interview: "I've really enjoyed in the past when people have made stories or insights clear for me, and so it's a great pleasure to work to make things equally clear for others."

Biographical and Critical Sources

PERIODICALS

Appraisal, summer, 1987, Lavinia C. Demos, review of *The Secret House: Twenty-four Hours in the Strange and Unexpected World in Which We Spend Our Nights and Days,* p. 21.

Astronomy, January, 2001, review of *E=mc2: A Biography of the World's Most Famous Equation,* p. 112.

Booklist, August, 1997, Donna Seaman, review of *The Secret Family: Twenty-four Hours inside the Mysterious World of Our Minds and Bodies,* p. 1864; August,

2000, Gilbert Taylor, review of *E=mc2,* p. 2088; August, 2000, Gilbert Taylor, review of *E=mc2,* p. 209; January 1, 2002, review of *The Secret House,* p. 979; February 1, 2005, Gilbert Taylor, review of *Electric Universe,* p. 925.

Chicago Sun-Times, November 27, 2000, Mike Thomas, interview with Bodanis.

Chicago Tribune, March 16, 2005, Patrick T. Reardon, review of *Electric Universe.*

Choice, December, 1984, S.E. Gunstream, review of *The Body Book: A Fantastic Voyage to the World Within,* p. 580; April, 2001, M. Mounts, review of *E=mc2,* p. 1495; December, 2005, M. Schaab, review of *Electric Universe,* p. 698.

Contemporary Review, May, 2005, review of *Electric Universe,* p. 319.

Daily Mail (London, England), February 11, 2005, Peter Forbes, review of *Electric Universe,* p. 72.

Discover, February, 1998, Sarah Richardson, review of *The Secret Family,* p. 88; October, 2000, Eric Powell, review of *E=mc2,* p. 104.

Economist, February 12, 2005, review of *Electric Universe,* p. 83.

Encounter, March, 1989, review of *Web of Words: The Ideas behind Politics,* p. 55.

Engineer, March 29, 2005, review of *Electric Universe,* p. 20.

Entertainment Weekly, August 22, 1997, Alexandra Jacobs, review of *The Secret Garden,* p. 128; February 25, 2005, Wook Kim, review of *Electric Universe,* p. 105.

Globe & Mail (Toronto, Ontario, Canada), November 25, 2000, review of *E=mc2,* p. D28.

Guardian (London, England), January 15, 2005, Pedro G. Ferreira, review of *Electric Universe,* p. 10.

Independent Sunday (London, England), January 29, 2006, Laurence Phelan, review of *Electric Universe,* p. 30.

Kirkus Reviews, June 15, 1997, review of *The Secret Family,* p. 922; January 15, 2005, review of *Electric Universe,* p. 94.

Kliatt, July, 2005, Edna Boardman, review of *Electric Universe,* p. 61.

Library Journal, September 15, 1984, Carla La Croix, review of *The Body Book,* p. 1764; July, 1997, Mark L. Shelton, review of *The Secret Family,* p. 118; November 1, 2000, James Olson, review of *E=mc2,* p. 124; January, 2001, review of *E=mc2,* p. 52; March 1, 2001, review of *E=mc2,* p. 48; December 1, 2004, Ian Gordon, review of *Electric Universe,* p. 154; September 1, 2005, review of *Electric Universe,* p. 192.

Los Angeles Times Book Review, December 26, 1993, Charles Solomon, review of *The Secret Garden: Dawn to Dusk in the Astonishing Hidden World of the Garden,* p. 11.

New Scientist, March 4, 1989, Roy Herbert, review of *The Secret House,* p. 60.

New Statesman and Society, February 3, 1989, Alan Brien, "Word Hunting," p. 45.

Observer (London, England), March 6, 2005, Mark Townsend, review of *Electric Universe,* p. 16; January 22, 2006, Oliver Robinson, review of *Electric Universe,* p. 29.

People, April 20, 1987, "They Say a Man's Home Is His Castle, but David Bodanis' Secret House Reveals the Creepy Truth," p. 133.

Publishers Weekly, June 8, 1984, review of *The Body Book,* p. 59; September 18, 2000, review of *E=mc2,* p. 98; December 6, 2004, review of *Electric Universe,* p. 50; April 4, 2005, review of *Electric Universe,* p. 22.

School Library Journal, December, 2000, Barbara A. Genco, review of *E=mc2,* p. 63.

Science Books and Films, March, 1993, David W. Kramer, review of *The Secret Garden,* p. 46; July, 2002, review of *E=mc2,* p. 450; November, 2002, review of *E=mc2,* p. 538; May-June, 2005, Parrish A. Staples, review of *Electric Universe,* p. 101.

Science News, April 16, 2005, review of *Electric Universe,* p. 255.

Spectator, November 4, 2000, Steve King, review of *E=mc2,* p. 53.

Sunday Times (London, England), March 6, 2005, William Peakin, review of *E=mc2,* p. 6.

Times Educational Supplement, November 10, 2000, review of *E=mc2,* p. 23; February 11, 2005, review of *Electric Universe,* pp. B18-B19.

Times Literary Supplement, January 30, 1998, A.M. Daniels, "The Last Explorers," p. 36.

U.S. News & World Report, December 18, 2000, Jay Tolson, review of *E=mc2,* p. 54.

Washington Post Book World, December 2, 1984, Carol Kurcoff, review of *The Body Book,* p. 14.

ONLINE

BookPage, http://www.bookpage.com/ (March, 2005), Michael Alec Rose, interview with Bodanis.

CollegeClub.com, http://www.collegeclub.com/ (September 13, 2001), "David Bodanis."

David Bodanis Home Page, http://www.davidbodanis.com (June 20, 2007).

*   *   *

BRADLEY, Kimberly Brubaker 1967-

Personal

Born 1967, in Fort Wayne, IN; married Bart Bradley, 1989; children: Matthew, Katie. *Education:* Smith College, B.S. (chemistry), 1989.

Addresses

Home—Bristol, TN. *E-mail*—mbbradley@planetc.com.

Career

Writer, 1993—. Worked as a research chemist, 1990-93.

Member

Society of Children's Book Writers and Illustrators.

Awards, Honors

National Science Teachers Association/Children's Book Council Outstanding Trade Book for Children designation, for "Let's-Read-and-Find-Out Science" series; Bank Street College Best Children's Book of the Year designation, 2000, for *Weaver's Daughter;* Top-Ten Historical Fiction for Youth listee, 2003, and Amelia Bloomer Project Feminist Books for Youth listee, 2004, both for *For Freedom: The Story of a French Spy.*

Writings

JUVENILE NOVELS

Ruthie's Gift, illustrated by Dave Kramer, Delacorte Press (New York, NY), 1998.

One-of-a-Kind Mallie, Delacorte Press (New York, NY), 1999.

Weaver's Daughter, Delacorte Press (New York, NY), 2000.

Halfway to the Sky, Delacorte Press (New York, NY), 2002.

For Freedom: The Story of a French Spy, Delacorte Press (New York, NY), 2003.

The President's Daughter, Delacorte Press (New York, NY), 2004.

Leap of Faith, Dial (New York, NY), 2007.

The Lacemaker and the Princess, Margaret K. McElderry (New York, NY), 2007.

PICTURE BOOKS

Pop!: A Book about Bubbles, ("Let's-Read-and-Find-Out Science" series), illustrated by Margaret Miller, HarperCollins (New York, NY), 2001.

Energy Makes Things Happen, ("Let's-Read-and-Find-Out Science" series), illustrated by Paul Meisel, HarperCollins (New York, NY), 2003.

Favorite Things, illustrated by Laura Huliska-Beith, Dial (New York, NY), 2003.

Forces Make Things Move, ("Let's-Read-and-Find-Out Science" series), illustrated by Paul Meisel, HarperCollins (New York, NY), 2004.

Ballerino Nate, illustrated by R.W. Alley, Dial (New York, NY), 2006.

The Perfect Pony, illustrated by Shelagh McNicholas, Dial (New York, NY) 2007.

Ghost writer of numerous middle-grade novels in a riding series for Bantam; contributor to horse magazines.

Adaptations

For Freedom was adapted as an audiobook, 2000.

Sidelights

The author of fiction for elementary-grade readers, as well as of picture books for younger children, Kimberly Brubaker Bradley demonstrates a remarkable breadth of theme and subject matter. Her first three titles, *Ruthie's Gift, One-of-a-Kind Mallie,* and *Weaver's Daughter,* are

Cover of Kimberly Brubaker Bradley's young-adult novel **Halfway to the Sky,** *featuring a photograph by Dick Durrance II.* (Dell Yearling, 2002. Background photo © 1994 by Dick Durrance II/Corbis. Reproduced by permission of Dell Yearling, an imprint of Random House Children's Books, a division of Random House, Inc.)

geared for middle-grade readers, while *Halfway to the Sky, For Freedom: The Story of a French Spy,* and *The Lacemaker* feature young-adult themes. Each of Bradley's books are noted for their wealth of detail and the diverse characters that readers meet within their pages: from a lonely girl living in rural Indiana in the early years of the twentieth century to a brave French teen fighting for her country during World War II, to a young boy who dreams of being a dancer.

Born in 1967 in Fort Wayne, Indiana, Bradley grew up in a reading family. "I have always loved to read, and my parents always read, too," she noted on the Book Nuts Reading Club Web site. Favorite books included the "Little House on the Prairie" series by Laura Ingalls Wilder, as well as "any horse book I could find," the author added. In addition to books, Bradley was influenced by her grandmother's stories of growing up in the small Indiana town of Cedarville as the only daughter among her parents' seven children.

Bradley began writing while in college, contributing articles on horses to various magazines. However, writing

took second place to her dreams of a medical career. While attending Smith College, she majored in chemistry, a subject she later explained to *Publishers Weekly* interviewer Elizabeth Devereaux "'strikes me a lot like writing. You get a certain number of things you can control and a certain number you can't, and you combine them.'" In addition to her chemistry studies and horse articles, Bradley also began writing stories for children, reworking some of the tales her grandmother had told about life in Indiana during the first decades of the twentieth century. During her sophomore year, Bradley enrolled in a course on children's literature taught by Newbery medalist Patrician MacLachlan. When MacLachlan saw some of Bradley's writings, she was impressed and arranged for her student to attend a writing conference in a group led by Jane Yolen. This further encouraged Bradley, and she began sending out manuscripts to publishers even before graduating from college. Though none of these sold, a number of editors made helpful suggestions to the young writer.

After graduating from Smith College, Bradley married and both she and her husband enrolled in medical school. Soon, however, she discovered that medicine was not for her. Using her degree in another way, she worked as a research chemist for several years, continuing to write in her spare time. In a writing contest for middle-grade fiction, Bradley's work failed to win top honors, but the manuscript was passed on to an editor at Bantam who was looking for someone to ghost-write a series of novels on horses. Leaving chemistry behind, Bradley began turning out four such novels a year. "'I don't consider them mine,'" she later told Devereaux. "'They're not my characters and not my setting. . . . But it taught me discipline.'" Soon she was working on what would become her own debut novel, *Ruthie's Gift*.

Geared for preteen readers, *Ruthie's Gift* began as a picture book fictionalizing an incident involving Bradley's grandmother and her siblings. Editors suggested a longer approach, however, and Bradley turned the work into a novel-length tale of an eight-year-old tomboy who learns hard lessons about life. Ruthie lives in a small farming town in Indiana, where she is the only third-grader in her local school and the only girl in a family of six boys. Growing up in such a household, she has learned to be independent and strong; the other girls at school do not take to her because of this and accuse Ruthie of being unladylike. Even when she makes friends, she usually ends up alienating them due to her uncompromising behavior. However, in one memorable year, Ruthie learns not only to be strong but also to be selfless: making best friends with twins Hallie and Mallie, she suffers a bout of pneumonia that almost kills her and loses her beloved brother Joe, a soldier, during World War I.

A critic reviewing *Ruthie's Gift* for *Publishers Weekly* cited the book's "brisk pacing, affectionate humor and . . . unforgettable heroine," adding that Bradley's "funny . . . poignant and accessible" writing contrib-

utes to an "excellent novel." Similar praise came from *Booklist* reviewer Hazel Rochman, who called the book a "real tearjerker," not because "it wallows in sentiment but because it is honest about jealousy, disappointment, and mess in family life." Rochman also commended Bradley's characters, which the critic described as "drawn with affectionate realism." For Devereaux, *Ruthie's Gift* stands as a "robust middle-grade novel," and Marilyn Payne Philips, writing in *School Library Journal*, deemed the book to be "just the ticket for readers crossing the bridge to chapter books."

Returning readers to Cedarville, Indiana in *One-of-a-Kind Mallie*, Bradley casts twins Hallie and Mallie from *Ruthie's Gift* in the lead. Set once again during World War I, the novel explores the idea of being unique as a human. Mallie dislikes being a twin because she is forever compared to or mistaken for her sister Hallie. Determining that she needs to prove how different she is from her sister, Mallie goes to a Gypsy encampment and trades her look-alike dress for a red blouse that will set her apart from her sister. She also picks cherries to earn the money that will allow her to take piano lessons from Mr. Jenkins's new mail-order bride. Through it all, Mallie also learns to appreciate her sister more and accept Hallie as a separate person. Bradley manages to sprinkle her tale with historical details, mentioning Red Cross knitting circles, food rationing, victory gardens, and the world of horse-drawn carts and home-baked bread.

Although Rochman found *One-of-a-Kind Mallie* less compelling than *Ruthie's Gift*, she dubbed "satisfying" the ending in which the young girls recognize that they "like each other and have a lot in common, but that they are also very different." A contributor to *Publishers Weekly* also noted that Bradley's follow-up "lacks the dramatic tension and depth" of her debut, although "the characterizations are just as sharp and engaging." Calling *Ruthie's Gift* a "well-written, deliberately paced story," Susan Hepler wrote in *School Library Journal* that the sequel "stands well on its own with a good plot and strong characterization." Reviewing the same book for the *Christian Science Monitor*, Enicia Fisher deemed *One-of-a-Kind Mallie* "poignant and charming," adding that Bradley "brings to life a likeably real heroine and a town that would seem commonplace but, as we learn, is actually one of a kind."

Bradley transports readers further back in time in both *Weaver's Daughter* and *The Lacemaker and the Princess*. A tale set in 1791 in what was called the Southwest Territory and is now the state of Tennessee, *Weaver's Daughter* introduces Lizzy Baker, who is part of a pioneer family. Every day Lizzy's farmer father works in the fields while her mother, a weaver, spends hours at the family loom. Lizzy dreams of becoming a weaver just like her mother, but illness plagues her. Every autumn she becomes sick, and now, at age ten, her spells

of sickness are noticeably worse. As winter approaches, Lizzie worries that such bouts will take their final toll in the coming cold. No doctor or midwife is able to cure her (she would now be diagnosed with asthma and allergies), but she hopes for the best and decides to focus her attention on the present rather than the unknowable future. Her mind is also kept off melancholy thoughts by the arrival of visitors from Charleston. Miss Sarah Beaumont and her young, good-looking stepson have views very different from those of Lizzy and her family. When the Beaumonts offer to take Lizzie to their home in Charleston, where the sea air may help her, Lizzie must make a choice: whether to lose her family to save herself. A *Publishers Weekly* contributor felt that in *Weaver's Daughter* Bradley "conveys a comforting message through Lizzy's bittersweet experiences," while Rochman cited the plot's "aching sadness," as well as characters who are "drawn with some complexity." Rochman further commented that Bradley "is careful neither to sentimentalize nor exploit the illness." Writing in *School Library Journal*, Miriam Lang Budin also found much to like in what she dubbed a "surprisingly rich book." For Budin, Bradley's tale is "compelling" and her characters "are rounded enough to display conflicted sentiments."

The beauty of the French palace of Versailles and the wealth of the eighteenth-century court of Louis XVI and Marie Antoinette are the subject of *The Lacemaker and the Princess*, which finds eleven-year-old lace maker Isabelle chosen to be the playmate of the queen's daughter. With approval of the queen, Isabelle plays with Princess Marie-Therese in the afternoons, but spends the early part of the day working at her loom. As a member of the working class, the girl senses the growing resentment felt by many toward royalty, but her knowledge of the people living in Versailles give her a more compassionate view of the hated and ill-fated aristocratic family, all of whom will ultimately lose their lives. Noting that Bradley has "skillfully integrated historical facts" into her tale, *Booklist* reviewer Gillian Engberg dubbed *The Lacemaker and the Princess* an "engrossing, believable story" about a friendship "that crosses class boundaries." The author's endnotes add factual depth to the tale, a *Kirkus Reviews* writer added, citing in particular Bradley's "first-person narrative," which is "full of description and intriguing insight into the period."

Halfway to the Sky follows twelve-year-old runaway Dani on a journey of self-discovery as she sets out on her own to hike the more-than-2,000 miles of the Appalachian Trail. Sadness has spurred this journey: Dani's thirteen-year-old brother, Springer, died just months before from muscular dystrophy. Her family has fallen apart as a result of the tragedy: her parents are divorced and her father has remarried and already has a new child on the way. With only sadness at home, Dani

needs to do something monumental as a start to turning her own life around. Running away from home, she begins her hike along the well-traveled trail, which stretches from Georgia to Maine. After Dani's mom realizes where her daughter has gone, she tracks the girl down, and soon joins the preteen on her life-changing trek. Reviewing *Halfway to the Sky* for *School Library Journal,* Ellen Fader noted that Bradley's novel is "fairly standard coming-of-age" fare "with the added benefit of Dani's mother also growing and healing during their time together on the trail." A *Kirkus Reviews* critic had higher praise for the novel, calling it an "emotionally taut story" and predicting that "teenagers will readily relate to the angst and anger and be intrigued by the details about the Trail itself."

Bradley moves the action from the United States to Europe in *For Freedom.* Based on a true story related in a series of interviews with fellow Tennessean Suzanne David Hall, the novel tells the story of a young French woman during the Nazi occupation of France and of her thrilling and sometimes chilling experiences as a member of the French Resistance. Married to an American G.I. in 1945, Suzanne David Hall moved to Tennessee where she raised her family. Bradley, in telling Hall's

Cover of Bradley's historical novel **For Freedom,** *featuring artwork by* ***Kamil Vojnar.*** (Delacorte Press, 2003. Reproduced by permission of Random House Children's Books, a division of Random House, Inc.)

story, employs a fictional format. In 1940, when the Germans begin bombing Suzanne's native Cherbourg, she is a thirteen-year-old schoolgirl devoted to music. Then a pregnant neighbor is killed in front of her during a bombing raid, and suddenly the war that has seemed so distant to her now seems very real. Soon after, the Germans march in and the Davids are asked to leave their house so that it can be used as barracks. When given the chance, Suzanne joins the Resistance as a courier. As a voice student, she has the perfect excuse to be walking around, for she legitimately has lessons to attend as well as recitals and costume fittings. Although the secret messages she now carries are well hidden, capture would mean death at the hands of the Germans, and in a climate of suspicion there are many who would gain much by turning her in to the Nazi authorities.

Reviewing *For Freedom* in *School Library Journal,* Kimberly Monaghan described Bradley's book as a "suspenseful novel . . . [that] moves swiftly into action," and one that will "appeal to readers who enjoy history and espionage." Similarly, *Booklist* contributor Roger Leslie called the book a "taut, engrossing World War II novel [that] instantly immerses readers." While Leslie noted that *For Freedom* "resonates with authenticity, excitement, and heart," *Kliatt* critic Claire Rosser deemed the work a "powerful story" that "fill[s readers] . . . with admiration for Suzanne's strength and commitment." In the same vein, a *Kirkus Reviews* critic applauded *For Freedom* as an "exciting account of a girl's coming of age in a scary time," and a contributor to *Publishers Weekly* called Bradley's novel a "gripping, high-stakes adventure" and a "compelling look at the covert battle for freedom."

Sustaining her focus on the early twentieth century, Bradley returns to her own country in *The President's Daughter.* The book is a fictionalized portrayal of the experiences of President Theodore Roosevelt's ten-year-old daughter, Ethel, after her family's move into the White House in 1901, *The President's Daughter* features the author's characteristic pattern: a young, female protagonist meets life head on in a dramatic situation. Life in the White House was exciting due to Ethel's parents' varied interests and relaxed rules, and tomboy play and pets were both allowed. However, Ethel only lived at her new home on weekends; week days she was a boarder at Washington, DC's prestigious National Cathedral School. In her book Bradley brings to life the joys and stresses that must have been experienced by this young daughter of a U.S. president; as a *Kirkus Reviews* writer noted, "she makes Ethel a vivid and engaging presence and her struggles for acceptance at school ring true." Reviewing *The President's Daughter* for *Booklist,* Kay Weisman called the novel "fascinating," and Kristen Oravec wrote in *School Library Journal* that Bradley's story "rings true" due to its wealth of "historical details."

Shifting her focus to younger readers, Bradley has contributed several titles to the "Let's Read-and-Find-out Science" series. These books, which include *Pop!: A Book about Bubbles, Energy Makes Things Happen,* and *Forces Make Things Move,* have won awards as well as critical praise. A contributor for *Kirkus Reviews,* writing about *Pop!,* concluded that "young readers (and their parents) will have a good time learning new science thanks to this playful offering." *School Library Journal* contributor Pamela K. Bomboy called the book an example of "science learning at its best." Similarly, in a critical analysis of *Energy Makes Things Happen,* a writer for *Kirkus Reviews* noted that it takes a "rare talent" to explain scientific concepts in a way that is at once "interesting and understandable." For this reviewer, "Bradley successfully leaps over that bar in this lively exploration." Featuring what another *Kirkus Reviews* contributor described as "simple language and appealing illustrations," *Force Makes Things Move* combines a readable text and "happily multicultural cartoon" illustrations by Paul Meisel "to elucidate [a] . . . tricky concept."

Moving from fact to fancy, in *Favorite Things* Bradley serves up a "creative bedtime tale," as a *Kirkus Reviews* critic characterized the book. Also written for younger children, *The Perfect Pony* highlights the passion of a young horse-lover in what another *Kirkus Reviews* writer deemed an "accessible tale" writtaen in "a simple, direct style." Another book for the storytime set, *Ballerino Nate* "tackles gender stereotypes head-on with a plucky hero who prefers plies and pirouettes to Little League and Nintendo," in the opinion of a *Publishers Weekly* contributor. While noting that Bradley's story has some slow moments, *Booklist* contributor Jennifer Mattson praised *Ballerino Nate,* commenting that the author "writes smoothly and insightfully about Nate's experiences" as a boy dancer. Praising Bradley's persistent puppy-dog protagonist, *School Library Journal* contributor Rachel G. Payne added that R.W. Alley's

Bradley turns her attention to younger readers in her nonfiction picture book Energy Makes Things Happen, ***featuring cover art by Paul Meisel.*** (HarperCollins, 2003. Illustration © 2003 by Paul Meisel. Reproduced by permission of HarperCollins Children's Books, a division of HarperCollins Publishers.)

A young boy's love of the dance is brought to life in R.W. Alley's illustrations for Bradley's picture book **Ballerino Nate.** (Dial, 2006. Illustration © 2006 by R.W. Alley. Reproduced by permission of Dial Books for Young Readers, a division of Penguin Putnam Books for Young Readers.)

watercolor and ink drawings of Nate and his efforts to join an all-girl ballet class "have a playful energy that moves the story forward."

Biographical and Critical Sources

PERIODICALS

Booklist, January 1, 1998, Hazel Rochman, review of *Ruthie's Gift,* p. 809; August, 1999, Hazel Rochman, review of *One-of-a-Kind Mallie,* p. 2005; August, 2000, Hazel Rochman, review of *Weaver's Daughter* p. 2138; August, 2001, Carolyn Phelan, review of *Pop!: A Book about Bubbles,* p. 2124; February 1, 2003, Ilene Cooper, review of *Energy Makes Things Happen,* p. 996; April 1, 2003, Roger Leslie, review of *For Freedom: The Story of a French Spy,* p. 1396; February 15, 2005, Kay Weisman, review of *The President's Daughter,* p. 1080; September 15, 2005, Carolyn Phelan, review of *Forces Make Things Move,* p. 67; February 1, 2006, Jennifer Mattson, review of *Ballerino Nate,* p. 53; April 15, 2007, Gillian Engberg, review of *The Lacemaker and the Princess,* p. 50.

Bulletin of the Center for Children's Books, February, 2005, Karen Coats, review of *The President's Daughter,* p. 245; April, 2006, Deborah Stevenson, review of *Ballerino Nate,* p. 343.

Christian Science Monitor, September 2, 1999, Enicia Fisher, review of *One-of-a-Kind Mallie,* p. 20.

Horn Book, July-August, 2003, Roger Sutton, review of *For Freedom,* pp. 450-451.

Kirkus Reviews, August 1, 2001, review of *Pop!,* p. 1117; January 15, 2002, review of *Halfway to the Sky,* pp. 100-101; November 15, 2002, review of *Energy Makes Things Happen,* p. 1688; May 1, 2003, review of *For Freedom,* p. 674; June 1, 2003, review of *Favorite Things,* p. 800; November 1, 2004, review of *The President's Daughter,* p. 1043; July 1, 2005, review of *Forces Make Things Move,* p. 731; February 15, 2006, review of *Ballerino Nate,* p. 178; March 15, 2007, review of *The Perfect Pony;* May 1, 2007, review of *The Lacemaker and the Princess.*

Kliatt, May, 2003, Claire Rosser, review of *For Freedom,* p. 6.

Publishers Weekly, December 22, 1997, review of *Ruthie's Gift,* p. 59; June 29, 1998, Elizabeth Devereaux, "Kimberly Brubaker Bradley," p. 30; August 2, 1999, review of *One-of-a-Kind Mallie,* p. 85; October 11, 1999, review of *Ruthie's Gift,* p. 78; October 23, 2000, review of *Weaver's Daughter,* p. 75; May 19, 2003, review of *Favorite Things,* p. 73; June 2, 2003, review of *For Freedom,* p. 51; March 13, 2006, review of *Ballerino Nate,* p. 65.

School Library Journal, February, 1998, Marilyn Payne Phillips, review of *Ruthie's Gift,* pp. 78-79; September, 1999, Susan Hepler, review of *One-of-a-Kind Mallie,* p. 176; October, 2000, Miriam Lang Budin, review of *Weaver's Daughter,* p. 155; October, 2001, Emily Herman, review of *Weaver's Daughter,* p. 93, and Pamela K. Bomboy, review of *Pop!,* p. 136; April, 2002, Ellen Fader, review of *Halfway to the Sky,* p. 142; June, 2003, Kimberly Monaghan, review of *For Freedom,* p. 136; August, 2003, Marianne Saccardi, review of *Favorite Things,* pp. 122-123; November, 2004, Kristen Oravec, review of *The President's Daughter,* p. 134; March, 2006, Rachel G. Payne, review of *Ballerino Nate,* p. 175; May, 2007, Carol Schene, review of *The Perfect Pony,* p. 85.

ONLINE

Kimberly Brubaker Bradley Home Page, http://www.kimberlybrubakerbradley.com (May 15, 2007).

Kids@Random Web site, http://www.randomhouse.com/ (May 15, 2007).*

*   *   *

BROWN, Calef

Personal

Male. *Education:* Art Center College of Design, B.F.A.

Addresses

Home and office—Pasadena, CA. *E-mail*—calef@calef-brown.com.

Career

Author and illustrator. Freelance illustrator; instructor at Art Center College of Design and Otis School of Art and Design.

Writings

Polka-Bats and Octopus Slacks: 14 Stories, Houghton Mifflin (Boston, MA), 1998.

Dutch Sneakers and Flea-Keepers: 14 More Stories, Houghton Mifflin (Boston, MA), 2000.

(Illustrator) John Harris, *Greece! Rome! Monsters!,* J. Paul Getty Museum (Los Angeles, CA), 2002.

Tippintown: A Guided Tour, Houghton Mifflin (Boston, MA), 2003.

Flamingos on the Roof: Poems and Paintings, Houghton Mifflin (Boston, MA), 2006.

Sidelights

Calef Brown originally began his career as a freelance illustrator by creating works for such high-profile periodicals as the *New York Times, Rolling Stone,* and *Newsweek.* Brown became interested in writing and illustrating children's books when the fast-paced, deadline-oriented life of freelancing began to wear thin. As he explained in an online interview with *Illustration Mundo,* his intent in writing his first children's book was to "illustrate something of my own that would have a longer shelf life than the magazine pieces that I was doing." His aim was achieved: his first self-illustrated children's book, *Polka-Bats and Octopus Slacks: 14 Stories,* was published in 1998 and went into five printings. In this book, as well as Brown's other books for

young children, he mixes original poetry with his folk-art inspired illustrations. He commented to *Illustration Mundo* that his texts are designed to be "read aloud. I want them to be musical—some rhythmic, percussive and lively, others quiet and atmospheric."

Critics have acknowledged Brown's skill both as a writer and an illustrator. Susan Dove Lempke, in her evaluation of *Flamingos on the Roof: Poems and Paintings* for *Horn Book,* commented on his ability to balance a well-written text with engaging, colorful illustrations and noted that the book's "imaginative wordplay is matched by . . . [Brown's] acrylic paintings depicting people and places in unusual hues." Other reviewers have pinpointed the effortlessness of Brown's poems. A *Kirkus Reviews* critic cited his ability to create audibly pleasing poetry with child appeal. Noting that Brown's texts are "composed with a fine ear for consistent rhythms and silly wordplay," the critic concluded that books such as *Flamingos on the Roof* "will tempt readers into repeat visits."

Biographical and Critical Sources

PERIODICALS

Booklist, March 15, 1998, John Peters, review of *Polka-Bats and Octopus Slacks: 14 Stories,* p. 1243; April 1, 2000, Gillian Engberg, review of *Dutch Sneakers and Flea-Keepers: 14 More Stories,* p. 1456; April 15, 2003, Michael Cart, review of *Tippintown: A Guided Tour,* p. 1475; April 15, 2006, Hazel Rochman, review of *Flamingos on the Roof: Poems and Paintings,* p. 44.

Horn Book, May-June, 2006, Susan Dove Lempke, review of *Flamingos on the Roof,* p. 337.

Kirkus Reviews, March 15, 2006, review of *Flamingos on the Roof,* p. 286.

Publishers Weekly, March, 1998, review of *Polka-Bats and Octopus Slacks,* p. 67; April 17, 2000, review of *Dutch Sneakers and Flea-Keepers,* p. 78; April 9, 2001, review of *Polka-Bats and Octopus Slacks,* p. 28; October 7, 2002, review of *Greece! Rome! Monsters!,* p. 73; March 3, 2003, review of *Tippintown,* p. 75; March 20, 2006, review of *Flamingos on the Roof,* p. 55.

School Library Journal, April, 2000, Linda M. Kenton, review of *Dutch Sneakers and Flea-Keepers,* p. 118; May, 2003, Liza Graybill, review of *Tippintown,* p. 108; July, 2006, Susan Scheps, review of *Flamingos on the Roof,* p. 118.

ONLINE

Calef Brown Home Page, http://www.calefbrown.com (May 12, 2007).

Houghton Mifflin Web site, http://www.houghton mifflinbooks.com/ (May 12, 2007), "Calef Brown."

Illustration Mundo Web site, http://www.illustrationmundo. com/ (March 31, 2007), Nate Williams, interview with Brown.*

In **Flamingos on the Roof,** *Calef Brown brings to life a humorous story with his whimsical art.* (Houghton Mifflin, 2006. Illustration © 2006 by Calef Brown. Reproduced by permission of Houghton Mifflin Company.)

BUCK, Nola
See GODWIN, Laura

*   *   *

BURKE, Jim 1973-

Personal
Born 1973, in Manchester, NH; son of Tom (a business owner) and Marjorie (a teacher) Burke; married; wife's name Suzanne. *Education:* Syracuse University, B.F.A., 1996.

Addresses
Home and office—Brooklyn, NY. *E-mail*—jimburkeart@aol.com.

Career
Author and illustrator. Freelance illustrator; Pratt Institute, New York, NY, instructor in painting.

Member
Society of Illustrators.

Awards, Honors
Oppenheim Toy Portfolio Gold Award and Parent's Choice designation, both 2003, and Massachusetts Center for the Book Honor designation and Teacher's Choice Book Award, International Reading Association, both 2004, all for *My Brother's Flying Machine;* Platinum Award, Oppenheim Toy Portfolio, and Original Art Show Award of Excellence, both for *A Christmas Gift for Mama;* Society of Illustrators Gold Medal; awards of excellence from Print's Regional Design, *Communication Arts* magazine, New York Art Directors Club, and *Graphis* magazine.

Illustrator
Jonathan Levin, editor, *Poetry for Young People: Walt Whitman,* Sterling Pub. (New York, NY), 1997.

Clyde Robert Bulla, *Shoeshine Girl,* HarperTrophy (New York, NY), 2000.

Lauren Thompson, *A Christmas Gift for Mama,* Scholastic Press (New York, NY), 2003.

Jane Yolen, *My Brothers' Flying Machine: Wilbur, Orville, and Me,* Little, Brown (New York, NY), 2003.

Jack Norworth, lyricist, *Take Me out to the Ball Game: The Sensational Baseball Song,* Little, Brown (New York, NY), 2006.

Barbara Timberlake Russell, *Maggie's Amerikay,* Farrar, Straus & Giroux (New York, NY), 2006.

Jane Yolen, *Johnny Appleseed,* HarperCollins (New York, NY), 2008.

Sidelights
Jazz music is an important component of illustrator Jim Burke's creative process. During an apprenticeship with famed artist Mark English in Kansas City, Missouri,

Through his evocative paintings, Jim Burke presents an illustrated history of American baseball in Take Me out to the Ball Game. (Little, Brown, 2006. Paintings © 2006 by Jim Burke. Reproduced by permission.)

Burke attended his first live jazz performance, and the musical genre has greatly influenced his art work ever since. As Burke commented on his home page, as an artist he attempts to use the tools of his trade in the same way that musical performers employ their instruments: "There is an honest bond and trust between a musician and his instrument, as there is between a painter and his brush. It is my goal to capture this dynamic relationship on my canvases." As a freelance illustrator, Burke creates designs for a variety of clients and has also illustrated books for well-known children's author Jane Yolen.

Burke has been acknowledged by critics for his ability to create images that are lifelike, a reviewer for *Publishers Weekly* describing his illustrations for *Take Me out to the Ball Game: The Sensational Baseball Song* as "stunning, realistic oil paintings." Based on a song written by vaudevillian and songwriter Jack Norworth in 1908, *Take Me out to the Ball Game* incorporates the lyrics of Norworth's famous baseball-themed anthem into Burke's text about the famous and controversial match between the New York Giants and the Chicago Cubs. In addition to Norworth's lyrics, Burke also includes informative sidebars featuring facts about the 1908 game, aspects that "hits a line drive straight into baseball's storied past," in the opinion of a *Kirkus Reviews* critic. Marilyn Taniguchi, reviewing the work for *School Library Journal,* noted that with *Take Me out to*

the Ball Game Burke "has fashioned a sparkling introduction to an exhilarating period in baseball history."

Biographical and Critical Sources

PERIODICALS

Booklist, March 1, 2003, Carolyn Phelan, review of *My Brothers' Flying Machine: Wilbur, Orville, and Me,* p. 1208; September 1, 2003, Ilene Cooper, review of *A Christmas Gift for Mama,* p. 133; April 1, 2006, GraceAnne A. DeCandido, *Take Me out to the Ball Game: The Sensational Baseball Song,* p. 44; May 1, 2006, Hazel Rochman, review of *Maggie's Amerikay,* p. 93.

Bulletin of the Center for Children's Books, May, 2006, Elizabeth Bush, *Take Me out to the Ball Game,* p. 392.

Christian Science Monitor, April 3, 2003, review of *My Brothers' Flying Machine,* p. 20.

Kirkus Reviews, March 15, 2003, review of *My Brothers' Flying Machine,* p. 482; November 1, 2003, review of *A Christmas Gift for Mama,* p. 1320; February 1, 2006, *Take Me out to the Ball Game,* p. 135; April 15, 2006, review of *Maggie's Amerikay,* p. 415.

Publishers Weekly, March 24, 2003, review of *My Brothers' Flying Machine,* p. 75; September 22, 2003, review of *A Christmas Gift for Mama,* p. 71; March 6, 2006, review of *Take Me out to the Ball Game,* p. 73.

Reading Teacher, November, 2004, review of *My Brothers' Flying Machine,* p. 287.

School Library Journal, March, 2003, Harriett Fargnoli, review of *My Brothers' Flying Machine,* p. 225; October, 2003, Susan Patron, review of *A Christmas Gift for Mama,* p. 68; April, 2006, Marilyn Taniguchi, *Take Me out to the Ball Game,* p. 123; April, 2006, Barbara Auerbach, review of *Maggie's Amerikay,* p. 116.

ONLINE

Hachette Book Group Web site, http://www.hachettebookgroupusa.com/ (May 13, 2007), "Jim Burke."

Jim Burke Home Page, http://www.jimburkeart.com (May 13, 2007).

Manchester Artists Association Web site, http://www.manchester-artists.org/ (May 13, 2007), "Jim Burke."*

C

CANN, Helen 1969-

Personal

Born February 19, 1969, in Bristol, England; daughter of Peter and Gillian Cann. *Education:* University of Wales, B.A. (with honors), postgraduate diploma, 1993.

Addresses

Home and office—GFF 46 Goldstone Villas, Hove, E. Sussex BN3 3RS, England. *E-mail*—contact@helen-cann.co.uk.

Career

Children's book illustrator. *Exhibitions:* Work exhibited in galleries, including Pro Patria Gallery, Zurich, Switzerland, 1993; Buildhall Arts Centre, Gloucester, England, 1994; Horsham Arts Centre, London, England, 1995; Mary Kleinman Gallery, London, 1998; Downstairs at the Air Gallery, London, 2000; Guildhall Gallery, Guildford, England, 2003; Holburne Museum, Bath, England, 2004; and Art Institute of Chicago, Chicago, IL, 2006.

Member

Association of Illustrators.

Awards, Honors

United Kingdom Reading Association Award, 1998, for *A Calendar of Festivals;* Bank Street College of Education Best Children's Book of the Year designation, 2003, for *Brigid's Cloak;* CBC Children's Book of the Year designation, 2003, and Christian Book Awards (UK) Best Children's Book designation, 2004, both for *The Lion Bible for Children.*

Illustrator

Josephine Evetts-Secker, reteller, *The Barefoot Book of Mother and Daughter Tales,* Barefoot Books (Bath, England), 1996 published as *Mother and Daughter Tales,* Abbeville Kids (New York, NY), 1996.

Animal Worlds, Sandvik, 1997.

Bel Mooney, *The Green Man,* Barefoot Books (Bath, England), 1997.

Josephine Evetts-Secker, reteller, *The Barefoot Book of Father and Daughter Tales,* Barefoot Books (Bath, England), 1997 published as *Father and Daughter Tales,* Abbeville Kids (New York, NY), 1997.

Josephine Evetts-Secker, reteller, *The Barefoot Book of Father and Son Tales,* Barefoot Books (Bath, England), 1998.

Josephine Evetts-Secker, reteller, *The Barefoot Book of Mother and Son Tales,* Barefoot Books (Bath, England), 1998.

Cherry Gilchrist, *A Calendar of Festivals: Celebrations from around the World,* Barefoot Books (Bath, England), 1998, Barefoot Books (Cambridge, MA), 2005.

Joyce Denham, *A Child's Book of Celtic Prayers,* Loyola Press (Chicago, IL), 1998.

Jasmine Brook and Lianne McCabe, *The Dreamcatcher: Keep Your Dream Happy—Forever!,* Armadillo (Enderby, England), 1998.

Sarah Boss, *Mary's Story,* Barefoot Books (Bath, England), 1999.

Ann Pilling, *Who Laid the Cornerstone of the World?,* Lion Children's Books (Oxford, England), 1999.

Georgina Swinburne, reteller, *The Toy Soldier,* Pearson Educational (Harlow, England), 2000.

Cameron Fox, reteller, *The Ugly Duckling,* Pearson Educational (Harlow, England), 2000.

Rebecca Hazell, *The Barefoot Book of Heroic Children,* Barefoot Books (Bristol, England), 2000.

Saviour Pirotta, *Christian Festival Tales,* Raintree Steck-Vaughn (Austin, TX), 2000.

Anne Elizabeth Stickney, *The Loving Arms of God,* Eerdmans (Grand Rapids, MI), 2001.

Burleigh Mutén, reteller, *A Lady of a Thousand Names: Goddess Stories from Many Cultures,* Barefoot Books (New York, NY), 2001.

Arthur Scholey, reteller, *Baboushka: A Christmas Folktale from Russia,* third edition, Candlewick Press (Boston, MA), 2001.

Bryce Milligan, *Brigid's Cloak: An Ancient Irish Story,* Eerdman's (Grand Rapids, MI), 2002.

Murray Watts, reteller, *The Bible for Children from Good Books,* Good Books (Intercourse, PA), 2002.

Mary Joslin, *Saint Nicholas: The Story of the Real Santa Claus,* Lion (Oxford, England), 2003, Pauline Books & Media (Boston, MA), 2006.

Rina Singh, reteller, *A Forest of Stories: Magical Tree Tales from around the World,* Barefoot Books (Bath, England), 2003, Barefoot Books (Cambridge, MA), 2005.

Rebecca Winter, *The Lion Book of Prayers for Children,* Lion (Oxford, England), 2005, published as *Prayers for Children,* Good Books (Intercourse, PA), 2005.

Laurie Krebs, *We're Riding on a Caravan: An Adventure on the Silk Road,* Barefoot Books (Cambridge, MA), 2005.

Mary Joslin, *On That Christmas Night,* Good Books (Intercourse, PA), 2005.

Mary Joslin, *On That Easter Morning,* Good Books (Intercourse, PA), 2005.

Sidelights

British Illustrator Helen Cann has long been inspired by the artwork of people from many lands. Praised for creating stylized images that often incorporate ethnic motifs, rendered in watercolor, acrylics, and collage, Cann has created art for cards and gift books, as well as for books by children. Among the many titles that feature her illustrations are *Mary's Story,* by Sarah Boss, Arthur Scholey's adaptation *Baboushka: A Christmas Folktale from Russia,* Laurie Krebs' *We're Riding on a Caravan: An Adventure on the Silk Road,* and a selection of anthologies that collect myths, legends, biblical stories, and other tales for young readers. Praising Cann's work in *Baboushka* for its "softly textured beauty," a *Kirkus Reviews* writer added that her watercolor-and-collage art, with its rich colors and "wonderful patterns," "evoke the feeling of Russian folk art."

After receiving her art training at the University of Wales, Cann worked as a freelance illustrator. Her first book-illustration project, *The Barefoot Book of Mother and Daughter Tales*—published in the United States as *Mother and Daughter Tales*—contains ten folktales from around the world. According to a *Publishers Weekly* reviewer, the artist contributes an "inviting montage of motifs from various cultures." *The Barefoot Book of Father and Son Tales* also contains ten multicultural folktales, in this case revolving around fathers and sons, and here Cann's "watercolor illustrations . . . add to the drama of the tales," according to Karen K. Radtke in *School Library Journal.*

In illustrating Cherry Gilchrist's *A Calendar of Festivals: Celebrations from around the World,* Cann includes detailed watercolor images on each page, interpreting the legends and folktales related to eight different festivals, including Purim, Holi, Vesak, Halloween, Kwaanza, and the Russian New Year. "Cann subtly alters her palette and style to reflect the various geographical settings in her watercolor vignette and spot illustrations," observed a critic for *Publishers Weekly.* She uses a similar technique in her work for Joyce Denham's *A Child's Book of Celtic Prayers,* creating borders and pastoral motifs that, in the words of a *Publishers Weekly* reviewer, result in a "handsome volume." Cann's collage works for *We're Riding on a Caravan,* which opens a window onto China's historic trade route, "are bright and colorful, depicting a world much more beautiful than it is in reality," according to *School Library Journal* contributor Barbara Scotto.

A trip along the ancient Silk Road is brought to life in Helen Cann's illustrations for Laurie Krebs' picture book We're Riding on a Caravan. (Barefoot Books, 2005. Illustration © 2005 by Helen Cann. Reproduced by permission.)

Cann's stylized art is a perfect match with Josephine Evetts-Secker's retelling of ancient stories in **Mother and Daughter Tales.** (Abbeville Kids, 1996. Illustration © 1996 by Helen Cann. Reproduced by permission of Barefoot Books, Ltd.)

Many of the books featuring Cann's art involve biblical themes. In *Mary's Story,* a biography of the Virgin Mary by Sarah Boss, her watercolor and graphite paintings draw from medieval and Renaissance art and create a "distinct sense of time and place," according to a *Publishers Weekly* critic. Writing in *Booklist,* Ilene Cooper noted that "Cann's richly colored artwork adds depth" to Boss's text due to her use of "interesting perspectives and Italian Renaissance-style framings." *On That Easter Morning,* one of a pair of books Cann illustrated for Mary Joslin, include "graceful" images that "reflect the emotions elicited by each scene through the expressive faces of the biblical figures and the color palette," according to *School Library Journal* contributor Linda L. Walkins. Noting that Cann includes women and children in her "attractive, polished paintings," a *Kirkus Reviews* writer added that "Christ's crucifixion is handled delicately in both text and illustrations." "Cann's mixed-media pictures and add both authenticity and wonder to" *Brigid's Cloak: An Ancient Irish Story,* Bryce Milligan's melding of Christian and Druidic traditions.

Cann once told *SATA:* "My work is watercolor and collage with pencil over the top for depth and definition. I source papers for collage from around the world—Japanese and Indian newsprint, hand-made papers, even sweet/candy papers. This just makes for interesting patterns and surfaces. I am interested in composition and

often use grids and borders to offset the central image. I love using pattern in my artwork and research decorative motifs before beginning a picture. I have a large collection of reference material taken from textiles, ceramics, jewelry, and even body paint!"

Biographical and Critical Sources

PERIODICALS

Booklist, April 1, 1999, Karen Hutt, review of *The Barefoot Book of Mother and Son Tales,* p. 1404; October 1, 1999, Ilene Cooper, review of *Mary's Story,* p. 370; April 15, 2000, Ilene Cooper, review of *The Barefoot Book of Heroic Children,* p. 1540; October 15, 2002, Diane Foote, review of *Brigid's Cloak: An Ancient Irish Story,* p. 408; December 1, 2003, Gillian Engberg, review of *A Forest of Stories: Magical Tree Tales from around the World,* p. 683; June 1, 2005, Ilene Cooper, review of *Prayers for Children,* p. 1804; November 1, 2005, Jennifer Mattson, review of *We're Riding on a Caravan: An Adventure on the Silk Road,* p. 53.

Kirkus Reviews, October 1, 2001, review of *Baboushka,* p. 1433; September 15, 2003, review of *A Forest of Stories,* p. 1182; April 15, 2005, review of *Prayers for Children,* p. 484; September 1, 2005, review of *We're Riding on a Caravan,* p. 976; November 1, 2005, review of *On That Christmas Night,* p. 1194; March 15, 2006, review of *On That Easter Morning,* p. 293.

Publishers Weekly, October 28, 1996, review of *Mother and Daughter Tales,* p. 81; March 23, 1998, review of *A Child's Book of Celtic Prayers,* p. 95; September 28, 1998, review of *A Calendar of Festivals,* p. 102; January 4, 1999, "Story Time," p. 92; August 30, 1999, review of *Mary's Story,* p. 75; April 3, 2000, review of *The Barefoot Book of Heroic Children,* p. 82; September 9, 2002, review of *Brigid's Cloak,* p. 64; September 5, 2005, review of *We're Riding on a Caravan,* p. 61.

School Library Journal, December, 1998, Pam Gosner, review of *A Calendar of Festivals,* p. 102; June, 1999, Karen K. Radtke, review of *The Barefoot Book of Father and Son Tales,* p. 114; August, 2001, Patricia Pearl Dole, review of *The Loving Arms of God,* p. 173; February, 2003, Sally R. Dow, review of *Brigid's Cloak,* p. 136; January, 2004, Marlene Gawron, review of *A Forest of Stories,* p. 122; January, 2006, Barbara Scotto, review of *We're Riding on a Caravan,* p. 119; May, 2006, Linda L. Walkins, review of *On That Easter Morning,* p. 113.

ONLINE

Helen Cann Home Page, http://www.helencann.co.uk (May 15, 2007).

CATANESE, P.W. 1961-

Personal

Born April 19, 1961, in Mineola, NY; son of Ralph (a U.S. postal inspector) and Muriel Catanese; married; wife's name Lisa (a writer); children: Kristina, Michael, Andrew. *Education:* University of Connecticut, B.A. 1983.

Addresses

Home—CT. *Agent*—Peter Rubie, The Peter Rubie Literary Agency, 240 W. 35th St., Ste. 500, New York, NY 10001. *E-mail*—pwcatanese@aol.com.

Career

Children's book author and cartoonist. Writer for advertising, beginning 1984.

Writings

"FURTHER TALES ADVENTURE" NOVELS SERIES; FOR CHILDREN

The Thief and the Beanstalk, Simon & Schuster (New York, NY), 2005.

P.W. Catanese (Photo courtesy of P.W. Catanese.)

The Brave Apprentice, Simon & Schuster (New York, NY), 2005.
The Eye of the Warlock, Simon & Schuster (New York, NY), 2005.
The Mirror's Tale, Simon & Schuster (New York, NY), 2006.
The Riddle of the Gnome, Simon & Schuster (New York, NY), 2007.

Sidelights

In his novels for children, P.W. Catanese revisits the lives of well-known fairy-tale characters, but focuses on events as they unfold decades after the initial magic has transpired. In his first novel, *The Thief and the Beanstalk,* for instance, agile young Jack who climbed a beanstalk, outsmarted a giant, and won the goose that lays golden eggs has grown old. In Catanese's tale, Jack becomes the target of a group of thieves who want the riches in his lavish castle. When young Nick is recruited to venture into Jack's castle, he decides to climb the same beanstalk, but what he finds at the top is far more menacing than Jack's giant. The story of Hansel and Gretel is the starting-off point for *The Eye of the Warlock,* which follows three children on a journey that draws them into a magic world that they hope will yield its treasure. *The Brave Apprentice* finds another plucky lad determined to fill the shoes of the Brave Little Tailor half a century before, and vanquish a new generation of giants who are not intimidated by old stories. Noting that *The Brave Apprentice* benefits from "a brave young hero . . . and some really horrific trolls," *School Library Journal* contributor Susan L. Rogers added that Catanese's "characters are interestingly depicted." Reviewing *The Mirror's Tale,* which revisits the Snow White saga, Sue Giffard noted in the same periodical that, with the story's "exciting and action-filled climax,"the novel will appeal to readers seeking "fast-paced, easily read adventure fantasy." Also citing the series' appeal to reluctant readers, a *Publishers Weekly* reviewer explained of *The Thief and the Beanstalk* that, while "Catanese smartly plumbs this well-known story for all its moral ambiguity," his "plot brims with perilous battles, narrow escapes and truly icky elements."

Catanese told *SATA:* "I don't know how many writers can tell you the exact moment that led to them becoming an author, but I can. It happened several years ago. I'd been reading a lot of fairy tales to my kids at the time, including Jack and the Beanstalk. I thought it would be interesting to read a vividly descriptive scene of the giant beanstalk erupting from the ground—something that happens 'off-screen' in the original story. So, just to entertain myself really, I sat down and started to write it. And then I wanted some human reactions in the scene, so I wrote in a boy and some bad guys, without really knowing who they were or why they were there. And working backwards and forwards from that, I created the whole story around it.

"During that embryonic stage of creating the story, I decided almost immediately that I didn't want to do a

retelling of the original fairy tale. Instead, I chose to write about what occurs many years later, because it seemed like a fresher approach. And that became the basis for *The Thief and the Beanstalk,* and the rest of my first five novels—each tells about what happens forty, sixty, or one hundred years after the events of a classic fairy tale such as Hansel and Gretel, Snow White, or Rumpelstiltskin. I take the loose threads of the original story and use them to weave an exciting, fast-paced new adventure. My characters walk in the footsteps of the original heroes, and the echoes of the old stories are strong, but the stakes are higher, the action is grander, and the emotions run deeper."

Biographical and Critical Sources

PERIODICALS

Kliatt, November, 2005, Deirdre Root, review of *The Brave Apprentice,* p. 20.

Publishers Weekly, August 8, 2005, review of *The Thief and the Beanstalk,* p. 235.

School Library Journal, July, 2005, Beth Wright, review of *The Thief and the Beanstalk,* p. 100; October, 2005, Susan L. Rogers, review of *The Brave Apprentice,* p. 156; August, 2006, Sue Giffard, review of *The Mirror's Tale,* p. 117.

Voice of Youth Advocates, June, 2005, Melissa Moore, review of *The Thief and the Beanstalk,* p. 144; August, 2005, Melissa Moore, review of *The Brave Apprentice,* p. 231; April, 2007, Melissa Moore, review of *Riddle of the Gnome,* p. 62.

ONLINE

P.W. Catanese Home Page, http://www.pwcatanese.com (June 15, 2007).

* * *

CHRISTIE, Ann Philippa
See PEARCE, Philippa

* * *

CHURCH, Caroline Jayne

Personal

Born in Oxford, England; children: Ian, William. *Education:* Middlesex Polytechnic (design and illustration).

Addresses

Home and office—Farnham, Surrey, England. *Agent*—Eunice McMullen Children's Literary Agent, Ltd., Low Ibbotsholme Cottage, Off Bridge Lane, Troutbeck Bridge, Windmere, Cumbria LA23 1HU, England. *E-mail*—carolinejayne@lineone.net.

Career

Author and illustrator. Works variously as a greeting-card designer.

Awards, Honors

Kate Greenaway Award nomination, Publishing Design Award, and Stockport Book Award shortlist, all 2002, all for *Hungry Hen* by Richard Waring; Southampton Favourite Book to Share Award, Southampton Library Services, 2003.

Writings

SELF-ILLUSTRATED

Do Your Ears Hang Low?: A Love Story, Scholastic (New York, NY), 2002.

Farmyard Carousel: A Fold-out Pop-up Farmyard with Play Pieces, Marks & Spencer (Chester, England), 2004.

Pond Goose, Oxford University Press (Oxford, England), 2004.

Ballet School Carousel: A Fold-out Pop-up Ballet School with Play Pieces, Marks & Spencer (Chester, England), 2004.

One Smart Goose, Orchard Books (New York, NY), 2005.

Scruff Sheep, Oxford University Press (Oxford, England), 2006.

Digby Takes Charge, Margaret K. McElderry Books (New York, NY), 2007.

One More Hug, Orchard Books (London, England), 2008.

ILLUSTRATOR

Wendy Hobson, abridger, *Frankenstein: The Modern Prometheus,* P. Bedrick Books (New York, NY), 1989.

Sheila Lavelle, *Fish Stew,* Paperbird, 1990.

Kate Khadir and Sue Nash, *Little Ghost,* Barron's (Happauge, NY), 1991.

Alan Gibbons, *S.O.S. Save Our Santa,* Dent Children's Books (London, England), 1992.

Margaret Ryan, *Millie Morgan, Pirate,* Walker (London, England), 1992.

Iris Smith, *Little Witch,* Barron's (Happauge, NY), 1993.

Theodore Clymer, *Animal Tales,* Ginn (Aylesbury, England), 1993.

Stewart Cowley, *From My Window,* Reader's Digest Association (Pleasantville, NY), 1994.

Stewart Cowley, *What's That Sound?,* Reader's Digest Association (Pleasantville, NY), 1994.

Tony Bradman, *One Puzzled Parrot,* Collins Educational (London, England), 1994.

Stewart Cowley, *Getting Dressed,* Joshua Morris (Bath, England), 1994.

Stewart Cowley, *Yellow Fish, Blue Fish,* Joshua Morris (Bath, England), 1994.

Karen Dolby, *Chocolate Island,* Usborne (London, England), 1994.

Tessa Krailing, *Supersnail,* Puffin (London, England), 1994.

Stewart Cowley, *My Wild Animals,* Joshua Morris (Bath, England), 1995.

Stewart Cowley, *My Toy Garage,* Joshua Morris (Bath, England), 1995.

Stewart Cowley, *My Dolls' House,* Joshua Morris (Bath, England), 1995.

Stewart Cowley, *My Busy Farm,* Joshua Morris (Bath, England), 1995.

Karen Dolby, *The Usborne Book of Young Puzzle Adventures: Lucy and the Sea Monster, Chocolate Island, Dragon in the Cupboard,* Usborne (London, England), 1995.

Julia Eccleshare, *Stories to Share,* Hodder Children's (London, England), 1996.

Joanne Reay, *Hippo Pot and Hippo Tot,* Ginn (Aylesbury, England), 1996.

Tim Healey, *Real Magic: A First Story about Things That Change,* Reader's Digest Children's Books (Bath, England), 1997.

Tim Healey, *The Farmyard Band: A First Story about Sound,* Reader's Digest Children's Books (Bath, England), 1997.

Alison Prince, *Fatso's Rat,* Hodder Children's (London, England), 1997.

Alison Prince, *Fergus-Fabulous Ferret,* Hodder Children's (London, England), 1997.

Karolina Edge, *Freddy's Wish,* Heinemann Library (Oxford, England), 1998.

Martine Oborne, *I Love You More,* Tango (London, England), 1998.

Siobhán Brandon, *The Bird's Story; The Buffalo's Story,* Zero to Ten (Slough, England), 1999.

Siobhán Brandon, *The Honey Badger's Story; The Honey Guide's Story,* Zero to Ten (Slough, England), 1999.

Gill Davies, *Little Ladybird,* Reader's Digest Children's Books (Bath, England), 1999.

Linda Jennings, *Nine Naughty Kittens,* Little Tiger (London, England), 1999.

Miriam Moss, *What's That Shape?,* Macdonald Young Books (Hove, England), 1999.

Mandy Ross, *The Wiggly Worms,* Ladybird (London, England), 1999.

Moira Butterfield, *Whose Ears?,* Ladybird (London, England), 2000.

Moira Butterfield, *Whose Bottom?,* Ladybird (London, England), 2000.

Richard Waring, *Hungry Hen,* HarperCollins Publishers (New York, NY), 2001.

Nancy I. Sanders, *The Pet I'll Get,* Reader's Digest Children's Books (Bath, England), 2001.

Jonathan Emmett, *A Turtle in the Toilet: A Pop-up Book,* Tiger Tales (Wilton, CT), 2002.

Jonathan Emmett, *A Mouse in the Marmalade: A Pop-up Book,* Tiger Tales (Wilton, CT), 2002.

Karen Dolby, *Lucy and the Sea Monster,* Usborne (London, England), 2002.

Kath Smith, *Fairies Are Fun,* Marks & Spencer (London, England), 2002.

Kath Smith, *Princesses Are Pretty,* Marks & Spencer (London, England), 2002.

First Prayers, Marks & Spencer (London, England), 2003.

Pippa Goodhart, *Pudding,* Chicken House (London, England), 2003.

Ian Whybrow, *Wobble Bear,* Oxford University Press (Oxford, England), 2003.

Ian Whybrow, *Wobble Bear Says Yellow,* Oxford University Press (Oxford, England), 2003.

Pippa Goodhart, *Pudgy: A Puppy to Love,* Scholastic (New York, NY), 2003.

Francesca Simon, *Hugo and the Bullyfrogs,* Gullane Children's (London, England), 2005.

Kath Smith, *Mermaids Are Amazing,* Marks & Spencer (Chester, England), 2005.

Kath Smith, *Ballerinas Are Beautiful,* Marks & Spencer (Chester, England), 2005.

Bernadette Rossetti-Shustak, *I Love You through and Through,* Scholastic (New York, NY), 2005.

Michaela Morgan, *Dear Bunny: A Bunny Love Story,* Chicken House (Frome, England), 2006.

Laurie Berkner, *The Story of My Feelings,* Scholastic (New York, NY), 2007.

Sidelights

Award-winning British artist Caroline Jayne Church incorporates bright colors, pleasing shapes, and texture in the majority of her illustrations for children's books. Church's illustration work is inspired by American folk art, which influences the paper cut outs the artist uses to form her collage images. In addition to her work both illustrating and writing children's books, Church has also created a popular line of greeting cards, prints and posters.

Church's self-illustrated *One Smart Goose* showcases her talent for integrating her paper collage art within an engaging story. The book recounts the tale of a white goose who is outcast by his fellow flock members because of the muddy condition of his feathers. The tidy and well-groomed geese around him eventually come to realize that being unkempt has its benefits: their dirty friend is able to camouflage himself from the hungry wolf who menaces the flock during the summer night. During the winter the clever but dingy goose finally takes a bath, thereby blending with the winter snow to conceal himself from the wolf, but when he suggests to his now-dirty flockmates that they do the same, the silly geese refuse to listen. Ultimately, the wise white goose must use his wits to save his empty-headed friends from the stealthy predator. *Booklist* reviewer Carolyn Phelan labeled Church's story "clever," and went on to remark that the child-friendly "illustrations are the book's most striking feature." Rachel G. Payne noted in her *School Library Journal* review that Church's "simple, playful text is full of fun sound effects and repeated phrases," while her textured collages "give the images depth." A *Publishers Weekly* critic dubbed *One Smart Goose* an "uplifting outing" that applauds individuality and cleverness.

Author and artist Caroline Jayne Church inspires children with her love of nature through her picture book **One Smart Goose.** (Orchard Books, 2003. Illustration © 2003 by Caroline Jayne Church. Reproduced by permission of Scholastic, Inc.)

Biographical and Critical Sources

PERIODICALS

Booklist, January 1, 2002, Hazel Rochman, review of *Hungry Hen,* p. 868; March 1, 2005, Carolyn Phelan, review of *One Smart Goose,* p. 1202; February 1, 2006, Karin Snelson, review of *Dear Bunny: A Bunny Love Story,* p. 44.

Kirkus Reviews, November 1, 2001, review of *Hungry Hen,* p. 1555; December 1, 2001, review of *Do Your Ears Hang Low?,* p. 1682; April 1, 2003, review of *Pudgy: A Puppy to Love,* p. 534; April 1, 2005, review of *One Smart Goose,* p. 414; January 1, 2006, review of *Dear Bunny,* p. 44.

Publishers Weekly, December 12, 1994, review of *Getting Dressed,* p. 63; December 12, 1994, review of *Yellow Fish, Blue Fish,* p. 63; December 12, 1994, review of *What's That Sound?,* p. 63; December 12, 1994, review of *From My Window,* p. 63; December 20, 1999, review of *Hugo and the Bully Frogs,* p. 79; November 5, 2001, review of *The Bird's Story; The Buffalo's Story,* p. 70; November 26, 2001, review of *Hungry Hen,* p. 60; January 21, 2002, review of *Do Your Ears Hang Low?,* p. 88; December 23, 2003, review of *Pudgy,* p. 69; April 11, 2005, review of *One Smart Goose,* p. 54.

School Library Journal, March, 2000, Olga R. Barnes, review of *Hugo and the Bully Frogs,* p. 212; January, 2002, Mary Elam, review of *Hungry Hen,* p. 112; February, 2002, Blair Christolon, review of *Do Your Ears Hang Low?,* p. 118; April, 2003, Sally R. Dow, review of *Pudgy,* p. 120; February, 2004, Carolyn Janssen, review of *Cluck, Cluck Who's There?,* p. 118; April, 2005, Martha Topol, review of *I Love You through and Through,* p. 110; May, 2005, Rachel G. Payne, review of *One Smart Goose,* p. 79.

ONLINE

Art in a Click Web site, http://dev.artinaclick.com/ (May 16, 2007).

Bloomsbury Web site, http://www.bloomsbury.com/ (May 16, 2007), "Caroline Jayne Church."

Caroline Jayne Church Home Page, http://www.caroline-jaynechurch.com (May 16, 2007).

Eunice McMullen Children's Literary Agent Web site, http://www.eunicemcmullen.co.uk/ (May 16, 2007), "Caroline Jayne Church."

HarperCollins Children's Web site, http://www.harpercollinschildrens.com/ (May 16, 2007), "Caroline Jayne Church."*

*   *   *

COONEY, Caroline B. 1947-

Personal

Born May 10, 1947, in Geneva, NY; daughter of Dexter Mitchell (a purchasing agent) and Martha (a teacher) Bruce; married (divorced); children: Louisa, Sayre, Harold. *Education:* Attended Indiana University, 1965-66, Massachusetts General Hospital School of Nursing, 1966-67, and University of Connecticut, 1968. *Religion:* Congregational. *Hobbies and other interests:* Playing the piano and organ, singing.

Addresses

Home—Westbrook, CT. *Agent*—Curtis Brown Ltd., 10 Astor Pl., New York, NY 10003.

Career

Author, 1978—.

Member

Authors Guild, Authors League of America, Mystery Writers of America.

Awards, Honors

Award for Juvenile Literature, American Association of University Women, North Carolina chapter, 1980, for *Safe as the Grave;* Romantic Book Award, Teen Romance category, 1985, for body of work; International Reading Association/Children's Book Centre Choice designation, Pacific States Award, and Iowa Teen Award, all for *The Face on the Milk Carton;* Best Young-Adult Fiction Books citation, *Booklist,* 1993, for *Flight Number 116 Is Down;* American Library Association (ALA) Notable Children's Book designation, 1990, for *The Face on the Milk Carton,* 2001, for *The Ransom of Mercy Carter,* and 2002, for *Goddess of Yesterday.*

Writings

YOUNG-ADULT FICTION

Safe as the Grave, illustrated by Gail Owens, Coward, McCann (New York, NY), 1979.

The Paper Caper, illustrated by Gail Owens, Coward, McCann (New York, NY), 1981.

An April Love Story, Scholastic (New York, NY), 1981.

Nancy and Nick, Scholastic (New York, NY), 1982.

He Loves Me Not, Scholastic (New York, NY), 1982.

A Stage Set for Love, Archway (New York, NY), 1983.

Holly in Love, Scholastic (New York, NY), 1983.

I'm Not Your Other Half, Putnam (New York, NY), 1984.

Sun, Sea, and Boys, Archway (New York, NY), 1984.

Nice Girls Don't, Scholastic (New York, NY), 1984.

Rumors, Scholastic (New York, NY), 1985.

Trying Out, Scholastic (New York, NY), 1985.

Suntanned Days, Simon & Schuster (New York, NY), 1985.

Racing to Love, Archway (New York, NY), 1985.

The Bad and the Beautiful, Scholastic (New York, NY), 1985.

The Morning After, Scholastic (New York, NY), 1985.

All the Way, Scholastic (New York, NY), 1985.

Saturday Night, Scholastic (New York, NY), 1986.

Don't Blame the Music, Putnam (New York, NY), 1986.

Saying Yes, Scholastic (New York, NY), 1987.

Last Dance, Scholastic (New York, NY), 1987.

The Rah Rah Girl, Scholastic (New York, NY), 1987.

Among Friends, Bantam (New York, NY), 1987.

Camp Boy-Meets-Girl, Bantam (New York, NY), 1988.

New Year's Eve, Scholastic (New York, NY), 1988.

Summer Nights, Scholastic (New York, NY), 1988.

The Girl Who Invented Romance, Bantam (New York, NY), 1988, reprinted, Delacorte (New York, NY), 2006.

Camp Reunion, Bantam (New York, NY), 1988.

Family Reunion, Bantam (New York, NY), 1989, reprinted, Delacorte (New York, NY) 2004.

The Fog, Scholastic (New York, NY), 1989.

The Face on the Milk Carton, Bantam (New York, NY), 1990.

The Snow, Scholastic (New York, NY), 1990.

The Fire, Scholastic (New York, NY), 1990.

The Party's Over, Scholastic (New York, NY), 1991.

The Cheerleader, Scholastic (New York, NY), 1991.

Twenty Pageants Later, Bantam (New York, NY), 1991.

The Perfume, Scholastic (New York, NY), 1992.

Operation: Homefront, Bantam (New York, NY), 1992.

Freeze Tag, Scholastic (New York, NY), 1992.

The Return of the Vampire (sequel to *The Cheerleader*), Scholastic (New York, NY), 1992.

Flight Number 116 Is Down, Scholastic (New York, NY), 1992.

The Vampire's Promise (sequel to *The Return of the Vampire*), Scholastic (New York, NY), 1993.

Whatever Happened to Janie? (sequel to *The Face on the Milk Carton*), Scholastic (New York, NY), 1993.

Forbidden, Scholastic (New York, NY), 1993.

The Stranger, Scholastic (New York, NY), 1993.

Twins, Scholastic (New York, NY), 1994.

Emergency Room, Scholastic (New York, NY), 1994.

Driver's Ed, Bantam (New York, NY), 1994.

Flash Fire, Scholastic (New York, NY), 1995.

Night School, Scholastic (New York, NY), 1995.

The Voice on the Radio (sequel to *What Ever Happened to Janie?*), Delacorte Press (New York, NY), 1996.

The Terrorist, Scholastic (New York, NY), 1997.

Wanted!, Scholastic (New York, NY), 1997.

What Child Is This?: A Christmas Story, Delacorte Press (New York, NY), 1997.

Burning Up, Delacorte Press (New York, NY), 1999.

Tune in Anytime, Delacorte Press (New York, NY), 1999.

What Janie Found (sequel to *The Voice on the Radio*), Delacorte Press (New York, NY), 2000.

The Ransom of Mercy Carter, Delacorte Press (New York, NY), 2001.

Fatality, Scholastic (New York, NY), 2001.

Goddess of Yesterday, Delacorte (New York, NY), 2002.

Code Orange, Delacorte (New York, NY), 2005.

Hit the Road, Delacorte (New York, NY), 2005.

A Friend at Midnight, Delacorte (New York, NY), 2006.

Enter Three Witches: A Story of Macbeth, Scholastic (New York, NY), 2007.

Diamonds in the Shadows, Delacorte (New York, NY), 2007.

"TIME-TRAVEL" NOVEL SERIES; FOR YOUNG ADULTS

Both Sides of Time, Delacorte Press (New York, NY), 1995.

Out of Time, Delacorte Press (New York, NY), 1996.

Prisoner of Time, Delacorte Press (New York, NY), 1998.

For All Time, Delacorte Press (New York, NY), 2001.

Time Travelers, Volume One (contains *Both Sides of Time* and *Out of Time*), Laurel Leaf (New York, NY), 2006.

Time Travelers, Volume Two (contains *Prisoner of Time* and *For All Time*), Laurel Leaf (New York, NY), 2006.

OTHER

Rear View Mirror (adult novel), Random House (New York, NY), 1980.

Sand Trap (adult novel), Berkley (New York, NY), 1983.

Contributor of stories to periodicals, including *Seventeen, American Girl, Jack and Jill, Humpty Dumpty,* and *Young World.*

Adaptations

Rear View Mirror was adapted as a television movie starring Lee Remick, Warner Bros., 1984; *The Face on the Milk Carton* and *Whatever Happened to Janie?* were adapted as a television movie broadcast by CBS in 1995. Many of Cooney's books have been adapted as audiobooks.

Sidelights

A prolific author for young adults, Caroline B. Cooney has become known for her teen romances as well as for writing more edgy novels that explore the ways that the horrors of the world at large can infiltrate even the most mundane life of the average American adolescent. While she began her writing career focusing on adult readers, Cooney quickly learned that she had a gift for connecting with young adults, and this led her to "the type of writing that I could both be successful at and enjoy," as she once recalled. In addition to winning the respect of critics for their likeable protagonists, fast-moving plots, and relevant topical focus, her novels *The Face on the Milk Carton, The Ransom of Mercy Carter,* and *The Girl Who Invented Romance* are also considered must-reads by many teens.

Cooney began writing when she was a young homemaker raising three children. "Sitting home with the babies," the writer once commented, "I had to find a way to entertain myself. So I started writing with a pencil, between the children's naps—baby in one arm, notebook in the other." She had difficulty marketing her novel-length historical novels for adults, but found that the short stories she wrote for a young-adult readership were quickly accepted by magazines such as *Seventeen.* "Having already written eight books with no luck," Cooney once recalled, "I wasn't interested in wasting my time writing another unpublishable novel. So instead I wrote an outline [of a teen mystery novel] and mailed it along with my short story-resumé to a number of publishers, saying, 'Would you be interested in seeing this'—knowing, of course, that they wouldn't. Naturally, when they all said 'yes,' I was stunned; the only thing to do was to quick write the book." That book was published in 1979 as *Safe as the Grave.*

Safe as the Grave, in which a young girl encounters a secret in the family cemetery, was followed up by Cooney with the adult suspense novel *Rear View Mirror,* the story of a young woman who is kidnapped and

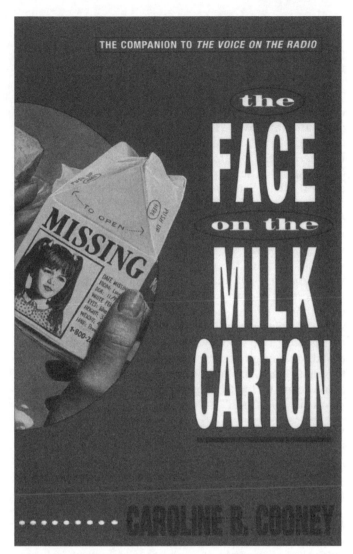

Cover of Caroline B. Cooney's well-known novel **The Face on the Milk Carton,** *featuring artwork by Derek James.* (Laurel-Leaf Books, 1990. Cover art © 1990 by Derek James. Reproduced by permission of Dell Publishing, a division of Random House, Inc.)

forced to drive two killers in her car. Michele Slung, reviewing Cooney's second novel for the *Washington Post,* called *Rear View Mirror* "so tightly written, so fast-moving, that it's easy not to realize until the last paragraph is over that one hasn't been breathing all the while." In 1984 *Rear View Mirror* was made into a television movie starring Lee Remick as the kidnapped woman.

Cooney returned to young-adult writing with *An April Love Story,* a romance novel published in 1981. Except for one more adult novel—1983's *Sand Trap*—her focus is now exclusively on a young-adult readership, and her original story ideas have been supplemented by plot suggestions from her editor as well as by her contribution to the "Cheerleader" and "Chrystal Falls" novel series. "It is exciting 'to write to order,'" Cooney once explained. "It often involves an idea or characters I've never thought about before, and I have to tackle it cold like any other assignment. Editors have such good

ideas! I also continue to write my own ideas, like *The Girl Who Invented Romance.* 'Romance' is a board game that Kelly designs and the board game [is] part of the book."

Though Cooney enjoys penning teen romances and stories of strong friendships such as the 2006 cross-generational novel *Hit the Road,* many of her books deal with serious topical issues that affect teens directly. In *Operation: Homefront,* a wife and mother with three children is called up for National Guard duty and shipped off to Saudi Arabia during the Gulf War, while *Family Reunion* focuses on a teen dealing with her parents' separation and divorce, as well as with her dad's remarriage. In *A Friend at Midnight* a teen must decide whether to betray a confidence when her older sister insists on inviting their abusive father to her wedding, while *Burning Up* finds an affluent Connecticut adolescent coming fact to face with prejudice after the inner-city church where she volunteers is torched by an arsonist. As Stephanie Zvirin noted in her *Booklist* review of *Burning Up,* Cooney excels at portraying both "the tentative boy-girl relationship between" her teen protagonists," and the "questioning and fervor that propels some teens to look beyond themselves and their families to larger issues."

While teens encounter divorce, prejudice, and separation within their own families and personal interactions, other, more abstract issues are made equally personal in several of Cooney's timely works of fiction. In *The Terrorist,* for example, she deals with the sobering subject of international terrorism, and, in the opinion of a *Publishers Weekly* contributor, "combines heartpounding suspense with some sobering reflections on the insular attitude characteristic of many Americans both at home and abroad." Terrorism of a different kind is the focus of *Code Orange,* a novel written in response to the nation's state of heightened vigilance following the September 11, 2001 terrorist attacks on its shores. While conducting research for a school paper on smallpox, slacker prep-school student Mitty Blake discovers an old envelope tucked into a book that contains 100-year-old smallpox scabs. As the Manhattan teen researches the highly contagious infectious disease, he realizes that he may have infected himself; in fact, he may be a danger to everyone he has contacted since first opening the envelope. Panic turns into a bumbling attempt to solve the problem as Mitty ultimately contacts both Federal authorities and inadvertantly attracts the notice of a terrorist group that has far darker motives. Praising *Code Orange* in *Horn Book,* Jeannine M. Chapman noted that Mitty's growing resourcefulness "is believably conveyed," as the "lighthearted tone" at the beginning of the novel builds to a "thrilling climax (with a twist)." A *Publishers Weekly* wrote that the author's "rat-a-tat delivery and hairpin turns keep the pages turning," and *Booklist* contributor John Peters cited the novel's "profoundly disturbing premise" and "its likable, ultimately heroic slacker protagonist."

Perhaps Cooney's most widely read novel, the critically acclaimed *The Face on the Milk Carton,* deals with the topic of child abduction. Janie Johnson is kidnapped when she is three years old by Hannah, a teenaged cult member; unaware of her past, she is raised by Hannah's parents. Janie's picture, displayed on a milk carton as that of a missing child, leads her to uncover her past. Cooney continues Janie's story in the novels *What Ever Happened to Janie?, The Voice on the Radio,* and *What Janie Found,* which follow the efforts of Cooney's determined young heroine to discover the truth about her family and her true identity. Citing Cooney's "skilled writing," a *Publishers Weekly* reviewer noted of *The Face on the Milk Carton* that the book's likeable protagonist and "suspenseful, impeccably-paced action add to this novel's appeal" among teen readers. "Cooney seems to have a special radar for adolescent longings and insecurities," noted another critic in the same periodical during a review of *The Voice on the Radio.* While the *Publishers Weekly* critic also noted the plot's lack of believability, this quality is more than outweighed by

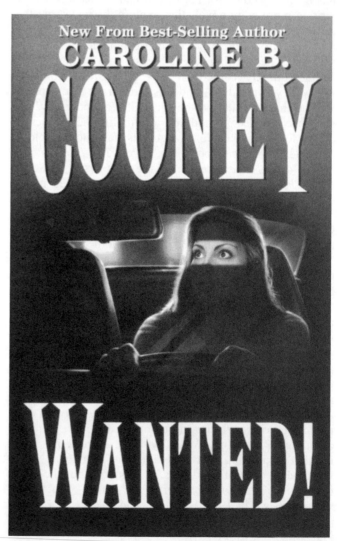

Cover of Cooney's teen thriller Wanted!, *which finds a teen accused of a murder she did not commit.* (Scholastic, Inc., 1997. Copyright © 1997 by Caroline B. Cooney. Reproduced by permission of Scholastic, Inc.)

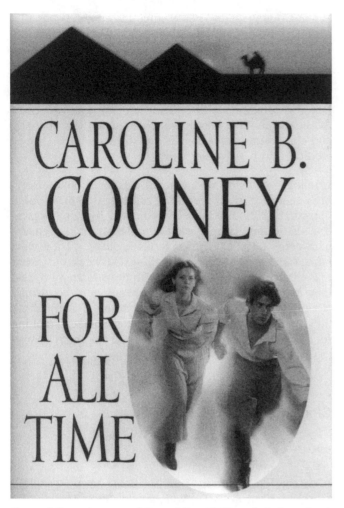

Cover of Cooney's young-adult novel For All Time, *featuring artwork by Craig White.* (Delacorte, 2001. Illustration © 2001 by Craig White. Reproduced by permission of Delacorte, a division of Random House, Inc.)

the novel's "psychological accuracy and well-aimed, gossipy views of teens," according to the reviewer.

Somewhat of a departure from her other books, Cooney's novel *Among Friends* features a unique structure. Six students have been given an assignment to write in journals during a three-month period. The entries from those journals, providing a variety of points of view, make up the novel. This approach, stated Mitzi Myers in the *Los Angeles Times,* provides "a more rounded interpretation than any single character could supply." Myers concluded: "It is a pleasure to find a book for young readers that not only individualizes characters through their writing but also has wise words to say about how writing offers very real help in coping with the problems of growing up."

Cooney mixes romance with science fiction with her "Time-Travel" novel series, which includes *Both Sides of Time, Out of Time, Prisoner of Time,* and *For All Time.* In *Both Sides of Time* readers meet high school graduate Annie Lockwood, whose romantic perspective would have made her better suited for life in the past. When Annie gets her wish and winds up in 1895, how-

ever, her twenty-first-century attitudes and expectations make her realize that living in the past means dealing with far more than long gowns, lavish balls, and dapper, respectful young gentlemen. However, when she falls in love with Strat, her link with the past is forever cemented, and she must learn to balance both her worlds. After revealing Annie's secret to his father in *Out of Time,* Strat is dismissed as insane and sent to a mental asylum. Despite the family problems in her modern life, Annie must now risk everything to return through time and bring her beloved to safety in her (for him) futuristic world. The series takes a new twist in *Prisoner of Time,* as Strat's sister Devonny finds herself betrothed to an unpleasant English noble and requires her brother's help in breaking the engagement. Surprise turns to romance when Annie's brother Tod Lockwood answers the call back through time. The series concludes in *For All Time,* as Annie's effort to control her travel through time misfires and she winds up at the right place but the wrong time . . . the very wrong time. Transported back into ancient times, Annie finds herself trapped in a Egyptian city. Meanwhile, her beloved Strat awaits her in the same city, three thousand years in the future, unaware of his time-traveling girlfriend's fate. In a review of *Both Sides of Time* for *Horn Book,* Sarah Guille deemed Cooney's story "suspenseful and poignant," noting that her heroine matures while learning an important lesson: "that real love has consequences and obligations that fantasies don't." Dubbing the series "a breathlessly romantic whirl through the centuries," a *Publishers Weekly* reviewer added that readers will be carried along by Cooney's "characteristically breezily, intimate style."

In *The Ransom of Mercy Carter,* Cooney offers readers another departure from her contemporary-theme novels: a historical fiction based on the 1704 raid on the English settlement at Deerfield, Massachusetts, when Kahnawake Mohawks destroyed the village and took more than 100 captives back to Canada. The novel focuses on young Mercy, a captive whose growing respect for the Native American culture into which she is forced must ultimately cause her to question her loyalty to her own family. Calling *The Ransom of Mercy Carter* a "gripping and thought-provoking account," a *Publishers Weekly* reviewer added that, though Cooney oversimplifies some historical elements, "the immediacy of Mercy's dilemma comes through." In her *Kliatt* review, Sally M. Tibbetts praised the author's detailed research, calling the novel "a great story about a young girl who learns to adapt and survive." Noting that Cooney raises "excellent questions" about how different cultures view what it means to be civilized or savage, *Booklist* contributor Gillian Engberg deemed *The Ransom of Mercy Carter* a "vivid, dramatic novel."

Another travel back through time is offered to readers of *Goddess of Yesterday,* which transports readers back to the classical world and the years leading up to the Trojan War. When readers meet Anaxandra, the six year old is living on an island in the Aegean sea until she is

sent as a hostage to the King of Siphnos. Six years later, her life is again thrown into turmoil when the king's palace is attacked and all are killed. By assuming the identity of the king's daughter, Callisto, Anaxandra is accepted at the palace of Sparta's King Menelaus, whose young wife is destined to become the fabled Helen of Troy. Charged with caring for the king's two-year-old son, Callisto/Anaxandra soon learns of the clandestine romantic affair between the boy's mother and Paris, prince of Troy. As the political tensions between Sparta and Troy mount, Helen's jealousy of her grows, forcing Callisto/Anaxandra to navigate the shifting allegiances in order to survive. Her destiny alters once again when she is ordered to accompany Helen and her young son on the deceitful queen's pivotal journey to Troy. There, in the company of her lover, the ill-fated Trojan prince Paris, one of the most dramatic battles of the ancient world will play out. Reviewing the novel for *Horn Book*, Kristi Elle Jemtegaard described *Goddess of Yesterday* as "by turns gruesome, dramatic, and tenderly domestic." In *Booklist*, Frances Bradburn praised Cooney for the "fresh perspective" from which she spins her "exciting, complex adventure story," although the critic added that the plot might confuse teens unfamiliar with the history of the Trojan War. In the opinion of *Kliatt* contributor Claire Rosser, *Goddess of Yesterday* stands as one of Cooney's "most ambitious" books for teen readers. Through the book's likeable fictional heroine, the novel "will make the ancient Greek world" come alive for teens, Rosser added, especially the actual men and women who figure in the tragedies preserved through the literary works of "Homer and the Greek dramatists." Noting that Cooney refashions the classic tale as a "grand adventure with a heroic girl at the center," Angela J. Reynolds predicted in *School Library Journal* that her "fine-tuned adventure . . . may leave middle-schoolers asking to read Homer."

History again mixes with literature in *Enter Three Witches: A Story of Macbeth*, which a *Publishers Weekly* contributor dubbed a "compulsively readable, behind-the-scenes peek into the rise and fall of Lord and Lady Macbeth." In bringing the Shakespearean drama to life for teens—revealing portions of the bard's text begin each chapter—Cooney mixes the play's characters with fictional ones such as Lady Mary, the fourteen-year-old ward of Lady Macbeth's until her father falls from grace and she is promised in marriage to a ruthless friend of the Scottish king. In her "engaging" retelling of the tragic story of how the lust for power can destroy lives and torment the soul, Cooney crafts prose with what *School Library Journal* reviewer Nancy Menaldi-Scanlan described as an "elevated tone." "While it may be difficult at first," the critic hastened to add, Cooney's text is "interesting and appropriate" enough to sustain reader interest. Although noting that fans of the original drama can most fully appreciate Cooney's "fascinating, humanizing" insight into each familiar character, Phelan added in *Booklist* that the likeable teen at the center of *Enter Three Witches* will engage fans of historical fiction and even inspire some to track out *Macbeth* in the original.

When Cooney started her writing career, she wrote in a spontaneous fashion. "I never used to know what was going to happen in the story until I wrote it," she once observed. "Then I began doing paperbacks for Scholastic and they required outlines, largely just to ensure that two writers didn't waste time and effort on similar ideas. Before, I'd always allowed the story to develop out of the characters, but the outlines demanded that the plot and characters evolve together at the same time. Now I wouldn't do it any other way."

Cooney's decision to create novels with compelling, high-energy stories, interesting protagonists, and strong, upbeat resolutions has been prompted by her observation that young people want stories that end on an upbeat note and a future that looks positive. "They want hope," she explained, "want things to work out, want reassurance that even were they to do something rotten, they and the people around them would still be alright. No matter what it is that they're doing, I don't think they want to have to read about it. Teenagers looking for books to read don't say, 'Oh, good, another depressing story.'"

Biographical and Critical Sources

BOOKS

Beacham's Guide to Literature for Young Adults, Thomson Gale (Detroit, MI), Volume 10, 2000, Volume 11, 2000.

Carroll, Pamela Sissi, *Caroline Cooney: Faith and Fiction* ("Scarecrow Studies in Young-Adult Literature" series), Scarecrow Press (Metuchen, NJ), 2002.

Drew, Bernard A., *The One Hundred Most Popular Young Adult Authors*, Libraries Unlimited (Englewood, CO), 1996.

St. James Guide to Young-Adult Writers, 2nd edition, St. James Press (Detroit, MI), 1999.

PERIODICALS

ALAN Review, winter, 1994.

Booklist, March 15, 1993, review of *Flight Number 116 Is Down*, p. 89; June 1, 1994, Stephanie Zvirin, review of *Driver's Ed*, p. 1809; November 1, 1995, Susan Dove Lempke, review of *Flash Fire*, p. 464; February 15, 1996, Sally Estes, review of *Out of Time*, p. 1004; July, 1997, Anne O'Malley, review of *The Terrorist*, p. 1810; June 1, 1998, Sally Estes, review of *Prisoner of Time*, p. 1745; December 1, 1998, Stephanie Zvirin, review of *Burning Up*, p. 661; April 1, 2001, Gillian Engberg, review of *The Ransom of Mercy Carter*, p. 1481; September 15, 2001, Debbie Carton, review of *For All Time*, p. 215; June 1, 2002, Frances Bradburn, review of *Goddess of Yesterday*, p. 1704; September 1, 2005, John Peters, review of *Code Orange*, p. 124; March 15, 2006, review of *Hit the Road*, p. 46; De-

cember 15, 2006, Jennifer Mattson, review of *A Friend at Midnight*, p. 44; March 1, 2007, Carolyn Phelan, review of *Enter Three Witches: A Story of Macbeth*, p. 73.

Bulletin of the Center for Children's Books, July-August, 1986, review of *Don't Blame the Music*, p. 205; April, 1991, review of *The Party's Over*, p. 187; December, 1992, review of *Operation: Homefront*, p. 108; September, 1994, review of *Driver's Ed*, p. 10; October, 1995, review of *Both Sides of Time*, p. 50; May, 1996, review of *Out of Time*, p. 296; November, 1999, review of *Tune in Anytime*, p. 87; March, 2000, review of *What Janie Found*, p. 241; November, 2001, review of *For All Time*, p. 97; July, 2002, review of *Goddess of Yesterday*, p. 397; June, 2006, Deborah Stevenson, review of *Hit the Road*, p. 448.

Horn Book, November-December, 1995, Sarah Guille, review of *Both Sides of Time*, p. 745; November-December, 2003, Kristi Elle Jemtegaard, review of *Goddess of Yesterday*, p. 774; September-October, 2005, Jeannine M. Chapman, review of *Code Orange*, p. 574.

Kirkus Reviews, June 15, 1993, p. 783; September 1, 2005, review of *Code Orange*, p. 970; March 1, 2007, review of *Enter Three Witches*, p. 218.

Kliatt, March, 1993, p. 4; May, 1993, p. 4; March, 2003, Sally M. Tibbetts, review of *The Ransom of Mercy Carter*, p. 21; September, 2003, Barbara McKee, review of *For All Time*, p. 24; January, 2004, Claire Rosser, review of *Goddess of Yesterday*, p. 16; September, 2005, Paula Rohrlick, review of *Code Orange*, p. 6.

Los Angeles Times, February 6, 1988, Mitzi Myers, "High Schoolers Learn about the Meaning of Friendship."

Publishers Weekly, June 18, 1979; August 25, 1989, review of *The Fog*, p. 65; January 12, 1990, review of *The Face on the Milk Carton*, p. 62; March 23, 1992, review of *Flight Number 116 Is Down*, p. 73; June 14, 1993, review of *Whatever Happened to Janie?*, p. 72; July 4, 1994, review of *Unforgettable*, p. 65; July 10, 1995, review of *Both Sides of Time*, p. 59; July 22, 1996, review of *The Voice on the Radio*, p. 242; July 28, 1997, review of *The Terrorist*, p. 75; October 6, 1997, review of *What Child Is This?*, p. 57; December 7, 1998, review of *Burning Up*, p. 61; July 26, 1999, review of *Tune In Anytime*, p. 92; January 3, 2000, review of *What Janie Found*, p. 77; February 12, 2001, review of *The Ransom of Mercy Carter*, p. 213; October 22, 2001, review of *For All Time*, p. 77; July 8, 2002, review of *Goddess of Yesterday*, p. 50; September 5, 2005, review of *Code Orange*, p. 63; May 22, 2006, review of *Hit the Road*, p. 54; November 6, 2006, review of *A Friend at Midnight*, p. 62; April 2, 2007, review of *Enter Three Witches*, p. 58.

School Library Journal, February, 1990, Tatiana Castleton, review of *The Face on the Milk Carton*, p. 109; February, 1992, review of *Flight Number 116 Is Down*, p. 107; November, 1992, Kenneth E. Kowen, review of *Operation: Homefront*, p. 88; June, 1993, Jacqueline Rose, review of *Whatever Happened to Janie?*, p. 126; August, 1994, Susan R. Farber, review of *Driver's Ed*, p. 168; July, 1995, Connie Tyrrell Burns, review of *Both Sides of Time*, p. 168; February, 1999, Claudia Moore, review of *The Voice on the Radio*, p. 69; August, 2001, Renee Steinberg, review of *The Ransom of Mercy Carter*, p. 213; June, 2002, Angela J. Reynolds, review of *Goddess of Yesterday*, p. 134; August, 2005, Blair Christolin, review of *The Ransom of Mercy Carter*, p. 48; October, 2005, Courtney Lewis, review of *Code Orange*, p. 156; November, 2006, Marie Orlando, review of *A Friend at Midnight*, p. 132; May, 2007, Nancy Menaldi-Scanlan, review of *Enter Three Witches*, p. 130.

Times Literary Supplement, May 20, 1988, review of *The Girl Who Invented Romance*.

Voice of Youth Advocates, February, 1990, review of *The Face on the Milk Carton*, p. 341; October, 1992, review of *Operation: Homefront*, p. 222; December, 1992, review of *The Return of the Vampire*, p. 291; April, 1993, review of *The Perfume*, pp. 20-21, 38; August, 1993, Samantha Hunt, review of *The Vampire's Promise*, p. 162; April, 1994, review of *The Stranger*, p. 36; August, 1994, review of *Emergency Room*, pp. 143-144; August, 1995, review of *Both Sides of Time*, p. 168; October, 1997, review of *The Terrorist*, p. 242; June, 1998, review of *What Child Is This?*, p. 128; February, 1999, review of *Burning Up*, p. 431; April, 2000, review of *What Janie Found*, p. 33; April 1, 2001, review of *The Ransom of Mercy Carter*, p. 36; June, 2001, review of *The Voice on the Radio*, p. 97; August, 2002, review of *Goddess of Yesterday*, p. 200; October, 2005, review of *Code Orange*, p. 298; December, 2006, review of *A Friend at Midnight*, p. 421.

Washington Post, June 1, 1980, Michele Slung, review of *Rear View Mirror*.

*　　*　　*

CORBMAN, Marjorie 1987-

Personal

Born 1987, in Morristown, NJ. *Education:* Attended Holy Cross College (MA). *Religion:* Eastern Orthodox.

Addresses

Home and office—Randolph, NJ. *E-mail*—lefteyeisanangel@aol.com.

Career

Author.

Writings

A Tiny Step away from Deepest Faith: A Teenager's Search for Meaning, Paraclete Press (Brewster, MA), 2005.

Biographical and Critical Sources

PERIODICALS

Booklist, October 1, 2005, Ilene Cooper, review of *A Tiny Step away from Deepest Faith: A Teenager's Search for Meaning*, p. 67.

Publishers Weekly, July 11, 2005, review of *A Tiny Step away from Deepest Faith,* p. 85; July, 25, 2005, review of *A Tiny Step from Deepest Faith,* p. 72.

Touchstone, January-February, 2006, Mother Macarta, review of *A Tiny Step away from Deepest Faith.*

United Church Observer, January, 2006, Janet Silman, review of *A Tiny Step away from Deepest Faith,* p. 48.

ONLINE

Holy Cross Web site, http://www.holycross.edu/ (May 16, 2007), "Marjorie Corbman, Debut Author."

Marjorie Corbman Home Page, http://www.marjoriecorbman.com (May 16, 2007).*

*   *   *

CRUISE, Robin 1951-

Personal

Born June 1, 1951 in Washington, DC; daughter of Robert Aloysius and Jessina Maria Cruise; married Richard S. Bayer (an attorney; divorced); children: Andrew, Henry, Hannah. *Hobbies and other interests:* Reading, writing, movies, long walks, spending time with family and friends, music, cooking, yoga.

Addresses

Home and office—San Diego, CA. *E-mail*—rcruisc2@san.rr.com.

Career

Author and editor. *Rocky Mountain News,* Denver, CO, former assistant editor and reporter; Harcourt, San Diego, CA, deputy publisher.

Writings

The Top-Secret Journal of Fiona Claire Jardin, Harcourt Brace (San Diego, CA), 1998.

Fiona's Private Pages, Harcourt Brace (San Diego, CA), 2000.

The Five Senses, Wright Group (DeSoto, TX), 2000.

Match Point, Artesian Press (Buena Park, CA), 2000.

The Nuclear Disaster at Chernobyl, Artesian Press (Buena Park, CA), 2000.

The Spooky Swamp Sound, Wright Group (DeSoto, TX), 2001.

Zoom!, Wright Group (DeSoto, TX), 2001.

(With Theresa Smythe) *Rainy Day Pals,* Harcourt Brace (San Diego, CA), 2002.

(With Theresa Smythe) *How a Book Gets Published,* Celebration Press (Parsippany, NJ), 2004.

Little Mamá Forgets, Farrar, Straus & Giroux (New York, NY), 2006.

Robin Cruise (Photograph courtesy of Robin Cruise.)

Only You, illustrated by Margaret Chodos-Irvine, Harcourt (Orlando, FL), 2006.

Contributor to periodicals, including *People, Travel & Leisure,* and *Allure.*

Sidelights

Robin Cruise has written a variety of books for young people, among them nonfiction, picture books, and several novels for young adults. Her young-adult novel *The Top-Secret Journal of Fiona Claire Jardin* follows the title character as she experiences the pressures of being a typical teen and also deals with her parents' divorce. Written in the first person, the book excerpts portions of the fictional Fiona's diary, allowing teen readers to fully empathize with the likable narrator. Helen T. Rosenberg, reviewing *The Top-Secret Journal of Fiona Claire Jardin* for *Booklist,* commented that Cruise's main character has a "voice [that] is at once lively, funny, and poignant." Fiona's saga continues in *Fiona's Private Pages,* which follows Fiona's life in the wake of her parents' divorce. Now Fiona and her brother are shuttled back and forth between each parent's new home, with the result that their friends become increasingly important. Linda L. Plevak remarked in her *School Library Journal* review of *Fiona's Private Pages* that Cruise, "like Judy Blume, . . . tackles serious issues but provides many opportunities for

laughter." *Booklist* contributor Susan Dove Lempke also praised the novel, noting that Cruise's "writing style is energetic and highly believable."

As she does in her teen novels, Cruise touches on real-life topics in her books for younger children. Praised as a "tender, heartfelt story" by *School Library Journal* contributor Catherine Callegari, *Little Mamá Forgets* describes the relationship a little girl named Lucy has with her grandmother now that the elderly woman suffers from Alzheimer's. The story is told from the point-of-view of Lucy as she shares time with her grandmother, Little Mamá. While Little Mamá will sometimes forget to tie her shoes and shows other lapses in memory, she never forgets to show her love to her granddaughter. Cruise also gives her poignant story a bilingual element by incorporating Spanish phrases throughout her text.

Biographical and Critical Sources

PERIODICALS

Booklist, April 15, 1998, Helen Rosenberg, review of *The Top-Secret Journal of Fiona Claire Jardin,* p. 1444; May 15, 2000, Susan Dove Lempke, review of *Fiona's Private Pages,* p. 1744; January 1, 2006, Ilene Cooper, review of *Little Mamá Forgets,* p. 92.

Kirkus Reviews, March 1, 2006, review of *Little Mamá Forgets,* p. 228.

Publishers Weekly, April 6, 1998, review of *The Top-Secret Journal of Fiona Claire Jardin,* p. 79; May 15, 2006, review of *Little Mamá Forgets,* p. 72.

Reading Teacher, March, 1999, review of *The Top-Secret Journal of Fiona Claire Jardin,* p. 627; February, 2001, review of *Fiona's Private Pages,* p. 542; April, 2001, Lynne T. Burke, review of *Fiona's Private Pages,* p. 32.

School Library Journal, April, 1998, Robin L. Gibson, review of *The Top-Secret Journal of Fiona Claire Jardin,* p. 128; June, 2000, review of *Fiona's Private Pages,* p. 142; August, 2006, Linda L. Plevak, review of *Little Mamá Forgets,* p. 78.

ONLINE

Robin Cruise Home Page, http://www.robincruise.com (May 16, 2007).

*   *   *

CYRUS, Kurt 1954-

Personal

Born August 17, 1954, in Redmond, OR; son of Warren H. and Joan Call Cyrus; partner of Linnea Lindberg. *Education:* Attended Oregon State University, 1974-76, and Art Center College of Design, 1978-80; Lane Community College, A.S. (respiratory therapy), 1985. *Hobbies and other interests:* Reforesting a twenty-acre tree farm.

Addresses

Home—Cottage Grove, OR. *E-mail*—kcyrus@efn.org.

Career

Children's book author and illustrator. Formerly worked as a fruit picker, forklift driver, and concrete mixer; Sacred Heart General Hospital, Eugene, OR, respiratory therapist, 1984-94; freelance author and illustrator, 1994—. SMART (Start Making A Reader Today) volunteer; Big Brother volunteer, 1998—.

Awards, Honors

Children's Choice Award, 1998, for *Tangle Town;* Christopher Award, 2000, for *The Mousery;* Pick of the Lists selection, American Booksellers Association, 2001, for *Oddhopper Opera;* PNBA Book Award, SSLI Honor, John Burroughs listee, *Skipping Stones* honor, and Beehive Award, all 2005, all for *Hotel Deep;* American Library Association Notable Book designation and Parents Choice honor, both 2006, both for *Mammoths on the Move* by Lisa Wheeler.

Writings

SELF-ILLUSTRATED

Tangle Town, Farrar, Straus & Giroux (New York, NY), 1997.

Slow Train to Oxmox, Farrar, Straus & Giroux (New York, NY), 1998.

Oddhopper Opera: A Bug's Garden of Verses, Harcourt (San Diego, CA), 2001.

Hotel Deep: Light Verse from Dark Water, Harcourt (Orlando, FL), 2005.

Tadpole Rex, Harcourt (Orlando, FL), 2008.

ILLUSTRATOR

Judith Mathews, *There's Nothing to D-o-o-o!,* Harcourt (San Diego, CA), 1999.

Charlotte Pomerantz, *The Mousery,* Harcourt (San Diego, CA), 2000.

Eve Bunting, *The Bones of Fred McFee,* Harcourt (San Diego, CA), 2002.

Lisa Wheeler, *Sixteen Cows,* Harcourt (San Diego, CA), 2002.

Lisa Wheeler, *Avalanche Annie: A Not-So-Tall Tale,* Harcourt (San Diego, CA), 2003.

M.T. Anderson, *Whales on Stilts,* Harcourt (Orlando, FL), 2005.

Anne Bustard, *Buddy: The Story of Buddy Holly,* Simon & Schuster (New York, NY), 2005.

Lisa Wheeler, *Mammoths on the Move,* Harcourt (Orlando, FL), 2006.

M.T. Anderson, *The Clue of the Linoleum Lederhosen* (sequel to *Whales on Stilts*), Harcourt (Orlando, FL), 2006.

Julia Durango, *Pest Fest,* Simon & Schuster (New York, NY), 2007.

Ann Whitford Paul, *Word Builder,* Simon & Schuster (New York, NY), 2008.

Sidelights

After years spent working odd jobs and almost a decade working as a respiratory therapist while developing his book-illustration career, Kurt Cyrus was able to leave his day job and pursue his first love full time. With 1997's *Tangle Town,* Cyrus made his picture book debut, and his more recent self-illustrated books, which include *Oddhopper Opera: A Bug's Garden of Verses* and *Tadpole Rex,* have been supplemented by illustration work for authors such as Lisa Wheeler, M.T. Anderson, Eve Bunting, and Anne Bustard. Reviewing Cyrus's work for Wheeler's prairie tale *Sixteen Cows,* a *Publishers Weekly* contributor wrote that the illustrator "uses the horizontal layouts to good effect in expansive watercolors of the golden prairie." Discussing *The Bones of Fred McFee,* a *Kirkus Reviews* critic concluded that Cyrus's mix of "smartly designed compositions and elongated perspectives creates an engrossingly eerie effect" in Bunting's Halloween-themed offering.

In *Tangle Town* Cyrus brings to life a place where everything is twisted up. When the mayor of Tangle Town cannot open his door because he is pushing when he should be pulling, he starts a chain reaction of misunderstandings similar to that caused during the children's game "Telephone." Ultimately, it takes a practical girl searching for a lost cow to straighten out the confusion in Tangle Town. Steven Engelfried, reviewing the book for *School Library Journal,* called Cyrus's illustrations "lively" and his story laden with "enough nonsense and wit to amuse most readers." Engelfried's opinion of Cyrus's debut picture book was borne out by *Tangle Town*'s selection as a Children's Choice Award in 1998.

In *Slow Train to Oxmox* Cyrus relates the story of Edwin Blink, who accidentally boards the wrong train one morning on the way to work. Instead of the express, Edwin finds himself aboard a slow train to nowhere. He is accompanied by a host of strange characters that help create a mood that a *Publishers Weekly* critic described as surrealist, dubbing *Slow Train to Oxmox* an "atmospheric tour de force." As the ride progresses, Edwin and his fellow travelers work to overcome a series of strange obstacles, yet they never reach a destination. In the opinion of Robin Tzannes, who reviewed *Slow Train to Oxmox* for the *New York Times Book Review,* Cyrus's drawings are "very fine" and "full of wit and clever detail." Tzannes judged that the "drawings alone make this book worthwhile."

Cyrus combines his intriguing illustrations with short poems in both *Oddhopper Opera* and *Hotel Deep: Light Verse from Dark Water. Oddhopper Opera* introduces a myriad of bugs—dung beetles, flies, spiders, katydids, and many more—while the twenty-one poems and accompanying pictures in *Hotel Deep* follow the saga of a lonely little sardine who becomes separated from his school in a coral reef. In his search for the way back home, the tiny sea creature is helped by a number of other unusual denizens of the deep. In reviewing *Oddhopper Opera,* a *Publishers Weekly* contributor noted that Cyrus's "bold, inventive artwork lends high spirits" to the storybook's "down-and-dirty view of the garden," while a *Kirkus Reviews* critic cited the illustrator's imaginative "page design," "with poems and pictures ingeniously wrapped together." Praising the "energetic scenes of underwater life" Cyrus brings to life in the pages of *Hotel Deep, School Library Journal* contributor Margaret Bush deemed the picture book a "cheerful tour for browsers," and a *Kirkus Reviews* writer maintained that Cyrus's "exactly rendered" sea creatures—identified by an author-provided appendix—balance a "witty" rhyming text that makes the book "equally suitable for a quick dip or full immersion."

"It's very important to have a well-organized work space that contains everything I need, but nothing else," Cyrus admitted to *SATA.* "I'm too easily distracted."

A single misstep can cause a major disaster in the world Kurt Cyrus brings to life in his self-illustrated picture book **Tangle Town.** (Farrar, Straus & Giroux, 1997. Illustration © 1997 by Kurt Cyrus. Reprinted by permission of Farrar, Straus & Giroux, a division of Farrar, Straus & Giroux, LLC.)

Cover of **Hotel Deep,** *a poetry collection written and illustrated by* **Cyrus.** (Harcourt, 2005. Illustration © by Kurt Cyrus. Reproduced by permission of Harcourt.)

Discussing his approach to crafting picture books in an interview with Logan Kaufman for the *Adventures Underground Web site,* the author/illustrator noted that his top priority is telling a compelling story. "I love doing a sequence of pictures tied to a narrative," Cyrus explained. "Magazine illustrations also tell stories, but they're usually designed to grab the reader's attention, have an immediate impact, and then be forgotten with the turn of a page. Books are less disposable. I like the idea that a kid might take the time to enter into this little world I'm creating, wander around in it, and return again some other day. That's how I used to read books."

Biographical and Critical Sources

PERIODICALS

Booklist, August, 1998, GraceAnne A. DeCandido, review of *Slow Train to Oxmox,* p. 2013; June 1, 1999, John Peters, review of *There's Nothing to D-o-o-o!,* p. 1842; March 15, 2001, Stephanie Zvirin, review of *Oddhopper Opera: A Bug's Garden of Verses,* p. 1394; February 15, 2005, John Peters, review of *Whales on Stilts!,* p. 173.

Kirkus Reviews, March 1, 2001, review of *Oddhopper Opera;* August 15, 2002, review of *The Bones of Fred McFee,* p. 1218; April 1, 2005, review of *Hotel Deep: Light Verse from Dark Water,* p. 415.

New York Times Book Review, November 15, 1998, Robin Tzannes, "Little Engines That Could," p. 46.

Publishers Weekly, July 20, 1998, review of *Slow Train to Oxmox,* p. 218; June 7, 1999, review of *There's Nothing to D-o-o-o!,* p. 81; July 31, 2000, review of *The Mousery,* p. 94; April 23, 2001, review of *Oddhopper Opera,* p. 77; March 25, 2002, review of *Sixteen Cows,* p. 63.

School Library Journal, March, 1997, Steven Engelfried, review of *Tangle Town,* pp. 149-150; May, 2001, Margaret Bush, review of *Oddhopper Opera,* p. 140; April, 2002, Helen Foster James, review of *Sixteen Cows,* p. 128; April, 2005, Margaret Bush, review of *Hotel Deep,* p. 120.

ONLINE

Adventures Underground Web site, http://www.advunderground.com/ (April, 2006), Logan Kaufman, interview with Cyrus.

D

DAVENIER, Christine 1961-

Personal

Born October 9, 1961, in France; daughter of Pierre (a teacher) and Michèle (a teacher) Davenier; companion of Philippe Harel (a film director); children: Joséphine.

Addresses

Home and office—30 rue de la Clef, Paris 75005, France. *Agent*—Judy Sue Goodwin-Sturges, 166 W. Newton St., Boston, MA 02118.

Career

School teacher in Paris, France, 1986-89; author and illustrator of children's books.

Writings

SELF-ILLUSTRATED

León et Albertine, Kaleidoscope (Paris, France), 1997, translation by Dominic Barth published as *Leon and Albertine,* Orchard Books (New York, NY), 1998, published as *Frankie and Albertine,* Walker Books (London, England), 1999.
Sleepy Sophie, Walker Books (London, England), 1999.

ILLUSTRATOR

Paul B. Janeczko, editor, *Very Best (Almost) Friends: Poems of Friendship,* Candlewick Press (Cambridge, MA), 1999.
C.M. Millen, *The Low-Down Laundry Line Blues,* Houghton Mifflin (Boston, MA), 1999.
Amy Hest, *Mabel Dancing,* Candlewick Press (Cambridge, MA), 2000.
Madeleine L'Engle, *The Other Dog,* SeaStar Books (New York, NY), 2000.

Steve Kroll, *That Makes Me Mad!,* SeaStar Books (New York, NY), 2002.
Susan Marie Swanson, *The First Thing My Mama Told Me,* Harcourt (San Diego, CA), 2002.
Carole Lexa Schaefer, *Full Moon Barnyard Dance,* Candlewick Press (Cambridge, MA), 2003.
Margaret Park Bridges, *I Love the Rain,* Chronicle Books (San Francisco, CA), 2005.
Juanita Havill, *I Heard It from Alice Zucchini: Poems about the Garden,* Chronicle Books (San Francisco, CA), 2006.
Cari Best, *Sally Jean, the Bicycle Queen,* Farrar, Straus & Giroux (New York, NY), 2006.
Norma Fox Mazer, *Has Anyone Seen My Emily Green?,* Candlewick Press (Cambridge, MA), 2007.
Jack Prelutsky, *Me I Am!,* Farrar, Straus & Giroux (New York, NY), 2007.
Kimberly Willis Holt, *Piper Reed, Navy Brat,* Henry Holt (New York, NY), 2007.

Contributor of illustrations to *In Every Tiny Grain of Sand: A Child's Book of Prayers and Praise,* edited by Reeve Lindbergh, Candlewick Press (Cambridge, MA), 2000.

ILLUSTRATOR; "IRIS AND WALTER" PICTURE-BOOK SERIES

Elissa Haden Guest, *Iris and Walter,* Harcourt (San Diego, CA), 2000.
Elissa Haden Guest, *Iris and Walter: Riding Rain,* Harcourt (San Diego, CA), 2001.
Elissa Haden Guest, *Iris and Walter and Baby Rose,* Harcourt (San Diego, CA), 2002.
Elissa Haden Guest, *Iris and Walter: the Sleepover,* Harcourt (San Diego, CA), 2002.
Elissa Haden Guest, *Iris and Walter: The School Play,* Harcourt (San Diego, CA), 2003.
Elissa Haden Guest, *Iris and Walter and Cousin Howie,* Harcourt (San Diego, CA), 2003.
Elissa Haden Guest, *Iris and Walter: Lost and Found,* Harcourt (San Diego, CA), 2004.
Elissa Haden Guest, *Iris and Walter and the Substitute Teacher,* Harcourt (San Diego, CA), 2004.

Elissa Haden Guest, *Iris and Walter and the Field Trip,* Harcourt (San Diego, CA), 2005.

Elissa Haden Guest, *Iris and Walter and the Birthday Party,* Harcourt (San Diego, CA), 2006.

Sidelights

Christine Davenier is a French illustrator whose pen-and-ink and watercolor drawings are considered charming and humorous by critics. "Like that of Rosemary Wells, Davenier's art evokes more emotion than seems possible," remarked Lisa Falk in a *School Library Journal* review of Davenier's self-illustrated picture-book debut, *Leon and Albertine.* While she has since narrowed her focus to illustrating the texts of other authors, such as Jack Prelutsky, Amy Hest, Steve Kroll, and Juanita Havill, Davenier has continued to gain a positive response from both readers and reviewers. Her "large, loosely rendered line and watercolor illustrations are expressive and packed with action," noted a *Kirkus Reviews* writer in appraising her early work, while in her *Booklist* review of *Iris and Walter and the Birthday Party* Hazel Rochman deemed Davenier's collaboration with author Elissa Haden Guest on the popular "Iris and Walter" series "both joyful and touching." In the *Times Educational Supplement,* fellow illustrator Ted Dewan also focused on the success of Davenier's illustrations, noting in his critique of the British version of *Leon and Albertine* that "Davenier's style is quite special; her stylish watercolours have an invigorating spontaneity. Eschewing painstaking craft in favour of scribbly economy is a daring decision for a picture book illustrator to take."

Leon and Albertine was first published in the author's native France and then released in translation in both the United States and England (where it was published as *Frankie and Albertine*). In her authorial debut, Davenier was praised for creating a universal story with a simple text that also lightly touches on an important theme. In the picture book Leon the pig falls in love with Albertine the hen, and the lovelorn swine seeks advice from the other farm animals on how to catch the eye of his beloved. After the rooster's advice on singing, the rabbit's advice on dancing, and the bull's advice on being strong all fail to impress the imperious Albertine, Leon gives up and goes off to play in the mud with a friend. The two pigs have such a good time that everyone in the barnyard soon decides to join in, even Albertine, who admires her muddy suitor for knowing how to have fun. Leon is emboldened to express his love and the two dance off into the sunset together.

Davenier brings the same breezy, expressive style she showcases in *Leon and Albertine* to the illustrations she creates for texts by other authors. In C.M. Millen's *The Low-Down Laundry Line Blues,* a younger sister tries to cajole her older sister out of a bad mood with a session of jumping rope. "The rhyme and the fluid watercolor illustrations, executed with real verve, successfully cap-

ture" the personalities of the sisters, noted Kate McClelland in appraising Davenier's contribution to the book for *School Library Journal.* In Paul B. Janeczko's anthology of poems, *Very Best (Almost) Friends: Poems of Friendship,* the artist's pen-and-ink and watercolor illustrations reflect the variety of feelings evoked by friendship, from joyous to angry and everything in between. "Clear blues and reds dominate the artist's palette, adding richness to the ink lines that sweep across the pages," observed Jane Marino in a review of *Very Best (Almost) Friends* for *School Library Journal.* Praising her "spontaneous, ebullient watercolors" as "reminiscent of the work of Marc Simont," *Booklist* contributor Jennifer Mattson concluded that in her illustrations for Cari Best's *Sally Jean, the Bicycle Queen,* Davenier "capture[s] the irresistible qualities of a little girl who knows how to make things happen." In her portraits of busy children that decorate the pages of Prelutsky's *Me I Am!,* Davenier's "delicate use of watercolors and her sketchy line create the feeling of gaiety and movement, yet elegantly convey [the] personality and emotion" of the book's young characters, according to *School Library Journal* contributor Carole Phillips.

In addition to capturing high spirits, Davenier's illustrations can also emphasize the softer side of human relations, as they do in works as Amy Hest's picture book *Mabel Dancing,* about a little girl who feels left out during her parents' dance party until the music floats her down the stairs and into her parents' accepting arms.

Christine Davenier captures the enthusiasm of a spirited young girl in her illustrations for Iris and Walter, *a picture book by Elissa Haden Guest.* (Gulliver Books, 2000. Illustration © 2000 by Christine Davenier. Reproduced by permission of Harcourt, Inc.)

The magical world of adults tantalizes the young heroine in Amy Hest's **Mabel Dancing,** *a story featuring Davenier's pen-and-ink and watercolor art.*
(Candlewick Press, 2000. Illustration © 2000 by Christine Davenier. Reproduced by permission of Candlewick Press, Inc., Cambridge, MA.)

Writing in the *New York Times Book Review,* Betsy Groban called this story "a dreamy, evocative portrait of parental love as it's supposed to be: all encompassing and unconditional." She takes a similarly lyrical approach the art she creates for Juanita Havill's *I Heard It from Alice Zucchini: Poems about the Garden,* and her "pencil, ink, and pastel illustrations lend a timeless quality" to Susan Marie Swanson's picture book *The First Thing My Mama Told Me,* in the opinion of *School Library Journal* contributor Martha Link.

Davenier once told *SATA:* "I don't feel really familiar with words and that's why I work with images. It is very hard for me to speak about my work. Each time I start to create a new story for a book, even if there is a chronology in what I have done and what I am doing at the moment, there is something I can't explain, something that escapes me. I will understand it or discover it through the children who will read or listen to my story. Maybe I create a story to share it with an audience and expect to understand why I did it from their reaction."

Biographical and Critical Sources

PERIODICALS

Booklist, July, 2002, Lauren Peterson, review of *The First Thing My Mama Told Me,* p. 1861; February 1, 2006, Hazel Rochman, review of *Iris and Walter and the Birthday Party,* p. 54; May 1, 2006, Jennifer Mattson, review of *Sally Jean, the Bicycle Queen,* p. 88.

Books for Keeps, September, 1999, George Hunt, review of *Frankie and Albertine,* p. 22.

Horn Book, May-June, 2005, Betty Carter, review of *Iris and Walter and the Field Trip,* p. 325.

Kirkus Reviews, January 1, 1998, review of *Leon and Albertine,* p. 56; September 1, 2003, review of *Full Moon Barnyard Dance,* p. 1130.

New York Times Book Review, March 11, 2001, Betsy Groban, "Mabel, the Night and the Music," p. 27; October 20, 2002, Abby McGanney Nolan, review of *The First Thing My Mama Told Me,* p. 23.

Publishers Weekly, June 10, 2002, review of *That Makes Me Mad!,* p. 60; June 26, 2006, review of *Sally Jean, the Bicycle Queen,* p. 51; March 5, 2007, review of *I Am Me!,* p. 59.

School Library Journal, March, 1998, Lisa Falk, review of *Leon and Albertine,* p. 168; January, 1999, Jane Marino, review of *Very Best (Almost) Friends: Poems of Friendship,* p. 143; May, 1999, Kate McClelland, review of *The Low-Down Laundry Line Blues,* p. 93; August, 2002, Martha Link, review of *The First Thing My Mama Told Me,* p. 170; November, 2003, Maryann H. Owen, review of *Full Moon Barnyard Dance,* p. 115; April, 2006, Teresa Pfeifer, review of *I Heard It from Alice Zucchini: Poems about the Garden,* p. 126; May, 2007, Carole Phillips, review of *I Am Me!,* p. 106.

Times Educational Supplement, August 27, 1999, Ted Dewan, review of *Frankie and Albertine,* p. 21.

ONLINE

Bulletin of the Center for Children's Books Online, http://www.bbcb.lis.uiuc.edu/ (March 1, 2001), Deborah Stevenson, "Christine Davenier."

Chronicle Books Web site, http://www.chroniclebooks.com/ (June 20, 2007), "Christine Davenier."*

*   *   *

De la CRUZ, Melissa 1971-

Personal

Born 1971, in Manila, Philippines; married Michael Hoch Johnston, October, 2002. *Education:* Columbia University, B.A. (English and art history).

Addresses

Agent—Richard Abate, International Creative Management, 40 W. 57th St., New York, NY 10019. *E-mail*—Melissa@Melissa-DeLacruz.com.

Career

Journalist and author. Computer programmer for an investment bank in NJ and in New York, NY; Morgan Stanley, New York, NY, senior consultant until 2001; *Hint* (online magazine), cofounder, senior fashion editor, and columnist, beginning 1998. Formerly worked as a child model.

Writings

YOUNG-ADULT NOVELS

The Au Pairs, Simon & Schuster (New York, NY), 2004.
Fresh off the Boat, HarperCollins (New York, NY), 2005.

The Au Pairs: Skinny-dipping, Simon & Schuster (New York, NY), 2005.
The Au Pairs: Sun-kissed, Simon & Schuster (New York, NY), 2006.
Blue Bloods, Hyperion (New York, NY), 2006.
Angels on Sunset Boulevard, Simon & Schuster (New York, NY), 2007.
The Au Pairs: Crazy Hot, Simon & Schuster (New York, NY), 2007.
Masquerade (sequel to *Blue Bloods*), Hyperion (New York, NY), 2007.

OTHER

Cat's Meow (adult novel), illustrated by Kim de Marco, Scribner's (New York, NY), 2001.
(With Karen Robinovitz) *How to Become Famous in Two Weeks or Less,* Ballantine (New York, NY), 2003.
(With Karen Robinovitz) *The Fashionista Files: Adventures in Four-Inch Heels and Faux Pas,* Ballantine Books (New York, NY), 2004.
(Editor with Tom Dolby) Girls Who Like Boys Who Like Boys: True Tales of Love, Lust, and Friendship between Straight Women and Gay Men, Dutton (New York, NY), 2007.

Contributor to anthologies, including *Mistletoe,* Scholastic (New York, NY), 2006; and *21 Proms,* edited by David Levithan and Dan Ehrenhaft, Scholastic, 2007. Contributor to periodicals, including *Allure, New York Times, Marie Claire, CosmoGirl, San Francisco Chronicle, Teen Vogue, Cosmopolitan, Seventeen, Glamour, Feed, McSweeneys, Hamptons Country, Nerve,* and *Manhattan Style.*

Sidelights

A computer programmer-turned-journalist whose articles have appeared in magazines such as *Glamour, Allure,* and *Seventeen,* Melissa De la Cruz is also the author of novels for older teens and twentysomethings that tap into the trendy materialism and interest in celebrity that characterize modern American popular culture. Initially focusing on an adult readership with *Cat's Meow,* De la Cruz has more recently won a loyal following among teen readers with her "Au Pairs" series about a group of teens who work and play in the affluent Hamptons during the summer months. In addition to her "Au Pairs" novels, she also moves into the horror genre with *Blue Bloods,* and tells an edgy contemporary story in *Angels on Sunset Boulevard.* Praised as a "witty, trendy, coming-of-age story" by a *Kirkus Reviews* writer, De la Cruz's *Fresh off the Boat* also brings a new perspective to teen culture through the story of fourteen-year-old Philippine teen Vicenza and her efforts to fit in with her peers at an exclusive prep school in San Francisco.

Living something of a celebrity lifestyle herself, De la Cruz also tantalizes readers with chronicles of her own experiences in the world of the well-heeled and well-

connected in books such as *The Fashionista Files: Adventures in Four-Inch Heels and Faux Pas,* and *How to Become Famous in Two Weeks or Less,* the latter coauthored with fellow journalist Karen Robinovitz.

De la Cruz found material for her first novel, *Cat's Meow,* in both her own life and the lives of those she has written about as a fashion journalist. The novel's protagonist, Cat McAllister, was a child actress, just as De la Cruz once was; and Cat's dreams of socialite celebrity reflect those the author recalls from her own childhood. In pursuit of a wealthy husband to help bolster her status among the New York social aristocracy—and to pay her mounting credit card bills—De la Cruz's pragmatic protagonist starts by throwing herself her fourth twenty-fifth birthday party and quickly adopts a Chinese orphan as a status symbol. When her money runs out and she loses her apartment, Cat is forced to look for work. Good fortune finally strikes when she finds a job at a fashion Web site (De la Cruz is an editor at an online fashion magazine) that sends her to runway shows in Paris and other posh locales. As a *Publishers Weekly* critic suggested of *Cat's Meow,* "society page addicts will no doubt enjoy its irreverent spin on the glamorous life."

The first young-adult novel by De la Cruz, *The Au Pairs* and its sequels were inspired by the vacations De la Cruz and her husband took in the Hamptons, a resort area frequented by wealthy Manhattan residents. "It is a magical place and a kind of over-the-top environment that was perfect for my kind of writing," the author told a *Teen Reads* online interviewer. "I love stories about social-climbing and outrageous behavior, and I wanted to show the *Upstairs/Downstairs* world. Also, a friend of ours who is a true blue Hamptonite told me about the 'hot nanny/au pair' phenomenon in the Hamptons, how these girls who worked there for the summer were the most-wanted girls in town . . . they had these crazy, glamorous lives even though they were babysitters."

In *The Au Pairs* readers meet Eliza, Mara, and Jacqui. Coming from different backgrounds—stuck-up Eliza hails from upstate New York, selfish and beautiful Jacqui is from Brazil, and Mara is a socially naïve, working-class girl from Massachusetts—the three teens have been hired to take care of the four spoiled offspring of the wealthy Perrys at the family's summer home in the Hamptons. Over the course of the summer, romance takes precedence over work, as Mara dates the dishy Ryan Perry and Jacqui pursues the handsome Luke. While noting that the teen sex, drug use, and celebrity will win *The Au Pairs* instant appeal for teen readers, Amanda MacGregor noted in *Kliatt* that De la Cruz's "strong writing and interesting characters help set this book apart."

Skinny-Dipping continues the "Au Pairs" saga, as Mara and Jacqui return to baby-sit the Perry children. Eliza, who is now dating Ryan, has found a interning position at the resort's popular Seventh Circle nightclub. Ro-

Cover of Melissa De la Cruz's young-adult novel **The Au Pairs,** *featuring a cover photograph by Tony Stone.* (Simon Pulse, 2005. Cover photograph © 2004 by Tony Stone/Getty Images. Reproduced by permission.)

mantic conflicts soon erupt, when Mara attempts to rekindle her romance with Ryan, and handsome French-born Philippe, Eliza's replacement au pair, attracts both Jacqui and Jacqui's employer, Mrs. Perry. In *Sun-kissed* the girls are spending their last summer before college, and Jacqui alone remains with the Perrys, hoping the couple's fragile marriage will hold together until the summer is over. Mara works as a reporter for *Hamptons* magazine, and the ambitious Eliza signs on as an assistant for a fashion designer hoping to regain the limelight by wooing celebrity clients. In a review of *Skinny-Dipping* in *School Library Journal,* Michele Capozzella wrote that the "Au Pairs" series would appeal to fans of Zoey Deans "A-List" novels and Cecily von Ziegesar's "Gossip Girl" saga due to its focus on "high fashion, fabulous parties, unlimited alcohol, sex, and celebrities." "Designer labels and movie star names fall like hailstones," quipped Ilene Cooper, adding in her *Booklist* review that teens will find *The Au Pairs* and its sequels "hard to put down."

The dark side of family history is at the core of *Blue Bloods,* as De la Cruz introduces a group of rich Manhattan teens who have powers that extend beyond their

good looks, family wealth, and social connections. Twins Mimi and Jack, intellectual Schuyler, and transplanted Texan Bliss are all students at Duchesne, a prestigious city school where the aggressive Mimi is at the top of the social pecking order. When the teens reach age fifteen, they also learn that they are immortal vampires who, in soul form, are reborn in a new infant body every generation. Now welcomed into the Conclave, a group led by the city's oldest vampire families, the teens learn the rules that allow them to remain undetected. They also feel invulnerable, until they realize that someone . . . or some thing . . . is deliberately targeting young vampires in a series of gruesome murders. "It's hard to resist a book that combines expensive clothes, modeling jobs, blood-sucking and even diary entries from a Mayflower vampire," wrote a *Publishers Weekly* contributor of the novel. A *Kirkus Reviews* writer called *Blue Bloods* "a juicy, voyeuristic peek into the lives of rich Manhattanites," a peek that is continued in *Masquerade.*

Life in the fast-lane party culture of modern Los Angeles is the focus of *Angels on Sunset Boulevard,* as a dangerous cult, spawned by the internet party site TAP—short for The Angels' Practice—hosts wild parties that attract teens with their "sex, drugs, and rock and roll" theme. Taj and Nick are fans of TAP, as well as of Johnny Silver, Taj's boyfriend and the new rock musician the site is promoting. Then Johnny goes missing, without a trace, followed by Nick's younger sister and a host of other teens. Now Taj and Nick find themselves drawn into a cult where dark rituals and danger await. Noting the novel's entertainment value, *School Library Journal* contributor Corinda J. Humphrey explained that De la Cruz's story is a "commentary on followers versus leaders and the ease with which teens are influenced by peer pressure." A *Kirkus Reviews* writer dubbed *Angels on Sunset Boulevard* a "Faustian morality tale" "with a twist," and a *Publishers Weekly* critic predicted that young-adult readers "will . . . be haunted by the story's provocative themes" about teen culture in De la Cruz's page-turner.

Biographical and Critical Sources

PERIODICALS

Booklist, July, 2004, Ilene Cooper, review of *The Au Pairs,* p. 1833; April 15, 2005, Debbie Carton, review of *Fresh off the Boat,* p. 1447; May 15, 2006, Jennifer Mattson, review of *Blue Bloods,* p. 56.

Bulletin of the Center for Children's Books, September, 2004, Karen Coats, review of *The Au Pairs,* p. 14; September, 2005, Karen Coats, review of *Fresh off the Boat,* p. 13; September, 2006, Karen Coats, review of *Blue Bloods,* p. 11.

Kirkus Reviews, June 1, 2004, review of *The Au Pairs,* p. 535; March, 2005, review of *Fresh off the Boat,* p. 350; April 1, 2006, review of *Blue Bloods,* p. 344; March 1, 2007, review of *Angels on Sunset Boulevard,* p. 220.

Kliatt, September, 2005, Amanda MacGregor, review of *The Au Pairs,* p. 18; September, 2006, Stephanie Squicciarini, review of *Fresh off the Boat,* p. 21.

Library Journal, May 15, 2007, Anna Katterjohn, review of *Girls Who Like Boys Who Like Boys: True Tales of Love, Lust, and Friendship between Straight Women and Gay Men,* p. 103.

Los Angeles Times Book Review, August 12, 2001, Mark Rozzo, review of *Cat's Meow,* p. 10.

New York Magazine, July 30, 2001, Amy Larocca, "Smart Set: Melissa De la Cruz."

Publishers Weekly, July 30, 2001, review of *Cat's Meow,* p. 63; May 9, 2005, review of *Fresh off the Boat,* p. 72; June 5, 2006, review of *Blue Bloods,* p. 64; March 5, 2007, review of *Angels on Sunset Boulevard,* p. 62; March 26, 2007, review of *Girls Who Like Boys Who Like Boys,* p. 76.

School Library Journal, June, 2004, Tracy Karbel, review of *The Au Pairs,* p. 136; April, 2005, Amy Patrick, review of *Fresh off the Boat,* p. 130; July, 2005, Michele Capozzella, review of *Skinny-dipping,* p. 101; June, 2006, Sharon Rawlins, review of *Blue Bloods,* and Jane Cronkhite, review of *Sun-kissed,* both p. 152; April, 2007, Corinda J. Humphrey, review of *Angels on Sunset Boulevard,* p. 130.

Voice of Youth Advocates, October, 2004, review of *The Au Pairs,* p. 293; August, 2005, Michelle Winship, review of *Fresh off the Boat,* p. 214; April, 2006, Vikki C. Terrile, review of *Blue Bloods,* p. 58.

ONLINE

Melissa De la Cruz Home Page, http://www.melissa-delacruz.com (May 15, 2007).

Teen Reads Web site, http://www.teenreads.com/ (July 1, 2005), interview with De la Cruz.*

*   *   *

DELESSERT, Étienne 1941-

Personal

Born January 4, 1941, in Lausanne, Switzerland; son of Ferdinand (a minister) and Berengère Delessert; married Rita Marshall (a graphic designer and art director), 1985; children: Adrien.

Addresses

Home—P.O. Box 1689, Lakeville, CT 06039. *E-mail*—Etienne@Etiennedelessert.com.

Career

Painter, graphic designer, illustrator, film director, publisher, and author. Freelance graphic designer and illustrator in Lausanne, Switzerland, and in Paris, France, 1962-65; freelance author and illustrator, 1965—. Good Book (publishing house), co-founder, with Herb Lubalin, 1969-74; Societe Carabosse (animated film produc-

tion company), Lausanne, co-founder, with Anne van der Essen, 1973-84; *Record* (children's magazine), Paris, art director, 1975-76; Editions Tournesol (publisher), co-founder, 1977. *Exhibitions:* One-man exhibitions include Art Alliance Gallery, Philadelphia, PA, 1970; California State College Gallery, Long Beach, 1972; Galerie Delpire, Paris, France, 1972; Galerie Melisa, Lausanne, Switzerland, 1974; Galerie Marquet, Paris, 1975; Musée des Arts Décoratifs du Louvre, Paris, 1975; Musée des Arts Décoratifs, Lausanne, 1976; Palais de l'Athenée, Geneva, Switzerland, 1976; Le Manoir, Martigny, France, 1985; Palazzio delle Espozizioni, Rome, Italy, 1991; Lustrare Gallery, New York, NY, 1991; Library of Congress, Washington, DC, 1994; Olympic Museum, Lausanne (touring retrospective), 1997; Tremaine Gallery, Lakeville, CT, 1997; School of Visual Arts, New York, NY, 1999; Galerie Cramer, Geneva, 2002, 2006; and Les Silos, Chaumont, France, 2003. Group exhibitions include Museum of American Illustration, New York, NY, beginning 1967; Galeríe Wolfsberg, Zurich, Switzerland, 1970; Brooklyn Museum, Brooklyn, NY, 1973-75; Galeríe Pauli, Lausanne, 1976; Centre Georges Pompidou, Paris, 1985; Art Institute, Boston, MA, 1985; Storyopolis Gallery, Los Angeles, CA, 1997; Hearst Center for the Arts, Cedar Falls, IA, 2002; Calcographia National, Madrid, Spain, 2004; and Norman Rockwell Museum, Stockbridge, MA, 2005.

Awards, Honors

American Society of Illustrators gold medals, 1967, 1972, 1976, 1978, and nine others, and twelve silver medals; *New York Times* Ten Best Illustrated Books of the Year designations, 1968, for *Story Number One for Children under Three Years of Age,* 1972, for *Just So Stories;* American Institute of Graphic Arts' Fifty Books of the Year inclusion, and Children's Book Show inclusion, 1971, for *How the Mouse Was Hit on the Head by a Stone and So Discovered the World,* and 1972, for *Just So Stories;* Brooklyn Art Books for Children citations, Brooklyn Museum/Brooklyn Public Library, 1973, 1974, and 1975, all for *How the Mouse Was Hit on the Head by a Stone and So Discovered the World;* Premio Europeo (Trente, Italy), 1977, for *Thomas et l'infini;* Gold Plaque, Biennale of Illustration, Bratislava, 1979, for *Les sept familles du lac Pipple-Popple* and *Die maus und was ihr bleibt,* and 1985, for *La belle et la bête;* Hans Christian Andersen Highly Commended Illustrator award, 1980; Prix Loisirs-Jeunes (Paris, France), 1981, for *Quinze gestes de Jésus,* and for *Story Number One for Children under Three Years of Age, How the Mouse Was Hit on the Head by a Stone and So Discovered the World, Le roman de Renart,* and *L'eau;* First Graphic Prize, International Bologna Book Fair, 1981, for "Yok-Yok" series, and 1989, for *A Long Long Song;* German Best Book of the Year awards for translations of *Story Number One for Children under Three Years of Age* and *Story Number Two for Children under Three Years of Age;* Hamilton King Award, 1996, for *I Hate to Read!* by Rita Marshall; Connecticut Book Award, 2005, for

Who Killed Cock Robin?; Hans Christian Andersen Award finalist, 2005.

Writings

FOR CHILDREN

L'arbre, illustrated by Eléonore Schmid, Harlan Quist/Ruy Vidal (Paris, France), 1966, translated as *The Tree,* Harlan Quist (New York, NY), 1966.

(With Eléonore Schmid; and illustrator) *Sans fin la fête,* Harlan Quist (Paris, France), 1967, revised edition translated by Jeffrey Tabberner as *The Endless Party,* Oxford University Press (New York, NY), 1981.

Comment la souris reçoit une pierre sur la tête ed découvre le monde, foreword by Jean Piaget, Ecole des Loisirs, (Paris, France), 1971, translated as *How the Mouse Was Hit on the Head by a Stone and So Discovered the World,* Doubleday (Garden City, NY), 1971.

(With Anne van der Essen) *La souris s'en va-t'en en Guerre,* Gallimard (Paris, France), 1978.

(With Christophe Gallaz) *L'amour-petit croque et ses amis,* Tournesol-Gallimard (Paris, France), 1982.

Happy Birthdays: A Notebook for Everyone's Birthday, designed by wife, Rita Marshall, Stewart, Tabori (New York, NY), 1986.

(And illustrator) *A Long Long Song,* Farrar, Straus (New York, NY), 1988.

(And illustrator) *Ashes, Ashes,* Stewart, Tabori (New York, NY), 1990.

(With Rita Marshall; and illustrator) *J'aime pas lire,* Gallimard (Paris, France), 1992, translated as *I Hate to Read!,* Creative Education (Mankato, MN), 1992.

(Adaptor) *The Seven Dwarves,* Creative Education (Mankato, MN), 2001.

(Adaptor) *Who Killed Cock Robin?* (folk song), Creative Editions (Mankato, MN), 2004.

(Adaptor) *A Was an Apple Pie: An English Nursery Rhyme,* Creative Editions (Mankato, MN), 2005.

Hungry for Numbers, Creative Editions (Mankato, MN), 2006.

Jeux d'enfant, Gallimard (Paris, France), 2006.

(Adaptor) *Humpty Dumpty,* Houghton Mifflin (New York, NY), 2006.

Alert!, Houghton Mifflin (Boston, MA), 2007.

Also author of animated films and children's films.

Author's works have been translated into fourteen languages.

ILLUSTRATOR; FOR CHILDREN

John Steinbeck, *Tortilla Flat* (French edition), Club Français du Livre (Paris, France), 1964.

Eugène Ionesco, *Story Number One for Children under Three Years of Age,* translated by Calvin K. Towle, Harlan Quist (New York, NY), 1968.

Betty Jean Lifton, *The Secret Seller,* Norton (New York, NY), 1968.

George Mendoza, *A Wart Snake in a Fig Tree,* Dial (New York, NY), 1968.

Eugène Ionesco, *Story Number Two for Children under Three Years of Age,* translated by Calvin K. Towle, Harlan Quist (New York, NY), 1970.

Rudyard Kipling, *Just So Stories* (anniversary edition), Doubleday (Garden City, NY), 1972.

Gordon Lightfoot, *The Pony Man,* Harper Magazine Press (New York, NY), 1972.

Joseph G. Raposo, *Being Green,* Western Publishing (Racine, WI), 1973.

Michel Déon, *Thomas et l'infini* (title means "Thomas and the Infinite"), Gallimard (Paris, France), 1975.

Anne van der Essen, *La souris et les papillons* (title means "The Mouse and the Butterflies"), Gallimard (Paris, France), 1975.

Anne van der Essen, *La souris et les poisons,* Gallimard (Paris, France), 1975, translation published as *The Mouse and the Poisons,* Middelhauve, 1977.

Anne van der Essen, *Die maus und der Lärm,* Middelhauve, 1975.

Anne van der Essen, *Die maus und was ihr bleibt,* Middlehauve, 1977, translation published as *Amelia Mouse and Her Great-Great-Grandchild,* Evans, 1978.

Oscar Wilde, *Le prince heureux* (translation of *The Happy Prince*), Gallimard (Paris, France), 1977.

Edgar Allan Poe, *Le scarabée d'or* (translation of *The Gold Bug*), Gallimard (Paris, France), 1977.

Edward Lear, *Les sept familles du lac Pipple-Popple* (translation of *The Seven Families from Lake Pipple-Popple*), Gallimard (Paris, France), 1978.

Andrienne Soutter-Perrot, *Les premiers livres de la nature* (title means "My First Nature Books"), 4 volumes, Tournesol-Gallimard (Paris, France), 1979, translated by Kitty Benedict as *The Earth, Water, Air,* and *Earthworm,* Creative Education (Mankato, MN), 1993.

Jacques Prévert, *Paroles,* Gallimard-Rombaldi (Paris, France), 1979.

Pierre-Marie Beaude and Jean Debruyne, *Quinze gestes de Jésus,* Centurion Jeunesse (Paris, France), 1981.

Jean Touvet Gallaz and François Baudier, *Petit croque et ses amis,* Tournesol (Paris, France), 1982.

Marie Catherine D'Aulnoy, *La belle et la bête,* Editions Grasset (Paris, France), 1983, translated as *Beauty and the Beast,* Creative Education (Mankato, MN), 1985, reprinted, 2000.

Truman Capote, *A Christmas Memory,* Creative Education (Mankato, MN), 1984.

Henri Dès, *Chanson pour mon chien,* Script & Mille-Pattes (Lausanne, Switzerland), 1986.

Henri Dès, *La petite Charlotte,* Script & Mille-Pattes (Lausanne, Switzerland), 1986.

Henri Dès, *On ne verra jamais,* Script & Mille-Pattes (Lausanne, Switzerland), 1986.

Willa Cather, *A Wagner Matinee,* Redpath Press (Minneapolis, MN), 1986.

Roald Dahl, *Taste,* Redpath Press (Minneapolis, MN), 1986.

A.A. Milne, *The Secret,* Redpath Press (Minneapolis, MN), 1986.

William Saroyan, *The Pheasant Hunter: About Fathers and Sons,* Redpath Press (Minneapolis, MN), 1986.

Zora Neale Hurston, *The Gilded Six-Bits,* Redpath Press (Minneapolis, MN), 1986.

Mark Twain (pseudonym of Samuel Clemens), *Baker's Bluejay Yarn,* Redpath Press (Minneapolis, MN), 1986.

Daniel Keyes, *Flowers for Algernon,* Creative Education (Mankato, MN), 1988.

Susan McCloskey, *The Joke,* D.C. Heath (Boston, MA), 1995.

Christophe Gallaz, *La Parole détruite,* Editions Zoé (Geneva, Switzerland), 1995.

Alistair Highet, *Lucas,* Creative Education (Mankato, MN), 2000.

Patricia Kirkpatrick, *John Keats,* Creative Editions (Mankato, MN), 2006.

Rita Marshall, *I Still Hate to Read!,* Creative Editions (Mankato, MN), 2007.

ILLUSTRATOR; "YOK-YOK" SERIES

Anne van der Essen, *The Caterpillar,* Tournesol-Gallimard (Paris, France), 1979, Merrill, 1980.

Anne van der Essen, *The Magician,* Tournesol-Gallimard (Paris, France), 1979, Merrill, 1980.

Anne van der Essen, *The Night,* Tournesol-Gallimard (Paris, France), 1979, Merrill, 1980.

Anne van der Essen, *The Blackbird,* Tournesol-Gallimard (Paris, France), 1979, Merrill, 1980.

Anne van der Essen, *The Frog,* Tournesol-Gallimard (Paris, France), 1979, Merrill, 1980.

Anne van der Essen, *The Rabbit,* Tournesol-Gallimard (Paris, France), 1979, Merrill, 1980.

Anne van der Essen, *The Shadow,* Tournesol-Gallimard (Paris, France), 1981.

Anne van der Essen, *The Circus,* Tournesol-Gallimard (Paris, France), 1981.

Anne van der Essen, *The Cricket,* Tournesol-Gallimard (Paris, France), 1981.

Anne van der Essen, *The Snow,* Tournesol-Gallimard (Paris, France), 1981.

Anne van der Essen, *The Violin,* Tournesol-Gallimard (Paris, France), 1981.

Anne van der Essen, *The Cherry,* Tournesol-Gallimard (Paris, France), 1981.

Anne van der Essen, *Le grand livre de Yok-Yok,* Tournesol-Gallimard (Paris, France), 1981.

Marie Agnès Gaudrat, *Yok-Yok et les secrets de la nuit,* Bayard Editions (Paris, France), 1998.

Marie Agnès Gaudrat, *Yok-Yok et les secrets des saisons,* Bayard Editions (Paris, France), 1998.

AND ILLUSTRATOR; "YOK-YOK" SERIES

Best Friends, Creative Education (Mankato, MN), 1994.

At Home, Creative Education (Mankato, MN), 1994.

Dance!, Creative Education (Mankato, MN), 1994.

For the Birds, Creative Education (Mankato, MN), 1994.

Let's Play, Creative Education (Mankato, MN), 1994.

Magic Tricks, Creative Education (Mankato, MN), 1994.

Moonlight, Creative Education (Mankato, MN), 1994.

Nonsense, Creative Education (Mankato, MN), 1994.

Nuts!, Creative Education (Mankato, MN), 1994.

Snowflakes, Creative Education (Mankato, MN), 1994.

Surprises, Creative Education (Mankato, MN), 1994.

Weird?, Creative Education (Mankato, MN), 1994.

What a Circus!, Creative Education (Mankato, MN), 1994.

ILLUSTRATOR; FOR ADULTS

Joel Jakubec, *Kafka contre l'absurde,* CRV (Lausanne, Switzerland), 1960.

Maurice Chappaz, *Le match Valais-Judée,* CRV (Lausanne, Switzerland), 1968, new edition, Plaisir de Lire-Empreintens (Lausanne, Switzerland), 1994.

Jacques Chessex, *La confession du Pasteur Burg,* Le livre du mois (Lausanne, Switzerland), 1970.

Le roman de Renard, Gallimard (Paris, France), 1977.

Maurice Chappaz, *Entre dieu et diable,* Editions Scarabée (Lausanne, Switzerland), 1981.

François Nourissier, *Le temps,* Le Verseau-Roth & Sauter (Lausanne, Switzerland), 1982.

Jacques Chessex, *Des cinq sens,* Le Verseau-Roth & Sauter (Lausanne, Switzerland), 1982.

Anne Morrow Lindbergh, *Hour of Lead: Sharing Sorrow,* Redpath Press (Minneapolis, MN), 1986.

Maya Angelou, *Mrs. Flowers: A Moment of Friendship,* Redpath Press (Minneapolis, MN), 1986.

Woody Allen, *The Lunatic's Tale,* Redpath Press (Minneapolis, MN), 1986.

Bob Greene, *Diary of a Newborn Baby,* Redpath Press (Minneapolis, MN), 1986.

P.G. Wodehouse, *The Clicking of Cuthbert,* Redpath Press (Minneapolis, MN), 1986.

John Updike, *A & P,* Redpath Press (Minneapolis, MN), 1986.

William Saroyan, *The Pheasant Hunter: About Fathers and Sons,* Redpath Press (Minneapolis, MN), 1986.

Sonoko Kondo, *The Poetical Pursuit of Food,* C.N. Potter (New York, NY), 1986.

Ogden Nash's Zoo, edited by Roy Finamore, Stewart, Tabori (New York, NY), 1987.

John Cheever, *Angel of the Bridge,* 1987.

Ernest Hemingway, *Christmas on the Roof of the World: A Holiday in the Swiss Alps,* Redpath Press (Minneapolis, MN), 1987.

Saki (pen name of H.H. Munro), *The Story-Teller,* Redpath Press (Minneapolis, MN), 1987.

Ogden Nash's Food, edited by Roy Finamore, Stewart, Tabori (New York, NY), 1989.

Mary Gordon and others, *Deadly Sins* (essay anthology), Morrow (New York, NY), 1994.

Les chats, Gallimard (Paris, France), 1998, translated as *The Cat Collection,* Creative Education (Mankato, MN), 1998.

Contributor of editorial illustrations to magazines, including *Atlantic Monthly, New York Times, Le Monde, Fortune, Rolling Stone, Redbook, McCall's, Fact,* and *Elle.*

Adaptations

How the Mouse Was Hit on the Head by a Stone and So Discovered the World was adapted for the stage by Nathalie Nath and produced in Geneva, Switzerland, then filmed for Swiss television; Delessert designed the production's costumes and sets.

Sidelights

An award-winning Swiss-born children's writer, illustrator, publisher, and filmmaker, Étienne Delessert is credited by many as one of the fathers of the modern picture book for children. Self-taught, Delessert has channeled his artistic talent, his vivid imagination, and his understanding of children into dozens of books. In addition to writing and illustrating such well-respected books as *How the Mouse Was Hit on the Head by a Stone and So Discovered the World, Humpty Dumpty,* and *The Long Long Song,* he has created the popular character Yok-Yok, star of both picture books and animated films, as well animation for the *Sesame Street* television program. Reviewing Delessert's illustrations for *I Hate to Read!,* a collaboration with the artist's wife, author Rita Marshall, a *Publishers Weekly* con-

Swiss illustrator Étienne Delessert brings his surreal perspective to Rita Marshall's humorous picture book **I Hate to Read!** (Creative Editions, 1993. Illustrations © 1992 by Étienne Delessert. Reproduced by permission of the illustrator.)

tributor characterized them as "inventive," noting that Delessert "wreaks playful havoc with perspective and scale, and features striking earthtone pastels punctuated with splashes of vibrant color." An internationally respected artist, Delessert has exhibited his work in museums and galleries around the world.

Born in Lausanne, Switzerland, in 1941, Delessert traces his interest in storytelling to his early childhood. "I was raised by my stepmother, who was a great storyteller, and who influenced my creative development tremendously . . . ," he once recalled. "The stories she told were of her own invention; she was best at dialogue and situation. I'm sure she would have made a fine playwright. We often acted out simple scenarios together . . .—no sets, no props, no costumes—just long, endless monologues in which I would attempt to become a tree or animal. . . . If my stepmother had to stop this activity to run an errand, I would go on for hours by myself. It was very good training for my imagination, and as an only child, it taught me how to play by myself."

As he grew into a reader, Delessert became interested in the fairy tales of Northern and Eastern Europe, and the rich images conjured up by these stories have continued to influence his artistic vision. "Much like in the northern fables," he once remarked, "I have looked into the shadows and the fog for monsters and witches." Delessert recaptured the mood of such stories in the late 1960s, when he co-founded the publishing house Good Book. At Good Book he collaborated with American-born graphic designer and art director Marshall to supervise the production of a series of fairy-tale books, illustrated by a stable of artists. Although Delessert left Good Book in the mid-1970s, he and Marshall have continued their collaboration in several picture books and the two were married in 1985. In his work, Delessert continues to draw inspiration from fairy tales.

One of Delessert's earliest original books, *How the Mouse Was Hit on the Head by a Stone and So Discovered the World,* was inspired by the work of noted Swiss educational psychologist Jean Piaget. Working from Piaget's stages of children's mental development, Delessert geared the book's illustrations and text to the cognitive level of five-and six-year-old children. In his story, Delessert describes features of the natural word, such as the sun and moon, using the same language as did the children Piaget interviewed during the 1950s. The book's text was read to several groups of children by Piaget's assistants, who checked for comprehension of single words and concepts. "One of the most interesting discoveries was that five and six year olds have their own interpretation of how the sun and moon rise and set," the author/illustrator recalled of the project, adding that these "interpretations . . . are somewhat similar to some ancient Mexican and African legends. Big hands, for example, throw the sun into the sky at dawn, and catch it back at sunset. We asked children to

Delessert's European influences and playful perspective combine in his illustrations for the original picture book **Dance!** (Creative Editions, 1994. Illustration © 1994 by Étienne Delessert. Reproduced by permission.)

make their own drawings illustrating the story we had built together. Without knowing it, the children made drawings very similar to my own."

Delessert takes between three and four months to produce the drawings needed for each picture book. "In some ways, I get more pleasure out of conceiving an idea than executing it," he once admitted. "I love to make the little thumbnail sketches. But after that, there is a long period which is simply craft—slowly executing what you intended—which sometimes makes me impatient. The very last part of drawing—the polishing, the 'making it work'—interests me again, but I don't like that in-between, very technical and painstaking stage." Although he has become experienced with computerized renderings, he prefers working with pen and ink and pastel. "I think that one of the basic satisfactions [of making art] is just to create a little object," he explained to *MacWeek* contributor Rick LePage. "This satisfaction doesn't exist when you work on a computer because [the image] is behind a glass. You cannot own it; you cannot have it; you cannot put it into your pocket."

In addition to experimenting with computerized graphics in his work, Delessert has also worked in animated feature-film production. Working with Anne van der Essen, he ran the Lausanne-based Carabosse Studios from

1973 to 1984, producing *Supersaxo,* an animated film adaptation of a fantasy novel by Swiss writer Maurice Chappaz. In *Phaedrus,* Denise Von Stockar observed that "many French-Swiss illustrators . . . started their careers at Delessert's studio," where they were given the chance to develop their own creative style. Reflecting on his interesting a variety of creative forms—another is sculpture—Delessert noted: "I'm a storyteller, and I love to tell stories. I was attracted to children's books because they are a medium in which I can develop a story through text and illustrations on several levels. Picture books are closely related to film, which also play with images and text."

One of Delessert's most enduring characters, Yok-Yok, had its start in the films of Carabosse. Picture-book adaptations were made of of the "Yok-Yok" films, 150 ten-second animated shorts which, according to the artist, "answer such questions as 'Why does a woodpecker tap on a tree trunk?' and 'What do frogs eat?' with animation." Featuring texts by van der Essen and illustrations by Delessert, the "Yok-Yok" books were published by Editions Tournesol, a company Delessert and van der Essen cofounded in 1977. Apart from the "Yok-Yok" books, which Delessert eventually wrote and illustrated, Tournesol also printed children's books by a host of other authors and illustrators, making a significant contribution to European picture books. Reviewing *Dance!,* a book in the "Yok-Yok" series, a *Publishers Weekly* contributor wrote that Delessert's "striking design and inventive art . . . effectively meshes soft pastels and brilliant hues."

Appearing in books for both children and adults that feature texts by writers as varied as Eugène Ionesco, Rudyard Kipling, Ogden Nash, Willa Cather, A.A. Milne, and Nora Zeale Hurston, Delessert's "bulbous-shouted, glittery-eyed creatures are instantly recognizable," according to a *Publishers Weekly* writer. His original self-illustrated picture books allow him even more creative latitude, and his quirky visual images pair with texts that weave darker, sometimes sinister fairy-tale elements into more lighthearted fare. A little mole overwhelmed by fears that his prized collection of tiny stones will be taken by robbers is the focus of *Alert!,* which features "expressionistic" illustrations that a *Kirkus Reviews* contributor insisted are "always worth a look." Life after the end of the fairy tail and marriage to the handsome prince is the focus of *The Seven Dwarves,* as Snow White's dwarf companions join her briefly at the palace before deciding that the life of a courtier is not for any one of them. Delessert attracts more sophisticated readers by creating "fanciful, cinematic" images that a *Publishers Weekly* critic described as "grotesque and delicate at the same time," while his "unique twist on the universally known tale will divert younger listeners." In *Booklist* GraceAnne A. DeCandido dubbed *The Seven Dwarves* a "compelling bridge from picture book to fairy tale" that features the author/illustrator's "signature combination of rubbery exaggeration, painstaking detail, and startling perspectives."

Traditional nursery rhymes and stories are adapted and brought to life in *A Was an Apple Pie: An English Nursery Rhyme, Humpty Dumpty,* and *Who Killed Cock Robin?* In *A Was an Apple Pie* the traditional text is "modernized with [Delessert's] vibrant fantastical figures," according to *School Library Journal* reviewer Carolyn Janssen, while in *Booklist* Gillian Engberg predicted that the artist's cast of "mysterious, expressive creatures may draw children's interest" to the centuries' old text. In *School Library Journal,* Robin L. Gibson described the visual landscape of Delessert's picture-book update on the well-known nursery rhyme about the roly-poly wall-sitter "surreal," and a *Publishers Weekly* reviewer dubbed *Humpty Dumpty* "a fascinating exercise in imagination." Called a "delightful version of a traditional ballad" by *School Library Journal* critic Marilyn Taniguchi, *Who Killed Cock Robin?* pairs the sad song of poor, unfortunate Cock Robin with paintings that depict smiling children in bird costumes, an "air of mystery" contained within Delessert's "alternately strange and lovely" art.

"Many fairy tales are illustrated and interpreted too sweetly, even when the story itself is quite strong," Delessert once explained, noting the importance of traditional stories among younger children. "I feel it is im-

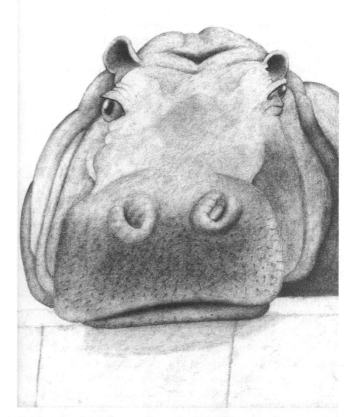

A talented artist, Delessert showcases his ability to tap the essence of his subject in his portraits that pair with the poetry in **Ogden Nash's Zoo.** (Creative Editions, 2005. Illustration © 2005 by Étienne Delessert. Reproduced by permission.)

Delessert presents his original adaptation of a traditional nursery rhyme in the large-format picture book **A Was an Apple Pie.**

portant to use visuals which are equivalent in strength to the text. Fairy tales usually work to open the reader up, to give him a kind of psychological help; while some images of the tale may be violent or bizarre, by the end, things are resolved and open. These great stories bring out the fears, loneliness, and violence that a person must face in order to move into peace and harmony." One "should not present children with sugar-coated versions of reality," the illustrator continued. "You have to expose them to all kinds of experiences, especially with a sense of humor and a sense of the bizarre with surrealistic situations which open them up to another kind of reality, another point of view. . . . After all, truth is not one-sided, not only what you see on T.V. or read in the papers, or what your parents tell you, or what you learn in school: truth is also what *you* see and how you perceive the unknown forces of the world, how you face birth, life, decay, and death. That has been, I believe, the essence of my books."

Biographical and Critical Sources

BOOKS

Catalogue du Musée des Arts décoratifs du Louvre, [Paris, France], 1975.

Chessex, Jacques, *Les dessins d'Étienne Delessert,* Bertil Galland (Lausanne, Switzerland), 1974.

Kingman, Lee, and others, compilers, *Illustrators of Children's Books: 1967-1976,* Horn Book (Boston, MA), 1978.

Marshall, Rita, *Étienne Delessert* (monograph), Stewart, Tabori (New York, NY), 1991.

Vassali, P., and A. Rausch, *Étienne Delessert,* Carte Segrete, 1992.

PERIODICALS

Booklist, November 15, 2000, review of *Beauty and the Beast,* p. 627; January 1, 2002, GraceAnne A. DeCandido, review of *The Seven Dwarves,* p. 851; January 1, 2006, Gillian Engberg, review of *A Was an Apple Pie: An English Nursery Rhyme,* p. 103.

Communication Arts, July, 1992, Amy Herndon, "Étienne Delessert," p. 190.

Graphis, number 128, 1967; number 208, 1979-80; number 235, 1985.

Horn Book, June, 1980, review of *How the Mouse Was Hit on the Head by a Stone and So Discovered the World,* p. 281; January-February, 2002, Roger Sutton, review of *The Seven Dwarves,* p. 66.

Idea (Japan), number 66, 1964; number 71, 1966.

Kirkus Reviews, April 1, 2006, review of *Humpty Dumpty,* p. 345; September 1, 2006, review of *Hungry for Numbers,* p. 902; January 15, 2007, review of *Alert!,* p. 71.

Library Journal, November 15, 1988, review of *Flowers for Algernon,* p. 28.

MacWeek, December 18, 1990, Rick LePage, "Artist Takes the Mac Back to School," p. 50.

New York Times, August 22, 1971.

New York Times Book Review, October 23, 1988, David Macaulay, review of *A Long Long Song,* p. 26; November 13, 2005, Karla Kuskin, review of *A Was an Apple Pie,* p. 28.

Novum gebrauchs graphik, January 1, 1976.

Phaedrus (annual), 1982, Denise Von Stockar, "From Töpffer to Delessert: The Picture Book Illustrators of French-speaking Switzerland," pp. 35-39.

Print, April, 1986; March-April, 1991, Rose de Neve, profile of Delesert.

Publishers Weekly, May 18, 1988, review of *A Long Long Song,* p. 85; June 29, 1990, review of *Ashes, Ashes,* p. 99; June 14, 1993, review of *I Hate to Read!,* p. 71; August 8, 1994, review of *Deadly Sins,* p. 406; September 26, 1994, review of *Dance!,* p. 70; June 26, 2006, review of *Humpty Dumpty,* p. 51; August 21, 2006, review of *Hungry for Numbers,* p. 68; January 22, 2007, review of *Alert!,* p. 183.

School Library Journal, March 20, 1981, Jean F. Mercier, review of *The Endless Party,* p. 63; January, 1982, review of *The Endless Party,* p. 62; September, 1988, Ruth K. MacDonald, review of *A Long Long Song,* p. 156; July, 1990, Christine Behrmann, review of *Ashes, Ashes,* p. 75; September 26, 1994, review of *Dance!,* p. 70; October 8, 2001, review of *The Seven Dwarves,* p. 63; January, 2006, Carolyn Janssen, review of *A Was an Apple Pie,* p. 96; January, 2005, Marilyn Taniguchi, review of *Who Killed Cock Robin?,* p. 118; August, 2006, Robin L. Gibson, review of *Humpty Dumpty,* p. 80; November, 2006, Wendy Lukehart, review of *Hungry for Numbers,* p. 87.

ONLINE

Étienne Delessert Home Page, http://www.etiennedelessert.com (April 15, 2007).

E

ELLIS, Sarah 1952-

Personal

Born May 19, 1952, in Vancouver, British Columbia, Canada; daughter of Joseph Walter (a clergyman) and Ruth Elizabeth (a nurse) Ellis. *Education:* University of British Columbia, B.A. (with honors), 1973, M.L.S., 1975; Simmons College, M.A. (children's literature), 1980.

Addresses

Home—Vancouver, British Columbia, Canada. *E-mail*—andyspandy@telus.net.

Career

Librarian and author. Toronto Public Library, Toronto, Ontario, Canada, librarian, c. 1975; Vancouver Public Library, Vancouver, British Columbia, children's librarian, 1976-81; North Vancouver District Library, North Vancouver, British Columbia, librarian, beginning 1981, now reference librarian. Writer-in-residence, Massey College, University of Toronto, 1999. Vermont College, teacher of writing. Speaker at schools, colleges, conferences, and workshops, including Children's Literature New England Summer Institute.

Member

Canadian Society of Children's Authors, Illustrators, and Performers, Writers' Union of Canada, Vancouver Society of Storytelling.

Awards, Honors

Sheila A. Egoff Awards, 1987, for *The Baby Project,* and 1997, for *Back of Beyond;* Governor-General's Award for Children's Literature, 1991, for *Pick-up Sticks;* Mr. Christie's Book Award, and Violet Downy Award, I.O.D.E., both 1994, both for *Out of the Blue;* Vicky Metcalf Award, Canadian Authors' Association, 1995, for body of work; Hackmatack Award nomina-

Sarah Ellis (Reproduced by permission.)

tion, and Sheila A. Egoff Children's Prize shortlist, both 2003, both for *A Prairie as Wide as the Sea;* Mr. Christie's Book Award Gold Seal honor and Governor General's Literary Award shortlist, both 2003, and Canadian Library Association Book of the Year shortlist and Violet Downy Award, both 2004, all for *The Several Lives of Orphan Jack;* Blue Spruce Award nominee, 2006, and Chocolate Lily Young Readers Choice Award nomination, 2007, both for *Ben over Night;*

Sheila A. Egoff Award, and Canadian Library Association Book of the Year nomination, both 2007, both for *Odd Man Out.*

Writings

The Baby Project, Groundwood Books (Toronto, Ontario, Canada), 1986, published as *A Family Project,* Macmillan (New York, NY), 1988.

Next-Door Neighbours, Groundwood Books (Toronto, Ontario, Canada), 1989, published as *Next-Door Neighbors,* Macmillan (New York, NY), 1990.

Putting up with Mitchell, illustrated by Barbara Wood, Brighouse Press, 1989.

Pick-up Sticks, Groundwood Books (Toronto, Ontario, Canada), 1991, Macmillan (New York, NY), 1992.

Out of the Blue, Groundwood Books (Toronto, Ontario, Canada), 1994, Simon & Schuster (New York, NY), 1995.

Back of Beyond: Stories of the Supernatural, Groundwood Books (Toronto, Ontario, Canada), 1996, Margaret K. McElderry Books (New York, NY), 1997.

The Young Writer's Companion, Douglas & McIntyre (Toronto, Ontario, Canada), 1999.

Next Stop! (picture book), illustrated by Ruth Ohi, Fitzhenry & Whiteside (Niagara Falls, NY), 2000.

From Reader to Writer: Teaching Writing through Classic Children's Books, Groundwood Books (Toronto, Ontario, Canada), 2000.

(Editor) *Girl's Own: An Anthology of Canadian Fiction for Young Readers,* Puffin Canada (Toronto, Ontario, Canada), 2001.

A Prairie as Wide as the Sea: The Immigrant Diary of Ivy Weatherall, Scholastic Canada (Markham, Ontario, Canada), 2001.

Big Ben, illustrated by Kim LaFave, Groundwood Books (Toronto, Ontario, Canada), 2001.

(With David Suzuki) *Salmon Forest,* illustrated by Sheena Lott, GreyStone Books (New York, NY), 2003.

The Several Lives of Orphan Jack, illustrated by Bruno St-Aubin, Douglas & McIntyre (Toronto, Ontario, Canada), 2003.

Ben over Night, illustrated by Kim LaFave, Groundwood Books (Toronto, Ontario, Canada), 2005.

Odd Man Out, Groundwood Books (Toronto, Ontario, Canada), 2006.

The Queen's Feet, illustrated by Dusan Petricic, Red Deer Press (Calgary, Alberta, Canada), 2006.

Also author of column "News from the North," published in *Horn Book,* 1984-98.

Ellis's works have been translated into French.

Sidelights

Writer, columnist, editor, and librarian Sarah Ellis has become one of the best-known children's authors in her native Canada due to the popularity of titles such as *The Baby Project, Pick-up Sticks, Back of Beyond: Sto-*

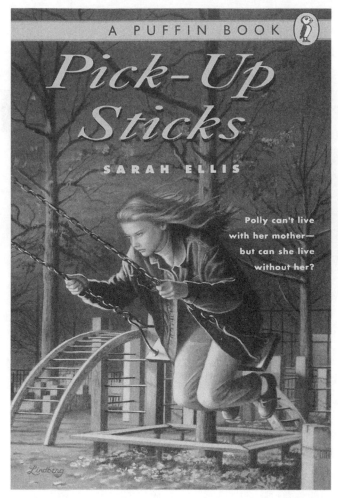

Cover of Ellis's young-adult novel **Pick-up Sticks,** *featuring artwork by Jeffrey Lindberg.* (Puffin Books, 1993. Cover illustration © 1993, by Jeffrey Lindberg. Reproduced by permission of Puffin Books, a division of Penguin Putnam Books for Young Readers.)

ries of the Supernatural, and *The Several Lives of Orphan Jack.* With her 1986 debut, *The Baby Project,* Ellis created "one of the most appealing and moving family stories to come along in ages," according to *Horn Book* contributor Hanna B. Zeiger, and the award-winning works she has produced since have been equally praised. In addition to young-adult novels, Ellis has also written for younger children, has edited several story collections, and has authored *From Reader to Writer: Teaching Writing through Classic Children's Books* to promote the craft of writing. Praised by *Booklist* contributor Hazel Rochman as "one of the best children's literature critics," Ellis "writes without condescension or pedantry. . . . Her prose is a delight: plain, witty, practical, wise."

Ellis was born in Vancouver, British Columbia, Canada, in 1952, the youngest of three children. As she once noted, "[my] joy in embroidering the truth probably comes from my own childhood. My father was a rich mine of anecdotes and jokes. He knew more variations on the 'once there were three men in a rowboat' joke than anyone I've encountered since. My mother was al-

ways willing to stop what she was doing to tell me about growing up on the prairies, stories of making doughnuts for the harvesters or how Aunt Florence threw eggs at the horses. I have one brother who collects tales of the absurd and another who is a born exaggerator. As youngest in the family I had to become a good storyteller just to hold my own at the dinner table."

Reading and tale-telling were important in Ellis's family while she was growing up, and books were also always close at hand in the Ellis home. "The first books I remember were a set of little yellow and black paperbound fairy tales, sent by Great-Aunt Lou in a Christmas parcel from England. My favorite was *The Wolf and the Seven Little Kids,*" the author once recalled. "Read-alouds in our house were picked to appeal to my older brothers, and that is how I first heard *Tom Sawyer,* in an edition with lovely pictures by Louis Slobodkin. (Later, in memory of those pictures, I gave one of my characters the last name of Slobodkin. Writers get to play these games.)

"When I got to school I discovered that you were allowed to take home one book a day from the library. So I did, every day. If it was raining (and it nearly always was in rainy Vancouver) the librarian would wrap the book in brown paper. It was like carrying home a present."

"Some of the books I read are still around—the 'Little House' books, *The Secret Garden, Half Magic.* I had *Peter Pan* read to me during a long stay in the hospital. I received *The Wizard of Oz* for Christmas when I was eight, and I read it all on Christmas afternoon. One summer I found a damp old copy of *Little Women* in the holiday cabin and for three days I lay on a top bunk, reading and weeping and happy, while the adults said, 'Wouldn't you like to go outside in the sun and play?'"

After graduating from high school, Ellis enrolled at the University of British Columbia, then went on to earn her degree in library science. After working for several years as children's librarian in North Vancouver, she traveled to Boston and earned an advanced degree in children's literature from Simmons College. While studying this curriculum as an enhancement to her work as a librarian, Ellis also did some of her first writing for children. However, it would be four more years before she would seriously undertake writing a children's book. In 1984 she took a leave from her job at the library and wrote, first articles, then short fiction, and finally a picture book. Although the story manuscript was rejected when she submitted it to a publisher, the publisher encouraged her to continue her efforts. Her next undertaking became *The Baby Project,* Ellis's first published work and the winner of the Sheila K. Egoff Award in 1987.

The Baby Project—published in the United States as *A Family Project*—is the story of how a young girl and her family deal with the expectation and ultimate loss of a new baby. Eleven-year-old Jessica eagerly awaits her new sister and even prepares a school project around the expected arrival. After the baby dies of crib death, Jessica must deal not only with her own feelings, but with her family's grief as well. Ellis creates a realistic and moving picture of a family in crisis, according to many critics. "She successfully focuses on the details of change, and in so doing creates an honest portrayal of family life," David Gale wrote in *School Library Journal.* The result, Gale added, is "a credible depiction of important family events, in turn funny and sad."

Much of the success of *The Baby Project* is due to the lifelike characters of Jessica and her family. Parents and siblings are portrayed as quirky, lovable people with a sense of humor. In addition, "although Jessica's point of view is consistently maintained, each complex character develops in a different way," Betsy Hearne observed in a review of the book for the *Bulletin of the Center for Children's Books.* Overall, Hearne added, "the cast is subtly portrayed." *Voice of Youth Advocates* contributor Mary Hedge also found the characters in *The Baby Project* to be believable, and praised "Jessica's courageous and cooperative attitude" in particular as "inspiring."

Next-Door Neighbors is also distinguished by "plausible characters in real life situations," according to Maria B. Salvadore in a review of Ellis's second novel for *School Library Journal.* The story takes place in 1957, when Peggy, the daughter of a minister, has just moved from the country to the city with her family. There she slowly makes friends with both George, the son of a refugee, and a Chinese gardener working for Peggy's wealthy, prejudiced neighbor. In recounting how Peggy learns about racism and responsibility, Ellis "has a deft descriptive touch, a way with a quirky phrase, and a convincing child's-eye view of hypocritical adults," Joan McGrath commented in *Quill & Quire.* The author "etches personalities that are likable amid their strengths and weaknesses and creates family dynamics that fit smoothly and believably into the plot," Barbara Elleman likewise wrote in *Booklist,* making her "ever in touch with her theme, her characters, her plot, and her audience."

Pick-up Sticks was inspired by a radio interview Ellis heard in which a homeless woman expressed her fear and frustration at not being able to care for her family. In the story, thirteen-year-old Polly must leave her single mom and go live with a financially secure uncle while her mother searches for proper housing in between holding down a job. In her new circumstances, Polly is confronted with the life she wished she could have had: a stable, comfortable home, in a nice neighborhood, where opportunities for friends and after-school activities are provided. Through her spoiled cousin and her new friends, she comes to learn that people of all walks of life experience discontent of some type, and that even her financially impoverished life with her mom is rich in many things.

In **The Several Lives of Orphan Jack** *Ellis introduces a resilient young hero who survives on his wits and his love of words.* (Groundwood Books, 2003. Illustration © 2003 by Bruno St-Aubin. Reproduced by permission of Groundwood Books/Douglas & McIntyre.)

In a change of pace, Ellis incorporates elements of fantasy into the story collection *Back of Beyond,* which is geared for older teens. Although her stories are based on traditional British folk tales, Ellis garbs them in modern dress, with the Internet, Mr. Potato Head, cults and gangs, and chat rooms figuring prominently. As John Burns noted in an article in *Canadian Review of Materials,* in *Back of Beyond* "mundane and magical worlds overlap. Ellis's protagonists have one foot in childhood and the other in adulthood; their transitional role means that anything can happen, and does." Praising the narrative voice as, by turns, "funny, cheeky, or probing," *Horn Book* contributor Marilyn Bousquin added that *Back of Beyond* is about "contemporary kids with . . . ordinary problems [who] realize new dimensions of themselves through their bone-chilling, sometimes heartwarming encounters with the otherworld."

Praised as "a small gem" by *Booklist* reviewer Ilene Cooper, Ellis's award-winning chapter book *The Several Lives of Orphan Jack* introduces a spirited twelve year old who loves words and whose most treasured possession is a page-worn dictionary that is missing the

"A" and"B" words. Excited by the prospect of being a bookkeeper's apprentice after leaving the Opportunities School for Orphans and Foundlings, the literal-minded youth becomes disillusioned when he learns that his new job focuses on numbers. Setting out into the real world armed with his trusty dictionary, Jack finds that his nimble mind and quick wit win him many new friends and numerous adventures, in a story Cooper noted embodies "both the joy of language and the vicissitudes of a life of possibilities." Reviewing *The Several Lives of Orphan Jack* for *Kirkus Reviews,* a contributor wrote that Ellis's "clean writing with a subtle humor weaves a tale that will inspire readers to learn new words," while Sharon Korbeck cited the author's "use of imagery, and alliteration" in her *School Library Journal* appraisal of the novel.

Another novel for older preteens, *Odd Man Out* focuses on twelve-year-old Kip. Sent to stay with his grandmother while his mother and her new husband go on a honeymoon, Kip finds himself outnumbered by five chatty, energetic, and very female cousins. Not surprisingly, the teen retires to the quiet refuge of his attic bedroom. Events that summer take a turn when he finds a book containing the teenage journal of his father, a man Kip never met but about whom he has many questions. Praising Kip as "an engaging protagonist," *Booklist* reviewer Michael Cart added that the boy's "search for the truth is suspenseful," while Terrie Dorio deemed *Odd Man Out* a "thoughtful and often funny" coming-of-age tale in which a teen is "challenged to think" about family members "in a different way."

Picture books by Ellis include *Next Stop!, Big Ben,* and *The Queen's Feet.* In *Next Stop!* readers meet Claire as she takes her weekly Saturday outing on the town bus. During her trip, the outgoing and imaginative Claire helps the driver, calling out the stops one by one, and greeting other regular riders. Ellis's text evokes the soothing regularity of a daily bus route; as *School Library Journal* contributor Steven Engelfried noted, "the repetitive pattern of the text suits the stop, start rhythm of a bus ride." Far more whimsical in tone, *The Queen's Feet* finds a royal monarch attached to two sets of toes that refuse to submit to the royal will. Although Queen Daisy may want to wear fancy shoes, her feet will only tolerate fuzzy slippers; when she wants to stand regally, they break into a spirited jig; and when she deigns to stroll in a garden, they carry her off and splash about in a nearby pond. As a *Kirkus Reviews* contributor advised, *The Queen's Feet* should be "required reading for all unruly little kickers, stompers, squirmers and scuffers."

In *Big Ben* and its sequel, *Ben over Night,* Ellis introduces readers to a young boy who is determined to keep pace with older children, even when it means being just a little bit scared or intimidated. In *Big Ben* the boy is frustrated because he is too little to do all the

The sights and sounds to be seen on a bus ride through a busy city are captured in Ruth Ohi's illustrations for Ellis's **Next Stop.** (Fitzhenry & Whiteside, 2000. Illustration © 2000 by Ruth Ohi. Reproduced by permission.)

things older siblings Joe and Robin can. His frustration is intensified on school report-card day, because Ben has no report card to share from preschool. However, the boy's older brothers are quick to recognize Ben's predicament; when Joe and Robin present the boy with a homemade report card of his own, Ben has been graded an "A-plus" little brother! Excitement over spending the night at best friend Peter's house is balanced by more than a few worries in *Ben over Night,* until Ben's family devises a way to help the little boy deal with his concerns. Joe and Robin's "affirmation is meaningful but not patronizing, and their delight in the remedy is as apparent as Ben's," noted a *Horn Book* reviewer of *Big Ben,* while a *Publishers Weekly* reviewer deemed *Ben over Night* a "thoughtful story" in which

Ellis's "compassionate and optimistic" spirit will inspire readers afraid of spending that first night away from home.

In addition to working part time as a reference librarian in her native Vancouver, Ellis devotes seven hours a day to her writing, and each of her young-adult novels takes about a year to complete. "When I was young I never once thought of becoming a writer," Ellis once noted. "Now, when I'm digging in the vegetable patch and I realize that I'm making up phrases for my gardening journal, or when I'm traveling and I find myself composing postcards at every new place, I wonder how I could ever not be a writer. Maybe I do want to record the events of my ordinary life, after all."

In his illustrations for **The Queen's Feet,** *Dušan Petričić reflects the silliness of Ellis's whimsical story.* (Red Deer Press, 2006. Illustration © 2006 by Dušan Petričić. Reproduced by permission.)

Biographical and Critical Sources

BOOKS

Children's Literature Review, Volume 42, Thomson Gale (Detroit, MI), 1997.

St. James Guide to Young-Adult Writers, 2nd edition, St. James Press (Detroit, MI), 1999.

PERIODICALS

Booklist, March 1, 1990, Barbara Elleman, review of *Next-Door Neighbors,* p. 1340; January 1, 1998, Chris Sherman, review of *Back of Beyond: Stories of the Supernatural,* p. 794; October 15, 2000, Hazel Rochman, review of *From Reader to Writer: Teaching Writing through Classic Children's Books,* p. 449; December 1, 2000, Hazel Rochman, review of *Next Stop!,* p. 718; December 1, 2003, Ilene Cooper, review of *The Several Lives of Orphan Jack,* p. 668; December 15, 2003, Gillian Engberg, review of *Salmon Forest,* p. 755; May 1, 2005, Carolyn Phelan, review of *Ben over Night,* p. 1589; May 1, 2006, Michael Cart, review of *The Queen's Feet,* p. 88; December 1, 2006, Michael Cart, review of *Odd Man Out,* p. 46.

Bulletin of the Center for Children's Books, April, 1988, Betsy Hearne, review of *A Family Project,* p. 154; December, 2003, Karen Coats, review of *The Several Lives of Orphan Jack,* p. 150, and Krista Hutley, review of *Salmon Forest,* p. 167; June, 2006, Karen Coats, review of *The Queen's Feet,* p. 449; December, 2006, Deborah Stevenson, review of *Odd Man Out,* p. 168.

Canadian Review of Materials, March 28, 1997, John Burns, "Sarah Ellis"; November 14, 2003, review of *The Several Lives of Orphan Jack.*

Horn Book, May-June, 1988, Hanna B. Zeiger, review of *A Family Project,* p. 350; November-December, 1997, Marilyn Bousquin, review of *Back of Beyond,* p. 680; May, 2001, Cathryn Mercer, review of *From Reader to Writer,* p. 289; March-April, 2002, review of *Big Ben,* p. 201; November-December, 2003, Christine M. Heppermann, review of *The Several Lives of Orphan Jack,* p. 742.

Kirkus Reviews, September 1, 2003, review of *The Several Lives of Orphan Jack,* p. 1122.

National Post, November 3, 2000, Elizabeth MacCallum, review of *Next Stop!,* p. B9.

Quill & Quire, September, 1989, Joan McGrath, review of *Next-Door Neighbors,* p. 23; December, 2001, Joanne Findon, review of *Big Ben.*

Publishers Weekly, May 23, 2005, review of *Ben over Night,* p. 78; February 27, 2006, review of *The Queen's Feet,* p. 59.

Resource Links, June, 2002, Joanne de Groot, review of *A Prairie as Wide as the Sea: The Immigrant Diary of Ivy Weatherall,* p. 11; February, 2004, Laura Reilly, review of *The Several Lives of Orphan Jack,* p. 12; October, 2006, Kathryn McNaughton, review of *The Queen's Feet,* p. 2; February, 2007, Moira Kirkpatrick, review of *Odd Man Out,* p. 12.

School Library Journal, March, 1988, David Thomson Gale, review of *A Family Project,* p. 188; March, 1990, Maria B. Salvadore, review of *Next-Door Neighbors,* p. 217; January, 2001, Steven Engelfried, review of *Next Stop!,* p. 93; September, 2001, Mary Lankford, review of *From Reader to Writer,* p. 262; December, 2003, Sharon Korbeck, review of *The Several Lives of Orphan Jack,* p. 149; June, 2005, Linda Ludke, review of *Ben over Night,* p. 108; April, 2006, Suzanne Myers Harold, review of *The Queen's Feet,* p. 105; December, 2006, Terrie Dorio, review of *Odd Man Out,* p. 138.

Voice of Youth Advocates, June, 1988, Mary Hedge, review of *A Family Project,* p. 85; February, 2007, Rachel L. Wadham, review of *Odd Man Out,* p. 524.

ONLINE

Canadian Children's Book Centre Web site, http:// collections.ic.gc.ca/ (November 29, 2001), "Sarah Ellis."

Friends of the CCBC Web site, http://www.education.wic. edu/ccbc/friends/ (June 10, 2007), Tana Elia, interview with Ellis.

Sarah Ellis Home Page, http://www.sarahellis.ca (June 10, 2007).

*   *   *

ELVGREN, Jennifer Riesmeyer

Personal

Married; husband's name Erik; children: William, Elizabeth, Sophia. *Hobbies and other interests:* Antiquing, horseback riding, playing the flute, playing with her children.

Addresses

Home and office—Barboursville, VA. *E-mail*—elvgren@earthlink.net.

Career

Author. Freelance feature writer for newspapers and magazines.

Awards, Honors

Bank Street College Best Books selection, and Americas Award for Children's and Young-Adult Literature, both 2007, both for *Josias, Hold the Book.*

Writings

If Nothing Happens. . . .: The Courtship Letters of Norman Wilson Ingerson and Stella May Murdock, 1982-1896, Chautauqua Region Press (Jamestown, NY), 2001.

Josias, Hold the Book, illustrated by Nicole Tadgell, Boyds Mills Press (Honesdale, PA), 2006.

Contributor to numerous periodicals, including *Victoria, Historic Traveler, Country Living, Highlights for Children, Spider, Ladybug,* and *Southern Living.*

Biographical and Critical Sources

PERIODICALS

Booklist, February 15, 2006, Ilene Cooper, review of *Josias, Hold the Book,* p. 101.

Kirkus Reviews, March 1, 2006, review of *Josias, Hold the Book,* p. 229.

Library Media Connection, November-December, 2006, Karen Sebesta, review of *Josias, Hold the Book,* p. 67.

School Library Journal, March, 2006, Catherine Callegari, review of *Josias, Hold the Book,* p. 187.

ONLINE

Jennifer Riesmeyer Elvgren Home Page, http://www.jenniferelvgren.com (May 16, 2007).

F

FALCONER, Ian 1959-

Personal
Born 1959, in Ridgefield, CT. *Education:* Attended New York University (art history), Parsons School of Design, (painting), and Otis Art Institute.

Addresses
Home—New York, NY.

Career
Set designer, children's book author and illustrator, and painter. Designer of stage sets and/or costumes for opera and stage productions, including (with David Hockney), *Tristan and Isolde,* 1987; *Turandot,* 1992; *Die Frau Ohne Schatten,* 1995; and *The Santaland Diaries,* 2002. Designer of sets and costumes for stage productions of New York City Ballet, Boston Ballet, and others; designer of float for Disneyland.

Awards, Honors
Parents' Choice Gold Award and Mittens Award Honor Book designation, both 2000, and Caldecott Honor Book designation, American Library Association (ALA), Marion Vannett Ridgway Award Honor Book designation, and White Ravens Award, all 2001, all for *Olivia;* Best Illustrated Book designation, *New York Times,* 2001, and ALA Notable Book designation, Bank Street College of Education Best Children's Book designation, American Booksellers Book Sense Book of the Year Award, and ABC Children's Booksellers Choices designation, all 2002, all for *Olivia Saves the Circus;* Book Sense Book of the Year nomination, American Booksellers Association, 2003, for *Olivia . . . and the Missing Toy;* Parent's Choice Gold Award for picture book, and National Association of Parenting Publications Gold Award, both 2003, and Bank Street College School of Education Best Children's Book designation, International Reading Association Children's

Choice designation, and Book Sense Book of the Year finalist, all 2004, all for *Olivia . . . and the Missing Toy;* works included on numerous state reading lists and award nomination lists.

Writings

SELF-ILLUSTRATED

Olivia, Atheneum (New York, NY), 2000.
Olivia Saves the Circus, Atheneum (New York, NY), 2001.
Olivia Counts, Atheneum (New York, NY), 2002.
Olivia's Opposites, Atheneum (New York, NY), 2002.
Olivia . . . and the Missing Toy, Atheneum (New York, NY), 2003.
Teatro Olivia (pop-up book), Atheneum (New York, NY), 2004.
Olivia Forms a Band, Athenum (New York, NY), 2006.
Olivia Dreams Big, Andrews McMeel (Kansas City, MO), 2006.

Contributor of illustrations to periodicals, including *New Yorker.*

Author's works have been translated into seventeen languages, including Latin.

Adaptations
Falconer's "Olivia" character has been used in merchandising, including as two dolls.

Sidelights
A theatrical set and costume designer who has also created cover designs for the popular *New Yorker* magazine, Ian Falconer made an unusual sidestep in his career when he decided to make a picture book for his four-year-old niece. In the self-illustrated *Olivia,* he first introduced his heroine, a fashion-savvy piglet who has gone on to gain a position within the pantheon of popu-

In Olivia, *Ian Falconer first introduced the stylish pig that sparked his career as a children's book author and illustrator.* (Atheneum, 2000. Illustration © 2000 by Ian Falconer. Reproduced by permission of Atheneum Books for Young Readers, an imprint of Simon & Schuster Children's Publishing Division.)

lar young picture-book heroines. Brought to life in Falconer's text and line drawings, Olivia is exuberant, intelligent, and unstoppable; in fact, as Jennifer M. Brown remarked in *Publishers Weekly,* "one could argue that Olivia's precociousness grows out of a three year old's relentless curiosity and unselfconscious belief that she can accomplish whatever she sets her mind to." Coupled with Falconer's laconic text and his bold, graphic art, Olivia's spirit quickly captured the hearts of reviewers and readers, and she has gone on to make more conquests in follow-up volumes such as *Olivia Forms a Band* and *Olivia's Opposites.*

Born in Connecticut, Falconer studied art history at New York University, then attended Parsons School of Design and the Otis Art Institute to pursue his interest in painting. Exhibiting a talent for design, he worked with artist David Hockney, who was then designing sets and costumes for stage productions produced in New York City, Los Angeles, Chicago, and London. Falconer began work on his first picture book after meeting his young niece. Hoping to capture the real-life Olivia's energy and can-do attitude, Uncle Ian decided to create an original picture book for the young girl's Christmas gift. Inspired by the black-and-white illustrations of Dr. Seuss, Falconer gave his book a sophisticated, minimalist look. Although the finished work intrigued one New York City publisher to whom it was shown in 1997, it

would be several more years until *Olivia* won the heart of an editor at Simon &Schuster. Published in 2000, the book earned its author the praise of critics and readers alike, as well as a coveted Caldecott honor for illustration.

Falconer's illustrations are notable for his use of graphite line on white paper, his vignette-style approach, and his use of only one or two clear, gouache accent colors within each book. In *Olivia,* for example, he uses dashes of bright red to convey the young piglet's boundless energy and her many interests, such as her love of art (particularly paintings featuring the color red), her dreams of becoming a prima ballerina, her enthusiasm for constructing amazing sand castles, and her pleasure in trying on all seventeen of the outfits in her closet (all in her favorite color of red!). Discussing his decision to use only a single accent color, Falconer explained to *Publishers Weekly* interviewer Jennifer M. Brown: "I think black-and-white can be just as arresting as color. It can also be much less information going into your eye, your brain, so that you pay attention to subtler detail in, say, facial expressions."

Although *Olivia* is built around a series of vignettes rather than a linear story, Ilene Cooper noted in her *Booklist* review that Falconer's "strong, clever art," his unusual design approach, his subtle humor, and his use of decorative endpapers that expand the plot all work together to reveal the escapades of the imaginative Olivia and her younger brother Ian. The author's "text is brief, funny, and sometimes ironic in relation to the highly amusing illustrations," commented Marianne Saccardi in *School Library Journal.* "Falconer's choice to suggest Olivia with a minimum of details and a masterful black line allows readers to readily identify with her . . . ," observed a *Publishers Weekly* critic; "There's a little bit of Olivia in everyone."

The irrepressible Olivia, along with her accommodating mom, returns in several more picture-book outings, among them *Olivia Saves the Circus, Olivia . . . and the Missing Toy,* and *Olivia Forms a Band.* Falconer introduces a little pig brother named William in *Olivia Saves the Circus,* which finds the multi-talented Olivia dazzling her schoolmates by recounting how she saved the day during an outing to the circus. Because the trapeze artists, the tattooed lady, the lion tamers, the bareback riders, and the trampoline jumpers are all sick in bed due to ear infections, the amazing Olivia bravely moves from show to show, putting on all the fancy circus outfits in turn and entertaining the crowds gathered to watch the show under the big top.

Most children can relate to the absolute panic a missing favorite toy can cause, and Falconer captures this sensation in *Olivia . . . and the Missing Toy.* Varying his characteristic black, white, and red art with a dash of green, the author/illustrator follows the spunky piglet as she conquers her fears and goes in search of her favorite rag doll during a particularly dark and very stormy

night. Apart from the missing toy—which has been adopted by the family's young puppy and is eventually discovered looking rather the worse for wear—Olivia must deal with an even more tragic fact: the soccer uniform assigned to Olivia's team is an unflattering shade of green! The determined Olivia continues to take charge in *Olivia Forms a Band,* using her creativity and a dash of turquoise to concoct the collection of instruments needed to sound out a much-needed marching-band accompaniment to a local fireworks display. According to Cooper, *Olivia . . . and the Missing Toy* matches a "simple yet compelling" story with illustrations that *School Library Journal* contributor Jane Barrer dubbed "stylish and witty." Wendy Lukehart noted in her *School Library Journal* review of *Olivia Forms a Band* that Falconer orchestrates an engaging text and detailed art to convey "the logic, invention, and humor emanating from a talented youngster, serious about the mission of the moment." Calling the author/illustrator "a master of antic line and situation," Michael Cart praised the series' "irrepressible" heroine in his *Booklist* review, while a *Kirkus Reviews* writer predicted that "every deft facial nuance" in *Olivia Forms a Band* "will be met with squeals of approval for the most popular pig in America."

Falconer wins over even younger fans with the board books *Olivia's Opposites* and *Olivia Counts.* In addition to the traditional "up, down" and "open, closed" pairings, the fashion-conscious pig uses skirt lengths, a tutu, hair accessories, and a favorite beach ball to illustrate relationships between concepts such as "plain" and "fancy" and "quiet" and "loud" in *Olivia's Opposites.* Meanwhile, toddlers can join the well-dressed piglet in counting an assortment of balls, bows, and paint pots in the companion volume.

Although the world of the stage remains Falconer's first love, he considers his work as a children's book writer more than just an entertaining sideline. As he explained to an online interviewer for Childrenslit.com, "I've always felt that children's books are for the most part condescending toward children and miss how smart children are. Their little hands and mouths may not be able to articulate what is going on in their sharp little brains. Writing children's books is [my] . . . opportunity to express this, and it seems to be appreciated by both children and adults."

Biographical and Critical Sources

PERIODICALS

Booklist, August, 2000, Ilene Cooper, review of *Olivia,* p. 2134; March 1, 2002, Ilene Cooper, review of *Olivia Saves the Circus,* p. 1146; July, 2002, Ilene Cooper, review of *Olivia Counts,* p. 1857; September 1, 2003, Ilene Cooper, review of *Olivia . . . and the Missing Toy,* p. 122; June 1, 2002, Michael Cart, review of *Olivia Forms a Band,* p. 82.
BP Report, July 16, 2001, "Olivia Takes Over the World."
Bulletin of the Center for Children's Books, November, 2001, review of *Olivia Saves the Circus,* p. 100; June, 2002, review of *Olivia's Opposites,* p. 362; December, 2003, Deborah Stevenson, review of *Olivia . . . and the Missing Toy,* p. 150; September, 2006, Karen Coats, review of *Olivia Forms a Band,* p. 12.
California, October, 1988, Donna Keene, "Ian Falconer: Work in Progress," p. 13.
Entertainment Weekly, December 8, 2000, Clarissa Cruz, "Bound for Glory: A Bevy of Books Suitable for Gift Giving Speaks Volumes about the Eclectic Pitch to Readers," p. 85.
Horn Book, November-December, 2001, review of *Olivia Saves the Circus,* p. 735; January-February, 2004, Roger Sutton, review of *Olivia . . . and the Missing Toy,* p. 69.
Interview, August, 1987, "Art and Comedy," p. 38; September, 1988, Greg Gorman, "Ian Falconer," p. 44.
New York, June 21, 1999, Tobi Tobias, "School of American Ballet," p. 66.
Kirkus Reviews, September 1, 2001, review of *Olivia Saves the Circus,* p. 1289; May 1, 2002, reviews of *Olivia's Opposites* and *Olivia Counts,* p. 653; September 15, 2003, review of *Olivia . . . and the Missing Toy,* p. 1173.
New York Times Book Review, November 19, 2000, M.P. Dunleavy, "Renaissance Pig: Meet Olivia, Who Dreams of Becoming a Dancer, or a Diva, or a Painter, or . . . ," p. 66; November 15, 2003, review of *Olivia . . . and the Missing Toy,* p. 45; May 1, 2006, review of *Olivia Forms a Band,* p. 457.
People, February 4, 2002, "Pig Tales," p. 123.
Publishers Weekly, July 17, 2000, review of *Olivia,* p. 193; November 20, 2000, "The Little Pig That Could," p. 19; December 18, 2000, Jennifer M. Brown, "Ian Falconer," p. 26; August 27, 2001, review of *Olivia Saves the Circus,* p. 83; September 1, 2003, review of *Olivia . . . and the Missing Toy,* p. 87; April 3, 2006, review of *Olivia Forms a Band,* p. 73.
School Library Journal, September, 2000, Marianne Saccardi, review of *Olivia,* p. 196; December, 2000, review of *Olivia,* p. 53; September 10, 2001, Gayle Feldman, "A Star Is Born," p. 54; October, 2001, Dorian Chong, review of *Olivia Saves the Circus,* p. 114; July, 2002, Sally R. Dow, review of *Olivia Counts,* p. 94; October, 2003, Jane Barrer, review of *Olivia . . . and the Missing Toy,* p. 188; June, 2006, Wendy Lukehart, review of *Olivia Forms a Band,* p. 110.

ONLINE

Children's Literature Web site, http://www.childrenslit.com/ (May 20, 2007), "Ian Falconer."*

*   *   *

FIRTH, Barbara

Personal

Female. *Education:* London College of Fashion, degree (pattern cutting).

Barbara Firth (Reproduced by permission.)

Addresses

Home and office—Harrow, Middlesex, England.

Career

Illustrator. Worked previously for *Vogue* knitting books.

Awards, Honors

Kate Greenaway Medal and Nestlé Smarties' Book Prize, both 1988, both for *Can't Sleep Little Bear?*

Illustrator

Judy Allen, *Exciting Things to Do with Nature Materials,* Lippincott (Philadelphia, PA), 1977.

Rosemary Verey, *The Herb Growing Book,* Little, Brown (Boston, MA), 1980.

Sue Tarsky, *The Potted Plant Book,* Walker (London, England), 1980.

Gerald Marshall Hall, *Pressing,* Warne (London, England), 1982.

Gerald Marshall Hall, *Fitting,* Warne (London, England), 1982.

Toni Naldrett, *Cutting Out,* Warne (London, England), 1982.

Toni Naldrett, *The Sewing Machine,* Warne (London, England), 1982.

Sue John, *The Special Days Cookbook,* Philomel (New York, NY), 1982.

Margaret Lane, *The Spider,* Dial Press (New York, NY), 1982.

Henry Smith, *Amazing Air,* Lothrop, Lee & Shepard (New York, NY), 1982.

Wendy Boase, *Country Animals,* Walker (London, England), 1983.

Wendy Boase, *Park Animals,* Walker (London, England), 1983.

Meriel Tilling, *Embroidery,* Warne (London, England), 1983.

David Lloyd, *Jack the Dog,* Walker (London, England), 1984.

David Lloyd, *Mot the Mouse,* Walker (London, England), 1984.

David Lloyd, *Lady Loudly the Goose,* Walker (London, England), 1984.

David Lloyd, *Romeo and Juliet the Lovebirds,* Walker (London, England), 1985.

David Lloyd, *Waldo the Tortoise,* Walker (London, England), 1985.

David Lloyd, *Tumult the Rabbit,* Walker (London, England), 1985.

Charles Causley, *"Quack!" Said the Billy-Goat,* Harper & Row (New York, NY), 1986.

William Mayne, *Leapfrog,* Walker (London, England), 1987.

Jonathan Gathorne-Hardy, *The Munros' New House,* Walker (London, England), 1987.

Martin Waddell, *The Park in the Dark,* Lothrop, Lee & Shepard (New York, NY), 1989.

Sarah Hayes, *The Grumpalump,* Clarion Books (New York, NY), 1990.

William Mayne, *Barnabas Walks,* Walker (London, England), 1990.

Martin Waddell, *Sam Vole and His Brothers,* Candlewick Press (Cambridge, MA), 1992.

Karen Wallace, *Bears in the Forest,* Candlewick Press (Cambridge, MA), 1994.

Peter Hansard, *Wag, Wag, Wag,* Candlewick Press (Cambridge, MA), 1994.

Wendy Durell, *Don't Open Your Mouth,* London Borough of Harrow (London, England), 1994.

Vivian French, *A Song for Little Toad,* Walker (London, England), 1995.

Martin Waddell, *We Love Them,* Candlewick Press (Cambridge, MA), 1997.

Jonathan London, *At the Edge of the Forest,* Candlewick Press (Cambridge, MA), 1998.

Charles Causley, *"Quack!" Said the Billy-Goat,* Candlewick Press (Cambridge, MA), 1999.

Martin Waddell, *Tom Rabbit,* Candlewick Press (Cambridge, MA), 2001.

Martin Waddell, *Hi, Harry!: The Moving Story of How One Slow Tortoise Slowly Made a Friend,* Candlewick Press (Cambridge, MA), 2003.

Emily Gibson, *The Original Million Dollar Mermaid: The Annette Kellerman,* Allen & Unwin (Crows Nest, New South Wales, Australia), 2005.

"BIG AND LITTLE BEAR" SERIES

Martin Waddell, *Can't You Sleep, Little Bear?,* Candlewick Press (Cambridge, MA), 1992.

Martin Waddell, *Let's Go Home, Little Bear,* Candlewick Press (Cambridge, MA), 1993.

Martin Waddell, *You and Me, Little Bear,* Candlewick Press (Cambridge, MA), 1996.

Martin Waddell, *Good Job, Little Bear!,* Candlewick Press (Cambridge, MA), 1999.

Martin Waddell, *Well Done, Little Bear,* Walker (London, England), 1999.

Martin Waddell, *The Little Bear Stories,* Walker (London, England), 2001.

Martin Waddell, *Sleep Tight, Little Bear!,* Candlewick Press (Cambridge, MA), 2005.

Adaptations

Can't Sleep Little Bear was adapted for audiobook by Candlewick Press, 2004.

Sidelights

As an illustrator, Barbara Firth prefers to draw things relating to nature, a habit that began in childhood when she sketched the wildlife surrounding her family's rural English home. Working in collaboration with writer Martin Waddell, Firth helped create the popular "Big and Little Bear" picture-book series. Reviewing her career during an interview posted on the Walker Books Web site, Firth noted the delight she has gained from illustrating the "Big and Little Bear" series: "I have always been biased toward illustrating natural history," she admitted, "so it was a joy to be able to draw pages and pages of bears." Titles from the "Big and Little Bear" series include *Can't You Sleep, Little Bear?, Let's Go Home, Little Bear,* and *You and Me, Little Bear.*

Martin Waddell's award-winning picture book **Can't You Sleep, Little Bear?** *features engaging illustrations by Firth.* (Candlewick Press, 1988. Illustration © 1988 by Barbara Firth.)

Firth uses warm-toned watercolors and colored pencil to illustrate the "Big and Little Bear" series, delicately conveying the special relationship Big Bear and Little Bear share. Jennifer Mattson, in an assessment of *Sleep Tight, Little Bear* for *Booklist,* commented that "Firth's expressive artwork, washed in muted tones of pebble, wood, and sky, harnesses the emotional undercurrents" of her two main characters. Discussing the same book in *School Library Journal,* Lauralyn Persson wrote of Firth's original artwork that its "soft colors and artful lines add appeal, character, and atmosphere." Firth's incorporation of delicate details is another aspect that is characteristic of her art. For example, in her work with Waddell, she portrays Big Bear in an apron while Little Bear is illustrated carrying a "teddy-boy." A *Kirkus Reviews* critic acknowledged Firth's inclusion of details in *Sleep Tight, Little Bear,* adding that the illustrator's "soft, expressive watercolors are delightfully engaging with some amusing subtle touches."

Biographical and Critical Sources

PERIODICALS

Booklist, September 15, 1992, Janice del Negro, review of *Sam Vole and His Brothers,* p. 158; May 1, 1993, Carolyn Phelan, review of *Let's Go Home, Little Bear,* p. 1597; June 1, 1994, Ellen Mandel, review of *Wag, Wag, Wag,* p. 1838; October 1, 1996, April Judge, review of *You and Me, Little Bear,* p. 360; December 1, 1998, April Judge, review of *At the Edge of the Forest,* p. 671; August, 1999, Carolyn Phelan, review of *Good Job, Little Bear,* p. 2067; March 1, 2001, Carolyn Phelan, review of *Tom Rabbit,* p. 1289; March 1, 2003, Ilene Cooper, review of *Hi Harry!: The Moving Story of How One Slow Tortoise Slowly Made a Friend,* p. 1205; January 1, 2006, Jennifer Mattson, review of *Sleep Tight, Little Bear,* p. 119.

Horn Book, June, 1981, Mary M. Burns, review of *The Herb Growing Book,* p. 321; March-April, 1993, Ellen Fader, review of *Let's Go Home, Little Bear,* p. 202; November, 1995, review of *A Song for Little Toad,* p. 768; March, 1999, Ellen Fader, review of *Good Job, Little Bear,* p. 203; March-April, 2003, Kitty Flynn, review of *Hi Harry!,* p. 207; January-February, 2004, review of *Hi Harry!,* p. 10; January-February, 2006, Susan Dove Lempke, review of *Sleep Tight, Little Bear,* p. 72.

Kirkus Reviews, March 15, 2003, review of *Hi Harry!,* p. 480; October 15, 2003, review of *Sleep Tight, Little Bear,* p. 1148.

Publishers Weekly, February 10, 1989, review of *The Park in the Dark,* p. 69; December 6, 1991, review of *Can't You Sleep, Little Bear?,* p. 73; August 17, 1998, review of *At the Edge of the Forest,* p. 72; March 24, 2003, review of *Hi Harry!,* p. 74; March 30, 1990, review of *We Love Them,* p. 60; March 22, 1993, review of *Let's Go Home, Little Bear,* p. 78; July 31,

1995, review of *A Song for Little Toad,* p. 80; July 8, 1996, review of *You and Me, Little Bear,* p. 83.

School Library Journal, March, 1983, Margaret Bush, review of *The Spider,* p. 164; March, 1983, Katherine Stemmer, review of *The Special Days Cookbook,* p. 178; July, 1989, Reva Pitch Margolis, review of *The Park in the Dark,* p. 77; August, 1990, Patricia Pearl, review of *We Love Them,* p. 135; September 1, 1991, Anna DeWind, review of *Grumpalump,* p. 233; September, 1995, Patricia Pearl Dole, review of *A Song for Little Toad,* p. 176; April, 2001, Kathy M. Newby, review of *Tom Rabbit,* p. 124; April, 2003, Piper L. Nyman, review of *Hi Harry!,* p. 142; December, 2005, Lauralyn Persson, review of *Sleep Tight, Little Bear,* p. 122.

Times Educational Supplement, March 24, 1989, Ann Thwaite, review of *The Park in the Dark,* p. 25; June 29, 1990, John Lawrence, review of *We Love Them,* p. 34; May 15, 1992, review of *Grumpalump,* p. 23; October 18, 1996, review of *You and Me, Little Bear,* p. 12.

Tribune Books (Chicago, IL), April 1, 2001, review of *Tom Rabbit,* p. 4.

ONLINE

Carnegie Greenaway Web site, http://www.carnegiegreenaway.org.uk/ (May 18, 2007), "Celebrating the Carnegie and Greenaway Winners."

Houghton Mifflin Web site, http://www.houghtonmifflin.com/ (May 18, 2007), "Barbara Firth."

Images of Delight, http://www.imagesofdelight.com/ (May 18, 2007).

Walker Books Web site, http://www.walkerbooks.com.uk/ (May 18, 2007), "Barbara Firth."*

*   *   *

FRIEDMAN, Laurie 1964-

Personal

Born January 28, 1964, in Fayetteville, AR; daughter of Kenneth (a lawyer) and Annette (a business executive) Baim; married David Friedman (a real estate developer), November 4, 1989; children: Rebecca, Adam. *Education:* Attended Sorbonne, University of Paris, 1984; Tulane University, B.A. (English and French), 1986. *Hobbies and other interests:* Cooking, reading, spending time with family, dog walking.

Addresses

Home—Miami, FL. *Agent*—Susan Cohen, Rosenstone/ Wender, 38 E. 29th St., 10th Fl., New York, NY 10016. *E-mail*—Lfriedman@aol.com.

Career

Children's book author. Grey Advertising, New York, NY, advertising account executive, 1986-88; Ogilvy & Mather Advertising, Houston, TX, account executive, 1990-92; N.W. Ayer Advertising, Houston, account executive, 1988-90; writer. Speaker at schools.

Member

Society of Children's Book Writers and Illustrators.

Awards, Honors

First-place award in children's division, writing competition of South Florida chapter, National Writer's Association, 1999, for *A Big Bed for Jed;* Bank Street College Children's Book Committee Best Children's Book designation, 2004, for *Mallory on the Move;* International Reading Association/Children's Book Council Children's Choice designation, 2005, for both *I'm Not Afraid of This Haunted House* and *Mallory vs. Max;* Society of School Librarians Honor designation, 2005, for *Mallory vs. Max.*

Writings

PICTURE BOOKS

A Big Bed for Jed, illustrated by Lisa Jahn-Clough, Dial Books for Young Readers (New York, NY), 2002.

A Style All Her Own, illustrated by Sharon Watts, Lerner (Minneapolis, MN), 2005.

I'm Not Afraid of This Haunted House, illustrated by Teresa Murfin, Carolrhoda (Minneapolis, MN), 2005.

Love, Ruby Valentine, illustrated by Lynn Avril Cravath, Carolrhoda (Minneapolis, MN), 2006.

"MALLORY" CHAPTER-BOOK SERIES

Mallory on the Move, illustrated by Tamara Schmitz, Carolrhoda (Minneapolis, MN), 2004.

Back to School, Mallory, illustrated by Tamara Schmitz, Carolrhoda (Minneapolis, MN), 2004.

Mallory vs. Max, illustrated by Tamara Schmitz, Carolrhoda (Minneapolis, MN), 2005.

Happy Birthday, Mallory!, illustrated by Tamara Schmitz, Carolrhoda (Minneapolis, MN), 2005.

In Business with Mallory, illustrated by Barbara Pollak, Carolrhoda (Minneapolis, MN), 2006.

Heart-to-Heart with Mallory, illustrated by Barbara Pollak, Carolrhoda (Minneapolis, MN), 2006.

Mallory on Board, illustrated by Barbara Pollak, Carolrhoda (Minneapolis, MN), 2007.

Sidelights

Children's book author Laurie Friedman is best known for her "Mallory" series of chapter books, which are geared for readers in the younger elementary grades. Praised by her humor and engaging young characters, Friedman has also shared her humorous slant on childhood with younger readers in the picture books *A Big Bed for Jed.* Here she gives the familiar transition from crib to bed an "amusing treatment" in a rhyming text that "will provoke smiles," according to *Booklist* contributor Ilene Cooper. Another picture book, *Love, Ruby*

Valentine, finds a young girl bemoaning the fact that she slept through her favorite day, until her pet cockatoo, Lovebird, reminds her that she can show her affection for others every day, not just on Valentine's Day. The author spins another holiday-themed offering in *I'm Not Afraid of This Haunted House,* while *A Style All Her Own* combines Friedman's text and Sharon Watts's illustrations into what *School Library Journal* contributor Carolyn Janssen dubbed "a fun bit of fluff for fashion-focused girls."

Readers meet eight-year-old Mallory MacDonald in *Mallory on the Move,* which finds the girl moving to a new town and making the transition between old and new friends. She weathers her stint as the new girl in class in *Back to School, Mallory,* helped by the fact that her mom is directing the school's end-of-year play. Sibling rivalry—more accurately, a competition for attention with her older brother's new dog—is the focus of *Mallory vs. Max,* and the need for financial independence inspires the girl to find gainful employment in *In Business with Mallory.* A secret admirer brightens the girl's mood in *Heart to Heart with Mallory,* while another step toward independence is taken in *Mallory on Board,* as Mallory goes on a cruise with her two best friends Joey and Mary Ann . . . and without her parents. Each of the "Mallory" books are written in a first-person narrative, and "Friedman's engaging writing style makes for enjoyable reading," according to *School Library Journal* contributor Tracy Karbel in a review of *Back to School, Mallory.* The author "finds a true voice for her likable but somewhat self-centered character," Sharon R. Pearce noted in her *School Library Journal* review of *Heart to Heart with Mallory,* while *Booklist* critic Shelle Rosenfeld dubbed Friedman's protagonist "lively" and "appealing." As Rosenfeld added, the "first-person narrative in *Mallory on the Move,* "written in short, descriptive sentences, is accessible and entertaining."

Friedman once told *SATA:* "My first book, *A Big Bed for Jed,* is a rhyming picture book about a little boy who conquers his fears and makes 'the big switch' from his crib to a bed. For me, imagination and a bit of real-life frustration were the key to writing *A Big Bed for Jed.* My own son's reluctance to move from a crib to a bed inspired me to come up with a solution that, along with a little dash of reverse psychology, proved surprisingly effective and served as the basis for Jed's fun and quirky story line.

"I like writing about change and transition, and the 'Mallory' books are all about learning to accept change. Change is hard to deal with. I hope my books will give kids a fresh and funny way to look at having to make changes and help them realize that change doesn't have to be bad, just different.

"I live in Miami, Florida, where I enjoy spending time with my husband, David, and our two children, Becca and Adam. I start each day with a walk, thinking about what my characters might do or say, then I go home and put all those thoughts and ideas on paper. I love what I do, and I am hard at work on lots more books for kids of all ages."

Biographical and Critical Sources

PERIODICALS

Booklist, January 1, 2002, Ilene Cooper, review of *A Big Bed for Jed,* p. 864; September 1, 2005, Connie Fletcher, review of *I'm Not Afraid of This Haunted House,* p. 144.
Bulletin of the Center for Children's Books, September, 2004, Hope Morrison, review of *Back to School, Mallory,* p. 16; September, 2005, Elizabeth Bush, review of *I'm Not Afraid of This Haunted House,* p. 16.
Kirkus Reviews, January 1, 2002, review of *A Big Bed for Jed,* p. 46; March 15, 2004, review of *Mallory on the Move,* p. 269; February 15, 2005, review of *Mallory vs. Max,* p. 228; July 1, 2005, review of *I'm Not Afraid of This Haunted House,* p. 734; September 1, 2006, review of *Love, Ruby Valentine,* p. 903.
Publishers Weekly, January 7, 2002, review of *A Big Bed for Jed,* p. 63; March 1, 2004, review of *Mallory on the Move,* p. 69; January 31, 2005, review of *A Style all Her Own,* p. 67; August 1, 2005, review of *I'm Not Afraid of This Haunted House,* p. 64; October 9, 2006, review of *Love, Ruby Valentine,* p. 55.
School Library Journal, July, 2002, Rosalyn Pierini, review of *A Big Bed for Jed,* p. 90; April, 2004, Debbie Stewart Hoskins, review of *Mallory on the Move,* p. 110; August, 2004, Tracy Karbel, review of *Back to School, Mallory,* p. 86; April, 2005, Carolyn Janssen, review of *A Style All Her Own,* and Sharon R. Pearce, review of *Mallory vs. Max,* both p. 97; September, 2005, Tina Zubak, review of *Happy Birthday, Mallory!,* p. 170; January, 2007, Sharon R. Pearce, review of *Heart to Heart with Mallory,* p. 94.*

*   *   *

FROST, Elizabeth
See FROST-KNAPPMAN, Elizabeth

*   *   *

FROST-KNAPPMAN, Elizabeth 1943-
(Elizabeth Frost)

Personal

Born October 1, 1943, in Washington, DC; daughter of Edward Laurie Frost and Lorena Ameter; married Edward William Knappman (a publisher and literary agent), November 6, 1965; children: Amanda Lee. *Education:* George Washington University, B.A., 1965;

Elizabeth Frost-Knappman (Photograph courtesy of Elizabeth Frost-Knappman.)

graduate study at University of Wisconsin—Madison, and New York University, 1966. *Politics:* Democrat. *Hobbies and other interests:* Tennis, knitting, reading, travel.

Addresses

Home—P.O. Box 805, Higganum, CT 06441. *Office*—New England Publishing Associates, Inc., P.O. Box 361, Chester, CT 06412. *E-mail*—elizabeth@nepa.com.

Career

Editor, agent, and author. Natural History Press, New York, NY, associate editor, 1967-69; William Collins & Sons, London, England, natural-history editor, 1970-71; Doubleday & Co., New York, NY, editor, then senior nonfiction editor, 1972-80; William Morrow & Co., New York, NY, senior nonfiction editor, 1980-82; New England Publishing Associates, Inc. (literary agency and book packager), Chester, CT, founder and president, 1983-2007. Lecturer at colleges, libraries, and organizations.

Awards, Honors

Choice Outstanding Academic Books designation, 1994, for *Clio Companion to Women's Progress in America.*

Writings

(Under name Elizabeth Frost) *The Quotable Lawyer,* Facts on File (New York, NY), 1986, revised edition, with David S. Shrager and Scarlet Riley, Checkmark Books (New York, NY), 1998.

(With Kathryn Cullen-DuPont) *Women Suffrage in America: An Eyewitness History,* Facts on File (New York, NY), 1992, revised edition, 2005.

The World Almanac of Presidential Quotations, World Almanac, 1993.

The ABC-Clio Companion to Women's Progress in America, American Bibliographical Center-Clio Press (Santa Barbara, CA), 1994.

American Journey: Women in America (CD-ROM), Primary Source Media, 1995.

(With Kathryn Cullen-DuPont) *Women's Rights on Trial: 101 Historic Trials from Ann Hutchinson to the Virginia Military Institute Cadets,* Thomson Gale (Detroit, MI), 1997.

(Editor, with husband, Edward W. Knappman, and Lisa Paddock) *Courtroom Drama: 120 of the World's Most Notable Trials,* UXL (Detroit, MI), 1998.

Sidelights

Elizabeth Frost-Knappman told *SATA:* "The year 1983 was a turning point for me. Recently, I had adopted my daughter, Amanda, and was at home after many years working as an editor. The women's movement was in the news and I became interested in its history. My reading eventually led to the publication of several books on women and law.

"My curiosity about law in general came from my mother, Lorena, a legal secretary, and my uncle Norman, an attorney working in Washington, DC, where I grew up. Uncle Norman's firm, Frost & Towers, had played a role in a case involving the letters of former first lady Mary Todd Lincoln, and I followed his interesting career in the newspapers. Then, in 1964-65, he employed me part time to help me pay for my courses at George Washington University. I collected information for his cases at the Library of Congress. Years later, writing my own books, I felt at home tracking down diaries, legal cases, letters, and speeches, which I relied on heavily in my writing.

"In 1983 I also started New England Publishing Associates, Inc., a literary agency. I worked out of an office in my home in Brooklyn, New York, until 1990, when my family and I moved to Haddam, Connecticut. My husband, Ed, and I expanded NEPA to include editorial services, such as writing, editing, indexing, and other aspects of book production.

"Looking back, I think that taking time out to raise my daughter gave me the time to broaden my interests from corporate publishing to writing and entrepreneurship, two very educational and enjoyable enterprises."

Biographical and Critical Sources

PERIODICALS

Choice, December, 1994, B.K. Lacks, review of *The ABC-Clio Companion to Women's Progress in America,* p. 573; June, 1997, review of *Women's Rights on Trial:*

101 Historic Trials from Ann Hutchinson to the Virginia Military Institute Cadets, p. 1734; April, 1999, review of *The Quotable Lawyer,* p. 1440.

Feminist Collections, summer, 2005, Martin Garnar, review of *Women's Suffrage in America,* p. 31.

School Library Journal, May, 1997, John Peters, review of *Women's Rights on Trial,* p. 158; August, 1998, Priscilla Bennett, review of *Courtroom Drama: 120 of the World's Most Notable Trials,* p. 188; October, 2005, Herman Sutter, review of *Women's Suffrage in America,* p. 88.

ONLINE

New England Publishing Associates Web site, http://www.nepa.com/ (June 10, 2007), "Elizabeth Frost-Knappman."

G

GAY, Marie-Louise 1952-

Personal

Born June 17, 1952, in Québec City, Québec, Canada; daughter of Bernard Roland Gay (a sales representative) and Colette Fontaine (a homemaker); married, c. 1972 (husband died, c. 1975); companion of David Toby Homel (an author and translator); children: (with Homel) Gabriel Reubens, Jacob Paul. *Education:* Attended Institute of Graphic Arts of Montréal, 1970-71; Montréal Museum of Fine Arts School, graduated, 1973; attended Academy of Art College (San Francisco, CA), 1977-79.

Addresses

Home—Montréal, Québec, Canada.

Career

Author, illustrator, graphic artist, cartoonist, animator, sculptor, and set, costume, and clothing designer. Actress on Canadian television and in local theater, c. 1961-62. Editorial illustrator for Canadian and American periodicals, 1972-87; graphic designer for magazines *Perspectives* and *Decormag,* 1974-76; La Courte Echelle (publishing company), Montréal, Québec, Canada, art director, 1980; University of Québec—Montréal, lecturer in illustration, beginning 1981; visiting lecturer in illustration, Ahuntsic College, 1984-85. Speaker at workshops and conferences at schools and libraries. Designer of children's clothing, beginning 1985; set designer for animated film *La Boite,* 1989. *Exhibitions:* Work exhibited in group and solo shows throughout Canada as well as internationally, including at Humor Pavillion, Montréal, Québec, Canada, 1974; Montréal Museum of Contemporary Art, 1979; Galerie 858, Montréal, 1980; Communication-Jeunnesse, Montréal, 1981-86; Toronto Art Directors' Club Show, Toronto, Ontario, Canada, 1982-83; Galerie Articule and Centre Culturel NDG, Montréal, 1984-86; Vancouver Art Gallery, Vancouver, British Columbia, Canada, 1988-90; Mable's Fable's, Toronto, 1990; and Ceperley House Gallery, Burnaby, British Columbia, 2000.

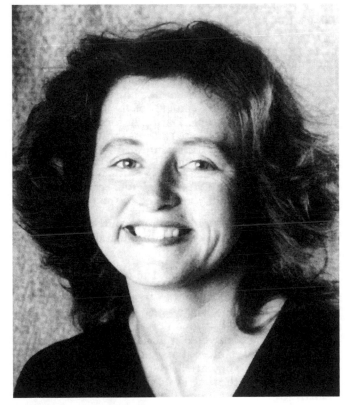

Marie-Louise Gay (Reproduced by permission.)

Member

Canadian Children's Book Center, IBBY Canada.

Awards, Honors

Claude Neon National Billboard Award, 1972; Western Art Directors Club Award, San Francisco, 1978; Society of Illustrators Award, 1979; Toronto Art Directors Club Award, 1983, 1985; Alvine-Belisle Prize for best French-Canadian children's book of the year, 1984, for *La soeur de Robert;* Canada Council Children's Literature Prize for illustration, 1984, for "Drôle d'école" series (French-Canadian prize) and for *Lizzy's Lion* (English-Canadian prize); Amelia Frances Howard-

Gibbon Illustrator's Award, Canadian Association of Children's Librarians, 1986, for *Moonbeam on a Cat's Ear;* Governor General's Literary Award for Children's Literature—Illustration, 1987, and Amelia Frances Howard-Gibbon Illustrator's Award, 1988, both for *Rainy Day Magic;* Governor General's Literary Award for Children's Literature—Illustration shortlist, 1989, for *Angel and the Polar Bear,* 1996, for *Berthold et Lucréce;* White Ravens Award selection, International Youth Library (Munich), 1993, for *Mademoiselle Moon;* Ehrenliste zum Osterreichiscchen Kinder-und Jugenbuchpreis, 1995, for *Fat Charlie's Circus* (German edition); Governor General's Literary Award for Children's Literature—Illustration shortlist, Mr. Christie's Book Award, and Storytelling World Awards Honor designation, all 1997, all for *The Fabulous Song;* Governor General's Literary Award for Children's Literature—Illustration shortlist, and Mr. Christie's Book Award shortlist, both 1998, both for *Rumpelstiltskin;* second prize, Alcuin Citations, Design Citations for Canadian Publishers, 1999, for *Dreams Are More Real than Bathtubs;* Governor General's Literary Award (Children's Literature—Illustration), 2000, for *Yuck: A Love Story;* shortlisted, Governor General's Literary Award (Children's Literature—Illustration), 2000, for *Sur mon île* (French edition); Ruth Schwartz Children's Book Award, Ontario Arts Council, Mr. Christie's Book Award, Amelia Howard-Gibbon Illustrator's Award nomination, and IBBY Honours List designation, all 2000, all for *Stella, Star of the Sea;* Governor General's Literary Award Children's Literature—Illustration, and Canadian Booksellers Association Illustrator of the Year Award shortlist, both 2000, both for *Yuck: A Love Story;* Ruth Schwartz Award shortlist, Mr. Christie's Book Award nomination, Elizabeth Mazrik-Cleaver Award, and Talking Book of the Year Award, all 2001, all for *Stella, Queen of the Snow;* named Children's Illustrator of the Year, Canadian Booksellers Association, 2000; Astrid Lindgren Memorial Award nomination, 2006.

Writings

SELF-ILLUSTRATED PICTURE BOOKS

De zéro à minuit (title means "From Zero to Midnight"), La Courte Echelle (Montréal, Québec, Canada), 1981.

La soeur de Robert (title means "Robert's Sister"), La Courte Echelle (Montréal, Québec, Canada), 1983.

Voyage au Clair de Lune, Heritage (Saint-Lambert, Canada), 1986, translated as *Moonbeam on a Cat's Ear,* Silver Burdett (Morristown, NJ), 1986, reissued with new design, Stoddart (Toronto, Ontario, Canada), 1992.

Magie d'un jour de pluie, Héritage (Saint-Lambert, Québec, Canada), 1986, translated as *Rainy Day Magic,* Stoddart (Dons Mills, Ontario, Canada), 1987, Albert Whitman (Morton Grove, IL), 1989.

Angèle et l'ours polaire, Heritage (Saint-Lambert, Québec, Canada), 1988, translated as *Angel and the Polar Bear,*

Stoddart (Dons Mills, Ontario, Canada), 1988, Kane/Miller (Brooklyn, NY), 1997.

Le cirque de Charlie Chou, Héritage (Saint-Lambert, Québec, Canada), 1989, translated as *Fat Charlie's Circus,* Stoddart (Dons Mills, Ontario, Canada), 1989.

Willy Nilly (adapted from the author's puppet play, *Bonne fête Willy;* also see below), Albert Whitman (Morton Grove, IL), 1990.

Mademoiselle Moon, Stoddart (Dons Mills, Ontario, Canada), 1992.

Lapin bleu, Heritage (Saint-Lambert, Québec, Canada), 1993, translated as *Rabbit Blue,* Stoddart (Dons Mills, Ontario, Canada), 1993.

Mimi-la-nuit, Heritage (Saint-Lambert, Québec, Canada), 1994, translation published as *Midnight Mimi,* Stoddart (Dons Mills, Ontario, Canada), 1994.

Qui a peur de Loulou?: théâtre (adapted from the author's puppet play; also see below), Editions VLB (Montréal, Québec, Canada), 1994.

(Reteller) *The Three Little Pigs,* Groundwood Books (Toronto, Ontario, Canada), 1994, Publishers Group West, 1996.

(Reteller) *Rumpelstiltskin,* Groundwood Books (Toronto, Ontario, Canada), 1997.

Princesse Pistache, Dominique et Cie. (Montréal, Québec, Canada), 1999.

Le jardin de Babel: théâtre (adapted from the author's puppet play; also see below), Lanctot (Outremont, Québec, Canada), 1999.

Sur mon île, 1999, translated as *On My Island,* Groundwood Books (Toronto, Ontario, Canada), 2000.

Caramba!, Dominique et Cie. (Saint-Lambert, Québec, Canada), 2007, English translation, Groundwood Books (Toronto, Ontario, Canada), 2007.

Les malheurs de princesse Pistache, Dominique et Cie. (Montréal, Québec, Canada), 2007.

"DRÔLE D'ÉCOLE" BOARD-BOOK SERIES; SELF-ILLUSTRATED

Rond comme ton visage, Ovale (Québec, Canada), 1984.

Blanc comme neige, Ovale (Québec, Canada), 1984.

Petit et grand, Ovale (Québec, Canada), 1984.

Un léopard dans mon placard, Ovale (Québec, Canada), 1984.

Mon Potager, Ovale (Québec, Canada), 1985, translated as *The Garden,* Lorimer (Toronto, Ontario, Canada), 1985.

"STELLA AND SAM" SERIES; SELF-ILLUSTRATED

Stella, étoille de la mer, Dominique et Cie. (Saint-Lambert, Québec, Canada), 1999, translated as *Stella, Star of the Sea,* Groundwood Books (Toronto, Ontario, Canada), 1999.

Stella, reine des neiges, Dominique et Cie. (Saint-Lambert, Québec, Canada), 2000, translated as *Stella, Queen of the Snow,* Groundwood Books (Toronto, Ontario, Canada), 2000.

Stella, fée de forêts, Dominique et Cie. (Saint-Lambert, Québec, Canada), 2002, translated as *Stella, Fairy of the Forest,* Groundwood Books (Toronto, Ontario, Canada), 2002.

Good Night Sam, Groundwood Books (Berkeley, CA), 2003.

Good Morning Sam, Groundwood Books (Berkeley, CA), 2003.

Stella, Princess of the Sky, Allen & Unwin (Crows Nest, New South Wales, Canada), 2004.

Que fais-tu, là, Sacha?, Dominique et Cie. (Saint-Lambert, Québec, Canada), 2006, translated as *What Are You Doing, Sam?,* Groundwood Books (Toronto, Ontario, Canada), 2006.

ILLUSTRATOR; FOR CHILDREN

Bernard Gauthier, *Hou Ilva* (picture book), La Tamanoir (Montréal, Québec, Canada), 1976.

Bernard Gauthier, *Dou Ilvien* (picture book; sequel to *Hou Ilva*), La Courte (Montréal, Québec, Canada), 1978.

Bernard Gauthier, *Hébert Lué* (picture book; sequel to *Dou Ilvien*), La Courte Echelle (Montréal, Québec, Canada), 1980.

Dennis Lee, *Lizzy's Lion,* Stoddart (Dons Mills, Ontario, Canada), 1984.

Tim Wynne-Jones, *The Last Piece of Sky,* Groundwood Books (Toronto, Ontario, Canada), 1993.

Don Gillmor, *When Vegetables Go Bad!,* Doubleday Canada (Toronto, Ontario, Canada), 1993, Firefly Books (Buffalo, NY), 1998.

Christiane Duchesne, *Berthold & Lucrèce,* Québec-Amerique Jeunesse (Montréal, Québec, Canada), 1994.

Don Gillmor, *The Fabulous Song,* Stoddart (Dons Mills, Ontario, Canada), 1996, Kane-Miller (Brooklyn, NY), 1998.

Lucie Papineau, *Monsier Soleil,* Dominique et Cie. (Saint-Lambert, Québec, Canada), 1997.

Sylvie Nicolas, *Le beurre de Doudou,* Héritage (Saint-Lambert, Québec, Canada), 1997.

Lois Wyse and Molly Rose Goldman, *How to Take Your Grandmother to the Museum,* Workman (New York, NY), 1998.

Don Gillmor, *The Christmas Orange,* Stoddart Kids (Toronto, Ontario, Canada), 1998, General Distribution Services, 1999.

Susan Musgrave, *Dreams Are More Real than Bathtubs,* Orca Book Publishers (Custer, WA), 1999.

Don Gillmor, *Yuck: A Love Story,* Stoddart Kids (Dons Mills, Ontario, Canada), 2000.

Marilyn Singer, *Didi and Daddy on the Promenade,* Clarion (New York, NY), 2001.

David Homel, *Travels with My Family,* Groundwood Books (Toronto, Ontario, Canada), 2005.

James Howe, *Houndsley and Catina,* Candlewick Press (Cambridge, MA), 2006.

James Howe, *Houndsley and Catina and the Birthday Surprise,* Candlewick Press (Cambridge, MA), 2006.

Frieda Wishinsky, *Please, Louise,* Groundwood Books (Toronto, Ontario, Canada), 2007.

Contributor of illustrations to books, including *La vache et d'autres animaux,* La Courte Echelle (Montréal, Québec, Canada), 1982, and *Mother Goose: A Cana-* *dian Sampler,* Groundwood (Toronto, Ontario, Canada), 1994, and to periodicals, including *Mother Jones, Psychology Today,* and *Saturday Night.*

ILLUSTRATOR; "SOPHIE/MADDIE" SERIES; PRIMARY-GRADE FICTION

Louise Leblanc, *Ça suffit, Sophie,* La Courte Echelle (Montréal, Québec, Canada), 1990, translated as *That's Enough, Maddie,* Formac (Halifax, Nova Scotia, Canada), 1990.

Louise Leblanc, *Sophie lance et compte,* La Courte Echelle (Montréal, Québec, Canada), 1991, translated as *Maddie in Goal,* Formac (Halifax, Nova Scotia, Canada), 1991.

Louise Leblanc, *Ça va mal pour Sophie,* La Courte Echelle (Montréal, Québec, Canada), 1992, translated as *Maddie Wants Music,* Formac (Halifax, Nova Scotia, Canada), 1993.

Louise Leblanc, *Sophie part en voyage,* La Courte Echelle (Montréal, Québec, Canada), 1993, translated as *Maddie Goes to Paris,* Formac (Halifax, Nova Scotia, Canada), 1993.

Louise Leblanc, *Sophie est en danger,* La Courte Echelle (Montréal, Québec, Canada), 1994, translated as *Maddie in Danger,* Formac (Halifax, Nova Scotia, Canada), 1994.

Louise Leblanc, *Sophie fait des folies,* La Courte Echelle (Montréal, Québec, Canada), 1995, translated as *Maddie in Hospital,* Formac (Halifax, Nova Scotia, Canada), 1995.

Louise Leblanc, *Sophie vit un cauchemar,* La Courte Echelle (Montréal, Québec, Canada), 1996, translated as *Sophie in Trouble,* Formac (Halifax, Nova Scotia, Canada), 1996.

Louise Leblanc, *Sophie devient sage . . . ,* La Courte Echelle (Montréal, Québec, Canada), 1997, translated by Sarah Cummins as *Maddie Tries to Be Good,* Formac (Halifax, Nova Scotia, Canada), 2000.

Louise Leblanc, *Sophie prend le grands moyens,* La Courte Echelle (Montréal, Québec, Canada), 1998, translated by Sarah Cummins as *Maddie Wants New Clothes,* Formac (Halifax, Nova Scotia, Canada), 2001.

Louise Leblanc, *Sophie veut vivre sa vie,* La Courte Echelle (Montréal, Québec, Canada), 1999, translated by Sarah Cummins as *Maddie Needs Her Own Life,* Formac (Halifax, Nova Scotia, Canada), 2001.

Louise Leblanc, *Ca suffit, Sophie!,* La Courte Echelle (Montréal, Québec, Canada), 1999.

Louise Leblanc, *Sophie court apres la fortune,* La Courte Echelle (Montréal, Québec, Canada), 2001, translated by Sarah Cummins as *Maddie's Millionaire Dreams,* Formac (Halifax, Nova Scotia, Canada), 2002.

Louise Leblanc, *Sophie déouvre l'envers du décor,* La Courte Echelle (Montréal, Québec, Canada), 2001, translated by Sarah Cummins as *Maddie on TV,* Formac (Halifax, Nova Scotia, Canada), 2003.

Louise Leblanc, *Sophie part en orbite,* La Courte Echelle (Montréal, Québec, Canada), 2004, translated by Sarah Cummins as *Maddie Surfs for Cyber-Pals,* Formac (Halifax, Nova Scotia, Canada), 2004.

Louise Leblanc *Sophie est la honte de la famille,* Diffusion du livre Mirabel (Saint-Laurent, Québec, Canada), 2005, translated by Sarah Cummins as *Maddie's Big Test,* Formac (Halifax, Nova Scotia, Canada), 2005.

Louise Leblanc, *Sophie défend les petits fantômes,* La Courte Echelle (Montréal, Québec, Canada), 2005, translated by Sarah Cummins as *Maddie Stands Tall,* Formac (Halifax, Nova Scotia, Canada), 2005.

ILLUSTRATOR; "JULIA" SERIES; PRIMARY-GRADE FICTION

Christiane Duschesne, *Julia et le chef des Pois,* Québec-Amerique Jeunesse (Montréal, Québec, Canada), 1997.

Christiane Duschesne, *Julia et les fantômes,* Boreal (Montréal, Québec, Canada), 1999.

Christiane Duschesne, *Julia et le voleur de nuit,* Boreal (Montréal, Québec, Canada), 2000.

Christiane Duschesne, *Julia et le premier cauchemar,* Boreal (Montréal, Québec, Canada), 2001.

OTHER

(Illustrator) Anne Taylor, *Hands On: A Media Resource Book for Teachers* (nonfiction) National Film Board of Canada (Montréal, Canada), 1977.

Graphic designer of *Crapauds et autres animaux* by Francine Tougas and others, 1981. Author and designer of puppet plays *Bonne fête Willy,* 1989; *Qui a peur de Loulou?,* 1993; and *Le jardin de Babel,* 1999, all produced in Québec, Canada.

Gay's books have been published in several languages, including Dutch, Danish, Norwegian, Spanish, Swedish, German, Portuguese, Greek, and Korean.

Sidelights

Well known in both French-and English-speaking Canada as an author and artist, Marie-Louise Gay is among her country's most prominent contemporary creators of children's literature. She directs her picture books—humorous, action-filled works as well as more-contemplative volumes—to youngsters ranging from preschool to the early primary grades. She has also provided the art for picture books and stories by writers as Dennis Lee, Tim Wynne-Jones, Don Gillmor, Susan Musgrave, James Howe, and Marilyn Singer, and has collaborated with writer Louise Leblanc on the popular "Sophie/Maddie" series. Introduced in books that highlight their author's originality, imagination, and an understanding of children and their world, Gay's young protagonists launch themselves into amazing adventures that transport them to such places as the sky or under the sea before they return home safely. While books such as *Caramba!* and her "Stella and Sam" picture books celebrate children's natural joyfulness and love of exuberant, often chaotic, play, other works by Gay depict the less-sunny parts of life, such as embarrass-

In addition to her own books, Gay brings to life a tale by popular writer James Howe in her artwork for **Houndsley and Catina.** (Candlewick Press, 2006. Illustration © 2006 by Marie-Louise Gay. Reproduced by permission of Candlewick Press, Inc., Cambridge, MA.)

ment, terror, loneliness, and the need for emotional support. Through both imaginative play and exploration of the world around them, her characters ultimately confront their fears and experience personal growth in engaging stories relayed in simple but lively prose and verse.

In her art Gay uses watercolor, pen and ink, colored pencil, and collage, and she renders her characters in a cartoon-like style that stresses their large bodies, broad faces, tiny limbs, and spiked hair. In addition to the energy, freshness, and colorful, expressionistic quality of her art, she is also noted for her inventive page designs and distinctive use of perspective. Although sometimes faulted for creating books without morals or tales featuring questionable adult role models, Gay's works captivate young readers. Dubbing the author/illustrator "the mistress of 'what-if'" in a *Canadian Children's Literature* review, Joan McGrath added that Gay's "perfect recall of a child's free-ranging, fresh-eyed delight coupled with the adult artistry to bring joyful fantasy to life . . . makes her work a nursery treasure." According to *Quill & Quire* contributor Janet McNaughton, "at her

best, . . . Gay captures the whimsical side of childhood in a way that few author/illustrators can," and a *St. James Guide to Children's Writers* essayist dubbed the author/illustrator "one of Canada's foremost interpreters of young children's perceptions of important real and imaginary elements of their lives."

Born in French-speaking Québec City, Québec, Gay moved with her family to Oakville, Ontario, at age five and there taught herself to read—in English. "That was the beginning of my addiction to reading," she later admitted in a *Something about the Author Autobiography Series (SAAS)* essay. "With books, I could find friends wherever we went." At age seven the family moved again, this time to a more rural home in West Vancouver, British Columbia. During trips to the public library, Gay stocked up on books, fueling a passion for reading she has retained as an adult. As Gay admitted to Marie Davis for *Canadian Children's Literature:* "I am an avid reader—I need a fix. I have to read all the time. And I have been like that since I was five years old."

While living in Vancouver, Gay became involved in the amateur theatrical group where her parents both appeared. Starting with small stage roles, she eventually acted in the children's television series *Tidewater Tramp* and *Friday Morning Series.* However, as she recalled in *SAAS,* "after a heady year of stardom, our family moved again, back to Montréal. A promising career bit the dust."

In Montréal, Gay attended a French private school, but was not happy there. During her teens, reading became a refuge, particularly science fiction by authors such as C.S. Lewis, Ursula K. Le Guin, and John Wyndham, as well as the novels of Colette, Lawrence Durrell, and Gabriel García Márquez. Gay also became interested in art, inspired "by a type of literature which came mainly from France and Belgium: *la bande dessinée,* illustrated albums, astonishing because of their innovative visual impact and highly humorous and intellectual content. I pored over these drawings and realize now that they had an enormous influence on my style of illustration." In school, she began to cover her notebooks with "all manner of strange cartoon creatures flying in between math equations, weaving in and out of grammar rules, skiing down equilateral triangles, or squashing chemistry problems to death." Sent to art school by her perceptive mother, Gay "stepped into another world. A world that suited me."

After leaving high school, Gay attended the Institute of Graphic Arts of Montréal, where she studied typography, perspective, and art history. Transferring to the Montréal Museum of Fine Arts School, she discovered animation, drawing and painting a variety of creatures that starred in her animated films. A year later she successfully began marketing her art to magazines in order to finance her filmmaking and her school tuition. In the process, Gay explained, "I . . . learned two very important things: to be very critical about my own work

and not to be afraid of throwing a drawing away and redoing it." At age twenty she married a fellow artist, but he tragically died three years later. Leaving Montréal, she moved to San Francisco and enrolled at the Academy of Arts College, where she studied anatomy, life drawing, portraits, and illustration techniques. During her three years there, Gay worked sporadically as an editorial illustrator, and also illustrated textbooks.

Returing to Montréal after graduation, Gay learned the ins and out of children's-book publishing through her job as art director and production manager of La Courte Echelle. Her first illustration work came when she provided art for three French-language children's books by Bernard Gauthier. In 1981 she produced her first original self-illustrated book, *De zéro à minuit.* Her second, the picture book *La soeur de Robert,* won the Alvine-Belisle Prize for best French-Canadian picture book, while her "Drôle d'école" board-book series won the Canada Council Children's Literature Prize in illustration. Gay was propelled to national attention through her work for *Lizzy's Lion,* a picture book in verse by well-known Canadian poet Dennis Lee. Because of the story, in which a hungry lion gobbles up a burglar, the work became one of the most censored books in Canada. Reviewing *Lizzy's Lion* for *Books in Canada,* Mary Ainslie Smith called Gay's illustrations "funny and eccentric," while John Bemrose concluded in *Maclean's* that her "mischievously exaggerated" interpretation of Lee's story "prevent sober judgment from spoiling the fun." Gay's illustrations for *Lizzy's Lion* earned the Canada Council Literature Prize in illustration for an English-language book in 1984, the same year she won for her "Drôle d'école" series. Her joint win of this coveted prize made her the first author to receive this award in both the French-language and English-language categories. Most of Gay's books are now published in both English and French editions.

Among Gay's other award-winning original picture books are *Moonbeam on a Cat's Ear, Rainy Day Magic, Caramba,* and *On My Island.* In the rhyming text of *Moonbeam on a Cat's Ear* Rose and Toby Toby lasso and ride the moon before being driven back inside by a thunderstorm. A popular story, the book was reissued in 1986, winning Gay the Amelia Frances Howard-Gibbon Illustrator's Award. A reviewer for the *Children's Book News* called the original version "a lovely book" possessing "all the elements of a classic picturebook," while *Books in Canada* reviewer Rhea Tregebov cited the interplay of layout, text, and illustrations in the revision as "not merely coherent, but brilliant," and described Gay's text as "marvelous poetry" in which the "use of rhyme and metre is so effective that the words have an inevitable feel to them, a hypnotic effect that only such poets as Dennis Lee and Gay seem able to create."

In the award-winning *Rainy Day Magic,* friends Victor and Joey use their imaginations to transport themselves to the jungle and under the sea after being sent to the

One of Gay's most popular picture books, **Rainy Day Magic** *encourages young readers to use their imagination.* (Stoddart Publishing Co., Ltd., 1987. Illustration © 1987 by Marie-Louise Gay. Reproduced by permission of the illustrator.)

basement by their parents as punishment for being too loud. When the children are called back upstairs for dinner, Joey sports a mauve starfish in her hair, a souvenir of her aquatic adventure. Another story that brings to life the travails of childhood unfolds in *Caramba,* as a small kitten learns to accept his limitations as well as his differences. While older cats can fly—at least their graceful leaps look that way to little Caramba—the young kitten's efforts to mimic their actions only find him face down and embarrassed. Ultimately the support of best-friend Portia the Pig and an accidental dunking reveals Caramba's special ability: unlike most kitties, he is unafraid of water. Calling Gay's feline protagonist "a charmingly self-deprecating cutie," a *Publishers Weekly* reviewer also praised the author/illustrator's "dreamy, gossamer watercolors," while *Resource Links* critic Lori Lavalle predicted that, with its "imaginative and unpredictable storyline," *Caramba* "is sure to become a classic."

The title character in *Fat Charlie's Circus* wants to be a famous circus performer when he grows up. The ambitious and resourceful lad is soon practicing stunts at home: lion-taming with his cat, walking the clothesline for a tightrope, training his goldfish to jump through a hoop, and juggling dinner plates. Unfortunately, the chaos resulting from the boy's practice causes Fat Charlie's parents to become upset. Hoping to assure them that his training is not in vain, Charlie decides to perform a diving act: he intends to jump from the tallest tree in his backyard into a tiny glass of water. Once he is in the tree, however, the boy realizes that he is too scared to dive. He is also too scared to come down from the tree. Crestfallen and in a predicament, the boy is rescued by his loving grandmother, who climbs the tree with the claim that she intends to jump with Char-

lie. When she becomes fearful of the same jump from the lofty height, Charlie retains his dignity by helping the older woman down. Reviewing *Fat Charlie's Circus* in *Canadian Children's Literature,* Marie Davis commented that the book has "an unusual depth—both in the carefully-shaded illustrations and the subtlety of the text," while *Canadian Review of Materials* contributor Alison Mews called it a "wonderful story that begs to be shared with children."

In the picture book *On My Island* Gay transports readers to a small island where a young boy and his animal companions—three ants, two cats, a wolf, and a bat—live, surrounded by the sea. Although the boy complains that his life is boring, readers can see the fantastic events taking place all around him: a dragon swims past, colorful kites climb into the sky, giant elephants parachute, canonball-like, into the water, and a train circles the island. As readers are gleefully aware, the bored young boy and his friends are always looking the other way when such amazing activities take place. In her watercolor-and-collage illustrations, Gay incorporates flower petals, fabrics, and bits of newspaper, and her use of font size takes on different configurations depending on the level of activity—for example, when the narrator shouts over a stiff wind, the text is huge. As *Booklist* contributor Carolyn Phelan wrote of *On My Island,* "the short, direct text, the well-composed double-page spreads, and the abundance of action in the illustrations combine" in a "satisfying and enjoyable" picture book. In *School Library Journal,* Holly Belli noted that, while it may be parents who appreciate the irony of Gay's tale, "children will pore over the pictures and imagine islands of their own."

Inspired by her childhood memories, Gay's "Sam and Stella" picture-book series—which includes *Stella, Star*

of the Sea, Stella, Queen of the Snow, Good Night, Sam, and *What Are You Doing, Sam?*—have brought her special recognition. In the award-winning series opener, *Stella, Star of the Sea,* red-headed Stella and her younger brother, Sam, spend a day at the seashore. Sam is afraid of the water but curious about it. Since Stella had been to the beach once before, she helpfully answers his many questions with replies that blend realism with imagination, and encourage Sam in entering the water. As with her other books, Gay incorporates watercolor and collage in her detailed illustrations, creating what a *Publishers Weekly* critic described as "an air of holiday abandon." In *Canadian Review of Materials,* Helen Norrie predicted of the book that "children will identify with the reluctant Sam and enjoy both his questions and Stella's answers."

The adventures of the two siblings continue in *Stella, Queen of the Snow,* as Sam experiences his first snowstorm and asks question after question about it. Big sister Stella, the self-proclaim Queen of the Snow, an-

A little kitten with big trepidations discovers his unique talents in Gay's endearing picture book **Caramba.** (Groundwood Books, 2005. Illustration © 2005 by Marie-Louise Gay. Reproduced by permission of Groundwood Books/Douglas & McIntyre.)

An older sister's imaginative stories inspire a little brother's courage in Gay's engaging picture book Stella, Star of the Sea. (Groundwood Books, 2001. Illustration © 1999 by Marie-Louise Gay. Reproduced by permission of Groundwood Books/Douglas & McIntyre.)

swers Sam's queries with her characteristically humorous mix of fantasy and fact. The children eat snowflakes, have a snowball fight, and make snow angels, among other activities, and by story's end Sam assures Stella that he can hear the snow angels singing. *Good Morning, Sam* and *Good Night, Sam* find the toddler learning to get dressed and undressed, and prepare for bed, all with the help of sister Stella as well as the family dog. *Stella, Princess of the Sky* finds the siblings outside contemplating the night sky, as Sam wonders out loud where the Sun sleeps and how the Moon rises up so high. A journey into a nearby woodland in search of the tiny fairies Stella assures her brother are under every leaf and twig is the focus of *Stella, Fairy of the Forest,* which *School Library Journal* contributor Mary Elam dubbed "a visual treasure for reading aloud."

Writing in *School Library Journal,* Grace Oliff called *Stella, Queen of the Snow* "a charming story of successful sibling mentoring, simply but effectively told" in which Gay's line-and-watercolor illustrations "complement both the humor and the message of the tale." In a review of *Good Morning, Sam* for *School Library Journal,* Martha Topol noted that in the "Stella and Sam" books Gay introduces "sweet, enduring characters who are bound to strike a familiar chord with readers," and *Booklist* contributor Stephanie Zvirin maintained that the "freewheeling ink-and-watercolor illustrations are delightful." According to *School Library Journal* writer Lisa Gangemi, a tale full of "charm and whimsy" is recounted in *Stella, Princess of the Night Sky,* and Zoe Johnstone wrote in her *Resource Links* review of the same book that Gay's illustrations "express energy, movement, and wonder." In *Horn Book* Jennifer Brabander noted of the 'Stella and Sam" books that Gay's "skillful interplay of text and art showcases [her] . . . agility in allowing both words and pictures to tell the story."

In addition to original stories, Gay has illustrated her retelling of several familiar stories. *The Three Little Pigs* incorporates several techniques used in oral storytelling, such as colloquial expressions and asides to the audience. Discussing Gay's watercolor illustrations for the work, Joanne Findon wrote in *Quill & Quire* that the images "are filled with colour and energy," and that "small details—leaves flying and raindrops blowing out of the illustrations and across the adjacent white spaces—create a satisfying sense of the oneness of words and pictures." Findon concluded by calling *The Three Little Pigs* a "lovely book that breathes life into a well-known tale." Gay's version of *Rumpelstiltskin* has received similar praise for the originality of its presentation. As Dave Jenkinson noted in *Canadian Review of Materials,* the author/illustrator's "text and illustrations soften the story for the intended audience," and *School Library Journal* contributor Jeanne Clancy Watkins concluded that, "in this age of the lavishly illustrated fairy tale, Gay gives readers a version of the well-worn Grimm tale that is surprisingly and refreshingly childlike." *Rumpelstiltskin* was shortlisted for the Governor General's Literary Award for illustration in 1997.

While working as a professional author and illustrator, Gay met her life partner, David Homel, an award-winning American writer and translator. The couple's two sons, Gabriel and Jacob, have served as the inspiration for several of Gay's original stories. In *Travels with My Family* she and Homel collaborate on one such a story, as their young narrator recounts a family road trip through North America and Mexico. While the boy and his younger brother vote for the proverbial trip to Disneyland, Mom and Dad decide to explore the region via alternate routes that result in a series of mishaps, adventures, and surprising discoveries. Noting that *Travels with My Family* is written in "simple language and adorned with amusing cartoon sketches," *School Li-*

brary Journal contributor Corinda J. Humphrey cited the chapter book as "a good choice" for less-experienced readers, while Shelle Rosenfeld noted in *Booklist* that the "droll, first-person" perspective of the book's young narrator is "often comical and sometimes suspenseful."

In addition to creating picture books, Gay has illustrated textbooks and posters, designed children's clothing and sets for animated films, and also written three puppet plays for Québec's Theatre de l'oeil that featured original puppets, costumes, and sets. In addition to teaching illustration to students at the university level, she is also a regular speaker at schools and in conferences on children's literature. As she once told *SATA:* "I feel that I'm concentrating on a particular medium because it's for kids. I am geared towards kids in what I want to talk about to them and how to make them laugh, whether in clothing design, in the plays, or in the books. I'm happy about that. I finally got to where I don't have to worry about the rush of the adult world and the quick throwaway feeling you have."

Regarding her work as an author/illustrator, Gay wrote in an essay for *SAAS:* "When I write and illustrate for children, my primary concern is to tell a good story, a story that will capture their heart and minds. I want to create characters and emotional situations that children will recognize. I want children to identify with the joy, anger, frustration, laughter, fear, loneliness, doubt, and happiness of my characters. I accomplish this in two ways: the first, of course, is the story itself, which in most cases is inspired by an ordinary event, a domestic situation. . . . The other way to ensure emotional identification is through illustration. I want children to identify visually with my characters. That's why I've created a series of rather funny-looking kids . . . not particularly pretty kids, but real kids!" "When I hear people (adults, of course) saying that children are more interested in videos, electronic games and so on, and that books will disappear altogether in a few decades, I do not believe it for one minute," Gay added. "What's disappearing is the time to read books, the time to tell stories. Children are naturally curious, open to new ideas, ready to trade reality for fiction. They are still open to other ways of thinking, their prejudices yet to come. If children are exposed to a wide range of books, reading will eventually become an important aspect of their lives. I, for my part, will continue writing for them."

Biographical and Critical Sources

BOOKS

St. James Guide to Children's Writers, fifth edition, St. James Press (Detroit, MI), 1999.
Something about the Author Autobiography Series, Volume 21, Thomson Gale (Detroit, MI), 1996.

PERIODICALS

Booklist, March 15, 2001, Carolyn Phelan, review of *On My Island,* p. 1403; April 1, 2001, Shelle Rosenfeld, review of *Didi and Daddy on the Promenade,* p. 1480; March 15, 2002, Stephanie Zvirin, review of *Stella, Fairy of the Forest,* p. 1261; March 15, 2003, Todd Morning, review of *Good Morning, Sam,* p. 1331; October 1, 2005, John Peters, review of *Caramba,* p. 62; May 15, 2006, Shelle Rosenfeld, review of *Travels with My Family,* p. 45; September 1, 2006, Ilene Cooper, review of *What Are You Doing, Sam?,* p. 135.

Books in Canada, December, 1984, Mary Ainslie Smith, review of *Lizzy's Lion,* p. 12; summer, 1992, Rhea Tregebov, review of *Moonbeam on a Cat's Ear,* p. 37.

Bulletin of the Center for Children's Books, March, 2002, review of *Stella, Fairy of the Forest,* p. 240; September, 2003, Janice Del Negro, review of *Good Night, Sam,* p. 13; October, 2004, Hope Morrison, review of *Stella, Princess of the Sky,* p. 73; September, 2006, Maggie Hommel, review of *Houndsley and Catina,* p. 19.

Canadian Children's Literature, number 54, 1989, Joan McGrath, review of *Moonbeam on a Cat's Ear,* pp. 67-69; number 59, 1990, Marie Davis, "The Fantastic and the Familiar in *Fat Charlie's Circus,*" pp. 75-77.

Children's Book News, June, 1986, review of *Moonbeam on a Cat's Ear,* p. 4.

Canadian Review of Materials, March, 1989, Leacy O'Brien, interview with Gay, pp. 54-55; March, 1990, Alison Mews, review of *Fat Charlie's Circus,* p. 64; November 28, 1997, Dave Jenkinson, review of *Rumpelstiltskin;* November 28, 1999, Helen Norrie, review of *Stella, Star of the Sea.*

Horn Book, July-August, 2003, Jennifer M. Brabander, review of *Good Morning, Sam,* p. 442; January-February, 2006, Jennifer M. Brabander, review of *Caramba,* p. 68.

Kirkus Reviews, September 1, 2003, review of *Good Night, Sam,* p. 1123; August 15, 2005, review of *Caramba,* p. 914; March 15, 2006, review of *Houndsley and Catina,* p. 292.

Maclean's, December 10, 1984, John Bemrose and others, review of *Lizzy's Lion,* pp. 62-63.

Publishers Weekly, July 28, 1997, review of *Rumpelstiltskin,* p. 74; March 29, 1999, review of *Stella, Star of the Sea,* p. 102; November 20, 2000, review of *Yuck: A Love Story,* p. 67; February 12, 2001, review of *Didi and Daddy on the Promenade,* p. 210; March 26, 2001, review of *On My Island,* p. 92; September 1, 2003, review of *Good Night, Sam,* p. 91; October 10, 2005, review of *Caramba,* p. 59.

Quill & Quire, December, 1989, Callie Israel, review of *Fat Charlie's Circus,* p. 22; number 60, 1990, Marie Davis, interview with Gay, pp. 52-74; December, 1993, Janet McNaughton, review of *Rabbit Blue,* p. 33; October, 1994, Joanne Findon, review of *The Three Little Pigs,* p. 41.

Resource Links, February, 2005, Zoe Johnstone, review of *Stella, Princess of the Sky,* p. 4; February, 2006, Lori Lavallee, review of *Caramba,* p. 3; October, 2006, Moira Kirkpatrick, review of *Travels with My Family,* p. 10.

School Library Journal, November, 1997, Jeanne Clancy Watkins, review of *Rumpelstiltskin,* p. 107; October, 2000, Grace Oliff, review of *Stella, Queen of the Snow,* p. 125; July, 2001, Holly Belli, review of *On My Island,* p. 75; June, 2002, Mary Elam, review of *Stella, Fairy of the Forest,* p. 96; April, 2003, Martha Topol, review of *Good Morning, Sam,* p. 1331; November, 2003, Marge Loch-Wouters, review of *Good Night, Sam,* p. 94; October, 2004, Lisa Gangemi, review of *Stella, Princess of the Sky,* p. 113; September, 2006, Maryann H. Owen, review of *What Are You Doing, Sam?,* p. 171; October, 2006, Maren Ostergard, review of *The Fabulous Song,* p. 77; November, 2006, Julie Roach, review of *Caramba,* p. 120.

ONLINE

Canadian Children's Book Centre Web site, http://www3. sympatico.ca/ (June 29, 2001), "Marie-Louise Gay."
Groundwood Books Web site, http://www. groundwoodbooks.com/ (June 9, 2007), "Authors: Marie-Louise Gay."
National Library of Canada, http://www.nlc-bnc.ca/ (June 28, 2001), "Cartoon Art: Marie-Louise Gay."

OTHER

Meet the Author/Illustrator: Marie-Louise Gay (video), School Services of Canada, 1991.*

*   *   *

GODWIN, Laura 1956-
(Nola Buck)

Personal

Born 1956, in Alberta, Canada. *Education:* Attended Calgary University. *Hobbies and other interests:* Photography, poetry.

Addresses

Home—New York, NY.

Career

Author and editor.

Writings

FOR CHILDREN

Forest, illustrated by Stacey Schuett, HarperCollins (New York, NY), 1998.
Little White Dog, illustrated by Dan Yaccarino, Hyperion (New York, NY), 1998.

The Flower Girl, illustrated by John Wallace, Hyperion (New York, NY), 2000.
Barnyard Prayers, illustrated by Brian Selznick, Hyperion (New York, NY), 2000.
Happy and Honey, illustrated by Jane Chapman, Margaret K. McElderry Books (New York, NY), 2000.
Honey Helps, illustrated by Jane Chapman, Margaret K. McElderry Books (New York, NY), 2000.
(With Ann M. Martin) *The Doll People,* illustrated by Brian Selznick, Hyperion (New York, NY), 2000.
The Best Fall of All, illustrated by Jane Chapman, Margaret K. McElderry Books (New York, NY), 2002.
Central Park Serenade, illustrated by Barry Root, Harper-Collins (New York, NY), 2002.
Happy Christmas, Honey!, illustrated by Jane Chapman, Margaret K. McElderry Books (New York, NY), 2002.
What the Baby Hears, illustrated by Mary Morgan, Hyperion (New York, NY), 2002.
(With Ann M. Martin) *The Meanest Doll in the World,* illustrated by Brian Selznick, Hyperion (New York, NY), 2003.
The Ring Bearer, illustrated by John Wallace, Hyperion (New York, NY), 2006.

FOR CHILDREN; UNDER PSEUDONYM NOLA BUCK

The Basement Stairs: A Spooky Pop-up Book, illustrated by Jonathan Lambert, HarperFestival (New York, NY), 1994.
Gotcha!: A Spooky Pop-up Book, illustrated by Jonathan Lambert, HarperFestival (New York, NY), 1994.
Halloween Parade: A Spooky Pop-up Book, illustrated by Jonathan Lambert, HarperFestival (New York, NY), 1994.
The Littlest Witch: A Spooky Pop-up Book, illustrated by Jonathan Lambert, HarperFestival (New York, NY), 1994.
Creepy Crawly Critters and Other Halloween Tongue Twisters, illustrated by Sue Truesdell, HarperCollins (New York, NY), 1995.
Sid and Sam, illustrated by G. Brian Karas, HarperCollins (New York, NY), 1996.
Morning in the Meadow, illustrated by Holly Keller, HarperFestival (New York, NY), 1997.
Oh, Cats!, illustrated by Nadine Bernard Westcott, Harper-Collins (New York, NY), 1997.
Santa's Short Suit Shrunk, and Other Christmas Tongue Twisters, illustrated by Sue Truesdell, HarperCollins (New York, NY), 1997.
How a Baby Grows, illustrated by Pamela Paparone, HarperFestival (New York, NY), 1998.
Hey, Little Baby!, illustrated by R.W. Alley, HarperFestival (New York, NY), 1999.

Sidelights

Laura Godwin is the author of several critically acclaimed picture books for children, including *Happy and Honey* and *Central Park Serenade,* as well as collaborating with Ann M. Martin on *The Doll People* and its follow-up chapter book *The Meanest Doll in the World.* Under the pseudonym Nola Buck, Godwin has

also penned a number of easy readers for the early-elementary grades as well as entertaining interactive titles such as *Gotcha!: A Spooky Pop-up Book.*

A native of Alberta, Godwin set her picture book *Forest* on a Canadian farm. While planting potatoes in a forest clearing, a young girl named Jeannie hears a newborn fawn bleating for its mother in the nearby woods. When her parents realize that the doe will not return, they allow Jeannie to care for the fawn overnight and then take it to a wildlife refuge. "Jeannie's attachment and concern for the abandoned fawn is palpable," observed *Horn Book* contributor Lauren Adams, and Carolyn Phelan wrote in *Booklist* that Godwin's "writing respects both the child's love of the deer and the best interests of the animal." In the verse collection *Barnyard Prayers,* a little boy enters a fantasy world as he puts the animals in his toy farm to bed. "Each poem is an exercise in empathy," wrote Joanna Rudge Long in *Horn Book,* the critic adding that the prayers "evoke not only the care between child and toy, farmer and animal, and parent and child, but also that between Creator and creature."

In *Happy and Honey* Godwin introduces a lively, tiger-striped kitten named Honey and her sleepy canine pal, Happy. To get her dozing puppy companion up and about, Honey offers Happy a toy, kisses him, and washes his tail and nose before he finally wakes. The two friends playfully tussle over a bone in *Honey Helps.* After Happy buries the bone in a big hole, Honey digs a smaller hole and retrieves the bone for her companion. Happy and Honey frolic together on a chilly autumn day in a further book in the series, *The Best Fall of All,* while *Happy Christmas, Honey!* follows the kitten's disastrous efforts to prepare for the holiday, including decorating the tree, baking cookies, wrapping presents, and singing carols. Both *Happy and Honey* and *Honey Helps* "have simple story lines," according to *School Library Journal* reviewer Wendy S. Carroll, the reviewer describing the titles as "good choices for youngsters just learning to read." "The limited vocabulary and intentional repetition may well make it easier for youngsters to recognize words," added a critic in *Publishers Weekly.* In *Booklist,* Kathy Broderick remarked that the "word repetition, simple sentences, and familiar language" in *Honey Helps* will appeal to beginning readers. "Kids may see a bit of themselves in the helpful Honey," Ilene Cooper stated in her *Booklist* review of *Happy Christmas, Honey!*

Using rhymed couplets, Godwin presents an ode to a famous New York City refuge in *Central Park Serenade.* "With very few words, the author creates a living picture of the city and its green space," noted Susan Marie Pitard in a review of the picture book for *School Library Journal.* Brought to life in illustrations by Barry Root, Godwin's story follows a young boy as he spends a day at the boating pond with his father and friends. "Offering a melodic read-aloud, this aptly titled, buoyant book should please young city-and country-dwellers alike," predicted a critic in *Publishers Weekly.*

Featuring illustrations by artust Brian Selznick, *The Doll People* concerns a family of antique English dolls who have lived in the same Victorian dollhouse for one hundred years. When Annabelle Doll finds a journal that may hold a clue to her Aunt Sarah's disappearance forty-five years earlier, she enlists the help of her new neighbor, the all-plastic Tiffany Funcraft, to locate the missing relative. Godwin and Martin "provide plenty of action and suspense, yet it is their skillfully crafted details about the dolls' personalities and daily routines that prove most memorable," noted a *Publishers Weekly* reviewer. In the sequel, *The Meanest Doll in the World,* Annabelle and Tiffany encounter the wicked Princess Mimi, who rules other dolls through fear and intimidation. A critic in *Kirkus Reviews* praised the "indelible mingling of wit, action, characterization, and art," and *School Library Journal* contributor Eva Mitnick stated that Godwin and Martin's "fantasy is destined to be a favorite for years to come."

Biographical and Critical Sources

PERIODICALS

Booklist, September 15, 1995, Hazel Rochman, review of *Creepy Crawly Critters and Other Halloween Tongue Twisters,* p. 168; August 1, 1996, Hazel Rochman, review of *Sid and Sam,* p. 1910; November 15, 1996, Stephanie Zvirin, review of *Oh, Cats!,* p. 596; September 15, 1997, Hazel Rochman, review of *Santa's Short Suit Shrunk, and Other Christmas Tongue Twisters,* p. 237; December 1, 1997, Roger Sutton, review of *Santa's Short Suit Shrunk, and Other Christmas Tongue Twisters,* p. 695; May 1, 1998, Carolyn Phelan, review of *Forest,* p. 1524; May 15, 1998, John Peters, review of *Little White Dog,* p. 1631; February 1, 1999, Hazel Rochman, review of *Hey, Little Baby!,* p. 978; August 1, 2000, Ilene Cooper, review of *The Doll People,* p. 2140; May 1, 2002, Shelley Townsend-Hudson, review of *What the Baby Hears,* p. 1532; June 1, 2002, Lauren Peterson, review of *Central Park Serenade,* p. 1737; November 1, 2002, Ilene Cooper, review of *Happy Christmas, Honey!,* p. 507; December 1, 2002, Kathy Broderick, review of *The Best Fall of All,* p. 674; October 15, 2003, Karin Snelson, review of *The Meanest Doll in the World,* p. 412.

Horn Book, May-June, 2000, Lauren Adams, review of *Forest,* p. 343; March-April, 2000, Joann Rudge Long, review of *Barnyard Prayers,* p. 205; September-October, 2002, Karla Kuskin, review of *Central Park Serenade,* p. 552.

Kirkus Reviews, March 1, 2002, review of *What the Baby Hears,* p. 335; March 15, 2002, review of *Central Park Serenade,* p. 411; November 1, 2002, review of *Happy Christmas, Honey!,* p. 1618; August 1, 2003, review of *The Meanest Doll in the World,* p. 1020; January 15, 2006, review of *The Ring Bearer,* p. 85.

New York Times Book Review, November 19, 2000, Krystyna Goddu, review of *The Doll People,* p. 45; January 18, 2004, Jane Margolies, review of *The Meanest Doll in the World,* p. 18.

Publishers Weekly, September 19, 1994, reviews of *The Littlest Witch: A Spooky Pop-up Book, Gotcha!: A Spooky Pop-up Book,* and *The Basement Stairs: A Spooky Pop-up Book,* p. 25; May 25, 1998, review of *Little White Dog,* p. 88; July 3, 2000, review of *The Doll People,* p. 71; October 9, 2000, review of *Happy and Honey* and *Honey Helps,* p. 86; February 25, 2002, reviews of *Central Park Serenade* and *What the Baby Hears,* p. 64; August 11, 2003, review of *The Meanest Doll in the World,* p. 280; October 6, 2003, review of *The Doll People,* p. 87; November 10, 2003, review of *The Meanest Doll in the World,* p. 37.

School Library Journal, December, 2000, Wendy S. Carroll, reviews of *Happy and Honey* and *Honey Helps,* p. 108; March, 2000, Barbara Chatton, review of *Barnyard Prayers,* p. 225; November, 2000, Kathie Meizner, review of *The Doll People,* p. 128; February, 2001, Kathleen Kelly MacMillan, review of *The Flower Girl,* p. 100; October, 2002, Mara Alpert, review of *Happy Christmas, Honey!,* p. 59, and Pamela K. Bomboy, review of *The Best Fall of All,* p. 111; May, 2002, Susan Marie Pitard, review of *Central Park Serenade,* p. 114; June, 2002, Joy Fleishhacker, review of *What the Baby Hears,* p. 96; October, 2003, Eva Mitnick, review of *The Meanest Doll in the World,* p. 130.*

*   *   *

GOOTMAN, Marilyn E. 1944-

Personal

Born 1944; married; husband's name Elliot (a math professor); children: Elissa, Jennifer, Michael. *Education:* Simmons College, B.A., 1967; Brandeis University, M.A., 1969; Ph.D. (education), 1976.

Addresses

Home and office—Athens, GA.

Career

Author. Gootman Education Associates, founder; worked previously as an elementary school teacher; University of Georgia, former instructor in department of elementary education.

Writings

(With Pamela Espeland) *When a Friend Dies: A Book for Teens about Grieving and Healing,* Free Spirit (Minneapolis, MN), 1994, revised and updated edition, 2005.

The Loving Parents' Guide to Discipline: How to Teach Your Child to Behave, with Kindness, Understanding, and Respect, Berkley Books (New York, NY), 1995, new edition, 2000.

The Caring Teacher's Guide to Discipline: Helping Young Students Learn Self-Control, Responsibility, and Respect, Corwin Press (Thousand Oaks, CA), 1997, new edition, 2005.

Cover of Marilyn E. Gootman's nonfiction work **When a Friend Dies.** (Free Spirit, 2005. © 1994, 2005 by Marilyn E. Gootman, Ed.D. Reproduced by permission.)

Contributor of articles to *Atlanta Journal Constitution, Humanist,* and *Redbook;* author of pamphlets for National Committee for the Prevention of Child Abuse.

Sidelights

Marilyn E. Gootman is the founder of Gootman Education Associates, a consulting company that provides educational strategies for teachers and parents. With a career history in education, Gootman has penned several instructive titles that help teachers and parents to solve disciplinary issues with their students and children. She has also written a guide geared toward young adults titled *When a Friend Dies: A Book for Teens about Grieving and Healing.* Gootman wrote the guide when her teenaged daughter lost a close friend. To help the teen cope with her grief, Gootman tried to find a book on the subject that was written specifically for teens. Having difficulty finding such a book, she was inspired to write her own guide for young-adult readers working through the grieving process.

When a Friend Dies includes quotes from teenagers who have experienced the loss of a friend; it also includes comments from well-known writers and philosophers that relate to the grieving process. The book concludes with a list of resources and readings that can also assist teens. *Kliatt* reviewer Olivia Durant, in her

assessment of *When a Friend Dies,* acknowledged the author for creating a straightforward text, commenting that "Gootman speaks in clear, reassuring language to teens." Durant concluded that the book "does not talk down" to teenaged readers, and an *NEA Today* critic deemed Gootman's guide a "non-preachy and compassionate book" that effectively handles a sensitive subject. Maryann H. Owen, reviewing *When a Friend Dies* for *School Library Journal,* regarded Gootman's book as a "compassionate, user-friendly" guide for teens and suggested that the list of suggested resources and readings compiled by Gootman "be made available to teens."

Biographical and Critical Sources

PERIODICALS

Booklist, February 15, 1995, Kathryn Carpenter, review of *The Loving Parents' Guide to Discipline: How to Teach Your Child to Behave, with Kindness, Understanding, and Respect,* p. 1045.

Kliatt, January, 2006, Olivia Durant, review of *When a Friend Dies: A Book for Teens about Grieving and Healing,* p. 29.

NEA Today, October, 2005, review of *When a Friend Dies,* p. 57.

School Library Journal, October, 2005, Maryann H. Owen, review of *When a Friend Dies,* p. 188.

Voice of Youth Advocates, August, 1994, review of *When a Friend Dies,* p. 166.

ONLINE

Corwin Press Web site, http://www.corwinpress.com/ (May 19, 2007), "Marilyn E. Gootman."

University of Georgia Center for Continuing Education Web site, http://www.georgiacenter.uga.edu/ (May 19, 2007), "Faculty Spotlight: Marilyn E. Gootman, Department of Elementary Education."*

H

HAFNER, Marylin 1925-

Personal

Born December 14, 1925, in Brooklyn, NY; daughter of Mark (an artist) and Francis Hafner; married Harvey B. Cushman, June 9, 1950 (marriage ended); married Rudolf G. de Reyna (a painter and writer), August 17, 1970; children: (first marriage) Abigail, Jennifer, Amanda. *Education:* Pratt Institute, B.Sc., 1947; attended New School for Social Research (now New School University), 1948-50, School of Visual Arts, Silvermine School of Art, and Slade School. *Politics:* Democrat. *Religion:* Unitarian Universalist. *Hobbies and other interests:* Cooking, antiques, travel, gardening, music.

Addresses

Home—Cambridge, MA.

Career

Artist, illustrator, and designer. *McCall's* magazine, New York, NY, art director, 1950-54; Famous Schools, Inc., Westport, CT, art instructor, 1968-70. Has taught art to children, designed advertising materials and textiles, and worked in graphic design.

Member

Society of Illustrators, Westport Artists Guild, Silvermine Guild of Artists.

Awards, Honors

New York Herald Tribune Children's Spring Book Festival award, 1949, for *Bonnie Bess: The Weathervane Horse* by Alvin Tresselt.

Writings

FOR CHILDREN; SELF-ILLUSTRATED

Mommies Don't Get Sick, Candlewick Press (Boston, MA), 1995.

A Year with Molly and Emmett, Candlewick Press (Boston, MA), 1997.

Molly and Emmett's Camping Adventure, McGraw-Hill, 2000.

Molly and Emmett's Surprise Garden, McGraw-Hill (Columbus, OH), 2001.

Emmett's Dream, McGraw-Hill (Columbus, OH), 2002.

Contributor of monthly comic-strip story for *Ladybug* magazine.

ILLUSTRATOR

Alvin Tresselt, *Bonnie Bess: The Weathervane Horse,* Lothrop (Boston, MA), 1949.

Hal Dareff, *Fun with ABC and 1-2-3,* Parents' Magazine Press, 1965.

Mabel Watts, *The Story of Zachary Zween,* Parents' Magazine Press, 1967.

Marguerite Staunton, *That's What* (poetry), Random House (New York, NY), 1968.

Charlotte Reynolds and Barbara Parker, *Poetry Please,* Random House (New York, NY), 1968.

Eleanor Felder, *X Marks the Spot,* Coward, 1971.

Lou A. Gaeddert, *Too Many Girls,* Coward, 1972.

Sally Cartwright, *Water Is Wet,* Coward, 1973.

Sally Cartwright, *Sunlight,* Coward, 1974.

Anne Edwards, *P.T. Barnum,* Putnam (New York, NY), 1977.

Charlotte Pomerantz, *The Mango Tooth* Greenwillow (New York, NY), 1977.

Jack Prelutsky, *It's Halloween,* Greenwillow (New York, NY), 1977.

Pauline Watson, *Cricket's Cookery,* Random House (New York, NY), 1977.

Peggy Parish, *Mind Your Manners!,* Greenwillow (New York, NY), 1978.

Velma and Barry Berkey, *Robbers, Bones, and Mean Dogs,* Addison Wesley, 1978.

Janet Schulman, *Jenny and the Tennis Nut,* Greenwillow (New York, NY), 1978.

Wilson Gage, *Mrs. Gaddy and the Ghost* (also see below), Greenwillow (New York, NY), 1979.

Barbara Power, *I Wish Laura's Mommy Was My Mommy*, Lippincott (Philadelphia, PA), 1979.

Steven Kroll, *The Candy Witch*, Holiday House (New York, NY),1979.

Janet Schulman, *Camp KeeWee's Secret Weapon*, Greenwillow (New York, NY), 1979.

Patricia Reilly Giff, *Next Year I'll Be Special*, Dutton (New York, NY), 1980.

Peggy Parish, *I Can—Can You?*, Greenwillow (New York, NY), 1980.

Jack Prelutsky, *Rainy Rainy Saturday*, Greenwillow (New York, NY), 1980.

Pat Ross, *Meet M & M*, Putnam (New York, NY), 1980.

Pat Ross, *M & M and the Haunted House Game*, Pantheon (New York, NY), 1980.

Marjorie Weinman Sharmat, *Little Devil Gets Sick*, Doubleday (New York, NY), 1980.

Marjorie Weinman Sharmat, *Rollo and Juliet Forever!*, Doubleday (New York, NY), 1981.

Meredith Tax, *Families*, Little, Brown (Boston, MA), 1981.

Jack Prelutsky, *It's Christmas*, Greenwillow (New York, NY), 1981.

Pat Ross, *M & M and the Big Bag*, Pantheon (New York, NY), 1981.

Morse Hamilton, *Big Sisters Are Bad Witches*, Greenwillow (New York, NY), 1981.

Florence Parry Heide, *Time's Up!*, Holiday House (New York, NY),1982.

Jack Prelutsky, *It's Thanksgiving*, Greenwillow (New York, NY), 1982.

Steven Kroll, *Are You Pirates?*, Pantheon (New York, NY), 1982.

Joan M. Lexau, *The Poison Ivy Case*, Dial (New York, NY), 1983.

Elizabeth Winthrop, *Katharine's Doll*, Dutton (New York, NY), 1983.

Nanette Newman, *That Dog!*, Crowell, 1983.

Pat Ross, *M & M and the Bad News Babies*, Pantheon (New York, NY), 1983.

Wilson Gage, *The Crow and Mrs. Gaddy* (also see below), Greenwillow (New York, NY), 1984.

Florence Parry Heide, *Time Flies!*, Holiday House (New York, NY),1984.

Wilson Gage, *Mrs. Gaddy and the Fast-growing Vine* (also see below), Greenwillow (New York, NY), 1985.

Melvin Berger, *Germs Make Me Sick!*, Crowell, 1985.

Steven Kroll, *Happy Mother's Day*, Holiday House (New York, NY),1985.

Joan Lexau, *The Dog Food Caper*, Dial (New York, NY), 1985.

Pat Ross, *M & M and the Mummy Mess*, Viking (New York, NY), 1985.

Pat Ross, *M & M and the Santa Secrets*, Viking (New York, NY), 1985.

Joanna Cole and Stephanie Calmenson, compilers, *The Laugh Book: A New Treasury of Humor for Children*, Doubleday (New York, NY), 1986.

Joan Robins, *My Brother, Will*, Greenwillow (New York, NY), 1986.

Terry Wolfe Phelan, *Best Friends, Hands Down*, Shoe Tree (Belvidere, NJ), 1986.

David A. Adler, *The Purple Turkey, and Other Thanksgiving Riddles*, Holiday House (New York, NY),1986.

Peggy Charren and Carol Hulsizer, *The TV-Smart Book for Kids*, Putnam (New York, NY), 1986.

Pat Ross, *M & M and the Super Child Afternoon*, Viking (New York, NY), 1987.

Steven Kroll, *Happy Father's Day*, Holiday House (New York, NY), 1988.

Jean Rogers, *Dinosaurs Are 568*, Greenwillow (New York, NY), 1988.

Vicki Cobb, *Feeding Yourself*, Lippincott (Philadelphia, PA), 1989.

Everett Hafner, *Sports Riddles*, Viking (New York, NY), 1989.

Vicki Cobb, *Getting Dressed*, Lippincott (Philadelphia, PA), 1989, revised as *Snap, Button Zip: Inventions to Keep Your Clothes On*, HarperCollins (New York, NY), 1993.

Vicki Cobb, *Keeping Clean*, Lippincott (Philadelphia, PA), 1989, revised as *Brush, Comb, Scrub: Inventions to Keep You Clean*, HarperCollins (New York, NY), 1993.

Vicki Cobb, *Writing It Down*, Lippincott (Philadelphia, PA), 1989.

Joanna Cole, *Bully Trouble*, Random House (New York, NY), 1989, reprinted, 2003.

Jean Rogers, *Raymond's Best Summer*, Greenwillow (New York, NY), 1990.

Marjorie Weinman Sharmat, *I'm Santa Claus and I'm Famous*, Holiday House (New York, NY), 1990.

Roni Schotter, *Hanukkah!*, Joy Street (New York, NY), 1990, board-book edition, Little, Brown (New York, NY), 2003.

Wilson Gage, *My Stars, It's Mrs. Gaddy!: The Three Mrs. Gaddy Stories* (contains *Mrs. Gaddy and the Ghost*, *Mrs. Gaddy and the Fast-growing Vine*, and *The Crow and Mrs. Gaddy*), Greenwillow (New York, NY), 1991.

Pat Ross, *M & M and the Halloween Monster*, Viking (New York, NY), 1991.

Mary Ann Hoberman, *Fathers, Mothers, Sisters, Brothers: A Collection of Family Poems*, Joy Street (New York, NY), 1991.

Riki Levinson, *Me Baby!*, Dutton (New York, NY), 1991.

Edith Kunhardt, *Red Day, Green Day*, Greenwillow (New York, NY), 1992.

Martine Davison, *Kevin and the School Nurse*, Random House (New York, NY), 1992.

Martine Davison, *Maggie and the Emergency Room*, Random House (New York, NY), 1992.

Nancy Evans Cooney, *Chatter-Box Jamie*, Putnam (New York, NY), 1993.

Jake Wolf, *And Then What?*, Greenwillow (New York, NY), 1993.

Judith Mathews, *An Egg and Seven Socks*, HarperCollins, 1993.

Pat Lowery Collins, *Don't Tease the Guppies*, Putnam (New York, NY), 1994.

Joanna Cole and Stephanie Calmenson, compilers, *A Pocketful of Laughs: Stories, Poems, Jokes, and Riddles*, Doubleday (New York, NY), 1995.

Roni Schotter, *Passover Magic,* Little, Brown (Boston, MA), 1995.

Kathryn Lasky, *Lunch Bunnies,* Little, Brown (Boston, MA), 1996.

Jake Wolf, *Daddy, Could I Have an Elephant?,* Greenwillow (New York, NY), 1996.

Roni Schotter, *Purim Play,* Little, Brown (Boston, MA), 1997.

Kathryn Lasky, *Show and Tell Bunnies,* Candlewick Press (Boston, MA), 1998.

Kathryn Lasky, *Science Fair Bunnies,* Candlewick Press (Boston, MA), 2000.

Kathryn Lasky, *Lucille's Snowsuit,* Crown (New York, NY), 2000.

Sid Fleischman, *A Carnival of Animals,* Greenwillow (New York, NY), 2000.

Johanna Hurwitz, *Ethan at Home,* Candlewick Press (Boston, MA), 2001.

Kathryn Lasky, *Starring Lucille,* Crown (New York, NY), 2001.

Johanna Hurwitz, *Ethan Out and About,* Candlewick Press (Boston, MA), 2001.

Lucille Camps In, Knopf (New York, NY), 2003.

The Pepins and Their Problems, Farrar, Straus & Giroux (New York, NY), 2004.

Joanna Cole, *The Missing Tooth,* Random House (New York, NY), 2004.

Bobbi Katz, selector, *Pocket Poems,* Dutton (New York, NY), 2004.

Kathryn Lasky, *Tumble Bunnies,* Candlewick Press (New York, NY), 2005.

Dayle Ann Dodds, *Teacher's Pets,* Candlewick Press (Cambridge, MA), 2006.

Hafner's illustrations have appeared in periodicals, including *Good Housekeeping* and *Humpty Dumpty.*

A collection of Hafner's papers and other materials is housed at the Thomas J. Dodd Research Center, University of Connecticut at Storrs.

Sidelights

During her long career as an illustrator, Marylin Hafner has brought to life the works of such noted children's

A girl learns to appreciate the important role her mother plays in her life in Marylin Hafner's self-illustrated picture book Mommies Don't Get Sick!
(Candlewick Press, 1997. Illustration © 1995 by Marylin Hafner. Reproduced by permission of Candlewick Press, Inc., Cambridge, MA.)

book authors as Florence Parry Heide, Steven Kroll, Kathryn Lasky, and Marjorie Weinman Sharmat through her drawings and paintings. In addition to her work as an artist, Hafner has also created original stories that carry the same light, humorous touch as her drawings. With the original self-illustrated picture book *Mommies Don't Get Sick,* as well as her picture-book series featuring the exploits of young Molly and her orange kitty, Emmett, Hafner added a whole new dimension to her work for the ready-to-read set. *Mommies Don't Get Sick* features watercolor images that "capture . . . family affection as well as . . . comic disorder," in the opinion of *Booklist* critic Hazel Rochman.

Born in Brooklyn, New York, in 1925, Hafner attended the Pratt Institute and the New School for Social Research before getting a job at *McCall's* magazine as an art director in 1950. Four years later she left to raise her three children; by 1968 she was back at work teaching at a correspondence school and doing freelance design work. Her first picture-book effort, Alvin Tresselt's *Bonnie Bess: The Weathervane Horse,* had been published years before, in 1949. Awarded the *New York Herald Tribune*'s Children's Spring Book Festival award, the newly illustrated *Bonnie Bess* signaled to Hafner that she had found her niche; in the decades since, she has contributed to dozens of books by a varied group of writers.

Hafner's characteristic round-edged, softly shaded style and her use of a variety of media—from pen and ink to watercolor to pencil—enhance three books by author Wilson Gage, among them *The Crow and Mrs. Gaddy.* "Hafner makes the happenings visible," commented a *Publishers Weekly* critic, who enjoyed the artist's "softly shaded drawings." Her ability to adapt her soft-edged style to each new illustration project has contributed to Hafner's success: in Patricia Reilly Giff's *Next Year I'll Be Special,* for example, the "rosy tones in Hafner's buoyant pictures match the dreams of glory" harbored by Giff's young protagonist, according to a *Publishers Weekly* reviewer. *School Library Journal* contributor Carolyn Noah praised the artist's treatment of Steven Kroll's *Are You Pirates?* by noting that Hafner's "black-and-sepia pen-and-ink illustrations are full of wily detail and bring the pirate antics to life." The illustrator's images for Jake Wolf's *Daddy, Could I Have an Elephant?* "never forsake their appealing down-to-earth quality, even when depicting the most outrageous scenarios," noted one *Publishers Weekly* contributor, while another noted that for Lasky's *Lunch Bunnies* she contributes "bustling illustrations [that] imbue the characters with a great deal of personality." "The cheery ink, watercolor and colored pencil illustrations" the artist contributes to Dayle Ann Dodds' *Teacher's Pets* "warm the pages with a playful vibrancy," in the opinion of yet another reviewer for *Publishers Weekly.*

In Vicki Cobb's *Feeding Yourself,* the author's discussion about the use of eating utensils around the world is enhanced by Hafner's interpretation of "their origins

Hafner's illustrations pop up in a large number of books, among them Sid Fleischman's story collection **A Carnival of Animals.** (Greenwillow Books, 2000. Illustration © 2000 by Marylin Hafner. Reproduced by permission of HarperCollins Children's Books, a division of HarperCollins Publishers.)

and uses in many cultures" through humorous and "lively watercolor illustrations," according to *School Library Journal* contributor Janie Schomberg. Hafner's pen-and-ink illustrations for Joanna Cole's *The Laugh Book* portray "comic characters running pell-mell over the pages; . . . just the kind of silly stuff kids love," remarked a *Publishers Weekly* contributor. *School Library Journal* critic Jane Saliers praised the artist's use of a quite different medium in *Happy Father's Day,* a collaboration with author Kroll that features "colorful line and wash illustrations . . . filled with active people, pets, and homey details." *Horn Book* reviewer Mary M. Burns also found appropriate Hafner's use of an full-color palette in illustrating Morse Hamilton's *Big Sisters Are Bad Witches,* remarking that the artist's "slightly caricatured figures and vivid use of color complement [the protagonist's] personality without losing the sense of warmth appropriate to a family story."

Featuring characters originally introduced to youngsters in comic-strip tales published in *Ladybug* magazine, Hafner's original picture books *A Year with Molly and Emmett, Molly and Emmett's Camping Adventure, Molly and Emmett's Surprise Garden,* and *Emmett's Dream* are each composed of a collection of short vignettes that bring to life Molly's adventures with her pet. *A Year with Molly and Emmett* follows the pair as they

Young readers gain a positive view of the school experience through Hafner's illustrations for Dayle Ann Dodds' picture book **Teacher's Pets.** (Candlewick Press, 2006. Illustration © 2006 by Marylin Hafner. Reproduced by permission of Candlewick Press, Inc., Cambridge, MA.)

take a camping trip, participate in a holiday-season toy drive, and cook breakfast, while *Molly and Emmett's Camping Adventure* finds the duo pitching a tent in Molly's backyard. The orange puss takes center state in

Emmett's Dream, after Molly becomes immersed in researching her family history and inspires Emmett to seek out the famous felines in his own family. "Toddlers will find comfort in Molly's consistently reassur-

ing tone," noted a *Publishers Weekly* contributor in a review of *A Year with Molly and Emmett.* Praising Hafner's "spunky, good-natured characters," another *Publishers Weekly* critic wrote that they "have a great dynamic and handily convey humor and a sense of discovery" in *Molly and Emmett's Camping Adventure.* Noting the gardening basics that Hafner includes in *Molly and Emmett's Surprise Garden,* Judith Constandtinides dubbed the book "thoroughly delightful" in her *School Library Journal* review.

Hafner once told *SATA,* "My most important influences in my work are Saul Steinberg, Ronald Searle, André François, and John Birmingham. I do not apply a 'formula' to illustration (using the same style or technique for every book)—but instead let the author's concept and general attitude decide what 'look' the book should have. I try to use the limitations of budget and color, etc., as a challenge to create a unity between words and pictures. My feeling about picture books is that the pictures can add another dimension without overpowering the author's intention."

Biographical and Critical Sources

PERIODICALS

Booklist, June 15, 1992, Deborah Abbott, review of *Red Day, Green Day,* p. 1847; May 1, 1993, Kay Weisman, review of *Chatterbox Jamie,* pp. 1601-1602; December 1, 1993, Elizabeth Bush, review of *And Then What?,* p. 1993; September 1, 1995, Hazel Rochman, review of *Mommies Don't Get Sick,* p. 86; November, 1995, Susan Dove Lempke, review of *Mommies Don't Get Sick,* p. 91; September 15, 1996, Leone McDermott, review of *Lunch Bunnies,* p. 247; December 1, 2000, Carolyn Phelan, review of *Molly and Emmett's Camping Adventure,* p. 720; July, 2003, Gillian Engberg, review of *Lucille Camps In,* p. 1897; February 1, 2004, Hazel Rochman, review of *Pocket Poems,* p. 978.

Horn Book, August, 1980, review of *Meet M & M,* p. 402, and *Next Year I'll Be Special,* p. 397; October, 1980, Paul Heins, review of *Rainy, Rainy Saturday,* p. 533; August, 1981, Mary M. Burns, review of *Big Sisters Are Bad Witches,* p. 414; December, 1981, Karen M. Klockner, review of *It's Christmas,* p. 654; December, 1983, Karen Jameson, review of *Katharine's Doll,* p. 706; July-August, 1986, review of *Germs Make Me Sick,* p. 474; January-February, 1992, Hanna B. Zeiger, review of *Hanukkah!,* p. 95; January-February, 2005, review of *The Pepins and Their Problems,* p. 15.

Kirkus Reviews, April 15, 2006, review of *Teacher's Pets,* p. 404.

Publishers Weekly, February 15, 1980, review of *Little Devil Gets Sick,* p. 110; May 16, 1980, review of *Next Year, I'll Be Special,* p. 211; June 6, 1980, review of *Meet M & M,* p. 82; May 1, 1981, review of *Families,* p. 67; December 22, 1982, review of *Rollo and Juliet Forever,* p. 63; February 3, 1984, review of *The Crow and Mrs. Gaddy,* p. 403; August 22, 1986, review of *The TV-Smart Book for Kids,* p. 102; October 31, 1986, review of *The Laugh Book: A New Treasury of Humor for Children,* pp. 68-69; July 1, 1996, review of *Daddy, Could I Have an Elephant?,* p. 59; August 5, 1996, review of *Lunch Bunnies,* p. 441; April 28, 1997, review of *A Year with Molly and Emmett,* p. 75; February 23, 1998, review of *Purim Play,* p. 67; November 9, 1998, review of *Show and Tell Bunnies,* p. 75; October 23, 2000, review of *Molly and Emmett's Camping Adventure,* p. 75; August, 2001, Judith Constantinides, review of *Molly and Emmett's Surprise Garden,* p. 147; June 12, 2006, review of *Teacher's Pets,* p. 52.

School Librarian, November, 1997, Catriona Nicholson, review of *A Year with Molly and Emmett,* p. 186.

School Library Journal, January, 1980, Reva Pitch, review of *The Candy Witch,* p. 57; May, 1980, Kathy Coffey, review of *Little Devil Gets Sick* and *Meet M & M,* pp. 83-84; July, 1980, Nancy Palmer, review of *I Wish Laura's Mommy Was My Mommy,* p. 124; February, 1983, Carolyn Noah, review of *Are You Pirates?,* p. 68; May, 1984, Nancy Palmer, review of *The Poison Ivy Case,* p. 98; May, 1986, Carolyn Noah, review of *My Brother, Will,* p. 84; November, 1986, Annette Curtis Klause, review of *The Purple Turkey, and Other Thanksgiving Riddles,* p. 71; January, 1987, Craighton Hippenhammer, review of *The Laugh Book,* p. 72; May, 1988, Jane Saliers, review of *Happy Father's Day!,* p. 85; December, 1988, Lisa Smith, review of *Dinosaurs Are 568,* p. 92; October, 1989, Janie Schomberg, reviews of *Feeding Yourself* and *Writing It Down,* pp. 102-103; October, 1990, Susan Hepler, review of *Hanukkah!,* p. 39; December, 1991, Alexandra Marris, review of *M & M and the Halloween Monster,* p. 100; April, 1998, Libby K. White, review of *Purim Play,* p. 110; July, 2000, June Roberts, review of *Science Fair Bunnies,* p. 81; October, 2000, Grace Oliff, review of *A Carnival of Animals,* p. 124; October, 2004, review of *Pocket Poems,* p. 28; April, 2005, Joy Fleishhacker, review of *Tumble Bunnies,* p. 105; May, 2006, Gloria Koster, review of *Teacher's Pets,* p. 86.

ONLINE

University of Connecticut Library Web site, http://www.lib.uconn.edu/ (May 15, 2007), "Marylin Hafner Papers."*

*   *   *

HALE, Christy 1955-
(Christine Hale Apostolou)

Personal

Born January 21, 1955, in Southbridge, MA; daughter of Harold Charles (a mechanical engineer) and Eunice Sherman (a draftsperson) Hale; married Scott Julian

Apostolou, August 31, 1991; children: one daughter. *Education:* Lewis and Clark College, B.A. (fine arts), 1977, M.A.T., 1980; Pratt Institute, B.F.A. (illustration and graphic design), 1986. *Politics:* Democrat. *Religion:* Protestant. *Hobbies and other interests:* Letterpress printing, playing guitar, traveling, and speaking Spanish.

Addresses

Home—Palo Alto, CA. *Agent*—Christina A. Tugeau, 3009 Margaret Jones La., Williamsburg, VA 23185. *E-mail*—christyh@christyhale.com.

Career

Willamette Middle School, West Linn, OR, art instructor, 1978-84; E.P. Dutton, New York, NY, art assistant, 1986-87; Aperture, New York, NY, designer, 1987-88; Putnam/Philomel, New York, NY, senior designer, 1987-89; Bradbury Press, New York, NY, interim art director, 1989; Macmillan, New York, NY, interim art director, 1989-90; Four Winds Press, New York, NY, art director, 1990-94; freelance designer and illustrator.

Awards, Honors

Award of Excellence, AIGA Cover Show, 1988; two Merit Awards for photo design, 1988-89; first place award, Bookbinder's Guild, 1989, for special trade book; honorable mention, *How* magazine, 1990, for illustration.

Writings

CHILDREN'S NONFICTION

Art Activities for Little Learners, Scholastic (New York, NY), 2004.
Quilting Activities for Young Learners, Scholastic (New York, NY), 2005.
Collaborative Art and Writing Projects for Young Learners, Scholastic (New York, NY), 2006.

Contributor to periodicals, including *Instructor.*

ILLUSTRATOR

William Stafford, *How to Hold Your Arms When It Rains,* Confluence Press (Lewiston, ID), 1990.
Felix Pitre, reteller, *Juan Bobo and the Pig,* Lodestar (New York, NY), 1993.
May Swenson, *The Complete Poems to Solve,* Macmillan (New York, NY), 1993.
T. Obinkaram Echewa, *The Ancestor Tree,* Lodestar (New York, NY), 1994.
Felix Pitre, reteller, *Paco and the Witch,* Lodestar (New York, NY), 1995.

Ali Wakefield, *Those Calculating Crows!,* Simon & Schuster (New York, NY), 1996.
Stephanie Stuve-Bodeen, *Elizabeti's Doll,* Lee & Low (New York, NY), 1998.
Stephanie Stuve-Bodeen, *Mama Elizabeti,* Lee & Low (New York, NY), 2000.
Betsy Hearne, *Who's in the Hall? A Mystery in Four Chapters,* Greenwillow (New York, NY), 2000.
Alice Mead, *Billy and Emma,* Farrar, Straus (New York, NY), 2000.
Eileen Spinelli, *A Safe Place Called Home,* Marshall Cavendish (New York, NY), 2001.
Stephanie Stuve-Bodeen, *Elizabeti's School,* Lee & Low (New York, NY), 2002.
Lillian Morrison, *It Rained All Day That Night: Autograph Album Verses and Inscriptions,* August House (Little Rock, AK), 2003.
Connie Ann Kirk, *Sky Dancers,* Lee & Low (New York, NY), 2004.
Molly Friedrich, *You Are Not My Real Mother!,* Little, Brown (New York, NY), 2004.
Lillian Morrison, *Guess Again!: Riddle Poems,* August House (Little Rock, AK), 2006.

Books featuring Hale's illustrations have been translated into Spanish.

Sidelights

Illustrator Christy Hale has created artwork for a variety of books for young readers. Teaming up with author Felix Pitre, she contributed art to picture-book retellings of traditional Puerto Rican folktales in *Juan Bobo and the Pig* and *Paco and the Witch,* providing "a unique and playful look at the folk heroes of another culture," according to a *Publishers Weekly* critic. In *Juan Bobo and the Pig* Juan is left to care for the family pig while his mother attends church. Considered a traditional "wise fool" character in Puerto Rican legend, Juan does not known how to quiet the unhappy swine, but eventually he realizes what the pig wants: he dresses it up and sends it off to church as well. A Puerto Rican version of the Rumpelstiltskin tale, *Paco and the Witch* finds young Paco falling under the spell of an old witch who will keep him captive unless he can guess her name correctly. If he cannot guess her name in time, Paco will become the main ingredient in witch's stew. Fortunately, Paco is saved from this fate by a crab who helps the boy name the witch and escape. Calling Hale's illustrations for *Juan Bobo and the Pig* "brightly colored and vigorous," *Booklist* reviewer Julie Corsaro also cited the art's "fifties . . . feeling," while *School Library Journal* contributor Lauren Mayer remarked that the "linoleum block prints . . . in bleached yet vibrant colors" reflect "the sun-drenched Caribbean" setting. Reviewing *Paco and the Witch,* a *Publishers Weekly* contributor cited Hale's "distinctive, sultry palette of purples, greens and golden browns," and *School Library Journal* critic Maria Redburn observed that the "illustrations are full of color, relating the ever-changing mood of the story."

Christy Hale collaborates with author Stephanie Stuve-Bodeen on the picture book **Mama Elizabeti,** *part of a series about a young Tanzanian girl.*
(Lee & Low Books, Inc., 2000. Illustration © 2000 by Christy Hale. Reproduced by permission of Lee & Low Books, Inc.)

Hale has also working with several other writers, among them Stephanie Stuve-Bodeen, Lillian Morrison, and Molly Friedrich. In *Elizabeti's Doll,* the first of several collaborations between Stuve-Bodeen and Hale, a young Tanzanian girl wishes for a doll of her own, to care for just as her mother cares for her new baby brother. Searching for a suitable doll, Elizabeti finds a smooth rock and names it Eva, bathing, diapering, and burping it just like a real baby. When Eva is mistakenly used by Elizabeti's older sister in the cooking fire, the young girl is distraught, but eventually she regains her doll and sings the stone toy to sleep. Hale "deftly captures

Working with teachers, Hale shares ideas for creative fun in books such as **Quilting Activities for Young Learners.** (Scholastic, 2005. © 2005 by Christy Hale.
Reproduced by permission of Scholastic, Inc.)

the story's mood in softly shaded mixed-media illustrations," claimed a *Publishers Weekly* reviewer, and *Booklist* contributor GraceAnne A. DeCandido dubbed *Elizabeti's Doll* "another triumph for the illustrator."

Elizabeti's story continues in *Mama Elizabeti* and *Elizabeti's School,* the latter which finds the young girl venturing forth on her first day away from home. Called "a perfect book for mothers hoping to spend some quality reading time with their daughters" by *Black Issues Book Review* critic Khafre Abif, *Mama Elizabeti* finds Elizabeti helping to care for toddler brother Obedi after their mother has another baby. Thinking that she has plenty of experience after taking care of Eva, the young girl discovers that a wiggly boy is much harder to care for than a lifeless rock. After momentarily losing track of Obedi, Elizabeti fears for his safety, but her worries are quickly relieved as he toddles back to her, walking for the first time. Claiming that Hale's "illustrations bring this book alive," *School Library Journal* reviewer Martha Topol wrote that the book's artwork "perfectly captures the spontaneity and totality of a toddler's love." Reviewing *Elizabeti's School* for *Horn Book,* Martha V. Parravano noted that "Hale's mixed-media illustrations are once again striking" and balance Stuve-Bodeen's "intimate . . . text, with effective use of close-ups and warm family groupings."

Hale has also provided the illustrations for Betsy Hearne's picture book *Who's in the Hall? A Mystery in Four Chapters,* an "excellent blend of good writing and fine illustration," remarked Marlene Gawron in a *School Library Journal* review. Describing the book as a "dandy choice for newly independent readers," *Horn Book* contributor Joanna Rudge Long observed that Hale's "dynamic cartoon-style illustrations pick up the story's humor" as well as provide a way for readers to keep track of all the characters in the story. Her ink and watercolor works for Lillian Morrison's *It Rained All Day That Tight: Autographs, Rhymes, and Inscriptions* "dance across each page, extending the sentiment. . . . implicit in each verse," noted *School Library Journal* reviewer Kathleen Whalin, and in *Kirkus Reviews* a reviewer noted that the art for Connie A. Kirk's *Sky Dancers* "captures the energy and excitement of the trip" a young Native-American boy makes to see his father walking on the high beams during the construction of the Empire State Building.

"I have been interested in "making books since I can remember," Hale once told *SATA.* "I decided at ten to become a writer and illustrator; although, the writer part hasn't happened yet. I entered into book design through letterpress printing, fine print edition-ing, paper making, and book binding and am just getting started on my illustration career. From the printer's need to make multiples, I have worked mainly in linoleum and woodcut. I have worked with poets on small chapbooks, and this medium (linocut) has allowed me to become the publisher of limited-edition books along with several small books of poetry and illustration.

"I enjoy the research involved in illustration. My picture books have been set in other cultures with great riches for me to draw from."

Biographical and Critical Sources

PERIODICALS

Black Issues Book Review, July, 2000, Khafre Abif, review of *Mama Elizabeti,* p. 74.

Booklist, June 1, 1993, Carolyn Phelan, review of *The Complete Poems to Solve,* p. 1805; October 15, 1993, Julie Corsaro, review of *Juan Bobo and the Pig,* p. 447; October 1, 1994, Hazel Rochman, review of *The Ancestor Tree,* p. 331; May 15, 1995, Hazel Rochman, review of *Paco and the Witch,* p. 1650; November 15, 1996, Kay Weisman, review of *Those Calculating Crows!,* p. 596; October 1, 1998, GraceAnne A. DeCandido, review of *Elizabeti's Doll,* p. 336; February 15, 2001, Henrietta M. Smith, review of *Elizabeti's Doll,* p. 1161; October 1, 2001, Carolyn Phelan, review of *A Safe Place Called Home,* p. 330; November 15, 2004, Hazel Rochman, review of *You're Not My Real Mother!,* p. 589, and Jennifer Mattson, review of *Sky Dancers,* p. 590; May 1, 2006, Carolyn Phelan, review of *Guess Again!: Riddle Poems,* p. 87.

Horn Book, May-June, 1993, Nancy Vasilakis, *The Complete Poems to Solve,* p. 341; July, 2000, review of *Mama Elizabeti,* p. 448; November, 2000, Joanna Rudge Long, review of *Who's in the Hall? A Mystery in Four Chapters,* p. 746; November-December, 2002, Martha V. Parravano, review of *Elizabeti's School,* p. 741.

Kirkus Reviews, October 15, 2004, review of *Sky Dancers,* p. 1009.

New York Times Book Review, January 15, 1995, review of *The Ancestor Tree,* p. 25; January 21, 2001, DeRaismes Combes, review of *Who's in the Hall?,* p. 25.

Publishers Weekly, July 12, 1993, review of *Juan Bobo and the Pig,* p. 447; May 29, 1995, review of *Paco and the Witch,* p. 84; July 15, 1996, review of *Those Calculating Crows!,* p. 73; August 24, 1998, review of *Elizabeti's Doll,* p. 56; July 3, 2000, review of *Who's in the Hall?,* p. 70.

School Library Journal, May, 1993, Lee Bock, *The Complete Poems to Solve,* p. 122; November, 1993, Lauren Mayer, review of *Juan Bobo and the Pig,* p. 101; February, 1995, Marilyn Iarusso, review of *The Ancestor Tree,* p. 73; August, 1995, Maria Redburn, review of *Paco and the Witch,* p. 137; December, 1996, JoAnn Rees, review of *Those Calculating Crows!,* p. 109; September, 1998, Martha Topol, review of *Elizabeti's Doll,* p. 183; May, 2000, Susan Hepler, review of *Billy and Emma,* p. 150; July, 2000, Martha Topol, review of *Mama Elizabeti,* p. 88; August, 2000, Marlene Gawron, review of *Who's in the Hall?,* p. 156; January, 2004, Kathleen Whalin, review of *It Rained All Day That Night: Autographs, Rhymes, and Inscriptions,* p. 154; January, 2005, Kathy Krasniewicz, review of *Sky Dancers,* p. 94.

ONLINE

Christy Hale Home Page, http://www.christyhale.com (June 15, 2007).

*   *   *

HARPER, Charise
See HARPER, Charise Mericle

*   *   *

HARPER, Charise Mericle
(Charise Harper)

Personal

Married; children: one daughter.

Addresses

Home—Mamaroneck, NY. *E-mail*—charise@charise-harper.com.

Career

Author, illustrator, and cartoonist.

Writings

SELF-ILLUSTRATED

When I Grow Up, Chronicle Books (San Francisco, CA), 2001.
Imaginative Inventions: The Who, What, Where, When, and Why of Roller Skates, Potato Chips, Marbles, and Pie and More!, Little, Brown (Boston, MA), 2001.
There Was a Bold Lady Who Wanted a Star, Little, Brown (Boston, MA), 2002.
The Trouble with Normal, Houghton Mifflin (Boston, MA), 2003.
Itsy Bitsy the Smart Spider, Dial Books for Young Readers (New York, NY), 2003.
Yes, No, Maybe So, Dial Books for Young Readers (New York, NY), 2004.
The Monster Show: Everything You Never Knew about Monsters, Houghton Mifflin (Boston, MA), 2004.
(Under name Charise Harper) *Baby Time: A Fast, Fun Keepsake Album,* Chronicle Books (San Francisco, CA), 2004.
The Invisible Mistakecase, Houghton Mifflin (Boston, MA), 2005.
The Little Book of Not So, Houghton Mifflin (Boston, MA), 2005.
Fashion Kitty (graphic novel), Hyperion (New York, NY), 2005.
Flush!: The Scoop on Poop throughout the Ages, Little, Brown (New York, NY), 2006.
Amy and Ivan: What's in That Truck?, Tricycle Press (Berkeley, CA), 2006.
Fashion Kitty versus the Fashion Queen (graphic novel), Hyperion (New York, NY), 2007.
When Randolph Turned Rotten, Knopf (New York, NY), 2007.
Just Grace, Houghton Mifflin (Boston, MA), 2007.
Still Just Grace, Houghton Mifflin (Boston, MA), 2007.

OTHER

(Illustrator) Amy Krouse Rosenthal, *Spoken Gems: A Journal for Recording the Funny, Odd, and Poignant Things Your Child Says,* Andrews McMeel (Kansas City, MO), 2000.
(Illustrator) Kathleen O'Dell, *Agnes Parker . . . Girl in Progess,* Dial Books (New York, NY), 2003.
(Illustrator) Kathleen O'Dell, *Agnes Parker . . . Happy Camper?,* Dial Books (New York, NY), 2005.
(Illustrator) Sandra Markle, *Chocolate: A Sweet History,* Grosset & Dunlap (New York, NY), 2005.
Flashcards of My Life (young-adult novel), Little, Brown (Boston, MA), 2006.

Contributor of illustrations to *New York Times, Chicago Tribune, Village Voice,* and *San Francisco Examiner.* Creator of *Eye-Spy,* weekly alternative syndicated comic strip, 1996—.

Sidelights

Charise Mericle Harper is the author of several highly acclaimed picture books for children, producing her self-illustrated debut work, *When I Grow Up,* in 2001. To complete the phrase "When I grow up, I want to be . . .," each double-page spread offers a positive characteristic such as "generous" or "brave," along with an illustration to highlight that particular attribute. "Every page is framed and the textured, vibrant illustrations have a tactile element," noted *School Library Journal* contributor Shawn Brommer. "Most memorably," wrote a *Publishers Weekly* critic, "Harper uses black-and-white photos of children's faces, seemingly snipped from a grade school yearbook, as collage elements." *Imaginative Inventions: The Who, What, Where, When, and Why of Roller Skates, Potato Chips, Marbles, and Pie and More!* explores, in verse, the origins of everyday items such as chewing gum and piggy banks. Reviewing the work in *Booklist,* GraceAnne A. DeCandido praised Harper's "puckish and offbeat visual imagery." A reviewer in *Publishers Weekly* similarly remarked of *Imaginative Inventions* that, "with its crazy-quilt visual patterns, bouncy stanzas and fun facts, this miscellany zigzags between informational and whimsical."

There Was a Bold Lady Who Wanted a Star, Harper's take on the folk song "I Know an Old Lady Who Swallowed a Fly," follows an adventurous woman's efforts to capture a star for her young son. She uses a number of modes of transportation to reach the heavenly body,

including driving a convertible and piloting an airplane. "Acrylic cartoons in bright colors lend a zany feel" to Harper's story, noted Leslie Barban in *School Library Journal,* and a *Kirkus Reviews* critic stated that "the repetitive pattern and cumulative effect follow that of the original and the jaunty illustration style fits the tale." In *The Trouble with Normal,* Finnigan the squirrel pursues his dream of becoming a Secret Service agent with the help of his human companion, Doug. According to a *Publishers Weekly* contributor, Harper "illustrates in hilarious mixed-media collages and writes in a wry deadpan," and *Booklist* reviewer Connie Fletcher dubbed the work "funny and fun, with an underlying friendship theme."

Inspired by her own daughter's love of a favorite nursery rhyme, Harper published *Itsy Bitsy the Smart Spider,* a "spirited take on a much-loved classic," according to a *Kirkus Reviews* critic. In the work, Itsy tires of being washed out by the rain and goes to great lengths to stay dry. "This book will make a fun read-aloud for children familiar with the original verse," observed Wendy Woodfill in *School Library Journal.* Another picture book by Harper, *Yes, No, Maybe So* features "a clever, discussion-opening" story "about acceptable and unacceptable behavior—and the gray areas in between," according to *Horn Book* reviewer Martha V. Parravano. In her story, Harper looks at familiar daily activities, such as eating, sharing, and getting dressed. In the words of a *Kirkus Reviews* critic, "the concept is explored with giggle-inducing humor."

A top-hatted emcee educates his audience about a variety of colorful creatures in *The Monster Show: Everything You Never Knew about Monsters.* Readers learn that monsters eat pizza, keep pets, and look silly in underwear. "The tone of the text remains reassuring throughout," remarked Mary Elam in *School Library Journal.* In *Fashion Kitty,* "Harper brings her comedic sense and flat, droll cartoons together in a graphic novel for young girls," noted a contributor in *Kirkus Reviews.* The work, which concerns an eight-year-old feline superhero with a flair for style, continues in *Fashion Kitty versus the Fashion Queen.* According to Jennifer Feigelman, reviewing *Fashion Kitty* in *School Library Journal,* Harper's "pictures are artistically appealing and visually spectacular."

A teen records her thoughts about friendship and identity in Harper's first young-adult novel, *Flashcards of My Life.* After Emily receives an unusual birthday gift, she begins chronicling the trials and triumphs of her middle-school world, including her encounters with catty girlfriends and unrequited love. "Harper's tale will elicit nods of recognition—and a few chuckles," observed a *Publishers Weekly* critic in a review of the novel.

Biographical and Critical Sources

PERIODICALS

Booklist, December 15, 2001, GraceAnne A. DeCandido, review of *Imaginative Inventions: The Who, What, Where, When, and Why of Roller Skates, Potato Chips, Marbles, and Pie and More!,* p. 734; November 15, 2002, Diane Foote, review of *There Was a Bold Lady Who Wanted a Star,* p. 605; May 1, 2003, Connie Fletcher, review of *The Trouble with Normal,* p. 1605; February 1, 2006, Jennifer Hubert, review of *Flashcards of My Life,* p. 50; May 15, 2006, Jennifer Mattson, review of *Amy and Ivan,* p. 49.

Bulletin of the Center for Children's Books, November, 2002, review of *There Was a Bold Lady Who Wanted a Star,* p. 109; December, 2005, review of *Fashion Kitty,* p. 183.

Horn Book, Martha V. Parravano, review of *Yes, No, Maybe So,* p. 313.

Kirkus Reviews, August 1, 2001, review of *Imaginative Inventions,* p. 1123; August 15, 2002, review of *There Was a Bold Lady Who Wanted a Star,* p. 1224; February 1, 2003, review of *The Trouble with Normal,* p. 230; February 1, 2004, review of *Itsy Bitsy the Smart Spider,* p. 134; March 15, 2004, review of *Yes, No, Maybe So,* p. 270; July 15, 2004, review of *The Monster Show: Everything You Never Knew about Monsters,* p. 686; February 1, 2005, review of *Agnes Parker . . . Happy Camper?,* p. 179; August 1, 2005, review of *Fashion Kitty,* p. 848; January 1, 2006, review of *Flashcards of My Life,* p. 41.

Publishers Weekly, February 12, 2001, review of *When I Grow Up,* p. 209; August 20, 2001, review of *Imaginative Inventions,* p. 79; September 16, 2002, review of *There Was a Bold Lady Who Wanted a Star,* p. 67; February 10, 2003, review of *The Trouble with Normal,* p. 186; August 9, 2004, review of *The Monster Show,* p. 250; October 3, 2005, review of *Fashion Kitty,* p. 71; January 9, 2006, review of *Flashcards of My Life,* p. 54.

School Library Journal, July, 2001, Shawn Brommer, review of *When I Grow Up,* p. 82; October, 2001, Lynda Ritterman, review of *Imaginative Inventions,* p. 140; September, 2002, Leslie Barban, review of *There Was a Bold Lady Who Wanted a Star,* p. 213; February, 2003, Susan Patron, review of *Agnes Parker . . . Girl in Progress,* p. 146; April, 2003, Wanda Meyers-Hines, review of *The Trouble with Normal,* p. 122; March, 2004, Wendy Woodfill, review of *Itsy Bitsy the Smart Spider,* p. 169; July, 2004, Kathleen Kelly MacMillan, review of *Yes, No, Maybe So,* p. 77; September, 2004, Mary Elam, review of *The Monster Show,* p. 161; March, 2005, Debbie Whitbeck, review of *Agnes Parker . . . Happy Camper?,* p. 216; June, 2005, Margaret Bush, review of *The Little Book of Not So,* p. 116; November, 2005, Jennifer Feigelman, review of *Fashion Kitty,* p. 174; December, 2005, Lisa S. Schindler, review of *The Invisible Mistakecase,* p. 114; January, 2006, Diana Pierce, review of *Flashcards of*

My Life, p. 133; September, 2006, Catherine Threadgill, review of *Amy and Ivan,* p. 173, and Julie Roach, review of *Flush!: The Scoop on Poop throughout the Ages,* p. 192.

Voice of Youth Advocates, February, 2006, Kelly Czarnecki, review of *Flashcards of My Life,* p. 485.

ONLINE

Charise Mericle Harper Home Page, http://www.charise-harper.com (May 10, 2007).*

* * *

HARVEY, Roland 1945-

Personal

Born December 11, 1945, in Melbourne, Victoria, Australia; son of Herbert Bruce (a graphic artist) and Eveline Anne (a graphic artist) Harvey; married Rona Judith Sharpe (a teacher and astrologer), 1977; children: Sally Christina, Timothy Piers, Roland James, Sara Jane. *Education:* Royal Melbourne Institute of Technology, B.S. (environmental science), 1974, studied architecture, 1973-77. *Politics:* "Green." *Hobbies and other interests:* Cooking, music, physical exercise.

Addresses

Home—Kew, Victoria, Australia.

Career

Worked as a cadet executive for a corporation in Victoria, Australia, 1964-68; affiliated with Colonial Sugar Refining Co., Victoria, 1968-72; Roland Harvey Studios/The Five Mile Press, Collingwood, Victoria, managing director, 1977-90; Roland Harvey Studios/ The Periscope Press, Hawthorn, Victoria, managing director, beginning 1991; writer and illustrator; speaker at conferences.

Member

Black and White Illustrators Club, Icicles Ski Club, Gippsland Lakes Yacht Club.

Awards, Honors

Commendation, Children's Book Council of Australia (CBCA), 1984, and shortlisted for best picture story book, Young Australians Best Book Award Council, 1986, both for *The Friends of Emily Culpepper;* Clifton Pugh Award, CBCA, and Junior Book of the Year Award shortlist, CBCA, both 1986, both for *Burke and Wills;* Children's Picture Book of the Year finalist, and Honour Book designation, both CBCA, both 1989, both for *My Place in Space;* Wilderness Society Environment Award, 1999, for *Islands in My Garden;* Eve Pownall Award for Information Books shortlist, CBCA,

2001, for *Sick As;* Children's Book of the Year Awards shortlist in Picture-Book Category, Speech Pathology Australia Book of the Year shortlist for Best Book for Language Development, and APA Book Design Award for Children's Picture Book, all 2005, all for *At the Beach.*

Writings

SELF-ILLUSTRATED

Roland Harvey's Book of Christmas, Five Mile Press (Canterbury, Victoria, Australia), 1982.

Roland Harvey's First Ever Book of Things to Make and Do, Roland Harvey Studios, 1982.

Roland Harvey's Second Ever Book of Things to Make and Do, Roland Harvey Studios, 1983.

Roland Harvey's Incredible Book of Almost Everything, Five Mile Press (Canterbury, Victoria, Australia), 1985.

Burke and Wills, Five Mile Press (Canterbury, Victoria, Australia), 1985.

Roland Harvey's New Book of Christmas, Five Mile Press (Canterbury, Victoria, Australia), 1986.

Roland Harvey's Only Joking Take-Away Fun Book!, Ashton Scholastic, 1987.

The Real Me Book, Five Mile Press (Canterbury, Victoria, Australia), 1989.

(With Scott Riddle) *Crisis on Christmas Eve,* Periscope Press, 1991.

Roland Harvey's Drawing Book, Scholastic Australia (Sydney, New South Wales, Australia), 1996.

The Secret Record of Me, Roland Harvey Books (Port Melbourne, Victoria, Australia), 1997.

At the Beach: Postcards from Crabby Spit, Allen & Unwin (Crows Nest, New South Wales, Australia), 2004.

Outlaws of the World, National Museum of Australia (Canberra, Australia Capital Territory, Australia), 2004.

In the Bush: Our Holiday at Wombat Flat, Allen & Unwin (Crows Nest, New South Wales, Australia), 2005.

ILLUSTRATOR

Lorraine Milne, *The Fix-It Man: Songs for Schools,* Macmillan, 1979.

Michael Dugan, compiler, *More Stuff and Nonsense,* Collins, 1980.

Alan Boardman, *Eureka Stockade,* Five Mile Press (Canterbury, Victoria, Australia), 1981.

Alan Boardman, *The First Fleet,* Five Mile Press (Canterbury, Victoria, Australia), 1982.

Jean Chapman, *The Great Candle Scandal,* Hodder & Stoughton, 1982.

Ann Coleridge, *The Friends of Emily Culpepper,* Five Mile Press (Canterbury, Victoria, Australia), 1983, Putnam (New York, NY), 1987.

Alan Boardman, *The Crossing of the Blue Mountains,* Five Mile Press (Canterbury, Victoria, Australia), 1984, reprinted, Scholastic (Sydney, New South Wales, Australia), 1997.

Alan Boardman, *Great Events in Australia's History,* Five Mile Press (Canterbury, Victoria, Australia), 1985.

Jim Converse, *The Book of Australian Trivia,* Five Mile Press (Canterbury, Victoria, Australia), 1985.

Nette Hilton, *Dirty Dave the Bushranger,* Five Mile Press (Canterbury, Victoria, Australia), 1987, published as *Dirty Dave,* Orchard Books (New York, NY), 1990.

(With Joe Levine) Robin Hirst and Sally Hirst, *My Place in Space,* Five Mile Press (Canterbury, Victoria, Australia), 1988, Orchard Books (New York, NY), 1990.

Marcia Vaughan, *Milly Fitzwilly's Mousecatcher,* Periscope Press, 1991.

Jim Howes, *Islands in My Garden,* Roland Harvey Books (Port Melbourne, Victoria, Australia), 1998.

Cathy Dodson, *Bass and Flinders,* Scholastic (Sydney, New South Wales, Australia), 1999.

Nette Hilton, *What's a Bunyip?,* Roland Harvey Books (Port Melbourne, Victoria, Australia), 1999.

Gwenda Smyth, *The Six Wonders of Wobbly Bridge,* Roland Harvey Books (Port Melbourne, Victoria, Australia), 1999.

Kate Ryan, *Belvedere Dreaming,* Roland Harvey Books (Port Melbourne, Victoria, Australia), 2000.

Gael Jennings, *Sick As: Bloody Moments in the History of Medicine,* Roland Harvey Books (Port Melbourne, Victoria, Australia), 2000, published as *Bloody Moments: Highlights from the Astonishing History of Medicine,* Annick Press (Toronto, Ontario, Canada), 2000.

Kate Ryan, *Belvedere in the City,* Roland Harvey Books (Port Melbourne, Victoria, Australia), 2000.

Kay Keck and Denise Phillips, *Heritage Masks,* Scholastic Australia (Sydney, New South Wales, Australia), 2001.

Vashti Farrer, *Letters Back Home: A Play,* Pearson Educational (South Melbourne, Victoria, Australia), 2002.

Kate Ryan, *Belvedere Is Beached,* Puffin (Camberwell, Victoria, Australia), 2002.

Michelle Schwarz, *The Super Sailing Sea Restaurant,* Viking (Camberwell, Victoria, Australia, 2002, published as *The Best Restaurant in the World,,* Dutton (New York, NY), 2004.

Mary Small, *The Monster Hole,* Puffin (Camberwell, Victoria, Australia), 2003.

Pam Harvey, *Climbing Mount Sugarbin,* Puffin (Camberwell, Victoria, Australia), 2003.

Alison Lester, *Bonnie & Sam: The Circus Pony Brumby,* Allen & Unwin (Crows Nest, New South Wales, Australia), 2007.

Alison Lester, *Bonnie & Sam: The Shadow Brumby,* Allen & Unwin (Crows Nest, New South Wales, Australia), 2007.

Sidelights

Humor is the main ingredient in the stories and illustrations of Roland Harvey. Trained as an architect, Harvey has won a popular following among young readers in his native Australia due to the detailed art work he contributes to texts by authors such as Gael Jennings, Allan Boardman, Alison Lester, and Nette Hilton. A history buff, Harvey delights in capturing the attention of young readers with historically accurate visual details, bringing readers back to the nineteenth century in his art for Boardman's *Eureka Stockade* and *The Voyage of the First Fleet,* and creating shivers of delight through his deliciously gross art for Jennings' *Sick As: Bloody Moments in the History of Medicine.* Often compared to the work of Quentin Blake and Babette Cole, Harvey's "whimsical" drawings also appear alongside those of fellow illustrator Joe Levine in *My Place in Space,* a guide to the solar system by coauthors Robin and Sally Hirst that a *Publishers Weekly* reviewer praised as "instructive and entertaining." In addition to children's books, Harvey's art has also appeared on calendars and greeting cards.

Moving from fact to fancy, Harvey has also illustrated a number of fanciful stories, such as Scott Riddle's *Crisis on Christmas Eve,* Michelle Schwartz's *The Best Restaurant in the World,* and Hilton's *Dirty Dave. Crisis on Christmas Eve* finds a red-faced Santa Claus stranded in Australia on the BIG DAY when his reindeer go on strike, until the helpful residents of Green's Station do what it takes to keep Christmas Day fun for all. An outback vagabond cashes in on a dark and horribly embarrassing family secret—his dear old dad designs and sews each of his stylish outlaw outfits—in *Dirty Dave.* Published in Australia as *The Super Sailing Sea Restaurant, The Best Restaurant in the World* features a floating café where candy, gum, and other yummy treats replace far-more-sensible—and unpleasantly healthy—ingredients on the menu. Dubbing *The Best Restaurant in the World* a "madcap book that's packed with kid appeal," Bina Williams wrote in *School Library Journal* that Harvey's "wacky" pen-and-ink and watercolor art brings to life his "frothy, exuberant tale," while *Booklist* contributor Julie Cummins cited the picture book's "wispy watercolors" and "clever, imaginative" story. In similar fashion, *Dirty Dave* was praised by a *Publishers Weekly* critic for featuring "quirky, intricately detailed" illustrations "full of sly humor," while *Magpies* contributor Cathryn Crowe heralded *Crisis on Christmas Eve* as a "highly original and hilarious offering which will give young readers hours of pleasure."

Harvey allows his imagination—and his sense of whimsy—full rein when pairing his drawings with an original text, as he does in the picture books *At the Beach: Postcards from Crabby Spit* and *In the Bush: Our Holiday at Wombat Flat. At the Beach* pairs busy illustrations with a text that reads like a series of postcards. With each turn of the page, readers are increasingly caught up in the adventures of Franky as he describes to his Grandma the fun he has swimming, surfing, making bonfires, and crabbing, while also casually mentioning vacation highlights that involve such tantalizing things as UFO sightings and falling bird poo. Another family jaunt inspires another sequence of correspondence, this time as Franky and family venture into the Australia outback, with its desert terrain, interesting animals, erratic weather, campfire stories, and more. In a *Kirkus Reviews* appraisal, a critic described

Roland Harvey helps young readers understand the cosmic puzzle through his artwork for Robin and Sally Hirst's picture book My Place in Space. (Orchard, 1992. Illustration © 1988, by The Five Miles Press. Airbrushed astronomical painting copyright 1988 by Joe Levine. Reproduced by permission of Scholastic, Inc.)

the two companion volumes as "rollicking" fun for young readers.

In addition to fictional stories, Harvey shares his art techniques with young readers in *Roland Harvey's First Ever Book of Things to Make and Do* and *Roland Harvey's Drawing Book*. As in his illustrations for middle-grade histories, the artwork in *Roland Harvey's Drawing Book* provides opportunities for laughter as well as learning, while the author/illustrator's clearly written asides and captions convey a tremendous amount of information about drawing techniques such as perspective, light and tone, and shape. Special attention is paid to techniques used in drawing people and animals. "In short," concluded Kevin Steinberger in a *Magpies* review, *Roland Harvey's Drawing Book* "is quite the most thorough and engaging drawing manual for children I've ever seen."

"My parents were both graphic artists, which gave me a lot of confidence in my drawing," Harvey once told *SATA*. "It also stalled my entry into the real world of illustrating: my mum and dad had suffered in the Great Depression. So I tried a number of other careers and finally architecture, which I loved. Ironically, another depression in the building trade pushed me from architecture into illustrating, then writing and illustrating, and then publishing, writing, and illustrating. I love that even more.

"My first real success came with an attempt to present history in an interesting way. It was on that project that I discovered I work best in a team. *Eureka Stockade*,

the true story of the Gold Rush in Australia and the miners' struggle against repression, was developed with Alan Boardman and was really the birth of my 'style.' In the illustrations of that book, little challenges and questions lurk in every corner, tiny tragedies and comedies are enacted off center stage. I have also worked on other history books, as well as on *My Place in Space*, an interesting collaboration between two astronomers (Robin and Sally Hirst), an airbrush wizard (Joe Levine), and me.

"I don't feel bound to book illustrating; a lot of my time goes toward developing my very Australian cards, kids' calendars, posters and 'other things.' I listen a lot to what my kids say about my books, such as 'Dad— you can't say that!' or 'The reindeer wouldn't be rude to Santa!' I also notice kids laugh at anything to do with toilets."

Biographical and Critical Sources

PERIODICALS

Booklist, May 15, 2004, Julie Cummins, review of *The Best Restaurant in the World*, p. 1627.

Bulletin of the Center for Children's Books, March, 1990, review of *My Place in Space*, p. 163.

Canadian Review of Materials, May 11, 2001, review of *Bloody Moments: Highlights from the Astonishing History of Medicine*.

Horn Book, March-April, 1990, Hanna B. Zeiger, review of *Dirty Dave,* p. 189; May-June, 1990, Hanna B. Zeiger, review of *My Place in Space,* p. 325.

Kirkus Reviews, March 15, 2006, review of *At the Beach: Postcards from Crabby Spit,* p. 291; October 15, 2006, review of *In the Bush: Our Holiday at Wombat Flat,* p. 1072.

Magpies, November, 1992, Cathryn Crowe, review of *Crisis on Christmas Eve,* p. 28; July, 1996, Kevin Steinberger, review of *Roland Harvey's Drawing Book,* pp. 40-41; March, 1997, Rayma Turton, reviews of *The First Fleet, Eureka Stockade,* and *Burke and Wills,* p. 24.

Publishers Weekly, October 9, 1987, review of *The Friends of Emily Culpepper,* p. 51; January 19, 1990, review of *My Place in Space,* p. 108; March 30, 1990, review of *Dirty Dave,* p. 60.

School Library Journal, March, 1988, Lee Bock, review of *The Friends of Emily Culpepper,* p. 164; April, 1990, Marcia Hupp, review of *Dirty Dave,* p. 91; November, 2000, Mary R. Hofmann, review of *Bloody Moments,* p. 170; October, 2004, Bina Williams, review of *The Best Restaurant in the World,* p. 129.

Resource Links, October, 2000, review of *The Secret Record of Me,* p. 15; December, 2000, review of *Bloody Moments,* p. 20.

ONLINE

Allen & Unwin Web site, http://www.allen-unwin.com/ (May 20, 2006), "Roland Harvey."

*　　*　　*

HEMPHILL, Helen 1955-

Personal

Born 1955, in Bridgeport, TX. *Education:* Undergraduate degree (speech and drama); Belmont University, M.A. (English); Vermont College, M.F.A. (writing for children and young adults).

Addresses

Home and office—P.O. Box 150203, Nashville, TN 37215. *E-mail*—readermail@helenhemphill.com.

Career

Author. Worked previously as a teacher.

Member

Authors Guild, Authors League, Tennessee Writers Alliance.

Awards, Honors

Martha Whitmore Hickman Award in Fiction honorable mention, Tennessee Writers' Alliance, 1999; Teacher Award, Frist Foundation, 2000.

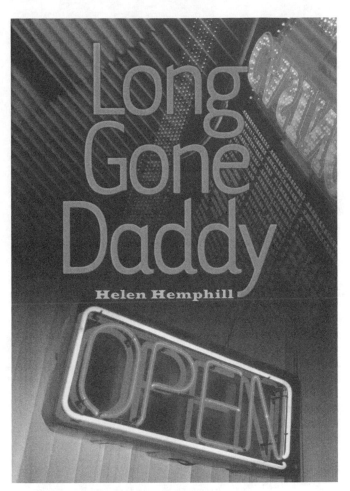

*Cover of Helen Hemphill's young-adult novel **Long Gone Daddy**, which takes readers on an unusual trip of self-discovery.* (Front Street, an imprint of Boyds Mills Press, 2006. Illustration © 2006 by Helen Hemphill. Reproduced by permission of Boyd Mills Press.)

Writings

Long Gone Daddy, Front Street (Asheville, NC), 2006.
Runaround, Front Street (Asheville, NC), 2007.

Sidelights

Helen Hemphill's young-adult novel *Long Gone Daddy* explores the tense relationship between a fourteen-year-old boy and his preacher father. The novel takes place in the South, and in an interview with Teri S. Lesesne for *Teacher Librarian,* Hemphill noted how important setting is in her writing. "Place has a pretty deep hold in my psyche," she explained, "and it is most often the point around which ideas about character identity and plot seem to crystallize." Hemphill also commented in an interview for the *Assembly on Literature for Adolescents Web site* that her own setting, in regards to her writing process, is usually "at home in my office with my books and lots of pictures" because "I like visual images while I'm working."

The comedy of *Long Gone Daddy* is found in its three main characters: Harlan Q, Harlan R, and Warrior. Harlan Q and his father, Harlan R, are forced to take a road

trip to Las Vegas to deliver the corpse of Harlan Q's grandfather to family members in his hometown of Las Vegas. During the road trip they pick up Warrior, a wanna-be actor who helps to rekindle the estranged relationship between Harlan Q and his father. Reviewing Hemphill's novel, several critics cited the humorous tone the author takes, noting that it effectively engages young readers. A *Publishers Weekly* contributor dubbed Hemphill "a writer to watch," citing her ability to create "laugh-out-loud scenes." In *Booklist*, Gillian Engberg wrote that in *Long Gone Daddy* "Hemphill strikes a confident balance between deep heartache and sharply irreverent humor."

Biographical and Critical Sources

PERIODICALS

Booklist, May 1, 2006, Gillian Engberg, review of *Long Gone Daddy*, p. 81.

Bulletin of the Center for Children's Books, June, 2006, Deborah Stevenson, review of *Long Gone Daddy*, p. 454.

Kirkus Reviews, May 1, 2006, review of *Long Gone Daddy*, p. 460.

Kliatt, May, 2006, Claire Rosser, review of *Long Gone Daddy*, p. 10.

Publishers Weekly, June 26, 2006, review of *Long Gone Daddy*, p. 53.

School Library Journal, July, 2006, Susan Oliver, review of *Long Gone Daddy*, p. 104.

Teacher Librarian, October, 2006, Teri S. Lesesne, interview with Hemphill, p. 58.

ONLINE

Assembly on Literature for Adolescents Web site, http://alan-ya.org/ (May 19, 2007), David Gill, "Helen Hemphill."

Cynthia Leitich-Smith Blog, http://cynthialeitichsmith.blogspot.com/ (June 5, 2006), "Helen Hemphill on *Long Gone Daddy*" (interview).

Helen Hemphill Home Page, http://www.helenhemphill.com (May 19, 2007).*

*   *   *

HIMELBLAU, Linda (?)-2005

Personal

Died 2005, in Carmel Valley, CA; married Irving Himelblau.

Career

Educator and writer. Fifth-grade school teacher at Central Elementary School, San Diego, CA, 1974-99.

Awards, Honors

Channel 10 Leadership Award, Sempra Energy/ Lead San Diego, for work with immigrant students; San Diego Book Award, San Diego Book Award Association, 2005, for unpublished novel *Far from Ordinary;* San Diego Book Award finalist, 2006, for *The Trouble Begins.*

Writings

The Trouble Begins, Delacorte Press (New York, NY), 2005.

Sidelights

As a fifth-grade school teacher at San Diego's Central Elementary school Linda Himelblau spent a great deal of time with the school's immigrant students, who came to America from Latin America, Africa, and Southeast Asia. After teaching for fifteen years, Himelblau retired to focus on writing for young readers. *The Trouble Begins*, a middle-grade novel that was published just prior to her death in 2005, ranked as a finalist in the San Diego Book Awards in 2006.

The Trouble Begins introduces eleven-year-old Du Nguyen, a boy based on one of Himelblau's former students. In fact, many of the characters found within the novel were inspired by the students Himelblau encountered during her teaching career. Framed as a first-person narrative, the novel follows Du as he emigrates with his grandmother from a refugee camp in the Philippines to the United States, where he reunites with his parents and siblings. Now in a new country, and living with family members he has not seen for a decade, Du learns that assimilating to a new lifestyle is not easy. In addition to troubles at home, he also faces difficulties at his new elementary school where classmates tease him and teachers misunderstand him. In *The Trouble Begins* Himelblau details Du's experiences as he slowly progresses from a frustrated and angry outsider to an accepted family member and well-respected student.

Reviewing Himelblau's book, a *Kirkus Reviews* critic described *The Trouble Begins* as "a completely convincing picture of the immigrant experience from the point of view of a small boy." Gerry Larson, writing in *School Library Journal*, remarked that "Du's voice is energetic, descriptive, and direct" and added that the first-person viewpoint of the novel's likeable narrator will "help sensitize readers to the cultural and emotional hurdles facing many immigrant classmates." Leigh Fenly, in an assessment of *The Trouble Begins* for the *San Diego Union Tribune Online*, noted that "Himelblau has achieved something rare: She's created a believable, struggling family of refugees and placed at its center an unforgettable character."

Biographical and Critical Sources

PERIODICALS

Bulletin of the Center for Children's Books, December, 2005, review of *The Trouble Begins,* p. 185.

Horn Book, January-February, 2006, Jennifer M. Brabander, review of *The Trouble Begins,* p. 79.

Kirkus Reviews, October 15, 2005, review of *The Trouble Begins,* p. 1139.

School Library Journal, February, 2006, Gerry Larson, review of *The Trouble Begins,* p. 132.

ONLINE

Random House Web site, http://www.randomhouse.ca/ (May 19, 2007), "Linda Himelblau."

San Diego Union Tribune Online, http://www.signonsandiego.com/ (January 15, 2006), Leigh Fenly, review of *The Trouble Begins.**

*　　*　　*

HINDLEY, Judy 1940-

Personal

Born December 24, 1940, in Lompoe, CA; daughter of Vernon Kelly (a lab technician) and Virginia Mae Phelps; married Brian Hindley, February 11, 1961 (divorced 1982); children: John, Anna. *Education:* University of Chicago, B.A. (English; with honors), 1963. *Politics:* "Radical green."

Addresses

Home and office—The Flat, 46 Kingsbury St., Marlborough, Wiltshire SN8 1JE, England. *E-mail*—jmhindley@hotmail.com.

Career

Writer and activist. Usborne Publishing Ltd., London, England, former editor. Activist, involved in local, environmental, and human rights issues; Results (lobby group), member of management team, 1990-93; Marlborough Climate Pledge, founder, 2006.

Member

Survival International, U.N.A., Campaign against the Arms Trade.

Awards, Honors

Times Educational Supplement Junior Information Book Award, 1990; Outstanding Science Trade Book designation, 1990; Oppenheim Toy Portfolio Gold Award, 2000, 2001, 2002; Oppenheim Toy Portfolio Platinum Award, 2002.

Judy Hindley (Reproduced by permission of Judy Hindley.)

Writings

FOR CHILDREN

(With Anabelle Curtis) *The Know-How Book of Paper Fun,* illustrated by Colin King, Usborne (London, England), 1975, Corwin (New York, NY), 1976.

The Know-How Book of Spycraft, Usborne (London, England), 1975, published as *The Know-how Book of Codes, Secret Agents, and Spies,* Corwin (New York, NY), 1976.

How Your Body Works, illustrated by Colin King, Usborne (London, England), 1975, new edition, 1995.

The Time-Traveler Book of Knights and Castles, illustrated by Toni Goffe, Usborne (London, England), 1976, published as *Knights and Castles,* 1997, included in *The Usborne Time Traveller,* edited by Philippa Wingate, 1998.

(With Donald Rumbelow) *The Know-How Book of Detection,* illustrated by Colin King, Usborne (London, England), 1978.

The Good Spy Guide to Secret Messages, Usborne (London, England), 1978.

The Good Spy Guide to Tracking and Trailing, Usborne (London, England), 1978.

The Good Detective's Guide to Fakes and Forgeries, Usborne (London, England), 1979.

The Counting Book, Usborne (London, England), 1979.

Pete and Jim, illustrated by Colin West, Hardy/Clarke, 1985.

The Brave Explorers, Hardy/Clarke, 1985.

Polly's Dance, illustrated by Jill Bennett, Hardy/Clarke, 1985.

Jane's Amazing Woolly Jumper, illustrated by Jill Bennett, Hardy/Clarke, 1985.

The Animal Parade, Collins (London, England), 1985.

The Alphabet Game, illustrated by Colin West, Collins (London, England), 1985.

Isn't It Time?, Collins (London, England), 1985, illustrated by Nick Sharratt, Candlewick Press (Cambridge, MA), 1996.

How Big? How Tall?, Collins (London, England), 1985.

The Big Red Bus, Collins (London, England), 1985, illustrated by William Benedict, Candlewick Press (Cambridge, MA), 1995.

The Little Yellow Truck, Collins (London, England), 1985.

If I Had a Car, Collins (London, England), 1985.

The Train Stops Here, Collins (London, England), 1985.

Once There Was a House: And You Can Make It!, illustrated by Robert Bartelt, Collins (London, England), 1986, Random House (New York, NY), 1987.

Once There Was a Knight: And You Can Be One Too!, illustrated by Robert Bartelt, Collins (London, England), 1987, Random House (New York, NY), 1988.

Make, Bake, Grow, and Sew, illustrated by Judy Bastyra, HarperCollins (New York, NY), 1989.

Mrs. Mary Malarky's Seven Cats, illustrated by Denise Teasdale, ABC (London, England), 1989, Orchard (New York, NY), 1990.

The Little Train, illustrated by Robert Kendall, ABC (London, England), 1989, Orchard (New York, NY), 1990.

The Tree, illustrated by Alison Wisenfeld, C.N. Potter (New York, NY), 1990.

My Own Story Book, ABC (London, England), 1990.

The Sleepy Book: A Lullaby, illustrated by Patrice Aggs, ABC (London, England), 1990, Orchard (New York, NY), 1991.

Uncle Harold and the Green Hat, illustrated by Peter Utton, Farrar, Straus (New York, NY), 1991.

How Many Twos?, illustrated by Steve Bland, ABC (London, England), 1991.

My Own Fairy Story Book, illustrated by Toni Goffe, Kingfisher (London, England), 1991.

Soft and Noisy, illustrated by Patrice Aggs, Hyperion (New York, NY), 1992.

Zoom on a Broom! Six Fun-filled Stories, illustrated by Toni Goffe, Kingfisher (New York, NY), 1992.

What If It's a Pirate?, illustrated by Selina Young, ABC (London, England), 1992, published as *Maybe It's a Pirate,* Thomasson-Grant (Charlottesville, VA), 1992.

A Piece of String Is a Wonderful Thing, illustrated by Margaret Chamberlain, Candlewick Press (Cambridge, MA), 1993.

Robbers and Witches, illustrated by Toni Goffe, Kingfisher (London, England), 1993.

Giants and Princesses, illustrated by Toni Goffe, Kingfisher (London, England), 1993.

Feathery Furry Tales, illustrated by Toni Goffe, Kingfisher (London, England), 1993.

Into the Jungle, illustrated by Melanie Epps, Candlewick Press (Cambridge, MA), 1994.

The Wheeling and Whirling-around Book, illustrated by Margaret Chamberlain, Candlewick Press (Cambridge, MA), 1994.

Funny Walks, illustrated by Alex Ayliffe, BridgeWater Books (Mahwah, NJ), 1994.

One by One, illustrated by Nick Sharratt, Walker (London, England), 1994, Candlewick Press (Cambridge, MA), 1996.

Little and Big, illustrated by Nick Sharratt, Walker (London, England), 1994, Candlewick Press (Cambridge, MA), 1996.

Crazy ABC, illustrated by Nick Sharratt, Walker (London, England), 1994, Candlewick Press (Cambridge, MA), 1996.

Princess Rosa's Winter, illustrated by Margaret Chamberlain, Kingfisher (Boston, MA), 1997.

A Song of Colors, illustrated by Mike Bostock, Candlewick Press (Cambridge, MA), 1998.

Ten Bright Eyes, illustrated by Alison Bartlett, Peachtree (Atlanta, GA), 1998.

The Best Thing about a Puppy, illustrated by Pat Casey, Candlewick Press (Cambridge, MA), 1998.

Eyes, Nose, Fingers, and Toes: A First Book All about You, illustrated by Brita Granström, Candlewick Press (Cambridge, MA), 1999.

Hurry, Scurry, Mousie, Reader's Digest (Pleasantville, NY), 1999.

Leap, Froggie, Leap!, Reader's Digest (Pleasantville, NY), 1999.

The Perfect Little Monster, illustrated by Jonathan Lycett-Smith, Walker (London, England), 2000, Candlewick Press (Cambridge, MA), 2001.

The Little Book of Cats, illustrated by Margaret Chamberlain, Red Fox (London, England), 2000.

Mama, Did You Miss Me?, Bloomsbury (London, England), 2001.

The Best Thing about a Kitten, Walker (London, England), 2001.

Dogs Are My Favorite Things, illustrated by Margaret Chamberlain, Random House (New York, NY), 2001.

What's in Baby's Morning?, illustrated by Jo Burroughs, Walker (London, England), 2001, Candlewick Press (Cambridge, MA), 2004.

The Very Silly Duck, Walker (London, England), 2001.

Rosy's House, illustrated by Helen Craig, Walker (London, England), 2001.

Does a Cow Say Boo?, illustrated by Brita Granström, Candlewick Press (Cambridge, MA), 2002.

Do like a Duck Does!, illustrated by Ivan Bates, Candlewick Press (Cambridge, MA), 2002.

Rosy's Visitors, illustrated by Helen Craig, Candlewick Press (Cambridge, MA), 2002.

Can You Move like an Elephant?, illustrated by Manya Stojic, Barron's Educational (Hauppauge, NY), 2003.

Sleepy Places, illustrated by Tor Freeman, Candlewick Press (Cambridge, MA), 2006.

Baby Talk: A Book of First Words and Phrases, illustrated by Brita Granström, Candlewick Press (Cambridge, MA), 2006.

Contributor to books, including *Bedtime Stories for the Very Young,* Kingfisher, 1991; *The Crocodile Book,* Hutchinson, 1992; *Animal Stories for the Very Young,* Kingfisher, 1994; and *Pirates,* Transworld, 1999.

Sidelights

Judy Hindley is the author of numerous books for young children. Her works range from toddler-sized volumes that teach the basics of color, shape, and size to stories focusing on the interests and concerns of slightly older children. In *Sleepy Places* her readers discover where each of Earth's creatures rest, while life in exotic locations is showcased in the pages of *In the Jungle.* *Princess Rosa's Winter,* a beginning reader also penned by Hindley, even smuggles a history lesson into its engaging storyline about a young girl attempting to overcome her dislike of winter. According to *Booklist* contributor Ilene Cooper, "despite its easy style" Hindley's tale successfully introduces children to the ups and downs of life as it was lived in the Middle Ages. Enhanced by illustrations by artists such as Nick Sharratt, Toni Goffe, and Margaret Chamberlain, Hindley's nonfiction books and story picture books are written in "a lean rhythmic prose," according to a *Kirkus Reviews* writer.

While growing up in the United States, Hindley channeled her active imagination into games of pretend, into a love of reading, and into performing off-the-cuff plays with her friends. She moved to England after she married, and began her writing career while raising her two children. As the author explained on the Walker Books Web site, "I was very happy when I started working on children's books because although it can be very hard work, sometimes it's just like making things up—except that you get something real in the end."

In stories such as *The Perfect Little Monster* and *Rosy's Visitors* Hindley draws on the imaginary games that filled her own childhood years. Related in a "lively, rhythmic text [that] is well suited to reading aloud," *The Perfect Little Monster* introduces a baby that scowls and yells and behaves in every way like every parent's nightmare . . . except that in this case the doting parents are monsters themselves. Focusing on a little girl who creates an imaginary world within a stone's throw of her home's back door, *Rosy's Visitors* was praised as a "sweet, summery tale" by *Booklist* reviewer GraceAnne A. DeCandido. The author "deftly expresses a child's delight in secret places, cozy nooks, and role-play," noted a *Kirkus Reviews* contributor, and *School Library Journal* critic Laurie Von Mehren deemed *Rosy's Visitors* a "peaceful" tale that creates "a sweet, gentle mood" when paired with Helen Craig's warm-toned illustrations.

Reflecting Hindley's enjoyment in making things up, many of her stories feature animal characters that exhibit likeable human characteristics. In *Do like a Duck Does!,* for example, a fox pretends to be a duck and tag along with a family of ducklings in the hopes that he will end up with a snack. While putting this new duckling through its paces, Mama Duck sees through the fox's ploy, as will young readers. As Joy Fleishhacker remarked in her *School Library Journal* review, although "tension builds throughout the story, . . . the tone remains light, and there is never any doubt that Mama Duck has things firmly under control." In a *Booklist* review of *Do like a Duck Does!,* Ilene Cooper noted that the story features "a clever premise, a bouncy text, and sunny, funny pictures" by illustrator Ivan Bates, while a *Kirkus Reviews* writer concluded that the "rhyming text filled with repetitive phrases make" Hindley's picture book "a natural for reading aloud."

In addition to taking on unusual characteristics, animals can also act predictably like animals in Hindley's stories *Does a Cow Say Boo?, Sleepy Places,* and *Mrs. Mary Malarky's Seven Cats.* In *Does a Cow Say Boo?,* featuring pencil-and-watercolor artwork by Brita Granström, Hindley creates a series of rhymes that build into an animal chorus and present readers with what a *Kirkus Reviews* writer deemed "a fresh approach to a popular topic." *Mrs. Mary Malarky's Seven Cats*—a "warm, cozy story" that *School Library Journal* contributor Susan Hepler predicted would find a satisfied audience among "owners of cats, stuffed or real"—finds a little boy quizing his babysitter about the seven cats that have temporarily decided to share the woman's home. On her next visit, Mrs. Malarky informs her quizzical charge that all the cats but one have moved on. The boy is sad that Mrs. Malarky must be alone in her quiet, lonely house . . . that is, until she shows him a picture of the remaining cat, surrounded by its litter of young kittens.

In *The Best Thing about a Puppy* a young boy catalogues his own puppy's good and bad points, but wisely concludes: "The best thing is, a puppy is a friend." Praising the book's simple text, Maura Bresnahan noted in her appraisal for *School Library Journal* that "children will be charmed by the antics of [the] . . . lovable pup" that scampers through the pages of Hindley's "inviting" tale. A *Kirkus Reviews* writer added that the author "masterfully captures the abundant energy and mischievousness" of the young dog as it becomes "the delight and exasperation of its new owner."

In *Into the Jungle* Hindley leads readers from their comfortable relationships with docile pets and takes them for a walk on the wild side. "When you go into the jungle, go carefully," Hindley warns in her engaging text. As her story unfolds, two children wander through an imaginary jungle, surrounded by unseen beasts: chimps, tigers, crocodiles, and exotic birds. "The exuberance and the suspense and the wondering of what jungle creature to expect all combine to make this conversation book a delight," pronounced Cynthia Anthony in a review of *Into the Jungle* for *Magpies.*

The Big Red Bus and *The Little Train* find Hindley focusing on vehicles rather than animals. In *The Big Red Bus* the trusty bus gets one of its wheels stuck in a deep pothole. Soon, a line of cars is stopped behind the bus, until a tractor helps the bus out of its predicament and a truck and steamroller repair the pothole. *School Library Journal* contributor Martha Topol deemed *The Big Red Bus* a story that "begs to be read aloud . . . to toddlers who . . . won't be able to resist participating." A *Books for Keeps* reviewer called Hindley's work "a clearly told, lively story" that is "ideal for storytelling time." Similarly, *The Little Train* was praised by *School Library Journal* reviewer Jeanne Marie Clancy for being "lyrically told in a language both simple and spare."

In addition to picture books, Hindley has created several toddler "concept" books that showcase her abilities as a poet. In *A Song of Colors* she focuses her rhythmic verses on twelve different colors: blue for dragonflies, red for poppies and cherries, and the like. The concept of counting is introduced in both *One by One* and *Ten Bright Eyes*. "The simple rhyming text works wonderfully with the eye-catching, childlike pictures," commented *School Library Journal* contributor Rachel Fox of the collaboration between Hindley and artist Alison Bartlett that resulted in *Ten Bright Eyes*. Another valuable introduction to basic concepts, *Baby Talk: A Book of First Words and Phrases* follows a young child throughout one day, pairing a "bouncy rhyme" in which Hindley features familiar objects such as "blanket" and "bath" with Granström's "adorable" artwork to build beginning vocabularies, according to Cooper. "Toddlers will enjoy pointing out familiar items," wrote *Horn Book* reviewer Bridget T. McCaffrey of the work.

Among the most interesting of Hindley's books for young people are those that inspire curiosity and encourage creativity. In *Once There Was a House: And You Can Make It!* she joins designer Gregg Reyes in demonstrating how to construct a house—in fact, a whole town—out of discarded cardboard boxes, tape, plastic detergent bottles, old newspapers, and other commonplace materials. Praising *Once There Was a House* as ideal for children with "bounce and initiative," *Growing Point* reviewer Margery Fisher voiced similar approval for the companion volume *Once There Was a Knight: And You Can Be One Too!* In this volume, Hindley and Reyes introduce a boy and girl who create their own mini Renaissance Fair, complete with jousting knights, a terrifying dragon, and a king and queen. "Illustrations . . . show the busy young . . . exercising imagination and ingenuity," commented Fisher, the critic noting in particular the historical accuracy of the crafts presented. Other idea books for creative-minded young readers that Hindley has authored include *Make, Bake, Grow, and Sew*, which teaches basic skills for everything from sewing on a button to building simple wood furniture.

Biographical and Critical Sources

PERIODICALS

Booklist, August, 1994, Mary Harris Veeder, review of *Into the Jungle*, p. 2048; October 15, 1995, Hazel Rochman, review of *The Big Red Bus*, p. 411; November 1, 1998, Stephanie Zvirin, review of *The Best Thing about a Puppy*, p. 502; January 1, 2000, review of *Eyes, Nose, Fingers, and Toes: A First Book about You*, p. 824; March 1, 2002, Ilene Cooper, review of *Do like a Duck Does!*, p. 1133; May 1, 2002, GraceAnne A. DeCandido, review of *Rosy's Visitors*, p. 1533; June 1, 2002, Diane Foote, review of *Does a Cow Say Boo?*, p. 1738; September 15, 2004, Ilene Cooper, review of *What's in Baby's Morning?*, p. 250; March 15, 2005, Ilene Cooper, review of *Princess Rosa's Winter*, p. 1299; February 15, 2006, Ilene Cooper, review of *Baby Talk: A Book of First Words and Phrases*, p. 102; April 15, 2006, Gillian Engberg, review of *Sleepy Places*, p. 51.

Books for Keeps, November, 1986, review of *Once There Was a House: And You Can Make It!*, pp. 20-21; May, 1993, review of *A Piece of String Is a Wonderful Thing*, p. 4; November, 1995, review of *Into the Jungle*, p. 6; March, 1996, review of *Crazy ABC*, p. 6; November, 1996, review of *The Big Red Bus*, p. 6; September, 1998, Judith Sharman, review of *The Best Thing about a Puppy*, pp. 19-20.

Books for Your Children, spring, 1985, Margaret Carter, review of *Animal Parade*, p. 14; autumn-winter, 1990, p. 23.

Bulletin of the Center for Children's Books, May, 1993, Betsy Hearne, review of *A Piece of String Is a Wonderful Thing*, p. 274; September, 1994, review of *The Wheeling and Whirling-around Book*, p. 14; April, 2002, review of *Do like a Duck Does!*, p. 282; October, 2002, review of *Does a Cow Say Boo?*, p. 60; August, 2006, Deborah Stevenson, review of *Sleepy Places*, p. 500.

Growing Point, September, 1976, review of *How Your Body Works*, p. 2947; March, 1980, review of *The Counting Book*, p. 3663; September, 1986, review of *Once There Was a House*, p. 4685; November, 1987, Margery Fisher, review of *Once There Was a Knight: And You Can Be One Too!*, p. 4891.

Horn Book, May-June, 2006, Bridget T. McCaffrey, review of *Baby Talk*, p. 297.

Junior Bookshelf, June, 1990, review of *Make, Bake, Grow, and Sew*, p. 135; October, 1990, review of *The Tree*, p. 221; December, 1994, review of *Crazy ABC*, p. 215.

Kirkus Reviews, August 15, 1995, review of *The Big Red Bus*, pp. 1188-1189; August 1, 1998, review of *The Best Thing about a Puppy*, p. 1118; May 15, 1999, review of *Eyes, Nose, Fingers, and Toes*, p. 801; January 15, 2002, review of *Do like a Duck Does!*, p. 105; May 1, 2002, review of *Rosy's Visitors* and *Does a Cow Say Boo?*, p. 656; July 1, 2004, review of *What's in Baby's Morning?*, p. 630; March 15, 2006, review of *Baby Talk*, p. 292; April 15, 2006, review of *Sleepy Places*, p. 407.

Magpies, March, 1995, Cynthia Anthony, review of *Into the Jungle,* p. 21.

Publishers Weekly, February 9, 1990, Diane Roback, review of *Mrs. Mary Malarky's Seven Cats,* p. 59; November 9, 1992, review of *Maybe It's a Pirate,* p. 82; June 27, 1994, review of *Into the Jungle,* p. 76; March 2, 1998, review of *A Song of Colors,* p. 68; June 21, 1999, review of *Eyes, Nose, Fingers, and Toes,* p. 66; December 4, 2000, review of *The Perfect Little Monster,* p. 72; January 28, 2002, review of *Do like a Duck Does!,* p. 289; March, 20, 2002, review of *Rosy's Visitors,* p. 64; May 13, 2002, review of *Does a Cow Say Boo?,* p. 69; July 12, 2004, review of *What's in Baby's Morning?,* p. 62; April 17, 2006, review of *Sleepy Places,* p. 186.

School Librarian, winter, 2003, review of *Can You Move like an Elephant?,* p. 187.

School Library Journal, March, 1990, Susan Hepler, review of *Mrs. Mary Malarky's Seven Cats,* p. 193; August, 1990, Jeanne Marie Clancy, review of *The Little Train,* p. 130; January, 1992, Lori A. Janick, review of *Uncle Harold and the Green Hat,* p. 90; May, 1992, Judith Gloyer, review of *The Sleepy Book,* p. 89; July, 1992, Nancy A. Gifford, review of *How Many Twos?,* p. 69; November, 1992, Jody McCoy, review of *Zoom on a Broom!,* p. 71; February, 1993, Nancy Seiner, review of *Soft and Noisy,* pp. 83-84; July, 1993, Patricia Pearl Doyle, review of *A Piece of String Is a Wonderful Thing,* p. 79; September, 1994, Patricia Pearl, review of *Funny Walks,* p. 186; January, 1995, Sandra Welzenbach, review of *The Wheeling and Whirling-around Book,* p. 104; January, 1996, Martha Topol, review of *The Big Red Bus,* p. 85; May, 1998, Lauralyn Persson, review of *A Song of Colors,* p. 113; October, 1998, Maura Bresnahan, review of *The Best Thing about a Puppy,* p. 102; November, 1998, Rachel Fox, review of *Ten Bright Eyes,* p. 86; July, 1999, Olga R. Barnes, review of *Eyes, Nose, Fingers, and Toes,* p. 73; June, 2001, Melinda Piehler, review of *The Perfect Little Monster,* p. 118; April, 2002, Joy Fleishhacker, review of *Do like a Duck Does!,* p. 112; August, 2002, Laurie Von Mehren, review of *Rosy's Visitors,* p. 158; September, 2002, Amy Lilien-Harper, review of *Does a Cow Say Boo?,* p. 194; March, 2006, Gay Lynn Van Vleck, review of *Baby Talk,* p. 192.

ONLINE

Candlewick Books Web site, http://www.candlewick.com/ (June 21, 2007), "Judy Hindley."

Walker Books Web site, http://www.walkerbooks.co.uk/ (March 28, 2007), "Judy Hindley."

*   *   *

HOLT, Kimberly Willis 1960-

Personal

Born September 9, 1960, in Pensacola, FL; daughter of Julian Ray (a data processing manager) and Brenda (a

Kimberly Willis Holt (Photograph courtesy of Diane Bondareff, AP Images.)

teacher) Willis; married Jerry William Holt (director of Amarillo CVC), February 23, 1985; children: Shannon. *Education:* Attended University of New Orleans, 1978-79, and Louisiana State University, 1979-81.

Addresses

Home—Amarillo, TX. *Office*—P.O. Box 20135, Amarillo, TX 79114. *Agent*—Flannery Literary Agency, 114 Wickfield Ct., Naperville, IL 60563.

Career

Radio news director, 1980-82; worked in advertising and marketing, 1982-87; interior decorator, 1987-93; writer, 1994—.

Awards, Honors

Boston Globe/Horn Book Award for Fiction, 1998, and American Library Association (ALA) Notable Book selection and Top Ten Best Books for Young Adults selection, both 1999, all for *My Louisiana Sky;* National Book Award for Young People's Literature, 1999, for *When Zachary Beaver Came to Town.*

Writings

YOUNG-ADULT NOVELS

My Louisiana Sky, Holt (New York, NY), 1998.
Mister and Me, Putnam (New York, NY), 1998.
When Zachary Beaver Came to Town, Holt (New York, NY), 1999.
Dancing in Cadillac Light, Putnam (New York, NY), 2001.

OTHER

Waiting for Gregory, illustrated by Gabi Swiatkowska, Holt (New York, NY), 2006.
Part of Me: Stories of a Louisiana Family, Holt (New York, NY), 2006.
Skinny Brown Dog, illustrated by Donald Saaf, Henry Holt (New York, NY), 2007.
Piper Reed, Navy Brat, illustrated by Christine Davenier, Holt (New York, NY), 2007.

Adaptations

Holt's novels have been adapted as audiobooks.

Sidelights

Kimberly Willis Holt writes poignant coming-of-age fiction for young readers, and her novels and short stories hum with the sleepy rhythms of small-town life. Since publishing her first novel, *My Louisiana Sky,* in 1994, she has continued to expand her focus, moving from the American South west to Texas, and including picture books as well as the anthology *Part of Me: Stories of a Louisiana Family* in her list of published works. Holt has won a number of awards, including two American Library Association citations and a prestigious National Book Award for Young People's Literature, the last for her novel *When Zachary Beaver Came to Town.* Her fiction has been praised for its realistic depiction of life in the rural South, and for the iconoclastic, but sympathetic characters she creates within her fictional world.

Holt was born in 1960, in Pensacola, Florida, the site of a large naval base. Her father worked for many years as a chef for the U.S. Navy, and her mother was a teacher. Julian Willis's job took the family to several far-flung places during Holt's young life, including France and the Pacific Ocean territory of Guam. They also lived in a number of American states, but always made Forest Hill, Louisiana, their spiritual home. Holt's grandmother lived there, and the future author loved spending time in a place where her roots ran so deep. She began to consider writing as a career at the age of twelve, when she read Carson McCullers's *The Heart Is a Lonely Hunter.* This 1940 work, like others by the Georgia native, explored human isolation and life in the South through the vantage point of an eloquent outsider, and the style of fiction moved the young Holt. "It was just

life-changing because of the characters," she told *School Library Journal* writer Kathleen T. Horning. "That was the first time I read a book where the characters seemed like real people to me."

Holt studied broadcast journalism at the University of New Orleans in the late 1970s and Louisiana State University until 1981, but left school to work as a news director for a radio station. The work was far from challenging, however, and so she took another job at the station selling advertising time. She also worked as an interior decorator for six years before thinking about writing for publication. As a teen and young adult, she had always envisioned a life as an author, but never pursued it in earnest. Part of the reason she abandoned her calling was due to a tough writing teacher she once had, who refused to provide her with any encouraging feedback. "In all fairness to her, she was a great teacher, but she would praise other people's writing but not mine," Holt told Horning in the *School Library Journal* interview. "I was very shy and insecure and I took it as though I really wasn't meant to be a writer."

Around 1994, Holt—by then married and raising a young child—moved to Amarillo, Texas, for her husband's job. In the sudden isolation, she discovered a surprising opportunity to begin writing for children. "I didn't know a soul there and I thought, 'If I'm ever going to do it, this is the time,'" she told Horning. The result was *My Louisiana Sky,* published by Holt in 1998. Set in a small town in central Louisiana, the story was inspired by a memorable incident that occurred when Holt was just nine. She had been traveling through rural Louisiana with her parents, and saw a woman carrying groceries walking on the side of the road. "This lady looked strange to me," Holt recalled in the interview with Horning. "She just had a different look about her on her face and I mentioned her to my mom and my mom said, 'That lady's mentally retarded and her husband is mentally retarded and they have a lot of kids.' It haunted me for the rest of my life."

Tiger Ann Parker is the unlikely heroine of *My Louisiana Sky,* which takes place in a town called Saitter in 1957. Tiger, who is twelve years old, does well in both school and athletics, but feels a certain degree of social ostracism because of her parents. Her father, who works in a local plant nursery, cannot even do simple math and Tiger's mother is even more developmentally challenged. As a young child, it used to delight Tiger that her mother played games with her so enthusiastically, but entering adolescence and yearning for a more "normal" life, the girl begins to feels embarrassed by her parents' limitations. She knows that some townspeople view the family as odd and are of the opinion that the Parkers should have never been allowed to marry and start a family. Fortunately, Tiger also lives with her astute, practical grandmother, who helps the teen face the teasing of others. Things begin to change in sleepy Saitter, however: Tiger's baseball-playing pal surprises her with a kiss one day, and then her beloved grand-

Cover of Holt's award-winning young-adult novel **My Louisiana Sky,**
featuring artwork by Matt Archambault. (Yearling Books, 1998. Reproduced by
permission of Dell Publishing, a division of Random House, Inc.)

mother dies. Tiger's sophisticated aunt comes to Saitter
in the midst of the crisis, and offers to take the teen
with her to live in the city of Baton Rouge. Tiger is
torn between staying with her parents, who love her
dearly, and going with the glamorous Dorie Kay and
experiencing a world of new opportunities far from the
town's small-mindedness. When a natural disaster
strikes, Tiger begins to realize the more positive aspects
of life in Saitter.

Betsy Hearne, reviewing *My Louisiana Sky* for the *Bulletin of the Center for Children's Books,* wrote that in
Tiger, Holt creates a character "with a distinctive voice"
as well as "a credible resolution showing Tiger's values
to be as strong as her family ties." In her *School Library Journal* review, Cindy Darling Codell asserted
that "Holt has nicely portrayed the rhythms, relationships, and sometimes harsh realities of small-town life."
Marilyn Bousquin, reviewing the novel for *Horn Book,*
found that Holt "eases the action along with a low-key,
unpretentious plot, never resorting to over-dramatization
or sentimentality in developing her uncannily credible
characters." In *Booklist* Hazel Rochman opined that "all
the characters, including Tiger's parents, are drawn

with warmth but no patronizing reverence," while a
Publishers Weekly critic asserted that Holt "presents
and handles a sticky dilemma with remarkable grace."

Just eighty pages in length, *Mister and Me* is aimed at
readers aged seven to eleven, and won praise for its depiction of a time and place that had long passed. The
book's protagonist, Jolene Johnson, knows no other
world except the sometimes-challenging, segregated
South of the World War II era. An African-American
child, Jolene lives with her widowed mother and grandfather in a Louisiana logging town. Life begins to
change a bit too quickly for the girl when Mister Leroy
Redfield, a logger new to town, begins courting Jolene's
mom. Dealing with a rival for her busy mother's affection makes Jolene miss her deceased father even more.
Although the girl attempts to rid the man from their
lives, her strategies only backfire. When her mother and
grandfather leave on a hurried trip to New Orleans,
Jolene is left with Leroy for caretaking, and a truce between the two leads to a new beginning. Lynda Short,
writing in *School Library Journal,* called *Mister and
Me* a "touching short novel" that depicts Jolene's coming to terms with the presence of a "man whose love
and patience allow her to expand her notion of family."
A *Publishers Weekly* review wrote that "the warmth and
love in the Johnson household envelops the novel," and
Kay Weisman noted in *Booklist* that Holt's "heartfelt
story is filled with richly developed characters who deal
with all-too-real problems."

The plot of Holt's National Book Award-winning *When
Zachary Beaver Came to Town* originated with another
memorable event in the author's life. At age thirteen,
she went to the Louisiana state fair and paid two dollars
to see a youth billed as "the fattest boy in the world."
He sat in a small trailer and, in a manner somewhat out
of character for the shy Holt, she asked him several
questions about himself. He answered them, but he was
understandably a bit surly about it. Years later, Holt met
another woman who recalled meeting the boy, but also
recalled eating her lunch with him. In Holt's story, the
action takes place in the fictional small town of Antler,
Texas, during the summer of 1971, when young teens
Toby Wilson and friend Cal watch the trailer bearing
Zachary Beaver, "the world's fattest teenaged boy,"
drive into town. The boys dream of life outside of Antler, and when they visit the 643-pound Zachary they
ask him numerous questions. Zachary seems to possess
an oddly encyclopedic knowledge of the world, but re-
lies on his legal guardian—who disappears shortly after
Zachary's trailer arrives in the parking lot of the local
Dairy Maid. In their sleuthing, the curious Toby and
Cal discover one of Zachary's secrets, and then help
him fulfill a dream while also coming to terms with
their own limited reality.

In *When Zachary Beaver Came to Town* "Holt tenderly
captures small-town life and deftly fills it with decent
characters who ring true," wrote Linnea Lannon in her
New York Times Book Review appraisal. "Picturesque

images . . . drive home the point that everyday life is studded with memorable moments," stated a *Publishers Weekly* contributor.

Set in the late 1960s, in the small town of Moon, Texas, *Dancing in Cadillac Light* follows the story of Jaynell Lambert, an eleven-year-old tomboy whose life changes after her independent-minded grandfather comes to stay with her family. While Grandpap's behaviors seem odd to the girl—he lets the low-class Pickens family live in his old house free of charge, pays cash for a gaudy, green 1962 Cadillac, and shuffles around town with no destination in mind—Jaynell finds her views about character and the meaning of poverty changing after the old man's passing. Calling *Dancing in Cadillac Light* "a solid page-turner," *School Library Journal* reviewer Wiliam McLoughlin added that the story clearly showcases Holt's "remarkable gift for creating endearingly eccentric characters as well as witty dialogue rich in dialect and idiom." Jaynell is enjoyable and serves as a "spunky and tough" narrator, in the opinion of a *Publishers Weekly* contributor, the critic adding that *Dancing in Cadillac Light* "captures a child's sense that time stretches endlessly before her."

Thirteen-year-old Isabel Moreno center stage in *Keeper of the Night*. Living on the island of Guam with her family, Isabel must still learn to cope with tragedy and her troubled siblings after her mother commits suicide and the family starts to come apart. Noting that Isabel "comes through as a thoroughly believable eighth grader," Kathleen Isaacs described *Keeper of the Night* as "a beautifully written description of sorrow and recovery that should appeal to a wide audience." *Kliatt* contributor Michele Winship dubbed the novel an engaging coming-of-age tale.

In addition to novels, Holt has also authored several picture books. In *Waiting for Gregory,* which feature paintings by Polish-born artist Gabi Swiatkowska, a young girl eagerly awaits the birth of her baby cousin. After Iris asks various relatives factual questions about childbirth, she finds that everyone gives her a different answer in Holt's amusing tale. In *Skinny Brown Dog,* Holt's story about a stray dog who adopts a reluctant small-town baker is brought to life in artwork by Donald Saaf. Reviewing *Waiting for Gregory* in *Booklist,* Hazel Rochman wrote that Holt's mix of the everyday and the magical . . . captures the longing, mystery, and joy" of childhood, while a *Kirkus Reviews* writer concluded that the author's "child's-eye take on the passage of time is concrete and comforting" to young readers.

When asked by *School Library Journal* interviewer Horning about the eccentricity of her characters, Holt replied: "I'm attracted to people like that. I like the flaws in people. . . . And I also love the people that seem normal on the surface and then they're really not.

I find that a high compliment when people say that they think my characters are eccentric or quirky, because I guess that's what I love about life."

Biographical and Critical Sources

PERIODICALS

Booklist, April 15, 1998, Hazel Rochman, review of *My Louisiana Sky,* p. 1438; November 15, 1998, Kay Weisman, review of *Mister and Me,* p. 590; January 1, 2000, review of *When Zachary Beaver Came to Town,* p. 820; February 1, 2001, Hazel Rochman, review of *Dancing in Cadillac Light,* p. 1053; February 1, 2006, Hazel Rochman, review of *Waiting for Gregory,* p. 55; September 1, 2006, Carolyn Phelan, review of *Part of Me: Stories of a Louisiana Family,* p. 128.

Bulletin of the Center for Children's Books, June, 1998, Betsy Hearne, review of *My Louisiana Sky,* p. 364; March, 2001, review of *Dancing in Cadillac Light,* p. 263; August, 2006, Karen Coats, review of *Waiting for Gregory,* p. 502; November, 2006, Karen Coats, review of *Part of Me,* p. 127.

Horn Book, July-August, 1998, Marilyn Bousquin, review of *My Louisiana Sky,* p. 489; November, 1999, Marilyn Bousquin, review of *When Zachary Beaver Came to Town,* p. 741; March, 2001, Susan P. Brabander, review of *Dancing in Cadillac Light,* p. 207; May-June, 2003, Lauren Adams, review of *Keeper of the Night,* p. 349; November-December, 2006, Christine M. Heppermann, review of *Part of Me,* p. 713.

Kirkus Reviews, May 1, 2003, review of *Keeper of the Night,* p. 677; April 1, 2006, review of *Waiting for Gregory,* p. 348; August 15, 2006, review of *Part of Me,* p. 843.

Kliatt, May, 2003, Michele Winship, review of *Keeper of the Night,* p. 10; September, 2006, Claire Rosser, review of *Part of Me,* p. 13.

New York Times Book Review, December 19, 1999, Linnea Lannon, review of *When Zachary Beaver Came to Town.*

Publishers Weekly, May 4, 1998, review of *My Louisiana Sky,* p. 213; August 31, 1998, review of *Mister and Me,* p. 76; November 1, 1999, review of *When Zachary Beaver Came to Town,* p. 85; January 29, 2001, review of *Dancing in the Cadillac Light,* p. 90; May 12, 2003, review of *Keeper of the Night,* p. 68; April 24, 2006, review of *Waiting for Gregory,* p. 59; July 17, 2006, review of *Part of Me,* p. 158; May 28, 2007, review of *Skinny Brown Dog,* p. 60.

School Library Journal, July, 1998, Cindy Darling Codell, review of *My Louisiana Sky,* pp. 95-96; November, 1998, Lynda Short, review of *Mister and Me,* p. 122; February, 2000, Kathleen T. Horning, "Small Town Girl," pp. 43-45; March, 2001, William McLoughlin, review of *Dancing in the Cadillac Light,* p. 250; May, 2003, Kathleen Isaacs, review of *Keeper of the Night,* p. 153; March, 2006, Marianne Saccardi, review of

Waiting for Gregory, p. 194; September, 2006, Melissa Moore, review of *Part of Me,* p. 208; May, 2007, Elizabeth Willoughby, review of *Part of Me,* p. 74.

Texas Monthly, December, 1999, Mike Shea, review of *When Zachary Beaver Came to Town,* p. 34.

Voice of Youth Advocates, August, 1998, Lynn Evarts, review of *My Louisiana Sky,* p. 202; February, 1999, review of *My Louisiana Sky,* p. 411; April, 2001, Diane Tuccilllo, review of *Dancing in the Cadillac Light,* p. 42; June, 2003, review of *Keeper of the Night,* p. 405; April, 2007, Lisa A. Hazlett, review of *Part of Me,* p. 50.

ONLINE

Kimberley Willis Holt Home Page, http://www.kimberly-willisholt.com (June 10, 2007).*

*   *   *

HORT, Lenny

Personal

Married; children: three daughters.

Addresses

Home—Fort Lee, NJ.

Career

Author and educator. Former children's book editor.

Writings

(Reteller) *The Boy Who Held Back the Sea,* illustrated by Thomas Locker, Dial Books (New York, NY), 1987.

(Reteller) Wilhelm Hauff, *The Tale of Caliph Stork,* illustrated by Friso Hensta, Dial Books (New York, NY), 1989.

(Reteller) Alexander Nikolayevich Afanasyev, *The Fool and the Fish: A Tale from Russia,* illustrated by Gennady Spirin, Dial Books (New York, NY), 1990.

How Many Stars in the Sky?, illustrated by James E. Ransome, Tambourine Books (New York, NY), 1991.

(Reteller) *The Goatherd and the Shepherdess: A Tale from Ancient Greece,* illustrated by Lloyd Bloom, Dial Books (New York, NY), 1995.

The Seals on the Bus, illustrated by G. Brian Karas, Holt (New York, NY), 2000.

Tie Your Socks and Clap Your Feet: Mixed Up Poems, illustrated by Stephen Kroninger, Atheneum (New York, NY), 2000.

Treasure Hunts! Treasure Hunts!, illustrated by Cary Pillo, HarperCollins (New York, NY), 2000.

We're Going on Safari, illustrated by Tony Arma, Harry N. Abrams (New York, NY), 2002.

We're Going on a Treasure Hunt, illustrated by Tony Arma, Harry N. Abrams (New York, NY), 2003.

(Adaptor) Beatrice Masini, *The Wedding Dress Mess,* illustrated by Anna Laura Cantone, Watson-Guptill (New York, NY), 2003.

George Washington: A Photographic Story of a Life, Dorling Kindersley (New York, NY), 2005.

(With Laaren Brown) *Nelson Mandela: A Photographic Story of a Life,* Dorling Kindersley (New York, NY), 2006.

Did Dinosaurs Eat Pizza?: Mysteries Science Hasn't Solved, illustrated by John O'Brien, Holt (New York, NY), 2006.

Sidelights

Lenny Hort is a children's book author whose varied output has allowed him to work as a biographer, historian, and reteller of folktales and legends. In *The Boy Who Held Back the Sea,* an adaptation of a tale that appears in *Hans Brinker; or, The Silver Skates* by nineteenth-century children's book author Mary Mapes Dodge, Hort recounts the story of a young troublemaker who saves his Dutch village from disaster by using his finger to plug a hole in a leaky dike. The author creates new characters and lengthens the original 1865 tale by "removing the story "from the realm of fable and placing it into fiction," noted *School Library Journal* critic Karen K. Radtke. In *The Tale of Caliph Stork,* Hort moves from the Netherlands to Persia, retelling a fairy tale in which a ruler of Baghdad finds himself unable to revert to human form after an evil sorcerer transforms him into a stork. "Hort's retelling is accessible and full of sly humor," observed Ruth Smith in a review of *The Tale of Caliph Stork* for *School Library Journal.*

The Fool and the Fish: A Tale from Russia, an adaptation of a folktale by Alexander Nikolayevich Afanasyev, concerns the misadventures of a lazy young man named Ivan who discovers a magical fish that grants his every wish. According to *School Library Journal* contributor Denise Anton Wright, the work "captures the flavor of Tsarist Russia and the contrast between the social classes." In *The Goatherd and the Shepherdess: A Tale from Ancient Greece* Hort "transforms and condenses a sexy pastoral romance from third-century Greece into a tragic but ultimately uplifting story" about Chloe, her lover Daphnis, and his rival Dorcon, noted a reviewer in *Publishers Weekly.*

In *Tie Your Socks and Clap Your Feet: Mixed Up Poems* Hort collects eighteen absurd rhymes that describe such oddities as a groundhog delivering valentines, a purple-skinned orange, and a basement that serves as a garage. According to Stephanie Zvirin, writing in *Booklist,* "the words have the ring of children's own nonsense poetry." Based on the popular preschool song "The Wheels on the Bus," Hort's *The Seals on the Bus* follows a family of four on their wild bus ride, during which the driver picks up a variety of unusual passen-

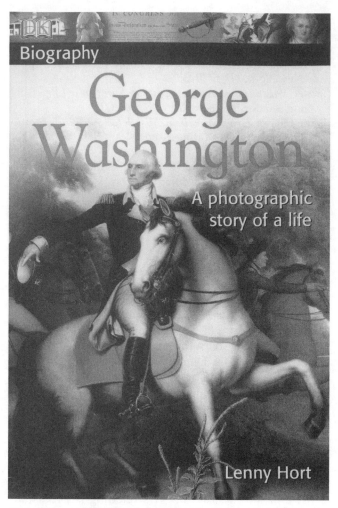

Cover of Lenny Hort's nonfiction work George Washington, *a profile of the first U.S. president that is told through pictures.* (DK Publishing, 2005. Cover art © 2005 by Richard T. Nowitz/Corbis.)

gers, including seals, geese, monkeys, vipers, and skunks. In the words of a *Horn Book* reviewer, "the interaction between animal and human passengers . . . is pure jubilation."

Other adaptations by Holt include Beatrice Masini's *The Wedding Dress Mess,* a humorous tale about an Italian seamstress and her neglected fiancée. Filomena is known far and wide as an expert designer of wedding gowns, and after Filippo proposes marriage to her, she immediately begins constructing her own dress, an ambitious creation that takes all of her time. When Filomena finally dons the outfit for her wedding day, the overdone monstrosity so frightens Filippo that he flees the altar. "Hort's translation . . . has considerable tongue-in-cheek zip," noted a *Kirkus Reviews* critic, while *School Library Journal* contributor Be Astengo praised "the story's droll turn of phrase and jaunty pace." According to a *Publishers Weekly* reviewer, "Filomena's story offers a charmingly offbeat setting for the lesson that love beats all."

Holt moves from folktales to nonfiction in books such as *George Washington: A Photographic Story of a Life*

and *Did Dinosaurs Eat Pizza?: Mysteries Science Hasn't Solved.* In *Did Dinosaurs Eat Pizza?,* a work aimed at early readers, Hort examines a series of unanswered questions about the prehistoric creatures. Calling the book "refreshing," *Booklist* reviewer Carolyn Phelan added that Hort "steers clear of both tooth-and-blood illustrations and the pretense that science has all the answers." A critic for *Publishers Weekly* described the text as "an entertaining way to consider how science is a field of raising questions and pursuing the answers, even if they are inconclusive."

Biographical and Critical Sources

PERIODICALS

Booklist, February 1, 1995, Carolyn Phelan, review of *The Goatherd and the Shepherdess: A Tale from Ancient Greece,* p. 1010; March 15, 2000, Stephanie Zvirin, review of *Tie Your Socks and Clap Your Feet: Mixed Up Poems,* p. 1383; June 1, 2000, Carolyn Phelan, review of *Treasure Hunts! Treasure Hunts!,* p. 1884; April 1, 2000, Carolyn Phelan, review of *The Seals on the Bus,* p. 1463; November 1, 2002, Karin Snelson, review of *We're Going on Safari,* p. 508; April 1, 2006, Carolyn Phelan, review of *Did Dinosaurs Eat Pizza?: Mysteries Science Hasn't Solved,* p. 45.

Horn Book, May, 2000, review of *The Seals on the Bus,* p. 294.

Kirkus Reviews, March 15, 2003, review of *The Wedding Dress Mess,* p. 473; February 1, 2006, review of *Did Dinosaurs Eat Pizza?,* p. 132.

Kliatt, May, 2005, Patricia Moore, review of *George Washington: A Photographic Story of a Life,* p. 41; November, 2006, Mary Ellen Snodgrass, review of *Nelson Mandela: A Photographic Story of a Life,* p. 34.

New York Times Book Review, November 11, 1990, D.M. Thomas, review of *The Fool and the Fish: A Tale from Russia,* p. 50.

Publishers Weekly, August 14, 1987, Diane Roback, review of *The Boy Who Held Back the Sea,* p. 100; August 31, 1990, review of *The Fool and the Fish,* p. 65; April 5, 1991, review of *How Many Stars in the Sky?,* p. 145; January 9, 1995, review of *The Goatherd and the Shepherdess,* p. 63; April 17, 2000, review of *Tie Your Socks and Clap Your Feet,* p. 79; October 14, 2002, review of *We're Going on Safari,* p. 82; March 10, 2003, review of *The Wedding Dress Mess,* p. 71; February 27, 2006, review of *Did Dinosaurs Eat Pizza?,* p. 60.

School Library Journal, November, 1987, Karen K. Radtke, review of *The Boy Who Held Back the Sea,* p. 91; November, 1990, Denise Anton Wright, review of *The Fool and the Fish,* p. 101; April, 2000, Barbara Chatton, review of *Tie Your Socks and Clap Your Feet,* p. 120; November, 2000, Rita Hunt Smith, review of *Treasure Hunts! Treasure Hunts!,* p. 143; May, 2000, John Sigwald, review of *The Seals on the Bus,* p. 161;

November, 2002, Laurie von Mehren, review of *We're Going on a Safari,* p. 126; May, 2003, Be Astengo, review of *The Wedding Dress Mess,* p. 125; January, 2004, Martha Topol, review of *We're Going on a Treasure Hunt,* p. 98; March, 2006, Mary Elam, review of *Did Dinosaurs Eat Pizza?,* p. 209.*

J-K

JAFFE, Michele 1970-
(Michele Sharon Jaffe)

Personal

Born 1970. *Education:* Harvard University, B.A., 1991, Ph.D. (comparative literature), 1998.

Addresses

Home—Las Vegas, NV. *E-mail*—michele@michelejaffe. com.

Career

Huntington Library, San Marino, CA, staff member; Harvard University, Cambridge, MA, instructor in Shakespeare.

Writings

FOR YOUNG ADULTS

Bad Kitty, HarperCollins (New York, NY), 2006.
Prom Nights from Hell, HarperCollins (New York, NY), 2007.

ROMANCE NOVELS

The Stargazer, Pocket Books (New York, NY), 1999.
The Water Nymph, Pocket Books (New York, NY), 2000.
Lady Killer, Ballantine Books (New York, NY), 2002.
Secret Admirer, Ballantine Books (New York, NY), 2002.
Bad Girl, Ballantine Books (New York, NY), 2003.
Loverboy, Ballantine Books (New York, NY), 2004.

OTHER

The Story of O: Prostitutes and Other Good-for-Nothings in the Renaissance (dissertation), Harvard University Press (Cambridge, MA), 1999.

Sidelights

Michele Jaffe earned her Ph.D. in comparative literature, then abandoned academia to pursue a career as a romance novelist. In an interview for *Beatrice* online, she explained of her surprising shift in career goals: "It first started when it became startlingly clear that I didn't want to be an academic. But I loved doing research, I loved what I was studying, and I wanted another outlet for the fascinating facts that I was finding, the interesting people I was meeting in my research." Set in the Renaissance, her novels *The Stargazer, The Water Nymph, Lady Killer,* and *Secret Admirer* comprise a series that follows the romantic exploits of six male cousins, while *Loverboy* moves into mystery as Jaffe details the exploits of an F.B.I. agent battling a modern-day serial killer.

In *The Stargazer* Jaffe transports readers to Venice, where Bianca Salva stumbles across the body of Isabella Bellochio, who was stabbed with a dagger belonging to aristocrat Ian Foscari. Having received a note from Isabella, Ian goes to visit her and, walking in just as Bianca pulls the dagger from Isabella's lifeless body, assumes Bianca to be the killer. Won over by her claims of innocence, Ian brings Bianca to his castle and gives her one week to prove that she is no killer. As a cover-up he tells everyone that she is his fiancée, which pleases his family since they want him to be married. Bianca, the daughter of a doctor, agrees to the ruse as long as she can perform an autopsy on her murdered friend. As Bianca and Ian work to find the true murderer, they fall passionately in love. *Booklist* contributor Patty Engelmann concluded of *The Stargazer* that "Jaffe's characters are intriguing, and the plot's many twists and turns are wonderfully entertaining."

The Water Nymph is set in England during the reign of Queen Elizabeth I. Crispin Foscari, the earl of Sandal, is dismissed from his position as part of the queen's secret service after being accused of treason. He has two weeks to discover the identity of the person making allegations against him. During his investigation, Crispin

meets Sophie Champion, a businesswoman who has questions about the suspicious death of her father. As the paths of Crispin and Sophie cross, they develop a mutual admiration and love for each other. In her *Booklist* review, Margaret Flanagan described *The Water Nymph* as "fast-paced historical fiction fairly crackling with passion and suspense."

Secret Admirer and *Lady Killer* are also set in London, England, in the late 1500s. In *Secret Admirer* Lady Tuesday Arlington discovers that painting the scenes of her deathly nightmares helps her to deal with them, but when her husband is murdered her dream paintings incriminate her as the killer. Investigator Lawrence Pickering begins to believe that Tuesday is not the real killer and falls in love with her. At the same time the murderer sets his sights on Pickering. As *Lady Killer* opens, it is three years since Miles Loredon killed the vampire of London in front of numerous witnesses. When Lady Clio Thornton finds the body of a woman that appears to have the marks of a vampire bite, she approaches Miles with her findings. As Clio and Miles work to solve the case, they fall in love, despite the fact that Miles is betrothed to Clio's cousin. Reviewing *Secret Admirer* for *Romantic Times* online, Kathe Robin claimed that the author "creates a masterful and highly suspenseful mystery with enough red herrings and stunning surprises to keep any fan enthralled," going on to dub *Lady Killer* "a compelling, hard-to-put-down read."

In the novels *Bad Girl* and *Loverboy* Jaffe turns from romance to the thriller genre. In *Loverboy* she introduces Imogen Page, a federal agent who sees life differently due to an unusual medical condition called synesthesia. Because she has the ability to translate what she sees and hears into tastes, Imogen is unusually sensitive to her surroundings. She uses her gift as head of the F.B.I.'s Cognitive Sciences unit, where it comes in handy as she tracks down a brutal serial killer known as Loverboy. After kidnaping his victim, the brazen five-time killer creates collages of his planned crime scene, then sends them to police in advance of his deadly attack. When a brilliant nuclear physicist seems to be the subject of the latest collage received by Las Vegas police, Imogen is called in and must channel all her concentration into deciphering the clues imbedded in the sinister work. A *Kirkus Reviews* writer called *Loverboy*'s female sleuth "smart, tough, and cute as a button," and in *Booklist* Joanne Wilkinson wrote that Jaffe salts her plot with "fascinating secondary characters, plenty of sprightly sexual banter, . . . and plot twists aplenty."

In Jaffe's first novel for teen readers, *Bad Kitty,* readers meet seventeen-year-old Californian Jasmine Callihan, the novel's narrator and a girl whose dream has always been to become a detective. Her wish comes true while she and her family are vacationing at Las Vegas's Venetian Hotel, for she quickly finds herself knee-deep in mystery. After being attacked by a frightened three-legged cat, the accident-prone teen disrupts a nearby wedding celebration, then becomes enmeshed in a murder that points to the husband of a famous model. Helped by the model's eight-year-old son, as well as by her three newly arrived friends from back home, Jasmine sets to work, her amusing banter fueling a plot that a *Publishers Weekly* reviewer characterized as "confusing" but "cinematic." Noting the presence of a suitable love interest and the appeal of Jaffe's "quirky characters," the critic predicted of *Bad Kitty* that teen mystery fans "will likely find themselves quickly clawing their way through this fun novel." Calling Jasmine's unique narrative voice "the book's greatest asset," a *Kirkus Reviews* writer added that Jaffe's sometimes confusing storyline "manages to hang onto its fizz until the enjoyably twisty ending." In addition to the "hilarious dialogue" among the teen friends, readers "will be entertained by Jaffe's inclusion of footnotes to the plot twists on each page," explained *School Library Journal* contributor Kathryn Childs, the critic adding that *Bad Kitty* provides "plenty of amusement" for mystery buffs.

Biographical and Critical Sources

PERIODICALS

Booklist, May 1, 1999, Patty Engelmann, review of *The Stargazer,* p. 1581; June 1, 2000, Margaret Flanagan, review of *The Water Nymph,* p. 1857; May 1, 2004, Joanne Wilkinson, review of *Loverboy,* p. 1510; January 1, 2006, Krista Huntley, review of *Bad Kitty,* p. 84.

Bulletin of the Center for Children's Books, April, 2006, Karen Coats, review of *Bad Kitty,* p. 359.

Kirkus Reviews, April 15, 2000, review of *The Water Nymph,* p. 511; April 1, 2004, review of *Loverboy,* p. 288; January 15, 2006, review of *Bad Kitty,* p. 86.

Library Journal, May 1, 1999, Kim Uden Rutter, review of *The Stargazer,* p. 110; October 1, 1999, review of *The Stargazer,* p. 51; May 15, 2000, Kim Uden Rutter, review of *The Water Nymph,* p. 125.

Publishers Weekly, June 7, 1999, review of *The Stargazer,* p. 71; June 21, 1999, "Love Ain't What It Used to Be," p. 26; May 1, 2000, review of *The Water Nymph,* p. 50; May 20, 2002, reviews of *Lady Killer* and *Secret Admirer,* p. 53; May 3, 2004, review of *Loverboy,* p. 168; January 30, 2006, review of *Bad Kitty,* p. 71.

Renaissance Quarterly, autumn, 2000, David Marsh, review of *The Story of O: Prostitutes and Other Good-for-Nothings in the Renaissance,* p. 906.

School Library Journal, February, 2006, Kathryn Childs, review of *Bad Kitty,* p. 132.

Seventeenth-Century News, fall, 2000, Edward H. Thompson, review of *The Story of O,* pp. 232-235.

Voice of Youth Advocates, February, 2006, Amy Alessio, review of *Bad Kitty,* p. 487.

ONLINE

Beatrice Online, http://www.beatrice.com/ (September 5, 2002), interview with Jaffe.

Michele Jaffe Home Page, http://http://www.michelejaffe. com (May 20, 2007).

Romance Reader Online, http://www.theromancereader. com/ (September 5, 2002), Cathy Sova, review of *The Stargazer.*

Romantic Times, http://www.romantictimes.com/ (September 5, 2002), Kathryn Falk, review of *The Stargazer;* Kathe Robin, review of *The Stargazer, The Water Nymph, Secret Admirer,* and *Lady Killer.*

*   *   *

JAFFE, Michele Sharon
See JAFFE, Michele

*   *   *

JUAN, Ana 1961-

Personal
Born 1961, in Valencia, Spain. *Education:* Attended Fine Arts University of Valencia.

Addresses
Home—Madrid, Spain. *E-mail*—anajuan@anajuan.net.

Career
Artist and illustrator. *Exhibitions:* Work exhibited at Notuno Gallery, Geneva, Switzerland, 1988; 121 Green Street Green Galeria, New York, NY, 1994; Art Miami, 1994; Galeria Tiempos Modernos, Madrid, Spain, 1997; Galeria Sen, Madrid, 1999; and Gallery Maria José Castellví, Barcelona, Spain, 2003.

Awards, Honors
Awards from Society of Newspaper Design; Notable Book selection, American Library Association, Américas Award Honor designation, and *Parenting* magazine Best Book designation, all 2002, all for *Frida;* Ezra Jack Keats New Illustrator Award, 2005, for *The Night Eater.*

Writings

SELF-ILLUSTRATED

The Night Eater, Arthur A. Levine Books (New York, NY), 2004.

ILLUSTRATOR

Cuentos populares españoles, Anaya (Madrid, Spain), 2002.

Jonah Winter, *Frida,* Arthur A. Levine Books (New York, NY), 2002.

Ana Juan (Photo courtesy of Ana Juan.)

Jacob and Wilhelm Grimm, *La bella durmiente,* Anaya (Madrid, Spain), 2003.

Campbell Geeslin, *Elena's Serenade,* Atheneum (New York, NY), 2004.

Rudyard Kipling, *Los libros de la selva,* translation by Gabriela Bustelo, Anaya (Madrid, Spain), 2004.

Tranquita tragaleguas y otros cuentos, Alfagura (Madrid, Spain), 2004.

Kelly Cunnane, *For You Are a Kenyan Child,* Atheneum (New York, NY), 2006.

Monique de Varennes, *The Jewel Box Ballerinas,* Atheneum (New York, NY), 2007.

Contributor of illustrations to magazines and newspapers, including *New Yorker, Madriz, Geo, Vibe, Marie Claire, American Spectator,* and *Boston Globe.*

Author's works have been translated into Spanish.

Sidelights
Ana Juan is the author and illustrator of the award-winning picture book *The Night Eater.* A native of Valencia, Spain, Juan developed an early interest in the arts. "During my childhood, I spent hours over hours drawing or making copies from old illustrations," she remarked on the *Scholastic* Web site. Juan recalled that she was especially fascinated by a treasured copy of *One Thousand and One Nights,* a volume of Persian tales. "The stories were full of magic, and the beautiful old illustrations caught me," she explained.

After graduating from art school, Juan began work on a variety of projects, including paintings for gallery exhibitions, book illustrations, movie posters, album jackets,

and magazine work. She became a regular contributor to the *New Yorker,* and her stunning covers drew the attention of editors at Scholastic, who asked her if she would consider book illustration. Her first children's-book project, Jonah Winter's *Frida,* is a biography of celebrated Mexican artist Frida Kahlo. Born in 1907, Kahlo was stricken with polio as a child and at age eighteen was nearly killed in a devastating bus accident. Crippled and suffering from chronic pain, Kahlo was bedridden for long periods of time, and she turned to art for solace. Her brightly colored paintings, combining elements of symbolism and surrealism, were greatly influenced by Mexican culture. According to *New York Times Book Review* contributor Martha Davis Beck, "Juan captures the spirit of the artist's environment and personality" in "dreamlike paintings . . . inspired by the folk art that surrounded Kahlo as a child and that she collected as an adult, including a devil, a jaguar and a dancing candy skull." In the *Bulletin of the Center for Children's Books,* Deborah Stevenson noted that Juan's acrylic illustrations have "a slightly softened, wide-eyed air that gives them their own mood

rather than being merely imitative," while "the child Frida has a round yet austere face, her expression distant and her eyes downcast as she focuses on the world of her visions rather than the real world." Nancy Menaldi-Scanlan, reviewing *Frida* for *School Library Journal,* also praised Juan's artwork, stating that her "brilliant colors and expressionistic style convey the sense of daring and the excitement that Kahlo demonstrated" in her own life and works.

Juan also served as the illustrator for Campbell Geeslin's *Elena's Serenade* and Kelly Cunnane's *For You Are a Kenyan Child.* Set in Mexico, *Elena's Serenade* concerns a young girl who decides to enter the male-dominated world of glassblowing and discovers that she possesses some amazing talents. "Juan's lush illustrations in desert tones, textured with scratches and splatters of ink, make the story's fantastical elements soar," noted a reviewer in *Publishers Weekly,* and Tracy Bell commented in *School Library Journal* that the artist "uses striking color combinations and shifting perspective to keep attention focused on the child and her

Juan's evocative, stylized paintings capture the spirit of Kelly Cunnane's gentle story in **For You Are a Kenyan Child.** (Illustration © 2006 by Ana Juan. Reprinted by permission of Atheneum Books for Young Readers, an imprint of Simon & Schuster Children's Publishing Division.)

A fine artist as well as an illustrator, Juan's paintings include the work "Tipobella." (Illustration courtesy of Ana Juan.)

changing emotions." A boy's daily activities in his village are the focus of *For You Are a Kenyan Child,* and here Juan's illustrations "show a colorful, richly pastel Kenya imbued with gently pink skies, lush green farms, and rainbow-hued animals," according to *Horn Book* critic Anita L. Burkam.

Juan received the Ezra Jack Keats New Illustrator Award for *The Night Eater,* "an unusual, enchanting blend of sophistication and simple storytelling," in the opinion of *Booklist* contributor Ilene Cooper. Each night, a mischievous, roly-poly figure wearing a sleeping cap and a beaked nose tucks behind the moon and gobbles up the darkness, paving the way for the sun to rise again. When the moon points out that the Night Eater has gained weight, the chubby fellow refuses to eat, sending the world into darkness. The story's "sense of magic realism . . . is matched in Juan's richly colored acrylic-and-wax paintings," noted *School Library Journal* reviewer Robin L. Gibson, while a *Publishers Weekly* critic wrote that the artist's "uncanny imagery is the stuff of dreams."

Biographical and Critical Sources

PERIODICALS

Booklist, March 1, 2002, Hazel Rochman, review of *Frida,* p. 1148; March 1, 2004, Jennifer Mattson, review of *Elena's Serenade,* p. 1194; December 15, 2004, Ilene Cooper, review of *The Night Eater,* p. 738; February 1, 2006, Gillian Engberg, review of *For You Are a Kenyan Child,* p. 66.

Bulletin of the Center for Children's Books, February, 2002, Deborah Stevenson, review of *Frida;* December, 2004, Deborah Stevenson, review of *The Night Eater,* p. 173; March, 2006, Elizabeth Bush, review of *For You Are a Kenyan Child,* p. 306.

Horn Book, March-April, 2002, Nell D. Beram, review of *Frida,* p. 233; March-April, 2006, Anita L. Burkam, review of *For You Are a Kenyan Child,* p. 170.

Kirkus Reviews, December 1, 2001, review of *Frida,* p. 1691; January 15, 2004, review of *Elena's Serenade,* p. 82; October 15, 2004, review of *The Night Eater,* p. 1008; December 1, 2005, review of *For You Are a Kenyan Child,* p. 1273.

New York Times Book Review, May 19, 2002, Martha Davis Beck, "They're Somebody! Who Are You?," review of *Frida.*

Publishers Weekly, December 10, 2001, review of *Frida,* p. 69; January 26, 2004, review of *Elena's Serenade,* p. 253; November 22, 2004, review of *The Night Eater,* p. 60; January 2, 2006, review of *For You Are a Kenyan Child,* p. 61.

School Library Journal, March, 2002, Nancy Menaldi-Scanlan, review of *Frida,* p. 224; March, 2004, Tracy Bell, review of *Elena's Serenade,* p. 158; January, 2005, Robin L. Gibson, review of *The Night Eater,* p. 94; January, 2006, Mary N. Oluonye, review of *For You Are a Kenyan Child,* p. 94.

ONLINE

Ana Juan Home Page, http://www.anajuan.net (May 10, 2007).

Scholastic Web site, http://content.scholastic.com/ (May 10, 2007), "Ana Juan."

SCBWI France Web site, http://www.kidbookpros.com/ (May, 2003), Ann Jacobus, "Meet the Pros: Ana Juan."

*   *   *

KANTNER, Seth 1965-

Personal

Born February 18, 1965, in Kapakavik, AK; son of Howard (a farmer) and Erna (an acupuncturist) Kantner; married Stacey L. Glaser (a librarian) February 15, 1995; children: China (daughter). *Education:* University of Montana at Missoula, B.A. (photojournalism); coursework at University of Alaska, Fairbanks.

Addresses

Office—P.O. Box 804, Kotzebue, AK 99752. *E-mail*—sethkantner@yahoo.com.

Career

Writer and photographer. Has worked variously as a trapper, fisherman, gardener, mechanic, and igloo builder. University of Alaska, Chukchi, adjunct professor of creative writing, 2000—.

Seth Kantner (Photo courtesy of Seth Kantner.)

Awards, Honors

Milkweed National Fiction Prize, *Publishers Weekly* Best Books designation, and Quality Paperback Book Club New Voices Award, all 2004, and Whiting Writer's Award, 2005, all for *Ordinary Wolves.*

Writings

Ordinary Wolves (novel), Milkweed Editions (Minneapolis, MN), 2004.

Contributor of writings and photographs to anthologies and to periodicals, including *Alaska, Prairie Schooner, Orion, Outside, Switch!, Reader's Digest,* and *Alaska Geographic.* Columnist for *Anchorage Daily News,* beginning 2004; contributing writer to *Ruralite,* beginning 2002.

Sidelights

Seth Kantner was born in a sod igloo in Alaska and was home schooled by his parents. Since childhood, he has photographed the vast region where he learned to hunt and fish and where he communed with the native peoples. Kantner has contributed photographs and essays to a number of periodicals, and with his debut

novel, *Ordinary Wolves,* he presents a detailed picture of life growing up in Alaska. Milkweed Editions purchased the novel and worked with Kantner to refine it and make it publishable. Each spring, Kantner sent Emilie Buchwald, the book's editor, a draft, and later in the summer, Buchwald returned it with editorial comments. Kantner revised over the winter and sent the next draft to Buchwald after the ice melted and he could travel to the post office. This went on for four years.

A *Publishers Weekly* contributor called *Ordinary Wolves* "a tour de force" and perhaps "the best treatment of the Northwest and its people since Jack London's works." This observation is a telling one: as Kantner said in an interview posted on *Milkweed Editions Online.,* the early-twentieth-century novelist was his main inspiration for becoming a writer. "He said when you spat or pissed it crackled and froze before it hit the ground. It never did that when I was a kid, reading Jack—it got to seventy-eight below one time, and it never did that. But the whole world believed it did because of London."

In *Ordinary Wolves* artist Abe Hawley comes to Alaska to find his bush-pilot father, falls in love with the wilderness, and stays. His wife cannot bear the isolation and hardship, however, and leaves Abe to raise their three children alone. The youngest child, who is known by his Inupiaq name, Cutuk, watches his brother, Jerry, leave for Fairbanks, and his sister, Iris, go off to college in Anchorage to become a teacher. Cutuk, who feels out of place in both native and white cultures, becomes curious about life away from the tundra and travels to Anchorage, where he is overcome with sensory overload. He eventually returns to Takunak and Dawna, a young woman he has loved since childhood and the woman who may become his future companion.

Library Journal reviewer Jim Coan felt that the "real depth" in *Ordinary Wolves* is found in the scenes in which Cutak is alone, hunting, stalking wolves, driving a dog team, and negotiating an environment "that, while harsh, is nevertheless in many ways more amenable than contemporary urban America." *Booklist* contributor Donna Seaman called Kantner an "impressively fluent and probing first-time novelist."

Biographical and Critical Sources

PERIODICALS

Alaska, September, 2004, Nick Jans, "The Real Thing" (profile).

Anchorage Daily News, May 28, 2004, Cinthia Ritchie, "Hunting Metaphors."

Booklist, May 1, 2004, Donna Seaman, review of *Ordinary Wolves,* p. 1545.

Kirkus Reviews, April 15, 2004, review of *Ordinary Wolves,* p. 350.

Library Journal, March 15, 2004, Jim Coan, review of *Ordinary Wolves,* p. 106.

Publishers Weekly, May 3, 2004, review of *Ordinary Wolves,* p. 170; May 24, 2004, Claire Kirch, "Awards and Bookseller Buzz Propel Alaskan Novel," p. 26.

ONLINE

Kapvik Photography Web site, http://www. kapvicphotography.com/ (June 20, 2007), "Seth Kantner."

Milkweed Editions Web site, http://www.milkweed.org/ (July 23, 2004), interview with Kantner.*

* * *

KATZ, Bobbi 1933-

Personal

Born May 2, 1933, in Newburgh, NY; daughter of George and Margaret Shapiro; married Harold D. Katz (an optometrist), July 15, 1956; children: Joshua, Lori. *Education:* Goucher College, B.A. (with honors), 1954; also studied at Hebrew University. *Politics:* Democrat. *Religion:* Unitarian.

Addresses

Home—Cornwall, NY. *E-mail*—Bobbikatz@aol.com.

Career

Freelance writer and fashion editor in New York, NY, 1954-55; Department of Welfare, Newburgh, NY, social worker, 1956-59; Headstart, Newburgh, social worker, 1966-67. Greater Cornwall School District, creative writing consultant; *Arts in Action* radio program, host, 1969-71; Newburgh NAACP, education chairman, 1964-47; Orange County SANE and Citizens for Peace, chairman, 1960-61.

Member

Authors Guild, Phi Beta Kappa.

Awards, Honors

National Council of Teachers of English Notable Book designation, 2001, for *A Rumpus of Rhymes.*

Writings

FOR CHILDREN

I'll Build My Friend a Mountain, Scholastic Book Services (New York, NY), 1972.

Nothing but a Dog, Feminist Press (New York, NY), 1972.

Upside-Down and Inside-Out, Franklin Watts (New York, NY), 1973.

The Manifesto and Me—Meg, Franklin Watts (New York, NY), 1974.

1,001 Words, Franklin Watts (New York, NY), 1974.

Rod and Reel Trouble, Albert Whitman (Morton Grove, IL), 1974.

Snow Bunny, illustrated by Michael Norman, Albert Whitman (Morton Grove, IL), 1976.

Volleyball Jinx, illustrated by Michael Norman, Albert Whitman (Morton Grove, IL), 1977.

(Selector) *Bedtime Bear's Book of Bedtime Poems,* illustrated by Dora Leder, Random House (New York, NY), 1983.

Birthday Bear's Book of Birthday Poems, illustrated by Louise Walton and Deborah Borgo, Random House (New York, NY), 1983.

Month by Month: A Care Bear Book of Poems, illustrated by Bobbi Barto, Random House (New York, NY), 1984.

Play with the Care Bears, illustrated by Bobbi Bardo, Random House (New York, NY), 1985.

A Popple in Your Pocket, and Other Funny Poems, illustrated by Joe Ewers, Random House (New York, NY), 1986.

Little Wrinkle's Surprise, illustrated by Guy Gilchrist, Happy House (New York, NY), 1987.

Peekaboo Animals, illustrated by Robin Kramer, Random House (New York, NY), 1989.

The Old Woman's Counting Book, illustrated by Pat Sustendal, Random House (New York, NY), 1989.

The Creepy, Crawly Book, illustrated by S.D. Schindler, Random House (New York, NY), 1989.

Poems for Small Friends, illustrated by Gyo Fujikawa, Random House (New York, NY), 1989.

The Care Bears and the Big Cleanup, illustrated by Richard Kolding, Random House (New York, NY), 1991.

Teenage Mutant Ninja Turtles: Don't Do Drugs: A Rap Song, illustrated by Isidre Mones, Random House (New York, NY), 1991.

Ghosts and Goose Bumps: Poems to Chill Your Bones, illustrated by Debra Kogan Ray, Random House (New York, NY), 1991.

Puddle Wonderful: Poems to Welcome Spring, illustrated by Mary Morgan, Random House (New York, NY), 1992.

A Family Hanukkah, illustrated by Caryl Herzfeld, Random House (New York, NY), 1992.

Meet Nelson Mandela, Random House (New York, NY), 1995.

The Story of Hanukkah, illustrated by Linda Dockey Graves, Random House (New York, NY), 1995.

Germs! Germs! Germs!, illustrated by Steve Björkman, Scholastic (New York, NY), 1996.

The Story of Passover, illustrated by Diane Paterson, Random House (New York, NY), 1996.

Could We Be Friends?: Poems for Pals, illustrated by Joung Un Kim, Mondo (Greenvale, NY), 1997.

Truck Talk: Rhymes on Wheels, Scholastic (New York, NY), 1997.

Lots of Lice, illustrated by Steve Björkman, Scholastic (New York, NY), 1998.

American History Poem, Scholastic (New York, NY), 1998.

Make Way for Tooth Decay, illustrated by Steve Björkman, Scholastic New York, NY), 1999.

We the People: Poems, illustrated by Nina Crews, Greenwillow (New York, NY), 2000.

A Rumpus of Rhymes: A Book of Noisy Poems, illustrated by Susan Estelle Kwas, Dutton (New York, NY), 2001.

(Selector) *Pocket Poems,* illustrated by Marylin Hafner, Dutton (New York, NY), 2004.

Once around the Sun, illustrated by LeUyen Pham, Harcourt (Orlando, FL), 2006.

Trailblazers: Poems of Exploration, illustrated by Carin Berger, Greenwillow (New York, NY), 2007.

Also author of educational materials for Scholastic Professional. Contributor of poetry to anthologies and magazines. Contributor of essay to *Period Pieces: Stories for Girls,* HarperCollins (New York, NY), 2001.

Adaptations

A Family Hanukkah was adapted as an audiocassette, Random House, 1993.

Sidelights

A prolific author who began writing for children in the early 1970s, Bobbi Katz is primarily known for her poetry collections. In *Once around the Sun* she takes readers on a voyage through time from a child's perspective, following the changes that can be seen as the twelve months cycle through the calendar during the course of a single year. Praising LeUyen Pham's illustrations for the work as "brightly colored and full of energy," Hazel Rochman added in her *Booklist* review that *Once around the Sun* features a simple vocabulary that makes the collection "great for reading aloud." Katz's verses match Pham's art in their "visual and aural imagery as well as emotional intensity," noted Teresa Pfeifer in a *School Library Journal* review of the work, and a *Kirkus Reviews* contributor wrote that "Katz's dozen poetic paeans are accessible tumbles of imagery."

Inspired by Katz's research into diaries, letters, and other original written source material, *We the People: Poems* introduces sixty-five notable Americans through first-person poems that illuminate the people, places, and events that comprise the country's history. Similar in concept, *Trailblazers: Poems of Exploration* allows readers to meet everyone from conquistadors to scientists as they bravely tread new ground. *Could We Be Friends? Poems for Pals* contains twenty-four poems that, with humor and an occasional whiff of sadness, focus on the close bonds between friends, family mem-

Designed to be carried about and quoted, Bobbi Katz's **Pocket Poems** *includes entertaining drawings by Marylin Hafner.* (Dutton Children's Books, 2004. Illustration © 2004 by Marylin Hafner. Reproduced by permission of Dutton Children's Books, a division of Penguin Putnam Books for Young Readers.)

bers, and neighbors, while in *Pocket Poems* Katz collects over fifty favorite childhood verses designed for easy memorization. In addition to five of her own works, *Pocket Poems* includes verse by a wide variety of authors, from nineteenth-century poets Emily Dickinson and Lewis Carroll to modern-day rhymers Jack Prelutsky, Aileen Fisher, and William Cole. Decorated with watercolor-and-ink cartoons by Marylin Hafner, *Pocket Poems* was praised by *School Library Journal* contributor Lee Bock as a "child-friendly collection" perfectly sized to tuck into a pocket for use whenever the need for a short verse arises.

Commenting on Katz's work in the *New York Times Book Review,* Marighy Dupuy wrote: "Not only are her poems engaging and lively, but she puts the words themselves front and center." The words that appear "front and center" in the twenty-eight verses assembled in *A Rumpus of Rhymes: A Book of Noisy Poems* are particularly delightful; as Lauren Peterson noted in *Booklist,* they offer young readers a chance "to be loud and silly" due to "an abundance of onomatopoeia." Noting that Katz's "rambunctious collection begs to be shared out loud," *School Library Journal* contributor Margaret C. Howell also praised the book's varied fonts, as well as the variety of rhythms that appear in the work.

As she noted on her home page, Katz never lacks for ideas. "Our planet pulses with life; from teeny, tiny

Poet Katz joins illustrator Susan Estelle Kwas in encouraging noisemaking, wiggling, and jumping about in the verse collection **A Rumpus of Rhyme.**
(Dutton Children's Books, 2001. Illustration © 2001 by Susan Estelle Kwas. Reproduced by permission of Dutton Children's Books, a division of Penguin Putnam Books for Young Readers.)

germs to gigantic elephants and whales," she explained. "And people are the most amazing of all. Ideas are all around saying, 'Choose me!' 'Choose me!'" Discussing the difference between being a poet and writing prose,

she once told *SATA:* "My poetry always comes from inside—from my deep need to express a feeling. The child in me writes picture books. My fiction is almost not mine. The characters emerge and seem to tell their

own stories. Even when writing within rigid boundaries that editors sometimes set, I find the characters become very real to me. I care what happens to them."

"I write only for children because I desperately want to return childhood to them," Katz added. "I hope to join those writers and artists who delight, sensitize, and give hope to children."

Biographical and Critical Sources

PERIODICALS

Booklist, September 1, 2001, Lauren Peterson, review of *A Rumpus of Rhymes: A Book of Noisy Poems,* p. 111; October, 1, 2001, Isabel Schon, review of *Germs! Germs! Germs!,* p. 328; February 1, 2004, Hazel Rochman, review of *Pocket Poems,* p. 978; April 15, 2006, Hazel Rochman review of *Once around the Sun,* p. 49.

Bulletin of the Center for Children's Books, July-August, 2006, Deborah Stevenson, review of *Once around the Sun,* p. 504.

Kirkus Reviews, July 1, 2001, review of *A Rumpus of Rhymes,* p. 942; February 15, 2004, review of *Pocket Poems,* p. 180; March 15, 2006, review of *Once around the Sun,* p. 293.

New York Times Book Review, November 18, 2001, Marighy Dupuy, review of *A Book of Noisy Poems,* p. 37.

School Library Journal, November, 2001, Margaret C. Howell, review of *A Rumpus of Rhymes,* p. 146; February, 2004, Lee Bock, review of *Pocket Poems,* p. 132; April, 2006, Nina Lindsay, review of *We the People: Poems,* p. 57; May, 2006, Teresa Pfeifer, review of *Once around the Sun.*

ONLINE

Bobbi Katz Home Page, http://www.bobbikatz.com (June 15, 2007).*

*   *   *

KELLEY, True 1946-
(True Adelaide Kelley)

Personal

Born February 25, 1946, in Cambridge, MA; daughter of Mark E. (an illustrator) and Adelaide (an artist) Kelley; married Steven W. Lindblom (a writer and illustrator); children: Jada Winter Lindblom. *Education:* University of New Hampshire, B.A. (elementary education), 1968; attended Rhode Island School of Design, 1968-71. *Hobbies and other interests:* Skiing, biking, canoeing, travel.

Addresses

Home—Warner, NH.

Career

Freelance illustrator, 1971—; writer, 1978—.

Member

Society of Children's Book Writers and Illustrators, Authors Guild, Audubon Society, New Hampshire Writers and Publishers Project, Wackos and Tubbers.

Awards, Honors

Children's Choice designation, International Reading Association, 1982, for *A Valentine for Fuzzboom;* Outstanding Science Trade Book for Children citation, National Science Teachers Association/Children's Book Council, 1987, for *What the Moon Is Like;* Children's Books of the Year, Child Study Children's Book Committee, 1995, for *I've Got Chicken Pox;* 100 Best Titles selection, New York Public Library, and Parents' Choice Honor Book selection, both 1995, both for *Three Stories You Can Read to Your Dog;* Parents' Choice award, 1997, for *Stay! Keeper's Story;* Space Books and Films Best Book citation, 1998, and Outstanding Achievement in Books honor, 1999, both for *Floating in Space;* Oppenheim Toy Portfolio Gold awards, 2000, for *My Dog Toby, The International Space Station,* and *Three More Stories You Can Read to Your Dog;* Parents' Choice Honor Book designation, 2000 and Best Children's Books of the Year designation, Bank Street College School of Education, 2001, both for *Three More Stories You Can Read to Your Dog;* Golden Duck Award for Best Children's Illustrated Book, 2003, for *Hazel Nutt, Mad Scientist,* by David Elliott; California Young Readers Medal nomination, 2004, for *Blabber Mouse;* Book of the Year designation, Bank Street College School of Education, 2007, for *In the Doghouse.*

Writings

SELF-ILLUSTRATED

(With husband, Steven Lindblom) *The Mouses' Terrible Christmas,* Lothrop (Boston, MA), 1980.

(With Steven Lindblom) *The Mouses' Terrible Halloween,* Lothrop (Boston, MA), 1980.

A Valentine for Fuzzboom, Houghton (Boston, MA), 1981.

Buggly Bear's Hiccup Cure, Parents Magazine Press (New York, NY), 1982.

The Mystery of the Stranger in the Barn, Putnam (New York, NY), 1986.

Look, Baby! Listen, Baby! Do, Baby!, Dutton (New York, NY), 1987.

Let's Eat!, Dutton (New York, NY), 1989.

Day Care Teddy Bear, Random House (New York, NY), 1990.

(With Christel Kleitsch) *It Happened at Pickle Lake,* Dutton (New York, NY), 1993.

I've Got Chicken Pox, Dutton (New York, NY), 1994.

Hammers and Mops, Pencils and Pots: A First Book of Tools and Gadgets We Use around the House, Crown (New York, NY), 1994.

Look Again at Funny Animals, Candlewick Press (Cambridge, MA), 1996.

Look Again at My Funny Family, Candlewick Press (Cambridge, MA), 1996.

Blabber Mouse, Dutton (New York, NY), 2001.

Claude Monet: Sunshine and Waterlilies, Grosset & Dunlap (New York, NY), 2001.

Pablo Picasso: Breaking All the Rules, Grosset & Dunlap (New York, NY), 2002.

School Lunch, Holiday House (New York, NY), 2004.

Pierre-Auguste Renoir: Paintings That Smile, Grosset & Dunlap (New York, NY), 2005.

The Blabber Report, Dutton (New York, NY), 2007.

ILLUSTRATOR; FICTION

Ann Cole, Carolyn Haas, Faith Bushnell, and Betty Weinburger, *I Saw a Purple Cow,* Little, Brown (Boston, MA), 1976.

Michael Pellowski, *Clara Cow Joins the Circus,* Parents Magazine Press (New York, NY), 1981.

Steven Lindblom, *Let's Give Kitty a Bath,* Addison Wesley (Reading, MA), 1982.

Ann Cole, Carolyn Haas, and Betty Weinburger, *Purple Cow to the Rescue,* Little, Brown (Boston, MA), 1982.

Joanne Oppenheim, *James Will Never Die,* Dodd (New York, NY), 1982.

Riki Levinson, *Touch! Touch!,* Dutton (New York, NY), 1986.

Joanna Cole, *Mixed-up Magic,* Scholastic (New York, NY), 1987.

Debra Meryl, *Baby's Peek-a-Boo Album,* Putnam (New York, NY), 1989.

Susan Breslow and Sally Blakemore, *I Really Want a Dog,* Dutton (New York, NY), 1989.

A. F. Bauman, *Guess Where You're Going, Guess What You'll Do,* Houghton (Boston, MA), 1989.

Michaela Morgan, *Dinostory,* Dutton (New York, NY), 1991.

Wendy Lewison, *Where's Baby?,* Scholastic (New York, NY), 1992.

Wendy Lewison, *Uh-Oh Baby,* Scholastic (New York, NY), 1992.

Wendy Lewison, *Bye-Bye Baby,* Scholastic (New York, NY), 1992.

Stephanie Calmenson, *Rollerskates!,* Scholastic (New York, NY), 1992.

Raffi, *Spider on the Floor* (songbook), Crown (New York, NY), 1993, board-book edition, Knopf (New York, NY), 2002.

Patricia Brennan Demuth, *In Trouble with Teacher,* Dutton (New York, NY), 1995.

Sara Swan Miller, *Three Stories You Can Read to Your Dog,* Houghton (Boston, MA), 1995.

Sara Swan Miller, *Three Stories You Can Read to Your Cat,* Houghton (Boston, MA), 1996.

Jean Marzollo, *Football Friends,* Scholastic (New York, NY), 1997.

Lois Lowry, *Stay! Keeper's Story,* Houghton (Boston, MA), 1997.

Vikki Cobb and Kathy Darling, *Don't Try This at Home,* Morrow (New York, NY), 1998.

Carol Diggory Shields, *Month by Month a Year Goes 'Round,* Dutton (New York, NY), 1998.

Jean Marzollo and Dan Marzollo, *Hockey Hero,* Scholastic (New York, NY), 1998.

Carol Diggory Shields, *Day by Day a Week Goes 'Round,* Dutton (New York, NY), 1999.

Jean Marzollo and Dan Marzollo, *Basketball Buddies,* Scholastic (New York, NY), 1999.

Jean Marzollo, Dan Marzollo, and Dave Marzollo, *Baseball Brothers,* Scholastic (New York, NY), 1999.

David Clemesha and Andrea Zimmerman, *My Dog Toby,* Harcourt (San Diego, CA), 2000.

Marty Crisp, *My Dog, Cat,* Holiday House (New York, NY), 2000.

Sara Swan Miller, *Three More Stories You Can Read to Your Cat,* Houghton (Boston, MA), 2000.

Sara Swan Miller, *Three More Stories You Can Read to Your Dog,* Houghton (Boston, MA), 2000.

Claire Masurel, *That Bad, Bad Cat!,* Putnam (New York, NY), 2002.

David Elliott, *Hazel Nutt, Mad Scientist,* Holiday House (New York, NY), 2003.

Sara Swan Miller, *Three Stories You Can Read to Your Teddy Bear,* Houghton (Boston, MA), 2003.

David Elliott, *Hazel Nutt, Alien Hunter,* Holiday House (New York, NY), 2004.

Anna Jane Hays, *Ready, Set, Preschool!,* Knopf (New York, NY), 2005.

Leslie Kimmelman, *In the Doghouse: An Emma and Bo Story,* Holiday House (New York, NY), 2006.

Susanna Leonard Hill, *No Sword Fighting in the House,* Holiday House (New York, NY), 2007.

ILLUSTRATOR; NONFICTION

Franklyn M. Branley, *Sun Dogs and Shooting Stars: A Skywatcher's Calendar,* Houghton Mifflin (Boston, MA), 1980.

Gilda Berger and Melvin Berger, *The Whole World of Hands,* Houghton Mifflin (Boston, MA), 1982.

Franklyn M. Branley, *Water for the World,* Crowell (New York, NY), 1982.

The Scribblers Play Book: Sunshine and Snowflakes, Western Publishing (New York, NY), 1982.

Ben Schneiderman, *Let's Learn Basic,* Little, Brown (Boston, MA), 1984.

Joyce Mitchell, *My Mommy Makes Money,* Little, Brown (Boston, MA), 1984.

Franklyn M. Branley, *Shivers and Goosebumps: How We Keep Warm,* Crowell (New York, NY), 1984.

Joanna Cole, *Cuts, Breaks, and Bruises: How Your Body Heals,* Crowell (New York, NY), 1985.

Eric Arnold and Jeffrey Loeb, *Lights Out! Kids Talk about Summer Camp,* Little, Brown (Boston, MA), 1986.

Franklyn M. Branley, *What the Moon Is Like,* Crowell (New York, NY), 1986, revised edition, 2000.

Patricia Lauber, *Get Ready for Robots,* Crowell (New York, NY), 1986.

Franklyn M. Branley, *It's Raining Cats and Dogs: All Kinds of Weather and Why We Have It,* Houghton (Boston, MA), 1986.

James Deem, *How to Find a Ghost,* Houghton (Boston, MA), 1988.

Philip Balestrino, *The Skeleton inside You,* Crowell (New York, NY), 1989.

(With Steven Lindblom) Gregory Niles and Douglas Eldredge, *The Fossil Factory: A Kid's Guide to Digging up Dinosaurs, Exploring Evolution, and Finding Fossils,* Addison Wesley (Reading, MA), 1989.

Franklyn M. Branley, *Superstar: The Supernova of 1987,* Crowell (New York, NY), 1990.

Paul Showers, *How Many Teeth?,* Harper (New York, NY), 1991.

James Deem, *How to Catch a Flying Saucer,* Houghton (Boston, MA), 1991.

Judy Donnelly, *All around the World,* Grosset & Dunlap (New York, NY), 1991.

Paul Showers, *Look at Your Eyes,* Harper (New York, NY), 1992.

James Deem, *How to Hunt Buried Treasure,* Houghton (Boston, MA), 1992.

James Deem, *How to Read Your Mother's Mind,* Houghton (Boston, MA), 1994.

James Deem, *How to Make a Mummy Talk,* Houghton (Boston, MA), 1995.

Franklyn M. Branley, *What Makes a Magnet?,* Crowell (New York, NY), 1997.

Franklyn M. Branley, *Floating in Space,* HarperCollins (New York, NY), 1998.

Ann Banks and Nancy Evans, *Goodbye, House: A Kid's Guide to Moving,* Crown (New York, NY), 1999.

Vicki Cobb and Kathy Darling, *You Gotta Try This! Absolutely Irresistible Science,* Morrow (New York, NY), 1999.

Franklyn M. Branley, *Flash, Crash, Rumble, and Roll,* revised edition, HarperCollins (New York, NY), 1999.

Franklyn M. Branley, *The International Space Station,* HarperCollins (New York, NY), 2000.

Franklyn M. Branley, *Mission to Mars,* foreword by Neil Armstrong, HarperCollins (New York, NY), 2002.

Roberta Edwards, *Who Was Leonardo da Vinci?,* Grosset & Dunlap (New York, NY), 2005.

Fran Hodgkins, *How People Learned to Fly,* HarperCollins (New York, NY), 2006.

Roberta Edwards, *Who Was King Tut?,* Grosset & Dunlap (New York, NY), 2006.

Also illustrator of textbooks.

Sidelights

With a successful career as an illustrator spanning over three decades, True Kelley continues to write and illustrate nonfiction books, chapter books, picture books, and board books for children. Her pen-and-ink drawings, often enhanced by watercolor washes, are designed to delight babies, teach lessons about science, and charm young readers. Whether she illustrates the texts of others, collaborates with her husband, Steven Lindblom, or writes and illustrates her own books, Kelley maintains her reputation as the creator of humorous, expressive, and informative works.

As Kelley once told *SATA,* she developed an interest in illustration when she was a girl. "My mother illustrated children's books and my father was art director for *Child Life* magazine," she explained. "My first published self-illustrated story appeared there when I was four years old. After graduating from college with a degree in elementary education, I attended Rhode Island School of Design. I began working as an advertising illustrator and was greatly influenced by my father. My interest in children led me to doing textbook illustrations."

Kelley's illustrations for the texts of other authors have won her continuous praise throughout her career. In a review of Susan Breslow and Sally Blakemore's *I Really Want a Dog,* *Horn Book* contributor Hanna B. Zeiger concluded that "children will love the bright, humorous illustrations of dogs in every conceivable situation." The artist's canine portrayals in Sara Swan Miller's *Three Stories You Can Read to Your Dog* and its sequel, *Three More Stories You Can Read to Your Dog,* also received praise, a *Publishers Weekly* critic noting that Kelley demonstrates "familiarity with doggy expressions and gestures." Gale W. Sherman remarked in *School Library Journal* that Kelley's work for this book makes Miller's text "even funnier," and *Booklist* critic Ilene Cooper described the watercolor illustrations as "clever and full of vigor." Commenting on *Three Stories You Can Read to Your Cat,* *School Library Journal* contributor Joy Fleishhacker noted that the "repertoire of expressions" Kelley gives to Miller's feline narrator range from "pointedly disinterested to openly disdainful to perfectly contented." In a *Publishers Weekly* review, a critic wrote that Kelley's "uncomplicated pen-and-ink and watercolor images in *Three Stories You Can Read to Your Cat,* show an attention to familiar cat poses" while Marilyn Taniguchi noted of Miller's *Three Stories You Can Read to Your Teddy Bear* that the artist's "cartoon illustrations with their squiggly busy lines are full of movement and humorous detail." Reviewing Leslie Kimmelman's *In the Doghouse: An Emma and Bo Story,* Kelley's illustrations "aptly reflecting the action and supplying much of the humor" in Kimmelman's "woofy treat," according to a *Kirkus Reviews* writer.

Kelley's collaboration with Jean Marzollo and Marzollo's sons Dan and Dave has resulted in a series of engaging beginning readers focusing on sports topics. In *Football Friends* Kelley's "realistic" pen-and-ink and watercolor illustrations "add visual breaks" to the story of a young boy who channels his competitive energies away from playground fights and onto the football field, according to Gale W. Sherman in *School Library Journal.* Similarly effective in Jean and Dan Marzollo's *Basketball Buddies,* Kelley's artwork also drew praise from *School Library Journal* contributor Nancy A. Gifford for including "ethnically diverse teams of boys and

In her engaging cartoon art, True Kelley adds another dimension to Andrea Zimmerman and David Clemesha's picture-book text for My Dog Toby.
(Harcourt, 2000. Illustration © 2000 by True Kelley. Reproduced by permission.)

girls" in a story about teamwork and sportsmanship, while in *Booklist* Carolyn Phelan praised Kelley's "cartoonlike ink drawings, washed with cheerful colors."

As several critics have noted, Kelley's cartoon-like illustrations serve as excellent supplements to the texts of nonfiction works and make information more easily understood. *The Fossil Factory: A Kid's Guide to Digging up Dinosaurs, Exploring Evolution, and Finding Fossils,* for example, which Kelley illustrated with husband Steven Lindblom, provides children with accessible scientific information about the petrified remains of dinosaurs and other ancient animals that now remain only as

fossils. In the words of a *Publishers Weekly* reviewer, Kelley and Lindblom's work exhibits "a wealth of paleontological lore in a winning fashion," while *New York Times Book Review* critic Malcolm W. Browne praised the couple's drawings and diagrams as "simple and delightful." Kelley's contribution to Franklyn M. Branley's *What Makes a Magnet?,* one of several nonfiction collaborations between author and illustrator, were favorably noted by *Booklist* critic Denia Hester, the critic commenting that the book's "bright, splashy watercolors . . . make scientific exploration look like the fun it ought to be." Kelley's "bright and appealing" watercolor renderings enhance an updated edition of Bran-

Sara Swan Miller's picture book **Three Stories You Can Read to Your Dog** *gets a humorous boost from Kelley's illustrations.* (Houghton Mifflin Company, 1995. Illustration © 1995 by True Kelley. Reproduced by permission of Houghton Mifflin Company.)

ley's *Flash, Crash, Rumble, and Roll,* according to *School Library Journal* contributor Patricia Manning, and her depiction of space life in Branley's *Mission to Mars* "is as likely as the text to recruit the astronauts of tomorrow" through her mix of "adventure, technology, and certain homey comforts," according to Phelan.

In another collaborative effort, Kelley illustrates several books with texts by James Deem that explore unusual subjects. *How to Make a Mummy Talk* explains what mummies are and describes their historical and cultural significance. Kelley's illustrations for this volume—black-and-white cartoon-like sketches—were cited by Mary Harris Veeder in a *Booklist* review as adding a "sense of humor" to Deem's nonfiction prose. *How to Read Your Mother's Mind,* Deem's book on extrasensory perception, also benefits from the addition of Kelley's "witty" pen-and-ink cartoons which "further clarify the text," according to a critic for *Kirkus Reviews.* In *Booklist,* Ilene Cooper described the illustrations as "terrific," while *Bulletin of the Center for Children's Books* contributor Roger Sutton praised the artwork's "lively improvisational flair/"

In addition to illustrating texts by others, Kelley has also created art for several original stories. One of the first, *A Valentine for Fuzzboom,* introduces a rabbit in love. Lima Bean admires the haughty Fuzzboom and crafts assorted valentines for her beloved for months before finally sending him the best one. When Fuzzboom fails to send a valentine in return, Lima Bean is so upset she barely notices when she receives a lovely gift from another friend. Later, Lima Bean realizes her mistake and attempts to resolve her friendship issues. Geared for much younger children, *Look, Baby! Listen, Baby! Do, Baby!* encourages infants to look, listen, and then act. In the book's first section, a baby can look at pictures of different babies' mouths, noses, eyes, hands, and feet, all functioning in a variety of ways. The listening section provides an assortment of sounds accompanied by illustrations of the things or creatures that make them, while the "Do Baby!" section features infants crying, crawling, playing, and doing other things babies do. The drawings of babies are "droll and cheerful," according to *Booklist* critic Denise Wilms, and a *Publishers Weekly* critic praised the diverse "expressions and mannerisms" of Kelley's infants. *Do Baby!* is "definitely and delightfully a book for sharing . . . and enjoying many times over," according to the *Publishers Weekly* reviewer.

Cover of Pierre-August Renoir: Paintings That Smile, *a visual biography of the famous French painter by True Kelley.* (Grosset & Dunlap, 2005. Reproduced by permission of Grosset & Dunlap, a division of Penguin Putnam Books for Young Readers.)

Let's Eat! describes where our food comes from, where it is eaten, and how various groups of people eat it around the world. Kelley's short text is brought to life in illustrations which, in the words of *School Library Journal* contributor Louise L. Sherman, are "clear, whimsical, simple yet expressive watercolor and pen-and-ink." "Kelley has a marvelous eye for the funny and naughty little actions of children," Margaret A. Bush commented in a review for *Horn Book,* while Barbara Elleman concluded in *Booklist* that *Let's Eat!* is a "cornucopia of information to consume in nibbles or large bites."

Other original titles by Kelley include *I've Got Chicken Pox, School Lunch,* and *Blabber Mouse.* According to *Booklist* critic Phelan, *I've Got Chicken Pox* is a "first-rate" introduction to the common childhood disease that provides "Pox Facts" on each page in addition to Kelley's entertaining story. Jess, the narrator, is excited when she learns that, because she has chicken pox she will miss a week of school! Although she gets to drink ginger ale and eat ice cream, Jess quickly gets tired of the chicken pox: Not only is she feverish, itchy, and bored, but she is also tormented by her brother, who is jealous of her pox. The payoff for all this torment comes when Jess finally returns to school, and can detail the horrors of her illness to her amazed friends. Denise L. Moll pointed out in a *School Library Journal* review that Kelley's watercolor illustrations for *I've Got Chicken Pox* "are vibrant and appealing," and a *Publishers Weekly* writer dubbed the book a "humorously illustrated, jaunty tale."

A tiny rodent with lots to tell is the subject of *Blabber Mouse,* "an entertaining story with an unexpected ending" according to a *Publishers Weekly* contributor. Blabber just cannot seem to help himself; even when he promises to keep a secret, his need to chatter is a frustration to his family and friends. However, Blabber's buddies finally hit upon the perfect solution when they give him a special gift: A diary into which he can spill

The adventurous young heroine of David Elliott's Hazel Nutt, Alien Hunter, *is brought to life through Kelley's whimsical cartoon art.* (Holiday House, 2004. Illustration copyright © 2004 by True Kelley. All rights reserved. Reproduced by permission of Holiday House, Inc.)

all his ideas, secrets, and gossip without causing any problems. A problem of an entirely different sort is the focus of *School Lunch,* after Harriet, the popular cook at Lincoln School, is replaced by a series of unacceptable chefs specializing in particularly unhealthy cuisine when she finally takes a vacation. Along with illustrations employing Kelley's "loosely doodled, expressive charm," *School Lunch* will serve useful in "lighten[ing] up units on nutrition," according to *Booklist* reviewer Jennifer Mattson, and a *Kirkus Reviews* writer called the book "marvelously cute and clever." While Grace Oliff concluded in her *School Library Journal* review that the book's illustrations "are bright and cheerful and amplify the silliness of the situation," Holly T. Sneering wrote in the same periodical that *Blabber Mouse* also pairs a "charming cast of characters and an effective narrative to teach children about gossip" with Kelley's characteristic upbeat and brightly hued cartoon art.

Biographical and Critical Sources

PERIODICALS

Booklist, March 15, 1981, Barbara Elleman, review of *A Valentine for Fuzzboom,* pp. 1028, 1030; September 15, 1987, Denise M. Wilms, review of *Look, Baby! Listen, Baby! Do, Baby!,* p. 150; May 15, 1989, Barbara Elleman, review of *Let's Eat!,* p. 1650; January 1, 1993, p. 807; March 1, 1994, Ilene Cooper, review of *How to Read Your Mother's Mind,* p. 1256; March 15, 1994, Julie Corsaro, review of *Hammers and Mops, Pencils and Pots: A First Book of Gadgets We Use around the House,* p. 1368; May 15, 1994, Carolyn Phelan, review of *I've Got Chicken Pox,* p. 1683; April 15, 1995, Ilene Cooper, review of *Three Stories You Can Read to Your Dog,* p. 1500; September 15, 1995, Mary Harris Veeder, review of *How to Make a Mummy Talk;* November 1, 1996, Denia Hester, review of *What Makes a Magnet?;* March 1, 1997, Stephanie Zvirin, review of *Three Stories You Can Read to Your Cat,* p. 1164; December 1, 1998, Ilene Cooper, review of *Month by Month a Year Goes 'Round,* p. 672; December 15, 1998, Ilene Cooper, review of *Day by Day a Week Goes 'Round,* p. 756; March 15, 1999, Carolyn Phelan, review of *Basketball Buddies,* p. 1337; September 15, 2000, Carolyn Phelan, review of *The International Space Station,* p. 244; November 15, 2001, Gillian Engberg, review of *Claude Monet: Sunshine and Waterlilies,* p. 572; December 1, 2001, John Peters, review of *Blabber Mouse,* p. 649; June 1, 2002, Ilene Cooper, review of *That Bad, Bad Cat,* p. 1742; January 1, 2003, Carolyn Phelan, review of *Mission to Mars,* p. 894; September 15, 2005, Jennifer Mattson, review of *School Lunch,* p. 73; April 15, 2005, Carolyn Phelan, review of *In the Doghouse,* p. 52.

Bulletin of the Center for Children's Books, March, 1994, Roger Sutton, review of *How to Read Your Mother's Mind.*

Horn Book, May-June, 1989, Margaret A. Bush, review of *Let's Eat!,* pp. 385-386; July-August, 1990, Hanna B. Zeiger, review of *I Really Want a Dog,* p. 442.

Kirkus Reviews, March 1, 1981, p. 280; March 1, 1994, review of *How to Read Your Mother's Mind;* February 20, 1995, review of *Three Stories You Can Read to Your Dog,* p. 206; March 1, 2002, review of *Three More Stories You Can Read to Your Cat;* September 1, 2005, review of *School Lunch,* p. 976; March 15, 2006, review of *In the Doghouse,* p. 294.

New York Times Book Review, June 24, 1990, Malcolm W. Browne, review of *The Fossil Factory,* p. 28; May 22, 1994, Andrea Higbie, review of *I've Got Chicken Pox,* p. 34.

Publishers Weekly, February 6, 1980, review of *A Valentine for Fuzzboom,* p. 373; September 11, 1987, review of *Look, Baby! Listen, Baby! Do, Baby!,* p. 90; February 23, 1990, review of *The Fossil Factory,* p. 219; August 16, 1991, review of *Dinostory,* p. 58; May 2, 1994, review of *I've Got Chicken Pox,* p. 306; February 20, 1995, review of *Three Stories You Can Read to Your Dog,* p. 206; February 3, 1997, review of *Three Stories You Can Read to Your Cat,* p. 107; July 28, 1997, review of *Stay! Keeper's Story,* p. 75; July 9, 2001, review of *Blabber Mouse,* p. 67; July 25, 2005, review of *Pierre-August Renoir: Paintings That Smile,* p. 79.

School Library Journal, April 1, 1981, Mary B. Nickerson, review of *A Valentine for Fuzzboom,* p. 114; December, 1982, review of *Buggly Bear's Hiccup Cure,* p. 76; January, 1987, Jeanette Larson, review of *The Mystery of the Stranger in the Barn,* p. 65; October, 1987, p. 114; March, 1989, Louise L. Sherman, review of *Let's Eat!,* p. 164; March, 1991, Kathleen Towey, review of *Day-Care Teddy Bear,* p. 174; September, 1991, p. 263; July, 1993, Elaine Lesh Morgan, review of *It Happened at Pickle Lake,* p. 62; February, 1994, Joyce Richards, review of *Spider on the Floor,* p. 90; May, 1994, Joyce Richards, review of *Hammers and Mops, Pencils and Pots,* p. 108; June, 1994, Denise L. Moll, review of *I've Got Chicken Pox,* p. 107; April, 1995, Gale W. Sherman, review of *Three Stories You Can Read to Your Dog,* p. 113; May, 1995, p. 84; May, 1997, Joy Fleishhacker, review of *Three Stories You Can Read to Your Cat,* p. 108; March, 1998, Gale W. Sherman, review of *Football Friends,* p. 184; April, 1999, Nancy A. Gifford, review of *Basketball Buddies,* pp. 104-105; June, 1999, Patricia Manning, review of *Flash, Crash, Rumble, and Roll,* p. 111; November, 2000, Kay Bowes, review of *The International Space Station,* p. 139; January, 2001, Gay Lynn Van Vleck, review of *My Dog, Cat,* p. 92; October, 2001, Holly T. Sneeringer, review of *Blabber Mouse,* p. 122; November, 2001, Susan Lissim, review of *Claude Monet,* p. 143; May, 2002, Anne Knickerbocker, review of *Three More Stories You Can Read to Your Cat,* p. 123; October, 2003, review of *Mission to Mars,* p. 143; June, 2004, review of *Three Stories You Can Read to Your Teddy Bear,* p. 115; October, 2004, review of *Hazel Nutt, Alien Hunter,* p. 112; November, 2005, Grace Oliff, review of *School Lunch,* p. 96.

True Kelley Home Page, http://www.truekelley.com (May 20, 2007).

* * *

KELLEY, True Adelaide
See KELLEY, True

* * *

KUIJER, Guus 1942-

Personal

Name pronounced "Hoose Ky-yer"; born August 1, 1942, in Amsterdam, Netherlands.

Addresses

Home and office—Amsterdam, Netherlands.

Career

Children's book author.

Awards, Honors

Gouden Griffel/Gold Pencil Award (Netherlands), 1976, for *Met de poppen gooien,* 1979, for *Krassen in het tafelblad,* 2000, for *Voor altijd samen, amen,* 2005, for *Het boek van alle dingen;* Zilveren Griffel/Silver Pencil Award (Netherlands), 1977, for *Grote mensen, daar kun je beter soep van koken,* 1984, for *Eend voor eend,* 1988, for *Tin Toeval en de kunst van het verdwalen/Tin Toeval en het geheim van tweebeenseiland,* 2002, for *Met de wind mee naar de zee;* Staatsprijs voor kinder-en jeugdliteratuur, 1979; Woutertje Pieterseprijs, 2003, for *Ik ben Polleke hoor!;* Gouden Uil/Golden Owl Award (Flemish), 2005, and Astrid Lindgren Memorial Award nomination, Swedish Arts Council, and Marsh Award for Children's Literature in Translation shortlist, National Centre for Research in Children's Literature, both 2006, all for for *Het boek van alle dingen/The Book of Everything.*

Writings

FOR CHILDREN

Een gat in de grens, [Netherlands], 1975.
Met de poppen gooien, [Netherlands], 1975, translated by Patricia Crampton as *Daisy's New Head,* Viking Children's Books (New York, NY), 1980.
Drie verschrikkelijke dagen, [Netherlands], 1976.
Grote mensen, daar kan je beter soep van koken, Querido (Amsterdam, Netherlands), 1977.

Pappa is een hond, [Netherlands], 1977.
Op je kop in de prullenbak, illustrated by Mance Post, Querido (Amsterdam, Netherlands), 1977.
Krassen in het tafelblad, [Netherlands], 1978.
Madelief: Krassen in het tafelblad, illustrated by Mance Post, Querido (Amsterdam, Netherlands), 1978, reprinted, Querido (Amsterdam, Netherlands), 1998.
Hoe Mieke Mom haar maffe moeder vindt, illustrated by Mance Post, Querido (Amsterdam, Netherlands), 1978.
Ik woonde in een leunstoel, [Netherlands], 1979.
Een hoofd vol macaroni, illustrated by Mance Post, Querido (Amsterdam, Netherlands), 1979.
Het geminachte kind, [Netherlands], 1980.
De tranen knallen uit mijn kop, illustrated by Mance Post, Querido (Amsterdam, Netherlands), 1980.
Crisis en kaalhoofdigheid, Arbeiderspers (Amsterdam, Netherlands), 1983.
Het grote boek van Madelief, illustrated by Mance Post, Querido (Amsterdam, Netherlands), 1983, reprinted, 2004.
Eend voor eend, illustrated by Tjong Khing, Querido (Amsterdam, Netherlands), 1983.
De zwarte stenen, Querido (Amsterdam, Netherlands), 1984.
Het land van de neushoomvogel, [Netherlands], 1985.
De jonge prinsen, illustrated by Tjong Khing, Querido (Amsterdam, Netherlands), 1986.
Tin Toeval en de kunst van het verdwalen, illustrated by Mance Post, Querido (Amsterdam, Netherlands), 1987.
Tin Toeval en de het geheim van Tweebeens-eiland, illustrated by Mance Post, Querido (Amsterdam, Netherlands), 1987.
Tin Toeval en de kunst van Madelief, illustrated by Mance Post, Querido (Amsterdam, Netherlands), 1989.
Olle, [Netherlands], 1990.
Tin Toeval in de onderwereld, illustrated by Mance Post, Querido (Amsterdam, Netherlands), 1996.
Die grote Tin Toeval, illustrated by Mance Post, Querido (Amsterdam, Netherlands), 1996.
De verhalen van Jonathan, [Netherlands], 1996.
Voor altijd samen, amen, illustrated by Alice Hoogstad, Querido (Amsterdam, Netherlands), 1999.
In land der Nashornvoegel, Fischer Taschenbuch (Frankfurt, Germany), 1999.
Het is fijn om er te zijn, [Netherlands], 2000.
Het geluk komt als de donder, [Netherlands], 2000.
Reukorgel, [Netherlands], 2000.
Met de wind mee naar zee, [Netherlands], 2001.
Ik ben Polleke hoor!, illustrated by Alice Hoogstad, Querido (Amsterdam, Netherlands), 2001.
Polleke, illustrated by Alice Hoogstad, Querido (Amsterdam, Netherlands), 2003.
Het Boek van alle dingen (novel), Querido (Amsterdam, Netherlands), 2004, translated by John Nieuwenhuizen as *The Book of Everything,* Arthur A. Levine Books (New York, NY), 2006.
Hoe een klein rotgodje God vermoordde, [Netherlands], 2006.
Het doden van een mens, [Netherlands], 2007.

Author's works have been translated to Spanish, French, German, Italian, and English.

OTHER

Rose, met vrome wimpers, Meulenhoff (Amsterdam, Netherlands), 1971.
Het dochtertje van de wasrouw, Meulenhoff (Amsterdam, Netherlands), 1973.
De man met de hamer, Arbeiderspers (Amsterdam, Netherlands), 1975.
Wimpers, herziene druk van Rose, met vrome wimpers, [Netherlands], 1980.
De wonderdoener, [Netherlands], 1983.
Izebel van Tyrus, Arbeiderspers (Amsterdam, Netherlands), 1988.
De redder van Afrika (novel), Arbeiderspers (Amsterdam, Netherlands), 1989.
Het vogeltje van Amsterdam, [Netherlands], 1992.
Lazarillo de Tormes, [Netherlands], 2000.

Also author of short fiction and stage dramas.

Adaptations

Madelief: Krassen in het tafelblad and *Polleke* were adapted for film by Ineke Houtman in 1998 and 2003, respectively.

Sidelights

One of the most beloved authors of children's books in his native Netherlands, Guus Kuijer is a prolific writer whose works range from picture books and novels to short stories and plays. In 2006 Kuijer received the Golden Pencil Award—the Dutch equivalent of America's Newbery Award—for his children's novel *The Book of Everything.* Kuijer's children's titles have also been adapted into Dutch films, such as *Madelief: Krassen in het tafelblad* and *Polleke.* Kuijer, in his writings for children, tends to focus his works from a child's perspective and reinforces his philosophy that children should be unrestricted and allowed to develop independently.

The award-winning novel *The Book of Everything,* one of Kuijer's books to be translated into English, was described by a *Kirkus Reviews* critic as an "austere little example of Dutch magical realism." The setting of the novel is the 1950s, the place Amsterdam, a city recovering from the recent Nazi occupation. The protagonist of the novel is Thomas, a nine year old who experi-

ences domestic abuse at the hands of his father on a daily basis. Thomas's father is a stern Calvinist who dominates his family by beating his wife and son. In an attempt to escape the harsh reality of family life, Thomas takes solace in his observations of the magical things that happen around him, and he documents these daily observations, as well as his fears and wishes, in a volume he calls his Book of Everything. Christine M. Heppermann in her review of Kuijer's work for *Horn Book,* noted that the author's "fanciful details . . . add subtlety and lightness to the otherwise dark subject matter." Kuijer manages to balance the dark subject matter of his novel with the optimistic outlook of his young protagonist, according to *School Library Journal* reviewer Sadie Mattox. As Mattox also remarked, "Thomas is proof that there is beauty in dirty streets and that innocence cannot be destroyed."

Biographical and Critical Sources

PERIODICALS

Booklist, June 1, 2006, Linda Perkins, review of *The Book of Everything,* p. 62.
Bulletin of the Center for Children's Books, May, 2006, Deborah Stevenson, review of *The Book of Everything,* p. 407.
Horn Book, July-August, 2006, Christine M. Heppermann, review of *The Book of Everything,* p. 444.
Kirkus Reviews, March 1, 2006, review of *The Book of Everything,* p. 233.
Publishers Weekly, March 27, 2006, review of *The Book of Everything,* p. 79.
School Library Journal, July, 2006, Sadie Mattox, review of *The Book of Everything,* p. 106.
School Librarian, Summer, 2006, Michael Holloway, review of *The Book of Everything,* p. 99.

ONLINE

Allen & Unwin Web site, http://www.allenandunwin.com/ (May 19, 2007).
Arthur A. Levine Web site, http://www.arthuralevinebooks. com/ (May 19, 2007), "Guus Kuijer."
Foundation for the Production and Translation of Dutch Literature Web site, http://www.productiefonds.nl/ (May 19, 2007), "Guus Kuijer."
Schrijvers Web site, http://www.schrijversinfo.nl/ (May 19, 2007), "Guus Kuijer."*

L

LACHTMAN, Ofelia Dumas 1919-

Personal
Born July 9, 1919, in Los Angeles, CA; married; children: one son, one daughter. *Education:* Attended Los Angeles City College and University of California, Los Angeles.

Addresses
Home—Los Angeles, CA.

Career
Author, 1974—. Formerly worked as a medical stenographer; West Los Angeles-Beverly Hills YWCA, former executive director.

Member
PEN International, Society of Children's Book Writers and Illustrators, Sisters in Crime.

Awards, Honors
Skipping Stones Book Award, 1995, for *Pepita Talks Twice/Pepita habla dos veces;* Benjamin Franklin Award for best young-adult novel, 1996, for *The Girl from Playa Blanca.*

Writings

BILINGUAL PICTURE BOOKS

Pepita Talks Twice/Pepita habla dos veces, illustrated by Alex Pardo DeLange, Piñata Books (Houston, TX), 1995.

Big Enough/Bastante grande, illustrated by Enrique O. Sánchez, Spanish translation by Yanitzia Canetti, Piñata Books (Houston, TX), 1998.

Pepita Thinks Pink/Pepita y el color rosado, illustrated by Alex Pardo DeLange, Spanish translation by Yanitzia Canetti, Piñata Books (Houston, TX), 1998.

Pepita Takes Time/Pepita, siempre tarde, illustrated by Alex Pardo DeLange, Spanish translation by Alejandra Balestra, Piñata Books (Houston, TX), 2001.

Tina and the Scarecrow Skins/Tina y las pieles de espantapájaros, illustrated by Alex Pardo DeLange, Spanish translation by José Juan Colín, Piñata Books (Houston, TX), 2002.

Pepita Finds Out/Lo que Pepita descubre, illustrated by Alex Pardo DeLange, Spanish translation by Carolina Villarroel, Piñata Books (Houston, TX), 2004.

Pepita Packs Up/Pepita empaca, illustrated by Alex Pardo DeLange, Spanish translation by Gabriela Baeza Ventura, Piñata Books (Houston, TX), 2005.

YOUNG-ADULT NOVELS

Campfire Dreams, Harlequin (New York, NY), 1987.

The Girl from Playa Blanca, Piñata Books (Houston, TX), 1995.

Call Me Consuela, Arte Público Press (Houston, TX), 1997.

Leticia's Secret, Piñata Books (Houston, TX), 1997.

The Summer of El Pintor, Arte Público Press (Houston, TX), 2001.

A Good Place for Maggie, Piñata Books (Houston, TX), 2002.

Looking for La Única (sequel to *The Summer of El Pintor*), Arte Público Press (Houston, TX), 2004.

The Trouble with Tessa, Piñata Books (Houston, TX), 2005.

The Truth about Las Mariposas, Arte Público Press (Houston, TX), 2007.

Campfire Dreams was translated into French and German.

OTHER

A Shell for Angela (adult novel), Arte Público Press (Houston, TX), 1995.

Contributor to periodicals, including *Chicago Tribune, Christian Science Monitor, Boston Globe, Washington Times, Newsday, St. Petersburg Times, Dallas Morning News,* and *Detroit News.*

Sidelights

The daughter of Mexican immigrants, Ofelia Dumas Lachtman is the author of several bilingual picture books for children, among them *Pepita Talks Twice/ Pepita habla dos veces,* as well as *The Girl from Playa Blanca* and other young-adult novels. In *Pepita Talks Twice* the title character, an irrepressible young girl who speaks both Spanish and English, serves as a translator for her family and friends. According to *Skipping Stones* critic Dick Keis, Lachtman's book serves as "an affirmation of the value of speaking two languages and understanding more than one culture." Pepita returns in *Pepita Takes Time/Pepita, siempre tarde,* while a troublesome school journalism project is the subject of *Pepita Finds Out/Lo que Pepita descubre. School Library Journal* contributor Ann Welton observed that *Pepita Finds Out,* in which the girl interviews family members in hopes of finding an interesting story to share with her class, "has a sound message to impart about acceptance and love of family." In *Pepita Packs Up/Pepita empaca,* which finds the youngster and her family preparing to move to a new home, "Lachtman's text combines a traumatic event . . . with the comfort of loving family and neighbors," according to a *Kirkus Reviews* writer.

Lachtman received the Benjamin Franklin Award for *The Girl from Playa Blanca,* a gothic romance featuring Hispanic characters. When their father disappears, Elena and brother Carlos follow his trail to Los Angeles, where Elena takes a job at the estate of a mysterious doctor, his gorgeous wife, and their brooding son. "It's hard to imagine a teen who wouldn't enjoy this light read," commented *Booklist* critic Jeanne Triner. Another young-adult mystery, *The Summer of El Pintor,* introduces Monica Ramos, a privileged teen who is forced to move into the home of her deceased mother in the Los Angeles barrio. When Monica's neighbor, an enigmatic artist named El Pintor, vanishes, the girl decides to investigate in a story praised as "fast-paced, poignant, and vivid" by *Booklist* contributor Gillian Engberg. In the sequel, *Looking for La Única,* Monica becomes the chief suspect when a priceless guitar is stolen from a friend's store, and she sets out to convince everyone of her innocence. "Monica proves herself a smart, strong and resourceful heroine," noted *Kliatt* reviewer Kathryn Kulpa of Lachtman's novel.

A sixteen year old seeks a quieter life after her father dies in *A Good Place for Maggie,* "a sweet story that will appeal to young people," according to Sherri Forgash Ginsberg in *Kliatt.* Hoping to escape fast-paced Los Angeles, Maggie Cruz hops into her old Volk-

Cover of Ofelia Dumas Lachtman's middle-grade novel **The Trouble with Tessa,** *featuring artwork by Giovanni Mora.* (Piñata Books, 2005. Arte Público Press—University of Houston. Reproduced by permission.)

swagen and heads to her grandfather's house in Twisted Creek, a remote mountain village. At her new school, Maggie learns that a group of students hope to modernize their small town, and, despite her misgivings, she eventually joins forces with them against a wealthy family that exerts too much control over the inhabitants of Twisted Creek. According to Ashley Larsen, writing in *School Library Journal,* "Lachtman animates the story with believable dialogue and likable characters."

The Trouble with Tessa finds imaginative eleven-year-old Tessa del Campo sure that she is destined to become a witch after she discovers some papers containing a series of spells. When she successfully focuses her magic against her bothersome younger sister, Tessa decides to attempt a more powerful spell: wishing her parents would divorce each other. The youngster is horrified, though, when it appears she is unable to reverse her spell's unfortunate outcome. *School Library Journal* critic Tasha Saecker praised the "likable, spunky heroine" Lachtman creates in *The Trouble with Tessa,* and *Kliatt* reviewer Mary Melaugh called the book "an enjoyable story."

Lachtman shares a story of friendship and parting in **Pepita Packs Up,** *a bilingual picture book illustrated by Alex Pardo DeLange.* (Piñata Books, 2005. Illustration © 2005 by Alex Pardo DeLange. Arte Público Press/University of Houston. Reproduced by permission.)

Biographical and Critical Sources

BOOKS

Hispanic Literary Companion, Visible Ink Press (Detroit, MI), 1997.

PERIODICALS

Booklist, November 15, 1995, Jeanne Triner, review of *The Girl from Playa Blanca,* p. 544; August 1, 2001, Gillian Engberg, review of *The Summer of El Pintor,* p. 2107; February 15, 2003, John Peters, review of *Tina and the Scarecrow Skins/Tina y las pieles de espantapájaros,* p. 1069; January 1, 2005, Carolyn Phelan, review of *Looking for La Única,* p. 845.

Kirkus Reviews, November 15, 2005, review of *Pepita Packs Up/Pepita empaca,* p. 1234.

Kliatt, May, 2003, Sherri Forgash Ginsberg, review of *A Good Place for Maggie,* p. 18; July, 2005, Kathryn Kulpa, review of *Looking for La Única,* p. 22; January, 2006, Mary Melaugh, review of *The Trouble with Tessa,* p. 16.

Publishers Weekly, January 23, 1995, review of *A Shell for Angela,* p. 65; July 20, 1998, review of *Pepita Thinks Pink/Pepita y el color rosado,* p. 222; June 4, 2001, review of *The Summer of El Pintor,* p. 81.

School Library Journal, October, 1987, Kathy Fritts, review of *Campfire Dreams,* p. 150; October, 1995, Anne Connor, review of *The Girl from Playa Blanca,* p. 134; January, 1998, Sylvia V. Meisner, review of *Leticia's Secret,* p. 114; August, 1998, Denise E. Agnosto, review of *Big Enough/Bastante grande,* p. 142; December, 1998, Selene S. Vasquez, review of *Pepita Thinks Pink/Pepita y el color rosado,* p. 86; January, 2001, Ann Welton, review of *Pepita Takes Time/Pepita, siempre tarde,* p. 102; July, 2001, Leigh Ann Jones, review of *The Summer of El Pintor,* p. 110; December, 2002, Ashley Larsen, review of *A Good Place for Maggie,* p. 143; March, 2003, Ann Welton, review of *Tina and the Scarecrow Skins/Tina y las pieles de espantapájaros,* and *Pepita Finds Out/Lo que Pepita descubre,* p. 227; May, 2005, Tasha Saecker, review of *The Trouble with Tessa,* p. 132; February, 2006, Maria Otero-Boisvert, review of *Pepita Packs Up/Pepita empaca,* p. 126.

Skipping Stones, April-May, 1996, Dick Keis, review of *Pepita Talks Twice/Pepita habla dos veces,* p. 7.

Voice of Youth Advocates, October, 1988, review of *Campfire Dreams,* p. 188; December, 1995, review of *The Girl from Playa Blanca,* p. 303; December, 2001, review of *The Summer of El Pintor,* p. 360; October, 2003, review of *A Good Place for Maggie,* p. 313.

ONLINE

Arte Público Press Web site, http://www.arte.uh.edu/ (May 10, 2007), "Ofelia Dumas Lachtman."

Latino-American Experience Web site, http://testlae.greenwood.com/ (May 10, 2007), "Ofelia Dumas Lachtman."*

LERNER, Aaron 1920-2007
(Aaron Bunsen Lerner)

OBITUARY NOTICE— See index for *SATA* sketch: Born September 21, 1920, in Minneapolis, MN; died of complications from Alzheimer's disease, February 3, 2007, in New Haven, CT. Dermatologist, educator, and author. Lerner was best remembered as the discoverer of melatonin, as well as other hormones and proteins that affect the skin's health. He was a graduate of the University of Minnesota, earning a Ph.D. there in 1945 and an M.D. in 1946. While still a student, Lerner made his first medical discovery: a blood protein now known as cryoglobulin. After two years of service in the U.S. Army, he was an American Cancer Society fellow at what is now Case Western Reserve University for a year. During the early 1950s, Lerner taught at the University of Michigan and the University of Oregon before joining the staff of Yale University Medical School in 1955. He became a full professor of dermatology there in 1957, remaining at Yale until his 1995 retirement. He was chair of his department from 1958 until 1985. It was also in 1958 that Lerner and his team of researchers discovered melatonin, a hormone that affects the skin's ability to darken and, interestingly, is also involved in regulating the body's circadian rhythms. Later, Lerner also developed a technique to treat vitiligo, a disorder that destroys pigment cells in the skin. Lerner was the author, with his wife, Marguerite Lerner, of *Dermatologic Medications* (1954). He also cowrote the children's book *Infinity: What Is It?* (1969) and authored the young-adult biography *Einstein and Newton: A Comparison of the Two Greatest Scientists* (1973).

OBITUARIES AND OTHER SOURCES:

PERIODICALS

New York Times, February 20, 2007, p. A17.
Times (London, England), March 20, 2007, p. 61.

*   *   *

LERNER, Aaron Bunsen
See LERNER, Aaron

*   *   *

LLOYD-JONES, Sally 1960-

Personal

Born 1960, in Kampala, Uganda; moved to United States, 1989. *Education:* Sussex University, degree (art history and French); attended Sorbonne IV, University of Paris. *Religion:* Christian. *Hobbies and other interests:* Distance running, photography, movies, sailing, biking.

Sally Lloyd-Jones (Photograph courtesy of Sally Lloyd-Jones.)

Addresses

Home and office—New York, NY. *E-mail*—sallylj@mac.com.

Career

Author and editor. Oxford University Press, London, England, editorial assistant; Octopus Books, Michelin House, London, editor; Reader's Digest, New York, NY, publisher of Christian children's book list until 2000; full-time writer, beginning 2000.

Member

Authors Guild, Society of Children's Book Writers and Illustrators.

Awards, Honors

Golden Book Award, Evangelical Christian Publishers Association, for *Baby's First Bible*.

Writings

EDITOR AND DEVISER; NOVELTY-FORMAT BOOKS

Hidden Toys, illustrated by Amanda Leslie, Dial Books for Young Readers (New York, NY), 1989.

Who Can I Call?, illustrated by Paul Harvey, Egmont Children's Books (London, England), 1992.

What Do Ducklings Do?, illustrated by Paul Harvey and Amy Wulfing, Broadman & Holman (Nashville, TN), 1992.

Friends of God: Moving Picture Book, illustrated by Nancy Pistone, Standard Publishing (Cincinnati, OH), 1993.

The Hippo's Adventure Bible Playtime Book, illustrated by Bari Weissman, Standard Publishing (Cincinnati, OH), 1993.

In the Beginning: Moving Picture Book, illustrated by Nancy Pistone, Standard Publishing (Cincinnati, OH), 1993.

Three Special Journeys, illustrated by Bari Weissman, Standard Publishing (Cincinnati, OH), 1993.

Bible Stories: Reusable Stickers, illustrated by Stuart Trotter, Standard Publishing (Cincinnati, OH), 1994.

(With Etta Wilson) *Bible Encyclopedia: A First Reference Book,* Standard Publishing (Cincinnati, OH), 1995.

The Lord Is My Shepherd, Random House (New York, NY), 1995.

The Lord's Prayer, illustrated by Chris Demarest, Random House (New York, NY), 1995.

David and Goliath, illustrated by Don Page, Reader's Digest (Westport, CT), 1995.

Moses in the Bulrushes, illustrated by Don Page, Reader's Digest (Westport, CT), 1996.

(With Wendy Lloyd-Jones) *Noah and the Ark Board Book,* illustrated by Toni Goffe, Standard Publishing (Cincinnati, OH), 1997.

Noah's Ark: With Catholic Scripture, illustrated by Tracey Moroney, Regina Books (Claremont, CA), 1999.

What Do You Eat?, illustrated by Rick Brown, Zondervan (Grand Rapids, MI), 1999.

Where Do You Live?, illustrated by Rick Brown, Zondervan (Grand Rapids, MI), 1999.

Noah's Ark: A Little Bible Playbook about Trust, illustrated by Tracey Moroney, Standard Publishing (Cincinnati, OH), 1999.

The Whale's Tale Bible Playtime Book, illustrated by Bari Weissman, Standard Publishing (Cincinnati, OH), 2000.

Jesus Is Born, Reader's Digest (Westport, CT), 2000.

The Wise Men, illustrated by Maureen Roffey, Concordia Publishing House, (St. Louis, MO), 2000.

How Big Is God's Love: A Soft-Edges Photo Frame Book, Standard Publishing Company (Cincinnati, OH), 2000.

My First Magnetic Numbers: 24-Page Activity Book (includes magnets), illustrated by Sue Cong, Reader's Digest (Westport, CT), 2000.

Noah, illustrated by Maureen Roffey, Reader's Digest (Westport, CT), 2000.

(With Thomas Kinkade) *Colors,* Tommy Nelson (Nashville, TN), 2001.

(With Thomas Kinkade) *Numbers,* Tommy Nelson (Nashville, TN), 2001.

(With Thomas Kinkade) *Shapes,* Tommy Nelson (Nashville, TN), 2001.

(With Thomas Kinkade) *Animals,* Tommy Nelson (Nashville, TN), 2001.

Farmyard Boogie, illustrated by Simone Abel, Silver Dolphin (Berkeley, CA), 2001.

Jungle Jive, illustrated by Simone Abel, Silver Dolphin (Berkeley, CA), 2001.

Who Says That, illustrated by Tracy Moroney, Reader's Digest (Westport, CT), 2001.

My Promise Rainbow, illustrated by Patricia Jennings, Standard Publishing (Cincinnati, OH), 2002.

I Can Talk to God!, illustrated by Linda Clearwater, Standard Publishing (Cincinnati, OH), 2002.

(Editor) *My Merry Christmas, and the Real Reason for Christmas Joy,* illustrated by Linda Clearwater, Standard Publishing (Cincinnati, OH), 2003.

Sweet Dreams, illustrated by Patricia Jennings, Tyndale Kids (Carol Stream, IL), 2004.

Also creator of magnetic-board books, rhebus books, and other interactive books.

BIBLE STORYBOOKS; FOR CHILDREN

Baby's First Bible, illustrated by Colin and Moira MacLean, Reader's Digest (Westport, CT), 1997.

A Child's First Bible, illustrated by G. Brian Karas, Joshua Morris Pub. (Westport, CT), 1998.

The Lift-the-Flap Bible, illustrated by Tracy Moroney, Reader's Digest (Westport, CT), 1999.

Illustrator Jane Chapman adds her detailed paintings to Lloyd-Jones' quiet story in the bedtime tale **Time to Say Goodnight.** (HarperCollins, 2006. Illustration © 2006 by Jane Chapman. Reproduced by permission of HarperCollins Children's Books, a division of HarperCollins Publishers.)

The Jesus Storybook Bible: Every Story Whispers His Name, illustrated by Jago, Zonderkidz (Grand Rapids, MI), 2007.

Tiny Bear's Bible, illustrated by Jago, Zonderkidz (Grand Rapids, MI), 2007.

CHILDREN'S PICTURE BOOKS

Handbag Friends, illustrated by Sue Heap, David Fickling Books (Oxford, England), 2005, David Fickling (New York, NY), 2006.

Time to Say Goodnight, illustrated by Jane Chapman, HarperCollins (New York, NY), 2006.

Little One, We Knew You'd Come, illustrated by Jackie Morris, Little, Brown (New York, NY), 2006.

Old MacNoah Had an Ark, illustrated by Jill Newton, HarperCollins (New York, NY), 2007.

How to Be a Baby . . . By Me, the Big Sister, illustrated by Sue Heap, Schwartz & Wade (New York, NY), 2007.

Author's titles have been translated into over eleven languages, including Spanish, Korean, German, Dutch, and French.

Sidelights

A best-selling author for children, Sally Lloyd-Jones has penned over fifty books. As she explained to *SATA,* "I worked in children's publishing for several years, where my job was basically to come up with funny ideas for what books can do (pop, flap, bounce, rock, float, squeak, tick) and write stories and rhymes to go inside." In an online interview with Daniel William Cruver for *Eucatastrophe,* Lloyd-Jones commented on the craft of children's writing, particularly when retelling Bible stories, and noted that children's book authors are required to "distill everything down to its simplest form . . . using simple language [that] lets [the extraordinary] . . . through more powerfully."

As a Christian children's writer, Lloyd-Jones retells Biblical stories in a way that will encourage young children. In her *Eucatastrophe* interview, she discussed, in particular, her objective in creating *The Jesus Storybook Bible: Every Story Whispers His Name.* "Throughout the mapping out of the book and writing the stories," she noted, "I was resolute in my determination to avoid even a whiff of moralizing in terms of applying the stories." Instead, Lloyd-Jones' Biblical storybook emphasizes the narrative aspects of the Bible so that young readers can "meet this wonderful Hero in [its] . . . pages."

In 2000 Lloyd-Jones left publishing to write full time. "My job now is to tell stories," she noted. "You mostly get into trouble for that when you're little, but when you're a grown-up you can get away with it—sometimes even get paid to do it! So far I seem to be getting away with it."

Since leaving publishing, Lloyd-Jones now predominately writes children's literature for the general market. Her picture book *Time to Say Goodnight,* for example, depicts the nightly ritual of an assortment of forest-animal children as they prepare to go to bed. Writing in verse, Lloyd-Jones weaves "rhythmic, even hypnotic language" that *Booklist* reviewer Karin Snelson noted will calm young children. *School Library Journal* reviewer Robin L. Gibson dubbed the book a "a sweet rhyming story," and a *Publishers Weekly* critic praised "the soothing predictability" of Lloyd-Jones' rhythmic text.

Biographical and Critical Sources

PERIODICALS

Booklist, February 1, 2006, Karin Snelson, review of *Time to Say Goodnight,* p. 56; November 15, 2006, Ilene Cooper, review of *How to Be a Baby . . . By Me the Big Sister,* p. 44.

Bulletin of the Center for Children's Books, April, 2007, review of *How to Be a Baby . . . By Me the Big Sister.*

Horn Book, January-February, 2007, review of *How to Be a Baby . . . By Me the Big Sister.*

Kirkus Reviews, February 15, 2006, review of *Time to Say Goodnight,* p. 186; November 1, 2006, review of *Little One, We Knew You'd Come,* p. 113; January 15, 2007, review of *How to Be a Baby . . . By Me the Big Sister.*

Publishers Weekly, August 30, 1999, reviews of *What Do You Eat?,* and *A Child's Garden of Verses,* both p. 77; February 13, 2006, review of *Time to Say Goodnight,* p. 88; September 25, 2006, review of *Little One, We Knew You'd Come,* p. 70.

New York Times Book Review, May 13, 2007, Amy Krouse Rosenthal, review of *How to Be a Baby . . . By Me the Big Sister.*

School Library Journal, March, 2006, Robin L. Gibson, review of *Time to Say Goodnight,* p. 196; October, 2006, Eva Mitnick, review of *Little One, We Knew You'd Come,* p. 97; February, 2007, Linda L. Walkins, review of *How to Be a Baby . . . By Me the Big Sister.*

ONLINE

Children's Bookwatch Web site, http://www.midwestbookreview.com/ (October, 2006), review of *Handbag Friends.*

Eucatastrophe Web site, http://www.eucatastrophe.com/ (May 19, 2007), Daniel William Cruver, interview with Lloyd-Jones.

Random House Web site, http://www.randomhouse.com/ (May 19, 2007), "Sally Lloyd-Jones."

Sally Lloyd-Jones Home Page, http://sallylloyd-jones.com (May 19, 2007).

Sally Lloyd-Jones Blog, http://sallylloyd-jones.blogspot.com (May 19, 2007).

LONG, Sylvia 1948-

Personal

Born September 29, 1948, in Ithaca, NY; daughter of Frank J. Jr. (a soil scientist) and Marion (a homemaker) Carlisle; married Thomas Wayne Long (a physician), June 20, 1970 (divorced, 2001); children: Matthew Thomas, John Charles. *Education:* Maryland Institute of Art, B.F.A., 1970. *Hobbies and other interests:* Birdwatching, hiking, exploring and enjoying nature.

Addresses

Home—Scottsdale, AZ. *E-mail*—sylvia@sylvia-long.com.

Career

Illustrator of books for children. Designer, with images appearing on household products for children. *Exhibitions:* Work exhibited at Suzanne Brown Galleries, Scottsdale, AZ; Elizabeth Stone Gallery, Birmingham, MI; Every Picture Tells a Story, Los Angeles, CA; and Duley-Jones Gallery, Scottsdale, AZ.

Member

Society of Children's Book Writers and Illustrators, Author's Guild.

Awards, Honors

International Reading Association Children's Book Award, 1991, and California Book Award, both for *Ten Little Rabbits;* CLASP award and Best Book of the Year for Latin-American Studies designation, both for *Alejandro's Gift; Smithsonian* magazine Notable Book designation, 1996, for *Hawk Hill; Child* magazine Best Books designation, 1997, for *Hush Little Baby* Reading Magic Award, *Parenting* magazine, 1999, for *Bugs for Lunch;* Society of Illustrators Original Art Exhibition selection, Children's Literature Choice selection, and *School Library Journal* Best Books designation, all 1999, all for *Sylvia Long's Mother Goose;* Children's Book Sense Pick, Society of Illustrators Original Art Exhibition inclusion, Cuffie Award, Chicago Public Library Best-of-the-Best designation, and New York Public Library 100 Titles for Reading and Sharing inclusion, all 2006, and American Academy for the Advancement of Science Prize, and Orbis Pictus Recommended designation, both 2007, all for *An Egg Is Quiet* by Dianna Hutts Aston.

Writings

SELF-ILLUSTRATED

(Reteller) *Hush Little Baby,* Chronicle Books (San Francisco, CA), 1997, board-book edition, 2002.

(Reteller) *Sylvia Long's Mother Goose,* Chronicle Books (San Francisco, CA), 1999.

ILLUSTRATOR

Virginia Grossman, *Ten Little Rabbits,* Chronicle Books (San Francisco, CA), 1991.

Oliver Herford, *The Most Timid in the Land,* Chronicle Books (San Francisco, CA), 1992.

Jonathan London and Lanny Pinola, retellers, *Fire Race: A Karuk Coyote Tale,* Chronicle Books (San Francisco, CA), 1993.

Jonathan London, *Liplap's Wish,* Chronicle Books (San Francisco, CA), 1994.

Richard E. Albert, *Alejandro's Gift,* Chronicle Books (San Francisco, CA), 1994.

Matthew Long and Thomas Long, *Any Bear Can Wear Glasses: The Spectacled Bear and Other Curious Creatures,* Chronicle Books (San Francisco, CA), 1995.

Suzie Gilbert, *Hawk Hill,* Chronicle Books (San Francisco, CA), 1996.

My Baby Journal, Chronicle Books (San Francisco, CA), 1998.

Margery Facklam, *Bugs for Lunch,* Charlesbridge Publishing, 1999.

Deck the Hall: A Traditional Carol, Chronicle Books (San Francisco, CA), 2000.

Hush Little Baby, Chronicle Books (San Francisco, CA), 2000.

June Taylor reteller, *Twinkle, Twinkle, Little Star: A Traditional Lullaby,* Chronicle Books (San Francisco, CA), 2001.

Michael Elsohn Ross, *Snug as a Bug,* Chronicle Books (San Francisco, CA), 2004.

Barbara Anne Skalak, *Waddle, Waddle, Quack, Quack, Quack,* Chronicle Books (San Francisco, CA), 2005.

Dianne Hutts Aston, *An Egg Is Quiet,* Chronicle Books (San Francisco, CA), 2006.

Dianne Hutts Aston, *A Seed Is Sleepy,* Chronicle Books (San Francisco, CA), 2007.

Jennifer Ward, *Because You Are My Baby,* Rising Moon (Flagstaff, AZ), 2007.

Some of the books Long has illustrated have been translated into French, German, Italian, Japanese, and Korean.

Adaptations

Long's illustrations from *Sylvia Long's Mother Goose* were adapted as the educational toys *Sylvia Long's Mother Goose Nesting Blocks* and *Sylvia Long's Mother Goose Block Books* by Chronicle Books, 2001.

Sidelights

An established fine-arts painter prior to becoming an award-winning illustrator of children's picture books, Sylvia Long is known for her nostalgic, detailed images in which anthropomorphized animals—particularly rabbits—possess emotions with which young children can

relate. Noting that her "passion headed toward children's books," Long explained to *Phoenix Business Journal* interviewer Stephanie Balzer that, with her career shift into children's literature, "I feel like I can make a greater contribution that way." As an illustrator, she inspires young children with a love of nature through her detailed ink-and-watercolor paintings, and her approach ranges from the whimsical and celebratory to scientifically accurate nonfiction. Reviewing Long's illustrations for Barbara Anne Skalak's picture book *Waddle, Waddle, Quack, Quack, Quack,* which follows five freshly hatched ducklings on their first full day of adventure, *School Library Journal* contributor Kristine M. Casper wrote that the artist's "pen-and-ink and watercolor paintings add bright color and a realistic portrayal of animals and habitat to this charming story."

After earning a degree from the Maryland Institute of Art, Long forged a successful career as a fine artist while married and raising two sons. As she once recalled to *SATA:* "I created a children's book with a friend, just for fun. Some years later, it was published and I found I had the opportunity to illustrate additional books for children, which became my primary interest." That work, Virginia Grossman's *Ten Little Rabbits,* is a simple counting book that featured rabbits costumed in Native-American dress. As the pages turn, different bunnies take part in traditional Native-American rituals and subsistence activities. A *Publishers Weekly* review found *Ten Little Rabbits* in possession of "an unusual—and effective—balance between the real and the imaginary."

Another early illustration project, illustrating Oliver Herford's *The Most Timid in the Land,* is transported by Long's artwork into a medieval realm. The story revolves around rabbit Princess Bunita and her kingly father's offer of her hand (or paw) to the suitor who proves himself "the most timid in the land." The eligible bachelor hares strive to outdo one another until the day of the contest arrives. Then all predictably flee in fear, leaving the wise Bunita to await the one hare brave enough to return. A *Publishers Weekly* reviewer praised the rabbits' "delightfully expressive faces," explaining that their animated personalities and "imaginative antics. . . . make this a splendid visual treat."

Long also features her beloved rabbits in Jonathan London's picture book *Liplap's Wish,* which tells how the very first rabbits became stars that watch over the world below. According to *School Library Journal* contributor Martha Gordon, Long's illustrations for the book "reflect the poignancy of the tale with soft colors and thoughtful expressions" on the faces of Liplap, his mother, and the other rabbits involved. The collaboration between author and artist "create[s] an affecting work that will be especially meaningful to" young readers who have recently lost a grandparent, added a *Publishers Weekly* writer.

Fire Race: A Karuk Coyote Tale, a Native-American myth retold by London and coauthor Lanny Pinola,

Sylvia Long's love of nature is apparent in her detailed illustrations for Margery Facklam's **Bugs for Lunch.** (Charlesbridge, 1999. Illustration © 1999 by Sylvia Long. Used with permission by Charlesbridge Publishing, Inc. All rights reserved.)

finds a band of animals freezing because they do not yet know how to create fire. When it is discovered that the mean Yellow Jacket sisters keep a vital flame hidden on a mountaintop, clever Coyote devises a plan to steal some of the fire from them. In bringing the story to life with her illustrations, "Long creates impressively realistic animal characters with an inventive measure of whimsy," stated a *Publishers Weekly* reviewer. Other books illustrated by Long that focus on the animal world include Michael Elsohn Ross's *Snug as a Bug,* which follows the bedtime ritual of a number of nature's creatures.

An award-winning picture book by Richard E. Albert, *Alejandro's Gift* introduces an elderly man who lives alone in an adobe house in the desert. As depicted in Long's accompanying art, lonely Alejandro tends his gardens, his burro serving as his sole friend. One day, a squirrel appears in the man's garden and drinks from the water collected in its furrowed rows. Soon a host of other creatures follows suit. Welcoming the intrusion, the lonely man realizes that the creatures are there for water, rather than for his company, and so he digs a larger water hole in the hopes that even larger creatures will come. When animals fail to appear, Alejandro realizes that his hole was dug too close to the road, so he

digs yet another, this time in a quieter spot. Paired with Albert's environmentally conscious text, Long's "polished paintings . . . impressively recreate the muted colors and varied textures of the desert," observed a *Publishers Weekly* reviewer of *Alejandro's Gift,* while *School Library Journal* contributor Graciela Italiano noted that "Long's rich, detailed, and realistically rendered pictures provide the perfect visual setting" for Albert's empathetic story."

Suzie Gilbert's *Hawk Hill* features Long's paintings depicting birds and humans. The story, aimed at readers aged eight to ten, introduces a young boy who is unhappy over his family's recent move to a new town. Pete loves birds of prey, however, and he finds solace in watching a band of hawks circle a nearby hilltop. When he comes across a hospital for injured birds run by a taciturn older woman named Mary, Pete begins helping out at the hospital, and learns much about these majestic creatures, befriending Mary in the process. In addition to praising Long's depiction of owls, falcons, osprey, and other birds of prey, *Booklist* critic Julie Corsaro commended her portrait of Mary. "Long presents a convincing physical portrait—wrinkles and all—of a compassionate elderly person," noted the critic. She also brings to life Margery Facklam's rhyming verses for *Bugs for Lunch* in artwork that *Booklist* contributor Kay Weisman noted "conveys a great deal of scientific information without ever appearing cluttered." Patricia Manning, writing in *School Library Journal,* termed the same book "an attractive, high-interest book with . . . dramatic illustrations."

Praised for its "understated elegance" by a *Publishers Weekly* reviewer, Dianna Hutts Aston's picture book *An Egg Is Quiet* also benefits from Long's creative contribution. In the book, which is designed to mimic the diary of a naturalist, Aston focuses on the characteristics of creatures that bear young by nurturing eggs: hummingbirds, emperor penguins, ostriches, salmon, insects, and even sea turtles. The book's detailed illustrations serve as a guide to basic biology, revealing the growth from egg to creature and showcasing an assembly of eggs that *Booklist* reviewer Gillian Engberg cited as being "as brilliantly colored and polished as gems." Citing Long's "skilled use of contrast and compositional balance" as effective in sustaining the interest of younger readers, the *Publishers Weekly* contributor also noted the illustrator's use of "breathtaking color" in the image culminating Aston's tale. A second collaborative effort between Aston and Long, *A Seed Is Sleepy,* introduces young children to plant reproduction and the diversity among seeds. "Long's ink-and-watercolor sketches, full of rich color and intricate detail, merit high praise" in this work, according to *School Library Journal* reviewer Maura Bresnahan.

A family affair, the picture book *Any Bear Can Wear Glasses: The Spectacled Bear and Other Curious Creatures* is a collaboration between the illustrator, physician husband Thomas Long, and son Matthew Long.

Here, a host of animals with rather unusual names fill the pages and help elementary-aged readers learn about endangered species. With text that states, for instance, that "any crab can make music," Long pairs an illustration of four crabs playing instruments, while the opposite page reads, "but there's only one fiddler crab." Long's images, noted *School Library Journal* contributor Lisa Wu Stowe, "do not sacrifice accuracy, even when being silly," and a *Publishers Weekly* reviewer declared that the picture book's "lighthearted presentation successfully pulls youngsters into the crisply written text."

In several of her books, Long begins with traditional songs, then animates them with visual stories featuring rabbit characters. In *Hush Little Baby,* the classic children's nursery lullaby, Long found fault with the original text, in which a mother promises a wealth of treats if her child will just fall asleep. In her retelling, Long's bunny mother substitutes the material goods for both natural wonders and more personal awards, like a song, or a shooting star. Across the pages, she points out the wonders of nature at nightfall to her children, to remind them that it is time to retire for the day. "Long's song is gracious," wrote a reviewer for *Publishers Weekly,* and her pictures "both soothing and diverting." *Kirkus Reviews* also praised the work, and mentioned Long's "trademark rabbits frequently depicted in warm embraces" as one of the book's charms. Other traditional works that benefit from Long's attention include *Deck the Hall: A Traditional Carol* and *Twinkle, Twinkle Little Star: A Traditional Lullaby.* Reviewing *Deck the Hall,* Engberg cited "the sense of cozy excitement infusing each picture," while *Twinkle, Twinkle, Little Star* provides what a *Kirkus Reviews* writer deemed a "wonderfully soothing" bedtime-story experience due to Long's "beautiful, bright watercolor illustrations" portraying a variety of animals eating dinner, brushing their teeth, and pulling on their pajamas in preparation for sleep.

Sylvia Long's Mother Goose, one of the artist's most popular books, features India ink-and-watercolor images that bring to life the eighty-two verses of the classic work. As she did in *Hush Little Baby,* Long reworks several of the poems, removing menacing characters to generate a more-positive message. This approach won her laudatory reviews. In Long's version of the Humpty Dumpty tale, for example, the fall of the roly-poly title character does not end with his complete destruction; instead, a duckling emerges from Humpty Dumpty's cracked shell. When the bough breaks in another tale and sends a tree-top cradle plummeting earthward, a young bird is inspired to take his first solo flight. Patricia Pearl Dole, writing in *School Library Journal,* described Long's artwork here as "luminous" and "lively," while a *Publishers Weekly* contributor declared that in *Sylvia Long's Mother Goose* the illustrator "conjures up winsome animal characters" and "links the rhymes inventively."

Regarding her work as an artist, Long once told *SATA:* "I have been asked if it takes a lot of discipline to be

self-employed, working in a studio in my home. For me, discipline is required to accomplish all the other responsibilities of life—laundry, cooking, etc.—rather than my work in the studio. I love what I do and don't think my life would change much if I won the lottery tomorrow."

Biographical and Critical Sources

PERIODICALS

Booklist, April 15, 1994, Julie Corsaro, review of *Alejandro's Gift,* p. 1537; January 15, 1995, Janice Del Negro, review of *Liplap's Wish,* p. 937; November 1, 1996, Julie Corsaro, review of *Hawk Hill,* p. 497; June 1, 1997, Julie Corsaro, review of *Hush Little Baby,* p. 1708; February 1, 1999, Kay Weisman, review of *Bugs for Lunch,* p. 976; November 15, 1999, John Peters, review of *Sylvia Long's Mother Goose,* p. 631; September 1, 2000, Gillian Engberg, review of *Deck the Hall: A Traditional Carol,* p. 133; April 15, 2006, Gillian Engberg, review of *An Egg Is Quiet,* p. 48.

Child, December-January, 1998, Margot Slade, "Editor's Picks," p. 126.

Kirkus Reviews, March 15, 1997, review of *Hush Little Baby,* p. 464; October 15, 2001, review of *Twinkle, Twinkle, Little Star: A Traditional Lullaby,* p. 1487; April 1, 2004, review of *Snug as a Bug,* p. 337; March 1, 2005, review of *Waddle, Waddle, Quack, Quack, Quack,* p. 296; March 15, 2006, review of *An Egg Is Quiet,* p. 286.

Publishers Weekly, February 8, 1991, review of *Ten Little Rabbits,* p. 56; April 13, 1992, review of *The Most Timid in the Land,* p. 52; April 19, 1993, review of *Fire Race,* p. 59; February 14, 1994, review of *Alejandro's Gift,* p. 87; October 3, 1994, review of *Liplap's Wish,* p. 68; October 30, 1995, review of *Any Bear Can Wear Glasses,* p. 60; October 7, 1996, review of *Hawk Hill,* p. 74; January 20, 1997, review of *Hush Little Baby,* p. 400; August 18, 1997, p. 29; January 11, 1999, review of *Bugs for Lunch,* p. 71; October 4, 1999, review of *Sylvia Long's Mother Goose,* p. 72; February 14, 2005, review of *Waddle, Waddle, Quack, Quack, Quack,* p. 76; March 6, 2006, review of *An Egg Is Quiet,* p. 74.

School Library Journal, July, 1994, Graciela Italiano, review of *Alejandro's Gift,* p. 73; November, 1994, Martha Gordon, review of *Liplap's Wish,* p. 84; December, 1995, Lisa Wu Stowe, review of *Any Bear Can Wear Glasses,* p. 98; March, 1999, Patricia Manning, review of *Bugs for Lunch,* p. 192; December, 1999, Patricia Pearl Dole, review of *Sylvia Long's Mother Goose,* p. 122; January, 2002, Patricia Pearl Dole, review of *Twinkle, Twinkle, Little Star,* p. 111; June, 2004, Rachel G. Payne, review of *Snug as a Bug,* p. 118; May, 2005, Kristine M. Casper, review of *Waddle, Waddle, Quack, Quack, Quack,* p. 97; June, 2006, Patricia Manning, review of *An Egg Is Quiet,* p. 104; May, 2007, Maura Bresnahan, review of *A Seed Is Sleepy,* p. 113.

ONLINE

Chronicle Books Web site, http://www.chroniclebooks.com/ (June 22, 2007), interview with Long.

Sylvia Long Home Page, http://www.sylvia-long.com (June 22, 2007).

M

MALKIN, Nina 1959(?)-

Personal

Born c. 1959, in Brooklyn, NY; married; husband's name Jason.

Addresses

Home and office—Brooklyn, NY. *Agent*—Laura Dail Literary Agency, 350 7th Ave., Ste 2003, New York, NY 10001. *E-mail*—nina@6xtheband.com.

Career

Writer and editor. *Teen People* magazine, editor.

Writings

6X: The Uncensored Confessions (young-adult novel), Scholastic (New York, NY), 2005.
6X: Loud, Fast, and Out of Control (young-adult novel), Scholastic (New York, NY), 2005.
(With others) *Mistletoe* (four novellas), Scholastic (New York, NY), 2006.
An Unlikely Cat Lady: Feral Adventures in the Backyard Jungle, Lyons Press (Guilford, CT), 2007.

Contributor of articles to periodicals, including *Real Simple, Essence, Cosmopolitan, Teen, Women's Wear Daily, New York Times,* and *In Style.*

Sidelights

Teen People editor Nina Malkin has plenty of experience interviewing musicians, and she puts that experience to good use in creating the "6x" novel series: stories about a hot teen rock band as told from band members' perspective. As Malkin wrote on the *6X the Band Web site,* "I'm pretty passionate about music, but since I'm basically tone deaf, I write about it rather than try to make it."

6X: The Uncensored Confessions introduces readers to a fictional hot new band that was created by an entertainment lawyer eager to cash in on the next big thing. The four characters—nicknamed "The Boss," "The Body," "The Boy," and "The Voice"—take turns narrating a behind-the-scenes "video diary" which readers follow in book form. With its documentary feel, *6X: The Uncensored Confessions* has more of a confessional feel than does a traditional novel. "The book has no real plot, but doesn't particularly need one," explained *Kliatt* reviewer Amanda MacGregor, while a *Publishers Weekly* critic found Malkin's "premise . . . enticing, and the character's voices . . . truly distinct." The adventures of the band mates continue in *6X: Loud, Fast, and Out of Control.*

Malkin is also the author of a rather unusual memoir titled *An Unlikely Cat Lady: Feral Adventures in the Backyard Jungle.* Here she recounts her work with feral cats, including her efforts to keep wild cats safe and trap and neuter them to prevent more strays from being born. When asked about her writing process by Stacy N. Hackett for the *CatChannel.com,* Malkin revealed her creative philosophy: "Bang it out. Just relate the events. Since everything in *An Unlikely Cat Lady* actually happened, I didn't have to rely on my imagination. It's a bit trickier with fiction."

Biographical and Critical Sources

PERIODICALS

Kliatt, January, 2006, Amanda MacGregor, review of *6X: The Uncensored Confessions,* p. 16.
Library Journal, December 1, 2006, Edell M. Schaefer, review of *An Unlikely Cat Lady: Feral Adventures in the Backyard Jungle,* p. 148.
Publishers Weekly, September 5, 2005, review of *6X: The Uncensored Confessions,* p. 64; October 30, 2006, review of *An Unlikely Cat Lady,* p. 49.

ONLINE

6X the Band Web site, http://www.6xtheband.com/ (May 17, 2007).

Brooklyn Paper Online, http://brooklynpaper.com/ (February 24, 2007), Dana Rubenstein, "Nina Malkin."

CatChannel.com, http://www.catchannel.com/ (March 17, 2007), Stacy N. Hackett, "Meet Nina Malkin."

Laura Dail Literary Agency Web site, http://www.ldlainc.com/ (May 17, 2007).*

*   *   *

MANUEL, Lynn 1948-

Personal

Born January 21, 1948, in Hamilton, Ontario, Canada; daughter of Clarence Earl (a steelworker) and Verna Mary Maycock; children: Jennifer Vallee, David. *Education:* McMaster University, B.A. (history), 1969; Ontario Teacher Education College, B.Ed., 1975; University of British Columbia, M.F.A. (creative writing), 1993.

Addresses

Home—White Rock, British Columbia, Canada.

Career

Writer and proofreader.

Member

Writer's Union of Canada, Canadian Society of Children's Authors, Illustrators, and Performers.

Awards, Honors

Our Choice designation, Canadian Children's Book Center, 1997-98, for *The Night the Moon Blew Kisses,* 1998-99, for *Lucy Maud and the Cavendish Cat,* and 2003, for *The Lickety-Split Princess.*

Writings

FOR CHILDREN

Mystery at Cranberry Farm, illustrated by Sylvie Daigneault, Gage Educational Publishers (Scarborough, Ontario, Canada), 1981.

Mystery of the Ghostly Riders, illustrated by Sylvie Daigneault, Gage, Educational Publishers (Scarborough, Ontario, Canada), 1985.

The Ghost Ships That Didn't Belong, illustrated by Paul McCusker, Gage Educational Publishers (Scarborough, Ontario, Canada), 1987.

Return to Cranberry Farm, illustrated by Rob Johannsen, Gage Educational Publishers (Scarborough, Ontario, Canada), 1990.

The Princess Who Laughed in Colours, illustrated by J.O. Pennanen, Penumbra Press (Manotick, Ontario, Canada), 1995.

The Night the Moon Blew Kisses, illustrated by Robin Spowart, Houghton Mifflin (Boston, MA), 1996.

Fifty-five Grandmas and a Llama, illustrated by Carolyn Fisher, Gibbs Smith Publisher (Layton, UT), 1997.

Lucy Maud and the Cavendish Cat, illustrated by Janet Wilson, Tundra Books (Toronto, Ontario, Canada), 1997.

The Cherry Pit Princess, illustrated by Debbie Edlin, Coteau Books (Regina, Saskatchewan, Canada), 1997.

The Lickety-Split Princess, illustrated by Debbie Edlin, Coteau Books (Regina, Saskatchewan, Canada), 2001.

The Christmas Thingamajig, illustrated by Carol Benioff, Dutton (New York, NY), 2002.

Camels Always Do, illustrated by Kasia Charko, Orca Book (Victoria, British Columbia, Canada), 2004.

The Trouble with Tilly Trumble, illustrated by Diane Greenseid, Harry N. Abrams (New York, NY), 2006.

The Summer of the Marco Polo, illustrated by Kasia Charko, Orca Book (Custer, WA), 2007.

Sidelights

Lynn Manuel became a writer after moving to British Columbia, Canada, in the late 1970s. In mysteries such as *The Ghost Ships That Didn't Belong, Mystery at Cranberry Farm,* and *Return to Cranberry Farm,* as well as in *The Cherry Pit Princess* and its sequel, *The Lickety-Split Princess,* she introduces young protagonists whose imaginations and curiosity lead them into all sorts of page-turning adventures. Manuel spins wordplay, riddles, and tall tales into engaging stories geared for elementary-grade readers, and her skills as a writer have extended to picture-books such as *The Night the Moon Blew Kisses* and *Camels Always Do.* The latter, a "fun yet informative" book that was praised by *Resource Links* reviewer Victoria Pennell for providing young children with "a glimpse into an unusual and probably little-know incident in [nineteenth-century] Canadian history."

In Manuel's *The Cherry Pit Princess,* readers meet Dagney Comfort, a third grader who remains devoted to best friend Anna, even though Anna and her family have moved away. Although she makes a new friend in the artistically inclined Megan Canary, loyal Dagney believes that she must always hold Anna in highest regard. Then, during a summer holiday spent with Megan at her Aunt Allie's orchard, Dagney learns that each friend is unique and all can hold special places inside one's heart. The girls' adventures continue in *The Lickety-Split Princess,* as dreams of fame inspire Dagney and Megan to enter a local writing contest. At first confident that Dagney's vivid imagination will fuel their fiction, the girls find themselves without an ending and cast about for ways to jump-start Dagney's talent for storytelling as the contest deadline draws near. Praising Manuel for creating two "imaginative, light-hearted but thoughtful" protagonists in Dagney and Megan, *Re-*

source *Links* reviewer Janice Flander praised *The Cherry Pit Princess* as a good choice for beginning chapter-book readers who enjoy stories about "friendships, imagination and enterprise."

In *The Ghost Ships That Didn't Belong* Manuel takes confident readers on a spine-tingling adventure. Based on a true incident that took place during the Canadian Cariboo gold rush of the nineteenth century, the story introduces two ten-year-old cousins who encounter a group of glowing sailing ships in a field near their grandparents' house. Meeting with a spooky old woman who is the only other person able to see the ghostly flotilla, the children find themselves in a race against time as they attempt to solve a mystery before the ships bear down upon them. Gisela Sherman stated in *Canadian Children's Literature* that, with *The Ghost Ships That Didn't Belong* Manuel creates "an exciting modern ghost story, with vivid descriptions, some nice light spots and bits of history slipped in smoothly."

Manuel's first picture book, *The Night the Moon Blew Kisses,* follows a little girl and her grandmother as they take a walk on a snowy, moonlit night. The child blows kisses to the moon and the moon responds with snowflake kisses. Manuel's "text is fresh and gentle," noted Anne Louise Mahoney in a review for *Quill & Quire,* and *School Library Journal,* contributor Ruth K. MacDonald dubbed *The Night the Moon Blew Kisses* "a mystical, marvelous nighttime tour of a winter landscape."

In another picture book by Manuel, the whimsically titled *Fifty-five Grandmas and a Llama,* young Sam wishes desperately for a grandmother. Finally placing an ad in the newspaper, the boy gets more than he bargains for when fifty-five potential grandmas show up, one even toting a llama! "The lesson that too much of a good thing is not a good thing packs a big comic wallop here," asserted Pam McCuen in her review of *Fifty-five Grandmas and a Llama* for the *Bulletin of the Center for Children's Books.* Manuel focuses on yet another unusual woman in the entertaining *The Trouble with Tilly Trumble.* As brought to life in colorful paintings by Diane Greenseid, her unconventional protagonist is frustrated in her search for the perfect cozying-up-by-the-fireside chair. Finally, a scruffy stray dog adopts Tilly and warms up her cluttered home with his waggy-tailed presence. Praising "Tilly's whimsical lifestyle" and her grudging affection for her new houseguest, Shelle Rosenfeld added in *Booklist* that Manuel creates "a touching story of finding comfort when one least expects it." *The Trouble with Tilly Trumble* was described by *School Library Journal* Elaine Lesh Morgan as "a satisfying story of two unique individuals finding one another" that is given added impact by Manuel's "descriptive" and "creative" text.

The sadness of a young girl following the death of a beloved relative is the focus of *The Christmas Thingamajig,* a picture book in which "Manuel's warm, lyri-cal text ably touches on grief's complicated emotions," according to *Booklist* critic Townsend-Hudson. Praising Manuel's inclusion of an "upbeat ending" in her poignant tale, Linda Israelson added in her *School Library Journal* review that *The Christmas Thingamajig* is sure to "resonate with children . . . who have experienced a similar loss."

Growing up in Canada, Manuel was captivated by the stories of well-known Canadian writer Lucy Maud Montgomery, and Montgomery's *The Story Girl* and *The Golden Road* were among her favorite books. As the author later explained to *SATA,* "I knew that I wanted to write a picture book for children about Maud's life, especially the period when she was working on *Anne of Green Gables.* My problem was how to write an interesting and accurate account of such a lonely time. Maud lived a very isolated life while she was caring for her elderly grandmother in Cavendish, on Prince Edward Island. She was often deeply depressed." During her research, Manuel revealed, she "came to see how much [Montgomery's] . . . gray cat Daffy meant to her, and how constant was her love for him. That was when I decided to write about this time of her life through the eyes of her cat. In that way, the loneliness could be kept in the background, and the focus of the story could be Maud and her cat Daffy." According to *Resource Links* contributor Isobel Lang, in the picture book *Lucy Maud and the Cavendish Cat* Manuel achieves success at "the difficult task of weaving a winsome tale" from her in-depth research, providing "children and adults alike" a revealing look at the life of "an icon of Canadian literature."

Biographical and Critical Sources

PERIODICALS

Booklist, September 15, 2002, Shelley Townsend-Hudson, review of *The Christmas Thingamajig,* p. 246; April 15, 2006, Shelle Rosenfeld, review of *The Trouble with Tilly Trumble,* p. 53.
Bulletin of the Center for Children's Books, July-August, 1997, Pam McCuen, review of *Fifty-five Grandmas and a Llama,* pp. 402-403.
Canadian Book Review Annual, 2004, Anne Hutchings, review of *Camels Always Do,* p. 479.
Canadian Children's Literature, number 53, 1989, Gisela Sherman, review of *The Ghost Ships That Didn't Belong,* pp. 71-73.
Canadian Review of Materials, April 10, 1998, review of *Lucy Maud and the Cavendish Cat;* September 21, 2001, review of *The Lickety-Split Princess,* p. 1621.
Horn Book, November, 1997, review of *Lucy Maude and the Cavendish Cat,* p. 706.
Kirkus Reviews, June 1, 1996, review of *The Night the Moon Blew Kisses,* p. 827; November 1, 2002, review of *The Christmas Thingamajig,* p. 1621; March 15, 2006, review of *The Trouble with Tilly Trumble,* p. 295.

Publishers Weekly, July 15, 1996, review of *The Night the Moon Blew Kisses,* p. 73.

Quill & Quire, October, 1996, Anne Louise Mahoney, review of *The Night the Moon Blew Kisses,* p. 46.

Resource Links, February, 1998, review of *The Cherry Pit Princess,* p. 112; June, 1998, review of *Lucy Maud and the Cavendish Cat,* pp. 3-4; October, 2001, Zoe Johnstone Guha, review of *The Lickety-Split Princess,* p. 19; April, 2004, Victoria Pennell, review of *Camels Always Do,* p. 6.

School Library Journal, November, 1996, Ruth K. MacDonald, review of *The Night the Moon Blew Kisses,* p. 88; April, 1997, Kathy Piehl, review of *Fifty-five Grandmas and a Llama,* pp. 113-114; October, 2002, Linda Israelson, review of *The Christmas Thingamajig,* p. 61; November, 2004, Julie Roach, review of *Camels Always Do,* p. 112; December, 2006, Elaine Lesh Morgan, review of *The Trouble with Tilly Trumble,* p. 108.*

* * *

MARINO, Peter 1960-

Personal

Born July 21, 1960, in Amsterdam, NY; son of Giacchino "Jack" (a mortgage broker) and Noreen Grace (an office manager) Marino; married G.A. Broadwell (a linguistics professor) June 12, 2004. *Education:* State University of New York at Albany, M.A. (education), 1983. *Politics:* "Reasonable." *Religion:* Unitarian Universalist. *Hobbies and other interests:* Kayaking, biking, gardening, cooking, film festivals.

Addresses

Office—Adirondack Community College, 640 Bay Rd., Queensbury, NY 12804. *Agent*—John Hawkins and Assoc., 71, W. 23rd St., Ste. 1600, New York, NY 10010. *E-mail*—pmarino300@yahoo.com.

Career

Educator, playwright, and novelist. Adirondack Community College, Queensbury, NY, professor of English, 1990—. Unitarian Universalist Congregation of Saratoga Springs, member of social justice committee, 2002—. Actor in regional theatre; Mop and Bucket Company (improvisational troupe), founding member.

Member

Society of Children's Book Writers and Illustrators.

Awards, Honors

Chancellor's Award for Excellence in Scholarship and Creative Activities, State University of New York, 2005-06; Young Adult Library Services Association Best Book for Young Adults nomination, 2007, for *Dough Boy.*

Peter Marino (Photo courtesy of Peter Marino.)

Writings

Ralph Smith of Schenectady, New York's Coming Out to His Wife Options (one-act play), produced in New York, 2003.

Dough Boy (young-adult novel), Holiday House (New York, NY), 2005.

The Good Samaritan (one-act play), produced in Boston, MA, 2006.

Alice Blunt (young-adult novel), Holiday House (New York, NY), 2008.

Magic and Misery (young-adult novel), Holiday House (New York, NY), 2008.

Also author, with Tom Ecobelli, of play *The Grandma Show,* produced in Albany, NY.

Sidelights

"I wrote my first book when I was in third grade," author and playwright Peter Marino told *SATA.* "I can't remember the title now, but it was about a woman named Carrie who was in labor and had to get to the hospital. I must have been heavily influenced by the birth of triplets on the television program *My Three Sons.* I thought it was the coolest thing in nature that three babies could be exactly alike, so I ran with the idea and had Carrie deliver six.

"More important is the thrill I felt writing and illustrating my own book, and showing it off to friends and family. It was then I knew absolutely that I wanted to

be a writer. I wish I could tick off the subsequent awards and achievements that propelled me through childhood into the literary life, but there were none. I couldn't even get a piece in *Highlights* magazine. Someone else won the creative writing award at my high school graduation (and I hope he is reading this). I had much to learn about writing, and more significantly, much to learn about how to define the word 'writer.' It wasn't until the age of forty was creeping through my window that I realized I was a writer whether I got published or not. It's been said a thousand times if once, but it's true: Writing is a physical and emotional necessity— and it's the most fulfilling work I do.

"That's not to say my career as a composition professor is secondary. I love working with students at the community-college level. Teaching writing means I am a writer working with other writers all the time. Granted, most of my students do not consider themselves writers, but part of my job is to get them a little closer to that self-definition by treating them as peers in the work of words.

"My full-time teaching job affords me the basic necessities of life—housing, food, HBO—but fitting my writing in is always something akin to solving a crossword. Sometimes I get frustrated and leave the spaces blank. Then I realize a whole week has gone by and I've barely written a word in the face of so many student papers to read and plans to draw up and e-mails to send and answer. This is when my soul starts tapping its ethereal fingers, shyly at first, then with growing frustration, to remind me that, despite the hundred things I'm currently caught up in, I really need to do some work.

"When I first queried my agent about my young-adult novel *Dough Boy,* I told him that, despite my book being about childhood weight issues and school bullying, my intentions were not to cash in on fashionable themes. I had not studied the markets to see what publishers were looking for. I just wanted to tell the story of a fat boy with an ironic sense of humor, like the protagonists in novels by some of my favorite authors— William Sleator, Jerry Spinelli, Ron Koertge, and Isabelle Holland. Tristan's story evolved from the truth of my own teenage anxiety, and from my observations as a middle-school teacher. By writing, I wanted to see if I could discover some truth about Tristan, this character I had in my head whose journey I really had no plan for. By the end of the novel I discovered a few things about him, that he was going to have to accept the uniqueness of his own physical design and his own social station, and that neither of those were in conflict with achieving an individual degree of physical fitness.

"If you as an aspiring writer ask me for advice, I can suggest that you write regularly and without fail, because a priority is a priority. You can take the advice, and I do, of Peter Elbow, and not worry if your first drafts lack direction. They will take shape, eventually, if you keep working on them and get feedback from others before you go public. That's what's disappointing about advice. . . . It's always some species of common sense instead of the potions or antidotes we really want!

"I can also suggest you search for truth in your writing—not objective truth like 2+2=4, but truths unique to your characters. 'What if. . .' is an okay template if you're churning out formula fiction, but you won't find your own writer-self in the process. I learned that lesson the slow way, in the course of writing two of my plays, a one-act with a very long title, and a full-length comedy, *The Grandma Show,* the latter written with my lifelong friend Tom Ecobelli. In both cases, the first drafts were all about the jokes. But through the revision process, I (or we) discovered that a writer can't forfeit taking his characters seriously. The humor needs to derive from the essence of the characters, not be a character unto itself.

"Finally, although it sounds clichéed, give perseverance a try. Life continues to be unfair, so there are lots of talented writers who have had limited or no publishing experience, while many so-so or just plain lousy writers can afford heated backyards for their dogs. If you get discouraged by a lack of commercial success, think instead about your soul and what it needs, and you will keep writing."

Biographical and Critical Sources

PERIODICALS

Booklist, November 15, 2005, Jennifer Hubert, review of *Dough Boy,* p. 55.

Bulletin of the Center for Children's Books, November, 2005, Deborah Stevenson, review of *Dough Boy,* p. 146.

Kirkus Reviews, October 15, 2005, review of *Dough Boy,* p. 1142.

Publishers Weekly, October 17, 2005, review of *Dough Boy,* p. 69.

School Library Journal, November, 2005, Susan Riley, review of *Dough Boy,* p. 141.

Times Union (Albany, NY), Donna Liquori, "'Dough Boy' Deals with Weighty Teen Issues," p. J4.

Voice of Youth Advocates, February, 2006, Jay Wise, review of *Dough Boy,* p. 488.

*   *   *

MASSON, Sophie 1959-

Personal

Born 1959, in Jakarta, Indonesia; married David Leach; children: Philippa, Xavier, Bevis. *Education:* Earned B.A. and M.A.

Addresses

Home—New South Wales, Australia. *Agent*—Margaret Connolly, Margaret Connolly and Associates, P.O. Box 945, Wahroonga, New South Wales 2076, Australia. *E-mail*—smasson@northnet.com.au.

Career

Novelist and author of essays and short fiction. Worked various odd jobs in Australia; former journalist.

Member

Arthurian Association of Australia, Australian Society of Authors, Children's Book Council of Australia.

Writings

FOR CHILDREN

Fire in the Sky, Angus & Robertson (Sydney, New South Wales, Australia), 1990.

Birds of a Feather, Mammoth (Melbourne, Victoria, Australia), 1996.

The Troublemaker, Hodder Headline (Sydney, New South Wales, Australia), 1997.

Small World, Hodder Headline (Sydney, New South Wales, Australia), 2000.

(Editor) *The Road to Camelot* (children's fiction anthology), Random House Australia (Sydney, New South Wales, Australia), 2002.

Also author of *A River through Time* and *No Place like Home,* based on the television series *Guinevere Jones.*

"SEYRAC" NOVEL SERIES; FOR CHILDREN

The Opera Club, Mammoth (Melbourne, Victoria, Australia), 1993.

The Cousin from France, Mammoth (Melbourne, Victoria, Australia), 1994.

Winter in France, Mammoth (Melbourne, Australia), 1994.

The Secret, Mammoth (Melbourne, Victoria, Australia), 1996.

Family Business, Mammoth (Melbourne, Victoria, Australia), 2000.

YOUNG-ADULT NOVELS

Sooner or Later, University of Queensland Press (St. Lucia, Queensland, Australia), 1991.

A Blaze of Summer, University of Queensland Press (St. Lucia, Queensland, Australia), 1992.

The Sun Is Rising, University of Queensland Press (St. Lucia, Queensland, Australia), 1996.

The Gifting, HarperCollins (New York, NY), 1996.

The Tiger, HarperCollins (New York, NY), 1996.

Red City (sequel to *The Gifting*), HarperCollins (New York, NY), 1998.

Clementine, Hodder Headline (Sydney, New South Wales, Australia), 1999, St. Mary's (Winona, MN), 2000.

Family Business, Hodder Headline (Sydney, New South Wales, Australia), 2000.

The Green Prince, Hodder Headline (Sydney, New South Wales, Australia), 2000.

The Firebird, Hodder Headline (Sydney, New South Wales, Australia), 2001.

The Hand of Glory, Hodder Headline (Sydney, New South Wales, Australia), 2002.

The Lost Island, Hodder Children's Books (London, England), 2003.

Dame Ragnell, Hodder Children's Books (London, England), 2003.

The Tempestuous Voyage of Hopewell Shakespeare, Hodder Headline (Sydney, New South Wales, Australia), 2003.

In Hollow Lands, Hodder Headline (Sydney, New South Wales, Australia), 2004.

Snow, Fire, Sword, Hodder Headline (Sydney, New South Wales, Australia), 2004, Eos (New York, NY), 2006.

Malvolio's Revenge, Hodder Headline (Sydney, New South Wales, Australia), 2005.

The Tyrant's Nephew, Random House Australia Headline (Sydney, New South Wales, Australia), 2006.

The Maharajah's Ghost, Random House Australia Headline (Sydney, New South Wales, Australia), 2007.

The Secret Army, ABC Books (Sydney, New South Wales, Australia), 2008.

"STARMAKER" NOVEL SERIES; FOR YOUNG ADULTS

Carabas, Hodder Headline (Sydney, New South Wales, Australia), 1996, published as *Serafin,* St. Mary's (Winona, MN), 2000.

Cold Iron, Hodder Headline (Sydney, New South Wales, Australia), 1998, published as *Malkin,* St. Mary's (Winona, MN), 2000.

The First Day, St. Mary's (Winona, MN), 2000.

"THOMAS TREW" NOVEL SERIES; FOR YOUNG ADULTS

Thomas Trew and the Horns of Pan Hodder Headline (Sydney, New South Wales, Australia), 2006.

Thomas Trew and the Hidden People, Hodder Headline (Sydney, New South Wales, Australia), 2006.

"LAY LINES" ADULT FANTASY SERIES

The Knight by the Pool, Bantam (Sydney, New South Wales, Australia), 1998.

The Lady of the Flowers, Bantam (Sydney, New South Wales, Australia), 1999.

The Stone of Oakenfast, Bantam (Sydney, New South Wales, Australia), 2000.

The Forest of Dreams (omnibus), Bantam (Sydney, New South Wales, Australia), 2001.

OTHER

The House in the Rainforest (adult novel), University of Queensland Press (St. Lucia, Queensland, Australia), 1990.

The Hoax (adult novel), Mandarin Australia, 1997.

(Coauthor) *The Prince* (play), produced in Armidale, New South Wales, Australia, 2001.

Walking in the Garden of the Mind, Altair Australia (Blackwood, South Australia, Australia), 2005.

Contributor of reviews, short fiction, and essays, to numerous periodicals, anthologies, and Internet journals, including *Phantasies, Slightly Foxed, Good Readings, Magpies,* and *Quadrant.*

Adaptations

Several of Masson's novels have been adapted as audiobooks.

Sidelights

Sophie Masson is a writer of fairy tales and novels for young adults that have earned critical acclaim for the depth of their historical detail. Amidst settings that range from medieval France to a modern-day drama club, books such as *The Firebird,* her "StarMaker" fantasy series, and the modern-day fantasy *Snow, Fire, Sword* feature characters who struggle with their self-identity and seek to forge closer ties with others. Books for younger readers include her novel *Thomas Trew and the Hidden People,* which joins several other series installments in following a ten-year-old misfit who learns that he possesses a special skill when he discovers the secret world of the Hidden People. As the Australian-based Masson asserted, her primary goal in writing is "to tell a good story"; "to make readers escape into a wonderful world; to take them on amazing journeys, including into other people's hearts; to make them feel what it's like to be someone else. And to have fun."

The third of seven children, Masson was born in 1959, in Indonesia, where her father was then working. Before her first birthday, she was brought to her parents' native France, where she was raised by her grandmother until her parents' return five years later. Due to her father's job in international construction, Masson spent the rest of her childhood alternating between her family's home in rural France and their second home in Sydney, Australia. As the author later explained to an interviewer, "having to cope in two languages and two cultures was a good thing . . . , because it enriched my experience and my vocabulary."

"I was aware of stories from a very early age," Masson recalled. "I come from a family where stories are very important—stories of real life, of legends, of adventure, of all kinds. We know a lot about my dad's family particularly—they have traced it back to the sixteenth century—and so we grew up listening to stories of the ex-

Cover of **The First Day,** *part of Sophie Masson's "StarMaker" trilogy, featuring artwork by Sam Thiewes.* (Saint Mary's Press, 2000. Illustration © 2000 by Saint Mary's Press, 702 Terrace Heights, Winona, MN 55987-1320. Reproduced by permission.)

ploits of our ancestors. But also stories of the woods and rivers and mountains and villages of France. Dad would also make up scary stories for us, and tell us stories of the past, often in spots where great or tragic events had happened. . . . I loved stories with a passion, straight away; one of my earliest memories is of sitting in the sun in my grandmother's apartment in Toulouse, reading and dreaming over a book I had called *Le livre bleu de contes de fees*—the *Blue Book of Fairy Tales*—which had 'Rapunzel,' 'Sleeping Beauty,' and 'Toads and Diamonds' in it."

As a teen, Masson continued to indulge her childhood love of reading and also drew and spent time with friends. She also began writing "heaps of stories. You'd think being a writer of stories would be the first thing that would enter my head, but in fact it didn't. It wasn't until I was nearly at the end of high school that I realized I could do that. So you see not every writer, even if it's obvious to everyone else around them, actually knows they want to be that thing called a writer. . . .

Once I knew, though, from about the age of sixteen or seventeen, I started sending poetry and short stories off to magazines and newspapers. I mostly didn't get anywhere, but I kept trying. I also sent samples of my stuff to other writers, to famous poets for example, such as Les Murray or Bruce Dawe or A.D. Hope, who in Australia are really, really famous. And they took the trouble to write back. . . . They were so generous with their time and advice and encouragement for a young writer just starting out."

By the time Masson was a university student, she had amassed several publication credits. Paying for school required her to work a number of odd jobs—including stints in a Laundromat and a pizzeria, as a childcare worker, and delivering newspapers—while continuing to write. "There were days when I had to choose between having lunch and catching the bus home—and home was three hours' walk away from college!" she recalled. Taking time off from school to secure herself financially, Masson worked as a newspaper reporter and writer, finally finishing her degree several years later.

Masson's first published novel, *The House in the Rainforest,* had its origins in a short story she wrote at age sixteen. While working as a journalist, she expanded it into an adult novel about a young woman returning to the village where she was born. After submitting this manuscript to a publisher, she started right in on a second book: this one a children's time-travel novel in which the main characters move between modern Australia and medieval France. In 1990 both *The House in the Rainforest* and Masson's first children's book, *Fire in the Sky,* were published, starting her on her way to a career as a full-time writer.

Focusing most of her fiction on a young-adult readership, Masson has authored stand-alone novels as well as several installments in her "StarMaker" series. Her love of history as well as story allows her to range freely throughout time and place, and her characters frequently encounter hidden worlds. In *The Firebird* she mines Russian folklore to tell the tale of three brothers who go in search of the mythical Phoenix at the whim of their capricious and greedy father. *The Green Prince* revolves around Jack Fisher, an orphan living in medieval England. Visiting a local fair, Jack is fascinated by a half-man, half-fish creature named Vagan, who informs the young man that he must leave home to claim his inheritance. As it is soon revealed, Jack is actually the Champion of the Green Kingdom, an underwater land presided over by the Green Prince. The ensuing drama includes a struggle with the evil lord, Grimlow of the Abyss.

Praised by *Kliatt* contributor Leslie Farmer as "an accessible tale for younger YAs," *Snow, Fire, Sword* takes place in an island nation based on Indonesia and finds sixteen-year-old Adi and fellow traveler Dewi enmeshed in a struggle involving an evil sorcerer, a pantheon of petulant gods and spirits, and a group of fanatical

motorcycle-riding assassins known as the hantumu. Praising Masson's talent for evoking an "elaborate, vividly detailed setting" in her novel, a *Kirkus Reviews* writer added that the plot of *Snow, Fire, Sword* moves forward "with artful hints and misdirection to a satisfyingly decisive climax." Sue Giffard wrote in *School Library Journal* that Masson's fantasy tale "is exciting and action-packed."

Masson's "StarMaker" books include *The First Day, Carabas,* and *Cold Iron*—the last two published in the United States as *Serafin* and *Malkin* respectively. Here her teen protagonists find themselves in moral quandaries that force them to draw on their personal religious faith in order to triumph over adversity. *The First Day* centers upon Skye, who is auditioning for the part of Mary Magdalene in her school's planned stage production of *Jesus Christ Superstar.* The part is instead given to Judith, and Skye is cast as the apostle Peter. Skye now finds herself attracted to the play's lead, Marco, the only actor among the main characters who, like Skye, is also a committed Roman Catholic. Judith was raised among born-again Christians, while Skye's mother is a lapsed Catholic who neglected her daughter's religious education. Adding to the conflict, the

Cover of Masson's modern-day fantasy adventure Snow, Fire, Sword, *featuring artwork by Harvey Chan.* (Eos, 2006. Jacket art © 2006 by Harvey Chan. Reproduced by permission of HarperCollins Children's Books, a division of HarperCollins Publishers.)

play's Jewish director now lives with Skye's mom. "Characters are convincingly individuated, and no single perspective or pattern of belief is made to seem more valid than the others," noted a *Publishers Weekly* reviewer, the critic calling *The First Day* a "provocative" work of fiction.

Loosely based on the "Puss in Boots" fairy tale, *Serafin* takes place in early eighteenth-century France, and centers upon the teenaged Catou, who is an outcast in her village. Catou's neighbors believe that she possesses magical powers, and they attempt to lynch her as a witch. When the local miller's son, Frederic, comes to the girl's aid, both are exiled and decide to ask the king of France for help. Unbeknownst to her new friend, Catou does indeed possess supernatural powers, including the ability to change into a cat at will. However, she follows "the Law" and uses her powers only to do good. On their journey to the court of the Sun King, Louis XIV, Catou wields her power to obtain food and shelter for herself and Frederic, but feels a growing resentment because she must now look after the young man. Meanwhile, Frederic wonders why Catou is so mysterious about her activities. When the teens encounter Balze, a charismatic stranger who claims to work for Lord Tenebran, Catou senses that the man is a threat. Convincing Frederic to disguise himself as the marquis of Carabas, a purported Spanish aristocrat, Catou dons Frederic's clothes and passes as Carabas's servant boy, Serafin. Reaching the home of Lord Tenebran's brother, their host's daughter falls in love with Frederic in his marquis guise. Meanwhile, Catou, in feline form, secretly visits Tenebran and discovers that the lord has made arrangement with the Devil. "Both young people are prickly but likable characters," noted *School Library Journal* reviewer Elaine Fort Weischedel, the critic dubbing *Serafin* an "entertaining and thoughtful story."

In *Cold Iron* a disinherited, impoverished young woman named Tattercoats has been invited to the earl of Mairnsey's ball, and her friends Malkin the servant girl and Pug the gooseherd urge her to go. Helping her to escape the watchful eye of her autocratic grandfather on the night of the festivities, they also accompany Tattercoats on her arduous journey to the castle. In her novel Masson draws upon an English fairytale, "Tattercoats," as well as on the Cinderella story and Shakespeare's *A Midsummer Night's Dream,* for inspiration.

In *The Gifting* and its sequel, *Red City,* Masson takes readers even further back in time, setting her tale of mystery and adventure in the last years of the Roman empire. In *The Gifting,* after Sulia's merchant father dies, she decides to seek out her mother, who abandoned the family years ago when she crossed the seas and returned to her home country, Alainan. During her journey, Sulia meets Rufus, a disturbed boy, and the mysterious Lugan, who claims to have come from the mythic land known as the White Kingdom. Together, the trio become companions and Rufus and Lugan help

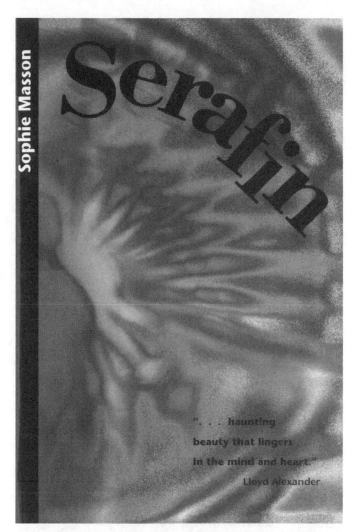

Cover of Masson's "StarMaker" novel **Serafin,** *which merges Shakespearean drama with the story of Puss in Boots.* (Saint Mary's Press, 2000. Illustration © 2000 by Saint Mary's Press, 702 Terrace Heights, Winona, MN 55987-1320. Reproduced by permission.)

Sulia in her search. In *Red City* Sulia reaches her destination and now must discover the city's key in order to locate her mother's whereabouts.

While most of her books are written with a young-adult readership in mind, Masson has penned several adult novels in addition to *The House in the Rainforest. The Hoax* revolves around an Australian writer and schoolteacher named Alex who was raised by his scholarly Uncle Julius after the tragic death of his parents. Summoned to his uncle's stately home to celebrate Julius's seventieth birthday, Alex finds his uncle busy working on a book about French composer Maurice Ravel. He also meets a fellow guests, the mysterious Charles Pym. As *The Hoax* progresses, Alex learns that Pym had written his uncle from France regarding his discovery of documents referencing Ravel's lost sonata, "Le Gouffre" ("The Abyss"). Ultimately, these documents are falsified, and the uncle's reputation is shattered after Pym vanishes.

Also geared for adult readers, Masson's "Lay Lines" trilogy, which includes *The Knight by the Pool, The*

Lady of the Flowers, and *The Stone of Oakenfast,* focus on Lady Marie de France. A poetess living in the Middle Ages, Marie encounters strange and sometimes frightening circumstances in her earthbound world as well as in the magical Otherworld. As the novels unfold, she must battle werewolves and other mythic creatures while also navigating the treacherous political intrigue of her day. Like many of her other novels, Masson mixes history with fiction, and actual historical figures make appearances within Marie's story.

"Usually an idea comes into my head months or even years before I work it up into a book," the prolific Masson once explained. "I keep a notebook in which I jot down ideas, impressions, bits and pieces of research and so on. I have to let an idea take its course; it has to 'ripen,' in a sense, it has to work away silently in my mind." Masson's writing process involves little planning. Instead, "I write fairly freely," she noted, "instinctively following threads, and though I have a general idea of where things are going, I don't usually have the details. The writing of the first draft usually takes me

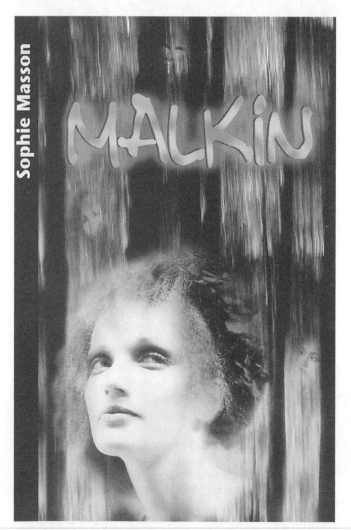

Cover of Masson's third "StarMaker" novel, Malkin, *known to Australian readers under the title* Cold Iron. (Saint Mary's Press, 2000. Illustration © 2000 by Saint Mary's Press, 702 Terrace Heights, Winona, MN 55987-1320. Reproduced by permission.)

anything from a month to five months; then I do second and third and whatever drafts, after I've had comments from other people. I need that input from others very early on, because I'm so close to my work and I write so instinctively. The whole process from starting to write to finishing the last revisions usually takes up to a year. But I'm often working on more than one book at any one time." Research is also important, and for Masson it is one of the exciting aspects of her work. "You often discover amazing things," she noted; "your education never stops! And quite often it leads you on to other ideas for books."

When asked why she decided to write for children, Masson explained that, "actually, writing for children chose me! I'd had such a good time reading as a child, and I really wanted to see if I could reproduce that pleasure myself! Also, many of the stories I wanted to write fitted children's and young people's books especially; it's a much freer, more fun, more magical atmosphere in children's literature, and I thoroughly enjoy it, though I also like writing for adults. The audience I have in mind is the child part of myself that loves stories and always has, though I also think of my kids a bit. The story takes over really and you forget about audiences.

"Young readers are freer, more open in their reading; they pick up all sorts of things but are also impatient if people are preachy or too descriptive. You have to remember to make your sentences strong, supple, but they can still be full of images; your characters must be convincing; the story must be good, a bit of suspense or mystery doesn't hurt, and so on. Young readers don't care if a book's won a prize or not—they are honest readers, who will tell you if they think a book is boring. Equally, though, I think young readers need to have their experience of the world widened; we learn a lot in our childhood books, without realizing it. One has to be aware of that. And I try to be. I think my work does speak to young readers on both those levels."

Biographical and Critical Sources

PERIODICALS

Booklist, May 15, 2006, Jennifer Mattson, review of *Snow, Fire, Sword,* p. 53.
Bulletin of the Center for Children's Books, July-August, 2006, April Spisak, review of *Snow, Fire, Sword,* p. 509.
Kirkus Reviews, April 15, 2006, review of *Snow, Fire, Sword,* p. 410.
Kliatt, May, 2006, Lesley Farmer, review of *Snow, Fire, Sword,* p. 11.
Magpies, March, 2006, Jo Goodman, review of *Malvolio's Revenge,* p. 40.
Publishers Weekly, March 13, 2000, review of *The First Day,* p. 82.

Quadrant, November, 1997, Clement Semmler, review of
The Hoax, p. 84.

School Library Journal, August, 2000, Elaine Fort Weischedel, review of *Serafin,* p. 186; October, 2006, Sue
Giffard, review of *Snow, Fire, Sword,* p. 162.

Shakespeare Newsletter, summer, 2003, Paula Glatzer, review of *The Tempestuous Voyage of Hopewell Shakespeare,* p. 53.

ONLINE

Sophie's Fantastic Castel (author's home page), http://
users.northnet.com.au/~smasson/ (June 20, 2007).

*   *   *

McCALL SMITH, Alexander 1948-
(Alexander Alasdair McCall Smith)

Personal

Born August 24, 1948, in Bulawayo, Rhodesia (now
Zimbabwe); married Elizabeth Parry (a physician),
1982; children: Lucy, Emily. *Education:* Attended Christian Brothers College (Bulawayo, Rhodesia); University
of Edinburgh, L.L.B., then Ph.D. *Religion:* Scottish
Presbyterian. *Hobbies and other interests:* Playing bas-
soon.

Addresses

Home and office—16A Napier Rd., Edinburgh EH10
5AY, Scotland. *E-mail*—alexander@alexandermccall-
smith.co.uk.

Career

Educator, author, and attorney. Queens University, Belfast, Northern Ireland, former professor; teacher in Swa-
ziland; University of Botswana, founder of law school
and professor of law, c. 1980; University of Edinburgh,
Edinburgh, Scotland, professor of medical law, 1984-
2005. Helped create a criminal code for Botswana. Human Genetics Commission of the United Kingdom, vice
chairman until 2004; United Nations Educational, Scientific, and Cultural Organization (UNESCO), former
member of International Bioethics Commission.

Awards, Honors

Chambers Award in children's fiction; Waterstone's Au-
thor of the Year designation; Dagger in the Library
Award, Crime Writers' Association; SAGA Award for
Wit, 2003; Author of the Year award, British Book
Awards, 2004; named commander, Order of the British
Empire, 2007.

Writings

FOR CHILDREN

The Perfect Hamburger, illustrated by Laszlo Acs, Hamish
Hamilton (London, England), 1982.

Alix and the Tigers, Corgi (London, England), 1988.

Alexander McCall Smith (Juda Ngwenya/Reuters/Landov. © 2004 Landov LLC.
All rights reserved. Reproduced by permission.)

Film Boy, illustrated by Joanna Carey, Methuen (London,
England), 1988.

Mike's Magic Seeds, illustrated by Kate Shannon, Young
Corgi (London, England), 1988.

(Editor) *Children of Wax: African Folk Tales,* Interlink,
1989.

Suzy Magician, Young Corgi (London, England), 1990.

The Five Lost Aunts of Harriet Bean, Blackie (London,
England), 1990, illustrated by Laura Rankin, Bloomsbury Children's Books (New York, NY), 2006.

The Tin Dog, illustrated by Jon Riley, Random House
(New York, NY), 1990.

Akimbo and the Crocodile Man, Methuen (London, England), 1993, illustrated by LeUyen Pham, Bloomsbury
Children's Books (New York, NY), 2006.

The Muscle Machine, illustrated by Terry McKenna,
Hamish Hamilton (London, England), 1995.

The Bubblegum Tree, illustrated by Georgien Overwater,
Hippo (London, England), 1996.

Bursting Balloons Mystery, illustrated by Georgien Overwater, Hippo (London, England), 1997.

The Popcorn Pirates, illustrated by Georgien Overwater,
Hippo (London, England), 1999.

Akimbo and the Elephants, illustrated by LeUyen Pham,
Bloomsbury Children's Books (New York, NY), 2005.

Akimbo and the Lions, illustrated by LeUyen Pham, Bloomsbury Children's Books (New York, NY), 2005.

Akimbo and the Snakes, illustrated by LeUyen Pham, Bloomsbury Children's Books (New York, NY), 2006.

The Cowgirl Aunt of Harriet Bean, illustrated by Laura Rankin, Bloomsbury Children's Books (New York, NY), 2006.

Harriet Bean and the League of Cheats, illustrated by Laura Rankin, Bloomsbury Children's Books (New York, NY), 2006.

Max and Maddy and the Chocolate Money Mystery, illustrated by Macky Pamintuan, Bloomsbury Children's (New York, NY), 2007.

Max and Maddy and the Bursting Balloons Mystery, illustrated by Macky Pamintuan, Bloomsbury Children's (New York, NY), 2007.

Also author of *The White Hippo,* Hamish Hamilton; *Marzipan Max,* Blackie; *The Ice-Cream Bicycle,* Viking Read Alone; *The Doughnut Ring,* Hamish Hamilton; *Paddy and the Ratcatcher,* Heinemann; and *The Princess Trick,* Puffin.

"NO. 1 LADIES' DETECTIVE AGENCY" NOVEL SERIES

The No. 1 Ladies' Detective Agency, D. Philip (Cape Town, South Africa), 1998, Anchor Books (New York, NY), 2005.

Tears of the Giraffe, Polygon (Edinburgh, Scotland), 2000, Anchor Books (New York, NY), 2002.

Morality for Beautiful Girls, Polygon (Edinburgh, Scotland), 2001, Anchor Books (New York, NY), 2002.

The Kalahari Typing School for Men, Pantheon (New York, NY), 2002.

The Full Cupboard of Life, Polygon (Edinburgh, Scotland), 2003, Pantheon (New York, NY), 2004.

In the Company of Cheerful Ladies, Pantheon (New York, NY), 2004.

Blue Shoes and Happiness, Pantheon (New York, NY), 2006.

The Good Husband of Zebra Drive, Pantheon (New York, NY), 2007.

The Miracle at Speedy Motors, Pantheon (New York, NY), 2008.

Series novels have been translate into over twenty-five other languages.

"SUNDAY PHILOSOPHY CLUB" NOVEL SERIES

The Sunday Philosophy Club, Pantheon (New York, NY), 2004.

Friends, Lovers, Chocolate, Pantheon (New York, NY), 2005.

The Right Attitude to Rain, Pantheon (New York, NY), 2006.

The Careful Use of Compliments, Pantheon (New York, NY), 2007.

"VON IGELFELD" NOVELS SERIES

The 2 1/2 Pillars of Wisdom, 2002.

At the Villa of Reduced Circumstances, illustrated by Iain McIntosh, Polygon (Edinburgh, Scotland), 2003, Anchor Books (New York, NY), 2005.

The Finer Points of Sausage Dogs, illustrated by Iain McIntosh, Polygon (Edinburgh, Scotland), 2003, Anchor Books (New York, NY), 2005.

Portuguese Irregular Verbs, illustrated by Iain McIntosh, Polygon (Edinburgh, Scotland), 2003, Anchor Books (New York, NY), 2005.

"SCOTLAND STREET" NOVEL SERIES

44 Scotland Street, illustrated by Iain McIntosh, Anchor Books (New York, NY), 2005.

Espresso Tales: The Latest from 44 Scotland Street, illustrated by Iain McIntosh, Polygon (Edinburgh, Scotland), 2005, Anchor Books (New York, NY), 2006.

The World according to Bertie, Little, Brown (London, England), 2007.

FICTION; FOR ADULTS

Heavenly Date, and Other Stories, Canongate (Edinburgh, Scotland), 1995, published as *Heavenly Date, and Other Flirtations,* Canongate (New York, NY), 2003.

The Girl Who Married a Lion, and Other Tales from Africa, Pantheon (New York, NY), 2004.

Fatty O'Leary's Dinner Party, Polygon (Edinburgh, Scotland), 2004.

Dream Angus: The Celtic God of Dreams, Canongate (New York, NY), 2006.

OTHER

(Editor with Tony Carty) *Power and Manoeuvrability,* Q Press (Edinburgh, Scotland), 1978.

(With John Kenyon Mason) *Butterworths Medico-Legal Encyclopedia,* Butterworths (Boston, MA), 1987.

(Editor with Elaine Sutherland) *Family Rights: Family Law and Medical Advances,* Edinburgh University Press (Edinburgh, Scotland), 1990.

(With John Kenyon Mason) *Law and Medical Ethics,* third edition, Butterworths (Austin, TX), 1991.

(With Kwame Frimpong) *The Criminal Law of Botswana,* Juta (Cape Town, South Africa), 1992.

(Editor with Michael A. Menlowe) *The Duty to Rescue: The Jurisprudence of Aid,* Dartmouth (Brookfield, VT), 1993.

(Editor with Colin Shapiro) *Forensic Aspects of Sleep,* Wiley (New York, NY), 1997.

(With Daniel W. Shuman) *Justice and the Prosecution of Old Crimes: Balancing Legal, Psychological, and Moral Concerns,* American Psychological Association (Washington, DC), 2000.

(With Alan Merry) *Errors, Medicine, and the Law,* Cambridge University Press (New York, NY), 2001.

Adaptations

The story "Children of Wax" was made into an animated film; other stories by Smith have been read on BBC Radio. A film adaptation of *The No. 1 Ladies' De-*

tective Agency was produced by Richard Sydney Pollack and directed by Anthony Minghella. McCall Smith's "No. 1 Ladies' Detective Agency" novels were adapted as audiobooks by Hachette Audio. Other books adapted as audiobooks include *44 Scotland Yard,* read by Ian MacKenzie, Recorded Books, 2005; *Espresso Tales,* read by MacKenzie, Recorded Books, 2006; and *Akimbo and the Elephants,* read by the author, Recorded Books, 2006.

Sidelights

A recognized expert on medical ethics, Alexander McCall Smith has become best known outside the academic world as the author of best-selling adult mysteries. In fact, McCall Smith began his writing career in the early 1980s as a children's book author. While working as a professor at the University of Edinburgh, the Scottish author was also producing such books as *The Perfect Hamburger, Akimbo and the Crocodile Man,* and *Harriet Bean and the League of Cheats,* some of which are set in the African country of Rhodesia, where McCall Smith grew up. It was only after his 1998 novel, *The No. 1 Ladies' Detective Agency,* gained best-seller status that the prolific author was able to retire from academia and focus on writing for both children and adults.

The youngest of four children, McCall Smith was born in 1948, when Rhodesia was still the British colony known as Zimbabwe. The Smith family was living in Africa because of the author's father's job as a public prosecutor for the colonial government, and McCall Smith remained in Rhodesia throughout his childhood. Attending the Christian Brothers College in his home city of Bulawayo, he moved to Scotland at age seventeen to continue his education. After earn both an L.L.B. and Ph.D. from the University of Edinburgh, he briefly taught at Queens University in Belfast, Northern Ireland, but the pull of family drew him back to Africa. While living in Botswana, McCall Smith helped found the University of Botswana Law School and taught law there for several years while also helping to build the country's criminal code. Years later, in 1992, he coauthored *The Criminal Law of Botswana,* one of several books in which he focuses on legal matters.

McCall Smith eventually returned to Scotland and became a professor of medical law at the University of Edinburgh. In addition to teaching, he wrote widely on his subject, gaining a reputation as an expert in medical legal ethics. He was given many prestigious positions; in addition to accepting several temporary professorships abroad, he also served as the deputy chairman of the British government's Human Genetics Commission as well as Britain's representative on the United Nations Educational, Scientific, and Cultural Organization (UNESCO) bioethics commission. What his colleagues may not have realized was that, while becoming a highly respected professor and ethics expert, McCall Smith was also establishing a secondary career as an author of fiction.

McCall Smith's interest in writing began in childhood, and by age eight he was attempting to find a publisher for his first novel. While pursuing a career in law, he continued writing as a hobby. Interestingly, when his real career as a writer began years later, it began almost by accident, when the young attorney won a children's fiction-writing contest run by Chambers publishing. Reflecting both Western and non-Western cultural influences, his children's books include *The White Hippo, The Muscle Machine, Akimbo and the Elephants, Max and Maddy and the Bursting Balloons Mystery,* and a series of novels featuring a young sleuth named Harriet Bean.

One of McCall Smith's earliest books for children, *The White Hippo,* is set in Gambia and focuses on the unsuccessful efforts of a group of villagers to protect an albino hippo from a white man claiming to be a photographer. More Western in theme, *The Perfect Hamburger* finds a boy named Joe joining forces with Mr. Borthwick to help the man save his family-run hamburger shop from being forced out of business by a chain restaurant. Returning to Africa in *Akimbo and the*

McCall Smith's earliest books for children include African stories such as Akimbo and the Elephants, *a chapter-book featuring artwork by LeUyen Pham.* (Bloomsbury Children's Books, 2005. Illustration © 2005 by LeUyen Pham. Reproduced by permission.)

Elephants, McCall Smith introduces the young Kenyan boy who also appears in *Akimbo and the Crocodile Man, Akimbo and the Lions,* and *Akimbo and the Snake.* A lover of nature, Akimbo witnesses the harm poachers cause in his family's game reserve as they kill adult elephants in order to steal their tusks. Determined to save the large, lumbering creatures, the boy decides to go undercover, convincing the poachers that he wants to learn the skills of their illegal trade. Noting that the series' short, fast-paced chapter-book format will appeal to reluctant readers, a *Publishers Weekly* contributor praised McCall Smith's "concise writing" as well as the "evocative" illustrations contributed by artist LeUyen Pham. In *Akimbo and the Crocodile Man* the boy helps a zoologist who has been injured on the family's game preserve, while *Akimbo and the Snakes* finds Akimbo facing a dangerous green mamba snake while accompanying Uncle Peter on a trip to a snake park. The boy's adoption of a young lion cub proves poignant in *Akimbo and the Lions* when Akimbo realizes that the wild creature has grown old enough to be set free. Reviewing the "Akimbo" stories, *Booklist* contributor Shelle Rosenfeld praised McCall Smith's "brave, caring protagonist" and explained that the series "convey[s] appreciation and respect for the African landscape, culture, and people."

In *The Five Lost Aunts of Harriet Bean* chapter-book readers are introduced to another spunky preteen, in this case nine-year-old Harriet Bean, who lives with her forgetful father, an inventor. When her dad suddenly recalls, after years of forgetting, that he has five older sisters, Harriet goes in search of her aunts and discovers that they share many of her personality traits: curious by nature, they lead eventful lives as detectives. In *Harriet Bean and the League of Cheats* the girl joins up with twin aunts Japonica and Thessalonika and goes undercover as a jockey in order to help racehorse trainer Mr. Fetlock discover who is cheating at a local racetrack. A trip to the United States is in store for Harriet in *The Cowgirl Aunt of Harriet Bean* when Japonica and Thessalonika decide to visit their sister. Formica's work as a cowgirl is having being made more difficult due to the activities of some wily cattle rustlers, and her sisters and Harriet set about finding a way to help her. Reviewing *The Cowgirl Aunt of Harriet Bean* in *School Library Journal,* Pat Leach praised the book as a enjoyable "romp of quirky personalities and unlikely situations" that is enhanced by illustrator Laura Rankin's "comic" drawings.

Of all McCall Smith's works, the prolific writer is best known for his "No. 1 Ladies' Detective Agency" series, which begins with the 1998 novel of the same name. The series' pivotal character is Mma Precious Ramotswe, a solidly built, divorced woman in her late thirties who works as a professional sleuth. Mma Ramostwe was inspired by a woman McCall Smith saw while visiting Botswana. "We were going to have chicken for lunch," he recalled to Marcel Berlins in the London *Guardian,* "and there was this woman in a red

McCall Smith entertains beginning readers with the exploits of an engaging young sleuth in **Harriet Bean and the League of Cheats,** *featuring artwork by Laura Rankin.* (Bloomsbury Children's Books, 2006. Illustration © 2006 by Laura Rankin. Reproduced by permission.)

dress who chased and chased the chicken and eventually caught it, and wrung its neck. I thought to myself: I would like to write about an enterprising woman like that."

When readers meet her in *The No. 1 Ladies' Detective Agency,* Mma Ramotswe is living in Gaborone, Botswana, a town in the cattle country bordering the Kalahari Desert. Liberated from her regular job by an inheritance of 180 heads of cattle she has received from her father, she decides to found the first all-female detective agency, and soon becomes embroiled in family conflicts such as cheating husbands, as well as employer-employee troubles. Helping Mma Ramotswe in her threadbare operation is Mma Makutsi, a secretarial college graduate who has lost better jobs to her prettier classmates. Another key figure is J.L.B. Matekoni, a mechanic who assists the women and eventually marries Mma Ramotswe as the series progresses. The bride-to-be is a rather unconventional detective, one who also serves as family counselor, comments on manners and the lack of them, and is less concerned with legally administered justice than with doing right by her clients. In her favorable review of *The No. 1 La-*

dies' Detective Agency for the *New York Times*, Alida Becker dubbed Mma Ramotswe the "Miss Marple of Botswana."

The adventures of the dynamic and resourceful Mma Ramotswe have continued to spin out in several other novels, among them *Tears of the Giraffe, The Kalahari Typing School for Men, In the Company of Cheerful Ladies, Blue Shoes and Happiness,* and *The Good Husband of Zebra Drive.* In each novel, Mma Ramotswe's professional challenges are supplemented by an unending supply of engaging concerns, inconveniences, and surprises, as well as by the insights of the forthright heroine herself. In *Blue Shoes and Happiness,* for example, Mme Ramotswe worries about her increasing girth while dealing with a local witch, a cook suspected of stealing food for her husband, and the relationship issues of loyal secretary Mma Makutsi. Noting that McCall Smith "renders brisk, seamless tales that are both wry and profound," *Booklist* contributor Allison Brick added of *Blue Shoes and Happiness* that, underlying the swirl of activity, "are eloquent descriptions of the serene African country that holds a special place in his heart." Reviewing *The No. 1 Ladies' Detective Agency,* Christine Jeffords noted in *Best Reviews* online that the author "succeeds in giving his story a lilting, lyrical flavor that makes the reader feel almost as if she is listening to a story being spun by a native tale-teller." *Spectator* critic Anthony Daniels praised him for "creating fictional characters who are decent, goodhearted but not in the least bit dull." "For all their apparent simplicity," Daniels added, "the Precious Ramotswe books are highly sophisticated." Noted Allison Block in *Booklist,* the "No. 1 Ladies' Detective Agency" series serves as McCall Smith's "love letter to a country whose salubrious climate is matched by the warmth and humanity of its people."

Inspired by a commission from the *Scotsman* newspaper to write a serialized novel published five days a week for six months, the first volume of McCall Smith's "44 Scotland Street" series features 800-word chapters and a narrative that was directed by reader input. In *44 Scotland Street* readers meet Pat, a young twenty-something whose life connects with those of the people who share the same Edinburgh boarding house address, as well as the characters she meets at her job in a local art gallery. Noting the popularity of the original serial, a *Publishers Weekly* critic praised the book's "large, well-drawn cast of characters, the intricate plot and the way Smith nimbly jumps from situation to situation" through varying point of view. Discussing the sequel, *Espresso Tales: The Latest from 44 Scotland Street,* another *Publishers Weekly* reviewer noted that the author's "pacing is impeccable: moving his focus from one character to another seamlessly, dropping in just the right amount of description, [and] keeping the talk light and sharp." Noting the book's appeal to young-adult readers due to characters such as Bertie Pollock, a precocious six year old who is being overscheduled by his ambitious yuppie parents, Will Marston wrote in *School Library Journal* that *Espresso Tales* "is a prose poem about the small things in life that are being threatened by globalization and mass entertainment."

Other works by McCall Smith include short-story collections such as *Heavenly Date, and Other Stories* and *The Girl Who Married a Lion, and Other Tales from Africa,* as well as *Dream Angus: The Celtic God of Dreams,* a work described by a *Publishers Weekly* reviewer as "an elegant contemporary reworking" of a Celtic myth about a young god who "presides over love and youth." His other series include the "von Ingelfeld" series as well as the "Sunday Philosophy Club" books, a "whimsical" set of novels in which "murder and moral obligation mingle," according to a *Publishers Weekly* contributor. Featuring Edinburgh-based moral philosopher-turned-detective Isabel Dalhousie, the "Sunday Philosophy Club" installments include *The Right Attitude to Rain* and *Friends, Lovers, Chocolate,* the latter in which a man is troubled by the memories of the donor of his recently implanted heart. *School Library Journal* reviewer Kim Dare noted of the series that McCall Smith's "characters and plots are thoughtful and thought-provoking, and will stay with readers well beyond the final page," as will the novel's vivid Edinburgh setting.

"McCall Smith's greatest gift as a writer . . . is that he can write likeable characters," explained Ruaridh Nicoll, echoing Dare's assessment of the "Sunday Philosophy Club" books while also summarizing the adult mystery novels that comprise the bulk of the author's work. "Kindness, combined with mischievousness, marks his heroines, while his villains are soused in self-importance . . . ," Nicoll added. "He likes foibles and eccentricities and is suspicious of slickness. He is somebody you enjoy spending time with, and that, rightly, makes him a bestseller."

Biographical and Critical Sources

PERIODICALS

Booklist, September 15, 2003, Mary Frances Wilkens, review of *Heavenly Date, and Other Flirtations,* p. 212; August, 2004, Allison Block, review of *The Sunday Philosophy Club,* p. 1872; November 1, 2004, Allison Block, review of *The Girl Who Married a Lion, and Other Tales from Africa,* p. 442; February 1, 2005, Allison Block, review of *In the Company of Cheerful Ladies,* p. 918; April 1, 2005, Allison Block, review of *44 Scotland Yard,* p. 1325; September 1, 2005, Shelle Rosenfeld, review of *Akimbo and the Elephants,* p. 135; July, 2006, Allison Block, review of *Friends, Lovers, Chocolate,* p. 1877; March 1, 2006, Allison Block, review of *Blue Shoes and Happiness,* p. 44; October 1, 2006, Allison Block, review of *The Right Attitude to Rain,* p. 6, and *Dream Angus: The Celtic God of Dreams,* p. 38; March 15, 2007, Allison Block, review of *The Good Husband of Zebra Drive,* p. 4.

Choice, February, 1992, P. Alden, review of *Children of Wax: African Folk Tales,* p. 903; July-August, 1994, M.A. Foley, review of *The Duty to Rescue: The Jurisprudence of Aid,* p. 1792.

Guardian (London, England), January 21, 2003, interview with McCall Smith, p. 8.

Kirkus Reviews, June 15, 1991, review of *Children of Wax,* p. 793; March 15, 2005, review of *44 Scotland Street,* p. 314, and *In the Company of Cheerful Ladies,* p. 12; July 1, 2005, review of *Friends, Lovers, Chocolate,* p. 712; July 15, 2005, review of *Akimbo and the Elephants,* p. 797; May 15, 2006, review of *Espresso Tales: The Latest from 44 Scotland Street,* p. 492.

Library Journal, July, 1991, Patricia Dooley, review of *Children of Wax,* p. 106.

New Statesman, September 6, 2004, Ruaridh Nicoll, "Applied Ethics," p. 52.

New York Times Book Review, January 27, 2002, Alida Becker, "Miss Marple of Botswana," p. 12.

Publishers Weekly, July 22, 2002, Charlotte Abbott, "From Africa, with Love," p. 75; April 25, 2003, review of *Heavenly Date, and Other Flirtations,* p. 38; August 2, 2004, review of *The Sunday Philosophy Club,* p. 51; April 25, 2005, review of *44 Scotland Street,* p. 35; July 18, 2005, review of *Friends, Lovers, Chocolate,* p. 177; September 5, 2005, review of *Akimbo and the Elephants,* p. 63; May 22, 2006, review of *Espresso Tales,* p. 31; August 21, 2006, *Dream Angus,* p. 49; August 28, 2006, review of *The Right Attitude to Rain,* p. 31.

Resource Links, October, 2006, Mavis Holder, review of *The Five Lost Aunts of Harriet Bean,* p. 12; December, 2006, Teresa Hughes, review of *Harriet Bean and the League of Cheats,* p. 20.

School Library Journal, September, 2005, Sheila Janega, review of *In the Company of Cheerful Ladies,* p. 244; November, 2005, Mary N. Oluonye, review of *Akimbo and the Elephants,* p. 108; December, 2005, Kim Dare, review of *Friends, Lovers, Chocolate,* p. 178; November, 2006, Will Marston, review of *Espresso Tales,* p. 171; December, 2006, Kathleen Meulen, review of *The Five Lost Aunts of Harriet Bean,* p. 108; January, 2007, Pat Leach, review of *The Cowgirl Aunt of Harriet Bean,* p. 98.

ONLINE

Alexander McCall Smith Home Page, http://www.AlexanderMcCallSmith.co.uk (June 15, 2007).

Best Reviews Online, http://thebestreviews.com/ (October 4, 2002), review of *The No. 1 Ladies' Detective Agency.*

BookLoons, http://bookloons.com/ (December 12, 2002), G. Hall, review of *The No. 1 Ladies' Detective Agency.**

* * *

McCALL SMITH, Alexander Alasdair
See McCALL SMITH, Alexander

McDONNELL, Patrick 1956-

Personal

Born March 17, 1956, in Elizabeth, NJ; married Karen O'Connell. *Education:* School of Visual Arts, B.F.A., 1978.

Addresses

Home—Edison, NJ.

Career

Cartoonist, animator, and illustrator. Creator of "Mutts" daily syndicated comic strip, 1994—. Creator of animated television commercial for New York Philharmonic, 1993. Guest curator for Charles M. Schulz Museum.

Member

National Cartoonists Society, Charles M. Schulz Museum, Humane Society of the United States (member of board of directors), Fund for Animals (member of board), HSUS Hollywood Office, Art for Animals, Neighborhood Cats, North Shore Animal League.

Awards, Honors

Adamson Statuette, Swedish Academy of Comic Art, 1997; Ark Trust Genesis Award, 1997, 1999; Harvey Award for best comic strip, 1997, 1999, 2001, 2002, 2003, 2005; Reuben Award, National Cartoonist Society, 1997, for comic strip of the year, and 1999, for cartoonist of the year; Max and Moritz Award for best international comic strip, 1998; People for the Ethical Treatment of Animals Humanitarian Award, 2001; HSUS Hollywood Genesis Award, 2002, 2005.

Writings

"MUTTS TREASURY" SERIES

Mutts, foreword by Charles M. Schulz, Andrews McMeel (Kansas City, MO), 1996.

Cats and Dogs: Mutts II, Andrews McMeel (Kansas City, MO), 1997.

More Shtuff, Andrews McMeel (Kansas City, MO), 1998.

Yesh!, Andrews McMeel (Kansas City, MO), 1999.

Mutts Sundays, Andrews McMeel (Kansas City, MO), 1999.

Our Mutts, Andrews McMeel (Kansas City, MO), 2000.

A Little Look-See, Andrews McMeel (Kansas City, MO), 2001.

Sunday Mornings, Andrews McMeel (Kansas City, MO), 2001.

What Now?, Andrews McMeel (Kansas City, MO), 2002.

I Want to Be the Kitty!, Andrews McMeel (Kansas City, MO), 2003.

Sunday Afternoons, Andrews McMeel (Kansas City, MO), 2003.

Dog-eared, Andrews McMeel (Kansas City, MO), 2004.

Who Let the Cat Out?, Andrews McMeel (Kansas City, MO), 2005.

Sunday Evenings, Andrews McMeel (Kansas City, MO), 2005.

Everyday Mutts, Andrews McMeel (Kansas City, MO), 2006.

Animal Friendly, Andrews McMeel (Kansas City, MO), 2007.

FOR CHILDREN; SELF-ILLUSTRATED

The Gift of Nothing, Little, Brown (New York, NY), 2005.

Just like Heaven, Little, Brown (New York, NY), 2006.

Art, Little, Brown (New York, NY), 2006.

Hug Time, Little, Brown (New York, NY), 2007.

OTHER

(With wife Karen O'Connell and Georgia Riley de Havenon) *Krazy Kat: The Comic Art of George Herriman,* Harry N. Abrams (New York, NY), 1986.

Bad Baby (comic-strip collection), Fawcett Columbine (New York, NY), 1988.

(Illustrator) *They Said It!: 200 of the Funniest Sports Quips and Quotes,* Oxmoor House (New York, NY), 2000.

Mutts: The Comic Art of Patrick McDonnell, essay by John Carlin, Harry N. Abrams (New York, NY), 2003.

Illustrator for Russell Baker's "Observer" column, *New York Times Magazine,* 1978-93; creator of *Jerseyana* cartoon for *New Jersey Monthly,* 1980s; creator of "Bad Baby" monthly strip for *Parents* magazine; illustrator for "Scorecard" column in *Sports Illustrated,* "Bright Ideas" in *Parade,* and "Laughter" in *Reader's Digest.*

Sidelights

Patrick McDonnell is the creator of the popular comic strip "Mutts," which appears in more than 700 newspapers worldwide and has garnered a host of awards. The humorous, understated cartoon revolves around the adventures of Earl the dog, Mooch the cat, and a cast of eccentric supporting characters. According to George Gene Gustines, writing in the *New York Times,* "Mutts is a throwback. Its daily tales . . . ooze an archaic innocence (and sometimes an anarchic knowingness) that would not have been out of place in a Sunday comics supplement from the 1920's. It's easy to imagine Earl and Mooch rubbing panels with classic strips like George Herriman's 'Krazy Kat' or E.C. Segar's 'Popeye.'"

Born in 1956, McDonnell attended the School of Visual Arts in New York City, and after graduation he began a career as a freelance illustrator. From 1978 to 1993 he drew Russell Baker's "Observer" column in the *New York Times Magazine,* and he also created "Bad Baby,"

Like its companion volumes, **Cats and Dogs** *collects the strips from Patrick McDonnell's popular "Mutts" comic strip.* (Andrews McMeel, 1997. Illustration © 1997 by Patrick McDonnell. Reproduced with permission.)

a monthly comic strip that ran in *Parents* magazine for ten years. During this time, McDonnell was also a regular contributor to *Sports Illustrated, Reader's Digest, Parade,* and other national magazines.

Despite his tremendous success, McDonnell decided to pursue his dream of writing and illustrating his own comic strip, and in 1994 he created "Mutts." At its heart is the friendship between Earl, the amiable canine who loves belly rubs, and Mooch, the curious feline who obsesses over little pink socks. According to David Astor, writing in *Editor & Publisher,* "McDonnell is not your typical modern-day cartoonist. While many of his peers produce comics with a hip, cynical edge, McDonnell prefers a kinder, gentler, 'stop-and-smell-the-roses' approach." As Astor continued, "McDonnell also bucks the trend of more topicality in comics by trying to keep the 'real world' from entering" his comic-strip fantasy. The animal cast of "Mutts" "think about food, sleep, the weather and other basics of life as they get in and out of all kinds of humorous situations." As McDonnell told *New Jersey Monthly* contributor Annemarie Conte, "a lot of cartoon animals are people in disguise. I want to keep my animals as animal-like as possible."

In addition to seeing his "Mutts" strip appear in daily syndication, McDonnell has produced a number of "Mutts" anthologies, among them *Mutts Sundays* and *Who Let the Cat Out?* He has also produced several children's books featuring the "Mutts" characters. In

Cover illustration of cartoonist McDonnell's self-illustrated picture book **The Gift of Nothing.** (Little, Brown, 2005. Illustration © 2005 by Patrick McDonnell. Mutts © 2005 by Patrick McDonnell, distributed by King Features Syndicate. Reproduced by permission.)

The Gift of Nothing, for example, McDonnell creates "a perfect meditation on gift giving and friendship," according to a critic in *Kirkus Reviews,* In the book, Mooch tries to find the perfect present for Earl on his special day. When readers reunite with Mooch in the pages of *Just like Heaven,* he awakens from a nap just as a fog rolls in and mistakenly believes he has arrived in Heaven. "The small, sketchy illustrations hold a great deal of charm," observed *School Library Journal* reviewer Julie Roach. McDonnell is also the author of *Art,* a self-illustrated work about a young boy's penchant for creating fanciful doodles, scribbles, and splotches. "The primary color illustrations are exuberant and joyful and seamlessly match the text," wrote a contributor in *Kirkus Reviews.*

A strong advocate for animal welfare, McDonnell serves on the board of directors for the Humane Society of the United States. "People really identify with that special bond we all have with our animal companions," the cartoonist and author remarked on the *King Features* Web site. "Animals have unique personalities all their own. In *Mutts,* I try to express the world from their point of view."

Biographical and Critical Sources

BOOKS

McDonnell, Patrick, *Mutts: The Comic Art of Patrick McDonnell,* essay by John Carlin, Harry N. Abrams (New York, NY), 2003.

PERIODICALS

Booklist, April 1, 2006, Gillian Engberg, review of *Art,* p. 48.

Childhood Education, fall, 2006, May Anne Hannibal, review of *Art,* p. 51.

Editor & Publisher, November 16, 1996, David Astor, "It's Reigning a Cat and Dog in Hit Strip," p. 40; February 1, 2004, Dave Astor, "Syndicates: Art Book Showcases Artistic *Mutts* strip."

Kirkus Reviews, September 15, 2005, review of *The Gift of Nothing,* p. 1030; March 15, 2006, review of *Art,* p. 296; September 15, 2006, review of *Just like Heaven,* p. 961.

New Jersey Monthly, April, 2006, Annemarie Conte, "His Name Is Earl."

New York Times, September 25, 2005, George Gene Gustines, "Where the Mild Things Are."

Publishers Weekly, November 21, 2005, review of *The Gift of Nothing,* p. 46; August 28, 2006, review of *Just like Heaven,* p. 52.

School Library Journal, January, 2006, Marianne Saccardi, review of *The Gift of Nothing,* p. 108; April, 2006, Marianne Saccardi, review of *Art,* p. 129; November, 2006, Julie Roach review of *Just like Heaven,* p. 105.

ONLINE

King Features Web site, http://www.kingfeatures.com/ (May 10, 2007), "Patrick McDonnell."

Patrick McDonnell Home Page, http://muttscomics.com (May 10, 2007).*

*   *   *

MONTHEI, Betty
(Betty Jane Sanders)

Personal

Married; husband's name Lee. *Hobbies and other interests:* Walking, SCUBA diving, drawing, painting, photography, sewing, reading.

Addresses

Home—AK. *Agent*—The Chudney Agency, 750 Kappock St., Ste. 808, Riverdale, NY 10463.

Career

Children's book author.

Writings

Looking for Normal, HarperCollins (New York, NY), 2005.

Contributor to *Alaska Women Write: Living, Laughing, and Loving on the Last Frontier,* edited by Dana Stabenow. Also author of romance novels *Marriage Is Just the Beginning* and *His Secret Son,* both under pseudonym Betty Jane Sanders.

Sidelights

Raised in the Pacific Northwest, Betty Monthei grew up with a love of writing. Beginning her career writing for adults, she published two romance novels under the pen name Betty Jane Sanders before turning her attention to younger readers. Monthei's young-adult novel *Looking for Normal* features a compelling story about a brother and sister whose world is rocked by a family tragedy when their father murders their mother and then kills himself.

Annie is twelve years old when her father's violent act makes her and her brother, Ted, orphans. Unfortunately, after the siblings move in with their grandparents, they find themselves once again embroiled in domestic abuse. Annie struggles to understand the reasons behind the violence, and attempts to let go of her hatred and forgive even those who have hurt her. "Annie's voice rings honest and true throughout as she searches for a normal life," wrote a *Kirkus Reviews* contributor. In another review of *Looking for Normal,* B. Allison Gray noted in *School Library Journal* that the author "is superb at describing the characters' moods and the oppression caused by sadness, fear, and shock." According to *Booklist* critic Cindy Dobrez, "Monthei writes a sensitive, poignant novel about dealing with the impact of just such horrific loss."

Biographical and Critical Sources

PERIODICALS

Booklist, June 1, 2005, Cindy Dobrez, review of *Looking for Normal,* p. 1813.

Children's Bookwatch, November, 2005, review of *Looking for Normal.*

Kirkus Reviews, March 1, 2005, review of *Looking for Normal,* p. 292.

School Library Journal, April, 2005, B. Allison Gray, review of *Looking for Normal,* p. 137.

ONLINE

Betty Monthei Home Page, http://www.bettymonthei.com (May 17, 2007).*

*   *   *

MONTIJO, Rhode

Personal

Male. *Education:* California College of Arts and Crafts, B.F.A., 1995.

Addresses

Home and office—Oakland, CA. *E-mail*—rhode@rhode-montijo.com.

Career

Author, illustrator, and creator of comic books.

Writings

SELF-ILLUSTRATED

Cloud Boy, Simon & Schuster Books for Young Readers (New York, NY), 2006.

Also author and illustrator of *Pablo's Inferno* comic-book series.

ILLUSTRATOR

Greg Trine, *The Curse of the Bologna Swandwich,* Henry Holt (New York, NY), 2006.
Greg Trine, *The Grateful Fred,* Henry Holt (New York, NY), 2006.
Greg Trine, *The Revenge of the McNasty Brothers,* Henry Holt (New York, NY), 2006.
Vicky Rubin, *The Three Swingin' Pigs,* Henry Holt (New York, NY), 2007.
Greg Trine, *The Fake Caper Caper,* Henry Holt (New York, NY), 2007.
Greg Trine, *Terror in Tights,* Henry Holt (New York, NY), 2007.

Biographical and Critical Sources

PERIODICALS

Kirkus Reviews, February 1, 2006, review of *Cloud Boy,* p. 134; June 1, 2006, review of *The Curse of the Bologna Sandwich,* p. 581.
Library Media Connection, February, 2007, Liz Deskins, review of *The Curse of the Bologna Sandwich,* p. 62.
Publishers Weekly, May 8, 2006, review of *Cloud Boy,* p. 64; July 31, 2006, review of *The Curse of the Bologna Sandwich,* p. 75.
School Library Journal, April, 2006, Roxanne Burg, review of *Cloud Boy,* p. 114; May, 2006, Rebecca Sheridan, review of *The Curse of the Bologna Sandwich,* p. 106; December, 2006, Adrienne Furness, review of *The Grateful Fred,* p. 116.
U.S. News & World Report, July 3, 2006, Vicky Hallett, "Books to Battle Brain Freeze," p. 64.

ONLINE

Rhode Montijo Home Page, http://www.rhodemontijo.com (May 26, 2007).*

MORRIS, Jennifer E. 1969-

Personal

Born January 31, 1969, in Union City, PA; daughter of Thomas Harvey and Molly Marsh; married Michael Morris; children: Robin Elizabeth, Leo Michael. *Education:* University of Pittsburgh, B.S. (computer science), 1990; Stevens Institute of Technology, M.S. (computer science), 1995. *Hobbies and other interests:* Sewing, gardening, cooking.

Addresses

Home—Lunenburg, MA. *Agent*—Carrie Hannigan, Russell & Volkening, 50 W. 29th St., New York, NY 10001. *E-mail*—jemorris@jemorris.com.

Career

Digital illustrator and designer. AT & T, software developer, 1991-95; CHS, senior software engineer, 1995-97; database consultant, 1997-98; graphic designer; freelance author and illustrator, 1998—.

Member

Society of Children's Book Writers and Illustrators.

Awards, Honors

Louie Awards, National Stationery Show, 2000, 2001, 2005; four Society of Children's Book Writers and Illustrators (SCBWI) illustration contest honors, 2005-06; New England SCBWI Conference Portfolio Exhibition Merit Award, 2006; Maryland Library Association Blue Crab Young Readers Award Honor Book designation, 2006, for *May I Please Have a Cookie?;* SCBWI Don Freeman memorial grant, 2007.

Writings

PICTURE BOOKS

(Self-illustrated) *May I Please Have a Cookie?,* Scholastic (New York, NY), 2005.
(Illustrator) Jean Marie Cochran, *If a Monkey Jumps on Your School Bus,* Pleasant St. Press, 2007.

Sidelights

Jennifer E. Morris told *SATA:* "Growing up in the small town of Bradford, Pennsylvania, I loved to draw. As an only child, I spent many hours entertaining myself drawing and looking through picture books. I was not a prolific reader as a child, but I would spend hours pouring over the illustrations. And from the time I was about six years old I wanted to become an artist myself.

"In college computer science seemed like the more practical major, but I took every art class I could, including a summer studying at the Chautauqua Institute. Even

Jennifer E. Morris brings to life a close family relationship in her self-illustrated picture book **May I Please Have a Cookie?** (Cartwheel Books, 2005. Reproduced by permission.)

after college when I went to work as a computer software developer, I always made time for art and I never lost my love of picture books. When my daughter was born, I took the opportunity to leave my computer career and pursue my artistic passions more seriously.

"At first, I created my artwork using traditional media (watercolors, acrylics, and colored pencil). But my background in computers and technology made the jump to digital media a logical progression. I find the computer gives me a freedom to experiment with color and composition that I never experienced with paint and paper. Although my work always starts with pencil drawings, I now use the computer to create my final paintings.

"My children, Robin and Leo, are the biggest inspiration for my work. The main character in my picture book *May I Please Have a Cookie?*, the cookie-loving alligator named Alfie, shares my children's love of sweets and their flair for the dramatic. I also see a lot of myself in Alfie's exasperated mother.

"To me, creating characters and stories that children can relate to and enjoy is nothing short of magical. And when a child says they enjoy my stories or even that they wish they could meet one of my characters, I feel that I've really accomplished something important."

Biographical and Critical Sources

PERIODICALS

Booklist, January 1, 2006, Hazel Rochman, review of *May I Please Have a Cookie?,* p. 118.

ONLINE

Jennifer E. Morris Home Page, http://www.jemorris.com (June 15, 2007).

*   *   *

MORTENSEN, Denise Dowling

Personal

Born in Garden City, NY; married; husband's name Scott; children: Erin, Brian, Andrew, Katie, Patrick. *Education:* St. Bonaventure University, B.S. (journalism). *Hobbies and other interests:* Gardening, reading.

Addresses

Home and office—Chatham, NJ. *E-mail*—info@denisemortensen.com.

Career

Children's book author, copyeditor, and proofreader. CBS News, New York, NY, member of staff; Condé Nast Publications, New York, NY, member of editorial staff.

Writings

PICTURE BOOKS

Good Night Engines, illustrated by Melissa Iwai, Clarion Books (New York, NY), 2003.
Ohio Thunder, illustrated by Kate Kiesler, Clarion Books (New York, NY), 2006.
Wake Up Engines, illustrated by Melissa Iwai, Clarion Books (New York, NY), 2007.

Biographical and Critical Sources

PERIODICALS

Booklist, December 15, 2003, Hazel Rochman, review of *Good Night Engines,* p. 754; April 15, 2006, Carolyn Phelan, review of *Ohio Thunder,* p. 54.
Kirkus Reviews, October 15, 2003, review of *Good Night Engines,* p. 1274; April 15, 2006, review of *Ohio Thunder,* p. 412.

Library Media Connection, August-September, 2006, Judith Beavers, review of *Ohio Thunder,* p. 84.

Publishers Weekly, November 3, 2003, review of *Good Night Engines,* p. 72.

School Library Journal, December, 2003, Shawn Brommer, review of *Good Night Engines,* p. 121; May, 2006, Kathy Piehl, review of *Ohio Thunder,* p. 96.

ONLINE

Denise Dowling Mortensen Home Page, http://www.denisemortensen.com (May 26, 2007).*

* * *

MOZELLE, Shirley

Personal

Female.

Addresses

Home and office—Jacksonville, FL.

Career

Children's book author.

Writings

Zack's Alligator, illustrated by James Watts, Harper & Row (New York, NY), 1989.

Zack's Alligator Goes to School, illustrated by James Watts, HarperCollins (New York, NY), 1994.

The Pig Is in the Pantry, the Cat Is on the Shelf, illustrated by Jennifer Plecas, Clarion (New York, NY), 2000.

The Bear Upstairs, illustrated by Doug Cushman, Holt (New York, NY), 2005.

The Kitchen Talks: Poems, illustrated by Petra Mathers, Holt (New York, NY), 2006.

Sidelights

Shirley Mozelle began her career as a writer for young children with the "I Can Read" titles *Zack's Alligator* and *Zack's Alligator Goes to School,* both of which feature the misadventures of Bridget the Alligator. She is also the author of picture books for young readers as well as a collection of poetry for the very young.

In *The Pig Is in the Pantry, the Cat Is on the Shelf* Mozelle tells the story of a farmer who leaves his house unlocked when he goes to town. When he returns, the man discovers that all of the animals on the farm have made themselves at home inside. Using "repetitive description, lots of numbers and animal sounds, plus a gentle tone," a reviewer for *Publishers Weekly* explained that Mozelle's book is designed to appeal to the "very young." While noting that the story is sometimes difficult to follow, Christine Lindsey wrote in *School Library Journal* that *The Pig Is in the Pantry, the Cat Is on the Shelf* is "filled with alliteration, animal antics, and opportunities to count and tell time." *Booklist* critic Connie Fletcher deemed the tale "a rollicking story line, filled with wordplay, animal noises, counting drills, and silly songs."

Valuing diversity and befriending people with different likes and dislikes are the themes of *The Bear Upstairs.* A writer bear is irritated when a noisy new neighbor moves in, banging and clanging throughout the day and disturbing her work. When she finally goes up to speak with him, she realizes that the clumsy neighbor is more than what she expected: he is a chef, and a huge fan of her cookbook. From her recipe, the chef creates an omelet that the two neighbors share together. "It's a familiar tale, but the message is upbeat," wrote a contributor to *Publishers Weekly,* while *School Library Journal* contributor Wendy Woodfill explained that Mozelle's "subtle message of acceptance and tolerance is conveyed with humor and wit and will surely strike a chord with many readers."

In *The Kitchen Talks: Poems* Mozelle includes twenty short poems that provide the perspective of familiar kitchen objects, from the refrigerator to the toaster. Teresa Pfeifer, reviewing the collection for *School Library Journal,* found the book to be "a playful take on commonplace objects," while Hazel Rochman wrote in *Booklist* that Mozelle's verses are "wonderful for reading aloud."

Biographical and Critical Sources

PERIODICALS

Booklist, August, 2000, Connie Fletcher, review of *The Pig Is in the Pantry, the Cat Is on the Shelf,* p. 2149; March 15, 2006, Hazel Rochman, review of *The Kitchen Talks: Poems,* p. 49.

Kirkus Reviews, August 1, 2005, review of *The Bear Upstairs,* p. 855; March 1, 2006, review of *The Kitchen Talks,* p. 236.

Publishers Weekly, March 27, 2000, review of *The Pig Is in the Pantry, the Cat Is on the Shelf,* p. 79; October 24, 2005, review of *The Bear Upstairs,* p. 56.

School Library Journal, May, 2000, Christine Lindsey, review of *The Pig Is in the Pantry, the Cat Is on the Shelf,* p. 150; November, 2005, Wendy Woodfill, review of *The Bear Upstairs,* p. 102; April, 2006, Teresa Pfeifer, review of *The Kitchen Talks,* p. 130.

ONLINE

Harper Collins Web site, http://www.harpercollins.com/ (May 18, 2007), "Sharon Mozelle."

Houghton Mifflin Web site, http://www.houghtonmifflinbooks.com/ (May 18, 2007), "Sharon Mozelle."*

O-P

OROZCO, José-Luis 1948-

Personal

Born May 6, 1948, in Mexico City, Distrito Federal, Mexico; immigrated to United States, c. 1967; children: four children. *Education:* University of California, Berkeley, B.A.; University of San Francisco, M.A.

Addresses

Home—P.O. Box 461900, Los Angeles, CA 90046. *E-mail*—info@joseluisorozco.com.

Career

Author, songwriter, and performer. Recordings include *Lirica Infantil: Latin-American Children's Music* (thirteen volumes), and *José-Luis Orozco canta 160 años de corrido mexicano y chicano,* 1981. Speaker and consultant at conferences and seminars.

Awards, Honors

Congressional Hispanic Caucus honor, 2003.

Writings

FOR CHILDREN

(Selector, arranger, and translator) *De Colores, and Other Latin-American Folk Songs for Children*, illustrated by Elisa Kleven, Dutton (New York, NY), 1994.

(Selector, arranger, and translator) *Diez deditos: Ten Little Fingers, and Other Play Rhymes and Action Songs from Latin America,* illustrated by Elisa Kleven, Dutton (New York, NY), 1997.

(Selector, arranger, and translator) *Fiestas: A Year of Latin-American Songs of Celebration* (includes compact disc), illustrated by Elisa Kleven, Dutton (New York, NY), 2002.

José-Luis Orozco (Photograph courtesy of Jose-Luis Orozco.)

Cantamos y apprendemos con José-Luis Orozco/Singing and Learning with José-Luis Orozco (DVD), 2003.

Rin, Rin, Rin . . . Do, Re, Mi: libro ilustrado en español e inglés: A Picture Book in Spanish and English, illustrated by David Diaz, Orchard Books (New York, NY), 2005.

Sidelights

José-Luis Orozco has built a successful career doing what he truly enjoys: singing for children. In addition to recording the thirteen-volume song collection *Lirica Infantil: Latin-American Children's Music,* he has written several books weaving story and song, as well as producing *Fiestas: A Year of Latin-American Songs of Celebration,* which contains an accompanying compact

David Diaz's folk-style artwork captures the sights and sounds of Orozco's bilingual picture book **Rin, Rin, Rin . . . Do, Re, Mi.** (Orchard Books, 2005. Illustration © 2005 by David Diaz. Reproduced by permission of Scholastic Inc.)

disc. Born in Mexico City, Mexico, Orozco learned many traditional songs from his paternal grandmother. At age eight, he joined the Mexico City Boys Choir, and toured with them throughout Europe, the Caribbean, and Central and South America. From his tour around the world, he gained the fascination for different cultures that would inspire his adult career. In an acknowledgment of Orozco's work promoting Latin culture among young people, the author and musician was invited to participate in the 2003 National Book Festival organized by First Lady Laura Bush.

Fiestas contains bilingual versions of over twenty celebration songs and rhymes gathered from a number of Spanish-speaking countries, allowing young listeners to celebrate with music throughout the year, while *De Colores, and Other Latin-American Folk Songs for Children* contains twenty-seven folk songs that *Booklist* reviewer Annie Ayres dubbed "truly a musical treasure." Also featuring a Latin flavor, the animated DVD *Cantamos y apprendemos con José-Luis Orozco/Singing and Learning with José-Luis Orozco* also motivates children to learn about the Spanish language and the rich tradition of Latin-American children's music. Noting the value of *Fiestas* in teaching Spanish to younger children, a *Kirkus Reviews* contributor maintained that "Orozco's community activism and social beliefs are demonstrated throughout the . . . attractive songbook."

Horn Book contributor Maeve Visser Knoth described *De Colores, and Other Latin-American Folk Songs for Children* as a "lovely and useful resource [that] will have children and adults singing, clapping, and dancing along," while Rudine Sims Bishop added in the same periodical that the book "can serve to enrich and expand the musical repertoire of children and teachers alike."

In the bilingual *Rin, Rin, Rin . . . Do, Re, Mi: libro ilustrado en español e inglés: A Picture Book in Spanish and English* Orozco tells the story of a young boy who enjoys counting, singing, practicing the alphabet, and reading with other members of his family. Featuring illustrations by award-winning illustrator David Diaz, the book was designed to build literacy skills among Latino children. Praising the book's "powerful, arresting" art by Diaz, *School Library Journal* contributor Maria Otero-Boisvert dubbed *Rin, Rin, Rin . . . Do, Re, Mi* a "romping, rhyming picture book."

Biographical and Critical Sources

PERIODICALS

Booklist, December 15, 1994, Annie Ayres, review of *De Colores, and Other Latin-American Folk Songs for Children,* p. 750; January 1, 1998, Karen Morgan, re-

view of *Diez dedidos: Ten Little Fingers, and Other Play Rhymes and Action Songs from Latin America,* p. 819; September 15, 2002, Linda Perkins, review of *Fiestas: A Year of Latin-American Songs of Celebration,* p. 229.

Bulletin of the Center for Children's Books, March, 1998, review of *Diez dedidos,* p. 254.

Hispanic, June-July, 2005, Ambar Hernandez, review of *Rin, Rin, Rin . . . Do, Re, Mi: libro ilustrado en español e inglés: A Picture Book in Spanish and English,* p. 68.

Horn Book, January-February, 1995, Maeve Visser Knoth, review of *De Colores, and Other Latin-American Folk Songs for Children,* p. 66; May-June, 1995, Rudine Sims Bishop, review of *De Colores, and Other Latin-American Folk Songs for Children,* p. 316; March-April, 1998, Elena Abos, review of *Diez dedidos,* p. 231.

Kirkus Reviews, September 1, 2002, review of *Fiestas,* p. 131; May 1, 2005, review of *Rin, Rin, Rin . . . Do, Re, Mi,* p. 543.

Publishers Weekly, December 8, 1997, review of *Diez dedidos,* p. 819; August 23, 1999, review of *De Colores, and Other Latin-American Folk Songs for Children,* p. 61.

School Library Journal, November, 2002, Ann Welton, review of *Fiestas,* p. 153: June, 2003, Maria Otero-Boisvert, review of *Fiestas,* p. 71; February, 2006, Maria Otero-Boisvert, review of *Rin, Rin, Rin . . . Do, Re, Mi,* p. 127.

ONLINE

José-Luis Orozco Home Page, http://www.joseluisorozco.com (May 21, 2007).*

*   *   *

PARR, Todd 1962-

Personal

Born 1962, in WY.

Addresses

Home—San Francisco, CA. *E-mail*—todd@toddparr.com.

Career

Children's book illustrator and author, and graphic artist. Commercial artist, with licensed designs appearing on clothing, toys, and furniture items. Creator of television program *ToddWorld,* airing on Discovery Kids Channel, beginning 2002. Active in reading programs through Reach Out and Read vand others. *Exhibitions:* Work exhibited at FAO Schwartz, New York, NY, and San Francisco, CA.

Todd Parr (Photograph courtesy of Jerry Giovanini.)

Awards, Honors

National Publication Awards Honors Book designation, 1999, for *This Is My Hair;* Daytime Academy Award nominations, 2005, 2006, 2007 for Outstanding Children's Animated Program, and 2007, for Original Song, all for *ToddWorld.*

Writings

SELF-ILLUSTRATED PICTURE BOOKS

Do's and Don'ts, Little, Brown (Boston, MA), 1999.
This Is My Hair, Little, Brown (Boston, MA), 1999.
The Okay Book, Little, Brown (Boston, MA), 1999.
Things That Make You Feel Good/Things That Make You Feel Bad, Little, Brown (Boston, MA), 1999.
The Best Friends Book, Little, Brown (Boston, MA), 2000.
Underwear Do's and Don'ts, Little, Brown (Boston, MA), 2000.
Zoo Do's and Don'ts, Little, Brown (Boston, MA), 2000.
The Feelings Book, Little, Brown (Boston, MA), 2000.
Big and Little (board book), Little, Brown (Boston, MA), 2001.
Black and White (board book), Little, Brown (Boston, MA), 2001.
It's Okay to Be Different, Little, Brown (Boston, MA), 2001.
My Really Cool Baby Book, Little, Brown (Boston, MA), 2001.
The Daddy Book, Little, Brown (Boston, MA), 2002.
The Mommy Book, Little, Brown (Boston, MA), 2002.
The Feel Good Book, Little, Brown (Boston, MA), 2002.
Funny Faces, Little, Brown (Boston, MA), 2002.
Going Places, Little, Brown (Boston, MA), 2002.

Otto Goes to School, Little, Brown (Boston, MA), 2003.
Otto Goes to Bed, Little, Brown (Boston, MA), 2003.
Otto Goes to the Beach, Little, Brown (Boston, MA), 2003.
Otto Goes to Camp, Little, Brown (Boston, MA), 2004.
Otto Has a Birthday Party, Little, Brown (Boston, MA), 2004.
The Peace Book, Little, Brown (Boston, MA), 2004.
Who's Your Best Friend?, LB Kids, Brown (New York, NY), 2005.
Let's Play Together, Little, Brown (Boston, MA), 2005.
Reading Makes You Feel Good, Little, Brown (New York, NY), 2005.
The Grandma Book, Little, Brown (New York, NY), 2006.
The Grandpa Book, Little, Brown (New York, NY), 2006.
It's a Colorful World, Little, Brown (New York, NY), 2006.
Giant Book of Friendship Fun! (interactive book), LB Kids (New York, NY), 2006.
Todd's Silly Book of Shapes, Little, Brown (New York, NY), 2006.
We Belong Together: A Book about Adoption and Families, Little, Brown (New York, NY), 2007.

Also author of *Be Hospitable,* privately published c. 2006, as part of a marketing campaign for Hilton Family of Hotels.

Parr's books have been translated into several languages, including Japanese, Spanish, French, Korean, Hebrew, Portuguese, and Dutch.

Adaptations

ToddWorld, a twenty-six-episode television series based on Parr's books, was developed for broadcast in 2002. Several novelty books were adapted from the series, and from Parr's work, by YAY! Design, among them *Stella's Different Ears, A Dog's Day,* and *Lights out, Todd!*

Sidelights

With engaging titles such as *Underwear Do's and Don'ts, The Okay Book,* and *Giant Book of Friendship Fun!,* the toddler-friendly books created by author/illustrator Todd Parr feature bright, saturated colors and graphic, heavily outlined shapes. While each of his books reflect Parr's childlike sense of whimsy, they also address difficult concepts, as in *The Peace Book,* which shrinks an abstract concept into child-friendly terms. Noting each volume's diminutive size and simple texts, *Children's Book Review Service* contributor Leanne D. Grace characterized Parr's literary output as "small books containing big ideas," while in *School Library Journal* Christy Norris Blanchette praised the author's "reassuring and kindhearted lessons." In a *Bookpage.com* interview, Parr explained that he includes three main ingredients in each of his popular books: "bright colors, bold lines, with simple feel-good messages about believing in yourself and being different."

Raised in Wyoming, Parr loved to draw as a child, and art class ranked as the best part of the school day. His two favorite books while growing up were *Green Eggs and Ham* by Dr. Seuss and both *Go, Dog, Go!* and *Are You My Mother?* by P.D. Eastman inspired his decision to become a children's book author and illustrator in the late 1990s. The same quirky humor used by Seuss and Eastman is embodied in Parr's own picture books, which a *Publishers Weekly* contributor characterized as "whimsical" and "upbeat" combinations of "advice and silliness." "One of my first book reviews said an actual child drew the illustrations," Parr recalled in an interview with Chris Mills for *Instructor* magazine. "At the time, I thought it was so embarrassing. I was wrecked. But I've really come to appreciate that comment over the years, because I think it's why kids relate so well to me and my books."

Parr's board books, in particular, are popular with the toddler set. In the titles *Black and White* and *Big and Little* his high-contrast illustrations help teach even the youngest toddler a basic concept using what a *Publishers Weekly* contributor characterized, in a review of *Black and White* as a "signature bold black line" that "pops from neon-bright pages." His "Otto" series, about a yellow puppy with one blue ear, also engages young page-turners with gentle stories full of toddler appeal. In *Otto Goes to Bed,* the puppy prepares for bed by barking at the moon, and in *Otto Goes to the Beach* he makes new friends during a trip to the seashore, among them a crabby crab, a condescending kitty, and a purple poodle sporting a bright pink hairstyle. *Otto Goes to School* finds the happy puppy fueling up with a banana-split breakfast before boarding the bus for his first day of school. While gaining an important lesson in safe tail-wagging, the likeable Otto gives children "support for a new experience," according to *Booklist* contributor Ilene Cooper. In *School Library Journal* Melinda Piehler predicted that the "Otto" books "will charm adults and children alike."

An early example of Parr's penchant for fun is *This Is My Hair,* which showcases the many things a child's hair can do, from blowing in the breeze to becoming flattened by a hat to being pulled back tight in pigtails. In addition to discussing hairstyle variations from short to long, Parr veers off into the world of the totally absurd by suggesting "It's okay to put fish in your hair," thereby winning the hearts of toddlers everywhere. "Best friends will let you make dinner for them even if you serve spaghetti and worms," Parr suggests in *The Best Friends Book.* A *Kirkus Reviews* writer praised *This Is My Hair* for both its "uplifting" conclusion and Parr's humorous illustrations. Calling *The Best Friends Book* "truly witty," another *Kirkus Reviews* contributor praised the author's "cheerfully, deliberately formulaic" approach, and added that the rules and advice Parr imparts in this book will be "of importance to children."

Parr's characteristic round-headed, smiling cartoon children make books such as **This Is My Hair** ***so appealing to the toddler set.*** (Little, Brown & Company, 1999. Reproduced by permission.)

Writing in *School Library Journal,* Olga R. Barnes also praised Parr's bright, stick-figure art and predicted that story-time participants will "laugh out loud" at the author/illustrator's "tongue-in-cheek" text.

While humor injects itself into all Parr's work, several of his books weave serious themes in with the fun. In *It's Okay to Be Different,* for example, a bright purple

elephant reminds toddlers that "It's okay to have a different nose," adding its voice to the diverse animal menagerie that give voice to childhood insecurities ranging from being in an embarrassing situation to having a visible disability. *The Family Book* broke new ground by including children growing up with same-sex parents, while *The Feel Good Book* promotes compassion, curiosity, and optimism. *Reading Makes You Feel Good*

touts the many joys to be found in books. Effective in its intent, *It's Okay to Be Different* is useful "for beginning a discussion on mutual respect," in the opinion of *School Library Journal* contributor Adele Greenlee, while a *Publishers Weekly* critic wrote that the book "focuses on acceptance and individuality and encourages readers to do the same." In a similar fashion, *The Family Book* "documents differences matter-of-factly," according to a *School Library Journal* critic, and *The Feel Good Book* was described as the "perfect pick-me-up for any child who is having a bad day" by *School*

Library Journal reviewer Linda Ludke. *Reading Makes You Feel Good* contains a "worthy message" paired with artwork featuring "rich colors and neatly drawn, thick-lined simplicity," according to *Booklist* contributor John Peters. In *School Library Journal,* Suzanne Myers Harold noted that Parr's inclusion of "fun details" and multi-colored animal characters "encourage children and adults to move beyond the text and discuss the pictures together," thereby strengthening each book's value.

Parr designs board books such as **The Silly Book of Shapes** ***to be perfect for toddler-sized hands.*** (Little, Brown, 2006. Illustration © 2006 by Todd Parr. Reproduced by permission.)

Parr shares the unique relationship children have with doting relatives in works such as **The Grandpa Book.** (Little, Brown, 2006. Illustration © 2006 by Todd Parr. Reproduced by permission.)

Designed to help young children record their growing-up years, *My Really Cool Baby Book* reflects the diversity among modern families, such as blended families and single-parent families. Along with a colorful growth chart, the book contains stickers, checklists, question-naires, photo pages, and fill-in-the-blank sections that help children and parents record the years from infancy to toddlerdom and beyond. Not only "first word" but "first burp" are included in a work a *Publishers Weekly* contributor praised for featuring Parr's characteristic "signature neon-bright colors, energetic humor, . . . and consideration of children's feelings." Families are also the focus of *The Grandma Book* and *The Grandpa Book,* which help children distinguish the many inter-esting and often amazing traits most loving grandpar-ents share, as well as *The Mommy Book* and *The Daddy Book.*

Parr, who lives and works in San Francisco, California, with his dog, Bully, enjoys his popularity as a chil-dren's book author and illustrator, and makes time in his schedule to attend the book tours that allow him to meet his many young fans. In addition to his "book work," he is a successful commercial designer whose artwork appears on everything from backpacks to toys and bath accessories. His books, which are enjoyed by children all around the world, from England and Aus-tralia to the Netherlands and Japan, have also inspired

Parr to create the animated television program, *ToddWorld*, which follows the adventures of a blue-faced seven year old named Todd who shares a fantasy world with talking animals and demonstrates the importance of tolerance and the benefits of diversity.

Biographical and Critical Sources

BOOKS

Parr, Todd, *This Is My Hair*, Little, Brown (Boston, MA), 1999.

Parr, Todd, *The Best Friends Book*, Little, Brown (Boston, MA), 2000.

Parr, Todd, *It's Okay to Be Different*, Little, Brown (Boston, MA), 2001.

PERIODICALS

Advocate, April 25, 2006, P.J. Gray, "Family Guy," p. 60.

Booklist, August, 2005, Ilene Cooper, review of *Otto Goes to School*, p. 2042; December 1, 2005, John Peters, review of *Reading Makes You Feel Good*, p. 55.

Children's Book Review Service, April, 1999, Leanne D. Grace, review of *The Okay Book, Do's and Don'ts, This Is My Hair*, and *Things That Make You Feel Good/Things That Make You Feel Bad*, p. 102.

Instructor, March-April, 2007, Chris Mills, interview with Parr, p. 72.

Kirkus Reviews, March 15, 1999, review of *This Is My Hair*, p. 454; January 15, 2000, review of *The Best Friends Book*, p. 122; September 1, 2001, review of *It's Okay to Be Different*, p. 1298; March 15, 2006, review of *The Grandpa Book*, p. 298.

Publishers Weekly, April 5, 1999, review of *The Okay Book*, p. 243; October 2, 2000, review of *Underwear Do's and Don'ts*, p. 83; April 2, 2001, review of *My Really Cool Baby Book*, p. 66; April 23, 2001, review of *Black and White*, p. 80; August 27, 2001, review of *It's Okay to Be Different*, p. 83.

School Library Journal, May, 1999, Christy Norris Blanchette, review of *Do's and Don'ts, The Okay Book, Things That Make You Feel Good/Things That Make You Feel Bad*, and *This Is My Hair*, p. 94; August, 2000, Olga R. Barnes, review of *The Best Friends Book* and *Zoo Do's and Don'ts*, p. 162; December, 2000, Holly Belli, review of *The Feelings Book* and *Underwear Do's and Don'ts*, pp. 122-123; October, 2001, Adele Greenlee, review of *It's Okay to Be Different*, p. 128; May, 2002, Shawn Brommer, review of *The Daddy Book* and *The Mommy Book*, p. 124; October, 2002, Linda Ludke, review of *The Feel Good Book*, p. 125; July, 2003, Melinda Piehler, review of *Otto Goes to Bed* and *Otto Goes to the Beach*, p. 146; December, 2003, Marilyn Taniguchi, review of *The Family Book*, p. 122; October, 2004, Olga R. Kuharets, review of *Otto Has a Birthday Party*, p. 126; November, 2004, Blair Christolon, review of *The Peace Book*, p. 114; September, 2005, Marge Loch-

Wouters, review of *Otto Goes to School*, and Suzanne Myers Harold, review of *Reading Makes You Feel Good*, p. 184; April, 2006, Linda Staskus, review of *The Grandma Book*, p. 115.

ONLINE

Bookpage.com, http://www.bookpage.com/ (February 4, 2002), interview with Parr.

Todd Parr Home Page, http://www.toddparr.com (May 20, 2007).*

* * *

PAYNE, C.F. 1956-
(Chris Fox Payne)

Personal

Born 1956, in Cincinnati, OH; married; wife's name Paula; children: Trevor, Evan. *Education:* Miami University (OH), B.F.A., 1976; postgraduate study at Illustrators Workshop.

Addresses

Home—Cincinnati, OH. *E-mail*—cfoxpayne@yahoo.com.

Career

Artist and illustrator. Worked for design studios in Akron, OH, and Chicago, IL, c. late 1970s; freelance illustrator, 1980—. Instructor at East Texas State University, Miami University, OH, and Syracuse University; Columbus College of Art and Design, Columbus, OH, chair of illustration department. Illustrators Partnership of America, founding member and member of board. *Exhibitions:* Work has been exhibited in numerous galleries, including National Portrait Gallery, Washington, DC; Norman Rockwell Museum, Stockbridge, MA; and Cincinnati Art Museum (solo show), Cincinnati, OH.

Member

Society of Illustrators (museum committee chair), Art Directors Club of Cincinnati (president, 1996).

Awards, Honors

Hamilton King Award, Gold Funny Bone, and gold and silver medals, all from Society of Illustrators; awards from *Communication Arts, Step-by-Step Graphics, Print*, and *How* magazines, and from Society of Publication Designers.

Writings

ILLUSTRATOR

Wayne W. Martin, *The Gospel of Mark: A New Translation for Children*, Upper Room (Nashville, TN), 1984.

Valerie Tripp, *Meet Molly: An American Girl,* Pleasant Company (Madison, WI), 1986.

Valerie Tripp, *Molly's Surprise: A Christmas Story,* Pleasant Company (Madison, WI), 1986.

Valerie Tripp, *Molly Learns a Lesson: A School Story,* Pleasant Company (Madison, WI), 1986.

Marissa Moss, *True Heart,* Silver Whistle (San Diego, CA), 1999.

John Lithgow, *The Remarkable Farkle McBride,* Simon & Schuster (New York, NY), 2000.

Marissa Moss, *Brave Harriet: The First Woman to Fly the English Channel,* Silver Whistle (San Diego, CA), 2001.

Ernest L. Thayer, *Casey at the Bat: A Ballad of the Republic Sung in the Year 1888,* Winslow House (Delray, FL), 2001.

John Lithgow, *Micawber,* Simon & Schuster (New York, NY), 2002.

Phil Bildner, *Shoeless Joe and Black Betsy,* Simon & Schuster (New York, NY), 2002.

Marissa Moss, *Mighty Jackie: The Strike-Out Queen,* Simon & Schuster (New York, NY), 2004.

Dan Shaughnessy, *The Legend of the Curse of the Bambino,* Simon & Schuster (New York, NY), 2005.

Phil Bildner, *The Shot Heard 'round the World,* Simon & Schuster (New York, NY), 2005.

Eve Bunting, *Pop's Bridge,* Harcourt (Orlando, FL), 2006.

Phil Bildner, *Turkey Bowl,* Simon & Schuster (New York, NY), 2006.

Illustrations have appeared in numerous periodicals, including *Atlantic Monthly, Rolling Stone, Esquire, Gentleman's Quarterly, Time, New Yorker,* and *Reader's Digest.*

Sidelights

C.F. Payne is an award-winning illustrator whose work has appeared in *Time, Esquire, Rolling Stone,* the *New Yorker,* and other national magazines. Payne's art "celebrates a slice of modern American life with provocative, relevant images of our culture," noted a contributor for the Reader's Digest Web site. "His work is reminiscent of the art of Norman Rockwell—contemporary and classic, timely and timeless." Payne has also illustrated a number of critically acclaimed children's books by such authors as Marissa Moss, John Lithgow, and Phil Bildner. His work has "made him one of the most admired and successful illustrators in the country," according to *American Artist* contributor M. Stephen Doherty.

Payne first teamed with Moss on *True Heart,* a work of historical fiction about a young woman's efforts to become a train engineer. "With extraordinary depth, Payne's brown-tone, full-page paintings combine realism and romance," observed *Booklist* reviewer Hazel Rochman. The pair have also collaborated on *Brave Harriet: The First Woman to Fly the English Channel,* the tale of pioneering female aviator Harriet Quimby. Payne's "mixed media artwork combines paints and pastels in a series of beautiful scenes," remarked Carolyn Phelan in *Booklist,* and a critic in *Publishers Weekly* wrote that the illustrations "resemble period photographs." In *Mighty Jackie: The Strike-Out Queen,* Moss looks at the legendary performance of Jackie Mitchell, a seventeen-year-old hurler who struck out New York Yankee superstars Babe Ruth and Lou Gehrig in a 1931 exhibition baseball game. "Payne's pictures mirror the text's immediacy," wrote a *Publishers Weekly* critic. "Close-ups show Ruth's face as he awaits Jackie's first pitch, then later his expression of dismay and outrage" after he is called out. Writing in *School Library Journal,* Grace Oliff noted that the artist's "mixed-media illustrations with their judicious use of sepia increase the nostalgic feel."

Payne combined his talents with Lithgow, an Emmy Award-winning actor, on *The Remarkable Farkle McBride,* a humorous verse tale about a musical prodigy who searches for the perfect musical instrument. A reviewer in *Publishers Weekly* complimented the artist's "outrageously droll . . . illustrations, with their blend of caricature and realism," and *School Library Journal* contributor Carol Ann Wilson remarked that Payne's compositions not only "contain whimsical details and lots of musical innuendoes," they also "deliver a visual punch." In *Micawber,* Lithgow introduces an art-loving squirrel who scampers around New York City's Central Park by day and, using his tail as a brush, creates his own masterpieces by night. Payne's "varying perspectives and occasionally paint-splattered backgrounds embrace all the exhilaration of Lithgow's words," noted a *Publishers Weekly* contributor.

In addition to *Mighty Jackie,* Payne has illustrated several other works about the sport of baseball. Using a mix of acrylics, watercolor, oil, ink, and colored pencil, he provided the artwork for *Casey at the Bat: A Ballad of the Republic Sung in the Year 1888,* a version of Ernest L. Thayer's classic poem. According to a critic in *Kirkus Reviews,* "every detail is both larger than life, and painted with crystal clarity." In *The Legend of the Curse of the Bambino,* Dan Shaughnessy examines the eighty-year string of bad luck that befell the Boston Red Sox after the team sold its star player, Babe Ruth, to the Yankees. "Payne visualizes a genial, mischievous Ruth impeding fielders and blowing on pop-ups to turn them into unexpected home runs," Marilyn Taniguchi remarked in *School Library Journal.* In *Shoeless Joe and Black Betsy,* Bildner looks at the career of early-twentieth-century ballplayer Joseph "Shoeless Joe" Jackson, who was aided by his cherished hickory-wood bat, Black Betsy. "Payne's portraits take on a tall-tale quality suffused with nostalgia; his strong-featured characters offer a riveting blend of humor and gravity," a *Publishers Weekly* reviewer commented. Bobby Thomson's home run, which awarded the New York Giants the 1951 National League pennant over their arch rivals, the Brooklyn Dodgers, is the subject of Bildner's *The Shot Heard 'round the World.* Payne's compositions "are bathed in attractive autumnal colors, suggest-

C.F. Payne creates detailed drawings that capture the energy of the budding squirrel artist that stars in *John Lithgow's* **Micawber.** (Aladdin Paperbacks, 2005. Illustration © 2002 by C.F. Payne. Reprinted by permission of Simon & Schuster Book for Young Readers, an imprint of Simon & Schuster Children's Publishing Division.)

ing the October setting as well as the melancholy of the Dodgers' defeat," wrote Bill Ott in *Booklist*.

Biographical and Critical Sources

BOOKS

Reed, Walt, *The Illustrator in America: 1860-2000*, Watson-Guptill (New York, NY), 2001.

PERIODICALS

American Artist, M. Stephen Doherty, "Using Mediums to Their Best Advantage," p. 32.

Booklist, April 1, 1999, Hazel Rochman, review of *True Heart*, p. 1424; July 1, 2001, Carolyn Phelan, review of *Brave Harriet: The First Woman to Fly the English Channel*, p. 2009; February 15, 2002, Bill Ott, review of *Shoeless Joe and Black Betsy*, p. 1014; February 1, 2003, Linda Perkins, review of *Casey at the Bat: A Ballad of the Republic Sung in the Year 1888*, p. 993; January 1, 2004, GraceAnne A. DeCandido, review of *Mighty Jackie: The Strike-Out Queen*, p. 868; March 1, 2005, Bill Ott, review of *The Shot Heard 'round the World*, p. 1199; March 15, 2005, Todd Morning, review of *The Legend of the Curse of the Bambino*, p. 1298.

Communication Arts, March-April, 1991, Rhodes Patterson, "C.F. Payne," p. 54.

Kirkus Reviews, December 15, 2001, review of *Shoeless Joe and Black Betsy*, p. 1754; August 1, 2002, review of *Micawber*, p. 1135; December 15, 2002, review of *Casey at the Bat*, p. 1858; January 15, 2004, review of *Mighty Jackie*, p. 87; February 15, 2005, review of *The Shot Heard 'round the World*, p. 226; review of March 15, 2005, review of *The Legend of Curse of the Bambino*, p. 357; April 15, 2006, review of *Pop's Bridge*, p. 402.

Publishers Weekly, July 24, 2000, review of *The Remarkable Farkle McBride*, p. 93; July 16, 2001, review of *Brave Harriet*, p. 180; January 7, 2002, review of *Shoeless Joe and Black Betsy*, p. 64; June 24, 2002, review of *Micawber*, p. 56; January 6, 2003, review of *Casey at the Bat*, p. 59; January 19, 2004, review of *Mighty Jackie*, p. 76; February 7, 2005, reviews of *The Shot Heard 'round the World* and *The Legend of the Curse of the Bambino*, p. 59.

School Library Journal, September, 2000, Carol Ann Wilson, review of *The Remarkable Farkle McBride*, p. 204; September, 2001, Ann Chapman Callaghan, review of *Brave Harriet*, p. 220; April, 2002, Wendy Lukehart, review of *Shoeless Joe and Black Betsy*, p. 100; September, 2002, Wendy Lukehart, review of *Micawber*, p. 198; March, 2003, Wendy Lukehart, review of *Casey at the Bat*, p. 224; February, 2004, Grace Oliff, review of *Mighty Jackie*, p. 134; May, 2005, Marilyn Taniguchi, reviews of *The Shot Heard*

'round the World, p. 77, and *The Legend of the Curse of the Bambino*, p. 97; March, 2006, John Peters, review of *Mighty Jackie*, p. 88; May, 2006, Marilyn Taniguchi, review of *Mighty Jackie*, p. 60; June, 2006, Marianne Saccardi, review of *Pop's Bridge*, p. 108.

Tribune Books (Chicago, IL), April 6, 2003, review of *Casey at the Bat*, p. 5.

ONLINE

Reader's Digest Web site, http://www.rd.com/ (May 10, 2007), "Meet C.F. Payne."

Richard Solomon Web site, http://www.richardsolomon.com/ (May 10, 2007), "C.F. Payne."*

*   *   *

PAYNE, Chris Fox
See PAYNE, C.F.

*   *   *

PEARCE, Philippa 1920-2006
(Ann Philippa Christie)

OBITUARY NOTICE— See index for *SATA* sketch: Born January 23, 1920, in Great Shelford, Cambridgeshire, England; died December 21, 2006. Editor and author. Pearce was an award-winning children's-book author famous for her classic 1958 tale, *Tom's Midnight Garden*. Educated at Girton College, Cambridge, where she studied English and history and earned a master's degree in 1942, she then joined the British civil service. After World War II, however, she pursued a more pleasurable career as a writer and producer for the school broadcasting department of the British Broadcasting Corporation (BBC). While working for the BBC, she released her first children's title, *Minnow on the Say* (1954), which was published in the United States four years later as *The Minnow Leads to Treasure*. Though it earned a Lewis Carroll Shelf Award, the success of this book was nothing compared to that of *Tom's Midnight Garden*, a fantasy tale that touched the hearts of millions. It was translated in versions all over the world and adapted several times to television. As with its predecessor, it also won a Lewis Carroll Shelf Award, but, in addition, a Carnegie Medal. The popularity of the book was such that Pearce left her job at the BBC, but returned part time in 1960. She had also worked as an editor in the education department at Clarendon Press for a year, and from 1960 to 1967 she was the editor of children's books for Andre Deutsch. Pearce published many more children's tales over the next four decades, including the Whitbread award-winning *The Battle of Bubble and Squeek* (1978). Among her other works are *What the Neighbours Did, and Other Stories* (1972), *A*

Picnic for Bunnykins (1984), *Children of Charlecote* (1989), *The Little White Hen* (1986), and *The Ghost in Annie's Room* (2000), *The Peddler of Swaffham* (2001), *Familiar and Haunting Collected Stories* (2002), and *Little Gentleman* (2004). Named to the Order of the British Empire for her literary contributions, she reflected on her childhood in the privately printed autobiography *Logbook* (2000).

OBITUARIES AND OTHER SOURCES:

BOOKS

Pearce, Philippa, *Logbook,* privately printed, 2000.

PERIODICALS

Times (London, England), December 21, 2006.

R

RAY, Delia 1963-

Personal

Born April 29, 1963, in Newport News, VA; daughter of Edward Joseph (an aeronautics engineer) and Roberta Olivia (a reading teacher) Ray; married Matthew Andrew Howard III (a neurosurgeon) June 28, 1986; children: Caroline O'Connell Howard, Susan Davis Howard, one other daughter. *Education:* University of Virginia, B.A., 1985. *Religion:* Roman Catholic.

Addresses

Home—Iowa City, IA. *E-mail*—deliarayhoward@aol.com.

Career

Vernon Publications, Inc. (periodicals publisher), Seattle, WA, staff writer, 1985; Laing Communications, Inc. (book publisher), Seattle, editor, 1986-89.

Member

Society of Children's Book Writers and Illustrators (Seattle chapter).

Awards, Honors

American Library Association (ALA) Notable Book designation, Bank Street College Children's Book of the Year designation, NCSS/Children's Book Council Notable Children's Trade Book in the Field of Social Studies, all 1991, all for *A Nation Torn;* New York Public Library Books for the Teen Age designation, and YALSA Recommended title, both 1992, both for *Behind the Blue and Gray;* Society of School Librarians International Book Award, 2004, and six state reading list nominations, all for *Ghost Girl.*

Writings

Gold! The Klondike Adventure, Lodestar (New York NY), 1989.

A Nation Torn: The Story of How the Civil War Began, Lodestar (New York, NY), 1990.
Behind the Blue and Gray: The Soldier's Life in the Civil War, Lodestar (New York, NY), 1991.
Ghost Girl: A Blue Ridge Mountain Story, Clarion (New York, NY), 2003.
Singing Hands, Clarion Books (New York, NY), 2006.

Sidelights

Delia Ray began her writing career as the author of several nonfiction books that bring to life interesting aspects of American history for younger readers. In more recent years she has moved into fiction while continuing to inspire her readers with her love of history; both her novels *Ghost Girl: A Blue Ridge Mountain Story* and *Singing Hands* take place in the American South during the early twentieth century. Praising *Ghost Girl,* a *Kirkus Reviews* writer noted that Ray's "loving attention to setting, character, and detail" enriches her story, which the critic called "a quiet and subtle evocation of a time and a place."

In her first book, *Gold! The Klondike Adventure,* Ray brings to life the Klondike Gold Rush of 1897 through the eyes of four intriguing men. Calling *Gold!* "a sophisticated portrait of the 1897 Klondike excitement," Henry Mayer wrote in the *New York Times Book Review* that this book "will help [elementary-grade students], as well as their middle-school compatriots east of the Sierra Nevada, sense the human drama of the gold rush phenomenon."

In both *A Nation Torn: The Story of How the Civil War Began* and *Behind the Blue and Gray: The Soldier's Life in the Civil War* Ray focuses on the conflict that divided the United States during the mid-nineteenth century: the U.S. Civil War. *A Nation Torn* follows the fateful chronology of events, from the actions of abolitionist John Brown at Harper's Ferry to the speeches of Henry Clay, that led to war, while eyewitness accounts and civil war-era photographs help evoke the day-to-day lives of the young men from both north and south

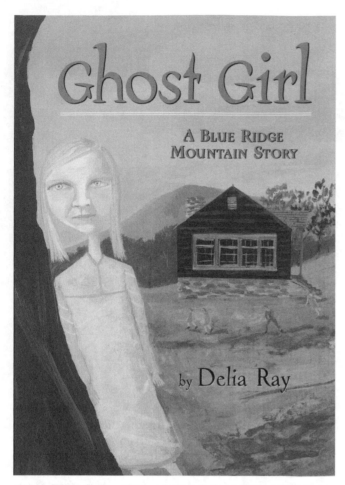

Cover of Delia Ray's middle-grade historical novel Ghost Girl, *featuring artwork by R. Gregory Christie.* (Clarion Books, 2003. Jacket illustration © 2003 by R. Gregory Christie. Reproduced by permission of Houghton Mifflin Company.)

who came together as their two world collided in *Behind the Blue and Gray.* Referencing the wealth of photographs in *A Nation Torn,* a *Horn Book* critic dubbed the work a "beautifully framed . . . presentation of the beginning of the Civil War [that] has been expertly crafted."

Ray moves to fiction in her more-recent books, which include *Ghost Girl.* Based on the letters of a young teacher named Christine Vest, the story introduces eleven-year-old April Sloane. Nicknamed Ghost Girl because of her white-blonde hair and waif-like appearance, April lives a hardscrabble life with her family in rural Virginia. While news comes that President and Mrs. Herbert Hoover plan to build a school near her home, April is excited by the possibility of learning to read. With the help of a supportive young teacher, April confronts a tragedy within her own family as well as the challenges she confronts at school, ultimately gaining a sense of her own strength and resilience. Reviewing *Ghost Girl* in *Horn Book,* Robin Smith praised the novel as "poignant, realistic, and somber" coming-of-age tale in which "nothing is pat or predictable." In her *School Library Journal* review of the book, Terrie Dorio called April "an engaging character," and noted that

Ray "seemlessly incorporated historical fact into the [novel's] narrative."

Again returning readers to the early twentieth century, *Singing Hands* is set in Birmingham, Alabama, in 1948, and introduces another preteen dealing with hardship. In this case it is Gussie Davis, a twelve year old whose confusion over her own identity as a hearing child in a deaf family results in unruly and rebellious behavior. For disrupting her deaf father's ministry at St. Jude's Church for the Deaf, Gussie must now assist at services, where she learns first hand about prejudice and also learns how to deal with the handicaps within her own family. While noting that the novel contains "an excess of subplots" involving Gussie's blossoming relationships with a variety of people, *School Library Journal* reviewer Kathleen Kelly MacMillan concluded that Ray's "exploration of Gussie's feelings" and her sense of disconnection from her family as a member of the hearing world, is presented in a "heartfelt" fashion. Praising the coming-of-age novel as "superb," a *Kirkus Reviews* writer cited Ray's "realistically sympathetic characters" as well as the "kindness, humor, and playfulness" of the story's young heroine. *Singing Hands* was inspired by Ray's mother and especially by her grandfather, a deaf man who worked as an advocate for other deaf people during the same time and in the same place wherein which the novel takes place.

Ray once told *SATA:* "When I was young, writing came easily. My best friend and I spent our summer vacations writing dozens of poems and then collecting them into little, staple-bound books. When we had finished reading all of the Greek myths in our library books, we invented our own gods and goddesses and copied down complicated stories about them, full of wild love affairs and adventures. In the sixth grade, I wrote the school Christmas play during lunch and science class. And in high school, I was unfortunately the one who was chosen to write the poem for our senior-prom program. By the time I reached college, I was enrolling in all of the creative writing classes I could find and naturally telling myself that some day I was going to be a 'real' writer.

"But as graduation rolled closer, I finally admitted to myself that twelve short stories and a few school magazine articles were not going to earn me my dream career. Even more important, I had to turn my skills into something that could pay my monthly rent. So I enrolled in the Radcliffe Publishing Course, which covered all aspects of making books and magazines, hoping to find some answers.

"While most of the other graduates migrated to the publishing capital of New York City, I followed my husband to Seattle, Washington, where he was facing an eight-year residency in neurosurgery. Since the publishing industry in Seattle is limited to a few small companies, I knew I was lucky to find an editing job in a

start-up firm run by one of my instructors from Radcliffe. In the next three years, I edited every type of manuscript, from gory tales of Alaska bear maulings to reports on nuclear waste management.

"Suddenly, the miracle opportunity struck. The editors at Lodestar had seen an adult book that my company produced about the Klondike Gold Rush and wanted one for children on the same subject. And . . . my boss was going to trust me to write it.

"Looking back now, I know writing nonfiction for ten to fourteen year olds was the best crash course in authorship I could have had. The task forced me to organize my ideas scrupulously. I had to explain complex concepts, such as gold-panning methods and the Missouri Compromise, in the clearest and simplest terms. I was also determined to make history exciting, perhaps to make up for all the dull history books that I was forced to read as a child. I wanted my factual accounts to read like fiction, with descriptions of how people looked and felt, with dialogue and anecdotes that captured the fever of the times and pulled the reader in."

Biographical and Critical Sources

PERIODICALS

Booklist, November 15, 2003, Hazel Rochman, review of *Ghost Girl: A Blue Ridge Mountain Story,* p. 610; May 1, 2006, Cindy Dobrez, review of *Singing Hands,* p. 85.

Bulletin of the Center for Children's Books, November, 2003, Karen Coats, review of *Ghost Girl,* p. 122; June, 2006, Deborah Stevenson, review of *Singing Hands,* p. 467.

Horn Book, September-October, 1990, review of *A Nation Torn: The Story of How the Civil War Began,* pp. 623-624; July-August, 1991, Anita Silvey, review of *Behind the Blue and Gray,* p. 482; January-February, 2004, Robin Smith, review of *Ghost Girl,* p. 91; May-June, 2006, Deirdre F. Baker, review of *Singing Hands,* p. 326.

Kirkus Reviews, September 1, 2003, review of *Ghost Girl,* p. 1129; April 1, 2006, review of *Singing Hands,* p. 355.

New York Times Book Review, November 12, 1989, Henry Mayer "American Treasure Hunts," p. 44.

School Library Journal, December, 1990, Trevelyn Jones, review of *A Nation Torn,* p. 224; August, 1991, review of *Behind the Blue and Gray,* p. 207; November, 2003, Terrie Dorio, review of *Ghost Girl,* p. 146; July, 2006, Kathleen Kelly MacMillan, review of *Singing Hands,* p. 110.

ONLINE

Delia Ray Home Page, http://www.deliaray.com (June 15, 2007).*

REYNOLDS, Peter H. 1961-

Personal

Born March 16, 1961, in Weston, Ontario, Canada; son of Keith H. (a treasurer) and Hazel E. (a bookkeeper) Reynolds; children: Sarah. *Education:* Attended Fitchburg State College, 1978-83, and Massachusetts College of Art, 1979-80.

Addresses

Office—The Blue Bunny, 577 High St., Dedham, MA 02026. *Agent*—Pippin Properties, 155 E. 38th St., Ste. 2H, New York, NY 10016.

Career

Tom Snyder Productions, Cambridge, MA, vice president and creative director, for thirteen years; FableVision Studios, Boston, MA, cofounder (with brother, Paul Reynolds) and creative director. Creative Journey Retreat, founder and organizer; speaker at events.

Awards, Honors

Media and Methods Excellence in Education Award, *Parenting* magazine award, Parents' Choice Award, Educom Distinguished Software award, and Technology and Learning Award of Excellence, for work on Tom Snyder Productions projects; Telly Award second place, ASIFA-East, and BDA International Design Silver Award, both for *The Blue Shoe;* ASIFA-East third-place honor and ASIFA-Hollywood Annie nomination, both 1999, both for *Living Forever;* National Education Association Top 100 Books listee, 2000, for *The North Star;* named Shaper of the Future 2000, *Converge* magazine; Christopher Award, Oppenheim Toy Portfolio Platinum Award, Irma S. and James H. Black Honor Book, Bank Street College of Education, Chicago Public Library Best Book designation, and Chapman Award for Best Classroom Read-aloud, all 2004, all for *The Dot.*

Writings

SELF-ILLUSTRATED PICTURE BOOKS

Fizz and Martina in the Incredible Not-for-Profit Pet Resort Mystery, Tom Snyder Productions (Watertown, MA), 1993.

The North Star, FableVision Press (Watertown, MA), 1997.

(With Sue Pandiani) *North Star Inspiration for the Classroom,* FableVision Press (Watertown, MA), 1999.

Sydney's Star, Simon & Schuster (New York, NY), 2001.

The Dot, Candlewick Press (Cambridge, MA), 2003.

Ish, Candlewick Press (Cambridge, MA), 2004.

So Few of Me, Candlewick Press (New York, NY), 2006.

The Best Kid in the World, Atheneum (New York, NY), 2006.

Has created more than twenty interactive children's stories for the online service Prodigy, including *The Three Wolf Architects, The Adventures of Pewter Pan, Snow White and the Seven Accounts, Hilary and the Beast,* and *The Gingerbread Channel.*

ILLUSTRATOR

Megan McDonald, *Judy Moody,* Candlewick Press (Cambridge, MA), 1999.

Donald H. Graves, *The Portfolio Standard,* Heinemann (Portsmouth, NH), 2000.

Tobi Tobias, *Serendipity,* Simon & Schuster (New York, NY), 2000.

Megan McDonald, *Judy Moody Gets Famous!,* Candlewick Press (Cambridge, MA), 2001.

Megan McDonald, *Judy Moody Saves the World,* Candlewick Press (Cambridge, MA), 2002.

Ellen Potter, *Olivia Kidney,* Philomel Books (New York, NY), 2003.

Megan McDonald, *Judy Moody Predicts the Future,* Candlewick Press (Cambridge, MA), 2003.

Megan McDonald, *Judy Moody, M.D.: The Doctor Is In!,* Candlewick Press (Cambridge, MA), 2004.

Megan McDonald, *Judy Moody Declares Independence,* Candlewick Press (Cambridge, MA), 2005.

Ellen Potter, *Olivia Kidney and the Exit Academy,* Philomel Books (New York, NY), 2005.

Megan McDonald, *Stink: The Incredible Shrinking Kid,* Candlewick Press (Cambridge, MA), 2005.

Megan McDonald, *Judy Moody's Double-Rare Way-Not-Boring Book of Fun Stuff to Do,* Candlewick Press (Cambridge, MA), 2005.

Megan McDonald, *Judy Moody: Around the World in 8 1/2 Days,* Candlewick Press (Cambridge, MA), 2006.

Megan McDonald, *Stink and the Incredible Super-Galactic Jawbreaker,* Candlewick Press (Cambridge, MA), 2006.

Megan McDonald, *Stink and the World's Worst Super-Stinky Sneakers,* Candlewick Press (Cambridge, MA), 2007.

Alison McGhee, *Someday,* Atheneum (New York, NY), 2007.

Also illustrator of texts and book covers for other children's books.

Adaptations

Ish was adapted for video, Weston Woods, 2005.

Sidelights

An author, illustrator, designer, filmmaker, and motivational speaker, Peter H. Reynolds began his career in advertising, but quickly moved on to become a pivotal player in Tom Snyder Productions, one of the early computer software companies specializing in educational products. As creative director, author, and/or artist, Reynolds contributed to the firm's short films, public service announcements, interactive software programs, and online stories, all with a goal of encouraging creativity in young people while making learning fun. Reynolds' view of life as a journey of learning is detailed in his book *The North Star,* a work that eventually inspired a guidebook for teachers interested in bringing the North Star approach into their classrooms. Earning respect for his inspiring picture books such as *The Dot* and *Ish,* Reynolds is also the cofounder, with twin brother Paul Reynolds, of the educational media company FableVision.

In *The Dot* Reynolds focuses on Vashti, a young girl who seems to have no natural artistic ability. However, when she completes a drawing assignment by marking her paper with one single dot, Vashti's clever art teacher expresses enthusiasm, asks Vashti to sign her work, and hangs it prominently in the classroom. Soon, Vashti is making all sizes, colors, and patterns of dots, and when a little boy has the same frustration over a lack of drawing skill the girl takes on the role of encouraging teacher in reaction to his own simple, unschooled mark. A similar tale is the focus of *Ish,* in which Ramon loves to draw anywhere and any time, until teasing from his older brother makes Ramon yield to his inner critic. Discarding drawing after drawing, the boy soon discovers that his little sister sees something special in Ramon's un-realistic pictures, giving the budding artist renewed confidence.

Calling *The Dot* "simplicity itself," Ilene Cooper added in her *Booklist* review that Reynolds' "small book carries a big message." According to *School Library Journal* reviewer Kathy Krasniewicz, in *The Dot* Reynolds pairs spare, gestured images rendered in "fluid pen-and-ink, watercolor, and tea" with a simple text to recount a journey "of self-expression, artistic experimentation, and success," while a *Kirkus Reviews* writer predicted that *Ish* "may speak to formerly artistic young readers who are selling their own abilities short." A *Publishers Weekly* contributor also praised *Ish,* noting that the author/illustrator's "minimalist pen-and-ink illustrations" bring to life the book's "tidy lesson in the importance of . . . drawing . . . outside the box and believing in one's own abilities despite others' reactions." As Cooper noted in *Booklist,* the "great emotion and warmth" in *Ish* will appeal to young children, while a *Kirkus Reviews* writer predicted that Reynolds' book "will encourage other little artists."

Reynolds packs a message relevant to adults as well as children in *So Few of Me.* Poor Leo is a busy boy, and when he wishes the wish of all very-busy people—that there was another "him" to help get everything on his to-do list completed—he gets his wish. Soon, in fact, ten Leos crowd the page, each one rushing to get something done. All those Leos need supervision, however, and after a time the original young boy decides that perhaps one Leo is quite enough. Citing Reynolds' characteristic simple line-and-wash art, a *Kirkus Reviews* writer noted that the book's "spare portraits glow amid backgrounds that are softly colored yet clearly defined and set against crisp, white space." According to a *Pub-*

Cover of Peter H. Reynolds' award-winning picture book **The Dot,** *which shows that creativity takes many forms.* (Candlewick Press, 2003. Jacket illustration © 2003 by Peter H. Reynolds. Reproduced by permission of Candlewick Press, Inc., Cambridge, MA.)

lishers Weekly contributor, *So Few of Me* is "an engaging and eye-opening tale for over-programmed kids and the adults who set their schedules."

My Very Big Little World and *The Best Kid in the World* highlight the relationship between Sugarloaf and Spoke, two siblings in a close-knit family, as they deal with typical events and feelings. In *My Very Big Little World* readers meet toddler Sugarloaf, who lives in the shadow of her likeable older brother Spoke. Sibling jealousy is the focus of *The Best Kid in the World,* which finds Sugarloaf jealous after Spoke returns home from at school with a special medal acknowledging his helpfulness. Praising Reynolds' "clear, simple sentences" in her *School Library Journal* review of *The Best Kid in the World,,* Linda L. Watkins added that the author/

illustrator's "breezy watercolor illustrations depict the child's undertakings with humor and charm." A *Kirkus Reviews* writer concluded that the book's "watercolor characters are delightfully expressive."

Reynolds' first illustration project, creating art for Megan McDonald's *Judy Moody,* was welcomed as the inaugural appearance of a likeable new heroine for first readers. The book's third-grade title character approaches the first day of school with some trepidation, and things only get worse when she finds herself assigned to the desk next to a boy well known for his habit of eating paste. McDonald's ability to capture both the way children think and the way they talk makes for an entertaining read, remarked Shelle Rosenfeld in a review of *Booklist,* adding that children will "also like

the witty, detailed drawings (especially the picture of Judy's unique collage)." Janice M. Del Negro, writing in the *Bulletin of the Center for Children's Books,* similarly commented: "Each chapter is amiably illustrated with . . . full-page and spot art that extends the friendly feeling of the humorous text."

Reynolds has gone on to illustrate several more "Judy Moody" books, as well as several books by McDonald that focus on Judy's seven-year-old sibling Stinky Moody. He has also contributed art to Alison McGhee's *Someday* and Tobi Tobias's *Serendipity,* the latter a picture book that defines the tongue-twisting word of the title with both humor and sentimentality, according to critics. In *Serendipity* "Reynolds provides sweetnatured and airy watercolor and ink cartoons," according to a reviewer in *Publishers Weekly,* while Sue Sherif wrote in *School Library Journal* that "teachers will undoubtedly use [*Serendipity*] . . . as a starting point for writing exercises." Reynolds' ink and watercolor images for *Someday* "have the same soft sentimentality" as McGhee's story, noted Carolyn Janssen in *School Library Journal,* and a *Publishers Weekly* contributor praised the author/illustrator's "spare, wispy pen-and-ink and watercolor" art.

On his home page, Reynolds explained that the inspiration behind his work as an author and illustrator of picture books was a math teacher named Mr. Matson.

One of Reynolds' most popular collaborations are his books with author Megan McDonald, which include **Judy Moody Predicts the Future.** (Candlewick Press, 2003. Illustration © 2003 by Peter H. Reynolds. Reproduced by permission of Candlewick Press, Inc., Cambridge, MA.)

When Mr. Matson discovered Reynolds doodling during math class, instead of punishing the young student he gave him a job: to combine his art skills and storytelling to make a comic book that illustrated math concepts. "My journey has been dedicated to helping kids, especially the 'off the path' kids," Reynolds explained. "I was one of them myself. Not every student is lucky enough to have a teacher, or adult, see his or her potential."

"When I visit students in schools they ask me what my hobbies are. I say thinking, dreaming. If my art and stories can help inspire others to do the same, I'll feel my life had meaning."

Biographical and Critical Sources

PERIODICALS

Booklist, July, 2000, Shelle Rosenfeld, review of *Judy Moody,* pp. 2028, 2030; December 15, 2001, Todd Morning, review of *Sydney's Star,* p. 741; November 1, 2003, Ilene Cooper, review of *The Dot,* p. 513; November 1, 2004, Ilene Cooper, review of *Ish,* p. 498.

Bulletin of the Center for Children's Books, May, 2000, Janice M. Del Negro, review of *Judy Moody,* pp. 324-325.

Horn Book, September, 2001, review of *Judy Moody Gets Famous!,* p. 589.

Kirkus Reviews, October 1, 2001, review of *Sydney's Star,* p. 1432; October 1, 2003, review of *The Dot,* p. 1229; July 15, 2004, review of *Ish,* p. 693; August 1, 2006, review of *So Few of Me,* p. 795.

Publishers Weekly, April 17, 2000, review of *Judy Moody,* p. 81; August 28, 2000, review of *Serendipity,* p. 82; July 30, 2001, review of *Judy Moody Gets Famous!,* p. 85; November 12, 2001, review of *Sydney's Star,* p. 59; October 20, 2003, review of *The Dot,* p. 54; October 11, 2004, review of *Ish,* p. 79; October 16, 2006, review of *So Few of Me,* p. 51; February 12, 2007, review of *Someday,* p. 84.

School Library Journal, July, 2000, Janie Schomberg, review of *Judy Moody,* p. 83; Sue Sherif, November, 2000, review of *Serendipity,* p. 135; October, 2001, Sharon R. Pearce, review of *Judy Moody Gets Famous!,* p. 124; December, 2001, Maryann H. Owen, review of *Sydney's Star,* p. 110; November, 2003, Kathy Krasniewicz, review of *The Dot,* p. 114; July, 2004, Lisa G. Kropp, review of *The Dot,* p. 44; January, 2005, Shawn Brommer, review of *Ish,* p. 97; May, 2005, Caroline Ward, review of *Olivia Kidney and the Exit Academy,* 138; July, 2006, Sharon Rawlins, review of *The Dot,* p. 86; August, 2006, Linda L. Walkins, review of *The Best Kid in the World,* p. 96; December, 2006, review of *So Few of Me,* p. 114; March, 2007, Carolyn Janssen, review of *Someday,* p. 176.

ONLINE

Digital MASS, http://www.boston.com/ (April, 2000), Tim Allik, "Peter Reynolds, FableVision: He Hasn't Forgotten the 'Little' People."

FableVision Web site, http://www.fablevision.com/ (February 2, 2002), "Peter Reynolds."

Peter H. Reynolds Home Page, http://www.peterhreynolds.com (June 15, 2007).*

*   *   *

REYNOLDS, Susan

Personal

Married; husband's name Matt. *Hobbies and other interests:* Distance walking, travel, photography.

Addresses

Home and office—P.O. Box 393, Hillsboro, NM 88042-0393. *E-mail*—Pheidippides@journeyheretothere.com.

Career

Artist, event promoter, and writer. Here to There, LLC, Hillsboro, NM, owner.

Writings

The First Marathon: The Legend of Pheidippides, illustrated by Daniel Minter, Albert Whitman (Morton Grove, IL), 2006.

Also author of *Walking outside the Box,* Outskirts Press.

Sidelights

On her home page, artist and author Susan Reynolds explained the inspiration for her children's book *The First Marathon: The Legend of Pheidippides.* She had just finished walking her first marathon in San Diego, California, and was flying home. A marathon is a road race with a set distance of 26.2 miles; it is named in honor of a Greek soldier who, legend holds, ran without stopping from the town of Marathon to the city of Athens to bring news of a Persian defeat in the famed Battle of Marathon. As Reynolds recalled, she "was in a state of fatigue such as I've never experienced—before or since. That fatigue, coupled with the general pain I was in, had me nearly asleep as I stifled groans and tried to settle into something of a comfortable position. I was just about off to dreamland when inspiration struck . . . that little voice from deep within simply said, 'You should tell the story of the marathon and do it for kids.'"

In *The First Marathon* Reynolds takes readers back 2,500 years, to one of the most important battles of the ancient world. As a small group of Greek soldiers collided with Persian troops on the plains of Marathon, young Pheidippides ran the 140 miles to Sparta to request reinforcements, then returned to the battlefield. Following the Greek victory, the soldier then ran to

The story of the most famous run of ancient times is captured in Daniel Minter's illustrations for Susan Reynolds' picture book The First Marathon.
(Albert Whitman, 2006. Illustration © 2006 by Daniel Minter. Reproduced by permission.)

Athens to relay the news, dying shortly thereafter. Although the story "involves armies and an empire, a heroic herald, and brave soldiers," Reynolds added on her home page that *The First Marathon* "is most of all a story of courage, the kind of courage ordinary people like you and I can still find deep within ourselves to do things that are not so ordinary." Praising the "strong, rhythmic movement" expressed in Daniel Minter's bold illustrations for the book, *Booklist* contributor Hazel Rochman cited Reynolds' "long, fascinating afterword," which features the history of the popular marathon road race as it has evolved in modern times. In her *School Library Journal* review, Ann Welton called Pheidippides "an engaging young hero," and noted that Reynolds' text "would read aloud quite well."

Biographical and Critical Sources

PERIODICALS

Booklist, February 15, 2006, Hazel Rochman, review of *The First Marathon: The Legend of Pheidippides,* p. 100.
Kirkus Reviews, January 15, 2006, review of *The First Marathon,* p. 89.
School Library Journal, March, 2006, Ann Welton, review of *The First Marathon,* p. 212.

ONLINE

Susan Reynolds Home Page, http://www.journeyheretothere.com (May 15, 2007).*

*   *   *

RUSSON, Penni 1974-

Personal

Born 1974, in Tasmania, Australia; married May 17, 2002; children: two. *Education:* Attended Monash University and RMIT University.

Addresses

Home and office—Melbourne, Victoria, Australia.

Career

Writer and editor.

Writings

(Editor with Jill Allan) *Ranthology* (short stories and poetry), Rant (Clifton Hill, Victoria, Australia), 2000.

Undine, Random House (Milsons Point, New South Wales, Australia), 2004, Greenwillow (New York, NY), 2006.
Breathe, Random House (Milsons Point, New South Wales, Australia), 2005, Greenwillow (New York, NY), 2007.
Drift, Random House (North Sydney, New South Wales, Australia), 2007.

Sidelights

Australian freelance writer and editor Penni Russon began writing poetry because she felt the length was "more manageable," according to her home page. Eventually, however, she "discovered novels were a lot more forgiving," and has gone on to create the "Undine Trilogy" for teen readers. In this series of young-adult novels, Russon draws on chaos and string theory, as well as traditional sources such as Hans Christian Andersen's *The Little Mermaid,* Shakespeare's *The Tempest,* and the German myth about Undine, an immortal water nymph who loses her ability to live forever after she falls in love with a mortal man. Recasting the story for a contemporary audience, the author recreates Undine as a modern teen who just wants a normal life.

In *Undine,* the main character slowly realizes that she possesses strange powers that draw upon the ocean. Although her mother has told her that her father disappeared long ago, Undine now hears a voice in her head that she is certain belongs to her missing dad. "The language is vivid and rich, full of references to [Shakespeare's play] *The Tempest* in an Australian setting," wrote a *Kirkus Reviews* contributor. June H. Keuhn, reviewing the novel for *School Library Journal,* also noted the strength of Russon's prose, and concluded that *Undine* "offers readers a new and interesting magical twist as well as a surprise ending," while *Booklist* critic Gillian Engberg deemed the book "an impressive debut from a writer to watch."

Breathe finds Undine exploring her father's home in Greece, and there she is tempted to use her magic. Trout, the teen's best friend and love interest, is nearly killed by Undine's magic; nonetheless, he is drawn to learn more about the powers he fears. As a result, Trout becomes a pawn of Max, another girl obsessed with magic. "In this mesmerizing story, Trout is the real protagonist and his search to find himself stands in contrast to Undine and her desire to lose herself in magic," explained Janis Flint-Ferguson in a *Kliatt* review of *Breathe.* "Russon's bracing, poetic voice and earthy, likable characters ground the story's esoteric symbolism," wrote Engberg in praise of the trilogy's second volume. The saga concludes in *Drift,* which finds Undine missing and Trout hoping to forget about her—until her shadow begins appearing in his photographs.

Discussing her work on the "Undine Trilogy," Russon noted on her home page that she has "grown to care deeply for all my characters." She also offered the following advice for young authors: "Write honestly, write what you know and understand. This doesn't mean you

can't use fantasy scenarios (like a spy or future world), but your characters' psychology needs to be in your grasp, the emotions should be real."

Biographical and Critical Sources

PERIODICALS

Booklist, February 15, 2006, Gillian Engberg, review of *Undine,* p. 93; February 15, 2007, Gillian Engberg, review of *Breathe,* p. 73.

Horn Book, March-April, 2006, Claire E. Gross, review of *Undine,* p. 194; March-April, 2007, Claire E. Gross, review of *Breathe,* p. 201.

Kirkus Reviews, January 15, 2006, review of *Undine,* p. 89.

Kliatt, January, 2006, Lesley Farmer, review of *Undine,* p. 12; January, 2007, Janis Flint-Ferguson, review of *Breathe,* p. 18.

Publishers Weekly, March 6, 2006, review of *Undine,* p. 76.

School Library Journal, February, 2006, June H. Keuhn, review of *Undine,* p. 136; January, 2007, June H. Keuhn, review of *Breathe,* p. 138.

ONLINE

Penni Russon Blog Site, http://eglantinescake.blogspot. com/ (May 17, 2007).

Penni Russon Home Page, http://www.pennirusson.com (May 18, 2007).

Random House Australia Web site, http://www. randomhouse.com.au/ (May 18, 2007), "Penni Russon."

S

SANDERS, Betty Jane
    See MONTHEI, Betty

*   *   *

SHORE, Diane Z.
   (Diane ZuHone Shore)

Personal

Married; husband's name John; children: Jennifer, Sam.

Addresses

Home and office—Marietta, GA. *E-mail*—DZShore@ bellsouth.net.

Career

Children's book author.

Awards, Honors

History Feature of the Year Award, *Highlights* magazine, 2002, for article "Presidential Dreams"; Children's Choice Award, and Georgia Author of the Year nomination, both 2004, both for *Bus-a-saurus Bop;* Georgia Author of the Year nomination, 2006, and Kansas Reads choice, 2007, both for *Look Both Ways;* Georgia Author of the Year nomination, 2007, for *This Is the Dream.*

Writings

Bus-a-saurus Bop, illustrated by David Clark, Bloomsbury Children's Books (New York, NY), 2003.
Rosa Loves to Read, Children's Press (New York, NY), 2004.
Look Both Ways: A Cautionary Tale, illustrated by Teri Weidner, Bloomsbury Children's Books (New York, NY), 2005.

This Is the Dream, HarperCollins (New York, NY), 2006.

Contributor to numerous periodicals, including *Highlights for Children, Humpty Dumpty, Jack & Jill, Turtle, Children's Playmate, Spider, Cricket,* and *Boys' Quest.*

Biographical and Critical Sources

PERIODICALS

Black Issues Book Review, January-February, 2006, review of *This Is the Dream,* p. 37.
Booklinks, March, 2006, Carolyn Phelan, review of *This Is the Dream,* p. 8.
Booklist, February 1, 2006, Carolyn Phelan, review of *This Is the Dream,* p. 69.
Bulletin of the Center for Children's Books, February, 2006, Deborah Stevenson, review of *This Is the Dream,* p. 285.
Chicago Tribune, January 8, 2006, Mary Harris Russell, review of *This Is the Dream,* p. 2.
Children's Bookwatch, September, 2005, review of *Look Both Ways: A Cautionary Tale.*
Horn Book, March-April, 2006, Martha V. Parravano, review of *This Is the Dream,* p. 205.
Kirkus Reviews, June 15, 2003, review of *Bus-a-saurus Bop,* p. 864; July 1, 2005, review of *Look Both Ways,* p. 744; December 1, 2005, review of *This Is the Dream,* p. 1280.
Publishers Weekly, July 21, 2003, review of *Bus-a-saurus Bop,* p. 194; November 21, 2005, review of *This Is the Dream,* p. 46.
School Library Journal, August, 2004, Bethany L.W. Hankinson, review of *Jenny's Socks,* p. 90; July, 2005, Corrina Austin, review of *Look Both Ways,* p. 82; January, 2006, Teresa Pfeifer, review of *This Is the Dream,* p. 124.

ONLINE

Diane Shore Home Page, http://www.dianezshore.com/ (May 26, 2007).

Bloomsbury Press Web site, http://www.bloomsburyusa. com/ (May 26, 2007), "Diane Z. Shore."

*   *   *

SHORE, Diane ZuHone
See SHORE, Diane Z.

*   *   *

SLATER, Dashka 1963-

Personal
Born 1963; daughter of Philip Slater (an author and playwright) and Dori Appel (a playwright); married; children: one son. *Education:* University of California, Berkeley, graduate (with honors).

Addresses
Home and office—Oakland, CA. *E-mail*—info@dash-kaslater.com.

Career
Journalist, novelist, and children's book author.

Awards, Honors
Golden Medallion Media Award, State Bar of California, 1993, and first prize, California Newspaper Publishers Association, 1994, both for for "The Death Squad"; Media Alliance Meritorious Achievement Award, 1994; PASS Award, National Council on Crime and Delinquency, 1995, for "Reading, Writing and Rhythm"; Sundance Institute Writers Program nominee, 2001; National Endowment for the Arts creative writing fellowship, 2004.

Writings

The Wishing Box (adult novel), Chronicle Books (San Francisco, CA), 2000.
Lights, Camera, Alcatraz: Hollywood's View of an American Landmark, Golden Gate National Parks Conservancy (San Francisco, CA), 2005.
Firefighters in the Dark (for children), Houghton Mifflin (Boston, MA), 2006.
Baby Shoes (for children), illustrated by Hiroe Nakata, Bloomsbury Children's Books (New York, NY), 2006.
The Sea Serpent and Me, illustrated by Catia Chien, Houghton Mifflin (Boston, MA), 2008.

Contributor to numerous periodicals, including *More, Salon, Mother Jones, Sierra, Dallas Morning News,* and *San Francisco Chronicle Magazine.*

Biographical and Critical Sources

PERIODICALS

Booklist, May 1, 2006, Carolyn Phelan, review of *Baby Shoes,* p. 84.
Kirkus Reviews, April 1, 2006, review of *Baby Shoes,* p. 357; October 1, 2006, review of *Firefighters in the Dark,* p. 1025.
Publishers Weekly, October 9, 2006, review of *Firefighters in the Dark,* p. 54.
School Library Journal, May, 2006, Linda Zeilstra Sawyer, review of *Baby Shoes,* p. 104; October, 2006, Jayne Damron, review of *Firefighters in the Dark,* p. 126.

ONLINE

Dashka Slater Home Page, http://www.dashkaslater.com (May 26, 2007).
Wishing Box Web site, http://www.chroniclebooks.com/ (May 26, 2007), interview with Slater.

*   *   *

SMITH, Lane 1959-

Personal
Born August 25, 1959, in Tulsa, OK; son of Lewis (an accountant) and Mildred Annette (a homemaker) Smith; married Molly Leach (a designer), 1996. *Education:* Art Center College of Design (Pasadena, CA), B.F.A. (illustration), 1983.

Addresses
Home—Washington Depot, CT. *E-mail*—lane@lane-smithbooks.com.

Career
Illustrator and author. Freelance illustrator, 1983—. Art director for film adaptation of *James and the Giant Peach,* Disney, 1996; contributed design work to *Monsters, Inc.,* Pixar, 2000. *Exhibitions:* Works exhibited at Master Eagle Gallery, New York, NY; Brockton Children's Museum, Brockton, MA; Joseloff Gallery, Hartford, CT; Bruce Museum; and in American Institute of Graphic Artists touring show.

Awards, Honors
New York Times Ten Best Illustrated Books of the Year citation, *School Library Journal* Best Book of the Year citation, *Horn Book* Honor List inclusion, *Booklist* Editor's Choice listee, and Silver Buckeye Award, all 1987, all for *Halloween ABC;* Silver Medal, Society of Illustrators, *New York Times* Best Books of the Year citation, American Library Association (ALA) Notable Chil-

dren's Book citation, Maryland Black-eyed Susan Picture-Book Award, and *Parenting* Reading Magic Award, all 1989, all for *The True Story of the Three Little Pigs!;* Golden Apple Award, Bratislava International Biennial of Illustrations, 1990, Society of Illustrators Silver Medal, 1991, and first-place award, New York Book Show, all for *The Big Pets; Parent's Choice* Award for Illustration, *New York Times* Best Books of the Year citation, and ALA Notable Children's Book citation, all 1991, all for *Glasses—Who Needs 'Em?;* ALA Caldecott Honor Book designation *New York Times* Best Illustrated Books of the Year citation and Notable Children's Book citation, and *School Library Journal* Best Books of the Year citation, all 1992, all for *The Stinky Cheese Man, and Other Fairly Stupid Tales; Publishers Weekly,* Best Children's Book citation, and *Booklist* Editors' Choice citation, both 1995, and ALA Best Book for Young Adults citation, 1996, all for *Math Curse; New York Times* Best Illustrated Book of the Year and Notable Book designations, *Child* magazine Best Book of the Year designation, National Parenting Publication Gold Award, Oppenheim Toy Portfolio Platinum Book Award, Quills Award nomination, *School Library Journal, Horn Book, Publishers Weekly, Parenting,* and *Child* magazine Best Book of the Year designations, and Bookbinder's Guild New York Book Show Merit Award, all 2006, all for *John, Paul, George, and Ben.*

Writings

SELF-ILLUSTRATED

Flying Jake, Macmillan (New York, NY), 1989.
The Big Pets, Viking (New York, NY), 1990.
Glasses—Who Needs 'Em?, Viking (New York, NY), 1991.
The Happy Hocky Family!, Viking (New York, NY), 1993.
Pinocchio: The Boy, Viking (New York, NY), 2002.
The Happy Hocky Family Moves to the Country!, Viking (New York, NY), 2003.
John, Paul, George, and Ben, Hyperion (New York, NY), 2006.

ILLUSTRATOR

Eve Merriam, *Halloween ABC,* Macmillan (New York, NY), 1987, revised edition published as *Spooky ABC,* Simon & Schuster (New York, NY), 2002.
Jon Scieszka, *The True Story of the Three Little Pigs!,* Viking (New York, NY), 1989.
Jon Scieszka, *The Stinky Cheese Man, and Other Fairly Stupid Tales,* Viking (New York, NY), 1992.
Jon Scieszka, *Math Curse,* Viking (New York, NY), 1995.
Karey Kirkpatrick, *Disney's James and the Giant Peach,* Disney Press (New York, NY), 1996.
Roald Dahl, *James and the Giant Peach: A Children's Story,* Knopf (New York, NY), 1996.

Dr. Seuss and Jack Prelutsky, *Hooray for Diffendoofer Day!,* Knopf (New York, NY), 1998.
Jon Scieszka, *Squids Will Be Squids: Fresh Morals, Beastly Fables,* Viking (New York, NY), 1998.
George Saunders, *The Very Persistent Gappers of Frip,* Villard (New York, NY), 2000.
Jon Scieszka, *Baloney, (Henry P.),* Viking (New York, NY), 2001.
Jon Scieszka, *Science Verse,* Viking (New York, NY), 2004.
Jon Scieszka, *Seen Art?,* Viking/Museum of Modern Art (New York, NY), 2005.
Jon Scieszka, *Cowboy and Octopus,* Viking (New York, NY), 2007.

Contributor of illustrations to periodicals, including *Rolling Stone, Time, Ms., Newsweek, New York Times, Atlantic Monthly,* and *Esquire.*

ILLUSTRATOR; "TIME WARP TRIO" SERIES

Jon Scieszka, *Knights of the Kitchen Table,* Viking (New York, NY), 1991.
Jon Scieszka, *The Not-So-Jolly Roger,* Viking (New York, NY), 1991.
Jon Scieszka, *The Good, the Bad, and the Goofy,* Viking (New York, NY), 1992.
Jon Scieszka, *Your Mother Was a Neanderthal,* Viking (New York, NY), 1993.
Jon Scieszka, *2095,* Viking (New York, NY), 1995.
Jon Scieszka, *Tut, Tut,* Viking (New York, NY), 1996.
Jon Scieszka, *Summer Reading Is Killing Me!,* Viking (New York, NY), 1998.
Jon Scieszka, *It's All Greek to Me,* Viking (New York, NY), 1999.

Adaptations

The "Tim Warp Trio" books were adapted as a television series, which itself has been novelized.

Sidelights

Children's book aficionados of all ages are likely acquainted with the work of Lane Smith, whose satirical illustrations range from downright goofy to more than a bit unsettling. The winner of numerous awards and the author of several original self-illustrated picture books, Smith is best known for his long-time collaboration with writer Jon Scieszka (pronounced "shes-ka"), which has produced such popular children's books as *The True Story of the Three Little Pigs!, The Stinky Cheese Man, and Other Fairly Stupid Tales, Squids Will Be Squids: Fresh Morals, Beastly Fables, Science Verse,* and the multi-volume "Time Warp Trio" series. Smith's illustrations have also appeared in magazines such as *Rolling Stone, Time,* and *Ms.,* and he designed the characters for the Disney film adaptation of Roald Dahl's classic children's book *James and the Giant Peach.*

Smith is noted for creating figures with large heads and small bodies, and in his picture-book worlds the laws of physics often do not apply. He paints in oils, using dark

pigments that give his figures a distinctively strange, otherworldly quality. In an essay for *Children's Books and Their Creators* Smith explained that he is frequently asked by adults why his work is so dark. "I am not quite sure why myself," he continued. "All I can say is when I was a child, I *liked* dark things. I liked the night. I liked being inside with my family and listening to the sound the wind made outside. I liked the scratching of the clawlike branches against the roof. I liked thunderstorms. I liked building tents and castles out of blankets and chairs, then crawling under them. I liked telling ghost stories. I liked Halloween."

Born in Oklahoma, Smith grew up in Corona, California, with his parents and brother Shane. Influenced by the humor in his household, he developed an early fascination for the offbeat and the absurd. During summer trips back to Oklahoma along Route 66, he enjoyed discovering unusual sights along the way. "I think that's where my bizarre sense of design comes from," he once revealed. "Once you've seen a 100-foot cement buffalo on top of a doughnut stand in the middle of nowhere, you're never the same."

Smith's artistic talent became evident during grade school and junior high school. As he admitted in an essay for *Talking with Artists,* his career was determined by his lack of mathematical ability: "I guess I really knew I wanted to be an artist when my fourth-grade math test came back with a big 'D' on it." While Smith spent his time drawing and writing stories, he also read extensively. "I think one of my fondest memories is of lying stretched out on the library floor at Parkridge Elementary, reading Eleanor Cameron's *Wonderful Flight to the Mushroom Planet,*" he recalled in the same essay. "I loved the story and the art. To this day, whenever I smell hard-boiled eggs I think of how Chuck and David saved the planet with the sulfur-smelling eggs. From then on I drew only space stuff."

After high school Smith enrolled at the prestigious Art Center College of Design in Pasadena, California, where he studied illustration. To earn money for tuition, he worked as a night janitor at nearby Disneyland, maintaining park attractions such as the Haunted Mansion and the Revolving Teacup. When he developed an interest in pop art and European illustration, one of his teachers warned Smith that, with those influences, he would never find a job in the United States. In 1984, the year after he earned his degree, Smith moved to New York City and, contrary to his teacher's prediction, was soon selling his illustrations to some of the nation's most popular magazines. As Smith admitted in *Horn Book,* although he was initially worried about employment prospects in New York, "the punk/new-wave movement came, and my work seemed to fit acceptably into that category."

While working on assignments for *Ms., Time, Rolling Stone,* and other magazines by day, Smith developed his oil-painting technique at night. In college he had

In his early career, Lane Smith created cover art for books, such as Paul Jennings' humorous Australian import, **Unreal!** (Viking, 1985. Cover illustration © 1991 by Lane Smith. Reproduced by permission of Viking Penguin, a division of Penguin Putnam Books for Young Readers.)

concentrated on drawing, so oils were a new medium for him. His first substantial project was a series of thirty Halloween-themed paintings that illustrated the letters of the alphabet. He submitted the finished work to the children's book department at Macmillan. Impressed by his work, the publisher hired children's author Eve Merriam to compose poems for each of the thirty illustrations. Smith enjoyed his first experience in collaboration, finding that Merriam's poetry gave him new ideas. For instance, as he commented in his *Horn Book* essay, "I had V for 'Vampire,' and she came up with 'Viper,' which I liked a lot because I could use the V for the viper's open mouth." When *Halloween ABC* was published in 1987, reviewers responded positively to Smith's illustrations. Although the book was banned in some places because it was considered "Satanic," it received several awards.

In the mid-1980s Smith met Scieszka, a teacher and aspiring children's author. In addition to sharing Smith's wacky sense of humor—they both enjoyed "Monty Python" films and *Mad* magazine—Scieszka liked Smith's art, so they collaborated on the book *The True Story of*

A traditional story gets a new twist as Smith brings to life Jon Scieszka's text for **The True Story of the Three Little Pigs!** (Puffin Books, 1989. Illustration © 1989, by Lane Smith. Reproduced by permission of Puffin Books, a division of Penguin Putnam Books for Young Readers.)

the Three Little Pigs! In this version of the traditional tale (told from the wolf's point of view), Alexander T. Wolf is jailed in the Pig Pen and charged with killing the three pigs. Claiming that he has been misunderstood and victimized by the media, Alexander maintains that he called on the pigs only to borrow a cup of sugar to make a birthday cake for his grandmother. At the time he had a bad cold, and his sneeze blew their houses down. Alexander is quick to add that if the houses had not been so poorly constructed they would not have collapsed. In *Horn Book* Smith explained his approach to illustrating Scieszka's story: "I think Jon thought of the wolf as a con artist trying to talk his way out of a situation. But I really believed the wolf, so I portrayed him with glasses and a little bow tie and tried to make him a victim of circumstance."

When *The True Story of the Three Little Pigs!* was published, it sold out within a few weeks, and children, teachers, and librarians all praised the contemporary twist the book gave to an old story. While a *Publishers Weekly* reviewer predicted that Smith's pictures might seem "mystifyingly adult," other critics delighted in his quirky style. In their review of the book for *Wilson Library Bulletin*, Donnarae MacCann and Olga Richard observed that by "using minimal but subtly changing browns and ochres, he combines a great variety of creative modes: fanciful, realist, surreal, cartoonish."

In 1989 Smith also wrote and illustrated *Flying Jake,* the first of several solo picture books he has produced. He dedicated the work to his high school art teacher, Mr. Baughman, who taught him to experiment with different media when expressing various moods. His sec-

ond original work, *The Big Pets,* he described in *Children's Books and Their Creators* as "a surreal nighttime journey of a little girl and her giant cat." In Smith's story, the girl and her cat travel to the Milk Pool, where children swim and other cats happily drink along the pool's edge, and also encounter the Bone Garden and the Hamster Hole. In *Children's Books and Their Creators* Smith recalled that, "when I wrote *Big Pets* . . . I was expanding on my own childhood fantasies of slipping out into the night for fantastic adventures while knowing there was a home base of security to come back to." Reviewers were charmed by the book's illustrations, finding them to be less threatening than those in *The True Story of the Three Little Pigs!* As a *Publishers Weekly* reviewer noted, Smith's "enticing illustrations . . . provide the perfect landscape for this nocturnal romp."

Another original work, *Glasses—Who Needs 'Em?* describes a boy's visit to the eye doctor to be fitted for his first pair of eyeglasses and is based on Smith's own experience getting glasses in the fifth grade. As he told *Publishers Weekly* interviewer Amanda Smith, he wanted the book's young protagonist to be "a little reluctant about [getting glasses] but still be kind of cool, so kids who wear glasses empathize and get some laughs out of the book, too." Writing in *Children's Books and Their Creators,* he also credited his wife, book designer Molly Leach, with giving *Glasses—Who*

Cover of Smith's self-illustrated picture book **The Big Pets,** *a quirky bedtime tale in which giant pets see eye-to-eye with their pint-sized owners.* (Viking Penguin, 1991. Illustration © 1991 by Lane Smith. Reproduced by permission of Viking Penguin, a division of Penguin Putnam Books for Young Readers.)

In his '50s-style art, Smith tells a '50s-style story in the picture book
The Happy Hocky Family Moves to the Country! (Puffin Books, 2003. Illustration © 2003 by Lane Smith. Reproduced by permission of Puffin Books, a division
of Penguin Putnam Books for Young Readers.)

Needs 'Em? the right visual effect by creating the opening lines of the story in the form of an eye examination
chart. The words in the first line are in large letters,
then they shrink down to the type size used in the rest
of the book. "Not only did this device draw the reader
into the story and establish the proper framework,"
Smith observed, "it also looked smashing!" Leach has
designed several of Smith's other books.

Both *The Happy Hocky Family!* and *The Happy Hocky
Family Moves to the Country!* are playful spoofs on the
beginner-level schoolbooks of the 1950s. The seventeen-
episode plot in *The Happy Hocky Family!* is designed
to help young readers understand the disappointments,
mistakes, and accidents—as well as the positive experiences—that can happen in life. In his illustrations, Smith
uses stick figures, basic outline shapes, and primary
colors. In reviewing the book for the *New York Times
Book Review,* Edward Koren noted that "Smith's drafts-
manship, wonderfully expressive, still manages to create a family that is general and unspecific, one that
could be of any racial or ethnic group." Moving from
primary to brown tones for *The Happy Hocky Family
Moves to the Country!,* Smith contrasts the city ameni-
ties with their country counterparts through visual images; for example, "Milk" is shown as a cow rather
than a supermarket container, and "garbage collector" is
a raccoon rather than a city employee. Noting the retro-
appeal of the work, *School Library Journal* contributor

Barbara Auerbach dubbed *The Happy Hocky Family
Moves to the Country!* "an irreverent look at country
life."

With *John, Paul, George, and Ben* Smith attracted both
the attention of educators and numerous picture-book
honors. With a title that plays on popular culture, the
book focuses on the Founding Fathers, who achieved
America's independence from England despite an amusing collection of personal foibles illustrated by Smith in
a somewhat shaky historical accuracy. For example,
George Washington's legendary admission to chopping
down cherry trees prompted the establishment of the
nation's capital in New York, where few cherry trees
would tempt the president's axe. "While children will
love the off-the-wall humor" in *John, Paul, George,
and Ben, School Library Journal* contributor Marianne
Saccardi added that "there is plenty for adult readers to
enjoy" as well. While Carolyn Phelan wrote in *Booklist*
that Smith's un-history might "confuse children unfamiliar with the period," the book's illustrations are
"deftly drawn, witty, and instantly appealing." "Humor,
both broad . . . and sly . . . reminds readers that books
hold many discoveries, and quite a bit of ye olde fun,"
wrote *Horn Book* reviewer Betty Carter in praise of
Smith's patriotic picture-book effort.

The success of Smith's collaborations with Scieszka
have made both men popular guests in schools. During
their visits to classrooms, they read from the stories
Scieszka has published. Not surprisingly, a particular
favorite of many children is "The Stinky Cheese Man,"
which appears in the 1992 story collection *The Stinky
Cheese Man, and Other Fairly Stupid Tales.* As Smith
noted in *Horn Book,* the story usually elicits "a huge reaction" from children. They "would just roll in the
aisles. And then for the rest of the day you wouldn't
hear anything else. . . . they would raise their hand
and say, 'How about "The Stinky Car"?' Or they would
come up after class and say, 'How about "The Stinky
Cat"?' Because you know you are not supposed to talk
about things being stinky."

The Stinky Cheese Man, and Other Fairly Stupid Tales
contains "updated" versions of such classic stories as
"Chicken Little," "The Ugly Duckling," "The Princess
and the Frog," and "The Princess and the Pea." As part
of Scieszka's updating, however, Chicken Little becomes Chicken Licken, and while the animals the
chicken warns are indeed crushed, the crusher is the
book's table of contents rather than a falling sky. In another updated retelling, the ugly duckling grows up to
be an ugly duck, not a lovely swan, and the frog prince
is revealed to be . . . just a frog. Sustaining the ironic
theme, "The Princess and the Pea" is retitled "The Princess and the Bowling Ball."

The Stinky Cheese Man, and Other Fairly Stupid Tales
was an immediate hit, receiving praise from readers and

reviewers alike. Smith received a 1993 Caldecott Honor Book award as well as several other citations for his illustrations, and Mary M. Burns, writing in *Horn Book,* lauded it as "another masterpiece from the team that created *The True Story of the Three Little Pigs!*" *New York Times Book Review* contributor Signe Wilkinson predicted that the book will appeal not only to children but to readers of all ages: "Kids, who rejoice in anything stinky, will no doubt enjoy the blithe, mean-spirited anarchy of these wildly spinning stories," while "for those who are studying fairy tales at the college level, 'The Stinky Cheese Man' would be a perfect key to the genre."

Among Smith and Scieszka's many popular works is their "Time Warp Trio" novel series, which includes *Knights of the Kitchen Table, The Not-So-Jolly Roger, The Good, the Bad, and the Goofy, Your Mother Was a Neanderthal, 2095, Tut, Tut, Summer Reading Is Killing Me!,* and *It's All Greek to Me.* In the series, Joe, Sam, and Fred travel back in time and, with the aid of a magical book, encounter fantastic adventures. When they are transported to medieval England in *Knights of the Kitchen Table,* they save King Arthur's Camelot. Using their magic power to read, the three friends are able to defeat an evil knight, a giant, and a dragon. In *The Not-So-Jolly Roger,* the boys meet Blackbeard and his band of pirates, who threaten to kill Joe, Sam, and

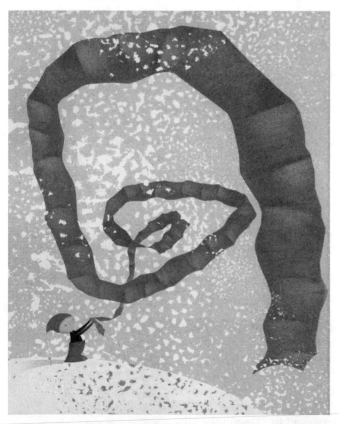

Smith twists a well-known story into a new sort of tale in his engaging picture book **Pinocchio: The Boy.** (Viking, 2002. Illustration © 2002 by Lane Smith. Reproduced by permission of Viking, a division of Penguin Putnam Books for Young Readers.)

Fred and make them walk the plank. The trio's good fortunes fade in *Your Mother Was a Neanderthal,* which finds the boys transported back to the Stone Age. Once there, they discover that, not only are they naked, they also do not have their magic book. After Sam fashions suitable garments, the boys embark on a series of escapades as they try to flee cavegirls, ultimately escaping to a happy ending. In *2095* Joe, Fred, and Sam are launched into the future, courtesy of their magic book. Starting out in the 1920s room of the Natural History Museum, their move forward in time lands them in the equally dated 1990s exhibition room, where they meet their great-grandchildren and try to return to their own present. A 266-pound chicken presents a substantial threat to the trio in *Summer Reading Is Killing Me!,* after Joe thoughlessly puts his summer reading list in The Book and summons forth a host of famous picture-book characters.

The "Time Warp Trio" series received positive responses from reviewers who, like Smith-Scieszka fans, have looked forward to each new installment. In the *New York Times Book Review* Elizabeth-Ann Sachs dubbed *Knights of the Kitchen Table* a "rollicking good story," and a *Publishers Weekly* critic predicted that fans would "gobble up" *The Good, the Bad, and the Goofy* "as they eagerly await the next" "Time Warp Trio" adventure. In her *Booklist* review, Janice Del Negro praised *Your Mother Was a Neanderthal,* noting that Smith's illustrations "add a rollicking, somewhat riotous air to the proceedings." "This is the kind of book that kids tell one another to read," Gale W. Sherman noted of the same book in her review for *School Library Journal.* Julie Yates Walton, in a review of *2095* for *Booklist,* praised Smith's black-pencil illustrations, which are "brimming with zany, adolescent hyperbole." "The farce is as furious and silly as ever," announced *Booklist* contributor Hazel Rochman in a review of Scieszka and Smith's *Summer Reading Is Killing Me!*

In *The Stinky Cheese Man, and Other Fairly Stupid Tales* Smith and Scieszka turn the tables on Mother Goose; with *Squids Will Be Squids* they take Aesop to task in eighteen contemporary wacky fables and tales. In another humorous collaboration, *Math Curse,* a girl wakes up one morning to find that every event during the day—from getting dressed to eating breakfast and going to school—transformed into a math problem that must be solved. She decides her teacher, Mrs. Fibonacci, has put a math curse on her, but that night she dreams of a way to get rid of the curse. *Seen Art?* takes readers to the halls of the newly (as of 2004) redesigned Museum of Modern Art (MoMA), as the narrator recounts his search for his friend Art within its walls. With a story similar to that in *Math Curse, Science Verse* assembles what a *Kirkus Reviews* contributor described as a "madcap collection of science poetry that lampoons familiar songs" as technoterminology infiltrates a child's everyday world. A reviewer for *Publishers Weekly* praised Smith's illustrations for *Squids Will Be Squids,* writing that his artwork "ardently keeps pace with Sci-

eszka's leaps of fancy." Reviewing *Math Curse* for *Booklist,* Carolyn Phelan wrote that, both "bold in design and often bizarre in expression, Smith's paintings clearly express the child's feelings of bemusement, frustration, and panic as well as her eventual joy when she overcomes the math curse." The "muted background tones" Smith incorporates into his images for *Seen Art?* serve as "an effective foil for the well-reproduced if sometimes diminutive artwork" the illustrator creates to reproduce MoMA's world-famous collection, Phelan added.

In addition to his work with Scieszka, Smith has also provided illustrations for *Hooray for Diffendoofer Day!,* a book begun by Dr. Seuss (Theodore Geisel) and completed following Geisel's death by poet Jack Prelutsky. Describing the artist's contribution to the work, *Horn Book* critic Joanna Rudge Long wrote that Smith's "satirical renditions, [rendered] in his own distinctive, sophisticated style," contain "such zany folk and weirdly expressive settings as" the late pseudonymous author "might have dreamed up" himself. Working with short-story writer George Saunders, Smith also provided illustrations for *The Very Persistent Gappers of Frip,* "a delightful story, lavishly illustrated," as Susan Salpini commented in *School Library Journal.* Something of a departure for Smith, *The Very Persistent Gappers of Frip* is geared mainly for adult readers. Caitlin Dover, reviewing the book in *Print* magazine, applauded Smith's "perceptive, eclectic paintings" and concluded of the sophisticated offering: "This may be Smith's first foray into adult fiction, but we doubt it will be his last."

Biographical and Critical Sources

BOOKS

Cummings, Pat, compiler and editor, *Talking with Artists,* Bradbury Press (New York, NY), 1992, pp. 72-75.
Silvey, Anita, editor, *Children's Books and Their Creators,* Houghton (Boston, MA), 1995.

PERIODICALS

Booklist, October 1, 1993, Janice Del Negro, review of *Your Mother Was a Neanderthal,* p. 346; July 1 & 15, 1995, Julie Yates Walton, review of *2095,* p. 1773; November 1, 1995, Carolyn Phelan, review of *Math Curse,* p. 472; May 1, 1996, Ilene Cooper, reviews of *Disney's James and the Giant Peach* and *James and the Giant Peach,* p. 1511; October 1, 1997, p. 352; May 1, 1998, p. 1522; June 1, 1998, Hazel Rochman, review of *Summer Reading Is Killing Me!,* p. 1769; September 15, 1998, p. 232; January 1, 2000, p. 988; April 15, 2005, Gillian Engberg, review of *Seen Art?,* p. 1456; February 15, 2006, Carolyn Phelan, review of *John, Paul, George, and Ben,* p. 104.
Bulletin of the Center for Children's Books, May, 2006, Elizabeth Bush, review of *John, Paul, George, and Ben,* p. 424.

Entertainment Weekly, November 19, 1999, p. 135.
Horn Book, November-December, 1992, Mary M. Burns, review of *The Stinky Cheese Man, and Other Fairly Stupid Tales,* p. 720; January-February, 1993, Lane Smith, "The Artist at Work," pp. 64-70; November-December, 1995, p. 738; July-August, 1998, Joanna Rudge Long, review of *Hooray for Diffendoofer Day!,* pp. 479-481; May-June, 2001, p. 316.
New York, April 8, 1996, Barbara Ensor, "Mr. Smith Goes to Hollywood," pp. 50, 51-53; September-October, 2004, Peter D. Sieruta, review of *Science Verse,* p. 574; May-June, 2006, Betty Carter, review of *John, Paul, George, and Ben,* p. 349.
Kirkus Reviews, August 15, 2004, review of *Science Verse,* p. 813; April 15, 2005, review of *Seen Art?,* p. 481; March 15, 2006, review of *John, Paul, George, and Ben,* p. 301.
New Yorker, December 25, 1995, pp. 45-46.
New York Times Book Review, October 6, 1991, Elizabeth-Ann Sachs, reviews of *Knights of the Kitchen Table* and *The Not-So-Jolly Roger,* p. 23; November 8, 1992, Signe Wilkinson, "No Princes, No White Horses, No Happy Endings," pp. 29, 59; November 14, 1993, Edward Koren, review of *The Happy Hocky Family!,* p. 44.
Print, November, 2000, Caitlin Dover, review of *The Very Persistent Gappers of Frip,* p. 16.
Publishers Weekly, July 28, 1989, review of *The True Story of the Three Little Pigs!,* p. 218; December 21, 1990, review of *The Big Pets,* p. 55; July 26, 1991, Amanda Smith, "Jon Scieszka and Lane Smith," pp. 220-221; May 11, 1992, review of *The Good, the Bad, and the Goofy,* p. 72; February 9, 1998, p. 24; May 18, 1998, review of *Squids Will Be Squids: Fresh Morals, Beastly Fables,* p. 78; May 25, 1998, p. 28; July 10, 2000, p. 45; April 30, 2001, p. 76; July 16, 2001, p. 84; May 2, 2005, review of *Seen Art?,* p. 198; January 23, 2006, review of *John, Paul, George, and Ben,* p. 207.
School Library Journal, October, 1993, Gale W. Sherman, review of *Your Mother Was a Neanderthal,* p. 130; September, 1995, Lucinda Snyder Whitehurst, review of *Math Curse,* p. 215; June, 1998, pp. 121-122; August, 1998, p. 145; October, 1999, pp. 126-127; January, 2001, Susan Salpini, review of *The Very Persistent Gappers of Frip,* p. 160; May, 2001, Mary Ann Carich, review of *Baloney (Henry P.),* p. 134; June, 2004, Steven Engelfried, review of *Baloney (Henry P.),* p. 58; May, 2005, Carol Ann Wilson, review of *Seen Art?,* p. 96; June, 2005, Steven Engelfried, review of *Science Verse,* p. 56; March, 2006, Marianne Saccardi, review of *John, Paul, George, and Ben,* p. 214; January, 2007, Alison Grant, review of *You Can't but Ghengis Khan,* p. 108.
Time, December 21, 1992, "Kid-Lit Capers," pp. 69-70.
Wilson Library Bulletin, June, 1992, Donnarae MacCann, and Olga Richard, review of *The True Story of the Three Little Pigs!,* p. 118.

ONLINE

Lane Smith Home Page, http://www.lanesmithbooks.com (June 21, 2007).

STEMPLE, Jason

Personal

Son of David Stemple (a professor) and Jane Yolen (a children's book author). *Education:* Greenfield Community College, A.A. (graphic design); Western State College of Colorado, B.A. (business).

Addresses

Home and office—Charleston, SC. *Agent*—Elizabeth Harding, Curtis Brown, 10 Astor Place, New York, NY 10003. *E-mail*—stemplej@bellsouth.net.

Career

Photographer, author, and graphic designer. Formerly worked as a photo lab technician, ski photographer, and fly-fishing guide.

Illustrator

PHOTOGRAPHER

Jane Yolen, *A Letter from Phoenix Farm*, R.C. Owen Publishers (Katonah, NY), 1992.

Jane Yolen, *Water Music: Poems for Children*, Wordsong/ Boyds Mills Press (Honesdale, PA), 1995.

Jane Yolen, *Once upon Ice, and Other Frozen Poems*, Wordsong/Boyds Mills Press (Honesdale, PA), 1997.

Jane Yolen, *House, House*, Marshall Cavendish (New York, NY), 1998.

Jane Yolen, *Snow, Snow: Winter Poems for Children*, Wordsong (Honesdale, PA), 1998.

Jane Yolen, *Color Me a Rhyme: Nature Poems for Young People*, Wordsong (Honesdale, PA), 2000.

Jane Yolen, *Horizons: Poems as Far as the Eye Can See*, Wordsong/Boyds Mills Press (Honesdale, PA), 2002.

Jane Yolen, *Wild Wings: Poems for Young People*, Wordsong/Boyds Mills Press (Honesdale, PA), 2002.

Jane Yolen, *Least Things: Poems about Small Natures*, Wordsong/Boyds Mills Press (Honesdale, PA), 2003.

Jane Yolen, *Fine Feathered Friends: Poems for Young People*, Wordsong (Honesdale, PA), 2004.

Jane Yolen, *Count Me a Rhyme: Animal Poems by the Numbers*, Wordsong (Honesdale, PA), 2005.

Jane Yolen, *Shape Me a Rhyme: Nature's Forms in Poetry*, Wordsong (Honesdale, PA), 2007.

Biographical and Critical Sources

PERIODICALS

Booklinks, July, 2005, Rebecca Rupp, review of *Color Me a Rhyme: Nature Poems for Young People*, p. 60; November, 2006, review of *Least Things: Poems about Small Natures*, p. 18.

Booklist, May 15, 2002, Susan Dove Lempke, review of *Wild Wings: Poems for Young People*, p. 1596; November 1, 2004, GraceAnne A. DeCandido, review of *Fine Feathered Friends: Poems for Young People*, p. 478; April 1, 2006, Carolyn Phelan, review of *Count Me a Rhyme: Animal Poems by the Numbers*, p. 38.

Children's Bookwatch, April, 2006, review of *Count Me a Rhyme*.

Kirkus Reviews, March 1, 2002, review of *Wild Wings*, p. 349; September 1, 2003, review of *Least Things*, p. 1133; February 1, 2006, review of *Count Me a Rhyme*, p. 139.

Library Media Connection, January, 2003, review of *Horizons: Poems as Far as the Eye Can See*, p. 95; November-December, 2006, Kare Sebesta, review of *Count Me a Rhyme*, p. 87.

Publishers Weekly, August 25, 2003, "Back to Basics," p. 66.

School Library Journal, June, 2002, Sharon Korbeck, review of *Wild Wings*, p. 127; October, 2002, Nina Lindsay, review of *Horizons*, p. 152; October, 2003, Donna Cardon, review of *Least Things*, p. 157; December, 2004, Susan Scheps, review of *Fine Feathered Friends*, p. 172; April, 2006, Lee Bock, review of *Count Me a Rhyme*, p. 132.

Science Books and Films, May, 2003, review of *Wild Wings*, p. 105.

Tribune Books (Chicago, IL), September 22, 2002, review of *Horizons*, p. 4.

ONLINE

Jason Stemple Home Page, http://www.jasonstemple.com (June 9, 2007).*

* * *

STEPHENSON, Lynda 1941-

Personal

Born December 31, 1941, in Shamrock, TX; daughter of Thurman (an attorney) and Jerome Stanley (a grade-school teacher) Adkins; married Carl Gene Stephenson (a math teacher), June 8, 1963; children: Amy S. Patterson, Tom A. Stephenson. *Education:* Attended Trinity University (San Antonio, TX); Oklahoma University, B.A., M.A, A.B.D. (English). *Politics:* Democrat. *Religion:* Presbyterian. *Hobbies and other interests:* Reading, collecting art, home design, travel.

Addresses

Home—Edmond, OK. *E-mail*—gendastep@sbcglobal.net.

Career

Educator and author. East Central University, Ada, OK, professor of English composition, literature, and humanities, 1965-89.

Lynda Stephenson (Photograph courtesy of Lynda Stephenson.)

Member

Oklahoma Writers Federation, Oklahoma City Writers.

Awards, Honors

Oklahoma Book Award finalist, International Reading Association Notable Book designation, and *ForeWord* magazine Book of the Year Award honorable mention, all 2006, and Kappa Delta Gamma Book of the Year designation, 2007, all for *Dancing with Elvis.*

Writings

Dancing with Elvis (young-adult novel), Eerdman's Publishing (Grand Rapids, MI), 2005.

Author of one-act play *One Sunday Morning,* produced in San Antonio, TX. Contributor of short fiction to periodicals, including *Byline,* and of humorous essays to *Edmond Sun* newspaper.

Sidelights

Lynda Stephenson told *SATA:* "I grew up in the small Texas Panhandle town of Shamrock during the 1950s, and I have written all my life, beginning with poetry at

age four. As an undergraduate at Trinity University in San Antonio, I wrote a one-act play titled *One Sunday Morning,* which was performed by the drama department, and I also wrote poetry published in student periodicals.

"After receiving a B.A., and M.A., and A.B.D. in English from Oklahoma University, I taught English composition and literature at East Central University in Ada, Oklahoma, for over twenty years. Much of that time, I served as the faculty sponsor of *The Originals,* the university's art and literature magazine. Also, I wrote church-related literature, essays, short stories, art reviews, and poetry.

"My husband, Gene, and I moved to Clarksville, Arkansas, in 1989, and as the president's wife at the University of the Ozarks, I served as head of church relations and helped write and edit various college publications.

"When we moved to Edmond, Oklahoma, I served as a volunteer docent at the Western Arts and Heritage Museum and started a Books and Culture reading group at the First Presbyterian Church. While taking a creative writing class from University of Central Oklahoma artist-in-residence Rilla Askew, author of *The Mercy Seat* and *Fire in Beulah,* I began writing in earnest. Over the next few semesters I enrolled in several creative writing classes.

"*Dancing with Elvis* started out as a short story, which I read to a fiction seminar at the Calvin College Festival of Faith in Writing in 2002. After my presentation several workshop participants told me my story wasn't finished. They wanted to know what would happen to the main character, Frankilee Baxter. I decided to stick with Frankilee and see her through her troubles, and the young-adult novel was the result.

"I wrote about a self-conscious, unattractive but privileged girl growing up during the 'fifties, a time of enormous historical importance. Thus, the book is about teenaged angst set against the backdrop of racial tension sparked by the 1955 *Brown vs. Board of Education* Supreme Court ruling. I wanted to say, 'Hey, the fifties weren't a happy time for everybody.'

"Although I write mostly to educate and entertain, I also want to challenge myself. With every writing project, I think, 'Let's see if I can do this.' I've known for a long time that I could write fairly entertaining poetry and short stories, but with *Dancing with Elvis* I wanted to see if I could write a novel. After finishing it, I wanted to see if I could sell it to a publisher. Then I wanted to see if I could promote it. Now I want to see if I can write another novel, and start the same process all over again.

"My writing habits are erratic. I'm constantly writing in my head, and scribble on scraps of paper frequently, sometimes late at night and sometimes in public places.

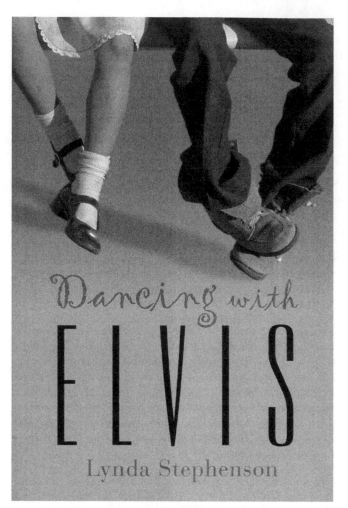

Cover of Stephenson's young-adult novel Dancing with Elvis, *which brings readers back to pre-civil-rights-era Texas.* (Eerdmans Books for Young Readers, 2005. Reproduced by permission.)

When I'm at the computer, I spend big blocks of time working, occasionally from eight to ten hours at a time. I'm fairly lazy and procrastinate often, but when I'm into a project, I work until I'm exhausted.

"*Dancing with Elvis* was influenced in style, subject matter, humor, and depth by the coming-of-age stories of Jane Austen, Charles Dickens, Mark Twain, Mary Karr, J.D. Salinger, Carson McCullers, Harper Lee, and Frank McCourt. Others who have influenced me include Kent Haruf, Eudora Welty, Flannery O'Conner, Ernest Hemingway, F. Scott Fitzgerald, William Faulkner, and the authors of the 'Nancy Drew' mystery stories.

"If I were to give advice to another writer, I'd say 'Take classes from professors you trust, and listen to their criticism. Be prepared to rewrite everything you've written. Join a writers' group of people who have published and will appreciate and understand your work. Most of all, write because you love to write and enjoy the challenge. Send your work out but expect nothing. Then you'll be surprised when something good comes your way."

Biographical and Critical Sources

PERIODICALS

Booklist, November 15, 2005, Ilene Cooper, review of *Dancing with Elvis,* p. 57.

Kirkus Reviews, August 1, 2005, review of *Dancing with Elvis,* p. 859.

Publishers Weekly, September 19, 2005, review of *Dancing with Elvis,* p. 67.

School Library Journal, January, 2006, Sharon Morrison, review of *Dancing with Elvis,* p. 143.

Voice of Youth Advocates, April, 2006, Jamie Hansen, review of *Dancing with Elvis,* p. 52.

ONLINE

Eerdmans Books for Young Readers Web site, http://www.eerdmans.com/ (January, 2006), interview with Stephenson.

Plano Profile Online, http://www.wishbonegraphics.com/ (November, 2005), Cindy Boykin, interview with Stephenson.

*　　*　　*

STOHNER, Anu 1952-

Personal

Born 1952, in Helsinki, Finland.

Addresses

Home and office—Munich, Germany.

Career

Children's book author and translator.

Writings

PICTURE BOOKS

Santa's Littlest Helper (originally published in the German as *Der kleine Weinachtsmann*), illustrated by Henrike Wilson, Bloomsbury (New York, NY), 2004.

Brave Charlotte (originally published in the German as *Scaf Charlotte*), illustrated by Henrike Wilson, Bloomsbury (New York, NY), 2005.

Santa's Littlest Helper Travels the World, illustrated by Henrike Wilson, Bloomsbury (New York, NY), 2007.

Biographical and Critical Sources

PERIODICALS

Booklist, August, 2005, Ilene Cooper, review of *Brave Charlotte,* p. 2036.

Children's Bookwatch, November, 2005, review of _Brave Charlotte_.

Horn Book, January-February, 2006, Roget Sutton, review of _Brave Charlotte_, p. 70.

Kirkus Reviews, October 1, 2005, review of _Brave Charlotte_, p. 1090.

Publishers Weekly, November 21, 2005, review of _Brave Charlotte_, p. 47.

School Library Journal, January, 2006, Donna Cardon, review of _Brave Charlotte_, p. 114.

Washington Post Book World, December 11, 2005, Elizabeth Ward, review of _Brave Charlotte_, p. 8.

ONLINE

Bloomsbury Press Web site, http://www.bloomsbury.com/ (June 9, 2007), "Anu Stohner."*

*   *   *

SULLIVAN, Sarah G. 1953-

Personal

Born July 21, 1953, in Fairmont, WV; daughter of John L., Jr. (a district sales manager) and Sarah (a homemaker) Sullivan; married Ricklin Brown (an attorney), September 4, 1992; children: Jack (deceased); (stepchildren) Marshall, Jennifer, Christiana. _Education:_ Tufts University, A.B. (French), 1975; attended Sorbonne, University of Paris, 1973-74; West Virginia University, J.D., 1980; Vermont College, M.F.A. (writing for children and young adults), 2005. _Politics:_ Democrat. _Religion:_ Presbyterian. _Hobbies and other interests:_ Canoeing, skiing, hiking, biking, reading, travel.

Addresses

Home—Charleston, WV. _Agent_—Adams Literary, 7845 Colony Rd., C4 No. 215, Charlotte, NC 28226. _E-mail_—sarahglenn1@verizon.net.

Career

Attorney and author. Jackson & Kelly (law firm), Charleston, WV, associate attorney, 1980-85; U.S. Attorney's Office and U.S. Trustee's Office for Southern District of West Virginia, Charleston, U.S. attorney, 1984-87, staff attorney, 1987-92; Lewis, Friedberg, Glasser, Casey & Rollins, Charleston, associate attorney, 1992-94. Substitute high-school teacher in English and creative writing. Read Aloud West Virginia, Founding member and member of advisory committee, 1999-2003; conducts writing workshops.

Member

Society of Children's Book Writers and Illustrators, Authors Guild, West Virginia Writers.

Sarah G. Sullivan (Photograph courtesy of Sarah Sullivan.)

Awards, Honors

West Virginia Commission on the Arts individual artists fellowship, 2001; Oppenheim Toy Portfolio Gold Award, 2005, for _Dear Baby_.

Writings

FOR CHILDREN

Root Beer and Banana, illustrated by Greg Shed, Candlewick Press (Cambridge, MA), 2005.

Dear Baby: Letters from Your Big Brother, illustrated by Paul Meisel, Candlewick Press (Cambridge, MA), 2005.

Passing the Music Down, Candlewick Press (Cambridge, MA), 2008.

Contributor to periodicals, including _Journal of Children's Literature_ and _Cricket_.

Sidelights

Sarah G. Sullivan told _SATA:_ "I like stories with a strong sense of place, which probably comes from having moved around a lot while I was growing up. I was always trying to fit in. I guess I still am. I also like humor. Life is so much easier when we can settle back and have a good laugh at ourselves.

Based on memories of childhood summers, Sarah Sullivan's **Root Beer and Bananas** *is enhanced by Gred Shed's evocative illustrations.* (Candlewick Press, 2005. Illustration © 2005 by Greg Shed. Reproduced by permission of Candlewick Press, Inc., Cambridge, MA.)

"My first picture book, *Root Beer and Banana,* came directly out of a writing exercise I did at a workshop led by George Ella Lyon. The story was inspired by memories of summers I spent with my grandparents in

a small town on the Rappahannock River in Virginia, though it is not, strictly speaking, autobiographical."

Biographical and Critical Sources

PERIODICALS

Booklist, May 1, 2005, Hazel Rochman, review of *Root Beer and Banana,* p. 1594; September 15, 2005, Hazel Rochman, review of *Dear Baby: Letters from Your Big Brother,* p. 75.
Kirkus Reviews, May 15, 2005, review of *Root Beer and Banana,* p. 597; August 1, 2005, review of *Dear Baby,* p. 859.
School Library Journal, July 1, 2005, Linda Staskus, review of *Root Beer and Banana,* p. 83; September 1, 2005, Kara Schaff, review of *Dear Baby,* p. 187.

ONLINE

Sarah G. Sullivan Home Page, http://www.sarahsullivan-books.com (June 20, 2007).

*   *   *

SYMES, Ruth Louise 1962-

Personal

Born 1962, in England; married Eric Wainwright.

Addresses

Home—London, England. *E-mail*—info@ruthsymes. com.

Career

Children's book author and editor. Formerly taught children with special needs; former aerobics instructor; worked as an actor. Writing coach for British Broadcasting Corporation; judge for short-story competition.

Awards, Honors

Carnegie Medal nomination, 1997, for *Master of Secrets; Cosmopolitan* Women of Achievement Award finalist, 1999; Paws TV Drama Award, 2000, for adaptation of *Frankie's Romeo;* Sir Peter Ustinov Screenwriting Award runner up, 2001, for *The Mum Trap.*

Writings

(Editor, with Trev Lynn) *The Governess: An Anthology,* St. Martin's Press (New York, NY), 1997.

Ruth Louise Symes (Photograph courtesy of Ruth Louise Symes.)

Play If You Dare, illustrated by Stephen Player, Macdonald Young (Hove, England), 1999.
The Sheep Fairy: When Wishes Have Wings, illustrated by David Sim, Scholastic (New York, NY), 2003.
Floppy Ears, illustrated by Tony Kenyon, Orion (London, England), 2004.
Mondays at Monster School, Orion (London, England), 2005.
Little Tail, Orion (London, England), 2006.
Harriet Dancing, illustrated by Caroline Jayne Church, Scholastic (New York, NY), 2007.

Also author of children's books *The Twelfth-Floor Kids, Chip's Dad, Smelly Sock Soup,* and *The Sarah Song.*

NOVELS

Master of Secrets, Puffin (London, England), 1997.
The Mum Trap (also see below), Andersen (London, England), 2002.
Frankie's Romeo (also see below), Dolphin (London, England), 2002.

OTHER

Adapted *Frankie's Romeo* as a teleplay, produced 2000; adapted *The Mum Trap* as the teleplay *Pizzas, Pimples, and Polly.* Author of television scripts for series *The Hoobs* and *PicMe.*

Sidelights

When growing up in England, being a writer was only one of the many things Ruth Louise Symes wanted to do. "I changed my mind a lot," she explained to an interviewer for the *Chicken House Web site,* "but mainly I think I wanted to be an actor, singer and teacher but most of all a writer—and I got to do all of those things and am still doing them." In addition to writing books for the very young, Symes has also penned middle-grade and young-adult novels as well as scripts produced on British network television.

In her novel *Master of Secrets* Symes describes a teen's experiences when his class engages in an unusual English project. When Raj joins the other students in his class in exchanging anonymous letters, he quickly discovers that the mysterious person writing to him is actually the school bully. Believing himself to be anonymous, the letter writer admits to suffering from abuse at home, and shares his worries about what to do to change his life. *Master of Secrets* was nominated for the Carnegie Medal in 1997.

Symes moves from a teen readership to a younger audience in *The Sheep Fairy: When Wishes Have Wings,* a picture book in which Wendy Woolcoat enjoys her life as a sheep, but admits to a fairy that she would love to have the chance to fly. The fairy grants Wendy's wish, and for one night the sheep takes to the skies. The book is "destined to be a champion read-aloud, and a surefire way to give young listeners wings of their own," according to a *Kirkus Reviews* contributor. A *Liverpool Echo* reviewer recommended Woolcoat's tale as one "guaranteed to put a smile on any five and under's face." In another picture-book offering, *Floppy Ears,* Symes introduces a rabbit who, although considered too small, ultimately saves the day when Fox sneaks up on the rabbit's friends. A *Liverpool Echo* contributor dubbed *Floppy Ears* "ideal for reading aloud."

Asked by an interviewer from the Wordpool Web site to comment on her career writing for children, Symes explained: "I like the variety—working on a picture book one day, a novel the next, [then] TV and film." After living in such places as Singapore, Israel, Australia, and New Zealand, Symes came full circle, and now makes her home in London, England, where she grew up.

Biographical and Critical Sources

PERIODICALS

Booklist, October 1, 2003, Lauren Peterson, review of *The Sheep Fairy: When Wishes Have Wings,* p. 329.
Independent on Sunday (London, England), January 25, 1998, Jonathan Sale, review of *The Governess,* p. 26.
Journal of Women's History, spring, 2000, Birgitte Soland, review of *The Governess,* p. 198.
Kirkus Reviews, October 1, 2003, review of *The Sheep Fairy,* p. 1231; March 15, 2005, review of *Floppy Ears,* p. 359.
Liverpool Echo (Liverpool, England), review of *The Sheep Fairy,* p. 22; March 15, 2005, review of *Floppy Ears,* p. 24.
MBR Bookwatch, June, 2005, Diane C. Conovan, review of *Floppy Ears.*
Publishers Weekly, November 24, 2003, review of *The Sheep Fairy,* p. 63.
School Library Journal, December, 2003, Jody McCoy, review of *The Sheep Fairy,* p. 128.

ONLINE

Chicken House Web site, http://www.doublecluck.com/ (May 18, 2007), interview with Symes.
Ruth Louise Symes Home Page, http://www.ruthsymes.com (May 17, 2007).
Wordpool Web site, http://www.wordpool.co.uk/ (May 17, 2007), interview with Symes.

T-Y

TRUEIT, Trudi
See TRUEIT, Trudi Strain

* * *

TRUEIT, Trudi Strain 1963-
(Trudi Trueit)

Personal
Born 1963, in Seattle, WA; married Bill Trueit. *Education:* Pacific Lutheran University, B.A. *Hobbies and other interests:* Drawing, painting, photography.

Addresses
Home and office—Everett, WA. *Agent*—Rosemary Stimola, Stimola Literary Studio, 308 Chase Ct., Edgewater, NJ 07020. *E-mail*—trudi@truditrueit.com.

Career
Trueit Media, president and chief executive officer. Formerly worked as a television news reporter, weather forecaster, journalist, media specialist, and news anchor.

Writings

NONFICTION; FOR CHILDREN

The Water Cycle, Franklin Watts (New York, NY), 2002.
Storm Chaser, Franklin Watts (New York, NY), 2002.
Clouds, Franklin Watts (New York, NY), 2002.
Octopuses, Squids, and Cuttlefish, Franklin Watts (New York, NY), 2002.
Rain, Hail, and Snow, Franklin Watts (New York, NY), 2002.
Fossils, Franklin Watts (New York, NY), 2003.
Eating Disorders, Franklin Watts (New York, NY), 2003.

Earthquakes, Franklin Watts (New York, NY), 2003.
Lizards, Children's Press (New York, NY), 2003.
Rocks, Gems, and Minerals, Franklin Watts (New York, NY), 2003.
Snakes, Children's Press (New York, NY), 2003.
Turtles, Children's Press (New York, NY), 2003.
Volcanoes, Franklin Watts (New York, NY), 2003.
Alligators and Crocodiles, Children's Press (New York, NY), 2003.
Keeping a Journal, Franklin Watts (New York, NY), 2004.
ADHD, Franklin Watts (New York, NY), 2004.
Dreams and Sleep, Franklin Watts (New York, NY), 2004.
The Boston Tea Party, Children's Press (New York, NY), 2005.
Gunpowder, Franklin Watts (New York, NY), 2005.
The Camera, Franklin Watts (New York, NY), 2006.
Surviving Divorce: Teens Talk about What Helps and What Hurts, Scholastic (New York, NY), 2006.
Diwali, Children's Press (New York, NY), 2006.
Mississippi, Children's Press (New York, NY), 2007.
Martin Luther King, Jr. Day, Children's Press (New York, NY), 2007.
Chanukah, Children's Press (New York, NY), 2007.
Earth Day, Children's Press (New York, NY), 2007.
Thanksgiving, Children's Press (New York, NY), 2007.
Kwanzaa, Children's Press (New York, NY), 2007.
Utah, Children's Press (New York, NY), 2007.
Valentine's Day, Children's Press (New York, NY), 2007.
Halloween, Children's Press (New York, NY), 2007.
Independence Day, Children's Press (New York, NY), 2007.
Massachusetts, Children's Press (New York, NY), 2007.
Easter, Child's World (Mankato, MN), 2007.
Christmas, Child's World (Mankato, MN), 2007.
Hanukkah, Child's World (Mankato, MN), 2007.
President's Day, Child's World (Mankato, MN), 2007.
Memorial Day, Child's World (Mankato, MN), 2007.
Martin Luther King, Jr. Day, Child's World (Mankato, MN), 2007.

"JULEP O'TOOLE" NOVEL SERIES; UNDER NAME TRUDI TRUEIT

Julep O'Toole: Confessions of a Middle Child, Dutton Children's Books (New York, NY), 2005.
Julep O'Toole: Miss Independent, Dutton Children's Books (New York, NY), 2006.
Julep O'Toole: What I Really Want to Do Is Direct, Dutton Children's Books (New York, NY), 2007.

Sidelights

Trudi Strain Trueit told *SATA:* "Whether it was writing plays in elementary school or reporting of a television news organization as an adult, writing has always been an important part of my life. I have the best of both worlds, publishing fiction, which feeds my creative side, and nonfiction, which keeps me constantly learning and growing. If you can uncover and pursue your passion in life, whatever that might be, you are, indeed, fortunate."

Biographical and Critical Sources

PERIODICALS

Booklist, October 1, 2005, Shelle Rosenfeld, review of *Julep O'Toole: Confessions of a Middle Child,* p. 60; April 12, 2006, Shelle Rosenfeld, review of *Julep O'Toole: Miss Independent,* p. 48; January 1, 2007, Gillian Engberg, review of *Surviving Divorce: Teens Talk about What Helps and What Hurts,* and Ilene Cooper, review of *Valentine's Day,* both p. 86.
Kirkus Reviews, September 1, 2005, review of *Julep O'Toole: Confessions of a Middle Child,* p. 984; March 15, 2006, review of *Julep O'Toole: Miss Independent,* p. 302; January 15, 2007, review of *Julep O'Toole: What I Really Want to Do Is Direct,* p. 82.
School Library Journal, January, 2004, Kathryn Kosiorek, review of *Rocks, Gems, and Minerals,* p. 161; July, 2004, Linda Beck, review of *ADHD,* p. 116; March, 2005, Sharton A. Neal, review of *Keeping a Journal,* p. 236; April, 2005, Elaine Landau, review of *Dyslexia,* p. 51; October, 2005, Faith Brautigam, review of *Julep O'Toole: Confessions of a Middle Child,* p. 176; March, 2006, Rita Soltan, review of *Julep O'Toole: Miss Independent,* p. 230; October, 2006, Teri Markson, review of *Chanukah,* p. 101.
Voice of Youth Advocates, October, 2003, reviews of *Earthquakes* and *Volcanoes,* p. 339; June, 2005, Elaine McGuire, reviews of *Death and Dying* and *Keeping a Journal,* p. 168.

ONLINE

Trudi Trueit Home Page, http://www.truditrueit.com (June 9, 2007).
Penguin Group Web site, http://us.penguingroup.com/ (June 9, 2007), "Trudi Trueit."

Van STOCKUM, Hilda 1908-2006

OBITUARY NOTICE— See index for *SATA* sketch: Born February 9, 1908, in Rotterdam, Netherlands; died of a stroke, November 1, 2006, in Berkhamsted, England. Author. Van Stockum was a popular author and illustrator of children's books. Born in the Netherlands, she spent some of her childhood years in Ireland, and in adulthood she lived in the United States, Canada, and England. All of these settings would eventually work their way into Van Stockum's stories. Her first book, *A Day on Skates: The Story of a Dutch Picnic* (1934), included a foreword by her aunt, noted poet Edna St. Vincent Millay. After attending the Corcoran School of Art in Washington, DC, in the mid-1930s, she continued to release more self-illustrated children's titles, among them *Francie on the Run* (1939), *Pegeen* (1941), and *The Mitchells* (1945). Van Stockum's books are typically gentle stories of family life, but in some cases, as with *The Winged Watchman* (1962) and *The Borrowed House* (1975), she focused on serious topics, such as World War II and the Holocaust. Also a translator and illustrator of books by other authors, such as Catherine C. Coblentz and Louisa May Alcott, Van Stockum published over twenty of her own titles. Among her other works are *Canadian Summer* (1948), *Little Old Bear* (1962), *Rufus Round and Round* (1973), and *The Mitchells: Five for Victory* (1995). Van Stockum was an accomplished still-life painter, too, and she was honored in 1993 when one of her paintings was reproduced on an Irish postage stamp.

OBITUARIES AND OTHER SOURCES:

BOOKS

Twentieth-Century Children's Writers, 3rd edition, St. James Press (Detroit, MI), 1989.

PERIODICALS

New York Times, November 4, 2006, p. B15.

*   *   *

VIZZINI, Ned 1981-

Personal

Born April 4, 1981, in New York, NY; son of James D. (an executive vice president) and Emma (a chief executive officer) Vizzini. *Education:* Hunter College, B.S. (computer science and English), 2003.

Addresses

Home—New York, NY. *Agent*—Jay Mandel, William Morris Agency, 1325 Avenue of the Americas, New York, NY 10019. *E-mail*—ned.vizzini@gmail.com.

Career

Journalist. *New York Press,* New York, NY, contributing writer, 2001-02; freelance writer, 2002-03. Former computer programmer at New York Cityscape, Computer Associates, Edison Price Lighting, and Brain Bridge. Quiktrak, New York, NY, former bike messenger.

Writings

Teen Angst? Naaah . . . : A Quasi-Autobiography, Free Spirit Publishing (Minneapolis, MN), 2000.
Be More Chill, Miramax (New York, NY), 2004.
It's Kind of a Funny Story, Miramax (New York, NY), 2006.

Contributor of short fiction to anthologies, including *Sixteen, Not like I'm Jealous or Anything, Guys Write for Guys Read,* and *21 Proms,* 2006. Contributor of articles to newspapers and magazines, including *Teen* and *New York Times Magazine.* Author of "Since When?" (weekly column), for *New York Press.*

Author's works have been translated into several languages, including Dutch, German, Italian, French, Hebrew, Indonesian, and Spanish.

Adaptations

Vizzini's books have been adapted for audiobook by Harper Audio. Film rights to *Be More Chill* were acquired by Depth of Field Productions. Film rights to *It's Kind of a Funny Story* were acquired by Paramount Pictures, 2006.

Sidelights

Ned Vizzini's first published work was an essay he submitted to the *New York Press,* about winning a school literary prize. As a freelance writer for the paper, he wrote about everything from family vacations to getting drunk in the street with dangerous urban youth. The success of Vizzini's work earned him an invitation to contribute a teen-focused article to the *New York Times.* His *New York Press* columns eventually became the core of his first book, *Teen Angst? Naaah . . . : A Quasi-Autobiography,* which was published when its author was nineteen years old. Vizzini then moved into fiction with the young-adult novels *Be More Chill* and *It's Kind of a Funny Story.* He has more recently moved into literary reviews and writing short fiction outside of the young-adult realm.

According to critical consensus, in the columns included in *Teen Angst?* Vizzini comes across as geeky, intelligent, and funny, although a mature perspective is revealed in his comic asides and in the book's index. Vizzini's "wonderfully sardonic voice . . . suggests a wisdom beyond his years," remarked Laura Glaser in a review of the book for *School Library Journal.* Other reviewers emphasized the humorous aspect of Vizzini's unglamorous tales of high school life. "He's gifted but gawky, adventurous yet filled with anxiety. Most of all, he shows a real talent for self-deprecating humor," wrote a reviewer for *Publishers Weekly.* Although *Booklist* contributor Todd Morning claimed that Vizzini's humor "occasionally . . . seems forced," the critic added that both teens and adults would find much common ground in *Teen Angst?*

Featuring what a *Publishers Weekly* reviewer described as an "over-the-top plot and tangy narrative," *Be More Chill* introduces geeky high schooler Jeremy Heere, who wisely recognizes that he needs all the help he can get to win the heart of the ultra-bright Christine. After secretly cashing in 600 dollars worth of his aunt's Beanie Baby collection, the awkward teen purchases a squib, a microscopic supercomputer implant that is guaranteed to raise Jeremy's hip-ness rating. While the device makes good on its promises, and Jeremy's popularity rises, as Christine gets within his sites the squib begins to push Jeremy to take some eyebrow-raising actions that reflect poorly on his character. The *Publishers Weekly* critic, while noting the novel's teen appeal, also praised Vizzini's "wry, nearly anthropological observations of the high school caste system," and Loren Adams described *Be More Chill* as a "teenage boy's fairy tale come true" in her *Horn Book* review. Calling the novel "a witty send-up of high school hierarchies," *Kliatt* reviewer Amanda MacGregor predicted that the author's "engaging satire on popularity will appeal to the geeks, the cool kids, and everyone in between." In his review for the *New York Times Book Review,* Simon Rodberg was clear: *Be More Chill* "is so accurate that it should come with a warning."

It's Kind of a Funny Story is based on Vizzini's five-day stay in Brooklyn's Methodist Hospital psychiatric ward. The book recounts fifteen-year-old Craig Gilner's battle with suicidal depression as a result of a taxing school year at Manhattan's Executive Pre-Professional High School that exacerbates his feelings of social inadequacy. Although Craig gets support from his parents and sister, but the friends that surface in his narration are too caught up in their own problems to help him. Eventually, long-dormant talents resurface as Craig gains a newfound ability to connect to others during his hospitalization. In the novel he shows himself to be a typical Vizzini protagonist: "good kids at sea in a confusing world," as Claire Rosser noted in *Kliatt.* Craig comes across as a "sensitive teen," wrote *School Library Journal* reviewer Diane P. Tuccillo, and his "well-paced narrative . . . is filled with humor and pathos." While calling the novel's plot somewhat unrealistic, Ilene Cooper praised Vizzini's narrative voice as "intimate, real, funny, ironic, and one kids will come closer to hear," concluding that *It's Kind of a Funny Story* "offers hope in a package that readers will find enticing."

Discussing the writing life with *Boston Herald* reviewer Lauren Beckham Falcone, Vizzini had the following ad-

vice for aspiring authors: "Write what you know, and kill your darlings, which means get rid of the stuff that sounds good to you and you alone. That's the hard part. The easy part is submitting. Prepare to be rejected, but, really, just have the guts to do it."

Biographical and Critical Sources

BOOKS

Vizzini, Ned, *Teen Angst? Naaah . . . . : A Quasi-Autobiography,* Free Spirit Publishing (Minneapolis, MN), 2000.

PERIODICALS

Booklist, October 15, 2000, Todd Morning, review of *Teen Angst?,* pp. 428, 431; August, 2004, Debbie Carton, review of *Be More Chill,* p. 1921; February 1, 2006, Ilene Cooper, review of *It's Kind of a Funny Story,* p. 49.

Boston Herald, June 12, 2000, Lauren Beckham Falcone, "Write-Minded" (interview with Vizzini).

Bulletin of the Center for Children's Books, September, 2004, Janice Del Negro, review of *Be More Chill,* p. 43; May, 2006, Loretta Gaffney, review of *It's Kind of a Funny Story,* p. 427.

Horn Book, September-October, 2004, Lauren Adams, review of *Be More Chill,* p. 600; May-June, 2006, Jennifer M. Brabander, review of *It's Kind of a Funny Story,* p. 336.

Journal of Adolescent and Adult Literacy, May, 2005, James Blasingame, review of *Be More Chill,* p. 716; April, 2007, James Blasingame, interview with Vizzini, p. 607.

Kirkus Reviews, June 1, 2004, review of *Be More Chill,* p. 542; April 1, 2006, review of *It's Kind of a Funny Story,* p. 358.

Kliatt, May, 2004, Paula Rohrlick, review of *Be More Chill,* p. 14; January, 2006, Amanda MacGregor, review of *Be More Chill,* p. 22; March, 2006, Claire Rosser, review of *It's Kind of a Funny Story,* p. 18.

New York Times Book Review, May 16, 2004, Simon Rodberg, review of *Be More Chill,* p. 24; June 18, 2006, Tanya Lee Stone, review of *It's Kind of a Funny Story,* p. 15.

Publishers Weekly, July 31, 2000, review of *Teen Angst?,* p. 97; March 10, 2003, John F. Baker, "Two-Book Deal for Teen Cult Writer," p. 12; June 28, 2004, review of *Be More Chill,* p. 51; April 10, 2006, review of *It's Kind of a Funny Story,* p. 74.

School Library Journal, November, 2000, Laura Glaser, review of *Teen Angst?,* p. 177; April, 2006, Diane P. Tuccillo, review of *It's Kind of a Funny Story,* p. 49.

Voice of Youth Advocates, June, 2004, Walter Hogan, review of *Be More Chill,* p. 148; April, 2006, David Goodale, review of *It's Kind of a Funny Story,* p. 54.

ONLINE

Ned Vizzini Home Page, http://www.nedvizzini.com (June 15, 2007).

WINTER, Jonah 1962-

Personal

Born 1962, in Fort Worth, TX; son of Jeanette Winter (a writer and illustrator).

Addresses

Home and office—Brooklyn, NY.

Career

Author, illustrator, and poet. Worked variously as a llama rancher, a flower deliverer, and a children's book editor; George Mason University, VA, former instructor. Performer in musical band Ed's Redeeming Qualities.

Awards, Honors

Cohen Award, *Ploughshares* magazine, 2000, for "Sestina: Bob"; Slope Editions Book Prize, 2001, for *Maine: Poems*; Parent's Choice Gold Medal, 2002, for *Frida*; *Kirkus Reviews* Best Children's Books citation, 2006, and *Booklist* Top-Ten Black History Books for Youth selection, 2007, both for *Dizzy.*

Writings

Diego, illustrated by mother, Jeanette Winter, Knopf (New York, NY), 1991.

Wyatt Earp and the Showdown at Tombstone, Disney Press (New York, NY), 1995.

(Self-illustrated) *Fair Ball!: Fourteen Great Stars from Baseball's Negro Leagues,* Scholastic (New York, NY), 1999.

Once upon a Time in Chicago: The Story of Benny Goodman, illustrated by Jeanette Winter, Hyperion (New York, NY), 2000.

Béisbol!: Latino Baseball Pioneers and Legends, introduction by Bruce Markusen Rodríguez, Lee & Low (New York, NY), 2001.

Wild Women of the Wild West, illustrated by Mary Morgan, Holiday House (New York, NY), 2002.

Frida, illustrated by Ana Juan, Arthur A. Levine (New York, NY), 2002.

Paul Revere and the Bell Ringers, Aladdin (New York, NY), 2003.

Roberto Clemente: Pride of the Pittsburgh Pirates, illustrated by Raúl Colón, Atheneum (New York, NY), 2005.

The 39 Apartments of Ludwig van Beethoven, illustrated by Barry Blitt, Schwartz & Wade (New York, NY), 2006.

Dizzy, illustrated by Sean Qualls, Arthur A. Levine (New York, NY), 2006.

The Secret World of Hildegard, illustrated by Jeanette Winter, Arthur A. Levine (New York, NY), 2007.

Muhammad Ali: Champion of the World, illustrated by François Roca, Schwartz & Wade (New York, NY), 2008.

Steel Town, illustrated by Terry Widener, Atheneum (New York, NY), 2008.

POETRY FOR ADULTS

Maine: Poems, selected by David Lehman, Slope Editions (Raymond, NH), 2002.
Amnesia (poetry), Oberlin College Press (Oberlin, OH), 2004.

Contributor of poetry to periodicals, including *Ploughshares, Prairie Schooner,* and *Literary Review.*

Authors works have been translated into Spanish.

Sidelights

Jonah Winter began his career as a poet, publishing his work in adult magazines as early as the age of seven. After graduating from college, however, Winter found the market for his poetry more competitive. Persisting in his efforts, he was ultimately rewarded for his perseverance when he received a Pushcart Prize for a ten-year-old poem that had been rejected by a number of periodicals.

Jonah Winter introduces readers to the life of an eccentric but very famous composer in **The 39 Apartments of Ludwig van Beethoven,** *a picture book with art by Barry Blitt.* (Schwartz & Wade Books, 2006. Illustration © 2006 by Barry Blitt. Reproduced by permission of Schwartz & Wade Books, an imprint of Random House Children's Books, a division of Random House, Inc.)

Alongside his poetry for adults, Winter has written several picture books for young readers. From jazz musicians to baseball players to artists, Winter introduces young readers to important people in history in biographies such as *Diego,* which recounts the childhood of Mexican muralist Diego Rivera. Featuring illustrations by the author's mother, Jeanette Winter, as well as a bilingual text, the book's "crisp text" and "dynamic illustrations successfully convey the spirit of the man and his work," according to a *Publishers Weekly* contributor. Winter continues his focus on the lives of Mexican artists in *Frida,* which gives readers an introduction to Frida Kahlo, the wife of Rivera and an artist in her own right. A *Publishers Weekly* contributor considered the book "an outstanding introduction to an influential artist," and Nell D. Beram wrote in *Horn Book* that "Winter consistently manages to convey much" about his subject's life "with a few well-chosen words." Jane P. Marshall, writing in the *Albany Times Union,* cited the "poetic sparseness" of Winter's text. Another biography, *Roberto Clemente: Pride of the Pittsburgh Pirates,* provides young readers with what a *Kirkus Reviews* contributor dubbed "a well-constructed introduction to a compassionate, dignified, multi-talented sports hero."

Winter's long interest in baseball began as a child, when he collected baseball cards. For his self-illustrated *Fair Ball!: Fourteen Great Stars from Baseball's Negro Leagues* he creates nostalgic paintings that mimic these old-time sports collectibles. "Winter's distinctive, painterly illustrations make the strongest statements in the book," Carolyn Phelan wrote in a favorable *Booklist* review of the book. Along with providing the history of fourteen major stars of the historical Negro Leagues, "Winter also slips amusing lore into his conversational text," explained a *Publishers Weekly* contributor. *Béisbol!: Latino Baseball Pioneers and Legends* is similar in theme, focusing on fourteen legendary Latino baseball players. "This title will be a welcome addition to any baseball collection," predicted Blair Christolon in a review of *Béisbol!* for *School Library Journal.*

In a departure from his fact-based titles, Winter creates a picture book in the style of a "mockumentary" in *The 39 Apartments of Ludwig van Beethoven.* Based on fact-based trivia that includes the number of legless pianos Beethoven owned and the large number of apartments where the composer resided, Winter imagines how Beethoven might have moved those pianos from one place to another. "Older readers will enjoy its tongue-in-cheek lampoon of portentous documentaries," wrote a *Publishers Weekly* contributor, the critic concluding that "this irreverent account of a brilliant musician is full of satiric pleasures." Of Winter's characterization of Beethoven, a *Kirkus Reviews* contributor wrote that, "through it all, Beethoven looms larger than life, as well he should."

Moving from classical music to jazz, Winter presents a picture-book biography of jazz legend Dizzy Gillespie in *Dizzy.* As a *Kirkus Reviews* contributor noted, Win-

ter's prose "breaks into ecstatic scat," providing "syncopated rhythms of bebop [that] form the backbeat" of the biography. According to *School Library Journal* contributor Lee Bock, "through a powerful marriage of rhythmic text and hip and surprising illustrations, the unorthodox creator of Bebop comes to life." *School Library Journal* contributor Ilene Cooper noted that, by inspiring an interest in "trumpet revolutionary Dizzy Gillespie," Winter inspires readers "to learn more about his music."

Biographical and Critical Sources

PERIODICALS

Albany Times Union (Albany, NY), Jane P. Marshall, "Life Stories Make Great Tales for Children to Read," p. J5.
Booklist, April 15, 1999, Carolyn Phelan, review of *Fair Ball!: Fourteen Great Stars from Baseball's Negro Leagues,* p. 1528; September 1, 1999, Sally Estes, review of *Fair Ball!,* p. 132; October 1, 2001, Annie Ayres, review of *Béisbol!: Latino Baseball Pioneers and Legends,* p. 317; March 1, 2002, Hazel Rochman, review of *Frida,* p. 1148; February 15, 2005, Bill Ott, review of *Roberto Clemente: Pride of the Pittsburgh Pirates,* p. 1082; August 1, 2006, Hazel Rochman, review of *The 39 Apartments of Ludwig van Beethoven,* p. 79; November 1, 2006, Ilene Cooper, review of *Dizzy,* p. 63.
Children's Bookwatch, December, 2006, review of *The 39 Apartments of Ludwig van Beethoven.*
Christian Century, December 4, 2002, review of *Frida,* p. 34.
Horn Book, March-April, 2002, Nell D. Beram, review of *Frida,* p. 233; November-December, 2006, Lolly Robinson, review of *Dizzy,* p. 738.
Kirkus Reviews, December 1, 2001, review of *Frida,* p. 1691; February 15, 2005, review of *Roberto Clemente,* p. 238; August 15, 2006, review of *The 39 Apartments of Ludwig van Beethoven,* p. 854; September 15, 2006, review of *Dizzy,* p. 970.
Publishers Weekly, August 9, 1991, review of *Diego,* p. 57; May 10, 1999, review of *Fair Ball!,* p. 68; December 10, 2001, review of *Frida,* p. 69; April 21, 2003, review of *Maine,* p. 58; July 17, 2006, review of *The 39 Apartments of Ludwig van Beethoven,* p. 157.
School Library Journal, July, 2001, Blair Christolon, review of *Beisbol!,* p. 101; March, 2002, Nancy Menaldi-Scanlan, review of *Frida,* p. 224; February, 2004, Gina Powell, review of *Paul Revere and the Bell Ringers,* p. 136; February 7, 2005, review of *Roberto Clemente,* p. 59; May, 2005, Marilyn Taniguchi, review of *Roberto Clemente,* p. 116; July, 2005, Coop Renner, review of *Frida,* p. 44; October, 2006, Joy Fleishhacker, review of *The 39 Apartments of Ludwig van Beethoven,* p. 130; October, 2006, Lee Bock, review of *Dizzy,* p. 143.

ONLINE

Arthur A. Levine Web site, http://www.arthuralevinebooks. com/ (May 18, 2007), "Jonah Winter."

Oberlin College Web site, http://www.oberlin.edu/alummag/ (winter, 2003), Katie Hubbard, "Winning Words."*

*   *   *

YOURGRAU, Barry

Personal

Born in South Africa. *Hobbies and other interests:* Old-school Latin music, world soccer, gangster films in many cultures.

Addresses

Home and office—New York, NY. *Agent*—Ellen Levine, Trident Media Group, 41 Madison Ave., 36th Fl., New York, NY 10010. *E-mail*—barry@yourgrau.com.

Career

Performance artist, commentator, actor, and writer. Has appeared on National Public Radio and on MTV. Actor, appearing in films *Fatman and Littleboy, Don't Look under the Bed,* and *Terminal Justice.*

Awards, Honors

Drama-Logue Award for *Wearing Dad's Head.*

Writings

FOR ADULTS

A Man Jumps out of an Airplane: Stories, SUN (New York, NY), 1984.
Wearing Dad's Head, Peregrine Smith Books (Salt Lake City, UT), 1987.
The Sadness of Sex, Delta Trade Paperbacks (New York, NY), 1995.
Haunted Traveller: An Imaginary Memoir, Arcade Pub. (New York, NY), 1999.

Author's works have been included in several anthologies. Contributor of short fiction and articles to periodicals, including *Paris Review, Bomb, Nerve, Story, Los Angeles Times, New York Times, Spin, Salon,* and *New York.*

FOR CHILDREN

My Curious Uncle Dudley, illustrated by Tony Auth, Candlewick Press (Cambridge, MA), 2004.
Nastybook, illustrated by Robert DeJesus, HarperCollins (New York, NY), 2005.
Another Nastybook: The Curse of the Tweeties (An Entire Novel), art by Robert DeJesus, Joanna Cotler Books (New York, NY), 2006.

Biographical and Critical Sources

PERIODICALS

Booklist, April 15, 1999, Donna Seaman, review of *Haunted Traveller: An Imaginary Memoir,* p. 1516; September 15, 2004, Debbie Carton, review of *My Curious Uncle Dudley,* p. 246; April 15, 2005, Ilene Cooper, review of *Nastybook,* p. 1450.
Bulletin of the Center for Children's Books, May, 2005, review of *Nastybook,* p. 414.
Entertainment Weekly, March 20, 1992, Margot Mifflin, review of *A Man Jumps out of an Airplane,* p. 64.
Kirkus Reviews, July 15, 2004, review of *My Curious Uncle Dudley,* p. 695; April 15, 2005, review of *Nastybook,* p. 485; April 1, 2006, review of *Another NastyBook: The Curse of the Tweeties,* p. 359.
Library Journal, May 15, 1999, Thomas O'Connell, review of *Haunted Traveller,* p. 97.
Publishers Weekly, January 16, 1995, review of *The Sadness of Sex,* p. 453; March 22, 1999, review of *Haunted Traveller,* p. 68; July 26, 2004, review of *My Curious Uncle Dudley,* p. 55; June 6, 2005, review of *Nastybook,* p. 65.
School Library Journal, January, 2005, Edith Ching, review of *My Curious Uncle Dudley,* p. 100; June, 2005, Elaine E. Knight, review of *Nastybook,* p. 173; August, 2006, Elaine Lesh Morgan, review of *Another Nastybook,* p. 132.
Voice of Youth Advocates, June, 2005, Walter Hogan, review of *Nastybook,* p. 156.

ONLINE

Barry Yourgrau Home Page, http://www.yourgrau.com (June 9, 2007).

Illustrations Index

(In the following index, the number of the *volume* in which an illustrator's work appears is given *before* the colon, and the *page number* on which it appears is given *after* the colon. For example, a drawing by Adams, Adrienne appears in Volume 2 on page 6, another drawing by her appears in Volume 3 on page 80, another drawing in Volume 8 on page 1, and so on and so on. . . .)

YABC

Index references to *YABC* refer to listings appearing in the two-volume *Yesterday's Authors of Books for Children,* also published by The Gale Group. *YABC* covers prominent authors and illustrators who died prior to 1960.

A

Aas, Ulf *5:* 174
Abbe, S. van
  See van Abbe, S.
Abel, Raymond *6:* 122; *7:* 195; *12:* 3; *21:* 86; *25:* 119
Abelliera, Aldo *71:* 120
Abolafia, Yossi *60:* 2; *93:* 163; *152:* 202
Abrahams, Hilary *26:* 205; *29:* 24, 25; *53:* 61
Abrams, Kathie *36:* 170
Abrams, Lester *49:* 26
Abulafia, Yossi *154:* 67; *177:* 3
Accorsi, William *11:* 198
Acs, Laszlo *14:* 156; *42:* 22
Adams, Adrienne *2:* 6; *3:* 80; *8:* 1; *15:* 107; *16:* 180; *20:* 65; *22:* 134, 135; *33:* 75; *36:* 103, 112; *39:* 74; *86:* 54; *90:* 2, 3
Adams, Connie J. *129:* 68
Adams, John Wolcott *17:* 162
Adams, Lynn *96:* 44
Adams, Norman *55:* 82
Adams, Pam *112:* 1, 2
Adams, Sarah *98:* 126; *164:* 180
Adamson, George *30:* 23, 24; *69:* 64
Addams, Charles *55:* 5
Ade, Rene *76:* 198
Adinolfi, JoAnn *115:* 42; *176:* 2
Adkins, Alta *22:* 250
Adkins, Jan *8:* 3; *69:* 4; *144:* 2, 3, 4
Adler, Peggy *22:* 6; *29:* 31
Adler, Ruth *29:* 29
Adlerman, Daniel *163:* 2
Adragna, Robert *47:* 145
Agard, Nadema *18:* 1
Agee, Jon *116:* 8, 9, 10; *157:* 4
Agre, Patricia *47:* 195
Aguirre, Alfredo *152:* 218
Ahl, Anna Maria *32:* 24
Ahlberg, Allan *68:* 6, 7, 9; *165:* 5
Ahlberg, Janet *68:* 6, 7, 9
Aicher-Scholl, Inge *63:* 127
Aichinger, Helga *4:* 5, 45
Aitken, Amy *31:* 34
Akaba, Suekichi *46:* 23; *53:* 127
Akasaka, Miyoshi *YABC 2:* 261
Akino, Fuku *6:* 144
Alain *40:* 41
Alajalov *2:* 226
Alborough, Jez *86:* 1, 2, 3; *149:* 3

Albrecht, Jan *37:* 176
Albright, Donn *1:* 91
Alcala, Alfredo *91:* 128
Alcantará, Felipe Ugalde *171:* 186
Alcorn, John *3:* 159; *7:* 165; *31:* 22; *44:* 127; *46:* 23, 170
Alcorn, Stephen *110:* 4; *125:* 106; *128:* 172; *150:* 97; *160:* 188; *165:* 48
Alcott, May *100:* 3
Alda, Arlene *44:* 24; *158:* 2
Alden, Albert *11:* 103
Aldridge, Andy *27:* 131
Aldridge, George *105:* 125
Alejandro, Cliff *176:* 75
Alex, Ben *45:* 25, 26
Alexander, Ellen *91:* 3
Alexander, Lloyd *49:* 34
Alexander, Martha *3:* 206; *11:* 103; *13:* 109; *25:* 100; *36:* 131; *70:* 6, 7; *136:* 3, 4, 5; *169:* 120
Alexander, Paul *85:* 57; *90:* 9
Alexeieff, Alexander *14:* 6; *26:* 199
Alfano, Wayne *80:* 69
Aliki
  See Brandenberg, Aliki
Allamand, Pascale *12:* 9
Allan, Judith *38:* 166
Alland, Alexandra *16:* 255
Allen, Gertrude *9:* 6
Allen, Graham *31:* 145
Allen, Jonathan *131:* 3, 4; *177:* 8, 9, 10
Allen, Joy *168:* 185
Allen, Pamela *50:* 25, 26, 27, 28; *81:* 9, 10; *123:* 4, 5
Allen, Rowena *47:* 75
Allen, Thomas B. *81:* 101; *82:* 248; *89:* 37; *104:* 9
Allen, Tom *85:* 176
Allender, David *73:* 223
Alley, R.W. *80:* 183; *95:* 187; *156:* 100, 153; *169:* 4, 5; *179:* 17
Allison, Linda *43:* 27
Allon, Jeffrey *119:* 174
Allport, Mike *71:* 55
Almquist, Don *11:* 8; *12:* 128; *17:* 46; *22:* 110
Aloise, Frank *5:* 38; *10:* 133; *30:* 92
Althea
  See Braithwaite, Althea
Altschuler, Franz *11:* 185; *23:* 141; *40:* 48; *45:* 29; *57:* 181
Alvin, John *117:* 5

Ambrus, Victor G. *1:* 6, 7, 194; *3:* 69; *5:* 15; *6:* 44; *7:* 36; *8:* 210; *12:* 227; *14:* 213; *15:* 213; *22:* 209; *24:* 36; *28:* 179; *30:* 178; *32:* 44, 46; *38:* 143; *41:* 25, 26, 27, 28, 29, 30, 31, 32; *42:* 87; *44:* 190; *55:* 172; *62:* 30, 144, 145, 148; *86:* 99, 100, 101; *87:* 66, 137; *89:* 162; *134:* 160
Ames, Lee J. *3:* 12; *9:* 130; *10:* 69; *17:* 214; *22:* 124; *151:* 13
Amon, Aline *9:* 9
Amoss, Berthe *5:* 5
Amstutz, Andre *152:* 102
Amundsen, Dick *7:* 77
Amundsen, Richard E. *5:* 10; *24:* 122
Ancona, George *12:* 11; *55:* 144; *145:* 7
Anderson, Alasdair *18:* 122
Andersen, Bethanne *116:* 167; *162:* 189; *175:* 17
Anderson, Bob *139:* 16
Anderson, Brad *33:* 28
Anderson, C.W. *11:* 10
Anderson, Carl *7:* 4
Anderson, Catherine Corley *72:* 2
Anderson, Cecil *127:* 152
Anderson, David Lee *118:* 176
Anderson, Derek *169:* 9; *174:* 180
Anderson, Doug *40:* 111
Anderson, Erica *23:* 65
Anderson, Laurie *12:* 153, 155
Anderson, Lena *99:* 26
Anderson, Peggy Perry *179:* 2
Anderson, Sara *173:* 3
Anderson, Scoular *138:* 13
Anderson, Susan *90:* 12
Anderson, Wayne *23:* 119; *41:* 239; *56:* 7; *62:* 26; *147:* 6
Andreasen, Daniel *86:* 157; *87:* 104; *103:* 201, 202; *159:* 75; *167:* 106, 107; *168:* 184
Andrew, Ian *111:* 37; *116:* 12; *166:* 2
Andrew, John *22:* 4
Andrews, Benny *14:* 251; *31:* 24; *57:* 6, 7
Andrews, Vaughn *166:* 28
Anelay, Henry *57:* 173
Angel, Marie *47:* 22
Angelo, Valenti *14:* 8; *18:* 100; *20:* 232; *32:* 70
Anglund, Joan Walsh *2:* 7, 250, 251; *37:* 198, 199, 200
Anholt, Catherine *74:* 8; *131:* 7; *141:* 5
Anholt, Laurence *141:* 4

Anno, Mitsumasa 5: 7; 38: 25, 26, 27, 28, 29, 30, 31, 32; 77: 3, 4; 157: 10, 11
Antal, Andrew 1: 124; 30: 145
Antram, David 152: 133
Apostolou, Christy Hale
  See Hale, Christy
Apple, Margot 33: 25; 35: 206; 46: 81; 53: 8; 61: 109; 64: 21, 22, 24, 25, 27; 71: 176; 77: 53; 82: 245; 92: 39; 94: 180; 96: 107; 152: 4, 5; 162: 192, 194; 173: 44
Appleyard, Dev 2: 192
Aragones, Sergio 48: 23, 24, 25, 26, 27
Araneus 40: 29
Arbo, Cris 103: 4
Archambault, Matt 85: 173; 138: 19, 20; 143: 33; 145: 144; 179: 103
Archer, Janet 16: 69; 178: 156
Ardizzone, Edward 1: 11, 12; 2: 105; 3: 258; 4: 78; 7: 79; 10: 100; 15: 232; 20: 69,178; 23: 223; 24: 125; 28: 25, 26, 27, 28, 29, 30, 31,33, 34, 35, 36, 37; 31: 192, 193; 34: 215, 217; 60: 173; 64: 145; 87: 176; YABC 2: 25
Arena, Jill 176: 49
Arenella, Roy 14: 9
Argent, Kerry 103: 56; 138: 17; 158: 134
Arisman, Marshall 162: 50
Armer, Austin 13: 3
Armer, Laura Adams 13: 3
Armer, Sidney 13: 3
Armitage, David 47: 23; 99: 5; 155: 4
Armitage, Eileen 4: 16
Armstrong, George 10: 6; 21: 72
Armstrong, Shelagh 102: 114
Arno, Enrico 1: 217; 2: 22, 210; 4: 9; 5: 43; 6: 52; 29: 217, 219; 33: 152; 35: 99; 43: 31, 32, 33; 45: 212, 213, 214; 72: 72; 74: 166; 100: 169
Arnold, Caroline 174: 5
Arnold, Emily 76: 7, 9, 10
Arnold, Katya 115: 11; 168: 2, 3
Arnold, Tedd 116: 14; 133: 152; 160: 5
Arnosky, James Edward 22: 20; 70: 9, 10, 11; 118: 3, 5; 160: 8, 10
Arnsteen, Katy Keck 105: 97; 116: 145
Arrowood, Clinton 12: 193; 19: 11; 65: 210
Artell, Mike 89: 8
Arting, Fred J. 41: 63
Artzybasheff, Boris 13: 143; 14: 15; 40: 152, 155
Aruego, Ariane 6: 4
Aruego, José 4: 140; 6: 4; 7: 64; 33: 195; 35: 208; 68: 16, 17; 75: 46; 93: 91, 92; 94: 197; 109: 65, 67; 125: 2, 3, 4, 5; 127: 188; 143: 25; 178: 17, 19, 74
Arzoumanian, Alik 177: 12
Asare, Meshack 86: 9; 139: 19
Ascensios, Natalie 105: 139
Asch, Frank 5: 9; 66: 2, 4, 6, 7, 9, 10; 102: 18, 19,21; 154: 12
Ashby, Gail 11: 135
Ashby, Gil 146: 4
Ashby, Gwynneth 44: 26
Ashley, C.W. 19: 197
Ashmead, Hal 8: 70
Aska, Warabe 56: 10
Assel, Steven 44: 153; 77: 22, 97
Astrop, John 32: 56
Atene, Ann 12: 18
Atherton, Lisa 38: 198
Atkinson, Allen 60: 5
Atkinson, J. Priestman 17: 275
Atkinson, Janet 86: 147; 103: 138
Atkinson, Mike 127: 74
Atkinson, Wayne 40: 46
Attebery, Charles 38: 170
Atwell, Debby 150: 6
Atwood, Ann 7: 9
Aubrey, Meg Kelleher 77: 159
Auch, Herm 173: 7, 8
Auch, Mary Jane 173: 7
Augarde, Steve 25: 22; 159: 7

Austerman, Miriam 23: 107
Austin, Margot 11: 16
Austin, Robert 3: 44
Austin, Virginia 81: 205; 127: 221
Auth, Tony 51: 5
Avendano, Dolores 158: 74
Avedon, Richard 57: 140
Averill, Esther 1: 17; 28: 39, 40, 41
Axeman, Lois 2: 32; 11: 84; 13: 165; 22: 8; 23: 49; 61: 116; 101: 124
Axtel, David 155: 110
Ayer, Jacqueline 13: 7
Ayer, Margaret 15: 12; 50: 120
Ayers, Alan 91: 58; 107: 169
Ayliffe, Alex 95: 164
Ayto, Russell 111: 5; 112: 54
Azarian, Mary 112: 9, 10; 114: 129; 117: 171; 137: 163; 171: 4, 5

B

B.T.B.
  See Blackwell, Basil T.
Babbitt, Bradford 33: 158
Babbitt, Natalie 6: 6; 8: 220; 68: 20; 70: 242, 243
Baca, Maria 104: 5
Bacchus, Andy 94: 87
Bacha, Andy 109: 169
Bachem, Paul 48: 180; 67: 65; 144: 206
Back, Adam 63: 125
Back, George 31: 161
Backhouse, Colin 78: 142
Bacon, Bruce 4: 74
Bacon, Paul 7: 155; 8: 121; 31: 55; 50: 42; 56: 175; 62: 82, 84
Bacon, Peggy 2: 11, 228; 46: 44
Baek, Matthew J. 169: 95
Baer, Julie 161: 2
Baicker-McKee, Carol 177: 15
Bailey, Peter 58: 174; 87: 221
Bailey, Sheila 155: 11
Baker, Alan 22: 22; 61: 134; 93: 11, 12; 146: 6, 7, 10
Baker, Charlotte 2: 12
vBaker, Garin 89: 65
Baker, Jeannie 23: 4; 88: 18, 19, 20
Baker, Jim 22: 24
Baker, Joe 82: 188; 111: 55; 124: 70
Baker, Keith 179: 6, 7
Baker, Leslie 112: 214; 132: 103, 246
Baldridge, Cyrus LeRoy 19: 69; 44: 50
Baldus, Zachary 152: 231
Balet, Jan 11: 22
Balian, Lorna 9: 16; 91: 16
Balit, Christina 102: 24; 159: 9; 162: 118, 119
Ballantyne, R.M. 24: 34
Ballis, George 14: 199
Balouch, Kristen 176: 11
Baltzer, Hans 40: 30
Banbery, Fred 58: 15
Banfill, A. Scott 98: 7; 112: 59
Bang, Molly Garrett 24: 37, 38; 69: 8, 9, 10; 111: 7,9, 10, 11; 140: 11; 158: 37, 38, 39
Banik, Yvette Santiago 21: 136
Banner, Angela
  See Maddison, Angela Mary
Bannerman, Helen 19: 13, 14
Bannon, Laura 6: 10; 23: 8
Bantock, Nick 74: 229; 95: 6
Baptist, Michael 37: 208
Baracca, Sal 135: 206
Barasch, Lynne 126: 16
Barbarin, Lucien C., Jr. 89: 88
Barbour, Karen 96: 5; 74: 209; 170: 16
Bare, Arnold Edwin 16: 31
Bare, Colleen Stanley 32: 33
Barger, Jan 147: 11
Bargery, Geoffrey 14: 258

Barkat, Jonathan 149: 177; 164: 254
Barker, Carol 31: 27
Barker, Cicely Mary 49: 50, 51
Barkley, James 4: 13; 6: 11; 13: 112
Barks, Carl 37: 27, 28, 29, 30, 31, 32, 33, 34
Barling, Joy 62: 148
Barling, Tom 9: 23
Barlow, Gillian 62: 20
Barlow, Perry 35: 28
Barlowe, Dot 30: 223
Barlowe, Wayne 37: 72; 84: 43; 105: 5
Barnard, Bryn 88: 53; 13: 55; 169: 13
Barner, Bob 29: 37; 128: 33; 136: 19, 20; 177: 27
Barnes, Hiram P. 20: 28
Barnes, Tim 137: 28
Barnes-Murphy, Rowan 88: 22
Barnett, Charles II 175: 150
Barnett, Ivan 70: 14
Barnett, Moneta 16: 89; 19: 142; 31: 102; 33: 30, 31, 32; 41: 153; 61: 94, 97
Barney, Maginel Wright 39: 32, 33, 34; YABC 2: 306
Barnum, Jay Hyde 11: 224; 20: 5; 37: 189, 190
Baron, Alan 80: 3; 89: 123
Barr, George 60: 74; 69: 64
Barragan, Paula S. 134: 116
Barrall, Tim 115: 152
Barrauds 33: 114
Barrer-Russell, Gertrude 9: 65; 27: 31
Barret, Robert 85: 134
Barrett, Angela 40: 136, 137; 62: 74; 75: 10; 76: 142; 144: 137; 145: 14
Barrett, Jennifer 58: 149
Barrett, John E. 43: 119
Barrett, Moneta 74: 10
Barrett, Peter 55: 169; 86: 111
Barrett, Robert 62: 145; 77: 146; 82: 35
Barrett, Ron 14: 24; 26: 35
Barron, John N. 3: 261; 5: 101; 14: 220
Barrow, Ann 136: 27
Barrows, Walter 14: 268
Barry, Ethelred B. 37: 79; YABC 1: 229
Barry, James 14: 25
Barry, Katharina 2: 159; 4: 22
Barry, Robert E. 6: 12
Barry, Scott 32: 35
Bartenbach, Jean 40: 31
Barth, Ernest Kurt 2: 172; 3: 160; 8: 26; 10: 31
Bartlett, Alison 101: 88; 165: 93
Barton, Byron 8: 207; 9: 18; 23: 66; 80: 181; 90: 18, 19, 20, 21; 126: 29, 30
Barton, Harriett 30: 71
Barton, Jill 129: 108; 135: 120; 145: 185, 189
Bartram, Robert 10: 42
Bartsch, Jochen 8: 105; 39: 38
Bascove, Barbara 45: 73
Base, Graeme 101: 15, 16, 17, 18; 162: 8, 10, 12
Baseman, Gary 174: 12
Bash, Barbara 132: 9
Baskin, Leonard 30: 42, 43, 46, 47; 49: 125, 126, 128, 129,133; 173: 120
Bass, Saul 49: 192
Bassett, Jeni 40: 99; 64: 30
Basso, Bill 99: 139
Batchelor, Joy 29: 41, 47, 48
Bate, Norman 5: 16
Bates, Leo 24: 35
Batet, Carmen 39: 134
Batherman, Muriel 31: 79; 45: 185
Battaglia, Aurelius 50: 44
Batten, John D. 25: 161, 162
Batten, Mary 162: 14, 15
Battles, Asa 32: 94, 95
Bauer, Jutta 150: 32
Bauernschmidt, Marjorie 15: 15
Baum, Allyn 20: 10
Baum, Willi 4: 24, 25; 7: 173

Bauman, Leslie *61:* 121
Baumann, Jill *34:* 170
Baumhauer, Hans *11:* 218; *15:* 163, 165, 167
Baxter, Glen *57:* 100
Baxter, Leon *59:* 102
Baxter, Robert *87:* 129
Bayley, Dorothy *37:* 195
Bayley, Nicola *40:* 104; *41:* 34, 35; *69:* 15; *129:* 33, 34, 35
Baylin, Mark *158:* 233
Baynes, Pauline *2:* 244; *3:* 149; *13:* 133, 135,137, 141; *19:* 18, 19, 20; *32:* 208, 213, 214; *36:* 105, 108; *59:* 12, 13, 14, 16, 17, 18, 20; *100:* 158, 159, 243; *133:* 3, 4
Beach, Lou *150:* 150
Beame, Rona *12:* 40
Bear's Heart *73:* 215
Beard, Dan *22:* 31, 32
Beard, J.H. *YABC 1:* 158
Bearden, Romare *9:* 7; *22:* 35
Beardshaw, Rosalind *169:* 22
Beardsley, Aubrey *17:* 14; *23:* 181; *59:* 130, 131
Bearman, Jane *29:* 38
Beaton, Cecil *24:* 208
Beaton, Clare *125:* 28
Beauce, J.A. *18:* 103
Beaujard, Sophie *81:* 54
Beck, Charles *11:* 169; *51:* 173
Beck, Ian *138:* 27
Beck, Ruth *13:* 11
Becker, Harriet *12:* 211
Beckett, Sheilah *25:* 5; *33:* 37, 38
Beckhoff, Harry *1:* 78; *5:* 163
Beckman, Kaj *45:* 38, 39, 40, 41
Beckman, Per *45:* 42, 43
Beddows, Eric *72:* 70
Bedford, F.D. *20:* 118, 122; *33:* 170; *41:* 220, 221,230, 233
Bee, Joyce *19:* 62
Beeby, Betty *25:* 36
Beech, Carol *9:* 149
Beek *25:* 51, 55, 59
Beeke, Tiphanie *177:* 127
Beekman, Doug *125:* 146, 148
Beerbohm, Max *24:* 208
Beeson, Bob *108:* 57
Begin, Maryjane *82:* 13
Beha, Philippe *172:* 85
Behr, Joyce *15:* 15; *21:* 132; *23:* 161
Behrens, Hans *5:* 97
Beier, Ellen *135:* 170; *139:* 47
Beinicke, Steve *69:* 18
Beisner, Monika *46:* 128, 131; *112:* 127
Belden, Charles J. *12:* 182
Belina, Renate *39:* 132
Bell, Corydon *3:* 20
Bell, Graham *54:* 48
Bell, Julia *151:* 214
Bell, Julie *159:* 172; *165:* 18
Bell, Thomas P. *76:* 182
Bellamy, Glen *127:* 15
Beltran, Alberto *43:* 37
Bemelmans, Ludwig *15:* 19, 21; *100:* 27
Ben-Ami, Doron *75:* 96; *84:* 107; *108:* 132; *110:* 63; *159:* 157
Bendall-Brunello, John *150:* 4; *157:* 163
Benda, Wladyslaw T. *15:* 256; *30:* 76, 77; *44:* 182
Bender, Robert *77:* 162; *79:* 13; *160:* 23
Bendick, Jeanne *2:* 24; *68:* 27, 28
Benioff, Carol *121:* 42; *175:* 23
Benner, Cheryl *80:* 11
Bennett, Charles H. *64:* 6
Bennett, Erin Susanne *165:* 216
Bennett, F.I. *YABC 1:* 134
Bennett, James *146:* 240
Bennett, Jill *26:* 61; *41:* 38, 39; *45:* 54
Bennett, Rainey *15:* 26; *23:* 53
Bennett, Richard *15:* 45; *21:* 11, 12, 13; *25:* 175

Bennett, Susan *5:* 55
Benny, Mike *142:* 78
Benoit, Elise *77:* 74
Benson, Linda *60:* 130; *62:* 91; *75:* 101; *79:* 156; *134:* 129
Benson, Patrick *68:* 162; *147:* 17, 18, 19, 20
Bentley, Carolyn *46:* 153
Bentley, James *149:* 30
Bentley, Roy *30:* 162
Benton, Jim *172:* 22
Benton, Thomas Hart *2:* 99
Berelson, Howard *5:* 20; *16:* 58; *31:* 50
Berenstain, Jan *12:* 47; *64:* 33, 34, 36, 37, 38, 40, 42, 44; *135:* 25, 28, 31, 35
Berenstain, Stan *12:* 47; *64:* 33, 34, 36, 37, 38, 40, 42, 44; *135:* 25, 28, 31, 35
Berenzy, Alix *65:* 13; *73:* 6; *78:* 115
Berg, Joan *1:* 115; *3:* 156; *6:* 26, 58
Berg, Ron *36:* 48, 49; *48:* 37, 38; *67:* 72
Bergen, David *115:* 44
Berger, Barbara *77:* 14
Berger, William M. *14:* 143; *YABC 1:* 204
Bergherr, Mary *74:* 170; *151:* 123
Bergin, Mark *114:* 8, 9; *143:* 95; *160:* 26, 27
Bergstreser, Douglas *69:* 76
Bergum, Constance R. *121:* 14, 15
Bering, Claus *13:* 14
Berkeley, Jon *139:* 218
Berkowitz, Jeanette *3:* 249
Berman, Paul *66:* 14
Bernal, Richard *154:* 176
Bernadette
    See Watts, Bernadette
Bernardin, James *112:* 24; *167:* 94
Bernath, Stefen *32:* 76
Bernhard, Durga *80:* 13
Bernstein, Michel J. *51:* 71
Bernstein, Ted *38:* 183; *50:* 131
Bernstein, Zena *23:* 46
Berridge, Celia *86:* 63
Berrill, Jacquelyn *12:* 50
Berry, Erick
    See Best, Allena
Berry, William D. *14:* 29; *19:* 48
Berry, William A. *6:* 219
Berson, Harold *2:* 17, 18; *4:* 28, 29, 220; *9:* 10; *12:* 19; *17:* 45; *18:* 193; *22:* 85; *34:* 172; *44:* 120; *46:* 42; *80:* 240
Berton, Patsy *99:* 16
Bertschmann, Harry *16:* 1
Besco, Don *70:* 99
Beskow, Elsa *20:* 13, 14, 15
Bess, Clayton *63:* 94
Best, Allena *2:* 26; *34:* 76
Betera, Carol *74:* 68
Bethell, Thomas N. *61:* 169
Bethers, Ray *6:* 22
Bettina
    See Ehrlich, Bettina
Betts, Ethel Franklin *17:* 161, 164, 165; *YABC 2:* 47
Betz, Rudolf *59:* 161
Bewick, Thomas *16:* 40, 41, 43, 44, 45, 47; *54:* 150; *YABC 1:* 107
Beyer, Paul J. III *74:* 24
Bezencon, Jacqueline *48:* 40
Biamonte, Daniel *40:* 90
Bianchi, John *91:* 19
Bianco, Pamela *15:* 31; *28:* 44, 45, 46
Bible, Charles *13:* 15
Bice, Clare *22:* 40
Bierman, Don *57:* 184
Biggers, John *2:* 123
Bileck, Marvin *3:* 102; *40:* 36, 37
Bilibin, Ivan *61:* 8, 9, 12, 13, 14, 15, 151, 152, 154, 162
Billington, Patrick *98:* 71
Billout, Guy *144:* 38, 39
Bimen, Levent *5:* 179
Binch, Caroline *81:* 18; *140:* 15, 16; *144:* 115
Binder, Hannes *169:* 163

Bing, Christopher *126:* 34
Binger, Bill *121:* 46
Binks, Robert *25:* 150
Binzen, Bill *24:* 47
Birch, Reginald *15:* 150; *19:* 33, 34, 35, 36; *37:* 196,197; *44:* 182; *46:* 176; *YABC 1:* 84; *2:* 34, 39
Birchall, Mark *123:* 188
Bird, Esther Brock *1:* 36; *25:* 66
Birdsong, Keith *167:* 85
Birkett, Rachel *78:* 206
Birling, Paul *109:* 30
Birmingham, Christian *132:* 243; *143:* 114
Birmingham, Lloyd P. *12:* 51; *83:* 13
Biro, Val *1:* 26; *41:* 42; *60:* 178; *67:* 23, 24; *84:* 242, 243
Bischoff, Ilse *44:* 51
Bishop, Gavin *97:* 17, 18; *144:* 42, 44
Bishop, Kathleen Wong *115:* 67
Bishop, Rich *56:* 43
Bite, I. *60:* 14
Bittinger, Ned *93:* 117
Bjorklund, Lorence *3:* 188, 252; *7:* 100; *9:* 113; *10:* 66; *19:* 178; *33:* 122, 123; *35:* 36, 37, 38, 39,41, 42, 43; *36:* 185; *38:* 93; *47:* 106; *66:* 194; *YABC 1:* 242
Bjorkman, Steve *91:* 199; *160:* 110
Black Sheep *164:* 100
Blackburn, Loren H. *63:* 10
Blackford, John *137:* 105
Blackwell, Basil T. *YABC 1:* 68, 69
Blackwood, Gary L. *118:* 17
Blades, Ann *16:* 52; *37:* 213; *50:* 41; *69:* 21; *99:* 215
Blair, Jay *45:* 46; *46:* 155
Blaisdell, Elinore *1:* 121; *3:* 134; *35:* 63
Blake, Robert J. *160:* 28, 29
Blake, Quentin *3:* 170; *10:* 48; *13:* 38; *21:* 180; *26:* 60; *28:* 228; *30:* 29, 31; *40:* 108; *45:* 219; *46:* 165, 168; *48:* 196; *52:* 10, 11, 12,13, 14, 15, 16, 17; *73:* 41, 43; *78:* 84, 86; *80:* 250, 251; *84:* 210, 211, 212; *87:* 177; *96:* 24, 26, 28; *124:* 79; *125:* 32, 34
Blake, Robert J. *37:* 90; *53:* 67; *54:* 23
Blake, William *30:* 54, 56, 57, 58, 59, 60
Blanchard, N. Taylor *82:* 140
Blass, Jacqueline *8:* 215
Blazek, Scott R. *91:* 71
Bleck, Cathie *118:* 116
Blegvad, Erik *2:* 59; *3:* 98; *5:* 117; *7:* 131; *11:* 149; *14:* 34, 35; *18:* 237; *32:* 219; *60:* 106; *66:* 16, 17, 18, 19; *70:* 233; *76:* 18; *82:* 106; *87:* 45; *100:* 188; *129:* 125; *132:* 17, 18, 19, 20; *176:* 14; *YABC 1:* 201
Blessen, Karen *93:* 126
Bliss, Corinne Demas *37:* 38
Blitt, Barry *179:* 199
Bloch, Lucienne *10:* 12
Blondon, Herve *129:* 48
Bloom, Lloyd *35:* 180; *36:* 149; *47:* 99; *62:* 117; *68:* 231; *72:* 136; *75:* 185; *83:* 99; *108:* 19
Bloom, Suzanne *172:* 23, 24
Blossom, Dave *34:* 29
Blumenschein, E.L. *YABC 1:* 113, 115
Blumer, Patt *29:* 214
Blundell, Kim *29:* 36
Bluthenthal, Diana Cain *93:* 32; *104:* 106; *177:* 26
Blythe, Benjamin *128:* 7
Blythe, Gary *112:* 52
Boake, Kathy *176:* 185
Board, Perry *171:* 99
Boardman, Gwenn *12:* 60
Bober, Richard *125:* 145; *132:* 40
Bobri *30:* 138; *47:* 27
Bock, Vera *1:* 187; *21:* 41
Bock, William Sauts *8:* 7; *14:* 37; *16:* 120; *21:* 141; *36:* 177; *62:* 203
Bodecker, N(iels) M(ogens) *8:* 13; *14:* 2; *17:* 55, 56, 57; *73:* 22, 23, 24

Boehm, Linda *40:* 31
Bogacki, Tomek *138:* 31, 32; *144:* 123
Bogdan, Florentina *107:* 43
Bohdal, Susi *22:* 44; *101:* 20
Bohlen, Nina *58:* 13
Boies, Alex *96:* 53
Bolam, Emily *101:* 216; *159:* 12
Bolian, Polly *3:* 270; *4:* 30; *13:* 77; *29:* 197
Bolle, Frank *87:* 100
Bollen, Roger *79:* 186; *83:* 16
Bolling, Vickey *114:* 44
Bollinger, Peter *101:* 7; *128:* 198; *172:* 26
Bolognese, Don *2:* 147, 231; *4:* 176; *7:* 146; *17:* 43; *23:* 192; *24:* 50; *34:* 108; *36:* 133; *71:* 24, 25; *103:* 131; *129:* 39, 40
Bolton, A.T. *57:* 158
Bond, Arnold *18:* 116
Bond, Barbara Higgins *21:* 102
Bond, Bruce *52:* 97
Bond, Felicia *38:* 197; *49:* 55, 56; *89:* 170; *90:* 171; *126:* 37
Bond, Higgins *177:* 22, 23
Bonn, Pat *43:* 40
Bonners, Susan *41:* 40; *85:* 36; *94:* 99, 100; *151:* 105, 106
Bonsall, Crosby *23:* 6
Boon, Debbie *103:* 6; *144:* 188
Boon, Emilie *86:* 23, 24
Boone, Debbie *165:* 77
Boore, Sara *60:* 73
Bootman, Colin *155:* 13; *159:* 35; *174:* 192
Booth, Franklin *YABC 2:* 76
Booth, Graham *32:* 193; *37:* 41, 42
Borda, Juliette *102:* 188
Bordier, Georgette *16:* 54
Boren, Tinka *27:* 128
Borges, Jose Francisco *119:* 62
Borja, Robert *22:* 48
Born, Adolf *49:* 63
Bornstein, Ruth *14:* 44; *88:* 45, 46; *107:* 30
Borten, Helen *3:* 54; *5:* 24
Bosin, Blackbear *69:* 104
Bossom, Naomi *35:* 48
Bostock, Mike *83:* 221; *114:* 14
Boston, Peter *19:* 42
Bosustow, Stephen *34:* 202
Boszko, Ron *75:* 47
Bottner, Barbara *14:* 46
Boucher, Joelle *41:* 138
Boulat, Pierre *44:* 40
Boulet, Susan Seddon *50:* 47
Bouma, Paddy *118:* 25; *128:* 16
Bour, Daniele *66:* 145
Bourke-White, Margaret *15:* 286, 287; *57:* 102
Boutet de Monvel, M. *30:* 61, 62, 63, 65
Bowen, Betsy *105:* 222
Bowen, Richard *42:* 134
Bowen, Ruth *31:* 188
Bower, Ron *29:* 33
Bowers, David *95:* 38; *115:* 20; *127:* 169, 170; *165:* 57
Bowman, Claire *174:* 177
Bowman, Eric *151:* 23
Bowman, Leslie *85:* 203; *105:* 108; *116:* 76; *128:* 234
Bowman, Peter *146:* 214, 215; *150:* 115
Bowser, Carolyn Ewing *22:* 253
Boxall, Ed *178:* 28
Boyd, Aaron *158:* 242
Boyd, Patti *45:* 31
Boyle, Eleanor Vere *28:* 50, 51
Boynton, Sandra *57:* 13, 14, 15; *107:* 36, 37; *152:* 12, 13, 14
Bozzo, Frank *4:* 154
Brabbs, Derry *55:* 170
Brace, Eric *132:* 193, 194; *152:* 71
Brackers de Hugo, Pierre *115:* 21
Bradford, June *158:* 138
Bradford, Ron *7:* 157
Bradley, David P. *69:* 105
Bradley, Richard D. *26:* 182

Bradley, William *5:* 164
Brady, Irene *4:* 31; *42:* 37; *68:* 191
Bragg, Michael *32:* 78; *46:* 31
Bragg, Ruth Gembicki *77:* 18
Brainerd, John W. *65:* 19
Braithwaite, Althea *23:* 12, 13; *119:* 16
Brak, Syd *146:* 187
Bralds, Braldt *90:* 28; *91:* 151
Bram, Elizabeth *30:* 67
Bramley, Peter *4:* 3
Brandenberg, Aliki *2:* 36, 37; *24:* 222; *35:* 49, 50, 51,52, 53, 54, 56, 57; *75:* 15, 17; *92:* 205; *113:* 18, 19, 20; *157:* 28; *156:* 111
Brandenburg, Alexa *75:* 19
Brandenburg, Jim *47:* 58; *150:* 212
Brandi, Lillian *31:* 158
Brandon, Brumsic, Jr. *9:* 25
Bransom, Paul *17:* 121; *43:* 44
Braren, Loretta Trezzo *87:* 193
Braun, Wendy *80:* 17, 18
Brautigam, Don *115:* 175, 176
Brazell, Derek *75:* 105; *79:* 9
Breathed, Berkeley *86:* 27, 28, 29; *161:* 13, 14
Brennan, Steve *83:* 230; *101:* 184
Brenner, Fred *22:* 85; *36:* 34; *42:* 34
Brett, Bernard *22:* 54
Brett, Harold M. *26:* 98, 99, 100
Brett, Jan *30:* 135; *42:* 39; *71:* 31, 32; *130:* 23, 24, 25, 26, 27; *171:* 15, 16
Brewer, Paul *106:* 115; *145:* 202
Brewer, Sally King *33:* 44
Brewster, Patience *40:* 68; *45:* 22, 183; *51:* 20; *66:* 144; *89:* 4; *97:* 30, 31
Brick, John *10:* 15
Brickman, Robin D. *131:* 88; *142:* 150; *155:* 18; *178:* 109
Bridge, David R. *45:* 28
Bridgman, L.J. *37:* 77
Bridwell, Norman *4:* 37; *138:* 36, 37, 40
Brierley, Louise *91:* 22; *96:* 165
Briggs, Harry *172:* 187
Briggs, Raymond *10:* 168; *23:* 20, 21; *66:* 29, 31, 32; *131:* 28, 29
Brigham, Grace A. *37:* 148
Bright, Robert *24:* 55
Brighton, Catherine *107:* 39
Brinckloe, Julie *13:* 18; *24:* 79, 115; *29:* 35; *63:* 140; *81:* 131
Brion *47:* 116
Brisley, Joyce L. *22:* 57
Brisson, James F. *110:* 60
Brittingham, Geoffrey *88:* 37
Brix-Henker, Silke *81:* 194
Brock, Charles E. *15:* 97; *19:* 247, 249; *23:* 224, 225; *36:* 88; *42:* 41, 42, 43, 44, 45; *100:* 189; *YABC 1:* 194, 196, 203
Brock, Emma *7:* 21
Brock, Henry Matthew *15:* 81; *16:* 141; *19:* 71; *34:* 115; *40:* 164; *42:* 47, 48, 49; *49:* 66
Brocksopp, Arthur *57:* 157
Broda, Ron *136:* 180; *174:* 123
Brodkin, Gwen *34:* 135
Brodovitch, Alexi *52:* 22
Bromhall, Winifred *5:* 11; *26:* 38
Bromley, Lizzy *159:* 179
Bronson, Linda *150:* 210; *174:* 133
Brooke, L. Leslie *16:* 181, 182, 183, 186; *17:* 15, 16, 17; *18:* 194
Brooker, Christopher *15:* 251
Brooker, Krysten *111:* 94; *140:* 28; *162:* 111; *175:* 108
Brooks, Erik *166:* 52
Brooks, Maya Itzna *92:* 153
Brooks, Ron *94:* 15
Brooks, S.G. *178:* 127
Broomfield, Maurice *40:* 141
Brotman, Adolph E. *5:* 21
Brown, Buck *45:* 48
Brown, Calef *179:* 18
Brown, Christopher *62:* 124, 125, 127, 128
Brown, Craig McFarland *73:* 28; *84:* 65

Brown, Dan *61:* 167; *115:* 183, 184; *116:* 28, 29
Brown, David *7:* 47; *48:* 52
Brown, Denise *11:* 213
Brown, Don *172:* 29
Brown, Ford Madox *48:* 74
Brown, Judith Gwyn *1:* 45; *7:* 5; *8:* 167; *9:* 182, 190; *20:* 16, 17, 18; *23:* 142; *29:* 117; *33:* 97; *36:* 23, 26; *43:* 184; *48:* 201, 223; *49:* 69; *86:* 227; *110:* 188; *153:* 7
Brown, Kathryn *98:* 26
Brown, Laurie Krasny *99:* 30
Brown, Marc (Tolon) *10:* 17, 197; *14:* 263; *51:* 18; *53:* 11, 12, 13, 15, 16, 17; *75:* 58; *80:* 24, 25, 26; *82:* 261; *99:* 29; *145:* 22, 23, 25, 27; *162:* 198
Brown, Marcia *7:* 30; *25:* 203; *47:* 31, 32, 33, 34, 35,36, 37, 38, 39, 40, 42, 43, 44; *YABC 1:* 27
Brown, Margery W. *5:* 32, 33; *10:* 3
Brown, Martin *101:* 43
Brown, Mary Barrett *97:* 74
Brown, Palmer *36:* 40
Brown, Paul *25:* 26; *26:* 107
Brown, Richard *61:* 18; *67:* 30
Brown, Rick *78:* 71; *150:* 154
Brown, Robert S. *85:* 33
Brown, Rod *157:* 142
Brown, Ruth *55:* 165; *86:* 112, 113; *105:* 16, 17, 18; *171:* 178
Brown, Trevor *99:* 160; *139:* 247
Browne, Anthony *45:* 50, 51, 52; *61:* 21, 22, 23, 24, 25; *105:* 21, 22, 23, 25
Browne, Dik *8:* 212; *67:* 32, 33, 35, 37, 39
Browne, Gordon *16:* 97; *64:* 114, 116, 117, 119, 121
Browne, Hablot K. *15:* 65, 80; *21:* 14, 15, 16, 17, 18, 19,20; *24:* 25
Browne, Jane *165:* 222
Browning, Coleen *4:* 132
Browning, Mary Eleanor *24:* 84
Bruce, Robert *23:* 23
Brude, Dick *48:* 215
Bruel, Nick *166:* 41
Brule, Al *3:* 135
Brumbeau, Jeff *157:* 29
Bruna, Dick *43:* 48, 49, 50; *76:* 27, 28
Brundage, Frances *19:* 244
Brunhoff, Jean de *24:* 57, 58
Brunhoff, Laurent de *24:* 60; *71:* 35, 36, 37
Brunkus, Denise *84:* 50; *123:* 117; *178:* 209
Brunson, Bob *43:* 135
Bryan, Ashley *31:* 44; *72:* 27, 28, 29; *107:* 92; *116:* 192; *132:* 24; *178:* 33, 34, 35
Bryant, Laura J. *176:* 36
Bryant, Michael *93:* 74
Brychta, Alex *21:* 21
Bryer, Diana *107:* 121
Bryson, Bernarda *3:* 88, 146; *39:* 26; *44:* 185; *131:* 40
Buba, Joy *12:* 83; *30:* 226; *44:* 56
Buchanan, George *166:* 198
Buchanan, Lilian *13:* 16
Buchanan, Rachel *171:* 71
Bucholtz-Ross, Linda *44:* 137
Buchs, Thomas *40:* 38
Buck, Margaret Waring *3:* 30
Buckhardt, Marc *172:* 59
Buckley, Mike *166:* 180
Budwine, Greg *175:* 172
Buehner, Mark *104:* 12, 15; *105:* 160; *119:* 98; *157:* 188; *159:* 39, 40, 43
Buehr, Walter *3:* 31
Buff, Conrad *19:* 52, 53, 54
Buff, Mary *19:* 52, 53
Bull, Charles Livingston *18:* 207; *88:* 175, 176
Bullen, Anne *3:* 166, 167
Bullock, Kathleen *77:* 24
Bumgarner-Kirby, Claudia *77:* 194
Burbank, Addison *37:* 43

Burchard, Peter Duncan *3:* 197; *5:* 35; *6:* 158, 218; *143:* 17
Burckhardt, Marc *94:* 48; *110:* 89
Burger, Carl *3:* 33; *45:* 160, 162
Burgeson, Marjorie *19:* 31
Burgess, Anne *76:* 252
Burgess, Gelett *32:* 39, 42
Burgess, Mark *157:* 31
Burke, Jim *179:* 19
Burke, Phillip *95:* 117
Burkert, Nancy Ekholm *18:* 186; *22:* 140; *24:* 62, 63,64, 65; *26:* 53; *29:* 60, 61; *46:* 171; *YABC 1:* 46
Burkhardt, Bruce *142:* 86
Burkhardt, Melissa A. *142:* 86
Burleson, Joe *104:* 35; *172:* 139
Burn, Doris *6:* 172
Burn, Jeffrey *89:* 125; *152:* 132
Burn, Ted
    See Burn, Thomas E.
Burn, Thomas E. *151:* 41
Burnard, Damon *115:* 23
Burnett, Virgil *44:* 42
Burningham, John *9:* 68; *16:* 60, 61; *59:* 28, 29, 30,31, 32, 33, 35; *111:* 18, 19, 21; *160:* 37
Burns, Howard M. *12:* 173
Burns, Jim *47:* 70; *86:* 32; *91:* 197; *123:* 16
Burns, M.F. *26:* 69
Burns, Raymond *9:* 29
Burns, Robert *24:* 106
Burr, Dan *65:* 28; *108:* 134; *164:* 203
Burr, Dane *12:* 2
Burra, Edward *YABC 2:* 68
Burrell, Galen *56:* 76
Burri, Rene *41:* 143; *54:* 166
Burridge, Marge Opitz *14:* 42
Burris, Burmah *4:* 81
Burroughs, John Coleman *41:* 64
Burroughs, Studley O. *41:* 65
Burton, Marilee Robin *46:* 33
Burton, Virginia Lee *2:* 43; *44:* 49, 51; *100:* 46, 47; *YABC 1:* 24; *147:* 56
Busoni, Rafaello *1:* 186; *3:* 224; *6:* 126; *14:* 5; *16:* 62, 63
Butchkes, Sidney *50:* 58
Butler, Geoff *94:* 20
Butler, Ralph *116:* 212
Butterfield, Ned *1:* 153; *27:* 128; *79:* 63
Butterworth, Nick *106:* 43, 44; *149:* 34
Buxton, John *123:* 12
Buzelli, Christopher *105:* 149
Buzonas, Gail *29:* 88
Buzzell, Russ W. *12:* 177
Byard, Carole *39:* 44; *57:* 18, 19, 20; *60:* 60; *61:* 93, 96; *69:* 210; *78:* 246; *79:* 227
Byars, Betsy *46:* 35
Byfield, Barbara Ninde *8:* 18
Byfield, Graham *32:* 29
Bynum, Janie *176:* 50
Byrd, Robert *13:* 218; *33:* 46; *158:* 70
Byrd, Samuel *123:* 104

C

Cabat, Erni *74:* 38
Cabban, Vanessa *138:* 73; *176:* 39
Cabrera, Jane *103:* 24; *152:* 27
Caddy, Alice *6:* 41
Cady, Harrison *17:* 21, 23; *19:* 57, 58
Caffrey, Aileen *72:* 223; *141:* 154
Cairns, Julia *177:* 37
Caldecott, Randolph *16:* 98, 103; *17:* 32, 33, 36, 38, 39; *26:* 90; *100:* 49, 50; *YABC 2:* 172
Calder, Alexander *18:* 168
Calderón, Gloria *179:* 5
Calderon, W. Frank *25:* 160
Caldwell, Ben *105:* 75; *149:* 60

Caldwell, Clyde *98:* 100; *116:* 39
Caldwell, Doreen *23:* 77; *71:* 41
Caldwell, John *46:* 225
Call, Greg *126:* 135; *165:* 49
Callahan, Kevin *22:* 42
Callahan, Philip S. *25:* 77
Callan, Jamie *59:* 37
Calvin, James *61:* 92
Camburn-Bracalente, Carol A. *118:* 22
Cameron, Julia Margaret *19:* 203
Cameron, Scott *99:* 18
Camm, Martin *140:* 208, 209, 210
Campbell, Ann *11:* 43; *123:* 182
Campbell, Bill *89:* 39
Campbell, Ken *126:* 143
Campbell, Robert *55:* 120
Campbell, Rod *51:* 27; *98:* 34
Campbell, Walter M. *YABC 2:* 158
Camps, Luis *28:* 120, 121; *66:* 35
Cann, Helen *124:* 50; *141:* 78; *170:* 138; *179:* 22, 23
Cannon, Janell *78:* 25; *128:* 40
Canright, David *36:* 162
Canty, Thomas *85:* 161; *92:* 47; *113:* 192; *134:* 60
Canyon, Christopher *150:* 44; *151:* 112
Caporale, Wende *70:* 42
Capp, Al *61:* 28, 30, 31, 40, 41, 43, 44
Cappon, Manuela *154:* 64
Caras, Peter *36:* 64
Caraway, Caren *57:* 22
Caraway, James *3:* 200, 201
Carbe, Nino *29:* 183
Cares, Linda *67:* 176
Carigiet, Alois *24:* 67
Carle, Eric *4:* 42; *11:* 121; *12:* 29; *65:* 32,33, 34, 36; *73:* 63, 65; *163:* 55, 56
Carling, Amelia Lau *164:* 46
Carlino, Angela *168:* 43
Carlson, Nancy L. *41:* 116; *56:* 25; *90:* 45; *144:* 48, 50
Carlluccio, Maria *175:* 129
Carmi, Giora *79:* 35; *149:* 40
Carpenter, Nancy *76:* 128; *86:* 173; *89:* 171; *131:* 186; *134:* 8; *138:* 215; *153:* 204; *159:* 93; *165:* 232
Carr, Archie *37:* 225
Carrick, Donald *5:* 194; *39:* 97; *49:* 70; *53:* 156; *63:* 15, 16, 17, 18, 19, 21; *80:* 131; *86:* 151; *118:* 24
Carrick, Malcolm *28:* 59, 60
Carrick, Paul *118:* 26
Carrick, Valery *21:* 47
Carrier, Lark *71:* 43
Carroll, Jim *88:* 211; *140:* 177; *153:* 99
Carroll, Lewis
    See Dodgson, Charles L.
Carroll, Michael *72:* 5
Carroll, Pamela *84:* 68; *128:* 214
Carroll, Ruth *7:* 41; *10:* 68
Carter, Abby *81:* 32; *97:* 121; *102:* 61; *163:* 139; *164:* 125
Carter, Barbara *47:* 167, 169
Carter, David A. *114:* 24, 25; *170:* 42, 43
Carter, Don *124:* 54
Carter, Harry *22:* 179
Carter, Helene *15:* 38; *22:* 202, 203; *YABC 2:* 220, 221
Carter, Penny *173:* 91
Cartlidge, Michelle *49:* 65; *96:* 50, 51
Cartwright, Reg *63:* 61, 62; *78:* 26; *143:* 4
Cartwright, Shannon *176:* 81
Carty, Leo *4:* 196; *7:* 163; *58:* 131
Cary *4:* 133; *9:* 32; *20:* 2; *21:* 143
Cary, Page *12:* 41
Casale, Paul *71:* 63; *109:* 122; *136:* 28
Case, Sandra E. *16:* 2
Caseley, Judith *87:* 36; *159:* 47, 48, 49
Casilla, Robert *78:* 7; *167:* 124
Casino, Steve *85:* 193

Cassel, Lili
    See Wronker, Lili Cassel
Cassel-Wronker, Lili
    See Wronker, Lili Cassel
Cassels, Jean *8:* 50; *150:* 119; *173:* 37
Cassen, Melody *140:* 51
Cassity, Don *104:* 24
Cassler, Carl *75:* 137, 138; *82:* 162
Casson, Hugh *65:* 38, 40, 42, 43
Castellon, Federico *48:* 45, 46, 47, 48
Castle, Jane *4:* 80
Castro, Antonio *84:* 71
Catalano, Dominic *94:* 79; *163:* 60, 61; *162:* 54
Catalanotto, Peter *63:* 170; *70:* 23; *71:* 182; *72:* 96; *74:* 114; *76:* 194, 195; *77:* 7; *79:* 157; *80:* 28, 67; *83:* 157; *85:* 27; *108:* 11; *113:* 30, 31, 33, 34, 36; *114:* 27, 28, 29; *117:* 53; *124:* 168; *159:* 54, 55
Catania, Tom *68:* 82
Cather, Carolyn *3:* 83; *15:* 203; *34:* 216
Catrow, David *117:* 179; *152:* 31, 33; *173:* 24
Cauley, Lorinda Bryan *44:* 135; *46:* 49
Cayard, Bruce *38:* 67
Cazet, Denys *52:* 27; *99:* 39, 40; *163:* 65, 66
Cecil, Randy *127:* 132, 133
Cellini, Joseph *2:* 73; *3:* 35; *16:* 116; *47:* 103
Cepeda, Joe *90:* 62; *109:* 91; *134:* 172; *159:* 57, 58, 164
Chabrian, Debbi *45:* 55
Chabrian, Deborah *51:* 182; *53:* 124; *63:* 107; *75:* 84; *79:* 85; *82:* 247; *89:* 93; *101:* 197
Chagnon, Mary *37:* 158
Chalmers, Mary *3:* 145; *13:* 148; *33:* 125; *66:* 214
Chamberlain, Christopher *45:* 57
Chamberlain, Margaret *46:* 51; *106:* 89
Chamberlain, Nigel *78:* 140
Chambers, C.E. *17:* 230
Chambers, Dave *12:* 151
Chambers, Jill *134:* 110
Chambers, Mary *4:* 188
Chambliss, Maxie *42:* 186; *56:* 159; *93:* 163, 164; *103:* 178
Champlin, Dale *136:* 124
Chan, Harvey *96:* 236; *99:* 153; *143:* 218; *179:* 144
Chandler, David P. *28:* 62
Chaney, Howard *139:* 27
Chang, Warren *101:* 209
Chapel, Jody *68:* 20
Chapman, C.H. *13:* 83, 85, 87
Chapman, Frederick T. *6:* 27; *44:* 28
Chapman, Gaynor *32:* 52, 53
Chapman, Jane *145:* 186; *150:* 56; *166:* 220; *174:* 202; *176:* 43, 44; *179:* 131
Chapman, Lynne *175:* 31
Chappell, Warren *3:* 172; *21:* 56; *27:* 125
Charles, Donald *30:* 154, 155
Charlip, Remy *4:* 48; *34:* 138; *68:* 53, 54; *119:* 29, 30
Charlot, Jean *1:* 137, 138; *8:* 23; *14:* 31; *48:* 151; *56:* 21
Charlot, Martin *64:* 72
Charlton, Michael *34:* 50; *37:* 39
Charmatz, Bill *7:* 45
Chartier, Normand *9:* 36; *52:* 49; *66:* 40; *74:* 220; *145:* 169; *168:* 91; *177:* 108
Chase, Lynwood M. *14:* 4
Chast, Roz *97:* 39, 40
Chastain, Madye Lee *4:* 50
Chateron, Ann *152:* 19
Chatterton, Martin *68:* 102; *152:* 19
Chau, Tungwai *140:* 35
Chauncy, Francis *24:* 158
Chayka, Doug *145:* 97; *177:* 150
Chee, Cheng-Khee *79:* 42; *81:* 224
Chen, Chih-sien *90:* 226
Chen, Tony *6:* 45; *19:* 131; *29:* 126; *34:* 160
Cheney, T.A. *11:* 47
Cheng, Judith *36:* 45; *51:* 16

Chermayeff, Ivan *47:* 53
Cherry, David *93:* 40
Cherry, Lynne *34:* 52; *65:* 184; *87:* 111; *99:* 46, 47
Chesak, Lina *135:* 118
Chess, Victoria *12:* 6; *33:* 42, 48, 49; *40:* 194; *41:* 145; *69:* 80; *72:* 100; *92:* 33, 34; *104:* 167
Chessare, Michele *41:* 50; *56:* 48; *69:* 145
Chesterton, G.K. *27:* 43, 44, 45, 47
Chestnutt, David *47:* 217
Chesworth, Michael *75:* 24, 152; *88:* 136; *94:* 25; *98:* 155; *160:* 42
Chetham, Celia *134:* 34
Chetwin, Grace *86:* 40
Cheung, Irving *158:* 96
Chevalier, Christa *35:* 66
Chew, Ruth *7:* 46; *132:* 147
Chewning, Randy *92:* 206
Chichester Clark, Emma *72:* 121; *77:* 212; *78:* 209; *87:* 143; *117:* 37, 39, 40; *144:* 138; *156:* 24, 25
Chifflart *47:* 113, 127
Child, Lauren *119:* 32
Chin, Alex *28:* 54
Chitwood, Susan Tanner *163:* 16
Cho, Shinta *8:* 126
Chodos-Irvine, Margaret *52:* 102, 103, 107; *152:* 44
Choi, Yangsook *171:* 134; *173:* 135; *178:* 38, 39, 40
Chollat, Emilie *170:* 203
Chollick, Jay *25:* 175
Choma, Christina *99:* 169
Chorao, Kay *7:* 200, 201; *8:* 25; *11:* 234; *33:* 187; *35:* 239; *69:* 35; *70:* 235; *123:* 174
Chowdhury, Subrata *62:* 130; *162:* 22, 23
Christelow, Eileen *38:* 44; *83:* 198, 199; *90:* 57, 58
Christensen, Bonnie *93:* 100; *153:* 67
Christensen, Gardell Dano *1:* 57
Christensen, James C. *140:* 226
Christiana, David *90:* 64; *135:* 13; *171:* 7
Christiansen, Per *40:* 24
Christie, R. Gregory *116:* 107; *127:* 20, 21; *162:* 179; *164:* 114; *165:* 137; *174:* 157; *179:* 172
Christy, Howard Chandler *17:* 163, 164, 165, 168, 169; *19:* 186, 187; *21:* 22, 23, 24, 25
Chronister, Robert *23:* 138; *63:* 27; *69:* 167
Church, Caroline Jayne *179:* 27
Church, Frederick *YABC 1:* 155
Chute, Marchette *1:* 59
Chwast, Jacqueline *1:* 63; *2:* 275; *6:* 46, 47; *11:* 125; *12:* 202; *14:* 235
Chwast, Seymour *3:* 128, 129; *18:* 43; *27:* 152; *92:* 79; *96:* 56, 57, 58; *146:* 32, 33
Cieslawksi, Steve *101:* 142; *127:* 116; *158:* 169, 171
Cinelli, Lisa *146:* 253
Cirlin, Edgard *2:* 168
Clairin, Georges *53:* 109
Clapp, John *105:* 66; *109:* 58; *126:* 7; *129:* 148; *130:* 165
Clark, Brenda *119:* 85; *153:* 55
Clark, David *77:* 164; *134:* 144, 145
Clark, Emma Chichester
    See Chichester Clark, Emma
Clark, Victoria *35:* 159
Clarke, Greg *169:* 134
Clarke, Gus *72:* 226; *134:* 31
Clarke, Harry *23:* 172, 173
Clarke, Peter *75:* 102
Claverie, Jean *38:* 46; *88:* 29
Clayton, Elaine *159:* 60
Clayton, Robert *9:* 181
Cleaver, Elizabeth *8:* 204; *23:* 36
Cleland, T.M. *26:* 92
Clemens, Peter *61:* 125
Clement, Charles *20:* 38
Clement, Rod *97:* 42

Clement, Stephen *88:* 3
Clementson, John *84:* 213
Clevin, Jorgen *7:* 50
Clifford, Judy *34:* 163; *45:* 198
Clokey, Art *59:* 44
Clouse, James *84:* 15
Clouse, Nancy L. *78:* 31; *114:* 90
Clover, Peter *152:* 45
Cneut, Carll *156:* 166; *165:* 67
Coalson, Glo *9:* 72, 85; *25:* 155; *26:* 42; *35:* 212; *53:* 31; *56:* 154; *94:* 37, 38, 193
Cober, Alan E. *17:* 158; *32:* 77; *49:* 127
Cober-Gentry, Leslie *92:* 111
Cocca-Leffler, Maryann *80:* 46; *136:* 60; *139:* 193
Cochran, Bobbye *11:* 52
CoConis, Ted *4:* 41; *46:* 41; *51:* 104
Cocozza, Chris *87:* 18; *110:* 173; *111:* 149
Cockcroft, Jason *152:* 20
Coerr, Eleanor *1:* 64; *67:* 52
Coes, Peter *35:* 172
Cogancherry, Helen *52:* 143; *69:* 131; *77:* 93; *78:* 220; *109:* 204; *110:* 129
Coggins, Jack *2:* 69
Cohen, Alix *7:* 53
Cohen, Miriam *155:* 23, 24
Cohen, Nancy R. *165:* 35
Cohen, Santiago *164:* 26
Cohen, Sheldon *105:* 33, 34; *166:* 46, 47
Cohen, Vincent O. *19:* 243
Cohen, Vivien *11:* 112
Coker, Paul *51:* 172
Colbert, Anthony *15:* 41; *20:* 193
Colby, C.B. *3:* 47
Cole, Babette *58:* 172; *96:* 63, 64; *155:* 29
Cole, Brock *68:* 223; *72:* 36, 37, 38, 192; *127:* 23; *136:* 64, 65
Cole, Gwen *87:* 185
Cole, Henry *178:* 120
Cole, Herbert *28:* 104
Cole, Michael *59:* 46
Cole, Olivia H.H. *1:* 134; *3:* 223; *9:* 111; *38:* 104
Colin, Paul *102:* 59; *123:* 118; *126:* 152
Collicott, Sharleen *98:* 39; *143:* 29, 30
Collier, Bryan *126:* 54; *151:* 166; *174:* 16, 17, 18
Collier, David *13:* 127
Collier, John *27:* 179
Collier, Steven *50:* 52
Collier-Morales, Roberta *168:* 61
Collins, Heather *66:* 84; *67:* 68; *81:* 40; *98:* 192, 193; *129:* 95, 96, 98
Collins, Matt *167:* 90
Collins, Ross *140:* 23, 24
Colman, Audrey *146:* 161
Colon, Raul *108:* 112; *113:* 5; *117:* 167; *134:* 112; *146:* 23; *159:* 92; *166:* 73
Colonna, Bernard *21:* 50; *28:* 103; *34:* 140; *43:* 180; *78:* 150
Comport, Sally Wern *117:* 169; *169:* 104
Conde, J.M. *100:* 120
Condon, Grattan *54:* 85 Condon, Ken *161:* 44
Cone, Ferne Geller *39:* 49
Cone, J. Morton *39:* 49
Conklin, Paul *43:* 62
Connolly, Howard *67:* 88
Connolly, Jerome P. *4:* 128; *28:* 52
Connolly, Peter *47:* 60
Conoly, Walle *110:* 224
Conover, Chris *31:* 52; *40:* 184; *41:* 51; *44:* 79
Contreras, Gerry *72:* 9
Converse, James *38:* 70
Conway *62:* 62
Conway, Michael *69:* 12; *81:* 3; *92:* 108
Cook, G.R. *29:* 165
Cook, Joel *108:* 160
Cookburn, W.V. *29:* 204
Cooke, Donald E. *2:* 77
Cooke, Tom *52:* 118
Coomaraswamy, A.K. *50:* 100

Coombs, Charles *43:* 65
Coombs, Deborah *139:* 175
Coombs, Patricia *2:* 82; *3:* 52; *22:* 119; *51:* 32, 33, 34, 35, 36, 37, 38, 39, 40, 42, 43
Cooney, Barbara *6:* 16, 17, 50; *12:* 42; *13:* 92; *15:* 145; *16:* 74, 111; *18:* 189; *23:* 38, 89, 93; *32:* 138; *38:* 105; *59:* 48, 49, 51, 52, 53; *74:* 222; *81:* 100; *91:* 25; *96:* 71, 72, 74; *100:* 149; *YABC2:* 10
Cooper, Elisha *157:* 38, 39
Cooper, Floyd *79:* 95; *81:* 45; *84:* 82; *85:* 74; *91:* 118; *96:* 77, 78; *103:* 149; *144:* 54; *145:* 151; *159:* 198; *176:* 133, 134
Cooper, Heather *50:* 39
Cooper, Helen *102:* 42, 43, 44
Cooper, Mario *24:* 107
Cooper, Marjorie *7:* 112
Cope, Jane *61:* 201; *108* 52
Copelman, Evelyn *8:* 61; *18:* 25
Copley, Heather *30:* 86; *45:* 57
Corbett, Grahame *30:* 114; *43:* 67
Corbino, John *19:* 248
Corcos, Lucille *2:* 223; *10:* 27; *34:* 66
Corey, Robert *9:* 34
Corlass, Heather *10:* 7
Cornell, James *27:* 60
Cornell, Jeff *11:* 58
Cornell, Laura *94:* 179; *95:* 25
Corrigan, Barbara *8:* 37
Corrigan, Patrick *145:* 149
Corwin, Judith Hoffman *10:* 28
Cory, Fanny Y. *20:* 113; *48:* 29
Cosentino, Ralph *169:* 32
Cosgrove, Margaret *3:* 100; *47:* 63; *82:* 133
Costabel, Eva Deutsch *45:* 66, 67
Costanza, John *58:* 7, 8, 9
Costello, Chris *86:* 78
Costello, David F. *23:* 55
Cote, Nancy *126:* 139; *156:* 101; *174:* 101
Couch, Greg *94:* 124; *110:* 13; *162:* 31; *168:* 149
Councell, Ruth Tietjen *79:* 29
Courtney, Cathy *58:* 69, 144; *59:* 15; *61:* 20, 87
Courtney, R. *35:* 110
Counihan, Claire *133:* 106
Cousineau, Normand *89:* 180; *112:* 76
Cousins, Lucy *172:* 53, 54
Couture, Christin *41:* 209
Covarrubias, Miguel *35:* 118, 119, 123, 124, 125
Coville, Katherine *32:* 57; *36:* 167; *92:* 38
Covington, Neverne *113:* 87
Cowdrey, Richard *169:* 170; *178:* 205
Cowell, Cressida *140:* 39
Cowell, Lucinda *77:* 54
Cox *43:* 93
Cox, Charles *8:* 20
Cox, David *56:* 37; *90:* 63; *119:* 38
Cox, Palmer *24:* 76, 77
Cox, Steve *140:* 96
Coxe, Molly *69:* 44
Coxon, Michele *158:* 80
Crabb, Gordon *70:* 39
Crabtree, Judith *98:* 42
Craft, Kinuko *22:* 182; *36:* 220; *53:* 122, 123, 148, 149; *74:* 12; *81:* 129; *86:* 31; *89:* 139; *127:* 27, 28, 29; *132:* 142; *139:* 38
Craig, Dan *177:* 67
Craig, David *136:* 198
Craig, Helen *49:* 76; *62:* 70, 71, 72; *69:* 141; *94:* 42, 43, 44; *112:* 53; *135:* 101, 102
Crane, Alan H. *1:* 217
Crane, H.M. *13:* 111
Crane, Jack *43:* 183
Crane, Jordan *174:* 21
Crane, Walter *18:* 46, 47, 48, 49, 53, 54, 56, 57, 59, 60, 61; *22:* 128; *24:* 210, 217; *100:* 70, 71
Cravath, Lynne W. *98:* 45
Crawford, Denise *137:* 213

Crawford, Will *43:* 77
Credle, Ellis *1:* 69
Czernecki, Stefan *154:* 104; *178:* 68, 69
Crespi, Francesca *87:* 90
Cressy, Michael *124:* 55
Crews, Donald *32:* 59, 60; *76:* 42, 43, 44
Crews, Nina *97:* 49
Crichlow, Ernest *74:* 88; *83:* 203
Croft, James *150:* 57
Crofut, Bob *80:* 87; *81:* 47
Crofut, Susan *23:* 61
Croll, Carolyn *80:* 137; *102:* 52
Cross, Peter *56:* 78; *63:* 60, 65
Crowe, Elizabeth *88:* 144
Crowell, Pers *3:* 125
Cruikshank, George *15:* 76, 83; *22:* 74, 75, 76, 77, 78, 79,80, 81, 82, 84, 137; *24:* 22, 23
Crump, Fred H. *11:* 62
Cruz, Ray *6:* 55; *70:* 234; *123:* 173; *172:* 192
Csatari, Joe *44:* 82; *55:* 152; *63:* 25, 28; *102:* 58
Cuetara, Mittie *158:* 85
Cuffari, Richard *4:* 75; *5:* 98; *6:* 56; *7:* 13,84, 153; *8:* 148, 155; *9:* 89; *11:* 19; *12:* 55, 96,114; *15:* 51, 202; *18:* 5; *20:* 139; *21:* 197; *22:* 14, 192; *23:* 15, 106; *25:* 97; *27:* 133; *28:* 196; *29:* 54; *30:* 85; *31:* 35; *36:* 101; *38:* 171; *42:* 97; *44:* 92, 192; *45:* 212, 213; *46:* 36, 198; *50:* 164; *54:* 80, 136, 137, 145; *56:* 17; *60:* 63; *66:* 49, 50; *70:* 41; *71:* 132; *77:* 157; *78:* 58, 149; *79:* 120; *85:* 2, 152
Cugat, Xavier *19:* 120
Cumings, Art *35:* 160
Cummings, Chris *29:* 167
Cummings, Michael *159:* 142
Cummings, Pat *42:* 61; *61:* 99; *69:* 205; *71:* 57,58; *78:* 24, 25; *93:* 75; *107:* 49, 50; *164:* 259
Cummings, Richard *24:* 119
Cunette, Lou *20:* 93; *22:* 125
Cunningham, Aline *25:* 180
Cunningham, David *11:* 13
Cunningham, Imogene *16:* 122, 127
Cunningham, Kelley *176:* 159
Cupples, Pat *107:* 12; *126:* 109
Curlee, Lynn *98:* 48; *141:* 39
Curry, John Steuart *2:* 5; *19:* 84; *34:* 36; *144:* 126
Curry, Tom *127:* 131
Curtis, Bruce *23:* 96; *30:* 88; *36:* 22
Curtis, Neil *167:* 30
Cusack, Margaret *58:* 49, 50, 51
Cushman, Doug *65:* 57; *101:* 39, 40; *133:* 179; *157:* 45
Cyrus, Kurt *132:* 39; *179:* 36, 37
Czechowski, Alicia *95:* 21; *171:* 37
Czernecki, Stefan *117:* 173

D

Dabcovich, Lydia *25:* 105; *40:* 114; *99:* 75, 76
Dacey, Bob *82:* 175; *152:* 65
d'Achille, Gino *127:* 175, 176
Dailey, Don *78:* 197
Dain, Martin J. *35:* 75
Dale, Penny *127:* 224; *151:* 57; *160:* 89
Dale, Rae *72:* 197
Daley, Joann *50:* 22
Dalton, Anne *40:* 62; *63:* 119
Daly, Deborah M. *74:* 213
Daly, Jim *103:* 60; *150:* 48
Daly, Jude *138:* 118, 119
Daly, Nicholas *37:* 53; *76:* 48, 49
Daly, Niki *107:* 15; *114:* 38, 39, 40; *164:* 86
Daly, Paul *97:* 205
Dalziel, Brothers *33:* 113
D'Amato, Alex *9:* 48; *20:* 25
D'Amato, Janet *9:* 48; *20:* 25; *26:* 118
D'Amico, Steve *170:* 52

Danalis, Johnny *167:* 27
Daniel, Alan *23:* 59; *29:* 110; *76:* 50, 53, 55, 56; *153:* 76 115: 74; *134:* 70
Daniel, Lea *76:* 53, 55; *153:* 76
Daniel, Lewis C. *20:* 216
Daniels, Beau *73:* 4
Daniels, Steve *22:* 16
Daniels, Stewart *56:* 12
Dann, Bonnie *31:* 83
Dann, Penny *82:* 128
Danska, Herbert *24:* 219
Danyell, Alice *20:* 27
Darley, F.O.C. *16:* 145; *19:* 79, 86, 88, 185; *21:* 28,36; *35:* 76, 77, 78, 79, 80, 81; *YABC 2:* 175
Darling, Lois *3:* 59; *23:* 30, 31
Darling, Louis *1:* 40, 41; *2:* 63; *3:* 59; *23:* 30,31; *43:* 54, 57, 59; *121:* 53
Darrow, David R. *84:* 101
Darrow, Whitney, Jr. *13:* 25; *38:* 220, 221
Darwin, Beatrice *43:* 54
Darwin, Len *24:* 82
Dastolfo, Frank *33:* 179
Dauber, Liz *1:* 22; *3:* 266; *30:* 49
Daugherty, James *3:* 66; *8:* 178; *13:* 27, 28, 161; *18:* 101; *19:* 72; *29:* 108; *32:* 156; *42:* 84; *YABC 1:* 256; *2:* 174
d'Aulaire, Edgar Parin *5:* 51; *66:* 53
d'Aulaire, Ingri Parin *5:* 51; *66:* 53
Davalos, Felipe *99:* 197; *159:* 66; *174:* 163
Davenier, Christine *125:* 88; *127:* 32; *128:* 152; *179:* 39, 40
Davick, Linda *151:* 124
David, Jonathan *19:* 37
Davidson, Kevin *28:* 154
Davidson, Raymond *32:* 61
Davie, Helen K. *77:* 48, 49
Davis, Allen *20:* 11; *22:* 45; *27:* 222; *29:* 157; *41:* 99; *47:* 99; *50:* 84; *52:* 105
Davis, Bette J. *15:* 53; *23:* 95
Davis, Dimitris *45:* 95
Davis, Hendon *151:* 122
Davis, Jack E. *145:* 139; *175:* 84, 85
Davis, Jim *32:* 63, 64
Davis, Katie *152:* 52, 53, 54
Davis, Lambert *110:* 23, 24; *176:* 58
Davis, Marguerite *31:* 38; *34:* 69, 70; *100:* 34; *YABC 1:* 126, 230
Davis, Nelle *69:* 191
Davis, Paul *78:* 214
Davis, Yvonne LeBrun *94:* 144
Davisson, Virginia H. *44:* 178
DaVolls, Andy *85:* 53
Dawson, Diane *24:* 127; *42:* 126; *52:* 130; *68:* 104
Day, Alexandra *67:* 59; *97:* 54; *166:* 65; *169:* 40
Day, Larry *169:* 88
Day, Rob *94:* 110; *127:* 24
Dean, Bob *19:* 211
de Angeli, Marguerite *1:* 77; *27:* 62, 65, 66, 67, 69, 70, 72; *100:* 75, 76; *YABC 1:* 166
DeArmond, Dale *70:* 47
Deas, Michael *27:* 219, 221; *30:* 156; *67:* 134; *72:* 24; *75:* 155; *84:* 206; *88:* 124
Debon, Nicolas *151:* 60; *177:* 46
de Bosschere, Jean *19:* 252; *21:* 4
De Bruyn, M(onica) G. *13:* 30, 31
Decker, C.B. *172:* 120
De Cuir, John F. *1:* 28, 29
Deeter, Catherine *74:* 110; *103:* 150; *137:* 50
Degen, Bruce *40:* 227, 229; *57:* 28, 29; *56:* 156; *75:* 229; *76:* 19; *81:* 36, 37; *92:* 26; *93:* 199; *97:* 56, 58, 59; *124:* 40; *147:* 39, 40, 41; *168:* 23
De Grazia *14:* 59; *39:* 56, 57
DeGrazio, George *88:* 40
deGroat, Diane *9:* 39; *18:* 7; *23:* 123; *28:* 200, 201; *31:* 58, 59; *34:* 151; *41:* 152; *43:* 88; *46:* 40, 200; *49:* 163; *50:* 89; *52:* 30, 34; *54:* 43; *63:* 5; *70:* 136; *71:* 99; *73:* 117,156; *77:*

34; *85:* 48; *86:* 201; *87:* 142; *90:* 72, 73, 143; *95:* 182; *111:* 123; *118:* 160; *126:* 8; *130:* 130; *138:* 93, 94; *169:* 46, 47
de Groot, Lee *6:* 21
Deines, Brian *110:* 139
DeJohn, Marie *89:* 78
Dekhteryov, B. *61:* 158
de Kiefte, Kees *94:* 107
Delacre, Lulu *36:* 66; *156:* 35
Delaney, A. *21:* 78
Delaney, Molly *80:* 43
Delaney, Ned *28:* 68; *56:* 80; *102:* 11
DeLange, Alex Pardo *179:* 128
DeLapine, Jim *79:* 21
De La Roche Saint Andre, Anne *75:* 37
de Larrea, Victoria *6:* 119, 204; *29:* 103; *72:* 203; *87:* 199
Delessert, Étienne *7:* 140; *46:* 61, 62, 63, 65, 67, 68; *130:* 38, 39, 40, 41, 42; *179:* 46, 47, 48, 49; *YABC 2:* 209
DeLorenzo, Christopher *154:* 149
Delulio, John *15:* 54
DeLuna, Tony *88:* 95
Demarest, Chris L. *45:* 68, 69, 70; *73:* 172, 173, 176; *78:* 106; *82:* 48, 49; *89:* 212; *92:* 86; *128:* 57, 58; *175:* 46, 48
De Mejo, Oscar *40:* 67
Demi *11:* 135; *15:* 245; *66:* 129, 130; *89:* 216; *102:* 66, 67, 68
Denetsosie, Hoke *13:* 126; *82:* 34
Denise, Christopher *147:* 43, 44; *176:* 101
Dennis, Morgan *18:* 68, 69; *64:* 89
Dennis, Wesley *2:* 87; *3:* 111; *11:* 132; *18:* 71, 72, 73, 74; *22:* 9; *24:* 196, 200; *46:* 178; *69:* 94, 96; *129:* 62
Denslow, W.W. *16:* 84, 85, 86, 87; *18:* 19, 20, 24; *29:* 211; *100:* 21
Denton, Kady MacDonald *110:* 82; *130:* 70
Denton, Terry *72:* 163; *174:* 26
DePalma, Mary Newell *132:* 114; *139:* 75
de Paola, Tomie *8:* 95; *9:* 93; *11:* 69; *25:* 103; *28:* 157; *29:* 80; *39:* 52, 53; *40:* 226; *46:* 187; *59:* 61, 62, 63, 64, 65, 66, 67, 68, 69, 71, 72, 74; *62:* 19; *108:* 63, 67, 68, 70; *155:* 62, 64, 66
Deraney, Michael J. *77:* 35; *78:* 148
deRosa, Dee *70:* 48; *71:* 210; *91:* 78
Dervaux, Isabelle *111:* 117
De Saulles, Tony *119:* 39
de Seve, Peter *146:* 261
Deshaprabhu, Meera Dayal *86:* 192
Desimini, Lisa *86:* 68; *94:* 47; *96:* 7; *104:* 107; *125:* 194; *131:* 180; *172:* 56
de St. Menin, Charles *70:* 17
Detmold, Edward J. *22:* 104, 105, 106, 107; *35:* 120; *64:* 5; *YABC 2:* 203
Detrich, Susan *20:* 133
Deutermann, Diana *77:* 175
DeVelasco, Joseph E. *21:* 51
de Veyrac, Robert *YABC 2:* 19
DeVille, Edward A. *4:* 235
de Visser, John *55:* 119
Devito, Bert *12:* 164
Devlin, Harry *11:* 74; *74:* 63, 65; *136:* 77, 78
Dewan, Ted *108:* 73; *157:* 55; *165:* 129
Dewar, Nick *133:* 122
Dewey, Ariane *7:* 64; *33:* 195; *35:* 208; *68:* 16,17; *75:* 46; *93:* 91; *94:* 197; *109:* 65, 66, 67; *125:* 2, 3, 4, 5; *127:* 188; *143:* 25; *178:* 17, 19, 74
Dewey, Jennifer (Owings) *58:* 54; *64:* 214; *65:* 207; *88:* 169; *103:* 45
Dewey, Kenneth *39:* 62; *51:* 23; *56:* 163
de Zanger, Arie *30:* 40
Diakité, Baba Wagué *174:* 28
Diamond, Donna *21:* 200; *23:* 63; *26:* 142; *35:* 83, 84, 85, 86, 87, 88, 89; *38:* 78; *40:* 147; *44:* 152; *50:* 144; *53:* 126; *69:* 46, 47, 48, 201; *71:* 133; *123:* 19
Dias, Ron *71:* 67

Diaz, David *80:* 213; *96:* 83, 84; *108:* 228; *110:* 29; *149:* 106; *150:* 63; *179:* 160
Dibley, Glin *138:* 83; *141:* 128
DiCesare, Joe *70:* 38; *71:* 63, 106; *79:* 214; *93:* 147; *116:* 217; *143:* 111; *166:* 57
Dick, John Henry *8:* 181
Dickens, Frank *34:* 131
Dickey, Robert L. *15:* 279
Dickson, Mora *84:* 21
Didier, Sam *166:* 114
Dietz, James *128:* 223
di Fate, Vincent *37:* 70; *90:* 11; *93:* 60; *109:* 219, 220
Di Fiori, Lawrence *10:* 51; *12:* 190; *27:* 97; *40:* 219; *93:* 57; *130:* 45
Digby, Desmond *97:* 180
Di Grazia, Thomas *32:* 66; *35:* 241
Dillard, Annie *10:* 32
Dillard, Sarah *136:* 186
Dillon, Corinne B. *1:* 139
Dillon, Diane *4:* 104, 167; *6:* 23; *13:* 29; *15:* 99; *26:* 148; *27:* 136, 201; *51:* 29, 48, 51, 52, 53, 54,55, 56, 57, 58, 59, 60, 61, 62; *54:* 155; *56:* 69; *58:* 127,128; *61:* 95; *62:* 27; *64:* 46; *68:* 3; *69:* 209; *74:* 89; *79:* 92; *86:* 89; *92:* 28, 177; *93:* 7, 210; *94:* 239, 240; *97:* 167; *106:* 58, 59,61, 64; *107:* 3; *139:* 246; *167:* 77
Dillon, Leo *4:* 104, 167; *6:* 23; *13:* 29; *15:* 99; *26:* 148; *27:* 136, 201; *51:* 29, 48, 51, 52, 53, 54,55, 56, 57, 58, 59, 60, 61, 62; *54:* 155; *56:* 69; *58:* 127,128; *61:* 95; *62:* 27; *64:* 46; *68:* 3; *69:* 209; *74:* 89; *79:* 92; *86:* 89; *92:* 28, 177; *93:* 7, 210; *94:* 239, 240; *97:* 167; *106:* 58, 59,61, 64; *107:* 3; *139:* 246; *167:* 77
Dillon, Sharon Saseen *59:* 179, 188
DiMaccio, Gerald *121:* 80
DiMaggio, Joe *36:* 22
DiMassi, Gina *169:* 17
Dinan, Carol *25:* 169; *59:* 75
Dines, Glen *7:* 66, 67
Dinesen, Thomas *44:* 37
Dinh, Pham Viet *167:* 184
Dinnerstein, Harvey *42:* 63, 64, 65, 66, 67, 68; *50:* 146
Dinsdale, Mary *10:* 65; *11:* 171
Dinyer, Eric *86:* 148; *109:* 163; *110:* 239; *124:* 11; *150:* 69; *170:* 4; *171:* 30
Dion, Nathalie *170:* 124
DiSalvo-Ryan, DyAnne *59:* 77; *62:* 185; *117:* 46; *144:* 64; *150:* 153
Disney, Walt *28:* 71, 72, 73, 76, 77, 78, 79, 80, 81, 87, 88, 89,90, 91, 94
DiTerlizzi, Tony *105:* 7; *147:* 22; *154:* 31, 32, 33
Divito, Anna *83:* 159
Dixon, Don *74:* 17; *109:* 196
Dixon, Larry *127:* 125
Dixon, Maynard *20:* 165
Doares, Robert G. *20:* 39
Dobias, Frank *22:* 162
Dobrin, Arnold *4:* 68
Dobson, Steven Gaston *102:* 103
Dockray, Tracy *139:* 77
Docktor, Irv *43:* 70
Dodd, Ed *4:* 69
Dodd, Julie *74:* 73
Dodd, Lynley *35:* 92; *86:* 71; *132:* 45, 46, 47
Dodge, Bill *96:* 36; *118:* 7, 8, 9; *133:* 135
Dodgson, Charles L. *20:* 148; *33:* 146; *YABC 2:* 98
Dodson, Bert *9:* 138; *14:* 195; *42:* 55; *54:* 8; *60:* 49; *101:* 125
Dodson, Liz Brenner *105:* 117; *111:* 15
Dohanos, Stevan *16:* 10
Dolce, J. Ellen *74:* 147; *75:* 41
Dolch, Marguerite P. *50:* 64
Dolesch, Susanne *34:* 49
Dollar, Diane *57:* 32
Dolobowsky, Mena *81:* 54

Dolson, Hildegarde *5:* 57
Domanska, Janina *6:* 66, 67; *YABC 1:* 166
Domi *134:* 113
Dominguez, El *53:* 94
Domjan, Joseph *25:* 93
Domm, Jeffrey C. *84:* 69; *135:* 70
Donahey, William *68:* 209
Donahue, Dorothy *76:* 170
Donahue, Vic *2:* 93; *3:* 190; *9:* 44
Donald, Elizabeth *4:* 18
Donalty, Alison *149:* 195, 196, 197
Donato *85:* 59; *149:* 204
Doney, Todd L.W. *87:* 12; *93:* 112; *98:* 135; *101:* 57; *104:* 40; *118:* 163; *135:* 162, 163; *151:* 18
Donna, Natalie *9:* 52
Donohue, Dorothy *95:* 2; *132:* 30; *176:* 54, 55; *178:* 77, 78, 79
Dooling, Michael *82:* 19; *105:* 55; *106:* 224; *125:* 135; *171:* 46; *172:* 12; *176:* 120
Doran, Ben-Ami *128:* 189
Dore, Gustave *18:* 169, 172, 175; *19:* 93, 94, 95, 96, 97, 98,99, 100, 101, 102, 103, 104, 105; *23:* 188; *25:* 197, 199
Doremus, Robert *6:* 62; *13:* 90; *30:* 95, 96, 97; *38:* 97
Dorfman, Ronald *11:* 128
Doriau *86:* 59; *91:* 152
Dorros, Arthur *78:* 42, 43; *91:* 28
Doruyter, Karel *165:* 105
dos Santos, Joyce Audy *57:* 187, 189
Doty, Roy *28:* 98; *31:* 32; *32:* 224; *46:* 157; *82:* 71; *142:* 7
Doucet, Bob *132:* 238; *169:* 159
Dougherty, Charles *16:* 204; *18:* 74
Doughty, Rebecca *177:* 174
Doughty, Thomas *118:* 31; *140:* 60
Douglas, Aaron *31:* 103
Douglas, Carole Nelson *73:* 48
Douglas, Goray *13:* 151
Dow, Brian *150:* 92
Dowd, Jason *132:* 51, 52; *164:* 244
Dowd, Vic *3:* 244; *10:* 97
Dowden, Anne Ophelia *7:* 70, 71; *13:* 120
Dowdy, Mrs. Regera *29:* 100
Downing, Julie *60:* 140; *81:* 50; *86:* 200; *99:* 129
Doyle, Janet *56:* 31
Doyle, Richard *21:* 31, 32, 33; *23:* 231; *24:* 177; *31:* 87
Draper, Angie *43:* 84
Drath, Bill *26:* 34
Drawson, Blair *17:* 53; *126:* 65
Dray, Matt *177:* 47
Drescher, Henrik *105:* 60, 62, 63; *172:* 72
Drescher, Joan *30:* 100, 101; *35:* 245; *52:* 168; *137:* 52
Drew, Patricia *15:* 100
Drummond, V.H. *6:* 70
Drury, Christian Potter *105:* 97
Dubanevich, Arlene *56:* 44
Ducak, Danilo *99:* 130; *108:* 214
Duchesne, Janet *6:* 162; *79:* 8
Duda, Jana *102:* 155
Dudash, Michael *32:* 122; *77:* 134; *82:* 149
Duer, Douglas *34:* 177
Duffy, Daniel Mark *76:* 37; *101:* 196; *108:* 147, 148
Duffy, Joseph *38:* 203
Duffy, Pat *28:* 153
Dugin, Andrej *77:* 60
Dugina, Olga *77:* 60
Duke, Chris *8:* 195; *139:* 164
Duke, Kate *87:* 186; *90:* 78, 79, 80, 81
Duke, Marion *165:* 87
Dulac, Edmund *19:* 108, 109, 110, 111, 112, 113, 114, 115, 117; *23:* 187; *25:* 152; *YABC 1:* 37; *2:* 147
Dulac, Jean *13:* 64
Dumas, Philippe *52:* 36, 37, 38, 39, 40, 41, 42, 43, 45; *119:* 40, 41, 42

Dunaway, Nancy *108:* 161
Dunbar, James *76:* 63
Duncan, Beverly *72:* 92
Duncan, John *116:* 94
Dunn, H.T. *62:* 196
Dunn, Harvey *34:* 78, 79, 80, 81
Dunn, Iris *5:* 175
Dunn, Phoebe *5:* 175
Dunne, Jeanette *72:* 57, 173, 222
Dunnick, Regan *176:* 51; *178:* 83, 84
Dunnington, Tom *3:* 36; *18:* 281; *25:* 61; *31:* 159; *35:* 168; *48:* 195; *79:* 144; *82:* 230
Dunn-Ramsey, Marcy *117:* 131
Dunrea, Olivier *59:* 81; *118:* 53, 54; *124:* 43
Duntze, Dorothee *88:* 28; *160:* 76
Dupasquier, Philippe *86:* 75; *104:* 76; *151:* 63
DuQuette, Keith *90:* 83; *155:* 73, 74
Duroussy, Nathalie *146:* 150
Durrell, Julie *82:* 62; *94:* 62
Dutz *6:* 59
Duvoisin, Roger *2:* 95; *6:* 76, 77; *7:* 197; *28:* 125; *30:* 101, 102, 103, 104, 105, 107; *47:* 205; *84:* 254
Dyer, Dale *141:* 71
Dyer, Jane *75:* 219; *129:* 28; *147:* 49, 50, 51; *168:* 121
Dypold, Pat *15:* 37

E

E.V.B.
See Boyle, Eleanor Vere (Gordon)
Eachus, Jennifer *29:* 74; *82:* 201; *164:* 153
Eadie, Bob *63:* 36
Eagle, Bruce *95:* 119
Eagle, Ellen *82:* 121; *89:* 3
Eagle, Jeremy *141:* 71
Eagle, Michael *11:* 86; *20:* 9; *23:* 18; *27:* 122; *28:* 57; *34:* 201; *44:* 189; *73:* 9; *78:* 235; *85:* 43
Earl-Bridges, Michele *159:* 128
Earle, Edwin *56:* 27
Earle, Olive L. *7:* 75
Earle, Vana *27:* 99
Early, Lori *132:* 2
Early, Margaret *72:* 59
East, Stella *131:* 223
Eastman, P.D. *33:* 57
Easton, Reginald *29:* 181
Eaton, Tom *4:* 62; *6:* 64; *22:* 99; *24:* 124
Ebel, Alex *11:* 89
Ebert, Len *9:* 191; *44:* 47
Echevarria, Abe *37:* 69
Eckersley, Maureen *48:* 62
Eckert, Horst *72:* 62
Ede, Janina *33:* 59
Edens, Cooper *49:* 81, 82, 83, 84, 85; *112:* 58
Edens, John *109:* 115
Edgar, Sarah E. *41:* 97
Edliq, Emily S. *131:* 107
Edrien *11:* 53
Edwards, Freya *45:* 102
Edwards, George Wharton *31:* 155
Edwards, Gunvor *2:* 71; *25:* 47; *32:* 71; *54:* 106
Edwards, Jeanne *29:* 257
Edwards, Linda Strauss *21:* 134; *39:* 123; *49:* 88, 89
Edwards, Michelle *152:* 62, 63
Edwards, Wallace *170:* 55
Egan, Tim *155:* 76, 77, 78
Egge, David *102:* 71
Eggenhofer, Nicholas *2:* 81
Eggleton, Bob *74:* 40; *81:* 190, 191; *105:* 6; *121:* 183; *149:* 203; *166:* 215
Egielski, Richard *11:* 90; *16:* 208; *33:* 236; *38:* 35; *49:* 91, 92, 93, 95, 212, 213, 214, 216; *79:* 122; *106:* 67, 68, 69; *134:* 135; *144:* 244; *163:* 82, 84

Ehlert, Lois *35:* 97; *69:* 51; *112:* 7; *113:* 208; *128:* 63, 64, 65; *172:* 77, 79, 80
Ehrlich, Bettina *1:* 83
Eitan, Ora *160:* 165
Eichenberg, Fritz *1:* 79; *9:* 54; *19:* 248; *23:* 170; *24:* 200; *26:* 208; *50:* 67, 68, 69, 70, 71, 72, 73,74, 75, 77, 79, 80, 81; *60:* 165; *100:* 137; *YABC 1:* 104, 105; *2:* 213
Einsel, Naiad *10:* 35; *29:* 136
Einsel, Walter *10:* 37
Einzig, Susan *3:* 77; *43:* 78; *67:* 155; *129:* 154
Eisner, Will *165:* 82, 83
Eitzen, Allan *9:* 56; *12:* 212; *14:* 226; *21:* 194; *38:* 162; *76:* 218
Eldridge, H. *54:* 109
Eldridge, Harold *43:* 83
Elgaard, Greta *19:* 241
Elgin, Kathleen *9:* 188; *39:* 69
Ellacott, S.E. *19:* 118
Elliott, Mark *93:* 69; *105:* 108; *107:* 123; *140:* 53; *165:* 189; *173:* 67
Elliott, Sarah M. *14:* 58
Ellis, Dianne *130:* 208
Ellis, Jan Davey *88:* 50; *115:* 80
Ellis, Richard *130:* 47, 48
Ellison, Pauline *55:* 21
Elmer, Richard *78:* 5
Elmore, Larry *90:* 8
Elwell, Tristan *110:* 39; *121:* 182; *127:* 46; *137:* 144; *141:* 173; *151:* 236; *158:* 264; *167:* 119, 120, 121; *169:* 20
Elzbieta *88:* 80, 81
Emberley, Ed *8:* 53; *70:* 53, 54; *146:* 65, 69, 70
Emberley, Michael *34:* 83; *80:* 72; *119:* 47, 48; *147:* 100; *158:* 115
Emerling, Dorothy *104:* 27
Emery, Leslie *49:* 187
Emmett, Bruce *49:* 147; *80:* 175; *101:* 206
Emry-Perrott, Jennifer *61:* 57
Emshwiller, Ed *174:* 45
Engel, Diana *70:* 57
Engle, Mort *38:* 64
Englebert, Victor *8:* 54
English, Mark *101:* 207
Enik, Ted *142:* 39
Enos, Randall *20:* 183
Enright, Maginel Wright *19:* 240, 243; *39:* 31, 35, 36
Enrique, Romeo *34:* 135
Epstein, Stephen *50:* 142, 148
Erdogan, Buket *174:* 179
Erdrich, Louise *141:* 62
Erhard, Walter *1:* 152
Erickson, Phoebe *11:* 83; *59:* 85
Erikson, Mel *31:* 69
Eriksson, Eva *63:* 88, 90, 92, 93
Ering, Timothy Basil *131:* 100; *176:* 63, 64
Ernst, Lisa Campbell *47:* 147; *95:* 47; *154:* 46, 47, 48; *164:* 88
Esco, Jo *61:* 103
Escourido, Joseph *4:* 81
Escriva, Vivi *119:* 51
Este, Kirk *33:* 111
Estep, David *73:* 57
Estes, Eleanor *91:* 66
Estoril, Jean *32:* 27
Estrada, Pau *74:* 76
Estrada, Ric *5:* 52, 146; *13:* 174
Etchemendy, Teje *38:* 68
Etheredges, the *73:* 12
Etienne, Kirk-Albert *145:* 184
Ets, Marie Hall *2:* 102
Ettlinger, Doris *171:* 98
Eulalie *YABC 2:* 315
Evans, Greg *73:* 54, 55, 56; *143:* 40, 41
Evans, Katherine *5:* 64
Evans, Leslie *144:* 227
Evans, Shane W. *159:* 142; *160:* 190; *168:* 39
Everitt, Betsy *151:* 110
Ewart, Claire *76:* 69; *145:* 59, 60

Ewing, Carolyn *66:* 143; *79:* 52
Ewing, Juliana Horatia *16:* 92
Eyolfson, Norman *98:* 154

F

Fabian, Limbert *136:* 114
Facklam, Paul *132:* 62
Falconer, Ian *125:* 66; *179:* 59
Falconer, Pearl *34:* 23
Falkenstern, Lisa *70:* 34; *76:* 133; *78:* 171; *127:* 16
Falls, C.B. *1:* 19; *38:* 71, 72, 73, 74
Falter, John *40:* 169, 170
Falwell, Cathryn *118:* 77; *137:* 185
Fancher, Lou *138:* 219; *141:* 64; *144:* 199; *177:* 51
Fanelli, Sara *89:* 63; *126:* 69
Faria, Rosana *150:* 143
Farmer, Andrew *49:* 102
Farmer, Peter *24:* 108; *38:* 75
Farnsworth, Bill *93:* 189; *116:* 147; *124:* 8; *135:* 52; *146:* 242, 243, 244
Farquharson, Alexander *46:* 75
Farrell, David *40:* 135
Farris, David *74:* 42
Fasolino, Teresa *118:* 145
Fatigati, Evelyn *24:* 112
Faul-Jansen, Regina *22:* 117
Faulkner, Jack *6:* 169
Faulkner, Matt *161:* 174; *167:* 75
Fava, Rita *2:* 29
Fax, Elton C. *1:* 101; *4:* 2; *12:* 77; *25:* 107
Fay *43:* 93
Fearnley, Jan *153:* 82, 83
Fearrington, Ann *146:* 80
Federspiel, Marian *33:* 51
Fedorov, Nickolai Ivanovich *110:* 102
Feelings, Tom *5:* 22; *8:* 56; *12:* 153; *16:* 105; *30:* 196; *49:* 37; *61:* 101; *69:* 56, 57; *93:* 74; *105:* 88
Fehr, Terrence *21:* 87
Feiffer, Jules *3:* 91; *8:* 58; *61:* 66, 67, 70, 74, 76,77, 78; *111:* 47, 48, 49, 50; *132:* 122; *157:* 62
Feigeles, Neil *41:* 242
Feldman, Elyse *86:* 7
Feller, Gene *33:* 130
Fellows, Muriel H. *10:* 42
Felstead, Cathie *116:* 85
Felts, Shirley *33:* 71; *48:* 59
Fennell, Tracy *171:* 69
Fennelli, Maureen *38:* 181
Fenton, Carroll Lane *5:* 66; *21:* 39
Fenton, Mildred Adams *5:* 66; *21:* 39
Ferguson, Peter *177:* 30, 31
Ferguson, Walter W. *34:* 86
Fernandes, Eugenie *77:* 67
Fernandes, Stanislaw *70:* 28
Fernandez, Fernando *77:* 57
Fernandez, Laura *77:* 153; *101:* 117; *131:* 222; *170:* 119; *175:* 182
Ferrington, Susan *172:* 22
Fetz, Ingrid *11:* 67; *12:* 52; *16:* 205; *17:* 59; *29:* 105; *30:* 108, 109; *32:* 149; *43:* 142; *56:* 29; *60:* 34; *85:* 48; *87:* 146
Fiammenghi, Gioia *9:* 66; *11:* 44; *12:* 206; *13:* 57, 59; *52:* 126, 129; *66:* 64; *85:* 83; *91:* 161; *166:* 169
Fiedler, Joseph Daniel *96:* 42; *113:* 173; *129:* 164; *146:* 17; *159:* 68; *162:* 104
Field, Rachel *15:* 113
Fielding, David *70:* 124
Fieser, Stephen *152:* 36
Fine, Howard *145:* 159; *159:* 64; *165:* 134; *174:* 129
Fine, Peter K. *43:* 210
Finger, Helen *42:* 81
Fink, Sam *18:* 119

Finlay, Winifred *23:* 72
Finney, Pat *79:* 215
Fiore, Peter *99:* 196; *125:* 139; *144:* 225; *160:* 169
Fiorentino, Al *3:* 240
Firehammer, Karla *174:* 202
Firmin, Charlotte *29:* 75; *48:* 70
Firmin, Peter *58:* 63, 64, 65, 67, 68, 70, 71
Firth, Barbara *81:* 208; *127:* 218; *179:* 62
Fischel, Lillian *40:* 204
Fischer, Hans *25:* 202
Fischer-Nagel, Andreas *56:* 50
Fischer-Nagel, Heiderose *56:* 50
Fisher, Carolyn *154:* 50
Fisher, Chris *79:* 62; *158:* 248
Fisher, Cynthia *117:* 45; *137:* 118
Fisher, Jeffrey *142:* 80
Fisher, Leonard Everett *3:* 6; *4:* 72, 86; *6:* 197; *9:* 59; *16:* 151, 153; *23:* 44; *27:* 134; *29:* 26; *34:* 87, 89, 90, 91, 93, 94, 95, 96; *40:* 206; *50:* 150; *60:* 158; *73:* 68, 70, 71, 72, 73; *176:* 71, 72, 73; *YABC 2:* 169
Fisher, Lois *20:* 62; *21:* 7
Fisher, Valorie *177:* 55
Fisk, Nicholas *25:* 112
Fitschen, Marilyn *2:* 20, 21; *20:* 48
Fitz-Maurice, Jeff *175:* 2
Fitzgerald, F.A. *15:* 116; *25:* 86, 87
Fitzhugh, Louise *1:* 94; *9:* 163; *45:* 75, 78
Fitzgerald, Joanne *157:* 153, 154
Fitzhugh, Susie *11:* 117
Fitzpatrick, Jim *109:* 130
Fitzpatrick, Marie-Louise *125:* 69, 70
Fitzsimmons, Arthur *14:* 128
Fix, Philippe *26:* 102
Flack, Marjorie *21:* 67; *100:* 93; *YABC 2:* 122
Flagg, James Montgomery *17:* 227
Flavin, Teresa *132:* 115
Flax, Zeona *2:* 245
Fleetwood, Tony *171:* 51
Fleishman, Seymour *14:* 232; *24:* 87
Fleming, Denise *71:* 179; *81:* 58; *126:* 71, 72, 73; *173:* 52, 53
Fleming, Guy *18:* 41
Flesher, Vivienne *85:* 55
Fletcher, Claire *80:* 106; *157:* 159
Flint, Russ *74:* 80
Floate, Helen *111:* 163
Floca, Brian *155:* 88, 89
Floethe, Richard *3:* 131; *4:* 90
Floherty, John J., Jr. *5:* 68
Flook, Helen *160:* 81
Flora, James *1:* 96; *30:* 111, 112
Florczak, Robert *166:* 51
Florian, Douglas *19:* 122; *83:* 64, 65; *125:* 71, 72, 74, 76; *128:* 130; *177:* 58, 60
Flory, Jane *22:* 111
Flower, Renee *125:* 109
Floyd, Gareth *1:* 74; *17:* 245; *48:* 63; *62:* 35,36, 37, 39, 40, 41; *74:* 245; *79:* 56
Fluchere, Henri A. *40:* 79
Flynn, Barbara *7:* 31; *9:* 70
Fogarty, Thomas *15:* 89
Folger, Joseph *9:* 100
Folkard, Charles *22:* 132; *29:* 128, 257, 258
Foott, Jeff *42:* 202
Forberg, Ati *12:* 71, 205; *14:* 1; *22:* 113; *26:* 22; *48:* 64, 65
Ford, George *24:* 120; *31:* 70, 177; *58:* 126; *81:* 103; *107:* 91; *136:* 100
Ford, H.J. *16:* 185, 186
Ford, Jason *174:* 119
Ford, Pamela Baldwin *27:* 104
Fordham, John *168:* 160, 161
Foreman, Michael *2:* 110, 111; *67:* 99; *73:* 78, 79, 80,81, 82; *93:* 146; *135:* 55, 56, 57
Forrester, Victoria *40:* 83
Forsey, Chris *140:* 210
Fortnum, Peggy *6:* 29; *20:* 179; *24:* 211; *26:* 76, 77, 78; *39:* 78; *58:* 19, 21, 23, 27; *YABC 1:* 148

Foster, Brad W. *34:* 99
Foster, Genevieve *2:* 112
Foster, Gerald *7:* 78
Foster, Jon *146:* 18
Foster, Laura Louise *6:* 79
Foster, Marian Curtis *23:* 74; *40:* 42
Foster, Sally *58:* 73, 74
Foucher, Adele *47:* 118
Foust, Mitch *168:* 50
Fowler, Mel *36:* 127
Fowler, Richard *87:* 219
Fowles, Selley *165:* 127
Fox, Charles Phillip *12:* 84
Fox, Jim *6:* 187
Fox-Davies, Sarah *76:* 150
Frace, Charles *15:* 118
Frailey, Joy *72:* 108
Frame, Paul *2:* 45, 145; *9:* 153; *10:* 124; *21:* 71; *23:* 62; *24:* 123; *27:* 106; *31:* 48; *32:* 159; *34:* 195; *38:* 136; *42:* 55; *44:* 139; *60:* 39, 40, 41, 42, 43, 44, 46; *73:* 183
Frampton, David *85:* 72; *102:* 33; *139:* 182; *152:* 37
Francois, Andre *25:* 117
Francoise
    See Seignobosc, Francoise
Frank, Lola Edick *2:* 199
Frank, Mary *4:* 54; *34:* 100
Franke, Phil *45:* 91
Frankel, Alona *66:* 70
Frankel, Julie *40:* 84, 85, 202
Frankenberg, Robert *22:* 116; *30:* 50; *38:* 92, 94, 95; *68:* 111
Frankfeldt, Gwen *84:* 223; *110:* 92
Frankland, David *169:* 137
Franklin, Ashton *165:* 144
Franklin, John *24:* 22
Franson, Leanne R. *111:* 57, 58; *151:* 7
Frascino, Edward *9:* 133; *29:* 229; *33:* 190; *48:* 80, 81, 82, 83, 84, 85, 86
Frasconi, Antonio *6:* 80; *27:* 208; *53:* 41, 43, 45, 47,48; *68:* 145; *73:* 226; *131:* 68
Fraser, Betty *2:* 212; *6:* 185; *8:* 103; *31:* 72,73; *43:* 136; *111:* 76
Fraser, Eric *38:* 78; *41:* 149, 151
Fraser, F.A. *22:* 234
Fraser, James *171:* 68
Fraser, Mary Ann *137:* 63
Frasier, Debra *69:* 60; *112:* 67
Fraustino, Lisa Rowe *146:* 87
Frazee, Marla *72:* 98; *105:* 79, 80; *151:* 67, 68; *164:* 165; *171:* 190, 191
Frazetta, Frank *41:* 72; *58:* 77, 78, 79, 80, 81, 82, 83
Frazier, Craig *177:* 63
Freas, John *25:* 207
Fredrickson, Mark *103:* 33
Freeland, Michael J. *118:* 115
Freeman, Don *2:* 15; *13:* 249; *17:* 62, 63, 65, 67, 68; *18:* 243; *20:* 195; *23:* 213, 217; *32:* 155; *55:* 129
Freeman, Irving *67:* 150
Freeman, Laura *144:* 111
Freeman, Pietri *140:* 223
Freeman, Tom *167:* 118
Freeman, Tor *164:* 93
Fregosi, Claudia *24:* 117
Fremaux, Charlotte Murray *138:* 29; *141:* 95
French, Fiona *6:* 82, 83; *75:* 61; *109:* 170; *132:* 79, 80, 81, 82
French, Martin *163:* 4
Frendak, Rodney *126:* 97, 98
Freschet, Gina *175:* 73
Freynet, Gilbert *72:* 221
Friedman, Judith *43:* 197; *131:* 221
Friedman, Marvin *19:* 59; *42:* 86
Frinta, Dagmar *36:* 42
Frith, Michael K. *15:* 138; *18:* 120
Fritz, Ronald *46:* 73; *82:* 124
Fromm, Lilo *29:* 85; *40:* 197

Frost, A.B. *17:* 6, 7; *19:* 123, 124, 125, 126, 127, 128, 129,130; *100:* 119; *YABC 1:* 156, 157, 160; *2:* 107
Frost, Kristi *118:* 113
Frost, Michael *151:* 209
Froud, Brian *150:* 82, 83
Froud, Wendy *151:* 237
Fry, Guy *2:* 224
Fry, Rosalie *3:* 72; *YABC 2:* 180, 181
Fry, Rosalind *21:* 153, 168
Fryer, Elmer *34:* 115
Fuchs, Bernie *110:* 10; *162:* 46
Fuchs, Erich *6:* 84
Fuchshuber, Annegert *43:* 96
Fufuka, Mahiri *32:* 146
Fuge, Charles *144:* 91, 93
Fujikawa, Gyo *39:* 75, 76; *76:* 72, 73, 74
Fulford, Deborah *23:* 159
Fuller, Margaret *25:* 189
Fulweiler, John *93:* 99
Funai, Mamoru *38:* 105
Funk, Tom *7:* 17, 99
Furchgott, Terry *29:* 86
Furness, William Henry, Jr. *94:* 18
Furukawa, Mel *25:* 42
Fusari, Erika *164:* 227

G

Gaadt, David *78:* 212; *121:* 166
Gaadt, George *71:* 9
Gaber, Susan *99:* 33; *115:* 57, 58; *164:* 195; *169:* 61, 62, 63
Gaberell, J. *19:* 236
Gabler, Mirko *99:* 71
Gackenbach, Dick *19:* 168; *41:* 81; *48:* 89, 90, 91, 92,93, 94; *54:* 105; *79:* 75, 76, 77
Gad, Victor *87:* 161
Gaetano, Nicholas *23:* 209
Gaffney-Kessell, Walter *94:* 219; *174:* 188
Gag, Flavia *17:* 49, 52
Gag, Wanda *100:* 101, 102; *YABC 1:* 135, 137, 138, 141, 143
Gagnon, Cecile *11:* 77; *58:* 87
Gal, Laszlo *14:* 127; *52:* 54, 55, 56; *65:* 142; *68:* 150; *81:* 185; *96:* 104, 105
Galazinski, Tom *55:* 13
Galdone, Paul *1:* 156, 181, 206; *2:* 40, 241; *3:* 42,144; *4:* 141; *10:* 109, 158; *11:* 21; *12:* 118, 210; *14:* 12; *16:* 36, 37; *17:* 70, 71, 72, 73, 74; *18:* 111, 230; *19:* 183; *21:* 154; *22:* 150, 245; *33:* 126; *39:* 136, 137; *42:* 57; *51:* 169; *55:* 110; *66:* 80, 82, 139; *72:* 73; *100:* 84
Gale, Cathy *140:* 22; *143:* 52
Gall, Chris *176:* 79, 80
Gallagher, S. Saelig *105:* 154
Gallagher, Sears *20:* 112
Galloway, Ewing *51:* 154
Galouchko, Annouchka Gravel *95:* 55
Galster, Robert *1:* 66
Galsworthy, Gay John *35:* 232
Galvez, Daniel *125:* 182
Gamble, Kim *112:* 64, 65; *124:* 77
Gammell, Stephen *7:* 48; *13:* 149; *29:* 82; *33:* 209; *41:* 88; *50:* 185, 186, 187; *53:* 51, 52, 53, 54, 55, 56,57, 58; *54:* 24, 25; *56:* 147, 148, 150; *57:* 27, 66; *81:* 62, 63; *87:* 88; *89:* 10; *106:* 223; *126:* 2; *128:* 71, 73, 74, 77; *154:* 34
Gamper, Ruth *84:* 198
Gampert, John *58:* 94
Ganly, Helen *56:* 56
Gannett, Ruth Chrisman *3:* 74; *18:* 254; *33:* 77, 78
Gantschev, Ivan *45:* 32
Garafano, Marie *73:* 33
Garbot, Dave *131:* 106
Garbutt, Bernard *23:* 68

Garcia *37:* 71
Garcia, Manuel *74:* 145
Garcia-Franco, Rebecca *173:* 46
Gardiner, Lindsey *178:* 128
Gardner, Earle *45:* 167
Gardner, Joan *40:* 87
Gardner, Joel *40:* 87, 92
Gardner, John *40:* 87
Gardner, Lucy *40:* 87
Gardner, Richard
    See Cummings, Richard
Gardner, Sally *171:* 177; *177:* 66, 68
Gargiulo, Frank *84:* 158
Garland, Michael *36:* 29; *38:* 83; *44:* 168; *48:* 78, 221, 222; *49:* 161; *60:* 139; *71:* 6, 11; *72:* 229; *74:* 142; *89:* 187; *93:* 183; *104:* 110; *131:* 55; *139:* 209; *168:* 56
Garland, Peggy *60:* 139
Garland, Sarah *62:* 45; *135:* 67, 68; *171:* 118
Garn, Aimee *75:* 47
Garner, Joan *128:* 170
Garneray, Ambroise Louis *59:* 140
Garnett, Eve *3:* 75
Garnett, Gary *39:* 184
Garns, Allen *80:* 125; *84:* 39; *165:* 231
Garraty, Gail *4:* 142; *52:* 106
Garrett, Agnes *46:* 110; *47:* 157
Garrett, Edmund H. *20:* 29
Garrett, Tom *107:* 194
Garrick, Jacqueline *67:* 42, 43; *77:* 94
Garrison, Barbara *19:* 133; *104:* 146; *109:* 87
Garro, Mark *108:* 131; *128:* 210
Garvey, Robert *98:* 222
Garza, Carmen Lomas *80:* 211
Gates, Frieda *26:* 80
Gaughan, Jack *26:* 79; *43:* 185
Gaver, Becky *20:* 61
Gawing, Toby *72:* 52
Gay, Marie-Louise *68:* 76, 77, 78; *102:* 136; *126:* 76, 78, 81, 83; *127:* 55, 56; *179:* 70, 72, 73, 74
Gay, Zhenya *19:* 135, 136
Gaydos, Tim *62:* 201
Gazsi, Ed *80:* 48
Gazso, Gabriel *73:* 85
Geary, Clifford N. *1:* 122; *9:* 104; *51:* 74
Geary, Rick *142:* 44, 46
Gee, Frank *33:* 26
Geehan, Wayne *157:* 181
Geer, Charles *1:* 91; *3:* 179; *4:* 201; *6:* 168; *7:* 96; *9:* 58; *10:* 72; *12:* 127; *39:* 156,157, 158, 159, 160; *42:* 88, 89, 90, 91; *55:* 111, 116
Geerinck, Manuel *173:* 128
Gehm, Charlie *36:* 65; *57:* 117; *62:* 60, 138
Geisel, Theodor Seuss *1:* 104, 105, 106; *28:* 108, 109, 110,111, 112, 113; *75:* 67, 68, 69, 70, 71; *89:* 127, 128; *100:* 106, 107, 108
Geisert, Arthur *92:* 67, 68; *133:* 72, 73, 74; *165:* 97, 98; *171:* 64, 65
Geldart, William *15:* 121; *21:* 202
Genia *4:* 84
Gentry, Cyrille R. *12:* 66
Genzo, John Paul *136:* 74
George, Jean *2:* 113
George, Lindsay Barrett *95:* 57; *155:* 97, 98
Geraghty, Paul *130:* 60, 61
Gerard, Jean Ignace *45:* 80
Gerard, Rolf *27:* 147, 150
Gerber, Mark *61:* 105
Gerber, Mary Jane *112:* 124; *171:* 56
Gerber, Stephanie *71:* 195
Gerdstein, Mordecai *169:* 105
Gergely, Tibor *54:* 15, 16
Geritz, Franz *17:* 135
Gerlach, Geff *42:* 58
Gerrard, Roy *47:* 78; *90:* 96, 97, 98, 99
Gerritsen, Paula *177:* 69
Gershinowitz, George *36:* 27
Gerstein, Mordicai *31:* 117; *47:* 80, 81, 82, 83, 84, 85, 86; *51:* 173; *69:* 134; *107:* 122; *142:* 49, 52; *165:* 209; *176:* 119; *178:* 95, 97, 99

Gervase *12:* 27
Geter, Tyrone *146:* 249; *150:* 86
Getz, Arthur *32:* 148
Gewirtz, Bina *61:* 81
Giancola, Donato *95:* 146; *164:* 226
Gibbons, Gail *23:* 78; *72:* 77, 78, 79; *82:* 182; *104:* 65; *160:* 99, 100
Gibbs, Tony *40:* 95
Gibran, Kahlil *32:* 116
Gider, Iskender *81:* 193
Giebfried, Rosemary *170:* 135
Giesen, Rosemary *34:* 192, 193
Giffard, Hannah *83:* 70
Giguere, George *20:* 111
Gilbert, John *19:* 184; *54:* 115; *YABC 2:* 287
Gilbert, W.S. *36:* 83, 85, 96
Gilbert, Yvonne *116:* 70; *128:* 84; *149:* 119
Gilchrist, Jan Spivey *72:* 82, 83, 84, 85, 87; *77:* 90; *105:* 89, 91; *130:* 63, 64; *155:* 105, 107
Giles, Will *41:* 218
Gili, Phillida *70:* 73
Gill, Margery *4:* 57; *7:* 7; *22:* 122; *25:* 166; *26:* 146, 147
Gillen, Denver *28:* 216
Gillette, Henry J. *23:* 237
Gilliam, Stan *39:* 64, 81
Gillies, Chuck *62:* 31
Gilliland, Jillian *87:* 58
Gillman, Alec *98:* 105
Gilman, Esther *15:* 124
Gilman, Phoebe *104:* 70, 71
Ginsberg, Sari *111:* 184
Ginsburg, Max *62:* 59; *68:* 194 Girard, Roge *161:* 30
Girouard, Patrick *155:* 100
Giovanopoulos, Paul *7:* 104; *60:* 36
Giovine, Sergio *79:* 12; *93:* 118; *139:* 118
Githens, Elizabeth M. *5:* 47
Gladden, Scott *99:* 108; *103:* 160
Gladstone, Gary *12:* 89; *13:* 190
Gladstone, Lise *15:* 273
Glanzman, Louis S. *2:* 177; *3:* 182; *36:* 97, 98; *38:* 120, 122; *52:* 141, 144; *71:* 191; *91:* 54, 56
Glaser, Byron *154:* 59, 60
Glaser, Milton *3:* 5; *5:* 156; *11:* 107; *30:* 26; *36:* 112; *54:* 141; *151:* 70
Glass, Andrew *36:* 38; *44:* 133; *48:* 205; *65:* 3; *68:* 43, 45; *90:* 104, 105; *150:* 89
Glass, Marvin *9:* 174
Glasser, Judy *41:* 156; *56:* 140; *69:* 79; *72:* 101
Glattauer, Ned *5:* 84; *13:* 224; *14:* 26
Glauber, Uta *17:* 76
Gleeson, J.M. *YABC 2:* 207
Glegg, Creina *36:* 100
Glienke, Amelie *63:* 150
Gliewe, Unada *3:* 78, 79; *21:* 73; *30:* 220
Gliori, Debi *72:* 91; *138:* 82; *162:* 37
Glovach, Linda *7:* 105
Gobbato, Imero *3:* 180, 181; *6:* 213; *7:* 58; *9:* 150; *18:* 39; *21:* 167; *39:* 82, 83; *41:* 137, 251; *59:* 177
Goble, Paul *25:* 121; *26:* 86; *33:* 65; *69:* 68, 69; *131:* 79, 80
Goble, Warwick *46:* 78, 79
Godal, Eric *36:* 93
Godkin, Celia *145:* 84, 86
Godfrey, Michael *17:* 279
Godon, Ingrid *166:* 163
Goembel, Ponder *42:* 124
Goffe, Toni *61:* 83, 84, 85; *89:* 11; *90:* 124; *178:* 118
Goffstein, M.B. *8:* 71; *70:* 75, 76, 77
Golbin, Andre *15:* 125
Gold, Robert *166:* 151, 152
Goldfeder, Cheryl *11:* 191
Goldsborough, June *5:* 154, 155; *8:* 92, *14:* 226; *19:* 139; *54:* 165
Goldsmith, Robert *110:* 77

Goldstein, Leslie *5:* 8; *6:* 60; *10:* 106
Goldstein, Nathan *1:* 175; *2:* 79; *11:* 41, 232; *16:* 55
Goldstrom, Robert *98:* 36; *145:* 51, 52
Golembe, Carla *79:* 80, 81; *136:* 91; *144:* 113
Golin, Carlo *74:* 112
Gomez, Elizabeth *127:* 70; *133:* 76
Gomi, Taro *64:* 102; *103:* 74, 76
Gon, Adriano *101:* 112
Gonsalve, Ron *178:* 213
Gonzalez, Maya Christina *104:* 3; *136:* 92
Goodall, John S. *4:* 92, 93; *10:* 132; *66:* 92, 93; *YABC 1:* 198
Goode, Diane *15:* 126; *50:* 183; *52:* 114, 115; *76:* 195; *84:* 94; *99:* 141; *114:* 76, 77, 78; *170:* 99, 101
Goodelman, Aaron *40:* 203
Goodenow, Earle *40:* 97
Goodfellow, Peter *62:* 95; *94:* 202
Goodman, Joan Elizabeth *50:* 86
Goodman, Vivienne *82:* 251; *146:* 181, 182
Goodnow, Patti *117:* 33
Goodwin, Harold *13:* 74
Goodwin, Philip R. *18:* 206
Goor, Nancy *39:* 85, 86
Goor, Ron *39:* 85, 86
Gorbachev, Valeri *89:* 96; *112:* 97; *143:* 63, 64
Gordon, Gwen *12:* 151
Gordon, Margaret *4:* 147; *5:* 48, 49; *9:* 79
Gordon, Mike *101:* 62, 63, 64
Gordon, Russell *136:* 204; *137:* 214
Gordon, Walter *138:* 9
Gore, Leonid *89:* 51; *94:* 74; *136:* 8; *158:* 117; *166:* 136; *168:* 36; *170:* 107
Gorecka-Egan, Erica *18:* 35
Gorey, Edward *1:* 60, 61; *13:* 169; *18:* 192; *20:* 201; *29:* 90, 91, 92, 93, 94, 95, 96, 97, 98, 99, 100; *30:* 129; *32:* 90; *34:* 200, *65:* 48; *68:* 24, 25; *69:* 79; *70:* 80, 82, 83, 84, 85; *136:* *127:* 62
Gorsline, Douglas *1:* 98; *6:* 13; *11:* 113; *13:* 104; *15:* 14; *28:* 117, 118; *YABC 1:* 15
Gorton, Julia *108:* 94; *178:* 81, 82
Gosfield, Josh *118:* 165, 166; *149:* 67
Gosner, Kenneth *5:* 135
Gosney, Joy *167:* 142
Gotlieb, Jules *6:* 127
Goto, Scott *115:* 86; *136:* 69
Gottlieb, Dale *67:* 162; *107:* 16; *149:* 6
Goudey, Ray *97:* 86
Gough, Alan *91:* 57
Gough, Philip *23:* 47; *45:* 90
Gould, Chester *49:* 112, 113, 114, 116, 117, 118
Gould, Jason *151:* 232
Gourbault, Martine *177:* 159
Govern, Elaine R. *26:* 94
Gower, Teri *102:* 184
Gowing, Toby *60:* 25; *63:* 33; *78:* 70, 252; *83:* 228; *86:* 187; *93:* 145; *108:* 133; *110:* 217
Grabianski *20:* 144
Grabianski, Janusz *39:* 92, 93, 94, 95
Graboff, Abner *35:* 103, 104
Graef, Renee *61:* 188; *72:* 207
Grafe, Max *156:* 173; *178:* 237
Graham, A.B. *11:* 61
Graham, Bob *101:* 66, 67, 68; *151:* 74, 75
Graham, L. *7:* 108
Graham, Margaret Bloy *11:* 120; *18:* 305, 307
Graham, Mark *88:* 208; *159:* 153
Grahame-Johnstone, Janet *13:* 61
Grahame-Johnstone, Anne *13:* 61
Grainger, Sam *42:* 95
Gralley, Jean *166:* 86
Gramatky, Hardie *1:* 107; *30:* 116, 119, 120, 122, 123
Gran, Julie *168:* 118
Granahan, Julie *84:* 84
GrandPre, Mary *84:* 131; *109:* 199; *118:* 76
Grandström, Brita *176:* 139

Grandville, J.J. *45:* 81, 82, 83, 84, 85, 86, 87, 88; *47:* 125; *64:* 10
Granger, Paul *39:* 153
Granström, Brita *162:* 35; *167:* 46
Grant, (Alice) Leigh *10:* 52; *15:* 131; *20:* 20; *26:* 119; *48:* 202
Grant, Gordon *17:* 230, 234; *25:* 123, 124, 125, 126; *52:* 69; *YABC 1:* 164
Grant, Melvyn *159:* 186, 187; *170:* 48, 49
Grant, Renee *77:* 40
Grant, Shirley *109:* 45
Graves, Elizabeth *45:* 101
Graves, Keith *167:* 89
Gray, Harold *33:* 87, 88
Gray, Les *82:* 76; *83:* 232
Gray, Reginald *6:* 69
Greder, Armin *76:* 235
Green, Ann Canevari *62:* 48
Green, Eileen *6:* 97
Green, Elizabeth Shippen *139:* 109
Green, Jonathan *86:* 135; *105:* 109
Green, Ken *111:* 68
Green, Michael *32:* 216
Green, Robina *87:* 138
Green, Jonathan *157:* 105
Greene, Jeffrey *117:* 93
Greenaway, Kate *17:* 275; *24:* 180; *26:* 107; *41:* 222, 232; *100:* 115, 116; *YABC 1:* 88, 89; *2:* 131, 133, 136, 138, 139, 141
Greenberg, Melanie Hope *72:* 93; *80:* 125; *101:* 174; *133:* 180
Greenseid, Diane *178:* 106, 107
Greenstein, Elaine *150:* 100
Greenwald, Sheila *1:* 34; *3:* 99; *8:* 72
Greger, Carol *76:* 86
Gregorian, Joyce Ballou *30:* 125
Gregory, Emilian *177:* 146
Gregory, Fran *130:* 4; *140:* 93
Gregory, Frank M. *29:* 107
Greiffenhagen, Maurice *16:* 137; *27:* 57; *YABC 2:* 288
Greiner, Robert *6:* 86
Gretter, J. Clemens *31:* 134
Gretz, Susanna *7:* 114
Gretzer, John *1:* 54; *3:* 26; *4:* 162; *7:* 125; *16:* 247; *18:* 117; *28:* 66; *30:* 85, 211; *33:* 235; *56:* 16
Grey, Mini *166:* 90
Grey Owl *24:* 41
Gri *25:* 90
Grieder, Walter *9:* 84
Griesbach/Martucci *59:* 3
Grifalconi, Ann *2:* 126; *3:* 248; *11:* 18; *13:* 182; *46:* 38; *50:* 145; *66:* 99, 100, 101, 104, 106; *69:* 38; *70:* 64; *87:* 128; *90:* 53; *93:* 49; *128:* 48; *133:* 79, 81
Griffin, Gillett Good *26:* 96
Griffin, James *30:* 166
Griffin, John Howard *59:* 186
Griffin, Rachel *131:* 23
Griffith, Gershom *94:* 214
Griffiths, Dave *29:* 76
Griffiths, Dean *168:* 180; *169:* 182
Grimsdell, Jeremy *83:* 75
Grimwood, Brian *82:* 89
Gringhuis, Dirk *6:* 98; *9:* 196
Gripe, Harald *2:* 127; *74:* 98
Grisha *3:* 71
Grohmann, Susan *84:* 97
Gropper, William *27:* 93; *37:* 193
Gros *60:* 199
Grose, Helen Mason *YABC 1:* 260; *2:* 150
Grossman, Nancy *24:* 130; *29:* 101
Grossman, Robert *11:* 124; *46:* 39
Groth, John *15:* 79; *21:* 53, 54; *83:* 230
Grover, Lorie Ann *168:* 59
Grubb, Lisa *160:* 116
Gruelle, Johnny *35:* 107
Gschwind, William *11:* 72
Guay, Rebecca *110:* 95, 96; *135:* 240
Guback, Georgia *88:* 102

Guerguerion, Claudine *105:* 73
Guevara, Susan *97:* 87; *167:* 49
Guggenheim, Hans *2:* 10; *3:* 37; *8:* 136
Guida, Lisa Chauncy *172:* 188
Guilbeau, Honore *22:* 69
Guillette, Joseph *137:* 37
Guisewite, Cathy *57:* 52, 53, 54, 56, 57
Gukova, Julia *95:* 104; *154:* 103; *168:* 195
Gundersheimer, Karen *35:* 240; *82:* 100
Gunderson, Nick *57:* 120
Gurney, James *76:* 97; *86:* 32
Gurney, John Steven *75:* 39, 82; *110:* 175; *143:* 67, 68; *169:* 172
Gusman, Annie *38:* 62
Gustafson, Scott *34:* 111; *43:* 40
Gustavson, Adam *104:* 10; *171:* 183; *176:* 87
Guthridge, Bettina *108:* 79
Guthrie, R. Dale *64:* 143
Guthrie, Robin *20:* 122
Gutierrez, Akemi *172:* 87
Gutierrez, Alan *136:* 31, 32
Gutierrez, Rudy *97:* 162
Gutmann, Bessie Pease *73:* 93, 94
Gwynne, Fred *41:* 94, 95
Gyberg, Bo-Erik *38:* 131

H

Haas, Irene *17:* 77; *87:* 46; *96:* 117
Hack, Konrad *51:* 127
Hader, Berta H. *16:* 126
Hader, Elmer S. *16:* 126
Haeffele, Deborah *76:* 99
Haemer, Alan *62:* 109
Hafner, Marylin *22:* 196, 216; *24:* 44; *30:* 51; *35:* 95; *51:* 25, 160, 164; *86:* 16; *105:* 196; *121:* 93, 94; *149:* 208, 209; *179:* 82, 83, 84, 115
Hagerty, Sean *62:* 181
Hague, Michael *32:* 128; *48:* 98, 99, 100, 101, 103, 105, 106, 107, 108, 109, 110; *49:* 121; *51:* 105; *64:* 14, 15; *79:* 134; *80:* 91, 92; *83:* 135; *100:* 241; *102:* 29; *129:* 101, 103, 104
Hair, Jonathan *115:* 135
Halas, John *29:* 41, 47, 48
Haldane, Roger *13:* 76; *14:* 202
Hale, Christy *79:* 124; *84:* 200; *114:* 201; *128:* 2, 3; *146:* 203; *158:* 243; *167:* 99; *179:* 87
Hale, Irina *26:* 97
Hale, James Graham *88:* 207
Hale, Kathleen *17:* 79; *66:* 114, 116, 118
Haley, Gail E. *43:* 102, 103, 104, 105; *78:* 65, 67; *136:* 106, 107
Hall, Amanda *96:* 110
Hall, Chuck *30:* 189
Hall, Douglas *15:* 184; *43:* 106, 107; *86:* 100; *87:* 82; *129:* 72
Hall, H. Tom *1:* 227; *30:* 210
Hall, Melanie *116:* 48, 49; *169:* 77, 78
Hall, Sydney P. *31:* 89
Hall, Tim *164:* 196
Hall, Vicki *20:* 24
Hallinan, P.K. *39:* 98
Hallman, Tom *98:* 166
Hally, Greg *101:* 200; *151:* 224
Halperin, Wendy Anderson *96:* 151; *125:* 96, 97, 98, 99; *139:* 22; *140:* 84
Halpern, Joan *10:* 25
Halpern, Shari *174:* 172
Halsey, Megan *96:* 172; *114:* 185
Halstead, Virginia *125:* 105
Halverson, Janet *49:* 38, 42, 44
Hallensleben, Georg *134:* 5, 6; *172:* 17
Hamanaka, Sheila *71:* 100
Hamann, Brad *78:* 151
Hamann, Sigune *104:* 115
Hamberger, John *6:* 8; *8:* 32; *14:* 79; *34:* 136; *88:* 78
Hamil, Tom *14:* 80; *43:* 163

Hamilton, Bill and Associates *26:* 215
Hamilton, Helen S. *2:* 238
Hamilton, J. *19:* 83, 85, 87
Hamilton, Laurie *116:* 210
Hamilton, Todd Cameron *84:* 15
Hamlin, Janet *97:* 136; *124:* 90; *137:* 157
Hamlin, Louise *71:* 135
Hammond, Chris *21:* 37
Hammond, Elizabeth *5:* 36, 203
Hampshire, Michael *5:* 187; *7:* 110, 111; *48:* 150; *51:* 129
Hampson, Denman *10:* 155; *15:* 130
Hampton, Blake *41:* 244
Handford, Martin *64:* 105, 106, 107, 109
Handforth, Thomas *42:* 100, 101, 102, 103, 104, 105, 107
Handville, Robert *1:* 89; *38:* 76; *45:* 108, 109
Hane, Roger *17:* 239; *44:* 54
Haney, Elizabeth Mathieu *34:* 84
Hanke, Ted *71:* 10
Hanley, Catherine *8:* 161
Hann, Jacquie *19:* 144
Hanna, Cheryl *91:* 133
Hanna, Wayne A. *67:* 145
Hannon, Mark *38:* 37
Hansen, Gabby *159:* 11
Hansen, Mia *149:* 76
Hanson, Joan *8:* 76; *11:* 139
Hanson, Peter E. *52:* 47; *54:* 99, 100; *73:* 21; *84:* 79; *116:* 144
Hansson, Gunilla *64:* 111, 112
Hardcastle, Nick *121:* 82; *175:* 185
Hardy, David A. *9:* 96; *119:* 74
Hardy, Paul *YABC 2:* 245 *Haring, Keith 145:* 65
Harlan, Jerry *3:* 96
Harlin, Greg *89:* 194; *103:* 82; *118:* 161; *121:* 167
Harness, Cheryl *106:* 80; *131:* 87; *178:* 111
Harnischfeger *18:* 121
Harper, Arthur *YABC 2:* 121
Harper, Betty *126:* 90
Harper, Jamie *174:* 71
Harper, Piers *79:* 27; *105:* 102; *161:* 67
Harrington, Glenn *82:* 18; *94:* 66, 68
Harrington, Jack *83:* 162
Harrington, Richard *5:* 81
Harris, Jim *127:* 130
Harris, John *83:* 25
Harris, Nick *86:* 177
Harris, Susan Yard *42:* 121
Harrison, Florence *20:* 150, 152
Harrison, Harry *4:* 103
Harrison, Jack *28:* 149
Harrison, Mark *105:* 157; *165:* 190
Harrison, Ted *56:* 73
Harsh, Fred *72:* 107
Harston, Jerry *105:* 143
Hart, Lewis *98:* 115
Hart, William *13:* 72
Hartland, Jessie *171:* 80, 81
Hartung, Susan Kathleen *150:* 107, 108; *173:* 106; *175:* 106
Hartelius, Margaret *10:* 24
Hartshorn, Ruth *5:* 115; *11:* 129
Harvey, Amanda *145:* 44
Harvey, Bob *48:* 219
Harvey, Gerry *7:* 180
Harvey, Lisa *97:* 21
Harvey, Paul *88:* 74
Harvey, Roland *71:* 88; *123:* 63; *179:* 94
Hassall, Joan *43:* 108, 109
Hassell, Hilton *YABC 1:* 187
Hassett, John *162:* 59
Hasselriis, Else *18:* 87; *YABC 1:* 96
Hastings, Glenn *89:* 183
Hastings, Ian *62:* 67
Hauman, Doris *2:* 184; *29:* 58, 59; *32:* 85, 86, 87
Hauman, George *2:* 184; *29:* 58, 59; *32:* 85, 86, 87

Hausherr, Rosmarie *15:* 29
Hawkes, Kevin *78:* 72; *104:* 198; *105:* 197; *112:* 109; *126:* 87; *144:* 88; *149:* 210; *150:* 110, 135; *156:* 94; *164:* 35
Hawkins, Jacqui *112:* 86; *162:* 64
Hawkinson, John *4:* 109; *7:* 83; *21:* 64
Hawkinson, Lucy *21:* 64
Hawthorne, Mike *140:* 228
Haxton, Elaine *28:* 131
Haydock, Robert *4:* 95
Hayes, Geoffrey *26:* 111; *44:* 133; *91:* 85
Haynes, Max *72:* 107
Hays, Michael *73:* 207; *83:* 93; *139:* 197; *146:* 202, 250
Haywood, Carolyn *1:* 112; *29:* 104
Heale, Jonathan *104:* 117
Healy, Daty *12:* 143
Healy, Deborah *58:* 181, 182; *101:* 111
Heap, Sue *102:* 207; *150:* 113, 114
Hearn, Diane Dawson *79:* 99; *113:* 13
Hearon, Dorothy *34:* 69
Heaslip, William *57:* 24, 25
Hechtkopf, H. *11:* 110
Heck, Ed *173:* 81
Hedderwick, Mairi *30:* 127; *32:* 47; *36:* 104; *77:* 86; *145:* 91, 93, 95
Hefferman, Phil *146:* 197
Hefter, Richard *28:* 170; *31:* 81, 82; *33:* 183
Hehenberger, Shelly *126:* 91
Heigh, James *22:* 98
Heighway, Richard *25:* 160; *64:* 4
Heighway-Bury, Robin *159:* 89
Heine, Helme *67:* 86; *135:* 91, 92
Heinly, John *45:* 113
Hellard, Susan *81:* 21
Hellebrand, Nancy *26:* 57
Heller, Linda *46:* 86
Heller, Ruth M. *66:* 125; *77:* 30, 32
Hellmuth, Jim *38:* 164
Helms, Georgeann *33:* 62
Helquist, Brett *142:* 203; *146:* 133, 134; *156:* 10; *173:* 25
Helweg, Hans *41:* 118; *50:* 93; *58:* 22, 26
Hemphill, Helen *179:* 95
Henba, Bobbie *90:* 195
Henderson, Dave *73:* 76; *75:* 191, 192, 193, 194; *82:* 4
Henderson, Douglas *103:* 68
Henderson, Kathy *55:* 32; *155:* 118
Henderson, Keith *35:* 122
Henderson, Meryl *127:* 58, 60; *169:* 81
Hendry, Linda *80:* 104; *83:* 83; *164:* 216
Hengeveld, Dennis *142:* 86
Henkes, Kevin *43:* 111; *108:* 106, 107, 108
Henneberger, Robert *1:* 42; *2:* 237; *25:* 83
Henriksen, Harold *35:* 26; *48:* 68
Henriquez, Celeste *103:* 137
Henriquez, Elsa *82:* 260
Henriquez, Emile F. *89:* 88
Henry, Everett *29:* 191
Henry, Matthew *117:* 58
Henry, Paul *93:* 121
Henry, Thomas *5:* 102
Hensel *27:* 119
Henshaw, Jacqui *141:* 127
Henstra, Friso *8:* 80; *36:* 70; *40:* 222; *41:* 250; *73:* 100, 101
Henterly, Jamichael *93:* 4
Heo, Yumi *89:* 85, 86; *94:* 89, 90; *146:* 40, 137, 138; *163:* 227
Hepple, Norman *28:* 198
Herbert, Helen *57:* 70
Herbert, Wally *23:* 101
Herbster, Mary Lee *9:* 33
Herge
    See Remi, Georges
Hermansen, Pal *133:* 113
Hermanson, Dennis *10:* 55
Hermes, Gertrude *54:* 161
Herr, Margo *57:* 191
Herr, Susan *83:* 163

Herriman, George *140:* 74, 75, 76, 77, 78
Herriman, Lisa *87:* 190
Herring, Michael *121:* 76
Herrington, Roger *3:* 161
Herscovici, C. *165:* 240
Hescox, Richard *85:* 86; *90:* 30; *139:* 35
Heslop, Mike *38:* 60; *40:* 130
Hess, Lydia J. *85:* 17
Hess, Mark *111:* 146; *113:* 207
Hess, Paul *134:* 47; *166:* 133
Hess, Richard *42:* 31
Hester, Ronnie *37:* 85
Heuser, Olga J. *121:* 116
Heusser, Sibylle *168:* 195
Heustis, Louise L. *20:* 28
Hewitson, Jennifer *74:* 119; *124:* 167
Hewitt, Kathryn *80:* 126; *149:* 105
Hewitt, Margaret *84:* 112
Heyduck-Huth, Hilde *8:* 82
Heyer, Carol *74:* 122; *130:* 72, 73
Heyer, Hermann *20:* 114, 115
Heyer, Marilee *102:* 108
Heyman, Ken *8:* 33; *34:* 113
Heyne, Ulrike *146:* 151
Heywood, Karen *48:* 114
Hickling, P.B. *40:* 165
Hickman, Stephen *85:* 58; *136:* 33; *171:* 128
Hierstein, Judy *56:* 40; *162:* 168
Higashi, Sandra *154:* 59, 60
Higginbottom, J. Winslow *8:* 170; *29:* 105, 106
Higgins, Chester *101:* 79
Higham, David *50:* 104
Hilb, Nora *176:* 8
Hildebrandt, Greg *8:* 191; *55:* 35, 36, 38, 39, 40, 42, 46; *172:* 110
Hildebrandt, Tim *8:* 191; *55:* 44, 45, 46
Hilder, Rowland *19:* 207
Hill, Eric *66:* 127, 128; *133:* 91
Hill, Gregory *35:* 190
Hill, Pat *49:* 120
Hillenbrand, Will *84:* 115; *92:* 76, 80; *93:* 131; *104:* 168; *128:* 137; *145:* 187; *146:* 184; *147:* 105, 106, 107; *152:* 59
Hillier, Matthew *45:* 205
Hillman, Priscilla *48:* 115
Hills, Tad *113:* 4; *137:* 147; *173:* 83
Himler, Ronald *6:* 114; *7:* 162; *8:* 17, 84, 125; *14:* 76; *19:* 145; *26:* 160; *31:* 43; *38:* 116; *41:* 44, 79; *43:* 52; *45:* 120; *46:* 43; *54:* 44, 83; *58:* 180; *59:* 38; *68:* 146; *69:* 231; *70:* 98; *71:* 177, 178; *77:* 219; *79:* 212; *83:* 62; *89:* 5; *91:* 160; *92:* 91, 92, 93; *94:* 93; *95:* 69, 174, 194; *99:* 99, 112; *113:* 92; *118:* 114; *137:* 73, 74, 77, 167; *163:* 99; *165:* 138; *178:* 9, 220
Himmelman, John *47:* 109; *65:* 87; *94:* 96, 97; *159:* 85
Hinds, Bill *37:* 127, 130
Hines, Anna Grossnickle *51:* 90; *74:* 124; *95:* 78, 79,80, 81
Hines, Bob *135:* 149, 150
Hiroko *99:* 61
Hiroshige *25:* 71
Hirsh, Marilyn *7:* 126
Hiscock, Bruce *137:* 80, 81
Hissey, Jane *103:* 90; *130:* 81
Hitch, Jeff *99:* 206; *128:* 86
Hitz, Demi *11:* 135; *15:* 245; *66:* 129, 130; *152:* 94, 95
Hnizdovsky, Jacques *32:* 96; *76:* 187
Ho, Kwoncjan *15:* 132
Hoban, Lillian *1:* 114; *22:* 157; *26:* 72; *29:* 53; *40:* 105, 107, 195; *41:* 80; *69:* 107, 108; *71:* 98; *77:* 168; *106:* 50; *113:* 86; *136:* 118
Hoban, Tana *22:* 159; *104:* 82, 83, 85
Hobbs, Leigh *166:* 95
Hoberman, Norman *5:* 82
Hobson, Sally *77:* 185
Hockerman, Dennis *39:* 22; *56:* 23
Hodgell, P.C. *42:* 114

Hodges, C. Walter *2:* 139; *11:* 15; *12:* 25; *23:* 34; *25:* 96; *38:* 165; *44:* 197; *45:* 95; *100:* 57; *YABC 2:* 62, 63
Hodges, David *9:* 98
Hodgetts, Victoria *43:* 132
Hofbauer, Imre *2:* 162
Hoff, Syd *9:* 107; *10:* 128; *33:* 94; *72:* 115,116, 117, 118; *138:* 114, 115
Hoffman, Rosekrans *15:* 133; *50:* 219; *63:* 97
Hoffman, Sanford *38:* 208; *76:* 174; *88:* 160, 161; *151:* 156
Hoffmann, Felix *9:* 109
Hoffnung, Gerard *66:* 76, 77
Hofsinde, Robert *21:* 70
Hogan, Inez *2:* 141
Hogarth, Burne *41:* 58; *63:* 46, 48, 49, 50, 52, 53, 54, 55,56
Hogarth, Paul *41:* 102, 103, 104; *YABC 1:* 16
Hogarth, William *42:* 33
Hogenbyl, Jan *1:* 35
Hogner, Nils *4:* 122; *25:* 144
Hogrogian, Nonny *3:* 221; *4:* 106, 107; *5:* 166; *7:* 129; *15:* 2; *16:* 176; *20:* 154; *22:* 146; *25:* 217; *27:* 206; *74:* 127, 128, 129, 149, 152; *127:* 99; *YABC 2:* 84, 94
Hokanson, Lars *93:* 111; *172:* 137
Hokusai *25:* 71
Hol, Colby *126:* 96
Holberg, Richard *2:* 51
Holbrook, Kathy *107:* 114
Holdcroft, Tina *38:* 109
Holden, Caroline *55:* 159
Holder, Heidi *36:* 99; *64:* 9
Holder, Jimmy *151:* 224
Holiday, Henry *YABC 2:* 107
Holl, F. *36:* 91
Holland, Brad *45:* 59, 159
Holland, Gay W. *128:* 105
Holland, Janice *18:* 118
Holland, Marion *6:* 116
Holldobler, Turid *26:* 120
Holliday, Keaf *144:* 236
Holling, Holling C. *15:* 136, 137
Hollinger, Deanne *12:* 116
Holm, Sharon Lane *114:* 84; *115:* 52
Holmes, B. *3:* 82
Holmes, Bea *7:* 74; *24:* 156; *31:* 93
Holmes, Dave *54:* 22
Holmes, Lesley *135:* 96
Holmgren, George Ellen *45:* 112
Holmlund, Heather D. *150:* 140
Holt, Norma *44:* 106
Holt, Pater *151:* 188
Holtan, Gene *32:* 192
Holub, Joan *149:* 72
Holyfield, John *149:* 231
Holz, Loretta *17:* 81
Hom, Nancy *79:* 195
Homar, Lorenzo *6:* 2
Homer, Winslow *128:* 8; *YABC 2:* 87
Honey, Elizabeth *112:* 95, 96; *137:* 93, 94
Honeywood, Varnette P. *110:* 68, 70
Hong, Lily Toy *76:* 104
Honigman, Marian *3:* 2
Honore, Paul *42:* 77, 79, 81, 82
Hood, Alun *69:* 145, 218; *72:* 41; *80:* 226; *87:* 4; *95:* 139
Hood, Susan *12:* 43
Hook, Christian *104:* 103
Hook, Frances *26:* 188; *27:* 127
Hook, Jeff *14:* 137; *103:* 105
Hook, Richard *26:* 188
Hooks *63:* 30
Hooper, Hadley *177:* 145
Hoover, Carol A. *21:* 77
Hoover, Russell *12:* 95; *17:* 2; *34:* 156
Hope, James *141:* 116
Hopkins, Chris *99:* 127
Hopman, Philip *178:* 184
Hoppin, Augustus *34:* 66
Horacek, Petr *163:* 117

Horder, Margaret *2:* 108; *73:* 75
Horen, Michael *45:* 121
Horne, Daniel *73:* 106; *91:* 153; *109:* 127; *110:* 232; *164:* 176
Horne, Richard *111:* 80
Horse, Harry *128:* 195; *169:* 86
Horvat, Laurel *12:* 201
Horvath, Ferdinand Kusati *24:* 176
Horvath, Maria *57:* 171
Horwitz, Richard *57:* 174
Hotchkiss, De Wolfe *20:* 49
Hough, Charlotte *9:* 112; *13:* 98; *17:* 83; *24:* 195
Houlihan, Ray *11:* 214
Housman, Laurence *25:* 146, 147
Houston, James *13:* 107; *74:* 132, 134, 135
Hovland, Gary *88:* 172; *171:* 148
Hoyt, Eleanor *158:* 231
How, W.E. *20:* 47
Howard, Alan *16:* 80; *34:* 58; *45:* 114
Howard, Arthur *165:* 111, 112
Howard, J.N. *15:* 234
Howard, John *33:* 179
Howard, Kim *116:* 71
Howard, Paul *142:* 126, 129; *144:* 187
Howard, Rob *40:* 161
Howarth, Daniel *170:* 34
Howe, John *115:* 47; *176:* 106
Howe, John F. *79:* 101; *80:* 150
Howe, Phillip *79:* 117; *175:* 115
Howe, Stephen *1:* 232
Howell, Karen *119:* 123
Howell, Pat *15:* 139
Howell, Troy *23:* 24; *31:* 61; *36:* 158; *37:* 184; *41:* 76, 235; *48:* 112; *56:* 13; *57:* 3; *59:* 174; *63:* 5; *74:* 46; *89:* 188; *90:* 231; *95:* 97; *98:* 130; *99:* 189; *153:* 156, 157, 158; *176:* 104
Howes, Charles *22:* 17
Hoyt, Ard *145:* 141
Hranilovich, Barbara *127:* 51
Hu, Ying-Hwa *116:* 107; *152:* 236; *173:* 171
Huang, Benrei *137:* 55
Huang, Zhong-Yang *117:* 30, 32
Hubbard, Woodleigh Marx *98:* 67; *115:* 79; *160:* 138
Hubley, Faith *48:* 120, 121, 125, 130, 131, 132, 134
Hubley, John *48:* 125, 130, 131, 132, 134
Hudak, Michal *143:* 74
Hudnut, Robin *14:* 62
Huerta, Catherine *76:* 178; *77:* 44, 45; *90:* 182
Huffaker, Sandy *10:* 56
Huffman, Joan *13:* 33
Huffman, Tom *13:* 180; *17:* 212; *21:* 116; *24:* 132; *33:* 154; *38:* 59; *42:* 147
Hughes, Arthur *20:* 148, 149, 150; *33:* 114, 148, 149
Hughes, Darren *95:* 44
Hughes, David *36:* 197
Hughes, Shirley *1:* 20, 21; *7:* 3; *12:* 217; *16:* 163; *29:* 154; *63:* 118; *70:* 102, 103, 104; *73:* 169; *88:* 70; *110:* 118, 119; *159:* 103
Hugo, Victor *47:* 112
Hull, Cathy *78:* 29
Hull, Richard *95:* 120; *123:* 175; *172:* 195
Hulsmann, Eva *16:* 166
Hummel, Berta *43:* 137, 138, 139
Hummel, Lisl *29:* 109; *YABC 2:* 333, 334
Humphrey, Henry *16:* 167
Humphreys, Graham *25:* 168
Humphries, Tudor *76:* 66; *80:* 4; *124:* 4, 5
Hunt, James *2:* 143
Hunt, Jonathan *84:* 120
Hunt, Paul *119:* 104; *129:* 135; *139:* 160; *173:* 112
Hunt, Robert *110:* 206, 235; *147:* 136, 137; *170:* 3
Hunter, Anne *133:* 190; *178:* 150
Hurd, Clement *2:* 148, 149; *64:* 127, 128, 129, 131, 133, 134,135, 136; *100:* 37, 38

Hurd, Peter *24:* 30, 31,; *YABC 2:* 56
Hurd, Thacher *46:* 88, 89; *94:* 114, 115, 116; *123:* 81, 82, 84
Hurlimann, Ruth *32:* 99
Hussar, Michael *114:* 113; *117:* 159
Hustler, Tom *6:* 105
Hutchins, Laurence *55:* 22
Hutchins, Pat *15:* 142; *70:* 106, 107, 108; *178:* 131, 132
Hutchinson, Sascha *95:* 211
Hutchinson, William M. *6:* 3, 138; *46:* 70
Hutchison, Paula *23:* 10
Hutton, Clarke *YABC 2:* 335
Hutton, Kathryn *35:* 155; *89:* 91
Hutton, Warwick *20:* 91
Huyette, Marcia *29:* 188
Hyatt, John *54:* 7
Hyatt, Mitch *178:* 162
Hyde, Maureen *82:* 17; *121:* 145, 146
Hyman, David *117:* 64
Hyman, Trina Schart *1:* 204; *2:* 194; *5:* 153; *6:* 106; *7:* 138, 145; *8:* 22; *10:* 196; *13:* 96; *14:* 114; *15:* 204; *16:* 234; *20:* 82; *22:* 133; *24:* 151; *25:* 79, 82; *26:* 82; *29:* 83; *31:* 37, 39; *34:* 104; *38:* 84, 100, 128; *41:* 49; *43:* 146; *46:* 91, 92, 93, 95, 96, 97, 98, 99, 100, 101, 102, 103, 104, 105,108, 109, 111, 197; *48:* 60, 61; *52:* 32; *60:* 168; *66:* 38; *67:* 214; *72:* 74; *75:* 92; *79:* 57; *82:* 95, 238; *89:* 46; *95:* 91, 92, 93; *100:* 33, 199; *132:* 12; *147:* 33, 35, 36; *167:* 58, 60; *177:* 189, 190

I

Ibarra, Rosa *147:* 91
Ibatoulline, Bagram *156:* 48; *174:* 33, 82
Ichikawa, Satomi *29:* 152; *41:* 52; *47:* 133, 134,135, 136; *78:* 93, 94; *80:* 81; *146:* 143, 145, 146
Ide, Jacqueline *YABC 1:* 39
Ilsley, Velma *3:* 1; *7:* 55; *12:* 109; *37:* 62; *38:* 184
in den Bosch, Nicole *150:* 204
Inga *1:* 142
Ingman, Bruce *134:* 50
Ingpen, Robert *109:* 103, 104; *132:* 138; *137:* 177; *166:* 103
Ingraham, Erick *21:* 177; *84:* 256; *103:* 66
Inkpen, Mick *99:* 104, 105; *106:* 44
Innerst, Stacy *149:* 104
Innocenti, Roberto *21:* 123; *96:* 122; *159:* 111, 197
Inoue, Yosuke *24:* 118
Iofin, Michael *97:* 157
Iosa, Ann *63:* 189
Ipcar, Dahlov *1:* 124, 125; *49:* 137, 138, 139, 140, 141, 142,143, 144, 145; *147:* 122, 124, 126
Irvin, Fred *13:* 166; *15:* 143, 144; *27:* 175
Irving, Jay *45:* 72
Irving, Laurence *27:* 50
Isaac, Joanne *21:* 76
Isaacs, Gary *170:* 188
Isadora, Rachel *43:* 159, 160; *54:* 31; *79:* 106, 107,108; *121:* 100, 102; *165:* 116, 117
Ishmael, Woodi *24:* 111; *31:* 99
Ives, Ruth *15:* 257
Iwai, Melissa *149:* 233

J

Jabar, Cynthia *101:* 201
Jackness, Andrew *94:* 237
Jackson, Julian *91:* 104, 106
Jackson, Michael *43:* 42
Jackson, Shelley *79:* 71; *99:* 109

Jacob, Murv *89:* 30
Jacobi, Kathy *62:* 118
Jacobs, Barbara *9:* 136
Jacobs, Lou, Jr. *9:* 136; *15:* 128
Jacobson, Laura *176:* 98; *177:* 85, 86
Jacobson, Rick *131:* 222; *170:* 119
Jacobus, Tim *79:* 140; *109:* 126; *129:* 180
Jacques, Robin *1:* 70; *2:* 1; *8:* 46; *9:* 20; *15:* 187; *19:* 253; *32:* 102, 103, 104; *43:* 184; *73:* 135; *YABC 1:* 42
Jaffee, Al *66:* 131, 132
Jagr, Miloslav *13:* 197
Jahn-Clough, Lisa *88:* 114; *152:* 104
Jahnke, Robert *84:* 24
Jainschigg, Nicholas *80:* 64; *91:* 138; *95:* 63; *99:* 25; *108:* 50; *171:* 41
Jakesavic, Nenad *85:* 102
Jakobsen, Kathy *116:* 83
Jakubowski, Charles *14:* 192
Jambor, Louis *YABC 1:* 11
James, Ann *73:* 50; *82:* 113; *158:* 61
James, Brian *140:* 91
James, Derek *35:* 187; *44:* 91; *61:* 133; *74:* 2; *80:* 57; *86:* 88; *130:* 30; *179:* 29
James, Gilbert *YABC 1:* 43
James, Harold *2:* 151; *3:* 62; *8:* 79; *29:* 113; *51:* 195; *74:* 90
James, Kennon *126:* 211
James, Robin *50:* 106; *53:* 32, 34, 35
James, Will *19:* 150, 152, 153, 155, 163
Janosch
  See Eckert, Horst
Janovitch, Marilyn *68:* 168
Janovitz, Marilyn *87:* 187; *130:* 198
Jansons, Inese *48:* 117
Jansson, Tove *3:* 90; *41:* 106, 108, 109, 110, 111, 113, 114
Jaques, Faith *7:* 11, 132, 133; *21:* 83, 84; *69:* 114,116; *73:* 170
Jaques, Frances Lee *29:* 224
Jauss, Anne Marie *1:* 139; *3:* 34; *10:* 57, 119; *11:* 205; *23:* 194
Jay, Alison *158:* 97, 98
Jeffers, Oliver *175:* 111
Jeffers, Susan *17:* 86, 87; *25:* 164, 165; *26:* 112; *50:* 132, 134, 135; *70:* 111, 112, 113; *137:* 107, 108, 109, 110, 111
Jefferson, Louise E. *4:* 160
Jenkin-Pearce, Susie *78:* 16
Jenkins, Debra Reid *85:* 202; *114:* 89; *173:* 134
Jenkins, Jean *98:* 79, 102
Jenkins, Leonard *157:* 169; *167:* 128
Jenkins, Patrick *72:* 126
Jenkins, Steve *124:* 177; *154:* 90, 91, 92, 93
Jenks, Aleta *73:* 117; *124:* 225
Jenkyns, Chris *51:* 97
Jensen, Bruce *95:* 39
Jensinius, Kirsten *56:* 58
Jeram, Anita *89:* 135; *102:* 122, 123; *129:* 112; *154:* 96, 97, 98; *164:* 154
Jernigan, E. Wesley *85:* 92
Jerome, Karen A. *72:* 194
Jeruchim, Simon *6:* 173; *15:* 250
Jeschke, Susan *20:* 89; *39:* 161; *41:* 84; *42:* 120
Jessel, Camilla *29:* 115
Jessell, Tim *159:* 3; *177:* 87
Jiang, Cheng An *109:* 108
Jiang, Wei *109:* 108
Jimenez, Maria *77:* 158; *93:* 127
Jobling, Curtis *138:* 74
Jocelyn, Marthe *118:* 83; *137:* 219; *163:* 119, 120
Joerns, Consuelo *38:* 36; *44:* 94
John, Diana *12:* 209
John, Helen *1:* 215; *28:* 204
Johns, Elizabeth *127:* 33
Johns, Jasper *61:* 172
Johns, Jeanne *24:* 114
Johnson, Adrian *143:* 50

Johnson, Bruce *9:* 47
Johnson, Cathy *92:* 136
Johnson, Crockett
  See Leisk, David
Johnson, D. William *23:* 104
Johnson, David *175:* 18
Johnson, Gillian *119:* 175; *164:* 217
Johnson, Harper *1:* 27; *2:* 33; *18:* 302; *19:* 61; *31:* 181; *44:* 46, 50, 95
Johnson, Ingrid *37:* 118
Johnson, James Ralph *1:* 23, 127
Johnson, James David *12:* 195
Johnson, Jane *48:* 136
Johnson, Joel Peter *98:* 18; *128:* 111
Johnson, John E. *34:* 133
Johnson, Kevin *72:* 44
Johnson, Kevin Eugene *109:* 215
Johnson, Larry *47:* 56; *123:* 107; *159:* 203
Johnson, Margaret S. *35:* 131
Johnson, Meredith Merrell *71:* 181; *83:* 158; *89:* 103; *104:* 88
Johnson, Milton *1:* 67; *2:* 71; *26:* 45; *31:* 107; *60:* 112; *68:* 96
Johnson, Pamela *16:* 174; *52:* 145; *62:* 140; *73:* 116; *85:* 64
Johnson, Paul Brett *83:* 95; *132:* 119
Johnson, Stephen T. *80:* 15; *131:* 35; *141:* 96; *145:* 40; *164:* 187; *175:* 32
Johnson, Steve *138:* 219; *141:* 64; *144:* 199; *177:* 51
Johnson, William R. *38:* 91
Johnson-Petrov, Arden *115:* 206
Johnston, David McCall *50:* 131, 133
Johnston, Lynne *118:* 85, 87, 89
Johnstone, Anne *8:* 120; *36:* 89
Johnstone, Janet Grahame *8:* 120; *36:* 89
Jonas, Ann *50:* 107, 108, 109; *135:* 113
Jones, Bob *71:* 5; *77:* 199
Jones, Carol *5:* 131; *72:* 185, 186; *153:* 111, 112
Jones, Chuck *53:* 70, 71
Jones, Davy *89:* 176
Jones, Elizabeth Orton *18:* 124, 126, 128, 129
Jones, Harold *14:* 88; *52:* 50
Jones, Holly *127:* 3
Jones, Jeff *41:* 64
Jones, Laurian *25:* 24, 27
Jones, Margaret *74:* 57
Jones, Randy *131:* 104
Jones, Richard *127:* 222
Jones, Robert *25:* 67
Jones, Wilfred *35:* 115; *YABC 1:* 163
Jordan, Charles *89:* 58
Jordan, Jess *158:* 136
Jordan, Martin George *84:* 127
Jordan, Richard *84:* 36
Jorgenson, Andrea *91:* 111
Jorisch, Stéphane *153:* 56, 193; *177:* 29; *178:* 138, 139
Joseph, James *53:* 88
Joudrey, Ken *64:* 145; *78:* 6
Joyce, William *72:* 131, 132, 133, 134; *73:* 227; *145:* 37
Joyner, Jerry *34:* 138
Juan, Ana *175:* 38; *179:* 111, 112
Jucker, Sita *5:* 93
Judkis, Jim *37:* 38
Juhasz, Victor *31:* 67
Jullian, Philippe *24:* 206; *25:* 203
Jung, Tom *91:* 217
Junge, Walter *67:* 150
Jupo, Frank *7:* 148, 149
Jurisch, Stephane *154:* 105
Justice, Martin *34:* 72

K

Kabatova-Taborska, Zdenka *107:* 153
Kachik, John *165:* 230
Kaczman, James *156:* 98
Kahl, David *74:* 95; *97:* 35; *109:* 174; *110:* 213
Kahl, M.P. *37:* 83
Kahl, Virginia *48:* 138
Kahn, Katherine Janus *90:* 135
Kakimoo, Kozo *11:* 148
Kalett, Jim *48:* 159, 160, 161
Kalin, Victor *39:* 186
Kalman, Maira *96:* 131, 132; *137:* 115
Kalmenoff, Matthew *22:* 191
Kalow, Gisela *32:* 105
Kamen, Gloria *1:* 41; *9:* 119; *10:* 178; *35:* 157; *78:* 236; *98:* 82
Kaminsky, Jef *102:* 153
Kandell, Alice *35:* 133
Kane, Henry B. *14:* 90; *18:* 219, 220
Kane, Robert *18:* 131
Kanfer, Larry *66:* 141
Kappes, Alfred *28:* 104
Karalus, Bob *41:* 157
Karas, G. Brian *80:* 60; *99:* 179; *115:* 41; *118:* 50; *136:* 168; *145:* 166; *149:* 245; *159:* 65; *171:* 192; *178:* 142, 143
Karasz, Ilonka *128:* 163
Karlin, Eugene *10:* 63; *20:* 131
Karlin, Nurit *63:* 78; *103:* 110
Karpinski, Tony *134:* 160
Kasamatsu, Shiro *139:* 155
Kasparavicius, Kestutis *139:* 210
Kassian, Olena *64:* 94
Kastner, Jill *79:* 135; *117:* 84, 85
Kasuya, Masahiro *41:* 206, 207; *51:* 100
Katona, Robert *21:* 85; *24:* 126
Katz, Karen *158:* 123
Kauffer, E. McKnight *33:* 103; *35:* 127; *63:* 67
Kaufman, Angelika *15:* 156
Kaufman, Joe *33:* 119
Kaufman, John *13:* 158
Kaufman, Stuart *62:* 64; *68:* 226; *137:* 44
Kaufmann, John *1:* 174; *4:* 159; *8:* 43, 1; *10:* 102; *18:* 133, 134; *22:* 251
Kaye, Graham *1:* 9; *67:* 7, 8
Kaye, M.M. *62:* 95
Kazalovski, Nata *40:* 205
Keane, Bil *4:* 135
Kearney, David *72:* 47; *121:* 83
Keating, Pamel T. *77:* 37
Keats, Ezra Jack *3:* 18, 105, 257; *14:* 101, 102; *33:* 129; *57:* 79, 80, 82, 83, 84, 87
Keegan, Charles *166:* 211
Keegan, Marcia *9:* 122; *32:* 93
Keeler, Patricia A. *81:* 56
Keely, Jack *119:* 95
Keely, John *26:* 104; *48:* 214
Keen, Eliot *25:* 213
Keep, Richard C. *170:* 122
Keeping, Charles *9:* 124, 185; *15:* 28, 134; *18:* 115; *44:* 194, 196; *47:* 25; *52:* 3; *54:* 156; *69:* 123, 124; *74:* 56; *155:* 9
Keeter, Susan *168:* 46
Keith, Eros *4:* 98; *5:* 138; *31:* 29; *43:* 220; *52:* 91, 92, 93, 94; *56:* 64, 66; *60:* 37; *79:* 93
Keleinikov, Andrei *65:* 101, 102
Kelen, Emery *13:* 115
Keller, A.J. *62:* 198
Keller, Arthur I. *26:* 106
Keller, Dick *36:* 123, 125
Keller, Holly *45:* 79; *76:* 118, 119, 120, 121; *108:* 137, 138, 140; *157:* 117, 118, 119
Keller, Katie *79:* 222; *93:* 108
Keller, Ronald *45:* 208
Kelley, True *41:* 114, 115; *42:* 137; *75:* 35; *92:* 104, 105; *124:* 62; *130:* 100, 101; *179:* 120, 121, 122

Kellogg, Steven *8:* 96; *11:* 207; *14:* 130; *20:* 58; *29:* 140, 141; *30:* 35; *41:* 141; *57:* 89, 90, 92,93, 94, 96; *59:* 182; *73:* 141; *77:* 129; *130:* 105, 106; *177:* 94, 95, 96, 97; *YABC 1:* 65, 73
Kelly, Billy *158:* 143
Kelly, Geoff *97:* 196; *112:* 25
Kelly, Irene *147:* 134
Kelly, Joseph *174:* 94
Kelly, Kathleen M. *71:* 109
Kelly, Laura *89:* 217
Kelly, True *163:* 87
Kelly, Walt *18:* 136, 137, 138, 139, 140, 141, 144, 145, 146, 148, 149
Kemble, E.W. *34:* 75; *44:* 178; *YABC 2:* 54, 59
Kemp-Welsh, Lucy *24:* 197; *100:* 214
Kendall, Jane *150:* 105
Kendall, Peter *152:* 85
Kendrick, Dennis *79:* 213
Kennaway, Adrienne *60:* 55, 56; *171:* 88, 89
Kennedy, Paul Edward *6:* 190; *8:* 132; *33:* 120
Kennedy, Richard *3:* 93; *12:* 179; *44:* 193; *100:* 15; *YABC 1:* 57
Kent, Jack *24:* 136; *37:* 37; *40:* 81; *84:* 89; *86:* 150; *88:* 77
Kent, Rockwell *5:* 166; *6:* 129; *20:* 225, 226, 227,229; *59:* 144
Kenyon, Tony *81:* 201; *127:* 74
Kepes, Juliet *13:* 119
Kerins, Anthony *76:* 84
Kerr, Judity *24:* 137
Kerr, Phyllis Forbes *72:* 141
Kessler, Leonard *1:* 108; *7:* 139; *14:* 107, 227; *22:* 101; *44:* 96; *67:* 79; *82:* 123
Kest, Kristin *168:* 99; *173:* 23
Kesteven, Peter *35:* 189
Ketcham, Hank *28:* 140, 141, 142
Kettelkamp, Larry *2:* 164
Key, Alexander *8:* 99
Khalsa, Dayal Kaur *62:* 99
Kiakshuk *8:* 59
Kidd, Chip *94:* 23
Kidd, Richard *152:* 110
Kidd, Tom *64:* 199; *81:* 189
Kiddell-Monroe, Joan *19:* 201; *55:* 59, 60; *87:* 174; *121:* 112
Kidder, Harvey *9:* 105; *80:* 41
Kidwell, Carl *43:* 145
Kieffer, Christa *41:* 89
Kiesler, Kate *110:* 105; *136:* 142
Kiff, Ken *40:* 45
Kilbride, Robert *37:* 100
Kilby, Don *141:* 144
Kim, Glenn *99:* 82
Kimball, Anton *78:* 114; *119:* 105
Kimball, Yeffe *23:* 116; *37:* 88
Kimber, Murray *171:* 91
Kimmel, Warren *176:* 112
Kincade, Orin *34:* 116
Kindersley, Barnabas *96:* 110
Kindred, Wendy *7:* 151
King, Colin *53:* 3
King, Robin *10:* 164, 165
King, Stephen Michael *141:* 31
King, Tara Calahan *139:* 172
King, Tony *39:* 121
Kingman, Dong *16:* 287; *44:* 100, 102, 104
Kingsley, Charles *YABC 2:* 182
Kingston, Julie *147:* 14
Kingston, Maxine Hong *53:* 92
Kipling, John Lockwood *YABC 2:* 198
Kipling, Rudyard *YABC 2:* 196
Kipniss, Robert *29:* 59
Kirchherr, Astrid *55:* 23
Kirchhoff, Art *28:* 136
Kirk, Daniel *153:* 115, 116, 117; *173:* 101
Kirk, David *117:* 88, 89; *161:* 97, 98
Kirk, Ruth *5:* 96
Kirk, Steve *170:* 37
Kirk, Tim *32:* 209, 211; *72:* 89; *83:* 49

Kirmse, Marguerite *15:* 283; *18:* 153
Kirsch, Vincent X. *124:* 207
Kirschner, Ruth *22:* 154
Kish, Ely *73:* 119; *79:* 2
Kitamura, Satoshi *62:* 102; *98:* 91; *101:* 147; *138:* 2; *143:* 83, 85, 86
Kiss, Andrew *168:* 115
Kitchel, JoAnn E. *133:* 32
Kitchen, Herbert Thomas *70:* 126
Kittelsen, Theodor *62:* 14
Kiuchi, Tatsuro *114:* 71
Kiwak, Barbara *172:* 135
Klahr, Susan *176:* 196
Klapholz, Mel *13:* 35
Klein, Bill *89:* 105
Klein, Robert *55:* 77
Klein, Suzanna *63:* 104
Kleinman, Zalman *28:* 143
Kleven, Elisa *173:* 96, 97
Kliban, B. *35:* 137, 138
Kline, Michael *127:* 66
Knabel, Lonnie *73:* 103; *75:* 187, 228
Kneen, Maggie *140:* 139
Knight, Ann *34:* 143
Knight, Christopher *13:* 125
Knight, Hilary *1:* 233; *3:* 21; *15:* 92, 158, 159; *16:* 258, 259, 260; *18:* 235; *19:* 169; *35:* 242; *46:* 167; *52:* 116; *69:* 126, 127; *132:* 129; *YABC 1:* 168, 169, 172
Knorr, Peter *126:* 92, 93
Knotts, Howard *20:* 4; *25:* 170; *36:* 163
Knutson, Barbara *112:* 134
Knutson, Kimberley *115:* 90
Kobayashi, Ann *39:* 58
Kocsis, J.C.
  See Paul, James
Koehler, Hanne Lore *176:* 203
Koehn, Ilse *34:* 198; *79:* 123
Koelsch, Michael *99:* 182; *107:* 164; *109:* 239; *138:* 142; *150:* 94; *176:* 105
Koering, Ursula *3:* 28; *4:* 14; *44:* 5; *64:* 140,141; *85:* 46
Koerner, Henry
  See Koerner, W.H.D.
Koerner, W.H.D. *14:* 216; *21:* 88, 89, 90, 91; *23:* 211
Koetsch, Mike *166:* 68
Koffler, Camilla *36:* 113
Kogan, Deborah Ray *161:* 101, 102
Koide, Yasuko *50:* 114
Kolado, Karen *102:* 228
Komoda, Kiyo *9:* 128; *13:* 214
Kompaneyets, Marc *169:* 92
Konashevich, Vladimir *61:* 160
Konashevicha, V. *YABC 1:* 26
Konigsburg, E.L. *4:* 138; *48:* 141, 142, 144, 145; *94:* 129, 130; *126:* 129, 130, 131
Kono, Erin Eitter *177:* 99
Kooiker, Leonie *48:* 148
Koonook, Simon *65:* 157
Koontz, Robin Michal *136:* 155
Koopmans, Loek *101:* 121
Kopelke, Lisa *154:* 107
Kopper, Lisa *72:* 152, 153; *105:* 135, 136
Korach, Mimi *1:* 128, 129; *2:* 52; *4:* 39; *5:* 159; *9:* 129; *10:* 21; *24:* 69
Koren, Edward *5:* 100; *65:* 65, 67
Kosaka, Fumi *164:* 130
Koscielniak, Bruce *99:* 122; *153:* 120, 121, 122
Koshkin, Alexander *92:* 180
Kossin, Sandy *10:* 71; *23:* 105
Kostin, Andrej *26:* 204
Kosturko, Bob *164:* 56
Kotzky, Brian *68:* 184
Kovacevic, Zivojin *13:* 247
Kovalski, Maryann *58:* 120; *84:* 88; *97:* 124, 125, 126; *158:* 3
Krahn, Fernando *2:* 257; *34:* 206; *49:* 152
Kramer, Anthony *33:* 81
Kramer, David *96:* 162; *109:* 132; *150:* 220

Kramer, Frank 6: 121
Krantz, Kathy 35: 83
Kratter, Paul 139: 65
Kraus, Robert 13: 217; 65: 113; 93: 93, 94
Krause, Jon 176: 62
Krauss, Trisha 174: 10
Kredel, Fritz 6: 35; 17: 93, 94, 95, 96; 22: 147; 24: 175; 29: 130; 35: 77; YABC 2: 166, 300
Krementz, Jill 17: 98; 49: 41
Krenina, Katya 117: 106; 125: 133; 176: 117
Kresin, Robert 23: 19
Krieger, Salem 54: 164
Kriegler, Lyn 73: 29
Krommes, Beth 128: 141; 149: 136
Krone, Mike 101: 71
Kronheimer, Ann 135: 119
Krosoczka, Jarrett J. 155: 142
Kruck, Gerald 88: 181
Krupinski, Loretta 67: 104; 102: 131; 161: 105, 106
Krupp, Robin Rector 53: 96, 98
Krush, Beth 1: 51, 85; 2: 233; 4: 115; 9: 61; 10: 191; 11: 196; 18: 164, 165; 32: 72; 37: 203; 43: 57; 60: 102, 103, 107, 108, 109
Krush, Joe 2: 233; 4: 115; 9: 61; 10: 191; 11: 196; 18: 164, 165; 32: 72, 91; 37: 203; 43: 57; 60: 102, 103, 107, 108, 109
Krych, Duane 91: 43
Krykorka, Vladyana 96: 147; 143: 90, 91; 168: 14
Kubick, Dana 165: 91
Kubinyi, Laszlo 4: 116; 6: 113; 16: 118; 17: 100; 28: 227; 30: 172; 49: 24, 28; 54: 23; 167: 149
Kubricht, Mary 73: 118
Kucharik, Elena 139: 31
Kuchera, Kathleen 84: 5
Kuhn, Bob 17: 91; 35: 235
Kulikov, Boris 163: 185
Kukalis, Romas 90: 27; 139: 37
Kuklin, Susan 63: 82, 83, 84
Kunhardt, Dorothy 53: 101
Kunhardt, Edith 67: 105, 106
Kunstler, Mort 10: 73; 32: 143
Kurchevsky, V. 34: 61
Kurczok, Belinda 121: 118
Kurelek, William 8: 107
Kuriloff, Ron 13: 19
Kurisu, Jane 160: 120
Kuskin, Karla 2: 170; 68: 115, 116; 111: 116
Kutzer, Ernst 19: 249
Kuzma, Steve 57: 8; 62: 93
Kuznetsova, Berta 74: 45
Kvasnosky, Laura McGee 93: 103; 142: 83
Kwas, Susan Estelle 179: 116
Kyong, Yunmee 165: 139

L

LaBlanc, Andre 24: 146
Laboccetta, Mario 27: 120
LaBrose, Darcie 157: 134
Labrosse, Darcia 58: 88; 108: 77; 178: 89
LaCava, Vince 95: 118
Laceky, Adam 32: 121
Lacis, Astra 85: 117
Lacome, Julie 174: 96, 97
La Croix YABC 2: 4
Ladwig, Tim 98: 212; 117: 76
La Farge, Margaret 47: 141
LaFave, Kim 64: 177; 72: 39; 97: 146; 99: 172; 106: 123; 149: 126
Lafontaine, Roger 167: 158
Lagarrigue, Jerome 136: 102
Laimgruber, Monika 11: 153
Laite, Gordon 1: 130, 131; 8: 209; 31: 113; 40: 63; 46: 117
Laliberté, Louise-Andrée 169: 98

LaMarche, Jim 46: 204; 61: 56; 94: 69; 114: 22; 129: 163; 162: 78, 80
Lamb, Jim 10: 117
Lambase, Barbara 101: 185; 150: 221; 166: 234
Lambert, J.K. 38: 129; 39: 24
Lambert, Sally Anne 133: 191
Lambert, Saul 23: 112; 33: 107; 54: 136
Lambert, Stephen 109: 33; 174: 99
Lambo, Don 6: 156; 35: 115; 36: 146
Lamontagne, Jacques 166: 227
Lamut, Sonja 57: 193
Lamut, Sonya 85: 102
Landa, Peter 11: 95; 13: 177; 53: 119
Landau, Jacob 38: 111
Landis, Joan 104: 23
Landon, Lucinda 79: 31
Landshoff, Ursula 13: 124
Landström, Lena 146: 165, 166
Landström, Olof 146: 166, 168; 170: 22
Lane, Daniel 112: 60
Lane, John R. 8: 145
Lane, John 15: 176, 177; 30: 146
Lane, Nancy 166: 74
Lang, G.D. 48: 56
Lang, Gary 73: 75
Lang, Jerry 18: 295
Lange, Dorothea 50: 141
Langley, Jonathan 162: 128
Langner, Nola 8: 110; 42: 36
Lanino, Deborah 105: 148
Lantz, Paul 1: 82, 102; 27: 88; 34: 102; 45: 123
Larkin, Bob 84: 225
Laroche, Giles 126: 140; 146: 81
LaRochelle, David 171: 97
Larrecq, John 44: 108; 68: 56
Larsen, Suzanne 1: 13
Larson, Gary 57: 121, 122, 123, 124, 125, 126, 127
Larsson, Carl 35: 144, 145, 146, 147, 148, 149, 150, 152, 153, 154
Larsson, Karl 19: 177
Lartitegui, Ana G. 105: 167
LaRue, Jenna 167: 20
La Rue, Michael D. 13: 215
Lasker, Joe 7: 186, 187; 14: 55; 38: 115; 39: 47; 83: 113, 114, 115
Latham, Barbara 16: 188, 189; 43: 71
Lathrop, Dorothy 14: 117, 118, 119; 15: 109; 16: 78, 79, 81; 32: 201, 203; 33: 112; YABC 2: 301
Lattimore, Eleanor Frances 7: 156
Lauden, Claire 16: 173
Lauden, George, Jr. 16: 173
Laune, Paul 2: 235; 34: 31
Laure, Jason 49: 53; 50: 122
Lauter, Richard 63: 29; 67: 111; 77: 198
Lavallee, Barbara 74: 157; 92: 154; 96: 126; 145: 193; 166: 125, 126
Lave, Fitz Hugh 59: 139
Lavis, Stephen 43: 143; 87: 137, 164, 165
Layton, Neal 152: 120, 121
Lawrason, June 168: 30
Lawrence, John 25: 131; 30: 141; 44: 198, 200
Lawrence, Stephen 20: 195
Lawson, Carol 6: 38; 42: 93, 131; 174: 56
Lawson, George 17: 280
Lawson, Robert 5: 26; 6: 94; 13: 39; 16: 11; 20: 100, 102, 103; 54: 3; 66: 12; 100: 144, 145; YABC 2: 222, 224, 225, 227, 228, 229, 230, 231, 232, 233, 234, 235, 237, 238, 239, 240, 241
Layfield, Kathie 60: 194
Lazare, Jerry 44: 109; 74: 28
Lazarevich, Mila 17: 118
Lazarus, Claire 103: 30
Lazarus, Keo Felker 21: 94
Lazzaro, Victor 11: 126
Lea, Bob 166: 208

Lea, Tom 43: 72, 74
Leacroft, Richard 6: 140
Leaf, Munro 20: 99
Leake, Donald 70: 41
Leander, Patricia 23: 27
Lear, Edward 18: 183, 184, 185
Lear, Rebecca 149: 46
Lebenson, Richard 6: 209; 7: 76; 23: 145; 44: 191; 87: 153
Le Cain, Errol 6: 141; 9: 3; 22: 142; 25: 198; 28: 173; 68: 128, 129; 86: 49
Lechon, Daniel 113: 211
Leder, Dora 129: 172
Leduc, Bernard 102: 36
Lee, Alan 62: 25, 28
Lee, Bryce 99: 60; 101: 195
Lee, Dom 83: 118, 120; 93: 123; 121: 121, 126; 146: 174, 175, 206, 207; 174: 204
Lee, Doris 13: 246; 32: 183; 44: 111
Lee, Hector Viveros 115: 96
Lee, Jeanne M. 158: 56
Lee, Jared 93: 200; 157: 229
Lee, Jody 81: 121; 82: 225; 91: 155; 100: 182
Lee, Jody A. 127: 124, 126, 127
See also Lee, Jody
Lee, Manning de V. 2: 200; 17: 12; 27: 87; 37: 102, 103, 104; YABC 2: 304
Lee, Marie G. 138: 157
Lee, Paul 97: 100; 105: 72, 209; 109: 177; 128: 113
Lee, Robert J. 3: 97; 67: 124
Lee, Victor 96: 228; 105: 182; 140: 196
Leech, Dorothy 98: 76
Leech, John 15: 59
Leedy, Loreen 84: 142; 128: 144, 145, 146; 175: 125, 126, 127
Leeman, Michael 44: 157
Leeming, Catherine 87: 39
Lees, Harry 6: 112
LeFever, Bill 88: 220, 221
Legenisel 47: 111
Legrand, Edy 18: 89, 93
Lehman, Barbara 73: 123; 170: 130
Lehrman, Rosalie 2: 180
Leichman, Seymour 5: 107
Leighton, Clare 25: 130; 33: 168; 37: 105, 106, 108,109
Leisk, David 1: 140, 141; 11: 54; 30: 137, 142, 143,144
Leister, Brian 89: 45; 106: 37; 114: 67; 149: 236
Leloir, Maurice 18: 77, 80, 83, 99
Lematire, Pascal 144: 175; 176: 130
Lemieux, Michele 100: 148; 139: 153
Lemke, Horst 14: 98; 38: 117, 118, 119
Lemke, R.W. 42: 162
Lemon, David Gwynne 9: 1
LeMoult, Adolph 82: 116
Lenn, Michael 136: 89
Lennon, John 114: 100
Lennox, Elsie 95: 163; 143: 160
Lenski, Lois 1: 144; 26: 135, 137, 139, 141; 100: 153, 154
Lent, Blair 1: 116, 117; 2: 174; 3: 206, 207; 7: 168, 169; 34: 62; 68: 217; 133: 101
Leonard, Richard 91: 128
Leone, Leonard 49: 190
Lerner, Carol 86: 140, 141, 142
Lerner, Judith 116: 138
Lerner, Sharon 11: 157; 22: 56
Leroux-Hugon, Helene 132: 139
Leslie, Cecil 19: 244
Lessac, Frane 80: 182, 207; 96: 182
Lessing, Erich 167: 52; 173: 60
Le Tord, Bijou 49: 156; 95: 112
Leutz, Emanuel 165: 27
Levai, Blaise 39: 130
Levin, Ted 12: 148
Levine, David 43: 147, 149, 150, 151, 152; 64: 11

Levine, Joe *71:* 88
Levine, Marge *81:* 127
Levinson, David *178:* 232
Levit, Herschel *24:* 223
Levstek, Ljuba *131:* 192; *134:* 216; *149:* 65; *168:* 180
Levy, Jessica Ann *19:* 225; *39:* 191
Levy, Lina *117:* 126
Lewin, Betsy *32:* 114; *48:* 177; *90:* 151; *91:* 125; *92:* 85; *115:* 105; *169:* 110, 111; *178:* 47
Lewin, Ted *4:* 77; *8:* 168; *20:* 110; *21:* 99,100; *27:* 110; *28:* 96, 97; *31:* 49; *45:* 55; *48:* 223; *60:* 20, 119, 120; *62:* 139; *66:* 108; *71:* 12; *72:* 21; *74:* 226; *76:* 139, 140; *77:* 82; *79:* 87; *85:* 49, 177; *86:* 55; *88:* 182; *93:* 28, 29; *94:* 34, 182, 194; *99:* 156; *104:* 8; *115:* 123; *118:* 74; *119:* 114, 116; *131:* 54; *145:* 99; *165:* 151; *177:* 75; *178:* 42
Lewis, Allen *15:* 112
Lewis, E.B. *88:* 143; *93:* 109; *119:* 79; *124:* 113; *128:* 49; *151:* 167; *168:* 110; *173:* 121; *174:* 66; *176:* 7
Lewis, H.B. *170:* 124
Lewis, J. Patrick *162:* 83
Lewis, Jan *81:* 22
Lewis, Kim *136:* 165
Lewis, Richard W. *52:* 25
Lewis, Robin Baird *98:* 193
Leydon, Rita Floden *21:* 101
Lichtenheld, Tom *152:* 125, 126
Lieblich, Irene *22:* 173; *27:* 209, 214
Lieder, Rick *108:* 197
Lies, Brian *92:* 40; *141:* 101; *150:* 138
Liese, Charles *4:* 222
Life, Kay *79:* 49
Lifton, Robert Jay *66:* 154
Lightburn, Ron *86:* 153; *91:* 122
Lightfoot, Norman R. *45:* 47
Lignell, Lois *37:* 114
Lill, Debra *121:* 70
Lilly, Charles *8:* 73; *20:* 127; *48:* 53; *72:* 9,16; *77:* 98; *102:* 94
Lilly, Ken *37:* 224
Lim, John *43:* 153
Limona, Mercedes *51:* 183
Liu, Grace *143:* 217; *162:* 86, 87; *174:* 185
Lincoln, Patricia Henderson *27:* 27; *78:* 127
Lindahn, Ron *84:* 17
Lindahn, Val *84:* 17
Lindberg, Howard *10:* 123; *16:* 190
Lindberg, Jeffrey *64:* 77; *77:* 71; *79:* 54; *80:* 149; *174:* 109; *179:* 52
Linden, Seymour *18:* 200, 201; *43:* 140
Lindenbaum, Pija *144:* 143
Linder, Richard *27:* 119
Lindman, Maj *43:* 154
Lindsay, Norman *67:* 114
Lindsay, Vachel *40:* 118
Lindstrom, Jack *145:* 118
Line, Les *27:* 143
Linell
   See Smith, Linell
Lionni, Leo *8:* 115; *72:* 159, 160, 161
Lipinsky, Lino *2:* 156; *22:* 175
Lippincott, Gary A. *70:* 35; *119:* 118
Lippman, Peter *8:* 31; *31:* 119, 120, 160
Lisi, Victoria *89:* 145
Lisker, Emily *169:* 114
Lisker, Sonia O. *16:* 274; *31:* 31; *44:* 113, 114
Lisowski, Gabriel *47:* 144; *49:* 157
Lissim, Simon *17:* 138
Little, Ed *89:* 145; *151:* 53
Little, Harold *16:* 72
Little, Mary E. *28:* 146
Littlewood, Karen *165:* 126
Litty, Julie *111:* 63
Litzinger, Rosanne *151:* 101; *176:* 118
Liu, Lesley *143:* 72
Livesly, Lorna *19:* 216
Livingston, Susan *95:* 22

Liwska, Renata *164:* 113
Llerena, Carlos Antonio *19:* 181
Lloyd, Errol *11:* 39; *22:* 178
Lloyd, Megan *77:* 118; *80:* 113; *97:* 75; *117:* 94, 95
Lo, Beth *165:* 154
Lo, Koon-chiu *7:* 134
Loates, Glen *63:* 76
Lobel, Anita *6:* 87; *9:* 141; *18:* 248; *55:* 85,86, 87, 88, 93, 104; *60:* 67; *78:* 263; *82:* 110; *96:* 157, 159; *101:* 84; *132:* 35; *162:* 93, 94
Lobel, Arnold *1:* 188, 189; *5:* 12; *6:* 147; *7:* 167, 209; *18:* 190, 191; *25:* 39, 43; *27:* 40; *29:* 174; *52:* 127; *55:* 89, 91, 94, 95, 97, 98, 99, 100, 101, 102,103, 105, 106; *60:* 18, 31; *66:* 181, 183; *75:* 57; *82:* 246; *136:* 146
Locker, Thomas *109:* 134
Lodge, Bernard *107:* 125, 126; *153:* 93
Loeb, Jeph *153:* 177
Lodge, Jo *112:* 119
Loefgren, Ulf *3:* 108
Loescher, Ann *20:* 108
Loescher, Gil *20:* 108
Loew, David *93:* 184; *171:* 120
Lofting, Hugh *15:* 182, 183; *100:* 161, 162
Lofts, Pamela *60:* 188
Loh, George *38:* 88
Lomberg, Jon *58:* 160
Lonette, Reisie *11:* 211; *12:* 168; *13:* 56; *36:* 122; *43:* 155
Long, Ethan *168:* 146; *178:* 12
Long, Laurel *162:* 135
Long, Loren *99:* 176; *172:* 65
Long, Melinda *152:* 128
Long, Miles *115:* 174
Long, Sally *42:* 184
Long, Sylvia *74:* 168; *132:* 63; *179:* 134
Longoni, Eduardo *73:* 85
Longtemps, Ken *17:* 123; *29:* 221; *69:* 82
Looser, Heinz *YABC 2:* 208
Lopshire, Robert *6:* 149; *21:* 117; *34:* 166; *73:* 13
Lord, John Vernon *21:* 104; *23:* 25; *51:* 22
Lorenz, Albert *40:* 146; *115:* 127
Loretta, Sister Mary *33:* 73
Lorraine, Walter H. *3:* 110; *4:* 123; *16:* 192; *103:* 119
Los, Marek *146:* 22
Loss, Joan *11:* 163
Louderback, Walt *YABC 1:* 164
Lousada, Sandra *40:* 138
Louth, Jack *149:* 252; *151:* 191, 192
Love, Judy *173:* 43
Low, Joseph *14:* 124, 125; *18:* 68; *19:* 194; *31:* 166; *80:* 239
Low, William *62:* 175; *80:* 147; *112:* 194; *150:* 202; *169:* 175; *177:* 110
Lowe, Vicky *177:* 130
Lowenheim, Alfred *13:* 65, 66
Lowenstein, Sallie *116:* 90, 91
Lowitz, Anson *17:* 124; *18:* 215
Lowrey, Jo *8:* 133
Lubach, Vanessa *142:* 152
Lubell, Winifred *1:* 207; *3:* 15; *6:* 151
Lubin, Leonard B. *19:* 224; *36:* 79, 80; *45:* 128, 129,131, 132, 133, 134, 135, 136, 137, 139, 140, 141; *70:* 95; *YABC2:* 96
Lucht, Irmgard *82:* 145
Ludwig, Helen *33:* 144, 145
Lufkin, Raymond *38:* 138; *44:* 48
Luhrs, Henry *7:* 123; *11:* 120
Lujan, Tonita *82:* 33
Lupo, Dom *4:* 204
Lustig, Loretta *30:* 186; *46:* 134, 135, 136, 137
Luthardt, Kevin *172:* 125, 126
Luxbacher, Irene *153:* 145
Luzak, Dennis *52:* 121; *99:* 142
Lydbury, Jane *82:* 98
Lydecker, Laura *21:* 113; *42:* 53
Lynch, Charles *16:* 33

Lynch, Marietta *29:* 137; *30:* 171
Lynch, P.J. *126:* 228; *129:* 110; *132:* 247
Lyon, Carol *102:* 26
Lyon, Elinor *6:* 154
Lyon, Fred *14:* 16
Lyon, Tammie *175:* 170
Lyons, Oren *8:* 193
Lyster, Michael *26:* 41

M

Maas, Dorothy *6:* 175
Maas, Julie *47:* 61
Macaulay, David *46:* 139, 140, 141, 142, 143, 144, 145, 147, 149, 150; *72:* 167, 168, 169; *137:* 129, 130, 131, 132
MacCarthy, Patricia *69:* 141
Macdonald, Alister *21:* 55
Macdonald, Roberta *19:* 237; *52:* 164
MacDonald, Norman *13:* 99
MacDonald, Suse *54:* 41; *109* 138; *130:* 156
Mace, Varian *49:* 159
Macguire, Robert Reid *18:* 67
Machetanz, Fredrick *34:* 147, 148
MacInnes, Ian *35:* 59
MacIntyre, Elisabeth *17:* 127, 128
Mack, Jeff *161:* 128
Mack, Stan *17:* 129; *96:* 33
Mackay, Donald *17:* 60
MacKaye, Arvia *32:* 119
Mackenzie, Stuart *73:* 213
MacKenzie, Garry *33:* 159
Mackie, Clare *87:* 134
Mackinlay, Miguel *27:* 22
MacKinstry, Elizabeth *15:* 110; *42:* 139, 140, 141, 142, 143,144, 145
MacLeod, Lee *91:* 167
Maclise, Daniel *YABC 2:* 257
Madden, Don *3:* 112, 113; *4:* 33, 108, 155; *7:* 193; *78:* 12; *YABC 2:* 211
Maddison, Angela Mary *10:* 83
Madsen, Jim *146:* 259; *152:* 237
Maestro, Giulio *8:* 124; *12:* 17; *13:* 108; *25:* 182; *54:* 147; *59:* 114, 115, 116, 117, 118, 121, 123, 124, 125,126, 127; *68:* 37, 38; *106:* 129, 130, 131, 136, 137, 138
Maffia, Daniel *60:* 200
Maggio, Viqui *58:* 136, 181; *74:* 150; *75:* 90; *85:* 159; *90:* 158; *109:* 184
Magnus, Erica *77:* 123
Magnuson, Diana *28:* 102; *34:* 190; *41:* 175
Magovern, Peg *103:* 123
Maguire, Sheila *41:* 100
Magurn, Susan *91:* 30
Mahony, Will *37:* 120
Mahony, Will *85:* 116
Mahood, Kenneth *24:* 141
Mahurin, Matt *164:* 225; *175:* 95
Maik, Henri *9:* 102
Maione, Heather Harms *106:* 5; *178:* 8
Maisto, Carol *29:* 87
Maitland, Antony *1:* 100, 176; *8:* 41; *17:* 246; *24:* 46; *25:* 177, 178; *32:* 74; *60:* 65, 195; *67:* 156; *87:* 131; *101:* 110
Majewski, Dawn W. *169:* 95
Mak, Kam *72:* 25; *75:* 43; *87:* 186; *97:* 24; *102:* 154; *149:* 195
Makie, Pam *37:* 117
Maktima, Joe *116:* 191
Maland, Nick *99:* 77
Male, Alan *132:* 64
Malone, James Hiram *84:* 161
Malone, Nola Langner *82:* 239
Malsberg, Edward *51:* 175
Malvern, Corinne *2:* 13; *34:* 148, 149
Manchess, Gregory *165:* 241
Mancusi, Stephen *63:* 198, 199
Mandelbaum, Ira *31:* 115
Manders, John *138:* 152, 155

Manet, Edouard 23: 170
Mangiat, Jeff 173: 127
Mangurian, David 14: 133
Manham, Allan 42: 109; 77: 180; 80: 227
Manley, Matt 103: 167; 117: 98; 172: 49
Manna, Giovanni 178: 44
Manniche, Lise 31: 121
Manning, Jane 96: 203
Manning, Jo 63: 154
Manning, Mick 176: 139
Manning, Samuel F. 5: 75
Mantel, Richard 57: 73; 63: 106; 82: 255
Maraja 15: 86; YABC 1: 28; 2: 115
Marcellino, Fred 20: 125; 34: 222; 53: 125;
  58: 205; 61: 64, 121, 122; 68: 154, 156,
  157, 158, 159; 72: 25; 86: 184; 98: 181;
  118: 129, 130, 131; 149: 218
Marchesi, Stephen 34: 140; 46: 72; 50: 147;
  66: 239; 70: 33; 73: 18, 114, 163; 77: 47,
  76,147; 78: 79; 80: 30; 81: 6; 89: 66; 93:
  21,130; 94: 94; 97: 66; 98: 96; 114: 115,
  116
Marchiori, Carlos 14: 60
Marciano, John Bemelmans 118: 133; 167:
  110, 111, 112
Marcus, Barry David 139: 248; 145: 18
Margules, Gabriele 21: 120
Mariana
  See Foster, Marian Curtis
Mariano, Michael 52: 108
Marino, Dorothy 6: 37; 14: 135
Mario, Heide Stetson 101: 202
Maris, Ron 71: 123
Maritz, Nicolaas 85: 123
Mark, Mona 65: 105; 68: 205; 116: 213
Markham, R.L. 17: 240
Marks, Alan 104: 104; 109: 182; 164: 92
Marks, Cara 54: 9
Marokvia, Artur 31: 122
Marquez, Susan 108: 121
Marrella, Maria Pia 62: 116
Marriott, Pat 30: 30; 34: 39; 35: 164, 165,
  166; 44: 170; 48: 186, 187, 188, 189, 191,
  192, 193; 91: 92
Mars, W.T. 1: 161; 3: 115; 4: 208, 225; 5: 92,
  105, 186; 8: 214; 9: 12; 13: 121; 27: 151;
  31: 180; 38: 102; 48: 66; 62: 164, 165; 64:
  62; 68: 229; 79: 55
Marschall, Ken 85: 29
Marsh, Christine 3: 164
Marsh, James 73: 137
Marsh, Reginald 17: 5; 19: 89; 22: 90, 96
Marshall, Anthony D. 18: 216
Marshall, Felicia 170: 190
Marshall, James 6: 160; 40: 221; 42: 24, 25,
  29; 51: 111, 112, 113, 114, 115, 116, 117,
  118, 119, 120, 121; 64: 13; 75: 126, 127,
  128, 129; 102: 10, 12
Marshall, Janet 97: 154
Marstall, Bob 55: 145; 84: 153, 170; 104: 145;
  154: 166, 167, 168
Martchenko, Michael 50: 129, 153, 155, 156,
  157; 83: 144,145; 154: 137, 138, 139
Marten, Ruth 129: 52
Martin, Charles E. 70: 144
Martin, David Stone 24: 232; 62: 4
Martin, Fletcher 18: 213; 23: 151
Martin, Rene 7: 144; 42: 148, 149, 150
Martin, Richard E. 51: 157; 131: 203
Martin, Ron 32: 81
Martin, Stefan 8: 68; 32: 124, 126; 56: 33
Martin, Whitney 166: 137
Martinez, Ed 58: 192; 72: 231; 77: 33; 80:
  214; 167: 123
Martinez, John 6: 113; 118: 13; 139: 143
Martinez, Sergio 158: 190
Martiniere, Stephan 171: 130
Marton, Jirina 95: 127, 128; 144: 145
Martorell, Antonio 84: 6; 97: 161
Martucci, Griesbach 52: 106
Marvin, Frederic 83: 86

Marx, Robert F. 24: 143
Masefield, Judith 19: 208, 209
Masheris, Robert 78: 51
Mason, George F. 14: 139
Mason, Robert 84: 96
Massey, Barbara 68: 142
Massie, Diane Redfield 16: 194
Massie, Kim 31: 43
Mataya, David 121: 66
Mathers, Petra 119: 135; 163: 104; 176: 143,
  144
Mathewuse, James 51: 143
Mathieu, Joseph 14: 33; 39: 206; 43: 167; 56:
  180; 79: 126; 94: 147
Matje, Martin 169: 177, 178; 172: 180
Matsubara, Naoko 12: 121
Matsuda, Shizu 13: 167
Matte, L'Enc 22: 183
Mattelson, Marvin 36: 50, 51
Matthews, F. Leslie 4: 216
Mattingly, David 71: 76, 77; 82: 64; 91: 216,
  217; 109: 25
Matulay, Laszlo 5: 18; 43: 168
Matus, Greta 12: 142
Mauldin, Bill 27: 23
Mauterer, Erin Marie 119: 5
Mawicke, Tran 9: 137; 15: 191; 47: 100
Mawson, Matt 74: 115
Max, Peter 45: 146, 147, 148, 149, 150
Maxie, Betty 40: 135
Maxwell, John Alan 1: 148
Mayan, Earl 7: 193
Mayer, Danuta 117: 103
Mayer, Marianna 32: 132
Mayer, Mercer 11: 192; 16: 195, 196; 20: 55,
  57; 32: 129, 130, 132, 133, 134; 41: 144,
  248, 252; 58: 186; 73: 140, 142, 143; 137:
  137, 138
Mayforth, Hal 166: 77
Mayhew, James 85: 121; 138: 187; 149: 140
Mayhew, Richard 3: 106
Mayo, Gretchen Will 38: 81; 84: 166
Mays, Victor 5: 127; 8: 45, 153; 14: 245; 23:
  50; 34: 155; 40: 79; 45: 158; 54: 91; 66:
  240
Mazal, Chanan 49: 104
Maze, Deborah 71: 83
Mazellan, Ron 75: 97, 98
Mazetti, Alan 112: 72
Mazille, Capucine 96: 168
Mazza, Adriana Saviozzi 19: 215
Mazzella, Mary Jo 82: 165
Mazzetti, Alan 45: 210
McAfee, Steve 135: 146; 167: 176
McAlinden, Paul 112: 128
McBride, Angus 28: 49; 103: 40
McBride, Will 30: 110
McCaffery, Janet 38: 145
McCallum, Graham 78: 78
McCallum, Stephen 141: 143; 156: 5; 166:
  228
McCann, Gerald 3: 50; 4: 94; 7: 54; 41: 121
McCarthy, Dan 174: 74
McCarthy, Linda 177: 128
McCarthy, Meghan 168: 134
McCauley, Adam 157: 36
McCay, Winsor 41: 124, 126, 128, 129, 130,
  131; 134: 77, 79
McClary, Nelson 1: 111
McClintock, Barbara 57: 135; 95: 130; 146:
  190
McClintock, Theodore 14: 141
McCloskey, Robert 1: 184, 185; 2: 186, 187;
  17: 209; 39: 139, 140, 141, 142, 143, 146,
  147, 148; 85: 150, 151; 100: 172, 173, 174
McClung, Robert 2: 189; 68: 166, 167
McClure, Gillian 31: 132; 150: 53
McConnel, Jerry 31: 75, 187
McConnell, Mary 102: 49
McCord, Kathleen Garry 78: 236
McCormack, John 66: 193

McCormick, A.D. 35: 119
McCormick, Dell J. 19: 216
McCrady, Lady 16: 198; 39: 127
McCrea, James 3: 122; 33: 216
McCrea, Ruth 3: 122; 27: 102; 33: 216
McCue, Lisa 65: 148, 149; 77: 54; 80: 132;
  175: 33; 177: 133, 136
McCully, Emily Arnold 2: 89; 4: 120, 121,
  146, 197; 5: 2, 129; 7: 191; 11: 122; 15:
  210; 33: 23; 35: 244; 37: 122; 39: 88; 40:
  103; 50: 30,31, 32, 33, 34, 35, 36, 37; 52:
  89, 90; 57: 6; 62: 3; 70: 195; 86: 82; 96:
  192; 97: 93; 110: 143,144; 117: 47; 167: 96
McCurdy, Michael 13: 153; 24: 85; 81: 160;
  82: 157, 158; 86: 125; 97: 92; 117: 178;
  132: 6; 147: 159, 160
McCusker, Paul 99: 19
McDaniel, Jerry 132: 135
McDaniel, Preston 160: 206; 170: 139
McDermott, Beverly Brodsky 11: 180
McDermott, Gerald 16: 201; 74: 174, 175;
  163: 150, 151
McDermott, Mike 96: 187
McDonald, Jill 13: 155; 26: 128
McDonald, Mercedes 169: 118
McDonald, Ralph J. 5: 123, 195
McDonnell, Flora 146: 199, 200
McDonnell, Patrick 179: 153, 154
McDonough, Don 10: 163
McElmurry, Jill 137: 148; 163: 141
McElrath-Eslick, Lori 129: 145; 142: 21; 173:
  123
McEntee, Dorothy 37: 124
McEwan, Keith 88: 116; 165: 122, 123
McEwen, Katharine 169: 34
McFall, Christie 12: 144
McFeely, Daniel 160: 213
McGaw, Laurie 109: 243; 143: 216
McGee, Barbara 6: 165
McGee, Marni 163: 153
McGillvray, Kim 158: 171; 165: 213
McGinley-Nally, Sharon 131: 19
McGinnis, Robert 110: 113; 177: 80
McGovern, Tara 98: 171
McGraw, Sheila 83: 146
McGregor, Malcolm 23: 27
McGuirk, Leslie 152: 159
McHale, John 138: 190
McHugh, Tom 23: 64
McIntosh, Jon 42: 56
McKay, Donald 2: 118; 32: 157; 45: 151, 152
McKean, Dave 150: 71; 174: 156
McKeating, Eileen 44: 58
McKee, David 10: 48; 21: 9; 70: 154, 155;
  107: 139, 140, 141; 134: 218; 158: 148, 149,
  150, 151
McKee, Diana 109: 185
McKelvey, Patrick 164: 141
McKendry, Joe 170: 136
McKeveny, Tom 164: 60; 173: 79
McKie, Roy 7: 44
McKillip, Kathy 30: 153
McKinney, Ena 26: 39
McKinnon, James 136: 75
McKowen, Scott 172: 63
McLachlan, Edward 5: 89
McLaren, Chesley 133: 53
McLaren, Kirsty 123: 99; 124: 226
Mclean, Andrew 113: 117, 118, 120, 121; 172:
  130, 131
Mclean, Janet 172: 130
McLean, Meg 94: 196
McLean, Sammis 32: 197
McLean, Wilson 90: 29; 113: 195
McLoughlin, John C. 47: 149
McLoughlin, Wayne 102: 230; 134: 178
McMahon, Robert 36: 155; 69: 169
McManus, Shawn 85: 71
McMenemy, Sarah 156: 139
McMillan, Bruce 22: 184

McMullan, James *40:* 33; *67:* 172; *87:* 142; *99:* 63, 64
McMullen, Nigel *146:* 177
McNeely, Tom *162:* 55
McNaught, Harry *12:* 80; *32:* 136
McNaughton, Colin *39:* 149; *40:* 108; *92:* 144, 145, 146; *134:* 104, 106
McNicholas, Maureen *38:* 148
McNicholas, Shelagh *173:* 61
McPhail, David *14:* 105; *23:* 135; *37:* 217, 218, 220,221; *47:* 151, 152, 153, 154, 155, 156, 158, 159, 160, 162, 163, 164; *71:* 211; *81:* 139, 140, 142; *86:* 123; *132:* 150; *140:* 129, 131, 132
McPhee, Richard B. *41:* 133
McPheeters, Neal *78:* 132; *86:* 90; *99:* 162; *111:* 141; *142:* 162
McQuade, Jacqueline *124:* 223
McQueen, Lucinda *28:* 149; *41:* 249; *46:* 206; *53:* 103
McQuillan, Mary *153:* 97
McVay, Tracy *11:* 68
McVicker, Charles *39:* 150
Mead, Ben Carlton *43:* 75
Meade, Holly *90:* 102; *94:* 101; *149:* 8; *151:* 107
Mecray, John *33:* 62
Meddaugh, Susan *20:* 42; *29:* 143; *41:* 241; *77:* 50; *84:* 173, 174, 175, 176, 177, 178; *125:* 160, 161, 162; *176:* 148, 149, 150, 151
Meehan, Dennis B. *56:* 144
Meents, Len W. *73:* 147, 150
Meers, Tony *99:* 113
Meisel, Paul *98:* 137; *124:* 18; *162:* 180; *179:* 16
Melanson, Luc *149:* 229
Melendez, Francisco *72:* 180
Melnychuk, Monika *153:* 65
Melo, John *16:* 285; *58:* 203
Meloni, Maria Teresa *98:* 62
Meltzer, Ericka
    See O'Rourke, Ericka
Menasco, Milton *43:* 85
Mendelson, Steven T. *86:* 154
Mendelssohn, Felix *19:* 170
Mendola, Christopher *88:* 223
Meng, Heinz *13:* 158
Merian, Maria Sibylla *140:* 88
Mero, Lee *34:* 68
Merrill, Frank T. *16:* 147; *19:* 71; *YABC 1:* 226, 229,273
Merriman, Rachel *98:* 108; *114:* 122; *149:* 142
Meryman, Hope *27:* 41
Meryweather, Jack *10:* 179
Meseldzija, Petar *168:* 97
Messick, Dale *64:* 150, 151, 152
Meth, Harold *24:* 203
Meyer, Herbert *19:* 189
Meyer, Renate *6:* 170
Meyers, Bob *11:* 136
Meyers, Nancy *172:* 124
Meynell, Louis *37:* 76
Micale, Albert *2:* 65; *22:* 185
Miccuci, Charles *82:* 163; *144:* 150
Micich, Paul *164:* 163
Middleton, Jeffrey *177:* 173
Middleton-Sandford, Betty *2:* 125
Mieke, Anne *45:* 74
Mighell, Patricia *43:* 134
Miglio, Paige *101:* 203; *151:* 223
Mikolaycak, Charles *9:* 144; *12:* 101; *13:* 212; *21:* 121; *22:* 168; *30:* 187; *34:* 103, 150; *37:* 183; *43:* 179; *44:* 90; *46:* 115, 118, 119; *49:* 25; *78:* 121, 122, 205, 207; *81:* 4
Milelli, Pascal *129:* 66; *135:* 153
Miles, Elizabeth *117:* 77
Miles, Jennifer *17:* 278
Milgrim, David *158:* 157
Milhous, Katherine *15:* 193; *17:* 51
Millais, John E. *22:* 230, 231
Millar, H.R. *YABC 1:* 194, 195, 203

Millard, C.E. *28:* 186
Millard, Kerry *105:* 124
Miller, Don *15:* 195; *16:* 71; *20:* 106; *31:* 178
Miller, Edna *29:* 148
Miller, Edward *115:* 64
Miller, Frank J. *25:* 94
Miller, Grambs *18:* 38; *23:* 16
Miller, Ian *99:* 128
Miller, Jane *15:* 196
Miller, Marcia *13:* 233
Miller, Marilyn *1:* 87; *31:* 69; *33:* 157
Miller, Mitchell *28:* 183; *34:* 207
Miller, Phil *175:* 150
Miller, Shane *5:* 140
Miller, Virginia *81:* 206
Millman, Isaac *172:* 18
Mills, Elaine *72:* 181
Mills, Judith Christine *130:* 168, 169
Mills, Lauren *92:* 170
Mills, Yaroslava Surmach *35:* 169, 170; *46:* 114
Millsap, Darrel *51:* 102
Milone, Karen *89:* 169
Milord, Susan *147:* 163, 164
Milton, Debbie *162:* 161
Mims, Ashley *170:* 51
Miner, Julia *98:* 69
Minor, Wendell *39:* 188; *52:* 87; *56:* 171; *58:* 116; *62:* 56; *66:* 109; *74:* 93; *78:* 129; *94:* 67; *117:* 12, 13; *124:* 84, 86; *136:* 121; *164:* 168, 169; *170:* 71
Minter, Daniel *176:* 154; *179:* 177
Mirocha, Paul *81:* 133
Mitchell, Judith *109:* 117
Mitchell, Mark *91:* 208
Mitgutsch, Ali *76:* 161
Mitsuhashi, Yoko *45:* 153
Miyake, Yoshi *38:* 141
Mizumura, Kazue *10:* 143; *18:* 223; *36:* 159
Mochi, Ugo *8:* 122; *38:* 150
Mock, Paul *55:* 83; *123:* 32
Modarressi, Mitra *90:* 236; *126:* 168; *173:* 165, 166
Modell, Frank *39:* 152
Mogenson, Jan *74:* 183
Mohn, Susan *89:* 224
Mohr, Mark *133:* 201
Mohr, Nicholasa *8:* 139; *113:* 127
Molan, Christine *60:* 177; *84:* 183
Moldon, Peter L. *49:* 168
Molk, Laurel *92:* 150
Momaday, N. Scott *48:* 159
Mombourquette, Paul *112:* 91; *126:* 142
Monks, Julie *165:* 231
Montgomery, Lucy *150:* 126
Montgomery-Higham, Amanda *169:* 131
Montiel, David *69:* 106; *84:* 145
Montresor, Beni *2:* 91; *3:* 138; *38:* 152, 153, 154,155, 156, 157, 158, 159, 160; *68:* 63
Montserrat, Pep *128:* 135
Moon, Carl *25:* 183, 184, 185
Moon, Eliza *14:* 40
Moon, Ivan *22:* 39; *38:* 140
Moore, Adrienne *67:* 147
Moore, Agnes Kay Randall *43:* 187
Moore, Cyd *117:* 107, 108; *159:* 137, 138
Moore, Gustav *127:* 181, 182; *170:* 162, 163
Moore, Jackie *128:* 79
Moore, Janet *63:* 153
Moore, Margie *176:* 156
Moore, Mary *29:* 160
Moore, Yvette *101:* 11, 12; *154:* 141
Mora, Giovanni *179:* 127
Mora, Raul Mina *20:* 41
Moraes, Odilon *102:* 144
Morales, Yuyi *154:* 144
Moran, Rosslyn *111:* 26
Moran, Tom *60:* 100
Mordvinoff, Nicolas *15:* 179
Moreno, René King *169:* 59
Morgan, Barbara *169:* 116

Morgan, Jacqui *58:* 57
Morgan, Mary *114:* 133, 134, 135; *123:* 11
Morgan, Tom *42:* 157
Morgan, Pierr *173:* 148
Morgenstern, Michael *158:* 7, 57; *171:* 103; *174:* 60
Morice, Dave *93:* 142
Morin, Paul *73:* 132; *79:* 130; *88:* 140; *137:* 143
Moriuchi, Mique *177:* 203
Morozumi, Atsuko *110:* 155
Morrill, Leslie *18:* 218; *29:* 177; *33:* 84; *38:* 147; *42:* 127; *44:* 93; *48:* 164, 165, 167, 168, 169, 170,171; *49:* 162; *63:* 136, 180; *70:* 72; *71:* 70, 91,92; *72:* 228; *80:* 163, 164, 165; *90:* 121; *121:* 88; *178:* 117
Morrill, Rowena A. *84:* 16; *98:* 163
Morris *47:* 91
Morris, Frank *55:* 133; *60:* 28; *76:* 2
Morris, Harry O. *119:* 138
Morris, Jackie *128:* 194; *144:* 119; *151:* 146
Morris, Jennifer E. *179:* 157
Morris, Oradel Nolen *128:* 180
Morris, Tony *62:* 146; *70:* 97
Morrison, Bill *42:* 116; *66:* 170; *69:* 40
Morrison, Gordon *87:* 150; *113:* 93; *128:* 181, 182
Morrison, Frank *169:* 162
Morrison, Taylor *159:* 144, 145
Morrow, Gray *2:* 64; *5:* 200; *10:* 103, 114; *14:* 175
Morton, Lee Jack *32:* 140
Morton, Marian *3:* 185
Mosberg, Hilary *117:* 195; *118:* 164; *149:* 55
Moser, Barry *56:* 68, 117, 118, 119, 120, 121, 122, 123, 124; *59:* 141; *60:* 160; *79:* 91, 147, 149, 151, 152; *82:* 81; *90:* 118; *91:* 35; *95:* 210; *97:* 91, 93; *102:* 152; *126:* 4; *128:* 175; *133:* 141; *138:* 167, 171, 174; *153:* 205; *174:* 130
Moser, Cara *90:* 118; *138:* 167
Moses, Grandma *18:* 228
Moses, Will *178:* 170, 171
Moskof, Martin Stephen *27:* 152
Mosley, Francis *57:* 144
Moss, Donald *11:* 184
Moss, Geoffrey *32:* 198
Moss, Marissa *71:* 130; *104:* 127; *163:* 156
Most, Bernard *48:* 91; *142, 143; *134:* 120
Mowry, Carmen *50:* 62
Moxley, Sheila *96:* 174; *169:* 26
Moyers, William *21:* 65
Moyler, Alan *36:* 142
Mozley, Charles *9:* 87; *20:* 176, 192, 193; *22:* 228; *25:* 205; *33:* 150; *43:* 170, 171, 172, 173, 174; *YABC2:* 89
Mueller, Hans Alexander *26:* 64; *27:* 52, 53
Mugnaini, Joseph *11:* 35; *27:* 52, 53; *35:* 62
Mujica, Rick *72:* 67; *88:* 95; *111:* 53
Muller, Robin *86:* 161
Muller, Steven *32:* 167
Muller, Jorg *35:* 215; *67:* 138, 139
Mulock, Julie *163:* 112
Mullins, Edward S. *10:* 101
Mullins, Patricia *51:* 68
Multer, Scott *80:* 108
Munari, Bruno *15:* 200
Munch, Edvard *140:* 143
Munowitz, Ken *14:* 148; *72:* 178, 179
Munro, Roxie *58:* 134; *136:* 177; *137:* 218
Munsinger, Lynn *33:* 161; *46:* 126; *71:* 92; *82:* 80; *89:* 218; *92:* 125; *94:* 157, 158, 159, 160; *98:* 196; *103:* 198; *142:* 143; *145:* 133, 134, 136; *153:* 203; *176:* 162; *177:* 140, 141, 142
Munson, Russell *13:* 9
Munster, Sebastian *166:* 107
Munoz, William *42:* 160
Munzar, Barbara *149:* 75
Murdocca, Salvatore *73:* 212; *98:* 132; *111:* 168; *157:* 228; *164:* 257

Murphy, Bill 5: 138; *130:* 170
Murphy, Jill 37: 142; *70:* 166; *142:* 132, 134
Murphy, Kelly *130:* 212; *143:* 119; *176:* 158
Murr, Karl 20: 62
Murray, Joe *175:* 37
Murray, Ossie 43: 176
Mussino, Attilio 29: 131; *100:* 164
Mutchler, Dwight *1:* 25
Myers, Bernice 9: 147; *36:* 75; *81:* 146, 147, 148
Muth, Jon J. *165:* 169; *167:* 109
Myers, Duane O. 99: 145
Myers, Tim *147:* 168
Myers, V.G. *142:* 41
Myers, Lou *11:* 2

N

Nachreiner, Tom 29: 182
Nacht, Merle 65: 49
Nadler, Ellis 88: 91
Najaka, Marlies 62: 101
Nakai, Michael 30: 217; *54:* 29
Nakata, Hiroe *157:* 156; *162:* 30
Nakatani, Chiyoko 12: 124
Narahashi, Keiko 77: 188; *82:* 213; *115:* 142, 143, 144
Nascimbene, Yan *133:* 128; *173:* 132, 133
Nash, Lesa 87: 135
Nash, Linell 46: 175
Nash, Scott *130:* 36
Naso, John 33: 183
Nason, Thomas W. *14:* 68
Nasser, Muriel 48: 74
Nast, Thomas 21: 29; *28:* 23; *51:* 132, 133, 134, 135,136, 137, 138, 139, 141
Nasta, Vincent 78: 185
Natale, Vincent 76: 3; *78:* 125; *112:* 47; *166:* 81; *174:* 189
Natchev, Alexi 96: 177
Nathan, Charlott *125:* 151
Nathan, Cheryl *150:* 104
Natti, Susanna 20: 146; *32:* 141, 142; *35:* 178; *37:* 143; *71:* 49; *93:* 98; *125:* 166, 168; *126:* 228; *151:* 6; *178:* 8
Navarra, Celeste Scala 8: 142
Naylor, Penelope 10: 104
Nazz, James 72: 8
Nebel, M. *45:* 154
Neebe, William 7: 93
Needler, Jerry 12: 93
Neel, Alice 31: 23
Neely, Beth *119:* 184
Neely, Keith R. 46: 124
Neff, Leland 78: 74
Negri, Rocco 3: 213; *5:* 67; *6:* 91, 108; *12:* 159
Negrin, Fabian *174:* 125; *175:* 15
Neidigh, Sherry *128:* 53
Neill, John R. *18:* 8, 10, 11, 21, 30; *100:* 22
Neilsen, Cliff *158:* 131; *177:* 112, 121
Neilsen, Terese *116:* 74
Nelson, Craig 62: 151; *153*
Nelson, Gail White 68: 140
Nelson, Jennifer *129:* 152
Nelson, Kadir *151:* 185; *154:* 146, 147; *157:* 189, 222
Nelson, S.D. *131:* 34
Ness, Evaline *1:* 164, 165; *2:* 39; *3:* 8; *10:* 147; *12:* 53; *26:* 150, 151, 152, 153; *49:* 30, 31, 32; *56:* 30; *60:* 113
Neubecker, Robert *170:* 143
Neville, Vera 2: 182
Nevwirth, Allan 79: 168
Newberry, Clare Turlay *1:* 170
Newbold, Greg *108:* 125; *145:* 199; *151:* 23
Newfeld, Frank *14:* 121; *26:* 154
Newman, Andy *149:* 61
Newman, Ann 43: 90

Newsham, Ian *143:* 162
Newsom, Carol 40: 159; *44:* 60; *47:* 189; *65:* 29; *70:* 192; *80:* 36; *85:* 137, 138; *92:* 167
Newsom, Tom 49: 149; *71:* 13, 62; *75:* 156; *91:* 113
Newton, Jill 83: 105
Ng, Michael 29: 171
Ng, Simon *167:* 7
Nicholson, William 15: 33, 34; *16:* 48
Nickens, Bessie *104:* 153
Nicklaus, Carol 45: 194; *62:* 132, 133
Nickless, Will 16: 139
Nicholas, Corasue *154:* 20
Nicolas 17: 130, 132, 133; *YABC 2:* 215
Niebrugge, Jane 6: 118
Nielsen, Jon 6: 100; *24:* 202
Nielsen, Kay 15: 7; *16:* 211, 212, 213, 215, 217; *22:* 143; *YABC 1:* 32, 33
Nielson, Cliff 95: 207, 208; *105:* 58; *114:* 112; *124:* 12; *125:* 91, 92; *132:* 224; *135:* 187; *136:* 40; *137:* 168; *145:* 54; *149:* 28; *158:* 129; *165:* 64, 158; *168:* 169; *170:* 6; *175:* 114, 116
Niland, Deborah 25: 191; *27:* 156; *135:* 50; *172:* 143
Niland, Kilmeny 25: 191; *75:* 143
Nino, Alex 59: 145
Ninon *1:* 5; *38:* 101, 103, 108
Nissen, Rie 44: 35
Nithael, Mark *158:* 237
Nivola, Claire A. 78: 126; *140:* 147
Nixon, K. *14:* 152
Noble, Louise 61: 170
Noble, Marty 97: 168; *125:* 171
Noble, Trinka Hakes 39: 162; *84:* 157
Noda, Takayo *168:* 143
Noguchi, Yoshie 30: 99
Nolan, Dennis 42: 163; *67:* 163; *78:* 189; *82:* 225; *83:* 26; *92:* 169, 170; *103:* 166; *111:* 35; *112:* 213; *127:* 171; *166:* 161
Noll, Sally 82: 171
Nolte, Larry *121:* 63, 65
Nones, Eric Jon 61: 111; *76:* 38; *77:* 177
Noonan, Daniel *100:* 224
Noonan, Julia 4: 163; *7:* 207; *25:* 151; *91:* 29; *95:* 149
Norcia, Ernie *108:* 155; *140:* 47
Nordenskjold, Birgitta 2: 208
Noreika, Robert *173:* 20
Norling, Beth *149:* 153, 154
Norman, Elaine 77: 72, 176; *94:* 35; *136:* 63; *178:* 42
Norman, Mary 36: 138, 147
Norman, Michael 12: 117; *27:* 168
Northway, Jennifer 85: 96
Nostlinger, Christiana *162:* 131
Novak, Linda *166:* 205
Novak, Matt *104:* 132, 133; *165:* 173, 174
Novelli, Luca 61: 137
Nugent, Cynthia *106:* 189
Numeroff, Laura Joffe 28: 161; *30:* 177
Nurse, Chris *164:* 91
Nussbaumer, Paul 16: 219; *39:* 117
Nutt, Ken 72: 69; *97:* 170
Nyce, Helene 19: 219
Nygren, Tord 30: 148; *127:* 164

O

Oakley, Graham 8: 112; *30:* 164, 165; *84:* 188,189, 190, 191, 192
Oakley, Thornton *YABC 2:* 189
Oberheide, Heide *118:* 37
Obligado, Lilian 2: 28, 66, 67; *6:* 30; *14:* 179; *15:* 103; *25:* 84; *61:* 138, 139, 140, 141, 143
Obrant, Susan *11:* 186
O'Brien, Anne Sibley 53: 116, 117; *155:* 115
O'Brien, John 41: 253; *72:* 12; *89:* 59, 60; *98:* 16; *161:* 185; *169:* 16

O'Brien, Teresa 87: 89
O'Brien, Tim 93: 25; *136:* 94; *164:* 57; *169:* 57; *173:* 55; *175:* 86
O'Clair, Dennis *127:* 25
Odell, Carole 35: 47
Odem, Mel 99: 164; *167:* 84, 87
O'Donohue, Thomas 40: 89
Oechsli, Kelly 5: 144, 145; *7:* 115; *8:* 83, 183; *13:* 117; *20:* 94; *81:* 199
Offen, Hilda 42: 207
Ogden, Bill 42: 59; *47:* 55
Ogg, Oscar 33: 34
Ogle, Nancy Gray *163:* 144
Ohi, Ruth 90: 175, 177; *131:* 63; *135:* 106; *175:* 107; *179:* 55
Ohlsson, Ib 4: 152; *7:* 57; *10:* 20; *11:* 90; *19:* 217; *41:* 246; *82:* 106; *92:* 213
Ohtomo, Yasuo 37: 146; *39:* 212, 213
O'Keefe, Jennifer *136:* 184
O'Kelley, Mattie Lou 36: 150
Olbinski, Rafal *149:* 27; *158:* 77
Oliver, Isaac *171:* 182
Oliver, Jenni 23: 121; *35:* 112
Oliver, Narelle *152:* 192
Oller, Erika *128:* 186; *134:* 126
Olschewski, Alfred 7: 172
Olsen, Ib Spang 6: 178, 179; *81:* 164
Olson, Alan 77: 229
Olugebefola, Ademola 15: 205
O'Malley, Kevin 94: 180; *106:* 8; *113:* 108; *136:* 70; *157:* 193
O'Neil, Dan IV 7: 176
O'Neill, Catharine 72: 113; *84:* 78; *134:* 153
O'Neill, Jean 22: 146
O'Neill, Michael J. 54: 172
O'Neill, Rose 48: 30, 31
O'Neill, Steve 21: 118
Ono, Chiyo 7: 97
Orbaan, Albert 2: 31; *5:* 65, 171; *9:* 8; *14:* 241; *20:* 109
Orbach, Ruth 21: 112
Orfe, Joan 20: 81
Org, Ed 119: 93
Ormai, Stella 72: 129
Ormerod, Jan 55: 124; *70:* 170, 171; *90:* 39; *132:* 172, 173, 174; *147:* 98
Ormsby, Virginia H. *11:* 187
O'Rourke, Ericka *108:* 216; *117:* 194; *111:* 142; *119:* 194; *137:* 152; *150:* 134; *167:* 64; *172:* 164
O'Rourke, Ericka Meltzer
  See O'Rourke, Ericka
Orozco, Jose Clemente 9: 177
Orr, Forrest W. 23: 9
Orr, N. *19:* 70
Ortiz, Vilma 88: 158
Osborn, Cathy *152:* 232
Osborn, Robert 65: 49
Osborne, Billie Jean 35: 209
Osmond, Edward 10: 111
O'Sullivan, Tom 3: 176; *4:* 55; *78:* 195
Otani, June *124:* 42; *156:* 53
Ottley, Matt *147:* 221; *171:* 133
Otto, Svend 22: 130, 141; *67:* 188, 189
Oudry, J.B. *18:* 167
Oughton, Taylor 5: 23; *104:* 136
Overeng, Johannes 44: 36
Overlie, George *11:* 156
Owens, Carl 2: 35; *23:* 521
Owens, Gail 10: 170; *12:* 157; *19:* 16; *22:* 70; *25:* 81; *28:* 203, 205; *32:* 221, 222; *36:* 132; *46:* 40; *47:* 57; *54:* 66, 67, 68, 69, 70, 71, 72, 73; *71:* 100; *73:* 64; *77:* 157; *80:* 32; *82:* 3; *99:* 226
Owens, Mary Beth *113:* 202, 203
Owens, Nubia 84: 74
Oxenbury, Helen 3: 150, 151; *24:* 81; *68:* 174, 175,176; *81:* 209; *84:* 213, 245; *129:* 56; *149:* 159
Oz, Robin 88: 167

P

Padgett, Jim *12:* 165
Page, Homer *14:* 145
Page, Mark *162:* 70
Paget, Sidney *24:* 90, 91, 93, 95, 97
Paget, Walter *64:* 122
Paillot, Jim *173:* 89
Pajouhesh, Noushin *160:* 121
Pak *12:* 76
Pak, Yu Cha *86:* 174
Paladino, Lance *134:* 30
Palazzo, Tony *3:* 152, 153
Palecek, Josef *56:* 136; *89:* 158
Palen, Debbie *135:* 88
Palencar, John Jude *84:* 12, 45; *85:* 87; *92:* 187; *99:* 128; *110:* 204; *150:* 122; *171:* 86
Palin, Nicki *81:* 201; *89:* 161
Palladini, David *4:* 113; *40:* 176, 177, 178, 179, 181,224, 225; *50:* 138; *78:* 186
Pallarito, Don *43:* 36
Palmer, Carol *158:* 230
Palmer, Heidi *15:* 207; *29:* 102
Palmer, Jan *42:* 153; *82:* 161
Palmer, Judd *153:* 160, 161
Palmer, Juliette *6:* 89; *15:* 208
Palmer, Kate Salley *104:* 143; *154:* 169
Palmer, Lemuel *17:* 25, 29
Palmisciano, Diane *110:* 62; *162:* 26
Palmquist, Eric *38:* 133
Panesis, Nicholas *3:* 127
Panton, Doug *52:* 99
Paparone, Pamela *129:* 174
Papas, William *11:* 223; *50:* 160
Papin, Joseph *26:* 113
Papish, Robin Lloyd *10:* 80
Paradis, Susan *40:* 216
Paraquin, Charles H. *18:* 166
Paris, Peter *31:* 127
Parisi, Elizabeth B. *141:* 82; *164:* 57
Park, Nick *113:* 143
Park, Seho *39:* 110
Park, W.B. *22:* 189
Parker, Ant *82:* 87, 88; *104:* 121
Parker, Lewis *2:* 179
Parker, Nancy Winslow *10:* 113; *22:* 164; *28:* 47, 144; *52:* 7; *69:* 153; *91:* 171, 174; *132:* 175
Parker, Robert *4:* 161; *5:* 74; *9:* 136; *29:* 39
Parker, Robert Andrew *11:* 81; *29:* 186; *39:* 165; *40:* 25; *41:* 78; *42:* 123; *43:* 144; *48:* 182; *54:* 140; *74:* 141; *91:* 24; *111:* 115; *151:* 201; *154:* 156
Parker-Rees, Guy *149:* 145
Parkin, Trevor *140:* 151
Parkins, David *114:* 123; *146:* 176; *176:* 168
Parkinson, Kathy *71:* 143; *144:* 234
Parkinson, Keith *70:* 66
Parks, Gordon, Jr. *33:* 228
Parnall, Peter *5:* 137; *16:* 221; *24:* 70; *40:* 78; *51:* 130; *69:* 17, 155; *136:* 22, 23, 24
Parnall, Virginia *40:* 78
Parow, Lorraine *158:* 127
Parr, Todd *134:* 139, 140; *179:* 163, 164, 165
Parrish, Anne *27:* 159, 160
Parrish, Dillwyn *27:* 159
Parrish, Maxfield *14:* 160, 161, 164, 165; *16:* 109; *18:* 12, 13; *YABC 1:* 149, 152, 267; *2:* 146, 149
Parry, David *26:* 156
Parry, Marian *13:* 176; *19:* 179
Partch, Virgil *45:* 163, 165
Pascal, David *14:* 174
Paschkis, Julie *177:* 153, 154
Pasquier, J.A. *16:* 91
Pasternak, Robert *119:* 53
Paterson, Diane *13:* 116; *39:* 163; *59:* 164, 165, 166,167; *72:* 51, 53; *129:* 175; *177:* 156, 157
Paterson, Helen *16:* 93

Patkau, Karen *112:* 123
Paton, Jane *15:* 271; *35:* 176
Patrick, John *139:* 190
Patrick, Pamela *90:* 160; *93:* 211; *105:* 12
Patterson, Geoffrey *54:* 75
Patterson, Robert *25:* 118
Patz, Nancy *111:* 40; *154:* 161
Paul, James *4:* 130; *23:* 161
Paul, Korky *102:* 85
Paull, Grace *24:* 157; *87:* 127
Paulsen, Ruth Wright *79:* 160, 164
Pavlov, Elena *80:* 49
Payne, Adam S. *135:* 166
Payne, C.F. *145:* 138, 140; *179:* 168
Payne, Joan Balfour *1:* 118
Payne, Tom *170:* 27
Payson, Dale *7:* 34; *9:* 151; *20:* 140; *37:* 22
Payzant, Charles *21:* 147
Peacock, Ralph *64:* 118
Peake, Mervyn *22:* 136, 149; *23:* 162, 163, 164; *YABC2:* 307
Pearson, Larry *38:* 225
Pearson, Tracey Campbell *64:* 163, 164, 167, 168, 169; *118:* 51; *156:* 169, 171, 172; *163:* 140
Peat, Fern B. *16:* 115
Peck, Anne Merriman *18:* 241; *24:* 155
Peck, Beth *66:* 242; *79:* 166; *80:* 136; *91:* 34; *95:* 9; *101:* 77; *164:* 197
Pedersen, Judy *66:* 217; *121:* 36; *172:* 67
Pedersen, Vilhelm *YABC 1:* 40
Pederson, Sharleen *12:* 92
Pedlar, Elaine *161:* 45
Peek, Merle *39:* 168
Peet, Bill *2:* 203; *41:* 159, 160, 161, 162, 163; *78:* 158, 159, 160, 161
Peguero, Adrian *116:* 133
Peguero, Gerard *116:* 133
Pels, Winslow Pinney *55:* 126
Peltier, Leslie C. *13:* 178
Penberthy, Mark *171:* 78
Pendle, Alexy *7:* 159; *13:* 34; *29:* 161; *33:* 215; *86:* 62
Pendola, Joanne *76:* 203; *81:* 125; *105:* 181; *178:* 152, 153
Pene du Bois, William *4:* 70; *10:* 122; *26:* 61; *27:* 145, 211; *35:* 243; *41:* 216; *68:* 180, 181; *73:* 45
Penfound, David *102:* 185
Pennington, Eunice *27:* 162
Peppe, Mark *28:* 142
Peppe, Rodney *4:* 164, 165; *74:* 187, 188, 189
Pepper, Hubert *64:* 143
Percy, Graham *63:* 2
Pericoli, Matteo *178:* 177
Perini, Ben *173:* 77
Perkins, David *60:* 68
Perkins, Lucy Fitch *72:* 199
Perkins, Lynne Rae *172:* 146
Perl, Susan *2:* 98; *4:* 231; *5:* 44, 45, 118; *6:* 199; *8:* 137; *12:* 88; *22:* 193; *34:* 54, 55; *52:* 128; *YABC 1:* 176
Perrone, Donna *78:* 166
Perry, Marie Fritz *165:* 180
Perry, Patricia *29:* 137; *30:* 171
Perry, Roger *27:* 163
Perske, Martha *46:* 83; *51:* 108, 147
Persson, Stina *175:* 166
Pesek, Ludek *15:* 237
Petach, Heidi *149:* 166
Peters, David *72:* 205
Petersham, Maud *17:* 108, 147, 148, 149, 150, 151, 152, 153
Petersham, Miska *17:* 108, 147, 148, 149, 150, 151, 152, 153
Peterson, Eric *109:* 125
Peterson, Nisse *99:* 27
Peterson, R.F. *7:* 101
Peterson, Russell *7:* 130
Petie, Haris *2:* 3; *10:* 41, 118; *11:* 227; *12:* 70

Petricic, Dusan *153:* 75, 76, 77; *170:* 12; *172:* 13; *176:* 170; *179:* 56
Petrides, Heidrun *19:* 223
Petrone, Valeria *159:* 160; *171:* 92
Petrosino, Tamara *177:* 40
Petruccio, Steven James *67:* 159; *127:* 5
Pettingill, Ondre *64:* 181; *70:* 64
Peyo *40:* 56, 57
Peyton, K.M. *15:* 212
Pfeifer, Herman *15:* 262
Pfister, Marcus *83:* 165, 166, 167; *146:* 152; *150:* 160
Pfloog, Jan *124:* 60
Pham, LeUyen *160:* 48; *175:* 154, 156; *179:* 149
Phillips, Craig *70:* 151
Phillips, Douglas *1:* 19
Phillips, F.D. *6:* 202
Phillips, Louise *133:* 67
Phillips, Thomas *30:* 55
Philpot, Glyn *54:* 46
Phiz
    See Browne, Hablot K.
Piatti, Celestino *16:* 223
Pica, Steve *115:* 181
Picarella, Joseph *13:* 147
Picart, Gabriel *121:* 165
Pichon, Liz *174:* 139
Pickard, Charles *12:* 38; *18:* 203; *36:* 152
Picken, George A. *23:* 150
Pickens, David *22:* 156
Pienkowski, Jan *6:* 183; *30:* 32; *58:* 140, 141, 142,143, 146, 147; *73:* 3; *87:* 156, 157; *131:* 189
Pignataro, Anna *163:* 220 *Pileggi, Steve 145:* 122
Pilkey, Dav *68:* 186; *115:* 164, 166; *166:* 173, 174, 175
Pimlott, John *10:* 205
Pincus, Harriet *4:* 186; *8:* 179; *22:* 148; *27:* 164, 165; *66:* 202
Pini, Wendy *89:* 166
Pinkett, Neil *60:* 8
Pinkney, Brian *81:* 184, 185; *94:* 107; *113:* 146, 147; *117:* 121, 166; *132:* 145; *158:* 108, 191; *160:* 189
Pinkney, Jerry *8:* 218; *10:* 40; *15:* 276; *20:* 66; *24:* 121; *33:* 109; *36:* 222; *38:* 200; *41:* 165, 166, 167, 168, 169, 170, 171, 173, 174; *44:* 198; *48:* 51; *53:* 20; *56:* 61, 68; *58:* 184; *60:* 59; *61:* 91; *71:* 146, 148, 149; *72:* 17; *73:* 149; *74:* 159,192; *75:* 45; *80:* 206; *81:* 44; *85:* 144; *95:* 50; *107:* 158, 159, 160; *108:* 164; *112:* 114, 115; *133:* 58
Pinkwater, Daniel Manus *46:* 180, 181, 182, 185, 188, 189, 190; *151:* 161 *76:* 178, 179, 180
Pinkwater, Manus *8:* 156; *46:* 180
    See also Pinkwater, Daniel Manus
Pinkwater, Jill *114:* 160, 161; *158:* 179
Pinto, Ralph *10:* 131; *45:* 93
Pinon, Mark *74:* 22
Piven, Hanoch *173:* 142
Pistolesi *73:* 211
Pittman, Helena Clare *71:* 151
Pitz, Henry C. *4:* 168; *19:* 165; *35:* 128; *42:* 80; *YABC 2:* 95, 176
Pitzenberger, Lawrence J. *26:* 94
Player, Stephen *82:* 190
Plecas, Jennifer *84:* 201; *106:* 124; *149:* 168
Plowden, David *52:* 135, 136
Plume, Ilse *170:* 149
Plummer, William *32:* 31
Podwal, Mark *56:* 170, 173; *101:* 154, 155, 157; *149:* 176; *160:* 199
Pogany, Willy *15:* 46, 49; *19:* 222, 256; *25:* 214; *44:* 142, 143, 144, 145, 146, 147, 148
Pohrt, Tom *67:* 116; *104:* 80; *152:* 199
Poirson, V.A. *26:* 89
Polacco, Patricia *74:* 195, 196, 197, 198; *123:* 121, 122, 123

Polgreen, John *21:* 44
Politi, Leo *1:* 178; *4:* 53; *21:* 48; *47:* 173,174, 176, 178, 179, 180, 181
Pollema-Cahill, Phyllis *123:* 126
Pollen, Samson *64:* 80
Polonsky, Arthur *34:* 168
Polseno, Jo *1:* 53; *3:* 117; *5:* 114; *17:* 154; *20:* 87; *32:* 49; *41:* 245
Pomaska, Anna *117:* 148
Ponter, James *5:* 204
Poole, Colin *111:* 27
Poortvliet, Rien *6:* 212; *65:* 165, 166, 167
Popp, Wendy *72:* 122; *158:* 68
Poppel, Hans *71:* 154, 155
Porfirio, Guy *76:* 134
Portal, Colette *6:* 186; *11:* 203
Porter, George *7:* 181
Porter, Janice Lee *136:* 175; *164:* 37
Porter, John *113:* 47
Porter, Pat Grant *84:* 112; *125:* 101
Porter, Sue *146:* 246, 247
Porter, Walter *124:* 175
Posen, Michael *175:* 82
Posthuma, Sieb *150:* 163
Postma, Lidia *79:* 17
Potter, Beatrix *100:* 194, 195; *132:* 179, 180, 181, 182; *YABC 1:* 208, 209, 210, 212, 213
Potter, Giselle *117:* 123; *143:* 44; *144:* 170, 197; *149:* 7; *150:* 165
Potter, Katherine *104:* 147; *171:* 135; *173:* 136
Potter, Miriam Clark *3:* 162
Poulin, Stephane *98:* 140, 141
Poullis, Nick *146:* 210
Powell, Constance Buffington *174:* 141
Powell, Gary *151:* 208
Powell, Ivan *67:* 219
Power, Margaret *105:* 122
Powers, Daniel *161:* 173
Powers, Richard M. *1:* 230; *3:* 218; *7:* 194; *26:* 186
Powledge, Fred *37:* 154
Powzyk, Joyce *74:* 214
Poydar, Nancy *96:* 149
Pracher, Richard *91:* 166
Prachaticka, Marketa *126:* 126
Prap, Lila *177:* 165
Prater, John *103:* 142, 143, 144; *149:* 172
Pratt, Charles *23:* 29
Pratt, George *116:* 208
Pratt, Pierre *150:* 73; *166:* 183; *168:* 172
Prebenna, David *73:* 174
Preiss-Glasser, Robin *123:* 176; *152* 40; *172:* 194
Press, Jenny *116:* 95
Preston, Mark *152:* 162
Pretro, Korinna *91:* 126
Price, Christine *2:* 247; *3:* 163, 253; *8:* 166
Price, Cynthia *118:* 156
Price, Edward *33:* 34
Price, Garrett *1:* 76; *2:* 42
Price, Hattie Longstreet *17:* 13
Price, Norman *YABC 1:* 129
Price, Willard *48:* 184
Priceman, Marjorie *81:* 171; *136:* 169; *156:* 200; *168:* 153, 154
Priestley, Alice *168:* 33
Primavera, Elise *26:* 95; *58:* 151; *73:* 37; *80:* 79; *86:* 156; *105:* 161
Primrose, Jean *36:* 109
Prince, Alison *86:* 188, 189
Prince, Leonora E. *7:* 170
Pritchett, Shelley *116:* 148
Prittie, Edwin J. *YABC 1:* 120
Proimos, James *176:* 4
Proimos, John *173:* 144
Prosmitsky, Jenya *132:* 33
Provensen, Alice *37:* 204, 215, 222; *70:* 176, 177, 178, 180, *71:* 213; *147:* 184
Provensen, Martin *37:* 204, 215, 222; *70:* 176, 177, 178, 180; *71:* 213
Pucci, Albert John *44:* 154

Pudlo *8:* 59
Pulver, Harry, Jr. *129:* 159
Pulver, Robin *160:* 4
Punchatz, Don *99:* 57
Purdy, Susan *8:* 162
Pursell, Weimer *55:* 18
Purtscher, Alfons *97:* 6
Puskas, James *5:* 141
Pyk, Jan *7:* 26; *38:* 123
Pyle, Chuck *99:* 149
Pyle, Howard *16:* 225, 226, 227, 228, 230, 231, 232, 235; *24:* 27; *34:* 124, 125, 127, 128; *59:* 132; *100:* 198

Q

Quackenbush, Robert *4:* 190; *6:* 166; *7:* 175, 178; *9:* 86; *11:* 65, 221; *41:* 154; *43:* 157; *70:* 185, 186; *71:* 137; *85:* 47; *92:* 148; *133:* 154, 164, 169
Qualls, Sean *177:* 167, 168
Quennell, Marjorie (Courtney) *29:* 163, 164
Quidor, John *19:* 82
Quirk, John *62:* 170
Quirk, Thomas *12:* 81

R

Rackham, Arthur *15:* 32, 78, 214-227; *17:* 105, 115; *18:* 233; *19:* 254; *20:* 151; *22:* 129, 131, 132, 133; *23:* 175; *24:* 161, 181; *26:* 91; *32:* 118; *64:* 18; *100:* 9, 16, 203, 204; *YABC 1:* 25, 45, 55, 147; *2:* 103, 142, 173, 210
Racz, Michael *56:* 134
Radcliffe, Andrew *82:* 215
Rader, Laura *101:* 219
Radunsky, Vladimir *177:* 170
Rafilson, Sidney *11:* 172
Raglin, Tim *125:* 24
Raible, Alton *1:* 202, 203; *28:* 193; *35:* 181; *110:* 207
Raine, Patricia *82:* 74; *88:* 154
Rama, Sue *173:* 45
Ramhorst, John *117:* 11
Ramirez, Gladys *177:* 19
Ramsey, James *16:* 41
Ramsey, Marcy Dunn *82:* 11
Ramus, Michael *51:* 171
Rand, Paul *6:* 188
Rand, Ted *67:* 9, 10, 121, 123; *74:* 190; *84:* 170; *103:* 170; *112:* 6; *114:* 73; *139:* 168; *143:* 194; *156:* 154; *161:* 9, 10
Randazzo, Tony *81:* 98
Randell, William *55:* 54
Rane, Walter *93:* 144; *143:* 109
Rankin, Joan *163:* 40
Rankin, Laura *176:* 173, 174; *179:* 150
Ransome, Arthur *22:* 201
Ransome, James E. *74:* 137; *75:* 80; *84:* 181; *94:* 108; *117:* 115; *123:* 128, 129, 130; *158:* 101, 102; *159:* 205; *178:* 188, 189, 190
Rantz, Don *119:* 184
Rao, Anthony *28:* 126
Raphael, Elaine *23:* 192; *71:* 24, 25
Rappaport, Eva *6:* 190
Raschka, Chris *80:* 187, 189, 190; *97:* 211; *115:* 210; *117:* 151, 152, 153, 154; *143:* 195; *145:* 153; *166:* 190, 191; *170:* 114
Rash, Andy *158:* 178; *162:* 172
Raskin, Ellen *2:* 208, 209; *4:* 142; *13:* 183; *22:* 68; *29:* 139; *36:* 134; *38:* 173, 174, 175, 176, 177, 178,179, 180, 181; *60:* 163; *86:* 81
Rathmann, Peggy *93:* 32; *94:* 168; *157:* 212, 214
Ratkus, Tony *77:* 133

Ratzkin, Lawrence *40:* 143
Rau, Margaret *9:* 157
Raverat, Gwen *YABC 1:* 152
Ravid, Joyce *61:* 73
Ravielli, Anthony *1:* 198; *3:* 168; *11:* 143
Ravilious, Robin *77:* 169
Rawlins, Donna *72:* 198; *73:* 15, 129
Rawlins, Janet *76:* 79
Rawlings, Steve *143:* 139; *151:* 54
Rawlinson, Debbie *75:* 132
Ray, Deborah Kogan *8:* 164; *29:* 238; *50:* 112, 113; *62:* 119; *78:* 191
Ray, Jane *96:* 166; *97:* 104; *152:* 208
Ray, Ralph *2:* 239; *5:* 73
Rayann, Omar *162:* 205
Rayevsky, Robert *64:* 17; *70:* 173; *80:* 204; *117:* 79
Raymond, Larry *31:* 108; *97:* 109
Rayner, Hugh *151:* 170
Rayner, Mary *22:* 207; *47:* 140; *72:* 191; *87:* 171, 172
Rayner, Shoo
    See Rayner, Hugh
Raynes, John *71:* 19
Raynor, Dorka *28:* 168
Raynor, Paul *24:* 73
Rayyan, Omar *110:* 222; *112:* 17; *125:* 131
Razzi, James *10:* 127
Read, Alexander D. *20:* 45
Reader, Dennis *71:* 157
Reasoner, Charles *53:* 33, 36, 37
Reczuch, Karen *115:* 132; *145:* 131
Redlich, Ben *163:* 221
Reed, Joseph *116:* 139
Reed, Lynn Rowe *115:* 173; *171:* 146
Reed, Tom *34:* 171
Reeder, Colin *74:* 202; *77:* 113
Rees, Mary *134:* 219
Reese, Bob *60:* 135
Reeve, Philip *171:* 50
Reeves, Eira B. *130:* 173, 174; *141:* 151
Regan, Dana *117:* 116
Regan, Laura *103:* 198; *153:* 206
Reichert, Renée *169:* 127
Reid, Barbara *82:* 178; *92:* 17; *93:* 169, 170
Reid, Stephen *19:* 213; *22:* 89
Reim, Melanie *104:* 151; *150:* 98
Reinert, Kirk *89:* 138
Reinertson, Barbara *44:* 150; *62:* 103
Reiniger, Lotte *40:* 185
Reisberg, Mira *119:* 2
Reisch, Jesse *158:* 130
Reiser, Lynn *81:* 175; *138:* 184
Reiss, John J. *23:* 193
Relf, Douglas *3:* 63
Relyea, C.M. *16:* 29; *31:* 153
Remi, Georges *13:* 184
Remington, Frederic *19:* 188; *41:* 178, 179, 180, 181, 183,184, 185, 186, 187, 188; *62:* 197
Remkiewicz, Frank *67:* 102; *77:* 171; *80:* 130; *113:* 107; *152:* 116; *152:* 211, 212; *157:* 148
Rendon, Maria *116:* 141; *192:* *134:* 152
Renfro, Ed *79:* 176
Renlie, Frank *11:* 200
Reschofsky, Jean *7:* 118
Rethi *60:* 181
Rethi, Lili *2:* 153; *36:* 156
Reusswig, William *3:* 267
Rex, Adam *156:* 172; *169:* 91
Rex, Michael *157:* 147
Rey, H.A. *1:* 182; *26:* 163, 164, 166, 167, 169; *69:* 172, 173, 174, 175; *86:* 195, 196, 197; *100:* 211; *YABC 2:* 17
Reynolds, Doris *5:* 71; *31:* 77
Reynolds, Peter H. *142:* 12; *179:* 175, 176
Rhead, Louis *31:* 91; *100:* 228
Rhodes, Andrew *38:* 204; *50:* 163; *54:* 76; *61:* 123, 124; *87:* 200
Ribbons, Ian *3:* 10; *37:* 161; *40:* 76
Ricci, Regolo *93:* 22; *164:* 148

Rice, Elizabeth 2: 53, 214
Rice, Eve 34: 174, 175; 91: 172
Rice, James 22: 210; 93: 173
Richards, Chuck 170: 154
Richards, George 40: 116, 119, 121; 44: 179
Richards, Henry YABC 1: 228, 231
Richardson, Ernest 2: 144
Richardson, Frederick 18: 27, 31
Richardson, John 110: 88
Richman, Hilda 26: 132
Richmond, George 24: 179
Riddell, Chris 114: 170, 195; 166: 179
Riddle, Tohby 74: 204; 151: 179
Riding, Peter 63: 195
Rieniets, Judy King 14: 28
Riger, Bob 2: 166
Riggio, Anita 73: 191; 85: 63; 137: 184; 172: 165
Riley, Jon 74: 70
Riley, Kenneth 22: 230
Riley-Webb, Charlotte 153: 143
Rinaldi, Angelo 165: 60, 69
Ringgold, Faith 71: 162; 114: 173, 174, 176
Ringi, Kjell 12: 171
Rios, Tere
    See Versace, Marie
Ripper, Charles L. 3: 175
Ripplinger, Henry 117: 31
Ritchie, William 74: 183
Ritter, John 175: 14
Ritz, Karen 41: 117; 72: 239; 87: 125; 102: 7; 106: 6
Rivers, Ruth 178: 193
Rivkin, Jay 15: 230
Rivoche, Paul 45: 125
Roach, Marilynne 9: 158
Robbin, Jodi 44: 156, 159
Robbins, Frank 42: 167
Robbins, Ken 147: 191, 192
Robbins, Ruth 52: 102
Roberts, Cliff 4: 126
Roberts, David 154: 4, 6
Roberts, Doreen 4: 230; 28: 105
Roberts, Jim 22: 166; 23: 69; 31: 110
Roberts, Tony 109: 195, 214
Roberts, W. 22: 2, 3
Robins, Arthur 137: 172; 151: 225
Robinson, Aminah Brenda Lynn 86: 205; 103: 55; 159: 175
Robinson, Charles [1870-1937] 17: 157, 171, 172, 173, 175, 176; 24: 207; 25: 204; YABC 2: 308, 309, 310, 331
Robinson, Charles 3: 53; 5: 14; 6: 193; 7: 150; 7: 183; 8: 38; 9: 81; 13: 188; 14: 248, 249; 23: 149; 26: 115; 27: 48; 28: 191; 32: 28; 35: 210; 36: 37; 48: 96; 52: 33; 53: 157; 56: 15; 62: 142; 77: 41; 111: 148
Robinson, Jerry 3: 262
Robinson, Joan G. 7: 184
Robinson, Lolly 90: 227
Robinson, T.H. 17: 179, 181, 182, 183; 29: 254
Robinson, W. Heath 17: 185, 187, 189, 191, 193, 195, 197, 199, 202; 23: 167; 25: 194; 29: 150; YABC 1: 44; 2: 183
Roche, Christine 41: 98
Roche, Denis 99: 184
Roche, P.K. 57: 151, 152
Rocker, Fermin 7: 34; 13: 21; 31: 40; 40: 190,191
Rocklen, Margot 101: 181
Rockwell, Anne 5: 147; 33: 171, 173; 71: 166, 167,168; 114: 183, 184
Rockwell, Gail 7: 186
Rockwell, Harlow 33: 171, 173, 175
Rockwell, Lizzy 114: 182; 162: 182
Rockwell, Norman 23: 39, 196, 197, 199, 200, 203, 204, 207; 41: 140, 143; 123: 47; YABC 2: 60
Rockwood, Richard 119: 75
Rodanas, Kristina 156: 183, 184

Rodegast, Roland 43: 100
Rodgers, Frank 69: 177
Rodriguez, Joel 16: 65
Rodriguez, Robert 145: 145
Rodriguez-Howard, Pauline 177: 18
Roeckelein, Katrina 134: 223
Roennfeldt, Robert 66: 243
Roever, J.M. 4: 119; 26: 170
Roffey, Maureen 33: 142, 176, 177
Rogasky, Barbara 46: 90
Rogé 173: 160
Rogers, Carol 2: 262; 6: 164; 26: 129
Rogers, Chris M. 150: 59
Rogers, Forest 87: 160; 101: 76
Rogers, Frances 10: 130
Rogers, Gregory 104: 76; 126: 57; 171: 26
Rogers, Jacqueline 78: 249; 80: 34; 86: 54
    103: 70; 115: 72; 129: 173; 131: 57, 225;
    143: 211; 153: 100
Rogers, Walter S. 31: 135, 138; 67: 65, 168;
    100: 81
Rogers, William A. 15: 151, 153, 154; 33: 35
Rogoff, Barbara 95: 20
Rohmann, Eric 103: 152
Rojankovsky, Feodor 6: 134, 136; 10: 183; 21:
    128,129, 130; 25: 110; 28: 42; 68: 120
Rolfsen, Alf 62: 15
Romain, Trevor 134: 157
Roman, Barbara J. 103: 171
Romas 114: 111; 165: 63
Romano, Robert 64: 68
Roos, Maryn 168: 198
Root, Barry 80: 212; 90: 196; 146: 78; 156:
    165; 159: 161
Root, Kimberly Bulcken 86: 72; 98: 21; 108:
    111; 127: 114; 159: 162; 176: 134
Roper, Bob 65: 153
Roraback, Robin 111: 156
Rorer, Abigail 43: 222; 85: 155
Rosales, Melodye 80: 35
Rosamilia, Patricia 36: 120
Rose, Carl 5: 62
Rose, David S. 29: 109; 70: 120
Rose, Gerald 68: 200, 201; 86: 48
Rose, Ted 93: 178
Rosenbaum, Jonathan 50: 46
Rosenberg, Amye 74: 207, 208
Rosenberry, Vera 87: 22, 26; 144: 212, 213;
    158: 120
Rosenblum, Richard 11: 202; 18: 18
Rosier, Lydia 16: 236; 20: 104; 21: 109; 22:
    125; 30: 151, 158; 42: 128; 45: 214; 77:
    227, 228
Rosing, Jens 85: 142
Ross
    See Thomson, Ross
Ross, Christine 83: 172, 173
Ross, Clare Romano 3: 123; 21: 45; 48: 199
Ross, Dave 32: 152; 57: 108
Ross, Herbert 37: 78
Ross, John 3: 123; 21: 45
Ross, Johnny 32: 190
Ross, Larry 47: 168; 60: 62
Ross, Ruth 109: 233
Ross, Tony 17: 204; 56: 132; 65: 176, 177,
    179; 90: 123; 123: 186, 187, 190; 130: 188,
    190, 191, 192; 132: 242; 174: 159; 176: 181,
    182, 183
Rossetti, Dante Gabriel 20: 151, 153
Roth, Arnold 4: 238; 21: 133
Roth, Marci 135: 223
Roth, Rob 105: 98; 146: 41
Roth, Robert 176: 159
Roth, Roger 61: 128
Roth, Stephanie 136: 171, 172
Roth, Susan L. 80: 38; 93: 78; 134: 165, 166
Rothenberg, Joani Keller 162: 190, 191
Rothman, Michael 139: 62 Rotman, Jeffrey L.
    145: 30
Rotondo, Pat 32: 158
Roughsey, Dick 35: 186

Rouille, M. 11: 96
Rounds, Glen 8: 173; 9: 171; 12: 56; 32: 194;
    40: 230; 51: 161, 162, 166; 56: 149; 70:
    198, 199; YABC 1: 1, 2, 3; 112: 163
Roundtree, Katherine 114: 88; 168: 102
Rowan, Evadne 52: 51
Rowe, Eric 111: 161
Rowe, Gavin 27: 144; 72: 47; 88: 201
Rowe, John 132: 70, 71
Rowell, Kenneth 40: 72
Rowen, Amy 52: 143
Rowena 116: 101
Rowland, Andrew 164: 136
Rowland, Jada 83: 73
Rowles, Daphne 58: 24
Roy, Jeroo 27: 229; 36: 110
Royo 118: 32; 144: 105, 106, 108; 165: 19;
    166: 166
Rubel, Nicole 18: 255; 20: 59; 81: 66, 67; 95:
    169, 170; 119: 60; 135: 177, 179, 180; 169:
    68
Rubel, Reina 33: 217
Rud, Borghild 6: 15
Ruddell, Gary 110: 238; 116: 207
Rudolph, Norman Guthrie 17: 13
Rue, Leonard Lee III 37: 164
Ruelle, Karen Gray 126: 193
Ruff, Donna 50: 173; 72: 203; 78: 49; 80:
    120,121; 93: 162; 164: 121
Ruffins, Reynold 10: 134, 135; 41: 191, 192,
    193, 194, 195, 196; 125: 187, 188, 189; 162:
    197
Ruhlin, Roger 34: 44
Ruiz, Art 95: 154; 110: 91
Runnerstroem, Bengt Arne 75: 161
Ruse, Margaret 24: 155
Rush, Ken 98: 74
Rush, Peter 42: 75
Russell, Charles M. 167: 171
Russell, E.B. 18: 177, 182
Russell, Jim 53: 134
Russell, P. Craig 80: 196; 146: 102; 162: 186
Russo, Marisabina 84: 51; 106: 164; 151: 183
Russo, Susan 30: 182; 36: 144
Russon, Mary 87: 145
Ruth, Rod 9: 161
Rutherford, Alexa 110: 108
Rutherford, Jenny 78: 5
Rutherford, Meg 25: 174; 34: 178, 179; 69:
    73; 72: 31
Rutland, Jonathan 31: 126
Ruurs, Margriet 147: 195
Ruzzier, Sergio 159: 176, 177; 163: 184
Ryan, Will 86: 134
Ryden, Hope 8: 176
Rylant, Cynthia 112: 170, 172
Rymer, Alta M. 34: 181
Ryniak, Christopher 178: 11
Rystedt, Rex 49: 80

                    S

Saaf, Chuck 49: 179
Saaf, Donald 101: 220; 124: 180
Sabaka, Donna R. 21: 172
Sabin, Robert 45: 35; 60: 30; 99: 161
Sabuda, Robert 170: 166, 167, 168
Sacker, Amy 16: 100
Saelig, S.M. 129: 73; 173: 59
Saffioti, Lino 36: 176; 48: 60
Saflund, Birgitta 94: 2
Sagsoorian, Paul 12: 183; 22: 154; 33: 106;
    87: 152
Sahara, Tony 168: 106; 177: 181; 178: 228
Sahlberg, Myron 57: 165
Saidens, Amy 145: 162
Saint Exupery, Antoine de 20: 157
Saint James, Synthia 152: 220
Saldutti, Denise 39: 186; 57: 178

Sale, Morton *YABC 2:* 31
Sale, Tim *153:* 177
Salerno, Steven *150:* 79; *176:* 188
Salter, George *72:* 128, 130
Saltzberg, Barney *135:* 184, 185
Saltzman, David *86:* 209
Salwowski, Mark *71:* 54
Salzman, Yuri *86:* 12
Sambourne, Linley *YABC 2:* 181
Sampson, Katherine *9:* 197
Samson, Anne S. *2:* 216
San Souci, Daniel *40:* 200; *96:* 199, 200; *113:* 171; *157:* 149; *170:* 69
Sancha, Sheila *38:* 185
Sanchez, Enrique O. *155:* 84
Sand, George X. *45:* 182
Sandberg, Lasse *15:* 239, 241
Sanders, Beryl *39:* 173
Sanderson, Ruth *21:* 126; *24:* 53; *28:* 63; *33:* 67; *41:* 48, 198, 199, 200, 201, 202, 203; *43:* 79; *46:* 36,44; *47:* 102; *49:* 58; *62:* 121, 122; *85:* 3; *109:* 207, 208, 209, 210; *172:* 157, 158
Sandia *119:* 74
Sandin, Joan *4:* 36; *6:* 194; *7:* 177; *12:* 145,185; *20:* 43; *21:* 74; *26:* 144; *27:* 142; *28:* 224, 225; *38:* 86; *41:* 46; *42:* 35; *59:* 6; *80:* 136; *94:* 188; *140:* 116; *153:* 179, 180
Sandland, Reg *39:* 215
Sandoz, Edouard *26:* 45, 47
Sanford, John *66:* 96, 97
Sankey, Tom *72:* 103
sano, Kazuhiko *153:* 208
Santore, Charles *54:* 139
Santoro, Christopher *74:* 215
Santos, Jesse J. *99:* 24
Sapieha, Christine *1:* 180
Saport, Linda *123:* 137, 138
Sara
   See De La Roche Saint Andre, Anne
Sardinha, Rick *175:* 151
Sarg, Tony *YABC 2:* 236
Sargent, Claudia *64:* 181
Sargent, Robert *2:* 217
Saris *1:* 33
Sarony *YABC 2:* 170
Sasaki, Goro *170:* 46
Sasek, Miroslav *16:* 239, 240, 241, 242
Sassman, David *9:* 79
Satty *29:* 203, 205
Sauber, Robert *40:* 183; *76:* 256; *78:* 154; *87:* 92
Saunders, Dave *85:* 163, 164, 165
Savadier, Elivia *84:* 50; *145:* 45; *164:* 206
Savage, Naomi *56:* 172
Savage, Steele *10:* 203; *20:* 77; *35:* 28
Savage, Stephen *174:* 182
Savio *76:* 4
Savitt, Sam *8:* 66, 182; *15:* 278; *20:* 96; *24:* 192; *28:* 98
Sawyer, Kem Knapp *84:* 228, 229
Say, Allen *28:* 178; *69:* 182, 183, 232; *110:* 194, 195,196; *161:* 154, 155
Sayles, Elizabeth *82:* 93; *105:* 155; *109:* 116
Scabrini, Janet *13:* 191; *44:* 128
Scanlan, Peter *83:* 27; *153:* 165
Scanlon, Paul *83:* 87
Scannell, Reece *105:* 105
Scarry, Huck *35:* 204, 205
Scarry, Richard *2:* 220, 221; *18:* 20; *35:* 193, 194, 195,196, 197, 198, 199, 200, 201, 202; *75:* 165, 167, 168
Schachner, Judith Byron *88:* 180; *92:* 163; *93:* 102; *142:* 82; *178:* 199, 200
Schaeffer, Mead *18:* 81, 94; *21:* 137, 138, 139; *47:* 128
Schaffer, Amanda *90:* 206
Schanzer, Rosalyn *138:* 192, 193
Scharl, Josef *20:* 132; *22:* 128
Scheel, Lita *11:* 230
Scheib, Ida *29:* 28

Schermer, Judith *30:* 184
Schick, Eleanor *82:* 210, 211; *144:* 222
Schick, Joel *16:* 160; *17:* 167; *22:* 12; *27:* 176; *31:* 147, 148; *36:* 23; *38:* 64; *45:* 116, 117; *52:* 5, 85; *104:* 159
Schields, Gretchen *75:* 171, 203
Schindelman, Joseph *1:* 74; *4:* 101; *12:* 49; *26:* 51; *40:* 146; *56:* 158; *73:* 40
Schindler, Edith *7:* 22
Schindler, S.D. *38:* 107; *46:* 196; *74:* 162; *75:* 172, 173; *99:* 133; *112:* 177; *118:* 185, 186; *121:* 71; *136:* 159; *143:* 45; *149:* 120; *156:* 30; *169:* 135; *171:* 161, 162, 163; *172:* 9
Schlesinger, Bret *7:* 77
Schmid, Eleanore *12:* 188; *126:* 196, 197
Schmiderer, Dorothy *19:* 224
Schmidt, Bill *73:* 34; *76:* 220, 222, 224
Schmidt, Elizabeth *15:* 242
Schmidt, George Paul *132:* 122
Schmidt, Karen Lee *54:* 12; *71:* 174; *92:* 56; *94:* 190, 191; *127:* 103
Schmidt, Lynette *76:* 205
Schneider, Christine M. *171:* 165
Schneider, Rex *29:* 64; *44:* 171
Schnurr, Edward *170:* 62
Schoberle, Cecile *80:* 200; *92:* 134
Schoenherr, Ian *32:* 83; *173:* 41
Schoenherr, John *1:* 146, 147, 173; *3:* 39, 139; *17:* 75; *29:* 72; *32:* 83; *37:* 168, 169, 170; *43:* 164, 165; *45:* 160, 162; *51:* 127; 66; 196, 197, 198; *68:* 83; *72:* 240; *75:* 225; *88:* 176
Scholder, Fritz *69:* 103
Schomburg, Alex *13:* 23
Schongut, Emanuel *4:* 102; *15:* 186; *47:* 218, 219; *52:* 147, 148, 149, 150
Schoonover, Frank *17:* 107; *19:* 81, 190, 233; *22:* 88,129; *24:* 189; *31:* 88; *41:* 69; *YABC 2:* 282, 316
Schories, Pat *164:* 210
Schottland, Miriam *22:* 172
Schramm, Ulrik *2:* 16; *14:* 112
Schreiber, Elizabeth Anne *13:* 193
Schreiber, Ralph W. *13:* 193
Schreiter, Rick *14:* 97; *23:* 171; *41:* 247; *49:* 131
Schroeder, Binette *56:* 128, 129
Schroeder, E. Peter *12:* 112
Schroeder, Ted *11:* 160; *15:* 189; *30:* 91; *34:* 43
Schrotter, Gustav *22:* 212; *30:* 225
Schubert, Dieter *101:* 167, 168
Schubert-Gabrys, Ingrid *101:* 167, 168
Schucker, James *31:* 163
Schuett, Stacey *72:* 137
Schulder, Lili *146:* 29
Schulke, Debra *57:* 167
Schulke, Flip *57:* 167
Schulz, Barbara *167:* 24
Schulz, Charles M. *10:* 137, 138, 139, 140, 141, 142; *118:* 192, 193, 194, 196, 199
Schutzer, Dena *109:* 32
Schwark, Mary Beth *51:* 155; *72:* 175
Schwartz, Amy *47:* 191; *82:* 100; *83:* 178, 179, 180,181; *129:* 107; *131:* 197, 198
Schwartz, Carol *124:* 41; *130:* 199
Schwartz, Charles *8:* 184
Schwartz, Daniel *46:* 37
Schwartz, Joanie *124:* 170
Schwartzberg, Joan *3:* 208
Schweitzer, Iris *2:* 137; *6:* 207
Schweninger, Ann *29:* 172; *82:* 246; *159:* 202; *168:* 166
Schwinger, Laurence *84:* 44; *91:* 61
Scofield, Penrod *61:* 107; *62:* 160
Scott, Anita Walker *7:* 38
Scott, Art *39:* 41
Scott, Frances Gruse *38:* 43
Scott, Julian *34:* 126
Scott, Roszel *33:* 238
Scott, Sally *87:* 27

Scott, Steve *166:* 230, 231; *171:* 93
Scott, Trudy *27:* 172
Scrace, Carolyn *143:* 95, 96
Scribner, Joanne *14:* 236; *29:* 78; *33:* 185; *34:* 208; *78:* 75; *164:* 237
Scrofani, Joseph *31:* 65; *74:* 225
Seaman, Mary Lott *34:* 64
Searle, Ronald *24:* 98; *42:* 172, 173, 174, 176, 177, 179; *66:* 73, 74; *70:* 205, 206, 207
Searle, Townley *36:* 85
Sebree, Charles *18:* 65
Sedacca, Joseph M. *11:* 25; *22:* 36
Seder, Jason *108:* 102
Seeger, Laura Vaccaro *172:* 162
Seegmiller, Don *174:* 57
Seely, David *164:* 173
Seeley, Laura L. *97:* 105
Segal, John *178:* 202
Segar, E.C. *61:* 179, 181
Segur, Adrienne *27:* 121
Seibold, J. Otto *83:* 188, 190, 191; *149:* 212, 214, 215, 216
Seignobosc, Francoise *21:* 145, 146
Sejima, Yoshimasa *8:* 187
Selig, Sylvie *13:* 199
Seltzer, Isadore *6:* 18; *133:* 59
Seltzer, Meyer *17:* 214
Selven, Maniam *144:* 133
Selway, Martina *169:* 157
Selznick, Brian *79:* 192; *104:* 25; *117:* 175; *126:* 156; *134:* 171; *158:* 76, 78; *169:* 70; *171:* 172, 173
Sempe, Jean-Jacques *47:* 92; *YABC 2:* 109
Sendak, Maurice *1:* 135, 190; *3:* 204; *7:* 142; *15:* 199; *17:* 210; *27:* 181, 182, 183, 185, 186, 187, 189,190, 191, 192, 193, 194, 195, 197, 198, 199, 203; *28:* 181, 182; *32:* 108; *33:* 148, 149; *35:* 238; *44:* 180, 181; *45:* 97, 99; *46:* 174; *73:* 225; *91:* 10, 11 *YABC1:* 167; *113:* 163, 165, 167, 168; *118:* 153; *127:* 161
Sengler, Johanna *18:* 256
Senn, Steve *60:* 145
Seredy, Kate *1:* 192; *14:* 20, 21; *17:* 210
Sergeant, John *6:* 74
Servello, Joe *10:* 144; *24:* 139; *40:* 91; *70:* 130, 131; *146:* 159
Seton, Ernest Thompson *18:* 260-269, 271
Seuss, Dr.
   See Geisel, Theodor
Severin, John Powers *7:* 62
Sewall, Marcia *15:* 8; *22:* 170; *37:* 171, 172, 173; *39:* 73; *45:* 209; *62:* 117; *69:* 185, 186; *71:* 212; *90:* 232; *96:* 127; *102:* 101; *107:* 129; *119:* 176, 177, 178, 180
Seward, James *70:* 35
Seward, Prudence *16:* 243
Sewell, Helen *3:* 186; *15:* 308; *33:* 102; *38:* 189, 190, 191, 192
Seymour, Stephen *54:* 21
Shachat, Andrew *82:* 179
Shahn, Ben *39:* 178; *46:* 193
Shalansky, Len *38:* 167
Shanks, Anne Zane *10:* 149
Shannon, David *57:* 137; *107:* 184; *112:* 216; *135:* 12; *152:* 223, 224, 225; *158:* 192
Sharp, Paul *52:* 60
Sharp, William *6:* 131; *19:* 241; *20:* 112; *25:* 141
Sharratt, Nick *102:* 207, 208; *104:* 163; *153:* 198; *175:* 176
Shaw, Barclay *74:* 14, 16; *118:* 138
Shaw, Charles *21:* 135; *38:* 187; *47:* 124; *126:* 219
Shaw, Charles G. *13:* 200
Shaw-Smith, Emma *144:* 117
Shea, Edmund *56:* 19
Shearer, Ted *43:* 193, 194, 195, 196
Shecter, Ben *16:* 244; *25:* 109; *33:* 188, 191; *41:* 77

Shed, Greg *74:* 94; *84:* 204; *129:* 149, *167:* 91; *179:* 192
Sheeban, Chris *144:* 190; *158:* 163
Shefcik, James *48:* 221, 222; *60:* 141
Shefelman, Karl *58:* 168
Shefts, Joelle *48:* 210
Shein, Bob *139:* 189
Shekerjian, Haig *16:* 245
Shekerjian, Regina *16:* 245; *25:* 73
Shemie, Bonnie *96:* 207
Shenton, Edward *45:* 187, 188, 189; *YABC 1:* 218, 219, 221
Shepard, Ernest H. *3:* 193; *4:* 74; *16:* 101; *17:* 109; *25:* 148; *33:* 152, 199, 200, 201, 202, 203, 204, 205, 206,207; *46:* 194; *98:* 114; *100:* 111, 178, 179, 217, 219, 220,221; *YABC 1:* 148, 153, 174, 176, 180, 181
Shepard, Mary *4:* 210; *22:* 205; *30:* 132, 133; *54:* 150, 152, 153, 157, 158; *59:* 108, 109, 111; *100:* 246
Shepherd, Irana *171:* 112
Shepperson, Rob *96:* 153; *177:* 163; *178:* 204
Sherman, Theresa *27:* 167
Sherwan, Earl *3:* 196
Shields, Charles *10:* 150; *36:* 63
Shields, Leonard *13:* 83, 85, 87
Shiffman, Lena *139:* 167; *168:* 136
Shigley, Neil K. *66:* 219
Shillabeer, Mary *35:* 74
Shilston, Arthur *49:* 61; *62:* 58
Shimin, Symeon *1:* 93; *2:* 128, 129; *3:* 202; *7:* 85; *11:* 177; *12:* 139; *13:* 202, 203; *27:* 138; *28:* 65; *35:* 129; *36:* 130; *48:* 151; *49:* 59; *56:* 63, 65, 153
Shine, Andrea *104:* 165; *128:* 34
Shinn, Everett *16:* 148; *18:* 229; *21:* 149, 150, 151; *24:* 218
Shinn, Florence Scovel *63:* 133, 135
Shore, Robert *27:* 54; *39:* 192, 193; *YABC 2:* 200
Shortall, Leonard *4:* 144; *8:* 196; *10:* 166; *19:* 227, 228, 229, 230; *25:* 78; *28:* 66, 167; *33:* 127; *52:* 125; *73:* 12, 212
Shortt, T.M. *27:* 36
Shpitalnik, Vladimir *83:* 194
Shropshire, Sandy *170:* 191
Shtainments, Leon *32:* 161
Shulevitz, Uri *3:* 198, 199; *17:* 85; *22:* 204; *27:* 212; *28:* 184; *50:* 190, 191, 192, 193, 194, 195, 196,197, 198, 199, 201; *106:* 181, 182, 183; *165:* 203, 205; *166:* 138
Shupe, Bobbi *139:* 80, 81
Shute, A.B. *67:* 196
Shute, Linda *46:* 59; *74:* 118
Siberell, Anne *29:* 193
Sibley, Don *1:* 39; *12:* 196; *31:* 47
Sibthorp, Fletcher *94:* 111, 112
Sidjakov, Nicolas *18:* 274
Siebel, Fritz *3:* 120; *17:* 145
Siebold, J. Otto *158:* 227
Siegel, Hal *74:* 246
Siegl, Helen *12:* 166; *23:* 216; *34:* 185, 186
Sill, John *140:* 194; *141:* 157
Sills, Joyce *5:* 199
Silva, Simon *108:* 122
Silver, Maggie *85:* 210
Silveria, Gordon *96:* 44
Silverstein, Alvin *8:* 189
Silverstein, Shel *33:* 211; *92:* 209, 210
Silverstein, Virginia *8:* 189
Silvey, Joe *135:* 203
Simard, Remy *95:* 156
Simmons, Elly *110:* 2; *127:* 69; *134:* 181
Simon, Eric M. *7:* 82
Simon, Hilda *28:* 189
Simon, Howard *2:* 175; *5:* 132; *19:* 199; *32:* 163, 164, 165

Simont, Marc *2:* 119; *4:* 213; *9:* 168; *13:* 238,240; *14:* 262; *16:* 179; *18:* 221; *26:* 210; *33:* 189, 194; *44:* 132; *58:* 122; *68:* 117; *73:* 204, 205, 206; *74:* 221; *126:* 199, 200; *133:* 195; *164:* 128
Sims, Agnes *54:* 152
Sims, Blanche *44:* 116; *57:* 129; *75:* 179, 180; *77:* 92; *104:* 192; *152:* 117; *156:* 160; *160:* 70; *168:* 174, 175
Singer, Edith G. *2:* 30
Singer, Gloria *34:* 56; *36:* 43
Singer, Julia *28:* 190
Singh, Jen *178:* 146
Siomades, Lorianne *134:* 45
Simont, Marc *163:* 40
Siracusa, Catherine *68:* 135; *82:* 218
Sis, Peter *67:* 179, 181, 183, 184, 185; *96:* 96, 98; *106:* 193, 194, 195; *149:* 224, 226
Sivard, Robert *26:* 124
Sivertson, Liz *116:* 84
Skardinski, Stanley *23:* 144; *32:* 84; *66:* 122; *84:* 108
Slackman, Charles B. *12:* 201
Slade, Paul *61:* 170
Slark, Albert *99:* 212
Slater, Rod *25:* 167
Sloan, Joseph *16:* 68
Sloane, Eric *21:* 3; *52:* 153, 154, 155, 156, 157, 158, 160
Sloat, Teri *164:* 231
Slobodkin, Louis *1:* 200; *3:* 232; *5:* 168; *13:* 251; *15:* 13, 88; *26:* 173, 174, 175, 176, 178, 179; *60:* 180
Slobodkina, Esphyr *1:* 201
Slonim, David *166:* 167, 168
Small, David *50:* 204, 205; *79:* 44; *95:* 189, 190, 191; *126:* 203, 204; *136:* 119; *143:* 201, 202, 203; *144:* 246; *150:* 5; *161:* 176
Small, W. *33:* 113
Smalley, Janet *1:* 154
Smedley, William T. *34:* 129
Smee, David *14:* 78; *62:* 30
Smee, Nicola *167:* 156
Smith, A.G., Jr. *35:* 182
Smith, Alvin *1:* 31, 229; *13:* 187; *27:* 216; *28:* 226; *48:* 149; *49:* 60
Smith, Anne Warren *41:* 212
Smith, Barry *75:* 183
Smith, Carl *36:* 41
Smith, Cat Bowman *146:* 39; *164:* 219
Smith, Craig *97:* 197; *172:* 175
Smith, Donald A. *178:* 7
Smith, Doris Susan *41:* 139
Smith, Duane *171:* 152
Smith, E. Boyd *19:* 70; *22:* 89; *26:* 63; *YABC 1:* 4, 5, 240, 248, 249
Smith, Edward J. *4:* 224
Smith, Elwood H. *157:* 231
Smith, Eunice Young *5:* 170
Smith, Gary *113:* 216
Smith, George *102:* 169
Smith, Howard *19:* 196
Smith, J. Gerard *95:* 42
Smith, Jacqueline Bardner *27:* 108; *39:* 197
Smith, Jay J. *61:* 119
Smith, Jeff *93:* 191
Smith, Jessie Willcox *15:* 91; *16:* 95; *18:* 231; *19:* 57, 242; *21:* 29, 156, 157, 158, 159, 160, 161; *34:* 65; *100:* 223; *YABC 1:* 6; *2:* 180, 185, 191, 311, 325
Smith, Jos. A. *52:* 131; *72:* 120; *74:* 151; *84:* 147, 148; *85:* 146; *87:* 96; *94:* 219; *96:* 97; *104:* 33; *108:* 126, 127, 128; *111:* 140; *136:* 145
Smith, Kenneth R. *47:* 182
Smith, Kevin Warren *89:* 112
Smith, L.H. *35:* 174
Smith, Lane *76:* 211, 213; *88:* 115; *105:* 202, 203,204, 205; *131:* 207; *160:* 217, 221; *179:* 183, 184, 185, 186
Smith, Lee *29:* 32

Smith, Linell Nash *2:* 195
Smith, Maggie Kaufman *13:* 205; *35:* 191; *110:* 158; *178:* 226
Smith, Mavis *101:* 219
Smith, Moishe *33:* 155
Smith, Philip *44:* 134; *46:* 203
Smith, Ralph Crosby *2:* 267; *49:* 203
Smith, Robert D. *5:* 63
Smith, Sally J. *84:* 55
Smith, Susan Carlton *12:* 208
Smith, Terry *12:* 106; *33:* 158
Smith, Virginia *3:* 157; *33:* 72
Smith, William A. *1:* 36; *10:* 154; *25:* 65
Smith-Moore, J.J. *98:* 147
Smolinski, Dick *84:* 217
Smoljan, Joe *112:* 201
Smollin, Mike *39:* 203
Smyth, Iain *105:* 207
Smyth, M. Jane *12:* 15
Smythe, Fiona *151:* 213
Smythe, Theresa *141:* 37
Snair, Andy *176:* 4
Sneed, Brad *125:* 25
Snyder, Andrew A. *30:* 212
Snyder, Jerome *13:* 207; *30:* 173
Snyder, Joel *28:* 163
So, Meilo *162:* 201
Soentpiet, Chris K. *97:* 208; *110:* 33; *159:* 184; *161:* 10; *163:* 130
Sofia *1:* 62; *5:* 90; *32:* 166; *86:* 43
Sofilas, Mark *93:* 157
Sokol, Bill *37:* 178; *49:* 23
Sokolov, Kirill *34:* 188
Solbert, Ronni *1:* 159; *2:* 232; *5:* 121; *6:* 34; *17:* 249
Solomon, Michael *174:* 115
Solonevich, George *15:* 246; *17:* 47
Soma, Liana *81:* 118
Soman, David *90:* 122; *102:* 126; *140:* 120; 93
Sommer, Robert *12:* 211
Sorel, Edward *4:* 61; *36:* 82; *65:* 191, 193; *126:* 214
Sorensen, Henrik *62:* 16
Sorensen, Svend Otto *22:* 130, 141; *67:* 188, 189
Sorra, Kristin *155:* 80
Sotomayor, Antonio *11:* 215
Souhami, Jessica *112:* 128; *176:* 193
Souza, Diana *71:* 139
Sovak, Jan *115:* 190
Soyer, Moses *20:* 177
Spaenkuch, August *16:* 28
Spafford, Suzy *160:* 228
Spain, Valerie *105:* 76
Spain, Sunday Sahara *133:* 204
Spalenka, Greg *149:* 69; *151:* 228
Spanfeller, James *1:* 72, 149; *2:* 183; *19:* 230, 231,232; *22:* 66; *36:* 160, 161; *40:* 75; *52:* 166; *76:* 37
Sparks, Mary Walker *15:* 247
Speidel, Sandra *78:* 233; *94:* 178; *134:* 180
Speirs, John *67:* 178
Spence, Geraldine *21:* 163; *47:* 196
Spence, Jim *38:* 89; *50:* 102
Spencer, Laurie *113:* 12
Spencer, Mark *57:* 170
Spengler, Kenneth J. *146:* 256
Sperling, Andrea *133:* 182
Spiegel, Doris *29:* 111
Spiegelman, Art *109:* 227
Spier, Jo *10:* 30
Spier, Peter *3:* 155; *4:* 200; *7:* 61; *11:* 78; *38:* 106; *54:* 120, 121, 122, 123, 124, 125, 126, 127, 128, 129, 130,131, 132, 133, 134
Spilka, Arnold *5:* 120; *6:* 204; *8:* 131
Spirin, Gennady *95:* 196, 197; *113:* 172; *128:* 9; *129:* 49; *134:* 210; *153:* 9
Spivak, I. Howard *8:* 10; *13:* 172
Spohn, David *72:* 233
Spohn, Kate *87:* 195; *147:* 201, 202
Spollen, Christopher J. *12:* 214

Spooner, Malcolm *40:* 142
Spowart, Robin *82:* 228; *92:* 149; *133:* 131; *176:* 163; *177:* 183, 184
Sprague, Kevin *150:* 60
Sprattler, Rob *12:* 176
Spring, Bob *5:* 60
Spring, Ira *5:* 60
Springer, Harriet *31:* 92
Spudvilas, Anne *110:* 74
Spurll, Barbara *78:* 199; *88:* 141, 142; *99:* 215
Spurrier, Steven *28:* 198
Spuvilas, Anne *85:* 114
Spy
  See Ward, Leslie
Squires, Stuart *127:* 74
St. Aubin, Bruno *179:* 54
St. John, J. Allen *41:* 62
Stabin, Victor *101:* 131; *164:* 158
Stadler, John *62:* 33
Staffan, Alvin E. *11:* 56; *12:* 187
Stahl, Ben *5:* 181; *12:* 91; *49:* 122; *71:* 128; *87:* 206; *112:* 107
Stair, Gobin *35:* 214
Stallwood, Karen *73:* 126
Stamaty, Mark Alan *12:* 215
Stammen, JoEllen McAllister *113:* 14
Stampnick, Ken *51:* 142
Stanbridge, Joanne *150:* 91
Stanley, Diane *3:* 45; *37:* 180; *80:* 217, 219
Stanley, Sanna *145:* 228
Starcke, Helmut *86:* 217
Starr, Branka *73:* 25
Stasiak, Krystyna *49:* 181; *64:* 194
Staub, Leslie *103:* 54
Staunton, Ted *112:* 192
Stawicki, Matt *164:* 250
Stead, L. *55:* 51, 56
Steadman, Broeck *97:* 185, 186; *99:* 56; *121:* 48
Steadman, Ralph *32:* 180; *123:* 143, 145
Steckler, June *90:* 178
Steele, Robert Gantt *169:* 174
Steichen, Edward *30:* 79
Steig, William *18:* 275, 276; *70:* 215, 216, 217, 218; *111:* 173, 174, 175, 176, 177
Stein, Harve *1:* 109
Steinberg, Saul *47:* 193
Steinel, William *23:* 146
Steiner, Charlotte *45:* 196
Steiner, Joan *110:* 219
Steirnagel, Michael *80:* 56
Stemp, Eric *60:* 184
Stephens, Alice Barber *66:* 208, 209
Stephens, Charles H. *YABC 2:* 279
Stephens, Pat *126:* 110; *128:* 101
Stephens, William M. *21:* 165
Steptoe, Javaka *151:* 203, 204
Steptoe, John *8:* 197; *57:* 9; *63:* 158, 159, 160, 161,163, 164, 165, 166, 167; *96:* 4; *105:* 87
Stern, Simon *15:* 249, 250; *17:* 58; *34:* 192, 193
Sterret, Jane *53:* 27
Stetsios, Debbie *165:* 108, 109
Steven, Kat *158:* 237
Stevens, David *62:* 44
Stevens, Janet *40:* 126; *57:* 10, 11; *80:* 112; *90:* 221, 222; *109:* 156; *130:* 34; *166:* 202; *176:* 53, 116
Stevens, Mary *11:* 193; *13:* 129; *43:* 95
Stevenson, Harvey *66:* 143; *80:* 201, 221; *153:* 60
Stevenson, James *42:* 182, 183; *51:* 163; *66:* 184; *71:* 185, 187, 188; *78:* 262; *87:* 97; *113:* 182, 183,184; *161:* 182, 183
Stevenson, Sucie *92:* 27; *104:* 194, 195; *112:* 168; *160:* 202
Stewart, April Blair *75:* 210
Stewart, Arvis *33:* 98; *36:* 69; *60:* 118; *75:* 91; *127:* 4
Stewart, Charles *2:* 205
Stewart, Joel *151:* 205

Stieg, William *172:* 58
Stiles, Fran *26:* 85; *78:* 56; *82:* 150
Stillman, Susan *44:* 130; *76:* 83
Stimpson, Tom *49:* 171
Stinemetz, Morgan *40:* 151
Stinson, Paul *110:* 86
Stirnweis, Shannon *10:* 164
Stites, Joe *86:* 96
Stobbs, William *1:* 48, 49; *3:* 68; *6:* 20; *17:* 117, 217; *24:* 150; *29:* 250; *60:* 179; *87:* 204, 205,206
Stock, Catherine *37:* 55; *65:* 198; *72:* 7; *99:* 225; *114:* 197, 198, 199; *126:* 3; *145:* 161; *161:* 82; *173:* 149
Stockman, Jack *113:* 24
Stoeke, Janet Morgan *90:* 225; *136:* 196
Stoerrle, Tom *55:* 147
Stolp, Jaap *49:* 98
Stolp, Todd *89:* 195
Stone, David L. *87:* 154
Stone, David *9:* 173
Stone, David K. *4:* 38; *6:* 124; *9:* 180; *43:* 182; *60:* 70
Stone, Helen V. *6:* 209
Stone, Helen *44:* 121, 122, 126
Stone, Kazuko G. *134:* 43
Stone, Phoebe *86:* 212; *134:* 213; *162:* 188
Stone, Steve *166:* 213
Stone, Tony *150:* 34, 35
Stoud, Virginia A. *89:* 31
Stover, Jill *82:* 234
Stratton, Helen *33:* 151
Stratton-Porter, Gene *15:* 254, 259, 263, 264, 268, 269
Streano, Vince *20:* 173
Street, Janet Travell *84:* 235
Streeter, Clive *121:* 2
Stringer, Lauren *129:* 187; *154:* 172, 173; *161:* 127
Strodl, Daniel *47:* 95
Strogart, Alexander *63:* 139
Stromoski, Rick *111:* 179; *124:* 161, 190
Strong, Joseph D., Jr. *YABC 2:* 330
Stroyer, Poul *13:* 221
Strugnell, Ann *27:* 38
Struzan, Drew *117:* 6
Stubbs, William *73:* 196
Stubis, Talivaldis *5:* 182, 183; *10:* 45; *11:* 9; *18:* 304; *20:* 127
Stubley, Trevor *14:* 43; *22:* 219; *23:* 37; *28:* 61; *87:* 26
Stuck, Marion *104:* 44
Stuecklen, Karl W. *8:* 34, 65; *23:* 103
Stull, Betty *11:* 46
Stutzman, Mark *119:* 99
Stutzmann, Laura *73:* 185
Suarez, Maribel *162:* 208
Suba, Susanne *4:* 202, 203; *14:* 261; *23:* 134; *29:* 222; *32:* 30
Sueling, Barbara *98:* 185
Sueling, Gwenn *98:* 186
Sugarman, Tracy *3:* 76; *8:* 199; *37:* 181, 182
Sugimoto, Yugo *170:* 144
Sugita, Yutaka *36:* 180, 181
Suh, John *80:* 157
Sullivan, Dorothy *89:* 113
Sullivan, Edmund J. *31:* 86
Sullivan, James F. *19:* 280; *20:* 192
Sully, Tom *104:* 199, 200
Sumichrast, Jozef *14:* 253; *29:* 168, 213
Sumiko *46:* 57
Summers, Leo *1:* 177; *2:* 273; *13:* 22
Summers, Mark *118:* 144
Sutton, Judith *94:* 164
Svarez, Juan *56:* 113
Svolinsky, Karel *17:* 104
Swain, Carol *172:* 182
Swain, Su Zan Noguchi *21:* 170
Swan, Susan *22:* 220, 221; *37:* 66; *60:* 146; *145:* 205
Swann, Susan *86:* 55

Swanson, Karl *79:* 65; *89:* 186
Swayne, Sam *53:* 143, 145
Swayne, Zoa *53:* 143, 145
Swearingen, Greg *152:* 56; *165:* 135; *173:* 2
Sweat, Lynn *25:* 206; *57:* 176; *73:* 184; *168:* 178
Sweet, Darrell K. *60:* 9; *69:* 86; *74:* 15; *75:* 215; *76:* 130, 131; *81:* 96, 122; *82:* 253; *83:* 11; *84:* 14; *85:* 37; *89:* 140; *90:* 6; *91:* 137,139; *95:* 160, 161; *126:* 25
Sweet, Darrell K. *1:* 163; *4:* 136; *164:* 175
Sweet, Melissa *71:* 94; *72:* 172; *111:* 82; *139:* 53, 58; *141:* 88; *142:* 231; *155:* 121; *159:* 121, 122; *172:* 185
Sweet, Ozzie *31:* 149, 151, 152
Sweetland, Robert *12:* 194
Swiatkowska, Gabi *132:* 43; *175:* 139
Swope, Martha *43:* 160; *56:* 86, 87, 89
Sylvada, Peter *154:* 174
Sylvester, Natalie G. *22:* 222
Szafran, Gene *24:* 144
Szasz, Susanne *13:* 55, 226; *14:* 48
Szekeres, Cyndy *2:* 218; *5:* 185; *8:* 85; *11:* 166; *14:* 19; *16:* 57, 159; *26:* 49, 214; *34:* 205; *60:* 150, 151, 152, 153, 154; *73:* 224; *74:* 218; *131:* 213, 215
Szpura, Beata *81:* 68; *119:* 65; *168:* 201

T

Taback, Simms *40:* 207; *52:* 120; *57:* 34; *80:* 241; *104:* 202, 203; *170:* 176, 177
Taber, Patricia *75:* 124
Tabor, Nancy Maria Grande *89:* 210; *161:* 188
Taddei, Richard *112:* 13, 14
Tadgell, Nicole *150:* 77; *161:* 20; *177:* 186
Tadiello, Ed *133:* 200
Tafuri, Nancy *39:* 210; *75:* 199, 200; *92:* 75; *130:* 215, 216, 217
Tailfeathers, Gerald *86:* 85
Tait, Douglas *12:* 220; *74:* 105, 106
Takabayashi, Mari *113:* 112; *130:* 22; *156:* 169
Takahashi, Hideko *136:* 160
Takakjian, Portia *15:* 274
Takashima, Shizuye *13:* 228
Talarczyk, June *4:* 173
Talbott, Hudson *84:* 240; *163:* 100
Tallarico, Tony *116:* 197
Tallon, Robert *2:* 228; *43:* 200, 201, 202, 203, 204, 205,206, 207, 209
Tamas, Szecsko *29:* 135
Tamburine, Jean *12:* 222
Tandy, H.R. *13:* 69
Tandy, Russell H. *65:* 9; *100:* 30, 131
Tang, Charles *81:* 202; *90:* 192
Tang, Susan *80:* 174; *108:* 158
Tang, You-shan *63:* 100
Tankersley, Paul *69:* 206; *133:* 219
Tannenbaum, Robert *48:* 181
Tanner, Jane *87:* 13; *97:* 37
Tanner, Tim *72:* 192; *84:* 35
Tanobe, Miyuki *23:* 221
Tarabay, Sharif *110:* 149; *113:* 123; *169:* 83
Tarkington, Booth *17:* 224, 225
Tarlow, Phyllis *61:* 198
Tate, Don *159:* 141, 191
Tauss, Herbert *95:* 179
Tauss, Marc *117:* 160; *126:* 155; *178:* 221
Tavares, Matt *159:* 192, 193
Taylor, Ann *41:* 226
Taylor, Dahl *129:* 157
Taylor, Geoff *93:* 156
Taylor, Isaac *41:* 228
Taylor, Mike *143:* 99, 100
Teague, Mark *83:* 6; *139:* 241; *170:* 180, 181
Teale, Edwin Way *7:* 196
Teason, James *1:* 14
Teeple, Lyn *33:* 147
Tee-Van, Helen Damrosch *10:* 176; *11:* 182

Teicher, Dick *50:* 211
Teichman, Mary *77:* 220; *124:* 208; *127:* 22
Temertey, Ludmilla *96:* 232; *104:* 43, 45; *109:* 244
Tempest, Margaret *3:* 237, 238; *88:* 200
Temple, Frances *85:* 185, 186, 187
Temple, Herbert *45:* 201
Templeton, Owen *11:* 77
Tenggren, Gustaf *18:* 277, 278, 279; *19:* 15; *28:* 86; *YABC2:* 145
Tennent, Julie *81:* 105
Tenneson, Joyce *153:* 166
Tenney, Gordon *24:* 204
Tenniel, John *74:* 234, 235; *100:* 89; *YABC 2:* 99; *153:* 63
Tepper, Matt *116:* 80
Terkel, Ari *103:* 162
Terry, Will *131:* 73
Teskey, Donald *71:* 51
Thacher, Mary M. *30:* 72
Thackeray, William Makepeace *23:* 224, 228
Thamer, Katie *42:* 187
Tharlet, Eve *146:* 149
Thelwell, Norman *14:* 201
Theobalds, Prue *40:* 23
Theurer, Marilyn Churchill *39:* 195
Thiesing, Lisa *89:* 134; *95:* 202; *156:* 190; *159:* 195
Thiewes, Sam *133:* 114
Thistlethwaite, Miles *12:* 224
Thollander, Earl *11:* 47; *18:* 112; *22:* 224
Thomas, Allan *22:* 13
Thomas, Art *48:* 217
Thomas, Eric *28:* 49
Thomas, Harold *20:* 98
Thomas, Jacqui *125:* 95
Thomas, Mark *42:* 136
Thomas, Martin *14:* 255
Thomas, Middy *177:* 114
Thompson, Arthur *34:* 107
Thompson, Carol *85:* 189; *95:* 75; *102:* 86; *147:* 166
Thompson, Colin *95:* 204
Thompson, Ellen *51:* 88, 151; *60:* 33; *67:* 42; *77:* 148; *78:* 75, 219; *79:* 122, 170; *84:* 219; *85:* 97; *87:* 37; *88:* 192, 194; *89:* 80; *93:* 37; *98:* 59; *132:* 14
Thompson, George W. *22:* 18; *28:* 150; *33:* 135
Thompson, John *58:* 201; *102:* 226; *124:* 154; *128:* 228; *129:* 157; *150:* 49
Thompson, Julie *44:* 158
Thompson, Katherine *132:* 146
Thompson, K. Dyble *84:* 6
Thompson, Miles *152:* 77
Thompson, Sharon *74:* 113; *158:* 60; *165:* 87
Thomson, Arline K. *3:* 264
Thomson, Hugh *26:* 88
Thomson, Ross *36:* 179
Thorkelson, Gregg *95:* 183, 184; *98:* 58; *165:* 30, 31
Thornberg, Dan *104:* 125
Thornburgh, Rebecca McKillip *143:* 37
Thorne, Diana *25:* 212
Thornhill, Jan *77:* 213
Thorpe, Peter *58:* 109
Thorvall, Kerstin *13:* 235
Threadgall, Colin *77:* 215
Thurber, James *13:* 239, 242, 243, 245, 248, 249
Thurman, Mark *63:* 173; *168:* 116
Tibbles, Jean-Paul *115:* 200
Tibbles, Paul *45:* 23
Tibo, Gilles *67:* 207; *107:* 199, 201
Tichenor, Tom *14:* 207
Tichnor, Richard *90:* 218
Tiegreen, Alan *36:* 143; *43:* 55, 56, 58; *77:* 200; *94:* 216, 217; *121:* 54, 59
Tierney, Tom *113:* 198, 200, 201
Tilley, Debbie *102:* 134; *133:* 226; *137:* 101; *159:* 96

Tilney, F.C. *22:* 231
Timbs, Gloria *36:* 90
Timmins, Harry *2:* 171
Tinkelman, Murray *12:* 225; *35:* 44
Titherington, Jeanne *39:* 90; *58:* 138; *75:* 79; *135:* 161
Tobin, Nancy *145:* 197
Toddy, Irving *172:* 144
Tolbert, Jeff *128:* 69
Tolford, Joshua *1:* 221
Tolkien, J.R.R. *2:* 243; *32:* 215
Tolmie, Ken *15:* 292
Tomei, Lorna *47:* 168, 171
Tomes, Jacqueline *2:* 117; *12:* 139
Tomes, Margot *1:* 224; *2:* 120, 121; *16:* 207; *18:* 250; *20:* 7; *25:* 62; *27:* 78, 79; *29:* 81, 199; *33:* 82; *36:* 186, 187, 188, 189, 190; *46:* 129; *56:* 71; *58:* 183; *70:* 228; *75:* 73, 75; *80:* 80; *83:* 97; *90:* 205
Toner, Raymond John *10:* 179
Tong, Gary *66:* 215
Tongier, Stephen *82:* 32
Tooke, Susan *173:* 162
Toothill, Harry *6:* 54; *7:* 49; *25:* 219; *42:* 192
Toothill, Ilse *6:* 54
Topolski, Feliks *44:* 48
Torbert, Floyd James *22:* 226
Torgersen, Don *55:* 157
Torline, Kevin *169:* 171
Tormey, Bertram M. *75:* 3, 4
Torrecilla, Pablo *176:* 207
Torres, Leyla *156:* 199, 201
Torrey, Helen *87:* 41
Torrey, Marjorie *34:* 105
Toschik, Larry *6:* 102
Totten, Bob *13:* 93
Toy, Julie *128:* 112
Trachok, Cathy *131:* 16
Tracy, Libba *82:* 24
Trago, Keith *158:* 253
Trail, Lee *55:* 157
Trang, To Ngoc *167:* 180
Trang, Winson *89:* 151
Trapani, Iza *116:* 202
Travers, Bob *49:* 100; *63:* 145
Treatner, Meryl *95:* 180
Tremain, Ruthven *17:* 238
Tresilian, Stuart *25:* 53; *40:* 212
Trez, Alain *17:* 236
Trezzo, Loretta *86:* 45
Trier, Walter *14:* 96
Trimby, Elisa *47:* 199
Trinkle, Sally *53:* 27
Tripp, F.J. *24:* 167
Tripp, Wallace *2:* 48; *7:* 28; *8:* 94; *10:* 54,76; *11:* 92; *31:* 170, 171; *34:* 203; *42:* 57; *60:* 157; *73:* 182
Trivas, Irene *53:* 4; *54:* 168; *82:* 46, 101
Trnka, Jiri *22:* 151; *43:* 212, 213, 214, 215; *YABC 1:* 30, 31
Troughton, Joanna *37:* 186; *48:* 72
Troyer, Johannes *3:* 16; *7:* 18
Trudeau, G.B. *35:* 220, 221, 222; *48:* 119, 123, 126, 127,128, 129, 133; *168:* 189
Trueman, Matthew *165:* 208
Truesdell, Sue *55:* 142; *108:* 219, 220
Tryon, Leslie *84:* 7; *139:* 214; *143:* 10
Tseng, Jean *72:* 195; *94:* 102; *119:* 126; *151:* 106; *173:* 138, 139
Tseng, Mou-sien *72:* 195; *94:* 102; *119:* 126; *151:* 106; *173:* 138, 139
Tsinajinie, Andy *2:* 62
Tsugami, Kyuzo *18:* 198, 199
Tucker, Ezra *156:* 31
Tuckwell, Jennifer *17:* 205
Tudor, Bethany *7:* 103
Tudor, Tasha *18:* 227; *20:* 185, 186, 187; *36:* 111; *69:* 196, 198; *100:* 44; *YABC 2:* 46, 314; *160:* 234
Tuerk, Hanne *71:* 201
Tulloch, Maurice *24:* 79

Tunis, Edwin *1:* 218, 219; *28:* 209, 210, 211, 212
Tunnicliffe, C.F. *62:* 176; 177; 178; 179; 181
Turkle, Brinton *1:* 211, 213; *2:* 249; *3:* 226; *11:* 3; *16:* 209; *20:* 22; *50:* 23; *67:* 50; *68:* 65; *79:* 205, 206, 207; *128:* 47; *YABC 1:* 79
Turnbull, Christopher J. *143:* 99, 100
Turner, Gwenda *59:* 195
Turska, Krystyna *12:* 103; *31:* 173, 174, 175; *56:* 32,34; *100:* 66
Tusa, Tricia *72:* 242; *111:* 180, 181; *157:* 165; *164:* 186
Tusan, Stan *6:* 58; *22:* 236, 237
Tworkov, Jack *47:* 207
Tyers, Jenny *89:* 220
Tylden-Wright, Jenny *114:* 119
Tyrol, Adelaide Murphy *103:* 27
Tyrrell, Frances *107:* 204
Tzimoulis, Paul *12:* 104

U

Uchida, Yoshiko *1:* 220
Uderzo *47:* 88
Ueno, Noriko *59:* 155
Ulm, Robert *17:* 238
Ulrich, George *73:* 15; *75:* 136, 139; *99:* 150
Ulriksen, Mark *101:* 58
Unada *84:* 67
　　See Gliewe, Unada
Underhill, Liz *53:* 159
Underwood, Clarence *40:* 166
Unger, Jim *67:* 208
Ungerer, Tomi *5:* 188; *9:* 40; *18:* 188; *29:* 175; *33:* 221, 222, 223, 225; *71:* 48; *106:* 209, 210, 211, 212
Unwin, Nora S. *3:* 65, 234, 235; *4:* 237; *44:* 173, 174; *YABC 1:* 59; *2:* 301
Upitis, Alvis *145:* 179
Urban, Helle *149:* 243
Urbanovic, Jackie *86:* 86
Uris, Jill *49:* 188, 197
Ursell, Martin *50:* 51
Utpatel, Frank *18:* 114
Utz, Lois *5:* 190

V

Vagin, Vladimir *66:* 10; *142:* 215
Vaillancourt, Francois *107:* 199
Vainio, Pirkko *123:* 157, 158
Vallejo, Boris *62:* 130; *72:* 212; *91:* 38; *93:* 61
Van Abbe, S. *16:* 142; *18:* 282; *31:* 90; *YABC 2:* 157, 161
Van Allsburg, Chris *37:* 205, 206; *53:* 161, 162, 163, 165,166, 167, 168, 169, 170, 171; *105:* 215, 216, 217, 218; *156:* 176, 177, 178
Vance, James *65:* 28
Van Der Linde, Henry *99:* 17
van der Meer, Ron *98:* 204, 205
van der Meer, Atie *98:* 204, 205
Vandivert, William *21:* 175
Van Dongen, H.R. *81:* 97
Van Dusen, Chris W. *173:* 169
Van Everen, Jay *13:* 160; *YABC 1:* 121
Van Fleet, John *165:* 12, 13
Van Frankenhuyzen, Gijsbert *145:* 230; *149:* 164
van Genechten, Guido *165:* 226
Van Horn, William *43:* 218
van Lawick, Hugo *62:* 76, 79
Van Loon, Hendrik Willem *18:* 285, 289, 291
Van Munching, Paul *83:* 85
Van Rynbach, Iris *102:* 192
Van Sciver, Ruth *37:* 162
VanSeveren, Joe *63:* 182

Van Stockum, Hilda *5:* 193
Van Wely, Babs *16:* 50; *79:* 16
Van Wright, Cornelius *72:* 18; *102:* 208; *116:* 107; *152:* 236; *173:* 170, 171
Van Zyle, Jon *103:* 125; *160:* 181, 182; *176:* 199, 200
Vardzigulyants, Ruben *90:* 54
Varga, Judy *29:* 196
Vargo, Kurt *79:* 224
Varley, Susan *61:* 199; *63:* 176, 177; *101:* 148; *134:* 220
Vasconcellos, Daniel *80:* 42
Vasiliu, Mircea *2:* 166, 253; *9:* 166; *13:* 58; *68:* 42
Vaughn, Frank *34:* 157
Vavra, Robert *8:* 206
Vawter, Will *17:* 163
Vayas, Diana *71:* 61
Vazquez, Carlos *125:* 184
Veeder, Larry *18:* 4
Velasquez, Eric *45:* 217; *61:* 45; *63:* 110, 111; *88:* 162; *90:* 34, 144; *94:* 213; *107:* 147; *132:* 192; *138:* 213; *159:* 126
Velasquez, Jose A. *63:* 73
Velez, Walter *71:* 75; *91:* 154; *121:* 181; *168:* 49
Velthuijs, Max *110:* 228, 229
Vendrell, Carme Sole *42:* 205
Venezia, Mike *54:* 17
Venti, Anthony Bacon *124:* 103; *126:* 26
Venturo, Piero *61:* 194, 195
Ver Beck, Frank *18:* 16, 17
Verkaaik, Ben *110:* 209
Verling, John *71:* 27
Verney, John *14:* 225; *75:* 8
Verrier, Suzanne *5:* 20; *23:* 212
Versace, Marie *2:* 255
Verstraete, Randy *108:* 193
Vestal, H.B. *9:* 134; *11:* 101; *27:* 25; *34:* 158
Vicatan *59:* 146
Vickrey, Robert *45:* 59, 64
Victor, Joan Berg *30:* 193
Viereck, Ellen *3:* 242; *14:* 229
Vigna, Judith *15:* 293; *102:* 194, 195, 196, 197
Vilato, Gaspar E. *5:* 41
Villiard, Paul *51:* 178
Vimnera, A. *23:* 154
Vincent, Eric *34:* 98
Vincent, Felix *41:* 237
Vincent, Gabrielle *121:* 175
Vip *45:* 164
Viskupic, Gary *83:* 48
Vitale, Stefano *109:* 71, 107; *114:* 219, 220; *123:* 106; *138:* 232
Vivas, Julie *51:* 67, 69; *96:* 225
Voake, Charlotte *114:* 221, 222
Vo-Dinh, Mai *16:* 272; *60:* 191
Vogel, Ilse-Margret *14:* 230
Voigt, Erna *35:* 228
Vojnar, Kamil *95:* 31; *114:* 4; *115:* 62; *121:* 90; *124:* 72; *130:* 31; *141:* 81; *146:* 196; *150:* 123; *158:* 5, 6; *158:* 154; *171:* 119, 188; *179:* 15
Vojtech, Anna *42:* 190; *108:* 222, 223; *150:* 203; *174:* 173
von Buhler, Cynthia *149:* 237; *162:* 177; *177:* 205
von Roehl, Angela *126:* 191
von Schmidt, Eric *8:* 62; *50:* 209, 210
von Schmidt, Harold *30:* 80
Vosburgh, Leonard *1:* 161; *7:* 32; *15:* 295, 296; *23:* 110; *30:* 214; *43:* 181
Voss, Tom *127:* 104
Voter, Thomas W. *19:* 3, 9
Vroman, Tom *10:* 29
Vulliamy, Clara *72:* 65

W

Waber, Bernard *47:* 209, 210, 211, 212, 213, 214; *95:* 215, 216, 217; *156:* 203, 205, 206, 207
Wack, Jeff *95:* 140; *110:* 90
Wagner, John *8:* 200; *52:* 104
Wagner, Ken *2:* 59
Waide, Jan *29:* 225; *36:* 139
Wainwright, Jerry *14:* 85
Waites, Joan C. *171:* 2
Wakeen, Sandra *47:* 97
Wakiyama, Hanako *171:* 96
Waldherr, Kris *81:* 186
Waldman, Bruce *15:* 297; *43:* 178
Waldman, Neil *35:* 141; *50:* 163; *51:* 180; *54:* 78; *77:* 112; *79:* 162; *82:* 174; *84:* 5, 56, 106; *94:* 232, 233, 234; *96:* 41; *111:* 139; *113:* 9; *118:* 30; *142:* 220, 223
Waldrep, Richard *111:* 147
Walker, Brian *144:* 128
Walker, Charles *1:* 46; *4:* 59; *5:* 177; *11:* 115; *19:* 45; *34:* 74; *62:* 168; *72:* 218
Walker, Dugald Stewart *15:* 47; *32:* 202; *33:* 112
Walker, Gil *8:* 49; *23:* 132; *34:* 42
Walker, Jeff *55:* 154; *123:* 116
Walker, Jim *10:* 94
Walker, Mort *8:* 213
Walker, Norman *41:* 37; *45:* 58
Walker, Stephen *12:* 229; *21:* 174
Wallace, Beverly Dobrin *19:* 259
Wallace, Cly *87:* 93
Wallace, Ian *53:* 176, 177; *56:* 165, 166; *58:* 4; *98:* 4; *101:* 191; *112:* 124; *141:* 197, 198, 199, 200; *151:* 212
Wallace, John *105:* 228
Wallace, Nancy Elizabeth *141:* 204
Wallenta, Adam *123:* 180
Waller, S.E. *24:* 36
Wallner, Alexandra *15:* 120; *156:* 183
Wallner, John C. *9:* 77; *10:* 188; *11:* 28; *14:* 209; *31:* 56, 118; *37:* 64; *51:* 186, 187, 188, 189, 190, 191,192, 193, 194, 195; *52:* 96; *53:* 23, 26; *71:* 99; *73:* 158; *89:* 215; *141:* 9
Wallner, John *162:* 17
Wallower, Lucille *11:* 226
Walotsky, Ron *93:* 87
Walsh, Ellen Stoll *99:* 209; *147:* 219
Walsh, Rebecca *158:* 193
Walsh, Vivian *149:* 215; *158:* 227
Walters, Audrey *18:* 294
Walther, Tom *31:* 179
Walton, Garry *69:* 149
Walton, Tony *11:* 164; *24:* 209; *153:* 8; *177:* 73
Waltrip, Lela *9:* 195
Waltrip, Mildred *3:* 209; *37:* 211
Waltrip, Rufus *9:* 195
Wan *12:* 76
Warburton, Sarah *154:* 187
Wappers, G. *121:* 40
Ward, Fred *52:* 19
Ward, Helen *72:* 244; *144:* 240, 242
Ward, John *42:* 191; *96:* 54; *97:* 110; *123:* 105; *124:* 71; *173:* 66
Ward, Keith *2:* 107; *132:* 69
Ward, Leslie *34:* 126; *36:* 87
Ward, Lynd *1:* 99, 132, 133, 150; *2:* 108, 158, 196, 259; *18:* 86; *27:* 56; *29:* 79, 187, 253, 255; *36:* 199,200, 201, 202, 203, 204, 205, 206, 207, 209; *43:* 34; *56:* 28; *60:* 116; *100:* 65
Ward, Peter *37:* 116
Waring, Geoff *172:* 84
Warhola, James *92:* 5; *115:* 85, 87; *118:* 174, 175, 177; *176:* 84
Warner, Ben *159:* 171
Warner, Peter *14:* 87
Warnes, Tim *175:* 159

Warnick, Elsa *113:* 223
Warren, Betsy *2:* 101
Warren, Jim *85:* 81
Warren, Marion Cray *14:* 215
Warshaw, Jerry *30:* 197, 198; *42:* 165
Wasden, Kevin *102:* 162
Washington, Nevin *20:* 123
Washington, Phyllis *20:* 123
Wasserman, Amy L. *92:* 110
Waterman, Stan *11:* 76
Watkins-Pitchford, D.J. *6:* 215, 217
Watling, James *67:* 210; *78:* 112; *101:* 81; *117:* 189, 190; *127:* 119, 120
Watson, Aldren A. *2:* 267; *5:* 94; *13:* 71; *19:* 253; *32:* 220; *42:* 193, 194, 195, 196, 197, 198, 199, 200, 201; *YABC 2:* 202
Watson, G. *83:* 162
Watson, Gary *19:* 147; *36:* 68; *41:* 122; *47:* 139
Watson, J.D. *22:* 86
Watson, Karen *11:* 26
Watson, Mary *117:* 193
Watson, Richard Jesse *62:* 188, 189
Watson, Wendy *5:* 197; *13:* 101; *33:* 116; *46:* 163; *64:* 12; *74:* 242, 243; *91:* 21; *142:* 228
Watt, Melanie *136:* 206
Wattenberg, Jane *174:* 200
Watterson, Bill *66:* 223, 225, 226
Watts, Bernadette *4:* 227; *103:* 182, 183
Watts, James *59:* 197; *74:* 145; *86:* 124
Watts, John *37:* 149
Watts, Leslie Elizabeth *150:* 207; *165:* 106
Watts, Stan *116:* 205
Weatherby, Mark Alan *77:* 141
Webb, Jennifer *110:* 79
Webb, Lanny *142:* 175
Webb, Sophie *135:* 214
Webber, Helen *3:* 141
Webber, Irma E. *14:* 238
Weber, Erik *56:* 19, 20
Weber, Florence *40:* 153
Weber, Jill *127:* 227, 228
Weber, Roland *61:* 204
Weber, William J. *14:* 239
Webster, Jean *17:* 241
Weeks, Sarah *162:* 39
Wegman, William *78:* 243
Wegner, Fritz *14:* 250; *20:* 189; *44:* 165; *86:* 62
Weidenear, Reynold H. *21:* 122
Weigel, Jeff *170:* 193
Weihs, Erika *4:* 21; *15:* 299; *72:* 201; *107:* 207, 208
Weil, Lisl *7:* 203; *10:* 58; *21:* 95; *22:* 188,217; *33:* 193
Weiman, Jon *50:* 162, 165; *52:* 103; *54:* 78, 79, 81; *78:* 80; *82:* 107; *93:* 82; *97:* 69; *105:* 179
Weiner, Sandra *14:* 240
Weiner, Scott *55:* 27
Weinhaus, Karen Ann *53:* 90; *71:* 50; *86:* 124
Weisgard, Leonard *1:* 65; *2:* 191, 197, 204, 264, 265; *5:* 108; *21:* 42; *30:* 200, 201, 203, 204; *41:* 47; *44:* 125; *53:* 25; *85:* 196, 198, 200, 201; *100:* 139,207; *YABC 2:* 13
Weisman, David *173:* 47
Weiss, Ellen *44:* 202
Weiss, Emil *1:* 168; *7:* 60
Weiss, Harvey *1:* 145, 223; *27:* 224, 227; *68:* 214; *76:* 245, 246, 247
Weiss, Nicki *33:* 229
Weissman, Bari *49:* 72; *90:* 125; *139:* 142
Weitzman, David L. *172:* 199
Welch, Sheila Kelly *130:* 221
Welkes, Allen *68:* 218
Wellington, Monica *99:* 223; *157:* 259, 260, 261
Welliver, Norma *76:* 94
Wellner, Fred *127:* 53
Wells, Frances *1:* 183
Wells, H.G. *20:* 194, 200

Wells, Haru *53:* 120, 121
Wells, Rosemary *6:* 49; *18:* 297; *60:* 32; *66:* 203; *69:* 215, 216; *114:* 227; *118:* 149, 150; *156:* 188, 189, 190, 191
Wells, Rufus III *56:* 111, 113
Wells, Susan *22:* 43
Wendelin, Rudolph *23:* 234
Wengenroth, Stow *37:* 47
Werenskiold, Erik *15:* 6; *62:* 17
Werner, Honi *24:* 110; *33:* 41; *88:* 122
Werth, Kurt *7:* 122; *14:* 157; *20:* 214; *39:* 128
West, Harry A. *124:* 38
Westcott, Nadine Bernard *68:* 46; *84:* 49; *86:* 133; *106:* 199; *111:* 78; *113:* 111; *130:* 224; *139:* 54; *158:* 256
Westerberg, Christine *29:* 226
Westerduin, Anne *105:* 229
Westerman, Johanna *162:* 206
Weston, Martha *29:* 116; *30:* 213; *33:* 85, 100; *53:* 181, 182, 183, 184; *77:* 95; *80:* 152; *119:* 196,197, 198, 199; *127:* 189; *133:* 196
Wetherbee, Margaret *5:* 3
Wexler, Jerome *49:* 73; *150:* 129
Whalley, Peter *50:* 49
Wheatley, Arabelle *11:* 231; *16:* 276
Wheeler, Cindy *49:* 205
Wheeler, Dora *44:* 179
Wheelright, Rowland *15:* 81; *YABC 2:* 286
Whelan, Michael *56:* 108; *70:* 27, 29, 67, 68, 148; *74:* 18; *84:* 14; *91:* 195, 196; *95:* 147; *98:* 150, 151; *106:* 157; *113:* 218, 220; *116:* 99, 100
Whelan, Patrick *135:* 145
Whistler, Rex *16:* 75; *30:* 207, 208
White, Craig *110:* 130; *119:* 193; *130:* 33; *179:* 31
White, David Omar *5:* 56; *18:* 6
White, Joan *83:* 225
White, Martin *51:* 197; *85:* 127
Whitear *32:* 26
Whitehead, Beck *86:* 171
Whitehead, S.B. *154:* 132
Whithorne, H.S. *7:* 49
Whitney, George Gillett *3:* 24
Whitney, Jean *99:* 53
Whitson, Paul *102:* 161
Whittam, Geoffrey *30:* 191
Whyte, Mary *96:* 127
Wiberg, Harald *38:* 127; *93:* 215
Wick, Walter *77:* 128
Wickstrom, Sylvie *106:* 87; *169:* 180
Widener, Terry *105:* 230; *106:* 7; *163:* 23
Wiese, Kurt *3:* 255; *4:* 206; *14:* 17; *17:* 18, 19; *19:* 47; *24:* 152; *25:* 212; *32:* 184; *36:* 211,213, 214, 215, 216, 217, 218; *45:* 161; *100:* 92
Wiesner, David *33:* 47; *51:* 106; *57:* 67; *58:* 55; *64:* 78, 79, 81; *69:* 233; *72:* 247, 248, 249, 251,252, 253, 254; *83:* 134; *104:* 31; *117:* 197, 199, 200, 202; *139:* 223, 224; *151:* 51
Wiesner, William *4:* 100; *5:* 200, 201; *14:* 262
Wiggins, George *6:* 133
Wijngaard, Juan *111:* 36; *114:* 124
Wikkelsoe, Otto *45:* 25, 26
Wikland, Ilon *5:* 113; *8:* 150; *38:* 124, 125, 130; *127:* 162
Wikler, Madeline *114:* 233
Wilbur, C. Keith, M.D. *27:* 228
Wilburn, Kathy *53:* 102; *68:* 234
Wilcox, Cathy *105:* 123
Wilcox, J.A.J. *34:* 122
Wilcox, R. Turner *36:* 219
Wild, Jocelyn *46:* 220, 221, 222; *80:* 117
Wilde, George *7:* 139
Wildsmith, Brian *16:* 281, 282; *18:* 170, 171; *66:* 25; *69:* 224, 225, 227; *77:* 103; *83:* 218; *124:* 214,217, 219
Wildsmith, Mike *140:* 229
Wilhelm, Hans *58:* 189, 191; *73:* 157; *77:* 127; *135:* 229, 230, 233, 234

Wilkin, Eloise *36:* 173; *49:* 208, 209, 210
Wilkinson, Barry *50:* 213
Wilkinson, Gerald *3:* 40
Wilkon, Jozef *31:* 183, 184; *71:* 206, 207, 209; *133:* 222
Wilks, Mike *34:* 24; *44:* 203
Willems, Mo *154:* 245, 246, 247
Willey, Bee *103:* 129; *139:* 159; *173:* 115
Willhoite, Michael A. *71:* 214
William, Maria *168:* 51
Williams, Berkeley, Jr. *64:* 75
Williams, Ferelith Eccles *22:* 238
Williams, Garth *1:* 197; *2:* 49, 270; *4:* 205; *15:* 198, 302, 304, 307; *16:* 34; *18:* 283, 298, 299, 300, 301; *29:* 177, 178, 179, 232, 233, 241, 242, 243, 244, 245, 248; *40:* 106; *66:* 229, 230, 231, 233, 234; *71:* 192; *73:* 218, 219, 220; *78:* 261; *100:* 251, 252, 255; *136:* 117; *YABC 2:* 15, 16, 19
Williams, J. Scott *48:* 28
Williams, Jennifer *102:* 201
Williams, Jenny *60:* 202; *81:* 21; *88:* 71
Williams, Kit *44:* 206, 207, 208, 209, 211, 212
Williams, Marcia *97:* 214; *159:* 208, 209
Williams, Maureen *12:* 238
Williams, Patrick *14:* 218
Williams, Richard *44:* 93; *72:* 229; *74:* 133; *78:* 155, 237; *91:* 178; *110:* 212; *136:* 201, 202, 203; *152:* 115
Williams, Sam *124:* 222; *153:* 11; *177:* 201, 202
Williams, Sophy *135:* 236
Williams, Vera B. *53:* 186, 187, 188, 189; *102:* 201, 202, 203
Williamson, Alex *177:* 180
Williamson, Mel *60:* 9
Willingham, Fred *104:* 206; *154:* 157
Willmore, J.T. *54:* 113, 114
Wilson, Anne *160:* 114
Wilson, Charles Banks *17:* 92; *43:* 73
Wilson, Connie *113:* 179
Wilson, Dagmar *10:* 47
Wilson, Dawn *67:* 161; *81:* 120; *113:* 158
Wilson, Edward A. *6:* 24; *16:* 149; *20:* 220, 221; *22:* 87; *26:* 67; *38:* 212, 214, 215, 216, 217
Wilson, Forrest *27:* 231
Wilson, Gahan *35:* 234; *41:* 136
Wilson, George *76:* 87
Wilson, Helen Miranda *140:* 61
Wilson, Jack *17:* 139
Wilson, Janet *77:* 154; *96:* 114; *99:* 219, 220; *153:* 64 *106:* 122; *130:* 210; *145:* 178; *173:* 64
Wilson, John *22:* 240
Wilson, Maurice *46:* 224
Wilson, Patten *35:* 61
Wilson, Peggy *15:* 4; *84:* 20
Wilson, Rowland B. *30:* 170
Wilson, Sarah *50:* 215
Wilson, Tom *33:* 232
Wilson, W.N. *22:* 26
Wilson-Max, Ken *170:* 196
Wilton, Nicholas *103:* 52
Wilwerding, Walter J. *9:* 202
Wimmer, Mike *63:* 6; *70:* 121; *75:* 186; *76:* 21,22, 23; *91:* 114; *97:* 45, 68; *98:* 28; *107:* 130; *146:* 21; *149:* 47; *173:* 126
Winborn, Marsha *78:* 34; *99:* 70
Winch, John *165:* 233
Winchester, Linda *13:* 231
Wind, Betty *28:* 158
Windham, Kathryn Tucker *14:* 260
Winfield, Alison *115:* 78
Winfield, Wayne *72:* 23
Wing, Gary *64:* 147
Wing, Ron *50:* 85
Wingerter, Linda S. *132:* 199; *174:* 181
Winick, Judd *124:* 227, 228, 229
Winslow, Will *21:* 124
Winsten, Melanie Willa *41:* 41

Winter, Jeanette *151:* 240, 241, 242
Winter, Milo *15:* 97; *19:* 221; *21:* 181, 203, 204, 205; *64:* 19; *YABC 2:* 144
Winter, Paula *48:* 227
Winter, Susan *163:* 177
Winters, Greg *70:* 117
Winters, Nina *62:* 194
Wise, Louis *13:* 68
Wiseman, Ann *31:* 187
Wiseman, B. *4:* 233
Wishnefsky, Phillip *3:* 14
Wiskur, Darrell *5:* 72; *10:* 50; *18:* 246
Wisniewski, David *95:* 220, 221
Wisniewski, Robert *95:* 10; *119:* 192
Witschonke, Alan *153:* 149, 150
Witt, Dick *80:* 244
Wittmann, Patrick *162:* 204
Wittman, Sally *30:* 219
Wittner, Dale *99:* 43
Wittwer, Hala *158:* 267
Woehr, Lois *12:* 5
Wohlberg, Meg *12:* 100; *14:* 197; *41:* 255
Wohnoutka, Mike *137:* 68
Wojtowycz, David *167:* 168
Woldin, Beth Weiner *34:* 211
Wolf, Elizabeth *133:* 151
Wolf, J. *16:* 91
Wolf, Janet *78:* 254
Wolf, Linda *33:* 163
Wolfe, Corey *72:* 213
Wolff, Ashley *50:* 217; *81:* 216; *156:* 216, 217; *170:* 57; *174:* 174
Wolff, Glenn *178:* 230
Wolfsgruber, Linda *166:* 61
Wondriska, William *6:* 220
Wong, Janet S. *98:* 225; *152:* 43
Wong, Nicole *174:* 13
Wonsetler, John C. *5:* 168
Wood, Audrey *50:* 221, 222, 223; *81:* 219, 221
Wood, Don *50:* 220, 225, 226, 228, 229; *81:* 218, 220; *139:* 239, 240
Wood, Grant *19:* 198
Wood, Heather *133:* 108
Wood, Ivor *58:* 17
Wood, Muriel *36:* 119; *77:* 167; *171:* 55
Wood, Myron *6:* 220
Wood, Owen *18:* 187; *64:* 202, 204, 205, 206, 208, 210
Wood, Ruth *8:* 11
Woodbridge, Curtis *133:* 138
Wooding, Sharon L. *66:* 237
Woodruff, Liza *132:* 239
Woodruff, Thomas *171:* 73
Woods, John, Jr. *109:* 142
Woodson, Jack *10:* 201
Woodson, Jacqueline *94:* 242
Woodward, Alice *26:* 89; *36:* 81
Wool, David *26:* 27
Woolley, Janet *112:* 75
Woolman, Steven *106:* 47; *163:* 73
Wooten, Vernon *23:* 70; *51:* 170
Worboys, Evelyn *1:* 166, 167
Word, Reagan *103:* 204
Wormell, Christopher *154:* 251
Worth, Jo *34:* 143
Worth, Wendy *4:* 133
Wosmek, Frances *29:* 251
Wrenn, Charles L. *38:* 96; *YABC 1:* 20, 21
Wright, Barbara Mullarney *98:* 161
Wright, Cliff *168:* 203
Wright, Dare *21:* 206
Wright-Frierson, Virginia *58:* 194; *110:* 246
Wright, George *YABC 1:* 268
Wright, Joseph *30:* 160
Wronker, Lili Cassel *3:* 247; *10:* 204; *21:* 10
Wummer, Amy *154:* 181; *168:* 150; *176:* 85
Wyant, Alexander Helwig *110:* 19
Wyatt, David *97:* 9; *101:* 44; *114:* 194; *140:* 20; *167:* 13
Wyatt, Stanley *46:* 210
Wyeth, Andrew *13:* 40; *YABC 1:* 133, 134

Wyeth, Jamie *41:* 257
Wyeth, N.C. *13:* 41; *17:* 252, 253, 254, 255, 256, 257, 258, 259, 264, 265, 266, 267, 268; *18:* 181; *19:* 80, 191, 200; *21:* 57, 183; *22:* 91; *23:* 152; *24:* 28, 99; *35:* 61; *41:* 65; *100:* 206; *YABC1:* 133, 223; *2:* 53, 75, 171, 187, 317
Wyman, Cherie R. *91:* 42

X

Xuan, YongSheng *119:* 202, 207, 208; *140:* 36

Y

Yaccarino, Dan *141:* 208, 209; *147:* 171
Yakovetic, Joe *59:* 202; *75:* 85
Yalowitz, Paul *93:* 33
Yamaguchi, Marianne *85:* 118
Yamasaki, James *167:* 93
Yang, Belle *170:* 198
Yang, Jay *1:* 8; *12:* 239
Yap, Weda *6:* 176
Yaroslava
  See Mills, Yaroslava Surmach
Yashima, Taro *14:* 84
Yates, John *74:* 249, 250
Yayo *178:* 88
Yee, Cora *166:* 233
Yee, Wong Herbert *115:* 216, 217; *172:* 204, 205
Yeo, Brad *135:* 121
Yezerski, Thomas F. *162:* 29
Ylla
  See Koffler, Camilla
Yohn, F.C. *23:* 128; *YABC 1:* 269

Yorinks, Adrienne *144:* 248
Yorke, David *80:* 178
Yoshida, Toshi *77:* 231
Yoshikawa, Sachiko *168:* 104; *177:* 28
Youll, Paul *91:* 218
Youll, Stephen *92:* 227; *118:* 136, 137; *164:* 248
Young, Cybéle *167:* 9
Young, Ed *7:* 205; *10:* 206; *40:* 124; *63:* 142; *74:* 250, 251, 252, 253; *75:* 227; *81:* 159; *83:* 98; *94:* 154; *115:* 160; *137:* 162; *YABC 2:* 242; *173:* 174, 175, 176
Young, Mary O'Keefe *77:* 95; *80:* 247; *134:* 214; *140:* 213
Young, Noela *8:* 221; *89:* 231; *97:* 195
Young, Selina *153:* 12
Yun, Cheng Mung *60:* 143

Z

Zacharow, Christopher *88:* 98
Zacks, Lewis *10:* 161
Zadig *50:* 58
Zaffo, George *42:* 208
Zagwyn, Deborah Turney *138:* 227
Zaid, Barry *50:* 127; *51:* 201
Zaidenberg, Arthur *34:* 218, 219, 220
Zalben, Jane Breskin *7:* 211; *79:* 230, 231, 233; *170:* 202
Zallinger, Jean *4:* 192; *8:* 8, 129; *14:* 273; *68:* 36; *80:* 254; *115:* 219, 220, 222
Zallinger, Rudolph F. *3:* 245
Zakrajsek, Molly *177:* 146
Zebot, George *83:* 214
Zeck, Gerry *40:* 232
Zeifert, Harriet *154:* 265, 267
Zeiring, Bob *42:* 130
Zeldich, Arieh *49:* 124; *62:* 120

Zeldis, Malcah *86:* 239; *94:* 198; *146:* 265, 266
Zelinsky, Paul O. *14:* 269; *43:* 56; *49:* 218-223; *53:* 111; *68:* 195; *102:* 219, 222, 221, 222; *154:* 255, 256, 257; *171:* 141
Zelvin, Diana *72:* 190; *76:* 101; *93:* 207
Zemach, Kaethe *149:* 250
Zemach, Margot *3:* 270; *8:* 201; *21:* 210, 211; *27:* 204, 205, 210; *28:* 185; *49:* 22, 183, 224; *53:* 151; *56:* 146; *70:* 245, 246; *92:* 74
Zeman, Ludmila *153* 212
Zemsky, Jessica *10:* 62
Zepelinsky, Paul *35:* 93
Zerbetz, Evon *127:* 34; *158:* 109
Zhang, Ange *101:* 190; *172:* 41
Zhang, Son Nang *163:* 113; *170:* 206
Ziegler, Jack *84:* 134
Zimdars, Berta *129:* 155
Zimet, Jay *147:* 94; *152:* 74
Zimic, Tricia *72:* 95
Zimmer, Dirk *38:* 195; *49:* 71; *56:* 151; *65:* 214; *84:* 159; *89:* 26; *147:* 224
Zimmer, Tracie Vaughn *169:* 183
Zimmermann, H. Werner *101:* 223; *112:* 197
Zimnik, Reiner *36:* 224
Zinkeisen, Anna *13:* 106
Zinn, David *97:* 97
Zoellick, Scott *33:* 231
Zonia, Dhimitri *20:* 234, 235
Zorn, Peter A., Jr. *142:* 157
Zudeck, Darryl *58:* 129; *63:* 98; *80:* 52
Zug, Mark *88:* 131
Zulewski, Tim *164:* 95
Zuma *99:* 36
Zvorykin, Boris *61:* 155
Zweifel, Francis *14:* 274; *28:* 187
Zwerger, Lisbeth *54:* 176, 178; *66:* 246, 247, 248; *130:* 230, 231, 232, 233
Zwinger, Herman H. *46:* 227
Zwolak, Paul *67:* 69, 71, 73, 74

Author Index

The following index gives the number of the volume in which an author's biographical sketch, Autobiography Feature, Brief Entry, or Obituary appears.

This index includes references to all entries in the following series, which are also published by The Gale Group.

YABC—*Yesterday's Authors of Books for Children: Facts and Pictures about Authors and Illustrators of Books for Young People from Early Times to 1960*
CLR—*Children's Literature Review: Excerpts from Reviews, Criticism, and Commentary on Books for Children*
SAAS—*Something about the Author Autobiography Series*

A

Aaron, Chester 1923- 74
  Earlier sketch in SATA 9
  See also SAAS 12
Aaseng, Nate
  See Aaseng, Nathan
Aaseng, Nathan 1953- 172
  Brief entry 38
  Earlier sketches in SATA 51, 88
  See also CLR 54
  See also SAAS 12
Abbas, Jailan 1952- 91
Abbey, Lynn
  See Abbey, Marilyn Lorraine
Abbey, Marilyn Lorraine 1948- 156
Abbott, Alice
  See Borland, Kathryn Kilby
  and Speicher, Helen Ross S(mith)
Abbott, Jacob 1803-1879 22
Abbott, Manager Henry
  See Stratemeyer, Edward L.
Abbott, R(obert) Tucker 1919-1995 61
  Obituary 87
Abbott, Sarah
  See Zolotow, Charlotte (Gertrude) S(hapiro)
Abbott, Tony 1952- 159
Abdelsayed, Cindy 1962- 123
Abdul, Raoul 1929- 12
Abel, Raymond 1911- 12
Abell, Kathleen 1938- 9
Abelove, Joan 110
Abels, Harriette S(heffer) 1926- 50
Abercrombie, Barbara (Mattes) 1939- 16
Abercrombie, Lynn
  See Sorrells, Walter
Abernethy, Robert G(ordon) 1927- 5
Abisch, Roslyn Kroop 1927- 9
Abisch, Roz
  See Abisch, Roslyn Kroop
Abodaher, David J. (Naiph) 1919- 17
Abolafia, Yossi 1944-
  See Abulafia, Yossi
Abouzeid, Chris 175
Abrahall, Clare Hoskyns
  See Hoskyns-Abrahall, Clare (Constance Drury)
Abrahams, Hilary (Ruth) 1938- 29
Abrahams, Robert David 1905-1998 4

Abrams, Joy 1941- 16
Abrams, Lawrence F. 58
  Brief entry 47
Abrashkin, Raymond 1911-1960 50
Abulafia, Yossi 1944- 177
  Brief entry 46
  Earlier sketch in SATA 60
Acampora, Paul 175
Achebe, Albert Chinualumogu
  See Achebe, Chinua
Achebe, Chinua 1930- 40
  Brief entry 38
  Earlier sketch in SATA 38
  See also CLR 20
Ackerman, Diane 1948- 102
Ackerman, Eugene (Francis) 1888-1974 10
Ackerman, Karen 1951- 126
Ackerman, Susan Yoder 1945- 92
Ackison, Wendy Wassink 1956- 103
Ackley, Peggy Jo 1955- 58
Ackroyd, Peter 1949- 153
Acorn, John (Harrison) 1958- 79
Acredolo, Linda (Potter) 1947- 159
Acs, Laszlo (Bela) 1931- 42
  Brief entry 32
Acuff, Selma Boyd 1924- 45
Ada, Alma Flor 1938- 143
  Earlier sketches in SATA 43, 84
  See also CLR 62
Adair, Gilbert 1944- 98
Adair, Ian 1942- 53
Adair, Margaret Weeks (?)-1971 10
Adam, Cornel
  See Lengyel, Cornel Adam
Adam, Mark
  See Alexander, Marc
Adam, Robert 1948- 93
Adams, Adrienne 1906- 90
  Earlier sketch in SATA 8
  See also CLR 73
Adams, Andy 1859-1935
  See YABC 1
Adams, Barbara Johnston 1943- 60
Adams, Bruin
  See Ellis, Edward S(ylvester)
Adams, Captain Bruin
  See Ellis, Edward S(ylvester)
Adams, Captain J. F. C.
  See Ellis, Edward S(ylvester)

Adams, Dale
  See Quinn, Elisabeth
Adams, Daniel
  See Nicole, Christopher (Robin)
Adams, Debra
  See Speregen, Devra Newberger
Adams, Douglas 1952-2001 116
  Obituary 128
Adams, Douglas Noel
  See Adams, Douglas
Adams, Edith
  See Shine, Deborah
Adams, Florence 1932- 61
Adams, Harriet S(tratemeyer) 1892(?)-1982 .. 1
  Obituary 29
Adams, Harrison
  See Rathborne, St. George (Henry)
  and Stratemeyer, Edward L.
Adams, Hazard 1926- 6
Adams, Hazard Simeon
  See Adams, Hazard
Adams, John Anthony 1944- 67
Adams, Laurie 1941- 33
Adams, Lowell
  See Joseph, James (Herz)
Adams, Nicholas
  See Pine, Nicholas
Adams, Nicholas
  See Smith, Sherwood
Adams, Nicholas
  See Doyle, Debra
  and Macdonald, James D.
Adams, Pam 1919- 112
Adams, Pamela
  See Adams, Pam
Adams, Richard (George) 1920- 69
  Earlier sketch in SATA 7
  See also CLR 121
Adams, Ruth Joyce 14
Adams, William Taylor 1822-1897 28
Adam Smith, Janet (Buchanan) 1905-1999 .. 63
Adamson, Gareth 1925-1982(?) 46
  Obituary 30
Adamson, George (Worsley) 1913-2005 30
Adamson, Graham
  See Groom, Arthur William
Adamson, Joy(-Friederike Victoria)
  1910-1980 11
  Obituary 22

Adamson, Wendy Writson 1942- 22
Addona, Angelo F. 1925- 14
Addy, Sharon Hart 1943- 108
Addy, Ted
 See Winterbotham, R(ussell) R(obert)
Adelberg, Doris
 See Orgel, Doris
Adelson, Leone 1908- 11
Adinolfi, JoAnn 176
Adkins, Jan 1944- 144
 Earlier sketches in SATA *8, 69*
 See also CLR *77*
 See also SAAS *19*
Adler, C(arole) S(chwerdtfeger) 1932- 126
 Earlier sketches in SATA *26, 63, 102*
 See also CLR *78*
 See also SAAS *15*
Adler, David A. 1947- 178
 Earlier sketches in SATA *14, 70, 106, 151*
 See also CLR *108*
Adler, Irene
 See Penzler, Otto
 and Storr, Catherine (Cole)
Adler, Irving 1913- 29
 Autobiography Feature 164
 Earlier sketch in SATA *1*
 See also CLR *27*
 See also SAAS *15*
Adler, Larry 1939- 36
Adler, Peggy 22
Adler, Ruth 1915-1968 1
Adlerman, Daniel (Ezra) 1963- 163
 Earlier sketch in SATA *96*
Adlerman, Kim
 See Adlerman, Kimberly M(arie)
Adlerman, Kimberly M(arie) 1964- 163
 Earlier sketch in SATA *96*
Adoff, Arnold 1935- 96
 Earlier sketches in SATA *5, 57*
 See also CLR *7*
 See also SAAS *15*
Adoff, Jaime (Levi) 163
Adorjan, Carol (Madden) 1934- 71
 Earlier sketch in SATA *10*
Adrian, Frances
 See Polland, Madeleine A(ngela Cahill)
Adrian, Mary
 See Jorgensen, Mary Venn
Adshead, Gladys L(ucy) 1896-1985 3
Aesop 620(?)B.C.-560(?)B.C. 64
 See also CLR *14*
Aesop, Abraham
 See Newbery, John
Affabee, Eric
 See Stine, R.L.
Agapida, Fray Antonio
 See Irving, Washington
Agard, John 1949- 138
Agard, Nadema 1948- 18
Agarwal, Deepa 1947- 141
Agee, Jon 1960- 157
 Earlier sketch in SATA *116*
Agell, Charlotte 1959- 150
 Earlier sketch in SATA *99*
Agent Orange
 See Moseley, James W(illett)
Aghill, Gordon
 See Garrett, (Gordon) Randall (Phillip)
 and Silverberg, Robert
Agle, Nan Hayden 1905- 3
 See also SAAS *10*
Agnew, Edith J(osephine) 1897-1988 11
Agonito, Joseph 177
Agonito, Rosemary 1937- 177
Ahern, Margaret McCrohan 1921- 10
Ahl, Anna Maria 1926- 32
Ahlberg, Allan 1938- 165
 Brief entry 35
 Earlier sketches in SATA *68, 120*
 See also CLR *18*

Ahlberg, Janet 1944-1994 120
 Brief entry 32
 Obituary 83
 Earlier sketch in SATA *68*
 See also CLR *18*
Aichinger, Helga 1937- 4
Aiken, Clarissa (M.) Lorenz 1899-1992 12
 Obituary 109
Aiken, Conrad (Potter) 1889-1973 30
 Earlier sketch in SATA *3*
Aiken, Joan (Delano) 1924-2004 73
 Autobiography Feature 109
 Obituary 152
 Earlier sketches in SATA *2, 30*
 See also CLR *90*
 See also SAAS *1*
Ainsley, Alix
 See Steiner, Barbara A(nnette)
Ainsworth, Catherine Harris 1910- 56
Ainsworth, Norma 1911-1987 9
Ainsworth, Ruth (Gallard) 1908- 73
 Earlier sketch in SATA *7*
Ainsworth, William Harrison 1805-1882 24
Aistrop, Jack 1916- 14
Aitken, Amy 1952- 54
 Brief entry 40
Aitken, Dorothy 1916- 10
Aitmatov, Chingiz (Torekulovich) 1928- 56
 See Aytmatov, Chingiz
Akaba, Suekichi 1910- 46
Akers, Floyd
 See Baum, L(yman) Frank
Aks, Patricia 1926-1994 68
Alagoa, Ebiegberi Joe 1933- 108
Alain
 See Brustlein, Daniel
Alan, David
 See Horsfield, Alan
Alan, Robert
 See Silverstein, Robert Alan
Alarcon, Francisco X(avier) 1954- 104
Albert, Burton 1936- 22
Albert, Louise 1928- 157
Albert, Richard E. 1909-1999 82
Albert, Susan Wittig 1940- 107
Alberts, Frances Jacobs 1907-1989 14
Albertson, Susan
 See Wojciechowski, Susan
Albion, Lee Smith 29
Alborough, Jez 1959- 149
 Earlier sketch in SATA *86*
Albrecht, Lillie (Vanderveer H.)
 1894-1985 12
Albyn, Carole Lisa 1955- 83
Alcock, Gudrun 1908- 56
 Brief entry 33
Alcock, Vivien (Dolores) 1924-2003 76
 Brief entry 38
 Obituary 148
 Earlier sketch in SATA *45*
 See also CLR *26*
Alcorn, John 1935- 31
 Brief entry 30
Alcorn, Stephen 1958- 110
Alcott, Louisa May 1832-1888 100
 See also YABC *1*
 See also CLR *109*
Alda, Arlene 1933- 158
 Brief entry 36
 Earlier sketches in SATA *44, 106*
 See also CLR *93*
Alden, Isabella (Macdonald) 1841-1930 115
 See also YABC *2*
Alden, Sue
 See Francis, Dorothy Brenner
Alderman, Clifford Lindsey 1902-1988 3
Alderson, Sue Ann 1940- 59
 Brief entry 48
Alding, Peter
 See Jeffries, Roderic
Aldis, Dorothy (Keeley) 1896-1966 2

Aldiss, Brian W. 1925- 34
Aldiss, Brian Wilson
 See Aldiss, Brian W.
Aldon, Adair
 See Meigs, Cornelia Lynde
Aldous, Allan (Charles) 1911- 27
Aldrich, Ann
 See Meaker, Marijane
Aldrich, Bess Streeter 1881-1954
 See CLR *70*
Aldrich, Thomas (Bailey) 1836-1907 114
 Earlier sketch in SATA *17*
Aldridge, (Harold Edward) James 1918- 87
Aldridge, Josephine Haskell 14
Alegria, Ricardo E(nrique) 1921- 6
Aleksin, Anatolii Georgievich 1924- 36
Alenov, Lydia 1948- 61
Alex, Ben (a pseudonym) 1946- 45
Alex, Marlee (a pseudonym) 1948- 45
Alexander, Anna B(arbara Cooke) 1913- 1
Alexander, Anne
 See Alexander, Anna B(arbara Cooke)
Alexander, Ellen 1938- 91
Alexander, Frances (Laura) 1888-1979 4
Alexander, Jocelyn Anne Arundel 1930- 22
Alexander, Linda 1935- 2
Alexander, Lloyd 1924-2007 135
 Earlier sketches in SATA *3, 49, 81, 129*
 See also CLR *48*
 See also SAAS *19*
Alexander, Lloyd Chudley
 See Alexander, Lloyd
Alexander, Marc 1929- 117
Alexander, Martha 1920- 136
 Earlier sketches in SATA *11, 70*
Alexander, Rae Pace
 See Alexander, Raymond Pace
Alexander, Raymond Pace 1898-1974 22
Alexander, Rod
 See Pellowski, Michael (Joseph)
Alexander, Sally Hobart 1943- 84
Alexander, Sue 1933- 136
 Earlier sketches in SATA *12, 89*
 See also SAAS *15*
Alexeieff, Alexandre A. 1901-1979 14
Alger, Horatio, Jr.
 See Stratemeyer, Edward L.
Alger, Horatio, Jr. 1832-1899 16
 See also CLR *87*
Alger, Leclaire (Gowans) 1898-1969 15
Aliki
 See CLR *71*
 See Brandenberg, Aliki (Liacouras)
Alkema, Chester Jay 1932- 12
Al-Khalili, Jim 1962- 124
Alkiviades, Alkis 1953- 105
Allaby, John Michael
 See Allaby, Michael
Allaby, Michael 1933- 167
Allamand, Pascale 1942- 12
Allan, Mabel Esther 1915-1998 75
 Earlier sketches in SATA *5, 32*
 See also CLR *43*
 See also SAAS *11*
Allan, Nicholas 1956- 123
 Earlier sketch in SATA *79*
Allan-Meyer, Kathleen 1918- 51
 Brief entry 46
Allard, Harry
 See Allard, Harry G(rover), Jr.
Allard, Harry G(rover), Jr. 1928- 102
 Earlier sketch in SATA *42*
 See also CLR *85*
Allee, Marjorie Hill 1890-1945 17
Allen, Adam
 See Epstein, Beryl (M. Williams)
 and Epstein, Samuel
Allen, Alex B.
 See Heide, Florence Parry
Allen, Allyn
 See Eberle, Irmengarde

Allen, Betsy
  See Harrison, Elizabeth (Allen) Cavanna
Allen, Bob 1961- 76
Allen, Gertrude E(lizabeth) 1888-1984 9
Allen, Grace
  See Hogarth, Grace (Weston Allen)
Allen, Jeffrey (Yale) 1948- 42
Allen, John
  See Perry, Ritchie (John Allen)
Allen, Jonathan 1957- 177
  Earlier sketch in SATA *131*
Allen, Jonathan Dean
  See Allen, Jonathan
Allen, Judy (Christina) 1941- 124
  Earlier sketch in SATA *80*
Allen, Kenneth S. 1913-1981 56
Allen, Leroy 1912- 11
Allen, Linda 1925- 33
Allen, Marjorie 1931- 22
Allen, Maury 1932- 26
Allen, Merritt Parmelee 1892-1954 22
Allen, Nancy Kelly 1949- 171
  Earlier sketch in SATA *127*
Allen, Nina (Stroemgren) 1935- 22
Allen, Pamela (Kay) 1934- 123
  Earlier sketches in SATA *50, 81*
  See also CLR *44*
Allen, Rodney F. 1938-1999 27
Allen, Roger MacBride 1957- 105
Allen, Ruth
  See Peterson, Esther (Allen)
Allen, Samuel W(ashington) 1917- 9
Allen, T. D.
  See Allen, Terril Diener
Allen, Terril Diener 1908- 35
  See Allen, T. D.
Allen, Terry D.
  See Allen, Terril Diener
Allen, Thomas B(enton) 1929- 140
  Earlier sketch in SATA *45*
Allen, Tom
  See Allen, Thomas B(enton)
Allende, Isabel 1942- 163
  See also CLR *99*
Allerton, Mary
  See Govan, (Mary) Christine Noble
Alley, Robert W.
  See Alley, R.W.
Alley, R.W. 169
Alleyn, Ellen
  See Rossetti, Christina
Allington, Richard L(loyd) 1947- 39
  Brief entry 35
Allison, Amy 1956- 138
Allison, Bob 14
Allison, Diane Worfolk 78
Allison, Jennifer 173
Allison, Linda 1948- 43
Allman, Barbara 1950- 137
Allmendinger, David F(rederick), Jr. 1938- . 35
Allred, Alexandra Powe 1965- 144
Allred, Gordon T(hatcher) 1930- 10
Allsop, Kenneth 1920-1973 17
Almedingen, E. M. 3
  See Almedingen, Martha Edith von
Almon, Russell
  See Clevenger, William R.
  and Downing, David A(lmon)
Almond, David 1951- 158
  Earlier sketch in SATA *114*
  See also CLR *85*
Almquist, Don 1929- 11
Alphin, Elaine Marie 1955- 139
  Autobiography Feature 139
  Earlier sketches in SATA *80, 130*
Alsop, Mary O'Hara 1885-1980 34
  Obituary 24
  Earlier sketch in SATA *2*
  See O'Hara, Mary
Alter, Anna 1974- 135

Alter, Judith (MacBain) 1938- 101
  Earlier sketch in SATA *52*
Alter, Judy
  See Alter, Judith (MacBain)
Alter, Robert Edmond 1925-1965 9
Althea
  See Braithwaite, Althea
Altman, Linda Jacobs 1943- 21
Altman, Suzanne
  See Orgel, Doris
  and Schecter, Ellen
Alton, Steve 169
Altshuler, Franz 1923- 45
Altsheler, Joseph A(lexander) 1862-1919
  See YABC *1*
Alvarez, John
  See del Rey, Lester
Alvarez, Joseph A. 1930- 18
Alvarez, Julia 1950- 129
al-Windawi, Thura
  See Windawi, Thura al-
Alyer, Philip A.
  See Stratemeyer, Edward L.
Amann, Janet 1951- 79
Amato, Carol A. 1942- 92
Amato, Mary 1961- 178
  Earlier sketch in SATA *140*
Ambrose, Stephen E. 1936-2002 138
  Earlier sketch in SATA *40*
Ambrose, Stephen Edward
  See Ambrose, Stephen E.
Ambrus, Gyozo Laszlo 1935- 41
  See Ambrus, Victor G.
Ambrus, Victor G. 1
  See also SAAS *4*
  See Ambrus, Gyozo Laszlo
Amend, Bill 1962- 147
Amerman, Lockhart 1911-1969 3
Ames, Evelyn 1908-1990 13
  Obituary 64
Ames, Gerald 1906-1993 11
  Obituary 74
Ames, Lee J(udah) 1921- 151
  Earlier sketch in SATA *3*
Ames, Mildred 1919-1994 85
  Earlier sketches in SATA *22, 81*
Amico, Tom 1960(?)- 176
Ammon, Richard 1942- 124
Amon, Aline 1928- 9
Amoss, Berthe 1925- 112
  Earlier sketch in SATA *5*
Anastasio, Dina 1941- 94
  Brief entry 30
  Earlier sketch in SATA *37*
Anckarsvard, Karin Inez Maria 1915-1969 6
Ancona, George 1929- 145
  Earlier sketches in SATA *12, 85*
  See also SAAS *18*
Anders, C. J.
  See Bennett, Cherie
Anders, Isabel 1946- 101
Anders, Lou 176
Andersdatter, Karla M(argaret) 1938- 34
Andersen, Hans Christian 1805-1875 100
  See also YABC *1*
  See also CLR *113*
Andersen, Ted
  See Boyd, Waldo T.
Andersen, Yvonne 1932- 27
Anderson, Bernice G(oudy) 1894-1997 33
Anderson, Bob 1944- 139
  Earlier sketch in SATA *136*
Anderson, Brad(ley Jay) 1924- 33
  Brief entry 31
Anderson, C. C.
  See Anderson, Catherine Corley
Anderson, C(larence) W(illiam) 1891-1971 . 11
Anderson, Catherine C.
  See Anderson, Catherine Corley
Anderson, Catherine Corley 1909-2001 72

Anderson, Clifford
  See Gardner, Richard (M.)
Anderson, Daryl Shon 1963- 93
Anderson, Dave
  See Anderson, David (Poole)
Anderson, David (Poole) 1929- 60
Anderson, Derek 1969- 169
Anderson, Eloise Adell 1927- 9
Anderson, George
  See Groom, Arthur William
Anderson, Grace Fox 1932- 43
Anderson, J(ohn) R(ichard) L(ane)
  1911-1981 15
  Obituary 27
Anderson, Joy 1928- 1
Anderson, Kevin J. 1962- 117
  Earlier sketch in SATA *74*
Anderson, Kevin James
  See Anderson, Kevin J.
Anderson, Kirsty 1978- 108
Anderson, Laurie Halse 1961- 132
  Earlier sketch in SATA *95*
Anderson, LaVere Francis Shoenfelt
  1907-1998 27
Anderson, Leone Castell 1923- 53
  Brief entry 49
Anderson, Lisa G. 1963- 108
Anderson, Lonzo 2
  See Anderson, John L(onzo)
Anderson, Lucia (Lewis) 1922- 10
Anderson, Madelyn Klein 1926-2005 28
Anderson, Margaret J(ean) 1931- 27
  See also SAAS *8*
Anderson, Marilyn D. 1943- 144
Anderson, Mary 1939- 82
  Earlier sketch in SATA *7*
  See also SAAS *23*
Anderson, Matthew Tobin
  See Anderson, M.T.
Anderson, Mona 1910-2004 40
Anderson, Mrs. Melvin
  See Anderson, Catherine Corley
Anderson, M.T. 1968- 146
  Earlier sketch in SATA *97*
Anderson, Norman Dean 1928- 22
Anderson, Peggy Perry 1953- 179
  Earlier sketch in SATA *84*
Anderson, Poul 1926-2001 90
  Autobiography Feature 106
  Brief entry 39
  See also CLR *58*
Anderson, Poul William
  See Anderson, Poul
Anderson, Rachel 1943- 86
  Earlier sketch in SATA *34*
  See also SAAS *18*
Anderson, Richard
  See Anderson, J(ohn) R(ichard) L(ane)
Anderson, Sara 173
Anderson, (Tom) Scoular 138
Anderson, Susan 1952- 90
Anderson, W. B.
  See Schultz, James Willard
Anderson, Wayne 1946- 147
  Earlier sketch in SATA *56*
Andre, Evelyn M(arie) 1924- 27
Andreassen, Karl
  See Boyd, Waldo T.
Andreassi, K. Robert
  See DeCandido, Keith R.A.
Andrew, Ian 1962- 166
  Earlier sketch in SATA *116*
Andrew, Ian Peter
  See Andrew, Ian
Andrew, Prudence (Hastings) 1924- 87
Andrews, Benny 1930-2006 31
  Obituary 178
Andrews, Eleanor Lattimore
  See Lattimore, Eleanor Frances
Andrews, Elton V.
  See Pohl, Frederick

Andrews, F(rank) Emerson 1902-1978 .... *22*
Andrews, J(ames) S(ydney) 1934- *4*
Andrews, Jan 1942- *167*
  Brief entry *49*
  Earlier sketches in SATA *58, 98*
Andrews, Julie 1935- *153*
  Earlier sketch in SATA *7*
  See also CLR *85*
Andrews, Roy Chapman 1884-1960 .... *19*
Andrews, Tamra 1959- *129*
Andrews, Wendy
  See Sharmat, Marjorie Weinman
Andrews, William G(eorge) 1930- *74*
Andrezel, Pierre
  See Blixen, Karen (Christentze Dinesen)
Andriani, Renee
  See Williams-Andriani, Renee
Andrist, Ralph K. 1914-2004 .... *45*
Andryszewski, Tricia 1956- *148*
  Earlier sketch in SATA *88*
Angel, Carl *178*
Angel, Marie 1923- *47*
Angeles, Peter A. 1931- *40*
Angeletti, Roberta 1964- *124*
Angeli, Marguerite (Lofft) de
  See de Angeli, Marguerite (Lofft)
Angell, Madeline 1919- *18*
Angelo, Valenti 1897- *14*
Angelou, Maya 1928- *136*
  Earlier sketch in SATA *49*
  See also CLR *53*
Angier, Bradford -1997 .... *12*
Anglund, Joan Walsh 1926- *2*
  See also CLR *94*
Ango, Fan D.
  See Longyear, Barry B(rookes)
Angrist, Stanley W(olff) 1933- *4*
Anholt, Catherine 1958- *131*
  Earlier sketch in SATA *74*
Anholt, Laurence 1959- *141*
  Earlier sketch in SATA *74*
Anita
  See Daniel, Anita
Anmar, Frank
  See Nolan, William F(rancis)
Annett, Cora
  See Scott, Cora Annett (Pipitone)
Annie-Jo
  See Blanchard, Patricia
  and Suhr, Joanne
Annixter, Jane
  See Sturtzel, Jane Levington
Annixter, Paul
  See Sturtzel, Howard A(llison)
Anno, Mitsumasa 1926- *157*
  Earlier sketches in SATA *5, 38, 77*
  See also CLR *122*
Anrooy, Francine Van
  See Van Anrooy, Francine
Ansary, Mir Tamim 1948- *140*
Anstey, Caroline 1958- *81*
Antell, Will D. 1935- *31*
Anthony, Barbara
  See Barber, Antonia
Anthony, C. L.
  See Smith, Dorothy Gladys
Anthony, Edward 1895-1971 .... *21*
Anthony, John
  See Beckett, Ronald Brymer
  and Ciardi, John (Anthony)
  and Sabini, John Anthony
Anthony, Joseph Patrick 1964- *103*
Anthony, Patricia 1947- *109*
Anthony, Piers 1934- *129*
  Autobiography Feature *129*
  Earlier sketch in SATA *84*
  See also CLR *118*
  See also SAAS *22*
Anthony, Susan C(arol) 1953- *87*
Anticaglia, Elizabeth 1939- *12*
Antle, Nancy 1955- *102*

Anton, Michael J(ames) 1940- *12*
Antonacci, Robert J(oseph) 1916- *45*
  Brief entry *37*
Anvil, Christopher
  See Crosby, Harry C., Jr.
Aoki, Hisako 1942- *45*
Apfel, Necia H(alpern) 1930- *51*
  Brief entry *41*
Aphrodite, J.
  See Livingston, Carole
Apikuni
  See Schultz, James Willard
Apostolou, Christine Hale 1955- *128*
  Earlier sketch in SATA *82*
  See Hale, Christy
Appel, Allen (R.) 1945- *115*
Appel, Benjamin 1907-1977 .... *39*
  Obituary *21*
Appel, Martin E(liot) 1948- *45*
Appel, Marty
  See Appel, Martin E(liot)
Appelbaum, Diana Muir Karter 1953- *132*
Appelt, Kathi 1954- *129*
  Earlier sketch in SATA *83*
Apperley, Dawn 1969- *135*
Appiah, Peggy 1921-2006 .... *84*
  Earlier sketch in SATA *15*
  See also SAAS *19*
Apple, Margot *152*
  Brief entry *42*
  Earlier sketch in SATA *64*
Applebaum, Stan 1922- *45*
Applegate, K. A.
  See CLR *90*
  See Applegate, Katherine (Alice)
Applegate, Katherine (Alice) 1956- *162*
  Earlier sketch in SATA *109*
  See Applegate, K. A.
Appleton, Victor *67*
  Earlier sketch in SATA *1*
  See Barrett, Neal, Jr.
  and Doyle, Debra
  and Macdonald, James D.
  and Stratemeyer, Edward L.
  and Vardeman, Robert E(dward)
Appleton, Victor II *67*
  Earlier sketch in SATA *1*
  See Goulart, Ron(ald Joseph)
Apsler, Alfred 1907-1982 .... *10*
Aragones, Sergio 1937- *48*
  Brief entry *39*
Araujo, Frank P. 1937- *86*
Arbo, Cris 1950- *103*
Arbuthnot, May Hill 1884-1969 .... *2*
Archambault, John *163*
  Earlier sketches in SATA *67, 112*
Archbold, Rick 1950- *97*
Archer, Colleen Rutherford 1949- *164*
Archer, Jules 1915- *85*
  Earlier sketch in SATA *4*
  See also SAAS *5*
Archer, Marion Fuller 1917- *11*
Archibald, Joe
  See Archibald, Joseph S(topford)
Archibald, Joseph S(topford) 1898-1986 .... *3*
  Obituary *47*
Ardagh, Philip 1961- *154*
Ardai, Charles 1969- *85*
Arden, Barbi
  See Stoutenburg, Adrien (Pearl)
Arden, William
  See Lynds, Dennis
Ardizzone, Edward (Jeffrey Irving)
  1900-1979 .... *28*
  Obituary *21*
  Earlier sketch in SATA *1*
  See also CLR *3*
Ardley, Neil (Richard) 1937- *121*
  Earlier sketch in SATA *43*
Arehart-Treichel, Joan 1942- *22*
Arena, Felice 1968- *151*

Arenella, Roy 1939- *14*
Argent, Kerry 1960- *138*
Argueta, Jorge *179*
Arkin, Alan 1934- *59*
  Brief entry *32*
Arkin, Alan Wolf
  See Arkin, Alan
Arksey, Neil *158*
Arlen, Leslie
  See Nicole, Christopher (Robin)
Arley, Robert
  See Jackson, Mike
Armer, Alberta (Roller) 1904-1986 .... *9*
Armer, Laura Adams 1874-1963 .... *13*
Armistead, John 1941- *130*
Armitage, David 1943- *155*
  Brief entry *38*
  Earlier sketch in SATA *99*
Armitage, Frank
  See Carpenter, John (Howard)
Armitage, Ronda (Jacqueline) 1943- *155*
  Brief entry *38*
  Earlier sketches in SATA *47, 99*
Armour, Richard (Willard) 1906-1989 .... *14*
  Obituary *61*
Armstrong, Alan 1939- *172*
Armstrong, Alan W.
  See Armstrong, Alan
Armstrong, George D. 1927- *10*
Armstrong, Gerry (Breen) 1929- *10*
Armstrong, Jeannette (C.) 1948- *102*
Armstrong, Jennifer 1961- *165*
  Autobiography Feature *120*
  Earlier sketches in SATA *77, 111*
  See also CLR *66*
  See also SAAS *24*
Armstrong, Louise *43*
  Brief entry *33*
Armstrong, Martin Donisthorpe
  1882-1974 .... *115*
Armstrong, Ralph Richard
  See Armstrong, Richard
Armstrong, Richard 1903-1986 .... *11*
Armstrong, William H(oward) 1914-1999 ..... *4*
  Obituary *111*
  See also CLR *117*
  See also SAAS *7*
Armstrong-Ellis, Carey (Fraser) 1956- *145*
Arndt, Ursula (Martha H.) *56*
  Brief entry *39*
Arneson, D(on) J(on) 1935- *37*
Arnett, Caroline
  See Cole, Lois Dwight
Arnett, Jack
  See Goulart, Ron(ald Joseph)
Arnette, Robert
  See Silverberg, Robert
Arno, Enrico 1913-1981 .... *43*
  Obituary *28*
Arnold, Caroline 1944- *174*
  Brief entry *34*
  Earlier sketches in SATA *36, 85, 131*
  See also CLR *61*
  See also SAAS *23*
Arnold, Elizabeth 1944- *164*
Arnold, Elliott 1912-1980 .... *5*
  Obituary *22*
Arnold, Emily 1939- *76*
  Earlier sketch in SATA *50*
  See McCully, Emily Arnold
Arnold, Katya 1947- *168*
  Earlier sketches in SATA *82, 115*
Arnold, Louise *175*
Arnold, Marsha Diane 1948- *147*
  Earlier sketch in SATA *93*
Arnold, Nick 1961- *113*
Arnold, Oren 1900-1980 .... *4*
Arnold, Susan (Riser) 1951- *58*
Arnold, Tedd 1949- *160*
  Earlier sketches in SATA *69, 116*

Arnoldy, Julie
  See Bischoff, Julia Bristol
Arnosky, James Edward 1946- 160
  Earlier sketch in SATA 22
  See also CLR 93
  See Arnosky, Jim
Arnosky, Jim 118
  Earlier sketch in SATA 70
  See also CLR 93
  See Arnosky, James Edward
Arnott, Kathleen 1914- 20
Arnov, Boris, Jr. 1926- 12
Arnow, Harriette (Louisa) Simpson
  1908-1986 42
  Obituary 47
Arnsteen, Katy Keck 1934- 68
Arnstein, Helene S(olomon) 1915- 12
Arntson, Herbert E(dward) 1911-1982 12
Aroner, Miriam 82
Aronson, Marc 1950- 175
  Earlier sketch in SATA 126
Aronson, Virginia 1954- 122
Arora, Shirley (Lease) 1930- 2
Arrasmith, Patrick 176
Arrigan, Mary 1943- 142
Arrington, Stephen L. 1948- 97
Arrington, Stephen Lee
  See Arrington, Stephen L.
Arrley, Richmond
  See Delany, Samuel R., Jr.
Arrowood, (McKendrick Lee) Clinton
  1939- 19
Artell, Mike 1948- 134
  Earlier sketch in SATA 89
Arthur, Robert, (Jr.) 1909-1969 118
  See Arthur, Robert (Andrew)
Arthur, Robert (Andrew) 1909-1969
  See Arthur, Robert, (Jr.)
Arthur, Ruth M(abel) 1905-1979 26
  Earlier sketch in SATA 7
Artis, Vicki Kimmel 1945- 12
Artzybasheff, Boris (Miklailovich)
  1899-1965 14
Aruego, Ariane
  See Dewey, Ariane
Aruego, Jose 1932- 178
  Earlier sketches in SATA 6, 68, 125
  See also CLR 5
Aruego, Jose Espiritu
  See Aruego, Jose
Arundel, Honor (Morfydd) 1919-1973 4
  Obituary 24
  See also CLR 35
Arundel, Jocelyn
  See Alexander, Jocelyn Anne Arundel
Arvey, Michael 1948- 79
Arzoumanian, Alik 177
Asare, Meshack (Yaw) 1945- 139
  Earlier sketch in SATA 86
Asaro, Catherine 1955- 165
  Earlier sketch in SATA 101
  See Asaro, Catherine Ann
Asaro, Catherine Ann 1955-
  See Asaro, Catherine
Asay, Donna Day 1945- 127
Asbjornsen, Peter Christen 1812-1885 15
  See also CLR 104
  See Asbjornsen and Moe
Asch, Frank 1946- 154
  Earlier sketches in SATA 5, 66, 102
Ash, Jutta 1942- 38
Ashabranner, Brent 1921- 166
  Earlier sketches in SATA 1, 67, 130
  See also CLR 28
  See also SAAS 14
Ashabranner, Brent Kenneth
  See Ashabranner, Brent
Ashbless, William
  See Powers, Tim
Ashby, Gil 1958- 146
Ashby, Gwynneth 1922- 44

Ashby, Ruth 170
Ashby, Yvonne 1955- 121
Ashe, Arthur (Robert, Jr.) 1943-1993 65
  Obituary 87
Ashe, Geoffrey (Thomas) 1923- 17
  Autobiography Feature 125
Ashe, Mary Ann
  See Lewis, Mary (Christianna)
Asher, Sandra Fenichel 71
  Brief entry 34
  Earlier sketch in SATA 36
  See also SAAS 13
  See Asher, Sandy
Asher, Sandy 1942- 158
  Autobiography Feature 158
  Earlier sketch in SATA 118
  See Asher, Sandra Fenichel
Asheron, Sara
  See Moore, Lilian
Ashey, Bella
  See Breinburg, Petronella
Ashford, Daisy
  See Ashford, Margaret Mary
Ashford, Jeffrey
  See Jeffries, Roderic
Ashford, Margaret Mary 1881-1972 10
Ashley, Bernard (John) 1935- 155
  Brief entry 39
  Earlier sketches in SATA 47, 79
  See also CLR 4
Ashley, Elizabeth
  See Salmon, Annie Elizabeth
Ashley, Ray
  See Abrashkin, Raymond
Ashman, Linda 1960- 150
Ashton, Lorayne
  See Gottfried, Theodore Mark
Ashton, Warren T.
  See Adams, William Taylor
Asimov, Isaac 1920-1992 74
  Earlier sketches in SATA 1, 26
  See also CLR 79
Asinof, Eliot 1919- 6
Aska, Warabe 56
  See Masuda, Takeshi
Asprin, Robert L(ynn) 1946- 92
Asquith, Cynthia Mary Evelyn (Charteris)
  1887-1960 107
Asquith, Ros 153
Astley, Juliet
  See Lofts, Norah (Robinson)
Aston, Dianna Hutts 1964- 176
Aston, James
  See White, T(erence) H(anbury)
Ata, Te 1895-1995 119
Atene, Ann
  See Atene, (Rita) Anna
Atene, (Rita) Anna 1922- 12
Atheling, William, Jr.
  See Blish, James (Benjamin)
Atkins, Catherine 160
Atkins, Jeannine 1953- 172
  Earlier sketch in SATA 113
Atkinson, Allen G. 1953(?)-1987 60
  Brief entry 46
  Obituary 55
Atkinson, M. E.
  See Frankau, Mary Evelyn Atkinson
Atkinson, Margaret Fleming 14
Attema, Martha 1949- 156
  Earlier sketch in SATA 94
Atticus
  See Davies, Hunter
  and Fleming, Ian
  and Pawle, Gerald Strachan
  and Wilson, (Thomas) Woodrow
Atwater, Florence (Hasseltine Carroll)
  1896-1979 66
  Earlier sketch in SATA 16
  See also CLR 19
Atwater, Montgomery Meigs 1904-1976 15

Atwater, Richard (Tupper) 1892-1948 66
  Brief entry 27
  Earlier sketch in SATA 54
  See also CLR 19
Atwater-Rhodes, Amelia 1984- 170
  Earlier sketch in SATA 124
Atwell, Debby 1953- 150
  Earlier sketch in SATA 87
Atwood, Ann (Margaret) 1913-1992 7
Atwood, Margaret 1939- 170
  Earlier sketch in SATA 50
Atwood, Margaret Eleanor
  See Atwood, Margaret
Aubrey, Meg Kelleher 1963- 83
Aubry, Claude B. 1914-1984 29
  Obituary 40
Auch, Herm 173
Auch, Mary Jane 173
  Earlier sketch in SATA 138
Auch, M.J.
  See Auch, Mary Jane
Auch, M.J.
  See Auch, Mary Jane
Auclair, Joan 1960- 68
Auel, Jean M(arie) 1936- 91
Auer, Martin 1951- 77
Augarde, Steve 1950- 159
  Earlier sketch in SATA 25
Augelli, John P(at) 1921- 46
Augustine, Mildred
  See Benson, Mildred (Augustine Wirt)
Ault, Phil
  See Ault, Phillip H(alliday)
Ault, Phillip H(alliday) 1914- 23
Ault, Rosalie Sain 1942- 38
Ault, Roz
  See Ault, Rosalie Sain
Aung, (Maung) Htin 1909- 21
Aunt Weedy
  See Alcott, Louisa May
Auseon, Andrew 1976- 166
Austen, Carrie
  See Bennett, Cherie
Austin, Carrie
  See Seuling, Barbara
Austin, Elizabeth S. 1907-1977 5
Austin, Harry
  See McInerny, Ralph
Austin, Margot 1909(?)-1990 11
  Obituary 66
Austin, Michael 178
Austin, Oliver L(uther), Jr. 1903-1988 7
  Obituary 59
Austin, Patricia 1950- 137
Austin, R. G.
  See Gelman, Rita Golden
  and Lamb, Nancy
Austin, Virginia 1951- 152
  Earlier sketch in SATA 80
Auteur, Hillary
  See Gottfried, Theodore Mark
Auth, Tony
  See Auth, William Anthony, Jr.
Auth, William Anthony, Jr. 1942- 51
Autry, Gloria Diener
  See Allen, Terril Diener
Auvil, Peggy A 1954- 122
Auvil, Peggy Appleby
  See Auvil, Peggy A
Averill, Esther (Holden) 1902-1992 28
  Obituary 72
  Earlier sketch in SATA 1
Avery, A. A.
  See Montgomery, Rutherford George
Avery, Al
  See Montgomery, Rutherford George
Avery, Gillian (Elise) 1926- 137
  Autobiography Feature 137
  Earlier sketches in SATA 7, 75
  See also SAAS 6
Avery, Kay 1908- 5

Avery, Lorraine
  See Older, Effin
  and Older, Jules
Avery, Lynn
  See Cole, Lois Dwight
Avi 108
  Earlier sketch in SATA 71
  See also CLR 68
  See Wortis, Avi
Avishai, Susan 1949- 82
Awdry, Christopher Vere 1940- 67
Awdry, Wilbert Vere 1911-1997 94
  See also CLR 23
Axelrod, Amy 131
Axelsen, Stephen 1953- 165
Axton, David
  See Koontz, Dean R.
Ayars, James S(terling) 1898-1986 4
Aye, A. K.
  See Edwards, Hazel (Eileen)
Ayer, Eleanor H. 1947-1998 121
  Earlier sketch in SATA 78
Ayer, Jacqueline 1930- 13
Ayer, Margaret (?)-1981 15
Aylesworth, Jim 1943- 139
  Earlier sketches in SATA 38, 89
  See also CLR 89
Aylesworth, Thomas G(ibbons) 1927-1995 .. 88
  Earlier sketch in SATA 4
  See also CLR 6
  See also SAAS 17
Aylward, Marcus
  See Alexander, Marc
Aymar, Brandt 1911- 22
Ayme, Marcel (Andre) 1902-1967 91
  See also CLR 25
Ayres, Becky
  See Hickox, Rebecca (Ayres)
Ayres, Pam 1947- 90
Aytmatov, Chingiz
  See Aitmatov, Chingiz (Torekulovich)
Ayto, Russell 1960- 166
  Earlier sketch in SATA 111
Azaid
  See Zaidenberg, Arthur
Azar, Penny 1952- 121
Azarian, Mary 1940- 171
  Earlier sketch in SATA 112

B

Baastad, Babbis Friis
  See Friis-Baastad, Babbis Ellinor
Bab
  See Gilbert, W(illiam) S(chwenck)
Babbis, Eleanor
  See Friis-Baastad, Babbis Ellinor
Babbitt, Lucy Cullyford 1960- 85
Babbitt, Natalie (Zane Moore) 1932- 106
  Earlier sketches in SATA 6, 68
  See also CLR 53
  See also SAAS 5
Babcock, Chris 1963- 83
Babcock, Dennis Arthur 1948- 22
Baber, Carolyn Stonnell 1936- 96
Baca, Maria 1951- 104
Bach, Alice (Hendricks) 1942- 93
  Brief entry 27
  Earlier sketch in SATA 30
Bach, Bellamy
  See Windling, Terri
Bach, Mary 1960- 125
Bach, Richard 1936- 13
Bach, Richard David
  See Bach, Richard
Bache, Ellyn 1942- 124
Bachel, Beverly K. 1957- 142
Bachman, Fred 1949- 12

Bachman, Richard
  See King, Stephen
Bachrach, Deborah 80
Bacmeister, Rhoda W(arner) 1893-1991 11
Bacon, Betty
  See Bacon, Elizabeth
Bacon, Elizabeth 1914-2001 3
  Obituary 131
Bacon, Joan Chase
  See Bowden, Joan Chase
Bacon, Josephine Dodge (Daskam)
  1876-1961 48
Bacon, Margaret Frances
  Obituary 50
  See Bacon, Peggy
Bacon, Margaret Hope 1921- 6
Bacon, Martha Sherman 1917-1981 18
  Obituary 27
  See also CLR 3
Bacon, Melvin 1950- 93
Bacon, Melvin L.
  See Bacon, Melvin
Bacon, Peggy 1895-1987 2
  See Bacon, Margaret Frances
Bacon, R(onald) L(eonard) 1924- 84
  Earlier sketch in SATA 26
Baden, Robert 1936- 70
Baden-Powell, Robert (Stephenson Smyth)
  1857-1941 16
Badt, Karin L(uisa) 1963- 91
Baehr, Kingsley M. 1937- 89
Baehr, Patricia 1952- 65
Baehr, Patricia Goehner
  See Baehr, Patricia
Baer, Jill
  See Gilbert, (Agnes) Joan (Sewell)
Baer, Judy 1951- 71
Baer, Julie 1960- 161
Baer-Block, Roxanna 172
Baerg, Harry J(ohn) 1909-1996 12
Baeten, Lieve 1954- 83
Bagert, Brod 1947- 80
Baggette, Susan K. 1942- 126
Bagnold, Enid 1889-1981 25
  Earlier sketch in SATA 1
Bahlke, Valerie Worth 1933-1994 81
  See Worth, Valerie
Bahous, Sally 1939- 86
Bahr, Mary (Madelyn) 1946- 95
Bahr, Robert 1940- 38
Bahti, Tom 1926-1972 57
  Brief entry 31
Baicker-McKee, Carol 1958- 177
Bailey, Alice Cooper 1890-1978 12
Bailey, Anne 1958- 71
Bailey, Bernadine (Freeman) 1901-1995 14
Bailey, Carolyn Sherwin 1875-1961 14
Bailey, Debbie 1954- 123
Bailey, Donna (Veronica Anne) 1938- 68
Bailey, Jane H(orton) 1916- 12
Bailey, John (Robert) 1940- 52
Bailey, Linda 1948- 107
Bailey, Maralyn Collins (Harrison) 1941- 12
Bailey, Matilda
  See Radford, Ruby L(orraine)
Bailey, Maurice Charles 1932- 12
Bailey, Pearl (Mae) 1918-1990 81
Bailey, Ralph Edgar 1893-1982 11
Bailey, Sheila (Lucas) 1960- 155
Baillie, Allan 1943- 151
  Earlier sketch in SATA 87
  See also CLR 49
  See also SAAS 21
Baillie, Allan Stuart
  See Baillie, Allan
Baines, John (David) 1943- 71
Bains, Larry
  See Sabin, Louis
Baird, Alison 1963- 138
Baird, Bil 1904-1987 30
  Obituary 52

Baird, Thomas (P.) 1923-1990 45
  Brief entry 39
  Obituary 64
Baird, William Britton
  See Baird, Bil
Baity, Elizabeth Chesley 1907-1989 1
Baiul, Oksana 1977- 108
Bakeless, John (Edwin) 1894-1978 9
Bakeless, Katherine Little 1895-1992 9
Baker, Alan 1951- 146
  Earlier sketches in SATA 22, 93
Baker, Augusta 1911-1998 3
Baker, Betty Lou 1928-1987 73
  Obituary 54
  Earlier sketch in SATA 5
Baker, Carin Greenberg 1959- 79
Baker, Charlotte 1910- 2
Baker, Christopher W. 1952- 144
Baker, (Mary) Elizabeth (Gillette) 1923- 7
Baker, Gayle Cunningham 1950- 39
Baker, James W. 1924- 65
  Earlier sketch in SATA 22
Baker, James W. 1926- 122
Baker, Janice E(dla) 1941- 22
Baker, Jeanette 178
Baker, Jeannie 1950- 156
  Earlier sketches in SATA 23, 88
  See also CLR 28
Baker, Jeffrey J(ohn) W(heeler) 1931- 5
Baker, Jim
  See Baker, James W.
Baker, Keith 1953- 179
Baker, Ken 1962- 133
Baker, Laura Nelson 1911- 3
Baker, Margaret 1890-1965 4
Baker, Margaret J(oyce) 1918- 12
  See also SAAS 8
Baker, Mary Gladys Steel 1892-1974 12
Baker, (Robert) Michael (Graham) 1938- 4
Baker, Nina (Brown) 1888-1957 15
Baker, Pamela J. 1947- 66
Baker, Rachel 1904-1978 2
  Obituary 26
Baker, Rosalie F. 1945- 166
Baker, Samm Sinclair 1909-1997 12
  Obituary 96
Baker, Susan (Catherine) 1942-1991 29
Balaam
  See Lamb, G(eoffrey) F(rederick)
Balan, Bruce 1959- 113
Balcavage, Dynise 1965- 137
Balch, Glenn 1902-1989 3
  Obituary 83
  See also SAAS 11
Balderose, Nancy Ward 1952- 93
Balderson, Margaret 1935- 151
Baldry, Cherith 1947- 167
  Earlier sketch in SATA 72
Balducci, Carolyn (Feleppa) 1946- 5
Baldwin, Alex
  See Griffin, W.E.B.
Baldwin, Anne Norris 1938- 5
Baldwin, Clara 11
Baldwin, Gordo
  See Baldwin, Gordon C(ortis)
Baldwin, Gordon C(ortis) 1908-1983 12
Baldwin, James 1841-1925 24
Baldwin, James 1924-1987 9
  Obituary 54
Baldwin, Louis 1919- 110
Baldwin, Margaret
  See Weis, Margaret
Baldwin, Stan(ley C.) 1929- 62
  Brief entry 28
Bales, Carol Ann 1940- 57
  Brief entry 29
Balet, Jan (Bernard) 1913- 11
Balgassi, Haemi 1971- 131
Balian, Lorna 1929- 91
  Earlier sketch in SATA 9

Balit, Christina 1961- 159
Earlier sketch in SATA 102
Ball, Duncan 1941- 73
Ball, Zachary
See Janas, Frankie-Lee
and Masters, Kelly R(ay)
Ballantine, Lesley Frost
See Frost, Lesley
Ballantyne, R(obert) M(ichael) 1825-1894 ... 24
Ballard, James Graham
See Ballard, J.G.
Ballard, Jane
See Gorman, Carol
Ballard, J.G. 1930- 93
Ballard, John 1945- 110
Ballard, Lowell C(lyne) 1904-1986 12
Obituary 49
Ballard, (Charles) Martin 1929- 1
Ballard, Mignon F(ranklin) 1934- 64
Brief entry 49
Ballard, Robert D(uane) 1942- 85
See also CLR 60
Ballard, Robin 1965- 126
Balliett, Blue 1955- 156
Ballinger, Bryan 1968- 161
Ballouhey, Pierre 1944- 90
Balogh, Penelope 1916-1975 1
Obituary 34
Balouch, Kristen 176
Balow, Tom 1931- 12
Baltazzi, Evan S(erge) 1921- 90
Baltimore, J.
See Catherall, Arthur
Baltzer, Hans (Adolf) 1900- 40
Bambara, Toni Cade 1939-1995 112
Bamfylde, Walter
See Bevan, Tom
Bamman, Henry A. 1918- 12
Banat, D. R.
See Bradbury, Ray
Bancroft, Griffing 1907-1999 6
Bancroft, Laura
See Baum, L(yman) Frank
Bandel, Betty 1912- 47
Baner, Skulda Vanadis 1897-1964 10
Banerjee, Anjali 174
Banfill, A. Scott 1956- 98
Bang, Betsy 1912- 48
Brief entry 37
Bang, Garrett
See Bang, Molly
Bang, Molly 1943- 158
Earlier sketches in SATA 24, 69, 111
See also CLR 8
Bang, Molly Garrett
See Bang, Molly
Bang-Campbell, Monika 140
Banjo, The
See Paterson, A(ndrew) B(arton)
Banke, Cecile de
See de Banke, Cecile
Banks, Kate 1960- 172
Earlier sketch in SATA 134
Banks, Lynne Reid
See CLR 86
See Reid Banks, Lynne
Banks, Michael A. 1951- 101
Banks, Paul 1952- 174
Banks, Sara (Jeanne Gordon Harrell) 26
See Harrell, Sara (Jeanne) Gordon
Bannatyne-Cugnet, Elizabeth Jo-Anne
See Bannatyne-Cugnet, Jo
Bannatyne-Cugnet, Jo 1951- 101
Banner, Angela
See CLR 24
See Maddison, Angela Mary
Bannerman, Helen (Brodie Cowan Watson)
1862(?)-1946 19
See also CLR 21
Banning, Evelyn I. 1903-1993 36
Bannon, Laura (?)-1963 6

Bannor, Brett 1959- 143
Bantock, Nick 1950(?)- 95
Barasch, Lynne 1939- 126
Earlier sketch in SATA 74
Barbalet, Margaret 1949- 77
Barbary, James
See Beeching, Jack
Barbash, Shepard 1957- 84
Barbe, Walter Burke 1926- 45
Barber, Antonia 1932- 163
Earlier sketch in SATA 29
Barber, Lynda
See Graham-Barber, Lynda
Barber, Lynda Graham
See Graham-Barber, Lynda
Barber, Richard (William) 1941- 35
Barbera, Joe 1911-2006 51
Obituary 179
Barbera, Joseph
See Barbera, Joe
Barbera, Joseph Roland
See Barbera, Joe
Barberis, Juan C(arlos) 1920- 61
Barbour, Karen 1956- 170
Earlier sketches in SATA 63, 121
Barbour, Ralph Henry 1870-1944 16
Barclay, Bill
See Moorcock, Michael
Barclay, Isabel
See Dobell, I(sabel) M(arian) B(arclay)
Barclay, William Ewert
See Moorcock, Michael
Bardhan-Quallen, Sudipta 168
Bare, Arnold Edwin 1920- 16
Bare, Colleen Stanley 32
Bargar, Gary W. 1947-1985 63
Barger, Jan 1948- 147
Barish, Matthew 1907-2000 12
Barkan, Joanne 127
Earlier sketch in SATA 77
Barker, Albert W. 1900- 8
Barker, Carol (Minturn) 1938- 31
Barker, Cicely Mary 1895-1973 49
Brief entry 39
See also CLR 88
Barker, Melvern 1907-1989 11
Barker, S(quire) Omar 1894-1985 10
Barker, Will 1913-1983 8
Barkin, Carol 1944- 52
Earlier sketch in SATA 42
Barklem, Jill 1951- 96
See also CLR 31
Barkley, Brad 178
Barkley, James Edward 1941- 6
Barks, Carl 1901-2000 37
Barley, Janet Crane 1934- 95
Barnaby, Ralph S(tanton) 1893-1986 9
Barnard, A. M.
See Alcott, Louisa May
Barnard, Bryn 1956- 169
Earlier sketch in SATA 115
Barne, Kitty
See Barne, Marion Catherine
Barne, Marion Catherine 1883-1957 97
See Barne, Kitty
Barner, Bob 1947- 136
Earlier sketch in SATA 29
Barnes, Dawn 1957- 175
Barnes, (Frank) Eric Wollencott 1907-1962 . 22
Barnes, Joyce Annette 1958- 85
Barnes, Laura T. 1958- 119
Barnes, Loutricia
See Barnes-Svarney, Patricia L(ou)
Barnes, Michael 1934- 55
Barnes-Murphy, Frances 1951- 88
Barnes-Murphy, Rowan 1952- 88
Barnes-Svarney, Patricia L(ou) 1953- 67
Barnet, Nancy 1954- 84
Barnett, Ivan 1947- 70
Barnett, Lincoln (Kinnear) 1909-1979 36
Barnett, Moneta 1922-1976 33

Barnett, Naomi 1927- 40
Barney, Maginel Wright 1881(?)-1966 39
Brief entry 32
Barnhart, Clarence L(ewis) 1900-1993 48
Obituary 78
Barnouw, Victor 1915-1989 43
Brief entry 28
Barnstone, Willis 1927- 20
Barnum, Jay Hyde 1888(?)-1962 20
Barnum, P. T., Jr.
See Stratemeyer, Edward L.
Barnum, Richard 67
Earlier sketch in SATA 1
Barnum, Theodore
See Stratemeyer, Edward L.
Baron, Kathy 1954- 90
Baron, Virginia Olsen 1931- 46
Brief entry 28
Barr, Donald 1921-2004 20
Obituary 152
Barr, George 1907-1992 2
Barr, Jene 1922-1985 16
Obituary 42
See Cohen, Jene Barr
Barr, Nevada 1952- 126
Earlier sketch in SATA 115
Barrer, Gertrude
See Barrer-Russell, Gertrude
Barrer-Russell, Gertrude 1921- 27
Barrett, Angela (Jane) 1955- 145
Earlier sketch in SATA 75
Barrett, Ethel 87
Brief entry 44
Barrett, Joyce Durham 1943- 138
Barrett, Judi
See Barrett, Judith
Barrett, Judith 1941- 26
See also CLR 98
Barrett, Robert T(heodore) 1949- 92
Barrett, Ron 1937- 14
Barrett, Susan (Mary) 1938- 113
Barrett, Tracy 1955- 156
Earlier sketches in SATA 84, 115
Barretta, Gene 176
Barrie, J(ames) M(atthew) 1860-1937 100
See also YABC 1
See also CLR 16
Barringer, William 1940-1996 153
Barrington, Michael
See Moorcock, Michael
Barris, George 1925- 47
Barrol, Grady
See Bograd, Larry
Barron, Rex 1951- 84
Barron, T(homas) A(rchibald) 1952- 126
Earlier sketch in SATA 83
See also CLR 86
Barron, Tom
See Barron, T(homas) A(rchibald)
Barrow, Lloyd H. 1942- 73
Barry, Dan 1958- 177
Barry, Dana (Marie Malloy) 1949- 139
Barry, James P(otvin) 1918- 14
Barry, Katharina Watjen 1936- 4
Barry, Robert (Everett) 1931- 6
Barry, Scott 1952- 32
Barry, Sheila Anne -2003 91
Bartell, Susan S. 175
Bartenbach, Jean 1918- 40
Barth, Edna 1914-1980 7
Obituary 24
Barth, Kelly L. 1964- 152
Barthelme, Donald 1931-1989 7
Obituary 62
Bartholomew, Barbara 1941- 86
Brief entry 42
Bartholomew, Jean
See Beatty, Patricia (Robbins)
Bartlett, Alison 153
Bartlett, Philip A. 1
Bartlett, Robert Merrill 1899-1995 12

Bartoletti, Susan Campbell 1958- *173*
Earlier sketches in SATA *88, 129, 135*
Barton, Byron 1930- *126*
Earlier sketches in SATA *9, 90*
Barton, Jill(ian) 1940- *75*
Barton, May Hollis *67*
Earlier sketch in SATA *1*
Barton, Pat *59*
See Arrowsmith, Pat
Bartos-Hoeppner, Barbara 1923- *5*
Bartram, Simon *156*
Bartsch, Jochen 1906- *39*
Baruch, Dorothy W(alter) 1899-1962 .... *21*
Barunga, Albert 1912(?)-1977 .... *120*
Bas, Rutger
See Rutgers van der Loeff-Basenau, An(na)
Maria Margaretha
Base, Graeme (Rowland) 1958- *162*
Earlier sketches in SATA *67, 101*
See also CLR *22*
Baseman, Gary 1960- *174*
Bash, Barbara 1948- *132*
Bashevis, Isaac
See Singer, Isaac Bashevis
Bashevis, Yitskhok
See Singer, Isaac Bashevis
Baskin, Leonard 1922-2000 .... *120*
Brief entry *27*
Earlier sketch in SATA *30*
Baskin, Nora Raleigh 1961- *129*
Bason, Lillian 1913- *20*
Bass, L. G.
See Geringer, Laura
Bassett, Jeni 1959- *64*
Brief entry *43*
Bassett, John Keith
See Keating, Lawrence A.
Bassett, Lisa 1958- *61*
Bassil, Andrea
See Nilsen, Anna
Bastyra, Judy *108*
Bat-Ami, Miriam 1950- *150*
Autobiography Feature *150*
Earlier sketches in SATA *82, 122*
Bate, Lucy 1939-1993 .... *18*
Bate, Norman (Arthur) 1916- *5*
Bateman, Colin 1962- *172*
Bateman, Teresa 1957- *168*
Earlier sketch in SATA *112*
Bates, Barbara S(nedeker) 1919- *12*
Bates, Betty *19*
See Bates, Elizabeth
Bates, Dianne 1948- *147*
Bates, Ivan *175*
Bates, Katharine Lee 1859-1929 .... *113*
See Lincoln, James
Bates, Martine
See Leavitt, Martine
Bateson, Catherine 1960- *157*
Batey, Tom 1946- *52*
Brief entry *41*
Bath, Kevin P.
See Bath, K.P.
Bath, K.P. *171*
Batherman, Muriel
See Sheldon, Muriel
Batson, Larry 1930- *35*
Batt, Tanya Robyn 1970- *131*
Battaglia, Aurelius 1910- *50*
Brief entry *33*
Batten, H(arry) Mortimer 1888-1958 .... *25*
Batten, Mary 1937- *162*
Earlier sketches in SATA *5, 102*
Batterberry, Ariane Ruskin 1935- *13*
Batterberry, Michael Carver 1932- *32*
Battle-Lavert, Gwendolyn 1951- *155*
Earlier sketch in SATA *85*
See Lavert, Gwendolyn Battle
Battles, (Roxy) Edith 1921- *7*
Baudouy, Michel-Aime 1909- *7*

Bauer, Caroline Feller 1935- *98*
Brief entry *46*
Earlier sketch in SATA *52*
See also SAAS *24*
Bauer, Fred 1934- *36*
Bauer, Helen 1900-1988 .... *2*
Bauer, Joan 1951- *160*
Earlier sketch in SATA *117*
Bauer, Jutta 1955- *150*
Bauer, Marion Dane 1938- *144*
Autobiography Feature *144*
Earlier sketches in SATA *20, 69, 113*
See also SAAS *9*
Bauer, Michael Gerard 1955(?)- *167*
Bauer, Steven 1948- *125*
Bauerschmidt, Marjorie 1926- *15*
Baughman, Dorothy 1940- *61*
Baum, Allyn Z(elton) 1924-1997 .... *98*
Earlier sketch in SATA *20*
Baum, L. Frank
See Thompson, Ruth Plumly
Baum, L(yman) Frank 1856-1919 .... *100*
Earlier sketch in SATA *18*
See also CLR *107*
Baum, Louis 1948- *64*
Brief entry *52*
Baum, Louis F.
See Baum, L(yman) Frank
Baum, Willi 1931- *4*
Baumann, Amy (Brown) Beeching 1922- *10*
Baumann, Hans 1914- *2*
See also CLR *35*
Baumann, Kurt 1935- *21*
Baumgartner, Barbara 1939- *86*
Baurys, Flo(rence) 1938- *122*
Bausum, Ann *173*
Bawden, Nina (Mary Mabey) 1925- *72*
Earlier sketch in SATA *4*
See also CLR *51*
See also SAAS *16*
See Kark, Nina Mary
Bay, Jeanette Graham 1928- *88*
Bayer, Harold
See Gregg, Andrew K.
Bayley, Nicola 1949- *129*
Earlier sketches in SATA *41, 69*
Baylor, Byrd 1924- *136*
Earlier sketches in SATA *16, 69*
See also CLR *3*
Baynes, Pauline (Diana) 1922- *133*
Earlier sketches in SATA *19, 59*
BB
See Watkins-Pitchford, Denys James
Beach, Charles
See Reid, (Thomas) Mayne
Beach, Charles Amory *1*
Beach, Edward L. 1918-2002 .... *12*
Obituary *140*
Beach, Edward Latimer
See Beach, Edward L.
Beach, Lisa 1957- *111*
Beach, Lynn
See Lance, Kathryn
Beach, Stewart T(aft) 1899-1979 .... *23*
Beachcroft, Nina 1931- *18*
Beagle, Peter S. 1939- *130*
Earlier sketch in SATA *60*
Beagle, Peter Soyer
See Beagle, Peter S.
Beaglehole, Helen 1946- *117*
Beale, Fleur *107*
Bealer, Alex W(inkler III) 1921-1980 .... *8*
Obituary *22*
Beales, Valerie 1915- *74*
Beals, Carleton 1893-1979 .... *12*
Beame, Rona 1934- *12*
Beamer, (George) Charles (Jr.) 1942- *43*
Bean, Normal
See Burroughs, Edgar Rice
Beaney, Jan
See Udall, Jan Beaney

Beaney, Jane
See Udall, Jan Beaney
Bear, Carolyn
See Rayban, Chloe
Bear, Greg(ory Dale) 1951- *105*
Earlier sketch in SATA *65*
Bearanger, Marie
See Messier, Claire
Beard, Charles A(ustin) 1874-1948 .... *18*
Beard, Dan(iel Carter) 1850-1941 .... *22*
Beard, Darleen Bailey 1961- *96*
Bearden, Romare (Howard) 1914(?)-1988 ... *22*
Obituary *56*
Beardmore, Cedric
See Beardmore, George
Beardmore, George 1908-1979 .... *20*
Beardsley, Martyn R. 1957- *150*
Bearman, Jane (Ruth) 1917- *29*
Beaton, Clare 1947- *125*
Beatty, Elizabeth
See Holloway, Teresa (Bragunier)
Beatty, Hetty Burlingame 1907-1971 .... *5*
Beatty, Jerome, Jr. 1918- *5*
Beatty, John (Louis) 1922-1975 .... *6*
Obituary *25*
Beatty, Patricia (Robbins) 1922-1991 .... *73*
Obituary *68*
Earlier sketches in SATA *1, 30*
See also SAAS *4*
Beaty, Mary (T.) 1947- *146*
Bechard, Margaret 1953- *164*
Earlier sketch in SATA *85*
Bechtel, Louise Seaman 1894-1985 .... *4*
Obituary *43*
Beck, Barbara L. 1927- *12*
Beck, Ian (Archibald) 1947- *138*
Beck, Peggy 1949- *171*
Becker, Beril 1901-1999 .... *11*
Becker, Deborah Zimmett 1955- *138*
Becker, Helaine 1961- *142*
Becker, John (Leonard) 1901- *12*
Becker, John E(mil) 1942- *148*
Becker, Joyce 1936- *39*
Becker, May Lamberton 1873-1958 .... *33*
Becker, Neesa 1951- *123*
Becker, Shari *174*
Beckett, Sheilah 1913- *33*
Beckman, Delores 1914-1994 .... *51*
Beckman, Gunnel 1910- *6*
See also CLR *25*
See also SAAS *9*
Beckman, Kaj
See Beckman, Karin
Beckman, Karin 1913- *45*
Beckman, Per (Frithiof) 1913- *45*
Bedard, Michael 1949- *154*
Earlier sketch in SATA *93*
See also CLR *35*
Beddows, Eric
See Nutt, Ken
Bedford, A. N.
See Watson, Jane Werner
Bedford, Annie North
See Watson, Jane Werner
Bedford, David *159*
Bedoukian, Kerop 1907-1981 .... *53*
Bee, Jay
See Brainerd, John W(hiting)
Beebe, B(urdetta) F(aye) *1*
See Johnson, B(urdetta) F(aye)
Beebe, (Charles) William 1877-1962 .... *19*
Beeby, Betty 1923- *25*
Beech, Webb
See Griffin, W.E.B.
Beecham, Jahnna *161*
Beechcroft, William
See Hallstead, William F(inn III)
Beeching, Jack 1922- *14*
Beeke, Tiphanie *163*
Beeler, Janet
See Shaw, Janet

Beeler, Nelson F(rederick) 1910-1978 .... *13*
Beere, Peter 1951- *97*
Beers, Dorothy Sands 1917- *9*
Beers, Lorna 1897-1989 .... *14*
Beers, V(ictor) Gilbert 1928- *130*
    Earlier sketch in SATA *9*
Beeton, Max
    See Redding, Robert Hull
Begay, Shonto 1954- *137*
Begaye, Lisa Shook
    See Beach, Lisa
Begin, Maryjane 1963- *82*
Begin-Callanan, Maryjane
    See Begin, Maryjane
Begley, Kathleen A(nne) 1948- *21*
Behan, Leslie
    See Gottfried, Theodore Mark
Behler, Deborah A. 1947- *145*
Behler, John L. 1943-2006 .... *145*
    Obituary *173*
Behler, John Luther
    See Behler, John L.
Behn, Harry 1898-1973 .... *2*
    Obituary *34*
Behnke, Frances L. *8*
Behr, Joyce 1929- *15*
Behrens, June York 1925- *19*
Behrman, Carol H(elen) 1925- *144*
    Earlier sketch in SATA *14*
Beifuss, John, (Jr.) 1959- *92*
Beil, Karen Magnuson 1950- *124*
Beiler, Edna 1923- *61*
Beinicke, Steve 1956- *69*
Beirne, Barbara 1933- *71*
Beiser, Arthur 1931- *22*
Beiser, Germaine 1931- *11*
Belair, Richard L. 1934- *45*
Belaney, Archibald Stansfeld 1888-1938 ...... *24*
    See Grey Owl
Belbin, David 1958- *164*
    Earlier sketch in SATA *106*
Belden, Wilanne Schneider 1925- *56*
Belfrage, Sally 1936-1994 .... *65*
    Obituary *79*
Belknap, B. H.
    See Ellis, Edward S(ylvester)
Belknap, Boynton
    See Ellis, Edward S(ylvester)
Belknap, Boynton M.D.
    See Ellis, Edward S(ylvester)
Bell, Anthea 1936- *148*
    Earlier sketch in SATA *88*
Bell, Clare (Louise) 1952- *99*
Bell, Corydon Whitten 1894-1980 .... *3*
Bell, David Owen 1949- *99*
Bell, Emerson
    See Stratemeyer, Edward L.
Bell, Emily Mary
    See Cason, Mabel Earp
Bell, Frank
    See Benson, Mildred (Augustine Wirt)
Bell, Gertrude (Wood) 1911-1987 .... *12*
Bell, Hilari 1958- *151*
Bell, Jadrien
    See Golden, Christie
Bell, Janet
    See Clymer, Eleanor
Bell, Janet Cheatham 1937- *127*
Bell, Krista (Anne Blakeney) 1950- *126*
Bell, Margaret E(lizabeth) 1898-1990 .... *2*
Bell, Mary Reeves 1946- *88*
Bell, Norman (Edward) 1899- *11*
Bell, Raymond Martin 1907-1999 .... *13*
Bell, Siobhan *177*
Bell, Thelma Harrington 1896-1985 .... *3*
Bell, William 1945- *90*
    See also CLR *91*
Bellairs, John (Anthony) 1938-1991 .... *160*
    Obituary *66*
    Earlier sketches in SATA *2, 68*
    See also CLR *37*

Beller, Susan Provost 1949- *128*
    Earlier sketch in SATA *84*
    See also CLR *106*
Bellingham, Brenda 1931- *99*
    Brief entry *51*
Bello, Rosario de
    See De Bello, Rosario
Belloc, (Joseph) Hilaire (Pierre Sebastien Rene
    Swanton) 1870-1953 .... *112*
    See also YABC *1*
    See also CLR *102*
Belloc, Joseph Peter Rene Hilaire
    See Belloc, (Joseph) Hilaire (Pierre Sebastien
    Rene Swanton)
Belloc, Joseph Pierre Hilaire
    See Belloc, (Joseph) Hilaire (Pierre Sebastien
    Rene Swanton)
Belloli, Andrea P. A. 1947- *86*
Bellville, Cheryl Walsh 1944- *54*
    Brief entry *49*
Belpre, Pura 1899-1982 .... *16*
    Obituary *30*
Belting, Natalia Maree 1915-1997 .... *6*
Belton, John Raynor 1931- *22*
Belton, Sandra (Yvonne) 1939- *134*
    Earlier sketch in SATA *85*
Beltran, Alberto 1923- *43*
Beltran-Hernandez, Irene 1945- *74*
Belvedere, Lee
    See Grayland, Valerie (Merle Spanner)
Bemelmans, Ludwig 1898-1962 .... *100*
    Earlier sketch in SATA *15*
    See also CLR *93*
Benander, Carl D. 1941- *74*
Benary, Margot
    See Benary-Isbert, Margot
Benary-Isbert, Margot 1889-1979 .... *2*
    Obituary *21*
    See also CLR *12*
Benasutti, Marion 1908-1992 .... *6*
Benatar, Raquel 1955- *167*
Benchley, Nathaniel (Goddard) 1915-1981 .. *25*
    Obituary *28*
    Earlier sketch in SATA *3*
Benchley, Peter 1940-2006 .... *164*
    Earlier sketches in SATA *3, 89*
Benchley, Peter Bradford
    See Benchley, Peter
Bender, Edna 1941- *92*
Bender, Esther 1942- *88*
Bender, Lucy Ellen 1942- *22*
Bender, Robert 1962- *160*
    Earlier sketch in SATA *79*
Bendick, Jeanne 1919- *135*
    Earlier sketches in SATA *2, 68*
    See also CLR *5*
    See also SAAS *4*
Bendick, Robert L(ouis) 1917- *11*
Benedict, Andrew
    See Arthur, Robert, (Jr.)
Benedict, Dorothy Potter 1889-1979 .... *11*
    Obituary *23*
Benedict, Lois Trimble 1902-1967 .... *12*
Benedict, Rex 1920-1995 .... *8*
Benedict, Stewart H(urd) 1924- *26*
Beneduce, Ann Keay *128*
Benet, Laura 1884-1979 .... *3*
    Obituary *23*
Benet, Stephen Vincent 1898-1943
    See YABC *1*
Benet, Sula 1906-1982 .... *21*
    Obituary *33*
Ben-Ezer, Ehud 1936- *122*
Benezra, Barbara (Beardsley) 1921- *10*
Benham, Leslie 1922- *48*
Benham, Lois (Dakin) 1924- *48*
Benham, Mary Lile 1914-1991 .... *55*
Benjamin, E. M. J.
    See Bache, Ellyn
Benjamin, Nora
    See Kubie, Nora Gottheil Benjamin

Benjamin, Saragail Katzman 1953- *86*
Benner, Cheryl 1962- *80*
Benner, Judith Ann 1942- *94*
Bennett, Alice
    See Ziner, Florence
Bennett, Cherie 1960- *158*
    Earlier sketch in SATA *97*
Bennett, Dorothea
    See Young, Dorothea Bennett
Bennett, James (W.) 1942- *153*
    Autobiography Feature *153*
    Earlier sketches in SATA *93, 148*
Bennett, Jay 1912- *87*
    Brief entry *27*
    Earlier sketch in SATA *41*
    See also SAAS *4*
Bennett, Jill (Crawford) 1934- *41*
Bennett, John 1865-1956
    See YABC *1*
Bennett, Penelope (Agnes) 1938- *94*
Bennett, Rachel
    See Hill, Margaret (Ohler)
Bennett, Rainey 1907-1998 .... *15*
    Obituary *111*
Bennett, Richard 1899- *21*
Bennett, Russell H(oradley) 1896- *25*
Bennett, Veronica 1953- *178*
Bennett, William (John) 1943- *102*
Benning, Elizabeth
    See Rice, Bebe Faas
Benson, Elizabeth P(olk) 1924- *65*
Benson, Kathleen 1947- *111*
    Earlier sketch in SATA *62*
Benson, Linda M(aria) 1959- *84*
Benson, Mildred (Augustine Wirt)
    1905-2002 .... *100*
    Obituary *135*
    Earlier sketch in SATA *65*
    See Keene, Carolyn
Benson, Mildred Wirt
    See Benson, Mildred (Augustine Wirt)
Benson, Millie
    See Benson, Mildred (Augustine Wirt)
Benson, Patrick 1956- *147*
Benson, Sally 1900-1972 .... *35*
    Obituary *27*
    Earlier sketch in SATA *1*
Bentley, Judith (McBride) 1945- *89*
    Earlier sketch in SATA *40*
Bentley, Nancy (L.) 1946- *78*
Bentley, Phyllis Eleanor 1894-1977 .... *6*
    Obituary *25*
Bentley, Roy 1947- *46*
Bentley, William (George) 1916- *84*
Benton, Jim 1963- *172*
ben Uzair, Salem
    See Horne, Richard Henry Hengist
Bercaw, Edna Coe 1961- *124*
Berck, Judith 1960- *75*
Berelson, Howard 1940- *5*
Berends, Polly Berrien 1939- *50*
    Brief entry *38*
Berenstain, Jan 1923- *135*
    Earlier sketches in SATA *12, 64, 129*
    See also CLR *19*
    See also SAAS *20*
Berenstain, Janice
    See Berenstain, Jan
Berenstain, Michael 1951- *45*
Berenstain, Stan 1923-2005 .... *135*
    Obituary *169*
    Earlier sketches in SATA *12, 64, 129*
    See also CLR *19*
    See also SAAS *20*
Berenstain, Stanley
    See Berenstain, Stan
Berenzy, Alix 1957- *168*
    Earlier sketch in SATA *65*
Beresford, Elisabeth 1928- *141*
    Earlier sketches in SATA *25, 86*
    See also SAAS *20*

Berg, Adriane G(ilda) 1948- 152
Berg, Dave
   See Berg, David
Berg, David 1920-2002 27
   Obituary 137
Berg, Elizabeth 1948- 104
Berg, Jean Horton 1913-1995 6
Berg, Joan
   See Victor, Joan Berg
Berg, Ron 1952- 48
Bergaust, Erik 1925-1978 20
Bergel, Colin J. 1963- 137
Bergen, Joyce 1949- 95
Berger, Barbara (Helen) 1945- 77
Berger, Gilda 1935- 88
   Brief entry 42
Berger, Josef 1903-1971 36
Berger, Melvin H. 1927- 158
   Autobiography Feature 124
   Earlier sketches in SATA 5, 88
   See also CLR 32
   See also SAAS 2
Berger, Phil 1942-2001 62
Berger, Samantha (Allison) 1969- 140
Berger, Terry 1933- 8
Bergey, Alyce (Mae) 1934- 45
Bergin, Mark 1961- 160
   Earlier sketch in SATA 114
Bergman, Donna 1934- 73
Bergman, Tamar 1939- 95
Bergsma, Jody Lynn 163
Bergum, Constance R. 1952- 121
Berkes, Marianne 173
Berkey, Barry Robert 1935- 24
Berkowitz, Freda Pastor 1908-1994 12
Berkus, Clara Widess 1909- 78
Berlan, Kathryn Hook 1946- 78
Berlfein, Judy Reiss 1958- 79
Berliner, Don 1930- 33
Berliner, Franz 1930- 13
Berlitz, Charles (L. Frambach) 1914-2003 ... 32
   Obituary 151
Berman, Linda 1948- 38
Berman, Paul (Lawrence) 1949- 66
Berna, Paul 1910-1994 15
   Obituary 78
   See also CLR 19
Bernadette
   See Watts, (Anna) Bernadette
Bernard, Bruce 1928-2000 78
   Obituary 124
Bernard, George I. 1949- 39
Bernard, Jacqueline (de Sieyes) 1921-1983 ... 8
   Obituary 45
Bernard, Patricia 1942- 106
Bernardin, James (B.) 1966- 112
Bernards, Neal 1963- 71
Bernays, Anne 1930- 32
Bernhard, Durga T. 1961- 80
Bernhard, Emery 1950- 80
Bernstein, Daryl (Evan) 1976- 81
Bernstein, Joanne E(ckstein) 1943- 15
Bernstein, Margery 1933- 114
Bernstein, Theodore M(enline) 1904-1979 ... 12
   Obituary 27
Berrien, Edith Heal
   See Heal, Edith
Berrill, Jacquelyn (Batsel) 1905- 12
Berrington, John
   See Brownjohn, Alan
Berry, B. J.
   See Berry, Barbara J.
Berry, Barbara J. 1937- 7
Berry, Erick
   See Best, (Evangel) Allena Champlin
Berry, James 1925- 110
   Earlier sketch in SATA 67
   See also CLR 22
Berry, Joy
   See Berry, Joy Wilt

Berry, Joy Wilt 1944- 58
   Brief entry 46
Berry, William D(avid) 1926- 14
Bersani, Shennen 1961- 164
Berson, Harold 1926- 4
Bertagna, Julie 1962- 151
Bertin, Charles-Francois
   See Berlitz, Charles (L. Frambach)
Bertolet, Paul
   See McLaughlin, Frank
Berton, Pierre (Francis de Marigny)
   1920-2004 99
   Obituary 158
Bertrand, Cecile 1953- 76
Bertrand, Diane Gonzales 1956- 177
   Earlier sketch in SATA 106
Bertrand, Lynne 1963- 164
   Earlier sketch in SATA 81
Beskow, Elsa (Maartman) 1874-1953 20
   See also CLR 17
Bess, Clayton
   See CLR 39
   See Locke, Robert
Best, (Evangel) Allena Champlin 1892-1974 . 2
   Obituary 25
Best, Cari 1951- 149
   Earlier sketch in SATA 107
Best, (Oswald) Herbert 1894-1980 2
Bestall, A(lfred) E(dmeades) 1892-1986 97
   Obituary 48
Betancourt, Jeanne 1941- 148
   Brief entry 43
   Earlier sketches in SATA 55, 96
Beth, Mary
   See Miller, Mary Beth
Bethancourt, T. Ernesto 11
   See also CLR 3
   See Paisley, Tom
Bethel, Dell 1929- 52
Bethell, Jean (Frankenberry) 1922- 8
Bethers, Ray 1902-1973 6
Bethke, Bruce Raymond 1955- 114
Bethlen, T. D.
   See Silverberg, Robert
Bethune, J. G.
   See Ellis, Edward S(ylvester)
Bethune, J. H.
   See Ellis, Edward S(ylvester)
Betteridge, Anne
   See Potter, Margaret (Newman)
Bettina
   See Ehrlich, Bettina Bauer
Bettmann, Otto Ludwig 1903-1998 46
Betts, James
   See Haynes, Betsy
Betz, Eva Kelly 1897-1968 10
Bevan, Tom 1868-1930(?)
   See YABC 2
Bewick, Thomas 1753-1828 16
Beyer, Audrey White 1916- 9
Beyer, Paul J. III 1950- 74
Beynon, John
   See Harris, John (Wyndham Parkes Lucas)
   Beynon
Bezencon, Jacqueline (Buxcel) 1924- 48
Bial, Morrison David 1917- 62
Bial, Raymond 1948- 165
   Earlier sketches in SATA 76, 116
Biala
   See Brustlein, Janice Tworkov
Biale, Rachel 1952- 99
Bialk, Elisa
   See Krautter, Elisa (Bialk)
Bianchi, John 1947- 91
Bianchi, Robert S(teven) 1943- 92
Bianco, Margery
   See Bianco, Margery Williams
Bianco, Margery Williams 1881-1944 15
   See also CLR 19
Bianco, Pamela 1906- 28
Bibby, Violet 1908- 24

Bible, Charles 1937- 13
Bibo, Bobette
   See Gugliotta, Bobette
Bice, Clare 1909-1976 22
Bickerstaff, Isaac
   See Swift, Jonathan
Biegel, Paul 1925- 79
   Earlier sketch in SATA 16
   See also CLR 27
   See also SAAS 18
Biemiller, Carl L(udwig), Jr.) 1912-1979 40
   Obituary 21
Bienenfeld, Florence L(ucille) 1929- 39
Bierhorst, John (William) 1936- 149
   Autobiography Feature 149
   Earlier sketches in SATA 6, 91
   See also SAAS 10
Biggar, Joan R(awlins) 1936- 120
Biggle, Lloyd, Jr. 1923-2002 65
Bilal, Abdel W(ahab) 1970- 92
Bilbrough, Norman 1941- 111
Bildner, Phil 173
Bileck, Marvin 1920- 40
Bilibin, Ivan (Iakolevich) 1876-1942 61
Bill, Alfred Hoyt 1879-1964 44
Billam, Rosemary 1952- 61
Billings, Charlene W(interer) 1941- 41
Billingsley, Franny 1954- 132
Billington, Elizabeth T(hain) 50
   Brief entry 43
Billout, Guy (Rene) 1941- 144
   Earlier sketch in SATA 10
   See also CLR 33
Bilson, Geoffrey 1938-1987 99
Binch, Caroline (Lesley) 1947- 140
   Earlier sketch in SATA 81
Bing, Christopher (H.) 126
Bingham, Caroline 1962- 158
Bingham, Jane M. 1941- 163
Bingham, Jane Marie
   See Bingham, Jane M.
Bingham, Sam(uel A.) 1944- 96
Bingley, Margaret (Jane Kirby) 1947- 72
Binkley, Anne
   See Rand, Ann (Binkley)
Binzen, Bill 24
   See Binzen, William
Birch, David (W.) 1913-1996 89
Birch, Reginald B(athurst) 1856-1943 19
Birchman, David 1949- 72
Birchmore, Daniel A. 1951- 92
Bird, Carmel 1940- 124
Bird, E(lzy) J(ay) 1911- 58
Birdsall, Jeanne 1952(?)- 170
Birdseye, Tom 1951- 148
   Earlier sketches in SATA 66, 98
Birenbaum, Barbara 1941- 65
Birmingham, Lloyd P(aul) 1924- 83
   Earlier sketch in SATA 12
Birmingham, Ruth
   See Sorrells, Walter
Birney, Betty G. 1947- 169
   Earlier sketch in SATA 98
Biro, B.
   See Biro, B(alint) S(tephen)
Biro, B(alint) S(tephen) 1921- 67
   See Biro, Val
Biro, Val 1
   See also CLR 28
   See also SAAS 13
   See Biro, B(alint) S(tephen)
Bischoff, Julia Bristol 1899-1970 12
Bishop, Bonnie 1943- 37
Bishop, Claire Huchet 1899(?)-1993 14
   Obituary 74
   See also CLR 80
Bishop, Courtney
   See Ruemmler, John D(avid)
Bishop, Curtis (Kent) 1912-1967 6
Bishop, Gavin 1946- 144
   Earlier sketch in SATA 97

Bishop, Kathleen Wong 1954- 120
Bishop, Kathy
  See Bishop, Kathleen Wong
Bishop, Nic 1955- 161
  Earlier sketch in SATA 107
Bisset, Donald 1910-1995 86
  Earlier sketch in SATA 7
Bisson, Terry 1942- 99
Bisson, Terry Ballantine
  See Bisson, Terry
Bitter, Gary G(len) 1940- 22
Bixby, William (Courtney) 1920-1986 6
  Obituary 47
Bjoerk, Christina 1938- 99
  Earlier sketch in SATA 67
  See also CLR 22
Bjork, Christina
  See Bjoerk, Christina
Bjorklund, Lorence F. 1913-1978 35
  Brief entry 32
Bjorkman, Steve 163
Black, Algernon David 1900-1993 12
  Obituary 76
Black, Holly 1971- 147
Black, Irma Simonton 1906-1972 2
  Obituary 25
Black, Mansell
  See Trevor, Elleston
Black, MaryAnn
  See Easley, MaryAnn
Black, Susan Adams 1953- 40
Blackall, Bernie 1956- 126
Blackburn, Claire
  See Altman, Linda Jacobs
Blackburn, John(ny) Brewton 1952- 15
Blackburn, Joyce Knight 1920- 29
Blackett, Veronica Heath 1927- 12
Blackie, Jean Cutler 1943- 79
Blacklin, Malcolm
  See Chambers, Aidan
Blacklock, Dyan 1951- 112
Blackman, Malorie 1962- 128
  Earlier sketch in SATA 83
Blackton, Peter
  See Wilson, Lionel
Blackwood, Alan 1932- 70
Blackwood, Gary L. 1945- 169
  Earlier sketches in SATA 72, 118
Blade, Alexander
  See Garrett, (Gordon) Randall (Phillip)
  and Hamilton, Edmond
  and Silverberg, Robert
Blades, Ann (Sager) 1947- 69
  Earlier sketch in SATA 16
  See also CLR 15
Bladow, Suzanne Wilson 1937- 14
Blaine, John
  See Goodwin, Harold L(eland)
Blaine, Marge
  See Blaine, Margery Kay
Blaine, Margery Kay 1937- 11
Blair, Alison
  See Lerangis, Peter
Blair, Anne Denton 1914-1993 46
Blair, David Nelson 1954- 80
Blair, Eric (Arthur) 1903-1950 29
  See Orwell, George
Blair, Jay 1953- 45
Blair, Lucile
  See Yeakley, Marjory Hall
Blair, Margaret Whitman 1951- 124
Blair, Pauline Hunter
  See Clarke, Pauline
Blair, Ruth Van Ness 1912-1999 12
Blair, Shannon
  See Kaye, Marilyn
Blair, Walter 1900-1992 12
  Obituary 72
Blaisdell, Bob
  See Blaisdell, Robert
Blaisdell, Robert 1959- 105

Blake, Bronwyn 1940- 149
Blake, Jon 1954- 171
  Earlier sketch in SATA 78
Blake, Olive
  See Supraner, Robyn
Blake, Quentin (Saxby) 1932- 125
  Earlier sketches in SATA 9, 52, 96
  See also CLR 31
Blake, Robert 1949- 42
Blake, Robert J. 160
Blake, Walker E.
  See Griffin, W.E.B.
Blake, William 1757-1827 30
  See also CLR 52
Blakely, Gloria 1950- 139
Blakely, Roger K. 1922- 82
Blakeney, Jay D.
  See Chester, Deborah
Blakey, Nancy 1955- 94
Blanc, Esther S. 1913-1997 66
Blanchard, Patricia 125
Blanchet, M(uriel) Wylie 1891-1961 106
Blanco, Richard L(idio) 1926- 63
Bland, E.
  See Nesbit, E(dith)
Bland, Edith Nesbit
  See Nesbit, E(dith)
Bland, Fabian
  See Nesbit, E(dith)
Blank, Clarissa Mabel 1915-1965 62
Blassingame, Wyatt Rainey 1909-1985 34
  Obituary 41
  Earlier sketch in SATA 1
Blatchford, Claire H. 1944- 94
Blauer, Ettagale 1940- 49
Bledsoe, Glen L. 1951- 108
Bledsoe, Glen Leonard
  See Bledsoe, Glen L.
Bledsoe, Karen E. 1962- 167
  Earlier sketch in SATA 108
Bledsoe, Karen Elizabeth
  See Bledsoe, Karen E.
Bledsoe, Lucy Jane 1957- 162
  Earlier sketch in SATA 97
Bleeker, Sonia 2
  Obituary 26
  See Zim, Sonia Bleeker
Blegen, Daniel M. 1950- 92
Blegvad, Erik 1923- 132
  Earlier sketches in SATA 14, 66
Blegvad, Lenore 1926- 176
  Earlier sketches in SATA 14, 66
Blish, James (Benjamin) 1921-1975 66
Blishen, Edward (William) 1920-1996 66
  Obituary 93
  Earlier sketch in SATA 8
Bliss, Corinne Demas 1947- 37
  See Demas, Corinne
Bliss, Frederick
  See Card, Orson Scott
Bliss, Gillian
  See Paton Walsh, Jill
Bliss, Harry 1964- 156
Bliss, Reginald
  See Wells, H(erbert) G(eorge)
Bliss, Ronald G(ene) 1942- 12
Bliven, Bruce, Jr. 1916-2002 2
Blixen, Karen (Christentze Dinesen)
  1885-1962 44
  See Dinesen, Isak
Blizzard, Gladys S. (?)-1992 79
Blobaum, Cindy 1966- 123
Bloch, Lucienne 1909-1999 10
Bloch, Marie Halun 1910-1998 6
  See also SAAS 9
Bloch, Robert (Albert) 1917-1994 12
  Obituary 82
Blochman, Lawrence G(oldtree)
  1900-1975 22

Block, Francesca Lia 1962- 158
  Earlier sketches in SATA 80, 116
  See also CLR 116
  See also SAAS 21
Block, Irvin 1917- 12
Blomgren, Jennifer (Alice) 1954- 136
Blood, Charles Lewis 1929- 28
Bloom, Barbara Lee 1943- 146
Bloom, Freddy 1914-2000 37
  Obituary 121
Bloom, Lloyd 1947- 108
  Brief entry 43
Bloom, Suzanne 1950- 172
Bloomfield, Michaela 1966- 70
Bloor, Edward (William) 1950- 155
  Earlier sketch in SATA 98
Blos, Joan W(insor) 1928- 153
  Autobiography Feature 153
  Brief entry 27
  Earlier sketches in SATA 33, 69, 109
  See also CLR 18
  See also SAAS 11
Blough, Glenn O(rlando) 1907-1995 1
Blue, Rose 1931- 166
  Autobiography Feature 117
  Earlier sketches in SATA 5, 91, 93
  See also SAAS 24
Blue, Zachary
  See Stine, R.L.
Bluggage, Oranthy
  See Alcott, Louisa May
Blumberg, Leda 1956- 59
Blumberg, Rhoda 1917- 123
  Earlier sketches in SATA 35, 70
  See also CLR 21
Blume, Judy (Sussman) 1938- 142
  Earlier sketches in SATA 2, 31, 79
  See also CLR 69
Blumenthal, Deborah 161
Blumenthal, Shirley 1943- 46
Blutig, Eduard
  See Gorey, Edward (St. John)
Bly, Janet (Chester) 1945- 43
Bly, Stephen A(rthur) 1944- 116
  Earlier sketch in SATA 43
Blyler, Allison Lee 1966- 74
Blyton, Carey 1932-2002 9
  Obituary 138
Blyton, Enid (Mary) 1897-1968 25
  See also CLR 31
Boardman, Fon Wyman, Jr. 1911-2000 6
Boardman, Gwenn R. 12
  See Petersen, Gwenn Boardman
Boase, Wendy 1944-1999 28
  Obituary 110
Boatner, Mark Mayo III 1921- 29
Bobbe, Dorothie de Bear 1905-1975 1
  Obituary 25
Bober, Natalie S. 1930- 134
  Earlier sketch in SATA 87
  See also SAAS 23
Bobette, Bibo
  See Gugliotta, Bobette
Bobritsky, Vladimir 47
  Brief entry 32
  See Bobri, Vladimir V.
Bochak, Grayce 1956- 76
Bock, Hal
  See Bock, Harold I.
Bock, Harold I. 1939- 10
Bock, William Sauts Netamux'we 1939- 14
Bodanis, David 179
Bode, Janet 1943-1999 96
  Obituary 118
  Earlier sketch in SATA 60
Bodecker, N(iels) M(ogens) 1922-1988 73
  Obituary 54
  Earlier sketch in SATA 8
Boden, Hilda
  See Bodenham, Hilda Morris
Bodenham, Hilda Morris 1901- 13

Bodett, Tom 70
  See Bodett, Thomas Edward
Bodie, Idella F(allaw) 1925- 89
  Earlier sketch in SATA 12
Bodker, Cecil 1927- 133
  Earlier sketch in SATA 14
  See also CLR 23
Bodker, Cecil 1927-
  See Bodker, Cecil
Bodsworth, (Charles) Fred(erick) 1918- 27
Boeckman, Charles 1920- 12
Boelts, Maribeth 1964- 163
  Earlier sketch in SATA 78
Boerst, William J. 1939- 170
  Earlier sketch in SATA 121
Boesch, Mark J(oseph) 1917- 12
Boesen, Victor 1908- 16
Bogacki, Tomek 1950- 138
Bogaerts, Gert 1965- 80
Bogan, Paulette 1960- 129
Bogart, Jo Ellen 1945- 92
  See also CLR 59
Boggs, Ralph Steele 1901-1994 7
Bograd, Larry 1953- 89
  Earlier sketch in SATA 33
  See also SAAS 21
Bohdal, Susi 1951- 101
  Earlier sketch in SATA 22
Bohlen, Nina 1931- 58
Bohlmeijer, Arno 1956- 94
Bohner, Charles (Henry) 1927- 62
Bohnhoff, Maya Kaathryn 1954- 88
Boiger, Alexandra 178
Boissard, Janine 1932- 59
Bojunga, Lygia
  See Nunes, Lygia Bojunga
Bojunga-Nunes, Lygia
  See Nunes, Lygia Bojunga
Boland, Janice 98
Bolden, Tonya 1959- 138
  Earlier sketch in SATA 79
Bolden, Tonya Wilyce
  See Bolden, Tonya
Boles, Paul Darcy 1916-1984 9
  Obituary 38
Bolian, Polly 1925- 4
Bollen, Roger 1941(?)- 83
  Brief entry 29
Bolliger, Max 1929- 7
Bollinger, Max 1929- 167
Bollinger, Peter 172
Bolognese, Don(ald Alan) 1934- 129
  Earlier sketches in SATA 24, 71
Bolotin, Norman (Phillip) 1951- 93
Bolton, Carole 1926- 6
Bolton, Elizabeth
  See St. John, Nicole
Bolton, Evelyn
  See Bunting, (Anne) Eve(lyn)
Bonar, Veronica
  See Bailey, Donna (Veronica Anne)
Bond, B. J.
  See Heneghan, James
Bond, Bruce 1939- 61
Bond, Felicia 1954- 126
  Earlier sketch in SATA 49
Bond, Gladys Baker 1912- 14
Bond, Higgins 1951- 177
  Earlier sketch in SATA 83
Bond, J. Harvey
  See Winterbotham, R(ussell) R(obert)
Bond, (Thomas) Michael 1926- 157
  Earlier sketches in SATA 6, 58
  See also CLR 95
  See also SAAS 3
Bond, Nancy 1945- 159
  Autobiography Feature 159
  Earlier sketches in SATA 22, 82
  See also CLR 11
  See also SAAS 13

Bond, Nancy Barbara
  See Bond, Nancy
Bond, Rebecca 1972- 130
Bond, Ruskin 1934- 87
  Earlier sketch in SATA 14
Bondie, J. D.
  See Cunningham, Chet
Bondoux, Anne-Laure 1971- 175
Bone, Ian 1956- 158
  Earlier sketch in SATA 117
Bonehill, Captain Ralph
  See Stratemeyer, Edward L.
Bonham, Barbara Thomas 1926- 7
Bonham, Frank 1914-1989 49
  Obituary 62
  Earlier sketch in SATA 1
  See also SAAS 3
Boniface, William 1963- 102
Bonn, Pat
  See Bonn, Patricia Carolyn
Bonn, Patricia Carolyn 1948- 43
Bonner, Mary Graham 1890-1974 19
Bonner, Mike 1951- 121
Bonners, Susan 1947- 85
  Brief entry 48
Bonnett-Rampersaud, Louise 173
Bonning, Tony 1948- 169
Bonsall, Crosby Barbara (Newell)
  1921-1995 23
  Obituary 84
Bonsall, Joseph S. 1948- 119
Bonsignore, Joan 1959- 140
Bontemps, Arna(ud Wendell) 1902-1973 44
  Obituary 24
  Earlier sketch in SATA 2
  See also CLR 6
Bonzon, Paul-Jacques 1908-1978 22
Boock, Paula 1964- 134
Booher, Dianna Daniels 1948- 33
Book, Rick 1949- 119
Book, Rita
  See Holub, Joan
Bookman, Charlotte
  See Zolotow, Charlotte (Gertrude) S(hapiro)
Boon, Debbie 1960- 103
Boon, Emilie (Laetitia) 1958- 86
Boone, Charles Eugene
  See Boone, Pat
Boone, Pat 1934- 7
Boorman, Linda (Kay) 1940- 46
Boorstin, Daniel J(oseph) 1914-2004 52
Booth, Ernest Sheldon 1915-1984 43
Booth, Graham (Charles) 1935- 37
Bootman, Colin 159
Borden, Louise (Walker) 1949- 141
  Autobiography Feature 141
  Earlier sketches in SATA 68, 104
Bordier, Georgette 1924- 16
Borgman, James
  See Borgman, Jim
Borgman, James Mark
  See Borgman, Jim
Borgman, Jim 1954- 122
  See Borgman, James Mark
Boring, Mel 1939- 168
  Earlier sketch in SATA 35
Borja, Corinne 1929- 22
Borja, Robert 1923- 22
Borland, Hal 5
  Obituary 24
  See Borland, Harold Glen
Borland, Kathryn Kilby 1916- 16
Borlenghi, Patricia 1951- 79
Born, Adolf 1930- 49
Bornstein, Ruth Lercher
  Autobiography Feature 107
  See Bornstein-Lercher, Ruth
Bornstein-Lercher, Ruth 1927- 88
  Earlier sketch in SATA 14
  See Bornstein, Ruth Lercher
Borski, Lucia Merecka 18

Borten, Helen Jacobson 1930- 5
Bortolotti, Dan 1969- 157
Borton, Elizabeth
  See Trevino, Elizabeth B(orton) de
Borton, Lady 1942- 98
Borton de Trevino, Elizabeth
  See Trevino, Elizabeth B(orton) de
Bortstein, Larry 1942- 16
Bortz, Alfred B(enjamin) 1944- 139
  Earlier sketch in SATA 74
Bortz, Fred
  See Bortz, Alfred B(enjamin)
Bosco, Jack
  See Holliday, Joseph
Boshell, Gordon 1908- 15
Boshinski, Blanche 1922- 10
Bosman, Paul 1929- 107
Bosse, Malcolm (Joseph, Jr.) 1926-2002 136
  Earlier sketch in SATA 35
Bosserman, (Charles) Phillip 1931- 84
Bossom, Naomi 1933- 35
Bostock, Mike 1962- 114
Boston, L(ucy) M(aria Wood) 1892-1990 19
  Obituary 64
  See also CLR 3
Bostrom, Kathleen (Susan) Long 1954- 139
Bostrom, Kathy
  See Bostrom, Kathleen (Susan) Long
Bosworth, J. Allan 1925- 19
Bothwell, Jean (?)-1977 2
Botkin, B(enjamin) A(lbert) 1901-1975 40
Botsford, Ward 1927-2004 66
Botting, Douglas (Scott) 1934- 43
Bottner, Barbara 1943- 170
  Autobiography Feature 121
  Earlier sketches in SATA 14, 93
  See also SAAS 26
Bottone, Frank G., Jr. 1969- 141
Bouchard, David 1952- 117
Boucher, (Clarence) Carter 1954- 129
Boudelang, Bob
  See Pell, Ed(ward)
Boughton, Richard 1954- 75
Boulet, Susan Seddon 1941- 50
Boulle, Pierre (Francois Marie-Louis)
  1912-1994 22
  Obituary 78
Boulton, Jane 1921- 91
Bouma, Paddy 1947- 128
Bour, Daniele 1939- 62
Bourdon, David 1934-1998 46
Bourgeois, Paulette 1951- 153
Bourne, Lesley
  See Marshall, Evelyn
Bourne, Miriam Anne 1931-1989 16
  Obituary 63
Boutet de Monvel, (Louis) M(aurice)
  1850(?)-1913 30
  See also CLR 32
Bova, Ben 1932- 133
  Earlier sketches in SATA 6, 68
  See also CLR 96
Bova, Benjamin William
  See Bova, Ben
Bovaird, Anne E(lizabeth) 1960- 90
Bow, Patricia 1946- 168
Bowden, Joan Chase 1925- 51
  Brief entry 38
Bowen, Alexandria Russell 97
Bowen, Andy Russell
  See Bowen, Alexandria Russell
Bowen, Anne 1952- 170
Bowen, Betty Morgan
  See West, Betty
Bowen, Catherine (Shober) Drinker
  1897-1973 7
Bowen, David
  See Bowen, Joshua David
Bowen, Fred 1953- 136
Bowen, Joshua David 1930- 22

Bowen, Rhys
See Quin-Harkin, Janet
Bowen, Robert Sydney 1900-1977 52
  Obituary 21
Bowermaster, Jon 1954- 135
  Earlier sketch in SATA 77
Bowers, Terrell L. 1945- 101
Bowers, Terry
See Bowers, Terrell L.
Bowie, C. W.
See Old, Wendie C(orbin)
  and Wirths, Claudine (Turner) G(ibson)
Bowie, Jim
See Norwood, Victor G(eorge) C(harles)
  and Stratemeyer, Edward L.
Bowkett, Stephen 1953- 67
Bowler, Jan Brett
See Brett, Jan
Bowler, Tim 1953- 149
Bowman, Crystal 1951- 105
Bowman, James Cloyd 1880-1961 23
Bowman, John S(tewart) 1931- 16
Bowman, Kathleen (Gill) 1942- 52
  Brief entry 40
Boxall, Ed 178
Boyce, George A(rthur) 1898- 19
Boyd, Candy Dawson 1946- 72
  See also CLR 50
Boyd, Pauline
See Schock, Pauline
Boyd, Selma
See Acuff, Selma Boyd
Boyd, Waldo T. 1918- 18
Boyden, Linda 1948- 143
Boyer, Allen B. 1963- 153
Boyer, Robert E(rnst) 1929- 22
Boyes, Vivien 1952- 106
Boyes, Vivien Elizabeth
See Boyes, Vivien
Boyle, Ann (Peters) 1916- 10
Boyle, Eleanor Vere (Gordon) 1825-1916 28
Boyle, Robert H. 1928- 65
Boylston, Helen Dore 1895-1984 23
  Obituary 39
Boynton, Sandra (Keith) 1953- 152
  Brief entry 38
  Earlier sketches in SATA 57, 107
  See also CLR 105
Boz
See Dickens, Charles (John Huffam)
Bracken, Charles
See Pellowski, Michael (Joseph)
Brackers de Hugo, Pierre 1960- 115
Brackett, Dolli Tingle 1911-1993 137
Brackett, Virginia 1950- 166
  Earlier sketch in SATA 121
Brackett, Virginia Roberts Meredith
See Brackett, Virginia
Bradbury, Bianca (Ryley) 1908-1982 56
  Earlier sketch in SATA 3
Bradbury, Edward P.
See Moorcock, Michael
Bradbury, Ray 1920- 123
  Earlier sketches in SATA 11, 64
Bradbury, Ray Douglas
See Bradbury, Ray
Bradby, Marie 161
Bradfield, Carl 1942- 91
Bradford, Ann (Liddell) 1917- 56
  Brief entry 38
Bradford, Barbara Taylor 1933- 66
Bradford, Karleen 1936- 96
  Earlier sketch in SATA 48
Bradford, Lois J(ean) 1936- 36
Bradford, Richard (Roark) 1932-2002 59
  Obituary 135
Bradley, Duane
See Sanborn, Duane
Bradley, Kimberly Brubaker 1967- 179

Bradley, Marion Zimmer 1930-1999 139
  Obituary 116
  Earlier sketch in SATA 90
See Chapman, Lee
  and Dexter, John
  and Gardner, Miriam
  and Ives, Morgan
  and Rivers, Elfrida
Bradley, Virginia 1912- 23
Bradley, Will
See Strickland, (William) Brad(ley)
Bradman, Tony 1954- 152
  Earlier sketch in SATA 81
Bradshaw, Gillian (Joan) 1949- 118
Bradshaw, Gillian 1956- 127
Bradshaw, Gillian Marucha
See Bradshaw, Gillian
Bradstreet, T. J.
See Thesman, Jean
Brady, Esther Wood 1905-1987 31
  Obituary 53
Brady, Irene 1943- 4
Brady, Kimberley S. 1953- 101
Brady, Kimberley Smith
See Brady, Kimberley S.
Brady, Lillian 1902- 28
Bragdon, Elspeth MacDuffie 1897-1980 6
Bragdon, Lillian Jacot 24
Brager, Bruce L. 1949- 146
Bragg, Mabel Caroline 1870-1945 24
Bragg, Michael 1948- 46
Bragg, Ruth Gembicki 1943- 77
Brahm, Sumishta 1954- 58
Brailsford, Frances
See Wosmek, Frances
Brainerd, John W(hiting) 1918- 65
Braithwaite, Althea 1940- 23
  Autobiography Feature 119
  See also SAAS 24
Bram, Elizabeth 1948- 30
Brancato, Robin F(idler) 1936- 97
  See also CLR 32
  See also SAAS 9
Branch, Muriel Miller 1943- 152
  Earlier sketch in SATA 94
Brand, Christianna
See Lewis, Mary (Christianna)
Brand, Rebecca
See Charnas, Suzy McKee
Brandel, Marc 1919- 71
Brandenberg, Alexa (Demetria) 1966- 97
Brandenberg, Aliki (Liacouras) 1929- 157
  Earlier sketches in SATA 2, 35, 75, 113
See Aliki
Brandenberg, Franz 1932- 75
  Earlier sketches in SATA 8, 35
Brandenburg, Jim 1945- 87
Brandhorst, Carl T(heodore) 1898-1988 23
Brandis, Marianne 1938- 149
  Earlier sketches in SATA 59, 96
Brandon, Brumsic, Jr. 1927- 9
Brandon, Curt
See Bishop, Curtis (Kent)
Brandreth, Gyles 1948- 28
  See Brandreth, Gyles Daubeney
Brandreth, Gyles Daubeney 1948-
  See Brandreth, Gyles
Brandt, Catharine 1905-1997 40
Brandt, Keith
See Sabin, Louis
Brandt, Sue R(eading) 1916- 59
Branfield, John (Charles) 1931- 11
Branford, Henrietta 1946-1999 106
Branley, Franklyn M(ansfield) 1915-2002 .. 136
  Earlier sketches in SATA 4, 68
  See also CLR 13
  See also SAAS 16
Branscum, Robbie (Tilley) 1937-1997 72
  Obituary 96
  Earlier sketch in SATA 23
  See also SAAS 17

Bransom, (John) Paul 1885-1979 43
Brashares, Ann 1967- 145
  See also CLR 113
Braswell, E.J.
See Lynn, Tracy
Braswell, Elizabeth J.
See Lynn, Tracy
Braswell, Liz
See Lynn, Tracy
Bratton, Helen 1899-1986 4
Bratun, Katy 1950- 160
  Earlier sketch in SATA 83
Braude, Michael 1936- 23
Braun, Lilian Jackson 1916(?)- 109
Brautigan, Richard (Gary) 1935-1984 56
Bray, Libba 159
Braymer, Marjorie Elizabeth 1911-1988 6
Breathed, Berke 1957- 161
  Earlier sketch in SATA 86
Breathed, Guy Berkeley
See Breathed, Berke
Brecht, Edith 1895-1975 6
  Obituary 25
Breck, Vivian
See Breckenfeld, Vivian Gurney
Breckenfeld, Vivian Gurney 1895-1992 1
Breda, Tjalmar
See DeJong, David C(ornel)
Bredeson, Carmen 1944- 163
  Earlier sketch in SATA 98
Breinburg, Petronella 1927- 11
  See also CLR 31
Breisky, William J(ohn) 1928- 22
Brenaman, Miriam 172
Brennan, Gale (Patrick) 1927- 64
  Brief entry 53
Brennan, Herbie
See Brennan, J(ames) H(erbert)
Brennan, J(ames) H(erbert) 1940- 140
Brennan, Jan
See Brennan, J(ames) H(erbert)
Brennan, Joseph Lomas 1903-2000 6
Brennan, Linda Crotta 1952- 130
Brenner, Anita 1905-1974 56
Brenner, Barbara (Johnes) 1925- 124
  Earlier sketches in SATA 4, 42, 76
  See also SAAS 14
Brenner, Fred 1920- 36
  Brief entry 34
Brent, Stuart 14
Breslin, Theresa 128
  Autobiography Feature 128
  Earlier sketch in SATA 70
Breslow, Maurice 1935- 72
Breslow, Maurice A
See Breslow, Maurice
Breslow, Susan 1951- 69
Brett, Bernard 1925- 22
Brett, Grace N(eff) 1900-1975 23
Brett, Jan 1949- 171
  Earlier sketches in SATA 42, 71, 130
  See also CLR 27
Brett, Jan Churchill
See Brett, Jan
Brett Bowler, Jan
See Brett, Jan
Brewer, James D. 1951- 108
Brewer, Sally King 1947- 33
Brewster, Benjamin
See Folsom, Franklin (Brewster)
Brewster, Hugh 1950- 95
Brewster, Patience 1952- 97
Brewton, John E(dmund) 1898-1982 5
Brian, Janeen (Paulette) 1948- 141
Brick, John 1922-1973 10
Brickman, Robin D. 1954- 155
Bride, Nadja
See Nobisso, Josephine

Bridgers, Sue Ellen 1942- 90
  Autobiography Feature 109
  Earlier sketch in SATA 22
  See also CLR 18
  See also SAAS 1
Bridges, Laurie
  See Bruck, Lorraine
Bridges, Ruby (Nell) 1954- 131
Bridges, William (Andrew) 1901-1984 5
Bridwell, Norman (Ray) 1928- 138
  Earlier sketches in SATA 4, 68
  See also CLR 96
Brier, Howard M(axwell) 1903-1969 8
Brierley, (Louise) 1958- 59
Briggs, Katharine Mary 1898-1980 101
  Obituary 25
Briggs, Peter 1921-1975 39
  Obituary 31
Briggs, Raymond 1934- 131
  Earlier sketches in SATA 23, 66
  See also CLR 10
Briggs, Raymond Redvers
  See Briggs, Raymond
Bright, Robert (Douglas Sr.) 1902-1988 63
  Obituary 60
  Earlier sketch in SATA 24
Bright, Sarah
  See Shine, Deborah
Brightfield, Richard 1927- 65
  Brief entry 53
Brightfield, Rick
  See Brightfield, Richard
Brighton, Catherine 1943- 107
  Earlier sketch in SATA 65
Brill, Marlene Targ 1945- 124
  Earlier sketch in SATA 77
Brimberg, Stanlee 1947- 9
Brimner, Larry Dane 1949- 170
  Autobiography Feature 112
  Earlier sketch in SATA 79
Brin, David 1950- 65
Brin, Ruth Firestone 1921- 22
Brinckloe, Julie (Lorraine) 1950- 13
Brindel, June (Rachuy) 1919- 7
Brindle, Max
  See Fleischman, Sid
Brindze, Ruth 1903-1984 23
Brink, Carol Ryrie 1895-1981 100
  Obituary 27
  Earlier sketches in SATA 1, 31
  See also CLR 30
Brinsmead, H. F.
  See Brinsmead, H(esba) F(ay)
Brinsmead, H. F(ay)
  See Brinsmead, H(esba) F(ay)
Brinsmead, H(esba) F(ay) 1922- 78
  Earlier sketch in SATA 18
  See also CLR 47
  See also SAAS 5
Briquebec, John
  See Rowland-Entwistle, (Arthur) Theodore
    (Henry)
Brisbane, Henry R.
  See Ellis, Edward S(ylvester)
Brisco, P. A.
  See Matthews, Patricia
Brisco, Patty
  See Matthews, Patricia
  and Matthews, Clayton (Hartley)
Briscoe, Jill (Pauline) 1935- 56
  Brief entry 47
Brisley, Joyce Lankester 1896-1978 22
  Obituary 84
Brissenden, Connie
  See Brissenden, Constance
Brissenden, Constance 1947- 150
Brisson, Pat 1951- 177
  Autobiography Feature 133
  Earlier sketches in SATA 67, 128, 133
Britt, Dell 1934- 1

Brittain, Bill
  See SAAS 7
  See Brittain, William (E.)
Brittain, C. Dale 1948- 82
Brittain, William (E.) 1930- 76
  Earlier sketch in SATA 36
  See Brittain, Bill
Brittingham, Geoffrey (Hugh) 1959- 76
Britton, Kate 49
  See Stegeman, Janet Allais
Britton, Louisa
  See McGuire, Leslie (Sarah)
Britton, Rick 1952- 82
Bro, Margueritte (Harmon) 1894-1977 19
  Obituary 27
Broach, Elise 1963- 173
Broadhead, Helen Cross 1913- 25
Brochmann, Elizabeth 1938- 41
Brock, Betty (Carter) 1923-2003 4
  Obituary 150
Brock, C(harles) E(dmund) 1870-1938 42
  Brief entry 32
Brock, Delia
  See Ephron, Delia
Brock, Emma L(illian) 1886-1974 8
Brock, H(enry) M(atthew) 1875-1960 42
Brockett, Eleanor Hall 1913-1967 10
Brockman, C(hristian) Frank 1902-1985 26
Brockmeier, Kevin 1972- 176
Broderick, Dorothy M. 1929- 5
Brodeur, Ruth Wallace
  See Wallace-Brodeur, Ruth
Brodie, Sally
  See Cavin, Ruth (Brodie)
Brodsky, Beverly
  See McDermott, Beverly Brodsky
Brody, Wendy
  See Staub, Wendy Corsi
Broeger, Achim 1944- 31
Broekel, Rainer Lothar 1923- 38
Broekel, Ray
  See Broekel, Rainer Lothar
Broekstra, Lorette 1964- 124
Broger, Achim
  See Broeger, Achim
Broida, Marian 154
Brokamp, Marilyn 1920- 10
Broman, Fred
  See Moseley, James W(illett)
Bromhall, Winifred 26
Brommer, Gerald F(rederick) 1927- 28
Brondfield, Jerome 1913-1998 22
Brondfield, Jerry
  See Brondfield, Jerome
Bronner, Stephen Eric 1949- 101
Bronowski, Jacob 1908-1974 55
Bronson, Lynn
  See Lampman, Evelyn Sibley
Brook, Judith (Penelope) 1926- 59
  Brief entry 51
Brook, Judy
  See Brook, Judith (Penelope)
Brooke, L(eonard) Leslie 1862-1940 17
  See also CLR 20
Brooke, William J. 1946- 139
Brooke-Haven, P.
  See Wodehouse, P(elham) G(renville)
Brookins, Dana 1931- 28
Brooks, Anita 5
  See Abramovitz, Anita (Zeltner Brooks)
Brooks, Bill 1939- 59
Brooks, Bruce 1950- 112
  Brief entry 53
  Earlier sketch in SATA 72
  See also CLR 25
Brooks, Caryl 1924- 84
Brooks, Charlotte K(endrick) 1918-1998 24
  Obituary 112
Brooks, Erik 1972- 152
Brooks, George
  See Baum, L(yman) Frank

Brooks, Gwendolyn 1917-2000 6
  Obituary 123
  See also CLR 27
Brooks, Gwendolyn Elizabeth
  See Brooks, Gwendolyn
Brooks, Jerome 1931- 23
Brooks, Kevin M. 1959- 150
Brooks, Lester 1924- 7
Brooks, Martha 1944- 134
  Autobiography Feature 134
  Earlier sketches in SATA 68, 121
Brooks, Maurice (Graham) 1900- 45
Brooks, Polly Schoyer 1912- 12
Brooks, Ron(ald George) 1948- 94
  Brief entry 33
Brooks, Terry 1944- 60
Brooks, Walter R(ollin) 1886-1958 17
Brooks-Hill, Helen (Mason) 1908-1994 59
Broome, Errol 1937- 158
  Earlier sketch in SATA 105
Brophy, Nannette 1963- 73
Brosnan, James Patrick 1929- 14
Brosnan, Jim
  See Brosnan, James Patrick
Brostoff, Anita 1931- 132
Brothers Grimm
  See Grimm, Jacob Ludwig Karl
  and Grimm, Wilhelm Karl
Brothers Hildebrandt, The
  See Hildebrandt, Greg
  and Hildebrandt, Tim
Broun, Emily
  See Sterne, Emma Gelders
Brouwer, S. W.
  See Brouwer, Sigmund (W.)
Brouwer, Sigmund (W.) 1959- 109
Brow, Thea 1934- 60
Brower, Millicent 8
Brower, Pauline 1929- 22
Browin, Frances Williams 1898-1986 5
Brown, Alexis
  See Baumann, Amy (Brown) Beeching
Brown, Anne Ensign 1937- 61
Brown, Beverly Swerdlow 97
Brown, Bill
  See Brown, William L(ouis)
Brown, Billye Walker
  See Cutchen, Billye Walker
Brown, Bob
  See Brown, Robert Joseph
Brown, Buck 1936- 45
Brown, Calef 1949- 179
Brown, Cassie 1919-1986 55
Brown, Conrad 1922- 31
Brown, Craig McFarland 1947- 73
Brown, David
  See Brown, David A(lan)
  and Myller, Rolf
Brown, Dee 1908-2002 110
  Obituary 141
  Earlier sketch in SATA 5
Brown, Dee Alexander
  See Brown, Dee
Brown, Don 1949- 172
Brown, Drew T. III 1955- 83
Brown, Drollene P. 1939- 53
Brown, Eleanor Frances 1908-1987 3
Brown, Elizabeth Ferguson 1937- 153
Brown, Elizabeth M(yers) 1915- 43
Brown, Fern G. 1918- 34
Brown, (Robert) Fletch 1923- 42
Brown, Fornan 1901-1996 71
  Obituary 88
Brown, George Earl 1883-1964 11
Brown, George Mackay 1921-1996 35
Brown, Irene Bennett 1932- 3
Brown, Irving
  See Adams, William Taylor
Brown, Ivor (John Carnegie) 1891-1974 5
  Obituary 26
Brown, Jane Clark 1930- 81

Brown, Janet Mitsui 87
Brown, Jo 1964- 170
Brown, Joanne 1933- 147
Brown, Joe David 1915-1976 44
Brown, Joseph E(dward) 1929- 59
　Brief entry 51
Brown, Judith Gwyn 1933- 20
Brown, Kathryn 1955- 168
　Earlier sketch in SATA 98
Brown, Kathy
　See Brown, Kathryn
Brown, Ken (James) 129
Brown, Kevin 1960- 101
Brown, Laurene Krasny 1945- 99
　Earlier sketch in SATA 54
Brown, Laurie Krasny
　See Brown, Laurene Krasny
Brown, Lloyd Arnold 1907-1966 36
Brown, Mahlon A.
　See Ellis, Edward S(ylvester)
Brown, Marc (Tolon) 1946- 145
　Earlier sketches in SATA 10, 53, 80
　See also CLR 29
Brown, Marcia (Joan) 1918- 47
　Earlier sketch in SATA 7
　See also CLR 12
Brown, Margaret Wise 1910-1952 100
　See also YABC 2
　See also CLR 107
Brown, Margery (Wheeler) 78
　Earlier sketch in SATA 5
Brown, Marion Marsh 1908-2001 6
Brown, Myra Berry 1918- 6
Brown, Palmer 1919- 36
Brown, Pamela (Beatrice) 1924-1989 5
　Obituary 61
Brown, Peter 1979- 178
Brown, Reeve Lindbergh
　See Lindbergh, Reeve
Brown, Richard E. 1946- 61
Brown, Robert Joseph 1907-1989 14
Brown, Roderick (Langmere) Haig-
　See Haig-Brown, Roderick (Langmere)
Brown, Rosalie 9
　See Moore, Rosalie (Gertrude)
Brown, Roswell
　See Webb, Jean Francis (III)
Brown, Roy (Frederick) 1921-1982 51
　Obituary 39
Brown, Ruth 1941- 170
　Earlier sketch in SATA 105
Brown, Scott 1971- 134
Brown, Sue Ellen 1954- 81
Brown, Tricia 1954- 114
Brown, Vinson 1912-1991 19
Brown, Walter R(eed) 1929- 19
Brown, Will
　See Ainsworth, William Harrison
Brown, William L(ouis) 1910-1964 5
Browne, Anthony 1946- 163
　Brief entry 44
　Earlier sketches in SATA 45, 61, 105
　See also CLR 19
Browne, Anthony Edward Tudor
　See Browne, Anthony
Browne, Dik
　See Browne, Richard Arthur Allen
Browne, Hablot Knight 1815-1882 21
Browne, Matthew
　See Rands, William Brighty
Browne, Nicky Matthews
　See Browne, N.M.
Browne, N.M. 1960- 167
Browne, Richard Arthur Allen 1917-1989 ... 67
　Brief entry 38
　See Browne, Dik
Browne, Vee F(rances) 1956- 90
Browning, Robert 1812-1889
　See YABC 1
　See also CLR 97
Brownjohn, Alan 1931- 6

Brownlee, Walter 1930- 62
Brownlie, Betty 1946- 159
Brownlow, Kevin 1938- 65
Brownridge, William R(oy) 1932- 94
Bruce, (William) Harry 1934- 77
Bruce, Mary 1927- 1
Bruchac, Joseph III
　See Bruchac, Joseph
Bruchac, Joseph 1942- 176
　Autobiography Feature 176
　Earlier sketches in SATA 42, 89, 131
　See also CLR 46
Bruck, Lorraine 1921- 55
　Brief entry 46
　See Bridges, Laurie
Bruel, Nick 166
Bruemmer, Fred 1929- 47
Brugman, Alyssa (F.) 1974- 152
Brumbeau, Jeff 1955- 157
Bruna, Dick 1927- 76
　Brief entry 30
　Earlier sketch in SATA 43
　See also CLR 7
Brunhoff, Jean de 1899-1937 24
　See also CLR 116
Brunhoff, Laurent de 1925- 150
　Earlier sketches in SATA 24, 71
　See also CLR 116
Brunskill, Elizabeth Ann Flatt 1966- 88
Brush, Karen A(lexandra) 1960- 85
Brussel-Smith, Bernard 1914- 58
Brust, Steven K. 1955- 121
　Earlier sketch in SATA 86
Brust, Steven K. Zoltan
　See Brust, Steven K.
Brustlein, Daniel 1904- 40
Brustlein, Janice Tworkov -2000 40
　Obituary 126
Brutschy, Jennifer 1960- 84
Bryan, Ashley 1923- 178
　Earlier sketches in SATA 31, 72, 132
　See also CLR 66
Bryan, Ashley F.
　See Bryan, Ashley
Bryant, Bernice (Morgan) 1908-1976 11
Bryant, Jen 1960- 175
　Earlier sketch in SATA 94
Bryant, Jennifer Fisher
　See Bryant, Jen
Bryant, Laura J. 176
Brychta, Alex 1956- 21
Brynie, Faith H. 1946- 113
Brynie, Faith Hickman
　See Brynie, Faith H.
Bryson, Bernarda 1903-2004 9
　See Shahn, Bernarda Bryson
Buba, Joy Flinsch 1904- 44
Buchan, Bryan 1945- 36
Buchan, John 1875-1940
　See YABC 2
Buchanan, Debby 1952- 82
Buchanan, Deborah Leevonne
　See Buchanan, Debby
Buchanan, Jane 1956- 160
Buchanan, Paul 1959- 116
Buchanan, Sue 1939- 139
Buchheimer, Naomi Barnett
　See Barnett, Naomi
Buchignani, Walter 1965- 84
Buchwald, Art 1925-2007 10
Buchwald, Arthur
　See Buchwald, Art
Buchwald, Emilie 1935- 7
Buck, Gisela 1941- 101
Buck, Lewis 1925- 18
Buck, Margaret Waring 1905-1997 3
Buck, Nola
　See Godwin, Laura
Buck, Pearl S(ydenstricker) 1892-1973 25
　Earlier sketch in SATA 1
Buck, Siegfried 1941- 101

Buckeridge, Anthony (Malcolm)
　1912-2004 85
　Earlier sketch in SATA 6
Buckholtz, Eileen (Garber) 1949- 54
　Brief entry 47
Buckler, Ernest 1908-1984 47
Buckless, Andrea K. 1968- 117
Buckley, Helen E(lizabeth) 1918- 90
　Earlier sketch in SATA 2
Buckley, James, Jr. 1963- 166
　Earlier sketch in SATA 114
Buckley, Michael 177
Buckmaster, Henrietta 6
　See Stephens, Henrietta Henkle
Bucks, Brad
　See Holub, Joan
Budd, E. S.
　See Sirimarco, Elizabeth
Budd, Lillian (Peterson) 1897-1989 7
Budhos, Marina 173
Buehler, Stephanie Jona 1956- 83
Buehner, Caralyn (M.) 1963- 159
　Earlier sketch in SATA 104
Buehner, Mark 1959- 159
　Earlier sketch in SATA 104
Buehr, Walter Franklin 1897-1971 3
Buell, Janet 1952- 106
Buergel, Paul-Hermann H. 1949- 83
Buettner, Dan 1960- 95
Buff, Conrad 1886-1975 19
Buff, Mary (E. Marsh) 1890-1970 19
Buffett, Jimmy 1946- 110
　Earlier sketch in SATA 76
Buffie, Margaret 1945- 161
　Earlier sketches in SATA 71, 107
　See also CLR 39
Bugni, Alice 1951- 122
Buhhos, Marina Tamar
　See Budhos, Marina
Buhhos, Marina Tamar
　See Budhos, Marina
Bujold, Lois McMaster 1949- 136
Bulfinch, Thomas 1796-1867 35
Bulion, Leslie 1958- 161
Bull, Angela (Mary) 1936- 45
Bull, Emma 1954- 99
　Autobiography Feature 103
Bull, Norman John 1916- 41
Bull, Schuyler M. 1974- 138
Bulla, Clyde Robert 1914-2007 139
　Earlier sketches in SATA 2, 41, 91
　See also SAAS 6
Bullard, Lisa 1961- 142
Bullock, Kathleen (Mary) 1946- 77
Bullock, Robert (D.) 1947- 92
Bulpin, (Barbara) Vicki 92
Bumstead, Kathleen Mary 1918-1987 53
Bundles, A'Lelia Perry 1952- 76
Bunin, Catherine 1967- 30
Bunin, Sherry 1925- 30
Bunkers, Suzanne L. 1950- 136
Bunting, A. E.
　See Bunting, (Anne) Eve(lyn)
Bunting, Eve
　See Bunting, (Anne) Eve(lyn)
Bunting, (Anne) Eve(lyn) 1928- 158
　Earlier sketches in SATA 18, 64, 110
　See also CLR 82
　See Bunting, Eve
Bunting, Glenn (Davison) 1957- 22
Burack, Sylvia K. 1916-2003 35
　Obituary 143
Burbank, Addison (Buswell) 1895-1961 37
Burch, Joann J(ohansen) 75
Burch, Robert J(oseph) 1925- 74
　Earlier sketch in SATA 1
　See also CLR 63
Burchard, Peter Duncan 1921- 143
　Earlier sketches in SATA 5, 74
　See also SAAS 13

Burchard, S. H.
　See Burchard, Sue
Burchard, Sue 1937- 22
Burchardt, Nellie 1921- 7
Burdett, Lois 117
Burdick, Eugene (Leonard) 1918-1965 22
Burford, Eleanor
　See Hibbert, Eleanor Alice Burford
Burgan, Michael 1960- 167
　Earlier sketch in SATA 118
Burger, Carl 1888-1967 9
Burgess, Ann Marie
　See Gerson, Noel Bertram
Burgess, Barbara Hood 1926- 69
Burgess, Em
　See Burgess, Mary Wyche
Burgess, (Frank) Gelett 1866-1951 32
　Brief entry 30
Burgess, Mark 157
Burgess, Mary Wyche 1916- 18
Burgess, Melvin 1954- 146
　Earlier sketch in SATA 96
Burgess, Michael
　See Gerson, Noel Bertram
Burgess, Robert F(orrest) 1927- 4
Burgess, Thornton Waldo 1874-1965 17
Burgess, Trevor
　See Trevor, Elleston
Burgwyn, Mebane Holoman 1914-1992 7
Burke, David 1927- 46
Burke, Diana G.
　See Gallagher, Diana G.
Burke, Diana Gallagher
　See Gallagher, Diana G.
Burke, Dianne O'Quinn 1940- 89
Burke, Janine 1952- 139
Burke, Jim 1973- 179
Burke, Katie 1953- 168
Burke, Patrick 1958- 114
Burke, Ralph
　See Garrett, (Gordon) Randall (Phillip)
　and Silverberg, Robert
Burkert, Nancy Ekholm 1933- 24
　See also SAAS 14
Burke-Weiner, Kimberly 1962- 95
Burks, Brian 1955- 95
Burland, Brian (Berkeley) 1931- 34
Burland, C. A.
　See Burland, Cottie (Arthur)
Burland, Cottie (Arthur) 1905-1983 5
Burleigh, Robert 1936- 146
　Earlier sketches in SATA 55, 98
Burlingame, (William) Roger 1889-1967 2
Burman, Ben Lucien 1896-1984 6
　Obituary 40
Burn, Doris 1923- 1
Burn, Ted
　See Burn, Thomas E.
Burn, Thomas E. 1940- 150
Burnard, Damon 1963- 115
Burnett, Constance Buel 1893-1975 36
Burnett, Frances (Eliza) Hodgson
　1849-1924 100
　See also YABC 2
　See also CLR 122
Burnford, Sheila (Philip Cochrane Every)
　1918-1984 3
　Obituary 38
　See also CLR 2
Burnham, Gretchen
　See Sprague, Gretchen
Burnham, Nicole 1970- 161
Burnham, Niki
　See Burnham, Nicole
Burnham, Sophy 1936- 65
Burningham, John (Mackintosh) 1936- 160
　Earlier sketches in SATA 16, 59, 111
　See also CLR 9
Burns, Diane L. 1950- 81
　See also SAAS 24

Burns, Eloise Wilkin
　See Wilkin, Eloise
Burns, Florence M. 1905-1988 61
Burns, Khephra 1950- 92
Burns, Marilyn 1941- 96
　Brief entry 33
Burns, Olive Ann 1924-1990 65
Burns, Paul C. 5
Burns, Ray
　See Burns, Raymond (Howard)
Burns, Raymond (Howard) 1924- 9
Burns, Theresa 1961- 84
Burns, William A. 1909-1999 5
Burr, Dan 1951- 65
Burr, Lonnie 1943- 47
Burrell, Roy E(ric) C(harles) 1923- 72
Burroughs, Edgar Rice 1875-1950 41
Burroughs, Jean Mitchell 1908- 28
Burroughs, Polly 1925- 2
Burroway, Janet (Gay) 1936- 23
Burstein, Chaya M(alamud) 1923- 64
Burstein, Fred 1950- 83
Burstein, John 1949- 54
　Brief entry 40
Burstein, Stanley M.
　See Burstein, Stanley Mayer
Burstein, Stanley Mayer 1941- 175
Bursztynski, Sue 1953- 114
Burt, Jesse Clifton 1921-1976 46
　Obituary 20
Burt, Olive Woolley 1894-1981 4
Burton, Gennett 1945- 95
Burton, Hester (Wood-Hill) 1913-2000 74
　Earlier sketch in SATA 7
　See also CLR 1
　See also SAAS 8
Burton, Leslie
　See McGuire, Leslie (Sarah)
Burton, Marilee Robin 1950- 82
　Earlier sketch in SATA 46
Burton, Maurice 1898-1992 23
Burton, Robert (Wellesley) 1941- 22
Burton, Virginia Lee 1909-1968 100
　Earlier sketch in SATA 2
　See also CLR 11
Burton, William H(enry) 1890-1964 11
Busby, Cylin 1970- 118
Buscaglia, (Felice) Leo(nardo) 1924-1998 ... 65
　See Buscaglia, Leo F.
Buscaglia, Leo F.
　See Buscaglia, (Felice) Leo(nardo)
Busch, Phyllis S. 1909- 30
Bush, Anne Kelleher
　See Kelleher, Anne
Bush, Catherine 1961- 128
Bushnell, Jack 1952- 86
Busoni, Rafaello 1900-1962 16
Buss, Helen M.
　See Clarke, Margaret
Busselle, Rebecca 1941- 80
Bustard, Anne 1951- 173
Butcher, Kristin 1951- 140
Butenko, Bohdan 1931- 90
Butler, Beverly Kathleen 1932- 7
Butler, Bill
　See Butler, William (Arthur) Vivian
　and Butler, Ernest Alton
　and Butler, William Huxford
Butler, Charles 1963- 175
　Earlier sketch in SATA 121
Butler, Charles Cadman
　See Butler, Charles
Butler, Dori Hillestad 1965- 164
Butler, Dorothy 1925- 73
Butler, Geoff 1945- 94
Butler, M. Christina 1934- 170
　Earlier sketch in SATA 72
Butler, Octavia E. 1947-2006 84
　See also CLR 65
Butler, Octavia Estelle
　See Butler, Octavia E.

Butler, Vivian
　See Butler, William (Arthur) Vivian
Butler, William
　See Butler, William (Arthur) Vivian
Butler, William (Arthur) Vivian 1927-1987 . 79
　See Marric, J. J.
Butters, Dorothy Gilman 5
　See Gilman, Dorothy
Butterworth, Emma Macalik 1928- 43
Butterworth, Nick 1946- 149
　Earlier sketch in SATA 106
Butterworth, Oliver 1915-1990 1
　Obituary 66
Butterworth, W.E.
　See Griffin, W.E.B.
Butterworth, William E.
　See Griffin, W.E.B.
Butterworth, William Edmund III
　See Griffin, W.E.B.
Butts, Ed 1951- 177
Butts, Edward P.
　See Butts, Ed
Butts, Ellen R(ubinstein) 1942- 93
Buxton, Ralph
　See Silverstein, Alvin
　and Silverstein, Virginia B(arbara Opshelor)
Buzzeo, Toni 1951- 135
Byalick, Marcia 1947- 141
　Earlier sketch in SATA 97
Byard, Carole (Marie) 1941- 57
Byars, Betsy 1928- 163
　Autobiography Feature 108
　Earlier sketches in SATA 4, 46, 80
　See also CLR 72
　See also SAAS 1
Byars, Betsy Cromer
　See Byars, Betsy
Byfield, Barbara Ninde 1930- 8
Byman, Jeremy 1944- 129
Bynum, Janie 133
Byrd, Elizabeth 1912-1989 34
Byrd, Nicole
　See Zach, Cheryl (Byrd)
Byrd, Robert (John) 1942- 158
　Earlier sketches in SATA 33, 112
Byrne, Mary Gregg 1951- 162

C

C. 3. 3.
　See Wilde, Oscar (Fingal O'Flahertie Wills)
Cabaniss, J(ames) Allen 1911-1997 5
Cabat, Erni 1914- 74
Cabban, Vanessa 1971- 176
Cable, Mary 1920- 9
Cabot, Meg 1967- 175
　Earlier sketch in SATA 127
　See also CLR 85
Cabot, Meggin
　See Cabot, Meg
Cabot, Meggin Patricia
　See Cabot, Meg
Cabot, Patricia
　See Cabot, Meg
Cabral, O. M.
　See Cabral, Olga
Cabral, Olga 1909- 46
Cabrera, Cozbi A. 1963- 177
Cabrera, Jane 1968- 152
　Earlier sketch in SATA 103
Cabrera, Marcela 1966- 90
Cade, Toni
　See Bambara, Toni Cade
Cadmus and Harmonia
　See Buchan, John
Cadnum, Michael 1949- 165
　Earlier sketches in SATA 87, 121
　See also CLR 78
Caduto, Michael J. 1955- 103

Cadwallader, Sharon 1936- 7
Cady, (Walter) Harrison 1877(?)-1970 19
Caffey, Donna (J.) 1954- 110
Cagle, Malcolm W(infield) 1918- 32
Cahn, Rhoda 1922- 37
Cahn, William 1912-1976 37
Cain, Arthur H(omer) 1913-1981 3
Caine, Geoffrey
  See Walker, Robert W(ayne)
Caines, Jeannette (Franklin) 1938- 78
  Brief entry 43
  See also CLR 24
Cairns, Trevor 1922- 14
Calabro, Marian 1954- 79
Caldecott, Moyra 1927- 22
Caldecott, Randolph (J.) 1846-1886 100
  Earlier sketch in SATA 17
  See also CLR 110
Calder, Charlotte 1952- 125
Calder, David 1932-1997 105
Calder, Lyn
  See Calmenson, Stephanie
Calder, Marie D(onais) 1948- 96
Calderone-Stewart, Lisa
  See Calderone-Stewart, Lisa-Marie
Calderone-Stewart, Lisa-Marie 1958- 123
Caldwell, Doreen (Mary) 1942- 71
Caldwell, John C(ope) 1913-1984 7
Caletti, Deb 1963- 171
Calhoun, B. B. 1961- 98
Calhoun, Chad
  See Barrett, Neal, Jr.
  and Cunningham, Chet
  and Goulart, Ron(ald Joseph)
Calhoun, Dia 1959- 129
Calhoun, Mary 2
  See also CLR 42
  See Wilkins, Mary Huiskamp
Calhoun, T.B.
  See Bisson, Terry
Calif, Ruth 1922- 67
Calkins, Franklin
  See Stratemeyer, Edward L.
Call, Hughie Florence 1890-1969 1
Callahan, Dorothy M(onahan) 1934- 39
  Brief entry 35
Callahan, Philip Serna 1923- 25
Callan, Jamie 1954- 59
Callaway, Bernice (Anne) 1923- 48
Callaway, Kathy 1943- 36
Callen, Larry
  See Callen, Lawrence Willard, Jr.
Callen, Lawrence Willard, Jr. 1927- 19
Calley, Karin 1965- 92
Calmenson, Stephanie 1952- 139
  Brief entry 37
  Earlier sketches in SATA 51, 84
Calvert, Elinor H.
  See Lasell, Elinor H.
Calvert, John
  See Leaf, (Wilbur) Munro
Calvert, Patricia 1931- 132
  Earlier sketches in SATA 45, 69
  See also SAAS 17
Camburn, Carol A.
  See Camburn-Bracalente, Carol A.
Camburn-Bracalente, Carol A. 1962- 118
Cameron, Ann 1943- 129
  Earlier sketches in SATA 27, 89
  See also SAAS 20
Cameron, Edna M. 1905-1999 3
Cameron, Eleanor (Frances) 1912-1996 25
  Obituary 93
  Earlier sketch in SATA 1
  See also CLR 72
  See also SAAS 10
Cameron, Elizabeth
  See Nowell, Elizabeth Cameron

Cameron, Elizabeth Jane 1910-1976 32
  Obituary 30
Cameron, Ian
  See Payne, Donald Gordon
Cameron, M(alcolm) G(ordon) Graham
  See Graham-Cameron, M(alcolm) G(ordon)
Cameron, M. Graham
  See Graham-Cameron, M(alcolm) G(ordon)
Cameron, Mike Graham
  See Graham-Cameron, M(alcolm) G(ordon)
Cameron, Polly 1928- 2
Cameron, Scott 1962- 84
Camp, Lindsay 1957- 133
Camp, Walter (Chauncey) 1859-1925
  See YABC 1
Campbell, (Elizabeth) Andrea 1963- 50
Campbell, Ann R. 1925- 11
Campbell, Bill 1960- 89
Campbell, Bruce
  See Epstein, Samuel
Campbell, Camilla 1905-1992 26
Campbell, Carole R. 1939- 125
Campbell, Hope 1925- 20
Campbell, Hugh 1930- 90
Campbell, Jane
  See Edwards, Jane Campbell
Campbell, Julie
  See Tatham, Julie Campbell
Campbell, Patricia J(ean) 1930- 45
Campbell, Patty
  See Campbell, Patricia J(ean)
Campbell, Peter A. 1948- 99
Campbell, R. W.
  See Campbell, Rosemae Wells
Campbell, Robin
  See Strachan, Ian
Campbell, Rod 1945- 98
  Brief entry 44
  Earlier sketch in SATA 51
Campbell, Rosemae Wells 1909- 1
Camper, Cathy 1956- 170
Campion, Nardi Reeder 1917- 22
Campling, Elizabeth 1948- 53
Campoy, F. Isabel (Coronado) 1946- 143
Camps, Luis 1928- 66
Canales, Viola 1957- 141
Canfield, Dorothea F.
  See Fisher, Dorothy (Frances) Canfield
Canfield, Dorothea Frances
  See Fisher, Dorothy (Frances) Canfield
Canfield, Dorothy
  See Fisher, Dorothy (Frances) Canfield
Canfield, Jack 1944- 164
Canfield, Jane White 1897-1984 32
  Obituary 38
Canfield, Muriel 1935- 94
Cann, Helen 1969- 179
  Earlier sketch in SATA 124
Cann, Kate 1954- 152
  Earlier sketch in SATA 103
Cannan, Joanna 82
  See Pullein-Thompson, Joanna Maxwell
Cannon, A(nn) E(dwards) 163
  Earlier sketch in SATA 93
Cannon, Bettie (Waddell) 1922- 59
Cannon, Curt
  See Hunter, Evan
Cannon, Eileen E(mily) 1948- 119
Cannon, Frank
  See Mayhar, Ardath
Cannon, Janell 1957- 128
  Earlier sketch in SATA 78
  See also CLR 120
Cannon, Marian G. 1923- 85
Cannon, Taffy
  See Cannon, Eileen E(mily)
Canusi, Jose
  See Barker, S(quire) Omar

Canyon, Christopher 1966- 150
  Earlier sketch in SATA 104
Capek, Michael 1947- 142
  Earlier sketch in SATA 96
Capes, Bernard (Edward Joseph)
  1854-1918 116
Caponigro, John Paul 1965- 84
Capote, Truman 1924-1984 91
Capp, Al 61
  See Caplin, Alfred Gerald
Cappel, Constance 1936- 22
Cappetta, Cynthia 1949- 125
Cappo, Nan Willard 1955- 143
Capps, Benjamin (Franklin) 1922- 9
Captain Kangaroo
  See Keeshan, Robert J.
Captain Wheeler
  See Ellis, Edward S(ylvester)
Captain Young of Yale
  See Stratemeyer, Edward L.
Capucilli, Alyssa Satin 1957- 163
  Earlier sketch in SATA 115
Capucine
  See Mazille, Capucine
Caraher, Kim(berley Elizabeth) 1961- 105
Caraker, Mary 1929- 74
Caras, Roger A(ndrew) 1928-2001 12
  Obituary 127
Caravantes, Peggy 1935- 140
Caraway, Caren 1939- 57
Carbone, Elisa 1954- 137
  Earlier sketch in SATA 81
  See Carbone, Elisa Lynn
Carbone, Elisa Lynn 173
  See Carbone, Elisa
Carbonnier, Jeanne 1894-1974 3
  Obituary 34
Card, Orson Scott 1951- 127
  Earlier sketch in SATA 83
  See also CLR 116
Carew, Jan (Rynveld) 1925- 51
  Brief entry 40
Carey, Bonnie
  See Marshall, Bonnie C.
Carey, Charles W., Jr. 1951- 170
Carey, Ernestine Gilbreth 1908-2006 2
  Obituary 177
Carey, Lisa 110
Carey, M. V.
  See Carey, Mary V(irginia)
Carey, Mary V(irginia) 1925-1994 44
  Brief entry 39
Carey, Peter 1943- 94
Carey, Valerie Scho 1949- 60
Carheden, Goorel Kristina
  See Naaslund, Goorel Kristina
Carigiet, Alois 1902-1985 24
  Obituary 47
  See also CLR 38
Carini, Edward 1923- 9
Carkeet, David 1946- 75
Carle, Eric 1929- 163
  Earlier sketches in SATA 4, 65, 120
  See also CLR 72
  See also SAAS 6
Carleton, Captain L. C.
  See Ellis, Edward S(ylvester)
Carleton, Captain Latham C.
  See Ellis, Edward S(ylvester)
Carleton, Latham C.
  See Ellis, Edward S(ylvester)
Carling, Amelia Lau 1949- 164
  Earlier sketch in SATA 119
Carlisle, Carolyn
  See Hawes, Louise
Carlisle, Clark
  See Holding, James (Clark Carlisle, Jr.)
Carlisle, Olga Andreyev 1930- 35
Carlsen, G(eorge) Robert 1917- 30

Carlsen, Ruth C(hristoffer) 1918- 2
Carlson, Bernice Wells 1910- 8
Carlson, Dale (Bick) 1935- 1
Carlson, Daniel (Bick) 1960- 27
Carlson, Laurie 1952- 173
  Earlier sketch in SATA 101
Carlson, Laurie Winn
  See Carlson, Laurie
Carlson, Melody 1956- 171
  Earlier sketch in SATA 113
Carlson, Nancy L.
  See Carlson, Nancy L(ee)
Carlson, Nancy L(ee) 1953- 144
  Brief entry 45
  Earlier sketches in SATA 56, 90
Carlson, Natalie Savage 1906-1997 68
  Earlier sketch in SATA 2
  See also SAAS 4
Carlson, Susan Johnston 1953- 88
Carlson, Vada F. 1897- 16
Carlstrom, Nancy White 1948- 156
  Brief entry 48
  Earlier sketches in SATA 53, 92
Carlton, Keith
  See Robertson, Keith (Carlton)
Carlyon, Richard 55
Carman, Patrick 161
Carmer, Carl (Lamson) 1893-1976 37
  Obituary 30
Carmer, Elizabeth Black 1904- 24
Carmi, Giora 1944- 149
  Earlier sketch in SATA 79
Carmichael, Carrie 40
  See Carmichael, Harriet
Carmody, Isobelle 1958- 161
Carmody, Isobelle Jane
  See Carmody, Isobelle
Carney, Mary Lou 1949- 170
Carol, Bill J.
  See Knott, William C(ecil, Jr.)
Caron, Romi
  See Caron-Kyselkova', Romana
Caron-Kyselkova', Romana 1967- 94
Caroselli, Remus F(rancis) 1916- 36
Carpelan, Bo (Gustaf Bertelsson) 1926- 8
Carpenter, (John) Allan 1917- 81
  Earlier sketch in SATA 3
Carpenter, Angelica Shirley 1945- 153
  Earlier sketch in SATA 71
Carpenter, Frances 1890-1972 3
  Obituary 27
Carpenter, John (Howard) 1948- 58
Carpenter, Johnny
  See Carpenter, John (Howard)
Carpenter, Patricia (Healy Evans) 1920- 11
Carr, Glyn
  See Styles, (Frank) Showell
Carr, Harriett H(elen) 1899-1977 3
Carr, Jan 1953- 132
  Earlier sketch in SATA 89
Carr, M. J.
  See Carr, Jan
Carr, Mary Jane 1899-1988 2
  Obituary 55
Carr, Philippa
  See Hibbert, Eleanor Alice Burford
Carr, Roger Vaughan 1937- 95
Carrel, Annette Felder 1929- 90
Carrick, Carol (Hatfield) 1935- 118
  Earlier sketches in SATA 7, 63
  See also SAAS 18
Carrick, Donald (F.) 1929-1989 63
  Earlier sketch in SATA 7
Carrick, Malcolm 1945- 28
Carrier, Lark 1947- 71
  Brief entry 50
Carrier, Roch 1937- 166
  Earlier sketch in SATA 105
Carrighar, Sally 1898-1985 24

Carrington, G. A.
  See Cunningham, Chet
Carrington, Marsha Gray 1954- 168
  Earlier sketch in SATA 111
Carris, Joan Davenport 1938- 44
  Brief entry 42
Carroll, Curt
  See Bishop, Curtis (Kent)
Carroll, Elizabeth
  See Barkin, Carol
  and James, Elizabeth
Carroll, Jenny
  See Cabot, Meg
Carroll, (Archer) Latrobe 1894-1996 7
Carroll, Laura
  See Parr, Lucy
Carroll, Lewis
  See CLR 108
  See Dodgson, Charles L(utwidge)
Carroll, Raymond 1924- 86
  Brief entry 47
Carruth, Hayden 1921- 47
Carryl, Charles E. 1841-1920 114
Carryl, Charles Edward
  See Carryl, Charles E.
Carse, Robert 1902-1971 5
Carson, J(ohn) Franklin 1920-1981 1
  Obituary 107
Carson, Mary Kay 1964- 150
Carson, Rachel
  See Carson, Rachel Louise
Carson, Rachel Louise 1907-1964 23
  See Carson, Rachel
Carson, Rosalind
  See Chittenden, Margaret
Carson, S. M.
  See Gorsline, (Sally) Marie
Carson, William C. 1928- 154
Carter, Alden R 1947- 137
  Earlier sketch in SATA 67
  See also CLR 22
  See also SAAS 18
Carter, Alden Richardson
  See Carter, Alden R
Carter, Andy 1948- 134
Carter, Angela 1940-1992 66
  Obituary 70
Carter, Angela Olive
  See Carter, Angela
Carter, Anne Laurel 1953- 135
Carter, Asa Earl
  See Carter, Forrest
Carter, Avis Murton
  See Allen, Kenneth S.
Carter, Bruce
  See Hough, Richard (Alexander)
Carter, Carol S(hadis) 1948- 124
Carter, David A. 1957- 170
  Earlier sketch in SATA 114
Carter, Don 1958- 124
Carter, Dorothy Sharp 1921- 8
Carter, Forrest 1927(?)-1979 32
Carter, Helene 1887-1960 15
Carter, (William) Hodding, Jr. 1907-1972 2
  Obituary 27
Carter, James Earl, Jr.
  See Carter, Jimmy
Carter, Jimmy 1924- 79
Carter, Katharine J(ones) 1905-1984 2
Carter, Lin(wood Vrooman) 1930-1988 91
Carter, Mike 1936- 138

Carter, Nick
  See Avallone, Michael (Angelo, Jr.)
  and Ballard, (Willis) Todhunter
  and Crider, Bill
  and Cassiday, Bruce (Bingham)
  and Chastain, Thomas
  and Dey, Frederic (Merrill) Van Rensselaer
  and Garside, (Clifford) Jack
  and Hayes, Ralph E(ugene)
  and Henderson, M(arilyn) R(uth)
  and Lynds, Dennis
  and Lynds, Gayle (Hallenbeck)
  and Randisi, Robert J.
  and Rasof, Henry
  and Stratemeyer, Edward L.
  and Smith, Martin Cruz
  and Swain, Dwight V(reeland)
  and Vardeman, Robert E(dward)
  and Wallmann, Jeffrey M(iner)
  and White, Lionel
Carter, Peter 1929- 57
Carter, Phyllis Ann
  See Eberle, Irmengarde
Carter, Samuel (Thomson) III 1904-1988 37
  Obituary 60
Carter, William E. 1926-1983 1
  Obituary 35
Cartlidge, Michelle 1950- 96
  Brief entry 37
  Earlier sketch in SATA 49
Cartner, William Carruthers 1910- 11
Cartwright, Ann 1940- 78
Cartwright, Reg(inald Ainsley) 1938- 64
Cartwright, Sally 1923- 9
Carusone, Al 1949- 89
Carvell, Marlene 172
Carver, John
  See Gardner, Richard (M.)
Carwell, L'Ann
  See McKissack, Patricia C.
Cary
  See Cary, Louis F(avreau)
Cary, Kate 1967(?)- 174
Cary, Louis F(avreau) 1915- 9
Caryl, Jean
  See Kaplan, Jean Caryl Korn
Casanova, Mary 1957- 136
  Earlier sketch in SATA 94
Cascone, A.G.
  See Cascone, Annette
  and Cascone, Gina
Cascone, Annette 1960- 103
Cascone, Gina 1955- 103
Case, Marshal T(aylor) 1941- 9
Case, Michael
  See Howard, Robert West
Caseley, Judith 1951- 159
  Brief entry 53
  Earlier sketch in SATA 87
Casewit, Curtis W(erner) 1922-2002 4
Casey, Barbara (Louise) 1944- 147
  Earlier sketch in SATA 79
Casey, Brigid 1950- 9
Casey, Tina 1959- 141
Cash, Megan Montague 160
Casilla, Robert 1959- 146
  Earlier sketch in SATA 75
Cason, Mabel Earp 1892-1965 10
Cass, Joan E(velyn) 1
Cass-Beggs, Barbara 1904- 62
Cassedy, Patrice (Rinaldo) 1953- 149
Cassedy, Sylvia 1930-1989 77
  Obituary 61
  Earlier sketch in SATA 27
  See also CLR 26
Cassel, Lili
  See Wronker, Lili Cassel
Cassels, Jean 173
Cassidy, Anne 1952- 166

Casson, Hugh Maxwell 1910-1999 65
    Obituary 115
Cassutt, Michael 1954- 78
Cassutt, Michael Joseph
    See Cassutt, Michael
Castaldo, Nancy Fusco 1962- 151
    Earlier sketch in SATA 93
Castaneda, Omar S. 1954- 71
Castell, Megan
    See Williams, Jeanne
Castellanos, Jane Mollie Robinson
    1913-2001 9
Castellon, Federico 1914-1971 48
Castellucci, Cecil 1969- 176
Castillo, Edmund L. 1924-2005 1
    Obituary 167
Castle, Lee
    See Ogan, George F.
    and Ogan, Margaret E. (Nettles)
Castle, Paul
    See Howard, Vernon (Linwood)
Castle, Robert
    See Hamilton, Edmond
Caswell, Brian 1954- 171
    Earlier sketch in SATA 97
Caswell, Helen (Rayburn) 1923- 12
Catalano, Dominic 1956- 163
    Earlier sketch in SATA 76
Catalano, Grace (A.) 1961- 99
Catalanotto, Peter 1959- 159
    Autobiography Feature 113
    Earlier sketches in SATA 70, 114
    See also CLR 68
    See also SAAS 25
Catanese, P.W. 1961- 179
Cate, Dick
    See Cate, Richard Edward Nelson
Cate, Richard Edward Nelson 1932- 28
Cather, Willa (Sibert) 1873-1947 30
    See also CLR 98
Catherall, Arthur 1906-1980 74
    Earlier sketch in SATA 3
    See Ruthin, Margaret
Cathon, Laura E(lizabeth) 1908-1991 27
Catlett, Elizabeth 1919(?)- 82
Catlin, Wynelle 1930- 13
Cato, Heather 105
Cato, Sheila 114
Catrow, David
    See Catrow, David J. III
Catrow, David J. III 152
Catt, Louis
    See French, Vivian
Cattell, James 1954- 123
Catton, (Charles) Bruce 1899-1978 2
    Obituary 24
Catz, Max
    See Glaser, Milton
Caudell, Marian 1930- 52
Caudill, Rebecca 1899-1985 1
    Obituary 44
Cauley, Lorinda Bryan 1951- 46
    Brief entry 43
Cauman, Samuel 1910-1971 48
Causley, Charles (Stanley) 1917-2003 66
    Obituary 149
    Earlier sketch in SATA 3
    See also CLR 30
Cavallaro, Ann (Abelson) 1918- 62
Cavallo, Diana 1931- 7
Cavanagh, Helen (Carol) 1939- 98
    Brief entry 37
    Earlier sketch in SATA 48
Cavanah, Frances 1899-1982 31
    Earlier sketch in SATA 1
Cavanna, Betty 30
    Earlier sketch in SATA 1
    See also SAAS 4
    See Harrison, Elizabeth (Allen) Cavanna
Cavanna, Elizabeth
    See Harrison, Elizabeth (Allen) Cavanna

Cave, Kathryn 1948- 123
    Earlier sketch in SATA 76
Cavendish, Peter
    See Horler, Sydney
Cavin, Ruth (Brodie) 1918- 38
Cavoukian, Raffi 1948- 68
Cawley, Winifred 1915- 13
Caxton, Pisistratus
    See Lytton, Edward G(eorge) E(arle) L(ytton)
    Bulwer-Lytton Baron
Cazeau, Charles J(ay) 1931- 65
Cazet, Denys 1938- 163
    Brief entry 41
    Earlier sketches in SATA 52, 99
Cazzola, Gus 1934- 73
Cebulash, Mel 1937- 91
    Earlier sketch in SATA 10
Ceder, Georgiana Dorcas -1985 10
Celenza, Anna Harwell 133
Celestino, Martha Laing 1951- 39
Cepeda, Joe 159
Cerf, Bennett (Alfred) 1898-1971 7
Cerf, Christopher (Bennett) 1941- 2
Cerullo, Mary M. 1949- 145
    Earlier sketch in SATA 86
Cervon, Jacqueline
    See Moussard, Jacqueline
Cetin, Frank Stanley 1921- 2
Chabon, Michael 1963- 145
Chaconas, D.J.
    See Chaconas, Dori
Chaconas, Dori 1938- 175
    Earlier sketch in SATA 145
Chaconas, Doris J.
    See Chaconas, Dori
Chadwick, Lester 67
    Earlier sketch in SATA 1
Chaffee, Allen 3
Chaffin, Lillie D(orton) 1925- 4
Chaikin, Miriam 1924- 152
    Earlier sketches in SATA 24, 102
Chall, Marsha Wilson 150
Challand, Helen J(ean) 1921- 64
Challans, Mary 1905-1983 23
    Obituary 36
    See Renault, Mary
Chalmers, Mary (Eileen) 1927- 6
    See also SAAS 14
Chamberlain, Margaret 1954- 46
Chamberlin, Kate 1945- 105
Chamberlin, Mary 1960- 177
Chamberlin, Rich 177
Chamberlin, Richard
    See Chamberlin, Rich
Chambers, Aidan 1934- 171
    Earlier sketches in SATA 1, 69, 108
    See also SAAS 12
Chambers, Catherine E.
    See St. John, Nicole
Chambers, John W. 1933- 57
    Brief entry 46
Chambers, Kate
    See St. John, Nicole
Chambers, Margaret Ada Eastwood 1911- 2
Chambers, Peggy
    See Chambers, Margaret Ada Eastwood
Chambers, Robert W(illiam) 1865-1933 107
Chan, Gillian 1954- 147
    Earlier sketch in SATA 102
Chance, James T.
    See Carpenter, John (Howard)
Chance, John T.
    See Carpenter, John (Howard)
Chance, Stephen
    See Turner, Philip (William)
Chandler, Caroline A(ugusta) 1906-1979 22
    Obituary 24
Chandler, David P(orter) 1933- 28
Chandler, Edna Walker 1908-1982 11
    Obituary 31

Chandler, Jennifer
    See Westwood, Jennifer
Chandler, Karen 1959- 122
Chandler, Linda S(mith) 1929- 39
Chandler, Pauline 175
Chandler, Robert 1953- 40
Chandler, Ruth Forbes 1894-1978 2
    Obituary 26
Chandonnet, Ann F. 1943- 92
Chaney, Jill 1932- 87
Chang, Chih-Wei 1966- 111
Chang, Cindy 1968- 90
Chang, Margaret 1941- 71
Chang, Margaret Scrogin
    See Chang, Margaret
Chang, Raymond 1939- 142
    Earlier sketches in SATA 71, 142 PEN
Chanin, Michael 1952- 84
Channel, A. R.
    See Catherall, Arthur
Chapian, Marie 1938- 29
Chapin, Tom 1945- 83
Chapman, Allen 67
    Earlier sketch in SATA 1
Chapman, Cheryl O(rth) 1948- 80
Chapman, (Constance) Elizabeth (Mann)
    1919- 10
Chapman, Gaynor 1935- 32
Chapman, Gillian 1955- 120
Chapman, Jane 1970- 176
    Earlier sketch in SATA 122
Chapman, Jean 104
    Earlier sketch in SATA 34
    See also CLR 65
Chapman, Lee
    See Bradley, Marion Zimmer
Chapman, Lynne F(erguson) 1963- 150
    Earlier sketch in SATA 94
Chapman, Vera (Ivy May) 1898-1996 33
Chapman, Walker
    See Silverberg, Robert
Chappell, Audrey 1954- 72
Chappell, Warren 1904-1991 68
    Obituary 67
    Earlier sketch in SATA 6
    See also SAAS 10
Charbonneau, Eileen 1951- 118
    Earlier sketch in SATA 84
Charbonnet, Gabrielle 1961- 81
Chardiet, Bernice (Kroll) 1927(?)- 27
Charles, Donald
    See Meighan, Donald Charles
Charles, Louis
    See Stratemeyer, Edward L.
Charles, Nicholas J.
    See Kuskin, Karla
Charles, Norma 153
Charlip, Remy 1929- 119
    Earlier sketches in SATA 4, 68
    See also CLR 8
Charlot, Jean 1898-1979 8
    Obituary 31
Charlot, Martin (Day) 1944- 64
Charlton, Michael (Alan) 1923- 34
Charmatz, Bill 1925-2005 7
Charnas, Suzy McKee 1939- 110
    Earlier sketch in SATA 61
Charosh, Mannis 1906- 5
Chartier, Normand L. 1945- 66
Chase, Alice
    See McHargue, Georgess
Chase, Alyssa 1965- 92
Chase, Andra 1942- 91
Chase, Emily
    See Aks, Patricia
    and Garwood, Julie
    and Sachs, Judith
    and White, Carol
Chase, Mary (Coyle) 1907-1981 17
    Obituary 29
Chase, Mary Ellen 1887-1973 10

Chase, Richard 1904-1988 .... *64*
   Obituary *56*
Chase, Samantha
   See Glick, Ruth (Burtnick)
Chast, Roz 1954- *97*
Chastain, Madye Lee 1908-1989 .... *4*
Chataway, Carol 1955- *140*
Chatterjee, Debjani 1952- *83*
Chauncy, Nan(cen Beryl Masterman)
   1900-1970 .... *6*
   See also CLR 6
Chaundler, Christine 1887-1972 .... *1*
   Obituary *25*
Chbosky, Stephen 1972- *164*
Chee, Cheng-Khee 1934- *79*
Cheese, Chloe 1952- *118*
Chekhonte, Antosha
   See Chekhov, Anton (Pavlovich)
Chekhov, Anton (Pavlovich) 1860-1904 .... *90*
Chen, Anthony 1929- *6*
Chen, Chih-Yuan 1975- *155*
Chen, Ju-Hong 1941- *78*
Chen, Sara
   See Odgers, Sally Farrell
Chen, Tony
   See Chen, Anthony
Chen, Yuan-tsung 1932- *65*
Chenault, Nell
   See Smith, Linell Nash
Chenery, Janet (Dai) 1923- *25*
Cheney, Cora 1916-1999 .... *3*
   Obituary *110*
Cheney, Glenn (Alan) 1951- *99*
Cheney, Lynne V. 1941- *152*
Cheney, Ted
   See Cheney, Theodore Albert
Cheney, Theodore A. Rees
   See Cheney, Theodore Albert
Cheney, Theodore Albert 1928- *11*
Cheng, Andrea 1957- *172*
   Earlier sketch in SATA *128*
Cheng, Christopher 1959- *173*
   Earlier sketch in SATA *106*
Cheng, Judith 1955- *36*
Cheng, Shan
   See Jiang, Cheng An
Cheripko, Jan 1951- *155*
   Earlier sketch in SATA *83*
Chermayeff, Ivan 1932- *47*
Chernoff, Dorothy A.
   See Ernst, (Lyman) John
Chernoff, Goldie Taub 1909- *10*
Cherry, Carolyn Janice *93*
   See Cherryh, C.J.
Cherry, Lynne 1952- *99*
   Earlier sketch in SATA *34*
Cherryh, C.J. 1942- *172*
   See Cherry, Carolyn Janice
Cherryholmes, Anne
   See Price, Olive
Cheshire, Simon *172*
Chesler, Bernice 1932-2002 .... *59*
Chess, Victoria (Dickerson) 1939- *92*
   Earlier sketch in SATA *33*
Chester, Deborah 1957- *85*
Chester, Kate
   See Guccione, Leslie Davis
Chesterton, G(ilbert) K(eith) 1874-1936 ...... *27*
Chesworth, Michael *160*
Chetin, Helen 1922- *6*
Chetwin, Grace *86*
   Brief entry *50*
Chevalier, Christa 1937- *35*
Chevalier, Tracy 1962- *128*
Chew, Ruth 1920- *7*
Chichester Clark, Emma 1955- *156*
   Earlier sketch in SATA *117*
   See Clark, Emma Chichester
Chidsey, Donald Barr 1902-1981 .... *3*
   Obituary *27*
Chiefari, Janet D. 1942- *58*

Chien-min, Lin
   See Rumford, James
Child, L. Maria
   See Child, Lydia Maria
Child, Lauren 1965- *160*
   Earlier sketch in SATA *119*
Child, Lincoln B. 1957- *113*
Child, Lydia Maria 1802-1880 .... *67*
Child, Mrs.
   See Child, Lydia Maria
Child, Philip 1898-1978 .... *47*
Children's Shepherd, The
   See Westphal, Arnold Carl
Childress, Alice 1920-1994 .... *81*
   Earlier sketches in SATA *7, 48*
   See also CLR 14
Childs, H(alla) Fay (Cochrane) 1890-1971 .... *1*
   Obituary *25*
Chilton, Charles (Frederick William)
   1917- *102*
Chimaera
   See Farjeon, Eleanor
Chin, Richard (M.) 1946- *52*
Chinery, Michael 1938- *26*
Chin-Lee, Cynthia D. 1958- *102*
Chippendale, Lisa A. *158*
Chipperfield, Joseph Eugene 1912-1980(?) .. *87*
   Earlier sketch in SATA *2*
Chisholm, P. F.
   See Finney, Patricia
Chislett, Gail (Elaine) 1948- *58*
Chittenden, Elizabeth F. 1903-1999 .... *9*
Chittenden, Margaret 1935- *28*
Chittum, Ida 1918- *7*
Chitwood, Suzanne Tanner 1958- *160*
Chmielarz, Sharon Lee 1940- *72*
Choate, Judith (Newkirk) 1940- *30*
Chocolate, Debbi 1954- *96*
Chocolate, Deborah M. Newton
   See Chocolate, Debbi
Chodos-Irvine, Margaret *152*
Choi, Sook Nyul 1937- *73*
   Autobiography Feature *126*
   See also CLR 53
Choi, Yangsook *178*
Choldenko, Gennifer 1957- *135*
Chorao, (Ann Mc)Kay (Sproat) 1936- *162*
   Earlier sketches in SATA *8, 69*
Choron, Sandra (Zena Samelson) 1950- *146*
Chown, Marcus 1959- *137*
Choyce, Lesley 1951- *165*
   Earlier sketch in SATA *94*
Chrisman, Arthur Bowie 1889-1953 .... *124*
   See also YABC 1
Christelow, Eileen 1943- *90*
   Autobiography Feature *120*
   Brief entry *35*
   Earlier sketch in SATA *38*
Christensen, Bonnie 1951- *157*
   Earlier sketch in SATA *110*
Christensen, Gardell Dano 1907-1991 .... *1*
Christensen, Laurie
   See Steding, Laurie
Christesen, Barbara 1940- *40*
Christgau, Alice Erickson 1902-1977 .... *13*
Christian, Mary Blount 1933- *9*
Christie, Agatha (Mary Clarissa)
   1890-1976 .... *36*
Christie, Gregory
   See Christie, R. Gregory
Christie, Philippa *129*
   Earlier sketches in SATA *1, 67*
   See also CLR 9
   See Pearce, Philippa
Christie, R. Gregory 1971- *127*
Christopher, John
   See CLR 2
   See Youd, (Christopher) Samuel
Christopher, Louise
   See Hale, Arlene

Christopher, Matt(hew Frederick)
   1917-1997 .... *80*
   Obituary *99*
   Earlier sketches in SATA *2, 47*
   See also CLR *119*
   See also SAAS 9
Christopher, Milbourne 1914(?)-1984 .... *46*
Christy, Howard Chandler 1873-1952 .... *21*
Chrustowski, Rick *176*
Chrystie, Frances N(icholson) 1904-1986 ..... *60*
Chu, Daniel 1933- *11*
Chukovsky, Kornei (Ivanovich) 1882-1969 . *34*
   Earlier sketch in SATA *5*
Church, Caroline Jayne *179*
Church, Richard 1893-1972 .... *3*
Churchill, E(lmer) Richard 1937- *11*
Churchill, Elizabeth
   See Hough, Richard (Alexander)
Chute, B(eatrice) J(oy) 1913-1987 .... *2*
   Obituary *53*
Chute, Marchette (Gaylord) 1909-1994 .... *1*
Chwast, Jacqueline 1932- *6*
Chwast, Seymour 1931- *146*
   Earlier sketches in SATA *18, 96*
Ciardi, John (Anthony) 1916-1986 .... *65*
   Obituary *46*
   Earlier sketch in SATA *1*
   See also CLR 19
   See also SAAS 26
Ciccone, Madonna Louise Veronica
   See Madonna
Ciment, James D. 1958- *140*
Cisneros, Sandra 1954-
   See CLR *123*
Citra, Becky 1954- *137*
Clair, Andree *19*
Clampett, Robert *44*
   See Clampett, Bob
Clapp, John 1968- *109*
Clapp, Patricia 1912- *74*
   Earlier sketch in SATA *4*
   See also SAAS 4
Clare, Ellen
   See Sinclair, Olga
Clare, Helen
   See Clarke, Pauline
Claremont, Chris 1950- *87*
Claremont, Christopher Simon
   See Claremont, Chris
Clark, Ann Nolan 1896-1995 .... *82*
   Obituary *87*
   Earlier sketch in SATA *4*
   See also CLR 16
   See also SAAS 16
Clark, Champ 1923-2002 .... *47*
Clark, Christopher (Anthony) Stuart
   See Stuart-Clark, Christopher (Anthony)
Clark, Clara Gillow 1951- *154*
   Earlier sketch in SATA *84*
Clark, David
   See Hardcastle, Michael
Clark, David Allen
   See Ernst, (Lyman) John
Clark, Emma Chichester *69*
   See Chichester Clark, Emma
Clark, Frank J(ames) 1922- *18*
Clark, Garel
   See Garelick, May
Clark, Halsey
   See Deming, Richard
Clark, Joan
   See Benson, Mildred (Augustine Wirt)
Clark, Joan 1934- *96*
   Earlier sketch in SATA *59*
Clark, Leonard 1905-1981 .... *30*
   Obituary *29*
Clark, M. R.
   See Clark, Mavis Thorpe
Clark, Margaret (D.) 1943- *126*
Clark, Margaret Goff 1913- *82*
   Earlier sketch in SATA *8*

Clark, Mary Higgins 1929- *46*
Clark, Mavis Thorpe 1909-1999 .... *74*
  Earlier sketch in SATA *8*
  See also CLR *30*
  See also SAAS *5*
Clark, Merle
  See Gessner, Lynne
Clark, Patricia Denise 1921- *117*
  See Lorrimer, Claire
Clark, Patricia Finrow 1929- *11*
Clark, Ronald William 1916-1987 .... *2*
  Obituary *52*
Clark, Sherryl 1956- *149*
Clark, Van D(eusen) 1909-1974 .... *2*
Clark, Virginia
  See Gray, Patricia (Clark)
Clark, Walter Van Tilburg 1909-1971 .... *8*
Clarke, Arthur C. 1917- *115*
  Earlier sketches in SATA *13, 70*
  See also CLR *119*
Clarke, Arthur Charles
  See Clarke, Arthur C.
Clarke, Clorinda 1917- *7*
Clarke, Gus 1948- *134*
Clarke, J.
  See Clarke, Judith
Clarke, James Hall
  See Rowland-Entwistle, (Arthur) Theodore
  (Henry)
Clarke, Joan B. 1921- *42*
  Brief entry *27*
Clarke, John
  See Laklan, Carli
  and Sontup, Dan(iel)
Clarke, Judith 1943- *164*
  Earlier sketches in SATA *75, 110*
  See also CLR *61*
Clarke, Julia 1950- *138*
Clarke, Kenneth 1957- *107*
Clarke, Lea
  See Rowland-Entwistle, (Arthur) Theodore
  (Henry)
Clarke, Margaret 1941-
  See CLR *99*
Clarke, Mary Stetson 1911-1994 .... *5*
Clarke, Michael
  See Newlon, (Frank) Clarke
Clarke, Pauline 1921- *131*
  See also CLR *28*
  See Clare, Helen
  and Hunter Blair, Pauline
Clarke-Rich, Elizabeth L. 1934- *103*
Clarkson, E(dith) Margaret 1915- *37*
Clarkson, Ewan 1929- *9*
Claudia, Susan
  See Goulart, Ron(ald Joseph)
  and Johnston, William
Claverie, Jean 1946- *38*
Clay, Patrice 1947- *47*
Claypool, Jane *103*
  See Miner, Jane Claypool
Clayton, Elaine 1961- *159*
  Earlier sketch in SATA *94*
Clayton, Lawrence (Otto, Jr.) 1945- *75*
Clayton, Sandra 1951- *110*
Cleary, Beverly 1916- *121*
  Earlier sketches in SATA *2, 43, 79*
  See also CLR *72*
  See also SAAS *20*
Cleary, Beverly Atlee Bunn
  See Cleary, Beverly
Cleary, Brian P. 1959- *132*
  Earlier sketch in SATA *93*
Cleaver, Bill *22*
  Obituary *27*
  See also CLR *6*
  See Cleaver, William J(oseph)
Cleaver, Carole 1934- *6*

Cleaver, Elizabeth (Ann Mrazik)
  1939-1985 .... *23*
  Obituary *43*
  See also CLR *13*
Cleaver, Hylton Reginald 1891-1961 .... *49*
Cleaver, Vera (Allen) 1919-1993 .... *76*
  Earlier sketch in SATA *22*
  See also CLR *6*
Cleishbotham, Jebediah
  See Scott, Sir Walter
Cleland, Mabel
  See Widdemer, Mabel Cleland
Clem, Margaret H(ollingsworth) 1923- *90*
Clemens, Samuel Langhorne 1835-1910 .... *100*
  See also YABC *2*
  See Twain, Mark
Clemens, Virginia Phelps 1941- *35*
Clement, Priscilla Ferguson 1942- *171*
Clement, Rod *97*
Clements, Andrew 1949- *158*
  Earlier sketch in SATA *104*
Clements, Bruce 1931- *178*
  Earlier sketches in SATA *27, 94*
Clemons, Elizabeth
  See Nowell, Elizabeth Cameron
Clerk, N. W.
  See Lewis, C.S.
Cleveland-Peck, Patricia *80*
Cleven, Cathrine
  See Cleven, Kathryn Seward
Cleven, Kathryn Seward *2*
Clevenger, William R. 1954- *84*
Clevenger, William Russell
  See Clevenger, William R.
Clevin, Joergen 1920- *7*
Clevin, Jorgen
  See Clevin, Joergen
Clewes, Dorothy (Mary) 1907-2003 .... *86*
  Obituary *138*
  Earlier sketch in SATA *1*
Clifford, David
  See Rosenberg, Eth(el) Clifford
Clifford, Eth *92*
  See also SAAS *22*
  See Rosenberg, Eth(el) Clifford
Clifford, Harold B(urton) 1893-1988 .... *10*
Clifford, Margaret Cort 1929- *1*
Clifford, Martin
  See Hamilton, Charles (Harold St. John)
Clifford, Mary Louise Beneway 1926- *23*
Clifford, Peggy
  See Clifford, Margaret Cort
Clifford, Rachel Mark
  See Lewis, Brenda Ralph
Clifton, Lucille 1936- *128*
  Earlier sketches in SATA *20, 69*
  See also CLR *5*
Clifton, Thelma Lucille
  See Clifton, Lucille
Climo, Shirley 1928- *166*
  Autobiography Feature *110*
  Brief entry *35*
  Earlier sketches in SATA *39, 77*
  See also CLR *69*
Clinton, Cathryn 1957- *136*
Clinton, Dirk
  See Silverberg, Robert
Clinton, Jon
  See Prince, J(ack) H(arvey)
Clish, (Lee) Marian 1946- *43*
Clive, Clifford
  See Hamilton, Charles (Harold St. John)
Clokey, Art 1921- *59*
Cloudsley-Thompson, J(ohn) L(eonard)
  1921- *19*
Clouse, Nancy L. 1938- *78*
Clover, Peter 1952- *152*
Clutha, Janet Paterson Frame 1924-2004 ... *119*
  See Frame, Janet

Clymer, Eleanor 1906-2001 .... *85*
  Obituary *126*
  Earlier sketch in SATA *9*
  See also SAAS *17*
Clyne, Patricia (Edwards) *31*
Coalson, Glo 1946- *94*
  Earlier sketch in SATA *26*
Coates, Anna 1958- *73*
Coates, Belle 1896-1986 .... *2*
Coates, Ruth Allison 1915- *11*
Coats, Alice M(argaret) 1905-1976 .... *11*
Coatsworth, Elizabeth (Jane) 1893-1986 .... *100*
  Obituary *49*
  Earlier sketches in SATA *2, 56*
  See also CLR *2*
Cobalt, Martin
  See Mayne, William (James Carter)
Cobb, Mary 1931- *88*
Cobb, Vicki 1938- *136*
  Autobiography Feature *136*
  Earlier sketches in SATA *8, 69, 131*
  See also CLR *2*
  See also SAAS *6*
Cobbett, Richard
  See Pluckrose, Henry (Arthur)
Cober, Alan E(dwin) 1935-1998 .... *7*
  Obituary *101*
Cobham, Sir Alan
  See Hamilton, Charles (Harold St. John)
Coburn, Jake 1978- *155*
Cocagnac, Augustin Maurice(-Jean) 1924- *7*
Cocca-Leffler, Maryann 1958- *136*
  Earlier sketch in SATA *80*
Cochran, Bobbye A. 1949- *11*
Cockett, Mary *3*
Coddell, Esme Raji
  See Codell, Esme Raji
Codell, Esme Raji 1968- *160*
Cody, C. S.
  See Waller, Leslie
Cody, Jess
  See Cunningham, Chet
Coe, Anne (E.) 1949- *95*
Coe, Douglas
  See Epstein, Beryl (M. Williams)
  and Epstein, Samuel
Coen, Rena Neumann 1925- *20*
Coerr, Eleanor (Beatrice) 1922- *67*
  Earlier sketch in SATA *1*
Cofer, Judith Ortiz 1952- *164*
  Earlier sketch in SATA *110*
  See Ortiz Cofer, Judith
Coffey, Brian
  See Koontz, Dean R.
Coffin, Geoffrey
  See Mason, F(rancis) van Wyck
Coffin, M. T.
  See Stanley, George Edward
Coffman, Ramon Peyton 1896-1989 .... *4*
Cogan, Karen 1954- *125*
Coggins, Jack (Banham) 1911-2006 .... *2*
Cohen, Barbara 1932-1992 .... *77*
  Obituary *74*
  Earlier sketch in SATA *10*
  See also SAAS *7*
Cohen, Daniel (E.) 1936- *70*
  Earlier sketch in SATA *8*
  See also CLR *43*
  See also SAAS *4*
Cohen, Jan Barger
  See Barger, Jan
Cohen, Jene Barr
  See Barr, Jene
Cohen, Joan Lebold 1932- *4*
Cohen, Judith Love 1933- *78*
Cohen, Miriam 1926-1955 .... *155*
  Earlier sketches in SATA *29, 106*
  See also SAAS *11*
Cohen, Nora *75*
Cohen, Paul S. 1945- *58*

Cohen, Peter Zachary 1931- 150
  Earlier sketch in SATA 4
Cohen, Robert Carl 1930- 8
Cohen, Sholom 1951- 94
Cohn, Angelo 1914-1997 19
Cohn, Rachel 1968- 161
Coit, Margaret Louise 1922-2003 2
  Obituary 142
Colato Lainez, Rene 1970- 176
Colbert, Anthony 1934- 15
Colbert, Nancy A. 1936- 139
Colby, C(arroll) B(urleigh) 1904-1977 35
  Earlier sketch in SATA 3
Colby, Jean Poindexter 1909-1993 23
Cole, Annette
  See Steiner, Barbara A(nnette)
Cole, Babette 1949- 155
  Earlier sketches in SATA 61, 96
Cole, Betsy 1940- 83
Cole, Brock 1938- 136
  Earlier sketch in SATA 72
  See also CLR 18
Cole, Davis
  See Elting, Mary
Cole, Hannah 1954- 74
Cole, Jack -1974
  See Stewart, John (William)
Cole, Jackson
  See Curry, Thomas Albert
  and Germano, Peter B.
  and Heckelmann, Charles N(ewman)
  and Newton, D(wight) B(ennett)
  and Schisgall, Oscar
Cole, Jennifer
  See Zach, Cheryl (Byrd)
Cole, Joanna 1944- 168
  Brief entry 37
  Earlier sketches in SATA 49, 81, 120
  See also CLR 40
Cole, Lois Dwight 1903-1979 10
  Obituary 26
Cole, Michael 1947- 59
Cole, Sheila R. 1939- 171
  Earlier sketches in SATA 24, 95
Cole, Sheila Rotenberg
  See Cole, Sheila R.
Cole, Stephen 1971- 161
Cole, William (Rossa) 1919-2000 71
  Earlier sketch in SATA 9
  See also SAAS 9
Coleman, Andrew
  See Pine, Nicholas
Coleman, Clare
  See Bell, Clare (Louise)
  and Easton, M(alcolm) Coleman
Coleman, Loren 1947- 164
Coleman, Loren Elwood, Jr.
  See Coleman, Loren
Coleman, Mary Ann 1928- 83
Coleman, Michael (Lee) 1946- 133
  Autobiography Feature 133
  Earlier sketch in SATA 108
Coleman, William L(eRoy) 1938- 49
  Brief entry 34
Coles, Robert (Martin) 1929- 23
Colfer, Eoin 1965- 148
  See also CLR 112
Colin, Ann
  See Ure, Jean
Collard, Sneed B. III 1959- 139
  Earlier sketch in SATA 84
Colledge, Anne 1939- 142
Collicott, Sharleen 1937- 143
  Earlier sketch in SATA 98
Collier, Bryan 174
  Earlier sketch in SATA 126
Collier, Christopher 1930- 70
  Earlier sketch in SATA 16
Collier, Ethel 1903-1999 22

Collier, James Lincoln 1928- 166
  Earlier sketches in SATA 8, 70
  See also CLR 3
  See also SAAS 21
Collier, Jane
  See Collier, Zena
Collier, Steven 1942- 61
Collier, Zena 1926- 23
  See Collier, Jane
Collings, Gillian 1939- 102
Collington, Peter 1948- 99
  Earlier sketch in SATA 59
Collins, Ace 1953- 82
Collins, Andrew J.
  See Collins, Ace
Collins, David R(aymond) 1940-2001 121
  Earlier sketch in SATA 7
Collins, Heather 1946- 81
Collins, Hunt
  See Hunter, Evan
Collins, Michael
  See Lynds, Dennis
Collins, Michael 1930- 58
Collins, Pat(ricia) Lowery 1932- 151
  Earlier sketch in SATA 31
Collins, Paul 1954- 126
Collinson, A. S.
  See Collinson, Alan S.
Collinson, Alan S. 1934- 80
Collinson, Roger (Alfred) 1936- 133
Collodi, Carlo
  See CLR 120
  See Lorenzini, Carlo
Colloms, Brenda 1919- 40
Colman, Hila 53
  Earlier sketch in SATA 1
  See also SAAS 14
Colman, Penny (Morgan) 1944- 160
  Autobiography Feature 160
  Earlier sketches in SATA 77, 114
Colman, Warren (David) 1944- 67
Colombo, John Robert 1936- 50
Colon, Raul 156
Colonius, Lillian 1911-1992 3
Colorado, Antonio J.
  See Colorado (Capella), Antonio J(ulio)
Colorado (Capella), Antonio J(ulio)
  1903-1994 23
  Obituary 79
Colquhoun, Glenn 1964- 165
Colston, Fifi E. 1960- 150
Colt, Martin
  See Epstein, Beryl (M. Williams)
  and Epstein, Samuel
Colum, Padraic 1881-1972 15
  See also CLR 36
Columbus, Chris 1959- 97
Columbus, Christopher
  See Columbus, Chris
Columella
  See Moore, Clement Clarke
Colver, Anne 1908- 7
Colvin, James
  See Moorcock, Michael
Colwell, Eileen (Hilda) 1904-2002 2
Coman, Carolyn 127
Combs, Lisa M.
  See McCourt, Lisa
Combs, Robert
  See Murray, John
Comfort, Jane Levington
  See Sturtzel, Jane Levington
Comfort, Mildred Houghton 1886-1976 3
Comins, Ethel M(ae) 11
Comins, Jeremy 1933- 28
Commager, Henry Steele 1902-1998 23
  Obituary 102
Compere, Mickie
  See Davidson, Margaret
Compestine, Ying Chang 1963- 140
Compton, Patricia A. 1936- 75

Comte, The Great
  See Hawkesworth, Eric
Comus
  See Ballantyne, R(obert) M(ichael)
Comyns, Nance
  See Comyns-Toohey, Nantz
Comyns-Toohey, Nantz 1956- 86
Conan Doyle, Arthur
  See Doyle, Sir Arthur Conan
Condit, Martha Olson 1913- 28
Condon, Bill 1949- 142
Condon, Judith 83
Condy, Roy 1942- 96
Cone, Ferne Geller 1921- 39
Cone, Molly (Lamken) 1918- 151
  Autobiography Feature 151
  Earlier sketches in SATA 1, 28, 115
  See also SAAS 11
Cone, Patrick 1954- 89
Coney, Michael G. 1932-2005 61
  Obituary 170
Coney, Michael Greatrex
  See Coney, Michael G.
Coney, Mike
  See Coney, Michael G.
Conford, Ellen 1942- 162
  Earlier sketches in SATA 6, 68, 110
  See also CLR 71
Conger, Lesley
  See Suttles, Shirley (Smith)
Conklin, Gladys Plemon 1903- 2
Conklin, Paul S. 1929(?)-2003 43
  Brief entry 33
  Obituary 147
Conkling, Hilda 1910-1986 23
Conlan, Kathleen Elizabeth 1950- 145
Conlan, Kathy
  See Conlan, Kathleen Elizabeth
Conley-Weaver, Robyn 1963- 125
Conlon-McKenna, Marita 1956- 71
Conly, Jane Leslie 1948- 164
  Earlier sketches in SATA 80, 112
Conly, Robert Leslie 1918(?)-1973 23
  See O'Brien, Robert C.
Connolly, Jerome P(atrick) 1931- 8
Connolly, Pat 1943- 74
Connolly, Peter 1935- 105
  Earlier sketch in SATA 47
Conover, Chris 1950- 31
Conquest, Owen
  See Hamilton, Charles (Harold St. John)
Conrad, Joseph 1857-1924 27
Conrad, Pam 1947-1996 133
  Brief entry 49
  Obituary 90
  Earlier sketches in SATA 52, 80
  See also CLR 18
  See also SAAS 19
Conroy, Jack 19
  See Conroy, John Wesley
Conroy, Robert
  See Goldston, Robert (Conroy)
Constable, Kate 1966- 172
Constant, Alberta Wilson 1908-1981 22
  Obituary 28
Conway, Diana C(ohen) 1943- 91
Conway, Gordon
  See Hamilton, Charles (Harold St. John)
Cook, Bernadine 1924- 11
Cook, Fred J(ames) 1911-2003 2
  Obituary 145
Cook, Glen 1944- 171
  Earlier sketch in SATA 108
Cook, Glen Charles
  See Cook, Glen
Cook, Hugh 1956- 85
Cook, Hugh, Walter Gilbert
  See Cook, Hugh
Cook, Jean Thor 1930- 94
Cook, Joel 1934- 79
Cook, Joseph Jay 1924- 8

Cook, Lisa Broadie 157
Cook, Lyn
    See Waddell, Evelyn Margaret
Cook, Roy
    See Silverberg, Robert
Cook, Trish 175
Cooke, Ann
    See Cole, Joanna
Cooke, Arthur
    See Lowndes, Robert A(ugustine) W(ard)
Cooke, Barbara
    See Alexander, Anna B(arbara Cooke)
Cooke, David Coxe 1917- 2
Cooke, Donald Ewin 1916-1985 2
    Obituary 45
Cooke, Frank E. 1920- 87
Cooke, Jean (Isobel Esther) 1929- 74
Cooke, John Estes
    See Baum, L(yman) Frank
Cooke, Trish 1962- 129
Cookson, Catherine (McMullen) 1906-1998 .. 9
    Obituary 116
Cooley, Regina Francoise 1940- 177
Coolidge, Olivia E(nsor) 1908- 26
    Earlier sketch in SATA *1*
Cooling, Wendy 169
    Earlier sketch in SATA *111*
Coombs, Charles I(ra) 1914-1994 43
    Earlier sketch in SATA *3*
    See also SAAS *15*
Coombs, Chick
    See Coombs, Charles I(ra)
Coombs, Patricia 1926- 51
    Earlier sketch in SATA *3*
    See also SAAS *22*
Cooney, Barbara 1917-2000 96
    Obituary 123
    Earlier sketches in SATA *6, 59*
    See also CLR *23*
Cooney, Caroline B. 1947- 179
    Brief entry 41
    Earlier sketches in SATA *48, 80, 113, 130*
Cooney, Nancy Evans 1932- 42
Coontz, Otto 1946- 33
Cooper, Ann (Catharine) 1939- 104
Cooper, Dutch
    See Kuyper, Sjoerd
Cooper, Elisha 1971- 157
    Earlier sketch in SATA *99*
Cooper, Elizabeth Keyser -1992 47
Cooper, Floyd 144
    Earlier sketch in SATA *96*
    See also CLR *60*
Cooper, Gordon 1932- 23
Cooper, Helen 1963- 169
    Earlier sketch in SATA *102*
Cooper, Henry S(potswood) F(enimore), Jr.
    1933- 65
Cooper, Ilene 1948- 145
    Earlier sketches in SATA *66, 97*
Cooper, James Fenimore 1789-1851 19
    See also CLR *105*
Cooper, John R. *1*
Cooper, Kay 1941- 11
Cooper, Lee Pelham 1926- 5
Cooper, Lester (Irving) 1919-1985 32
    Obituary 43
Cooper, Lettice (Ulpha) 1897-1994 35
    Obituary 82
Cooper, Louise 1952- 152
Cooper, M.E.
    See Lerangis, Peter
Cooper, M.E.
    See Davis, Maggie S.
Cooper, Melrose
    See Kroll, Virginia L.
Cooper, Michael L. 1950- 117
    Earlier sketch in SATA *79*
Cooper, Patrick 1949- 134

Cooper, Susan 1935- *151*
    Earlier sketches in SATA *4, 64, 104*
    See also CLR *67*
    See also SAAS *6*
Cooper, Susan Mary
    See Cooper, Susan
Cope, Jane U(rsula) 1949- 108
Copeland, Helen 1920- 4
Copeland, Paul W. 23
Coplans, Peta 1951- 84
Copley (Diana) Heather Pickering 1918- 45
Coppard, A(lfred) E(dgar) 1878-1957
    See YABC *1*
Copper, Melinda 1952- 172
Copper, Melinda McConnaughey
    See Copper, Melinda
Coralie
    See Anderson, Catherine Corley
Corbett, Grahame 43
    Brief entry 36
Corbett, Scott 1913- 42
    Earlier sketch in SATA *2*
    See also CLR *1*
    See also SAAS *2*
Corbett, Sue 174
Corbett, W(illiam) J(esse) 1938- 102
    Brief entry 44
    Earlier sketch in SATA *50*
    See also CLR *19*
Corbin, Sabra Lee
    See Malvern, Gladys
Corbin, William
    See McGraw, William Corbin
Corbman, Marjorie 1987- *179*
Corby, Dan
    See Catherall, Arthur
Corcoran, Barbara (Asenath) 1911- 77
    Autobiography Feature 125
    Earlier sketch in SATA *3*
    See also CLR *50*
    See also SAAS *20*
Corcos, Lucille 1908-1973 10
Cordell, Alexander
    See Graber, Alexander
Cordell, Alexander
    See Graber, (George) Alexander
Corder, Zizou
    See Young, Louisa
Corella, Joseph
    See Odgers, Sally Farrell
Coren, Alan 1938- 32
Corey, Dorothy 23
Corey, Shana 1974- 133
Corfe, Thomas Howell 1928- 27
Corfe, Tom
    See Corfe, Thomas Howell
Corfield, Robin Bell 1952- 74
Corlett, William 1938-2005 46
    Brief entry 39
Cormack, M(argaret) Grant 1913- 11
Cormack, Maribelle B. 1902-1984 39
Cormier, Robert 1925-2000 83
    Obituary 122
    Earlier sketches in SATA *10, 45*
    See also CLR *55*
Cormier, Robert Edmund
    See Cormier, Robert
Cornelius, Carol 1942- 40
Cornelius, Kay 1933- 157
Cornell, J.
    See Cornell, Jeffrey
Cornell, James (Clayton, Jr.) 1938- 27
Cornell, Jean Gay 1920- 23
Cornell, Jeffrey 1945- 11
Cornish, Sam(uel James) 1935- 23
Cornwall, Nellie
    See Sloggett, Nellie
Correy, Lee
    See Stine, G(eorge) Harry
Corrick, James A. 1945- 76
Corrigan, (Helen) Adeline 1909- 23

Corrigan, Barbara 1922- 8
Corrigan, Eireann 1977- 163
Corrin, Sara 1918- 86
    Brief entry 48
Corrin, Stephen 86
    Brief entry 48
Cort, M. C.
    See Clifford, Margaret Cort
Cort, Margaret
    See Clifford, Margaret Cort
Corwin, Judith H(offman) 1946- 10
Cory, Rowena
    See Lindquist, Rowena Cory
Cosby, Bill
    See Cosby, William Henry, Jr.
Cosby, William Henry, Jr. 1937- 110
    Earlier sketch in SATA *66*
    See also Cosby, Bill
Cosentino, Ralph 169
Cosgrove, Margaret (Leota) 1926- 47
Cosgrove, Stephen E(dward) 1945- 53
    Brief entry 40
Coskey, Evelyn 1932- 7
Cosner, Shaaron 1940- 43
Cossi, Olga 1921- 102
    Earlier sketch in SATA *67*
Costabel, Eva Deutsch 1924- 45
Costabel-Deutsch, Eva
    See Costabel, Eva Deutsch
Costello, David 174
Costello, David F(rancis) 1904-1990 23
Cott, Jonathan 1942- 23
Cottam, Clarence 1899-1974 25
Cottle, Joan 1960- 135
Cottler, Joseph 1899-1996 22
Cottonwood, Joe 1947- 92
Cottrell, Leonard 1913-1974 24
Cottringer, Anne 1952- 150
    Earlier sketch in SATA *97*
Coulman, Valerie 1969- 161
Couloumbis, Audrey 173
Counsel, June 1926- 70
Countryman, The
    See Whitlock, Ralph
Courlander, Harold 1908-1996 6
    Obituary 88
Coursen, Valerie 1965(?)- 102
Courtney, Dayle
    See Goldsmith, Howard
Cousins, Linda 1946- 90
Cousins, Lucy 1964- 172
Cousins, Margaret 1905-1996 2
    Obituary 92
Cousteau, Jacques-Yves 1910-1997 98
    Earlier sketch in SATA *38*
Couture, Christin 1951- 73
Coville, Bruce 1950- 155
    Autobiography Feature 155
    Earlier sketches in SATA *32, 77, 118*
Covington, Dennis 109
Covington, Linda
    See Windsor, Linda
Cowan, Catherine 121
Coward, Fiona 1963- 178
Cowell, Cressida 1966 140
Cowen, Eve
    See Werner, Herma
Cowen, Ida 1898-1993 64
Cowie, Leonard W(allace) 1919- 4
Cowles, Kathleen
    See Krull, Kathleen
Cowley, Cassia Joy
    See Cowley, Joy
Cowley, Joy 1936- 164
Cowley, (Cassia) Joy 1936- 90
    Autobiography Feature 118
    Earlier sketch in SATA *4*
    See also CLR *55*
    See also SAAS *26*
Cowley, Marjorie 1925- 111
Cox, (Christopher) Barry 1931- 62

Cox, Clinton 1934- 108
  Earlier sketch in SATA 74
Cox, David (Dundas) 1933- 56
Cox, Donald William 1921- 23
Cox, Jack
  See Cox, John Roberts
Cox, John Roberts 1915-1981 9
Cox, Judy 1954- 160
  Earlier sketch in SATA 117
Cox, Palmer 1840-1924 24
  See also CLR 24
Cox, Vic 1942- 88
Cox, Vicki 1945- 158
Cox, Victoria
  See Garretson, Victoria Diane
Cox, Wally 25
  See Cox, Wallace (Maynard)
Cox, William R(obert) 1901-1988 46
  Brief entry 31
  Obituary 57
  See Ward, Jonas
Coxe, Molly 1959- 101
  Earlier sketch in SATA 69
Coxon, Michele 1950- 158
  Earlier sketch in SATA 76
Coy, Harold 1902-1986 3
Coy, John 1958- 171
  Earlier sketch in SATA 120
Craats, Rennay 1973- 131
Crabtree, Judith 1928- 98
  Earlier sketch in SATA 63
Cracker, Edward E.B.
  See Odgers, Sally Farrell
Craft, K. Y.
  See Craft, Kinuko Y(amabe)
Craft, Kinuko
  See Craft, Kinuko Y(amabe)
Craft, Kinuko Y(amabe) 1940- 127
  Earlier sketch in SATA 65
Craft, Ruth 1935- 87
  Brief entry 31
Craig, A. A.
  See Anderson, Poul
Craig, Alisa
  See MacLeod, Charlotte (Matilda)
Craig, Helen 1934- 94
  Earlier sketches in SATA 46, 49
Craig, John Eland
  See Chipperfield, Joseph Eugene
Craig, John Ernest 1921- 23
Craig, Kit
  See Reed, Kit
Craig, M. F.
  See Craig, Mary (Francis) Shura
Craig, M. Jean 17
Craig, M. S.
  See Craig, Mary (Francis) Shura
Craig, Margaret (Maze) 1911-1964 9
Craig, Mary
  See Craig, Mary (Francis) Shura
Craig, Mary Shura
  See Craig, Mary (Francis) Shura
Craig, Mary (Francis) Shura 1923-1991 86
  Obituary 65
  Earlier sketch in SATA 6
  See also SAAS 7
Craig, Ruth 1922- 95
Craik, Mrs.
  See Craik, Dinah Maria (Mulock)
Craik, Dinah Maria (Mulock) 1826-1887 34
  See Craik, Mrs.
  and Mulock, Dinah Maria
Crandall, Court 1965- 175
Crandell, Rachel 1943- 152
Crane, Barbara (Joyce) 1934- 31
Crane, Caroline 1930- 11
Crane, Jordan 1973- 174
Crane, M. A.
  See Wartski, Maureen (Ann Crane)
Crane, Stephen (Townley) 1871-1900
  See YABC 2

Crane, Walter 1845-1915 100
  Earlier sketch in SATA 18
  See also CLR 56
Crane, William D(wight) 1892-1976 1
Cranfield, Ingrid 1945- 74
Cranshaw, Stanley
  See Fisher, Dorothy (Frances) Canfield
Crary, Elizabeth (Ann) 1942- 99
  Brief entry 43
Crary, Margaret (Coleman) 1906-1986 9
Cravath, Lynne W(oodcock) 1951- 148
  Earlier sketch in SATA 98
Craven, Thomas 1889-1969 22
Crawford, Charles P. 1945- 28
Crawford, Deborah 1922- 6
Crawford, John E(dmund) 1904-1971 3
Crawford, K(aren) Michael 1959- 155
Crawford, Mel 1925- 44
  Brief entry 33
Crawford, Phyllis 1899- 3
Crawley, Dave 177
Cray, Roberta
  See Emerson, Ru
Crayder, Dorothy 7
Crayder, Teresa
  See Colman, Hila
Crayon, Geoffrey
  See Irving, Washington
Craz, Albert G. 1926- 24
Crebbin, June 1938- 169
  Earlier sketch in SATA 80
Crecy, Jeanne
  See Williams, Jeanne
Credle, Ellis 1902-1998 1
Creech, Sharon 1945- 172
  Earlier sketches in SATA 94, 139
  See also CLR 89
Creeden, Sharon 1938- 91
Creighton, Jill 1949- 96
Crenson, Victoria 1952- 159
  Earlier sketch in SATA 88
Cresp, Gael 1954- 119
Crespo, George 1962- 82
Cresswell, Helen 1934-2005 79
  Obituary 168
  Earlier sketches in SATA 1, 48
  See also CLR 18
  See also SAAS 20
Cressy, Michael 1955- 124
Cressy, Mike
  See Cressy, Michael
Cretan, Gladys (Yessayan) 1921- 2
Cretzmeyer, Stacy (Megan) 1959- 124
Crew, Gary 1947- 163
  Earlier sketches in SATA 75, 110
  See also CLR 42
Crew, Helen (Cecilia) Coale 1866-1941
  See YABC 2
Crew, Linda (Jean) 1951- 137
  Earlier sketch in SATA 71
Crews, Donald 1938- 76
  Brief entry 30
  Earlier sketch in SATA 32
  See also CLR 7
Crews, Nina 1963- 158
  Earlier sketch in SATA 97
Crichton, John Michael
  See Crichton, Michael
Crichton, Michael 1942- 88
  Earlier sketch in SATA 9
Crider, Allen Billy
  See Crider, Bill
Crider, Bill 1941- 99
Crilley, Mark 1966- 148
  Autobiography Feature 148
  Earlier sketch in SATA 120
Crimi, Carolyn 1959- 176
Cripps, Enid Margaret
  See Appiah, Peggy
Crisman, Ruth 1914- 73
Crisp, Marta Marie 1947- 128

Crisp, Marty
  See Crisp, Marta Marie
Crispin, A(nn) C(arol) 1950- 86
Crist, James J. 168
Cristall, Barbara 79
Crist-Evans, Craig 1954- 153
Crofford, Emily (Ardell) 1927- 61
Crofut, William E. III 1934- 23
Croll, Carolyn 1945- 102
  Brief entry 52
  Earlier sketch in SATA 56
Croman, Dorothy Young
  See Rosenberg, Dorothy
Cromie, Alice Hamilton 1914-2000 24
Cromie, William J(oseph) 1930- 4
Crompton, Anne Eliot 1930- 73
  Earlier sketch in SATA 23
Crompton, Richmal
  See Lamburn, Richmal Crompton
Cronbach, Abraham 1882-1965 11
Crone, Ruth 1919-2003 4
Cronin, A(rchibald) J(oseph) 1896-1981 47
  Obituary 25
Cronin, Doreen (A.) 125
  See also CLR 105
Cronin, Doreen 1966(?)- 178
Cronin, Doreen A.
  See Cronin, Doreen
Crook, Beverly Courtney 38
  Brief entry 35
Crook, Connie Brummel 1930- 168
  Earlier sketch in SATA 98
Crook, Constance
  See Crook, Connie Brummel
Crosby, Alexander L. 1906-1980 2
  Obituary 23
Crosby, Harry C., Jr. 102
Crosby, Margaret
  See CLR 77
  See Rathmann, Peggy
Crosher, G. R. 14
Cross, Gilbert B. 1939- 60
  Brief entry 51
Cross, Gillian 1945- 178
  Autobiography Feature 178
  Earlier sketches in SATA 38, 71, 110, 165
  See also CLR 28
Cross, Gillian Clare
  See Cross, Gillian
Cross, Helen Reeder
  See Broadhead, Helen Cross
Cross, Peter 1951- 95
Cross, Tom 1954- 146
Cross, Verda 1914- 75
Cross, Wilbur Lucius III 1918- 2
Crossland, Caroline 1964- 83
Crossley-Holland, Kevin 1941- 165
  Earlier sketches in SATA 5, 74, 120
  See also CLR 84
  See also SAAS 20
Crossley-Holland, Kevin John William
  See Crossley-Holland, Kevin
Crouch, Marcus 1913-1996 4
Crout, George C(lement) 1917- 11
Crow, Donna Fletcher 1941- 40
Crowe, Andrew 111
Crowe, John
  See Lynds, Dennis
Crowe, (Bettina) Peter Lum 1911- 6
Crowell, Grace Noll 1877-1969 34
Crowell, Pers 1910-1990 2
Crowell, Robert Leland 1909-2001 63
Crowfield, Christopher
  See Stowe, Harriet (Elizabeth) Beecher
Crowley, Arthur McBlair 1945- 38
Crowley, John 1942- 140
  Earlier sketch in SATA 65
Crownfield, Gertrude 1867-1945
  See YABC 1
Crowther, James Gerald 1899-1983 14
Crowther, Robert 1948- 163

Cruikshank, George 1792-1878 22
  See also CLR 63
Cruise, Robin 1951- 179
Crum, Shutta 134
Crummel, Susan Stevens 1949- 176
  Earlier sketch in SATA 130
Crump, Fred H., Jr. 1931- 76
  Earlier sketch in SATA 11
Crump, J(ames) Irving 1887-1979 57
  Obituary 21
Crump, William D(rake) 1949- 138
Crunden, Reginald
  See Cleaver, Hylton Reginald
Crunk, T.
  See Crunk, Tony
Crunk, Tony 1956- 130
Crutcher, Chris 1946- 153
  Earlier sketches in SATA 52, 99
  See also CLR 28
Crutcher, Christopher C.
  See Crutcher, Chris
Cruz, Ray(mond) 1933- 6
Cruz Martinez, Alejandro (?)-1987 74
Crystal, Billy 1947- 154
Cuetara, Mittie 1957- 158
  Earlier sketch in SATA 106
Cuffari, Richard 1925-1978 66
  Obituary 25
  Earlier sketch in SATA 6
Cullen, Countee 1903-1946 18
Culliford, Pierre 1928-1992 40
  Obituary 74
Cullinan, Bernice E(llinger) 1926- 135
Culp, Louanna McNary 1901-1965 2
Culper, Felix
  See McCaughrean, Geraldine
Cumbaa, Stephen 1947- 72
Cumming, Peter 1951- 168
Cumming, Primrose Amy 1915- 24
Cumming, Robert 1945- 65
Cummings, Betty Sue 1918- 15
  See also SAAS 9
Cummings, Parke 1902-1987 2
  Obituary 53
Cummings, Pat (Marie) 1950- 107
  Earlier sketches in SATA 42, 71
  See also CLR 48
  See also SAAS 13
Cummings, Phil 1957- 123
  Earlier sketch in SATA 74
Cummings, Priscilla 1951- 170
  Earlier sketch in SATA 129
Cummings, Richard
  See Gardner, Richard (M.)
Cummins, Maria Susanna 1827-1866
  See YABC 1
Cuneo, Mary Louise -2001 85
Cunliffe, John Arthur 1933- 86
  Earlier sketch in SATA 11
Cunliffe, Marcus (Falkner) 1922-1990 37
  Obituary 66
Cunnane, Kelly 175
Cunningham, Bob
  See May, Julian
Cunningham, Captain Frank
  See Glick, Carl (Cannon)
Cunningham, Cathy
  See Cunningham, Chet
Cunningham, Chet 1928- 23
Cunningham, Dale S(peers) 1932- 11
Cunningham, Dru 91
Cunningham, E. V.
  See Fast, Howard
Cunningham, Julia (Woolfolk) 1916- 132
  Earlier sketches in SATA 1, 26
  See also SAAS 2
Cunningham, Lawrence J. 1943- 125
Cunningham, Virginia
  See Holmgren, Virginia C(unningham)
Curiae, Amicus
  See Fuller, Edmund (Maybank)

Curie, Eve 1904- 1
Curlee, Lynn 1947- 141
  Earlier sketch in SATA 98
Curley, Daniel 1918-1988 23
  Obituary 61
Curley, Marianne 1959- 175
  Earlier sketch in SATA 131
Currie, Robin 1948- 120
Currie, Stephen 1960- 132
  Earlier sketch in SATA 82
Curry, Ann (Gabrielle) 1934- 72
Curry, Jane L(ouise) 1932- 138
  Autobiography Feature 138
  Earlier sketches in SATA 1, 52, 90
  See also CLR 31
  See also SAAS 6
Curry, Peggy Simson 1911-1987 8
  Obituary 50
Curtis, Bruce (Richard) 1944- 30
Curtis, Chara M(ahar) 1950- 78
Curtis, Christopher Paul 1954(?)- 140
  Earlier sketch in SATA 93
  See also CLR 68
Curtis, Gavin 1965- 107
Curtis, Jamie Lee 1958- 144
  Earlier sketch in SATA 95
  See also CLR 88
Curtis, Marci 160
Curtis, Patricia 1921- 101
  Earlier sketch in SATA 23
Curtis, Peter
  See Lofts, Norah (Robinson)
Curtis, Philip (Delacourt) 1920- 62
Curtis, Richard (Alan) 1937- 29
Curtis, Richard Hale
  See Deming, Richard
  and Levinson, Leonard
  and Rothweiler, Paul Roger
Curtis, Wade
  See Pournelle, Jerry (Eugene)
Curtiss, A(rlene) B. 1934- 90
Cusack, Margaret 1945- 58
Cushman, Doug 1953- 157
  Earlier sketches in SATA 65, 101
Cushman, Jerome 2
Cushman, Karen 1941- 147
  Earlier sketch in SATA 89
  See also CLR 55
Cusick, Richie Tankersley 1952- 140
  Earlier sketch in SATA 67
Cutchen, Billye Walker 1930- 15
Cutchins, Judy 1947- 59
Cutler, Daniel S(olomon) 1951- 78
Cutler, Ebbitt 1923- 9
Cutler, Ivor 1923-2006 24
  Obituary 174
Cutler, Jane 1936- 162
  Earlier sketches in SATA 75, 118
Cutler, May Ebbitt
  See Cutler, Ebbitt
Cutler, Samuel
  See Folsom, Franklin (Brewster)
Cutlip, Kimbra L(eigh-Ann) 1964- 128
Cutrate, Joe
  See Spiegelman, Art
Cutt, W(illiam) Towrie 1898-1981 16
  Obituary 85
Cuyler, Margery S(tuyvesant) 1948- 156
  Earlier sketches in SATA 39, 99
Cuyler, Stephen
  See Bates, Barbara S(nedeker)
Cyrus, Kurt 1954- 179
  Earlier sketch in SATA 132
Czernecki, Stefan 1946- 178

D

Dabba Smith, Frank 174
Dabcovich, Lydia 99
  Brief entry 47
  Earlier sketch in SATA 58
Dace, Dolores B(oelens) 1929- 89
Dadey, Debbie 1959- 136
  Earlier sketch in SATA 73
Dahl, Borghild (Margarethe) 1890-1984 7
  Obituary 37
Dahl, Roald 1916-1990 73
  Obituary 65
  Earlier sketches in SATA 1, 26
  See also CLR 111
Dahlberg, Maurine F. 1951- 171
Dahlstedt, Marden (Stewart) 1921-1983 8
  Obituary 110
Dain, Martin J. 1924-2000 35
Dakos, Kalli 1950- 115
  Earlier sketch in SATA 80
Dale, Anna 1971- 170
Dale, Gary
  See Reece, Colleen L.
Dale, George E.
  See Asimov, Isaac
Dale, Jack
  See Holliday, Joseph
Dale, Kim 1957- 123
Dale, Margaret J(essy) Miller 1911- 39
Dale, Mitzi
  See Hemstock, Gillian
Dale, Norman
  See Denny, Norman (George)
Dale, Penny 1954- 151
  Earlier sketch in SATA 70
Daley, Michael J. 170
Dalgliesh, Alice 1893-1979 17
  Obituary 21
  See also CLR 62
Dalkey, Kara 1953- 132
Dalkey, Kara Mia
  See Dalkey, Kara
Dallas, Ruth
  See Mumford, Ruth
Dalmas, John
  See Jones, John R(obert)
Dalton, Annie 1948- 140
  Earlier sketch in SATA 40
Dalton, Kit
  See Cunningham, Chet
Dalton, Pamela
  See Johnson, Pamela
Dalton, Sean
  See Chester, Deborah
Dalton, Sheila 1949- 108
Daly, Jim
  See Stratemeyer, Edward L.
Daly, Jude 1951- 177
Daly, Kathleen N(orah) 124
  Brief entry 37
Daly, Maureen 1921-2006 129
  Obituary 176
  Earlier sketch in SATA 2
  See also CLR 96
  See also SAAS 1
Daly, Nicholas 1946- 164
  Earlier sketches in SATA 37, 76, 114
  See also CLR 41
  See Daly, Niki
Daly, Niki
  See SAAS 21
  See Daly, Nicholas
D'Amato, Alex 1919- 20
D'Amato, Janet (Potter) 1925- 9
Damerow, Gail 1944- 83
Damerow, Gail Jane
  See Damerow, Gail
D'Amico, Carmela 170
D'Amico, Steve 170
Damrell, Liz 1956- 77

Damrosch, Helen
  See Tee-Van, Helen Damrosch
Dana, Barbara 1940- 22
Dana, Richard Henry, Jr. 1815-1882 26
Danachair, Caoimhin O
  See Danaher, Kevin
Danaher, Kevin 1913-2002 22
Danakas, John 1963- 94
Dandi
  See Mackall, Dandi Daley
D'Andrea, Kate
  See Steiner, Barbara A(nnette)
Dangerfield, Balfour
  See McCloskey, (John) Robert
Daniel, Alan 1939- 76
  Brief entry 53
Daniel, Anita 1893(?)-1978 23
  Obituary 24
Daniel, Anne
  See Steiner, Barbara A(nnette)
Daniel, Becky 1947- 56
Daniel, Claire 1949- 164
Daniel, Colin
  See Windsor, Patricia
Daniel, Hawthorne 1890- 8
Daniel, (Donna) Lee 1944- 76
Daniel, Rebecca
  See Daniel, Becky
Daniels, Guy 1919-1989 11
  Obituary 62
Daniels, Lucy
  See Oldfield, Jenny
Daniels, Max
  See Gellis, Roberta
Daniels, Olga
  See Sinclair, Olga
Daniels, Patricia 1955- 93
Daniels, Zoe
  See Laux, Constance
Dank, Gloria Rand 1955- 56
  Brief entry 46
Dank, Leonard D(ewey) 1929- 44
Dank, Milton 1920- 31
Dann, Max 1955- 62
Danneberg, Julie 1958- 173
Dantz, William R.
  See Philbrick, Rodman
Danziger, Paula 1944-2004 149
  Brief entry 30
  Obituary 155
  Earlier sketches in SATA 36, 63, 102
  See also CLR 20
Darby, Gene Kegley
  See Darby, Jean (Kegley)
Darby, J. N.
  See Govan, (Mary) Christine Noble
Darby, Jean (Kegley) 1921- 68
Darby, Patricia (Paulsen) 14
Darby, Ray(mond) 1912-1982 7
d'Arcy, Willard
  See Cox, William R(obert)
Dare, Geena
  See McNicoll, Sylvia (Marilyn)
Darian, Shea 1959- 97
Daringer, Helen Fern 1892-1986 1
Darke, Marjorie 1929- 87
  Earlier sketch in SATA 16
Darley, F(elix) O(ctavius) C(arr)
  1822-1888 35
Darling, David J. 1953- 60
  Brief entry 44
Darling, Kathy
  See Darling, Mary Kathleen
Darling, Lois (MacIntyre) 1917-1989 3
  Obituary 64
Darling, Louis, (Jr.) 1916-1970 3
  Obituary 23
Darling, Mary Kathleen 1943- 124
  Earlier sketches in SATA 9, 79
Darling, Sandra Louise Woodward
  See Day, Alexandra

Darnell, K(athryn) L(ynne) 1955- 150
Darroll, Sally
  See Odgers, Sally Farrell
Darrow, Whitney, (Jr.) 1909-1999 13
  Obituary 115
Darwin, Len
  See Darwin, Leonard
Darwin, Leonard 1916- 24
Dasent, Sir George Webbe 1817-1896 62
  Brief entry 29
Dash, Joan 1925- 142
Daskam, Josephine Dodge
  See Bacon, Josephine Dodge (Daskam)
D'ath, Justin 1953- 174
  Earlier sketch in SATA 106
Dauer, Rosamond 1934- 23
Daugherty, Charles Michael 1914- 16
Daugherty, James (Henry) 1889-1974 13
  See also CLR 78
Daugherty, Richard D(eo) 1922- 35
d'Aulaire, Edgar Parin 1898-1986 66
  Obituary 47
  Earlier sketch in SATA 5
  See also CLR 21
d'Aulaire, Ingri (Mortenson Parin)
  1904-1980 66
  Obituary 24
  Earlier sketch in SATA 5
  See also CLR 21
Dave, Dave
  See Berg, David
Daveluy, Paule Cloutier 1919- 11
Davenier, Christine 1961- 179
  Earlier sketch in SATA 127
Davenport, John 1960- 156
Daves, Michael 1938- 40
David, A. R.
  See David, A(nn) Rosalie
David, A(nn) Rosalie 1946- 103
David, Jonathan
  See Ames, Lee J(udah)
David, Lawrence 1963- 165
  Earlier sketch in SATA 111
David, Rosalie
  See David, A(nn) Rosalie
Davidson, Alice Joyce 1932- 54
  Brief entry 45
Davidson, Basil 1914- 13
Davidson, (Marie) Diane 1924- 91
Davidson, Hugh
  See Hamilton, Edmond
Davidson, Jessica 1915-1986 5
Davidson, Judith 1953- 40
Davidson, Lionel 1922- 87
Davidson, Margaret 1936- 5
Davidson, Marion
  See Garis, Howard R(oger)
Davidson, Mary R. 1885-1973 9
Davidson, Mary S. 1940- 61
Davidson, Mickie
  See Davidson, Margaret
Davidson, Nicole
  See Jensen, Kathryn
Davidson, R.
  See Davidson, Raymond
Davidson, Raymond 1926- 32
Davidson, Rosalie 1921- 23
Davie, Helen K(ay) 1952- 148
  Earlier sketch in SATA 77
Davies, Andrew (Wynford) 1936- 27
Davies, Bettilu D(onna) 1942- 33
Davies, Hunter 1936- 55
  Brief entry 45
Davies, Jacqueline 1962- 155
Davies, Joan 1934- 50
  Brief entry 47
Davies, Nicola 1958- 150
  Earlier sketch in SATA 99
Davies, Peter J(oseph) 1937- 52
Davies, Sumiko 1942- 46
Davis, (A.) Aubrey 1949- 153

Davis, Barbara Steincrohn
  See Davis, Maggie S.
Davis, Bette J. 1923- 15
Davis, Burke 1913- 4
Davis, Christopher 1928- 6
Davis, D(elbert) Dwight 1908-1965 33
Davis, Daniel S(heldon) 1936- 12
Davis, David R. 1948- 106
Davis, Donald 1944- 169
  Earlier sketch in SATA 93
Davis, Donald D.
  See Davis, Donald
Davis, Emma
  See Davis, Maggie S.
Davis, Gibbs 1953- 102
  Brief entry 41
  Earlier sketch in SATA 46
Davis, Grania 1943- 88
  Brief entry 50
Davis, H(arold) L(enoir) 1896-1960 114
Davis, Hubert J(ackson) 1904-1997 31
Davis, James Robert 1945- 32
  See Davis, Jim
Davis, Jenny 1953- 74
Davis, Jim
  See Davis, James Robert
Davis, Julia 1900(?)-1993 6
  Obituary 75
Davis, Karen (Elizabeth) 1944- 109
Davis, Katie 1959(?)- 152
Davis, Lambert 176
Davis, Leslie
  See Guccione, Leslie Davis
Davis, Louise Littleton 1921- 25
Davis, Maggie S. 1943- 57
Davis, Marguerite 1889- 34
Davis, Mary L(ee) 1935- 9
Davis, Mary Octavia 1901-1976 6
Davis, Nelle 1958- 73
Davis, Ossie 1917-2005 81
  See also CLR 56
Davis, Paxton 1925-1994 16
Davis, Robert 1881-1949
  See YABC 1
Davis, Robin W(orks) 1962- 87
Davis, Russell Gerard 1922- 3
Davis, Tim(othy N.) 1957- 94
Davis, Verne Theodore 1889-1973 6
Davis, Yvonne 1927- 115
Davol, Marguerite W. 1928- 146
  Earlier sketch in SATA 82
DaVolls, Andy (P.) 1967- 85
DaVolls, Linda 1966- 85
Davys, Sarah
  See Manning, Rosemary (Joy)
Dawes, Claiborne 1935- 111
Dawson, Elmer A. 67
  Earlier sketch in SATA 1
Dawson, Imogen (Zoe) 1948- 126
  Earlier sketch in SATA 90
Dawson, Mary 1919- 11
Day, A(rthur) Grove 1904-1994 59
Day, Alexandra 1941- 169
  Earlier sketches in SATA 67, 97
  See also CLR 22
  See also SAAS 19
Day, Beth (Feagles) 1924- 33
Day, Donna
  See Asay, Donna Day
Day, Edward C. 1932- 72
Day, Jon 1936(?)- 79
Day, Nancy 1953- 140
Day, Nancy Raines 1951- 148
  Earlier sketch in SATA 93
Day, Shirley 1962- 94
Day, Thomas 1748-1789
  See YABC 1
Day, Trevor 1955- 124
Dazey, Agnes J(ohnston) 2
Dazey, Frank M. 2
Deacon, Alexis 1978- 139

Deacon, Eileen
See Geipel, Eileen
Deacon, Richard
See McCormick, (George) Donald (King)
Deak, Erzsi 1959- 152
Dean, Anabel 1915- 12
Dean, Carolee 1962- 148
Dean, Karen Strickler 1923- 49
Dean, Ruth (Brigham) 1947- 145
Dean, Zoey
See Bennett, Cherie
de Angeli, Marguerite (Lofft) 1889-1987 ... 100
Obituary 51
Earlier sketches in SATA *1, 27*
See also CLR *1*
Deans, Sis Boulos 1955- 136
Earlier sketch in SATA *78*
DeArmand, Frances Ullmann 1904(?)-1984 . 10
Obituary 38
DeArmond, Dale 1914- 70
DeArmond, Dale Burlison
See DeArmond, Dale
Deary, Terry 1946- 171
Brief entry 41
Earlier sketches in SATA *51, 101*
Deaver, Julie Reece 1953- 68
de Banke, Cecile 1889-1965 11
De Bello, Rosario 1923- 89
Debon, Nicolas 151
de Bono, Edward 1933- 66
de Brissac, Malcolm
See Dickinson, Peter (Malcolm de Brissac)
de Brunhoff, Jean
See Brunhoff, Jean de
De Brunhoff, Laurent
See Brunhoff, Laurent de
De Bruyn, Monica G. 1952- 13
De Bruyn, Monica Jean Grembowicz
See De Bruyn, Monica G.
DeBry, Roger K. 1942- 91
de Camp, Catherine Crook 1907-2000 83
Earlier sketch in SATA *12*
de Camp, L(yon) Sprague 1907-2000 83
Earlier sketch in SATA *9*
DeCandido, Keith R.A. 112
Dechausay, Sonia E. 94
Decker, C.B. 172
Decker, Cynthia B.
See Decker, C.B.
Decker, Duane 1910-1964 5
DeClements, Barthe (Faith) 1920- 131
Earlier sketches in SATA *35, 71*
See also CLR *23*
de Conte, Sieur Louis
See Clemens, Samuel Langhorne
Dedman, Stephen 108
Dee, Catherine 1964- 138
Dee, Ruby 77
See Wallace, Ruby Ann
Deedy, John 1923- 24
Deegan, Paul Joseph 1937- 48
Brief entry 38
Deem, James M. 1950- 134
Earlier sketch in SATA *75*
Deem, James Morgan
See Deem, James M.
Deeter, Catherine 1947- 137
DeFelice, Cynthia 1951- 165
Earlier sketches in SATA *79, 121*
DeFelice, Cynthia C.
See DeFelice, Cynthia
Defoe, Daniel 1660(?)-1731 22
See also CLR *61*
DeFord, Deborah H. 123
deFrance, Anthony
See DiFranco, Anthony (Mario)
Degen, Bruce 1945- 147
Brief entry 47
Earlier sketches in SATA *57, 97*
DeGering, Etta (Belle) Fowler 1898-1996 7

De Goldi, Kate
See De Goldi, Kathleen Domenica
De Goldi, Kathleen Domenica 1959- 123
De Grazia, Ted 39
See De Grazia, Ettore
deGroat, Diane 1947- 169
Earlier sketches in SATA *31, 90*
deGros, J. H.
See Villiard, Paul
de Grummond, Lena Young 62
Earlier sketch in SATA *6*
de Hamel, Joan Littledale 1924- 86
De Haven, Tom 1949- 72
de Hugo, Pierre
See Brackers de Hugo, Pierre
Deiss, Joseph Jay 1915- 12
de Jenkins, Lyll Becerra 1925-1997 102
DeJong, David C(ornel) 1905-1967 10
de Jong, Dola 1911-2003 7
Obituary 149
See de Jong, Dorothea Rosalie
DeJong, Meindert 1906-1991 2
Obituary 68
See also CLR *73*
DeJonge, Joanne E. 1943- 56
Deka, Connie
See Laux, Constance
de Kay, Ormonde (Jr.) 1923-1998 7
Obituary 106
de Kiriline, Louise
See Lawrence, Louise de Kiriline
Dekker, Carl
See Laffin, John (Alfred Charles)
and Lynds, Dennis
deKruif, Paul (Henry) 1890-1971 50
Earlier sketch in SATA *5*
Delacre, Lulu 1957- 156
Earlier sketch in SATA *36*
DeLaCroix, Alice 1940- 75
de la Cruz, Melissa 1971- 179
De la Garza, Phyllis 1942- 169
De Lage, Ida 1918- 11
de la Mare, Walter (John) 1873-1956 16
See also CLR *23*
Delaney, Harry 1932- 3
Delaney, Joseph 1945- 172
Delaney, Michael 1955- 96
Delaney, Ned 28
See Delaney, Thomas Nicholas III
Delano, Hugh 1933- 20
Delany, Samuel R., Jr. 1942- 92
Delany, Samuel Ray
See Delany, Samuel R., Jr.
De La Ramee, Marie Louise 1839-1908 20
See Ouida
de la Roche, Mazo 1879-1961 64
De La Roche Saint Andre, Anne 1950- 75
Delaune, (Jewel) Lynn (de Grummond) 7
DeLaurentis, Louise Budde 1920- 12
Delderfield, Eric R(aymond) 1909-1995 14
Delderfield, Ronald Frederick 1912-1972 20
DeLeeuw, Adele (Louise) 1899-1988 30
Obituary 56
Earlier sketch in SATA *1*
De Leon, Nephtali 1945- 97
Delessert, Etienne 1941- 179
Brief entry 27
Earlier sketches in SATA *46, 130*
See also CLR *81*
Delgado, James P. 1958- 122
de Lint, Charles 1951- 157
Earlier sketch in SATA *115*
de Lint, Charles Henri Diederick Hofsmit
See de Lint, Charles
Delmar, Roy
See Wexler, Jerome (LeRoy)
Deloria, Vine, Jr. 1933-2005 21
Obituary 171
Deloria, Vine Victor, Jr.
See Deloria, Vine, Jr.

del Rey, Lester 1915-1993 22
Obituary 76
Delrio, Martin
See Doyle, Debra
and Macdonald, James D.
Delton, Judy 1931-2001 77
Obituary 130
Earlier sketch in SATA *14*
See also SAAS *9*
Delulio, John 1938- 15
Delving, Michael
See Williams, Jay
Demarest, Chris L. 1951- 175
Brief entry 44
Earlier sketches in SATA *45, 82, 128*
Demarest, Christopher Lynn
See Demarest, Chris L.
Demarest, Doug
See Barker, Will
Demas, Corinne 131
See Bliss, Corinne Demas
Demas, Vida 1927- 9
De Mejo, Oscar 1911-1992 40
Demers, Dominique 1956- 177
de Messieres, Nicole 1930- 39
Demi
See Hitz, Demi
Demijohn, Thom
See Disch, Thomas M.
and Sladek, John
Deming, Richard 1915-1983 24
See Queen, Ellery
Demuth, Patricia Brennan 1948- 84
Brief entry 51
Dendinger, Roger E. 1952- 158
Denenberg, Barry 175
Dengler, Marianna (Herron) 1935- 103
Dengler, Sandy 1939- 54
Brief entry 40
Denim, Sue
See Pilkey, Dav
Denise, Christopher 1968- 147
Denmark, Harrison
See Zelazny, Roger
Dennard, Deborah 1953- 136
Earlier sketch in SATA *78*
Denney, Diana 1910-2000 25
Obituary 120
Dennis, Morgan 1891(?)-1960 18
Dennis, Wesley 1903-1966 18
Denny, Norman (George) 1901-1982 43
Denslow, Sharon Phillips 1947- 142
Earlier sketch in SATA *68*
Denslow, W(illiam) W(allace) 1856-1915 16
See also CLR *15*
Denton, Kady MacDonald 110
Earlier sketch in SATA *66*
See also CLR *71*
Denver, Walt
See Redding, Robert Hull
and Sherman, Jory (Tecumseh)
Denzel, Justin F(rancis) 1917-1999 46
Brief entry 38
Denzer, Ann Wiseman
See Wiseman, Ann (Sayre)
DePalma, Mary Newell 1961- 139
dePaola, Thomas Anthony 1934- 155
Earlier sketches in SATA *11, 59, 108*
See dePaola, Tomie
dePaola, Tomie
See CLR *81*
See also SAAS *15*
See dePaola, Thomas Anthony
dePaola, Paul 1949- 74
DePauw, Linda Grant 1940- 24
DeRan, David 1946- 76
Derby, Pat 1942- 172
Derby, Sally 1934- 132
Earlier sketch in SATA *89*

de Regniers, Beatrice Schenk (Freedman)
1914-2000 .... *68*
   Obituary *123*
   Earlier sketch in SATA 2
   See also SAAS 6
Dereske, Jo 1947- *72*
Derleth, August (William) 1909-1971 .... *5*
Derman, Martha (Winn) *74*
Derman, Sarah Audrey 1915- *11*
DeRoberts, Lyndon
   See Silverstein, Robert Alan
de Roo, Anne Louise 1931-1997 .... *84*
   Earlier sketch in SATA 25
   See also CLR 63
deRosa, Dee *70*
Derrick, Lionel
   See Cunningham, Chet
Derrickson, Jim 1959- *141*
Derry Down Derry
   See Lear, Edward
Dervaux, Isabelle 1961- *106*
Derwent, Lavinia *14*
Desai, Anita 1937- *126*
   Earlier sketch in SATA 63
De Saulles, Tony 1958- *119*
Desbarats, Peter 1933- *39*
de Selincourt, Aubrey 1894-1962 .... *14*
Deshpande, Chris 1950- *69*
Desimini, Lisa 1964- *148*
   Earlier sketch in SATA 86
Desjarlais, John 1953- *71*
Desjarlais, John J.
   See Desjarlais, John
Desmoinaux, Christel 1967- *149*
   Earlier sketch in SATA 103
Desmond, Adrian J(ohn) 1947- *51*
Desmond, Alice Curtis 1897-1990 .... *8*
DeSpain, Pleasant 1943- *87*
Desputeaux, Helene 1959- *95*
Dessen, Sarah 1970- *172*
   Earlier sketch in SATA 120
Detine, Padre
   See Olsen, Ib Spang
de Trevino, Elizabeth B.
   See Trevino, Elizabeth B(orton) de
de Trevino, Elizabeth Borton
   See Trevino, Elizabeth B(orton) de
Detwiler, Susan Dill 1956- *58*
Deuker, Carl 1950- *150*
   Earlier sketch in SATA 82
Deutsch, Babette 1895-1982 .... *1*
   Obituary *33*
Deutsch, Eva Costabel
   See Costabel, Eva Deutsch
Deutsch, Helen 1906-1992 .... *76*
Deutsch, Kurt
   See Singer, Kurt D.
Devaney, John 1926-1994 .... *12*
de Varennes, Monique 1947- *168*
de Varona, Frank J. 1943- *83*
Devereux, Frederick L(eonard), Jr.
1914-1993 .... *9*
Devi, Nila
   See Woody, Regina Jones
deVinck, Christopher 1951- *85*
DeVito, Cara 1956- *80*
Devlin, Dorothy Wende
   See Devlin, Wende
Devlin, Harry 1918-2001 .... *136*
   Earlier sketches in SATA 11, 74
Devlin, Wende 1918-2002 .... *74*
   Earlier sketch in SATA 11
Devon, Paddie 1953- *92*
Devons, Sonia 1974- *72*
Devorah-Leah *111*
de Vos, Gail 1949- *122*
DeVries, Douglas 1933- *122*
De Waard, E(lliott) John 1935- *7*
Dewan, Ted 1961- *157*
   Earlier sketch in SATA 108
Dewdney, Selwyn (Hanington) 1909-1979 ... *64*

DeWeese, Gene
   See DeWeese, Thomas Eugene
DeWeese, Jean
   See DeWeese, Thomas Eugene
DeWeese, Thomas Eugene 1934- *46*
   Brief entry *45*
Dewey, Ariane 1937- *178*
   Earlier sketches in SATA 7, 109
Dewey, Jennifer (Owings) 1941- *103*
   Brief entry *48*
   Earlier sketch in SATA 58
Dewey, Kenneth Francis 1940- *39*
deWit, Dorothy (May Knowles) 1916-1980 . *39*
   Obituary *28*
Dexter, Alison 1966- *125*
Dexter, John
   See Bradley, Marion Zimmer
Deyneka, Anita 1943- *24*
Deyrup, Astrith Johnson 1923- *24*
Dhami, Narinder 1958- *152*
Dhondy, Farrukh 1944- *152*
   Earlier sketch in SATA 65
   See also CLR 41
Diakite, Baba Wague 1961- *174*
Diakite, Penda 1993(?)- *174*
Diamond, Arthur 1957- *76*
Diamond, Donna 1950- *69*
   Brief entry *30*
   Earlier sketch in SATA 35
Diamond, Petra
   See Sachs, Judith
Diamond, Rebecca
   See Sachs, Judith
Dias, Earl Joseph 1916- *41*
Dias, Ron 1937- *71*
Diaz, David 1959(?)- *150*
   Earlier sketch in SATA 96
   See also CLR 65
DiCamillo, Kate 1964- *163*
   Earlier sketch in SATA 121
   See also CLR 117
Di Certo, J(oseph) J(ohn) 1933- *60*
DiCianni, Ron 1952- *107*
Dick, Trella Lamson 1889-1974 .... *9*
Dickens, Charles (John Huffam)
1812-1870 .... *15*
   See also CLR 95
Dickens, Frank
   See Huline-Dickens, Frank William
Dickens, Monica (Enid) 1915-1992 .... *4*
   Obituary *74*
Dickinson, Emily (Elizabeth) 1830-1886 ..... *29*
Dickinson, Mary 1949- *48*
   Brief entry *41*
Dickinson, Mary-Anne
   See Rodda, Emily
Dickinson, Peter (Malcolm de Brissac)
1927- *150*
   Earlier sketches in SATA 5, 62, 95
   See also CLR 29
Dickinson, Susan 1931- *8*
Dickinson, Terence 1943- *102*
Dickinson, W(illiam) Croft 1897-1963 .... *13*
Dickson, Gordon R(upert) 1923-2001 .... *77*
Dickson, Naida 1916- *8*
Diehn, Gwen 1943- *80*
Dieterich, Michele M. 1962- *78*
Dietz, David H(enry) 1897-1984 .... *10*
   Obituary *41*
Dietz, Lew 1907-1997 .... *11*
   Obituary *95*
Diffily, Deborah *159*
Di Fiori, Larry
   See Di Fiori, Lawrence
Di Fiori, Lawrence 1934- *130*
DiFranco, Anthony (Mario) 1945- *42*
Digby, Anne 1935- *72*
Digges, Jeremiah
   See Berger, Josef
Digman, Kristina 1959- *176*

D'Ignazio, Fred(erick) 1949- *39*
   Brief entry *35*
Di Grazia, Thomas (?)-1983 .... *32*
Dikty, Julian May
   See May, Julian
Dillard, Annie 1945- *140*
   Earlier sketch in SATA 10
Dillard, Kristine 1964- *113*
Dillard, Polly Hargis 1916- *24*
Diller, Harriett 1953- *78*
Dillon, Barbara 1927- *44*
   Brief entry *39*
Dillon, Diane (Claire) 1933- *106*
   Earlier sketches in SATA 15, 51
   See also CLR 44
Dillon, Eilis 1920-1994 .... *74*
   Autobiography Feature *105*
   Obituary *83*
   Earlier sketch in SATA 2
   See also CLR 26
Dillon, Jana (a pseudonym) 1952- *117*
Dillon, Leo 1933- *106*
   Earlier sketches in SATA 15, 51
   See also CLR 44
Dillon, Sharon Saseen
   See Saseen, Sharon (Dillon)
Dils, Tracey E. 1958- *83*
Dilson, Jesse 1914-1988 .... *24*
Dinan, Carolyn *59*
   Brief entry *47*
Dines, Carol 1956- *175*
Dines, (Harry) Glen 1925-1996 .... *7*
Dinesen, Isak
   See Blixen, Karen (Christentze Dinesen)
Dinessi, Alex
   See Schembri, Jim
Dinneen, Betty 1929- *61*
Dinnerstein, Harvey 1928- *42*
Dinsdale, Tim(othy Kay) 1924-1987 .... *11*
Diouf, Sylviane A. 1952- *168*
Diouf, Sylviane Anna
   See Diouf, Sylviane A.
DiPucchio, Kelly *159*
Dirk
   See Gringhuis, Richard H.
Dirks, Wilhelmina 1916- *59*
Dirks, Willy
   See Dirks, Wilhelmina
Dirtmeister
   See Tomecek, Steve
DiSalvo, DyAnne 1960- *144*
   Earlier sketch in SATA 59
DiSalvo-Ryan, DyAnne
   See DiSalvo, DyAnne
Disch, Thomas M. 1940- *92*
   See also CLR 18
   See also SAAS 15
   See Disch, Tom
Disch, Thomas Michael
   See Disch, Thomas M.
Disch, Tom
   See Disch, Thomas M.
Disher, Garry 1949- *125*
   Earlier sketch in SATA 81
Disney, Walt(er Elias) 1901-1966 .... *28*
   Brief entry *27*
DiTerlizzi, Tony 1969- *154*
Divakaruni, Chitra Banerjee 1956- *160*
Di Valentin, Maria (Amelia) Messuri
1911-1985 .... *7*
Dixon, Ann R(enee) 1954- *127*
   Earlier sketch in SATA 77
Dixon, Dougal 1947- *127*
   Earlier sketch in SATA 45

Dixon, Franklin W. *100*
  Earlier sketches in SATA *1, 67*
  See also CLR *61*
  See Barrett, Neal, Jr.
  and Goulart, Ron(ald Joseph)
  and Lantz, Francess L(in)
  and Lerangis, Peter
  and McFarlane, Leslie (Charles)
  and Stanley, George Edward
  and Stratemeyer, Edward L.
Dixon, Jeanne 1936- *31*
Dixon, Paige
  See Corcoran, Barbara (Asenath)
Dixon, Peter L(ee) 1931- *6*
Dixon, Rachel 1952- *74*
Djoleto, (Solomon Alexander) Amu 1929- ... *80*
d'lacey, Chris 1949- *165*
Doak, Annie
  See Dillard, Annie
Doane, Pelagie 1906-1966 .... *7*
Dobell, I(sabel) M(arian) B(arclay)
  1909-1998 .... *11*
Dobie, J(ames) Frank 1888-1964 .... *43*
Dobler, Lavinia G. 1910- *6*
Dobrin, Arnold 1928- *4*
Dobson, Jill 1969- *140*
Dobson, Julia 1941- *48*
Dobson, Mary 1954- *117*
Dockery, Wallene T. 1941- *27*
Dockray, Tracy 1962- *139*
Dockrey, Karen 1955- *103*
Doctor, Bernard
  See Doctor, Bernard Aquina
Doctor, Bernard Aquina 1950- *81*
Doctor X
  See Nourse, Alan E(dward)
Dodd, Ed(ward Benton) 1902-1991 .... *4*
  Obituary *68*
Dodd, Lynley (Stuart) 1941- *132*
  Earlier sketches in SATA *35, 86*
  See also CLR *62*
Dodd, Marty 1921- *142*
Dodd, Quentin 1972- *137*
Dodds, Bill 1952- *78*
Dodds, Dayle Ann 1952- *150*
  Earlier sketch in SATA *75*
Dodge, Bertha S(anford) 1902-1995 .... *8*
Dodge, Fremont
  See Grimes, Lee
Dodge, Gil
  See Hano, Arnold
Dodge, Mary (Elizabeth) Mapes
  1831(?)-1905 .... *100*
  Earlier sketch in SATA *21*
  See also CLR *62*
Dodgson, Charles L(utwidge) 1832-1898 ... *100*
  See also YABC *2*
  See also CLR *2*
  See Carroll, Lewis
Dodson, Kenneth MacKenzie 1907-1999 ..... *11*
Dodson, Susan 1941- *50*
  Brief entry *40*
Dogyear, Drew
  See Gorey, Edward (St. John)
Doherty, Berlie 1943- *111*
  Earlier sketch in SATA *72*
  See also CLR *21*
  See also SAAS *16*
Doherty, Charles Hugh 1913- *6*
Doherty, Craig A. 1951- *169*
  Earlier sketch in SATA *83*
Doherty, Katherine M(ann) 1951- *83*
Doherty, Kieran 1945- *164*
Dokey, Cameron 1956- *97*
Dolan, Edward F(rancis), Jr. 1924- *94*
  Brief entry *31*
  Earlier sketch in SATA *45*
Dolan, Ellen M(eara) 1929-1998 .... *88*
Dolan, Sean J. 1958- *74*
Dolce, J. Ellen 1948- *75*
Dolch, Edward William 1889-1961 .... *50*

Dolch, Marguerite Pierce 1891-1978 .... *50*
Dollar, Diane (Hills) 1933- *57*
Dolson, Hildegarde *5*
  See Lockridge, Hildegarde (Dolson)
Domanska, Janina 1913(?)-1995 .... *68*
  Obituary *84*
  Earlier sketch in SATA *6*
  See also CLR *40*
  See also SAAS *18*
Dominguez, Angel 1953- *76*
Domino, John
  See Averill, Esther (Holden)
Domjan, Joseph (Spiri) 1907-1992 .... *25*
Domm, Jeffrey C. 1958- *84*
Donahue, Dorothy *178*
Donald, Rhonda Lucas 1962- *147*
Donalds, Gordon
  See Shirreffs, Gordon D(onald)
Donaldson, Bryna
  See Stevens, Bryna
Donaldson, Gordon 1913-1993 .... *64*
  Obituary *76*
Donaldson, Joan 1953- *78*
Donaldson, Julia 1948- *132*
  Earlier sketch in SATA *82*
Donaldson, Stephen R(eeder) 1947- *121*
Doner, Kim 1955- *91*
Doney, Todd L. W. 1959- *104*
Donkin, Nance (Clare) 1915- *95*
Donna, Natalie 1934-1979 .... *9*
Donnelly, Elfie 1950-
  See CLR *104*
Donnelly, Jennifer 1963- *154*
Donnelly, Matt 1972- *148*
Donoghue, Emma 1969- *101*
Donoughue, Carol 1935- *139*
Donovan, John 1928-1992 .... *72*
  Brief entry *29*
  See also CLR *3*
Donovan, Mary Lee 1961- *86*
Donze, Mary Terese 1911- *89*
Doob, Leonard W(illiam) 1909-2000 .... *8*
Dooley, Norah 1953- *74*
Dooling, Michael 1958- *105*
Dor, Ana
  See Ceder, Georgiana Dorcas
Dore, (Louis Christophe Paul) Gustave
  1832-1883 .... *19*
Doremus, Robert 1913- *30*
Doren, Marion (Walker) 1928- *57*
Dorenkamp, Michelle 1957- *89*
Dorflinger, Carolyn 1953- *91*
Dorian, Edith M(cEwen) 1900-1983 .... *5*
Dorian, Harry
  See Hamilton, Charles (Harold St. John)
Dorian, Marguerite *7*
Dorin, Patrick C(arberry) 1939- *59*
  Brief entry *52*
Dorman, Michael 1932- *7*
Dorman, N. B. 1927- *39*
Dorris, Michael 1945-1997 .... *75*
  Obituary *94*
  See also CLR *58*
Dorris, Michael A.
  See Dorris, Michael
Dorris, Michael Anthony
  See Dorris, Michael
Dorritt, Susan
  See Schlein, Miriam
Dorros, Arthur 1950- *168*
  Earlier sketches in SATA *78, 122*
  See also CLR *42*
  See also SAAS *20*
Dorros, Arthur M.
  See Dorros, Arthur
Dorson, Richard M(ercer) 1916-1981 .... *30*
Doss, Helen (Grigsby) 1918- *20*
Doss, Margot Patterson *6*
Dothers, Anne
  See Chess, Victoria (Dickerson)

Dottig
  See Grider, Dorothy
Dotts, Maryann J. 1933- *35*
Doty, Jean Slaughter 1929- *28*
Doty, Roy 1922- *28*
Doubtfire, Dianne (Abrams) 1918- *29*
Doucet, Sharon Arms 1951- *144*
  Autobiography Feature *144*
  Earlier sketch in SATA *125*
Dougherty, Charles 1922- *18*
Dougherty, Terri (L.) 1964- *146*
Doughty, Rebecca 1955- *174*
Douglas, Blaise 1960- *101*
Douglas, Carole Nelson 1944- *73*
Douglas, Garry
  See Kilworth, Garry
Douglas, James McM.
  See Griffin, W.E.B.
Douglas, Kathryn
  See Ewing, Kathryn
Douglas, Leonard
  See Bradbury, Ray
Douglas, Marjory Stoneman 1890-1998 .... *10*
Douglas, Michael
  See Crichton, Michael
Douglas, Michael
  See Bright, Robert (Douglas Sr.)
Douglass, Barbara 1930- *40*
Douglass, Frederick 1817(?)-1895 .... *29*
Douglass, Keith
  See Cunningham, Chet
Douty, Esther M(orris) 1909-1978 .... *8*
  Obituary *23*
Dow, Emily R. 1904-1987 .... *10*
Dow, Vicki
  See McVey, Vicki
Dowd, John David 1945- *78*
Dowdell, Dorothy (Florence) Karns 1910- ... *12*
Dowden, Anne Ophelia Todd 1907-2007 .... *7*
  See also SAAS *10*
Dowdey, Landon Gerald 1923- *11*
Dowdy, Mrs. Regera
  See Gorey, Edward (St. John)
Dowell, Frances O'Roark *157*
Dowling, Terry 1947- *101*
Downer, Ann 1960- *155*
Downer, Marion 1892(?)-1971 .... *25*
Downey, Fairfax D(avis) 1893-1990 .... *3*
  Obituary *66*
Downie, John 1931- *87*
Downie, Mary Alice 1934- *171*
  Earlier sketches in SATA *13, 87*
Downie, Mary Alice Dawe
  See Downie, Mary Alice
Downing, David A(lmon) 1958- *84*
Downing, Julie 1956- *148*
  Earlier sketch in SATA *81*
Downing, Paula E. 1951- *80*
Downing, Warwick 1931- *138*
Downing, Wick
  See Downing, Warwick
Doyle, A. Conan
  See Doyle, Sir Arthur Conan
Doyle, Sir Arthur Conan 1859-1930 .... *24*
  See also CLR *106*
  See Conan Doyle, Arthur
Doyle, Brian 1935- *156*
  Earlier sketches in SATA *67, 104*
  See also CLR *22*
  See also SAAS *16*
Doyle, Charlotte 1937- *178*
  Earlier sketch in SATA *94*
Doyle, Charlotte Lackner
  See Doyle, Charlotte
Doyle, Conan
  See Doyle, Sir Arthur Conan
Doyle, Debra 1952- *165*
  Earlier sketch in SATA *105*
  See Appleton, Victor
Doyle, John
  See Graves, Robert

Doyle, Malachy 1954- 165
  Earlier sketch in SATA 120
  See also CLR 83
Doyle, Richard 1824-1883 21
Doyle, Sir A. Conan
  See Doyle, Sir Arthur Conan
Dr. A
  See Asimov, Isaac
  and Silverstein, Alvin
  and Silverstein, Virginia B(arbara Opshelor)
Dr. Alphabet
  See Morice, Dave
Dr. Fred
  See Bortz, Alfred B(enjamin)
Dr. Laura
  See Schlessinger, Laura (Catherine)
Dr. Seuss
  See CLR 100
  See Geisel, Theodor Seuss
  and LeSieg, Theo.
  and Seuss, Dr.
  and Stone, Rosetta
Dr. Zed
  See Penrose, Gordon
Drabble, Margaret 1939- 48
Drackett, Phil(ip Arthur) 1922- 53
Draco, F.
  See Davis, Julia
Dracup, Angela 1943- 74
Dragisic, Patricia 116
Dragonwagon, Crescent 1952- 133
  Earlier sketches in SATA 11, 41, 75
  See also SAAS 14
Drake, David 1945- 85
Drake, David Allen
  See Drake, David
Drake, Frank
  See Hamilton, Charles (Harold St. John)
Drake, Jane 1954- 82
Drakeford, Dale B 1952- 113
Drakeford, Dale Benjamin
  See Drakeford, Dale B
Draper, Hastings
  See Jeffries, Roderic
Draper, Sharon M. 146
  Autobiography Feature 146
  Earlier sketch in SATA 98
  See also CLR 57
Draper, Sharon Mills
  See Draper, Sharon M.
Drapier, M. B.
  See Swift, Jonathan
Drawson, Blair 1943- 126
  Earlier sketch in SATA 17
Dray, Matt 1967- 177
Dray, Matthew Frederick
  See Dray, Matt
Dresang, Eliza (Carolyn Timberlake) 1941- . 19
Drescher, Henrik 1955- 172
  Earlier sketches in SATA 67, 105
  See also CLR 20
Drescher, Joan E(lizabeth) 1939- 137
  Earlier sketch in SATA 30
Drew, Patricia (Mary) 1938- 15
Drewery, Mary 1918- 6
Drewery, Melanie 1970- 165
Drewry, Henry N(athaniel) 1924- 138
Dreyer, Ellen 177
Drial, J. E.
  See Laird, Jean E(louise)
Drimmer, Frederick 1916-2000 60
  Obituary 124
Driskill, J. Lawrence 1920- 90
Driskill, Larry
  See Driskill, J. Lawrence
Driving Hawk, Virginia
  See Sneve, Virginia Driving Hawk
Drucker, Malka 1945- 111
  Brief entry 29
  Earlier sketch in SATA 39
Drucker, Olga Levy 1927- 79

Drummond, V(iolet) H(ilda) 1911-2000 6
Drummond, Walter
  See Silverberg, Robert
Drury, Clare Marie
  See Hoskyns-Abrahall, Clare (Constance
  Drury)
Drury, Roger W(olcott) 1914-1996 15
Druse, Eleanor
  See King, Stephen
Dryden, Pamela
  See St. John, Nicole
D.T., Hughes
  See Hughes, Dean
Duane, Diane (Elizabeth) 1952- 145
  Brief entry 46
  Earlier sketches in SATA 58, 95
Dubanevich, Arlene 1950- 56
Dubelaar, Thea 1947- 60
du Blane, Daphne
  See Groom, Arthur William
Duble, Kathleen Benner 1958- 164
Du Bois, Shirley Graham 1907(?)-1977 24
  See Graham, Shirley
Du Bois, W(illiam) E(dward) B(urghardt)
  1868-1963 42
du Bois, William Pene
  See Pene du Bois, William (Sherman)
Duboise, Novella 1911-1999 88
Dubosarsky, Ursula (Bridget) 1961- 147
  Earlier sketch in SATA 107
DuBose, LaRocque (Russ) 1926- 2
Dubrovin, Vivian 1931- 139
  Earlier sketch in SATA 65
DuBurke, Randy 172
Ducey, Jean Sparks 1915- 93
Du Chaillu, Paul (Belloni) 1835(?)-1903 26
Ducharme, Dede Fox
  See Ducharme, Lilian Fox
Ducharme, Lilian Fox 1950- 122
Ducornet, Erica 1943- 7
  See Ducornet, Rikki
Ducornet, Rikki
  See Ducornet, Erica
Duden, Jane 1947- 136
Duder, Tessa 1940- 117
  Earlier sketch in SATA 80
  See also CLR 43
  See also SAAS 23
Dudley, Helen
  See Hope Simpson, Jacynth
Dudley, Nancy
  See Cole, Lois Dwight
Dudley, Robert
  See Baldwin, James
Dudley, Ruth H(ubbell) 1905-2001 11
Dudley-Smith, T.
  See Trevor, Elleston
Due, Linnea A. 1948- 64
Dueck, Adele 1955- 97
Dueland, Joy V(ivian) 27
Duerr, Gisela 1968- 89
Duey, Kathleen 1950- 132
Dufault, Joseph Ernest Nephtali
  See James, Will(iam Roderick)
Duff, Maggie
  See Duff, Margaret K(app)
Duff, Margaret K(app) 1916-2003 37
  Obituary 144
Duffey, Betsy (Byars) 1953- 131
  Earlier sketch in SATA 80
Duffie, Charles 1960- 144
Duffield, Katy S. 1961- 147
Duffy, Carol Ann 1955- 165
  Earlier sketch in SATA 95
Dugan, Jack
  See Griffin, W.E.B.
Dugan, John Kevin
  See Griffin, W.E.B.
Dugan, Michael (Gray) 1947- 15
Duggan, Alfred Leo 1903-1964 25

Duggan, Maurice (Noel) 1922-1974 40
  Obituary 30
Duggleby, John 1952- 94
Dugin, Andrej 1955- 77
Dugina, Olga 1964- 77
du Jardin, Rosamond Neal 1902-1963 2
Duke, Kate 1956- 148
  Earlier sketch in SATA 90
  See also CLR 51
Duke, Will
  See Gault, William Campbell
Dulac, Edmund 1882-1953 19
Dumas, Alexandre (pere) 1802-1870 18
Dumas, Jacqueline 1946- 55
Dumas, Philippe 1940- 119
  Earlier sketch in SATA 52
du Maurier, Daphne 1907-1989 27
  Obituary 60
Dumbleton, Mike 1948- 124
  Earlier sketch in SATA 73
Dunbar, Fiona 1961- 167
Dunbar, Joyce 1944- 162
  Earlier sketches in SATA 76, 112
Dunbar, Paul Laurence 1872-1906 34
Dunbar, Robert E(verett) 1926- 32
Duncan, Alexandra
  See Moore, Ishbel (Lindsay)
Duncan, Alice Faye 1967- 168
  Earlier sketch in SATA 95
Duncan, Gregory
  See McClintock, Marshall
Duncan, Jane
  See Cameron, Elizabeth Jane
Duncan, Julia K. 1
  See Benson, Mildred (Augustine Wirt)
Duncan, Lois 1934- 141
  Autobiography Feature 141
  Earlier sketches in SATA 1, 36, 75, 133
  See also CLR 29
  See also SAAS 2
Duncan, Norman 1871-1916
  See YABC 1
Duncan, Terence
  See Nolan, William F(rancis)
Duncombe, Frances (Riker) 1900-1994 25
  Obituary 82
Dunham, Montrew 1919- 162
Dunham, Montrew Goetz
  See Dunham, Montrew
Dunkle, Clare B. 1964- 155
Dunlap, Julie 1958- 84
Dunleavy, Deborah 1951- 133
Dunlop, Agnes M. R. (?)-1982 87
  See Kyle, Elisabeth
Dunlop, Eileen (Rhona) 1938- 76
  Earlier sketch in SATA 24
  See also SAAS 12
Dunn, Anne M. 1940- 107
Dunn, Harvey T(homas) 1884-1952 34
Dunn, Herb
  See Gutman, Dan
Dunn, John M. (III) 1949- 93
Dunn, Judy
  See Spangenberg, Judith Dunn
Dunn, Mary Lois 1930- 6
Dunnahoo, Terry Janson 1927- 7
Dunne, Jeanette 1952- 72
Dunne, Kathleen 1933- 126
Dunne, Marie
  See Clark, Ann Nolan
Dunne, Mary Collins 1914- 11
Dunne, Mary Jo
  See Dunne, Mary Collins
Dunnett, Kaitlyn
  See Emerson, Kathy Lynn
Dunnett, Margaret (Rosalind) 1909-1977 42
Dunnick, Regan 178
Dunrea, Olivier 1953- 160
  Brief entry 46
  Earlier sketches in SATA 59, 118

Dunrea, Olivier Jean-Paul Dominique
  See Dunrea, Olivier
Dunton, Dorothy 1912- 92
Dupasquier, Philippe 1955- 151
  Earlier sketch in SATA 86
DuPrau, Jeanne 1944- 144
Dupuy, T(revor) N(evitt) 1916-1995 4
  Obituary 86
DuQuette, Keith 1960- 155
  Earlier sketch in SATA 90
Duran, Gloria 1924- 171
Duran, Gloria Bradley
  See Duran, Gloria
Duranceau, Suzanne 1952- 162
Durango, Julia 1967- 173
Durant, Alan 1958- 165
  Earlier sketch in SATA 121
Durant, John 1902- 27
Durbin, William 1951- 174
  Earlier sketch in SATA 143
Durell, Ann 1930- 66
Durkee, Sarah 173
Durrant, Lynda 1954- 148
  Earlier sketch in SATA 96
Durrell, Gerald (Malcolm) 1925-1995 8
  Obituary 84
Durrell, Julie 1955- 94
Durrett, Deanne 1940- 144
  Earlier sketch in SATA 92
Du Soe, Robert C. 1892-1958
  See YABC 2
Dussling, Jennifer 1970- 143
  Earlier sketch in SATA 96
DuTemple, Lesley A. 1952- 113
Dutz
  See Davis, Mary Octavia
Duval, Katherine
  See James, Elizabeth
Duvall, Aimee
  See Thurlo, Aimee
  and Thurlo, David
Duvall, Evelyn Millis 1906- 9
Duvall, Jill D(onovan) 1932- 102
Duvoisin, Roger (Antoine) 1904-1980 30
  Obituary 23
  Earlier sketch in SATA 2
  See also CLR 23
Dwiggins, Don(ald J.) 1913-1988 4
  Obituary 60
Dwight, Allan
  See Cole, Lois Dwight
Dwyer, Deanna
  See Koontz, Dean R.
Dwyer, K. R.
  See Koontz, Dean R.
Dyck, Peter J. 1914- 75
Dyer, James (Frederick) 1934- 37
Dyer, Jane 147
Dyess, John (Foster) 1939- 76
Dygard, Thomas J. 1931-1996 97
  Obituary 92
  Earlier sketch in SATA 24
  See also SAAS 15
Dyke, John 1935- 35

E

E. V. L.
  See Lucas, E(dward) V(errall)
Eagar, Frances (Elisabeth Stuart)
  1940-1978 11
  Obituary 55
Eager, Edward (McMaken) 1911-1964 17
  See also CLR 43
Eager, George 1921- 56
  See Eager, George B.
Eager, George B.
  See Eager, George
Eagle, Ellen 1953- 61

Eagle, Kin
  See Adlerman, Daniel (Ezra)
  and Adlerman, Kimberly M(arie)
Eagle, Mike 1942- 11
Earle, Olive L(ydia) 1888-1982 7
Earle, William
  See Johns, W(illiam) E(arle)
Earls, Nick 1963- 156
  Earlier sketch in SATA 95
Early, Jack
  See Scoppettone, Sandra
Early, Jon
  See Johns, W(illiam) E(arle)
Early, Margaret 1951- 72
Earnshaw, Brian 1929- 17
Earnshaw, Micky
  See Earnshaw, Spencer Wright
Earnshaw, Spencer Wright 1939- 88
Easley, MaryAnn 94
Eastman, Charles A(lexander) 1858-1939
  See YABC 1
Eastman, P(hilip) D(ey) 1909-1986 33
  Obituary 46
Easton, Kelly 1960- 141
Eastwick, Ivy (Ethel) O(live) 3
Eaton, Anne T(haxter) 1881-1971 32
Eaton, Anthony 1971- 167
Eaton, George L.
  See Verral, Charles Spain
Eaton, Janet
  See Givens, Janet E(aton)
Eaton, Jeanette 1886-1968 24
Eaton, Tom 1940- 22
Ebel, Alex 1927- 11
Eber, Dorothy (Margaret) Harley 1930- 27
Eberle, Irmengarde 1898-1979 2
  Obituary 23
Eble, Diane 1956- 74
Eboch, Chris 113
Echlin, Kim 1955- 166
Eckblad, Edith Berven 1923- 23
Eckert, Allan W. 1931- 91
  Brief entry 27
  Earlier sketch in SATA 29
  See also SAAS 21
Eckert, Horst 1931- 72
  Earlier sketch in SATA 8
  See Janosch
Ecklar, Julia (Marie) 1964- 112
Eddings, David (Carroll) 1931- 91
Ede, Janina 1937- 33
Edell, Celeste 12
Edelman, Lily (Judith) 1915-1981 22
Edelson, Edward 1932- 51
Edens, Cooper 1945- 166
  Earlier sketches in SATA 49, 112
Edens, (Bishop) David 1926- 39
Edey, Maitland A(rmstrong) 1910-1992 25
  Obituary 71
Edgeworth, Maria 1768-1849 21
Edgy, Wardore
  See Gorey, Edward (St. John)
Edison, Theodore
  See Stratemeyer, Edward L.
Edler, Tim(othy) 1948- 56
Edmiston, Jim 1948- 80
Edmonds, I(vy) G(ordon) 1917- 8
Edmonds, Walter D(umaux) 1903-1998 27
  Obituary 99
  Earlier sketch in SATA 1
  See also SAAS 4
Edmund, Sean
  See Pringle, Laurence P(atrick)
Edsall, Marian (Stickney) 1920- 8
Edwards, Al
  See Nourse, Alan E(dward)
Edwards, Anne 1927- 35
Edwards, Audrey 1947- 52
  Brief entry 31
Edwards, Becky (Jane) 1966- 125

Edwards, Bertram
  See Edwards, Herbert Charles
Edwards, Bronwen Elizabeth
  See Rose, Wendy
Edwards, Cecile Pepin 1916- 25
Edwards, Dorothy 1914-1982 88
  Obituary 31
  Earlier sketch in SATA 4
Edwards, F. E.
  See Nolan, William F(rancis)
Edwards, Frank B. 1952- 93
Edwards, Gunvor 32
Edwards, Harvey 1929- 5
Edwards, Hazel (Eileen) 1945- 135
Edwards, Herbert Charles 1912- 12
Edwards, Jane Campbell 1932- 10
Edwards, Julia
  See Stratemeyer, Edward L.
Edwards, Julie
  See Andrews, Julie
Edwards, Julie Andrews
  See Andrews, Julie
Edwards, Linda Strauss 1948- 49
  Brief entry 42
Edwards, Michelle 1955- 152
  Earlier sketch in SATA 70
Edwards, Monica le Doux Newton
  1912-1998 12
Edwards, Olwen
  See Gater, Dilys
Edwards, Page (Lawrence, Jr.) 1941-1999 ... 59
Edwards, R. T.
  See Goulart, Ron(ald Joseph)
Edwards, Sally (Cary) 1929- 7
Edwards, Samuel
  See Gerson, Noel Bertram
Edwards, Wallace 1957(?)- 170
Egan, E(dward) W(elstead) 1922- 35
Egan, Kerry 175
Egan, Lorraine Hopping 1960- 134
  Earlier sketch in SATA 91
Egan, Tim 1957- 155
  Earlier sketch in SATA 89
Egermeier, Elsie E(milie) 1890-1986 65
Eggenberger, David 1918- 6
Eggleston, Edward 1837-1902 27
Egielski, Richard 1952- 163
  Earlier sketches in SATA 11, 49, 106
Egypt, Ophelia Settle 1903-1984 16
  Obituary 38
Ehlert, Lois 1934- 172
  Earlier sketches in SATA 35, 69, 128
  See also CLR 28
Ehlert, Lois Jane
  See Ehlert, Lois
Ehling, Katalin Olah 1941- 93
Ehrenfreund, Norbert 1921- 86
Ehrlich, Amy 1942- 132
  Earlier sketches in SATA 25, 65, 96
Ehrlich, Bettina Bauer 1903-1985 1
Ehrlich, H. M.
  See Ziefert, Harriet
Eichenberg, Fritz 1901-1990 50
  Earlier sketch in SATA 9
Eichler, Margrit 1942- 35
Eichner, James A. 1927- 4
Eidson, Thomas 1944- 112
Eifert, Virginia (Louise) S(nider) 1911-1966 . 2
Eige, (Elizabeth) Lillian 1915- 65
Eiken, J. Melia 1967- 125
Einsel, Naiad 10
Einsel, Walter 1926- 10
Einzig, Susan 1922- 43
Eiseman, Alberta 1925- 15
Eisenberg, Azriel (Louis) 1903-1985 12
Eisenberg, Lisa 1949- 155
  Brief entry 50
  Earlier sketch in SATA 57
Eisenberg, Phyllis Rose 1924- 41
Eisner, Vivienne
  See Margolis, Vivienne

Eisner, Will 1917-2005 165
  Earlier sketch in SATA 31
Eisner, William Erwin
  See Eisner, Will
Eitzen, Allan 1928- 9
Eitzen, Ruth (Carper) 1924- 9
Ekwensi, C. O. D.
  See Ekwensi, Cyprian (Odiatu Duaka)
Ekwensi, Cyprian (Odiatu Duaka) 1921- ... 66
Elam, Richard M(ace, Jr.) 1920- 9
Elborn, Andrew
  See Clements, Andrew
  and Clements, Andrew
Elboz, Stephen 1956- 152
Eldin, Peter 1939- 154
Eldon, Kathy 1946- 107
Elfman, Blossom 1925- 8
Elgin, Kathleen 1923- 39
Elia
  See Lamb, Charles
Eliot, A. D.
  See Jewett, (Theodora) Sarah Orne
Eliot, Alice
  See Jewett, (Theodora) Sarah Orne
Eliot, Anne
  See Cole, Lois Dwight
Eliot, Dan
  See Silverberg, Robert
Elish, Dan 1960- 129
  Earlier sketch in SATA 68
Elisha, Ron 1951- 104
Elkin, Benjamin 1911-1995 3
Elkins, Dov Peretz 1937- 5
Ellacott, S(amuel) E(rnest) 1911- 19
Elleman, Barbara 1934- 147
Ellen, Jaye
  See Nixon, Joan Lowery
Eller, Scott
  See Holinger, William (Jacques)
  and Shepard, Jim
Ellestad, Myrvin H. 1921- 120
Elliot, David 1952- 122
Elliott, Bruce
  See Field, Edward
Elliott, David 1952- 163
Elliott, Don
  See Silverberg, Robert
Elliott, Elizabeth Shippen Green
  See Green, Elizabeth Shippen
Elliott, Janice 1931-1995 119
Elliott, Joey
  See Houk, Randy
Elliott, Louise 111
Elliott, Odette 1939- 75
Elliott, Patricia 1946- 176
Elliott, Sarah M(cCarn) 1930- 14
Elliott, (Robert) Scott 1970- 153
Elliott, William
  See Bradbury, Ray
Ellis, (Mary) Amabel (Nassau Strachey)
  Williams
  See Williams-Ellis, (Mary) Amabel (Nassau
  Strachey)
Ellis, Anyon
  See Rowland-Entwistle, (Arthur) Theodore
  (Henry)
Ellis, Deborah 1960- 129
Ellis, E. S.
  See Ellis, Edward S(ylvester)
Ellis, Edward S(ylvester) 1840-1916
  See YABC 1
Ellis, Ella Thorp 1928- 127
  Earlier sketch in SATA 7
  See also SAAS 9
Ellis, Harry Bearse 1921-2004 9
Ellis, Herbert
  See Wilson, Lionel
Ellis, Mel(vin Richard) 1912-1984 7
  Obituary 39
Ellis, Richard 1938- 130

Ellis, Sarah 1952- 179
  Earlier sketches in SATA 68, 131
  See also CLR 42
Ellison, Emily 114
Ellison, Lucile Watkins 1907(?)-1979 50
  Obituary 22
Ellison, Virginia H(owell) 1910- 4
Ellsberg, Edward 1891-1983 7
Ellsworth, Mary Ellen (Tressel) 1940- 146
Elmer, Robert 1958- 154
  Earlier sketch in SATA 99
Elmore, (Carolyn) Patricia 1933- 38
  Brief entry 35
El-Moslimany, Ann P(axton) 1937- 90
Elspeth
  See Bragdon, Elspeth MacDuffie
Elster, Jean Alicia 1953- 150
Elting, Mary 1906- 88
  Earlier sketch in SATA 2
  See also SAAS 20
Elvgren, Jennifer Riesmeyer 179
Elwart, Joan Potter 1927- 2
Elwood, Ann 1931- 55
  Brief entry 52
Elwood, Roger 1943-2007 58
Elya, Susan M(iddleton) 1955- 159
  Earlier sketch in SATA 106
Elzbieta 88
Emberley, Barbara A(nne) 1932- 146
  Earlier sketches in SATA 8, 70
  See also CLR 5
Emberley, Ed(ward Randolph) 1931- 146
  Earlier sketches in SATA 8, 70
  See also CLR 81
Emberley, Michael 1960- 119
  Earlier sketches in SATA 34, 80
Embry, Margaret Jacob 1919-1975 5
Emecheta, Buchi 1944- 66
Emecheta, Florence Onye Buchi
  See Emecheta, Buchi
Emerson, Alice B. 67
  Earlier sketch in SATA 1
  See Benson, Mildred (Augustine Wirt)
Emerson, Kathy Lynn 1947- 63
Emerson, Ru 1944- 107
  Earlier sketch in SATA 70
Emerson, Sally 1952- 111
Emerson, William K(eith) 1925- 25
Emert, Phyllis R(aybin) 1947- 93
Emery, Anne (McGuigan) 1907- 33
  Earlier sketch in SATA 1
Emmens, Carol Ann 1944- 39
Emmett, Jonathan 1965- 138
Emory, Jerry 1957- 96
Emrich, Duncan (Black Macdonald)
  1908-1970(?) 11
Emshwiller, Carol 1921- 174
  Autobiography Feature 174
Emshwiller, Carol Fries
  See Emshwiller, Carol
Emslie, M. L.
  See Simpson, Myrtle L(illias)
Ende, Michael (Andreas Helmuth)
  1929-1995 130
  Brief entry 42
  Obituary 86
  Earlier sketch in SATA 61
  See also CLR 14
Enderle, Dotti 1954- 145
Enderle, Judith (Ann) Ross 1941- 89
  Autobiography Feature 114
  Earlier sketch in SATA 38
  See also SAAS 26
Enell, Trinka (Gochenour) 1951- 79
Enfield, Carrie
  See Smith, Susan Vernon
Engdahl, Sylvia Louise 1933- 4
  Autobiography Feature 122
  See also CLR 2
  See also SAAS 5
Engel, Diana 1947- 70

Engelbreit, Mary 1952- 169
Engelhart, Margaret S. 1924- 59
Engelmann, Kim (V.) 1959- 87
England, George Allan 1877-1936 102
Englart, Mindi Rose 1965- 146
Engle, Eloise 9
  See Paananen, Eloise (Katherine)
Englebert, Victor 1933- 8
English, James W(ilson) 1915- 37
Engstrom, Elizabeth 1951- 110
Enright, D(ennis) J(oseph) 1920-2002 25
  Obituary 140
Enright, Elizabeth (Wright) 1909-1968 9
  See also CLR 4
Ensor, Robert (T.) 1922- 93
Entwistle, (Arthur) Theodore (Henry) Rowland
  See Rowland-Entwistle, (Arthur) Theodore
  (Henry)
Enys, Sarah L.
  See Sloggett, Nellie
Epanya, Christian A(rthur Kingue) 1956- 91
Ephraim, Shelly S(chonebaum) 1952- 97
Ephron, Delia 1944- 65
  Brief entry 50
Epler, Doris M. 1928- 73
Epp, Margaret A(gnes) 1913- 20
Epple, Anne Orth 1927- 20
Epstein, Anne Merrick 1931- 20
Epstein, Beryl (M. Williams) 1910- 31
  Earlier sketch in SATA 1
  See also CLR 26
  See also SAAS 17
Epstein, Perle S(herry) 1938- 27
Epstein, Rachel S. 1941- 102
Epstein, Samuel 1909-2000 31
  Earlier sketch in SATA 1
  See also CLR 26
  See also SAAS 17
Erdman, Loula Grace 1905(?)-1976 1
Erdoes, Richard 1912- 33
  Brief entry 28
Erdrich, Karen Louise
  See Erdrich, Louise
Erdrich, Louise 1954- 141
  Earlier sketch in SATA 94
Erickson, Betty J. 1923- 97
Erickson, Betty Jean
  See Erickson, Betty J.
Erickson, John R. 1943- 136
  Earlier sketch in SATA 70
Erickson, Jon 1948- 141
Erickson, Phoebe 59
Erickson, Russell E(verett) 1932- 27
Erickson, Sabra Rollins 1912-1995 35
Erickson, Walter
  See Fast, Howard
Ericson, Walter
  See Fast, Howard
Ericsson, Jennifer A. 170
Erikson, Mel 1937- 31
Ering, Timothy Basil 176
Erlanger, Baba
  See Trahey, Jane
Erlbach, Arlene 1948- 160
  Earlier sketches in SATA 78, 115
Erlich, Lillian (Feldman) 1910-1983 10
Ermatinger, James W. 1959- 170
Ernst, (Lyman) John 1940- 39
Ernst, Kathleen A. 1959- 162
Ernst, Kathryn (Fitzgerald) 1942- 25
Ernst, Lisa Campbell 1957- 154
  Brief entry 44
  Earlier sketches in SATA 55, 95
Ervin, Janet Halliday 1923- 4
Erwin, Will
  See Eisner, Will
Esbaum, Jill 174
Esbensen, Barbara J(uster) 1925-1996 97
  Brief entry 53
  Earlier sketch in SATA 62
Eschbacher, Roger 160

Eseki, Bruno
　　See Mphahlele, Ezekiel
Eshmeyer, R. E. 29
　　See Eschmeyer, R(einhart) E(rnst)
Eskridge, Ann E. 1949- 84
Espeland, Pamela (Lee) 1951- 128
　　Brief entry 38
　　Earlier sketch in SATA 52
Espriella, Don Manuel Alvarez
　　See Southey, Robert
Espy, Willard R(ichardson) 1910-1999 38
　　Obituary 113
Essrig, Harry 1912- 66
Estep, Irene Compton 5
Esterl, Arnica 1933- 77
Estes, Eleanor (Ruth) 1906-1988 91
　　Obituary 56
　　Earlier sketch in SATA 7
　　See also CLR 70
Estoril, Jean
　　See Allan, Mabel Esther
Estrada, Pau 1961- 74
Etchemendy, Nancy 1952- 166
　　Earlier sketch in SATA 38
Etchemendy, Nancy Elise Howell
　　See Etchemendy, Nancy
Etchison, Birdie L(ee) 1937- 38
Etchison, Craig 1945- 133
Etherington, Frank 1945- 58
Ets, Marie Hall 1893-1984 2
　　See also CLR 33
Ettlinger, Doris 1950- 173
Eunson, (John) Dale 1904-2002 5
　　Obituary 132
Evan, Frances Y. 1951- 167
Evanoff, Vlad 1916- 59
Evans, Cambria 1981- 178
Evans, Douglas 1953- 144
　　Earlier sketch in SATA 93
Evans, Eva (Knox) 1905-1998 27
Evans, Freddi Williams 1957- 134
Evans, Greg 1947- 143
　　Earlier sketch in SATA 73
Evans, Hubert Reginald 1892-1986 118
　　Obituary 48
Evans, Katherine (Floyd) 1901-1964 5
Evans, Larry
　　See Evans, Laurence Chubb
Evans, Laurence Chubb 1939- 88
Evans, Lawrence Watt
　　See Watt-Evans, Lawrence
Evans, Mari 1923- 10
Evans, Mark 19
Evans, Nancy 1950- 65
Evans, Patricia Healy
　　See Carpenter, Patricia (Healy Evans)
Evans, (Alice) Pearl 1927- 83
Evans, Shirlee 1931- 58
Evans, Tabor
　　See Cameron, Lou
　　and Knott, William C(ecil, Jr.)
　　and Wallmann, Jeffrey M(iner)
　　and Whittington, Harry (Benjamin)
Evarts, Esther
　　See Benson, Sally
Evarts, Hal G., (Jr.) 1915-1989 6
Everett, Gail
　　See Hale, Arlene
Evernden, Margery 1916- 5
Eversole, Robyn 1971- 74
Eversole, Robyn H.
　　See Eversole, Robyn
Eversole, Robyn Harbert
　　See Eversole, Robyn
Evslin, Bernard 1922-1993 83
　　Brief entry 28
　　Obituary 77
　　Earlier sketch in SATA 45
Ewart, Claire 1958- 145
　　Earlier sketch in SATA 76

Ewen, David 1907-1985 4
　　Obituary 47
Ewing, Juliana (Horatia Gatty) 1841-1885 ... 16
　　See also CLR 78
Ewing, Kathryn 1921- 20
Eyerly, Jeannette (Hyde) 1908- 86
　　Earlier sketch in SATA 4
　　See also SAAS 10
Eyre, Dorothy
　　See McGuire, Leslie (Sarah)
Eyre, Katherine Wigmore 1901-1970 26
Ezzell, Marilyn 1937- 42
　　Brief entry 38

F

Fabe, Maxene 1943- 15
Faber, Doris (Greenberg) 1924- 78
　　Earlier sketch in SATA 3
Faber, Harold 1919- 5
Fabre, Jean Henri (Casimir) 1823-1915 22
Facklam, Margery (Metz) 1927- 132
　　Earlier sketches in SATA 20, 85
Fadiman, Clifton (Paul) 1904-1999 11
　　Obituary 115
Fahs, Sophia Blanche Lyon 1876-1978 102
Fair, David 1952- 96
Fair, Sylvia 1933- 13
Fairfax-Lucy, Brian (Fulke Cameron-Ramsay)
　　1898-1974 6
　　Obituary 26
Fairfield, Flora
　　See Alcott, Louisa May
Fairman, Joan A(lexandra) 1935- 10
Faithfull, Gail 1936- 8
Falcone, L(ucy) M. 1951- 155
Falconer, Ian 1959- 179
　　Earlier sketch in SATA 125
　　See also CLR 90
Falconer, James
　　See Kirkup, James
Falconer, Lee N.
　　See May, Julian
Falkner, Leonard 1900-1977 12
Fall, Andrew
　　See Arthur, Robert, (Jr.)
Fall, Thomas
　　See Snow, Donald Clifford
Falls, C(harles) B(uckles) 1874-1960 38
　　Brief entry 27
Falstein, Louis 1909-1995 37
Fancher, Lou 1960- 177
Fanelli, Sara 1969- 126
　　Earlier sketch in SATA 89
Fanning, Leonard M(ulliken) 1888-1967 5
Faralla, Dana 1909- 9
Faralla, Dorothy W.
　　See Faralla, Dana
Farb, Peter 1929-1980 12
　　Obituary 22
Farber, Norma 1909-1984 75
　　Obituary 38
　　Earlier sketch in SATA 25
Farish, Terry 1947- 146
　　Earlier sketch in SATA 82
Farjeon, (Eve) Annabel 1919-2004 11
　　Obituary 153
Farjeon, Eleanor 1881-1965 2
　　See also CLR 34
Farley, Carol (J.) 1936- 137
　　Earlier sketch in SATA 4
Farley, Terri 165
Farley, Walter (Lorimer) 1915-1989 132
　　Earlier sketches in SATA 2, 43
Farlow, James O(rville, Jr.) 1951- 75
Farmer, Nancy 1941- 161
　　Earlier sketches in SATA 79, 117
Farmer, Patti 1948- 79

Farmer, Penelope (Jane) 1939- 105
　　Brief entry 39
　　Earlier sketch in SATA 40
　　See also CLR 8
　　See also SAAS 22
Farmer, Peter 1950- 38
Farmer, Philip Jose 1918- 93
Farnham, Burt
　　See Clifford, Harold B(urton)
Farnsworth, Bill 1958- 135
　　Earlier sketch in SATA 84
Farquhar, Margaret C(utting) 1905-1988 13
Farquharson, Alexander 1944- 46
Farquharson, Martha
　　See Finley, Martha
Farr, Diana (Pullein-Thompson) 82
　　See Pullein-Thompson, Diana
Farr, Finis (King) 1904-1982 10
Farrar, Jill
　　See Morris, Jill
Farrar, Susan Clement 1917- 33
Farrell, Ben
　　See Cebulash, Mel
Farrell, Patrick
　　See Odgers, Sally Farrell
Farrell, Sally
　　See Odgers, Sally Farrell
Farrer, Vashti 167
Farrington, S(elwyn) Kip, Jr. 1904-1983 20
Farshtey, Greg(ory T.) 1965- 148
Farthing, Alison 1936- 45
　　Brief entry 36
Farthing-Knight, Catherine 1933- 92
Fassler, Joan (Grace) 1931- 11
Fast, Howard 1914-2003 7
　　Autobiography Feature 107
Fast, Howard Melvin
　　See Fast, Howard
Fasulo, Michael 1963- 83
Fatchen, Max 1920- 84
　　Earlier sketch in SATA 20
　　See also SAAS 20
Fate, Marilyn
　　See Collins, Paul
Father Goose
　　See Ghigna, Charles
Fatigati, (Frances) Evelyn 1948- 24
Fatio, Louise 1904-1993 6
Faulhaber, Martha 1926- 7
Faulkner, Anne Irvin 1906- 23
Faulkner, Frank
　　See Ellis, Edward S(ylvester)
Faulkner, Nancy
　　See Faulkner, Anne Irvin
Faulknor, Cliff(ord Vernon) 1913- 86
Favole, Robert J(ames) 1950- 125
Fax, Elton Clay 1909-1993 25
Faxon, Lavinia
　　See Russ, Lavinia (Faxon)
Feagles, Anita M(acRae) 1927- 9
Feagles, Elizabeth
　　See Day, Beth (Feagles)
Feague, Mildred H. 1915- 14
Fearnley, Jan 1965- 153
Fearrington, Ann (Peyton) 1945- 146
Fecher, Constance
　　See Heaven, Constance (Christina)
Feder, Chris Welles 1938- 81
Feder, Harriet K. 1928- 73
Feder, Paula (Kurzband) 1935- 26
Federici, Debbie 1965- 175
Federici, Debbie Tanner
　　See Federici, Debbie
Feelings, Muriel (Lavita Grey) 1938- 16
　　See also CLR 5
　　See also SAAS 8
Feelings, Thomas 1933-2003 8
　　Obituary 148
　　See Feelings, Tom

Feelings, Tom 69
  See also CLR 58
  See also SAAS 19
  See Feelings, Thomas
Fehler, Gene 1940- 74
Fehrenbach, T(heodore) R(eed, Jr.) 1925- 33
Feiffer, Jules 1929- 157
  Earlier sketches in SATA 8, 61, 111
Feiffer, Jules Ralph
  See Feiffer, Jules
Feiffer, Kate 1964- 170
Feig, Barbara Krane 1937- 34
Feikema, Feike
  See Manfred, Frederick (Feikema)
Feil, Hila 1942- 12
Feilen, John
  See May, Julian
Feinberg, Barbara Jane 1938- 58
  See Feinberg, Barbara Silberdick
Feinberg, Barbara Silberdick 123
  See Feinberg, Barbara Jane
Feinstein, John 1956- 163
Feldman, Anne (Rodgers) 1939- 19
Feldman, Elane 79
Felix
  See Vincent, Felix
Fell, Derek 1939- 167
Fell, Derek John
  See Fell, Derek
Fellows, Muriel H. 10
Fellows, Stan 1957- 177
Fellows, Stanley
  See Fellows, Stan
Felsen, Henry Gregor 1916-1995 1
  See also SAAS 2
Feltenstein, Arlene (H.) 1934- 119
Felton, Harold William 1902-1991 1
Felton, Ronald Oliver 1909- 3
Felts, Shirley 1934- 33
Fenderson, Lewis H., Jr. 1907-1983 47
  Obituary 37
Fenner, Carol (Elizabeth) 1929-2002 89
  Obituary 132
  Earlier sketch in SATA 7
  See also SAAS 24
Fenner, Phyllis R(eid) 1899-1982 1
  Obituary 29
Fensham, Elizabeth 169
Fenten, Barbara D(oris) 1935- 26
Fenten, D(onald) X. 1932- 4
Fenton, Carroll Lane 1900-1969 5
Fenton, Edward 1917-1995 7
  Obituary 89
Fenton, Mildred Adams 1899-1995 21
Fenwick, Patti
  See Grider, Dorothy
Feravolo, Rocco Vincent 1922- 10
Ferber, Edna 1887-1968 7
Fergus, Charles 114
Ferguson, Alane 1957- 85
Ferguson, Bob
  See Ferguson, Robert Bruce
Ferguson, Cecil 1931- 45
Ferguson, Robert Bruce 1927-2001 13
Ferguson, Sarah 1959- 110
  Earlier sketch in SATA 66
Ferguson, Sarah Margaret
  See Ferguson, Sarah
Ferguson, Walter (W.) 1930- 34
Fergusson, Erna 1888-1964 5
Fermi, Laura 1907-1977 6
  Obituary 28
Fern, Eugene A. 1919-1987 10
  Obituary 54
Fernandes, Eugenie 1943- 139
  Earlier sketch in SATA 77
Fernandez, Laura 1960- 171
Ferrari, Maria 123
Ferreiro, Carmen 1958- 158
Ferrell, Nancy Warren 1932- 70

Ferrier, Lucy
  See Penzler, Otto
Ferris, Helen Josephine 1890-1969 21
Ferris, James Cody 1
  See McFarlane, Leslie (Charles)
Ferris, Jean 1939- 149
  Brief entry 50
  Earlier sketches in SATA 56, 105
Ferris, Jeri Chase 1937- 84
Ferry, Charles 1927- 92
  Earlier sketch in SATA 43
  See also CLR 34
  See also SAAS 20
Fetz, Ingrid 1915- 30
Feydy, Anne Lindbergh
  Brief entry 32
  See Sapieyevski, Anne Lindbergh
Fiammenghi, Gioia 1929- 66
  Earlier sketch in SATA 9
Fiarotta, Noel 15
  See Ficarotta, Noel
Fiarotta, Phyllis 15
  See Ficarotta, Phyllis
Fichter, George S. 1922-1993 7
Fidler, Kathleen (Annie) 1899-1980 87
  Obituary 45
  Earlier sketch in SATA 3
Fiedler, Jean(nette Feldman) 4
Fiedler, Joseph Daniel 159
Field, Dorothy 1944- 97
Field, Edward 1924- 109
  Earlier sketch in SATA 8
Field, Eugene 1850-1895 16
Field, Gans T.
  See Wellman, Manly Wade
Field, James 1959- 113
Field, Peter
  See Drago, Harry Sinclair
  and Dresser, Davis
  and Mann, E(dward) B(everly)
Field, Rachel (Lyman) 1894-1942 15
  See also CLR 21
Fielding, Kate
  See Oldfield, Jenny
Fienberg, Anna 1956- 112
Fife, Dale (Odile Hollerbach) 1901- 18
Fighter Pilot, A
  See Johnston, H(ugh) A(nthony) S(tephen)
Figler, Jeanie 1949- 123
Figley, Marty Rhodes 1948- 158
  Earlier sketch in SATA 88
Figueredo, D(anilo) H. 1951- 155
Figueroa, Pablo 1938- 9
Fijan, Carol 1918- 12
Filderman, Diane E(lizabeth) 1959- 87
Files, Meg 1946- 107
Fillmore, Parker H(oysted) 1878-1944
  See YABC 1
Filstrup, Chris
  See Filstrup, E(dward) Christian
Filstrup, E(dward) Christian 1942- 43
Finchler, Judy 1943- 93
Finder, Martin
  See Salzmann, Siegmund
Findlay, Jamieson 1958- 169
Findon, Joanne 1957- 161
Fine, Anne 1947- 160
  Earlier sketches in SATA 29, 72, 111
  See also CLR 25
  See also SAAS 15
Fine, Edith Hope 169
Fine, Jane
  See Ziefert, Harriet
Finger, Charles J(oseph) 1869(?)-1941 42
Fink, William B(ertrand) 1916- 22
Finke, Blythe Foote 1922- 26
Finkel, George (Irvine) 1909-1975 8
Finkelstein, Norman H. 1941- 137
  Earlier sketch in SATA 73
Finlay, Alice Sullivan 1946- 82

Finlay, Winifred Lindsay Crawford
  (McKissack) 1910-1989 23
Finlayson, Ann 1925- 8
Finley, Martha 1828-1909 43
Finley, Mary Peace 1942- 83
Finney, Jack 109
  See Finney, Walter Braden
Finney, Patricia 1958- 163
Finney, Shan 1944- 65
Firer, Ben Zion
  See Firer, Benzion
Firer, Benzion 1914- 64
Fireside, Bryna J. 1932- 73
Firmin, Charlotte 1954- 29
Firmin, Peter 1928- 58
  Earlier sketch in SATA 15
Firth, Barbara 179
Fischbach, Julius 1894-1988 10
Fischer, John
  See Fluke, Joanne
Fischer, R.J.
  See Fluke, Joanne
Fischer-Nagel, Andreas 1951- 56
Fischer-Nagel, Heiderose 1956- 56
Fischler, Shirley (Walton) 66
Fischler, Stan(ley I.) 66
  Brief entry 36
Fisher, Aileen (Lucia) 1906-2002 73
  Obituary 143
  Earlier sketches in SATA 1, 25
  See also CLR 49
Fisher, Barbara 1940- 44
  Brief entry 34
Fisher, Carolyn 1968- 154
Fisher, Catherine 1957- 155
Fisher, Chris 1958- 80
Fisher, Clavin C(argill) 1912- 24
Fisher, Dorothy (Frances) Canfield 1879-1958
  See YABC 1
  See also CLR 71
Fisher, Gary L. 1949- 86
Fisher, John (Oswald Hamilton) 1909- 15
Fisher, Laura Harrison 1934- 5
Fisher, Leonard Everett 1924- 176
  Autobiography Feature 122
  Earlier sketches in SATA 4, 34, 73, 120
  See also CLR 18
  See also SAAS 1
Fisher, Lois I. 1948- 38
  Brief entry 35
Fisher, Margery (Turner) 1913-1992 20
  Obituary 74
Fisher, Marshall Jon 1963- 113
Fisher, Nikki
  See Strachan, Ian
Fisher, Robert (Tempest) 1943- 47
Fisher, Suzanne
  See Staples, Suzanne Fisher
Fisher, Valorie 177
Fishman, Cathy Goldberg 1951- 106
Fisk, Nicholas 25
  See Higginbottom, David
Fisk, Pauline 1948- 160
  Earlier sketch in SATA 66
Fiske, Tarleton
  See Bloch, Robert (Albert)
Fisscher, Catharina G. M. 1958- 142
Fisscher, Tiny
  See Fisscher, Catharina G. M.
Fitch, Clarke
  See Sinclair, Upton
Fitch, John IV
  See Cormier, Robert
Fitch, Sheree 1956- 178
  Earlier sketch in SATA 108
Fitschen, Dale 1937- 20
Fitzalan, Roger
  See Trevor, Elleston
Fitzgerald, Captain Hugh
  See Baum, L(yman) Frank
Fitzgerald, Dawn 175

Fitzgerald, Edward Earl 1919-2001 20
Fitzgerald, F(rancis) A(nthony) 1940- 15
Fitzgerald, John D(ennis) 1907(?)-1988 20
  Obituary 56
  See also CLR *1*
Fitzgerald, Merni Ingrassia 1955- 53
Fitzgibbon, Terry 1948- 121
Fitzhardinge, Joan Margaret 1912- 73
  Earlier sketch in SATA *2*
  See Phipson, Joan
Fitzhugh, Louise (Perkins) 1928-1974 45
  Obituary 24
  Earlier sketch in SATA *1*
  See also CLR *72*
Fitzhugh, Percy Keese 1876-1950 65
Fitzpatrick, Marie-Louise 1962- 125
FitzRalph, Matthew
  See McInerny, Ralph
Fitz-Randolph, Jane (Currens) 1915- 51
Fitzsimons, Cecilia 1952- 97
Fitzsimons, Cecilia A.L.
  See Fitzsimons, Cecilia
Flack, Marjorie 1897-1958 100
  See also YABC *2*
  See also CLR *28*
Flack, Naomi John White -1999 40
  Brief entry 35
Flake, Sharon G. 166
Flannery, Kate
  See De Goldi, Kathleen Domenica
Flatt, Lizann
  See Brunskill, Elizabeth Ann Flatt
Fleagle, Gail S(hatto) 1940- 117
Fleetwood, Jenni 1947- 80
Fleischer, Jane
  See Oppenheim, Joanne
Fleischhauer-Hardt, Helga 1936- 30
Fleischman, Albert Sidney
  See Fleischman, Sid
Fleischman, John 1948- 145
Fleischman, Paul 1952- 156
  Brief entry 32
  Earlier sketches in SATA *39, 72, 110*
  See also CLR *66*
  See also SAAS *20*
Fleischman, Sid 1920- 148
  Earlier sketches in SATA *8, 59, 96*
  See also CLR *15*
Fleischner, Jennifer 1956- 93
Fleisher, Paul 1948- 132
  Earlier sketch in SATA *81*
Fleisher, Robbin 1951-1977 52
  Brief entry 49
Fleishman, Seymour 1918- 66
  Brief entry 32
Fleming, A. A.
  See Arthur, Robert, (Jr.)
Fleming, Alice Mulcahey 1928- 9
Fleming, Candace 1962- 143
  Earlier sketch in SATA *94*
Fleming, Denise 1950- 173
  Earlier sketches in SATA *81, 126*
Fleming, Ian 1908-1964 9
Fleming, Ian Lancaster
  See Fleming, Ian
Fleming, Ronald Lee 1941- 56
Fleming, Sally
  See Walker, Sally M(acArt)
Fleming, Stuart
  See Knight, Damon (Francis)
Fleming, Susan 1932- 32
Fleming, Thomas 1927- 8
Fleming, Thomas James
  See Fleming, Thomas
Fleming, Virginia (Edwards) 1923- 84
Flesch, Y.
  See Flesch, Yolande (Catarina)
Flesch, Yolande (Catarina) 1950- 55
Fletcher, Charlie May Hogue 1897-1977 3
Fletcher, Colin 1922-2007 28

Fletcher, Dirk
  See Cunningham, Chet
Fletcher, George U.
  See Pratt, (Murray) Fletcher
Fletcher, Helen Jill 1910- 13
Fletcher, Ralph (J.) 1953- 149
  Earlier sketch in SATA *105*
  See also CLR *104*
Fletcher, Susan (Clemens) 1951- 110
  Earlier sketch in SATA *70*
Fleur, Paul
  See Pohl, Frederik
Flexner, James Thomas 1908-2003 9
Flinn, Alex 1966- 159
Flint, Helen 1952- 102
Flint, Russ 1944- 74
Flitner, David P(erkins), Jr. 1949- 7
Floca, Brian 155
Floethe, Louise Lee 1913-1988 4
Floethe, Richard 1901-1998 4
Floherty, John Joseph 1882-1964 25
Flood, Bo
  See Flood, Nancy Bo
Flood, Nancy Bo 1945- 130
Flood, Pansie Hart 1964- 140
Flood, William 1942- 129
Flooglebuckle, Al
  See Spiegelman, Art
Flora, James (Royer) 1914-1998 30
  Obituary 103
  Earlier sketch in SATA *1*
  See also SAAS *6*
Florian, Douglas 1950- 177
  Earlier sketches in SATA *19, 83, 125*
Flory, Jane Trescott 1917- 22
Flournoy, Valerie 1952- 95
Flournoy, Valerie Rose
  See Flournoy, Valerie
Flowerdew, Phyllis -1994 33
Flowers, Pam 1946- 136
Flowers, Sarah 1952- 98
Floyd, Gareth 1940- 62
  Brief entry 31
Fluchere, Henri 1914-1991 40
Fluke, Joanne 88
Flutsztejn-Gruda, Ilona 1930- 170
Flynn, Barbara 1928- 9
Flynn, Jackson
  See Bensen, Donald R.
  and Shirreffs, Gordon D(onald)
Flynn, Nicholas
  See Odgers, Sally Farrell
Flynn, Rachel 1953- 171
  Earlier sketch in SATA *109*
Flynn, Warren (G.) 1950- 154
Fodor, R(onald) V(ictor) 1944- 25
Fogelin, Adrian 1951- 175
  Earlier sketch in SATA *129*
Foley, (Anna) Bernice Williams 1902-1987 . 28
Foley, June 1944- 44
Foley, (Mary) Louise Munro 1933- 106
  Brief entry 40
  Earlier sketch in SATA *54*
Folke, Will
  See Bloch, Robert (Albert)
Folsom, Franklin (Brewster) 1907-1995 5
  Obituary 88
Folsom, Michael (Brewster) 1938-1990 40
  Obituary 88
Fontenot, Mary Alice 1910- 91
  Earlier sketch in SATA *34*
Fontes, Justine 172
Foon, Dennis 1951- 119
Fooner, Michael 22
Foote, Timothy (Gilson) 1926- 52
Forberg, Ati 22
Forberg, Beate Gropius
  See Forberg, Ati
Forbes, Anna 1954- 101
Forbes, Bryan 1926- 37
Forbes, Cabot L.
  See Hoyt, Edwin P(almer), Jr.

Forbes, Esther 1891-1967 100
  Earlier sketch in SATA *2*
  See also CLR *27*
Forbes, Graham B. 1
Forbes, Kathryn
  See McLean, Kathryn (Anderson)
Forbes, Robert
  See Arthur, Robert, (Jr.)
Ford, Albert Lee
  See Stratemeyer, Edward L.
Ford, Barbara 56
  Brief entry 34
Ford, Brian J(ohn) 1939- 49
Ford, Carolyn (Mott) 1938- 98
Ford, Christine 1953- 176
Ford, Elbur
  See Hibbert, Eleanor Alice Burford
Ford, Ellen 1949- 89
Ford, George (Jr.) 31
Ford, Hilary
  See Youd, (Christopher) Samuel
Ford, Hildegarde
  See Morrison, Velma Ford
Ford, Jerome W. 1949- 78
Ford, Jerry
  See Ford, Jerome W.
Ford, Juwanda G(ertrude) 1967- 102
Ford, Marcia
  See Radford, Ruby L(orraine)
Ford, Peter 1936- 59
Ford, S. M.
  See Uhlig, Susan
Forde, Catherine 1961- 170
Foreman, Michael 1938- 135
  Earlier sketches in SATA *2, 73, 129*
  See also CLR *32*
  See also SAAS *21*
Foreman, Wilmoth 1939- 153
Forest, Dial
  See Gault, William Campbell
Forest, Heather 1948- 120
Forester, C(ecil) S(cott) 1899-1966 13
Forman, Brenda 1936- 4
Forman, James
  See Forman, James D(ouglas)
Forman, James D(ouglas) 1932- 70
  Earlier sketch in SATA *8*
Forrest, Elizabeth
  See Salsitz, Rhondi Vilott
Forrest, Mary
  See Pausacker, Jenny
Forrest, Sybil
  See Markun, Patricia Maloney
Forrestal, Elaine 1941- 165
  Earlier sketch in SATA *117*
Forrester, Helen 48
  See Bhatia, Jamunadevi
Forrester, Jade
  See Pausacker, Jenny
Forrester, Marian
  See Schachtel, Roger
Forrester, Sandra 1949- 166
  Earlier sketch in SATA *90*
Forrester, Victoria 1940- 40
  Brief entry 35
Forsee, (Frances) Aylesa -1986 1
Forsey, Chris 1950- 59
Forshay-Lunsford, Cin 1965- 60
Forster, E(dward) M(organ) 1879-1970 57
Forsyth, Kate 1966- 154
Fort, Paul
  See Stockton, Francis Richard
Forte, Maurizio 1961- 110
Fortey, Richard (Alan) 1946- 109
Forth, Melissa D(eal) 96
Fortnum, Peggy 26
  See Nuttall-Smith, Margaret Emily Noel
Forward, Robert L(ull) 1932-2002 82
Foster, Alan Dean 1946- 70
Foster, Brad W. 1955- 34
Foster, Doris Van Liew 1899-1993 10

Foster, E(lizabeth) C(onnell) 1902- 9
Foster, Elizabeth 1902- 12
Foster, Elizabeth 1905-1963 10
Foster, F. Blanche 1919- 11
Foster, G(eorge) Allen 1907-1969 26
Foster, Genevieve (Stump) 1893-1979 2
   Obituary 23
   See also CLR 7
Foster, Hal
   See Foster, Harold (Rudolf)
Foster, Harold (Rudolf) 1892-1982 31
   See Foster, Hal
Foster, Jeanne
   See Williams, Jeanne
Foster, John
   See Foster, John L(ouis)
   and Furcolo, Foster
Foster, John (Thomas) 1925- 8
Foster, John L(ouis) 1941- 102
Foster, Laura Louise (James) 1918- 6
Foster, Leila Merrell 1929- 73
Foster, Lynne 1937- 74
Foster, Marian Curtis 1909-1978 23
Foster, Sally 58
Foulds, E. V.
   See Foulds, Elfrida Vipont
Foulds, Elfrida Vipont 1902-1992 52
   See Vipont, Elfrida
Fourie, Corlia 1944- 91
Fourth Brother, The
   See Aung, (Maung) Htin
Fowke, Edith (Margaret) 1913-1996 14
Fowles, John 1926-2005 22
   Obituary 171
Fowles, John Robert
   See Fowles, John
Fox, Aileen 1907-2005 58
   Obituary 170
Fox, Aileen Mary
   See Fox, Aileen
Fox, Annie 1950- 175
Fox, Charles Philip 1913-2003 12
   Obituary 150
Fox, Eleanor
   See St. John, Wylly Folk
Fox, Freeman
   See Hamilton, Charles (Harold St. John)
Fox, Geoffrey 1941- 73
Fox, Grace
   See Anderson, Grace Fox
Fox, Larry 30
Fox, Lorraine 1922-1976 27
   Earlier sketch in SATA 11
Fox, Louisa
   See Kroll, Virginia L.
Fox, Mary Virginia 1919- 152
   Brief entry 39
   Earlier sketches in SATA 44, 88
Fox, Mem 103
   See also CLR 23
   See Fox, Merrion Frances
Fox, Merrion Frances 1946- 155
   Earlier sketch in SATA 51
   See also CLR 80
   See Fox, Mem
Fox, Michael W(ilson) 1937- 15
Fox, Paula 1923- 167
   Earlier sketches in SATA 17, 60, 120
   See also CLR 96
Fox, Robert J. 1927- 33
Fradin, Dennis
   See Fradin, Dennis Brindell
Fradin, Dennis Brindell 1945- 135
   Earlier sketches in SATA 29, 90
Fradin, Judith (Bernette) Bloom 1945- 152
   Earlier sketch in SATA 90
Frailey, Paige (Menefee) 1965- 82
Frame, Janet
   See Clutha, Janet Paterson Frame

Frame, Paul 1913-1994 60
   Brief entry 33
   Obituary 83
Frances, Miss
   See Horwich, Frances R(appaport)
Franchere, Ruth 18
Francis, Charles
   See Holme, Bryan
Francis, Dee
   See Haas, Dorothy F.
Francis, Dorothy Brenner 1926- 127
   Earlier sketch in SATA 10
Francis, Jaye
   See Pausacker, Jenny
Francis, Pamela (Mary) 1926- 11
Franck, Eddie
   See Cooke, Frank E.
Franco, Betsy 150
Franco, Eloise (Bauder) 1910- 62
Franco, Johan (Henri Gustave) 1908-1988 ... 62
Franco, Marjorie 38
Francois, Andre 1915-2005 25
Francoise
   See Seignobosc, Francoise
Frank, Anne(lies Marie) 1929-1945 87
   Brief entry 42
   See also CLR 101
Frank, Daniel B. 1956- 55
Frank, Emily R.
   See Frank, E.R.
Frank, E.R. 1967- 157
Frank, Helene
   See Vautier, Ghislaine
Frank, Hillary 1976- 148
Frank, Josette 1893-1989 10
   Obituary 63
Frank, Lucy 1947- 166
   Earlier sketch in SATA 94
Frank, Mary 1933- 34
Frank, R., Jr.
   See Ross, Frank (Xavier), Jr.
Frankau, Mary Evelyn Atkinson 1899-1974 .. 4
Frankel, Alona 1937- 66
Frankel, Bernice 9
Frankel, Edward 1910- 44
Frankel, Ellen 1951- 78
Frankel, Julie 1947- 40
   Brief entry 34
Frankenberg, Robert 1911- 22
Franklin, Cheryl J. 1955- 70
Franklin, Harold 1926- 13
Franklin, Kristine L. 1958- 124
   Earlier sketch in SATA 80
Franklin, Lance
   See Lantz, Francess L(in)
Franklin, Max
   See Deming, Richard
Franklin, Steve
   See Stevens, Franklin
Franson, Leanne R. 1963- 111
Franzen, Nils-Olof 1916- 10
Frascino, Edward 48
   Brief entry 33
   See also SAAS 9
Frasconi, Antonio 1919- 131
   Earlier sketches in SATA 6, 53
   See also SAAS 11
Fraser, Betty
   See Fraser, Elizabeth Marr
Fraser, Elizabeth Marr 1928- 31
Fraser, Eric (George) 1902-1983 38
Fraser, Mary Ann 1959- 137
   Earlier sketch in SATA 76
   See also SAAS 23
Fraser, Wynnette (McFaddin) 1925- 90
Frasier, Debra 1953- 112
   Earlier sketch in SATA 69
Fraustino, Lisa Rowe 1961- 146
   Autobiography Feature 146
   Earlier sketch in SATA 84

Frazee, Marla 1958- 151
   Earlier sketch in SATA 105
Frazetta, Frank 1928- 58
Frazier, Craig 1955- 177
Frazier, Neta (Osborn) Lohnes 1890-1990 7
Frederic, Mike
   See Cox, William R(obert)
Fredericks, Anthony D. 1947- 113
Freed, Alvyn M. 1913-1993 22
Freedman, Benedict 1919- 27
Freedman, Jeff 1953- 90
Freedman, Nancy 1920- 27
Freedman, Russell 1929- 175
   Earlier sketches in SATA 16, 71, 123
   See also CLR 71
Freedman, Russell Bruce
   See Freedman, Russell
Freeman, Barbara C(onstance) 1906- 28
Freeman, Bill
   See Freeman, William Bradford
Freeman, Don 1908-1978 17
   See also CLR 90
Freeman, Ira Maximilian 1905-1987 21
Freeman, Lucy (Greenbaum) 1916-2004 24
Freeman, Mae (Blacker) 1907- 25
Freeman, Marcia S. 1937- 102
Freeman, Martha 1956- 152
   Earlier sketch in SATA 101
Freeman, Nancy 1932- 61
Freeman, Peter J.
   See Calvert, Patricia
Freeman, Sarah (Caroline) 1940- 66
Freeman, Tor 1977- 164
Freeman, VicToria
   See Freeman, Tor
Freeman, William Bradford 1938- 58
   Brief entry 48
Fregosi, Claudia (Anne Marie) 1946- 24
French, Allen 1870-1946
   See YABC 1
French, Dorothy Kayser 1926- 5
French, Fiona 1944- 132
   Earlier sketches in SATA 6, 75
   See also CLR 37
   See also SAAS 21
French, Jackie 139
   Autobiography Feature 139
   Earlier sketch in SATA 108
   See French, Jacqueline Anne
French, Kathryn
   See Mosesson, Gloria R(ubin)
French, Martin 176
French, Michael 1944- 49
   Brief entry 38
French, Paul
   See Asimov, Isaac
French, Simon 1957- 147
   Earlier sketch in SATA 86
French, Vivian 165
Frenette, Liza 126
Freschet, Gina 1960- 175
   Earlier sketch in SATA 139
Frewer, Glyn (M.) 1931- 11
Frey, Darcy 98
Freymann, Saxton 1958(?)- 178
Freymann-Weyr, (Rhoda) Garret (Michaela)
   1965- 145
Frick, C. H.
   See Irwin, Constance (H.) Frick
Frick, Constance
   See Irwin, Constance (H.) Frick
Fricke, Aaron 1962- 89
Fridell, Ron 1943- 124
Friedlander, Joanne K(ohn) 1930- 9
Friedman, Debra 1955- 150
Friedman, Estelle (Ehrenwald) 1920- 7
Friedman, Frieda 1905- 43
Friedman, Ina R(osen) 1926- 136
   Brief entry 41
   Earlier sketch in SATA 49

Friedman, Jerrold David
  See Gerrold, David
Friedman, Judi 1935- *59*
Friedman, Laurie 1964- *179*
  Earlier sketch in SATA *138*
Friedman, Marvin 1930- *42*
  Brief entry *33*
Friedman, Robin 1968- *162*
Friedmann, Stan 1953- *80*
Friedrich, Otto (Alva) 1929-1995 .... *33*
Friedrich, Priscilla 1927- *39*
Friendlich, Dick
  See Friendlich, Richard J.
Friendlich, Richard J. 1909- *11*
Friermood, Elisabeth Hamilton 1903-1992 .... *5*
Friesen, Bernice (Sarah Anne) 1966- *105*
Friesen, Gayle 1960- *109*
Friesner, Esther M. 1951- *168*
  Earlier sketch in SATA *71*
Friis-Baastad, Babbis Ellinor 1921-1970 .... *7*
Frimmer, Steven 1928- *31*
Frischmuth, Barbara 1941- *114*
Friskey, Margaret (Richards) 1901-1995 .... *5*
Fritts, Mary Bahr
  See Bahr, Mary (Madelyn)
Fritz, Jean (Guttery) 1915- *163*
  Autobiography Feature *122*
  Earlier sketches in SATA *1, 29, 72, 119*
  See also CLR *96*
  See also SAAS *2*
Froehlich, Margaret W(alden) 1930- *56*
Frois, Jeanne 1953- *73*
Froissart, Jean 1338(?)-1410(?) *28*
Froman, Elizabeth Hull 1920-1975 .... *10*
Froman, Robert (Winslow) 1917- *8*
Fromm, Lilo 1928- *29*
Frommer, Harvey 1937- *41*
Frost, A(rthur) B(urdett) 1851-1928 .... *19*
Frost, Elizabeth
  See Frost-Knappman, Elizabeth
Frost, Erica
  See Supraner, Robyn
Frost, Helen 1949- *157*
Frost, Lesley 1899-1983 .... *14*
  Obituary *34*
Frost, Robert 1874-1963 .... *14*
  See also CLR *67*
Frost, Robert Lee
  See Frost, Robert
Frost, Shelley 1960- *138*
Frost-Knappman, Elizabeth 1943- *179*
Froud, Brian 1947- *150*
Fry, Annette R(iley) *89*
Fry, Christopher 1907-2005 .... *66*
Fry, Edward Bernard 1925- *35*
Fry, Rosalie Kingsmill 1911-1992 .... *3*
  See also SAAS *11*
Fry, Virginia Lynn 1952- *95*
Frye, Sally
  See Moore, Elaine
Fuchs, Bernie 1932- *162*
  Earlier sketch in SATA *95*
Fuchs, Erich 1916- *6*
Fuchshuber, Annegert 1940- *43*
Fuerst, Jeffrey B. 1956- *143*
Fuertes, Gloria 1918-1998 .... *115*
Fuge, Charles 1966- *144*
  Earlier sketch in SATA *74*
Fujikawa, Gyo 1908-1998 .... *76*
  Brief entry *30*
  Obituary *110*
  Earlier sketch in SATA *39*
  See also CLR *25*
  See also SAAS *16*
Fujita, Tamao 1905-1999 .... *7*
Fujiwara, Kim 1957- *81*
Fujiwara, Michiko 1946- *15*
Fuller, Catherine Leuthold 1916- *9*
Fuller, Edmund (Maybank) 1914- *21*
Fuller, Iola
  See McCoy, Iola Fuller

Fuller, John G(rant, Jr.) 1913-1990 .... *65*
Fuller, Kathleen
  See Gottfried, Theodore Mark
Fuller, Lois Hamilton 1915- *11*
Fuller, Margaret
  See Ossoli, Sarah Margaret (Fuller)
Fuller, Maud
  See Petersham, Maud (Sylvia Fuller)
Fuller, Roy (Broadbent) 1912-1991 .... *87*
Fuller, Sarah Margaret
  See Ossoli, Sarah Margaret (Fuller)
Fuller, Sarah Margaret
  See Ossoli, Sarah Margaret (Fuller)
Fults, John Lee 1932- *33*
Funk, Thompson 1911- *7*
Funk, Tom
  See Funk, Thompson
Funke, Cornelia 1958- *174*
  Earlier sketch in SATA *154*
Funke, Cornelia Caroline
  See Funke, Cornelia
Funke, Lewis 1912-1992 .... *11*
Fuqua, Jonathon Scott 1966- *141*
Furbee, Mary R.
  See Furbee, Mary Rodd
Furbee, Mary Rodd 1954- *138*
Furchgott, Terry 1948- *29*
Furlong, Monica (Mavis) 1930-2003 .... *86*
  Obituary *142*
Furman, Gertrude Lerner Kerman 1909- *21*
Furniss, Tim 1948- *49*
Furrow, Robert 1985- *172*
Furukawa, Toshi 1924- *24*
Fusillo, Archimede 1962- *137*
Futcher, Jane P. 1947- *76*
Fyleman, Rose (Amy) 1877-1957 .... *21*
Fyson, J(enny) G(race) 1904- *42*

G

Gaan, Margaret 1914- *65*
Gaber, Susan 1956- *169*
  Earlier sketch in SATA *115*
Gaberman, Judie Angell 1937- *78*
  Earlier sketch in SATA *22*
  See also CLR *33*
Gabhart, Ann 1947- *75*
Gabler, Mirko 1951- *77*
Gabriel, Adriana
  See Rojany, Lisa
Gabrys, Ingrid Schubert
  See Schubert-Gabrys, Ingrid
Gackenbach, Dick 1927- *79*
  Brief entry *30*
  Earlier sketch in SATA *48*
Gadd, Jeremy 1949- *116*
Gaddis, Vincent H. 1913-1997 .... *35*
Gadler, Steve J. 1905-1985 .... *36*
Gaeddert, Lou Ann (Bigge) 1931- *103*
  Earlier sketch in SATA *20*
Gaeddert, Louann
  See Gaeddert, Lou Ann (Bigge)
Gaer, Joseph 1897-1969 .... *118*
Gaer, Yossef
  See Gaer, Joseph
Gaetz, Dayle Campbell 1947- *138*
Gaffney, Timothy R. 1951- *170*
  Earlier sketch in SATA *69*
Gaffron, Norma (Bondeson) 1931- *97*
Gag, Wanda (Hazel) 1893-1946 .... *100*
  See also YABC *1*
  See also CLR *4*
Gage, Brian *162*
Gage, Wilson
  See Steele, Mary Q(uintard Govan)
Gagliano, Eugene M. 1946- *150*
Gagnon, Cecile 1936- *58*

Gaiman, Neil 1960- *146*
  Earlier sketch in SATA *85*
  See also CLR *109*
Gaiman, Neil Richard
  See Gaiman, Neil
Gainer, Cindy 1962- *74*
Gaines, Ernest J. 1933- *86*
  See also CLR *62*
Gaines, Ernest James
  See Gaines, Ernest J.
Gaither, Gloria 1942- *127*
Gal, Laszlo 1933- *96*
  Brief entry *32*
  Earlier sketch in SATA *52*
  See also CLR *61*
Galbraith, Kathryn O(sebold) 1945- *85*
Galdone, Paul 1907(?)-1986 .... *66*
  Obituary *49*
  Earlier sketch in SATA *17*
  See also CLR *16*
Galinsky, Ellen 1942- *23*
Gall, Chris 1961- *176*
Gallagher, Diana G. 1946- *153*
Gallagher, Lurlene Nora
  See McDaniel, Lurlene
Gallant, Roy A(rthur) 1924- *110*
  Earlier sketches in SATA *4, 68*
  See also CLR *30*
Gallardo, Evelyn 1948- *78*
Gallaz, Christophe 1948- *162*
Gallego Garcia, Laura 1977- *173*
Gallico, Paul (William) 1897-1976 .... *13*
Gallo, Donald R. 1938- *112*
  Autobiography Feature *104*
Gallo, Donald Robert
  See Gallo, Donald R.
Galloway, Owateka (S.) 1981- *121*
Galloway, Priscilla 1930- *112*
  Earlier sketch in SATA *66*
Gallup, Joan 1957- *128*
Galouchko, Annouchka Gravel 1960- *95*
Galt, Thomas Franklin, Jr. 1908-1989 .... *5*
Galt, Tom
  See Galt, Thomas Franklin, Jr.
Galvin, Matthew R. 1950- *93*
Galvin, Matthew Reppert
  See Galvin, Matthew R.
Gamble, Kim 1952- *124*
  Earlier sketch in SATA *81*
Gambrell, Jamey *82*
Gamerman, Martha 1941- *15*
Gammell, Stephen 1943- *128*
  Earlier sketches in SATA *53, 81*
  See also CLR *83*
Ganly, Helen (Mary) 1940- *56*
Gannett, Ruth Chrisman (Arens)
  1896-1979 .... *33*
Gannett, Ruth Stiles 1923- *3*
Gannon, Robert Haines 1931- *8*
Gano, Lila 1949- *76*
Gans, Roma 1894-1996 .... *45*
  Obituary *93*
Gant, Matthew
  See Hano, Arnold
Gantner, Susan (Verble) 1939- *63*
Gantos, Jack 1951- *169*
  Earlier sketches in SATA *20, 81, 119*
  See also CLR *85*
Gantos, John Bryan, Jr.
  See Gantos, Jack
Ganz, Yaffa 1938- *61*
  Brief entry *52*
Garafano, Marie 1942- *84*
Garant, Andre J. 1968- *123*
Garbe, Ruth Moore
  See Moore, Ruth (Ellen)
Garcia, Yolanda P. 1952- *113*
Garcia, Yolanda Pacheco
  See Garcia, Yolanda P.
Gard, Janice
  See Latham, Jean Lee

Gard, Joyce
   See Reeves, Joyce
Gard, Robert Edward 1910-1992 .... *18*
   Obituary *74*
Gardam, Jane (Mary) 1928- *130*
   Brief entry *28*
   Earlier sketches in SATA *39, 76*
   See also CLR *12*
   See also SAAS *9*
Gardella, Tricia 1944- *96*
Garden, Nancy 1938- *147*
   Autobiography Feature *147*
   Earlier sketches in SATA *12, 77, 114*
   See also CLR *51*
   See also SAAS *8*
Gardiner, John Reynolds 1944-2006 .... *64*
   Obituary *174*
Gardiner, Lindsey 1971- *144*
Gardner, Craig Shaw 1949- *99*
Gardner, Dic
   See Gardner, Richard (M.)
Gardner, Graham *159*
Gardner, Jane Mylum 1946- *83*
Gardner, Jeanne LeMonnier 1925- *5*
Gardner, John, Jr. 1933-1982 .... *40*
   Obituary *31*
Gardner, John Champlin, Jr.
   See Gardner, John, Jr.
Gardner, Martin 1914- *142*
   Earlier sketch in SATA *16*
Gardner, Miriam
   See Bradley, Marion Zimmer
Gardner, Richard (M.) 1931- *24*
Gardner, Richard A(lan) 1931-2003 .... *13*
   Obituary *144*
Gardner, Sally *177*
Gardner, Sandra 1940- *70*
Gardner, Scot 1968- *143*
Gardner, Sheldon 1934- *33*
Gardner, Ted
   See Gardner, Theodore Roosevelt II
Gardner, Theodore Roosevelt II 1934- *84*
Garelick, May 1910-1989 .... *19*
Garfield, James B. 1881-1984 .... *6*
   Obituary *38*
Garfield, Leon 1921-1996 .... *76*
   Obituary *90*
   Earlier sketches in SATA *1, 32*
   See also CLR *21*
Garis, Howard R(oger) 1873-1962 .... *13*
Garland, Mark 1953- *79*
Garland, Mark A.
   See Garland, Mark
Garland, Michael 1952- *168*
Garland, Sarah 1944- *135*
   Earlier sketch in SATA *62*
Garland, Sherry 1948- *145*
   Autobiography Feature *145*
   Earlier sketches in SATA *73, 114*
Garner, Alan 1934- *69*
   Autobiography Feature *108*
   Earlier sketch in SATA *18*
   See also CLR *20*
Garner, David 1958- *78*
Garner, Eleanor Ramrath 1930- *122*
Garner, James Finn 1960(?)- *92*
Garnet, A. H.
   See Slote, Alfred
Garnett, Eve C. R. 1900-1991 .... *3*
   Obituary *70*
Garou, Louis P.
   See Bowkett, Stephen
Garraty, John A(rthur) 1920- *23*
Garren, Devorah-Leah
   See Devorah-Leah
Garret, Maxwell R. 1917- *39*
Garretson, Victoria Diane 1945- *44*
Garrett, Helen 1895- *21*
Garrett, Richard 1920- *82*
Garrigue, Sheila 1931- *21*

Garrison, Barbara 1931- *163*
   Earlier sketch in SATA *19*
Garrison, Frederick
   See Sinclair, Upton
Garrison, Mary 1952- *146*
Garrison, Webb B(lack) 1919-2000 .... *25*
Garrity, Jennifer Johnson 1961- *124*
Garrity, Linda K. 1947- *128*
Garst, Doris Shannon 1894-1981 .... *1*
Garst, Shannon
   See Garst, Doris Shannon
Garth, Will
   See Hamilton, Edmond
   and Kuttner, Henry
Garthwaite, Marion H(ook) 1893-1981 .... *7*
Garvie, Maureen 1944- *175*
Garvie, Maureen McCallum
   See Garvie, Maureen
Gascoigne, Bamber 1935- *62*
Gaskins, Pearl Fuyo 1957- *134*
Gasperini, Jim 1952- *54*
   Brief entry *49*
Gater, Dilys 1944- *41*
Gates, Doris 1901-1987 .... *34*
   Obituary *54*
   Earlier sketch in SATA *1*
   See also SAAS *1*
Gates, Frieda 1933- *26*
Gates, Susan 1950- *153*
Gates, Viola R. 1931- *101*
Gathorne-Hardy, Jonathan G. 1933- *124*
   Earlier sketch in SATA *26*
Gatti, Anne 1952- *103*
Gatty, Juliana Horatia
   See Ewing, Juliana (Horatia Gatty)
Gauch, Patricia Lee 1934- *80*
   Earlier sketch in SATA *26*
   See also CLR *56*
   See also SAAS *21*
Gaul, Randy 1959- *63*
Gault, Clare 1925- *36*
Gault, Frank 1926-1982 .... *36*
   Brief entry *30*
Gault, William Campbell 1910-1995 .... *8*
Gauthier, Gail 1953- *160*
   Earlier sketch in SATA *118*
Gaver, Becky
   See Gaver, Rebecca
Gaver, Rebecca 1952- *20*
Gavin, Jamila 1941- *125*
   Earlier sketch in SATA *96*
Gay, Amelia
   See Hogarth, Grace (Weston Allen)
Gay, Kathlyn 1930- *144*
   Earlier sketch in SATA *9*
Gay, Marie-Louise 1952- *179*
   Earlier sketches in SATA *68, 126*
   See also CLR *27*
   See also SAAS *21*
Gay, Michel 1947- *162*
Gay, Zhenya 1906-1978 .... *19*
Gaze, Gillian
   See Barklem, Jill
Gear, Kathleen M. O'Neal
   See Gear, Kathleen O'Neal
Gear, Kathleen O'Neal 1954- *166*
   Earlier sketch in SATA *71*
Gear, W. Michael 1955- *166*
   Earlier sketch in SATA *71*
Geary, Rick 1946- *142*
Geason, Susan 1946- *122*
Gedalof, Robin
   See McGrath, Robin
Gedge, Pauline (Alice) 1945- *101*
Gee, Maurice 1931- *101*
   Earlier sketch in SATA *46*
   See also CLR *56*
Gee, Maurice Gough
   See Gee, Maurice
Geehan, Wayne (E.) 1947- *107*

Geer, Charles 1922- *42*
   Brief entry *32*
Geeslin, Campbell 1925- *163*
   Earlier sketch in SATA *107*
Gehman, Mary W. 1923- *86*
Gehr, Mary 1910(?)-1997 .... *32*
   Obituary *99*
Geipel, Eileen 1932- *30*
Geis, Darlene Stern 1918(?)-1999 .... *7*
   Obituary *111*
Geisel, Helen 1898-1967 .... *26*
Geisel, Theodor Seuss 1904-1991 .... *100*
   Obituary *67*
   Earlier sketches in SATA *1, 28, 75*
   See also CLR *100*
   See Dr. Seuss
Geisert, Arthur 1941- *171*
   Brief entry *52*
   Earlier sketches in SATA *56, 92, 133*
   See also CLR *87*
   See also SAAS *23*
Geisert, Arthur Frederick
   See Geisert, Arthur
Geisert, Bonnie 1942- *165*
   Earlier sketch in SATA *92*
Geldart, William 1936- *15*
Gelinas, Paul J. 1904-1996 .... *10*
Gellis, Roberta 1927- *128*
Gellis, Roberta Leah Jacobs
   See Gellis, Roberta
Gellman, Marc *112*
Gelman, Amy 1961- *72*
Gelman, Jan 1963- *58*
Gelman, Rita Golden 1937- *131*
   Brief entry *51*
   Earlier sketch in SATA *84*
Gelman, Steve 1934- *3*
Gemming, Elizabeth 1932- *11*
Gennaro, Joseph F(rancis), Jr. 1924- *53*
Gentile, Petrina 1969- *91*
Gentle, Mary 1956- *48*
Gentleman, David (William) 1930- *7*
Geoghegan, Adrienne 1962- *143*
George, Barbara
   See Katz, Bobbi
George, Emily
   See Katz, Bobbi
George, Gail
   See Katz, Bobbi
George, Jean
   See George, Jean Craighead
George, Jean Craighead 1919- *170*
   Earlier sketches in SATA *2, 68, 124*
   See also CLR *1, 80*
George, John L(othar) 1916- *2*
George, Kristine O'Connell 1954- *156*
   Earlier sketch in SATA *110*
George, Lindsay Barrett 1952- *155*
   Earlier sketch in SATA *95*
George, S(idney) C(harles) 1898- *11*
George, Sally
   See Orr, Wendy
George, Twig C. 1950- *114*
Georgiou, Constantine 1927- *7*
Georgiou, Theo
   See Odgers, Sally Farrell
Geraghty, Paul 1959- *130*
Gerard, Jean Ignace Isidore 1803-1847 .... *45*
Geras, Adele 1944- *173*
   Earlier sketches in SATA *23, 87, 129*
   See also SAAS *21*
   See Geras, Adele Daphne Weston
Geras, Adele Daphne Weston 1944-
   See Geras, Adele
Gerber, Merrill Joan 1938- *170*
   Autobiography Feature *170*
   Earlier sketches in SATA *64, 127*
Gerber, Perren 1933- *104*
Gerberg, Mort 1931- *64*
Gergely, Tibor 1900-1978 .... *54*
   Obituary *20*

Geringer, Laura 1948- 164
  Earlier sketches in SATA 29, 94
Gerler, William R(obert) 1917-1996 47
Gerrard, Jean 1933- 51
Gerrard, Roy 1935-1997 90
  Brief entry 45
  Obituary 99
  Earlier sketch in SATA 47
  See also CLR 23
Gerritsen, Paula 1956- 177
Gerrold, David 1944- 144
  Earlier sketch in SATA 66
Gershator, Phillis 1942- 158
  Earlier sketch in SATA 90
Gerson, Corinne 1927- 37
Gerson, Mary-Joan 136
  Earlier sketch in SATA 79
Gerson, Noel Bertram 1914-1988 22
  Obituary 60
Gerstein, Mordicai 1935- 178
  Brief entry 36
  Earlier sketches in SATA 47, 81, 142
  See also CLR 102
Gertridge, Allison 1967- 132
Gervais, Bernadette 1959- 80
Gesner, Clark 1938-2002 40
  Obituary 143
Gessner, Lynne 1919- 16
Geter, Tyrone 150
Getz, David 1957- 91
Getzinger, Donna 1968- 128
Gevirtz, Eliezer 1950- 49
Gewe, Raddory
  See Gorey, Edward (St. John)
Ghan, Linda (R.) 1947- 77
Ghent, Natale 1962- 148
Gherman, Beverly 1934- 123
  Earlier sketch in SATA 68
Ghigna, Charles 1946- 153
  Earlier sketch in SATA 108
Giacobbe, Beppe 1953- 174
Giambastiani, Kurt R. A. 1958- 141
Giannini, Enzo 1946- 68
Gibbons, Alan 1953- 124
Gibbons, Faye 1938 103
  Earlier sketch in SATA 65
Gibbons, Gail 1944- 160
  Earlier sketches in SATA 23, 72, 104
  See also CLR 8
  See also SAAS 12
Gibbons, Gail Gretchen
  See Gibbons, Gail
Gibbons, Kaye 1960- 117
Gibbs, Adrea 1960- 126
Gibbs, Alonzo (Lawrence) 1915-1992 5
Gibbs, Tony
  See Gibbs, Wolcott, Jr.
Gibbs, Wolcott, Jr. 1935- 40
Giblin, James Cross 1933- 122
  Earlier sketches in SATA 33, 75
  See also CLR 29
  See also SAAS 12
Gibson, Andrew (William) 1949- 72
Gibson, Betty 1911- 75
Gibson, Jo
  See Fluke, Joanne
Gibson, William 1914- 66
Gibson, William Ford
  See Gibson, William
Gidal, Nachum
  See Gidal, Tim Nachum
Gidal, Sonia (Epstein) 1922- 2
Gidal, Tim Nachum 1909-1996 2
Gidalewitsch, Nachum
  See Gidal, Tim Nachum
Gideon, Melanie 1963- 175
Giegling, John A(llan) 1935- 17
Gifaldi, David 1950- 76
Giff, Patricia Reilly 1935- 160
  Earlier sketches in SATA 33, 70, 121
Giffard, Hannah 1962- 83

Gifford, Griselda 1931- 171
  Earlier sketch in SATA 42
Gifford, Kerri 1961- 91
Gilbert, Ann
  See Taylor, Ann
Gilbert, Anne Yvonne 1951- 128
Gilbert, Barbara Snow 1954- 97
Gilbert, Frances
  See Collings, Gillian
Gilbert, Harriett 1948- 30
Gilbert, (Agnes) Joan (Sewell) 1931- 10
Gilbert, John (Raphael) 1926- 36
Gilbert, Nan
  See Gilbertson, Mildred Geiger
Gilbert, Roby Goodale 1966- 90
Gilbert, Ruth Gallard Ainsworth
  See Ainsworth, Ruth (Gallard)
Gilbert, Sara (Dulaney) 1943- 82
  Earlier sketch in SATA 11
Gilbert, Sheri L. 157
Gilbert, Suzie 1956- 97
Gilbert, W(illiam) S(chwenck) 1836-1911 ... 36
Gilbert, Yvonne
  See Gilbert, Anne Yvonne
Gilbertson, Mildred Geiger 1908-1988 2
Gilbreath, Alice 1921- 12
Gilbreth, Frank B(unker), Jr. 1911-2001 2
Gilchrist, Jan Spivey 1949- 130
  Earlier sketch in SATA 72
Gilden, Mel 1947- 97
Giles, Gail 152
Gilfond, Henry 2
Gilge, Jeanette 1924- 22
Gili, Phillida 1944- 70
Gill, Derek (Lewis Theodore) 1919-1997 9
Gill, Margery Jean 1925- 22
Gill, Shelley 176
Gill, Stephen 1932- 63
Gillespie, Carol Ann 1951- 158
Gillett, Mary (Bledsoe) 7
Gillette, Henry Sampson 1915- 14
Gillette, J(an) Lynett 1946- 103
Gilley, Jeremy 1969- 174
Gillham, Bill
  See Gillham, W(illiam) E(dwin) C(harles)
Gillham, W(illiam) E(dwin) C(harles)
  1936- 42
Gilliam, Stan 1946- 39
  Brief entry 35
Gilliland, Alexis A(rnaldus) 1931- 72
Gilliland, (Cleburne) Hap 1918- 92
Gillmor, Don 1954- 127
Gilman, Esther 1925- 15
Gilman, Laura Anne 178
Gilman, Phoebe 1940-2002 104
  Obituary 141
  Earlier sketch in SATA 58
Gilmore, Iris 1900-1982 22
Gilmore, Kate 1931- 87
Gilmore, Mary (Jean Cameron) 1865-1962 . 49
Gilmore, Susan 1954- 59
Gilpin, Stephen 177
Gilroy, Beryl (Agatha) 1924- 80
Gilson, Barbara
  See Gilson, Charles James Louis
Gilson, Charles James Louis 1878-1943
  See YABC 2
Gilson, Jamie 1933- 176
  Brief entry 34
  Earlier sketches in SATA 37, 91
Ginsburg, Mirra 1909-2000 92
  Earlier sketch in SATA 6
  See also CLR 45
Giovanni, Nikki 1943- 107
  Earlier sketch in SATA 24
  See also CLR 73
Giovanopoulos, Paul (Arthur) 1939- 7
Gipson, Fred(erick Benjamin) 1908-1973 2
  Obituary 24
Girard, Linda (Walvoord) 1942- 41

Girion, Barbara 1937- 78
  Earlier sketch in SATA 26
  See also SAAS 14
Girouard, Patrick 1957- 155
Girzone, Joseph F. 1930- 76
Girzone, Joseph Francis
  See Girzone, Joseph F.
Gise, Joanne
  See Mattern, Joanne
Gittings, Jo (Grenville) Manton 1919- 3
Gittings, Robert (William Victor) 1911-1992 . 6
  Obituary 70
Givens, Janet E(aton) 1932- 60
Givner, Joan 1936- 171
Givner, Joan Mary
  See Givner, Joan
Gladstone, Eve
  See Werner, Herma
Gladstone, Gary 1935- 12
Gladstone, M(yron) J. 1923- 37
Glanville, Brian (Lester) 1931- 42
Glanzman, Louis S. 1922- 36
Glaser, Byron 1954- 154
Glaser, Dianne E(lizabeth) 1937- 50
  Brief entry 31
Glaser, Isabel Joshlin 1929- 94
Glaser, Milton 1929- 151
  Earlier sketch in SATA 11
Glaser, Shirley 151
Glaspell, Susan 1882(?)-1948
  See YABC 2
Glass, Andrew 1949- 150
  Brief entry 46
  Earlier sketch in SATA 90
Glass, Linzi 175
Glass, Linzi Alex
  See Glass, Linzi
Glasscock, Amnesia
  See Steinbeck, John (Ernst)
Glassman, Bruce 1961- 76
Glauber, Uta (Heil) 1936- 17
Glazer, Thomas (Zachariah) 1914-2003 9
Glazer, Tom
  See Glazer, Thomas (Zachariah)
Gleasner, Diana (Cottle) 1936- 29
Gleason, Judith 1929- 24
Gleason, Katherine (A.) 1960- 104
Gleeson, Libby 1950- 142
  Autobiography Feature 142
  Earlier sketches in SATA 82, 118
Gleiter, Jan 1947- 111
Gleitzman, Morris 1953- 156
  Earlier sketch in SATA 88
  See also CLR 88
Glen, Maggie 1944- 88
Glendinning, Richard 1917-1988 24
Glendinning, Sally
  See Glendinning, Sara W(ilson)
Glendinning, Sara W(ilson) 1913-1993 24
Glenn, Mel 1943- 93
  Brief entry 45
  Earlier sketch in SATA 51
  See also CLR 51
Glenn, Patricia Brown 1953- 86
Glenn, Sharlee 159
Glenn, Sharlee Mullins
  See Glenn, Sharlee
Glennon, Karen M. 1946- 85
Gles, Margaret Breitmaier 1940- 22
Glick, Carl (Cannon) 1890-1971 14
Glick, Ruth (Burtnick) 1942- 125
Gliewe, Unada (Grace) 1927- 3
Glimmerveen, Ulco 1958- 85
Glines, Carroll V(ane), Jr. 1920- 19
Gliori, Debi 1959- 138
  Earlier sketch in SATA 72
Globe, Leah Ain 1900- 41
Glori Ann
  See Blakely, Gloria
Glovach, Linda 1947- 105
  Earlier sketch in SATA 7

Glover, Denis (James Matthews) 1912-1980 . 7
Glubok, Shirley (Astor) 146
  Autobiography Feature 146
  Earlier sketches in SATA 6, 68
  See also CLR 1
  See also SAAS 7
Glyman, Caroline A. 1967- 103
Glynne-Jones, William 1907-1977 11
Gobbato, Imero 1923- 39
Gobbletree, Richard
  See Quackenbush, Robert M(ead)
Goble, Dorothy 26
Goble, Paul 1933- 131
  Earlier sketches in SATA 25, 69
  See also CLR 21
Goble, Warwick (?)-1943 46
Godden, (Margaret) Rumer 1907-1998 36
  Obituary 109
  Earlier sketch in SATA 3
  See also CLR 20
  See also SAAS 12
Gode, Alexander
  See Gode von Aesch, Alexander (Gottfried
    Friedrich)
Gode von Aesch, Alexander (Gottfried
    Friedrich) 1906-1970 14
Godfrey, Jane
  See Bowden, Joan Chase
Godfrey, Martyn
  See Godfrey, Martyn N.
  and Godfrey, Martyn N.
Godfrey, Martyn N. 1949-2000 95
  See also CLR 57
  See Godfrey, Martyn
Godfrey, William
  See Youd, (Christopher) Samuel
Godkin, Celia (Marilyn) 1948- 145
  Earlier sketch in SATA 66
Godwin, Laura 1956- 179
Goedecke, Christopher (John) 1951- 81
Goekler, Susan
  See Wooley, Susan Frelick
Goertzen, Glenda 172
Goettel, Elinor 1930- 12
Goetz, Delia 1898-1996 22
  Obituary 91
Goffe, Toni 1936- 61
Goffstein, Brooke
  See Goffstein, M(arilyn) B(rooke)
Goffstein, M(arilyn) B(rooke) 1940- 70
  Earlier sketch in SATA 8
  See also CLR 3
Goforth, Ellen
  See Francis, Dorothy Brenner
Gogol, Sara 1948-2004 80
Goh, Chan Hon 1969- 145
Going, Kelly L.
  See Going, K.L.
Going, K.L. 156
Golann, Cecil Paige 1921-1995 11
Golbin, Andree 1923- 15
Gold, Alison Leslie 1945- 104
Gold, Bernice 150
Gold, Phyllis 21
  See Goldberg, Phyllis
Gold, Robert S(tanley) 1924- 63
Gold, Sharlya 9
Gold, Susan
  See Gold, Susan Dudley
Gold, Susan Dudley 1949- 147
Goldberg, Grace 1956- 78
Goldberg, Herbert S. 1926- 25
Goldberg, Jacob 1943- 94
Goldberg, Jake
  See Goldberg, Jacob
Goldberg, Jan 123
  See Curran, Jan Goldberg
Goldberg, Stan J. 1939- 26
Goldberg, Susan 1948- 71
Goldberg, Whoopi 1955- 119

Golden, Christie 1963- 167
  Earlier sketch in SATA 116
Goldentyer, Debra 1960- 84
Goldfeder, Cheryl
  See Pahz, Cheryl Suzanne
Goldfeder, James
  See Pahz, James Alon
Goldfeder, Jim
  See Pahz, James Alon
Goldfrank, Helen Colodny 1912- 6
Goldin, Augusta 1906-1999 13
Goldin, Barbara Diamond 1946- 129
  Autobiography Feature 129
  Earlier sketch in SATA 92
  See also SAAS 26
Goldin, David 1963- 101
Golding, Theresa Martin 1960- 150
Golding, William 1911-1993
  See CLR 94
Golding, William Gerald
  See Golding, William
Goldman, Alex J. 1917- 65
Goldman, E(leanor) M(aureen) 1943- 103
Goldman, Elizabeth 1949- 90
Goldring, Ann 1937- 149
Goldsborough, June 1923- 19
Goldsmith, Connie 1945- 147
Goldsmith, Howard 1943- 108
  Earlier sketch in SATA 24
Goldsmith, Oliver 1730(?)-1774 26
Goldsmith, Ruth M. 1919- 62
Goldstein, Nathan 1927- 47
Goldstein, Philip 1910-1997 23
Goldston, Robert (Conroy) 1927- 6
Goldstone, Lawrence A.
  See Treat, Lawrence
Golembe, Carla 1951- 79
Golenbock, Peter 1946- 99
Goll, Reinhold W(eimar) 1897-1993 26
Gollub, Matthew 1960- 134
  Earlier sketch in SATA 83
Gomez, Elizabeth 133
Gomez-Freer, Elizabeth
  See Gomez, Elizabeth
Gomi, Taro 1945- 103
  Earlier sketch in SATA 64
  See also CLR 57
Gondosch, Linda 1944- 58
Gonzalez, Catherine Troxell 1917-2000 87
Gonzalez, Christina
  See Gonzalez, Maya Christina
Gonzalez, Gloria 1940- 23
Gonzalez, Julie 1958- 174
Gonzalez, Maya
  See Gonzalez, Maya Christina
Gonzalez, Maya Christina 1964- 175
  Earlier sketch in SATA 115
Gonzalez, Rigoberto 1970- 147
Goobie, Beth 1959- 128
Good, Alice 1950- 73
Goodall, Daphne Machin
  See Machin Goodall, Daphne (Edith)
Goodall, Jane 1934- 111
Goodall, John S(trickland) 1908-1996 66
  Obituary 91
  Earlier sketch in SATA 4
  See also CLR 25
Goodbody, Slim
  See Burstein, John
Goode, Diane 1949- 170
  Earlier sketches in SATA 15, 84, 114
Goode, Diane Capuozzo
  See Goode, Diane
Goode, Stephen Ray 1943- 55
  Brief entry 40
Goodenow, Earle 1913- 40
Goodhart, Pippa 1958- 153
Goodhue, Thomas W. 1949- 143
Goodin, Sallie (Brown) 1953- 74
Goodman, Alison 1966- 111

Goodman, Deborah Lerme 1956- 50
  Brief entry 49
Goodman, Elaine 1930- 9
Goodman, Joan Elizabeth 1950- 162
  Earlier sketches in SATA 50, 94
Goodman, Walter 1927-2002 9
Goodrich, Samuel Griswold 1793-1860 23
GoodWeather, Harley
  See King, Thomas
Goodwin, Hal
  See Goodwin, Harold L(eland)
Goodwin, Harold L(eland) 1914-1990 51
  Obituary 65
  Earlier sketch in SATA 13
Goodwin, William 1943- 117
Goor, Nancy (Ruth Miller) 1944- 39
  Brief entry 34
Goor, Ron(ald Stephen) 1940- 39
  Brief entry 34
Goossen, Agnes
  See Epp, Margaret A(gnes)
Gootman, Marilyn E. 1944- 179
Gopnik, Adam 1956- 171
Gorbachev, Valeri 1944- 143
  Autobiography Feature 143
  Earlier sketch in SATA 98
Gordion, Mark
  See Turtledove, Harry
Gordon, Ad
  See Hano, Arnold
Gordon, Amy 1949- 156
  Earlier sketch in SATA 115
Gordon, Bernard Ludwig 1931- 27
Gordon, Colonel H. R.
  See Ellis, Edward S(ylvester)
Gordon, Donald
  See Payne, Donald Gordon
Gordon, Dorothy 1893-1970 20
Gordon, Esther S(aranga) 1935- 10
Gordon, Frederick 1
Gordon, Gaelyn 1939-1997
  See CLR 75
Gordon, Gary
  See Edmonds, I(vy) G(ordon)
Gordon, Hal
  See Goodwin, Harold L(eland)
Gordon, Jeffie Ross
  See Enderle, Judith (Ann) Ross
  and Gordon, Stephanie Jacob
Gordon, John
  See Gesner, Clark
Gordon, John (William) 1925- 84
Gordon, Lew
  See Baldwin, Gordon C(ortis)
Gordon, Margaret (Anna) 1939- 9
Gordon, Mike 1948- 101
Gordon, Selma
  See Lanes, Selma Gordon
Gordon, Sheila 1927- 88
  See also CLR 27
Gordon, Shirley 1921- 48
  Brief entry 41
Gordon, Sol 1923- 11
Gordon, Stephanie Jacob 1940- 89
  Autobiography Feature 114
  Earlier sketch in SATA 64
  See also SAAS 26
Gordon, Stewart
  See Shirreffs, Gordon D(onald)
Gorelick, Molly C(hernow) 1920-2003 9
  Obituary 153
Gorey, Edward (St. John) 1925-2000 70
  Brief entry 27
  Obituary 118
  Earlier sketch in SATA 29
  See also CLR 36
Gorham, Charles Orson 1868-1936 36
Gorham, Michael
  See Folsom, Franklin (Brewster)
Gorman, Carol 150
Gorman, Jacqueline Laks 1955- 148

Gormley, Beatrice 1942- 127
  Brief entry 35
  Earlier sketch in SATA 39
Gorog, Judith (Katharine Allen) 1938- 75
  Earlier sketch in SATA 39
Gorrell, Gena K. 1946- 170
Gorrell, Gena Kinton
  See Gorrell, Gena K.
Gorsline, Douglas (Warner) 1913-1985 11
  Obituary 43
Gorsline, (Sally) Marie 1928- 28
Gorsline, S. M.
  See Gorsline, (Sally) Marie
Gorton, Kaitlyn
  See Emerson, Kathy Lynn
Goryan, Sirak
  See Saroyan, William
Goscinny, Rene 1926-1977 47
  Brief entry 39
  See also CLR 37
Goss, Clay(ton E.) 1946- 82
Goss, Gary 1947- 124
Gottesman, S. D.
  See Kornbluth, C(yril) M.
  and Lowndes, Robert A(ugustine) W(ard)
  and Pohl, Frederik
Gottfried, Ted
  See Gottfried, Theodore Mark
Gottfried, Theodore Mark 1928- 150
  Earlier sketch in SATA 85
Gottlieb, Gerald 1923- 7
Gottlieb, William P. 1917-2006 24
Gottlieb, William Paul
  See Gottlieb, William P.
Goudey, Alice E(dwards) 1898-1993 20
Goudge, Eileen 1950- 88
Goudge, Elizabeth (de Beauchamp)
  1900-1984 2
  Obituary 38
  See also CLR 94
Gough, Catherine 24
  See Mulgan, Catherine
Gough, Philip 1908- 45
Gough, Sue 1940- 106
Goulart, Ron(ald Joseph) 1933- 138
  Earlier sketch in SATA 6
  See Appleton, Victor II
  and Dixon, Franklin W.
  and Hope, Laura Lee
  and Keene, Carolyn
Gould, Alberta 1945- 96
Gould, Chester 1900-1985 49
  Obituary 43
Gould, Jean R(osalind) 1909-1993 11
  Obituary 77
Gould, Lilian 6
Gould, Marilyn 1928- 76
  Earlier sketch in SATA 15
Gould, Robert 154
Gould, Steven 1955- 95
Gould, Steven Charles
  See Gould, Steven
Gourley, Catherine 1950- 95
Gourse, (Roberta) Leslie 1939-2004 89
Govan, (Mary) Christine Noble 1898-1985 ... 9
Gove, Doris 1944- 72
Govern, Elaine 1939- 26
Gowen, L. Kris 1968- 156
Graaf, Peter
  See Youd, (Christopher) Samuel
Graber, Alexander 1914-1997 98
  Earlier sketch in SATA 7
Graber, (George) Alexander 1914-1997 98
Graber, Janet 1942- 170
Graber, Richard (Fredrick) 1927- 26
Grabianski, Janusz 1928-1976 39
  Obituary 30
Graboff, Abner 1919-1986 35
Grace, Fran(ces Jane) 45
Grace, Theresa
  See Mattern, Joanne

Gracza, Margaret Young 1928- 56
Graduate of Oxford, A
  See Ruskin, John
Graeber, Charlotte Towner 106
  Brief entry 44
  Earlier sketch in SATA 56
Graeme, Roderic
  See Jeffries, Roderic
Graf, Michael
  See Graf, Mike
Graf, (Mike) 1960- 164
Graff, Polly Anne Colver
  See Colver, Anne
Graff, (S.) Stewart 1908- 9
Graham, Ada 1931- 11
Graham, Alastair 1945- 74
Graham, Arthur Kennon
  See Harrison, David L(ee)
Graham, Bob 1942- 151
  Earlier sketches in SATA 63, 101
  See also CLR 31
Graham, Brenda Knight 1942- 32
Graham, Charlotte
  See Bowden, Joan Chase
Graham, Eleanor 1896-1984 18
  Obituary 38
Graham, Ennis
  See Molesworth, Mary Louisa
Graham, Frank, Jr. 1925- 11
Graham, Ian 1953- 112
Graham, John 1926- 11
Graham, Kennon
  See Harrison, David L(ee)
Graham, Larry
  See Graham, Lawrence (Otis)
Graham, Lawrence (Otis) 1962- 63
Graham, Linda
  See Graham-Barber, Lynda
Graham, Lorenz (Bell) 1902-1989 74
  Obituary 63
  Earlier sketch in SATA 2
  See also CLR 10
  See also SAAS 5
Graham, Margaret Bloy 1920- 11
Graham, Robin Lee 1949- 7
Graham, Shirley 1896(?)-1977
  See Du Bois, Shirley Graham
Graham-Barber, Lynda 1944- 159
  Earlier sketch in SATA 42
Graham-Cameron, M.
  See Graham-Cameron, M(alcolm) G(ordon)
Graham-Cameron, M(alcolm) G(ordon)
  1931- 53
  Brief entry 45
Graham-Cameron, Mike
  See Graham-Cameron, M(alcolm) G(ordon)
Grahame, Kenneth 1859-1932 100
  See also YABC 1
  See also CLR 5
Gralley, Jean 166
Gramatky, Hardie 1907-1979 30
  Obituary 23
  Earlier sketch in SATA 1
  See also CLR 22
Grambling, Lois G. 1927- 148
  Earlier sketch in SATA 71
Grambo, Rebecca L(ynn) 1963- 109
Grammer, June Amos 1927- 58
Grand, Samuel 1912-1988 42
Grandville, J. J.
  See Gerard, Jean Ignace Isidore
Grandville, Jean Ignace Isidore Gerard
  See Gerard, Jean Ignace Isidore
Granfield, Linda 1950- 160
  Earlier sketch in SATA 96
Grange, Peter
  See Nicole, Christopher (Robin)
Granger, Michele 1949- 88
Granowsky, Alvin 1936- 101
Granstaff, Bill 1925- 10

Granstrom, Brita 1969- 167
  Earlier sketch in SATA 111
Grant, Bruce 1893-1977 5
  Obituary 25
Grant, Cynthia D. 1950- 147
  Earlier sketches in SATA 33, 77
Grant, Eva 1907-1996 7
Grant, Gordon 1875-1962 25
Grant, Gwen(doline Ellen) 1940- 47
Grant, Katie M.
  See Grant, K.M.
Grant, K.M. 175
Grant, (Alice) Leigh 1947- 10
Grant, Matthew G.
  See May, Julian
Grant, Maxwell
  See Gibson, Walter B(rown)
  and Lynds, Dennis
Grant, Myrna (Lois) 1934- 21
Grant, Neil 1938- 154
  Earlier sketch in SATA 14
Grant, Nicholas
  See Nicole, Christopher (Robin)
Grant, Richard 1948- 80
Grant, Skeeter
  See Spiegelman, Art
Grater, Michael 1923- 57
Gravel, Fern
  See Hall, James Norman
Gravelle, Karen 1942- 166
  Earlier sketch in SATA 78
Graves, Charles Parlin 1911-1972 4
Graves, Keith 156
Graves, Robert 1895-1985 45
Graves, Robert von Ranke
  See Graves, Robert
Graves, Valerie
  See Bradley, Marion Zimmer
Gray, Betsy
  See Poole, Gray Johnson
Gray, Caroline
  See Nicole, Christopher (Robin)
Gray, Elizabeth Janet
  See Vining, Elizabeth Gray
Gray, Genevieve S(tuck) 1920-1995 4
Gray, Harold (Lincoln) 1894-1968 33
  Brief entry 32
Gray, Jenny
  See Gray, Genevieve S(tuck)
Gray, John Lee
  See Jakes, John
Gray, Judith A. 1949- 93
Gray, Judith Anne
  See Gray, Judith A.
Gray, Keith 151
Gray, Kes 1960- 153
Gray, Les 1929- 82
Gray, Libba Moore 1937- 83
Gray, Luli 1945- 149
  Earlier sketch in SATA 90
Gray, Marian
  See Pierce, Edith Gray
Gray, Nicholas Stuart 1922-1981 4
  Obituary 27
Gray, Nigel 1941- 104
  Earlier sketch in SATA 33
Gray, (Lucy) Noel (Clervaux) 1898-1983 47
Gray, Patricia (Clark) 7
Gray, Patsey
  See Gray, Patricia (Clark)
Graydon, Shari 1958- 158
Grayland, V. Merle
  See Grayland, Valerie (Merle Spanner)
Grayland, Valerie (Merle Spanner) 7
Grayson, Devin (Kalile) 1970- 119
Grayson, Kristine
  See Rusch, Kristine Kathryn
Grayson, Paul 1946- 79
Graystone, Lynn
  See Brennan, Joseph Lomas

Great Comte, The
   See Hawkesworth, Eric
Greaves, Margaret 1914-1995 87
   Earlier sketch in SATA 7
Greaves, Nick 1955- 77
Gree, Alain 1936- 28
Green, Adam
   See Weisgard, Leonard (Joseph)
Green, Anne Canevari 1943- 62
Green, Brian
   See Card, Orson Scott
Green, Cliff(ord) 1934- 126
Green, Connie Jordan 1938- 80
Green, D.
   See Casewit, Curtis W(erner)
Green, Elizabeth Shippen 1871-1954 139
Green, Hannah
   See Greenberg, Joanne (Goldenberg)
Green, Jane 1937- 9
Green, John 1978(?)- 170
Green, Mary Moore 1906- 11
Green, Morton 1937- 8
Green, Norma B(erger) 1925- 11
Green, Phyllis 1932- 20
Green, Roger (Gilbert) Lancelyn 1918-1987 . 2
   Obituary 53
Green, (James Le)Roy 1948- 89
Green, Sheila Ellen 1934- 148
   Earlier sketches in SATA 8, 87
Green, Timothy 1953- 91
Greenaway, Kate 1846-1901 100
   See also YABC 2
   See also CLR 111
Greenbank, Anthony Hunt 1933- 39
Greenberg, David T. 1954- 171
Greenberg, Harvey R. 1935- 5
Greenberg, Jan 1942- 125
   Earlier sketch in SATA 61
Greenberg, Joanne (Goldenberg) 1932- 25
Greenberg, Melanie Hope 1954- 72
Greenberg, Polly 1932- 52
   Brief entry 43
Greenblat, Rodney Alan 1960- 106
Greenburg, Dan 1936- 175
   Earlier sketch in SATA 102
Greene, Bette 1934- 161
   Earlier sketches in SATA 8, 102
   See also CLR 2
   See also SAAS 16
Greene, Carla 1916- 67
   Earlier sketch in SATA 1
Greene, Carol 102
   Brief entry 44
   Earlier sketch in SATA 66
Greene, Constance C(larke) 1924- 72
   Earlier sketch in SATA 11
   See also CLR 62
   See also SAAS 11
Greene, Edgar
   See Papademetriou, Lisa
Greene, Ellin 1927- 23
Greene, Graham 1904-1991 20
Greene, Graham Henry
   See Greene, Graham
Greene, Jacqueline Dembar 1946- 131
   Earlier sketch in SATA 76
Greene, Laura Offenhartz 1935- 38
Greene, Meg
   See Malvasi, Meg Greene
Greene, Michele 1962- 178
Greene, Michele Dominguez
   See Greene, Michele
Greene, Rhonda Gowler 1955- 160
   Earlier sketch in SATA 101
Greene, Stephanie 1953- 173
   Earlier sketch in SATA 127
Greene, Wade 1933- 11
Greene, Yvonne
   See Flesch, Yolande (Catarina)
Greenfeld, Howard (Scheinman) 1928- 140
   Earlier sketch in SATA 19

Greenfeld, Josh(ua Joseph) 1928- 62
Greenfield, Eloise 1929- 155
   Earlier sketches in SATA 19, 61, 105
   See also CLR 38
   See also SAAS 16
Greening, Hamilton
   See Hamilton, Charles (Harold St. John)
Greenlaw, M. Jean 1941- 107
Greenleaf, Barbara Kaye 1942- 6
Greenleaf, Peter 1910-1997 33
Greenlee, Sharon 1935- 77
Greeno, Gayle 1949- 81
Greenseid, Diane 1948- 178
   Earlier sketch in SATA 93
Greenspun, Adele Aron 1938- 142
   Earlier sketch in SATA 76
Greenstein, Elaine 1959- 150
   Earlier sketch in SATA 82
Greenwald, Sheila
   See Green, Sheila Ellen
Greenwood, Barbara 1940- 129
   Earlier sketch in SATA 90
Greenwood, Pamela D. 1944- 115
Greer, Richard
   See Garrett, (Gordon) Randall (Phillip)
   and Silverberg, Robert
Gregg, Andrew K. 1929- 81
Gregg, Charles T(hornton) 1927- 65
Gregg, Walter H(arold) 1919- 20
Gregor, Arthur 1923- 36
Gregor, Lee
   See Pohl, Frederik
Gregori, Leon 1919- 15
Gregorian, Joyce Ballou 1946-1991 30
   Obituary 83
Gregorich, Barbara 1943- 66
Gregorowski, Christopher 1940- 30
Gregory, Diana (Jean) 1933- 49
   Brief entry 42
Gregory, Harry
   See Gottfried, Theodore Mark
Gregory, Jean
   See Ure, Jean
Gregory, Kristiana 1951- 136
   Earlier sketch in SATA 74
Gregory, Nan 1944- 148
Gregory, Philippa 1954- 122
Gregory, Stephen
   See Penzler, Otto
Gregory, Valiska 1940- 82
Greisman, Joan Ruth 1937- 31
Grendon, Stephen
   See Derleth, August (William)
Grenville, Pelham
   See Wodehouse, P(elham) G(renville)
Gretz, Susanna 1937- 7
Gretzer, John 18
Grewdead, Roy
   See Gorey, Edward (St. John)
Grey, Carol
   See Lowndes, Robert A(ugustine) W(ard)
Grey, Jerry 1926- 11
Grey, Mini 166
Greybeard the Pirate
   See Macintosh, Brownie
Grey Owl
   See CLR 32
   See Belaney, Archibald Stansfeld
Gri
   See Denney, Diana
Gribbin, John 1946- 159
Gribbin, John R.
   See Gribbin, John
Grice, Frederick 1910-1983 6
Grider, Dorothy 1915- 31
Gridley, Marion E(leanor) 1906-1974 35
   Obituary 26
Grieco-Tiso, Pina 1954- 108
Grieder, Walter 1924- 9
Griego, Tony A. 1955- 77
Griese, Arnold A(lfred) 1921- 9

Griessman, Annette 1962- 170
   Earlier sketch in SATA 116
Grieve, James 1934- 146
Grifalconi, Ann 1929- 133
   Earlier sketches in SATA 2, 66
   See also CLR 35
   See also SAAS 16
Griffin, Adele 1970- 153
   Earlier sketch in SATA 105
Griffin, Elizabeth May 1985- 89
Griffin, Gillett Good 1928- 26
Griffin, Judith Berry 34
Griffin, Kitty 1951- 137
Griffin, Peni R(ae Robinson) 1961- 99
   Earlier sketch in SATA 67
Griffin, Steven A. 1953- 89
Griffin, Steven Arthur
   See Griffin, Steven A.
Griffin, W.E.B. 1929- 5
   See Butterworth, W.E.
Griffith, Connie 1946- 89
Griffith, Gershom 1960- 85
Griffith, Helen V(irginia) 1934- 87
   Autobiography Feature 107
   Earlier sketch in SATA 39
Griffith, Jeannette
   See Eyerly, Jeannette (Hyde)
Griffiths, Andy 1961- 152
Griffiths, Helen 1939- 86
   Earlier sketch in SATA 5
   See also CLR 75
   See also SAAS 5
Grigson, Jane (McIntire) 1928-1990 63
Grimes, Lee 1920- 68
Grimes, Nikki 1950- 174
   Earlier sketches in SATA 93, 136
   See also CLR 42
Grimm, Jacob Ludwig Karl 1785-1863 22
   See also CLR 112
   See Grimm Brothers
Grimm, Wilhelm Karl 1786-1859 22
   See also CLR 112
   See Grimm Brothers
Grimm, William C(arey) 1907-1992 14
Grimm and Grim
   See Grimm, Jacob Ludwig Karl
   and Grimm, Wilhelm Karl
Grimm Brothers
   See CLR 112
   See Grimm, Jacob Ludwig Karl
   and Grimm, Wilhelm Karl
Grimsdell, Jeremy 1942- 83
Grimshaw, Nigel (Gilroy) 1925- 23
Grimsley, Gordon
   See Groom, Arthur William
Grindley, (Jane) Sally 1953- 148
Gringhuis, Dirk
   See Gringhuis, Richard H.
Gringhuis, Richard H. 1918-1974 6
   Obituary 25
Grinnell, George Bird 1849-1938 16
Grinspoon, David
   See Grinspoon, David H.
Grinspoon, David H. 1959- 156
Grinspoon, David Harry
   See Grinspoon, David H.
Gripe, Maria 1923- 74
   Earlier sketch in SATA 2
   See also CLR 5
Gripe, Maria Kristina
   See Gripe, Maria
Groch, Judith (Goldstein) 1929- 25
Grode, Redway
   See Gorey, Edward (St. John)
Groener, Carl
   See Lowndes, Robert A(ugustine) W(ard)
Groening, Matt 1954- 116
   Earlier sketch in SATA 81
Grohmann, Susan 1948- 84
Grohskopf, Bernice 7
Grol, Lini R(icharda) 1913- 9

Grollman, Earl A. 1925- 22
Groom, Arthur William 1898-1964 10
Grooms, Duffy 1964- 169
Gross, Alan 1947- 54
  Brief entry 43
Gross, Ernie 1913- 67
Gross, Philip 1952- 164
  Earlier sketch in SATA 84
Gross, Philip John
  See Gross, Philip
Gross, Ruth Belov 1929- 33
Gross, Sarah Chokla 1906-1976 9
  Obituary 26
Grosser, Morton 1931- 74
Grosser, Vicky 1958- 83
Grossman, Bill 1948- 126
  Earlier sketch in SATA 72
Grossman, Nancy 1940- 29
Grossman, Patricia 1951- 73
Grossman, Robert 1940- 11
Grote, JoAnn A. 1951- 113
Groten, Dallas 1951- 64
Groth, John (August) 1908-1988 21
  Obituary 56
Groth-Fleming, Candace
  See Fleming, Candace
Grove, Vicki 1948- 151
  Autobiography Feature 151
  Earlier sketch in SATA 122
Grover, Lorie Ann 1964- 168
Grover, Wayne 1934- 69
Groves, Georgina
  See Symons, (Dorothy) Geraldine
Groves, Maketa 1950- 107
Groves, Seli 77
Grubb, Lisa 160
Gruber, Michael 1940- 173
Gruber, Terry (deRoy) 1953- 66
Gruelle, John (Barton) 1880-1938 35
  Brief entry 32
  See Gruelle, Johnny
Gruelle, Johnny
  See CLR 34
  See Gruelle, John (Barton)
Gruenberg, Sidonie Matsner 1881-1974 2
  Obituary 27
Gruhzit-Hoyt, Olga (Margaret) 1922- 127
  Earlier sketch in SATA 16
Grummer, Arnold E(dward) 1923- 49
Grunewalt, Pine
  See Kunhardt, Edith
Grunwell, Jeanne Marie 1971- 147
Grupper, Jonathan 137
Gryski, Camilla 1948- 72
Guarino, Dagmar
  See Guarino, Deborah
Guarino, Deborah 1954- 68
Guay, Georgette (Marie Jeanne) 1952- 54
Guback, Georgia 88
Guccione, Leslie Davis 1946- 111
  Earlier sketch in SATA 72
Guck, Dorothy 1913-2002 27
Guerny, Gene
  See Gurney, Gene
Guest, Elissa Haden 1953- 125
Guest, Jacqueline 1952- 135
Guevara, Susan 167
  Earlier sketch in SATA 97
Gugler, Laurel Dee 95
Gugliotta, Bobette 1918-1994 7
Guianan, Eve 1965- 102
Guiberson, Brenda Z. 1946- 124
  Earlier sketch in SATA 71
Guile, Melanie 1949- 152
  Earlier sketch in SATA 104
Guillaume, Jeanette G. Flierl 1899-1990 8
Guillot, Rene 1900-1969 7
  See also CLR 22
Guisewite, Cathy (Lee) 1950- 57
Gulbis, Stephen 1959- 142
Gulley, Judie 1942- 58

Gump, P. Q.
  See Card, Orson Scott
Gundrey, Elizabeth 1924- 23
Gunn, James E. 1923- 35
Gunn, James Edwin
  See Gunn, James E.
Gunn, Robin Jones 1955- 84
Gunning, Monica Olwen 1930- 161
Gunston, Bill
  See Gunston, William Tudor
Gunston, William Tudor 1927- 9
Gunther, John 1901-1970
Guravich, Dan 1918- 74
Gurko, Leo 1914- 9
Gurko, Miriam 1910(?)-1988 9
  Obituary 58
Gurney, Gene 1924- 65
Gurney, James 1958- 120
  Earlier sketch in SATA 76
Gurney, John Steven 1962- 143
  Earlier sketch in SATA 75
Gustafson, Sarah R.
  See Riedman, Sarah R(egal)
Gustafson, Scott 1956- 34
Gustavson, Adam 176
Guthrie, A(lfred) B(ertram), Jr. 1901-1991 .. 62
  Obituary 67
Guthrie, Anne 1890-1979 28
Guthrie, Donna W. 1946- 105
  Earlier sketch in SATA 63
Gutierrez, Akemi 172
Gutman, Bill 128
  Brief entry 43
  Earlier sketch in SATA 67
Gutman, Dan 1955- 139
  Earlier sketch in SATA 77
Gutmann, Bessie Pease 1876-1960 73
Guy, Geoffrey 1942- 153
Guy, Ginger Foglesong 1954- 171
Guy, Rosa (Cuthbert) 1925- 122
  Earlier sketches in SATA 14, 62
  See also CLR 13
Guy, Susan 1948- 149
Guymer, (Wilhelmina) Mary 1909- 50
Guzman, Lila 1952- 168
Guzman, Rick 1957- 168
Gwynne, Fred(erick Hubbard) 1926-1993 41
  Brief entry 27
  Obituary 75
Gwynne, Oscar A.
  See Ellis, Edward S(ylvester)
Gwynne, Oswald A.
  See Ellis, Edward S(ylvester)

H

Haab, Sherri 1964- 169
  Earlier sketch in SATA 91
Haar, Jaap ter
  See CLR 15
  See ter Haar, Jaap
Haas, Carolyn Buhai 1926- 43
Haas, Dan 1957- 105
Haas, Dorothy F. 46
  Brief entry 43
  See also SAAS 17
Haas, Irene 1929- 96
  Earlier sketch in SATA 17
Haas, James E(dward) 1943- 40
Haas, (Katherine) Jessie 1959- 135
  Autobiography Feature 135
  Earlier sketch in SATA 98
Habenstreit, Barbara 1937- 5
Haber, Karen 1955- 78
Haber, Louis 1910-1988 12
Hackett, John Winthrop 1910-1997 65
Haddix, Margaret Peterson 1964- 125
  Earlier sketch in SATA 94
Haddon, Mark 1962- 155

Hader, Berta (Hoerner) 1891(?)-1976 16
Hader, Elmer (Stanley) 1889-1973 16
Hadithi, Mwenye
  See Hobson, Bruce
Hadley, Franklin
  See Winterbotham, R(ussell) R(obert)
Hadley, Lee 1934-1995 89
  Brief entry 38
  Obituary 86
  Earlier sketch in SATA 47
  See also CLR 40
  See Irwin, Hadley
Haeffele, Deborah 1954- 76
Haenel, Wolfram 1956- 89
  See also CLR 64
Hafner, Marylin 1925- 179
  Earlier sketches in SATA 7, 121
Hager, Alan 1940- 176
Hager, Betty 1923- 89
Hager, Sarah 171
Hager, Thomas 1953- 119
Hager, Tom
  See Hager, Thomas
Haggard, H(enry) Rider 1856-1925 16
Haggerty, James J(oseph) 1920- 5
Hagon, Priscilla
  See Allan, Mabel Esther
Hague, (Susan) Kathleen 1949- 49
  Brief entry 45
Hague, Michael R. 1948- 129
  Brief entry 32
  Earlier sketches in SATA 48, 80
Hahn, Emily 1905-1997 3
  Obituary 96
Hahn, Hannelore 8
Hahn, James (Sage) 1947- 9
Hahn, (Mona) Lynn 1949- 9
Hahn, Mary Downing 1937- 157
  Autobiography Feature 157
  Brief entry 44
  Earlier sketches in SATA 50, 81, 138
  See also SAAS 12
Hahn, Michael T. 1953- 92
Haig-Brown, Roderick (Langmere)
  1908-1976 12
  See also CLR 31
Haight, Rip
  See Carpenter, John (Howard)
Haight, Sandy 1949- 79
Haij, Vera
  See Jansson, Tove (Marika)
Haines, Gail Kay 1943- 11
Haines, Margaret Ann Beck
  See Beck, Peggy
Haining, Peter (Alexander) 1940- 14
Hains, Harriet
  See Watson, Carol
Hajdusiewicz, Babs Bell 163
Hakim, Joy 1931- 173
  Earlier sketch in SATA 83
Halacy, D(aniel) S(tephen), Jr. 1919-2002 ... 36
  See Halacy, Dan
Halacy, Dan
  See SAAS 8
  See Halacy, D(aniel) S(tephen), Jr.
Halam, Ann
  See Jones, Gwyneth A(nn)
Haldane, Roger John 1945- 13
Hale, Arlene 1924-1982 49
Hale, Bruce 1957- 123
Hale, Christy 179
  See Apostolou, Christine Hale
Hale, Edward Everett 1822-1909 16
Hale, Glenn
  See Walker, Robert W(ayne)
Hale, Helen
  See Mulcahy, Lucille Burnett
Hale, Irina 1932- 26
Hale, Kathleen 1898-2000 66
  Obituary 121
  Earlier sketch in SATA 17

Hale, Linda (Howe) 1929- 6
Hale, Lucretia P.
    See Hale, Lucretia Peabody
Hale, Lucretia Peabody 1820-1900 26
    See also CLR *105*
Hale, Nancy 1908-1988 .... *31*
    Obituary *57*
Hale, Shannon *158*
Haley, Gail E(inhart) 1939- *161*
    Autobiography Feature *161*
    Brief entry *28*
    Earlier sketches in SATA *43, 78, 136*
    See also CLR *21*
    See also SAAS *13*
Haley, Neale *52*
Hall, Adam
    See Trevor, Elleston
Hall, Adele 1910- 7
Hall, Anna Gertrude 1882-1967 8
Hall, Barbara 1960- *68*
Hall, Beverly B. 1918- *95*
Hall, Borden
    See Yates, Raymond F(rancis)
Hall, Brian P(atrick) 1935- *31*
Hall, Cameron
    See del Rey, Lester
Hall, Caryl
    See Hansen, Caryl (Hall)
Hall, Donald 1928- *97*
    Earlier sketch in SATA *23*
Hall, Donald Andrew, Jr.
    See Hall, Donald
Hall, Douglas 1931- *43*
Hall, Elizabeth 1929- *77*
Hall, Elvajean 1910-1984 6
Hall, Francie 1940- *166*
Hall, James Norman 1887-1951 .... *21*
Hall, Jesse
    See Boesen, Victor
Hall, Katy
    See McMullan, Kate
Hall, Kirsten Marie 1974- *67*
Hall, Lynn 1937- *79*
    Earlier sketches in SATA *2, 47*
    See also SAAS *4*
Hall, Malcolm 1945- 7
Hall, Marjory
    See Yeakley, Marjory Hall
Hall, Melanie W. 1949- *169*
    Earlier sketches in SATA *78, 116*
Hall, Patricia 1940- *136*
Hall, Rosalys Haskell 1914- 7
Hall, Willis 1929-2005 .... *66*
Hallard, Peter
    See Catherall, Arthur
Hallas, Richard
    See Knight, Eric
Hall-Clarke, James
    See Rowland-Entwistle, (Arthur) Theodore
    (Henry)
Hallensleben, Georg 1958- *173*
Haller, Dorcas Woodbury 1946- *46*
Hallett, Mark 1947- *83*
Halliburton, Richard 1900-1939(?) *81*
Halliburton, Warren J. 1924- *19*
Halliday, Brett
    See Dresser, Davis
    and Johnson, (Walter) Ryerson
    and Terrall, Robert
Halliday, William R(oss) 1926- *52*
Hallin, Emily Watson 1916-1995 6
Hallinan, P(atrick) K(enneth) 1944- *39*
    Brief entry *37*
Hallman, Ruth 1929- *43*
    Brief entry *28*
Hallowell, Tommy
    See Hill, Thomas
Hall-Quest, (Edna) Olga W(ilbourne)
    1899-1986 .... *11*
    Obituary *47*
Halls, Kelly Milner 1957- *131*

Hallstead, William F(inn III) 1924- *11*
Hallward, Michael 1889-1982 .... *12*
Halperin, Michael *156*
Halperin, Wendy Anderson 1952- *125*
    Earlier sketch in SATA *80*
Halpin, Marlene 1927- *88*
Halsell, Grace (Eleanor) 1923-2000 .... *13*
Halter, Jon C(harles) 1941- *22*
Halvorson, Marilyn 1948- *123*
Hamalian, Leo 1920- *41*
Hamberger, John 1934- *14*
Hamblin, Dora Jane 1920- *36*
Hambly, Barbara 1951- *108*
Hamer, Martyn
    See Eldin, Peter
Hamerstrom, Frances 1907-1998 .... *24*
Hamil, Thomas Arthur 1928- *14*
Hamill, Ethel
    See Webb, Jean Francis (III)
Hamilton, (John) Alan 1943- *66*
Hamilton, Alice
    See Cromie, Alice Hamilton
Hamilton, Anita 1919- *92*
Hamilton, Buzz
    See Hemming, Roy G.
Hamilton, Carol (Jean Barber) 1935- *94*
Hamilton, Charles (Harold St. John)
    1876-1961 .... *13*
Hamilton, Charles 1913-1996 .... *65*
    Obituary *93*
Hamilton, Clive
    See Lewis, C.S.
Hamilton, Dorothy (Drumm) 1906-1983 ...... *12*
    Obituary *35*
Hamilton, Edith 1867-1963 .... *20*
Hamilton, Edmond 1904-1977 .... *118*
Hamilton, (Muriel) Elizabeth (Mollie)
    1906- *23*
Hamilton, Emma Walton 1962- *177*
Hamilton, Franklin
    See Silverberg, Robert
Hamilton, Gail
    See Corcoran, Barbara (Asenath)
    and Dodge, Mary Abigail
Hamilton, Kersten 1958- *134*
Hamilton, Martha 1953- *123*
Hamilton, Mary (E.) 1927- *55*
Hamilton, Mollie
    See Kaye, M.M.
Hamilton, Morse 1943-1998 .... *101*
    Earlier sketch in SATA *35*
Hamilton, Peter F. 1960- *109*
Hamilton, Priscilla
    See Gellis, Roberta
Hamilton, Ralph
    See Stratemeyer, Edward L.
Hamilton, Virginia 1936-2002 .... *123*
    Obituary *132*
    Earlier sketches in SATA *4, 56, 79*
    See also CLR *40*
Hamilton, Virginia Esther
    See Hamilton, Virginia
Hamilton-Paterson, James 1941- *82*
Hamlet, Ova
    See Lupoff, Richard A(llen)
Hamley, Dennis 1935- *69*
    Earlier sketch in SATA *39*
    See also CLR *47*
    See also SAAS *22*
Hamlin, Peter J. 1970- *84*
Hamm, Diane Johnston 1949- *78*
Hammer, Charles 1934- *58*
Hammer, Richard 1928- 6
Hammerman, Gay M(orenus) 1926- *9*
Hammond, Ralph
    See Hammond Innes, Ralph
Hammond, Winifred G(raham) 1899-1992 ... *29*
    Obituary *107*
Hammond Innes, Ralph 1913-1998 .... *116*
    See Innes, (Ralph) Hammond
Hammontree, Marie (Gertrude) 1913- *13*

Hample, Zack 1977- *161*
Hampshire, Joyce Gregorian
    See Gregorian, Joyce Ballou
Hampshire, Susan 1942- *98*
Hampson, (Richard) Denman 1929- *15*
Hampton, Wilborn *156*
Hamre, Leif 1914- 5
Hamsa, Bobbie 1944- *52*
    Brief entry *38*
Han, Jenny 1981- *175*
Han, Lu
    See Stickler, Soma Han
Han, Soma
    See Stickler, Soma Han
Han, Suzanne Crowder 1953- *89*
Hancock, Mary A. 1923- *31*
Hancock, Sibyl 1940- 9
Hand, Elizabeth 1957- *167*
    Earlier sketch in SATA *118*
Handford, Martin (John) 1956- *64*
    See also CLR *22*
Handforth, Thomas (Schofield) 1897-1948 .. *42*
Handville, Robert (Tompkins) 1924- *45*
Hanel, Wolfram
    See Haenel, Wolfram
Haney, Lynn 1941- *23*
Hanff, Helene 1916-1997 .... *97*
    Earlier sketch in SATA *11*
Hanley, Boniface Francis 1924- *65*
Hanlon, Emily 1945- *15*
Hann, Jacquie 1951- *19*
Hann, Judith 1942- *77*
Hanna, Bill
    See Hanna, William (Denby)
Hanna, Cheryl 1951- *84*
Hanna, Jack (Bushnell) 1947- *74*
Hanna, Nell(ie L.) 1908- *55*
Hanna, Paul R(obert) 1902-1988 9
Hanna, William (Denby) 1910-2001 .... *51*
    Obituary *126*
Hannam, Charles 1925- *50*
Hannigan, Katherine *170*
Hannon, Ezra
    See Hunter, Evan
Hann-Syme, Marguerite *127*
Hano, Arnold 1922- *12*
Hano, Renee Roth
    See Roth-Hano, Renee
Hanover, Terri
    See Huff, Tanya
Hansen, Ann Larkin 1958- *96*
Hansen, Brooks 1965- *104*
Hansen, Caryl (Hall) 1929- *39*
Hansen, Ian V. 1929- *113*
Hansen, Jennifer 1972- *156*
Hansen, Joyce 1942- *172*
    Autobiography Feature *172*
    Brief entry *39*
    Earlier sketches in SATA *46, 101*
    See also CLR *21*
    See also SAAS *15*
Hansen, Joyce Viola
    See Hansen, Joyce
Hansen, Mark Victor *112*
Hansen, Ron(ald Thomas) 1947- *56*
Hanser, Richard (Frederick) 1909-1981 ...... *13*
Hanson, Joan 1938- 8
Hanson, Warren 1949- *155*
Hansson, Gunilla 1939- *64*
Harald, Eric
    See Boesen, Victor
Hard, Charlotte (Ann) 1969- *98*
Hardcastle, Michael 1933- *47*
    Brief entry *38*
Harding, Lee 1937- *32*
    Brief entry *31*
Hardt, Helga Fleischhauer
    See Fleischhauer-Hardt, Helga
Hardwick, Richard Holmes, Jr. 1923- *12*
Hardy, Alice Dale *67*
    Earlier sketch in SATA *1*

Hardy, David A(ndrews) 1936- 9
Hardy, Jon 1958- 53
Hardy, LeAnne 1951- 154
Hardy, Stuart
    See Schisgall, Oscar
Hare, Norma Q(uarles) 1924- 46
    Brief entry 41
Harel, Nira 1936- 154
Harford, Henry
    See Hudson, W(illiam) H(enry)
Hargrave, Leonie
    See Disch, Thomas M.
Hargrove, James 1947- 57
    Brief entry 50
Hargrove, Jim
    See Hargrove, James
Hariton, Anca I. 1955- 79
Hark, Mildred
    See McQueen, Mildred Hark
Harkaway, Hal
    See Stratemeyer, Edward L.
Harkins, Philip 1912-1997 6
    Obituary 129
Harlan, Elizabeth 1945- 41
    Brief entry 35
Harlan, Glen
    See Cebulash, Mel
Harlan, Judith 1949- 135
    Earlier sketch in SATA 74
    See also CLR 81
Harland, Richard 1947- 152
Harlee, J. V.
    See Leese, Jennifer L.B.
Harler, Ann
    See Van Steenwyk, Elizabeth (Ann)
Harley, Bill 1954- 87
Harlow, Joan Hiatt 1932- 157
Harmelink, Barbara (Mary) 9
Harmer, Mabel 1894-1992 45
Harmon, Dan
    See Harmon, Daniel E(lton)
Harmon, Daniel E(lton) 1949- 157
Harmon, Margaret 1906- 20
Harmon, William (Ruth) 1938- 65
Harnan, Terry 1920- 12
Harness, Cheryl 1951- 178
    Earlier sketch in SATA 131
Harnett, Cynthia (Mary) 1893-1981 5
    Obituary 32
Harper, Anita 1943- 41
Harper, Betty 1946- 126
Harper, Charise
    See Harper, Charise Mericle
Harper, Charise Mericle 179
Harper, Elaine
    See Hallin, Emily Watson
Harper, Ellen
    See Noble, Marty
Harper, Jamie 174
Harper, Jessica (R.) 1949- 148
Harper, Jo 1932- 169
    Earlier sketch in SATA 97
Harper, Mary Wood
    See Dixon, Jeanne
Harper, Piers 1966- 161
    Earlier sketch in SATA 105
Harper, Wilhelmina 1884-1973 4
    Obituary 26
Harrah, Madge 1931- 154
Harrah, Michael 1940- 41
Harrah, Monique
    See Harrah, Madge
Harrar, George E. 1949- 124
Harrell, Beatrice Orcutt 1943- 93
Harrell, Janice 1945- 70
Harries, Joan 1922- 39
Harrill, Ronald 1950- 90
Harrington, Denis J(ames) 1932- 88
Harrington, Lyn 5
    See Harrington, Evelyn Davis
Harris, Alan 1944- 71

Harris, Aurand 1915-1996 37
    Obituary 91
Harris, Carol Flynn 1933- 135
Harris, Catherine
    See Ainsworth, Catherine Harris
Harris, Christie
    See Harris, Christie (Lucy) Irwin
Harris, Christie (Lucy) Irwin 1907-2002 74
    Autobiography Feature 116
    Earlier sketch in SATA 6
    See also CLR 47
    See also SAAS 10
Harris, Christine 1955- 105
Harris, Colver
    See Colver, Anne
Harris, David (William) 1942- 118
Harris, Dorothy Joan 1931- 153
    Earlier sketch in SATA 13
Harris, Geraldine (Rachel) 1951- 54
Harris, Jacqueline L. 1929- 62
Harris, Janet 1932-1979 4
    Obituary 23
Harris, Jesse
    See Standiford, Natalie
Harris, Joan 1946- 146
Harris, Joel Chandler 1848-1908 100
    See also YABC 1
    See also CLR 49
Harris, John (Wyndham Parkes Lucas) Beynon
    1903-1969 118
    See Wyndham, John
Harris, Johnson
    See Harris, John (Wyndham Parkes Lucas)
    Beynon
Harris, Jonathan 1921-1997 52
Harris, Larry Vincent 1939- 59
Harris, Lavinia
    See St. John, Nicole
Harris, Leon A., Jr. 1926-2000 4
Harris, Lorle K(empe) 1912-2001 22
Harris, Marilyn
    See Springer, Marilyn Harris
Harris, Mark Jonathan 1941- 84
    Earlier sketch in SATA 32
Harris, Mary K(athleen) 1905-1966 119
Harris, Robie H. 1940- 147
    Brief entry 53
    Earlier sketch in SATA 90
Harris, Robin
    See Shine, Deborah
Harris, Rosemary (Jeanne) 82
    Earlier sketch in SATA 4
    See also CLR 30
    See also SAAS 7
Harris, Ruth Elwin 1935- 164
Harris, Sherwood 1932- 25
Harris, Steven Michael 1957- 55
Harris, Trudy 1949- 128
Harris-Filderman, Diane
    See Filderman, Diane E(lizabeth)
Harrison, C(hester) William 1913-1994 35
Harrison, Carol
    See Harrison, Carol Thompson
Harrison, Carol Thompson 113
Harrison, David L(ee) 1937- 150
    Earlier sketches in SATA 26, 92
Harrison, Deloris 1938- 9
Harrison, Edward Hardy 1926- 56
Harrison, Elizabeth (Allen) Cavanna
    1909-2001 142
    See Cavanna, Betty
Harrison, Harry (Max) 1925- 4
Harrison, Mette Ivie 1970- 149
Harrison, Michael 1939- 106
Harrison, Molly (Hodgett) 1909-2002 41
Harrison, Sarah 1946- 63
Harrison, Ted
    See Harrison, Edward Hardy
Harsh, Fred (T.) 1925- 72
Harshaw, Ruth H(etzel) 1890-1968 27

Harshman, Marc 1950- 109
    Earlier sketch in SATA 71
Hart, Alison
    See Leonhardt, Alice
Hart, Bruce 1938-2006 57
    Brief entry 39
Hart, Carole 1943- 57
    Brief entry 39
Hart, Carolyn 1936- 74
Hart, Carolyn G.
    See Hart, Carolyn
Hart, Carolyn Gimpel
    See Hart, Carolyn
Hart, Jan Siegel 1940- 79
Hart, Joyce 1954- 148
Hart, Lenore 171
Hart, Virginia 1949- 83
Harte, (Francis) Bret(t) 1836(?)-1902 26
Harter, Debbie 1963- 107
Hartfield, Claire 1957- 147
Hartinger, Brent 1964- 174
    Earlier sketch in SATA 145
Hartland, Jessie 171
Hartley, Ellen (Raphael) 1915-1980 23
Hartley, Fred Allan III 1953- 41
Hartley, William B(rown) 1913-1980 23
Hartling, Peter
    See CLR 29
    See Hartling, Peter
Hartling, Peter 1933- 66
    See Hartling, Peter
Hartman, Evert 1937- 38
    Brief entry 35
Hartman, Jane E(vangeline) 1928- 47
Hartman, Louis F(rancis) 1901-1970 22
Hartman, Rachel 174
Hartman, Victoria 1942- 91
Hartnett, Sonya 1968- 176
    Earlier sketches in SATA 93, 130
Hartshorn, Ruth M. 1928- 11
Hartung, Susan Kathleen 150
Hartwig, Manfred 1950- 81
Harvey, Brett 1936- 61
Harvey, Karen D. 1935- 88
Harvey, Roland 1945- 179
    Earlier sketches in SATA 71, 123
Harwick, B. L.
    See Keller, Beverly L(ou)
Harwin, Brian
    See Henderson, LeGrand
Harwood, Pearl Augusta (Bragdon)
    1903-1998 9
Haseley, Dennis 1950- 157
    Brief entry 44
    Earlier sketches in SATA 57, 105
Hashmi, Kerri 1955- 108
Haskell, Arnold L(ionel) 1903-1981(?) 6
Haskins, James
    See Haskins, James S.
Haskins, James S. 1941-2005 132
    Autobiography Feature 132
    Earlier sketches in SATA 9, 69, 105
    See also CLR 39
    See Haskins, Jim
Haskins, Jim
    See SAAS 4
    See Haskins, James S.
Hasler, Joan 1931- 28
Hass, Robert 1941- 94
Hassall, Joan 1906-1988 43
    Obituary 56
Hassett, Ann 1958- 162
Hassett, John 162
Hassler, Jon 1933- 19
Hassler, Jon Francis
    See Hassler, Jon
Hastings, Beverly
    See Barkin, Carol
    and James, Elizabeth
Hastings, Graham
    See Jeffries, Roderic

Hastings, Ian 1912- *62*
Hatch, Lynda S. 1950- *90*
Hathaway, Barbara *164*
Hathorn, Libby 1943- *156*
   Autobiography Feature *156*
   Earlier sketches in SATA *74, 120*
   See Hathorn, Elizabeth Helen
Haugaard, Erik Christian 1923- *68*
   Earlier sketch in SATA *4*
   See also CLR *11*
   See also SAAS *12*
Haugaard, Kay *117*
Haugen, Hayley Mitchell 1968- *172*
Haugen, Tormod 1945- *66*
Hauman, Doris 1898-1984 .... *32*
Hauman, George 1890-1961 .... *32*
Hauptly, Denis J(ames) 1945- *57*
Hauser, Jill Frankel 1950- *127*
Hauser, Margaret L(ouise) 1909- *10*
Hausherr, Rosmarie 1943- *86*
Hausman, Gerald 1945- *132*
   Earlier sketches in SATA *13, 90*
   See also CLR *89*
Hausman, Gerry
   See Hausman, Gerald
Hauth, Katherine B. 1940- *99*
Hautman, Pete 1952- *173*
   Earlier sketches in SATA *82, 128*
Hautman, Peter Murray
   See Hautman, Pete
Hautzig, Deborah 1956- *106*
   Earlier sketch in SATA *31*
Hautzig, Esther Rudomin 1930- *148*
   Earlier sketches in SATA *4, 68*
   See also CLR *22*
   See also SAAS *15*
Havel, Geoff 1955- *152*
Havel, Jennifer
   See Havill, Juanita
Havelin, Kate 1961- *143*
Havighurst, Walter (Edwin) 1901-1994 .... *1*
   Obituary *79*
Haviland, Virginia 1911-1988 .... *6*
   Obituary *54*
Havill, Juanita 1949- *155*
   Earlier sketch in SATA *74*
Hawes, Judy 1913- *4*
Hawes, Louise 1943- *60*
Hawke, Rosanne 1953- *165*
   Earlier sketch in SATA *124*
Hawke, Rosanne Joy
   See Hawke, Rosanne
Hawkes, Kevin (Cliff) 1959- *150*
   Earlier sketch in SATA *78*
Hawkes, Nigel 1943- *119*
Hawkesworth, Eric 1921- *13*
Hawkins, Arthur 1903-1985 .... *19*
Hawkins, Colin 1945- *162*
   Earlier sketch in SATA *112*
Hawkins, Jacqui *162*
   Earlier sketch in SATA *112*
Hawkins, Laura 1951- *74*
Hawkins, (Helena Ann) Quail 1905-2002 ...... *6*
   Obituary *141*
Hawkinson, John (Samuel) 1912-1994 .... *4*
Hawkinson, Lucy (Ozone) 1924-1971 .... *21*
Hawks, Robert 1961- *85*
Hawley, Mabel C. *67*
   Earlier sketch in SATA *1*
Hawthorne, Captain R. M.
   See Ellis, Edward S(ylvester)
Hawthorne, Nathaniel 1804-1864
   See YABC *2*
   See also CLR *103*
Hay, Jeff T. *154*
Hay, John 1915- *13*
Hay, Timothy
   See Brown, Margaret Wise
Hayashi, Leslie Ann 1954- *115*
Hayashi, Nancy 1939- *80*
Haycock, Kate 1962- *77*

Haycraft, Howard 1905-1991 .... *6*
   Obituary *70*
Haycraft, Molly Costain 1911- *6*
Hayden, Gwendolen Lampshire 1904- *35*
Hayden, Robert C(arter), Jr. 1937- *47*
   Brief entry *28*
Hayden, Robert E(arl) 1913-1980 .... *19*
   Obituary *26*
Hayden, Torey L. 1951- *163*
   Earlier sketch in SATA *65*
Hayden, Torey Lynn
   See Hayden, Torey L.
Hayes, Carlton J(oseph) H(untley)
   1882-1964 .... *11*
Hayes, Daniel 1952- *109*
   Earlier sketch in SATA *73*
Hayes, Geoffrey 1947- *91*
   Earlier sketch in SATA *26*
Hayes, Joe 1945- *131*
   Earlier sketch in SATA *88*
Hayes, John F. 1904-1980 .... *11*
Hayes, Rosemary *158*
Hayes, Sheila 1937- *51*
   Brief entry *50*
Hayes, Will *7*
Hayes, William D(imitt) 1913-1976 .... *8*
Haynes, Betsy 1937- *94*
   Brief entry *37*
   Earlier sketch in SATA *48*
   See also CLR *90*
Haynes, David 1955- *97*
Haynes, Linda
   See Swinford, Betty (June Wells)
Haynes, Mary 1938- *65*
Haynes, Max 1956- *72*
Hays, H(offmann) R(eynolds) 1904-1980 .... *26*
Hays, Thomas Anthony 1957- *84*
Hays, Tony
   See Hays, Thomas Anthony
Hays, Wilma Pitchford 1909- *28*
   Earlier sketch in SATA *1*
   See also CLR *59*
   See also SAAS *3*
Hayward, Linda 1943- *101*
   Brief entry *39*
Haywood, Carolyn 1898-1990 .... *75*
   Obituary *64*
   Earlier sketches in SATA *1, 29*
   See also CLR *22*
Hazell, Rebecca (Eileen) 1947- *141*
Hazen, Barbara Shook 1930- *178*
   Earlier sketches in SATA *27, 90*
Head, Gay
   See Hauser, Margaret L(ouise)
Head, Tom 1978- *167*
Headley, Elizabeth
   See Harrison, Elizabeth (Allen) Cavanna
Headley, Justina Chen 1968- *176*
Headstrom, (Birger) Richard 1902-1985 .... *8*
Heady, Eleanor B(utler) 1917-1979 .... *8*
Heagy, William D. 1964- *76*
Heal, Edith 1903-1995 .... *7*
Heal, Gillian 1934- *89*
Heale, Jay (Jeremy Peter Wingfield) 1937- .. *84*
Healey, Brooks
   See Albert, Burton
Healey, Larry 1927- *44*
   Brief entry *42*
Heap, Sue 1954- *150*
Heaps, Willard A(llison) 1908-1987 .... *26*
Hearn, Diane Dawson 1952- *79*
Hearn, Emily
   See Valleau, Emily
Hearn, Julie 1958- *152*
Hearn, Lian
   See Rubinstein, Gillian (Margaret)
Hearn, Sneed
   See Gregg, Andrew K.
Hearne, Betsy Gould 1942- *146*
   Earlier sketches in SATA *38, 95*
Heath, Charles D(ickinson) 1941- *46*

Heath, Veronica
   See Blackett, Veronica Heath
Heaven, Constance (Christina) 1911- *7*
Hebert-Collins, Sheila 1948- *111*
Hecht, Henri Joseph 1922- *9*
Hechtkopf, Henryk 1910- *17*
Heck, Bessie (Mildred) Holland 1911-1995 . *26*
Heck, Ed 1963- *173*
Heckert, Connie K(aye Delp) 1948- *82*
Hedderwick, Mairi 1939- *145*
   Earlier sketches in SATA *30, 77*
Hedges, Sid(ney) G(eorge) 1897-1974 .... *28*
Hedrick, Irene Hope 1920- *175*
Heelan, Jamee Riggio 1965- *146*
Heerboth, Sharon
   See Leon, Sharon
Heffernan, John 1949- *168*
   Earlier sketch in SATA *121*
Heffron, Dorris 1944- *68*
Hefter, Richard 1942- *31*
Hegarty, Reginald Beaton 1906-1973 .... *10*
Hehenberger, Shelly 1968- *126*
Heidbreder, Robert K. 1947- *130*
Heide, Florence Parry 1919- *118*
   Earlier sketches in SATA *32, 69*
   See also CLR *60*
   See also SAAS *6*
Heiderstadt, Dorothy 1907-2001 .... *6*
Heidi Louise
   See Erdrich, Louise
Heidler, David S(tephen) 1955- *132*
Heidler, Jeanne T. 1956- *132*
Heilbroner, Joan Knapp 1922- *63*
Heiligman, Deborah 1958- *144*
   Earlier sketch in SATA *90*
Heilman, Joan Rattner *50*
Heimann, Rolf 1940- *164*
   Earlier sketch in SATA *120*
Hein, Lucille Eleanor 1915-1994 .... *20*
Heine, Helme 1941- *135*
   Earlier sketch in SATA *67*
   See also CLR *18*
Heinlein, Robert A. 1907-1988 .... *69*
   Obituary *56*
   Earlier sketch in SATA *9*
   See also CLR *75*
Heinlein, Robert Anson
   See Heinlein, Robert A.
Heins, Ethel L(eah) 1918-1997 .... *101*
Heins, Paul 1909- *13*
Heintze, Carl 1922- *26*
Heinz, Brian J(ames) 1946- *95*
Heinz, W(ilfred) C(harles) 1915- *26*
Heinzen, Mildred
   See Masters, Mildred
Heisel, Sharon E(laine) 1941- *125*
   Earlier sketch in SATA *84*
Heitzmann, William Ray 1948- *73*
Heitzmann, Wm. Ray
   See Heitzmann, William Ray
Helakoski, Leslie *178*
Helberg, Shirley Adelaide Holden 1919- ... *138*
Helfer, Ralph *177*
Helfman, Elizabeth S(eaver) 1911-2001 .... *3*
Helfman, Harry Carmozin 1910-1995 .... *3*
Hellberg, Hans-Eric 1927- *38*
Heller, Linda 1944- *46*
   Brief entry *40*
Heller, Mike
   See Hano, Arnold
Heller, Ruth M. 1924- *112*
   Earlier sketch in SATA *66*
Hellman, Hal
   See Hellman, Harold
Hellman, Harold 1927- *4*
Helman, Andrea (Jean) 1946- *160*
   Earlier sketch in SATA *107*
Helmer, Diana Star 1962- *86*
Helmer, Marilyn *160*
   Earlier sketch in SATA *112*

Helps, Racey 1913-1971 2
   Obituary 25
Helquist, Brett 146
Helweg, Hans H. 1917- 50
   Brief entry 33
Helyar, Jane Penelope Josephine 1933- 138
   Autobiography Feature 138
   Earlier sketch in SATA 82
   See Poole, Josephine
Hemmant, Lynette 1938- 69
Hemming, Roy G. 1928-1995 11
   Obituary 86
Hemphill, Helen 1955- 179
Hemphill, Kris (Harrison) 1963- 118
Hemphill, Martha Locke 1904-1973 37
Hemstock, Gillian 1956- 173
Henba, Bobbie 1926- 87
Henbest, Nigel 1951- 55
   Brief entry 52
Henderley, Brooks 1
Henderson, Aileen Kilgore 1921- 178
Henderson, Aileen Mary
   See Fox, Aileen
Henderson, Gordon 1950- 53
Henderson, Kathy 1949- 155
   Brief entry 53
   Earlier sketches in SATA 55, 95
Henderson, LeGrand 1901-1965 9
Henderson, Nancy Wallace 1916- 22
Henderson, Zenna (Chlarson) 1917-1983 5
Hendrickson, Walter Brookfield, Jr. 1936- 9
Hendry, Diana 1941- 106
   Earlier sketch in SATA 68
Hendry, Frances Mary 1941- 171
   Earlier sketch in SATA 110
Hendry, Linda (Gail) 1961- 83
Heneghan, James 1930- 160
   Earlier sketches in SATA 53, 97
Henkes, Kevin 1960- 154
   Earlier sketches in SATA 43, 76, 108
   See also CLR 108
Hennessy, Barbara G.
   See Hennessy, B.G.
Hennessy, Barbara Gulbrandsen
   See Hennessy, B.G.
Hennessy, B.G. 1951- 175
Henney, Carolee Wells 1928- 102
Henriod, Lorraine 1925- 26
Henriquez, Emile F. 1937- 170
   Earlier sketch in SATA 89
Henry, April 1959- 174
Henry, Ernest 1948- 107
Henry, Joanne Landers 1927- 6
Henry, Maeve 1960- 75
Henry, Marguerite 1902-1997 100
   Obituary 99
   See also CLR 4
   See also SAAS 7
Henry, Marie H. 1935- 65
Henry, Marilyn 1939- 117
Henry, Marion
   See del Rey, Lester
Henry, O.
   See Porter, William Sydney
Henry, Oliver
   See Porter, William Sydney
Henry, T. E.
   See Rowland-Entwistle, (Arthur) Theodore
      (Henry)
Henschel, Elizabeth Georgie 56
Henson, James Maury
   See Henson, Jim
Henson, Jim 1936-1990 43
   Obituary 65
Henstra, Friso 1928- 73
   Earlier sketch in SATA 8
   See also SAAS 14
Hentoff, Nat(han Irving) 1925- 133
   Brief entry 27
   Earlier sketches in SATA 42, 69
   See also CLR 52

Henty, G(eorge) A(lfred) 1832-1902 64
   See also CLR 76
Heo, Yumi 1964- 146
   Earlier sketch in SATA 94
Hepler, Heather 177
Herald, Kathleen
   See Peyton, Kathleen Wendy (Herald)
Herb, Angela M. 1970- 92
Herbert, Cecil
   See Hamilton, Charles (Harold St. John)
Herbert, Don 1917-2007 2
Herbert, Donald Jeffrey
   See Herbert, Don
Herbert, Frank 1920-1986 37
   Obituary 47
   Earlier sketch in SATA 9
Herbert, Frank Patrick
   See Herbert, Frank
Herbert, Helen (Jean) 1947- 57
Herbert, Janis 1956- 139
Herbert, Wally
   See Herbert, Walter William
Herbert, Walter William 1934-2007 23
Herbst, Judith 1947- 74
Herda, D.J. 1948- 80
Herge
   See CLR 114
   See Remi, Georges
Heritage, Martin
   See Horler, Sydney
Herkimer, L(awrence) R(ussell) 1925(?)- 42
Herlihy, Dirlie Anne 1935- 73
Herman, Charlotte 1937- 99
   Earlier sketch in SATA 20
Hermanson, Dennis (Everett) 1947- 10
Hermes, Jules 1962- 92
Hermes, Patricia (Mary) 1936- 141
   Earlier sketches in SATA 31, 78
Hernandez, Natalie Nelson 1929- 123
Herndon, Ernest 91
Herold, Ann Bixby 1937- 72
Herrera, Juan Felipe 1948- 127
Herrick, Steven 1958- 156
   Earlier sketch in SATA 103
Herriman, George (Joseph) 1880-1944 140
Herriot, James 1916-1995 135
   Earlier sketch in SATA 86
   See also CLR 80
   See Wight, James Alfred
Herrmanns, Ralph 1933- 11
Herrold, Tracey
   See Dils, Tracey E.
Herron, Edward A(lbert) 1912- 4
Herschler, Mildred Barger 130
Hersey, John 1914-1993 25
   Obituary 76
Hersey, John Richard
   See Hersey, John
   and Hersey, John
Hershberger, Priscilla (Gorman) 1951- 81
Hershenhorn, Esther 1945- 151
Hershey, Kathleen M. 1934- 80
Hershey, Mary 173
Hersom, Kathleen 1911- 73
Hertz, Grete Janus 1915- 23
Herzig, Alison Cragin 1935- 87
Herzog, Brad 1968- 131
Heslewood, Juliet 1951- 82
Hess, Lilo 1916- 4
Hess, Paul 1961- 134
Hesse, Hermann 1877-1962 50
Hesse, Karen 1952- 158
   Autobiography Feature 113
   Earlier sketches in SATA 74, 103
   See also CLR 54
   See also SAAS 25
Hest, Amy 1950- 129
   Earlier sketches in SATA 55, 82
Heuer, Kenneth John 1927- 44
Heuman, William 1912-1971 21
Heuston, Kimberley 1960- 167

Heuston, Kimberley Burton
   See Heuston, Kimberley
Hewes, Agnes Danforth 1874-1963 35
Hewett, Anita 1918-1989 13
Hewett, Joan 1930- 140
   Earlier sketch in SATA 81
Hewett, Richard 1929- 81
Hewitson, Jennifer 1961- 97
Hewitt, Margaret 1961- 84
Hewitt, Sally 1949- 127
Hext, Harrington
   See Phillpotts, Eden
Hey, Nigel S(tewart) 1936- 20
Heyduck-Huth, Hilde 1929- 8
Heyer, Carol 1950- 130
   Earlier sketch in SATA 74
Heyer, Marilee 1942- 102
   Earlier sketch in SATA 64
Heyerdahl, Thor 1914-2002 52
   Earlier sketch in SATA 2
Heyes, (Nancy) Eileen 1956- 150
   Earlier sketch in SATA 80
Heyliger, William 1884-1955
   See YABC 1
Heyman, Ken(neth Louis) 1930- 114
   Earlier sketch in SATA 34
Heyward, (Edwin) DuBose 1885-1940 21
Heywood, Karen 1946- 48
Hezlep, William (Earl) 1936- 88
Hibbert, Christopher 1924- 4
Hibbert, Eleanor Alice Burford 1906-1993 2
   Obituary 74
   See Holt, Victoria
Hickman, Estella (Lee) 1942- 111
Hickman, Janet 1940- 127
   Earlier sketch in SATA 12
Hickman, Martha Whitmore 1925- 26
Hickman, Pamela M. 1958- 128
Hickock, Will
   See Harrison, C(hester) William
Hickok, Lorena A. 1893-1968 20
Hickox, Rebecca (Ayres) 116
Hicks, Barbara Jean 1953- 165
Hicks, Clifford B. 1920- 50
Hicks, Eleanor B.
   See Coerr, Eleanor (Beatrice)
Hicks, Harvey
   See Stratemeyer, Edward L.
Hicks, Peter 1952- 111
Hicyilmaz, Gaye 1947- 157
   Earlier sketch in SATA 77
Hieatt, Constance B(artlett) 1928- 4
Hiebert, Ray Eldon 1932- 13
Higdon, Hal 1931- 4
Higginbottom, David 1923- 87
   See Fisk, Nicholas
Higginbottom, J(effrey) Winslow 1945- 29
Higgins, Joanna 1945- 125
Higgins, Simon (Richard) 1958- 105
Higginsen, Vy 79
High, Linda Oatman 1958- 145
   Earlier sketch in SATA 94
High, Philip E. 1914- 119
High, Philip Empson
   See High, Philip E.
Higham, David (Michael) 1949- 50
Higham, Jon Atlas
   See Higham, Jonathan Huw
Higham, Jonathan Huw 1960- 59
Highet, Helen
   See MacInnes, Helen (Clark)
Hightower, Florence Cole 1916-1981 4
   Obituary 27
Highwater, Jamake (Mamake)
   1942(?)-2001 69
   Brief entry 30
   Earlier sketch in SATA 32
   See also CLR 17
Hilb, Nora 1953- 178

Hildebrandt, Greg 1939- *172*
    Brief entry *33*
    Earlier sketch in SATA *55*
Hildebrandt, Tim 1939-2006 .... *55*
    Brief entry *33*
Hildebrandt, Timothy
    See Hildebrandt, Tim
Hildebrandts, The
    See Hildebrandt, Greg
    and Hildebrandt, Tim
Hilder, Rowland 1905-1993 .... *36*
    Obituary *77*
Hildick, E. W.
    See SAAS 6
    See Hildick, (Edmund) Wallace
Hildick, (Edmund) Wallace 1925-2001 .... *68*
    Earlier sketch in SATA *2*
    See Hildick, E. W.
Hilgartner, Beth 1957- *58*
Hill, Alexis
    See Craig, Mary (Francis) Shura
    and Glick, Ruth (Burtnick)
Hill, Anthony R. 1942- *164*
    Earlier sketch in SATA *91*
Hill, Anthony Robert
    See Hill, Anthony R.
Hill, David 1942- *152*
    Earlier sketch in SATA *103*
Hill, Donna (Marie) 1921- *124*
    Earlier sketch in SATA *24*
Hill, Douglas (Arthur) 1935-2007 .... *78*
    Earlier sketch in SATA *39*
Hill, Elizabeth Starr 1925- *143*
    Earlier sketch in SATA *24*
Hill, Eric 1927- *133*
    Brief entry *53*
    Earlier sketch in SATA *66*
    See also CLR *13*
Hill, Gordon
    See Eldin, Peter
Hill, Grace Brooks *67*
    Earlier sketch in SATA *1*
Hill, Grace Livingston 1865-1947
    See YABC 2
Hill, Helen M(orey) 1915- *27*
Hill, John
    See Koontz, Dean R.
Hill, Johnson
    See Kunhardt, Edith
Hill, Judy I. R.
    See Roberts, Judy I.
Hill, Kathleen Louise 1917- *4*
Hill, Kay
    See Hill, Kathleen Louise
Hill, Kirkpatrick 1938- *126*
    Earlier sketch in SATA *72*
Hill, Laban Carrick *170*
Hill, Lee Sullivan 1958- *96*
Hill, Lorna 1902-1991 .... *12*
Hill, Margaret (Ohler) 1915- *36*
Hill, Meg
    See Hill, Margaret (Ohler)
Hill, Meredith
    See Craig, Mary (Francis) Shura
Hill, Monica
    See Watson, Jane Werner
Hill, Pamela Smith 1954- *112*
Hill, Ralph Nading 1917-1987 .... *65*
Hill, Robert W(hite) 1919-1982 .... *12*
    Obituary *31*
Hill, Ruth A.
    See Viguers, Ruth Hill
Hill, Ruth Livingston
    See Munce, Ruth Hill
Hill, Thomas 1960- *82*
Hillcourt, William 1900-1992 .... *27*
Hillenbrand, Will 1960- *147*
    Earlier sketch in SATA *84*
Hiller, Ilo (Ann) 1938- *59*
Hillerman, Tony 1925- *6*

Hillert, Margaret 1920- *91*
    Earlier sketch in SATA *8*
Hillman, Elizabeth 1942- *75*
Hillman, John 1952- *120*
Hillman, Martin
    See Hill, Douglas (Arthur)
Hillman, Priscilla 1940- *48*
    Brief entry *39*
Hills, C.A.R. 1955- *39*
Hills, Charles Albert Reis
    See Hills, C.A.R.
Hills, Tad *173*
Hilton, Irene Pothus -1979 .... *7*
Hilton, James 1900-1954 .... *34*
Hilton, Margaret Lynette 1946- *105*
    Earlier sketch in SATA *68*
    See Hilton, Nette
Hilton, Nette
    See CLR *25*
    See also SAAS *21*
    See Hilton, Margaret Lynette
Hilton, Ralph 1907-1982 .... *8*
Hilton, Suzanne 1922- *4*
Hilton-Bruce, Anne
    See Hilton, Margaret Lynette
Himelblau, Linda -2005 .... *179*
Himelstein, Shmuel 1940- *83*
Himler, Ann 1946- *8*
Himler, Ronald (Norbert) 1937- *137*
    Earlier sketches in SATA *6, 92*
Himmelman, John C(arl) 1959- *159*
    Earlier sketches in SATA *47, 94*
Hinckley, Helen
    See Jones, Helen Hinckley
Hind, Dolores (Ellen) 1931- *53*
    Brief entry *49*
Hindin, Nathan
    See Bloch, Robert (Albert)
Hindley, Judy 1940- *179*
    Earlier sketch in SATA *120*
Hinds, P(atricia) Mignon *98*
Hines, Anna Grossnickle 1946- *141*
    Brief entry *45*
    Earlier sketches in SATA *51, 95*
    See also SAAS *16*
Hines, Gary (Roger) 1944- *136*
    Earlier sketch in SATA *74*
Hinojosa, Maria (de Lourdes) 1961- *88*
Hinton, Nigel 1941- *166*
Hinton, Sam 1917- *43*
Hinton, S.E. 1950- *160*
    Earlier sketches in SATA *19, 58, 115*
    See also CLR *23*
Hinton, Susan Eloise
    See Hinton, S.E.
Hintz, Martin 1945- *128*
    Brief entry *39*
    Earlier sketch in SATA *47*
Hintz, Stephen V. 1975- *129*
Hippopotamus, Eugene H.
    See Kraus, (Herman) Robert
Hirano, Cathy 1957- *68*
Hirsch, Karen 1941- *61*
Hirsch, Odo *157*
    Earlier sketch in SATA *111*
Hirsch, Phil 1926- *35*
Hirsch, S. Carl 1913-1990 .... *2*
    See also SAAS *7*
Hirschfelder, Arlene B. 1943- *138*
    Earlier sketch in SATA *80*
Hirschi, Ron 1948- *95*
    Earlier sketch in SATA *56*
Hirschmann, Linda (Ann) 1941- *40*
Hirsh, Marilyn 1944-1988 .... *7*
    Obituary *58*
Hirshberg, Al(bert Simon) 1909-1973 .... *38*
Hiscock, Bruce 1940- *137*
    Earlier sketch in SATA *57*
Hiser, Constance 1950- *71*
Hiser, Iona Seibert -1998 .... *4*
Hislop, Julia Rose Catherine 1962- *74*

Hissey, Jane 1952- *130*
    Autobiography Feature *130*
    Earlier sketches in SATA *58, 103*
Hissey, Jane Elizabeth
    See Hissey, Jane
Hitchcock, Alfred (Joseph) 1899-1980 .... *27*
    Obituary *24*
Hite, Sid 1954- *175*
    Earlier sketches in SATA *75, 136*
Hitte, Kathryn 1919- *16*
Hitz, Demi 1942- *152*
    Earlier sketches in SATA *11, 66, 102*
    See also CLR *58*
    See Demi
Hitzeroth, Deborah L. 1961- *78*
Hnizdovsky, Jacques 1915- *32*
Ho, Minfong 1951- *151*
    Earlier sketches in SATA *15, 94*
    See also CLR *28*
Hoagland, Edward (Morley) 1932- *51*
Hoare, Robert J(ohn) 1921-1975 .... *38*
Hoban, Lillian 1925-1998 .... *69*
    Obituary *104*
    Earlier sketch in SATA *22*
    See also CLR *67*
Hoban, Russell 1925- *136*
    Earlier sketches in SATA *1, 40, 78*
    See also CLR *69*
Hoban, Russell Conwell
    See Hoban, Russell
Hoban, Tana 1917(?)-2006 .... *104*
    Obituary *173*
    Earlier sketches in SATA *22, 70*
    See also CLR *76*
    See also SAAS *12*
Hobart, Lois (Elaine) *7*
Hobbie, Holly 1944- *178*
    See also CLR *88*
Hobbs, Leigh 1953- *166*
Hobbs, Valerie 1941- *145*
    Autobiography Feature *145*
    Earlier sketch in SATA *93*
Hobbs, Will 1947- *177*
    Autobiography Feature *127*
    Earlier sketches in SATA *72, 110*
    See also CLR *59*
Hobbs, William Carl
    See Hobbs, Will
Hoberman, Mary Ann 1930- *158*
    Earlier sketches in SATA *5, 72, 111*
    See also CLR *22*
    See also SAAS *18*
Hobson, Bruce 1950- *62*
Hobson, Burton (Harold) 1933- *28*
Hobson, Laura Z(ametkin) 1900-1986 .... *52*
Hobson, Sally 1967- *172*
    Earlier sketch in SATA *84*
Hoce, Charley E. *174*
Hochschild, Arlie Russell 1940- *11*
Hockaby, Stephen
    See Mitchell, Gladys (Maude Winifred)
Hockenberry, Hope
    See Newell, Hope Hockenberry
Hodge, Deborah 1954- *163*
    Earlier sketch in SATA *122*
Hodge, P. W.
    See Hodge, Paul W(illiam)
Hodge, Paul W(illiam) 1934- *12*
Hodgell, P(atricia) C(hristine) 1951- *42*
Hodges, C. Walter 1909-2004 .... *2*
    Obituary *158*
Hodges, Carl G. 1902-1964 .... *10*
Hodges, Cyril Walter
    See Hodges, C. Walter
Hodges, Elizabeth Jamison *1*
Hodges, Margaret
    See Hodges, Margaret Moore
Hodges, Margaret Moore 1911-2005 .... *167*
    Obituary *172*
    Earlier sketches in SATA *1, 33, 75, 117*
    See also SAAS *9*

Hodgetts, Blake Christopher 1967- *43*
Hodgson, Harriet (W.) 1935- *84*
Hoehne, Marcia 1951- *89*
Hoellwarth, Cathryn Clinton
    See Clinton, Cathryn
Hoestlandt, Jo 1948- *94*
Hoestlandt, Jocelyne
    See Hoestlandt, Jo
Hoexter, Corinne K. 1927- *6*
Hoeye, Michael 1947- *136*
Hoff, Carol 1900-1979 .... *11*
Hoff, Mary (King) 1956- *157*
    Earlier sketch in SATA *74*
Hoff, Syd(ney) 1912-2004 .... *138*
    Obituary *154*
    Earlier sketches in SATA *9, 72*
    See also CLR *83*
    See also SAAS *4*
Hoffman, Edwin D. *49*
Hoffman, Mary (Margaret) 1945- *144*
    Earlier sketches in SATA *59, 97*
    See also SAAS *24*
    See Lassiter, Mary
Hoffman, Mat 1972- *150*
Hoffman, Nina Kiriki 1955- *160*
Hoffman, Phyllis M(iriam) 1944- *4*
Hoffman, Rosekrans 1926- *15*
Hoffmann, E(rnst) T(heodor) A(madeus)
    1776-1822 .... *27*
Hoffmann, Felix 1911-1975 .... *9*
Hoffmann, Heinrich 1809-1894
    See CLR *122*
Hoffmann, Margaret Jones 1910- *48*
Hoffmann, Peggy
    See Hoffmann, Margaret Jones
Hofher, Catherine Baxley 1954- *130*
Hofher, Cathy
    See Hofher, Catherine Baxley
Hofmeyr, Dianne (Louise) *138*
Hofsepian, Sylvia A. 1932- *74*
Hofsinde, Robert 1902-1973 .... *21*
Hogan, Bernice Harris 1929- *12*
Hogan, Inez 1895-1973 .... *2*
Hogan, James P(atrick) 1941- *81*
Hogan, Linda 1947- *132*
Hogarth, Burne 1911-1996 .... *89*
    Earlier sketch in SATA *63*
Hogarth, Grace (Weston Allen) 1905-1995 .. *91*
Hogarth, Jr.
    See Kent, Rockwell
Hogarth, (Arthur) Paul 1917-2001 .... *41*
Hogg, Garry 1902-1976 .... *2*
Hogg, Gary 1957- *172*
    Earlier sketch in SATA *105*
Hogner, Dorothy Childs *4*
Hogner, Nils 1893-1970 .... *25*
Hogrogian, Nonny 1932- *74*
    Autobiography Feature *127*
    Earlier sketch in SATA *7*
    See also CLR *95*
    See also SAAS *1*
Hoh, Diane 1937- *102*
    Brief entry *48*
    Earlier sketch in SATA *52*
Hoke, John (Lindsay) 1925- *7*
Hol, Coby 1943- *126*
Holabird, Katharine 1948- *135*
    Earlier sketch in SATA *62*
Holaday, Bobbie 1922- *153*
Holbeach, Henry
    See Rands, William Brighty
Holberg, Ruth L(angland) 1889-1984 .... *1*
Holbrook, Kathy 1963- *107*
Holbrook, Peter
    See Glick, Carl (Cannon)
Holbrook, Sabra
    See Erickson, Sabra Rollins
Holbrook, Sara *131*
Holbrook, Stewart Hall 1893-1964 .... *2*
Holcomb, Jerry (Leona) Kimble 1927- *113*

Holcomb, Nan
    See McPhee, Norma H.
Holden, Elizabeth Rhoda
    See Lawrence, Louise
Holding, James (Clark Carlisle, Jr.)
    1907-1997 .... *3*
Holeman, Linda 1949- *136*
    Autobiography Feature *136*
    Earlier sketch in SATA *102*
Holinger, William (Jacques) 1944- *90*
Holisher, Desider 1901-1972 .... *6*
Holl, Adelaide Hinkle 1910- *8*
Holl, Kristi D(iane) 1951- *51*
Holland, Gay W. 1941- *128*
Holland, Isabelle (Christian) 1920-2002 .... *70*
    Autobiography Feature *103*
    Obituary *132*
    Earlier sketch in SATA *8*
    See also CLR *57*
Holland, Janice 1913-1962 .... *18*
Holland, John L(ewis) 1919- *20*
Holland, Joyce
    See Morice, Dave
Holland, Julia 1954- *106*
Holland, Lynda (H.) 1959- *77*
Holland, Lys
    See Gater, Dilys
Holland, Marion 1908-1989 .... *6*
    Obituary *61*
Hollander, John 1929- *13*
Hollander, Nicole 1940(?)- *101*
Hollander, Paul
    See Silverberg, Robert
Hollander, Phyllis 1928- *39*
Hollander, Zander 1923- *63*
Holldobler, Turid 1939- *26*
Holliday, Joe
    See Holliday, Joseph
Holliday, Joseph 1910- *11*
Holling, Holling C(lancy) 1900-1973 .... *15*
    Obituary *26*
    See also CLR *50*
Hollingsworth, Alvin C(arl) 1930- *39*
Hollingsworth, Mary 1947- *166*
    Earlier sketch in SATA *91*
Holloway, Teresa (Bragunier) 1906- *26*
Holm, (Else) Anne (Lise) 1922-1998 .... *1*
    See also CLR *75*
    See also SAAS *7*
Holm, Jennifer L. 1968(?)- *163*
    Earlier sketch in SATA *120*
Holm, Matthew 1974- *174*
Holm, Sharon Lane 1955- *114*
    Earlier sketch in SATA *78*
Holman, Felice 1919- *82*
    Earlier sketch in SATA *7*
    See also SAAS *17*
Holm and Hamel
    See Holm, Jennifer L.
Holme, Bryan 1913-1990 .... *26*
    Obituary *66*
Holmes, Barbara Ware 1945- *127*
    Earlier sketch in SATA *65*
Holmes, John
    See Souster, (Holmes) Raymond
Holmes, Marjorie (Rose) 1910-2002 .... *43*
Holmes, Martha 1961- *72*
Holmes, Mary Z(astrow) 1943- *80*
Holmes, Oliver Wendell 1809-1894 .... *34*
Holmes, Peggy 1898- *60*
Holmes, Raymond
    See Souster, (Holmes) Raymond
Holmes, Rick
    See Hardwick, Richard Holmes, Jr.
Holmgren, Helen Jean 1930- *45*
Holmgren, Sister George Ellen
    See Holmgren, Helen Jean
Holmgren, Virginia C(unningham) 1909- *26*
Holmquist, Eve 1921- *11*
Holt, Kimberly Willis 1960- *179*
    Earlier sketch in SATA *122*

Holt, Margaret 1937- *4*
Holt, Margaret Van Vechten (Saunders)
    1899-1963 .... *32*
Holt, Michael (Paul) 1929- *13*
Holt, Rackham
    See Holt, Margaret Van Vechten (Saunders)
Holt, Rochelle L. *41*
    See DuBois, Rochelle (Lynn) Holt
Holt, Stephen
    See Thompson, Harlan (Howard)
Holt, Victoria
    See Hibbert, Eleanor Alice Burford
Holton, Leonard
    See Wibberley, Leonard (Patrick O'Connor)
Holtze, Sally Holmes 1952- *64*
Holtzman, Jerome 1926- *57*
Holub, Joan 1956- *149*
    Earlier sketch in SATA *99*
Holub, Josef 1926- *175*
Holubitsky, Katherine 1955- *165*
    Earlier sketch in SATA *121*
Holyer, Erna Maria 1925- *22*
Holyer, Ernie
    See Holyer, Erna Maria
Holz, Loretta (Marie) 1943- *17*
Homel, David 1952- *97*
Homze, Alma C. 1932- *17*
Honey, Elizabeth 1947- *137*
    Autobiography Feature *137*
    Earlier sketch in SATA *112*
Honeycutt, Natalie 1945- *97*
Hong, Lily Toy 1958- *76*
Honig, Donald 1931- *18*
Honness, Elizabeth H. 1904- *2*
Hoobler, Dorothy 1941- *161*
    Earlier sketches in SATA *28, 109*
Hoobler, Thomas *161*
    Earlier sketches in SATA *28, 109*
Hood, Joseph F. 1925- *4*
Hood, Robert E. 1926- *21*
Hood, Sarah
    See Killough, (Karen) Lee
Hook, Brendan 1963- *105*
Hook, Frances 1912-1983 .... *27*
Hook, Geoffrey R(aynor) 1928- *103*
Hook, Jeff
    See Hook, Geoffrey R(aynor)
Hook, Martha 1936- *27*
Hooker, Richard
    See Heinz, W(ilfred) C(harles)
Hooker, Ruth 1920-1998 .... *21*
hooks, bell 1952(?)- *170*
    Earlier sketch in SATA *115*
Hooks, William H(arris) 1921- *94*
    Earlier sketch in SATA *16*
Hoon, Patricia Easterly 1954- *90*
Hooper, Mary 1944- *160*
Hooper, Maureen Brett 1927- *76*
Hooper, Meredith 1939- *159*
    Earlier sketches in SATA *28, 101*
Hooper, Meredith Jean
    See Hooper, Meredith
Hooper, Patricia 1941- *95*
Hoopes, Lyn Littlefield 1953- *49*
    Brief entry *44*
Hoopes, Ned E(dward) 1932- *21*
Hoopes, Roy 1922- *11*
Hoose, Phillip M. 1947- *137*
Hoover, H(elen) M(ary) 1935- *132*
    Brief entry *33*
    Earlier sketches in SATA *44, 83*
    See also SAAS *8*
Hoover, Helen (Drusilla Blackburn)
    1910-1984 .... *12*
    Obituary *39*
Hope, Christopher (David Tully) 1944- *62*
Hope, Laura Lee *67*
    Earlier sketch in SATA *1*
    See Goulart, Ron(ald Joseph)
    and Stanley, George Edward
Hope Simpson, Jacynth 1930- *12*

Hopf, Alice (Martha) L(ightner) 1904-1988 ... 5
   Obituary 55
Hopkins, C. M.
   See Hopkins, Cathy
Hopkins, Cathy 1953- 165
Hopkins, Cathy M.
   See Hopkins, Cathy
Hopkins, Ellen L. 1955- 128
Hopkins, Jackie
   See Hopkins, Jackie Mims
Hopkins, Jackie Mims 1952- 178
   Earlier sketch in SATA 92
Hopkins, Joseph G(erard) E(dward) 1909- ... 11
Hopkins, Lee Bennett 1938- 168
   Earlier sketches in SATA 3, 68, 125
   See also CLR 44
   See also SAAS 4
Hopkins, Lyman
   See Folsom, Franklin (Brewster)
Hopkins, Marjorie 1911-1999 9
Hopkins, Mary R(ice) 1956- 97
Hopkinson, Amanda 1948- 84
Hopkinson, Deborah 1952- 159
   Earlier sketches in SATA 76, 108
   See also CLR 118
Hopman, Philip 1961- 177
Hoppe, Joanne 1932- 42
Hoppe, Matthias 1952- 76
Hopper, Nancy J. 1937- 38
   Brief entry 35
Hopping, Lorraine Jean
   See Egan, Lorraine Hopping
Horacek, Petr 163
Horenstein, Henry 1947- 108
Horgan, Paul (George Vincent O'Shaughnessy)
   1903-1995 13
   Obituary 84
Horlak, E. E.
   See Tepper, Sheri S.
Horler, Sydney 1888-1954 102
Horn, Sandra Ann 1944- 154
Hornblow, Arthur, Jr. 1893-1976 15
Hornblow, Leonora 1920-2005 18
   Obituary 171
Hornblow, Leonora Schinasi
   See Hornblow, Leonora
Horne, Constance 1927- 149
Horne, Richard 1960-2007 169
   Earlier sketch in SATA 111
Horne, Richard Henry Hengist
   1802(?)-1884 29
Horner, Althea (Jane) 1926- 36
Horner, Dave 1934- 12
Horner, Jack
   See Horner, John R(obert)
Horner, John R(obert) 1946- 106
Hornik, Laurie Miller 159
Horniman, Joanne 1951- 167
   Earlier sketch in SATA 98
Hornos, Axel 1907-1994 20
Hornstein, Reuben Aaron 1912- 64
Horowitz, Anthony 1955- 137
Horowitz, Dave 1973(?)- 172
Horowitz, Ruth 1957- 136
Horrocks, Anita 1958- 169
Horse, Harry
   See Horne, Richard
Horsfield, Alan 1939- 153
Hort, Lenny 179
Horton, James O. 1943- 173
Horton, James Oliver
   See Horton, James O.
Horton, Madelyn (Stacey) 1962- 77
Horvath, Betty 1927- 4
Horvath, Polly 1957- 140
   Earlier sketch in SATA 85
   See also CLR 90
Horwich, Frances R(appaport) 1908-2001 11
   Obituary 130
Horwitz, Elinor Lander 45
   Brief entry 33

Horwood, William 1944- 85
Hosford, Dorothy (Grant) 1900-1952 22
Hosford, Jessie 1892-1990 5
Hoshi, Shin'ichi 1926- 101
Hoskyns-Abrahall, Clare (Constance
   Drury) 13
Hossack, Sylvia 1939- 83
Hossack, Sylvie Adams
   See Hossack, Sylvia
Hosseini, Khaled 1965- 156
Hossell, Karen Price
   See Price, Karen
Hostetler, Marian 1932- 91
Houck, Carter 1924- 22
Hough, (Helen) Charlotte 1924- 9
Hough, Judy Taylor 1932- 63
   Brief entry 51
   Earlier sketch in SATA 56
Hough, Richard (Alexander) 1922-1999 17
Houghton, Eric 1930- 7
Houk, Randy 1944- 97
Houlehen, Robert J. 1918- 18
Household, Geoffrey (Edward West)
   1900-1988 14
   Obituary 59
Housman, Laurence 1865-1959 25
Houston, Dick 1943- 74
Houston, Gloria 138
   Autobiography Feature 138
   Earlier sketch in SATA 81
Houston, James A(rchibald) 1921-2005 74
   Obituary 163
   Earlier sketch in SATA 13
   See also CLR 3
   See also SAAS 17
Houston, James D. 1933- 78
Houston, Jeanne Toyo Wakatsuki
   See Houston, Jeanne Wakatsuki
Houston, Jeanne Wakatsuki 1934- 168
   Autobiography Feature 168
   Earlier sketch in SATA 78
Houston, Juanita C. 1921- 129
Houton, Kathleen
   See Kilgore, Kathleen
Houts, Amy F. 164
Hovey, Kate 158
Howard, Alan 1922- 45
Howard, Alyssa
   See Buckholtz, Eileen (Garber)
   and Glick, Ruth (Burtnick)
   and Titchener, Louise
Howard, Arthur 1948- 165
Howard, Arthur Charles
   See Howard, Arthur
Howard, Elizabeth Fitzgerald 1927- 119
   Earlier sketch in SATA 74
Howard, Ellen 1943- 99
   Earlier sketch in SATA 67
Howard, Jane R(uble) 1924- 87
Howard, Norman Barry 1949- 90
Howard, P. M.
   See Howard, Pauline Rodriguez
Howard, Paul 1967- 118
Howard, Pauline Rodriguez 1951- 124
Howard, Prosper
   See Hamilton, Charles (Harold St. John)
Howard, Robert West 1908-1988 5
Howard, Todd 1964- 135
Howard, Tristan
   See Currie, Stephen
Howard, Vernon (Linwood) 1918-1992 40
   Obituary 73
Howard, Warren F.
   See Pohl, Frederik
Howarth, David (Armine) 1912-1991 6
   Obituary 68
Howarth, Lesley 1952- 94
Howe, Deborah 1946-1978 29
Howe, James 1946- 161
   Earlier sketches in SATA 29, 71, 111
   See also CLR 9

Howe, John F. 1957- 79
Howe, Norma 1930- 126
Howell, Pat 1947- 15
Howell, S.
   See Styles, (Frank) Showell
Howell, Virginia
   See Ellison, Virginia H(owell)
Howes, Barbara 1914-1996 5
Howie, Diana (Melson) 1945- 122
Howker, Janni 1957- 72
   Brief entry 46
   See also CLR 14
   See also SAAS 13
Howland, Ethan 1963- 131
Hoy, Linda 1946- 65
Hoy, Nina
   See Roth, Arthur J(oseph)
Hoyle, Geoffrey 1942- 18
Hoyt, Edwin P(almer), Jr. 1923- 28
Hoyt, Erich 1950- 140
   Earlier sketch in SATA 65
Hoyt, Olga
   See Gruhzit-Hoyt, Olga (Margaret)
Hrdlitschka, Shelley 1956- 167
   Earlier sketch in SATA 111
Hrdlitschka, Shelley Joanne
   See Hrdlitschka, Shelley
Htin Aung, U.
   See Aung, (Maung) Htin
Hu, Ying-Hwa 173
Huang, Benrei 1959- 86
Hubalek, Linda K. 1954- 111
Hubbard, Michelle Calabro 1953- 122
Hubbard, Patricia 1945- 124
Hubbard, Woodleigh Marx 160
   Earlier sketch in SATA 98
Hubbell, Patricia 1928- 132
   Earlier sketch in SATA 8
Hubley, Faith Elliot 1924-2001 48
   Obituary 133
Hubley, John 1914-1977 48
   Obituary 24
Huck, Charlotte S. 1922- 136
   Earlier sketch in SATA 82
Hudak, Michal 1956- 143
Hudson, Cheryl Willis 1948- 160
   Earlier sketch in SATA 81
Hudson, Jan 1954-1990 77
   See also CLR 40
Hudson, Jeffrey
   See Crichton, Michael
Hudson, (Margaret) Kirsty 1947- 32
Hudson, Margaret
   See Shuter, Jane (Margaret)
Hudson, W(illiam) H(enry) 1841-1922 35
Hudson, Wade 1946- 162
   Earlier sketch in SATA 74
Huelsmann, Eva 1928- 16
Huff, Barbara A. 1929- 67
Huff, Tanya 1957- 171
   Earlier sketch in SATA 85
Huff, Tanya Sue
   See Huff, Tanya
Huff, T.S.
   See Huff, Tanya
Huff, Vivian 1948- 59
Huffaker, Sandy 1943- 10
Huffman, Tom 24
Huggins, Nathan Irvin 1927-1989 63
Huggins, Peter 178
Hughes, Carol 1955- 108
Hughes, Dean 1943- 139
   Earlier sketches in SATA 33, 77
   See also CLR 76
Hughes, Eden
   See Griffin, W.E.B.
Hughes, Edward James
   See Hughes, Ted

Hughes, (James Mercer) Langston
　1902-1967 33
　Earlier sketch in SATA 4
　See also CLR 17
Hughes, Libby 71
Hughes, Matilda
　See MacLeod, Charlotte (Matilda)
Hughes, Monica 1925-2003 162
　Earlier sketches in SATA 15, 70, 119
　See also CLR 60
　See also SAAS 11
Hughes, Monica Ince
　See Hughes, Monica
Hughes, Richard (Arthur Warren)
　1900-1976 8
　Obituary 25
Hughes, Sara
　See Saunders, Susan
Hughes, Shirley 1927- 159
　Earlier sketches in SATA 16, 70, 110
　See also CLR 15
Hughes, Ted 1930-1998 49
　Brief entry 27
　Obituary 107
　See also CLR 3
　See Hughes, Edward James
Hughes, Thomas 1822-1896 31
Hughes, Virginia
　See Campbell, Hope
Hughes, Walter (Llewellyn) 1910-1993 26
Hughey, Roberta 1942- 61
Hugo, Pierre Brackers de
　See Brackers de Hugo, Pierre
Hugo, Victor (Marie) 1802-1885 47
Huline-Dickens, Frank William 1931- 34
Huling, Jan 172
Huliska-Beith, Laura 175
Hull, Eleanor (Means) 1913- 21
Hull, Eric Traviss
　See Harnan, Terry
Hull, H. Braxton
　See Jacobs, Helen Hull
Hull, Jesse Redding
　See Hull, Jessie Redding
Hull, Jessie Redding 1932- 51
Hull, Katharine 1921-1977 23
Hull, Lise (E.) 1954- 148
Hull, Maureen 1949- 142
Hulme, Joy N. 1922- 161
　Earlier sketches in SATA 74, 112
Hults, Dorothy Niebrugge 1898-2000 6
Humble, Richard 1945- 60
Hume, Lotta Carswell 7
Hume, Ruth Fox 1922-1980 26
　Obituary 22
Hume, Stephen Eaton 1947- 136
Hummel, Berta 1909-1946 43
Hummel, Sister Maria Innocentia
　See Hummel, Berta
Humphrey, Carol Sue 1956- 167
Humphrey, Henry (III) 1930- 16
Humphrey, Kate
　See Forsyth, Kate
Humphrey, Sandra McLeod 1936- 95
Humphreys, Martha 1943- 71
Humphreys, Susan L.
　See Lowell, Susan
Hundal, Nancy 1957- 128
Huneck, Stephen 1949- 129
Hungerford, Hesba Fay
　See Brinsmead, H(esba) F(ay)
Hungerford, Pixie
　See Brinsmead, H(esba) F(ay)
Hunkin, Timothy Mark Trelawney 1950- 53
Hunt, Angela Elwell 1957- 159
　Earlier sketch in SATA 75
Hunt, Francesca
　See Holland, Isabelle (Christian)
Hunt, Irene 1907-2001 91
　Earlier sketch in SATA 2
　See also CLR 1

Hunt, Janie Louise 1963- 102
Hunt, Jonathan 1966- 84
Hunt, Joyce 1927- 31
Hunt, Linda 1940- 39
Hunt, Lisa B(ehnke) 1967- 84
Hunt, Mabel Leigh 1892-1971 1
　Obituary 26
Hunt, Morton M(agill) 1920- 22
Hunt, Nigel
　See Greenbank, Anthony Hunt
Hunt, Peter (Leonard) 1945- 76
Hunter, Anne B. 1966- 118
Hunter, Bernice Thurman 1922-2002 85
　Brief entry 45
Hunter, Bobbi Dooley 1945- 89
Hunter, Captain Marcy
　See Ellis, Edward S(ylvester)
Hunter, Chris
　See Fluke, Joanne
Hunter, Clingham M.D.
　See Adams, William Taylor
Hunter, Edith Fisher 1919- 31
Hunter, Erin
　See Cary, Kate
Hunter, Evan 1926-2005 25
　Obituary 167
　See McBain, Ed
Hunter, George E.
　See Ellis, Edward S(ylvester)
Hunter, Hilda 1921- 7
Hunter, Jim 1939- 65
Hunter, Kristin
　See Lattany, Kristin (Elaine Eggleston) Hunter
Hunter, Leigh
　See Etchison, Birdie L(ee)
Hunter, Lieutenant Ned
　See Ellis, Edward S(ylvester)
Hunter, Mel 1927-2004 39
Hunter, Mollie 1922- 139
　Autobiography Feature 139
　Earlier sketches in SATA 54, 106
　See also CLR 25
　See also SAAS 7
　See McIlwraith, Maureen Mollie Hunter
Hunter, Ned
　See Ellis, Edward S(ylvester)
Hunter, Norman (George Lorimer)
　1899-1995 84
　Earlier sketch in SATA 26
Hunter, Ryan Ann
　See Greenwood, Pamela D.
　and Macalaster, Elizabeth G.
Hunter, Sara Hoagland 1954- 98
Hunter Blair, Pauline 3
　See Clarke, Pauline
Huntington, Amy 1956- 138
Huntington, Geoffrey 145
Huntington, Harriet E(lizabeth) 1909- 1
Huntsberry, William E(mery) 1916- 5
Hurd, Clement (G.) 1908-1988 64
　Obituary 54
　Earlier sketch in SATA 2
　See also CLR 49
Hurd, Edith Thacher 1910-1997 64
　Obituary 95
　Earlier sketch in SATA 2
　See also CLR 49
　See also SAAS 13
Hurd, (John) Thacher 1949- 94
　Autobiography Feature 123
　Brief entry 45
　Earlier sketch in SATA 46
Hurlimann, Bettina 39
　Obituary 34
　See Huerlimann, Bettina
Hurlimann, Ruth 32
　Brief entry 31
　See Huerlimann, Ruth
Hurmence, Belinda 1921- 77
　See also CLR 25
　See also SAAS 20

Hurst, Carol Otis 1933- 130
Hurt-Newton, Tania 1968- 84
Hurwitz, Johanna 1937- 175
　Earlier sketches in SATA 20, 71, 113
　See also SAAS 18
Hurwood, Bernhardt J. 1926-1987 12
　Obituary 50
Husain, Shahrukh 1950- 108
Huser, Glen 1943- 151
Hutchens, Paul 1902-1977 31
Hutchins, Carleen Maley 1911- 9
Hutchins, Hazel J. 1952- 175
　Brief entry 51
　Earlier sketches in SATA 81, 135
　See also SAAS 24
Hutchins, Pat 1942- 178
　Earlier sketches in SATA 15, 70, 111
　See also CLR 20
　See also SAAS 16
Hutchins, Ross Elliott 1906- 4
Hutchison, Linda 1942- 152
Huthmacher, J. Joseph 1929- 5
Hutto, Nelson (Allen) 1904-1985 20
Hutton, Kathryn 1915- 89
Hutton, Warwick 1939-1994 20
　Obituary 83
　See also SAAS 17
Huxley, Aldous (Leonard) 1894-1963 63
Huxley, Elspeth (Josceline Grant)
　1907-1997 62
　Obituary 95
Hyde, Catherine R(yan) 1955- 141
Hyde, Dayton O(gden) 9
Hyde, Hawk
　See Hyde, Dayton O(gden)
Hyde, Margaret O(ldroyd) 1917- 139
　Earlier sketches in SATA 1, 42, 76
　See also CLR 23
　See also SAAS 8
Hyde, Shelley
　See Reed, Kit
Hyde, Wayne Frederick 1922- 7
Hylander, Clarence J(ohn) 1897-1964 7
Hyman, Robin P(hilip) 1931- 12
Hyman, Trina Schart 1939-2004 95
　Obituary 158
　Earlier sketches in SATA 7, 46
　See also CLR 50
Hymes, Lucia M(anley) 1907-1998 7
Hyndman, Jane Andrews Lee 1912-1978 46
　Obituary 23
　Earlier sketch in SATA 1
Hyndman, Robert Utley 1906-1973 18
Hynes, Pat 98

I

Iannone, Jeanne 7
　See Balzano, Jeanne (Koppel)
Ibatoulline, Bagram 1965(?)- 174
Ibbitson, John Perrie 1955- 102
Ibbotson, Eva 1925- 156
　Earlier sketches in SATA 13, 103
Ibbotson, M. C(hristine) 1930- 5
Icenoggle, Jodi 1967- 168
Icenoggle, Jodi O.
　See Icenoggle, Jodi
Ichikawa, Satomi 1949- 146
　Brief entry 36
　Earlier sketches in SATA 47, 78
　See also CLR 62
Ignoffo, Matthew 1945- 92
Igus, Toyomi 1953- 112
　Earlier sketch in SATA 76
Ihimaera, Witi (Tame) 1944- 148
Ikeda, Daisaku 1928- 77
Ilowite, Sheldon A. 1931- 27
Ilsley, Velma (Elizabeth) 1918- 12
Imai, Miko 1963- 90

Imershein, Betsy 1953- 62
Immel, Mary Blair 1930- 28
Immell, Myra H. 1941- 92
Impey, Rose 1947- 152
  Earlier sketch in SATA 69
Ingelow, Jean 1820-1897 33
Ingermanson, Randall 1958- 134
Ingermanson, Randy
  See Ingermanson, Randall
Ingersoll, Norman 1928- 79
Ingham, Colonel Frederic
  See Hale, Edward Everett
Ingman, Bruce 1963- 134
Ingman, Nicholas 1948- 52
Ingold, Jeanette 128
Ingpen, Robert 1936- 166
  Earlier sketch in SATA 109
Ingpen, Robert Roger
  See Ingpen, Robert
Ingraham, Erick 1950- 145
Ingraham, Leonard W(illiam) 1913-2003 4
Ingram, Scott 1948- 167
  Earlier sketch in SATA 92
Ingram, W. Scott
  See Ingram, Scott
Ingrams, Doreen 1906-1997 97
  Earlier sketch in SATA 20
Ingrid, Charles
  See Salsitz, Rhondi Vilott
Ingves, Gunilla (Anna Maria Folkesdotter)
  1939- 101
Inkpen, Mick 1952- 154
  Earlier sketch in SATA 99
Innes, (Ralph) Hammond
  See Hammond Innes, Ralph
Innes, Ralph Hammond
  See Hammond Innes, Ralph
Innocenti, Roberto 1940- 159
  Earlier sketch in SATA 96
  See also CLR 56
Inyart, Gene 6
  See Namovicz, Gene Inyart
Ionesco, Eugene 1912-1994 7
  Obituary 79
Ipcar, Dahlov (Zorach) 1917- 147
  Autobiography Feature 147
  Earlier sketches in SATA 1, 49
  See also SAAS 8
Ireland, Karin 151
  Earlier sketch in SATA 101
Ironside, Jetske 1940- 60
Irvin, Fred 1914- 15
Irvine, Georgeanne 1955- 72
Irvine, Joan 1951- 80
Irving, Alexander
  See Hume, Ruth Fox
Irving, Robert
  See Adler, Irving
Irving, Washington 1783-1859
  See YABC 2
  See also CLR 97
Irwin, Ann(abelle Bowen) 1915-1998 89
  Brief entry 38
  Obituary 106
  Earlier sketch in SATA 44
  See also CLR 40
  See Irwin, Hadley
Irwin, Constance (H.) Frick 1913-1995 6
Irwin, Hadley
  See CLR 40
  See also SAAS 14
  See Hadley, Lee
  and Irwin, Ann(abelle Bowen)
Irwin, Keith Gordon 1885-1964 11
Isaac, Joanne 1934- 21
Isaacs, Anne 1949- 90
Isaacs, Jacob
  See Kranzler, George G(ershon)
Isaacson, Philip M(arshal) 1924- 87

Isadora, Rachel 1953(?)- 165
  Brief entry 32
  Earlier sketches in SATA 54, 79, 121
  See also CLR 7
Isbell, Rebecca T(emple) 1942- 125
Isham, Charlotte H(ickock) 1912- 21
Ishida, Jui 176
Ish-Kishor, Judith 1892-1972 11
Ish-Kishor, Sulamith 1896-1977 17
Ishmael, Woodi 1914-1995 31
  Obituary 109
Isle, Sue 1963- 105
Israel, Elaine 1945- 12
Iterson, S(iny) R(ose) Van
  See Van Iterson, S(iny) R(ose)
Ivanko, John D. 1966- 111
Ivanko, John Duane
  See Ivanko, John D.
Iversen, Jeremy 1980(?)- 174
Iversen, Jeremy Watt
  See Iversen, Jeremy
Iverson, Carol (L.) 1941- 145
Iverson, Diane 1950- 122
Iverson, Eric G.
  See Turtledove, Harry
Ivery, Martha M. 1948- 124
Ives, David 1951- 173
Ives, Morgan
  See Bradley, Marion Zimmer
Iwamatsu, Jun Atsushi 1908-1994 81
  Earlier sketch in SATA 14
  See Yashima, Taro
Iwasaki (Matsumoto), Chihiro 1918-1974
  See CLR 18

J

Jac, Lee
  See Morton, Lee Jack, Jr.
Jacka, Martin 1943- 72
Jackson, Alison 1953- 160
  Earlier sketches in SATA 73, 108
Jackson, C(aary) Paul 1902-1991 6
Jackson, Caary
  See Jackson, C(aary) Paul
Jackson, Dave
  See Jackson, J. David
Jackson, Ellen B. 1943- 167
  Earlier sketches in SATA 75, 115
Jackson, Garnet Nelson 1944- 87
Jackson, Gina
  See Fluke, Joanne
Jackson, Guida M. 1930- 71
Jackson, J. David 1944- 91
Jackson, Jacqueline 1928- 65
Jackson, Jacqueline Dougan
  See Jackson, Jacqueline
Jackson, Jesse 1908-1983 29
  Obituary 48
  Earlier sketch in SATA 2
  See also CLR 28
Jackson, Marjorie 1928- 127
Jackson, Melanie 1956- 141
Jackson, Mike 1946- 91
Jackson, Neta J. 1944- 91
Jackson, O. B.
  See Jackson, C(aary) Paul
Jackson, Rob 1961- 176
Jackson, Robert B(lake) 1926- 8
Jackson, Robert Bradley
  See Jackson, Rob
Jackson, Sally
  See Kellogg, Jean (Defrees)
Jackson, Shirley 1919-1965 2
Jackson, Woody 1948- 92
Jacob, Helen Pierce 1927- 21
Jacobin
  See Bisson, Terry

Jacobs, Flora Gill 1918-2006 5
  Obituary 178
Jacobs, Francine 1935- 150
  Brief entry 42
  Earlier sketch in SATA 43
Jacobs, Frank 1929- 30
Jacobs, Helen Hull 1908-1997 12
Jacobs, Joseph 1854-1916 25
Jacobs, Judy 1952- 69
Jacobs, Laurie A. 1956- 89
Jacobs, Leah
  See Gellis, Roberta
Jacobs, Leland Blair 1907-1992 20
  Obituary 71
Jacobs, Linda
  See Altman, Linda Jacobs
Jacobs, Lou(is), Jr. 1921- 2
Jacobs, Shannon K. 1947- 77
Jacobs, Susan
  See Quinn, Susan
Jacobs, William Jay 1933- 89
  Earlier sketch in SATA 28
Jacobsen, Laura 177
Jacobson, Daniel 1923- 12
Jacobson, Jennifer
  See Jacobson, Jennifer Richard
Jacobson, Jennifer Richard 1958- 170
Jacobson, Morris K(arl) 1906- 21
Jacobson, Rick 170
Jacopetti, Alexandra 14
  See Hart, Alexandra
Jacques, Brian 1939- 176
  Earlier sketches in SATA 62, 95, 138
  See also CLR 21
Jacques, Robin 1920-1995 32
  Brief entry 30
  Obituary 86
  See also SAAS 5
Jaekel, Susan M. 1948- 89
Jaffe, Michele 179
Jaffe, Michele Sharon
  See Jaffe, Michele
Jaffee, Al(lan) 1921- 66
  Earlier sketch in SATA 37
Jagendorf, Moritz (Adolf) 1888-1981 2
  Obituary 24
Jahn, Michael
  See Jahn, (Joseph) Michael
Jahn, (Joseph) Michael 1943- 28
Jahn, Mike
  See Jahn, (Joseph) Michael
Jahn-Clough, Lisa 1967- 152
  Earlier sketch in SATA 88
Jahsmann, Allan Hart 1916- 28
Jakes, John 1932- 62
Jakes, John William
  See Jakes, John
  and Jakes, John
James, Andrew
  See Kirkup, James
James, Ann 1952- 168
  Earlier sketches in SATA 82, 117
James, Brian 1976- 140
James, Bronte
  See Nash, Renea Denise
James, Captain Lew
  See Stratemeyer, Edward L.
James, Dynely
  See Mayne, William (James Carter)
James, Edwin
  See Gunn, James E.
James, Elizabeth 1942- 97
  Earlier sketches in SATA 39, 45, 52
James, Emily
  See Standiford, Natalie
James, Harry Clebourne 1896-1978 11
James, J. Alison 1962- 146
  Earlier sketch in SATA 83
James, Josephine
  See Sterne, Emma Gelders

James, Mary
　See Meaker, Marijane
James, Philip
　See del Rey, Lester
　and Moorcock, Michael
James, Robin 1953- *50*
James, Robin Irene
　See James, Robin
James, Tegan
　See Odgers, Sally Farrell
James, Will(iam Roderick) 1892-1942 .... *19*
Jameson, W. C. 1942- *93*
Jamieson, Ian R.
　See Goulart, Ron(ald Joseph)
Jamiolkowski, Raymond M. 1953- *81*
Jane, Mary Childs 1909- *6*
Jane, Pamela *158*
Janeczko, Paul B(ryan) 1945- *155*
　Earlier sketches in SATA *53, 98*
　See also CLR *47*
　See also SAAS *18*
Janes, Edward C. 1908- *25*
Janes, J(oseph) Robert 1935- *148*
　Brief entry *50*
　Earlier sketch in SATA *101*
Janeway, Elizabeth (Hall) 1913-2005 .... *19*
Janger, Kathleen N. 1940- *66*
Janice
　See Brustlein, Janice Tworkov
Janosch
　See CLR *26*
　See Eckcrt, Horst
Janover, Caroline (Davis) 1943- *141*
　Earlier sketch in SATA *89*
Jansen, Jared
　See Cebulash, Mel
Janson, Dora Jane (Heineberg) 1916- *31*
Janson, H(orst) W(oldemar) 1913-1982 .... *9*
Jansson, Tove (Marika) 1914-2001 .... *41*
　Earlier sketch in SATA *3*
　See also CLR *2*
Janus, Grete
　See Hertz, Grete Janus
Jaques, Faith 1923-1997 .... *97*
　Earlier sketches in SATA *21, 69*
Jaquith, Priscilla 1908- *51*
Jaramillo, Mari-Luci 1928- *139*
Jarman, Julia 1946- *133*
Jarman, Rosemary Hawley 1935- *7*
Jarrell, Mary Von Schrader 1914- *35*
Jarrell, Randall 1914-1965 .... *7*
　See also CLR *111*
Jarrett, Roxanne
　See Werner, Herma
Jarrow, Gail 1952- *84*
Jarvis, E. K.
　See Ellison, Harlan
Jaskol, Julie 1958- *127*
Jasner, W. K.
　See Watson, Jane Werner
Jassem, Kate
　See Oppenheim, Joanne
Jauss, Anne Marie 1902(?)-1991 .... *10*
　Obituary *69*
Javernick, Ellen 1938- *89*
Jayne, Lieutenant R. H.
　See Ellis, Edward S(ylvester)
Jaynes, Clare
　See Mayer, Jane Rothschild
Jeake, Samuel, Jr.
　See Aiken, Conrad (Potter)
Jean-Bart, Leslie 1954- *121*
Jeapes, Ben 1965- *174*
Jefferds, Vincent H(arris) 1916- *59*
　Brief entry *49*
Jefferies, (John) Richard 1848-1887 .... *16*
Jeffers, Oliver 1977- *175*
Jeffers, Susan 1942- *137*
　Earlier sketches in SATA *17, 70, 129*
　See also CLR *30*

Jefferson, Sarah
　See Farjeon, (Eve) Annabel
Jeffries, Roderic 1926- *4*
Jeffries, Roderic Graeme
　See Jeffries, Roderic
Jenkin-Pearce, Susie 1943- *80*
Jenkins, A.M. *174*
Jenkins, Amanda McRaney
　See Jenkins, A.M.
Jenkins, Debra Reid
　See Reid Jenkins, Debra
Jenkins, Emily 1967- *174*
　Earlier sketch in SATA *144*
Jenkins, Jean *98*
Jenkins, Jerry B. 1949- *149*
Jenkins, Jerry Bruce
　See Jenkins, Jerry B.
Jenkins, Marie M(agdalen) 1909- *7*
Jenkins, Patrick 1955- *72*
Jenkins, Steve 1952- *154*
Jenkins, William A(twell) 1922-1998 .... *9*
Jenkyns, Chris 1924- *51*
Jennings, Coleman A(lonzo) 1933- *64*
Jennings, Dana Andrew 1957- *93*
Jennings, Elizabeth (Joan) 1926-2001 .... *66*
Jennings, Gary (Gayne) 1928-1999 .... *9*
　Obituary *117*
Jennings, Patrick 1962- *160*
　Earlier sketch in SATA *96*
Jennings, Paul 1943- *165*
　Earlier sketch in SATA *88*
　See also CLR *40*
Jennings, Richard (W.) 1945- *136*
Jennings, Robert
　See Hamilton, Charles (Harold St. John)
Jennings, S. M.
　See Meyer, Jerome Sydney
Jennings, Sharon 1954- *95*
Jennings, Sharon Elizabeth
　See Jennings, Sharon
Jennison, C. S.
　See Starbird, Kaye
Jennison, Keith Warren 1911-1995 .... *14*
Jensen, Kathryn 1949- *81*
Jensen, Kristine Mary 1961- *78*
Jensen, Niels 1927- *25*
Jensen, Vickie (Dee) 1946- *81*
Jensen, Virginia Allen 1927- *8*
Jenson-Elliott, Cynthia L(ouise) 1962- *143*
Jeram, Anita 1965- *154*
　Earlier sketches in SATA *71, 102*
Jerman, Jerry 1949- *89*
Jernigan, E. Wesley 1940- *85*
Jernigan, Gisela (Evelyn) 1948- *85*
Jeschke, Susan 1942- *42*
　Brief entry *27*
Jessel, Camilla (Ruth) 1937- *143*
　Earlier sketch in SATA *29*
Jessell, Tim *177*
Jessey, Cornelia
　See Sussman, Cornelia Silver
Jewel
　See Kilcher, Jewel
Jewell, Nancy 1940- *109*
　Brief entry *41*
Jewett, Eleanore Myers 1890-1967 .... *5*
Jewett, (Theodora) Sarah Orne 1849-1909 ... *15*
Jezard, Alison 1919- *57*
　Brief entry *34*
Jiang, Cheng An 1943- *109*
Jiang, Ji-li 1954- *101*
Jiang, Zheng An
　See Jiang, Cheng An
Jiler, John 1946- *42*
　Brief entry *35*
Jimenez, Francisco 1943- *108*
Jinks, Catherine 1963- *155*
　Earlier sketch in SATA *94*
Jobb, Jamie 1945- *29*
Jobling, Curtis *131*
Jocelyn, Ann Henning 1948- *92*

Jocelyn, Marthe 1956- *163*
　Earlier sketch in SATA *118*
Joerns, Consuelo *44*
　Brief entry *33*
Joey D
　See Macaulay, Teresa (E.)
Johansen, K(rista) V(ictoria) 1968- *129*
Johansson, Philip *163*
John, Joyce *59*
Johns, Avery
　See Cousins, Margaret
Johns, Elizabeth 1943- *88*
Johns, Janetta
　See Quin-Harkin, Janet
Johns, Linda 1945- *173*
Johns, W(illiam) E(arle) 1893-1968 .... *55*
Johns, Captain W. E.
　See Johns, W(illiam) E(arle)
Johnson, A.
　See Johnson, Annabell (Jones)
Johnson, A. E.
　See Johnson, Annabell (Jones)
　and Johnson, Edgar (Raymond)
Johnson, Angela 1961- *150*
　Earlier sketches in SATA *69, 102*
　See also CLR *33*
Johnson, Annabel
　See Johnson, Annabell (Jones)
Johnson, Annabell (Jones) 1921- *72*
　Earlier sketch in SATA *2*
　See Johnson, Annabel
Johnson, Art 1946- *123*
Johnson, Benjamin F., of Boone
　See Riley, James Whitcomb
Johnson, Bettye 1858-1919
　See Rogers, Bettye
Johnson, Caryn
　See Goldberg, Whoopi
Johnson, Caryn E.
　See Goldberg, Whoopi
Johnson, Charles R. 1925- *11*
Johnson, Charlotte Buel *46*
　See von Wodtke, Charlotte Buel Johnson
Johnson, Chuck
　See Johnson, Charles R.
Johnson, Crockett
　See CLR *98*
　See Leisk, David (Johnson)
Johnson, D(onald) B. 1944- *146*
Johnson, D(ana) William 1945- *23*
Johnson, Daniel Shahid 1954- *73*
Johnson, Dinah *130*
　See Johnson, Dianne
Johnson, Dolores 1949- *69*
Johnson, Dorothy M(arie) 1905-1984 .... *6*
　Obituary *40*
Johnson, E(ugene) Harper *44*
Johnson, Edgar (Raymond) 1912-1990 .... *72*
　Earlier sketch in SATA *2*
Johnson, Elizabeth 1911-1984 .... *7*
　Obituary *39*
Johnson, Eric W(arner) 1918-1994 ....
　Obituary *82*
　Earlier sketch in SATA *8*
Johnson, Evelyne 1922- *20*
Johnson, Fred 19(?)-1982 .... *63*
Johnson, Gaylord 1884-1972 .... *7*
Johnson, Gerald White 1890-1980 .... *19*
　Obituary *28*
Johnson, Harper
　See Johnson, E(ugene) Harper
Johnson, James Ralph 1922- *1*
Johnson, James Weldon 1871-1938 .... *31*
　See also CLR *32*
Johnson, Jane 1951- *48*
Johnson, Joan J. 1942- *59*
Johnson, John E(mil) 1929- *34*
Johnson, Johnny 1901-1995
　See Johnson, (Walter) Ryerson
Johnson, La Verne B(ravo) 1925- *13*
Johnson, Lee Kaiser 1962- *78*

Johnson, Lissa H(alls) 1955- 65
Johnson, Lois Smith 1894-1993 6
Johnson, Lois Walfrid 1936- 130
  Earlier sketches in SATA 22, 91
Johnson, Margaret S(weet) 1893-1964 35
Johnson, Marguerite Annie
  See Angelou, Maya
Johnson, Meredith Merrell 1952- 104
Johnson, Milton 1932- 31
Johnson, Neil 1954- 135
  Earlier sketch in SATA 73
Johnson, Pamela 1949- 71
Johnson, Patricia Polin 1956- 84
Johnson, Paul Brett 1947- 132
  Earlier sketch in SATA 83
Johnson, Rebecca L. 1956- 147
  Earlier sketch in SATA 67
Johnson, Rick L. 1954- 79
Johnson, (Walter) Ryerson 1901-1995 10
  Obituary 106
  See Halliday, Brett
Johnson, Scott 1952- 119
  Earlier sketch in SATA 76
Johnson, Sherrie 1948- 87
Johnson, Shirley K(ing) 1927- 10
Johnson, Spencer 1938- 145
  Brief entry 38
Johnson, Stephen T. 1964- 141
  Earlier sketch in SATA 84
Johnson, Steve 1960- 177
Johnson, Sue Kaiser 1963- 78
Johnson, Sylvia A. 166
  Brief entry 52
  Earlier sketch in SATA 104
Johnson, William R. 38
Johnson, William Weber 1909-1992 7
Johnston, Agnes Christine
  See Dazey, Agnes J(ohnston)
Johnston, Annie Fellows 1863-1931 37
Johnston, Dorothy Grunbock 1915-1979 54
Johnston, Ginny 1946- 60
Johnston, H(ugh) A(nthony) S(tephen)
  1913-1967 14
Johnston, Janet 1944- 71
Johnston, Johanna 1914(?)-1982 12
  Obituary 33
Johnston, Julie 1941- 110
  Autobiography Feature 128
  Earlier sketch in SATA 78
  See also CLR 41
  See also SAAS 24
Johnston, Lynn (Beverley) 1947- 118
Johnston, Norma 29
  See St. John, Nicole
Johnston, Portia
  See Takakjian, Portia
Johnston, Susan Taylor 1942- 128
  Earlier sketch in SATA 83
  See Johnston, Tony
Johnston, Tim(othy Patrick) 1962- 146
Johnston, Tony 8
  See Johnston, Susan Taylor
Joinson, Carla 160
Jonas, Ann 1932- 135
  Brief entry 42
  Earlier sketch in SATA 50
  See also CLR 74
Jonell, Lynne 109
Jones, Adrienne 1915-2000 82
  Earlier sketch in SATA 7
  See also SAAS 10
Jones, Annabel
  See Lewis, Mary (Christianna)
Jones, Betty Millsaps 1940- 54
Jones, Carol 1942- 153
  Earlier sketch in SATA 79
Jones, Charles M(artin) 1912-2002 53
  Obituary 133
  See Jones, Chuck
Jones, Charlotte Foltz 1945- 122
  Earlier sketch in SATA 77

Jones, Chuck
  See Jones, Charles M(artin)
Jones, Constance 1961- 112
Jones, Diana Wynne 1934- 160
  Earlier sketches in SATA 9, 70, 108
  See also CLR 120
  See also SAAS 7
Jones, Douglas C(lyde) 1924-1998 52
Jones, Elizabeth McDavid 155
Jones, Elizabeth Orton 1910-2005 18
  Obituary 164
Jones, Evan 1915-1996 3
Jones, Geraldine
  See McCaughrean, Geraldine
Jones, Gillingham
  See Hamilton, Charles (Harold St. John)
Jones, Gwyneth A(nn) 1952- 159
Jones, Harold 1904-1992 14
  Obituary 72
Jones, Helen Hinckley 1903-1991 26
Jones, Hettie 1934- 42
  Brief entry 27
Jones, Hortense P. 1918- 9
Jones, J. Sydney 1948- 101
Jones, Jasmine
  See Papademetriou, Lisa
Jones, Jennifer (Berry) 1947- 90
Jones, John R(obert) 1926- 76
Jones, Jon Sydney
  See Jones, J. Sydney
Jones, Marcia Thornton 1958- 115
  Earlier sketch in SATA 73
Jones, Martha T(annery) 1931- 130
Jones, Mary Alice 1898(?)-1980 6
Jones, McClure 34
Jones, Patrick 1961- 136
Jones, Penelope 1938- 31
Jones, Rebecca C(astaldi) 1947- 99
  Earlier sketch in SATA 33
Jones, Robin D(orothy) 1959- 80
Jones, Sanford W.
  See Thorn, John
Jones, Terence Graham Parry 1942- 127
  See Jones, Terry
  and Monty Python
Jones, Terry 67
  Brief entry 51
  See Jones, Terence Graham Parry
Jones, Tim Wynne
  See Wynne-Jones, Tim
Jones, V(ictoria) M(ary) 1958- 147
Jones, Veda Boyd 1948- 119
Jones, Volcano
  See Mitchell, Adrian
Jones, Weyman (B.) 1928- 4
  See also SAAS 11
Jones, William Glynne
  See Glynne-Jones, William
Jonk, Clarence 1906-1987 10
Jonsberg, Barry 1951- 168
Joos, Francoise 1956- 78
Joos, Frederic 1953- 78
Joosse, Barbara M. 1949- 164
  Earlier sketches in SATA 52, 96
Joosse, Barbara Monnot
  See Joosse, Barbara M.
Jordan, Alexis Hill
  See Glick, Ruth (Burtnick)
  and Titchener, Louise
Jordan, Anne Devereaux 1943- 80
Jordan, Chris
  See Philbrick, Rodman
Jordan, Don
  See Howard, Vernon (Linwood)
Jordan, Hope Dahle 1905-1995 15
Jordan, Jael (Michal) 1949- 30
Jordan, June 1936-2002 136
  Earlier sketch in SATA 4
  See also CLR 10
Jordan, June Meyer
  See Jordan, June

Jordan, Lee
  See Scholefield, Alan
Jordan, Martin George 1944- 84
Jordan, Robert 1948- 95
  See Rigney, James Oliver, Jr.
Jordan, Sherryl 1949- 122
  Earlier sketch in SATA 71
  See also SAAS 23
Jordan, Shirley 1930- 154
Jordan, Tanis 1946- 84
Jorgensen, Mary Venn -1995 36
Jorgensen, Norman 1954- 157
Jorgenson, Ivar
  See Silverberg, Robert
Jorisch, Stephane 178
Joseph, Anne
  See Coates, Anna
Joseph, James (Herz) 1924- 53
Joseph, Joan 1939- 34
Joseph, Joseph M(aron) 1903-1979 22
Joseph, Patrick
  See O'Malley, Kevin
Josephs, Rebecca
  See Talbot, Toby
Josh
  See Clemens, Samuel Langhorne
Joshua, Peter
  See Stone, Peter
Joslin, Mary 1953- 176
Joslin, Sesyle 2
  See Hine, Sesyle Joslin
Joyce, Bill
  See Joyce, William
Joyce, J(ames) Avery 1902-1987 11
  Obituary 50
Joyce, Peter 1937- 127
Joyce, William 1957- 118
  Brief entry 46
  Earlier sketch in SATA 72
  See also CLR 26
Joyner, Jerry 1938- 34
Juan, Ana 1961- 179
Juby, Susan 1969- 156
Jucker, Sita 1921- 5
Judah, Aaron 1923- 118
Judd, Cyril
  See Kornbluth, C(yril) M.
  and Merril, Judith
  and Pohl, Frederik
Judd, Denis (O'Nan) 1938- 33
Judd, Frances K. 1
  See Benson, Mildred (Augustine Wirt)
Jude, Conny 81
Judson, Clara Ingram 1879-1960 38
  Brief entry 27
Judy, Stephen
  See Tchudi, Stephen N.
Judy, Stephen N.
  See Tchudi, Stephen N.
Juhasz, Victor 1954- 177
Jukes, Mavis 1947- 111
  Brief entry 43
  Earlier sketch in SATA 72
  See also SAAS 12
Jules, Jacqueline 1956- 148
Julian, Jane
  See Wiseman, David
Jumpp, Hugo
  See MacPeek, Walter G.
Jungman, Ann 165
Jupo, Frank J. 1904-1981 7
Jurmain, Suzanne 1945- 169
  Earlier sketch in SATA 72
Jurmain, Suzanne Tripp
  See Jurmain, Suzanne
Juster, Norton 1929- 132
  Earlier sketch in SATA 3
  See also CLR 112

Justus, May 1898-1989 .... *1*
  Obituary *106*
Juvenilia
  See Taylor, Ann

K

Kaaberbol, Lene
  See Kaaberbol, Lene
Kaaberbol, Lene 1960- *159*
Kabdebo, Tamas
  See Kabdebo, Thomas
Kabdebo, Thomas 1934- *10*
Kabibble, Osh
  See Jobb, Jamie
Kacer, Kathy 1954- *142*
Kaczman, James *156*
Kadesch, Robert R(udstone) 1922- *31*
Kadohata, Cynthia (Lynn) 1956(?)- *155*
  See also CLR *121*
Kaempfert, Wade
  See del Rey, Lester
Kaestner, Erich 1899-1974 .... *14*
  See also CLR *4*
  See Kastner, Erich
Kahl, Jonathan (D.) 1959- *77*
Kahl, M(arvin) P(hilip) 1934- *37*
Kahl, Virginia (Caroline) 1919-2004 .... *48*
  Brief entry *38*
  Obituary *158*
Kahn, Joan 1914-1994 .... *48*
  Obituary *82*
Kahn, Katherine Janus 1942- *167*
  Earlier sketch in SATA *90*
Kahn, Peggy
  See Katz, Bobbi
Kahn, Roger 1927- *37*
Kahukiwa, Robyn 1940- *134*
Kains, Josephine
  See Goulart, Ron(ald Joseph)
Kaizuki, Kiyonori 1950- *72*
Kakimoto, Kozo 1915- *11*
Kalashnikoff, Nicholas 1888-1961 .... *16*
Kalb, Jonah 1926- *23*
Kalbacken, Joan 1925 .... *96*
Kalechofsky, Roberta 1931- *92*
Kaler, James Otis 1848-1912 .... *15*
Kalish, Claire M. 1947- *92*
Kallen, Stuart A(rnold) 1955- *126*
  Earlier sketch in SATA *86*
Kallevig, Christine Petrell 1955- *164*
Kalman, Bobbie 1947- *63*
Kalman, Maira 1949- *137*
  Earlier sketch in SATA *96*
  See also CLR *32*
Kalnay, Francis 1899-1992 .... *7*
Kaloustian, Rosanne 1955- *93*
Kalow, Gisela 1946- *32*
Kalstein, Dave *175*
Kamen, Gloria 1923- *98*
  Earlier sketch in SATA *9*
Kamerman, Sylvia E.
  See Burack, Sylvia K.
Kamm, Josephine (Hart) 1905-1989 .... *24*
Kammerman, Sylvia K.
  See Burack, Sylvia K.
Kandel, Michael 1941- *93*
Kandell, Alice S. 1938- *35*
Kane, Bob 1916-1998 .... *120*
Kane, Henry Bugbee 1902-1971 .... *14*
Kane, L. A.
  See Mannetti, Lisa
Kane, Robert W. 1910- *18*
Kane, Wilson
  See Bloch, Robert (Albert)
Kanefield, Teri 1960- *135*
Kaner, Etta 1947- *126*
Kanetzke, Howard W(illiam) 1932- *38*

Kanoza, Muriel Canfield
  See Canfield, Muriel
Kantner, Seth 1965- *179*
Kanzawa, Toshiko
  See Furukawa, Toshi
Kaplan, Andrew 1960- *78*
Kaplan, Anne Bernays
  See Bernays, Anne
Kaplan, Bess 1927- *22*
Kaplan, Boche 1926- *24*
Kaplan, Elizabeth 1956- *83*
Kaplan, Elizabeth A.
  See Kaplan, Elizabeth
Kaplan, Irma 1900- *10*
Kaplan, Jean Caryl Korn 1926- *10*
Kaplow, Robert 1954- *70*
Karageorge, Michael
  See Anderson, Poul
Karas, G. Brian 1957- *178*
Karas, George Brian
  See Karas, G. Brian
Karen, Ruth 1922-1987 .... *9*
  Obituary *54*
Kark, Nina Mary 1925- *132*
  Earlier sketch in SATA *4*
  See Bawden, Nina (Mary Mabey)
Karl, Herb 1938- *73*
Karl, Jean E(dna) 1927-2000 .... *122*
  Earlier sketch in SATA *34*
  See also SAAS *10*
Karlin, Bernie 1927- *68*
Karlin, Eugene 1918- *10*
Karlin, Nurit *103*
  Earlier sketch in SATA *63*
Karnes, Frances A. 1937- *110*
Karp, Naomi J. 1926- *16*
Karpinski, J. Rick
  See Karpinski, John Eric
Karpinski, John Eric 1952- *81*
Karpinski, Rick
  See Karpinski, John Eric
Karr, Kathleen 1946- *127*
  Earlier sketch in SATA *82*
Karr, Phyllis Ann 1944- *119*
Karwoski, Gail 1949- *127*
Karwoski, Gail Langer
  See Karwoski, Gail
Kashiwagi, Isami 1925- *10*
Kassem, Lou 1931- *62*
  Brief entry *51*
Kastel, Warren
  See Silverberg, Robert
Kastner, Erich
  See Kaestner, Erich
Kastner, Jill (Marie) 1964- *117*
  Earlier sketch in SATA *70*
Kasuya, Masahiro 1937- *51*
Kasza, Keiko 1951- *124*
Kataphusin
  See Ruskin, John
Katchen, Carole 1944- *9*
Kathryn
  See Searle, Kathryn Adrienne
Katona, Robert 1949- *21*
Katsarakis, Joan Harries
  See Harries, Joan
Katz, Avner 1939- *103*
Katz, Bobbi 1933- *179*
  Earlier sketch in SATA *12*
Katz, Fred(eric Phillip) 1938- *6*
Katz, Jane B(resler) 1934- *33*
Katz, Karen 1947- *158*
Katz, Marjorie P.
  See Weiser, Marjorie P(hillis) K(atz)
Katz, Susan 1945- *156*
Katz, Welwyn Wilton 1948- *96*
  Autobiography Feature *118*
  Earlier sketch in SATA *62*
  See also CLR *45*
Katz, William 1940- *98*
Katz, William Loren 1927- *13*

Kaufman, Bel *57*
Kaufman, Jeff 1955- *84*
Kaufman, Joe 1911-2001 .... *33*
Kaufman, Joseph
  See Kaufman, Joe
Kaufman, Mervyn D. 1932- *4*
Kaufmann, Angelika 1935- *15*
Kaufmann, John 1931- *18*
Kaula, Edna Mason 1906-1987 .... *13*
Kaur Khalsa, Dayal
  See Khalsa, Dayal Kaur
Kavaler, Lucy 1930- *23*
Kavanagh, Jack 1920- *85*
Kavanagh, P(atrick) J(oseph Gregory)
  1931- *122*
Kavanaugh, Ian
  See Webb, Jean Francis (III)
Kay, Alan N. 1965- *144*
Kay, Elizabeth 1949- *165*
Kay, Guy Gavriel 1954- *167*
  Earlier sketch in SATA *121*
Kay, Helen
  See Goldfrank, Helen Colodny
Kay, Jackie 1961- *165*
  Earlier sketch in SATA *97*
Kay, Jacqueline Margaret
  See Kay, Jackie
Kay, Mara *13*
Kay, Verla 1946- *120*
Kaye, Geraldine (Hughesdon) 1925- *85*
  Earlier sketch in SATA *10*
Kaye, Judy
  See Baer, Judy
Kaye, Marilyn 1949- *110*
  Earlier sketch in SATA *56*
Kaye, Mary Margaret
  See Kaye, M.M.
Kaye, M.M. 1908-2004 .... *62*
  Obituary *152*
Kaye, Mollie
  See Kaye, M.M.
Kaye, Peggy 1948- *143*
Keach, James P. 1950- *125*
Keams, Geri 1951- *117*
Keane, Bil 1922- *4*
Keaney, Brian 1954- *106*
Kearney, Meg 1964- *178*
Kearny, Jillian
  See Goulart, Ron(ald Joseph)
Keating, Bern
  See Keating, Leo Bernard
Keating, Frank 1944- *143*
Keating, Lawrence A. 1903-1966 .... *23*
Keating, Leo Bernard 1915- *10*
Keats, Emma 1899(?)-1979(?) *68*
Keats, Ezra Jack 1916-1983 .... *57*
  Obituary *34*
  Earlier sketch in SATA *14*
  See also CLR *35*
Keefer, Catherine
  See Ogan, George F.
  and Ogan, Margaret E. (Nettles)
Keefer, Janice Kulyk *132*
  See Kulyk Keefer, Janice
Keegan, Marcia 1943- *104*
  Earlier sketch in SATA *9*
Keehn, Sally M. 1947- *165*
  Earlier sketch in SATA *87*
Keel, Frank
  See Keeler, Ronald F(ranklin)
Keeler, Ronald F(ranklin) 1913-1983 .... *47*
Keely, Jack 1951- *119*
Keen, Martin L. 1913-1992 .... *4*
Keenan, Sheila 1953- *95*
Keene, Ann T(odd) 1940- *86*

Keene, Carolyn 100
  Earlier sketch in SATA 65
  See also CLR 118
  See Benson, Mildred (Augustine Wirt)
  and Goulart, Ron(ald Joseph)
  and Lerangis, Peter
  and McFarlane, Leslie (Charles)
  and Stanley, George Edward
  and Stratemeyer, Edward L.
Keens-Douglas, Richardo 1953- 154
  Earlier sketch in SATA 95
Keep, Linda Lowery
  See Lowery, Linda
Keep, Richard 1949- 170
Keep, Richard Cleminson
  See Keep, Richard
Keeping, Charles (William James)
  1924-1988 69
  Obituary 56
  Earlier sketch in SATA 9
  See also CLR 34
Keeshan, Robert J. 1927-2004 32
  Obituary 151
Kehret, Peg 1936- 149
  Autobiography Feature 149
  Earlier sketches in SATA 73, 108
Keillor, Garrison 1942- 58
Keillor, Gary Edward
  See Keillor, Garrison
Keir, Christine
  See Pullein-Thompson, Christine
Keister, Douglas 1948- 88
Keith, Doug 1952- 81
Keith, Eros 1942- 52
Keith, Hal 1934- 36
Keith, Harold (Verne) 1903-1998 74
  Earlier sketch in SATA 2
Keith, Robert
  See Applebaum, Stan
Keleinikov, Andrei 1924- 65
Kelemen, Julie 1959- 78
Kelen, Emery 1896-1978 13
  Obituary 26
Kelleam, Joseph E(veridge) 1913-1975 31
Kelleher, Anne 1959- 97
Kelleher, Annette 1950- 122
Kelleher, Daria Valerian 1955- 79
Kelleher, Victor (Michael Kitchener)
  1939- 129
  Brief entry 52
  Earlier sketch in SATA 75
  See also CLR 36
Keller, Beverly L(ou) 91
  Earlier sketch in SATA 13
Keller, Charles 1942- 82
  Earlier sketch in SATA 8
Keller, Debra 1958- 94
Keller, Dick 1923- 36
Keller, Emily 96
Keller, Gail Faithfull
  See Faithfull, Gail
Keller, Holly 1942- 157
  Brief entry 42
  Earlier sketches in SATA 76, 108
  See also CLR 45
Keller, Irene (Barron) 1927-2002 36
  Obituary 139
Kelley, Leo P(atrick) 1928- 32
  Brief entry 31
Kelley, Patrick (G.) 1963- 129
Kelley, Patte 1947- 93
Kelley, True 1946- 179
Kelley, True (Adelaide) 1946- 130
  Brief entry 39
  Earlier sketches in SATA 41, 92
Kelley, True Adelaide
  See Kelley, True
Kellin, Sally Moffet 1932- 9
Kelling, Furn L. 1914-2000 37
Kellogg, Gene
  See Kellogg, Jean (Defrees)

Kellogg, Jean (Defrees) 1916-1978 10
Kellogg, Steven 1941- 177
  Earlier sketches in SATA 8, 57, 130
  See also CLR 6
Kellogg, Steven Castle
  See Kellogg, Steven
Kellow, Kathleen
  See Hibbert, Eleanor Alice Burford
Kelly, Clint 1950- 140
Kelly, Eric P(hilbrook) 1884-1960
  See YABC 1
Kelly, Fiona
  See Coleman, Michael (Lee)
  and Hendry, Frances Mary
  and Oldfield, Jenny
  and Welford, Sue
Kelly, Irene 1957- 147
Kelly, Jeff
  See Kelly, Jeffrey
Kelly, Jeffrey 1946- 65
Kelly, Joanne (W.) 1934- 87
Kelly, Kate 1958- 91
Kelly, Kathleen M. 1964- 71
Kelly, Katy 1955- 169
Kelly, Lauren
  See Oates, Joyce Carol
Kelly, Laurene 1954- 123
Kelly, Martha Rose 1914-1983 37
Kelly, Marty
  See Kelly, Martha Rose
Kelly, Mij 166
Kelly, Ralph
  See Geis, Darlene Stern
Kelly, Regina Z(immerman) 1898-1986 5
Kelly, Rosalie (Ruth) 43
Kelly, Walt(er Crawford) 1913-1973 18
Kelsey, Alice Geer 1896-1982 1
Kelsey, Elin 159
Kemnitz, Thomas Milton, Jr. 1984- 152
Kemnitz, Tom, Jr.
  See Kemnitz, Thomas Milton, Jr.
Kemp, Gene 1926- 75
  Earlier sketch in SATA 25
  See also CLR 29
Kempner, Mary Jean 1913-1969 10
Kempton, Jean Welch 1914- 10
Kenda, Margaret 1942- 71
Kendall, Carol (Seeger) 1917- 74
  Earlier sketch in SATA 11
  See also SAAS 7
Kendall, Katherine
  See Applegate, Katherine (Alice)
Kendall, Lace
  See Stoutenburg, Adrien (Pearl)
Kendall, Martha E. 87
Kendall, Russ 1957- 83
Kenealy, James P. 1927- 52
  Brief entry 29
Kenealy, Jim
  See Kenealy, James P.
Kennaway, Adrienne 1945- 171
  Earlier sketch in SATA 60
Kennedy, Brendan 1970- 57
Kennedy, Dana Forrest 1917- 74
Kennedy, Dorothy M(intzlaff) 1931- 53
Kennedy, Doug(las) 1963- 122
Kennedy, John Fitzgerald 1917-1963 11
Kennedy, Joseph Charles 1929- 130
  Autobiography Feature 130
  Earlier sketches in SATA 14, 86
  See Kennedy, X. J.
Kennedy, Pamela (J.) 1946- 87
Kennedy, Paul E(dward) 1929- 113
  Earlier sketch in SATA 33
Kennedy, (Jerome) Richard 1932- 22
Kennedy, Robert 1938- 63
Kennedy, T.A. 1953- 42
  Brief entry 35
Kennedy, Teresa
  See Kennedy, T.A.

Kennedy, Teresa A.
  See Kennedy, T.A.
Kennedy, William 1928- 57
Kennedy, William Joseph
  See Kennedy, William
Kennedy, X. J.
  See CLR 27
  See also SAAS 22
  See Kennedy, Joseph Charles
Kennell, Ruth Epperson 1893-1977 6
  Obituary 25
Kennemore, Tim 1957- 133
Kennett, David 1959- 121
Kenny, Herbert Andrew 1912-2002 13
Kenny, Jude
  See Daly, Jude
Kenny, Kathryn
  See Bowden, Joan Chase
  and Krull, Kathleen
  and Sanderlin, Owenita (Harrah)
  and Stack, Nicolete Meredith
Kenny, Kevin
  See Krull, Kathleen
Kensinger, George
  See Fichter, George S.
Kensington, Kathryn Wesley
  See Rusch, Kristine Kathryn
Kent, Alexander
  See Reeman, Douglas Edward
Kent, David
  See Lambert, David (Compton)
Kent, Deborah Ann 1948- 155
  Brief entry 41
  Earlier sketches in SATA 47, 104
Kent, Jack
  See Kent, John Wellington
Kent, John Wellington 1920-1985 24
  Obituary 45
Kent, Lisa 1942- 90
Kent, Mallory
  See Lowndes, Robert A(ugustine) W(ard)
Kent, Margaret 1894- 2
Kent, Rockwell 1882-1971 6
Kent, Sherman 1903-1986 20
  Obituary 47
Kenward, Jean 1920- 42
Kenworthy, Leonard S. 1912-1991 6
Kenyon, Karen (Smith) 1938- 145
Kenyon, Kate
  See Adorjan, Carol (Madden)
  and Ransom, Candice F.
Kenyon, Ley 1913-1990 6
Keown, Elizabeth 78
Kepes, Juliet A(ppleby) 1919-1999 13
Kerby, Mona 1951- 75
Kerigan, Florence 1896-1984 12
Kerley, Barbara 1960- 138
Kerman, Gertrude
  See Furman, Gertrude Lerner Kerman
Kerns, Thelma 1929- 116
Kerr, Bob 1951- 120
Kerr, Jessica 1901-1991 13
Kerr, (Anne-)Judith 1923-1970 24
Kerr, M. E.
  See CLR 29
  See also SAAS 1
  See Meaker, Marijane
Kerr, P.B.
  See Kerr, Philip
Kerr, Philip 1956- 168
Kerr, Phyllis Forbes 1942- 72
Kerr, Tom 1950- 77
Kerrin, Jessica Scott 174
Kerry, Frances
  See Kerigan, Florence
Kerry, Lois
  See Duncan, Lois
Kershen, (L.) Michael 1982- 82
Kerven, Rosalind 1954- 83

Ker Wilson, Barbara 1929- *121*
 Earlier sketches in SATA *20, 70*
 See also SAAS *18*
Keselman, Gabriela 1953- *128*
Kesey, Ken 1935-2001 .... *66*
 Obituary *131*
Kesey, Ken Elton
 See Kesey, Ken
Kesler, Jay 1935- *65*
Kessel, Joyce Karen 1937- *41*
Kessler, Ethel 1922- *44*
 Brief entry *37*
Kessler, Leonard P. 1921- *14*
Kest, Kristin 1967- *168*
 Earlier sketch in SATA *118*
Kesteven, G. R.
 See Crosher, G. R.
Ketcham, Hank
 See Ketcham, Henry King
Ketcham, Henry King 1920-2001 .... *28*
 Brief entry *27*
 Obituary *128*
Ketcham, Sallie 1963- *124*
Ketchum, Liza 1946- *132*
 See Murrow, Liza Ketchum
Ketner, Mary Grace 1946- *75*
Kettelkamp, Larry (Dale) 1933- *2*
 See also SAAS *3*
Ketteman, Helen 1945- *167*
 Earlier sketches in SATA *73, 115*
Kettle, Peter
 See Glover, Denis (James Matthews)
Kevles, Bettyann Holtzmann 1938- *23*
Key, Alexander (Hill) 1904-1979 .... *8*
 Obituary *23*
Key, Samuel M.
 See de Lint, Charles
Keyes, Daniel 1927- *37*
Keyes, Fenton 1915-1999 .... *34*
Keyes, Greg
 See Keyes, J. Gregory
Keyes, J. Gregory 1963- *116*
Keyser, Marcia 1933- *42*
Keyser, Sarah
 See McGuire, Leslie (Sarah)
Khalsa, Dayal Kaur 1943-1989 .... *62*
 See also CLR *30*
 See Kaur Khalsa, Dayal
Khan, Rukhsana 1962- *165*
 Earlier sketch in SATA *118*
Khanshendel, Chiron
 See Rose, Wendy
Kheirabadi, Masoud 1951- *158*
Khemir, Sabiha *87*
Kherdian, David 1931- *74*
 Autobiography Feature *125*
 Earlier sketch in SATA *16*
 See also CLR *24*
Kibbe, Pat (Hosley) *60*
Kidd, Diana 1933-2000 .... *150*
Kidd, Richard 1952- *152*
Kidd, Ronald 1948- *173*
 Earlier sketches in SATA *42, 92*
Kiddell, John 1922- *3*
Kiddell-Monroe, Joan 1908-1972 .... *55*
Kidwell, Carl 1910- *43*
Kiefer, Irene 1926- *21*
Kiefer, Kathleen Balmes 1957- *142*
Kierstead, Vera M. 1913- *121*
Kiesel, Stanley 1925- *35*
Kiesler, Kate (A.) 1971- *152*
 Earlier sketch in SATA *90*
Kihn, Greg 1952- *110*
Kikukawa, Cecily H(arder) 1919- *44*
 Brief entry *35*
Kilcher, Jewel 1974- *109*
Kile, Joan 1940- *78*
Kilgore, Kathleen 1946- *42*
Kilian, Crawford 1941- *35*
Killdeer, John
 See Mayhar, Ardath

Killien, Christi 1956- *73*
Killilea, Marie (Lyons) 1913-1991 .... *2*
Killingback, Julia 1944- *63*
Killough, (Karen) Lee 1942- *64*
Kilreon, Beth
 See Walker, Barbara (Jeanne) K(erlin)
Kilworth, Garry 1941- *94*
Kilworth, Garry D.
 See Kilworth, Garry
Kilworth, Garry Douglas
 See Kilworth, Garry
Kim, Helen 1899-1970 .... *98*
Kimball, Gayle 1943- *90*
Kimball, Violet T(ew) 1932- *126*
Kimball, Yeffe 1914-1978 .... *37*
Kimber, Murray 1964- *171*
Kimble, Warren *176*
Kimbrough, Emily 1899-1989 .... *2*
 Obituary *59*
Kimeldorf, Martin (R.) 1948- *121*
Kimenye, Barbara 1940(?)- *121*
Kimmel, Elizabeth Cody *170*
Kimmel, Eric A. 1946- *176*
 Earlier sketches in SATA *13, 80, 125*
Kimmel, Margaret Mary 1938- *43*
 Brief entry *33*
Kimmelman, Leslie (Grodinsky) 1958- *156*
 Earlier sketch in SATA *85*
Kincaid, Jamaica 1949-
 See CLR *63*
Kincher, Jonni 1949- *79*
Kindl, Patrice 1951- *128*
 Earlier sketch in SATA *82*
Kindred, Wendy (Good) 1937- *7*
Kines, Pat Decker 1937- *12*
King, Adam
 See Hoare, Robert J(ohn)
King, Alison
 See Martini, Teri
King, (Maria) Anna 1964- *72*
King, Billie Jean 1943- *12*
King, Christopher (L.) 1945- *84*
King, (David) Clive 1924- *144*
 Earlier sketch in SATA *28*
King, Colin 1943- *76*
King, Cynthia 1925- *7*
King, Daniel (John) 1963- *130*
King, Elizabeth 1953- *83*
King, Frank R. 1904-1999 .... *127*
King, Jane
 See Currie, Stephen
King, Jeanette (Margaret) 1959- *105*
King, Larry L. 1929- *66*
King, Laurie R. 1952- *88*
King, Marian 1900(?)-1986 .... *23*
 Obituary *47*
King, Martin Luther, Jr. 1929-1968 .... *14*
King, Mary Ellen 1958- *93*
King, Paul
 See Drackett, Phil(ip Arthur)
King, Paula
 See Downing, Paula E.
King, Stephen 1947- *161*
 Earlier sketches in SATA *9, 55*
King, Stephen Edwin
 See King, Stephen
King, Stephen Michael *157*
King, Steve
 See King, Stephen
King, Thomas 1943- *96*
King, Tony 1947- *39*
Kingman, Dong (Moy Shu) 1911-2000 .... *44*
Kingman, Lee *67*
 Earlier sketch in SATA *1*
 See also SAAS *3*
 See Natti, (Mary) Lee
Kingsland, Leslie William 1912- *13*
Kingsley, Charles 1819-1875
 See YABC *2*
 See also CLR *77*
Kingsley, Emily Perl 1940- *33*

King-Smith, Dick 1922- *135*
 Brief entry *38*
 Earlier sketches in SATA *47, 80*
 See also CLR *40*
Kingston, Maxine Hong 1940- *53*
Kingston, Maxine Ting Ting Hong
 See Kingston, Maxine Hong
Kinney, C. Cle(land) 1915- *6*
Kinney, Harrison 1921- *13*
Kinney, Jean Stout 1912- *12*
Kinsey, Elizabeth
 See Clymer, Eleanor
Kinsey, Helen 1948- *82*
Kinsey-Warnock, Natalie 1956- *167*
 Earlier sketches in SATA *71, 116*
Kinzel, Dorothy 1950- *57*
Kinzel, Dottie
 See Kinzel, Dorothy
Kipling, (Joseph) Rudyard 1865-1936 .... *100*
 See also YABC *2*
 See also CLR *65*
Kippax, Frank
 See Needle, Jan
Kirby, David K. 1944- *78*
Kirby, David Kirk
 See Kirby, David K.
Kirby, Margaret
 See Bingley, Margaret (Jane Kirby)
Kirby, Susan E. 1949- *62*
Kirk, Connie Ann 1957- *167*
Kirk, Daniel 1952- *153*
 Earlier sketch in SATA *107*
Kirk, David 1955- *161*
 Earlier sketch in SATA *117*
Kirk, Heather 1949- *166*
Kirk, Ruth (Kratz) 1925- *5*
Kirkham, Dinah
 See Card, Orson Scott
Kirkland, Will
 See Hale, Arlene
Kirkpatrick, Katherine (Anne) 1964- *113*
Kirkup, James 1918- *12*
Kirkwood, Kathryn
 See Fluke, Joanne
Kirshenbaum, Binnie *79*
Kirshner, David S. 1958- *123*
Kish, Eleanor M(ary) 1924- *73*
Kish, Ely
 See Kish, Eleanor M(ary)
Kishida, Eriko 1929- *12*
Kisinger, Grace Gelvin (Maze) 1913-1965 .. *10*
Kissin, Eva H. 1923- *10*
Kissinger, Rosemary K.
 See Updyke, Rosemary K.
Kistler, John M. 1967- *160*
Kitamura, Satoshi 1956- *143*
 Earlier sketches in SATA *62, 98*
 See also CLR *60*
Kitchen, Bert
 See Kitchen, Herbert Thomas
Kitchen, Herbert Thomas 1940- *70*
Kite, (L.) Patricia *78*
 See Kite, Pat
Kitt, Tamara
 See de Regniers, Beatrice Schenk (Freedman)
Kittinger, Jo S(usenbach) 1955- *148*
 Earlier sketch in SATA *96*
Kituomba
 See Odaga, Asenath (Bole)
Kitzinger, Sheila 1929- *57*
Kiwak, Barbara 1966- *103*
Kjelgaard, James Arthur 1910-1959 .... *17*
 See also CLR *81*
 See Kjelgaard, Jim
Kjelgaard, Jim
 See Kjelgaard, James Arthur
Kjelle, Marylou Morano 1954- *146*
Klagsbrun, Francine (Lifton) *36*
Klaits, Barrie 1944- *52*
Klaperman, Gilbert 1921- *33*

Klaperman, Libby Mindlin 1921-1982 .... *33*
   Obituary *31*
Klass, David 1960- *142*
   Earlier sketch in SATA *88*
Klass, Morton 1927-2001 .... *11*
Klass, Sheila Solomon 1927- *99*
   Autobiography Feature *126*
   Earlier sketch in SATA *45*
   See also SAAS *26*
Klause, Annette Curtis 1953- *175*
   Earlier sketch in SATA *79*
   See also CLR *104*
Klaveness, Jan O'Donnell 1939- *86*
Kleberger, Ilse 1921- *5*
Kleeberg, Irene (Flitner) Cumming 1932- *65*
Klein, Aaron E. 1930-1998 .... *45*
   Brief entry *28*
Klein, Bill 1945- *89*
Klein, David 1919-2001 .... *59*
Klein, Frederick C. 1938- *154*
Klein, Gerda Weissmann 1924- *44*
Klein, H(erbert) Arthur *8*
Klein, James 1932- *115*
Klein, Leonore (Glotzer) 1916- *6*
Klein, Mina C(ooper) 1906-1979 .... *8*
Klein, Norma 1938-1989 .... *57*
   Earlier sketch in SATA *7*
   See also CLR *19*
   See also SAAS *1*
Klein, Rachel S. 1953- *105*
Klein, Robin 1936- *164*
   Brief entry *45*
   Earlier sketches in SATA *55, 80*
   See also CLR *21*
Klemin, Diana *65*
Klemm, Barry 1945- *104*
Klemm, Edward G., Jr. 1910-2001 .... *30*
Klemm, Roberta K(ohnhorst) 1884-1975 ..... *30*
Kleven, Elisa 1958- *173*
   Earlier sketch in SATA *76*
   See also CLR *85*
Klevin, Jill Ross 1935- *39*
   Brief entry *38*
Kliban, B(ernard) 1935-1990 .... *35*
   Obituary *66*
Klimowicz, Barbara 1927- *10*
Kline, Christina Baker 1964- *101*
Kline, James
   See Klein, James
Kline, Jim
   See Kline, Jim
Kline, Lisa Williams 1954- *143*
Kline, Suzy 1943- *152*
   Brief entry *48*
   Earlier sketches in SATA *67, 99*
Kliros, Thea 1935- *106*
Klise, M. Sarah 1961- *128*
Klug, Ron(ald) 1939- *31*
Knaak, Richard A. 1961- *166*
   Earlier sketch in SATA *86*
Knaak, Richard Allen
   See Knaak, Richard A.
Knapp, Edward
   See Kunhardt, Edith
Knapp, Ron 1952- *34*
Knebel, Fletcher 1911-1993 .... *36*
   Obituary *75*
Kneeland, Linda Clarke 1947- *94*
Knickerbocker, Diedrich
   See Irving, Washington
Knifesmith
   See Cutler, Ivor
Knigge, Robert (R.) 1921(?)-1987 .... *50*
Knight, Anne (Katherine) 1946- *34*
Knight, Brenda *112*
Knight, Christopher G. 1943- *96*
Knight, Damon (Francis) 1922-2002 .... *9*
   Obituary *139*
Knight, David C(arpenter) 1925-1984 .... *14*
   See also CLR *38*
Knight, Eric 1897-1943 .... *18*

Knight, Eric Mowbray
   See Knight, Eric
Knight, Francis Edgar 1905- *14*
Knight, Frank
   See Knight, Francis Edgar
Knight, Hilary 1926- *132*
   Earlier sketches in SATA *15, 69*
Knight, Joan (MacPhail) *159*
   Earlier sketch in SATA *82*
Knight, Joan
   See Knight, Joan (MacPhail)
Knight, Kathryn Lasky
   See Lasky, Kathryn
Knight, Mallory T.
   See Hurwood, Bernhardt J.
Knight, Theodore O. 1946- *77*
Knobloch, Dorothea 1951- *88*
Knoepfle, John (Ignatius) 1923- *66*
Knott, Bill
   See Knott, William C(ecil, Jr.)
Knott, William C(ecil, Jr.) 1927- *3*
   See Knott, Bill
   and Mitchum, Hank
   and Sharpe, Jon
Knotts, Howard (Clayton, Jr.) 1922- *25*
Knowles, Anne 1933- *37*
Knowles, John 1926-2001 .... *89*
   Obituary *134*
   Earlier sketch in SATA *8*
   See also CLR *98*
Knox, Calvin M.
   See Silverberg, Robert
Knox, (Mary) Eleanor Jessie 1909-2000 ...... *59*
   Earlier sketch in SATA *30*
Knox, Elizabeth 1959- *176*
Knox, Elizabeth Fiona
   See Knox, Elizabeth
Knox, James
   See Brittain, William (E.)
Knox, Jolyne 1937- *76*
Knudsen, James 1950- *42*
Knudsen, Michelle *171*
Knudson, R. R.
   See SAAS *18*
   See Knudson, Rozanne
Knudson, Richard L(ewis) 1930- *34*
Knudson, Rozanne 1932- *79*
   Earlier sketch in SATA *7*
   See Knudson, R. R.
Knutson, Barbara 1959-2005 .... *166*
Knutson, Kimberley *115*
Knye, Cassandra
   See Disch, Thomas M.
Koch, Dorothy Clarke 1924- *6*
Koch, Kenneth 1925-2002 .... *65*
Koch, Kenneth Jay
   See Koch, Kenneth
Koch, Phyllis (Mae) McCallum 1911- *10*
Kocsis, J. C.
   See Paul, James
Koda-Callan, Elizabeth 1944- *140*
   Earlier sketch in SATA *67*
Koehler, Phoebe 1955- *85*
Koehler-Pentacoff, Elizabeth 1957- *160*
   Earlier sketch in SATA *96*
Koehn, Ilse
   See Van Zwienen, Ilse Charlotte Koehn
Koenig, Viviane 1950- *80*
Koering, Ursula 1921-1976 .... *64*
Koerner, W(illiam) H(enry) D(avid)
   1878-1938 .... *21*
Koertge, Ronald 1940- *131*
   Earlier sketches in SATA *53, 92*
Koestler-Grack, Rachel A. 1973- *156*
Koff, Richard Myram 1926- *62*
Koffinke, Carol 1949- *82*
Kogan, Deborah *50*
   See Kogan Ray, Deborah
Kogan Ray, Deborah 1940- *161*
   See Kogan, Deborah
   and Ray, Deborah

Kogawa, Joy Nozomi 1935- *99*
Kogler, Jennifer Anne 1982(?)- *174*
Kohl, Herbert 1937- *47*
Kohl, Herbert R.
   See Kohl, Herbert
Kohl, MaryAnn F(aubion) 1947- *144*
   Earlier sketch in SATA *74*
Kohn, Bernice *4*
   See Hunt, Bernice (Kohn)
Kohn, Rita (T.) 1933- *89*
Kohner, Frederick 1905-1986 .... *10*
   Obituary *48*
Koide, Tan 1938-1986 .... *50*
Koike, Kay 1940- *72*
Koja, Kathe 1960- *155*
Kolb, Larry J. 1953- *175*
Kolba, St. Tamara *22*
Kolibalova, Marketa
   See Kolibalova, Marketa
Kolibalova, Marketa 1953- *126*
Koller, Jackie French 1948- *157*
   Earlier sketches in SATA *72, 109*
   See also CLR *68*
Kolodny, Nancy J. 1946- *76*
Komaiko, Leah 1954- *164*
   Earlier sketch in SATA *97*
Komisar, Lucy 1942- *9*
Komoda, Beverly 1939- *25*
Komoda, Kiyo 1937- *9*
Kompaneyets, Marc 1974- *169*
Komroff, Manuel 1890-1974 .... *2*
   Obituary *20*
Konigsburg, E.L. 1930- *126*
   Earlier sketches in SATA *4, 48, 94*
   See also CLR *81*
Konigsburg, Elaine Lobl
   See Konigsburg, E.L.
Koningsberger, Hans *5*
   See Koning, Hans
Konkle, Janet Everest 1917- *12*
Kono, Erin Eitter 1973- *177*
Konzak, Burt 1946- *151*
Koob, Theodora (J. Foth) 1918- *23*
Kooiker, Leonie
   See Kooyker-Romijn, Johanna Maria
Koons, James
   See Pernu, Dennis
Koontz, Dean R. 1945- *165*
   Earlier sketch in SATA *92*
Koontz, Dean Ray
   See Koontz, Dean R.
Koontz, Robin Michal 1954- *136*
   Earlier sketch in SATA *70*
Kooyker, Leonie
   See Kooyker-Romijn, Johanna Maria
Kooyker-Romijn, Johanna Maria 1927- *48*
   See Kooyker, Leonie
Kooyker-Romyn, Johanna Maria
   See Kooyker-Romijn, Johanna Maria
Kopelke, Lisa 1963- *154*
Kopper, Lisa (Esther) 1950- *105*
   Brief entry *51*
Koppes, Steven N. 1957- *169*
Koppes, Steven Nelson
   See Koppes, Steven N.
Korach, Mimi 1922- *9*
Koralek, Jenny 1934- *140*
   Earlier sketch in SATA *71*
Korczak, Janusz *65*
   See Goldszmit, Henryk
Koren, Edward (Benjamin) 1935- *148*
   Earlier sketch in SATA *5*
Korinets, Iurii Iosifovich
   See Korinetz, Yuri (Iosifovich)
Korinetz, Yuri (Iosifovich) 1923- *9*
   See also CLR *4*
Korman, Bernice 1937- *78*
Korman, Gordon 1963- *167*
   Brief entry *41*
   Earlier sketches in SATA *49, 81, 119*
   See also CLR *25*

Korman, Gordon Richard
See Korman, Gordon
Korman, Justine 1958- 70
Kornblatt, Marc 1954- 147
Earlier sketch in SATA 84
Kornprobst, Jacques 1937- 177
Korte, Gene J. 1950- 74
Korty, Carol 1937- 15
Koscielniak, Bruce 1947- 153
Earlier sketches in SATA 67, 99
Koshin, Alexander (A.) 1952- 86
Kositsky, Lynne 1947- 158
Koskenmaki, Rosalie
See Maggio, Rosalie
Koss, Amy Goldman 1954- 158
Earlier sketch in SATA 115
Kossin, Sandy (Sanford) 1926- 10
Kossman, Nina 1959- 84
Kotzwinkle, William 1938- 146
Earlier sketches in SATA 24, 70
See also CLR 6
Kouhi, Elizabeth 1917- 54
Brief entry 49
Kouts, Anne 1945- 8
Koutsky, Jan Dale 1955- 146
Kovacs, Deborah 1954- 132
Earlier sketch in SATA 79
Kovalski, Maryann 1951- 175
Earlier sketches in SATA 58, 97
See also CLR 34
See also SAAS 21
Kowalski, Kathiann M. 1955- 151
Earlier sketch in SATA 96
Kraft, Betsy Harvey 1937- 157
Krahn, Fernando 1935- 49
Brief entry 31
See also CLR 3
Krakauer, Hoong Yee Lee 1955- 86
Krakauer, Jon 1954- 108
Kramer, George
See Heuman, William
Kramer, Nora 1896(?)-1984 26
Obituary 39
Kramer, Remi (Thomas) 1935- 90
Krantz, Hazel (Newman) 12
Kranzler, George G(ershon) 1916- 28
Kranzler, Gershon
See Kranzler, George G(ershon)
Krasilovsky, Phyllis 1926- 38
Earlier sketch in SATA 1
See also CLR 83
See also SAAS 5
Krasne, Betty
See Levine, Betty K(rasne)
Krasner, Steven 1953- 154
Krasno, Rena 1923- 104
Kratman, Tom 175
Kraus, Joanna Halpert 1937- 87
Kraus, (Herman) Robert 1925-2001 93
Obituary 130
Earlier sketches in SATA 4, 65
See also SAAS 11
Krauss, Ruth (Ida) 1911-1993 30
Obituary 75
Earlier sketch in SATA 1
See also CLR 42
Krautter, Elisa (Bialk) 1912(?)-1990 1
Obituary 65
Krautwurst, Terry 1946- 79
Kray, Robert Clement 1930- 82
Kredel, Fritz 1900-1973 17
Kreikemeier, Gregory Scott 1965- 85
Krementz, Jill 1940- 134
Earlier sketches in SATA 17, 71
See also CLR 5
See also SAAS 8
Kremer, Marcie
See Sorenson, Margo
Krenina, Katya 1968- 101

Krensky, Stephen 1953- 136
Brief entry 41
Earlier sketches in SATA 47, 93
Krensky, Stephen Alan
See Krensky, Stephen
Kresh, Paul 1919-1997 61
Obituary 94
Kress, Nancy 1948- 147
Autobiography Feature 147
Earlier sketch in SATA 85
Kricher, John C. 1944- 113
Krieger, Melanie 96
Kripke, Dorothy Karp 30
Krisher, Trudy (B.) 1946- 160
Earlier sketch in SATA 86
Krishnaswami, Uma 1956- 144
Kristof, Jane 1932- 8
Kroeber, Theodora (Kracaw) 1897-1979 1
Kroeger, Mary Kay 1950- 92
Krohn, Katherine E(lizabeth) 1961- 125
Earlier sketch in SATA 84
Kroll, Francis Lynde 1904-1973 10
Kroll, Steven 1941- 135
Autobiography Feature 135
Earlier sketches in SATA 19, 66, 125
See also SAAS 7
Kroll, Virginia L. 1948- 168
Earlier sketches in SATA 76, 114
Kroll, Virginia Louisa
See Kroll, Virginia L.
Krommes, Beth 1956- 128
Kronenwetter, Michael 1943- 62
Kroniuk, Lisa
See Berton, Pierre (Francis de Marigny)
Kropp, Paul (Stephan) 1948- 38
Brief entry 34
See also CLR 96
Krosoczka, Jarrett J. 1977- 155
Krovatin, Christopher 1985- 171
Kruess, James
See CLR 9
See Kruss, James
Krull, Kathleen 1952- 149
Autobiography Feature 106
Brief entry 39
Earlier sketches in SATA 52, 80
See also CLR 44
Krumgold, Joseph (Quincy) 1908-1980 48
Obituary 23
Earlier sketch in SATA 1
Krupinski, Loretta 1940- 161
Earlier sketches in SATA 67, 102
Krupnick, Karen 1947- 89
Krupp, E(dwin) C(harles) 1944- 123
Earlier sketch in SATA 53
Krupp, Robin Rector 1946- 53
Krush, Beth 1918- 18
Krush, Joe 1918- 18
See Krush, Joseph P.
Kruss, James 1926-1997 8
See Kruess, James
Krykorka, Vladyana 1945- 96
Kubie, Eleanor Gottheil
See Kubie, Nora Gottheil Benjamin
Kubie, Nora Benjamin
See Kubie, Nora Gottheil Benjamin
Kubie, Nora Gottheil Benjamin 1899-1988 . 39
Obituary 59
Kubinyi, Laszlo 1937- 94
Earlier sketch in SATA 17
Kudlinski, Kathleen V. 1950- 150
Kuenstler, Morton 1927- 10
Kuharski, Janice 1947- 128
Kuijer, Guus 1942- 179
Kuklin, Susan 1941- 163
Earlier sketches in SATA 63, 95
See also CLR 51
Kulikov, Boris 1966- 170
Kulling, Monica 1952- 89
Kullman, Harry 1919-1982 35
Kumin, Maxine 1925- 12

Kumin, Maxine Winokur
See Kumin, Maxine
Kunhardt, Dorothy (Meserve) 1901-1979 53
Obituary 22
Kunhardt, Edith 1937- 67
Kunjufu, Jawanza 1953- 73
Kunstler, Morton
See Kuenstler, Morton
Kuntz, J(ohn) L. 1947- 91
Kuntz, Jerry 1956- 133
Kupferberg, Herbert 1918-2001 19
Kuratomi, Chizuko 1939- 12
See also CLR 32
Kurczok, Belinda 1978- 121
Kurelek, William 1927-1977 8
Obituary 27
See also CLR 2
Kurian, George 1928- 65
Kurjian, Judi(th M.) 1944- 127
Kurland, Gerald 1942- 13
Kurland, Michael 1938- 118
Earlier sketch in SATA 48
Kurland, Michael Joseph
See Kurland, Michael
Kuroi, Ken 1947- 120
Kurokawa, Mitsuhiro 1954- 88
Kurten, Bjorn (Olof) 1924-1988 64
Kurtz, Jane 1952- 139
Earlier sketch in SATA 91
See also CLR 123
Kurtz, Katherine (Irene) 1944- 126
Earlier sketch in SATA 76
Kurz, Rudolf 1952- 95
Kushner, Donn (J.) 1927- 52
See also CLR 55
Kushner, Ellen 1955- 98
Kushner, Ellen Ruth
See Kushner, Ellen
Kushner, Jill Menkes 1951- 62
Kushner, Lawrence 1943- 169
Earlier sketch in SATA 83
Kushner, Tony 1956- 160
Kuskin, Karla 1932- 164
Earlier sketches in SATA 2, 68, 111
See also CLR 4
See also SAAS 3
Kuskin, Karla Seidman
See Kuskin, Karla
Kusugak, Michael (Arvaarluk) 1948- 143
Kuttner, Paul 1922- 18
Kuyper, Sjoerd 1952- 177
Kuzma, Kay 1941- 39
Kvale, Velma R(uth) 1898-1979 8
Kvasnosky, Laura McGee 1951- 142
Earlier sketch in SATA 93
Kwasney, Michelle D. 1960- 162
Kyle, Benjamin
See Gottfried, Theodore Mark
Kyle, Elisabeth
See Dunlop, Agnes M. R.
Kyte, Kathy S. 1946- 50
Brief entry 44

L

L., Barry
See Longyear, Barry B(rookes)
L., Tommy
See Lorkowski, Thomas V(incent)
Lace, William W. 1942- 126
Lachner, Dorothea
See Knobloch, Dorothea
Lachtman, Ofelia Dumas 1919- 179
Lackey, Mercedes R. 1950- 127
Earlier sketch in SATA 81
Lackey, Mercedes Ritchie
See Lackey, Mercedes R.
Lacoe, Addie 78

Lacome, Julie 1961- 174
  Earlier sketch in SATA 80
Lacy, Leslie Alexander 1937- 6
Ladd, Cheryl (Jean) 1951- 113
Ladd, Louise 1943- 97
Ladd, Veronica
  See Miner, Jane Claypool
Laden, Nina 1962- 148
  Earlier sketch in SATA 85
Lader, Lawrence 1919-2006 6
  Obituary 178
LaDoux, Rita C. 1951- 74
Lady, A
  See Taylor, Ann
Lady of Quality, A
  See Bagnold, Enid
La Farge, Oliver (Hazard Perry)
  1901-1963 19
La Farge, Phyllis 14
LaFaye, A. 1970- 156
  Earlier sketch in SATA 105
LaFaye, Alexandria R.T.
  See LaFaye, A.
Laffin, John (Alfred Charles) 1922- 31
LaFontaine, Bruce 1948- 176
  Earlier sketch in SATA 114
La Fontaine, Jean de 1621-1695 18
Lager, Claude
  See Lapp, Christiane (Germain)
Lager, Marilyn 1939- 52
Lagercrantz, Rose (Elsa) 1947- 39
Lagerloef, Selma (Ottiliana Lovisa)
  See Lagerlof, Selma (Ottiliana Lovisa)
Lagerlof, Selma (Ottiliana Lovisa)
  1858-1940 15
  See also CLR 7
  See Lagerloef, Selma (Ottiliana Lovisa)
Laguna, Sofie 1968- 158
LaHaye, Tim F. 1926- 149
LaHaye, Timothy F.
  See LaHaye, Tim F.
Laiken, Deirdre S(usan) 1948- 48
  Brief entry 40
Laimgruber, Monika 1946- 11
Lain, Anna
  See Lamb, Nancy
Laing, Alexander (Kinnan) 1903-1976 117
Laing, Martha
  See Celestino, Martha Laing
Laird, Christa 1944- 108
  Autobiography Feature 120
  See also SAAS 26
Laird, Elizabeth (Mary Risk) 1943- 159
  Earlier sketches in SATA 77, 114
  See also CLR 65
Laird, Jean E(louise) 1930- 38
Laite, Gordon 1925- 31
Lake, Harriet
  See Taylor, Paula (Wright)
Laklan, Carli 1907-1988 5
Laliberte, Louise-Andree 1958- 169
Lalicki, Barbara 61
Lally, Soinbhe 1945- 119
LaMarche, Jim 162
Lamb, Beatrice Pitney 1904-1997 21
Lamb, Charles 1775-1834 17
Lamb, Elizabeth Searle 1917- 31
Lamb, G(eoffrey) F(rederick) 10
Lamb, Harold (Albert) 1892-1962 53
Lamb, Lynton (Harold) 1907-1977 10
Lamb, Mary Ann 1764-1847 17
Lamb, Nancy 1939- 80
Lamb, Robert (Boyden) 1941- 13
Lambert, David (Compton) 1932- 84
  Brief entry 49
Lambert, Janet 1895(?)-1973 25
Lambert, Martha L. 113
Lambert, Saul 1928 23
Lambert, Stephen 174
Lamburn, Richmal Crompton 1890-1969 5
  See Crompton, Richmal

Lamensdorf, Len
  See Lamensdorf, Leonard
Lamensdorf, Leonard 1930- 120
Laminack, Lester L. 1956- 163
  Earlier sketch in SATA 120
Lamorisse, Albert (Emmanuel) 1922-1970 ... 23
Lampert, Emily 1951- 52
  Brief entry 49
Lamplugh, Lois 1921- 17
Lampman, Evelyn Sibley 1907-1980 87
  Obituary 23
  Earlier sketch in SATA 4
Lamprey, Louise 1869-1951
  See YABC 2
Lampton, Chris
  See Lampton, Christopher F.
Lampton, Christopher
  See Lampton, Christopher F.
Lampton, Christopher F. 67
  Brief entry 47
Lamstein, Sarah 1943- 174
  Earlier sketch in SATA 126
Lamstein, Sarah Marwil
  See Lamstein, Sarah
Lanagan, Mary 1960- 163
Lancaster, Bruce 1896-1963 9
Lance, Kathryn 1943- 76
Land, Barbara (Neblett) 1923- 16
Land, Jane
  See Borland, Kathryn Kilby
  and Speicher, Helen Ross S(mith)
Land, Myrick (Ebben) 1922-1998 15
Land, Ross
  See Borland, Kathryn Kilby
  and Speicher, Helen Ross S(mith)
Landau, Elaine 1948- 141
  Earlier sketches in SATA 10, 94
Landau, Jacob 1917- 38
Landeck, Beatrice 1904-1978 15
Landin, Les 1923- 2
Landis, J(ames) D(avid) 1942- 60
  Brief entry 52
Landis, James D.
  See Landis, J(ames) D(avid)
Landis, Jill Marie 1948- 101
Landmann, Bimba 1968- 176
Landon, Dena 1978(?)- 168
Landon, Lucinda 1950- 56
  Brief entry 51
Landon, Margaret (Dorothea Mortenson)
  1903-1993 50
Landshoff, Ursula 1908-1989 13
Landstrom, Lena 1943- 146
Landstrom, Olof 1943- 146
Lane, Carolyn 1926-1993 10
Lane, Connie
  See Laux, Constance
Lane, Dakota 1959- 166
  Earlier sketch in SATA 105
Lane, Jerry
  See Martin, Patricia Miles
Lane, John (Richard) 1932- 15
Lane, Margaret 1907-1994 65
  Brief entry 38
  Obituary 79
Lane, Rose Wilder 1887-1968 29
  Brief entry 28
Lanes, Selma Gordon 1929- 3
Lanfredi, Judy 1964- 83
Lang, Andrew 1844-1912 16
  See also CLR 101
Lang, Aubrey 169
Lang, Paul 1948- 83
Lang, Susan S. 1950- 68
Lang, T.T.
  See Taylor, Theodore
Langdo, Bryan 1973- 138
Lange, John
  See Crichton, Michael
Lange, Suzanne 1945- 5

Langley, Andrew 1949- 166
  Earlier sketch in SATA 104
Langley, Charles P(itman) III 1949- 103
Langley, Jonathan 1952- 122
Langley, Wanda 173
Langner, Nola 8
  See Malone, Nola Langner
Langone, John (Michael) 1929- 46
  Brief entry 38
Langreuter, Jutta 1944- 122
Langrish, Katherine 177
Langsen, Richard C. 1953- 95
Langstaff, John 1920-2005 68
  Obituary 172
  Earlier sketch in SATA 6
  See also CLR 3
Langstaff, John Meredith
  See Langstaff, John
Langstaff, Launcelot
  See Irving, Washington
Langton, Jane (Gillson) 1922- 140
  Autobiography Feature 140
  Earlier sketches in SATA 3, 68, 129
  See also CLR 33
  See also SAAS 5
Lanier, Sidney 1842-1881 18
Lanier, Sterling E(dmund) 1927-2007 109
Lanino, Deborah 1964- 123
Lankford, Mary D. 1932- 112
  Earlier sketch in SATA 77
Lannin, Joanne (A.) 1951- 121
Lansdale, Joe R. 1951- 116
Lansdale, Joe Richard
  See Lansdale, Joe R.
Lansing, Alfred 1921-1975 35
Lansing, Karen E. 1954- 71
Lansky, Vicki 1942- 177
Lantier-Sampon, Patricia 1952- 92
Lantz, Fran
  See Lantz, Francess L(in)
Lantz, Francess L(in) 1952-2004 153
  Autobiography Feature 153
  Obituary 159
  Earlier sketches in SATA 63, 109
  See Dixon, Franklin W.
Lantz, Paul 1908- 45
Lantz, Walter 1900-1994 37
  Obituary 79
Lanza, Barbara 1945- 101
Lapp, Christiane (Germain) 1948- 74
Lappin, Peter 1911-1999 32
Larbalestier, Justine 178
Lardy, Philippe 1963- 168
Larios, Julie 1949- 178
Larios, Julie Hofstrand
  See Larios, Julie
Larkin, Amy
  See Burns, Olive Ann
Larkin, Maia
  See Wojciechowska, Maia (Teresa)
Laroche, Giles 1956- 126
  Earlier sketch in SATA 71
LaRochelle, David 1960- 171
  Earlier sketch in SATA 115
LaRose, Linda 125
Larrabee, Lisa 1947- 84
Larrecq, John M(aurice) 1926-1980 44
  Obituary 25
Larrick (Crosby), Nancy 1910-2004 4
Larsen, Anita 1942- 78
Larsen, Egon 1904- 14
Larsen, Rebecca 1944- 54
Larson, Eve
  See St. John, Wylly Folk
Larson, Gary 1950- 57
Larson, Ingrid D(ana) 1965- 92
Larson, Jean Russell 1930- 121
Larson, Kirby 1954- 96
Larson, Norita D(ittberner) 1944- 29
Larson, William H. 1938- 10
Larsson, Carl (Olof) 1853-1919 35

LaSalle, Charles A.
　See Ellis, Edward S(ylvester)
LaSalle, Charles E.
　See Ellis, Edward S(ylvester)
Lasell, Elinor H. 1929- 19
Lasell, Fen H.
　See Lasell, Elinor H.
Lasenby, Jack 1931- 172
　Earlier sketches in SATA 65, 103
Laser, Michael 1954- 117
Lash, Joseph P. 1909-1987 43
Lasher, Faith B. 1921- 12
Lasker, David 1950- 38
Lasker, Joe 83
　See also SAAS 17
　See Lasker, Joseph Leon
Lasker, Joseph Leon 1919- 9
　See Lasker, Joe
Laski, Marghanita 1915-1988 55
Laskin, Pamela L. 1954- 75
Lasky, Kathryn 1944- 157
　Earlier sketches in SATA 13, 69, 112
　See also CLR 11
Lasky Knight, Kathryn
　See Lasky, Kathryn
Lass, Bonnie 131
Lassalle, C. E.
　See Ellis, Edward S(ylvester)
Lassiter, Mary 59
　See Hoffman, Mary (Margaret)
Lassiter, Rhiannon 1977- 157
Latham, Barbara 1896- 16
Latham, Frank B(rown) 1910-2000 6
Latham, Jean Lee 1902-1995 68
　Earlier sketch in SATA 2
　See also CLR 50
Latham, Mavis
　See Clark, Mavis Thorpe
Latham, Philip
　See Richardson, Robert S(hirley)
Lathrop, Dorothy P(ulis) 1891-1980 14
　Obituary 24
Lathrop, Francis
　See Leiber, Fritz (Reuter, Jr.)
Latimer, Jim 1943- 80
Latta, Rich
　See Latta, Richard
Latta, Richard 1946- 113
Latta, Sara L. 1960- 174
Lattany, Kristin
　See Lattany, Kristin (Elaine Eggleston) Hunter
Lattany, Kristin (Eggleston) Hunter 1931- . 154
　Autobiography Feature 154
　Earlier sketch in SATA 132
Lattany, Kristin (Elaine Eggleston) Hunter
　1931- 132
　Earlier sketch in SATA 12
　See also CLR 3
　See also SAAS 10
　See Hunter, Kristin
Lattimore, Eleanor Frances 1904-1986 7
　Obituary 48
Lattin, Ann
　See Cole, Lois Dwight
Lauber, Patricia (Grace) 1924- 138
　Earlier sketches in SATA 1, 33, 75
　See also CLR 16
Laugesen, Mary E(akin) 1906-1995 5
Laughbaum, Steve 1945- 12
Laughlin, Florence Young 1910-2001 3
Laughlin, Rosemary 1941- 123
Laure, Ettagale
　See Blauer, Ettagale
Laure, Jason 1940- 50
　Brief entry 44
Laurence, Ester Hauser 1935- 7
Laurie, Rona 1916- 55
Laurin, Anne
　See McLaurin, Anne
Lauritzen, Jonreed 1902-1979 13

Lauscher, Hermann
　See Hesse, Hermann
Lauture, Denize 1946- 86
Laux, Connie
　See Laux, Constance
Laux, Constance 1952- 97
Laux, Dorothy 1920- 49
Lavallee, Barbara 1941- 166
　Earlier sketch in SATA 74
Lavender, David (Sievert) 1910-2003 97
　Obituary 145
　Earlier sketch in SATA 64
Lavender, William D. 1921- 143
Laverne, Christine 175
Lavert, Gwendolyn Battle 1951- 131
　See Battle-Lavert, Gwendolyn
Laverty, Donald
　See Blish, James (Benjamin)
　and Knight, Damon (Francis)
Lavigne, Louis-Dominique 107
Lavine, David 1928- 31
Lavine, Sigmund Arnold 1908-1986 82
　Earlier sketch in SATA 3
　See also CLR 35
Lavond, Paul Dennis
　See Kornbluth, C(yril) M.
　and Lowndes, Robert A(ugustine) W(ard)
　and Pohl, Frederik
Lawhead, Stephen R. 1950- 109
Lawhead, Steve
　See Lawhead, Stephen R.
Lawlor, Laurie 1953- 137
　Earlier sketch in SATA 80
Lawrence, Ann (Margaret) 1942-1987 41
　Obituary 54
Lawrence, Iain 1955- 135
Lawrence, J. T.
　See Rowland-Entwistle, (Arthur) Theodore
　(Henry)
Lawrence, Jerome 1915-2004 65
Lawrence, John 1933- 30
Lawrence, Louise 1943- 119
　Earlier sketches in SATA 38, 78
Lawrence, Louise de Kiriline 1894-1992 13
Lawrence, Lynn
　See Garland, Sherry
Lawrence, Margery H. 1889-1969 120
Lawrence, Michael 1943- 132
Lawrence, Mildred Elwood 1907-1997 3
Lawrence, R(onald) D(ouglas) 1921- 55
Lawrinson, Julia 1969- 141
Lawson, Amy
　See Gordon, Amy
Lawson, Carol (Antell) 1946- 42
Lawson, Don(ald Elmer) 1917-1990 9
Lawson, Joan 1906- 55
Lawson, Julie 1947- 126
　Earlier sketch in SATA 79
　See also CLR 89
Lawson, Marion Tubbs 1896-1994 22
Lawson, Robert 1892-1957 100
　See also YABC 2
　See also CLR 73
Lawton, Clive A. 1951- 145
Laxdal, Vivienne 1962- 112
Laycock, George (Edwin) 1921- 5
Layne, Laura
　See Knott, William C(ecil, Jr.)
Layne, Steven L. 171
Layton, Neal (Andrew) 1971- 152
Lazare, Gerald John 1927- 44
Lazare, Jerry
　See Lazare, Gerald John
Lazarevich, Mila 1942- 17
Lazarus, Keo Felker 1913-1993 21
　Obituary 129
Lea, Alec 1907- 19
Lea, Joan
　See Neufeld, John (Arthur)
Leach, Maria 1892-1977 39
　Brief entry 28

Leacock, Elspeth 1946- 131
Leacroft, Helen (Mabel Beal) 1919- 6
Leacroft, Richard (Vallance Becher) 1914- 6
Leaf, (Wilbur) Munro 1905-1976 20
　See also CLR 25
Leaf, VaDonna Jean 1929- 26
Leah, Devorah
　See Devorah-Leah
Leakey, Richard E(rskine Frere) 1944- 42
Leander, Ed
　See Richelson, Geraldine
Lear, Edward 1812-1888 100
　Earlier sketch in SATA 18
　See also CLR 75
Lears, Laurie 1955- 127
Leasor, (Thomas) James 1923- 54
Leavitt, Jerome E(dward) 1916- 23
Leavitt, Martine 1953- 170
LeBar, Mary E(velyn) 1910-1982 35
LeBlanc, Annette M. 1965- 68
LeBlanc, L(ee) 1913- 54
LeBox, Annette 1943- 145
Lebrun, Claude 1929- 66
Le Cain, Errol (John) 1941-1989 68
　Obituary 60
　Earlier sketch in SATA 6
Lecourt, Nancy (Hoyt) 1951- 73
Ledbetter, Suzann 1953- 119
Leder, Jane Mersky 1945- 61
　Brief entry 51
Lederer, Muriel 1929- 48
Lederer, William J(ulius) 1912- 62
Lee, Amanda
　See Baggett, Nancy
　and Buckholtz, Eileen (Garber)
　and Glick, Ruth (Burtnick)
Lee, Benjamin 1921- 27
Lee, Betsy 1949- 37
Lee, Carol
　See Fletcher, Helen Jill
Lee, Cora
　See Anderson, Catherine Corley
Lee, Dennis (Beynon) 1939- 102
　Earlier sketch in SATA 14
　See also CLR 3
Lee, Dom 1959- 146
　Autobiography Feature 121
　Earlier sketch in SATA 83
　See also SAAS 26
Lee, Doris Emrick 1905-1983 44
　Obituary 35
Lee, Elizabeth Rogers 1940- 90
Lee, Harper 1926- 11
Lee, Hector Viveros 1962- 115
Lee, Howard N.
　See Goulart, Ron(ald Joseph)
Lee, Huy Voun 1969- 129
Lee, J(oseph) Edward 1953- 130
Lee, Jeanne M. 1943- 138
Lee, John R(obert) 1923-1976 27
Lee, Jordan
　See Scholefield, Alan
Lee, Julian
　See Latham, Jean Lee
Lee, Liz
　See Lee, Elizabeth Rogers
Lee, Lucy
　See Talbot, Charlene Joy
Lee, Lyn 1953- 128
Lee, Manning de Villeneuve 1894-1980 37
　Obituary 22
Lee, Marian
　See Clish, (Lee) Marian
Lee, Marie G. 1964- 178
　Earlier sketches in SATA 81, 130
Lee, Marie Myung-Ok
　See Lee, Marie G.
Lee, Mary Price 1934- 82
　Earlier sketch in SATA 8

Lee, Mildred 6
    See also SAAS *12*
    See Scudder, Mildred Lee
Lee, Nelle Harper
    See Lee, Harper
Lee, Richard S. 1927- 82
Lee, Robert C. 1931- 20
Lee, Robert E(dwin) 1918-1994 65
    Obituary 82
Lee, Robert J. 1921- 10
Lee, Sally 1943- 67
Lee, Tammie
    See Townsend, Thomas L.
Lee, Tanith 1947- 134
    Earlier sketches in SATA *8, 88*
Leech, Ben
    See Bowkett, Stephen
Leedy, Loreen 1959- 175
    Brief entry 50
    Earlier sketches in SATA *54, 84, 128*
Leedy, Loreen Janelle
    See Leedy, Loreen
Lee-Hostetler, Jeri 1940- 63
Leekley, Thomas B(riggs) 1910-2001 23
Leeming, Jo Ann
    See Leeming, Joseph
Leeming, Joseph 1897-1968 26
Leemis, Ralph B. 1954- 72
Leese, Jennifer L.B. 1970- 163
Leeson, Muriel 1920- 54
Leeson, R. A.
    See Leeson, Robert (Arthur)
Leeson, Robert (Arthur) 1928- 76
    Earlier sketch in SATA *42*
Leffland, Ella 1931- 65
Lefler, Irene (Whitney) 1917- 12
Le Gallienne, Eva 1899-1991 9
    Obituary 68
Legg, Gerald 1947- 143
LeGrand
    See Henderson, LeGrand
Le Guin, Ursula K. 1929- 149
    Earlier sketches in SATA *4, 52, 99*
    See also CLR *91*
Le Guin, Ursula Kroeber
    See Le Guin, Ursula K.
Legum, Colin 1919-2003 10
Lehman, Barbara 1963- 170
    Earlier sketch in SATA *115*
Lehman, Bob 91
Lehman, Elaine 91
Lehn, Cornelia 1920- 46
Lehne, Judith Logan 1947- 93
Lehr, Delores 1920- 10
Lehr, Norma 1930- 71
Leiber, Fritz (Reuter, Jr.) 1910-1992 45
    Obituary 73
Leibold, Jay 1957- 57
    Brief entry 52
Leichman, Seymour 1933- 5
Leigh, Nila K. 1981- 81
Leigh, Tom 1947- 46
Leigh-Pemberton, John 1911-1997 35
Leighton, Clare (Veronica Hope)
    1899-1989 37
Leighton, Margaret (Carver) 1896-1987 1
    Obituary 52
Leiner, Al(an) 1938- 83
Leiner, Katherine 1949- 93
Leipold, L. Edmond 1902-1983 16
Leisk, David (Johnson) 1906-1975 30
    Obituary 26
    Earlier sketch in SATA *1*
    See also CLR *98*
    See Johnson, Crockett
Leister, Mary 1917- 29
Leitch, Patricia 1933- 98
    Earlier sketch in SATA *11*
Leitner, Isabella 1924- 86
Leland, Bob 1956- 92

Leland, Robert E.
    See Leland, Bob
Lematre, Pascal 1967- 176
Lember, Barbara Hirsch 1941- 92
LeMieux, A.C. 1954- 125
    Earlier sketch in SATA *90*
    See LeMieux, Anne
LeMieux, Anne
    See LeMieux, A.C.
LeMieux, Anne Connelly
    See LeMieux, A.C.
Lemieux, Michele 1955- 139
Lemke, Horst 1922- 38
Lenanton, Carola Mary Anima Oman
    See Oman, Carola (Mary Anima)
L'Engle, Madeleine 1918- 128
    Earlier sketches in SATA *1, 27, 75*
    See also CLR *57*
    See also SAAS *15*
L'Engle, Madeleine Camp Franklin
    See L'Engle, Madeleine
Lengyel, Cornel Adam 1915- 27
Lengyel, Emil 1895-1985 3
    Obituary 42
Lennon, John (Ono) 1940-1980 114
Leno, Jay 1950- 154
LeNoir, Janice 1941- 89
Lens, Sidney 1912-1986 13
    Obituary 48
Lenski, Lois 1893-1974 100
    Earlier sketches in SATA *1, 26*
    See also CLR *26*
Lent, Blair 133
    Earlier sketch in SATA *2*
Lent, Henry Bolles 1901-1973 17
Lent, John 1948- 108
Leodhas, Sorche Nic
    See Alger, Leclaire (Gowans)
Leokum, Arkady 1916(?)- 45
Leon, Sharon 1959- 79
Leonard, Alison 1944- 70
Leonard, Constance (Brink) 1923- 42
    Brief entry 40
Leonard, Elmore 1925- 163
Leonard, Elmore John, Jr.
    See Leonard, Elmore
Leonard, Jonathan N(orton) 1903-1975 36
Leonard, Laura 1923- 75
Leong, Gor Yun
    See Ellison, Virginia H(owell)
Leonhardt, Alice 1950- 152
Lerangis, Peter 1955- 171
    Earlier sketch in SATA *72*
    See Dixon, Franklin W.
    and Keene, Carolyn
Lerner, Aaron 1920-2007 35
    Obituary 179
Lerner, Aaron Bunsen
    See Lerner, Aaron
Lerner, Carol 1927- 86
    Earlier sketch in SATA *33*
    See also CLR *34*
    See also SAAS *12*
Lerner, Gerda 1920- 65
Lerner, Harriet 1944- 101
Lerner, Marguerite Rush 1924-1987 11
    Obituary 51
Lerner, Sharon (Ruth) 1938-1982 11
    Obituary 29
Leroe, Ellen W(hitney) 1949- 99
    Brief entry 51
    Earlier sketch in SATA *61*
Leroux, Gaston 1868-1927 65
Leroux-Hugon, Helene 1955- 132
LeRoy, Gen 52
    Brief entry 36
LeShan, Eda J(oan) 1922-2002 21
    See also CLR *6*

LeSieg, Theo.
    See Dr. Seuss
    and Geisel, Theodor Seuss
    and Seuss, Dr.
    and Stone, Rosetta
Lesinski, Jeanne M. 1960- 120
Leslie, Robert Franklin 1911-1990 7
Leslie, Roger 1961- 168
Leslie, Roger James
    See Leslie, Roger
Leslie, Sarah
    See McGuire, Leslie (Sarah)
LeSourd, Catherine
    See Marshall, (Sarah) Catherine (Wood)
Lessac, Frane
    See Lessac, Frane
Lessac, Frane 1954- 148
    Earlier sketch in SATA *61*
Lessem, Dino Don
    See Lessem, Don
Lessem, Don 1951- 155
    Earlier sketch in SATA *97*
Lesser, Rika 1953- 53
Lester, Alison 1952- 129
    Earlier sketches in SATA *50, 90*
Lester, Helen 1936- 145
    Earlier sketches in SATA *46, 92*
Lester, Julius 1939- 157
    Earlier sketches in SATA *12, 74, 112*
    See also CLR *41*
Lester, Julius Bernard
    See Lester, Julius
Lester, Mike 1955- 131
Le Sueur, Meridel 1900-1996 6
Le Tord, Bijou 1945- 95
    Earlier sketch in SATA *49*
Letts, Billie 1938- 121
Leuck, Laura 1962- 146
    Earlier sketch in SATA *85*
Leutscher, Alfred (George) 1913- 23
Levai, Blaise 1919- 39
Levenkron, Steven 1941- 86
Leverich, Kathleen 1948- 103
LeVert, (William) John 1946- 55
Levete, Sarah 1961- 153
Levin, Betty 1927- 137
    Earlier sketches in SATA *19, 84*
    See also SAAS *11*
Levin, Ira 1929- 66
Levin, Marcia Obrasky 1918- 13
Levin, Meyer 1905-1981 21
    Obituary 27
Levin, Miriam (Ramsfelder) 1962- 97
Levine, Abby 1943- 54
    Brief entry 52
Levine, Betty K(rasne) 1933- 66
Levine, David 1926- 43
    Brief entry 35
Levine, Edna S(imon) 35
Levine, Evan 1962- 77
    Earlier sketch in SATA *74*
Levine, Gail Carson 1947- 161
    Earlier sketch in SATA *98*
    See also CLR *85*
Levine, I(srael) E. 1923-2003 12
    Obituary 146
Levine, Joan Goldman 11
Levine, Joseph 1910- 33
Levine, Marge 1934- 81
Levine, Rhoda 14
Levine, Sarah 1970- 57
Levine, Shar 1953- 131
Levine-Freidus, Gail
    See Provost, Gail Levine
Levinson, Nancy Smiler 1938- 140
    Earlier sketches in SATA *33, 80*
Levinson, Riki 99
    Brief entry 49
    Earlier sketch in SATA *52*
Levithan, David 1972- 166

Levitin, Sonia (Wolff) 1934- *131*
   Autobiography Feature *131*
   Earlier sketches in SATA *4, 68, 119*
   See also CLR *53*
   See also SAAS *2*
Levitt, Sidney (Mark) 1947- *68*
Levon, O. U.
   See Kesey, Ken
Levoy, Myron *49*
   Brief entry *37*
Levy, Barrie *112*
Levy, Constance 1931- *140*
   Earlier sketch in SATA *73*
   See also SAAS *22*
Levy, Elizabeth 1942- *169*
   Earlier sketches in SATA *31, 69, 107*
   See also SAAS *18*
Levy, Janice *172*
Levy, Marilyn 1937- *67*
Levy, Nathan 1945- *63*
Levy, Robert 1945- *82*
Lewees, John
   See Stockton, Francis Richard
Lewin, Betsy 1937- *169*
   Autobiography Feature *115*
   Earlier sketches in SATA *32, 90*
Lewin, Hugh 1939- *72*
   Brief entry *40*
   See also CLR *9*
Lewin, Ted 1935- *165*
   Autobiography Feature *115*
   Earlier sketches in SATA *21, 76, 119*
Lewis, Alice C. 1936- *46*
Lewis, Amanda 1955- *80*
Lewis, (Joseph) Anthony 1927- *27*
Lewis, Anthony 1966- *120*
Lewis, Barbara A. 1943- *73*
Lewis, Beverly 1949- *80*
Lewis, Brenda Ralph 1932- *72*
Lewis, Brian 1963- *128*
Lewis, Claudia (Louise) 1907-2001 .... *5*
Lewis, Clive Staples
   See Lewis, C.S.
Lewis, C.S. 1898-1963 .... *100*
   Earlier sketch in SATA *13*
   See also CLR *109*
Lewis, Cynthia Copeland 1960- *111*
Lewis, E. M. *123*
   Earlier sketch in SATA *20*
Lewis, Earl Bradley
   See Lewis, E.B.
Lewis, E.B. 1956- *168*
   Earlier sketches in SATA *93, 124*
Lewis, Elizabeth Foreman 1892-1958 .... *121*
   See also YABC *2*
Lewis, Francine
   See Wells, Helen
Lewis, J. Patrick 1942- *162*
   Earlier sketches in SATA *69, 104*
Lewis, Jack P(earl) 1919- *65*
Lewis, Jean 1924- *61*
Lewis, Julinda
   See Lewis-Ferguson, Julinda
Lewis, Kevin *173*
Lewis, Kim 1951- *136*
   Earlier sketch in SATA *84*
Lewis, Linda (Joy) 1946- *67*
Lewis, Lucia Z.
   See Anderson, Lucia (Lewis)
Lewis, Marjorie 1929- *40*
   Brief entry *35*
Lewis, Mary (Christianna) 1907(?)-1988 .... *64*
   Obituary *56*
   See Brand, Christianna
Lewis, Mervyn
   See Frewer, Glyn (M.)
Lewis, Michael
   See Untermeyer, Louis
Lewis, Naomi *144*
   Earlier sketch in SATA *76*
Lewis, Paeony 1960- *173*

Lewis, Paul
   See Gerson, Noel Bertram
Lewis, Richard 1935- *3*
Lewis, Rob 1962- *72*
Lewis, Roger
   See Zarchy, Harry
Lewis, Shannon
   See Llywelyn, Morgan
Lewis, Shari 1934-1998 .... *35*
   Brief entry *30*
   Obituary *104*
Lewis, Sylvan R.
   See Aronson, Virginia
Lewis, Thomas P(arker) 1936- *27*
Lewis, Wendy A. 1966- *150*
Lewis-Ferguson, Julinda 1955- *85*
Lewison, Wendy Cheyette *177*
Lewiton, Mina 1904-1970 .... *2*
Lexau, Joan M. *130*
   Earlier sketches in SATA *1, 36*
Ley, Willy 1906-1969 .... *2*
Leydon, Rita (Floden) 1949- *21*
Leyland, Eric (Arthur) 1911- *37*
Li, Xiao Jun 1952- *86*
Liatsos, Sandra Olson 1942- *103*
Libby, Barbara M. *153*
Libby, Bill
   See Libby, William M.
Libby, William M. 1927-1984 .... *5*
   Obituary *39*
Liberty, Gene 1924- *3*
Lichtenheld, Tom *152*
Liddell, Kenneth 1912-1975 .... *63*
Lidz, Jane *120*
Lieberman, E(dwin) James 1934- *62*
Liebers, Arthur 1913-1984 .... *12*
Lieblich, Irene 1923- *22*
Liers, Emil E(rnest) 1890-1975 .... *37*
Lies, Brian 1963- *131*
Liestman, Vicki 1961- *72*
Lietz, Gerald S. 1918- *11*
Life, Kay (Guinn) 1930- *83*
Lifton, Betty Jean *118*
   Earlier sketch in SATA *6*
Lifton, Robert Jay 1926- *66*
Lightburn, Ron 1954- *91*
Lightburn, Sandra 1955- *91*
Lightner, A. M.
   See Hopf, Alice (Martha) L(ightner)
Lightner, Alice
   See Hopf, Alice (Martha) L(ightner)
Lignell, Lois 1911- *37*
Liles, Maurine Walpole 1935- *81*
Lilley, Stephen R. 1950- *97*
Lilley, Stephen Ray
   See Lilley, Stephen R.
Lillington, Kenneth (James) 1916-1998 .... *39*
Lilly, Ray
   See Curtis, Richard (Alan)
Lim, John 1932- *43*
Liman, Ellen (Fogelson) 1936- *22*
Limb, Sue 1946- *158*
Limburg, Peter R(ichard) 1929- *13*
Lin, Grace 1974- *162*
   Earlier sketch in SATA *111*
Lincoln, C(harles) Eric 1924-2000 .... *5*
Lincoln, James
   See Bates, Katharine Lee
Lindbergh, Anne *81*
   See Sapieyevski, Anne Lindbergh
Lindbergh, Anne Morrow 1906-2001 .... *33*
   Obituary *125*
Lindbergh, Anne Spencer Morrow
   See Lindbergh, Anne Morrow
Lindbergh, Charles A(ugustus, Jr.)
   1902-1974 .... *33*
Lindbergh, Reeve 1945- *163*
   Earlier sketch in SATA *116*
Lindblom, Steven (Winther) 1946- *94*
   Brief entry *39*
   Earlier sketch in SATA *42*

Linde, Gunnel 1924- *5*
Lindenbaum, Pija 1955- *144*
   Earlier sketch in SATA *77*
Lindgren, Astrid (Anna Emilia Ericsson)
   1907-2002 .... *38*
   Obituary *128*
   Earlier sketch in SATA *2*
   See also CLR *119*
Lindgren, Barbro 1937- *120*
   Brief entry *46*
   Earlier sketch in SATA *63*
   See also CLR *86*
Lindman, Maj (Jan) 1886-1972 .... *43*
Lindop, Edmund 1925- *5*
Lindquist, Jennie Dorothea 1899-1977 .... *13*
Lindquist, Rowena Cory 1958- *98*
Lindquist, Willis 1908-1988 .... *20*
Lindsay, Norman Alfred William
   1879-1969 .... *67*
   See also CLR *8*
Lindsay, (Nicholas) Vachel 1879-1931 .... *40*
Lindsey, Kathleen D(orothy) 1949- *153*
Line, David
   See Davidson, Lionel
Line, Les 1935- *27*
Linfield, Esther *40*
Lingard, Joan (Amelia) 1932- *130*
   Autobiography Feature *130*
   Earlier sketches in SATA *8, 74, 114*
   See also CLR *89*
   See also SAAS *5*
Link, Martin 1934- *28*
Linn, Margot
   See Ziefert, Harriet
Linnea, Sharon 1956- *82*
Lion, Melissa 1976- *176*
Lionni, Leo(nard) 1910-1999 .... *72*
   Obituary *118*
   Earlier sketch in SATA *8*
   See also CLR *71*
Lipinsky de Orlov, Lino S. 1908- *22*
Lipkind, William 1904-1974 .... *15*
Lipman, David 1931- *21*
Lipman, Matthew 1923- *14*
Lippincott, Gary A. 1953- *119*
   Earlier sketch in SATA *73*
Lippincott, Joseph W(harton) 1887-1976 .... *17*
Lippincott, Sarah Lee 1920- *22*
Lippman, Peter J. 1936- *31*
Lipsyte, Robert 1938- *161*
   Earlier sketches in SATA *5, 68, 113*
   See also CLR *76*
Lipsyte, Robert Michael
   See Lipsyte, Robert
Lisandrelli, Elaine Slivinski 1951- *94*
Lisker, Sonia O. 1933- *44*
Lisle, Holly 1960- *98*
Lisle, Janet Taylor 1947- *150*
   Brief entry *47*
   Earlier sketches in SATA *59, 96*
   See also SAAS *14*
Lisle, Rebecca *162*
Lisle, Seward D.
   See Ellis, Edward S(ylvester)
Lisowski, Gabriel 1946- *47*
   Brief entry *31*
Liss, Howard 1922-1995 .... *4*
   Obituary *84*
Lisson, Deborah 1941- *110*
   Earlier sketch in SATA *71*
List, Ilka Katherine 1935- *6*
Liston, Robert A. 1927- *5*
Litchfield, Ada B(assett) 1916-1999 .... *5*
Litchfield, Jo 1973- *116*
Lithgow, John (Arthur) 1945- *145*
Litowinsky, Olga (Jean) 1936- *26*
Littke, Lael J. 1929- *140*
   Earlier sketches in SATA *51, 83*
Little, A. Edward
   See Klein, Aaron E.
Little, Douglas 1942- *96*

Little, (Flora) Jean 1932- 149
    Earlier sketches in SATA 2, 68, 106
    See also CLR 4
    See also SAAS 17
Little, Lessie Jones 1906-1986 60
    Obituary 50
Little, Mary E. 1912-1999 28
Littlechild, George 1958- 85
Littledale, Freya (Lota) 1929-1992 74
    Earlier sketch in SATA 2
Littlefield, Bill 1948- 83
Littlefield, Holly 1963- 97
Littlesugar, Amy 1953- 176
    Earlier sketch in SATA 122
Littleton, Mark R. 1950- 142
    Earlier sketch in SATA 89
Littman, Sarah Darer 175
Lively, Penelope 1933- 164
    Earlier sketches in SATA 7, 60, 101
    See also CLR 7
Lively, Penelope Margaret
    See Lively, Penelope
Liverakos, L.A.
    See Gilman, Laura Anne
Liversidge, (Henry) Douglas 1913- 8
Livesey, Claire (Warner) 1927- 127
Livingston, Carole 1941- 42
Livingston, (M.) Irene 1932- 150
Livingston, Myra Cohn 1926-1996 68
    Obituary 92
    Earlier sketch in SATA 5
    See also CLR 7
    See also SAAS 1
Livingston, Richard R(oland) 1922- 8
Livo, Norma J. 1929- 76
Llerena Aguirre, Carlos 1952- 19
Llerena Aguirre, Carlos Antonio
    See Llerena Aguirre, Carlos
Llewellyn, Claire 1954- 143
    Earlier sketch in SATA 77
Llewellyn, Grace 1964- 110
Llewellyn, Grace Katherine
    See Llewellyn, Grace
Llewellyn, Richard
    See Llewellyn Lloyd, Richard Dafydd Vivian
Llewellyn, Sam 1948- 95
Llewellyn Lloyd, Richard Dafydd Vivian
    1906-1983 11
    Obituary 37
    See Llewellyn, Richard
Llewelyn, T. Harcourt
    See Hamilton, Charles (Harold St. John)
Lloyd, Alan
    See Lloyd, A.R.
Lloyd, Alan Richard
    See Lloyd, A.R.
Lloyd, A.R. 1927- 168
    Earlier sketch in SATA 97
Lloyd, David
    See Lloyd, David T.
Lloyd, David T. 1954- 167
Lloyd, E. James
    See James, Elizabeth
Lloyd, Errol 1943- 22
Lloyd, Hugh
    See Fitzhugh, Percy Keese
Lloyd, James
    See James, Elizabeth
Lloyd, Megan 1958- 117
    Earlier sketch in SATA 77
Lloyd, (Mary) Norris 1908-1993 10
    Obituary 75
Lloyd-Jones, Sally 1960- 179
Lloyd Webber, Andrew 1948- 56
    See Webber, Andrew Lloyd
Llywelyn, Morgan 1937- 109
Lo, Ginnie 165
Lo, Virginia M.
    See Lo, Ginnie
Lobato, Jose Bento Monteiro 1882-1948 ... 114

Lobel, Anita (Kempler) 1934- 162
    Earlier sketches in SATA 6, 55, 96
Lobel, Arnold (Stark) 1933-1987 55
    Obituary 54
    Earlier sketch in SATA 6
    See also CLR 5
Lobsenz, Amelia 12
Lobsenz, Norman M(itchell) 1919- 6
Lochak, Michele 1936- 39
Lochlons, Colin
    See Jackson, C(aary) Paul
Locke, Clinton W. 1
Locke, Elsie (Violet) 1912-2001 87
Locke, Lucie 1904-1989 10
Locke, Robert 1944- 63
    See Bess, Clayton
Locker, Thomas 1937- 109
    Earlier sketch in SATA 59
    See also CLR 14
Lockhart, E.
    See Jenkins, Emily
Lockridge, Hildegarde (Dolson)
    1908-1981 121
    See Dolson, Hildegarde
Lockwood, Mary
    See Spelman, Mary
Lodge, Bernard 1933- 107
    Earlier sketch in SATA 33
Lodge, Jo 1966- 173
    Earlier sketch in SATA 112
Loeb, Jeffrey 1946- 57
Loeb, Robert H., Jr. 1917- 21
Loefgren, Ulf 1931- 3
Loehfelm, Bill 1969- 153
Loeper, John J(oseph) 1929- 118
    Earlier sketch in SATA 10
Loescher, Ann Dull 1942- 20
Loescher, Gil(burt Damian) 1945- 20
Loewer, Jean Jenkins
    See Jenkins, Jean
Loewer, (Henry) Peter 1934- 98
LoFaro, Jerry 1959- 77
Lofo
    See Heimann, Rolf
Lofting, Hugh (John) 1886-1947 100
    Earlier sketch in SATA 15
    See also CLR 19
Lofts, Norah (Robinson) 1904-1983 8
    Obituary 36
Logan, Jake
    See Knott, William C(ecil, Jr.)
    and Krepps, Robert W(ilson)
    and Pearl, Jacques Bain
    and Riefe, Alan
    and Rifkin, Shepard
    and Smith, Martin Cruz
Logan, Mark
    See Nicole, Christopher (Robin)
Logan, Rochelle 1954- 169
Logston, Anne 1962- 112
Logue, Christopher 1926- 23
Logue, Mary 1952- 161
    Earlier sketch in SATA 112
Loh, Morag 1935- 73
Lohans, Alison 1949- 101
Loken, Newton Clayton 1919- 26
Lomas, Steve
    See Brennan, Joseph Lomas
Lomask, Milton (Nachman) 1909-1991 20
Lombard, Jenny 178
Lombino, Salvatore
    See Hunter, Evan
LoMonaco, Palmyra 1932- 102
London, Jack 1876-1916 18
    See also CLR 108
    See London, John Griffith
London, Jane
    See Geis, Darlene Stern
London, Jonathan (Paul) 1947- 157
    Earlier sketches in SATA 74, 113
Lonergan, (Pauline) Joy (MacLean) 1909- ... 10

Lonette, Reisie (Dominee) 1924- 43
Long, Cathryn J. 1946- 89
Long, Earlene (Roberta) 1938- 50
Long, Emmett
    See Leonard, Elmore
Long, Helen Beecher 1
Long, Judith Elaine 1953- 20
Long, Judy
    See Long, Judith Elaine
Long, Kim 1949- 69
Long, Loren 1966(?)- 151
Long, Melinda 1960- 152
Long, Sylvia 1948- 179
    Earlier sketch in SATA 120
Longbeard, Frederick
    See Longyear, Barry B(rookes)
Longfellow, Henry Wadsworth 1807-1882 ... 19
    See also CLR 99
Longfellow, Layne (A.) 1937- 102
Longman, Harold S. 1919- 5
Longsworth, Polly 1933- 28
Longtemps, Kenneth 1933- 17
Longway, A. Hugh
    See Lang, Andrew
Longyear, Barry B(rookes) 1942- 117
Loomans, Diane 1955- 90
Loomis, Christine 160
    Earlier sketch in SATA 113
Loomis, Jennifer A. 1942- 101
Loomis, Robert D. 5
Lopez, Angelo (Cayas) 1967- 83
Lopez, Barry (Holstun) 1945- 67
Lopez, Jack 1950- 178
Lopshire, Robert M(artin) 1927- 6
Loraine, Connie
    See Reece, Colleen L.
Lorbiecki, Marybeth 1959- 172
    Earlier sketch in SATA 121
Lord, Athena V. 1932- 39
Lord, Beman 1924-1991 5
    Obituary 69
Lord, Bette Bao 1938- 58
Lord, (Doreen Mildred) Douglas 1904- 12
Lord, John Vernon 1939- 21
Lord, Nancy
    See Titus, Eve
Lord, Walter 1917-2002 3
Lorde, Diana
    See Reno, Dawn E(laine)
Lorenz, Albert 1941- 115
Lorenzini, Carlo 1826-1890 100
    Earlier sketch in SATA 29
    See Collodi, Carlo
Lorimer, Janet 1941- 60
Loring, Emilie (Baker) 1864(?)-1951 51
Lorkowski, Thomas V(incent) 1950- 92
Lorkowski, Tom
    See Lorkowski, Thomas V(incent)
Lorraine, Walter (Henry) 1929- 16
Lorrimer, Claire
    See Clark, Patricia Denise
Loss, Joan 1933- 11
Lothrop, Harriet Mulford Stone 1844-1924 . 20
Lottridge, Celia Barker 1936- 157
    Earlier sketch in SATA 112
LoTurco, Laura 1963- 84
Lotz, Wolfgang 1912-1981 65
Louie, Ai-Ling 1949- 40
    Brief entry 34
Louis, Pat
    See Francis, Dorothy Brenner
Louisburgh, Sheila Burnford
    See Burnford, Sheila (Philip Cochrane Every)
Louise, Anita
    See Riggio, Anita
Lourie, Helen
    See Storr, Catherine (Cole)
Lourie, Peter (King) 1952- 142
    Earlier sketch in SATA 82
Love, Ann 1947- 168
    Earlier sketch in SATA 79

Love, D. Anne 1949- *145*
  Earlier sketch in SATA 96
Love, Douglas 1967- 92
Love, Katherine (Isabel) 1907- 3
Love, Kathleen Ann
  See Love, Ann
Love, Sandra (Weller) 1940- 26
Lovejoy, Jack 1937- *116*
Lovelace, Delos Wheeler 1894-1967 7
Lovelace, Maud Hart 1892-1980 2
  Obituary 23
Lovell, Ingraham
  See Bacon, Josephine Dodge (Daskam)
Loverseed, Amanda (Jane) 1965- 75
Lovett, Margaret (Rose) 1915- 22
Low, Alice 1926- *156*
  Earlier sketches in SATA *11, 76*
Low, Elizabeth Hammond 1898-1991 5
Low, Joseph 1911-2007 14
Low, William *177*
Lowe, Jay, Jr.
  See Loeper, John J(oseph)
Lowell, Susan 1950- *127*
  Earlier sketch in SATA *81*
Lowenstein, Dyno 1914-1996 6
Lowenstein, Sallie 1949- *116*
Lowery, Linda 1949- *151*
  Earlier sketch in SATA 74
Lowitz, Anson C. 1901(?)-1978 18
Lowitz, Sadyebeth Heath 1901-1969 17
Lowndes, Robert A(ugustine) W(ard)
  1916-1998 .... *117*
Lowrey, Janette Sebring 1892-1986 43
Lowry, Lois 1937- *177*
  Autobiography Feature *127*
  Earlier sketches in SATA *23, 70, 111*
  See also CLR 72
  See also SAAS 3
Lowry, Lois Hammersberg
  See Lowry, Lois
Lowry, Peter 1953- 7
Loyie, Larry 1933- *150*
Lozansky, Edward D. 1941- 62
Lozier, Herbert 1915- 26
Lubar, David 1954- *133*
Lubell, Cecil 1912-2000 6
Lubell, Winifred (A. Milius) 1914- 6
Lubin, Leonard
  See Lubin, Leonard B.
Lubin, Leonard B. 1943-1994 45
  Brief entry 37
Lubka, S. Ruth 1948- *154*
Luby, Thia 1954- *124*
Lucado, Max (Lee) 1955- *104*
Lucas, Cedric 1962- *101*
Lucas, E(dward) V(errall) 1868-1938 20
Lucas, Eileen 1956- *113*
  Earlier sketch in SATA 76
Lucas, George 1944- 56
Lucas, Jerry 1940- 33
Lucas, Victoria
  See Plath, Sylvia
Lucashenko, Melissa 1967- *104*
Luccarelli, Vincent 1923- 90
Luce, Celia (Geneva Larsen) 1914- 38
Luce, Willard (Ray) 1914-1990 38
Lucht, Irmgard 1937- 82
Luckett, Dave 1951- *167*
  Earlier sketch in SATA *106*
Luckhardt, Mildred Corell 1898-1990 5
Ludel, Jacqueline 1945- 64
Ludlum, Mabel Cleland
  See Widdemer, Mabel Cleland
Ludwig, Helen 33
Ludwig, Lyndell 1923- 63
Ludwig, Trudy 1959- *166*
Lueders, Edward (George) 1923- 14
Luenn, Nancy 1954- 79
  Earlier sketch in SATA *51*
Lufkin, Raymond H. 1897- 38
Lugard, Flora Louisa Shaw 1852-1929 21

Luger, Harriett Mandelay 1914- 23
Luhrmann, Winifred B(ruce) 1934- *11*
Luis, Earlene W. 1929- *11*
Luke, Pauline *178*
Luke, Pauline R.
  See Luke, Pauline
Lum, Peter
  See Crowe, (Bettina) Peter Lum
Lumry, Amanda (R.) *159*
Lund, Deb *157*
Lund, Doris Herold 1919- 12
Lung, Chang
  See Jordan, Robert
Lunge-Larsen, Lise 1955- *138*
Lunn, Carolyn (Kowalczyk) 1960- 67
Lunn, Janet (Louise Swoboda) 1928- *110*
  Earlier sketches in SATA *4, 68*
  See also CLR 18
  See also SAAS 12
Lunsford, Cin Forshay
  See Forshay-Lunsford, Cin
Lupica, Mike *177*
  See Lupica, Michael
Lupoff, Dick
  See Lupoff, Richard A(llen)
Lupoff, Richard A(llen) 1935- 60
Lurie, Alison 1926- *112*
  Earlier sketch in SATA 46
Lurie, Morris 1938- 72
Lussert, Anneliese 1929- *101*
Lusted, Marcia Amidon 1962- *143*
Lustig, Arnost 1926- 56
Lustig, Loretta 1944- 46
Luthardt, Kevin 1973- *172*
Luther, Rebekah (Lyn) S(tiles) 1960- 90
Luttmann, Gail
  See Damerow, Gail
Luttrell, Guy L. 1938- 22
Luttrell, Ida (Alleene) 1934- 91
  Brief entry 35
  Earlier sketch in SATA 40
Luttrell, William (J. III) 1954- *149*
Lutz, Norma Jean 1943- *122*
Lutzeier, Elizabeth 1952- 72
Lutzker, Edythe 1904-1991 5
Luxbacher, Irene M. 1970- *153*
Luzadder, Patrick 1954- 89
Luzzati, Emanuele 1921-2007 7
Luzzatto, Paola Caboara 1938- 38
Lybbert, Tyler 1970- 88
Lydon, Michael 1942- *11*
Lyfick, Warren
  See Reeves, Lawrence F.
Lyle, Katie Letcher 1938- 8
Lynch, Chris 1962- *171*
  Earlier sketches in SATA *95, 131*
  See also CLR 58
Lynch, Lorenzo 1932- 7
Lynch, Marietta 1947- 29
Lynch, P(atrick) J(ames) 1962- *122*
  Earlier sketch in SATA 79
Lynch, Patricia (Nora) 1898-1972 9
Lynds, Dennis 1924-2005 47
  Brief entry 37
Lyngseth, Joan
  See Davies, Joan
Lynn, Elizabeth A(nne) 1946- 99
Lynn, Mary
  See Brokamp, Marilyn
Lynn, Patricia
  See Watts, Mabel Pizzey
Lynn, Tracy *175*
Lyon, Elinor 1921- 6
Lyon, George Ella 1949- *148*
  Autobiography Feature *148*
  Earlier sketches in SATA *68, 119*
Lyon, Lyman R.
  See de Camp, L(yon) Sprague
Lyons, Dorothy M(arawee) 1907-1997 3
Lyons, Grant 1941- 30

Lyons, Marcus
  See Blish, James (Benjamin)
Lyons, Mary E(velyn) 1947- *142*
  Earlier sketch in SATA 93
Lystad, Mary (Hanemann) 1928- *11*
Lytle, Elizabeth Stewart 1949- 79
Lytle, Robert A. 1944- *119*
Lyttle, Richard B(ard) 1927- 23
Lytton, Edward G(eorge) E(arle) L(ytton)
  Bulwer-Lytton Baron 1803-1873 23

M

Ma, Wenhai 1954- 84
Maar, Leonard (Frank, Jr.) 1927- 30
Maartens, Maretha 1945- 73
Maas, Selve -1997 14
Mabie, Grace
  See Mattern, Joanne
Mac
  See MacManus, Seumas
  and Maccari, Ruggero
Macalaster, Elizabeth G. 1951- *115*
MacAlister, Katie *159*
MacAodhagain, Eamon
  See Egan, E(dward) W(elstead)
MacArthur-Onslow, Annette Rosemary
  1933- 26
Macaulay, David (Alexander) 1946- *137*
  Brief entry 27
  Earlier sketches in SATA *46, 72*
  See also CLR 14
Macaulay, Teresa (E.) 1947- 95
Macavinta, Courtney *176*
MacBeth, George (Mann) 1932-1992 4
  Obituary 70
MacBride, Roger Lea 1929-1995 85
MacCarter, Don 1944- 91
MacClintock, Dorcas 1932- 8
MacCullough, Carolyn *174*
MacDonald, Amy 1951- *156*
  Autobiography Feature *156*
  Earlier sketches in SATA *76, 136*
MacDonald, Anne Elizabeth Campbell Bard
  -1958
  See MacDonald, Betty
MacDonald, Anson
  See Heinlein, Robert A.
MacDonald, Betty 1908-1958
  See YABC *1*
  See MacDonald, Anne Elizabeth Campbell
  Bard
Macdonald, Blackie
  See Emrich, Duncan (Black Macdonald)
Macdonald, Caroline 1948- 86
  Obituary *111*
  See also CLR 60
Macdonald, Dwight 1906-1982 29
  Obituary 33
MacDonald, George 1824-1905 .... *100*
  Earlier sketch in SATA 33
  See also CLR 67
MacDonald, Golden
  See Brown, Margaret Wise
Macdonald, James D. 1954- *165*
  Earlier sketches in SATA *81, 114*
  See Appleton, Victor
Macdonald, Marcia
  See Hill, Grace Livingston
MacDonald, Margaret Read 1940- *164*
  Earlier sketch in SATA 94
Macdonald, Marianne 1934- *113*
Macdonald, Mary
  See Gifford, Griselda
MacDonald, Maryann 1947- 72
Macdonald, Shelagh 1937- 25
MacDonald, Suse 1940- *109*
  Brief entry 52
  Earlier sketch in SATA 54

Macdonald, Zillah K(atherine) 1885-1979 ... *11*
MacDonnell, Megan
    See Stevens, Serita (Deborah)
MacDougal, John
    See Blish, James (Benjamin)
MacDougal, John
    See Blish, James (Benjamin)
    and Lowndes, Robert A(ugustine) W(ard)
Mace, Elisabeth 1933- *27*
Mace, Varian 1938- *49*
MacEwen, Gwendolyn (Margaret)
    1941-1987 .... *50*
    Obituary *55*
Macfarlan, Allan A. 1892-1982 .... *35*
MacFarlane, Iris 1922- *11*
MacGill-Callahan, Sheila 1926-2000 .... *78*
MacGregor, Carol Lynn *153*
MacGregor, Ellen 1906-1954 .... *39*
    Brief entry *27*
MacGregor-Hastie, Roy (Alasdhair Niall)
    1929- *3*
MacGrory, Yvonne 1948- *142*
Machado, Ana Maria 1941- *150*
MacHale, D.J. 1956- *175*
MacHale, Donald James
    See MacHale, D.J.
Machetanz, Frederick 1908- *34*
Machin Goodall, Daphne (Edith) *37*
Macht, Norman L(ee) 1929- *122*
MacInnes, Helen (Clark) 1907-1985 .... *22*
    Obituary *44*
Macintosh, Brownie 1950- *98*
MacIntyre, Elisabeth 1916- *17*
Mack, Stan(ley) *17*
Mack, Todd *168*
Mack, Tracy 1968- *128*
Mackall, Dandi D.
    See Mackall, Dandi Daley
Mackall, Dandi Daley 1949- *177*
    Earlier sketch in SATA *118*
Mackay, Claire 1930- *97*
    Autobiography Feature *124*
    Earlier sketch in SATA *40*
    See also CLR *43*
Mackay, Constance D'Arcy (?)-1966 .... *125*
Mackay, Donald 1914-2005 .... *81*
    Obituary *173*
Mackay, Donald Alexander
    See Mackay, Donald
MacKaye, Percy (Wallace) 1875-1956 .... *32*
Mackel, Kathryn 1950- *162*
Mackel, Kathy
    See Mackel, Kathryn
MacKellar, William 1914- *4*
Macken, Walter 1915-1967 .... *36*
MacKenzie, Jill (Kelly) 1947- *75*
Mackey, Ernan
    See McInerny, Ralph
Mackie, Maron
    See McNeely, Jeannette
Mackin, Edward
    See McInerny, Ralph
MacKinnon, Bernie 1957- *69*
MacKinnon Groomer, Vera 1915- *57*
MacKinstry, Elizabeth 1879-1956 .... *42*
Mackler, Carolyn 1973- *156*
MacLachlan, Patricia 1938- *168*
    Brief entry *42*
    Earlier sketches in SATA *62, 107*
    See also CLR *14*
MacLane, Jack
    See Crider, Bill
MacLean, Alistair (Stuart) 1922(?)-1987 ...... *23*
    Obituary *50*
Maclean, Art
    See Shirreffs, Gordon D(onald)
MacLean, Christine Kole *177*
MacLean, Glynne 1964- *150*
MacLeod, Beatrice 1910- *162*
    Earlier sketch in SATA *10*

MacLeod, Beatrice Beach
    See MacLeod, Beatrice
MacLeod, Charlotte (Matilda) 1922-2005 .... *28*
    Obituary *160*
MacLeod, Doug 1959- *60*
MacLeod, Elizabeth *158*
MacLeod, Ellen Jane (Anderson) 1916- *14*
MacManus, James
    See MacManus, Seumas
MacManus, Seumas 1869-1960 .... *25*
MacMaster, Eve (Ruth) B(owers) 1942- *46*
MacMillan, Annabelle
    See Quick, Annabelle
MacMillan, Dianne M(arie) 1943- *125*
    Earlier sketch in SATA *84*
Macneill, Janet
    See McNeely, Jeannette
MacPeek, Walter G. 1902-1973 .... *4*
    Obituary *25*
MacPhail, Catherine 1946- *130*
MacPherson, Margaret 1908-2001 .... *9*
    See also SAAS *4*
MacPherson, Winnie 1930- *107*
Macrae, Travis
    See Feagles, Anita M(acRae)
MacRaois, Cormac 1944- *72*
Macumber, Mari
    See Sandoz, Mari(e Susette)
Macy, Sue 1954- *134*
    Earlier sketch in SATA *88*
Madaras, Lynda 1947- *151*
Madden, Don 1927- *3*
Madden, Kerry 1961- *168*
Madden-Lunsford, Kerry
    See Madden, Kerry
Maddern, Eric 1950- *166*
Maddigan, Beth 1967- *174*
Maddison, Angela Mary 1923- *10*
    See Banner, Angela
Maddock, Reginald (Bertram) 1912-1994 .... *15*
Madenski, Melissa (Ann) 1949- *77*
Madian, Jon 1941- *9*
Madison, Arnold 1937- *6*
Madison, Winifred *5*
Madonna 1958- *149*
Madsen, Gunnar *171*
Madsen, Ross Martin 1946- *82*
Madsen, Susan A. 1954- *90*
Madsen, Susan Arrington
    See Madsen, Susan A.
Maestro, Betsy (Crippen) 1944- *106*
    Brief entry *30*
    Earlier sketch in SATA *59*
    See also CLR *45*
Maestro, Giulio 1942- *106*
    Earlier sketches in SATA *8, 59*
    See also CLR *45*
Maeterlinck, Maurice 1862-1949 .... *66*
Magee, Doug 1947- *78*
Magee, Wes 1939- *64*
Maggio, Rosalie 1943- *69*
Magid, Ken(neth Marshall) *65*
Magnus, Erica 1946- *77*
Magorian, James 1942- *92*
    Earlier sketch in SATA *32*
Magorian, Michelle 1947- *128*
    Earlier sketch in SATA *67*
Magorian, Michelle Jane
    See Magorian, Michelle
Magovern, Peg *103*
Maguire, Anne
    See Nearing, Penny
Maguire, Gregory 1954- *129*
    Earlier sketches in SATA *28, 84*
    See also SAAS *22*
Maguire, Gregory Peter
    See Maguire, Gregory
Maguire, Jack 1920-2000 .... *74*
Maguire, Jesse
    See Smith, Sherwood

Maguire, Jessie
    See Smith, Sherwood
Maher, Ramona 1934- *13*
Mahlqvist, (Karl) Stefan *30*
    See Maehlqvist, (Karl) Stefan
Mahon, Julia C(unha) 1916- *11*
Mahood, Kenneth 1930- *24*
Mahy, Margaret 1936- *171*
    Earlier sketches in SATA *14, 69, 119*
    See also CLR *78*
Mahy, Margaret May
    See Mahy, Margaret
Maiden, Cecil (Edward) 1902-1981 .... *52*
Maidoff, Ilka
    See List, Ilka Katherine
Maifair, Linda Lee 1947- *83*
Maik, Henri
    See Hecht, Henri Joseph
Maillu, David G(ian) 1939- *111*
Maine, Trevor
    See Catherall, Arthur
Mains, Randolph P. 1946- *80*
Maiorano, Robert 1946- *43*
Maisner, Heather 1947- *89*
Maison, Della
    See Katz, Bobbi
Maitland, Antony Jasper 1935- *25*
Maitland, Barbara *102*
Major, Kevin (Gerald) 1949- *134*
    Earlier sketches in SATA *32, 82*
    See also CLR *11*
Majure, Janet 1954- *96*
Makie, Pam 1943- *37*
Makowski, Silk
    See Makowski, Silvia Ann
Makowski, Silvia Ann 1940- *101*
Malam, John 1957- *152*
    Earlier sketch in SATA *89*
Malcolm, Dan
    See Silverberg, Robert
Malcolm, Jahnna N.
    See Beecham, Jahnna
Malcolmson, Anne
    See von Storch, Anne B.
Malcolmson, David 1899-1978 .... *6*
Maletta, Dr. Arlene
    See Feltenstein, Arlene (H.)
Mali, Jane Lawrence 1937-1995 .... *51*
    Brief entry *44*
    Obituary *86*
Malkin, Nina 1959(?)- *179*
Mallett, Jerry J. 1939- *76*
Mallory, Kenneth 1945- *128*
Mallowan, Agatha Christie
    See Christie, Agatha (Mary Clarissa)
Malmberg, Carl 1904-1979 .... *9*
Malmgren, Dallin 1949- *65*
Malo, John W. 1911-2000 .... *4*
Malone, James Hiram 1930- *84*
Malone, Patricia 1932- *155*
Maloney, Pat
    See Markun, Patricia Maloney
Malory, Sir Thomas 1410(?)-1471(?) *59*
    Brief entry *33*
Malvasi, Meg Greene *143*
Malvern, Corinne 1905-1956 .... *34*
Malvern, Gladys (?)-1962 .... *23*
Mama G.
    See Davis, Grania
Mammano, Julie (Lynn) 1962- *107*
Mamonova, Tatyana 1943- *93*
Manchel, Frank 1935- *10*
Manchester, William (Raymond)
    1922-2004 .... *65*
Mandel, Brett H. 1969- *108*
Mandel, Peter (Bevan) 1957-1998 .... *87*
Mandel, Sally (Elizabeth) 1944- *64*
Mandell, Muriel (Hortense Levin) 1921- *63*
Manders, John 1957- *175*

Manes, Stephen 1949- 99
  Brief entry 40
  Earlier sketch in SATA 42
Manfred, Frederick (Feikema) 1912-1994 30
Mangin, Marie France 1940- 59
Mangione, Jerre 6
  Obituary 104
  See Mangione, Gerlando
Mango, Karin N. 1936- 52
Mangurian, David 1938- 14
Mania, Cathy 1950- 102
Mania, Robert 1952- 102
Mania, Robert C., Jr.
  See Mania, Robert
Maniatty, Taramesha 1978- 92
Maniscalco, Joseph 1926- 10
Manley, Deborah 1932- 28
Manley, Seon 1921- 15
  See also CLR 3
  See also SAAS 2
Mann, Elizabeth 1948- 153
Mann, Josephine
  See Pullein-Thompson, Josephine (Mary
  Wedderburn)
Mann, Kenny 1946- 91
Mann, Pamela 1946- 91
Mann, Patrick
  See Waller, Leslie
Mann, Peggy 6
  See Houlton, Peggy Mann
Mannetti, Lisa 1953- 57
  Brief entry 51
Mannheim, Grete (Salomon) 1909-1986 10
Manniche, Lise 1943- 31
Manning, Mick 1959- 176
Manning, Rosemary (Joy) 1911-1988 10
  See Davys, Sarah
  and Voyle, Mary
Manning, Sarra 162
Manning-Sanders, Ruth (Vernon)
  1895(?)-1988 73
  Obituary 57
  Earlier sketch in SATA 15
Mannion, Diane
  See Paterson, Diane
Mannis, Celeste Davidson 173
Mansir, A. Richard 1932- 170
Manson, Ainslie Kertland 1938- 115
Manson, Beverlie 1945- 57
  Brief entry 44
Manthorpe, Helen 1958- 122
Mantinband, Gerda (B.) 1917- 74
Manton, Jo
  See Gittings, Jo (Grenville) Manton
Manuel, Lynn 1948- 179
  Earlier sketch in SATA 99
Manushkin, Fran 1942- 166
  Earlier sketches in SATA 7, 54, 93
Manushkin, Frances
  See Manushkin, Fran
Man Without a Spleen, A
  See Chekhov, Anton (Pavlovich)
Manzano, Sonia 1950- 167
Mapes, Mary A.
  See Ellison, Virginia H(owell)
Maple, Marilyn 1931- 80
Mappin, Strephyn 1956- 109
Mara, Barney
  See Roth, Arthur J(oseph)
Mara, Jeanette
  See Cebulash, Mel
Marasmus, Seymour
  See Rivoli, Mario
Marbach, Ethel
  See Pochocki, Ethel (Frances)
Marcal, Annette B.
  See Callaway, Bernice (Anne)
Marcelino
  See Agnew, Edith J(osephine)

Marcellino, Fred 1939-2001 118
  Obituary 127
  Earlier sketch in SATA 68
March, Carl
  See Fleischman, Sid
Marchant, Bessie 1862-1941
  See YABC 2
Marchant, Catherine
  See Cookson, Catherine (McMullen)
Marcher, Marion Walden 1890-1987 10
Marchesi, Stephen 1951- 114
Marchesi, Steve
  See Marchesi, Stephen
  and Older, Effin
  and Older, Jules
Marchetta, Melina 1965- 170
Marciano, John Bemelmans 1970- 167
Marciano, John Bemelmans 1970- 118
  See also CLR 93
Marco, Lou
  See Gottfried, Theodore Mark
Marcus, Leonard S. 1950- 133
Marcus, Paul 1953- 82
Marcus, Rebecca B(rian) 1907- 9
Marcuse, Aida E. 1934- 89
Margaret, Karla
  See Andersdatter, Karla M(argaret)
Margolin, Harriet
  See Ziefert, Harriet
Margolis, Jeffrey A. 1948- 108
Margolis, Richard J(ules) 1929-1991 86
  Obituary 67
  Earlier sketch in SATA 4
Margolis, Vivienne 1922- 46
Mariana
  See Foster, Marian Curtis
Marie, Geraldine 1949- 61
Mariner, Scott
  See Pohl, Frederik
Marino, Dorothy Bronson 1912- 14
Marino, Jan 1936- 114
Marino, Nick
  See Deming, Richard
Marino, Peter 1960- 179
Mario, Anna
  See Odgers, Sally Farrell
Marion, Henry
  See del Rey, Lester
Maris, Ron 71
  Brief entry 45
Mark, Jan 1943-2006 164
  Obituary 173
  Earlier sketches in SATA 22, 69, 114
  See also CLR 11
Mark, Janet Marjorie
  See Mark, Jan
Mark, Joan T. 1937- 122
Mark, Pauline (Dahlin) 1913-1997 14
Mark, Polly
  See Mark, Pauline (Dahlin)
Mark, Ted
  See Gottfried, Theodore Mark
Markel, Michelle 169
Marker, Sherry 1941- 76
Markert, Jennifer 1965- 83
Markert, Jenny
  See Markert, Jennifer
Markham, Lynne 1947- 102
Markham, Marion M. 1929- 60
Markins, W. S.
  See Jenkins, Marie M(agdalen)
Markle, Sandra L. 1946- 148
  Brief entry 41
  Earlier sketches in SATA 57, 92
Markle, Sandra Lee
  See Markle, Sandra L.
Marko, Katherine D(olores) 28
Markoosie
  See Patsauq, Markoosie
Marks, Alan 1957- 151
  Earlier sketch in SATA 77

Marks, Burton 1930- 47
  Brief entry 43
Marks, Graham 158
Marks, Hannah K.
  See Trivelpiece, Laurel
Marks, J.
  See Highwater, Jamake (Mamake)
Marks, J(ames) M(acdonald) 1921- 13
Marks, Laurie J. 1957- 68
Marks, Mickey Klar -1986 12
Marks, Peter
  See Smith, Robert Kimmel
Marks, Rita 1938- 47
Marks, Stan(ley) 14
Marks-Highwater, J.
  See Highwater, Jamake (Mamake)
Markun, Patricia Maloney 1924- 15
Markusen, Bruce (Stanley Rodriguez)
  1965- 141
Marley, Louise 1952- 173
  Earlier sketch in SATA 120
Marlin, Hilda
  See Van Stockum, Hilda
Marlow, Max
  See Nicole, Christopher (Robin)
Marlow, Susan K. 1953- 178
Marlowe, Amy Bell 67
  Earlier sketch in SATA 1
Marlowe, Jack
  See Deary, Terry
Marney, Dean 1952- 90
Marokvia, Artur 1909- 31
Marokvia, Mireille (Journet) 1918- 5
Marol, Jean-Claude 1946- 125
Marr, John S(tuart) 1940- 48
Marric, J. J.
  See Butler, William (Arthur) Vivian
  and Creasey, John
Marrin, Albert 1936- 126
  Brief entry 43
  Earlier sketches in SATA 53, 90
  See also CLR 53
Marriott, Alice Lee 1910-1992 31
  Obituary 71
Marriott, Janice 1946- 134
Marriott, Pat(ricia) 1920- 35
Marroquin, Patricio
  See Markun, Patricia Maloney
Mars, W. T.
  See Mars, Witold Tadeusz J.
Mars, Witold Tadeusz J. 1912-1985 3
Marsden, Carolyn 1950- 175
  Earlier sketch in SATA 140
Marsden, John 1950- 146
  Earlier sketches in SATA 66, 97
  See also CLR 34
  See also SAAS 22
Marsh, Carole 1946- 127
Marsh, Dave 1950- 66
Marsh, J. E.
  See Marshall, Evelyn
Marsh, James 1946- 73
Marsh, Jean
  See Marshall, Evelyn
Marsh, Joan F. 1923- 83
Marsh, Valerie 1954- 89
Marshall, Anthony D(ryden) 1924- 18
Marshall, Bonnie C. 1941- 141
  Earlier sketch in SATA 18
Marshall, Bridget M(ary) 1974- 103
Marshall, (Sarah) Catherine (Wood)
  1914-1983 2
  Obituary 34
Marshall, Douglas
  See McClintock, Marshall
Marshall, Edward
  See Marshall, James
Marshall, Evelyn 1897-1991 11
Marshall, Felicity 1950- 116
Marshall, Garry 1934- 60

Marshall, H. H.
  See Jahn, (Joseph) Michael
Marshall, James 1942-1992 75
  Earlier sketches in SATA *6, 51*
  See also CLR *21*
Marshall, James Edward
  See Marshall, James
Marshall, James Vance
  See Payne, Donald Gordon
Marshall, Janet (Perry) 1938- 97
Marshall, Jeff
  See Laycock, George (Edwin)
Marshall, Kim
  See Marshall, Michael (Kimbrough)
Marshall, Michael (Kimbrough) 1948- 37
Marshall, Percy
  See Young, Percy M(arshall)
Marshall, S(amuel) L(yman) A(twood)
  1900-1977 21
Marsoli, Lisa Ann 1958- 101
  Brief entry 53
Marsten, Richard
  See Hunter, Evan
Marston, Elsa 1933- 156
Marston, Hope Irvin 1935- 127
  Earlier sketch in SATA *31*
Marszalek, John F. 1939- 167
Marszalek, John Francis, Jr.
  See Marszalek, John F.
Marszalek, John Francis 1939-
  See Marszalek, John F.
Martchenko, Michael 1942- 154
  Earlier sketches in SATA *50, 95*
Martel, Aimee
  See Thurlo, Aimee
  and Thurlo, David
Martel, Suzanne 1924- 99
Martin, Ann M(atthews) 1955- 126
  Brief entry 41
  Earlier sketches in SATA *44, 70*
  See also CLR *32*
Martin, Bill, Jr. 67
  Brief entry 40
  See also CLR *97*
  See Martin, William Ivan, Jr.
Martin, Charles E(lmer) 70
  Earlier sketch in SATA *69*
  See Mastrangelo, Charles E(lmer)
Martin, Christopher
  See Hoyt, Edwin P(almer), Jr.
Martin, Claire 1933- 76
Martin, David Stone 1913-1992 39
Martin, Donald
  See Honig, Donald
Martin, Dorothy 1921- 47
Martin, Eugene 1
Martin, Eva M. 1939- 65
Martin, Frances M(cEntee) 1906-1998 36
Martin, Francesca 1947- 101
Martin, Fred 1948- 119
Martin, Fredric
  See Christopher, Matt(hew Frederick)
Martin, George Raymond Richard
  See Martin, George R.R.
Martin, George R.R. 1948- 118
Martin, J(ohn) P(ercival) 1880(?)-1966 15
Martin, Jacqueline Briggs 1945- 149
  Earlier sketch in SATA *98*
Martin, Jane Read 1957- 84
Martin, Jeremy
  See Levin, Marcia Obrasky
Martin, Les
  See Schulman, L(ester) M(artin)
Martin, Linda 1961- 82
Martin, Lynne 1923- 21
Martin, Marcia
  See Levin, Marcia Obrasky
Martin, Marvin 1926- 126
Martin, Melanie
  See Pellowski, Michael (Joseph)

Martin, Nancy
  See Salmon, Annie Elizabeth
Martin, Patricia Miles 1899-1986 43
  Obituary 48
  Earlier sketch in SATA *1*
Martin, Peter
  See Chaundler, Christine
Martin, Rene 1891-1977 42
  Obituary 20
Martin, Rupert (Claude) 1905- 31
Martin, S. R.
  See Mappin, Strephyn
Martin, Stefan 1936- 32
Martin, Vicky
  See Storey, Victoria Carolyn
Martin, Webber
  See Silverberg, Robert
Martin, Wendy
  See Martini, Teri
Martin, William Ivan, Jr. 1916-2004 145
  Earlier sketch in SATA *40*
  See Martin, Bill, Jr.
Martineau, Diane 1940- 178
Martineau, Harriet 1802-1876
  See YABC *2*
Martinet, Jeanne 1958- 80
Martinez, Agnes 167
Martinez, Ed(ward) 1954- 98
Martinez, Elizabeth Coonrod 1954- 85
Martinez, Victor 1954- 95
Martini, Teri 1930- 3
Martini, Therese
  See Martini, Teri
Martino, Alfred C. 1964- 174
Martinson, Janis
  See Herbert, Janis
Marton, Jirina 1946- 144
  Earlier sketch in SATA *95*
Marton, Pierre
  See Stone, Peter
Martson, Del
  See Lupoff, Richard A(llen)
Martyr, Paula (Jane) 57
  See Lawford, Paula Jane
Maruki, Toshi 1912-2000 112
  See also CLR *19*
Marvin, Isabel R(idout) 1924- 84
Marx, Patricia Windschill 1948- 160
  Earlier sketch in SATA *112*
Marx, Robert F(rank) 1936- 24
Marx, Trish
  See Marx, Patricia Windschill
Marzani, Carl (Aldo) 1912-1994 12
Marzollo, Jean 1942- 130
  Earlier sketches in SATA *29, 77*
  See also SAAS *15*
Masefield, John (Edward) 1878-1967 19
Masoff, Joy 1951- 118
Mason, Adrienne 1962- 163
Mason, Cherie 170
Mason, Ernst
  See Pohl, Frederik
Mason, F(rancis) van Wyck 1901-1978 3
  Obituary 26
Mason, Frank W.
  See Mason, F(rancis) van Wyck
Mason, George Frederick 1904-2000 14
Mason, Miriam E(vangeline) 1900-1973 2
  Obituary 26
Mason, Simon 1962- 178
Mason, Tally
  See Derleth, August (William)
Mason, Van Wyck
  See Mason, F(rancis) van Wyck
Mass, Wendy 1967- 158
Mass, William
  See Gibson, William
Masselman, George 1897-1971 19
Massie, Dianne Redfield 1938- 125
  Earlier sketch in SATA *16*
Massie, Elizabeth 108

Masson, Sophie 1959- 179
  Earlier sketch in SATA *133*
Masters, Anthony (Richard) 1940-2003 112
  Obituary 145
Masters, Kelly R(ay) 1897-1987 3
Masters, Mildred 1932- 42
Masters, William
  See Cousins, Margaret
Masters, Zeke
  See Bensen, Donald R.
  and Goulart, Ron(ald Joseph)
Matas, Carol 1949- 93
  Autobiography Feature 112
  See also CLR *52*
Matchette, Katharine E. 1941- 38
Math, Irwin 1940- 42
Mathabane, Mark 1960- 123
Mather, Kirtley F(letcher) 1888-1978 65
Mathers, Petra 1945- 176
  Earlier sketch in SATA *119*
  See also CLR *76*
Matheson, Richard (Christian) 1953- 119
Matheson, Shirlee Smith 1942- 155
Mathews, Janet 1914-1992 41
Mathews, Judith 80
  See Goldberger, Judith M.
Mathews, Louise
  See Tooke, Louise Mathews
Mathieu, Joe 1949- 94
  Brief entry 36
  Earlier sketch in SATA *43*
Mathieu, Joseph P.
  See Mathieu, Joe
Mathis, Sharon Bell 1937- 58
  Earlier sketch in SATA *7*
  See also CLR *3*
  See also SAAS *3*
Matloff, Gregory 1945- 73
Matott, Justin 1961- 109
Matranga, Frances Carfi 1922- 78
Matray, James I. 1948- 161
Matray, James Irving
  See Matray, James I.
Matson, Emerson N(els) 1926- 12
Matsui, Tadashi 1926- 8
Matsuno, Masako 6
  See Kobayashi, Masako Matsuno
Matte, (Encarnacion) L'Enc 1936- 22
Mattern, Joanne 1963- 122
Matthews, Andrew 1948- 138
Matthews, Caitlin 1952- 122
Matthews, Downs 1925- 71
Matthews, Ellen
  See Bache, Ellyn
Matthews, Ellen 1950- 28
Matthews, Harold Downs
  See Matthews, Downs
Matthews, Jacklyn Meek
  See Meek, Jacklyn O'Hanlon
Matthews, John (Kentigern) 1948- 116
Matthews, Liz
  See Pellowski, Michael (Joseph)
Matthews, Morgan
  See Pellowski, Michael (Joseph)
Matthews, Nicola
  See Browne, N.M.
Matthews, Patricia 1927-2006 28
Matthews, Patricia Anne
  See Matthews, Patricia
Matthews, William Henry III 1919- 45
  Brief entry 28
Matthiessen, Peter 1927- 27
Mattingley, Christobel (Rosemary) 1931- 85
  Earlier sketch in SATA *37*
  See also CLR *24*
  See also SAAS *18*
Matulay, Laszlo 1912- 43
Matus, Greta 1938- 12
Maugham, W. S.
  See Maugham, W(illiam) Somerset
Maugham, W(illiam) Somerset 1874-1965 .. 54

Maugham, William Somerset
 See Maugham, W(illiam) Somerset
Maurer, Diane Philippoff
 See Maurer-Mathison, Diane V(ogel)
Maurer, Diane Vogel
 See Maurer-Mathison, Diane V(ogel)
Maurer-Mathison, Diane V(ogel) 1944- 89
Mauser, Pat Rhoads
 See McCord, Patricia
Mauser, Patricia Rhoads 37
 See McCord, Patricia
Maves, Mary Carolyn 1916- 10
Maves, Paul B(enjamin) 1913-1994 10
Mavor, Salley 1955- 125
Mawicke, Tran 1911- 15
Max, Peter 1939- 45
Maxon, Anne
 See Best, (Evangel) Allena Champlin
Maxwell, Arthur S. 1896-1970 11
Maxwell, Edith 1923- 7
Maxwell, Gavin 1914-1969 65
Maxwell, Katie
 See MacAlister, Katie
Maxwell-Hyslop, Miranda 1968- 154
May, Charles Paul 1920- 4
May, Elaine Tyler 1947- 120
May, J. C.
 See May, Julian
May, Julian 1931- 11
May, Robert Stephen 1929-1996 46
May, Robin
 See May, Robert Stephen
Mayall, Beth 171
Mayberry, Florence V(irginia) Wilson 10
Maybury, Richard J. 1946- 72
Maybury, Rick
 See Maybury, Richard J.
Mayer, Agatha
 See Maher, Ramona
Mayer, Ann M(argaret) 1938- 14
Mayer, Danuta 1958- 117
Mayer, Jane Rothschild 1903-2001 38
Mayer, Marianna 1945- 132
 Earlier sketches in SATA *32, 83*
Mayer, Mercer 1943- 137
 Earlier sketches in SATA *16, 32, 73, 129*
 See also CLR *11*
Mayerson, Charlotte Leon 36
Mayerson, Evelyn Wilde 1935- 55
Mayfield, Katherine 1958- 118
Mayfield, Sue 1963- 146
 Earlier sketch in SATA *72*
Mayhar, Ardath 1930- 38
Mayhew, James (John) 1964- 149
 Earlier sketch in SATA *85*
Maynard, Olga 1920- 40
Mayne, William (James Carter) 1928- 122
 Earlier sketches in SATA *6, 68*
 See also CLR *123*
 See also SAAS *11*
Maynes, J. O. Rocky, Jr.
 See Maynes, J. Oscar, Jr.
Maynes, J. Oscar, Jr. 1929- 38
Mayo, Gretchen Will 1936- 163
 Earlier sketch in SATA *84*
Mayo, Margaret 1935- 165
 Earlier sketches in SATA *38, 96*
Mayo, Margaret Mary
 See Mayo, Margaret
Mays, Lucinda L(a Bella) 1924- 49
Mays, (Lewis) Victor (Jr.) 1927- 5
Mazer, Anne 1953- 105
 Earlier sketch in SATA *67*
Mazer, Harry 1925- 167
 Earlier sketches in SATA *31, 67, 105*
 See also CLR *16*
 See also SAAS *11*
Mazer, Norma Fox 1931- 168
 Earlier sketches in SATA *24, 67, 105*
 See also CLR *23*
 See also SAAS *1*

Mazille, Capucine 1953- 96
Mazza, Adriana 1928- 19
Mazzio, Joann 1926- 74
Mbugua, Kioi Wa 1962- 83
McAfee, Carol 1955- 81
McAllister, Amanda
 See Dowdell, Dorothy (Florence) Karns
 and Hager, Jean
 and Meaker, Eloise
McAllister, Margaret I. 1956- 169
 Earlier sketch in SATA *117*
McAllister, M.I.
 See McAllister, Margaret I.
McArthur, Nancy 96
McAvoy, Jim 1972- 142
McBain, Ed
 See Hunter, Evan
McBratney, Sam 1943- 164
 Earlier sketch in SATA *89*
 See also CLR *44*
McBrier, Michael
 See Older, Effin
 and Older, Jules
McCafferty, Jim 1954- 84
McCaffery, Janet 1936- 38
McCaffrey, Anne 1926- 152
 Autobiography Feature 152
 Earlier sketches in SATA *8, 70, 116*
 See also CLR *49*
 See also SAAS *11*
McCaffrey, Anne Inez
 See McCaffrey, Anne
McCaffrey, Mary
 See Szudek, Agnes S(usan) P(hilomena)
McCain, Becky Ray 1954- 138
McCain, Murray (David, Jr.) 1926-1981 7
 Obituary 29
McCall, Edith (Sansom) 1911- 6
McCall, Virginia Nielsen 1909-2000 13
McCall Smith, Alexander 1948- 179
 Earlier sketch in SATA *73*
McCall Smith, Alexander Alasdair
 See McCall Smith, Alexander
McCallum, Phyllis
 See Koch, Phyllis (Mae) McCallum
McCallum, Stephen 1960- 91
McCampbell, Darlene Z. 1942- 83
McCann, Edson
 See del Rey, Lester
 and Pohl, Frederik
McCann, Gerald 1916- 41
McCann, Helen 1948- 75
McCannon, Dindga 41
McCants, William D. 1961- 82
McCarter, Neely Dixon 1929- 47
McCarthy, Agnes 1933- 4
McCarthy, Colin (John) 1951- 77
McCarthy, Meghan 168
McCarthy, Ralph F. 1950- 139
McCarthy-Tucker, Sherri N. 1958- 83
McCarty, Rega Kramer 1904-1986 10
McCaslin, Nellie 1914-2005 12
McCaughrean, Geraldine 1951- 173
 Earlier sketches in SATA *87, 139*
 See also CLR *38*
McCaughren, Tom 1936- 75
McCauley, Adam 1965- 128
McCay, (Zenas) Winsor 1869-1934 134
 Earlier sketch in SATA *41*
McClafferty, Carla Killough 1958- 137
McCleery, Patsy R. 1925- 133
 Earlier sketch in SATA *88*
McClintock, Barbara 1955- 146
 Earlier sketches in SATA *57, 95*
McClintock, Marshall 1906-1967 3
McClintock, May Garelick
 See Garelick, May
McClintock, Mike
 See McClintock, Marshall
McClintock, Norah 178
McClintock, Theodore 1902-1971 14

McClinton, Leon 1933- 11
McCloskey, Kevin 1951- 79
McCloskey, (John) Robert 1914-2003 100
 Obituary 146
 Earlier sketches in SATA *2, 39*
 See also CLR *7*
McCloy, James F(loyd) 1941- 59
McClung, Robert M(arshall) 1916- 135
 Earlier sketches in SATA *2, 68*
 See also CLR *11*
 See also SAAS *15*
McClure, Gillian Mary 1948- 31
McColley, Kevin 1961- 80
 See also SAAS *23*
McConduit, Denise Walter 1950- 89
McConnell, James Douglas Rutherford
 1915-1988 40
 Obituary 56
McCord, Anne 1942- 41
McCord, David (Thompson Watson)
 1897-1997 18
 Obituary 96
 See also CLR *9*
McCord, Jean 1924- 34
McCord, Pat Mauser
 See McCord, Patricia
McCord, Patricia 1943- 159
 See Mauser, Patricia Rhoads
McCord, Patricia Sue Rhoads Mauser
 See McCord, Patricia
McCormick, Brooks
 See Adams, William Taylor
McCormick, Dell J. 1892-1949 19
McCormick, (George) Donald (King)
 1911-1998 14
McCormick, Edith (Joan) 1934- 30
McCormick, Kimberly A. 1960- 153
McCormick, Patricia 1956- 128
McCourt, Lisa 1964- 159
 Earlier sketch in SATA *117*
McCourt, Malachy 1931- 126
McCoy, Iola Fuller 3
McCoy, J(oseph) J(erome) 1917- 8
McCoy, Karen Kawamoto 1953- 82
McCoy, Lois (Rich) 1941- 38
McCrady, Lady 1951- 16
McCrea, James (Craig, Jr.) 1920- 3
McCrea, Ruth (Pirman) 1921- 3
McCreigh, James
 See Pohl, Frederik
McCrumb, Sharyn 1948- 109
McCue, Lisa 1959- 177
 Earlier sketch in SATA *65*
McCue, Lisa Emiline
 See McCue, Lisa
McCullen, Andrew
 See Arthur, Robert, (Jr.)
McCullers, (Lula) Carson (Smith)
 1917-1967 27
McCulloch, John Tyler
 See Burroughs, Edgar Rice
McCulloch, Sarah
 See Ure, Jean
McCullough, David 1933- 62
McCullough, David Gaub
 See McCullough, David
McCullough, Frances Monson 1938- 8
McCullough, Sharon Pierce 1943- 131
McCully, Emily Arnold 134
 Autobiography Feature 134
 Earlier sketches in SATA *5, 110*
 See also CLR *46*
 See also SAAS *7*
 See Arnold, Emily
McCune, Dan
 See Haas, Dorothy F.
McCunn, Ruthanne Lum 1946- 63
McCurdy, Michael (Charles) 1942- 147
 Earlier sketches in SATA *13, 82*
McCutcheon, Elsie (Mary Jackson) 1937- ... 60
McCutcheon, John 1952- 97

McDaniel, Becky Bring 1953- 61
McDaniel, Lurlene 1944- 146
  Earlier sketch in SATA 71
McDaniels, Pellom III 1968- 121
McDearmon, Kay 20
McDermott, Beverly Brodsky 1941- 11
McDermott, Eleni 156
McDermott, Gerald (Edward) 1941- 163
  Earlier sketches in SATA 16, 74
  See also CLR 9
McDermott, Michael 1962- 76
McDevitt, John Charles 155
  Earlier sketch in SATA 94
  See McDevitt, Jack
McDole, Carol
  See Farley, Carol (J.)
McDonald, Collin 1943- 79
McDonald, Gerald D(oan) 1905-1970 3
McDonald, Jamie
  See Heide, Florence Parry
McDonald, Janet 1953- 148
McDonald, Jill (Masefield) 1927-1982 13
  Obituary 29
McDonald, Joyce 1946- 164
  Earlier sketch in SATA 101
McDonald, Lucile Saunders 1898-1992 10
McDonald, Mary Ann 1956- 84
McDonald, Megan 1959- 151
  Autobiography Feature 151
  Earlier sketches in SATA 67, 99, 148
  See also CLR 94
McDonald, Meme 1954- 112
McDonald, Mercedes 1956- 169
  Earlier sketch in SATA 97
McDonell, Chris 1960- 138
McDonnell, Christine 1949- 115
  Earlier sketch in SATA 34
McDonnell, Flora (Mary) 1963- 146
  Earlier sketch in SATA 90
McDonnell, Lois Eddy 1914-2001 10
McDonnell, Patrick 1956- 179
McDonough, Yona Zeldis 1957- 73
McElligott, Matt(hew) 1968- 135
McElmeel, Sharron L. 1942- 128
McElmurry, Jill 159
McElrath, William N. 1932- 65
McElrath-Eslick, Lori 1960- 96
McEntee, Dorothy (Layng) 1902- 37
McFadden, Kevin Christopher 1961(?)- 156
  Earlier sketch in SATA 68
  See also CLR 29
  See Pike, Christopher
McFall, Christie 1918- 12
McFarlan, Donald M(aitland) 1915- 59
McFarland, Henry "Hammer"
  See McFarland, Henry O.
McFarland, Henry O. 1934- 143
McFarland, Kenton D(ean) 1920- 11
McFarland, Martha
  See Smith-Ankrom, M. E.
McFarlane, Leslie (Charles) 1902-1977 31
  See Dixon, Franklin W.
  and Ferris, James Cody
  and Keene, Carolyn
  and Rockwood, Roy
McFarlane, Peter (William) 1940- 95
McFarlane, Sheryl P. 1954- 86
McFarlane, Todd 1961- 117
McGaw, Jessie Brewer 1913-1997 10
McGee, Barbara 1943- 6
McGee, Marni 163
McGiffin, (Lewis) Lee (Shaffer) 1908-1978 ... 1
McGill, Alice 159
McGill, Ormond 1913- 92
McGinley, Jerry 1948- 116
McGinley, Phyllis 1905-1978 44
  Obituary 24
  Earlier sketch in SATA 2
McGinnis, Lila S(prague) 1924- 44
McGinty, Alice B. 1963- 134
McGivern, Justin 1985- 129

McGivern, Maureen Daly
  See Daly, Maureen
McGivern, Maureen Patricia Daly
  See Daly, Maureen
McGough, Elizabeth (Hemmes) 1934- 33
McGovern, Ann 1930- 132
  Earlier sketches in SATA 8, 69, 70
  See also CLR 50
  See also SAAS 17
McGowen, Thomas E. 1927- 109
  Earlier sketch in SATA 2
McGowen, Tom
  See McGowen, Thomas E.
McGrady, Mike 1933- 6
McGrath, Barbara Barbieri 1953- 169
  Earlier sketch in SATA 108
McGrath, Robin 1949- 121
McGrath, Thomas (Matthew) 1916-1990 41
  Obituary 66
McGraw, Eloise Jarvis 1915-2000 67
  Obituary 123
  Earlier sketch in SATA 1
  See also SAAS 6
McGraw, William Corbin 1916-1999 3
McGreal, Elizabeth
  See Yates, Elizabeth
McGregor, Barbara 1959- 82
McGregor, Craig 1933- 8
McGregor, Iona 1929- 25
McGuffey, Alexander Hamilton 1816-1896 . 60
McGuigan, Mary Ann 1949- 106
McGuire, Edna 1899- 13
McGuire, Leslie (Sarah) 1945- 94
  Brief entry 45
  Earlier sketch in SATA 52
McGuirk, Leslie (A.) 1960- 152
McGurk, Slater
  See Roth, Arthur J(oseph)
McHargue, Georgess 1941- 77
  Earlier sketch in SATA 4
  See also CLR 2
  See also SAAS 5
McHugh, (Berit) Elisabet 1941- 55
  Brief entry 44
McIlwraith, Maureen Mollie Hunter 2
  See Hunter, Mollie
McInerney, Judith W(hitelock) 1945- 49
  Brief entry 46
McInerny, Ralph 1929- 93
McInerny, Ralph Matthew
  See McInerny, Ralph
McKaughan, Larry (Scott) 1941- 75
McKay, Donald 1895- 45
McKay, Hilary (Jane) 1959- 145
  Earlier sketch in SATA 92
  See also SAAS 23
McKay, Lawrence, Jr. 1948- 114
McKay, Robert W. 1921- 15
McKay, Sharon E. 1954- 165
McKay, Simon
  See Nicole, Christopher (Robin)
McKeating, Eileen 1957- 81
McKee, David (John) 1935- 158
  Earlier sketches in SATA 70, 107
  See also CLR 38
McKee, Tim 1970- 111
McKeever, Marcia
  See Laird, Jean E(louise)
McKelvey, Carole A. 1942- 78
McKelvy, Charles 1950- 124
McKendrick, Melveena (Christine) 1941- 55
McKendry, Joe 1972- 170
McKenna, Colleen O'Shaughnessy 1948- .. 136
  Earlier sketch in SATA 76
McKenzie, Ellen Kindt 1928- 80
McKernan, Victoria 1957- 171
McKie, Robin 112
McKillip, Patricia A. 1948- 174
  Earlier sketches in SATA 30, 80, 126
McKillip, Patricia Anne
  See McKillip, Patricia A.

McKillip, Patricia Anne
  See McKillip, Patricia A.
McKim, Audrey Margaret 1909-1999 47
McKinley, Jennifer Carolyn Robin
  See McKinley, Robin
McKinley, Robin 1952- 130
  Brief entry 32
  Earlier sketches in SATA 50, 89
  See also CLR 81
McKinney, Barbara Shaw 1951- 116
McKinney, Nadine 1938- 91
McKissack, Fredrick L. 1939- 162
  Brief entry 53
  Earlier sketches in SATA 73, 117
  See also CLR 55
McKissack, Fredrick Lemuel
  See McKissack, Fredrick L.
McKissack, Patricia C. 1944- 162
  Earlier sketches in SATA 51, 73, 117
  See also CLR 55
McKissack, Patricia L'Ann Carwell
  See McKissack, Patricia C.
McKissack and McKissack
  See McKissack, Fredrick L.
  and McKissack, Patricia C.
McKown, Robin (?)-1976 6
McLaren, Clemence 1938- 158
  Earlier sketch in SATA 105
McLaughlin, Frank 1934- 73
McLaurin, Anne 1953- 27
McLean, Andrew 1946- 172
  Earlier sketch in SATA 113
McLean, J. Sloan
  See Gillette, Virginia M(ary)
  and Wunsch, Josephine (McLean)
McLean, Janet 1946- 113
McLean, Kathryn (Anderson) 1909-1966 9
McLean, Virginia Overton 1946- 90
McLean-Carr, Carol 1948- 122
McLeish, Kenneth 1940-1997 35
McLenighan, Valjean 1947- 46
  Brief entry 40
McLennan, Connie 171
McLennan, Will
  See Wisler, G(ary) Clifton
McLeod, Bob 1951- 173
McLeod, Chum 1955- 95
McLeod, Emilie Warren 1926-1982 23
  Obituary 31
McLeod, Kirsty
  See Hudson, (Margaret) Kirsty
McLeod, Margaret Vail
  See Holloway, Teresa (Bragunier)
McLerran, Alice 1933- 137
  Earlier sketch in SATA 68
McLoughlin, John C. 1949- 47
McManus, Patrick F. 1933- 46
McManus, Patrick Francis
  See McManus, Patrick F.
McMeekin, Clark
  See McMeekin, Isabel McLennan
McMeekin, Isabel McLennan 1895-1973 3
McMenemy, Sarah 1965- 156
McMillan, Bruce 1947- 129
  Earlier sketches in SATA 22, 70
  See also CLR 47
McMillan, Naomi
  See Grimes, Nikki
McMorey, James L.
  See Moyer, Terry J.
McMorrow, Annalisa 1969- 104
McMullan, Jim 1934- 150
  Earlier sketch in SATA 87
McMullan, K. H.
  See McMullan, Kate
McMullan, Kate
  See McMullan, Kate
McMullan, Kate 1947- 132
  Brief entry 48
  Earlier sketches in SATA 52, 87

McMullan, Kate Hall
  See McMullan, Kate
McMurtrey, Martin A(loysias) 1921- 21
McNabb, Linda 1963- 147
McNair, Kate 3
McNair, Sylvia 1924-2002 74
McNaught, Harry 32
McNaughton, Colin 1951- 134
  Earlier sketches in SATA 39, 92
  See also CLR 54
McNaughton, Janet 1953- 162
  Earlier sketch in SATA 110
McNeely, Jeannette 1918- 25
McNeer, May (Yonge) 1902-1994 81
  Earlier sketch in SATA 1
McNeese, Tim 1953- 139
McNeill, Janet 97
  Earlier sketch in SATA 1
  See Alexander, Janet
McNicoll, Sylvia (Marilyn) 1954- 113
  See also CLR 99
McNulty, Faith 1918-2005 168
  Earlier sketches in SATA 12, 84, 139
McPhail, David M(ichael) 1940- 140
  Brief entry 32
  Earlier sketches in SATA 47, 81
McPhee, Norma H. 1928- 95
McPhee, Richard B(yron) 1934- 41
McPherson, James M(unro) 1936- 141
  Earlier sketch in SATA 16
McQueen, Lucinda 1950- 58
  Brief entry 48
McQueen, Mildred Hark 1908-1978 12
McRae, Russell (William) 1934- 63
McShean, Gordon 1936- 41
Mc Swigan, Marie 1907-1962 24
McVeity, Jen 148
McVey, Vicki 1946- 80
McVicker, Charles (Taggart) 1930- 39
McVicker, Chuck
  See McVicker, Charles (Taggart)
McWhirter, A(lan) Ross 1925-1975 37
  Obituary 31
McWhirter, Norris (Dewar) 1925-2004 37
McWilliams, Karen 1943- 65
Mdurvwa, Hajara E. 1962- 92
Meacham, Margaret 1952- 95
Meachum, Virginia 1918- 133
  Earlier sketch in SATA 87
Mead, Alice 1952- 146
  Earlier sketch in SATA 94
Mead, Russell (M., Jr.) 1935- 10
Meade, Ellen 5
  See Roddick, Ellen
Meade, Marion 1934- 127
  Earlier sketch in SATA 23
Meader, Stephen W(arren) 1892-1977 1
Meadmore, Susan
  See Sallis, Susan (Diana)
Meadow, Charles T(roub) 1929- 23
Meadowcroft, Enid LaMonte
  See Wright, Enid Meadowcroft (LaMonte)
Meadows, Graham (W.) 1934- 161
Meaker, M. J.
  See Meaker, Marijane
Meaker, Marijane 1927- 160
  Autobiography Feature 111
  Earlier sketches in SATA 20, 61, 99
  See Aldrich, Ann
  and James, Mary
  and Kerr, M. E.
  and Packer, Vin
Meaker, Marijane Agnes
  See Meaker, Marijane
Means, Florence Crannell 1891-1980 1
  Obituary 25
  See also CLR 56
Mearian, Judy Frank 1936- 49
Mecca, Judy Truesdell 1955- 127
Medary, Marjorie 1890-1980 14

Meddaugh, Susan 1944- 176
  Earlier sketches in SATA 29, 84, 125
Medearis, Angela Shelf 1956- 123
  Earlier sketch in SATA 72
Medearis, Mary 1915- 5
Medina, Jane 1953- 167
  Earlier sketch in SATA 122
Medlicott, Mary 1946- 88
Mee, Charles L., Jr. 1938- 72
  Earlier sketch in SATA 8
Meek, Jacklyn O'Hanlon 1933- 51
  Brief entry 34
Meeker, Clare Hodgson 1952- 96
Meeker, Oden 1919(?)-1976 14
Meeker, Richard
  See Brown, Fornan
Meeks, Esther MacBain 1
Meggs, Libby Phillips 1943- 130
Mehdevi, Alexander (Sinclair) 1947- 7
Mehdevi, Anne (Marie) Sinclair 1947- 8
Meidell, Sherry 1951- 73
Meier, Minta 1906- 55
Meighan, Donald Charles 1929- 30
Meigs, Cornelia Lynde 1884-1973 6
  See also CLR 55
Meilach, Dona Z(weigoron) 1926- 34
Meilman, Philip W(arren) 1951- 79
Meinstereifel, Ronald L. 1960- 134
Melcher, Marguerite Fellows 1879-1969 10
Melendez, Francisco 1964- 72
Melin, Grace Hathaway 1892-1973 10
Mellersh, H(arold) E(dward) L(eslie)
  1897- 10
Melmoth, Sebastian
  See Wilde, Oscar (Fingal O'Flahertie Wills)
Melnikoff, Pamela (Rita) 97
Meltzer, Milton 1915- 128
  Autobiography Feature 124
  Earlier sketches in SATA 1, 50, 80
  See also CLR 13
  See also SAAS 1
Melville, Anne
  See Potter, Margaret (Newman)
Melville, Herman 1819-1891 59
Melwood, Mary
  See Lewis, E. M.
Melzack, Ronald 1929- 5
Memling, Carl 1918-1969 6
Mendel, Jo
  See Bond, Gladys Baker
  and Gilbertson, Mildred Geiger
Mendelson, Steven T. 1958-1995 86
Mendes, Valerie 1939- 157
Mendez, Raymond A. 1947- 66
Mendonca, Susan
  Brief entry 45
  See Smith, Susan Vernon
Mendoza, George 1934- 41
  Brief entry 39
  See also SAAS 7
Menendez, Shirley (C.) 1937- 146
Meng, Heinz (Karl) 1924- 13
Mennen, Ingrid 1954- 85
Menotti, Gian Carlo 1911-2007 29
Menuhin, Sir Yehudi 1916-1999 40
  Obituary 113
Menville, Douglas 1935- 64
Menzel, Barbara Jean 1946- 63
Mercati, Cynthia 164
Mercati, Cynthia J.
  See Mercati, Cynthia
Mercer, Charles (Edward) 1917-1988 16
  Obituary 61
Meredith, David William
  See Miers, Earl Schenck
Meringoff, Laurene Krasny
  See Brown, Laurene Krasny
Meriwether, Louise 1923- 52
  Brief entry 31
Merlin, Arthur
  See Blish, James (Benjamin)

Merlin, Christina
  See Heaven, Constance (Christina)
Merriam, Eve 1916-1992 73
  Earlier sketches in SATA 3, 40
  See also CLR 14
Merrill, Jane 1946- 42
Merrill, Jean (Fairbanks) 1923- 82
  Earlier sketch in SATA 1
  See also CLR 52
Merriman, Alex
  See Silverberg, Robert
Merriman, Rachel 1971- 149
  Earlier sketch in SATA 98
Merrit, Elizabeth
  See Goudge, Eileen
Merski, Patricia K.
  See Merski, P.K.
Merski, P.K. 172
Mertz, Barbara 1927- 49
Mertz, Barbara Gross
  See Mertz, Barbara
Meschel, Susan V. 1936- 83
Messenger, Charles (Rynd Milles) 1942- 59
Messick, Dale 1906-2005 64
  Brief entry 48
Messier, Claire 1956- 103
Messieres, Nicole de
  See de Messieres, Nicole
Messmer, Otto 1892(?)-1983 37
Metcalf, Doris H(unter) 91
Metcalf, Suzanne
  See Baum, L(yman) Frank
Metos, Thomas H(arry) 1932- 37
Metter, Bert(ram Milton) 1927- 56
Metzenthen, David 1958- 167
  Earlier sketch in SATA 106
Meyer, Barbara 1939- 77
Meyer, Carolyn (Mae) 1935- 142
  Autobiography Feature 142
  Earlier sketches in SATA 9, 70, 118
  See also SAAS 9
Meyer, Edith Patterson 1895-1993 5
Meyer, F(ranklyn) E(dward) 1932- 9
Meyer, Jean Shepherd 11
Meyer, Jerome Sydney 1895-1975 3
  Obituary 25
Meyer, June
  See Jordan, June
Meyer, L. A.
  See Meyer, Louis A(lbert), Jr.
Meyer, Louis A(lbert), Jr. 1942- 144
  Earlier sketch in SATA 12
Meyer, Renate 1930- 6
Meyer, Susan E. 1940- 64
Meyers, Susan 1942- 164
  Earlier sketches in SATA 19, 108
Meynier, Yvonne (Pollet) 1908- 14
Mezey, Robert 1935- 33
Micale, Albert 1913- 22
Michael, James
  See Scagnetti, Jack
Michael, Livi 1960- 172
Michael, Manfred
  See Winterfeld, Henry
Michael, Olivia
  See Michael, Livi
Michaels, Barbara
  See Mertz, Barbara
Michaels, Joanne Louise
  See Teitelbaum, Michael
Michaels, Kristin
  See Williams, Jeanne
Michaels, Molly
  See Untermeyer, Louis
Michaels, Neal
  See Teitelbaum, Michael
Michaels, Ski
  See Pellowski, Michael (Joseph)
Michaels, Steve 1955- 71
Michaels, William M. 1917- 77

Michel, Anna 1943- *49*
 Brief entry *40*
Michel, Francois 1948- *82*
Michelson, Richard *173*
Micich, Paul *74*
Micklish, Rita 1931- *12*
Micklos, John, Jr. 1956- *173*
 Earlier sketch in SATA *129*
Micklos J., John, Jr. 1956-
 See Micklos, John, Jr.
Micucci, Charles (Patrick, Jr.) 1959- *144*
 Earlier sketch in SATA *82*
Middleton, Haydn 1955- *152*
 Earlier sketch in SATA *85*
Miers, Earl Schenck 1910-1972 .... *1*
 Obituary *26*
Migdale, Lawrence 1951- *89*
Mikaelsen, Ben 1952- *173*
 Earlier sketches in SATA *73, 107*
Mikaelsen, Benjamin John
 See Mikaelsen, Ben
Miklowitz, Gloria D. 1927- *129*
 Earlier sketches in SATA *4, 68*
 See also SAAS *17*
Mikolaycak, Charles 1937-1993 .... *78*
 Obituary *75*
 Earlier sketch in SATA *9*
 See also SAAS *4*
Mild, Warren (Paul) 1922- *41*
Milelli, Pascal 1965- *135*
Miles, Betty 1928- *78*
 Earlier sketch in SATA *8*
 See also SAAS *9*
Miles, Miska
 See Martin, Patricia Miles
Miles, (Mary) Patricia 1930- *29*
Miles, Patricia A.
 See Martin, Patricia Miles
Milgrim, David *158*
Milgrom, Harry 1912-1978 .... *25*
Milhous, Katherine 1894-1977 .... *15*
Milich, Zoran *174*
Milios, Rita 1949- *79*
Militant
 See Sandburg, Carl (August)
Millais, Raoul 1901- *77*
Millar, Barbara F. 1924- *12*
Millar, Margaret (Ellis Sturm) 1915-1994 .... *61*
 Obituary *79*
Millbank, Captain H. R.
 See Ellis, Edward S(ylvester)
Millen, C(ynthia) M. 1955- *114*
Miller, Albert G(riffith) 1905-1982 .... *12*
 Obituary *31*
Miller, Alice Ann 1958- *150*
Miller, Alice P(atricia McCarthy) *22*
Miller, Debbie 1951- *160*
 Earlier sketch in SATA *103*
Miller, Debbie S.
 See Miller, Debbie
Miller, Deborah Uchill 1944- *61*
Miller, Don 1923- *15*
Miller, Doris R.
 See Mosesson, Gloria R(ubin)
Miller, Eddie
 See Miller, Edward
Miller, Edna Anita 1920- *29*
Miller, Edward 1905-1974 .... *8*
Miller, Elizabeth 1933- *41*
Miller, Ellanita 1957- *87*
Miller, Eugene 1925- *33*
Miller, Frances A. 1937- *52*
 Brief entry *46*
Miller, Helen M(arkley) -1984 .... *5*
Miller, Jane (Judith) 1925-1989 .... *15*
Miller, Jewel 1956- *73*
Miller, John
 See Samachson, Joseph
Miller, Judi *117*
Miller, Louise (Rolfe) 1940- *76*
Miller, M. L. *85*

Miller, Madge 1918- *63*
Miller, Margaret J.
 See Dale, Margaret J(essy) Miller
Miller, Marilyn (Jean) 1925- *33*
Miller, Marvin *65*
Miller, Mary Beth 1942- *9*
Miller, Maryann 1943- *73*
Miller, Natalie 1917-1976 .... *35*
Miller, Robert H. 1944- *91*
Miller, Ruth White
 See White, Ruth C.
Miller, Sandra
 See Miller, Sandy
Miller, Sandra Peden
 See Miller, Sandy
Miller, Sandy 1948- *41*
 Brief entry *35*
Miller, Sarah 1969- *175*
Miller, Virginia
 See Austin, Virginia
Miller, William R. 1959- *116*
Milligan, Bryce 1953- *170*
Milligan, Spike
 See CLR *92*
 See Milligan, Terence Alan
Milligan, Terence Alan 1918-2002 .... *29*
 Obituary *134*
 See Milligan, Spike
Millington, Ada
 See Deyneka, Anita
Millman, Isaac 1933- *140*
Mills, Adam
 See Stanley, George Edward
Mills, Claudia 1954- *145*
 Brief entry *41*
 Earlier sketches in SATA *44, 89*
Mills, Elaine (Rosemary) 1941- *72*
Mills, Joyce C. 1944- *102*
Mills, Judith Christine 1956- *130*
Mills, Yaroslava Surmach 1925- *35*
Millspaugh, Ben P. 1936- *77*
Millstead, Thomas E. *30*
Milne, A. A. 1882-1956 .... *100*
 See also YABC *1*
 See also CLR *108*
Milne, Alan Alexander
 See Milne, A. A.
Milne, Lorus J. *5*
 See also CLR *22*
 See also SAAS *18*
Milne, Margery *5*
 See also CLR *22*
 See also SAAS *18*
Milne, Terry
 See Milne, Theresa Ann
Milne, Theresa Ann 1964- *84*
Milnes, Irma McDonough 1924- *101*
Milonas, Rolf
 See Myller, Rolf
Milord, Susan 1954- *147*
 Earlier sketch in SATA *74*
Milotte, Alfred G(eorge) 1904-1989 .... *11*
 Obituary *62*
Milstein, Linda 1954- *80*
Milton, Ann *134*
Milton, Hilary (Herbert) 1920- *23*
Milton, John R(onald) 1924- *24*
Milton, Joyce 1946- *101*
 Brief entry *41*
 Earlier sketch in SATA *52*
Milverton, Charles A.
 See Penzler, Otto
Minahan, John A. 1956- *92*
Minar, Barbra (Goodyear) 1940- *79*
Minard, Rosemary 1939- *63*
Minarik, Else Holmelund 1920- *127*
 Earlier sketch in SATA *15*
 See also CLR *33*
Miner, Jane Claypool 1933- *38*
 Brief entry *37*
 See Claypool, Jane

Miner, Lewis S. 1909-1971 .... *11*
Mines, Jeanette 1948- *61*
Mines, Jeanette Marie
 See Mines, Jeanette
Minier, Nelson
 See Stoutenburg, Adrien (Pearl)
Minnitt, Ronda Jacqueline
 See Armitage, David
Minor, Wendell G. 1944- *164*
 Earlier sketches in SATA *78, 109*
Minter, Daniel 1961- *176*
Mintonye, Grace *4*
Miranda, Anne 1954- *109*
 Earlier sketch in SATA *71*
Mirsky, Jeannette 1903-1987 .... *8*
 Obituary *51*
Mirsky, Reba Paeff 1902-1966 .... *1*
Mishica, Clare 1960- *91*
Miskovits, Christine 1939- *10*
Miss Frances
 See Horwich, Frances R(appaport)
Miss Read
 See Saint, Dora Jessie
Mister Rogers
 See Rogers, Fred McFeely
Mitchard, Jacquelyn 1953- *168*
 Earlier sketch in SATA *98*
Mitchell, Adrian 1932- *166*
 Earlier sketch in SATA *104*
Mitchell, Allison
 See Griffin, W.E.B.
Mitchell, B(etty) J(o) 1931- *120*
Mitchell, Clyde
 See Ellison, Harlan
Mitchell, Cynthia 1922- *29*
Mitchell, (Sibyl) Elyne (Keith) 1913- *10*
Mitchell, Gladys (Maude Winifred)
 1901-1983 .... *46*
 Obituary *35*
Mitchell, Jay
 See Roberson, Jennifer
Mitchell, Joyce Slayton 1933- *142*
 Brief entry *43*
 Earlier sketch in SATA *46*
Mitchell, K. L.
 See Lamb, Elizabeth Searle
Mitchell, Kathy 1948- *59*
Mitchell, Lori 1961- *128*
Mitchell, Margaree King 1953- *84*
Mitchell, Marianne 1947- *145*
Mitchell, Rhonda *89*
Mitchelson, Mitch
 See Mitchelson, Peter Richard
Mitchelson, Peter Richard 1950- *104*
Mitchison, Naomi (Margaret Haldane)
 1897-1999 .... *24*
 Obituary *112*
Mitchnik, Helen 1901-1982 .... *41*
 Brief entry *35*
Mitchum, Hank
 See Knott, William C(ecil, Jr.)
 and Murray, Stuart A. P.
 and Newton, D(wight) B(ennett)
 and Sherman, Jory (Tecumseh)
Mitgutsch, Ali 1935- *76*
Mitsuhashi, Yoko *45*
 Brief entry *33*
Mitton, Jacqueline 1948- *162*
 Earlier sketches in SATA *66, 115*
Mitton, Simon 1946- *66*
Mitton, Tony 1951- *149*
 Earlier sketch in SATA *104*
Mizner, Elizabeth Howard 1907- *27*
Mizumura, Kazue *18*
Mobin-Uddin, Asma *172*
Mobley, Joe A. 1945- *91*
Moche, Dinah (Rachel) L(evine) 1936- *44*
 Brief entry *40*
Mochi, Ugo (A.) 1889-1977 .... *38*

Mochizuki, Ken 1954- 146
  Earlier sketch in SATA 81
  See also SAAS 22
Modarressi, Mitra 1967- 126
Modell, Frank B. 1917- 39
  Brief entry 36
Modesitt, Jeanne 1953- 143
  Earlier sketch in SATA 92
Modesitt, L.E., Jr. 1943- 164
  Earlier sketch in SATA 91
Modesitt, Leland Exton, Jr.
  See Modesitt, L.E., Jr.
Modrell, Dolores 1933- 72
Moe, Barbara 1937- 20
Moe, Jorgen (Ingebretsen) 1813-1882
  See CLR 104
  See Asbjornsen and Moe
Moed-Kass, Pnina 169
Moerbeek, Kees 1955- 98
Moeri, Louise 1924- 93
  Earlier sketch in SATA 24
  See also SAAS 10
Moffett, Jami 1952- 84
Moffett, Martha (Leatherwood) 1934- 8
Mogensen, Suzanne A(ncher) 1946- 129
Mohn, Peter B(urnet) 1934- 28
Mohn, Viola Kohl 1914- 8
Mohr, Nicholasa 1938- 97
  Autobiography Feature 113
  Earlier sketch in SATA 8
  See also CLR 22
  See also SAAS 8
Mok, Esther 1953- 93
Molan, Christine 1943- 84
Molarsky, Osmond 1909- 16
Moldon, Peter L(eonard) 1937- 49
Mole, John 1941- 103
  Earlier sketch in SATA 36
  See also CLR 61
Molesworth, Mary Louisa 1839-1921 98
Molin, Charles
  See Mayne, William (James Carter)
Molina, Silvia 1946- 97
Molk, Laurel 1957- 162
  Earlier sketch in SATA 92
Mollel, Tololwa M. 1952- 88
Molloy, Anne Baker 1907-1999 32
Molloy, Michael (John) 1940- 162
Molloy, Paul (George) 1924- 5
Moloney, James 1954- 144
  Autobiography Feature 144
  Earlier sketch in SATA 94
Momaday, N. Scott 1934- 48
  Brief entry 30
Momaday, Navarre Scott
  See Momaday, N. Scott
Monaco, Octavia 1963- 169
Monagle, Bernie 1957- 121
Moncure, Jane Belk 1926- 23
Monjo, F(erdinand) N(icholas III)
  1924-1978 16
  See also CLR 2
Monk, Isabell 1952- 136
Monroe, Lyle
  See Heinlein, Robert A.
Monsell, Helen Albee 1895-1971 24
Monson-Burton, Marianne 1975- 139
Montecalvo, Janet 177
Montenegro, Laura Nyman 1953- 95
Montero, Gloria 1933- 109
Montes, Marisa 1951- 144
Montgomerie, Norah (Mary) 1913- 26
Montgomery, Constance
  See Cappel, Constance
Montgomery, Elizabeth Rider 34
  Obituary 41
  Earlier sketch in SATA 3
  See Julesberg, Elizabeth Rider Montgomery
Montgomery, Hugh (Edward) 1962- 146

Montgomery, L(ucy) M(aud) 1874-1942 100
  See also YABC 1
  See also CLR 91
Montgomery, Raymond A. (Jr.) 1936- 39
Montgomery, Rutherford George 1894-1985 . 3
Montgomery, Sy 1958- 132
  Autobiography Feature 132
  Earlier sketch in SATA 114
Montgomery, Vivian 36
Monthei, Betty 179
Montijo, Rhode 179
Montpetit, Charles 1958- 101
Montresor, Beni 1926-2001 38
  Earlier sketch in SATA 3
  See also SAAS 4
Monty Python
  See Chapman, Graham
  and Cleese, John (Marwood)
  and Gilliam, Terry
  and Idle, Eric
  and Jones, Terence Graham Parry
  and Palin, Michael (Edward)
Moodie, Craig 1956- 172
Moodie, Fiona 1952- 133
Moody, Minerva
  See Alcott, Louisa May
Moody, Ralph Owen 1898-1982 1
Moon, Carl 1879(?)-1948 25
Moon, Grace (Purdie) 1877(?)-1947 25
Moon, Lily
  See Warnes, Tim
Moon, Nicola 1952- 147
  Earlier sketch in SATA 96
Moon, Pat 1946- 113
Moon, Sheila (Elizabeth) 1910-1991 5
  Obituary 114
Mooney, Bel 1946- 95
Mooney, Bill 122
  See Mooney, William F.
Moor, Emily
  See Deming, Richard
Moorcock, Michael 1939- 166
  Earlier sketch in SATA 93
  See Bradbury, Edward P.
Moore, Anne Carroll 1871-1961 13
Moore, Cheri
  See Ladd, Cheryl (Jean)
Moore, Clement Clarke 1779-1863 18
Moore, Cyd 1957- 133
  Earlier sketch in SATA 83
Moore, Elaine 1944- 86
Moore, Eva 1942- 103
  Earlier sketch in SATA 20
Moore, Ishbel (Lindsay) 1954- 140
Moore, Jack (William) 1941- 46
  Brief entry 32
Moore, Janet Gaylord 1905-1992 18
Moore, Jim 1946- 42
Moore, John Travers 1908- 12
Moore, Lilian 1909-2004 137
  Obituary 155
  Earlier sketch in SATA 52
  See also CLR 15
Moore, Liz
  See Moore, M. Elizabeth
Moore, M. Elizabeth 1959- 156
Moore, Margaret R(umberger) 1903- 12
Moore, Margie 176
Moore, Marianne (Craig) 1887-1972 20
Moore, Patrick (Alfred Caldwell) 1923- 49
  Brief entry 39
  See also SAAS 8
Moore, Peter 1963- 175
Moore, Regina
  See Dunne, Mary Collins
Moore, Ruth (Ellen) 1908-1989 23
Moore, Ruth Nulton 1923- 38
Moore, S(arah) E. 23
Moore, Sarah Margaret
  See Hodges, Margaret Moore
Moore, Tara 1950- 61

Moore, Yvette 1958- 154
  Earlier sketches in SATA 69, 70
Mooser, Stephen 1941- 75
  Earlier sketch in SATA 28
Mora, Francisco X(avier) 1952- 90
Mora, Pat 1942- 134
  Earlier sketch in SATA 92
  See also CLR 58
Mora, Patricia
  See Mora, Pat
Morales, Yuyi 154
Moran, Tom 1943- 60
Moranville, Sharelle Byars 152
Moray Williams, Ursula 1911-2006 142
  Obituary 177
  Earlier sketch in SATA 73
  See also SAAS 9
  See Williams, Ursula Moray
Mordvinoff, Nicolas 1911-1973 17
More, Caroline
  See Cone, Molly (Lamken)
  and Strachan, Margaret Pitcairn
Moreton, Andrew Esq.
  See Defoe, Daniel
Morey, Charles
  See Fletcher, Helen Jill
Morey, Walt(er Nelson) 1907-1992 51
  Obituary 70
  Earlier sketch in SATA 3
  See also SAAS 9
Morgan, Alfred P(owell) 1889-1972 33
Morgan, Alison (Mary) 1930- 85
  Earlier sketch in SATA 30
Morgan, Anne 1954- 121
Morgan, Douglas
  See Macdonald, James D.
Morgan, Ellen
  See Bumstead, Kathleen Mary
Morgan, Geoffrey 1916- 46
Morgan, Helen (Gertrude Louise)
  1921-1990 29
Morgan, Jane
  See Cooper, James Fenimore
  and Franklin, Jane (Morgan)
  and Moren, Sally M(oore)
Morgan, Lenore H. 1908-1976 8
Morgan, Mary 1957- 114
  Earlier sketch in SATA 81
Morgan, Nicola 1961- 161
Morgan, Nina 1953- 110
Morgan, Pierr 1952- 122
  Earlier sketch in SATA 77
Morgan, Robin (Evonne) 1941- 80
Morgan, Roxanne
  See Gentle, Mary
Morgan, Sarah (Nicola) 1959- 68
Morgan, Shirley 10
  See Kiepper, Shirley Morgan
Morgan, Stacy T(owle) 1959- 104
Morgan, Stevie
  See Davies, Nicola
Morgan, Tom 1942- 42
Morgan, Wendy
  See Staub, Wendy Corsi
Morgan-Vanroyen, Mary
  See Morgan, Mary
Morgenstern, Susie Hoch 1945- 133
Mori, Hana 1909-1990(?) 88
Mori, Kyoko 1957- 122
  Autobiography Feature 126
  See also CLR 64
  See also SAAS 26
Moriarty, Jaclyn 162
Moriarty, William J. 1930- 127
Morice, Dave 1946- 93
Morin, Isobel V. 1928- 110
Morley, Wilfred Owen
  See Lowndes, Robert A(ugustine) W(ard)
Morningstar, Mildred (Whaley) 1912-1997 .. 61
  Obituary 114
Morozumi, Atsuko 110

Morpurgo, Michael 1943- *143*
  Earlier sketch in SATA *93*
  See also CLR *51*
Morrah, Dave
  See Morrah, David Wardlaw, Jr.
Morrah, David Wardlaw, Jr. 1914-1991 .... *10*
Morreale-de la Garza, Phyllis
  See De la Garza, Phyllis
Morressy, John 1930-2006 .... *23*
Morrill, Leslie H(olt) 1934-2003 .... *48*
  Brief entry *33*
  Obituary *148*
  See also SAAS *22*
Morris, Chris(topher Crosby) 1946- *66*
Morris, Deborah 1956- *91*
Morris, Desmond 1928- *14*
Morris, Desmond John
  See Morris, Desmond
Morris, Don 1954- *83*
Morris, Gerald (Paul) 1963- *150*
  Earlier sketch in SATA *107*
Morris, Gilbert (Leslie) 1929- *104*
Morris, Jackie *151*
Morris, Janet (Ellen) 1946- *66*
Morris, Jay
  See Tatham, Julie Campbell
Morris, (Margaret) Jean 1924- *98*
Morris, Jeffrey B(randon) 1941- *92*
Morris, Jennifer E. 1969- *179*
Morris, Jill 1936- *165*
  Earlier sketch in SATA *119*
Morris, Juddi *85*
Morris, Judy K. 1936- *61*
Morris, Oradel Nolen *128*
Morris, Robert A(da) 1933- *7*
Morris, William 1913-1994 .... *29*
Morrison, Bill 1935- *66*
  Brief entry *37*
Morrison, Chloe Anthony Wofford
  See Morrison, Toni
Morrison, Dorothy Nafus *29*
Morrison, Gordon 1944- *128*
  Earlier sketch in SATA *87*
Morrison, Joan 1922- *65*
Morrison, Lillian 1917- *108*
  Earlier sketch in SATA *3*
Morrison, Lucile Phillips 1896- *17*
Morrison, Martha A. 1948- *77*
Morrison, Meighan 1966- *90*
Morrison, Richard
  See Lowndes, Robert A(ugustine) W(ard)
Morrison, Robert
  See Lowndes, Robert A(ugustine) W(ard)
Morrison, Roberta
  See Webb, Jean Francis (III)
Morrison, Susan Dudley
  See Gold, Susan Dudley
Morrison, Taylor 1971- *159*
  Earlier sketch in SATA *95*
Morrison, Toni 1931- *144*
  Earlier sketch in SATA *57*
  See also CLR *99*
Morrison, Velma Ford 1909- *21*
Morrison, Wilbur Howard 1915- *64*
Morrison, William
  See Samachson, Joseph
Morriss, James E(dward) 1932- *8*
Morrow, Barbara Olenyik 1952- *167*
Morrow, Betty
  See Bacon, Elizabeth
Morse, Carol
  See Yeakley, Marjory Hall
Morse, Flo 1921- *30*
Morse, Tony 1953- *129*
Mort, Vivian
  See Cromie, Alice Hamilton
Mortensen, Denise Dowling *179*
Mortimer, Anne 1958- *116*
Morton, Alexandra (Hubbard) 1957- *144*
Morton, Anthony
  See Arthur, Robert, (Jr.)

Morton, Jane 1931- *50*
Morton, Joseph C. 1932- *156*
Morton, Lee Jack, Jr. 1928- *32*
Morton, Miriam 1918(?)-1985 .... *9*
  Obituary *46*
Mosatche, Harriet (S.) 1949- *122*
Moscow, Alvin 1925- *3*
Mosel, Arlene (Tichy) 1921-1996 .... *7*
Moseley, James W(illett) 1931- *139*
Moseng, Elisabeth 1967- *90*
Moser, Barry (A.) 1940- *138*
  Earlier sketches in SATA *56, 79*
  See also CLR *49*
  See also SAAS *15*
Moser, Don(ald Bruce) 1932- *31*
Moses, Sheila P. 1961- *168*
Moses, Will 1956- *178*
  Earlier sketch in SATA *120*
Mosesson, Gloria R(ubin) *24*
Mosher, Richard 1949- *120*
Moskin, Marietta D(unston) 1928- *23*
Moskof, Martin Stephen 1930- *27*
Mosley, Francis 1957- *57*
Moss, Don(ald) 1920- *11*
Moss, Elaine (Dora) 1924- *57*
  Brief entry *31*
Moss, Jeff(rey) 1942-1998 .... *73*
  Obituary *106*
Moss, Marissa 1959- *163*
  Earlier sketches in SATA *71, 104*
Moss, Miriam 1955- *140*
  Earlier sketch in SATA *76*
Moss, Thylias 1954- *108*
Moss, Thylias Rebecca Brasier
  See Moss, Thylias
Most, Bernard 1937- *134*
  Brief entry *40*
  Earlier sketches in SATA *48, 91*
Mott, Evelyn Clarke 1962- *133*
  Earlier sketch in SATA *75*
Motz, Lloyd 1909- *20*
Mould, Edwin
  See Whitlock, Ralph
Mouly, Francoise *155*
Mountain, Robert
  See Montgomery, Raymond A. (Jr.)
Mountfield, David
  See Grant, Neil
Moussard, Jacqueline 1924- *24*
Mowat, Claire (Angel Wheeler) 1933- *123*
Mowat, Farley 1921- *55*
  Earlier sketch in SATA *3*
  See also CLR *20*
Mowat, Farley McGill
  See Mowat, Farley
Mowry, Jess 1960- *131*
  Autobiography Feature *131*
  Earlier sketch in SATA *109*
  See also CLR *65*
Moxley, Sheila 1966- *96*
Moyer, Terry J. 1937- *94*
Moyes, Patricia *63*
  See Haszard, Patricia Moyes
Moyler, Alan (Frank Powell) 1926- *36*
Mozelle, Shirley *179*
Mozley, Charles 1915- *43*
  Brief entry *32*
Mphahlele, Es'kia
  See Mphahlele, Ezekiel
Mphahlele, Ezekiel 1919- *119*
  See Mphahlele, Es'kia
Mr. McGillicuddy
  See Abisch, Roslyn Kroop
Mr. Sniff
  See Abisch, Roslyn Kroop
Mr. Tivil
  See Lorkowski, Thomas V(incent)
Mr. Wizard
  See Herbert, Don
Mrs. Fairstar
  See Horne, Richard Henry Hengist

Muchamore, Robert 1972- *175*
Muchmore, Jo Ann 1937- *103*
Mude, O.
  See Gorey, Edward (St. John)
Mudgeon, Apeman
  See Mitchell, Adrian
Mueller, Jorg 1942- *67*
  See also CLR *43*
Mueller, Virginia 1924- *28*
Muggs
  See Watkins, Lois
Muir, Diana
  See Appelbaum, Diana Muir Karter
Muir, Frank (Herbert) 1920-1998 .... *30*
Muir, Helen 1937- *65*
Mukerji, Dhan Gopal 1890-1936 .... *40*
  See also CLR *10*
Mulcahy, Lucille Burnett *12*
Mulford, Philippa G. 1948- *112*
  Earlier sketch in SATA *43*
Mulford, Philippa Greene
  See Mulford, Philippa G.
Mulila, Vigad G.
  See Maillu, David G(ian)
Mullen, Michael 1937- *122*
Muller, Billex
  See Ellis, Edward S(ylvester)
Muller, Jorg
  See Mueller, Jorg
Muller, (Lester) Robin 1953- *86*
Mullin, Caryl Cude 1969- *130*
Mullins, Edward S(wift) 1922- *10*
Mullins, Hilary 1962- *84*
Mulock, Dinah Maria
  See Craik, Dinah Maria (Mulock)
Mulvihill, William Patrick 1923- *8*
Mumford, Ruth 1919- *86*
  See Dallas, Ruth
Mumy, Bill 1954- *112*
Mun
  See Leaf, (Wilbur) Munro
Munari, Bruno 1907-1998 .... *15*
  See also CLR *9*
Munce, Ruth Hill 1898- *12*
Mundy, Simon 1954- *64*
Mundy, Simon Andrew James Hainault
  See Mundy, Simon
Munger, Nancy *170*
Munowitz, Ken 1935-1977 .... *14*
Munoz, William 1949- *92*
  Earlier sketch in SATA *42*
Munro, Alice 1931- *29*
Munro, Alice Anne
  See Munro, Alice
Munro, Eleanor 1928- *37*
Munro, Roxie 1945- *136*
  Earlier sketch in SATA *58*
Munsch, Bob
  See Munsch, Robert (Norman)
Munsch, Robert (Norman) 1945- *120*
  Brief entry *48*
  Earlier sketches in SATA *50, 83*
  See also CLR *19*
Munsinger, Lynn 1951- *177*
  Earlier sketches in SATA *33, 94*
Munson, Derek 1970- *139*
Munson, R. W.
  See Karl, Jean E(dna)
Munson-Benson, Tunie 1946- *15*
Munsterberg, Peggy 1921- *102*
Munthe, Nelly 1947- *53*
Munves, James (Albert) 1922- *30*
Munzer, Martha E. 1899-1999 .... *4*
Murch, Mel
  See Manes, Stephen
Murdoch, David H(amilton) 1937- *96*
Murhall, J(acqueline) J(ane) 1964- *143*
Murphy, Barbara Beasley 1933- *130*
  Earlier sketch in SATA *5*
Murphy, Claire Rudolf 1951- *137*
  Earlier sketch in SATA *76*

Murphy, E(mmett) Jefferson 1926- *4*
Murphy, Jill (Frances) 1949- *142*
  Earlier sketches in SATA *37, 70*
  See also CLR *39*
Murphy, Jim 1947- *124*
  Brief entry *32*
  Earlier sketches in SATA *37, 77*
  See also CLR *53*
Murphy, Joseph E., Jr. 1930- *65*
Murphy, Kelly 1977- *143*
Murphy, Louise 1943- *155*
Murphy, Pat
  See Murphy, E(mmett) Jefferson
Murphy, Patricia J. 1963- *132*
Murphy, Robert (William) 1902-1971 .... *10*
Murphy, Shirley Rousseau 1928- *126*
  Earlier sketches in SATA *36, 71*
  See also SAAS *18*
Murphy, Stuart J. 1942- *157*
  Earlier sketch in SATA *115*
Murphy, Tim
  See Murphy, Jim
Murray, John 1923- *39*
Murray, Kirsty 1960- *165*
  Earlier sketch in SATA *108*
Murray, Marguerite 1917- *63*
Murray, Marian *5*
Murray, Martine 1965- *125*
Murray, (Judith) Michele (Freedman)
  1933-1974 .... *7*
Murray, Ossie 1938- *43*
Murray, Peter
  See Hautman, Pete
Murrow, Liza Ketchum 1946- *78*
  See Ketchum, Liza
Musgrave, Florence 1902-1999 .... *3*
Musgrove, Margaret W(ynkoop) 1943- *124*
  Earlier sketch in SATA *26*
Mussey, Virginia Howell
  See Ellison, Virginia H(owell)
Mussey, Virginia T.H.
  See Ellison, Virginia H(owell)
Mutel, Cornelia F. 1947- *74*
Muth, Jon J. *165*
Mutz
  See Kuenstler, Morton
Mwangi, Meja 1948- *174*
My Brother's Brother
  See Chekhov, Anton (Pavlovich)
Myers, Anna *160*
Myers, Arthur 1917- *91*
  Earlier sketch in SATA *35*
Myers, Bernice *81*
  Earlier sketch in SATA *9*
Myers, Caroline Elizabeth Clark
  1887-1980 .... *28*
Myers, Christopher 1975-
  See CLR *97*
Myers, Edward 1950- *172*
  Earlier sketch in SATA *96*
Myers, Elisabeth P(erkins) 1918- *36*
Myers, (Mary) Hortense (Powner)
  1913-1987 .... *10*
Myers, Jack 1913-2006 .... *83*
  Obituary *178*
Myers, Jack Edgar
  See Myers, Jack
Myers, Lou 1915-2005 .... *81*
  Obituary *171*
Myers, Louis
  See Myers, Lou
Myers, R.E. 1924- *119*
Myers, Robert Eugene
  See Myers, R.E.
Myers, Tim 1953- *176*
  Earlier sketch in SATA *147*
Myers, Timothy Joseph
  See Myers, Tim

Myers, Walter Dean 1937- *157*
  Brief entry *27*
  Earlier sketches in SATA *41, 71, 109*
  See also CLR *110*
  See also SAAS *2*
  See Myers, Walter M.
Myers, Walter M.
  See Myers, Walter Dean
Myller, Rolf 1926-2006 .... *27*
  Obituary *175*
Myra, Harold L(awrence) 1939- *46*
  Brief entry *42*
Myracle, Lauren 1969- *162*
Myrus, Donald (Richard) 1927- *23*
Mysterious Traveler, The
  See Arthur, Robert, (Jr.)

N

Na, An *149*
Naaslund, Goorel Kristina 1940- *170*
Nadel, Laurie 1948- *74*
Naden, Corinne J. 1930- *166*
  Earlier sketch in SATA *79*
Nagel, Andreas Fischer
  See Fischer-Nagel, Andreas
Nagel, Heiderose Fischer
  See Fischer-Nagel, Heiderose
Nagle, Shane *176*
Naidoo, Beverley 1943- *135*
  Earlier sketch in SATA *63*
  See also CLR *29*
Naipaul, Shivadhar Srinivasa
  See Naipaul, Shiva
Nakae, Noriko 1940- *59*
Nakatani, Chiyoko 1930-1981 .... *55*
  Brief entry *40*
  See also CLR *30*
Nally, Susan W. 1947- *90*
Namioka, Lensey 1929- *157*
  Autobiography Feature *116*
  Earlier sketches in SATA *27, 89*
  See also CLR *48*
  See also SAAS *24*
Nanji, Shenaaz 1954- *131*
Nanogak Agnes 1925- *61*
Napier, Mark
  See Laffin, John (Alfred Charles)
Napoli, Donna Jo 1948- *137*
  Earlier sketch in SATA *92*
  See also CLR *51*
  See also SAAS *23*
Narahashi, Keiko 1959- *115*
  Earlier sketch in SATA *79*
Narayan, Rasipuram Krishnaswami
  See Narayan, R.K.
Narayan, R.K. 1906-2001 .... *62*
Nascimbene, Yan 1949- *173*
  Earlier sketch in SATA *133*
Nash, Bruce M(itchell) 1947- *34*
Nash, Linell
  See Smith, Linell Nash
Nash, Mary (Hughes) 1925- *41*
Nash, (Frediric) Ogden 1902-1971 .... *46*
  Earlier sketch in SATA *2*
Nash, Renea Denise 1963- *81*
Nast, Elsa Ruth
  See Watson, Jane Werner
Nast, Thomas 1840-1902 .... *51*
  Brief entry *33*
Nastick, Sharon 1954- *41*
Nathan, Amy *155*
  Earlier sketch in SATA *104*
Nathan, Dorothy (Goldeen) (?)-1966 .... *15*
Nathan, Robert (Gruntal) 1894-1985 .... *6*
  Obituary *43*
Nathanson, Laura Walther 1941- *57*
Natti, Susanna 1948- *125*
  Earlier sketch in SATA *32*

Naughtie, Eleanor
  See Updale, Eleanor
Naughton, Bill
  See Naughton, William John (Francis)
Naughton, James Franklin 1957- *85*
Naughton, Jim
  See Naughton, James Franklin
Naughton, William John (Francis)
  1910-1992 .... *86*
  See Naughton, Bill
Navarra, John Gabriel 1927- *8*
Naylor, Penelope 1941- *10*
Naylor, Phyllis 1933-
  See Naylor, Phyllis Reynolds
Naylor, Phyllis Reynolds 1933- *152*
  Autobiography Feature *152*
  Earlier sketches in SATA *12, 66, 102*
  See also CLR *17*
  See also SAAS *10*
  See Naylor, Phyllis
Nazarian, Nikki
  See Nichols, Cecilia Fawn
Nazaroff, Alexander I(vanovich) 1898-1981 .. *4*
Neal, Harry Edward 1906-1993 .... *5*
  Obituary *76*
Neal, Michael
  See Teitelbaum, Michael
Nearing, Penny 1916- *47*
  Brief entry *42*
Nebel, Gustave E. *45*
  Brief entry *33*
Nebel, Mimouca
  See Nebel, Gustave E.
Nee, Kay Bonner *10*
Needham, Kate 1962- *95*
Needle, Jan 1943- *98*
  Earlier sketch in SATA *30*
  See also CLR *43*
  See also SAAS *23*
Needleman, Jacob 1934- *6*
Neel, David 1960- *82*
Neel, Preston 1959- *93*
Negri, Rocco 1932- *12*
Neier, Aryeh 1937- *59*
Neigoff, Anne *13*
Neigoff, Mike 1920- *13*
Neilson, Frances Fullerton (Jones)
  1910-2001 .... *14*
Neimark, Anne E. 1935- *145*
  Earlier sketch in SATA *4*
Neimark, Paul G. 1934- *80*
  Brief entry *37*
Neitzel, Shirley 1941- *134*
  Earlier sketch in SATA *77*
Nell
  See Hanna, Nell(ie L.)
Nelson, Blake 1960- *177*
Nelson, Catherine Chadwick 1926- *87*
Nelson, Cordner (Bruce) 1918- *54*
  Brief entry *29*
Nelson, Drew 1952- *77*
Nelson, Esther L. 1928- *13*
Nelson, Jim A.
  See Stotter, Mike
Nelson, Julie L. 1970- *117*
Nelson, Kadir *154*
Nelson, Kris
  See Rusch, Kristine Kathryn
Nelson, Marilyn 1946- *151*
  See Waniek, Marilyn Nelson
Nelson, Mary Carroll 1929- *23*
Nelson, O. Terry 1941- *62*
Nelson, Peter N. 1953- *73*
Nelson, Richard K(ing) 1941- *65*
Nelson, Robin Laura 1971- *141*
Nelson, Roy Paul 1923- *59*
Nelson, Sharlene (P.) 1933- *96*
Nelson, Ted (W.) 1931- *96*
Nelson, Theresa 1948- *143*
  Autobiography Feature *143*
  Earlier sketch in SATA *79*

Nerlove, Miriam 1959- *53*
  Brief entry *49*
Nesbit, E(dith) 1858-1924 .... *100*
  See also YABC *1*
  See also CLR *70*
Nesbit, Troy
  See Folsom, Franklin (Brewster)
Nespojohn, Katherine V(eronica) 1912-1975 . *7*
Ness, Evaline (Michelow) 1911-1986 .... *26*
  Obituary *49*
  Earlier sketch in SATA *1*
  See also CLR *6*
  See also SAAS *1*
Nestor, Larry 1940- *149*
Nestor, William P(rodromos) 1947- *49*
Nethery, Mary *93*
Neubecker, Robert *170*
Neuberger, Julia (Babette Sarah) 1950- *142*
  Earlier sketch in SATA *78*
Neufeld, John (Arthur) 1938- *131*
  Autobiography Feature *131*
  Earlier sketches in SATA *6, 81*
  See also CLR *52*
  See also SAAS *3*
Neuhaus, David 1958- *83*
Neumeyer, Peter F(lorian) 1929- *13*
Neurath, Marie (Reidemeister) 1898-1986 ..... *1*
Neuschwander, Cindy 1953- *157*
  Earlier sketch in SATA *107*
Neusner, Jacob 1932- *38*
Neville, Charles
  See Bodsworth, (Charles) Fred(erick)
Neville, Emily Cheney 1919- *1*
  See also SAAS *2*
Neville, Mary
  See Woodrich, Mary Neville
Nevins, Albert (Francis) J(erome)
  1915-1997 .... *20*
Newberger, Devra
  See Speregen, Devra Newberger
Newberry, Clare Turlay 1903-1970 .... *1*
  Obituary *26*
Newbery, John 1713-1767 .... *20*
Newbery, Linda 1952- *142*
Newcombe, Jack *45*
  Brief entry *33*
  See Newcombe, Eugene A.
Newcome, Robert 1955- *91*
Newcome, Zita 1959- *88*
Newell, Crosby
  See Bonsall, Crosby Barbara (Newell)
Newell, Edythe W(eatherford) 1910-1989 .... *11*
Newell, Hope Hockenberry 1896-1965 .... *24*
Newfeld, Frank 1928- *26*
Newlon, (Frank) Clarke 1905(?)-1982 .... *6*
  Obituary *33*
Newman, Daisy 1904-1994 .... *27*
  Obituary *78*
Newman, Gerald 1939- *46*
  Brief entry *42*
Newman, Jerry 1935- *82*
Newman, Leslea 1955- *134*
  Earlier sketches in SATA *71, 128*
Newman, Margaret
  See Potter, Margaret (Newman)
Newman, Marjorie *146*
Newman, Matthew (Harrison) 1955- *56*
Newman, Nanette 1934- *162*
Newman, Robert (Howard) 1909-1988 .... *87*
  Obituary *60*
  Earlier sketch in SATA *4*
Newman, Shirlee P(etkin) *144*
  Earlier sketches in SATA *10, 90*
Newsom, Carol 1948- *92*
  Earlier sketch in SATA *40*
Newsom, Tom 1944- *80*
Newth, Mette 1942- *140*
Newton, David E(dward) 1933- *67*
Newton, James R(obert) 1935- *23*
Newton, Suzanne 1936- *77*
  Earlier sketch in SATA *5*

Ney, John 1923- *43*
  Brief entry *33*
Nez, John *155*
Ng, Franklin *82*
Nichol, B(arrie) P(hillip) 1944-1988 .... *66*
Nicholas, Louise D.
  See Watkins, Dawn L.
Nicholls, Judith (Ann) 1941- *61*
Nichols, Cecilia Fawn 1906-1987 .... *12*
Nichols, Grace 1950- *164*
  Earlier sketch in SATA *98*
Nichols, Janet (Louise) 1952- *67*
Nichols, Judy 1947- *124*
Nichols, Leigh
  See Koontz, Dean R.
Nichols, Paul
  See Hawks, Robert
Nichols, Peter
  See Youd, (Christopher) Samuel
Nichols, (Joanna) Ruth 1948- *15*
Nicholson, C. R.
  See Nicole, Christopher (Robin)
Nicholson, Christina
  See Nicole, Christopher (Robin)
Nicholson, Joyce Thorpe 1919- *35*
Nicholson, Lois P. 1949- *88*
Nicholson, Robin
  See Nicole, Christopher (Robin)
Nicholson, William 1872-1949
  See CLR *76*
Nickell, Joe 1944- *167*
  Earlier sketch in SATA *73*
Nickelsburg, Janet 1893-1983 .... *11*
Nickerson, Elizabeth *14*
  See Nickerson, Betty
Nickl, Barbara (Elisabeth) 1939- *56*
Nicklaus, Carol *62*
  Brief entry *33*
Nickless, Will 1902-1979(?) *66*
Nic Leodhas, Sorche
  See Alger, Leclaire (Gowans)
Nicol, Ann
  See Turnbull, Ann (Christine)
Nicolas
  See Mordvinoff, Nicolas
Nicolay, Helen 1866-1954
  See YABC *1*
Nicole, Christopher (Robin) 1930- *5*
Nicoll, Helen 1937- *87*
Nicolson, Cynthia Pratt 1949- *141*
Ni Dhuibhne, Eilis 1954- *91*
Niehaus, Paddy Bouma
  See Bouma, Paddy
Nields, Nerissa 1967- *166*
Nielsen, Kay (Rasmus) 1886-1957 .... *16*
  See also CLR *16*
Nielsen, Laura F(arnsworth) 1960- *93*
Nielsen, Nancy J. 1951- *77*
Nielsen, Virginia
  See McCall, Virginia Nielsen
Nieuwsma, Milton J(ohn) 1941- *142*
Nightingale, Sandy 1953- *76*
Nikolajeva, Maria 1952- *127*
Nikola-Lisa, W. 1951- *71*
Niland, Deborah 1951- *172*
  Earlier sketch in SATA *27*
Niland, Kilmeny *75*
Nilsen, Anna 1948- *174*
  Earlier sketch in SATA *96*
Nilsson, Eleanor 1939- *117*
  Earlier sketch in SATA *81*
  See also SAAS *23*
Nilsson, Per 1954- *159*
Nimmo, Jenny 1944- *144*
  Earlier sketch in SATA *87*
  See also CLR *44*
Niven, Larry 1938- *171*
  Earlier sketch in SATA *95*
  See Niven, Laurence VanCott
Niven, Laurence VanCott
  See Niven, Larry

Nivola, Claire A. 1947- *140*
  Earlier sketch in SATA *84*
Nix, Garth 1963- *143*
  Earlier sketch in SATA *97*
  See also CLR *68*
Nixon, Hershell Howard 1923- *42*
Nixon, Joan Lowery 1927-2003 .... *115*
  Obituary *146*
  Earlier sketches in SATA *8, 44, 78*
  See also CLR *24*
  See also SAAS *9*
Nixon, K.
  See Nixon, Kathleen Irene (Blundell)
Nixon, Kathleen Irene (Blundell)
  1894-1988(?) *14*
  Obituary *59*
Nobisso, Josephine 1953- *121*
  Earlier sketch in SATA *78*
Noble, Iris (Davis) 1922-1986 .... *5*
  Obituary *49*
Noble, Marty 1947- *125*
  Earlier sketch in SATA *97*
Noble, Trinka Hakes *123*
  Brief entry *37*
Noda, Takayo 1961- *168*
Nodelman, Perry 1942- *101*
Nodset, Joan L.
  See Lexau, Joan M.
Noel Hume, Ivor 1927- *65*
Noestlinger, Christine
  See Nostlinger, Christine
Noguere, Suzanne 1947- *34*
Nolan, Dennis 1945- *166*
  Brief entry *34*
  Earlier sketches in SATA *42, 92*
Nolan, Han 1956- *157*
  Earlier sketch in SATA *109*
Nolan, Janet 1956- *145*
Nolan, Jeannette Covert 1897-1974 .... *2*
  Obituary *27*
Nolan, Paul T(homas) 1919- *48*
Nolan, William F(rancis) 1928- *88*
  Brief entry *28*
Nolen, Jerdine 1953- *157*
  Earlier sketch in SATA *105*
Noll, Sally 1946- *82*
Noonan, Diana 1960- *146*
Noonan, Julia 1946- *148*
  Earlier sketches in SATA *4, 95*
Norac, Carl 1960- *166*
Nordan, Robert W(arren) 1934-2004 .... *133*
Nordhoff, Charles Bernard 1887-1947 .... *23*
Nordlicht, Lillian *29*
Nordstrom, Ursula 1910-1988 .... *3*
  Obituary *57*
Nordtvedt, Matilda 1926- *67*
Norling, Beth 1969- *149*
Norman, Charles 1904-1996 .... *38*
  Obituary *92*
Norman, Howard
  See Norman, Howard A.
Norman, Howard A. 1949- *81*
Norman, James
  See Schmidt, James Norman
Norman, Jay
  See Arthur, Robert, (Jr.)
Norman, Lilith 1927- *120*
  Earlier sketch in SATA *86*
Norman, Mary 1931- *36*
Norman, Steve
  See Pashko, Stanley
Norment, Lisa 1966- *91*
Norris, Gunilla Brodde 1939- *20*
North, Andrew
  See Norton, Andre
North, Anthony
  See Koontz, Dean R.
North, Captain George
  See Stevenson, Robert Louis (Balfour)
North, Captain George
  See Stevenson, Robert Louis (Balfour)

North, Howard
    See Trevor, Elleston
North, Joan 1920- 16
North, Milou
    See Erdrich, Louise
North, Robert
    See Withers, Carl A.
North, Sara
    See Bonham, Barbara Thomas
    and Hager, Jean
North, Sterling 1906-1974 45
    Obituary 26
    Earlier sketch in SATA *1*
Northeast, Brenda V(ictoria) 1948- 106
Northmore, Elizabeth Florence 1906-1974 . 122
Norton, Alice Mary 43
    Earlier sketch in SATA *1*
    See Norton, Andre
Norton, Andre 1912-2005 91
    See also CLR *50*
    See Norton, Alice Mary
Norton, Browning
    See Norton, Frank R. B(rowning)
Norton, Frank R. B(rowning) 1909-1989 10
Norton, Mary 1903-1992 60
    Obituary 72
    Earlier sketch in SATA *18*
    See also CLR *6*
Nosredna, Trebor
    See Anderson, Bob
Nostlinger, Christine 1936- 162
    Brief entry 37
    Earlier sketch in SATA *64*
    See also CLR *12*
Nourse, Alan E(dward) 1928-1992 48
    See also CLR *33*
Novak, Matt 1962- 165
    Brief entry 52
    Earlier sketches in SATA *60, 104*
Novelli, Luca 1947- 61
Nowell, Elizabeth Cameron 12
Noyes, Deborah
    See Wayshak, Deborah Noyes
Nugent, Nicholas 1949- 73
Numeroff, Laura Joffe 1953- 142
    Earlier sketches in SATA *28, 90*
    See also CLR *85*
Nunes, Lygia Bojunga 1932- 154
    Earlier sketch in SATA *75*
    See Bojunga, Lygia
Nunn, Laura (Donna) Silverstein 1968- 124
Nurnberg, Maxwell 1897-1984 27
    Obituary 41
Nussbaumer, Paul (Edmund) 1934- 16
Nutt, Ken 1951- 163
    Earlier sketch in SATA *97*
Nuygen, Mathieu 1967- 80
Nyberg, (Everett Wayne) Morgan 1944- 87
Nyce, (Nellie) Helene von Strecker
    1885-1969 19
Nyce, Vera 1862-1925 19
Nye, Naomi Shihab 1952- 147
    Earlier sketch in SATA *86*
    See also CLR *59*
Nye, Robert 1939- 6
Nyikos, Stacy A. 1969- 164
Nystrom, Carolyn 1940- 130
    Earlier sketch in SATA *67*

O

Oakes, Elizabeth H. 1964- 132
Oakes, Vanya 1909-1983 6
    Obituary 37
Oakley, Don(ald G.) 1927- 8
Oakley, Graham 1929- 84
    Earlier sketch in SATA *30*
    See also CLR *7*
Oakley, Helen (McKelvey) 1906- 10

Oana, Katherine 1929- 53
    Brief entry 37
Oates, Eddie H. 1943- 88
Oates, Joyce Carol 1938- 159
Oates, Stephen B(aery) 1936- 59
Obed, Ellen Bryan 1944- 74
Oberle, Joseph 1958- 69
Oberman, Sheldon 1949-2004 85
    Autobiography Feature 114
    Obituary 153
    See also CLR *54*
    See also SAAS *26*
Obligado, Lilian (Isabel) 1931- 61
    Brief entry 45
Obrant, Susan 1946- 11
O'Brian, E. G.
    See Clarke, Arthur C.
O'Brien, Anne Sibley 1952- 80
    Brief entry 48
    Earlier sketch in SATA *53*
O'Brien, Robert C.
    See CLR *2*
    See Conly, Robert Leslie
O'Brien, Thomas C(lement) 1938- 29
O'Callaghan, Julie 1954- 113
O'Callahan, Jay 1938- 88
O'Carroll, Ryan
    See Markun, Patricia Maloney
Ochiltree, Dianne 1953- 117
Ockham, Joan Price
    See Price, Joan
O'Connell, Margaret F(orster) 1935-1977 30
    Obituary 30
O'Connell, Peg
    See Ahern, Margaret McCrohan
O'Connell, Rebecca 1968- 130
O'Connor, Barbara 1950- 154
O'Connor, Francine M(arie) 1930- 90
O'Connor, Genevieve A. 1914- 75
O'Connor, Jane 1947- 150
    Brief entry 47
    Earlier sketches in SATA *59, 103*
O'Connor, Karen 1938- 89
    Earlier sketch in SATA *34*
O'Connor, Patrick
    See Wibberley, Leonard (Patrick O'Connor)
O'Conor, Jane 1958- 78
Odaga, Asenath (Bole) 1937- 130
    Earlier sketch in SATA *67*
    See also SAAS *19*
O Danachair, Caoimhin
    See Danaher, Kevin
Odanaka, Barbara 159
O'Daniel, Janet 1921- 24
O'Day, Cathy
    See Crane, Barbara (Joyce)
O'Dell, Scott 1898-1989 134
    Earlier sketches in SATA *12, 60*
    See also CLR *16*
Odenwald, Robert P(aul) 1899-1965 11
Odgers, Sally
    See Odgers, Sally Farrell
Odgers, Sally Farrell 1957- 139
    Earlier sketch in SATA *72*
O'Donnell, Dick
    See Lupoff, Richard A(llen)
    and Thompson, Don(ald Arthur)
Oechsli, Kelly 1918-1999 5
Oesterle, Virginia Rorby
    See Rorby, Ginny
Ofek, Uriel 1926- 36
    See also CLR *28*
Offenbacher, Ami 1958- 91
Offit, Sidney 1928- 10
Ofosu-Appiah, L(awrence) H(enry) 1920- ... 13
Ogan, George F. 1912-1983 13
Ogan, M. G.
    See Ogan, George F.
    and Ogan, Margaret E. (Nettles)
Ogan, Margaret E. (Nettles) 1923-1979 13

Ogburn, Charlton (Jr.) 1911-1998 3
    Obituary 109
Ogburn, Jacqueline K. 162
Ogilvie, Elisabeth May 1917-2006 40
    Brief entry 29
    Obituary 176
Ogilvy, Gavin
    See Barrie, J(ames) M(atthew)
Ogilvy, Ian 1943- 177
Ogilvy, Ian Raymond
    See Ogilvy, Ian
Ogletree, Charles J. 1952- 175
O'Green, Jennifer
    See Roberson, Jennifer
O'Green, Jennifer Roberson
    See Roberson, Jennifer
O'Hagan, Caroline 1946- 38
O'Hanlon, Jacklyn
    See Meek, Jacklyn O'Hanlon
O'Hara, Elizabeth
    See Ni Dhuibhne, Eilis
O'Hara, Kenneth
    See Morris, (Margaret) Jean
O'Hara, Mary
    See Alsop, Mary O'Hara
O'Hara (Alsop), Mary
    See Alsop, Mary O'Hara
O'Hare, Jeff(rey A.) 1958- 105
Ohi, Ruth 1964- 95
Ohiyesa
    See Eastman, Charles A(lexander)
Ohlsson, Ib 1935- 7
Ohmi, Ayano 1959- 115
Ohtomo, Yasuo 1946- 37
o huigin, sean 1942- 138
    See also CLR *75*
Oiseau
    See Moseley, James W(illett)
Oke, Janette 1935- 97
O'Keefe, Susan Heyboer 176
    Earlier sketch in SATA *133*
O'Keeffe, Frank 1938- 99
O'Kelley, Mattie Lou 1908-1997 97
    Earlier sketch in SATA *36*
Okimoto, Jean Davies 1942- 103
    Earlier sketch in SATA *34*
Okomfo, Amasewa
    See Cousins, Linda
Olaleye, Isaac O. 1941- 96
    See also SAAS *23*
Olcott, Frances Jenkins 1872(?)-1963 19
Old, Wendie C(orbin) 1943- 154
Old Boy
    See Hughes, Thomas
Oldenburg, E(gbert) William 1936-1974 35
Older, Effin 1942- 114
Older, Jules 1940- 156
    Earlier sketch in SATA *114*
Oldfield, Jenny 1949- 140
Oldfield, Margaret J(ean) 1932- 56
Oldfield, Pamela 1931- 86
Oldham, June 70
Oldham, Mary 1944- 65
Olds, Elizabeth 1896-1991 3
    Obituary 66
Olds, Helen Diehl 1895-1981 9
    Obituary 25
Oldstyle, Jonathan
    See Irving, Washington
O'Leary, Brian (Todd) 1940- 6
O'Leary, Patsy B(aker) 1937- 97
Oliphant, B. J.
    See Tepper, Sheri S.
Oliver, Burton
    See Burt, Olive Woolley
Oliver, Chad
    See Oliver, Symmes C(hadwick)
Oliver, John Edward 1933- 21
Oliver, Marilyn Tower 1935- 89
Oliver, Narelle 1960- 152
Oliver, Shirley (Louise Dawkins) 1958- 74

Oliver, Symmes C(hadwick) 1928-1993 .... *101*
  See Oliver, Chad
Oliviero, Jamie 1950- *84*
Olmsted, Lorena Ann 1890-1989 .... *13*
Olney, Ross R. 1929- *13*
Olschewski, Alfred (Erich) 1920- *7*
Olsen, Barbara *148*
Olsen, Carol 1945- *89*
Olsen, Ib Spang 1921- *81*
  Earlier sketch in SATA 6
Olsen, Violet (Mae) 1922-1991 .... *58*
Olson, Arielle North 1932- *67*
Olson, Gene 1922- *32*
Olson, Helen Kronberg *48*
Olson, Kay Melchisedech 1948- *175*
Olson, Marianne
  See Mitchell, Marianne
Olugebefola, Ademole 1941- *15*
Oluonye, Mary N(kechi) 1955- *111*
Om
  See Gorey, Edward (St. John)
O'Malley, Kevin 1961- *157*
Oman, Carola (Mary Anima) 1897-1978 ..... *35*
O'Mara, Carmel 1965- *166*
O'Mara-Horwitz, Carmel
  See O'Mara, Carmel
O'Meara, Walter (Andrew) 1897-1989 .... *65*
Ommanney, F(rancis) D(ownes) 1903-1980 . *23*
O Mude
  See Gorey, Edward (St. John)
Oneal, Elizabeth 1934- *82*
  Earlier sketch in SATA 30
  See Oneal, Zibby
O'Neal, Reagan
  See Jordan, Robert
Oneal, Zibby
  See CLR 13
  See Oneal, Elizabeth
O'Neill, Amanda 1951- *111*
O'Neill, Gerard K(itchen) 1927-1992 .... *65*
O'Neill, Judith (Beatrice) 1930- *34*
O'Neill, Mary L(e Duc) 1908(?)-1990 .... *2*
  Obituary *64*
Onslow, Annette Rosemary MacArthur
  See MacArthur-Onslow, Annette Rosemary
Onyefulu, Ifeoma 1959- *157*
  Earlier sketches in SATA 81, 115
Opie, Iona (Margaret Balfour) 1923- *118*
  Earlier sketches in SATA 3, 63
  See also SAAS 6
Opie, Peter (Mason) 1918-1982 .... *118*
  Obituary *28*
  Earlier sketches in SATA 3, 63
Oppel, Kenneth 1967- *153*
  Earlier sketch in SATA 99
Oppenheim, Joanne 1934- *174*
  Earlier sketches in SATA 5, 82, 136
Oppenheim, Shulamith Levey 1928- *177*
Oppenheimer, Joan L(etson) 1925- *28*
Oppong, Joseph Ransford 1953- *160*
Optic, Oliver
  See Adams, William Taylor
  and Stratemeyer, Edward L.
Oram, Hiawyn 1946- *101*
  Earlier sketch in SATA 56
Orbach, Ruth Gary 1941- *21*
Orczy, Emma
  See Orczy, Baroness Emmuska
Orczy, Emma Magdalena Rosalia Maria Josefa
  See Orczy, Baroness Emmuska
Orczy, Emmuska
  See Orczy, Baroness Emmuska
Orczy, Baroness Emmuska 1865-1947 .... *40*
  See Orczy, Emma
Orde, A. J.
  See Tepper, Sheri S.
O'Reilly, Jackson
  See Jordan, Robert
Orenstein, Denise Gosliner 1950- *157*

Orgel, Doris 1929- *148*
  Earlier sketches in SATA 7, 85
  See also CLR 48
  See also SAAS 19
Orleans, Ilo 1897-1962 .... *10*
Orlev, Uri 1931- *135*
  Earlier sketch in SATA 58
  See also CLR 30
  See also SAAS 19
Ormai, Stella *57*
  Brief entry *48*
Ormerod, Jan 1946- *132*
  Brief entry *44*
  Earlier sketches in SATA 55, 70
  See also CLR 20
Ormondroyd, Edward 1925- *14*
Ormsby, Virginia H(aire) 1906-1990 .... *11*
Orozco, Jose-Luis 1948- *179*
Orr, Katherine S(helley) 1950- *72*
Orr, Wendy 1953- *141*
  Earlier sketch in SATA 90
Orris
  See Ingelow, Jean
Orth, Richard
  See Gardner, Richard (M.)
Ortiz Cofer, Judith
  See Cofer, Judith Ortiz
Orwell, George
  See CLR 68
  See Blair, Eric (Arthur)
Orwin, Joanna 1944- *141*
Osborn, Elinor 1939- *145*
Osborn, Lois D(orothy) 1915- *61*
Osborne, Charles 1927- *59*
Osborne, Chester G(orham) 1915-1987 .... *11*
Osborne, David
  See Silverberg, Robert
Osborne, George
  See Silverberg, Robert
Osborne, Leone Neal 1914-1996 .... *2*
Osborne, Mary Pope 1949- *144*
  Earlier sketches in SATA 41, 55, 98
  See also CLR 88
Osceola
  See Blixen, Karen (Christentze Dinesen)
Osgood, William E(dward) 1926- *37*
O'Shaughnessy, Darren
  See Shan, Darren
O'Shaughnessy, Ellen Cassels 1937- *78*
O'Shea, Catherine Patricia Shiels
  See O'Shea, Pat
O'Shea, Pat 1931-2007 .... *87*
  See also CLR 18
Osmond, Edward 1900- *10*
Ossoli, Sarah Margaret (Fuller) 1810-1850 .. *25*
  See Fuller, Margaret
  and Fuller, Sarah Margaret
Ostendorf, (Arthur) Lloyd, (Jr.) 1921-2000 .. *65*
  Obituary *125*
Ostow, Micol 1976- *170*
Otfinoski, Steven 1949- *116*
  Earlier sketch in SATA 56
Otis, James
  See Kaler, James Otis
O'Toole, Thomas 1941- *71*
O'Trigger, Sir Lucius
  See Horne, Richard Henry Hengist
Otten, Charlotte F(ennema) 1926- *98*
Ottley, Matt 1962- *171*
  Earlier sketch in SATA 102
Ottley, Reginald Leslie 1909-1985 .... *26*
  See also CLR 16
Otto, Svend
  See Soerensen, Svend Otto
Oughton, Jerrie (Preston) 1937- *131*
  Earlier sketch in SATA 76
Oughton, (William) Taylor 1925- *104*
Ouida
  See De La Ramee, Marie Louise
Ousley, Odille 1896-1976 .... *10*
Outcalt, Todd 1960- *123*

Overmyer, James E. 1946- *88*
Overton, Jenny (Margaret Mary) 1942- *52*
  Brief entry *36*
Owen, Ann
  See Qualey, Marsha
Owen, Annie 1949- *75*
Owen, Caroline Dale
  See Snedeker, Caroline Dale (Parke)
Owen, Clifford
  See Hamilton, Charles (Harold St. John)
Owen, Dilys
  See Gater, Dilys
Owen, (Benjamin) Evan 1918-1984 .... *38*
Owen, (John) Gareth 1936-2002 .... *162*
  Earlier sketch in SATA 83
  See also CLR 31
  See also SAAS 14
Owens, Bryant 1968- *116*
Owens, Gail 1939- *54*
Owens, Thomas S(heldon) 1960- *86*
Owens, Tom
  See Owens, Thomas S(heldon)
Oxenbury, Helen 1938- *149*
  Earlier sketches in SATA 3, 68
  See also CLR 70
Oxendine, Bess Holland 1933- *90*
Oz, Frank (Richard) 1944- *60*
Ozer, Jerome S. 1927- *59*

P

Pace, Lorenzo 1943- *131*
Pace, Mildred Mastin 1907- *46*
  Brief entry *29*
Pachter, Hedwig (?)-1988 .... *63*
Pack, Janet 1952- *77*
Pack, Robert 1929- *118*
Packard, Edward 1931- *148*
  Earlier sketches in SATA 47, 90
Packer, Kenneth L. 1946- *116*
Packer, Vin
  See Meaker, Marijane
Pad, Peter
  See Stratemeyer, Edward L.
Page, Eileen
  See Heal, Edith
Page, Eleanor
  See Coerr, Eleanor (Beatrice)
Page, Jake 1936- *81*
Page, James Keena, Jr.
  See Page, Jake
Page, Lou Williams 1912-1997 .... *38*
Page, Mary
  See Heal, Edith
Page, Robin 1943- *154*
Pagnucci, Susan 1944- *90*
Pahz, Cheryl
  See Pahz, Cheryl Suzanne
Pahz, Cheryl Suzanne 1949- *11*
Pahz, James Alon 1943- *11*
Paice, Margaret 1920- *10*
Paige, Harry W(orthington) 1922- *41*
  Brief entry *35*
Paige, Richard
  See Koontz, Dean R.
Paige, Robin
  See Albert, Susan Wittig
Paine, Penelope Colville 1946- *87*
Paine, Roberta M. 1925- *13*
Paisley, Tom 1932- *78*
  See Bethancourt, T. Ernesto
Palatini, Margie *174*
  Earlier sketch in SATA 134
Palazzo, Anthony D.
  See Palazzo, Tony
Palazzo, Tony 1905-1970 .... *3*
Palder, Edward L. 1922- *5*
Palecek, Josef 1932- *56*
Palecek, Libuse 1937- *89*

Palin, Michael (Edward) 1943- 67
　See Monty Python
Palladini, David (Mario) 1946- 40
　Brief entry 32
Pallas, Norvin 1918-1983 23
Pallotta-Chiarolli, Maria 1960- 117
Palmer, Bernard (Alvin) 1914-1998 26
Palmer, C. Everard 1930- 14
Palmer, (Ruth) Candida 1926- 11
Palmer, Cyril Everard
　See Palmer, C. Everard
Palmer, Don
　See Benson, Mildred (Augustine Wirt)
Palmer, Hap 1942- 68
Palmer, Heidi 1948- 15
Palmer, Helen Marion
　See Geisel, Helen
Palmer, Jessica 1953- 120
Palmer, Judd 1972- 153
Palmer, Juliette 1930- 15
Palmer, Kate Salley 1946- 97
Palmer, Maria
　See Brennan, J(ames) H(erbert)
　and Strachan, Ian
Palmer, Robin 1909-2000 43
Paltrowitz, Donna 1950- 61
　Brief entry 50
Paltrowitz, Donna Milman
　See Paltrowitz, Donna
Paltrowitz, Stuart 1946- 61
　Brief entry 50
Pamintuan, Macky 178
Panagopoulos, Janie Lynn 149
Panati, Charles 1943 65
Panchyk, Richard 1970- 138
Panetta, George 1915-1969 15
Panetta, Joseph N. 1953- 96
Panik, Sharon 1952- 82
Panowski, Eileen Thompson 1920- 49
Pansy
　See Alden, Isabella (Macdonald)
Pantell, Dora (Fuchs) 39
Panter, Carol 1936- 9
Paolini, Christopher 1983- 157
　See also CLR 102
Papademetriou, Lisa 175
Papas, Bill
　See Papas, William
Papas, William 1927-2000 50
Papashvily, George 1898-1978 17
Papashvily, Helen (Waite) 1906-1996 17
Pape, D. L.
　See Pape, Donna (Lugg)
Pape, Donna (Lugg) 1930- 82
　Earlier sketch in SATA 2
Paperny, Myra (Green) 1932- 51
　Brief entry 33
Paradis, Adrian A(lexis) 1912- 67
　Earlier sketch in SATA 1
　See also SAAS 8
Paradis, Marjorie Bartholomew
　1886(?)-1970 17
Paradiz, Valerie 1963- 176
Parenteau, Shirley Laurolyn 1935- 47
　Brief entry 40
Parish, Margaret (Cecile) 1927-1988 73
　See Parish, Peggy
Parish, Margaret Holt
　See Holt, Margaret
Parish, Peggy 17
　Obituary 59
　See also CLR 22
　See Parish, Margaret (Cecile)
Park, Barbara 1947- 123
　Brief entry 35
　Earlier sketches in SATA 40, 78
　See also CLR 34
Park, Bill
　See Park, W(illiam) B(ryan)
Park, Frances 1955- 171
Park, Ginger 173

Park, Janie Jaehyun 150
Park, Jordan
　See Kornbluth, C(yril) M.
　and Pohl, Frederik
Park, Linda Sue 1960- 173
　Earlier sketch in SATA 127
　See also CLR 84
Park, Nick 1958- 113
Park, (Rosina) Ruth (Lucia) 1923(?)- 93
　Earlier sketch in SATA 25
　See also CLR 51
Park, W(illiam) B(ryan) 1936- 22
Parke, Marilyn 1928- 82
Parker, Barbara Keevil 1938- 157
Parker, Elinor Milnor 1906- 3
Parker, Julie F. 1961- 92
Parker, Kristy 1957- 59
Parker, Kim 1963- 174
Parker, Lois M(ay) 1912-1996 30
Parker, Margot M. 1937- 52
Parker, Marjorie Blain 1960- 145
Parker, Mary Jessie 1948- 71
Parker, Nancy Winslow 1930- 132
　Earlier sketches in SATA 10, 69
　See also SAAS 20
Parker, Richard 1915-1990 14
Parker, Robert
　See Boyd, Waldo T.
Parker, Toni Trent 1947-2005 142
　Obituary 169
Parkes, Lucas
　See Harris, John (Wyndham Parkes Lucas)
　Beynon
Parkhill, John
　See Cox, William R(obert)
Parkins, David 1955- 176
Parkinson, Ethelyn M(inerva) 1906-1999 11
Parkinson, Kathy 71
　See Parkinson, Kathryn N.
Parkinson, Siobhan
　See Parkinson, Siobhan
Parkinson, Siobhan 1954- 178
Parks, Deborah A. 1948- 133
　Earlier sketch in SATA 91
Parks, Edd Winfield 1906-1968 10
Parks, Gordon 1912-2006 108
　Obituary 175
　Earlier sketch in SATA 8
Parks, Gordon Roger Alexander
　See Parks, Gordon
Parks, Peggy J. 1951- 143
Parks, PJ
　See Parks, Peggy J.
Parks, Rosa 1913-2005 83
　Obituary 169
Parks, Rosa Louise Lee
　See Parks, Rosa
Parks, Van Dyke 1943- 62
Parley, Peter
　See Goodrich, Samuel Griswold
Parlin, John
　See Graves, Charles Parlin
Parnall, Peter 1936- 69
　Earlier sketch in SATA 16
　See also SAAS 11
Parotti, Phillip (Elliott) 1941- 109
Parr, Ann 1943- 144
Parr, Danny
　See Parr, Ann
Parr, Letitia (Evelyn) 1906-1985(?) 37
Parr, Lucy 1924- 10
Parr, Todd 179
　Earlier sketch in SATA 134
Parrish, Anne 1888-1957 27
Parrish, Mary
　See Cousins, Margaret
Parrish, Maxfield
　See Parrish, (Frederick) Maxfield
Parrish, (Frederick) Maxfield 1870-1966 14
Parry, Marian 1924- 13

Parson Lot
　See Kingsley, Charles
Parsons, Alexandra 1947- 92
Parsons, Ellen
　See Dragonwagon, Crescent
Parsons, Martin (Leslie) 1951- 116
Parsons-Yazzi, Evangeline 172
Partch, Virgil Franklin II 1916-1984 39
　Obituary 39
Parton, Dolly 1946- 94
Parton, Dolly Rebecca
　See Parton, Dolly
Partridge, Benjamin W., Jr. 1915-2005 28
　Obituary 163
Partridge, Benjamin Waring, Jr.
　See Partridge, Benjamin W., Jr.
Partridge, Cora Cheney
　See Cheney, Cora
Partridge, Elizabeth 134
Partridge, Jenny (Lilian) 1947- 52
　Brief entry 37
Pasachoff, Naomi 1947- 147
Pascal, David 1918- 14
Pascal, Francine 1938- 143
　Brief entry 37
　Earlier sketches in SATA 51, 80
　See also CLR 25
Paschal, Nancy
　See Trotter, Grace V(iolet)
Paschkis, Julie 1957- 177
Pascudniak, Pascal
　See Lupoff, Richard A(llen)
Pashko, Stanley 1913-1982 29
Passailaigue, Thomas E.
　See Paisley, Tom
Pateman, Robert 1954- 84
Patent, Dorothy Hinshaw 1940- 162
　Autobiography Feature 162
　Earlier sketches in SATA 22, 69, 120
　See also CLR 19
　See also SAAS 13
Paterson, A(ndrew) B(arton) 1864-1941 97
Paterson, Banjo
　See Paterson, A(ndrew) B(arton)
Paterson, Diane 1946- 177
　Brief entry 33
　Earlier sketch in SATA 59
Paterson, John (Barstow) 1932- 114
Paterson, Katherine 1932- 133
　Earlier sketches in SATA 13, 53, 92
　See also CLR 50
Paterson, Katherine Womeldorf
　See Paterson, Katherine
Patience, John 1949- 90
Patneaude, David 1944- 159
　Earlier sketch in SATA 85
Paton, Alan 1903-1988 11
　Obituary 56
Paton, Alan Stewart
　See Paton, Alan
Paton, Jane (Elizabeth) 1934- 35
Paton, Priscilla 1952- 98
Paton Walsh, Gillian
　See Paton Walsh, Jill
Paton Walsh, Jill 1937- 109
　Earlier sketches in SATA 4, 72
　See also CLR 65
　See also SAAS 3
　See Paton Walsh, Gillian
　and Walsh, Jill Paton
Patrick, Susan
　See Clark, Patricia Denise
Patron, Susan 1948- 76
Patsauq, Markoosie 1942-
　See CLR 23
Patschke, Steve 1955- 125
Patten, Brian 1946- 152
　Earlier sketch in SATA 29
Patterson, Charles 1935- 59
Patterson, Geoffrey 1943- 54
　Brief entry 44

Patterson, James 1947- *164*
Patterson, James B.
　See Patterson, James
Patterson, Lillie G. -1999 .... *88*
　Earlier sketch in SATA *14*
Patterson, Nancy Ruth 1944- *148*
　Earlier sketch in SATA *72*
Pattison, Darcy (S.) 1954- *126*
　Earlier sketch in SATA *72*
Pattou, Edith *164*
Patz (Blaustein), Nancy *154*
Paul, Aileen 1917- *12*
Paul, Ann Whitford 1941- *168*
　Earlier sketches in SATA *76, 110*
Paul, Elizabeth
　See Crow, Donna Fletcher
Paul, Hamish Vigne Christie 1951- *151*
　See also CLR *87*
Paul, James 1936- *23*
Paul, Korky
　See Paul, Hamish Vigne Christie
Paul, Robert
　See Roberts, John G(aither)
Paul, Tessa 1944- *103*
Pauli, Hertha (Ernestine) 1909-1973 .... *3*
　Obituary *26*
Paull, Grace A. 1898- *24*
Paulsen, Gary 1939- *158*
　Earlier sketches in SATA *22, 50, 54, 79, 111*
　See also CLR *82*
Paulson, Jack
　See Jackson, C(aary) Paul
Pauquet, Gina Ruck
　See Ruck-Pauquet, Gina
Pausacker, Jenny 1948- *72*
　See also SAAS *23*
Pausewang, Gudrun 1928- *165*
　Earlier sketch in SATA *104*
Pavel, Frances 1907- *10*
Paver, Michelle *170*
Paxton, Tom *70*
　See Paxton, Thomas R.
Payne, Alan
　See Jakes, John
Payne, Bernal C., Jr. 1941- *60*
Payne, C. D. 1949- *133*
Payne, C.F. 1956- *179*
Payne, Chris Fox
　See Payne, C.F.
Payne, Donald Gordon 1924- *37*
Payne, Emmy
　See West, Emily Govan
Payne, Nina *135*
Payne, Rachel Ann
　See Jakes, John
Payson, Dale 1943- *9*
Payzant, Charles *18*
Paz, A.
　See Pahz, James Alon
Paz, Zan
　See Pahz, Cheryl Suzanne
Peace, Mary
　See Finley, Mary Peace
Peake, Mervyn 1911-1968 .... *23*
Peale, Norman Vincent 1898-1993 .... *20*
　Obituary *78*
Pearce, Jacqueline 1962- *146*
Pearce, Margaret *104*
Peare, Catherine Owens 1911- *9*
Pearson, Gayle 1947- *119*
　Earlier sketch in SATA *53*
Pearson, Kit 1947- *77*
　Autobiography Feature *117*
　See also CLR *26*
Pearson, Mary E. 1955- *134*
Pearson, Susan 1946- *166*
　Brief entry *27*
　Earlier sketches in SATA *39, 91*
Pearson, Tracey Campbell 1956- *155*
　Earlier sketch in SATA *64*

Pease, (Clarence) Howard 1894-1974 .... *2*
　Obituary *25*
Peavy, Linda 1943- *54*
Peck, Anne Merriman 1884-1976 .... *18*
Peck, Beth 1957- *79*
Peck, Jan *159*
Peck, Jeanie J. 1967- *147*
Peck, Marshall III 1951- *92*
Peck, Richard 1934- *158*
　Autobiography Feature *110*
　Earlier sketches in SATA *18, 55, 97, 110*
　See also CLR *15*
　See also SAAS *2*
Peck, Richard Wayne
　See Peck, Richard
Peck, Robert Newton 1928- *156*
　Autobiography Feature *108*
　Earlier sketches in SATA *21, 62, 111*
　See also CLR *45*
　See also SAAS *1*
Peck, Sylvia 1953- *133*
Peck-Whiting, Jeanie J.
　See Peck, Jeanie J.
Pederson, Sharleen
　See Collicott, Sharleen
Peebles, Anne
　See Galloway, Priscilla
Peek, Merle 1938- *39*
Peel, John 1954- *79*
Peel, Norman Lemon
　See Hirsch, Phil
Peeples, Edwin A(ugustus, Jr.) 1915-1994 ..... *6*
Peers, Judi 1956- *119*
Peers, Judith May West
　See Peers, Judi
Peet, Bill
　See CLR *12*
　See Peet, William Bartlett
Peet, Creighton B. 1899-1977 .... *30*
Peet, Mal *171*
Peet, Malcolm
　See Peet, Mal
Peet, William Bartlett 1915-2002 .... *78*
　Obituary *137*
　Earlier sketches in SATA *2, 41*
　See Peet, Bill
Peguero, Leone *116*
Pelaez, Jill 1924- *12*
Pelham, David 1938- *70*
Pell, Ed(ward) 1950- *157*
Pellowski, Anne 1933- *20*
Pellowski, Michael (Joseph) 1949- *151*
　Brief entry *48*
　Earlier sketch in SATA *88*
Pellowski, Michael Morgan
　See Pellowski, Michael (Joseph)
Pelta, Kathy 1928- *18*
Peltier, Leslie C(opus) 1900-1980 .... *13*
Pemberton, John Leigh
　See Leigh-Pemberton, John
Pembury, Bill
　See Groom, Arthur William
Pemsteen, Hans
　See Manes, Stephen
Pendennis, Arthur Esquir
　See Thackeray, William Makepeace
Pender, Lydia Podger 1907- *61*
Pendery, Rosemary (Schmitz) *7*
Pendle, Alexy 1943- *29*
Pendleton, Don
　See Cunningham, Chet
　and Garside, (Clifford) Jack
　and Jagninski, Tom
　and Krauzer, Steven M(ark)
　and Obstfeld, Raymond
Pendziwol, Jean E. 1965- *177*
Pene du Bois, William (Sherman)
　1916-1993 .... *68*
　Obituary *74*
　Earlier sketch in SATA *4*
　See also CLR *1*

Penn, Ruth Bonn
　See Rosenberg, Eth(el) Clifford
Pennac, Daniel 1944- *155*
Pennage, E. M.
　See Finkel, George (Irvine)
Penner, Fred 1946- *169*
　Earlier sketch in SATA *67*
Penner, Frederick Ralph Cornelius
　See Penner, Fred
Penney, Grace Jackson 1904-2000 .... *35*
Penney, Ian 1960- *76*
Penney, Sue 1957- *152*
　Earlier sketch in SATA *102*
Pennington, Eunice 1923- *27*
Pennington, Lillian Boyer 1904- *45*
Penrose, Gordon 1925- *66*
Penson, Mary E. 1917- *78*
Penzler, Otto 1942- *38*
Pepe, Phil 1935- *20*
Pepe, Philip
　See Pepe, Phil
Peppe, Rodney (Darrell) 1934- *74*
　Earlier sketch in SATA *4*
　See also SAAS *10*
Percy, Charles Henry
　See Smith, Dorothy Gladys
Percy, Rachel 1930- *63*
Perdrizet, Marie-Pierre 1952- *79*
Perenyi, Constance 1954- *93*
Perenyi, Constance Marie
　See Perenyi, Constance
Perera, Hilda 1926- *105*
Perera, Thomas Biddle 1938- *13*
Peretti, Frank E. 1951- *141*
　Earlier sketch in SATA *80*
Perez, Lana
　See Perez, Marlene
Perez, Marlene *170*
Pericoli, Matteo 1968- *178*
Perkins, Al(bert Rogers) 1904-1975 .... *30*
Perkins, Lucy Fitch 1865-1937 .... *72*
Perkins, Lynne Rae *172*
　Earlier sketch in SATA *131*
Perkins, (Richard) Marlin 1905-1986 .... *21*
　Obituary *48*
Perkins, Mitali 1963- *88*
Perks, Anne-Marie 1955- *122*
Perl, Lila *72*
　Earlier sketch in SATA *6*
Perl, Susan 1922-1983 .... *22*
　Obituary *34*
Perlmutter, O(scar) William 1920-1975 .... *8*
Pernu, Dennis 1970- *87*
Perrault, Charles 1628-1703 .... *25*
　See also CLR *79*
Perret, Gene (Richard) 1937- *76*
Perrine, Mary 1913-1976 .... *2*
Perrins, Lesley 1953- *56*
Perrow, Angeli 1954- *121*
Perry, Andrea 1956- *148*
Perry, Barbara Fisher
　See Fisher, Barbara
Perry, Elizabeth 1959- *174*
Perry, Elizabeth Goodwin
　See Perry, Elizabeth
Perry, Marie Fritz *165*
Perry, Patricia 1949- *30*
Perry, Phyllis J(ean) 1933- *152*
　Earlier sketches in SATA *60, 101*
Perry, Ritchie (John Allen) 1942- *105*
Perry, Roger 1933- *27*
Perry, Steve(n Carl) 1947- *76*
Pershall, Mary K. 1951- *172*
　Earlier sketch in SATA *70*
Pershing, Marie
　See Schultz, Pearle Henriksen
Perske, Robert 1927- *57*
Persun, Morgan Reed
　See Watkins, Dawn L.
Petach, Heidi *149*

Peter
  See Stratemeyer, Edward L.
Peters, Alexander
  See Hollander, Zander
Peters, Andrew Fusek 1965- 169
  Earlier sketch in SATA *107*
Peters, Caroline
  See Betz, Eva Kelly
Peters, David 1954- 72
Peters, Elizabeth
  See Mertz, Barbara
Peters, Emma
  See Price, Karen
Peters, Gabriel
  See Matott, Justin
Peters, Julie Anne 1952- 128
  Earlier sketch in SATA *82*
Peters, Linda
  See Catherall, Arthur
Peters, Lisa Westberg 1951- 161
  Earlier sketches in SATA *74, 115*
Peters, Patricia 1953- 84
Peters, Russell M. 1929- 78
Peters, S. H.
  See Porter, William Sydney
  and Proffitt, Nicholas
Petersen, David 1946- 109
  Earlier sketch in SATA *62*
Petersen, Gwenn Boardman 1924- 61
  See Boardman, Gwenn R.
Petersen, P(eter) J(ames) 1941- 118
  Brief entry 43
  Earlier sketches in SATA *48, 83*
Petersen, Palle 1943- 85
Petersham, Maud (Sylvia Fuller)
  1890-1971 17
  See also CLR *24*
Petersham, Miska 1888-1960 17
  See also CLR *24*
Peterson, Cris 1952- 174
  Earlier sketches in SATA *84, 145*
Peterson, Dawn 1934- 86
Peterson, Esther (Allen) 1934- 35
Peterson, Hans 1922- 8
Peterson, Harold L(eslie) 1922-1978 8
Peterson, Helen Stone 1910- 8
Peterson, Jean Sunde 1941- 108
Peterson, Jeanne Whitehouse 1939- 159
  See Whitehouse, Jeanne
Peterson, Kathleen B. 1951- 119
Peterson, Lorraine 1940- 56
  Brief entry 44
Peterson, Shelley 1952- 146
Petie, Haris 10
  See Petty, Roberta
Petricic, Dusan 1946- 176
Petrides, Heidrun 1944- 19
Petrie, Catherine 1947- 52
  Brief entry 41
Petroski, Catherine (Ann Groom) 1939- 48
Petrovich, Michael B(oro) 1922- 40
Petrovskaya, Kyra
  See Wayne, Kyra Petrovskaya
Petruccio, Steven James 1961- 67
Petry, Ann (Lane) 1908-1997 5
  Obituary ...., 94
  See also CLR *12*
Pettit, Jayne 1932- 108
Pevsner, Stella 131
  Earlier sketches in SATA *8, 77*
  See also SAAS *14*
Peyo
  See Culliford, Pierre
Peyton, K. M.
  See CLR *3*
  See also SAAS *17*
  See Peyton, Kathleen Wendy (Herald)
Peyton, Kathleen Wendy (Herald) 1929- 157
  Earlier sketches in SATA *15, 62*
  See Peyton, K. M.
Pfanner, (Anne) Louise 1955- 68

Pfeffer, Susan Beth 1948- 83
  Earlier sketch in SATA *4*
  See also CLR *11*
  See also SAAS *17*
Pfeffer, Wendy 1929- 142
  Earlier sketch in SATA *78*
Pfeiffer, Janet (B.) 1949- 96
Pfister, Marcus 150
  Earlier sketch in SATA *83*
  See also CLR *42*
Pfitsch, Patricia Curtis 1948- 148
Pflieger, Pat 1955- 84
Pham, LeUyen 1973- 175
Phelan, Mary Kay 1914- 3
Phelan, Matt 1970- 172
Phelan, Terry Wolfe 1941- 56
Phelps, Ethel Johnston 1914-1984 35
Philbrick, Rodman 1951- 163
  Earlier sketch in SATA *122*
  See Philbrick, W. R.
Philbrick, W. R. 163
  See Philbrick, Rodman
Philbrick, W. Rodman
  See Philbrick, Rodman
Philbrook, Clem(ent E.) 1917- 24
Phillips, Aileen Paul
  See Paul, Aileen
Phillips, Betty Lou
  See Phillips, Elizabeth Louise
Phillips, Bob 1940- 95
Phillips, Douglas A. 1949- 161
Phillips, Elizabeth Louise 58
  Brief entry 48
Phillips, Irv(ing W.) 1905-2000 11
  Obituary 125
Phillips, Jack
  See Sandburg, Carl (August)
Phillips, Leon
  See Gerson, Noel Bertram
Phillips, Loretta (Hosey) 1893-1987 10
Phillips, Louis 1942- 102
  Earlier sketch in SATA *8*
Phillips, Mary Geisler 1881-1964 10
Phillips, Michael
  See Nolan, William F(rancis)
Phillips, (Woodward) Prentice 1894-1981 10
Phillpotts, Eden 1862-1960 24
Phin
  See Thayer, Ernest Lawrence
Phipson, Joan
  See CLR *5*
  See also SAAS *3*
  See Fitzhardinge, Joan Margaret
Phiz
  See Browne, Hablot Knight
Phleger, Fred B. 1909-1993 34
Phleger, Marjorie Temple 1908(?)-1986 1
  Obituary 47
Piatti, Celestino 1922- 16
Picard, Barbara Leonie 1917- 89
  Earlier sketch in SATA *2*
  See also SAAS *10*
Pichon, Liz 174
Pickard, Charles 1932- 36
Pickering, James Sayre 1897-1969 36
  Obituary 28
Pickering, Robert B. 1950- 93
Pielichaty, Helena 1955- 142
Pienkowski, Jan (Michal) 1936- 131
  Earlier sketches in SATA *6, 58*
  See also CLR *6*
Pierce, Edith Gray 1893-1977 45
Pierce, Katherine
  See St. John, Wylly Folk
Pierce, Meredith Ann 1958- 127
  Brief entry 48
  Earlier sketch in SATA *67*
  See also CLR *20*
Pierce, Ruth (Ireland) 1936- 5
Pierce, Sharon
  See McCullough, Sharon Pierce

Pierce, Tamora 1954- 153
  Brief entry 49
  Earlier sketches in SATA *51, 96*
Pierce, Terry 178
Pierik, Robert 1921- 13
Piers, Robert
  See Anthony, Piers
Pig, Edward
  See Gorey, Edward (St. John)
Pike, Bob
  See Pike, Robert W(ilson)
Pike, Christopher
  See McFadden, Kevin Christopher
Pike, Deborah 1951- 89
Pike, E(dgar) Royston 1896-1980 22
  Obituary 56
Pike, R. William 1956- 92
Pike, Robert W(ilson) 1931- 102
Pilarski, Laura 1926- 13
Pilgrim, Anne
  See Allan, Mabel Esther
Pilkey, Dav 1966- 166
  Earlier sketches in SATA *68, 115*
  See also CLR *48*
Pilkey, David Murray, Jr.
  See Pilkey, Dav
Pilkington, Francis Meredyth 1907- 4
Pilkington, Roger (Windle) 1915-2003 10
  Obituary 144
Pincus, Harriet 1938- 27
Pinczes, Elinor J(ane) 1940- 81
Pine, Nicholas 1951- 91
Pine, Tillie S(chloss) 1896-1999 13
Pini, Richard (Alan) 1950- 89
Pini, Wendy 1951- 89
Pinkett, Jada
  See Smith, Jada Pinkett
Pinkney, Andrea Davis 1963- 160
  Earlier sketch in SATA *113*
Pinkney, (Jerry) Brian 1961- 148
  Earlier sketch in SATA *74*
  See also CLR *54*
Pinkney, Gloria Jean 1941- 85
Pinkney, J. Brian
  See Pinkney, (Jerry) Brian
Pinkney, Jerry 1939- 151
  Brief entry 32
  Earlier sketches in SATA *41, 71, 107*
  See also CLR *43*
  See also SAAS *12*
Pinkney, John 97
Pinkney, Sandra L. 128
Pinkwater, D. Manus
  See Pinkwater, Daniel Manus
Pinkwater, Daniel
  See Pinkwater, Daniel Manus
Pinkwater, Daniel M.
  See Pinkwater, Daniel Manus
Pinkwater, Daniel Manus 1941- 158
  Earlier sketches in SATA *8, 46, 76, 114*
  See also CLR *4*
  See also SAAS *3*
Pinkwater, Manus
  See Pinkwater, Daniel Manus
Pinner, Joma
  See Werner, Herma
Pioneer
  See Yates, Raymond F(rancis)
Piowaty, Kim Kennelly 1957- 49
Piper, Roger
  See Fisher, John (Oswald Hamilton)
Pirner, Connie White 1955- 72
Piro, Richard 1934- 7
Pirot, Alison Lohans
  See Lohans, Alison
Pirsig, Robert M(aynard) 1928- 39
Pita
  See Rendon, Maria
Pitcher, Caroline (Nell) 1948- 128
Pitre, Felix 1949- 84
Pitrone, Jean Maddern 1920- 4

Pittman, Helena Clare 1945- 71
Pitz, Henry C(larence) 1895-1976 4
    Obituary 24
Piven, Hanoch 1963- 173
Pizer, Vernon 1918- 21
Place, Marian T(empleton) 1910- 3
Place, Robin (Mary) 1926- 71
Plaidy, Jean
    See Hibbert, Eleanor Alice Burford
Plain, Belva 1919- 62
Plath, Sylvia 1932-1963 96
Platt, Kin 1911- 86
    Earlier sketch in SATA *21*
    See also SAAS *17*
Platt, Randall 1948- 95
Platt, Randall Beth
    See Platt, Randall
Platt, Richard 1953- 166
    Earlier sketch in SATA *120*
Playfellow, Robin
    See Ellis, Edward S(ylvester)
Playsted, James
    See Wood, James Playsted
Plecas, Jennifer 1966- 149
    Earlier sketch in SATA *84*
Plimpton, George 1927-2003 10
    Obituary 150
Plimpton, George Ames
    See Plimpton, George
Plomer, William Charles Franklin
    1903-1973 24
Plotz, Helen Ratnoff 1913-2000 38
Plourde, Lynn 1955- 168
    Earlier sketch in SATA *122*
Plowden, David 1932- 52
Plowden, Martha Ward 1948- 98
Plowhead, Ruth Gipson 1877-1967 43
Plowman, Stephanie 1922- 6
Pluckrose, Henry (Arthur) 1931- 141
    Earlier sketch in SATA *13*
Plum, J.
    See Wodehouse, P(elham) G(renville)
Plum, Jennifer
    See Kurland, Michael
Plume, Ilse 170
    Brief entry 43
Plumme, Don E.
    See Katz, Bobbi
Plummer, Margaret 1911- 2
Pochocki, Ethel (Frances) 1925- 76
Podendorf, Illa (E.) 1903(?)-1983 18
    Obituary 35
Podwal, Mark 1945- 160
    Earlier sketch in SATA *101*
Poe, Edgar Allan 1809-1849 23
Poe, Ty (Christopher) 1975- 94
Pogany, William Andrew 1882-1955 44
    See Pogany, Willy
Pogany, Willy
    Brief entry 30
    See Pogany, William Andrew
Pohl, Frederik 1919- 24
Pohlmann, Lillian (Grenfell) 1902-1997 11
Pohrt, Tom 1953- 152
    Earlier sketch in SATA *67*
Pointon, Robert
    See Rooke, Daphne (Marie)
Points, Larry G. 1945- 177
    Earlier sketch in SATA *133*
Points, Larry Gene
    See Points, Larry G.
Pokeberry, P. J.
    See Mitchell, B(etty) J(o)
POLA
    See Watson, Pauline
Polacco, Patricia Ann 1944- 123
    Earlier sketch in SATA *74*
    See also CLR *40*
Polak, Monique 1960- 178
Polatnick, Florence T. 1923- 5

Polder, Markus
    See Kruss, James
Polese, Carolyn 1947- 58
Polese, James 1914- 87
Polette, Nancy (Jane) 1930- 42
Polhamus, Jean Burt 1928- 21
Policoff, Stephen Phillip 1948- 77
Polikoff, Barbara G. 1929- 162
    Earlier sketch in SATA *77*
Polikoff, Barbara Garland
    See Polikoff, Barbara G.
Polisar, Barry Louis 1954- 134
    Earlier sketch in SATA *77*
Politi, Leo 1908-1996 47
    Obituary 88
    Earlier sketch in SATA *1*
    See also CLR *29*
Polking, Kirk 1925- 5
Pollack, Jill S. 1963- 88
Polland, Barbara K(ay) 1939- 44
Polland, Madeleine A(ngela Cahill) 1918- ... 68
    Earlier sketch in SATA *6*
    See also SAAS *8*
Pollema-Cahill, Phyllis 1958- 123
Pollock, Bruce 1945- 46
Pollock, Mary
    See Blyton, Enid (Mary)
Pollock, Penny 1935- 137
    Brief entry 42
    Earlier sketch in SATA *44*
Pollowitz, Melinda Kilborn 1944- 26
Polner, Murray 1928- 64
Polonsky, Arthur 1925- 34
Polseno, Jo 17
Pomaska, Anna 1946- 117
Pomerantz, Charlotte 1930- 177
    Earlier sketches in SATA *20, 80*
Pomeroy, Pete
    See Roth, Arthur J(oseph)
Pond, Alonzo W(illiam) 1894-1986 5
Pontiflet, Ted 1932- 32
Poole, Gray Johnson 1906- 1
Poole, Josephine 5
    See also SAAS *2*
    See Helyar, Jane Penelope Josephine
Poole, (Jane Penelope) Josephine
    See Helyar, Jane Penelope Josephine
Poole, Lynn 1910-1969 1
Poole, Peggy 1925- 39
Poortvliet, Rien 1932- 65
    Brief entry 37
Pope, Elizabeth Marie 1917- 38
    Brief entry 36
Popescu, Christine
    See Pullein-Thompson, Christine
Poploff, Michelle 1956- 67
Popp, K. Wendy 91
Poppel, Hans 1942- 71
Portal, Colette 1936- 6
Porte, Barbara Ann 1943- 152
    Brief entry 45
    Earlier sketches in SATA *57, 93*
Porter, A(nthony) P(eyton) 1945- 68
Porter, Connie (Rose) 1959(?)- 129
    Earlier sketch in SATA *81*
Porter, Donald Clayton
    See Gerson, Noel Bertram
Porter, Eleanor H(odgman) 1868-1920
    See CLR *110*
Porter, Gene(va Grace) Stratton
    See Stratton-Porter, Gene(va Grace)
Porter, Janice Lee 1953- 108
    Earlier sketch in SATA *68*
Porter, Katherine Anne 1890-1980 39
    Obituary 23
Porter, Kathryn
    See Swinford, Betty (June Wells)
Porter, Sheena 1935- 24
    See also SAAS *10*
Porter, Sue
    See Limb, Sue

Porter, Sue 1951- 76
Porter, William Sydney 1862-1910
    See YABC 2
    See Henry, O.
Porto, Tony 1960- 153
Posell, Elsa Z(eigerman) -1995 3
Posten, Margaret L(ois) 1915- 10
Posthuma, Sieb 1960- 150
Potok, Chaim 1929-2002 106
    Obituary 134
    Earlier sketch in SATA *33*
    See also CLR *92*
Potok, Herbert Harold -2002
    See Potok, Chaim
Potok, Herman Harold
    See Potok, Chaim
Potter, Beatrix 1866-1943 132
    Earlier sketch in SATA *100*
    See also YABC *1*
    See also CLR *73*
Potter, Giselle 150
Potter, Helen Beatrix
    See Potter, Beatrix
Potter, Margaret (Newman) 1926-1998 21
    Obituary 104
    See Betteridge, Anne
Potter, Marian 1915- 9
Potter, Miriam Clark 1886-1965 3
Poulin, Stephane 1961- 98
    See also CLR *28*
Poulton, Kimberly 1957(?)- 136
Pournelle, Jerry (Eugene) 1933- 161
    Earlier sketches in SATA *26, 91*
Povelite, Kay 1955- 102
Pow, Tom 1950- 163
Powe-Allred, Alexandra
    See Allred, Alexandra Powe
Powell, A. M.
    See Morgan, Alfred P(owell)
Powell, Consie 174
Powell, E. Sandy 1947- 72
Powell, E.S.
    See Powell, E. Sandy
Powell, Pamela 1960- 78
Powell, Patricia Hruby 1966- 136
Powell, Randy 1956- 118
Powell, Richard Stillman
    See Barbour, Ralph Henry
Powell, Robert (Stephenson Smyth) Baden
    See Baden-Powell, Robert (Stephenson
    Smyth)
Powell, Stephanie 1953- 93
Power, Margaret (M.) 1945- 125
    Earlier sketch in SATA *75*
Powers, Anne
    See Schwartz, Anne Powers
Powers, Bill 1931- 52
    Brief entry 31
Powers, Daniel 1959- 164
Powers, Margaret
    See Heal, Edith
Powers, Tim 1952- 107
Powers, Timothy Thomas
    See Powers, Tim
Powledge, Fred 1935- 37
Poynter, Margaret 1927- 27
Prachaticka, Marketa
    See Kolibalova, Marketa
Prachatika, Marketa
    See Kolibalova, Marketa
Prager, Arthur 44
Prager, Ellen J. 1962- 136
Prange, Beckie 172
Prap, Lila 1955- 177
Pratchett, Terry 1948- 139
    Earlier sketch in SATA *82*
    See also CLR *64*
Prater, John 1947- 149
    Earlier sketches in SATA *72, 103*
Pratt, (Murray) Fletcher 1897-1956 102
Pratt, Kristin Joy 1976- 87

Pratt, Pierre 1962- *166*
  Earlier sketch in SATA *95*
Preiss, Byron 1953-2005 .... *166*
  Brief entry *42*
  Earlier sketch in SATA *47*
Preiss, Byron Cary
  See Preiss, Byron
Preller, James 1961- *88*
Prelutsky, Jack 1940- *171*
  Earlier sketches in SATA *22, 66, 118*
  See also CLR *115*
Prentice, Amy
  See Kaler, James Otis
Prescott, Casey
  See Morris, Chris(topher Crosby)
Presnall, Judith (Ann) Janda 1943- *96*
Pressler, Mirjam 1940- *155*
Preston, Douglas 1956- *113*
Preston, Edna Mitchell *40*
Preston, Lillian Elvira 1918- *47*
Preussler, Otfried 1923- *24*
Price, Beverley Joan 1931- *98*
Price, Christine (Hilda) 1928-1980 .... *3*
  Obituary *23*
Price, Jennifer
  See Hoover, Helen (Drusilla Blackburn)
Price, Joan 1931- *124*
Price, Jonathan (Reeve) 1941- *46*
Price, Karen 1957- *125*
Price, Kathy Z. 1957- *172*
Price, Lucie Locke
  See Locke, Lucie
Price, Olive 1903-1991 .... *8*
Price, Susan 1955- *128*
  Earlier sketches in SATA *25, 85*
Price, Willard 1887-1983 .... *48*
  Brief entry *38*
Price-Groff, Claire *127*
Priceman, Marjorie 1958- *168*
  Earlier sketches in SATA *81, 120*
Prichard, Katharine Susannah 1883-1969 ..... *66*
Prideaux, Tom 1908-1993 .... *37*
  Obituary *76*
Priestley, Alice 1962- *95*
Priestley, Lee (Shore) 1904-1999 .... *27*
Priestly, Doug 1954- *122*
Priestly, Douglas Michael
  See Priestly, Doug
Prieto, Mariana Beeching 1912-1999 .... *8*
Primavera, Elise 1954- *109*
  Brief entry *48*
  Earlier sketch in SATA *58*
Prime, Derek (James) 1931- *34*
Prince, Alison (Mary) 1931- *86*
  Earlier sketch in SATA *28*
Prince, J(ack) H(arvey) 1908- *17*
Prince, Maggie *102*
Pringle, Eric *138*
Pringle, Laurence P(atrick) 1935- *154*
  Earlier sketches in SATA *4, 68, 104*
  See also CLR *57*
  See also SAAS *6*
Prinz, Yvonne 1960- *175*
Prior, Natalie Jane 1963- *106*
Pritchett, Elaine H(illyer) 1920- *36*
Pritchett, Laura 1971- *178*
Pritchett, Laura Rose
  See Pritchett, Laura
Pritts, Kim Derek 1953- *83*
Prochazkova, Iva 1953- *68*
Proctor, Everitt
  See Montgomery, Rutherford George
Proeysen, Alf 1914-1970
  See CLR *24*
  See Proysen, Alf
Professor Scribbler
  See Hollingsworth, Mary
Proimos, James 1955- *173*
Prose, Francine 1947- *149*
  Earlier sketch in SATA *101*

Provensen, Alice 1918- *147*
  Earlier sketches in SATA *9, 70*
  See also CLR *11*
Provensen, Martin (Elias) 1916-1987 .... *70*
  Obituary *51*
  Earlier sketch in SATA *9*
  See also CLR *11*
Provenzo, Eugene (F., Jr.) 1949- *142*
  Earlier sketch in SATA *78*
Provost, Gail Levine 1944- *65*
Provost, Gary (Richard) 1944-1995 .... *66*
Proysen, Alf *67*
  See Proeysen, Alf
Pruett, Candace (J.) 1968- *157*
Pryor, Bonnie H. 1942- *69*
Pryor, Boori (Monty) 1950- *112*
Pryor, Helen Brenton 1897-1972 .... *4*
Pryor, Michael 1957- *153*
Pucci, Albert John 1920- *44*
Pudney, John (Sleigh) 1909-1977 .... *24*
Pugh, Ellen (Tiffany) 1920- *7*
Pullein-Thompson, Christine 1925-2005 .... *82*
  Obituary *172*
  Earlier sketch in SATA *3*
Pullein-Thompson, Diana *3*
  See Farr, Diana (Pullein-Thompson)
Pullein-Thompson, Josephine (Mary
  Wedderburn) *82*
  Earlier sketch in SATA *3*
Pullman, Philip 1946- *150*
  Earlier sketches in SATA *65, 103*
  See also CLR *84*
  See also SAAS *17*
Pullman, Philip Nicholas
  See Pullman, Philip
Pulver, Harry, Jr. 1960- *129*
Pulver, Robin 1945- *133*
  Earlier sketch in SATA *76*
Puner, Helen W(alker) 1915-1989 .... *37*
  Obituary *63*
Purdy, Carol 1943- *120*
  Earlier sketch in SATA *66*
Purdy, Susan G(old) 1939- *8*
Purmell, Ann 1953- *147*
Purnell, Idella 1901-1982 .... *120*
Purscell, Phyllis 1934- *7*
Purtill, Richard L. 1931- *53*
Pushker, Gloria 1927- *162*
  Earlier sketch in SATA *75*
Pushker, Gloria Teles
  See Pushker, Gloria
Pushkin, Aleksandr Sergeevich
  See Pushkin, Alexander (Sergeyevich)
Pushkin, Alexander (Sergeyevich)
  1799-1837 .... *61*
  See Pushkin, Aleksandr Sergeevich
Putnam, Alice 1916- *61*
Putnam, Arthur Lee
  See Alger, Horatio, Jr.
Putnam, Peter B(rock) 1920-1998 .... *30*
  Obituary *106*
Puttock, Simon *178*
Pyle, Howard 1853-1911 .... *100*
  Earlier sketch in SATA *16*
  See also CLR *117*
Pyle, Katharine 1863-1938 .... *66*
Pyne, Mable Mandeville 1903-1969 .... *9*
Pyrnelle, Louise-Clarke 1850-1907 .... *114*

Q

Quackenbush, Robert M(ead) 1929- *133*
  Autobiography Feature *133*
  Earlier sketches in SATA *7, 70*
  See also CLR *122*
  See also SAAS *7*
Qualey, Marsha 1953- *124*
  Earlier sketch in SATA *79*
Qualls, Sean *177*

Quammen, David 1948- *7*
Quark, Jason
  See Eldin, Peter
Quarles, Benjamin (Arthur) 1904-1996 .... *12*
Quatermass, Martin
  See Carpenter, John (Howard)
Quattlebaum, Mary 1958- *134*
  Earlier sketch in SATA *88*
Quay, Emma *173*
  Earlier sketch in SATA *119*
Queen, Ellery
  See Deming, Richard
  and Dannay, Frederic
  and Davidson, Avram (James)
  and Fairman, Paul W.
  and Flora, Fletcher
  and Hoch, Edward D(entinger)
  and Kane, Henry
  and Lee, Manfred B.
  and Marlowe, Stephen
  and Powell, (Oval) Talmage
  and Sheldon, Walter J(ames)
  and Sturgeon, Theodore (Hamilton)
  and Tracy, Don(ald Fiske)
  and Vance, Jack
Queen, Ellery, Jr.
  See Dannay, Frederic
  and Holding, James (Clark Carlisle, Jr.)
  and Lee, Manfred B.
Quennell, Marjorie Courtney 1884-1972 ...... *29*
Quentin, Brad
  See Bisson, Terry
Quest, (Edna) Olga W(ilbourne) Hall
  See Hall-Quest, (Edna) Olga W(ilbourne)
Quick, Annabelle 1922-1986 .... *2*
Quill, Monica
  See McInerny, Ralph
Quin-Harkin, Janet 1941- *165*
  Earlier sketches in SATA *18, 90, 119*
Quin-Harkin, Janet Elizabeth
  See Quin-Harkin, Janet
Quinlan, Susan E. 1954- *88*
Quinlan, Susan Elizabeth
  See Quinlan, Susan E.
Quinn, Elisabeth 1881-1962 .... *22*
Quinn, Pat 1947- *130*
Quinn, Patrick 1950- *73*
Quinn, Rob 1972- *138*
Quinn, Theodora K.
  See Kroeber, Theodora (Kracaw)
Quinn, Vernon
  See Quinn, Elisabeth
Quirk, Anne (E.) 1956- *99*
Quixley, Jim 1931- *56*
Quyth, Gabriel
  See Jennings, Gary (Gayne)

R

Ra, Carol F. 1939- *76*
Raab, Evelyn 1951- *129*
Rabe, Berniece (Louise) 1928- *148*
  Autobiography Feature *148*
  Earlier sketches in SATA *7, 77*
  See also SAAS *10*
Rabe, Olive H(anson) (?)-1968 .... *13*
Rabin, Staton 1958- *162*
  Earlier sketch in SATA *84*
Rabinowich, Ellen 1946- *29*
Rabinowitz, Sandy 1954- *52*
  Brief entry *39*
Rachlin, Carol K(ing) 1919- *64*
Rachlin, Harvey 1951- *47*
Rachlin, Harvey Brant
  See Rachlin, Harvey
Rachlin, Nahid *64*
Rackham, Arthur 1867-1939 .... *100*
  Earlier sketch in SATA *15*
  See also CLR *57*

Raczka, Bob 1963- *163*
Radencich, Marguerite C. 1952-1998 .... *79*
Radford, Ruby L(orraine) 1891-1971 .... *6*
Radin, Ruth Yaffe 1938- *107*
Brief entry *52*
Earlier sketch in SATA *56*
Radlauer, David 1952- *28*
Radlauer, Edward 1921- *15*
Radlauer, Ruth Shaw 1926- *98*
Earlier sketch in SATA *15*
Radley, Gail 1951- *112*
Earlier sketch in SATA *25*
Radunsky, Vladimir *177*
Rae, Gwynedd 1892-1977 .... *37*
Raebeck, Lois 1921- *5*
Rael, Elsa Okon 1927-
See CLR *84*
Raffi
See Cavoukian, Raffi
Raftery, Gerald (Bransfield) 1905-1986 .... *11*
Ragan-Reid, Gale 1956- *90*
Rahaman, Vashanti 1953- *98*
Rahn, Joan Elma 1929- *27*
Rai, Bali 1971- *152*
Raible, Alton (Robert) 1918- *35*
Raiff, Stan 1930- *11*
Raines, Shirley C(arol) 1945- *128*
Rainey, W. B.
See Blassingame, Wyatt Rainey
Rake, Jody 1961- *157*
Ralston, Jan
See Dunlop, Agnes M. R.
Ramal, Walter
See de la Mare, Walter (John)
Ramanujan, A(ttipat) K(rishnaswami)
1929-1993 .... *86*
Ramstad, Ralph L. 1919- *115*
Rana, Indi
See Rana, Indira Higham
Rana, Indira Higham 1944- *82*
Ranadive, Gail 1944- *10*
Rand, Ann (Binkley) *30*
Rand, Gloria 1925- *156*
Earlier sketch in SATA *101*
Rand, Paul 1914-1996 .... *6*
Randall, Carrie
See Ransom, Candice F.
Randall, David 1972- *167*
Randall, Florence Engel 1917-1997 .... *5*
Randall, Janet
See Young, Janet Randall
and Young, Robert W(illiam)
Randall, Robert
See Garrett, (Gordon) Randall (Phillip)
and Silverberg, Robert
Randall, Ruth (Elaine) Painter 1892-1971 ..... *3*
Randell, Beverley
See Price, Beverley Joan
Randle, Kristen D. 1952- *92*
Autobiography Feature *119*
See also SAAS *24*
Randle, Kristen Downey
See Randle, Kristen D.
Randolph, Boynton M.D.
See Ellis, Edward S(ylvester)
Randolph, Ellen
See Rawn, Melanie
Randolph, Geoffrey
See Ellis, Edward S(ylvester)
Randolph, J. H.
See Ellis, Edward S(ylvester)
Randolph, Lieutenant J. H.
See Ellis, Edward S(ylvester)
Rands, William Brighty 1823-1882 .... *17*
Raney, Ken 1953- *74*
Rankin, Joan 1940- *148*
Earlier sketch in SATA *88*
Rankin, Laura 1953(?)- *176*
Ranney, Agnes V. 1916-1985 .... *6*

Ransom, Candice F. 1952- *135*
Brief entry *49*
Earlier sketches in SATA *52, 89*
Ransome, Arthur (Michell) 1884-1967 .... *22*
See also CLR *8*
Ransome, James E. 1961- *178*
Earlier sketches in SATA *76, 123*
See also CLR *86*
Rant, Tol E.
See Longyear, Barry B(rookes)
Raphael, Elaine *23*
See Bolognese, Elaine (Raphael Chionchio)
Rapp, Adam 1968(?)- *148*
Rappaport, Doreen *151*
Rappaport, Eva 1924- *6*
Rappoport, Ken 1935- *167*
Earlier sketch in SATA *89*
Rarick, Carrie 1911-2002 .... *41*
Raschka, Chris 1959- *166*
Earlier sketches in SATA *80, 117*
Raschka, Christopher
See Raschka, Chris
Rascol, Sabina I. *159*
Rash, Andy *162*
Raskin, Edith Lefkowitz 1908-1987 .... *9*
Raskin, Ellen 1928-1984 .... *139*
Earlier sketches in SATA *2, 38*
See also CLR *12*
Raskin, Joseph 1897-1982 .... *12*
Obituary *29*
Rathjen, Carl Henry 1909-1984 .... *11*
Rathmann, Peggy 1953- *157*
Earlier sketch in SATA *94*
See Crosby, Margaret
Ratliff, Thomas M. 1948- *118*
Rattigan, Jama Kim 1951- *99*
Ratto, Linda Lee 1952- *79*
Rattray, Simon
See Trevor, Elleston
Ratz de Tagyos, Paul 1958- *76*
Rau, Dana Meachen 1971- *167*
Earlier sketch in SATA *94*
Rau, Margaret 1913- *168*
Earlier sketch in SATA *9*
See also CLR *8*
Raucher, Herman 1928- *8*
Raum, Elizabeth 1949- *155*
RavenWolf, Silver 1956- *155*
Ravielli, Anthony 1916-1997 .... *3*
Obituary *95*
Ravilious, Robin 1944- *77*
Rawding, F(rederick) W(illiam) 1930- *55*
Rawlings, Marjorie Kinnan 1896-1953 ...... *100*
See also YABC *1*
See also CLR *63*
Rawlinson, Julia *175*
Rawls, (Woodrow) Wilson 1913-1984 .... *22*
See also CLR *81*
Rawlyk, George Alexander 1935- *64*
Rawn, Melanie 1954- *98*
Rawn, Melanie Robin
See Rawn, Melanie
Ray, Carl 1943-1978 .... *63*
Ray, Deborah *8*
See Kogan Ray, Deborah
Ray, Delia 1963- *179*
Earlier sketch in SATA *70*
Ray, Irene
See Sutton, Margaret Beebe
Ray, Jane 1960- *152*
Earlier sketch in SATA *72*
Ray, JoAnne 1935- *9*
Ray, Mary (Eva Pedder) 1932- *127*
Earlier sketch in SATA *2*
Ray, Mary Lyn 1946- *154*
Earlier sketch in SATA *90*
Rayban, Chloe 1944- *167*
Rayevsky, Robert 1955- *81*
Raymond, Robert
See Alter, Robert Edmond
Rayner, Hugh *151*

Rayner, Mary 1933- *87*
Earlier sketch in SATA *22*
See also CLR *41*
Rayner, Shoo
See Rayner, Hugh
Rayner, William 1929- *55*
Brief entry *36*
Raynor, Dorka *28*
Rayson, Steven 1932- *30*
Razzell, Arthur (George) 1925- *11*
Razzell, Mary (Catherine) 1930- *102*
Razzi, James 1931- *10*
Read, Elfreida 1920- *2*
Read, Nicholas 1956- *146*
Read, Piers Paul 1941- *21*
Reade, Deborah 1949- *69*
Reader, Dennis 1929- *71*
Reading, Richard P(atrick) 1962- *161*
Readman, Jo 1958- *89*
Ready, Kirk L(ewis) 1943- *39*
Reaney, James 1926- *43*
Reaver, Chap 1935-1993 .... *69*
Obituary *77*
Reaver, Herbert R.
See Reaver, Chap
Reaves, J. Michael
See Reaves, (James) Michael
Reaves, (James) Michael 1950- *99*
Redding, Robert Hull 1919- *2*
Redekopp, Elsa *61*
Redway, Ralph
See Hamilton, Charles (Harold St. John)
Redway, Ridley
See Hamilton, Charles (Harold St. John)
Reece, Colleen L. 1935- *116*
Reece, Gabrielle 1970- *108*
Reed, Betty Jane 1921- *4*
Reed, E.
See Evans, Mari
Reed, Gwendolyn E(lizabeth) 1932- *21*
Reed, Kit 1932- *116*
Earlier sketch in SATA *34*
Reed, Lynn Rowe *171*
Reed, Neil 1961- *99*
Reed, Talbot Baines 1852-1893
See CLR *76*
Reed, Thomas (James) 1947- *34*
Reed, William Maxwell 1871-1962 .... *15*
Reeder, Carolyn 1937- *97*
Earlier sketch in SATA *66*
See also CLR *69*
Reeder, Colin (Dawson) 1938- *74*
Reeder, Colonel Red
See Reeder, Russell P(otter), Jr.
Reeder, Russell P(otter), Jr. 1902-1998 .... *4*
Obituary *101*
Reeder, Stephanie Owen 1951- *102*
Reed-Jones, Carol 1955- *112*
Reef, Catherine 1951- *128*
Earlier sketch in SATA *73*
Reekie, Jocelyn (Margaret) 1947- *145*
Reeman, Douglas Edward 1924- *63*
Brief entry *28*
Rees, Celia 1949- *124*
Rees, David (Bartlett) 1936-1993 .... *69*
Obituary *76*
Earlier sketch in SATA *36*
See also SAAS *5*
Rees, Douglas 1947- *169*
Rees, Ennis (Samuel, Jr.) 1925- *3*
Rees, (George) Leslie (Clarence)
1905-2000 .... *105*
Obituary *135*
Reese, Bob
See Reese, Robert A.
Reese, Della 1931(?)- *114*
Reese, Lyn
See Reese, Carolyn Johnson
Reese, Robert A. 1938- *60*
Brief entry *53*
Reese, (John) Terence 1913-1996 .... *59*

Reeve, Joel
  See Cox, William R(obert)
Reeve, Kirk 1934- 117
Reeve, Philip 170
Reeves, Faye Couch 1953- 76
Reeves, James 15
  See Reeves, John Morris
Reeves, Jeni 1947- 111
Reeves, John Morris 1909-1978 87
  See Reeves, James
Reeves, Joyce 1911- 17
Reeves, Lawrence F. 1926- 29
Reeves, Ruth Ellen
  See Ranney, Agnes V.
Regan, Dian Curtis 1950- 149
  Autobiography Feature 149
  Earlier sketches in SATA *75, 133*
Regehr, Lydia 1903-1991 37
Reger, James P. 1952- 106
Reggiani, Renee 1925- 18
Rehm, Karl M. 1935- 72
Reich, Ali
  See Katz, Bobbi
Reich, Susanna 1954- 113
Reiche, Dietlof 1941- 159
Reichert, Mickey Zucker
  See Reichert, Miriam Zucker
Reichert, Miriam Zucker 1962- 85
Reichert, Renee 172
Reichhold, Jane(t E.) 1937- 147
Reid, Alastair 1926- 46
Reid, Barbara 1922- 21
Reid, Barbara (Jane) 1957- 93
  See also CLR *64*
Reid, Desmond
  See Moorcock, Michael
  and McNeilly, Wilfred (Glassford)
Reid, Eugenie Chazal 1924- 12
Reid, John Calvin 21
Reid, (Thomas) Mayne 1818-1883 24
Reid, Meta Mayne 1905-1991 58
  Brief entry 36
Reid, Robin (Nicole) 1969- 145
Reid Banks, Lynne 1929- 165
  Earlier sketches in SATA *22, 75, 111*
  See also CLR *24*
  See Banks, Lynne Reid
Reider, Katja 1960- 126
Reid Jenkins, Debra 1955- 87
Reiff, Stephanie Ann 1948- 47
  Brief entry 28
Reig, June 1933- 30
Reigot, Betty Polisar 1924- 55
  Brief entry 41
Reim, Melanie (K.) 1956- 104
Reinach, Jacquelyn (Krasne) 1930-2000 28
Reiner, Carl 1922- 151
Reiner, William B(uck) 1910-1976 46
  Obituary 30
Reinfeld, Fred 1910-1964 3
Reinhardt, Dana 1971- 175
Reinhart, Matthew 161
Reiniger, Lotte 1899-1981 40
  Obituary 33
Reinsma, Carol 1949- 91
Reinstedt, Randall A. 1935- 101
Reinstedt, Randy
  See Reinstedt, Randall A.
Reisberg, Mira 1955- 82
Reisberg, Veg
  See Reisberg, Mira
Reiser, Lynn (Whisnant) 1944- 138
  Earlier sketch in SATA *81*
Reisgies, Teresa (Maria) 1966- 74
Reiss, Johanna (de Leeuw) 1929(?)- 18
  See also CLR *19*
Reiss, John J. 23
Reiss, Kathryn 1957- 144
  Earlier sketch in SATA *76*
Reit, Seymour Victory 1918-2001 21
  Obituary 133

Reit, Sy
  See Reit, Seymour Victory
Relf, Patricia 1954- 134
  Earlier sketch in SATA *71*
Remi, Georges 1907-1983 13
  Obituary 32
  See Herge
Remington, Frederic S(ackrider)
  1861-1909 41
Remkiewicz, Frank 1939- 152
  Earlier sketch in SATA *77*
Remy, Georges
  See Remi, Georges
Renaud, Bernadette 1945- 66
Renault, Mary
  See Challans, Mary
Rendell, Joan 28
Rendina, Laura (Jones) Cooper 1902- 10
Rendon, Marcie R. 1952- 97
Rendon, Maria 1965- 116
Renee, Janina 1956- 140
Renfro, Ed 1924- 79
Renick, Marion (Lewis) 1905-1983 1
Renken, Aleda 1907- 27
Renlie, Frank H. 1936- 11
Rennert, Richard Scott 1956- 67
Rennison, Louise 1951- 149
Reno, Dawn E(laine) 1953- 130
Rensie, Willis
  See Eisner, Will
Renton, Cam
  See Armstrong, Richard
Renvoize, Jean 5
Resciniti, Angelo G. 1952- 75
Resnick, Michael David
  See Resnick, Mike
Resnick, Mike 1942- 159
  Earlier sketches in SATA *38, 106*
Resnick, Seymour 1920- 23
Retla, Robert
  See Alter, Robert Edmond
Reuter, Bjarne (B.) 1950- 142
  Earlier sketch in SATA *68*
Reuter, Carol (Joan) 1931- 2
Revena
  See Wright, Betty Ren
Revsbech, Vicki
  See Liestman, Vicki
Rey, H(ans) A(ugusto) 1898-1977 100
  Earlier sketches in SATA *1, 26, 69*
  See also CLR *93*
Rey, Margret (Elisabeth) 1906-1996 86
  Obituary 93
  Earlier sketch in SATA *26*
  See also CLR *93*
Reyher, Becky
  See Reyher, Rebecca Hourwich
Reyher, Rebecca Hourwich 1897-1987 18
  Obituary 50
Reynolds, C. Buck 1957- 107
Reynolds, John
  See Whitlock, Ralph
Reynolds, Madge
  See Whitlock, Ralph
Reynolds, Malvina 1900-1978 44
  Obituary 24
Reynolds, Marilyn (M.) 1935- 121
  See also SAAS *23*
Reynolds, Marilynn 1940- 141
  Earlier sketch in SATA *80*
Reynolds, Pamela 1923- 34
Reynolds, Peter H. 1961- 128
Reynolds, Peter J. 1961- 179
Reynolds, Susan 179
Rhine, Richard
  See Silverstein, Alvin
  and Silverstein, Virginia B(arbara Opshelor)
Rhoades, Diane 1952- 90
Rhodes, Bennie (Loran) 1927- 35
Rhodes, Donna McKee 1962- 87
Rhodes, Frank Harold Trevor 1926- 37

Rhue, Morton
  See Strasser, Todd
Rhyne, Nancy 1926- 66
Rhynes, Martha E. 1939- 141
Ribbons, Ian 1924- 37
  Brief entry 30
  See also SAAS *3*
Ricciuti, Edward R(aphael) 1938- 10
Rice, Alice (Caldwell) Hegan 1870-1942 63
Rice, Bebe Faas 1932- 89
Rice, Dale R. 1948- 42
Rice, Dale Richard
  See Rice, Dale R.
Rice, Dick
  See Rice, R. Hugh
Rice, Earle (Wilmont), Jr. 1928- 151
  Earlier sketch in SATA *92*
Rice, Edward 1918-2001 47
  Brief entry 42
Rice, Elizabeth 1913-1976 2
Rice, Eve 1951- 91
  Earlier sketch in SATA *34*
Rice, Eve Hart
  See Rice, Eve
Rice, Inez 1907- 13
Rice, James 1934- 93
  Earlier sketch in SATA *22*
Rice, John F. 1958- 82
Rice, R. Hugh 1929- 115
Rice, Richard H.
  See Rice, R. Hugh
Rich, Barbara
  See Graves, Robert
Rich, Elaine Sommers 1926- 6
Rich, Josephine Bouchard 1912- 10
Rich, Louise Dickinson 1903-1991 54
  Obituary 67
Richard, Adrienne 1921- 5
  See also SAAS *9*
Richard, James Robert
  See Bowen, Robert Sydney
Richards, Chuck 1957- 170
Richards, Frank
  See Hamilton, Charles (Harold St. John)
Richards, Hilda
  See Hamilton, Charles (Harold St. John)
Richards, Jackie 1925- 102
Richards, Jean 1940- 135
Richards, Justin 169
Richards, Kay
  See Baker, Susan (Catherine)
Richards, Laura E(lizabeth Howe) 1850-1943
  See YABC *1*
  See also CLR *54*
Richards, Norman 1932- 48
Richards, R(onald) C(harles) W(illiam)
  1923- 59
  Brief entry 43
Richardson, Andrew (William) 1986- 120
Richardson, Carol 1932- 58
Richardson, Grace Lee
  See Dickson, Naida
Richardson, Jean (Mary) 59
Richardson, Judith Benet 1941- 77
Richardson, Robert S(hirley) 1902-1981 8
Richardson, Sandy 1949- 116
Richardson, Willis 1889-1977 60
Richelson, Geraldine 1922- 29
Richemont, Enid 1940- 82
Richler, Mordecai 1931-2001 98
  Brief entry 27
  Earlier sketch in SATA *44*
  See also CLR *17*
Richman, Sophia 1941- 142
Rich-McCoy, Lois
  See McCoy, Lois (Rich)
Richmond, Robin 1951- 75
Richoux, Pat(ricia) 1927- 7
Richter, Alice 1941- 30
Richter, Conrad (Michael) 1890-1968 3

Richter, Hans Peter 1925-1993 6
 See also CLR *21*
 See also SAAS *11*
Rickard, Graham 1949- *71*
Riddell, Chris 1962- *166*
 Earlier sketch in SATA *114*
Riddell, Christopher Barry
 See Riddell, Chris
Riddell, Edwina 1955- *82*
Ridden, Brian (John) 1934- *123*
Riddle, Tohby 1965- *151*
 Earlier sketch in SATA *74*
Riddles, Libby 1956- *140*
Ridge, Antonia (Florence) (?)-1981 .... *7*
 Obituary *27*
Ridge, Martin 1923-2003 .... *43*
Ridley, Philip *171*
 Earlier sketch in SATA *88*
Ridlon, Marci *22*
 See Balterman, Marcia Ridlon
Riedman, Sarah R(egal) 1902-1995 .... *1*
Riehecky, Janet 1953- *164*
Riesenberg, Felix, Jr. 1913-1962 .... *23*
Rieu, E(mile) V(ictor) 1887-1972 .... *46*
 Obituary *26*
Riffenburgh, Beau 1955- *175*
Rigg, Sharon
 See Creech, Sharon
Riggio, Anita 1952- *148*
 Earlier sketch in SATA *73*
Riggs, Stephanie 1964- *138*
Rigney, James Oliver, Jr.
 See Jordan, Robert
Rikhoff, Jean 1928- *9*
Rikki
 See Ducornet, Erica
Riley, James A. 1939- *97*
Riley, James Whitcomb 1849-1916 .... *17*
Riley, Jocelyn 1949- *60*
 Brief entry *50*
Riley, Jocelyn Carol
 See Riley, Jocelyn
Riley, Linda Capus 1950- *85*
Riley, Martin 1948- *81*
Rimes, (Margaret) LeAnn 1982- *154*
Rinaldi, Ann 1934- *161*
 Brief entry *50*
 Earlier sketches in SATA *51, 78, 117*
 See also CLR *46*
Rinard, Judith E(llen) 1947- *140*
 Earlier sketch in SATA *44*
Rinder, Lenore 1949- *92*
Ring, Elizabeth 1920- *79*
Ringdalh, Mark
 See Longyear, Barry B(rookes)
Ringgold, Faith 1930- *114*
 Earlier sketch in SATA *71*
 See also CLR *30*
Ringi, Kjell (Arne Soerensen) 1939- *12*
Rinkoff, Barbara Jean (Rich) 1923-1975 .... *4*
 Obituary *27*
Rinn, Miriam 1946- *127*
Riordan, James 1936- *95*
Riordan, Rick *174*
Rios, Tere
 See Versace, Marie Teresa Rios
Ripken, Cal, Jr. 1960- *114*
Ripken, Calvin Edward, Jr.
 See Ripken, Cal, Jr.
Ripley, Catherine 1957- *82*
Ripley, Elizabeth Blake 1906-1969 .... *5*
Ripper, Charles L(ewis) 1929- *3*
Ripper, Chuck
 See Ripper, Charles L(ewis)
Riq
 See Atwater, Richard (Tupper)
Rish, David 1955- *110*
Riskind, Mary 1944- *60*
Rissinger, Matt 1956- *93*
Rissman, Art
 See Sussman, Susan

Rissman, Susan
 See Sussman, Susan
Ritchie, Barbara Gibbons *14*
Ritter, Felix
 See Kruss, James
Ritter, John H. 1951- *137*
 Earlier sketch in SATA *129*
Ritter, Lawrence S(tanley) 1922-2004 .... *58*
 Obituary *152*
Ritthaler, Shelly 1955- *91*
Ritz, Karen 1957- *80*
Rivera, Geraldo (Miguel) 1943- *54*
 Brief entry *28*
Rivers, Elfrida
 See Bradley, Marion Zimmer
Rivers, Karen 1970- *131*
Riverside, John
 See Heinlein, Robert A.
Rivkin, Ann 1920- *41*
Rivoli, Mario 1943- *10*
Roach, Marilynne K. 1946- *9*
Roach, Marilynne Kathleen
 See Roach, Marilynne K.
Roach, Portia
 See Takakjian, Portia
Robb, Laura 1937- *95*
Robbins, Frank 1917-1994(?) *42*
 Brief entry *32*
Robbins, Ken 1945- *147*
 Brief entry *53*
 Earlier sketch in SATA *94*
Robbins, Raleigh
 See Hamilton, Charles (Harold St. John)
Robbins, Ruth 1917(?)- *14*
Robbins, Tony
 See Pashko, Stanley
Robbins, Wayne
 See Cox, William R(obert)
Robel, S. L.
 See Fraustino, Lisa Rowe
Roberson, Jennifer 1953- *72*
Roberson, John R(oyster) 1930- *53*
Robert, Adrian
 See St. John, Nicole
Roberts, Bethany *133*
Roberts, Bruce (Stuart) 1930- *47*
 Brief entry *39*
Roberts, Charles G(eorge) D(ouglas)
 1860-1943 .... *88*
 Brief entry *29*
 See also CLR *33*
Roberts, David
 See Cox, John Roberts
Roberts, Elizabeth 1944- *80*
Roberts, Elizabeth Madox 1886-1941 .... *33*
 Brief entry *27*
 See also CLR *100*
Roberts, Jim
 See Bates, Barbara S(nedeker)
Roberts, John G(aither) 1913-1993 .... *27*
Roberts, Judy I. 1957- *93*
Roberts, Katherine 1962- *152*
Roberts, M. L.
 See Mattern, Joanne
Roberts, Nancy Correll 1924- *52*
 Brief entry *28*
Roberts, Terence
 See Sanderson, Ivan T(erence)
Roberts, Willo Davis 1928-2004 .... *150*
 Autobiography Feature *150*
 Obituary *160*
 Earlier sketches in SATA *21, 70, 133*
 See also CLR *95*
 See also SAAS *8*
Robertson, Barbara (Anne) 1931- *12*
Robertson, Don 1929-1999 .... *8*
 Obituary *113*
Robertson, Dorothy Lewis 1912- *12*
Robertson, Ellis
 See Ellison, Harlan
 and Silverberg, Robert

Robertson, Janet (E.) 1935- *68*
Robertson, Jennifer Sinclair 1942-1998 .... *12*
Robertson, Jenny
 See Robertson, Jennifer Sinclair
Robertson, Keith (Carlton) 1914-1991 .... *85*
 Obituary *69*
 Earlier sketch in SATA *1*
 See also SAAS *15*
Robertson, Stephen
 See Walker, Robert W(ayne)
Robertus, Polly M. 1948- *73*
Robeson, Kenneth
 See Dent, Lester
 and Goulart, Ron(ald Joseph)
Robeson, Kenneth
 See Johnson, (Walter) Ryerson
Robinet, Harriette Gillem 1931- *104*
 Earlier sketch in SATA *27*
 See also CLR *64*
Robins, Deri 1958- *166*
 Earlier sketch in SATA *117*
Robins, Patricia
 See Clark, Patricia Denise
Robins, Rollo, Jr.
 See Ellis, Edward S(ylvester)
Robins, Seelin
 See Ellis, Edward S(ylvester)
Robinson, Adjai 1932- *8*
Robinson, Aminah Brenda Lynn 1940- *159*
 Earlier sketch in SATA *77*
Robinson, Barbara (Webb) 1927- *84*
 Earlier sketch in SATA *8*
Robinson, C(harles) A(lexander), Jr.
 1900-1965 .... *36*
Robinson, Charles 1870-1937 .... *17*
Robinson, Charles 1931- *6*
Robinson, Dorothy W. 1929- *54*
Robinson, Eve
 See Tanselle, Eve
Robinson, Glen 1953- *92*
Robinson, Glendal P.
 See Robinson, Glen
Robinson, Jan M. 1933- *6*
Robinson, Jean O. 1934- *7*
Robinson, Joan (Mary) G(ale Thomas)
 1910-1988 .... *7*
Robinson, Kim Stanley 1952- *109*
Robinson, Lee 1948- *110*
Robinson, Lloyd
 See Silverberg, Robert
Robinson, Lynda S(uzanne) 1951- *107*
Robinson, Marileta 1942- *32*
Robinson, Maudie Millian Oller 1914- *11*
Robinson, Nancy K(onheim) 1942-1994 ...... *91*
 Brief entry *31*
 Obituary *79*
 Earlier sketch in SATA *32*
Robinson, Ray(mond Kenneth) 1920- *23*
Robinson, Shari
 See McGuire, Leslie (Sarah)
Robinson, Sharon 1950- *162*
Robinson, Spider 1948- *118*
Robinson, Sue
 See Robinson, Susan Maria
Robinson, Susan Maria 1955- *105*
Robinson, Suzanne
 See Robinson, Lynda S(uzanne)
Robinson, T(homas) H(eath) 1869-1950 ...... *17*
Robinson, (Wanda) Veronica 1926- *30*
Robinson, W(illiam) Heath 1872-1944 .... *17*
Robison, Bonnie 1924- *12*
Robison, Nancy L(ouise) 1934- *32*
Robles, Harold E. 1948- *87*
Robottom, John 1934- *7*
Robson, Eric 1939- *82*
Roche, A. K.
 See Abisch, Roslyn Kroop
 and Kaplan, Boche
Roche, Denis (Mary) 1967- *99*
Roche, Luane 1937- *170*

Roche, P(atricia) K. 1935- 57
  Brief entry 34
Roche, Terry
  See Poole, Peggy
Rochman, Hazel 1938- 105
Rock, Lois
  See Joslin, Mary
Rock, Maxine 1940- 108
Rocker, Fermin 1907- 40
Rocklin, Joanne 1946- 134
  Earlier sketch in SATA 86
Rockwell, Anne F. 1934- 162
  Earlier sketches in SATA 33, 71, 114
  See also SAAS 19
Rockwell, Anne Foote
  See Rockwell, Anne F.
Rockwell, Bart
  See Pellowski, Michael (Joseph)
Rockwell, Harlow 1910-1988 33
  Obituary 56
Rockwell, Norman (Percevel) 1894-1978 23
Rockwell, Thomas 1933- 70
  Earlier sketch in SATA 7
  See also CLR 6
Rockwood, Joyce 1947- 39
Rockwood, Roy 67
  Earlier sketch in SATA 1
  See McFarlane, Leslie (Charles)
  and Stratemeyer, Edward L.
Rodanas, Kristina 1952- 155
Rodari, Gianni 1920-1980
  See CLR 24
Rodd, Kathleen Tennant 57
  Obituary 55
  See Rodd, Kylie Tennant
Rodda, Emily 1948- 146
  Earlier sketch in SATA 97
  See also CLR 32
Roddenberry, Eugene Wesley 1921-1991 45
  Obituary 69
  See Roddenberry, Gene
Roddenberry, Gene
  Obituary 69
  See Roddenberry, Eugene Wesley
Roddic, Shen 153
Roddy, Lee 1921- 57
Rodenas, Paula 73
Rodgers, Frank 1944- 69
Rodgers, Mary 1931- 130
  Earlier sketch in SATA 8
  See also CLR 20
Rodman, Emerson
  See Ellis, Edward S(ylvester)
Rodman, Eric
  See Silverberg, Robert
Rodman, Maia
  See Wojciechowska, Maia (Teresa)
Rodman, (Cary) Selden 1909-2002 9
Rodowsky, Colby 1932- 164
  Earlier sketches in SATA 21, 77, 120
  See also SAAS 22
Rodowsky, Colby F.
  See Rodowsky, Colby
Rodriguez, Alejo 1941- 83
Rodriguez, Christina 1981- 177
Rodriguez, Luis J. 1954- 125
Roeder, Virginia Marsh 1926- 98
Roehrig, Catharine H. 1949- 67
Roennfeldt, Robert 1953- 78
Roessel-Waugh, C. C.
  See Waugh, Carol-Lynn Rossel
  and Waugh, Charles G(ordon)
Roets, Lois F. 1937- 91
Roever, J(oan) M(arilyn) 1935- 26
Rofes, Eric 1954-2006 52
Rofes, Eric Edward 1954-2006
  See Rofes, Eric
Roffey, Maureen 1936- 33
Rogak, Lisa 1962- 80
Rogak, Lisa Angowski
  See Rogak, Lisa

Rogasky, Barbara 1933- 144
  Earlier sketch in SATA 86
Rogers, (Thomas) Alan (Stinchcombe)
  1937- 81
  Earlier sketch in SATA 2
Rogers, Bettye 1858-1919 103
Rogers, Cindy 1950- 89
Rogers, Emma 1951- 74
Rogers, Frances 1888-1974 10
Rogers, Fred McFeely 1928-2003 33
  Obituary 138
Rogers, Hal
  See Sirimarco, Elizabeth
Rogers, Jean 1919- 55
  Brief entry 47
Rogers, Matilda 1894-1976 5
  Obituary 34
Rogers, Pamela 1927- 9
Rogers, Paul 1950- 98
  Earlier sketch in SATA 54
Rogers, Robert
  See Hamilton, Charles (Harold St. John)
Rogers, W(illiam) G(arland) 1896-1978 23
Rohan, M. S.
  See Rohan, Michael Scott
Rohan, Michael Scott 1951- 98
Rohan, Mike Scott
  See Rohan, Michael Scott
Rohmann, Eric 1957- 171
  See also CLR 100
Rohmer, Harriet 1938- 56
Rohrer, Doug 1962- 89
Rojan
  See Rojankovsky, Feodor (Stepanovich)
Rojankovsky, Feodor (Stepanovich)
  1891-1970 21
Rojany, Lisa 94
Rokeby-Thomas, Anna E(lma) 1911- 15
Roland, Albert 1925-2002 11
Roland, Mary
  See Lewis, Mary (Christianna)
Roleff, Tamara L. 1959- 143
Rolerson, Darrell A(llen) 1946- 8
Roll, Winifred 1909-1998 6
Rollins, Charlemae Hill 1897-1979 3
  Obituary 26
Rollock, Barbara T(herese) 1924- 64
Romack, Janice Reed
  See LeNoir, Janice
Romain, Trevor 134
Romanenko, Vitaliy 1962- 101
Romano, Louis G. 1921- 35
Romano, Melora A. 1966- 118
Romano, Ray 1957- 170
Romano, Raymond
  See Romano, Ray
Romijn, Johanna Maria Kooyker
  See Kooyker-Romijn, Johanna Maria
Romyn, Johanna Maria Kooyker
  See Kooyker-Romijn, Johanna Maria
Rong, Yu 1970- 174
Rongen, Bjoern 1906- 10
Rongen, Bjorn
  See Rongen, Bjoern
Ronson, Mark
  See Alexander, Marc
Rood, Ronald (N.) 1920- 12
Rook, Sebastian
  See Jeapes, Ben
Rooke, Daphne (Marie) 1914- 12
Roop, Connie 1951- 167
  Brief entry 49
  Earlier sketches in SATA 54, 116
Roop, Constance Betzer
  See Roop, Connie
Roop, Peter 1951- 167
  Brief entry 49
  Earlier sketches in SATA 54, 116
Roop, Peter G.
  See Roop, Peter

Roop, Peter Geiger
  See Roop, Peter
Roos, Stephen 1945- 128
  Brief entry 41
  Earlier sketches in SATA 47, 77
Roose-Evans, James 1927- 65
Roosevelt, (Anna) Eleanor 1884-1962 50
Root, Betty 84
Root, Phyllis 1949- 145
  Brief entry 48
  Earlier sketches in SATA 55, 94
Roper, Laura (Newbold) Wood 1911-2003 .. 34
  Obituary 150
Roper, Robert 1946- 142
  Earlier sketch in SATA 78
Roraback, Robin (Ellan) 1964- 111
Rorby, Ginny 1944- 94
Rorer, Abigail 1949- 85
Rosamel, Godeleine de 1968- 151
Roscoe, D(onald) T(homas) 1934- 42
Rose, Anne 8
Rose, Deborah Lee 1955- 124
  Earlier sketch in SATA 71
Rose, Elizabeth (Jane Pretty) 1933- 68
  Brief entry 28
Rose, Florella
  See Carlson, Vada F.
Rose, Gerald (Hembdon Seymour) 1935- 68
  Brief entry 30
Rose, Malcolm 1953- 168
  Earlier sketch in SATA 107
Rose, Nancy A.
  See Sweetland, Nancy A(nn)
Rose, Ted 1940- 93
Rose, Wendy 1948- 12
Rosen, Lillian (Diamond) 1928- 63
Rosen, Marvin 1933- 161
Rosen, Michael (Wayne) 1946- 137
  Brief entry 40
  Earlier sketches in SATA 48, 84
  See also CLR 45
Rosen, Michael J(oel) 1954- 86
Rosen, Sidney 1916- 1
Rosen, Winifred 1943- 8
Rosenbaum, Maurice 1907- 6
Rosenberg, Amye 1950- 74
Rosenberg, Dorothy 1906- 40
Rosenberg, Eth(el) Clifford 1915- 3
  See Clifford, Eth
Rosenberg, Jane 1949- 58
Rosenberg, Liz 1958- 129
  Earlier sketch in SATA 75
Rosenberg, Maxine B(erta) 1939- 93
  Brief entry 47
  Earlier sketch in SATA 55
Rosenberg, Nancy (Sherman) 1931- 4
Rosenberg, Sharon 1942- 8
Rosenberry, Vera 1948- 144
  Earlier sketch in SATA 83
Rosenblatt, Arthur
  See Rosenblatt, Arthur S.
Rosenblatt, Arthur S. 1938- 68
  Brief entry 45
Rosenblatt, Lily 1956- 90
Rosenbloom, Joseph 1928- 21
Rosenblum, Richard 1928- 11
Rosenburg, John M. 1918- 6
Rosenfeld, Dina 1962- 99
Rosenthal, Amy Krouse 1965- 177
Rosenthal, Betsy R. 1957- 178
Rosenthal, Harold 1914-1999 35
Rosenthal, M(acha) L(ouis) 1917-1996 59
Rosenthal, Mark A(lan) 1946- 64
Rosman, Steven M 1956- 81
Rosman, Steven Michael
  See Rosman, Steven M
Rosoff, Meg 1956- 160
Ross, Alan
  See Warwick, Alan R(oss)
Ross, Christine 1950- 172
  Earlier sketch in SATA 83

Ross, Clare *111*
  Earlier sketch in SATA *48*
  See Romano, Clare
Ross, Dana Fuller
  See Cockrell, Amanda
  and Gerson, Noel Bertram
Ross, Dave *32*
  See Ross, David
Ross, David 1896-1975 .... *49*
  Obituary *20*
Ross, David 1949- *133*
  See Ross, Dave
Ross, Diana
  See Denney, Diana
Ross, Edward S(hearman) 1915- *85*
Ross, Eileen 1950- *115*
Ross, Frank (Xavier), Jr. 1914- *28*
Ross, Jane 1961- *79*
Ross, John 1921- *45*
Ross, Judy 1942- *54*
Ross, Katharine Reynolds
  See Ross, Kathy
Ross, Kathy 1948- *169*
  Earlier sketch in SATA *89*
Ross, Kent 1956- *91*
Ross, Lillian Hammer 1925- *72*
Ross, Michael Elsohn 1952- *170*
  Earlier sketches in SATA *80, 127*
Ross, Pat(ricia Kienzle) 1943- *53*
  Brief entry *48*
Ross, Ramon R(oyal) 1930- *62*
Ross, Stewart 1947- *134*
  Earlier sketch in SATA *92*
  See also SAAS *23*
Ross, Tom 1958- *84*
Ross, Tony 1938- *176*
  Earlier sketches in SATA *17, 65, 130*
Ross, Wilda 1915- *51*
  Brief entry *39*
Rossel, Seymour 1945- *28*
Rossel-Waugh, C. C.
  See Waugh, Carol-Lynn Rossel
Rossetti, Christina 1830-1894 .... *20*
  See also CLR *115*
Rossetti, Christina Georgina
  See Rossetti, Christina
Rossi, Joyce 1943- *116*
Rossotti, Hazel Swaine 1930- *95*
Rostkowski, Margaret I. 1945- *59*
Roth, Arnold 1929- *21*
Roth, Arthur J(oseph) 1925-1993 .... *43*
  Brief entry *28*
  Obituary *75*
  See also SAAS *11*
Roth, David 1940- *36*
Roth, Matthue 1978(?)- *174*
Roth, Susan L. *134*
Rothberg, Abraham 1922- *59*
Roth-Hano, Renee 1931- *85*
Rothkopf, Carol Z. 1929- *4*
Rothman, Joel 1938- *7*
Rotner, Shelley 1951- *169*
  Earlier sketch in SATA *76*
Rottman, S(usan) L(ynn) 1970- *157*
  Earlier sketch in SATA *106*
Roueche, Berton 1911-1994 .... *28*
Roughsey, Dick 1921(?)-1985 .... *35*
  See also CLR *41*
Roughsey, Goobalathaldin
  See Roughsey, Dick
Rounds, Glen (Harold) 1906-2002 .... *112*
  Obituary *141*
  Earlier sketches in SATA *8, 70*
Rourke, Constance Mayfield 1885-1941
  See YABC *1*
Rowan, Deirdre
  See Williams, Jeanne
Rowe, Jennifer
  See Rodda, Emily
Rowe, John A. 1949- *146*
Rowh, Mark 1952- *90*

Rowland, Florence Wightman 1900-1997 ...... *8*
  Obituary *108*
Rowland-Entwistle, (Arthur) Theodore (Henry)
  1925- *94*
  Earlier sketch in SATA *31*
Rowling, J.K. 1965- *174*
  Earlier sketch in SATA *109*
  See also CLR *112*
Rowling, Joanne Kathleen
  See Rowling, J.K.
Rowsome, Frank (Howard), Jr. 1914-1983 .. *36*
Roy, Gabrielle 1909-1983 .... *104*
Roy, Jacqueline 1954- *74*
Roy, Jennifer
  See Roy, Jennifer Rozines
Roy, Jennifer Rozines 1967- *178*
Roy, Liam
  See Scarry, Patricia (Murphy)
Roy, Ron(ald) 1940- *110*
  Brief entry *35*
  Earlier sketch in SATA *40*
Roybal, Laura 1956- *85*
Roybal, Laura Husby
  See Roybal, Laura
Royds, Caroline 1953- *55*
Royston, Angela 1945- *169*
  Earlier sketch in SATA *120*
Rozakis, Laurie E. 1952- *84*
Rubel, Nicole 1953- *135*
  Earlier sketches in SATA *18, 95*
Rubin, Eva Johanna 1925- *38*
Rubin, Susan Goldman 1939- *132*
  Earlier sketch in SATA *84*
Rubinetti, Donald 1947- *92*
Rubinstein, Gillian (Margaret) 1942- *158*
  Autobiography Feature *116*
  Earlier sketches in SATA *68, 105*
  See also CLR *35*
  See also SAAS *25*
Rubinstein, Patricia (Giulia Caulfield Kate)
  -2003 .... *29*
  Obituary *149*
  See Forest, Antonia
Rubinstein, Robert E(dward) 1943- *49*
Rublowsky, John M(artin) 1928- *62*
Rubright, Lynn 1936- *171*
Ruby, Laura *155*
Ruby, Lois (F.) 1942- *95*
  Autobiography Feature *105*
  Brief entry *34*
  Earlier sketch in SATA *35*
Ruchlis, Hy(man) 1913-1992 .... *3*
  Obituary *72*
Rucker, Mike 1940- *91*
Ruckman, Ivy 1931- *93*
  Earlier sketch in SATA *37*
Ruck-Pauquet, Gina 1931- *40*
  Brief entry *37*
Rudley, Stephen 1946- *30*
Rudolph, Marguerita 1908- *21*
Rudomin, Esther
  See Hautzig, Esther Rudomin
Rue, Leonard Lee III 1926- *142*
  Earlier sketch in SATA *37*
Ruedi, Norma Paul
  See Ainsworth, Norma
Ruelle, Karen Gray 1957- *126*
  Earlier sketch in SATA *84*
Ruemmler, John D(avid) 1948- *78*
Ruepp, Krista 1947- *143*
Ruffell, Ann 1941- *30*
Ruffins, Reynold 1930- *125*
  Earlier sketch in SATA *41*
Rugoff, Milton 1913- *30*
Ruhen, Olaf 1911-1989 .... *17*
Rumbaut, Hendle 1949- *84*
Rumford, James 1948- *116*
Rumsey, Marian (Barritt) 1928- *16*
Rumstuckle, Cornelius
  See Brennan, J(ames) H(erbert)
Runnerstroem, Bengt Arne 1944- *75*

Runyan, John
  See Palmer, Bernard (Alvin)
Runyon, Catherine 1947- *62*
Ruoff, A. LaVonne Brown 1930- *76*
Rusch, Kris
  See Rusch, Kristine Kathryn
Rusch, Kristine Kathryn 1960- *113*
Rush, Alison 1951- *41*
Rush, Peter 1937- *32*
Rushford, Patricia H(elen) 1943- *134*
Rushmore, Helen 1898-1994 .... *3*
Rushmore, Robert (William) 1926-1986 .... *8*
  Obituary *49*
Ruskin, Ariane
  See Batterberry, Ariane Ruskin
Ruskin, John 1819-1900 .... *24*
Russ, Lavinia (Faxon) 1904-1992 .... *74*
Russell, Charlotte
  See Rathjen, Carl Henry
Russell, Ching Yeung 1946- *107*
Russell, Franklin (Alexander) 1926- *11*
Russell, Gertrude Barrer
  See Barrer-Russell, Gertrude
Russell, Helen Ross 1915- *8*
Russell, James 1933- *53*
Russell, Jim
  See Russell, James
Russell, Joan Plummer 1930- *139*
Russell, P(hilip) Craig 1951- *162*
  Earlier sketch in SATA *80*
Russell, Patrick
  See Sammis, John
Russell, Paul (Gary) 1942- *57*
Russell, Sarah
  See Laski, Marghanita
Russell, Sharman Apt 1954- *123*
Russell, Solveig Paulson 1904-1985 .... *3*
Russo, Marisabina 1950- *151*
  Earlier sketch in SATA *106*
Russo, Monica J. 1950- *83*
Russo, Susan 1947- *30*
Russon, Penni 1974- *179*
Rutgers van der Loeff, An
  See Rutgers van der Loeff-Basenau, An(na)
  Maria Margaretha
Rutgers van der Loeff-Basenau, An(na) Maria
  Margaretha 1910- *22*
Ruth, Rod 1912-1987 .... *9*
Rutherford, Douglas
  See McConnell, James Douglas Rutherford
Rutherford, Meg 1932- *34*
Ruthin, Margaret *4*
  See Catherall, Arthur
Rutledge, Jill Zimmerman 1951- *155*
Rutz, Viola Larkin 1932- *12*
Ruurs, Margriet 1952- *147*
  Earlier sketch in SATA *97*
Ruzzier, Sergio 1966- *159*
Ryan, Betsy
  See Ryan, Elizabeth (Anne)
Ryan, Cheli Duran *20*
Ryan, Darlene 1958- *176*
Ryan, Elizabeth (Anne) 1943- *30*
Ryan, Jeanette
  See Mines, Jeanette
Ryan, John (Gerald Christopher) 1921- *22*
Ryan, Margaret 1950- *166*
  Earlier sketch in SATA *78*
Ryan, Mary E. 1953- *61*
Ryan, Mary Elizabeth
  See Ryan, Mary E.
Ryan, Pam(ela) Munoz *134*
Ryan, Patrick 1957- *138*
Ryan, Peter (Charles) 1939- *15*
Ryan-Lush, Geraldine 1949- *89*
Rybakov, Anatoli (Naumovich) 1911-1998 .. *79*
  Obituary *108*
  See Rybakov, Anatolii (Naumovich)
Rybakov, Anatolii (Naumovich)
  See Rybakov, Anatoli (Naumovich)
Rybolt, Thomas R. 1954- *62*

Rybolt, Thomas Roy
  See Rybolt, Thomas R.
Rybolt, Tom
  See Rybolt, Thomas R.
Rydberg, Ernest E(mil) 1901-1993 21
Rydberg, Lou(isa Hampton) 1908- 27
Rydell, Katy 1942- 91
Rydell, Wendell
  See Rydell, Wendy
Rydell, Wendy 4
Ryden, Hope 91
  Earlier sketch in SATA 8
Ryder, Joanne (Rose) 1946- 163
  Brief entry 34
  Earlier sketches in SATA 65, 122
  See also CLR 37
Ryder, Pamela
  See Lamb, Nancy
Rye, Anthony
  See Youd, (Christopher) Samuel
Rylant, Cynthia 1954- 160
  Brief entry 44
  Earlier sketches in SATA 50, 76, 112
  See also CLR 86
  See also SAAS 13
Rymer, Alta May 1925- 34

S

S. L. C.
  See Clemens, Samuel Langhorne
S., Svend Otto
  See Soerensen, Svend Otto
Saaf, Donald W(illiam) 1961- 124
Saal, Jocelyn
  See Sachs, Judith
Sabbeth, Carol (Landstrom) 1957- 125
Saberhagen, Fred 1930-2007 89
  Earlier sketch in SATA 37
Saberhagen, Fred Thomas
  See Saberhagen, Fred
Sabin, Edwin L(egrand) 1870-1952
  See YABC 2
Sabin, Francene 27
Sabin, Lou
  See Sabin, Louis
Sabin, Louis 1930- 27
Sabre, Dirk
  See Laffin, John (Alfred Charles)
Sabuda, Robert 1965- 170
Sabuda, Robert (James) 1965- 120
  Earlier sketch in SATA 81
Sabuda, Robert James
  See Sabuda, Robert
Sachar, Louis 1954- 154
  Brief entry 50
  Earlier sketches in SATA 63, 104
  See also CLR 79
Sachs, Elizabeth-Ann 1946- 48
Sachs, Judith 1947- 52
  Brief entry 51
Sachs, Marilyn 1927- 164
  Autobiography Feature 110
  Earlier sketches in SATA 3, 68
  See also CLR 2
  See also SAAS 2
Sachs, Marilyn Stickle
  See Sachs, Marilyn
Sackett, S(amuel) J(ohn) 1928- 12
Sackson, Sid 1920- 16
Sacre, Antonio 1968- 152
Saddler, Allen
  See Richards, R(onald) C(harles) W(illiam)
Saddler, K. Allen
  See Richards, R(onald) C(harles) W(illiam)
Sadie, Stanley (John) 1930-2005 14
Sadiq, Nazneen 1944- 101
Sadler, Catherine Edwards 1952- 60
  Brief entry 45

Sadler, Marilyn (June) 1950- 79
Sadler, Mark
  See Lynds, Dennis
Saffer, Barbara 144
Sagan, Carl 1934-1996 58
  Obituary 94
Sagan, Carl Edward
  See Sagan, Carl
Sage, Juniper
  See Brown, Margaret Wise
  and Hurd, Edith Thacher
Sagsoorian, Paul 1923- 12
Said, S.F. 1967- 174
Said, S.F. 1967- 174
Saidman, Anne 1952- 75
Saint, Dora Jessie 1913- 10
St. Anthony, Jane 175
St. Antoine, Sara L. 1966- 84
Saint-Exupery, Antoine de 1900-1944 20
  See also CLR 10
Saint-Exupery, Antoine Jean Baptiste Marie
  Roger de
  See Saint-Exupery, Antoine de
St. George, Judith 1931- 161
  Earlier sketches in SATA 13, 99
  See also CLR 57
  See also SAAS 12
St. James, Blakely
  See Gottfried, Theodore Mark
  and Platt, Charles
St. James, Blakely
  See Griffin, W.E.B.
Saint James, Synthia 1949- 152
  Earlier sketch in SATA 84
St. John, Nicole 143
  Autobiography Feature 143
  Earlier sketch in SATA 89
  See also CLR 46
  See also SAAS 7
  See Johnston, Norma
St. John, Philip
  See del Rey, Lester
St. John, Wylly Folk 1908-1985 10
  Obituary 45
St. Max, E. S.
  See Ellis, Edward S(ylvester)
St. Meyer, Ned
  See Stratemeyer, Edward L.
St. Mox, E. A.
  See Ellis, Edward S(ylvester)
St. Myer, Ned
  See Stratemeyer, Edward L.
St. Tamara
  See Kolba, St. Tamara
Saito, Michiko
  See Fujiwara, Michiko
Sakers, Don 1958- 72
Sakharnov, S.
  See Sakharnov, Svyatoslav
Sakharnov, Svyatoslav 1923- 65
Sakharnov, Svyatoslav Vladimirovich
  See Sakharnov, Svyatoslav
Saksena, Kate 148
Sakurai, Gail 1952- 153
  Earlier sketch in SATA 87
Salassi, Otto R(ussell) 1939-1993 38
  Obituary 77
Salat, Cristina 82
Saldutti, Denise 1953- 39
Sale, Tim 1956- 153
Salem, Kay 1952- 92
Salerno, Steven 176
Salinger, J.D. 1919- 67
  See also CLR 18
Salinger, Jerome David
  See Salinger, J.D.
Salisbury, Graham 1944- 161
  Earlier sketches in SATA 76, 108
Salisbury, Joyce E(llen) 1944- 138

Salkey, (Felix) Andrew (Alexander)
  1928-1995 118
  Earlier sketch in SATA 35
Salley, Coleen 166
Sallis, Susan (Diana) 1929- 55
Salmon, Annie Elizabeth 1899- 13
Salsi, Lynn 1947- 130
Salsitz, R. A. V.
  See Salsitz, Rhondi Vilott
Salsitz, Rhondi Vilott 115
  See Salsitz, R. A. V.
Salten, Felix
  See Salzmann, Siegmund
Salter, Cedric
  See Knight, Francis Edgar
Saltman, Judith 1947- 64
Saltzberg, Barney 1955- 135
Saltzman, David (Charles Laertes)
  1967-1990 86
Salvadori, Mario (George) 1907-1997 97
  Earlier sketch in SATA 40
Salwood, F. K.
  See Kilworth, Garry
Salzer, L. E.
  See Wilson, Lionel
Salzman, Marian 1959- 77
Salzmann, Siegmund 1869-1945 25
  See Salten, Felix
Samachson, Dorothy (Mirkin) 1914-1997 3
Samachson, Joseph 1906-1980 3
  Obituary 52
Sammis, John 1942- 4
Sampson, Emma (Keats) Speed 1868-1947 . 68
Sampson, Fay (Elizabeth) 1935- 151
  Brief entry 40
  Earlier sketch in SATA 42
Sampson, Michael 1952- 143
  Earlier sketch in SATA 95
Samson, Anne S(tringer) 1933- 2
Samson, Joan 1937-1976 13
Samson, Suzanne M. 1959- 91
Samuels, Charles 1902-1982 12
Samuels, Cynthia K(alish) 1946- 79
Samuels, Gertrude 1910(?)-2003 17
  Obituary 147
Sanborn, Duane 1914-1996 38
Sancha, Sheila 1924- 38
Sanchez, Alex 1957- 151
Sanchez, Sonia 1934- 136
  Earlier sketch in SATA 22
  See also CLR 18
Sanchez-Silva, Jose Maria 1911- 132
  Earlier sketch in SATA 16
  See also CLR 12
Sand, George X. 45
Sandak, Cass R(obert) 1950-2001 51
  Brief entry 37
Sandberg, (Karin) Inger 1930- 15
Sandberg, Karl C. 1931- 35
Sandberg, Lasse (E. M.) 1924- 15
Sandburg, Carl (August) 1878-1967 8
  See also CLR 67
Sandburg, Charles
  See Sandburg, Carl (August)
Sandburg, Charles A.
  See Sandburg, Carl (August)
Sandburg, Helga 1918- 3
  See also SAAS 10
Sandell, Lisa Ann 1977- 175
Sander, Heather L. 1947- 157
Sanderlin, George 1915- 4
Sanderlin, Owenita (Harrah) 1916- 11
Sanders, Betty Jane
  See Monthei, Betty
Sanders, Nancy I. 1960- 141
  Earlier sketch in SATA 90
Sanders, Scott Russell 1945- 109
  Earlier sketch in SATA 56
Sanders, Winston P.
  See Anderson, Poul
Sanderson, Irma 1912- 66

Sanderson, Ivan T(erence) 1911-1973 6
Sanderson, Margaret Love
    See Keats, Emma
    and Sampson, Emma (Keats) Speed
Sanderson, Ruth 1951- 172
    Earlier sketches in SATA 41, 109
Sanderson, Ruth L.
    See Sanderson, Ruth
Sandin, Joan 1942- 153
    Earlier sketches in SATA 12, 94
Sandison, Janet
    See Cameron, Elizabeth Jane
Sandler, Martin W. 160
Sandoz, Mari(e Susette) 1900-1966 5
Sanford, Agnes (White) 1897-1976 61
Sanford, Doris 1937- 69
Sanger, Marjory Bartlett 1920- 8
San Jose, Christine 1929- 167
Sankey, Alice (Ann-Susan) 1910- 27
San Souci, Daniel 96
San Souci, Robert D. 1946- 158
    Earlier sketches in SATA 40, 81, 117
    See also CLR 43
Santiago, Esmeralda 1948- 129
Santos, Helen
    See Griffiths, Helen
Santrey, Louis
    See Sabin, Louis
Santucci, Barbara 1948- 130
Sapieyevski, Anne Lindbergh 1940-1993 78
    Earlier sketch in SATA 35
    See Feydy, Anne Lindbergh
    and Lindbergh, Anne
Saport, Linda 1954- 123
Sapp, Allen 1929- 151
Sarac, Roger
    See Caras, Roger A(ndrew)
Sarah, Duchess of York
    See Ferguson, Sarah
Sarasin, Jennifer
    See Sachs, Judith
Sarg, Anthony Frederick
    See Sarg, Tony
Sarg, Tony 1882-1942
    See YABC 1
Sargent, Pamela 1948- 78
    Earlier sketch in SATA 29
Sargent, Robert 1933- 2
Sargent, Sarah 1937- 44
    Brief entry 41
Sargent, Shirley 1927-2004 11
Sarnoff, Jane 1937- 10
Saroyan, William 1908-1981 23
    Obituary 24
Sarton, Eleanor May
    See Sarton, May
Sarton, May 1912-1995 36
    Obituary 86
Saseen, Sharon (Dillon) 1949- 59
Sasek, Miroslav 1916-1980 16
    Obituary 23
    See also CLR 4
Sasso, Sandy Eisenberg 1947- 162
    Earlier sketches in SATA 86, 116
Sathre, Vivian 1952- 133
    Earlier sketch in SATA 79
Satterfield, Charles
    See del Rey, Lester
    and Pohl, Frederik
Sattgast, L. J.
    See Sattgast, Linda J.
Sattgast, Linda J. 1953- 91
Sattler, Helen Roney 1921-1992 74
    Earlier sketch in SATA 4
    See also CLR 24
Sauer, Julia Lina 1891-1983 32
    Obituary 36
Sauerwein, Leigh 1944- 155
Saul, Carol P. 1947- 117
    Earlier sketch in SATA 78
Saul, John (W. III) 1942- 98

Saul, (Ellen) Wendy 1946- 42
Saulnier, Karen Luczak 1940- 80
Saunders, Caleb
    See Heinlein, Robert A.
Saunders, Dave 1939- 85
Saunders, Julie 1939- 85
Saunders, (William) Keith 1910-1994 12
Saunders, Rubie (Agnes) 1929- 21
Saunders, Susan 1945- 96
    Brief entry 41
    Earlier sketch in SATA 46
Saunders-Smith, Gail 1952- 169
Sauvain, Philip Arthur 1933- 111
Savadier, Elivia 1950- 164
    Earlier sketch in SATA 79
Savage, Alan
    See Nicole, Christopher (Robin)
Savage, Blake
    See Goodwin, Harold L(eland)
Savage, Candace (M.) 1949- 142
Savage, Deborah 1955- 76
Savage, Jeff 1961- 97
Savageau, Cheryl 1950- 96
Savery, Constance (Winifred) 1897-1999 1
Saville, Andrew
    See Taylor, Andrew
Saville, (Leonard) Malcolm 1901-1982 23
    Obituary 31
Saviozzi, Adriana
    See Mazza, Adriana
Savitt, Sam 1917(?)-2000 8
    Obituary 126
Savitz, Harriet May 1933- 72
    Earlier sketch in SATA 5
    See also SAAS 26
Sawicki, Mary 1950- 90
Sawyer, (Frederick) Don(ald) 1947- 72
Sawyer, Kem Knapp 1953- 84
Sawyer, Robert J. 1960- 149
    Earlier sketch in SATA 81
Sawyer, Robert James
    See Sawyer, Robert J.
Sawyer, Ruth 1880-1970 17
    See also CLR 36
Saxby, H. M.
    See Saxby, (Henry) Maurice
Saxby, (Henry) Maurice 1924- 71
Saxon, Andrew
    See Arthur, Robert, (Jr.)
Saxon, Antonia
    See Sachs, Judith
Say, Allen 1937- 161
    Earlier sketches in SATA 28, 69, 110
    See also CLR 22
Sayers, Frances Clarke 1897-1989 3
    Obituary 62
Sayles, Elizabeth 1956- 163
    Earlier sketch in SATA 108
Saylor-Marchant, Linda 1963- 82
Sayre, April Pulley 1966- 131
    Earlier sketch in SATA 88
Sazer, Nina 1949- 13
Scabrini, Janet 1953- 13
Scagell, Robin 1946- 107
Scagnetti, Jack 1924- 7
Scamander, Newt
    See Rowling, J.K.
Scamell, Ragnhild 1940- 77
Scanlon, Marion Stephany 11
Scannell, Vernon 1922- 59
Scarborough, Elizabeth 171
    See Scarborough, Elizabeth Ann
Scarborough, Elizabeth Ann 1947- 171
    Earlier sketch in SATA 98
    See Scarborough, Elizabeth
Scarf, Maggi
    See Scarf, Maggie
Scarf, Maggie 1932- 5
Scariano, Margaret M. 1924- 86
Scarlett, Susan
    See Streatfeild, (Mary) Noel

Scarry, Huck
    See Scarry, Richard McClure, Jr.
Scarry, Patricia (Murphy) 1924- 2
Scarry, Patsy
    See Scarry, Patricia (Murphy)
Scarry, Richard (McClure) 1919-1994 75
    Obituary 90
    Earlier sketches in SATA 2, 35
    See also CLR 41
Scarry, Richard McClure, Jr. 1953- 35
Schachner, Judith Byron 1951- 178
    Earlier sketch in SATA 88
Schachner, Judy
    See Schachner, Judith Byron
Schachtel, Roger 1949- 38
Schachtel, Roger Bernard
    See Schachtel, Roger
Schaedler, Sally 116
Schaefer, Carole Lexa 173
Schaefer, Jack (Warner) 1907-1991 66
    Obituary 65
    Earlier sketch in SATA 3
Schaefer, Lola M. 1950- 144
    Earlier sketch in SATA 91
Schaeffer, Mead 1898- 21
Schaeffer, Susan Fromberg 1941- 22
Schaer, Brigitte 1958- 112
Schaller, George B(eals) 1933- 30
Schanzer, Rosalyn (Good) 1942- 138
    Earlier sketch in SATA 77
Schatell, Brian 66
    Brief entry 47
Schechter, Betty (Goodstein) 1921- 5
Schecter, Ellen 1944- 85
Scheeder, Louis 1946- 141
Scheer, Julian (Weisel) 1926-2001 8
Scheffer, Victor B(lanchard) 1906- 6
Scheffler, Ursel 1938- 81
Scheffrin-Falk, Gladys 1928- 76
Scheidl, Gerda Marie 1913- 85
Scheier, Michael 1943- 40
    Brief entry 36
Schell, Mildred 1922- 41
Schell, Orville (Hickok) 1940- 10
Scheller, Melanie 1953- 77
Schellie, Don 1932- 29
Schembri, Jim 1962- 124
Schemm, Mildred Walker 1905-1998 21
    Obituary 103
    See Walker, Mildred
Schenker, Dona 1947- 133
    Earlier sketch in SATA 68
Scher, Paula 1948- 47
Scherf, Margaret 1908-1979 10
Schermer, Judith (Denise) 1941- 30
Schertle, Alice 1941- 145
    Earlier sketches in SATA 36, 90
Schick, Alice 1946- 27
Schick, Eleanor 1942- 144
    Earlier sketches in SATA 9, 82
Schick, Joel 1945- 31
    Brief entry 30
Schields, Gretchen 1948- 75
Schiff, Ken(neth Roy) 1942- 7
Schiller, Andrew 1919- 21
Schiller, Barbara (Heyman) 1928- 21
Schiller, Pamela (Byrne) 127
Schindel, John 1955- 115
    Earlier sketch in SATA 77
Schindelman, Joseph 1923- 67
    Brief entry 32
Schindler, S.D. 1952- 171
    Brief entry 50
    Earlier sketches in SATA 75, 118
Schindler, Steven D.
    See Schindler, S.D.
Schinto, Jeanne 1951- 93
Schisgall, Oscar 1901-1984 12
    Obituary 38
Schlaepfer, Gloria G. 1931- 154

Schlee, Ann 1934- 44
    Brief entry 36
Schleichert, Elizabeth 1945- 77
Schlein, Miriam 1926-2004 130
    Obituary 159
    Earlier sketches in SATA 2, 87
    See also CLR 41
Schlesinger, Arthur M., Jr. 1917-2007 61
    See Schlesinger, Arthur Meier
Schlesinger, Arthur Meier 1888-1965
Schlessinger, Laura (Catherine) 1947- 160
    Earlier sketch in SATA 110
Schloat, G. Warren, Jr. 1914-2000 4
Schmid, Eleonore 1939- 126
    Earlier sketches in SATA 12, 84
Schmiderer, Dorothy 1940- 19
Schmidt, Annie M. G. 1911-1995 67
    Obituary 91
    See also CLR 22
Schmidt, Diane 1953- 70
Schmidt, Elizabeth 1915- 15
Schmidt, Gary D. 1957- 135
    Earlier sketch in SATA 93
Schmidt, James Norman 1912-1983 21
Schmidt, Karen Lee 1953- 94
Schmidt, Lynette 1952- 76
Schneider, Antonie 1954- 167
    Earlier sketch in SATA 89
Schneider, Christine M. 1972(?)- 171
    Earlier sketch in SATA 120
Schneider, Dick
    See Schneider, Richard H.
Schneider, Elisa
    See Kleven, Elisa
Schneider, Herman 1905-2003 7
    Obituary 148
Schneider, Laurie
    See Adams, Laurie
Schneider, Nina 1913- 2
Schneider, Rex 1937- 44
Schneider, Richard H. 1922- 171
Schneider, Richard Henry
    See Schneider, Richard H.
Schnirel, James R. 1931- 14
Schnitter, Jane T. 1958- 88
Schnitzlein, Danny 134
Schnur, Steven 1952- 144
    Earlier sketch in SATA 95
Schoberle, Cecile 1949- 80
Schock, Pauline 1928- 45
Schoell, William 1951- 160
Schoen, Barbara (Taylor) 1924-1993 13
Schoenherr, Ian 177
Schoenherr, John (Carl) 1935- 66
    Earlier sketch in SATA 37
    See also SAAS 13
Schofield, Sandy
    See Rusch, Kristine Kathryn
Scholastica, Sister Mary
    See Jenkins, Marie M(agdalen)
Scholefield, A. T.
    See Scholefield, Alan
Scholefield, Alan 1931- 66
Scholefield, Edmund O.
    See Griffin, W.E.B.
Scholey, Arthur 1932- 28
Schone, Virginia 22
Schongut, Emanuel 1936- 52
    Brief entry 36
Schoonover, Frank (Earle) 1877-1972 24
Schoor, Gene 1921- 3
Schories, Pat 1952- 164
    Earlier sketch in SATA 116
Schott, Jane A. 1946- 172
Schotter, Roni 149
    Earlier sketch in SATA 105
Schraff, Anne E(laine) 1939- 92
    Earlier sketch in SATA 27
Schram, Peninnah 1934- 119
Schrecengost, Maity 1938- 118

Schrecengost, S. Maitland
    See Schrecengost, Maity
Schrecker, Judie 1954- 90
Schreiber, Elizabeth Anne (Ferguson)
    1947- 13
Schreiber, Ralph W(alter) 1942- 13
Schreiner, Samuel A(gnew), Jr. 1921- 70
Schroeder, Alan 1961- 98
    Earlier sketch in SATA 66
Schroeder, Binette
    See Nickl, Barbara (Elisabeth)
Schroeder, Russell (K.) 1943- 146
Schubert, Dieter 1947- 101
    Earlier sketch in SATA 62
Schubert-Gabrys, Ingrid 1953- 101
    Earlier sketch in SATA 62
Schuerger, Michele R. 110
Schuett, Stacey 1960- 168
    Earlier sketch in SATA 75
Schulke, Flip Phelps Graeme 1930- 57
Schulman, Arlene 1961- 105
Schulman, Janet 1933- 137
    Earlier sketch in SATA 22
Schulman, L(ester) M(artin) 1934- 13
Schulte, Elaine L(ouise) 1934- 36
Schultz, Betty K(epka) 1932- 125
Schultz, Gwendolyn 21
Schultz, James Willard 1859-1947
    See YABC 1
Schultz, Pearle Henriksen 1918- 21
Schulz, Charles M. 1922-2000 10
    Obituary 118
Schulz, Charles Monroe
    See Schulz, Charles M.
Schumaker, Ward 1943- 96
Schuman, Michael A. 1953- 134
    Earlier sketch in SATA 85
Schur, Maxine
    See Schur, Maxine Rose
Schur, Maxine Rose 1948- 135
    Autobiography Feature 135
    Brief entry 49
    Earlier sketches in SATA 53, 98
Schurfranz, Vivian 1925- 13
Schutzer, A. I. 1922- 13
Schuyler, Pamela R. 1948- 30
Schwager, Tina 1964- 110
Schwandt, Stephen (William) 1947- 61
Schwark, Mary Beth 1954- 51
Schwartz, Alvin 1927-1992 56
    Obituary 71
    Earlier sketch in SATA 4
    See also CLR 89
Schwartz, Amy 1954- 131
    Brief entry 41
    Earlier sketches in SATA 47, 83
    See also CLR 25
    See also SAAS 18
Schwartz, Anne Powers 1913-1987 10
Schwartz, Carol 1954- 77
Schwartz, Charles W(alsh) 1914- 8
Schwartz, David M. 1951- 110
    Earlier sketch in SATA 59
Schwartz, David Martin
    See Schwartz, David M.
Schwartz, Elizabeth Reeder 1912- 8
Schwartz, Ellen 1949- 117
Schwartz, Jerome L.
    See Lawrence, Jerome
Schwartz, Joel L. 1940- 54
    Brief entry 51
Schwartz, Joyce R. 1950- 93
Schwartz, Julius 1907-2004 45
Schwartz, Perry 1942- 75
Schwartz, Sheila (Ruth) 1929- 27
Schwartz, Stephen (Lawrence) 1948- 19
Schwartz, Virginia Frances 1950- 131
Schwarz, (Silvia Tessa) Viviane 1977- 141
Schweitzer, Byrd Baylor
    See Baylor, Byrd

Schweitzer, Iris 59
    Brief entry 36
Schweninger, Ann 1951- 168
    Earlier sketches in SATA 29, 98
Schwerin, Doris H(alpern) 1922- 64
Scieszka, Jon 1954- 160
    Earlier sketches in SATA 68, 105
    See also CLR 107
Scillian, Devin 128
Scioscia, Mary (Hershey) 1926- 63
Scofield, Penrod 1933- 62
    Obituary 78
Scoggin, Margaret C(lara) 1905-1968 47
    Brief entry 28
Scoltock, Jack 1942- 141
    Earlier sketch in SATA 72
Scoppettone, Sandra 1936- 92
    Earlier sketch in SATA 9
    See Early, Jack
Scot, Michael
    See Rohan, Michael Scott
Scotland, Jay
    See Jakes, John
Scott, Alastair
    See Allen, Kenneth S.
Scott, Ann Herbert 1926- 140
    Autobiography Feature 140
    Brief entry 29
    Earlier sketches in SATA 56, 94
Scott, Bill
    See Scott, William N(eville)
Scott, Cora Annett (Pipitone) 1931- 11
Scott, Dan
    See Barker, S(quire) Omar
Scott, Elaine 1940- 164
    Earlier sketches in SATA 36, 90
Scott, Jack Denton 1915-1995 83
    Earlier sketch in SATA 31
    See also CLR 20
    See also SAAS 14
Scott, Jane (Harrington) 1931- 55
Scott, John 1912-1976 14
Scott, John Anthony 1916- 23
Scott, John M(artin) 1913- 12
Scott, Mary
    See Mattern, Joanne
Scott, Melissa 1960- 109
Scott, Richard
    See Rennert, Richard Scott
Scott, Roney
    See Gault, William Campbell
Scott, Sally 1909-1978 43
Scott, Sally 1948- 44
Scott, Sally Elisabeth
    See Scott, Sally
Scott, W. N.
    See Scott, William N(eville)
Scott, Sir Walter 1771-1832
    See YABC 2
Scott, Warwick
    See Trevor, Elleston
Scott, William N(eville) 1923- 87
Scotti, Anna
    See Coates, Anna
Scotton, Rob 1960- 177
Scribner, Charles, Jr. 1921-1995 13
    Obituary 87
Scribner, Joanne L. 1949- 33
Scribner, Kimball 1917- 63
Scrimger, Richard 1957- 164
    Earlier sketch in SATA 119
Scroder, Walter K. 1928- 82
Scruggs, Sandy 1961- 89
Scudder, Brooke 1959- 154
Scull, Marie-Louise 1943-1993 77
Scuro, Vincent 1951- 21
Seabrooke, Brenda 1941- 148
    Earlier sketches in SATA 30, 88
Seaman, Augusta Huiell 1879-1950 31
Seamands, Ruth 1916- 9

Searcy, Margaret Zehmer 1926- *54*
  Brief entry *39*
Searight, Mary W(illiams) 1918- *17*
Searle, Kathryn Adrienne 1942- *10*
Searle, Ronald (William Fordham) 1920- *70*
  Earlier sketch in SATA *42*
Sears, Stephen W. 1932- *4*
Sebastian, Lee
  See Silverberg, Robert
Sebestyen, Igen
  See Sebestyen, Ouida
Sebestyen, Ouida 1924- *140*
  Earlier sketch in SATA *39*
  See also CLR *17*
  See also SAAS *10*
Sebrey, Mary Ann 1951- *62*
Sechrist, Elizabeth Hough 1903-1991 .... *2*
Sedges, John
  See Buck, Pearl S(ydenstricker)
Sedgwick, Marcus 1968- *160*
Seed, Cecile Eugenie 1930- *86*
  See Seed, Jenny
Seed, Jenny *8*
  See also CLR *76*
  See Seed, Cecile Eugenie
Seeger, Laura Vaccaro *172*
Seeger, Pete 1919- *139*
  Earlier sketch in SATA *13*
Seeger, Peter R.
  See Seeger, Pete
Seeley, Laura L. 1958- *71*
Seever, R.
  See Reeves, Lawrence F.
Sefozo, Mary 1925- *82*
Sefton, Catherine
  See Waddell, Martin
Segal, John *178*
Segal, Joyce 1940- *35*
Segal, Lore 1928- *163*
  Earlier sketches in SATA *4, 66*
  See also SAAS *11*
Segal, Lore Groszmann
  See Segal, Lore
Segar, E(lzie) C(risler) 1894-1938 .... *61*
Seguin, Marilyn W(eymouth) 1951- *91*
Seguin-Fontes, Marthe 1924- *109*
Seibold, J. Otto 1960- *149*
  Earlier sketch in SATA *83*
  See also SAAS *22*
Seidel, Ross *95*
Seidelman, James Edward 1926- *6*
Seiden, Art(hur) *107*
  Brief entry *42*
Seidler, Ann (G.) 1925- *131*
Seidler, Tor 1952- *149*
  Brief entry *46*
  Earlier sketches in SATA *52, 98*
Seidman, Laurence Ivan 1925- *15*
Seigel, Kalman 1917-1998 .... *12*
  Obituary *103*
Seignobosc, Francoise 1897-1961 .... *21*
Seinfeld, Jerry 1954- *146*
Seitz, Jacqueline 1931- *50*
Seixas, Judith S. 1922- *17*
Sejima, Yoshimasa 1913- *8*
Selberg, Ingrid (Maria) 1950- *68*
Selden, George
  See CLR *8*
  See Thompson, George Selden
Selden, Neil R(oy) 1931- *61*
Self, Margaret Cabell 1902-1996 .... *24*
Selig, Sylvie 1942- *13*
Sellers, Naomi
  See Flack, Naomi John White
Selman, LaRue W. 1927- *55*
Selsam, Millicent E(llis) 1912-1996 .... *29*
  Obituary *92*
  Earlier sketch in SATA *1*
  See also CLR *1*
Seltzer, Meyer 1932- *17*
Seltzer, Richard 1946- *41*

Seltzer, Richard Warren, Jr.
  See Seltzer, Richard
Selvadurai, Shyam 1965(?)- *171*
Selway, Martina 1940- *169*
  Earlier sketch in SATA *74*
Selznick, Brian 1966- *171*
  Earlier sketches in SATA *79, 117*
Semel, Nava 1954- *107*
Semloh
  See Holmes, Peggy
Sendak, Jack 1924(?)-1995 .... *28*
Sendak, Maurice 1928- *165*
  Earlier sketches in SATA *1, 27, 113*
  See also CLR *74*
Sendak, Maurice Bernard
  See Sendak, Maurice
Sender, Ruth M(insky) 1926- *62*
Sengler, Johanna 1924- *18*
Senisi, Ellen B. 1951- *116*
Senisi, Ellen Babinec
  See Senisi, Ellen B.
Senn, J(oyce) A(nn) 1941- *115*
Senn, Steve 1950- *60*
  Brief entry *48*
Serage, Nancy 1924- *10*
Seredy, Kate 1899-1975 .... *1*
  Obituary *24*
  See also CLR *10*
Seroff, Victor I(ilyitch) 1902-1979 .... *12*
  Obituary *26*
Serraillier, Ian (Lucien) 1912-1994 .... *73*
  Obituary *83*
  Earlier sketch in SATA *1*
  See also CLR *2*
  See also SAAS *3*
Serros, Michele *175*
Serros, Michele M.
  See Serros, Michele
Servello, Joe 1932- *10*
Service, Pamela F. 1945- *64*
Service, Robert
  See Service, Robert W(illiam)
Service, Robert W(illiam) 1874(?)-1958 ...... *20*
  See Service, Robert
Serwadda, W(illiam) Moses 1931- *27*
Serwer-Bernstein, Blanche L(uria)
  1910-1997 .... *10*
Sescoe, Vincent E. 1938- *123*
Seth, Mary
  See Lexau, Joan M.
Seton, Anya 1904(?)-1990 .... *3*
  Obituary *66*
Seton, Ernest (Evan) Thompson 1860-1946 . *18*
  See also CLR *59*
Seton-Thompson, Ernest
  See Seton, Ernest (Evan) Thompson
Seuling, Barbara 1937- *145*
  Earlier sketches in SATA *10, 98*
  See also SAAS *24*
Seuss, Dr.
  See Dr. Seuss
  and Geisel, Theodor Seuss
  and LeSieg, Theo.
  and Stone, Rosetta
Severn, Bill
  See Severn, William Irving
Severn, David
  See Unwin, David S(torr)
Severn, William Irving 1914- *1*
Sewall, Marcia 1935- *119*
  Earlier sketches in SATA *37, 69*
Seward, Prudence 1926- *16*
Sewell, Anna 1820-1878 .... *100*
  Earlier sketch in SATA *24*
  See also CLR *17*
Sewell, Helen (Moore) 1896-1957 .... *38*
Sexton, Anne (Harvey) 1928-1974 .... *10*
Seymour, Alta Halverson *10*
Seymour, Jane 1951- *139*
Seymour, Tres 1966- *164*
  Earlier sketch in SATA *82*

Shachtman, Tom 1942- *49*
Shackleton, C. C.
  See Aldiss, Brian W.
Shader, Rachel
  See Sofer, Barbara
Shadow, Jak
  See Sutherland, Jon
Shadyland, Sal
  See Cooper, Louise
Shafer, Robert E(ugene) 1925- *9*
Shaffer, Terea 1968- *79*
Shahan, Sherry 1949- *134*
  Earlier sketch in SATA *92*
Shahn, Bernarda Bryson
  See Bryson, Bernarda
Shaik, Fatima *114*
Shalant, Phyllis 1949- *150*
Shan, Darren 1972- *168*
  Earlier sketch in SATA *129*
Shanberg, Karen
  See Shragg, Karen (I.)
Shane, Harold Gray 1914-1993 .... *36*
  Obituary *76*
Shange, Ntozake 1948- *157*
Shanks, Ann Zane (Kushner) *10*
Shannon, David 1959- *152*
  Earlier sketch in SATA *107*
  See also CLR *87*
Shannon, George (William Bones) 1952- ... *143*
  Earlier sketches in SATA *35, 94*
Shannon, Jacqueline *63*
Shannon, Margaret
  See Silverwood, Margaret Shannon
Shannon, Monica 1905(?)-1965 .... *28*
Shannon, Terry *21*
  See Mercer, Jessie
Shannon, Terry Miller 1951- *148*
Shapiro, Irwin 1911-1981 .... *32*
Shapiro, Milton J. 1926- *32*
Shapiro, Tricia
  See Andryszewski, Tricia
Shapp, Martha Glauber 1910- *3*
Sharfman, Amalie *14*
Sharma, Partap 1939- *15*
Sharma, Rashmi
  See Singh, Rashmi Sharma
Sharman, Alison
  See Leonard, Alison
Sharmat, Marjorie Weinman 1928- *133*
  Earlier sketches in SATA *4, 33, 74*
Sharmat, Mitchell 1927- *127*
  Earlier sketch in SATA *33*
Sharp, Anne Wallace 1947- *144*
Sharp, Luke
  See Alkiviades, Alkis
Sharp, Margery 1905-1991 .... *29*
  Obituary *67*
  Earlier sketch in SATA *1*
  See also CLR *27*
Sharpe, Jon
  See Duncan, Alice
  and Knott, William C(ecil, Jr.)
  and Messman, Jon
Sharpe, Mitchell R(aymond) 1924- *12*
Sharpe, Susan 1946- *71*
Sharratt, Nick 1962- *153*
  Earlier sketch in SATA *104*
Shasha, Mark 1961- *80*
Shattuck, Roger 1923-2005 .... *64*
  Obituary *174*
Shattuck, Roger Whitney
  See Shattuck, Roger
Shaw, Arnold 1909-1989 .... *4*
  Obituary *63*
Shaw, Carolyn V. 1934- *91*
Shaw, Charles (Green) 1892-1974 .... *13*
Shaw, Evelyn S. 1927- *28*
Shaw, Flora Louisa
  See Lugard, Flora Louisa Shaw

Shaw, Janet 1937- 146
  Earlier sketch in SATA 61
  See also CLR 96
Shaw, Janet Beeler
  See Shaw, Janet
Shaw, Lisa
  See Rogak, Lisa
Shaw, Margret 1940- 68
Shaw, Nancy 1946- 162
  Earlier sketch in SATA 71
Shaw, Ray 7
Shaw, Richard 1923- 12
Shawn, Frank S.
  See Goulart, Ron(ald Joseph)
Shay, Art
  See Shay, Arthur
Shay, Arthur 1922- 4
Shay, Lacey
  See Shebar, Sharon Sigmond
Shea, George 1940- 54
  Brief entry 42
Shea, Pegi Deitz 1960- 172
  Earlier sketches in SATA 77, 137
Shearer, John 1947- 43
  Brief entry 27
  See also CLR 34
Shearer, Ted 1919- 43
Shebar, Sharon Sigmond 1945- 36
Shecter, Ben 1935- 16
Shedd, Warner 1934- 147
  Earlier sketch in SATA 87
Sheedy, Alexandra Elizabeth 1962- 39
  Earlier sketch in SATA 19
Sheehan, Ethna 1908-2000 9
Sheehan, Patty 1945- 77
Sheehan, Sean 1951- 154
  Earlier sketch in SATA 86
Sheen, Barbara 1949- 143
Shefelman, Janice Jordan 1930- 129
  Earlier sketch in SATA 58
Shefelman, Tom (Whitehead) 1927- 58
Sheffer, H. R.
  See Abels, Harriette S(heffer)
Sheffield, Charles 1935-2002 109
Sheffield, Janet N. 1926- 26
Sheikh, Nazneen
  See Sadiq, Nazneen
Shekerjian, Regina Tor 16
Shelby, Anne 1948- 85
  Autobiography Feature 121
  See also SAAS 26
Sheldon, Ann 67
  Earlier sketch in SATA 1
Sheldon, Ann
  See Antle, Nancy
Sheldon, Aure 1917-1976 12
Sheldon, John
  See Bloch, Robert (Albert)
Sheldon, Muriel 1926- 45
  Brief entry 39
Shell, Barry 1951- 176
Shelley, Frances
  See Wees, Frances Shelley
Shelley, Mary Wollstonecraft (Godwin)
  1797-1851 29
Shelton, William Roy 1919-1995 5
  Obituary 129
Shemie, Bonnie (Jean Brenner) 1949- 96
Shemin, Margaretha (Hoeneveld) 1928- 4
Shen, Michele 1953- 173
Shenker, Michele
  See Shen, Michele
Shenton, Edward 1895-1977 45
Shepard, Aaron 1950- 113
  Earlier sketch in SATA 75
Shepard, Ernest Howard 1879-1976 100
  Obituary 24
  Earlier sketches in SATA 3, 33
  See also CLR 27
Shepard, James R.
  See Shepard, Jim

Shepard, Jim 1956- 164
  Earlier sketch in SATA 90
Shepard, Mary
  See Knox, (Mary) Eleanor Jessie
Shephard, Esther 1891-1975 5
  Obituary 26
Shepherd, Donna Walsh
  See Walsh Shepherd, Donna
Shepherd, Elizabeth 4
Shepherd, Irana 173
Shepherd, Roni
  See Shepherd, Irana
Shepperson, Rob 178
Sherburne, Zoa (Lillian Morin) 1912-1995 3
  See also SAAS 18
Sherlock, Patti 71
Sherman, D(enis) R(onald) 1934- 48
  Brief entry 29
Sherman, Diane (Finn) 1928- 12
Sherman, Elizabeth
  See Friskey, Margaret (Richards)
Sherman, Harold (Morrow) 1898-1987 37
  Obituary 137
Sherman, Josepha 163
  Earlier sketch in SATA 75
Sherman, Michael
  See Lowndes, Robert A(ugustine) W(ard)
Sherman, Nancy
  See Rosenberg, Nancy (Sherman)
Sherman, Pat 174
Sherman, Peter Michael
  See Lowndes, Robert A(ugustine) W(ard)
Sherrard, Valerie (Anne) 1957- 141
Sherrod, Jane
  See Singer, Jane Sherrod
Sherry, Clifford J. 1943- 84
Sherry, (Dulcie) Sylvia 1932- 122
  Earlier sketch in SATA 8
Sherwan, Earl 1917- 3
Sherwood, Jonathan
  See London, Jonathan (Paul)
Shetterly, Will 1955- 78
  Autobiography Feature 106
Shetterly, William Howard
  See Shetterly, Will
Shiefman, Vicky 1942- 22
Shields, Brenda Desmond (Armstrong)
  1914- 37
Shields, Carol Diggory 174
Shields, Charles 1944- 10
Shiels, Barbara
  See Adams, Barbara Johnston
Shiffman, Lena 1957- 101
Shiina, Makoto 1944- 83
Shimin, Symeon 1902-1984 13
Shine, Andrea 1955- 104
Shine, Deborah 1932- 71
Shinn, Everett 1876-1953 21
Shinn, Sharon 1957- 164
  Earlier sketch in SATA 110
Shippen, Katherine B(inney) 1892-1980 1
  Obituary 23
  See also CLR 36
Shippey, T(homas) A(lan) 1943- 143
Shipton, Eric Earle 1907-1977 10
Shiraz, Yasmin 173
Shirer, William L(awrence) 1904-1993 45
  Obituary 78
Shirley, Gayle C 1955- 96
Shirley, Gayle Corbett
  See Shirley, Gayle C
Shirley, Jean 1919- 70
Shirreffs, Gordon D(onald) 1914-1996 11
Shirts, Morris A(lpine) 1922- 63
Shlichta, Joe 1968- 84
Shmurak, Carole B. 1944- 118
Shore, Diane Z. 179
Shore, Diane ZuHone
  See Shore, Diane Z.
Shore, June Lewis 30
Shore, Nancy 1960- 124

Shore, Robert 1924- 39
Short, Michael 1937- 65
Short, Roger
  See Arkin, Alan
Shortall, Leonard W. 19
Shortt, Tim(othy Donald) 1961- 96
Shotwell, Louisa Rossiter 1902-1993 3
Shoup, Barbara 1947- 156
  Earlier sketch in SATA 86
  See also SAAS 24
Showalter, Jean B(reckinridge) 12
Showell, Ellen Harvey 1934- 33
Showers, Paul C. 1910-1999 92
  Obituary 114
  Earlier sketch in SATA 21
  See also CLR 6
  See also SAAS 7
Shpakow, Tanya 1959(?)- 94
Shpitalnik, Vladimir 1964- 83
Shragg, Karen (I.) 1954- 142
Shreeve, Elizabeth 1956- 156
Shreve, Susan
  See Shreve, Susan Richards
Shreve, Susan Richards 1939- 152
  Brief entry 41
  Earlier sketches in SATA 46, 95
Shriver, Jean Adair 1932- 75
Shriver, Maria 1955- 134
Shriver, Maria Owings
  See Shriver, Maria
Shrode, Mary
  See Hollingsworth, Mary
Shtainmets, Leon 32
Shub, Elizabeth 1915(?)-2004 5
Shuken, Julia 1948- 84
Shulevitz, Uri 1935- 165
  Earlier sketches in SATA 3, 50, 106
  See also CLR 61
Shulman, Alix Kates 1932- 7
Shulman, Dee 1957- 146
Shulman, Irving 1913-1995 13
Shulman, Neil B(arnett) 1945- 89
Shumsky, Zena
  See Collier, Zena
Shura, Mary Francis
  See Craig, Mary (Francis) Shura
Shusterman, Neal 1962- 140
  Autobiography Feature 140
  Earlier sketches in SATA 85, 121
Shuter, Jane (Margaret) 1955- 151
  Earlier sketch in SATA 90
Shuttlesworth, Dorothy Edwards 3
Shwartz, Susan (Martha) 1949- 94
Shyer, Christopher 1961- 98
Shyer, Marlene Fanta 13
Siberell, Anne 29
Sibley, Don 1922- 12
Siburt, Ruth 1951- 121
Siculan, Daniel 1922- 12
Sidgwick, Ethel 1877-1970 116
Sidjakov, Nicolas 1924- 18
Sidman, Joyce 1956- 145
Sidney, Frank
  See Warwick, Alan R(oss)
Sidney, Margaret
  See Lothrop, Harriet Mulford Stone
Siegal, Aranka 1930- 88
  Brief entry 37
Siegel, Beatrice 36
Siegel, Helen
  See Siegl, Helen
Siegel, Robert (Harold) 1939- 39
Siegelson, Kim L. 1962- 114
Siegl, Helen 1924- 34
Siepmann, Mary Aline
  See Wesley, Mary (Aline)
Sierra, Judy 1945- 162
  Earlier sketch in SATA 104
Sieswerda, Paul L. 1942- 147
Sievert, Terri
  See Dougherty, Terri (L.)

Silas
See McCay, (Zenas) Winsor
Silcock, Sara Lesley 1947- *12*
Sill, Cathryn 1953- *141*
Earlier sketch in SATA *74*
Sill, John 1947- *140*
Earlier sketch in SATA *74*
Sillitoe, Alan 1928- *61*
Sills, Leslie (Elka) 1948- *129*
Silly, E. S.
See Kraus, (Herman) Robert
Silsbe, Brenda 1953- *73*
Silva, Joseph
See Goulart, Ron(ald Joseph)
Silver, Ruth
See Chew, Ruth
Silverberg, Robert 1935- *91*
Autobiography Feature *104*
Earlier sketch in SATA *13*
See also CLR *59*
Silverman, Erica 1955- *165*
Earlier sketches in SATA *78, 112*
Silverman, Janis L. 1946- *127*
Silverman, Mel(vin Frank) 1931-1966 .... *9*
Silverman, Robin L. 1954- *96*
Silverman, Robin Landew
See Silverman, Robin L.
Silverstein, Alvin 1933- *124*
Earlier sketches in SATA *8, 69*
See also CLR *25*
Silverstein, Herma 1945- *106*
Silverstein, Robert Alan 1959- *124*
Earlier sketch in SATA *77*
Silverstein, Shel 1932-1999 .... *92*
Brief entry *27*
Obituary *116*
Earlier sketch in SATA *33*
See also CLR *96*
Silverstein, Sheldon Allan
See Silverstein, Shel
Silverstein, Virginia B(arbara Opshelor)
1937- *124*
Earlier sketches in SATA *8, 69*
See also CLR *25*
Silverthorne, Elizabeth 1930- *35*
Silverwood, Margaret Shannon 1966- *137*
Earlier sketch in SATA *83*
Silvey, Diane F. 1946- *135*
Sim, David 1953- *162*
Sim, Dorrith M. 1931- *96*
Simard, Remy 1959- *168*
Simmie, Lois (Ann) 1932- *106*
Simmonds, Posy 1945- *130*
See also CLR *23*
Simmons, Andra 1939- *141*
Simmons, Elly 1955- *134*
Simms, Laura 1947- *117*
Simner, Janni Lee *113*
Simon, Charlie May
See Fletcher, Charlie May Hogue
Simon, Francesca 1955- *111*
Simon, Gabriel 1972- *118*
Simon, Hilda Rita 1921- *28*
See also CLR *39*
Simon, Howard 1903-1979 .... *32*
Obituary *21*
Simon, Joe
See Simon, Joseph H.
Simon, Joseph H. 1913- *7*
Simon, Martin P(aul William) 1903-1969 .... *12*
Simon, Mina Lewiton
See Lewiton, Mina
Simon, Norma (Feldstein) 1927- *129*
Earlier sketches in SATA *3, 68*
Simon, Seymour 1931- *138*
Earlier sketches in SATA *4, 73*
See also CLR *63*
Simon, Shirley (Schwartz) 1921- *11*
Simon, Solomon 1895-1970 .... *40*
Simonetta, Linda 1948- *14*
Simonetta, Sam 1936- *14*

Simons, Barbara B(rooks) 1934- *41*
Simont, Marc 1915- *126*
Earlier sketches in SATA *9, 73*
Simpson, Colin 1908-1983 .... *14*
Simpson, Harriette
See Arnow, Harriette (Louisa) Simpson
Simpson, Jacynth Hope
See Hope Simpson, Jacynth
Simpson, Lesley 1963- *150*
Simpson, Margaret 1943- *128*
Simpson, Myrtle L(illias) 1931- *14*
Sims, Blanche *168*
Earlier sketch in SATA *75*
Sims, Blanche L.
See Sims, Blanche
Simundsson, Elva 1950- *63*
Sinclair, Clover
See Gater, Dilys
Sinclair, Emil
See Hesse, Hermann
Sinclair, Jeff 1958- *77*
Sinclair, Olga 1923- *121*
Sinclair, Rose
See Smith, Susan Vernon
Sinclair, Upton 1878-1968 .... *9*
Sinclair, Upton Beall
See Sinclair, Upton
Singer, A.L.
See Lerangis, Peter
Singer, Arthur 1917-1990 .... *64*
Singer, Isaac
See Singer, Isaac Bashevis
Singer, Isaac Bashevis 1904-1991 .... *27*
Obituary *68*
Earlier sketch in SATA *3*
See also CLR *1*
Singer, Jane Sherrod 1917-1985 .... *4*
Obituary *42*
Singer, Julia 1917- *28*
Singer, Kurt D. 1911-2005 .... *38*
Obituary *172*
Singer, Marilyn 1948- *158*
Autobiography Feature *158*
Brief entry *38*
Earlier sketches in SATA *48, 80, 125*
See also CLR *48*
See also SAAS *13*
Singer, Muff 1942-2005 .... *104*
Obituary *160*
Singer, Susan (Mahler) 1941- *9*
Singh, Rashmi Sharma 1952- *90*
Singleton, Linda Joy 1957- *166*
Earlier sketch in SATA *88*
Singleton, L.J.
See Singleton, Linda Joy
Sinykin, Sheri(l Terri) Cooper 1950- *142*
Autobiography Feature *142*
Earlier sketches in SATA *72, 133*
Sipiera, Paul P., (Jr.) 1948- *144*
Earlier sketch in SATA *89*
Siracusa, Catherine (Jane) 1947- *82*
Sirett, Dawn (Karen) 1966- *88*
Sirimarco, Elizabeth 1966- *158*
Sirof, Harriet 1930- *94*
Earlier sketch in SATA *37*
Sirois, Allen L. 1950- *76*
Sirvaitis (Chernyaev), Karen (Ann) 1961- ... *79*
Sis, Peter 1949- *106*
Earlier sketch in SATA *67*
See also CLR *110*
See Sis, Peter
Sis, Peter 1949- *149*
See also CLR *110*
See Sis, Peter
Sisson, Rosemary Anne 1923- *11*
Sister Mary Terese
See Donze, Mary Terese
Sita, Lisa 1962- *87*
Sitomer, Alan Lawrence *174*
Sitomer, Harry 1903-1985 .... *31*
Sitomer, Mindel 1903-1987 .... *31*

Sittenfeld, Curtis 1976(?)- *164*
Sive, Helen R(obinson) 1951- *30*
Sivulich, Sandra (Jeanne) Stroner 1941- *9*
Skarmeta, Antonio 1940- *57*
Skelly, James R(ichard) 1927- *17*
Skinner, Constance Lindsay 1877-1939
See YABC *1*
Skinner, Cornelia Otis 1901-1979 .... *2*
Skipper, G. C. 1939- *46*
Brief entry *38*
Sklansky, Amy E(dgar) 1971- *145*
Skofield, James *95*
Brief entry *44*
Skold, Betty Westrom 1923- *41*
Skorpen, Liesel Moak 1935- *3*
Skott, Maria
See Nikolajeva, Maria
Skrypuch, Marsha Forchuk 1954- *134*
Skultety, Nancy Laney 1960- *175*
Skurzynski, Gloria 1930- *145*
Autobiography Feature *145*
Earlier sketches in SATA *8, 74, 122*
See also SAAS *9*
Skurzynski, Gloria Joan
See Skurzynski, Gloria
Skutch, Robert 1925- *89*
Skye, Maggie
See Werner, Herma
Skye, Obert *170*
Slackman, Charles B. 1934- *12*
Slade, Arthur G(regory) 1967- *149*
Earlier sketch in SATA *106*
Slade, Richard 1910-1971 .... *9*
Slangerup, Erik Jon 1969- *130*
Slate, Joseph 1928- *174*
Earlier sketches in SATA *38, 122*
Slate, Joseph Frank
See Slate, Joseph
Slater, Dashka 1963- *179*
Slater, Ray
See Lansdale, Joe R.
Slaughter, Hope 1940- *84*
Slaughter, Jean
See Doty, Jean Slaughter
Slaughter, Tom 1955- *152*
Slavicek, Louise Chipley 1956- *144*
Slavin, Bill 1959- *148*
Earlier sketch in SATA *76*
Slaymaker, Melissa Eskridge 1958- *158*
Sleator, William (Warner III) 1945- *161*
Earlier sketches in SATA *3, 68, 118*
See also CLR *29*
Slegers, Liesbet 1975- *154*
Sleigh, Barbara 1906-1982 .... *86*
Obituary *30*
Earlier sketch in SATA *3*
Slepian, Jan 1921- *85*
Brief entry *45*
Earlier sketch in SATA *51*
See also SAAS *8*
Slepian, Janice B.
See Slepian, Jan
Slicer, Margaret O. 1920- *4*
Slier, Debby
See Shine, Deborah
Sloan, Brian 1966- *172*
Sloan, Carolyn 1937- *116*
Earlier sketch in SATA *58*
Sloan, Glenna (Davis) 1930- *120*
Sloane, Eric 1910(?)-1985 .... *52*
Obituary *42*
Sloane, Todd 1955- *88*
Sloat, Teri 1948- *164*
Earlier sketches in SATA *70, 106*
Slobodkin, Florence Gersh 1905-1994 .... *5*
Obituary *107*
Slobodkin, Louis 1903-1975 .... *26*
Earlier sketch in SATA *1*
Slobodkina, Esphyr 1908-2002 .... *1*
Obituary *135*
See also SAAS *8*

Sloggett, Nellie 1851-1923 .... *44*
Sloss, Lesley Lord 1965- *72*
Slote, Alfred 1926- *72*
  Earlier sketch in SATA *8*
  See also CLR *4*
  See also SAAS *21*
Slote, Elizabeth 1956- *80*
Small, David 1945- *126*
  Brief entry *46*
  Earlier sketches in SATA *50, 95*
  See also CLR *53*
Small, Ernest
  See Lent, Blair
Small, Mary 1932- *165*
Small, Terry 1942- *75*
Smallcomb, Pam 1954- *159*
Smalls, Irene
  See Smalls-Hector, Irene
Smalls-Hector, Irene 1950- *146*
  Earlier sketch in SATA *73*
  See also CLR *103*
Smaridge, Norah (Antoinette) 1903-1994 ...... *6*
Smee, Nicola 1948- *167*
  Earlier sketch in SATA *76*
Smiley, Virginia Kester 1923- *2*
Smith, Anne Warren 1938- *41*
  Brief entry *34*
Smith, Barry (Edward Jervis) 1943- *75*
Smith, Beatrice S(chillinger) *12*
Smith, Betsy Covington 1937- *55*
  Earlier sketch in SATA *43*
Smith, Betty (Wehner) 1904-1972 .... *6*
Smith, Bradford 1909-1964 .... *5*
Smith, Brenda 1946- *82*
Smith, C. Pritchard
  See Hoyt, Edwin P(almer), Jr.
Smith, Caesar
  See Trevor, Elleston
Smith, Charles R., (Jr.) 1969- *159*
Smith, Craig 1955- *172*
  Earlier sketches in SATA *81, 117*
Smith, Cynthia Leitich 1967- *152*
Smith, D. James 1955- *176*
Smith, Datus C(lifford), Jr. 1907-1999 .... *13*
  Obituary *116*
Smith, Debra 1955- *89*
Smith, Derek 1943- *141*
Smith, Dick King
  See King-Smith, Dick
Smith, Dodie
  See Smith, Dorothy Gladys
Smith, Doris Buchanan 1934-2002 .... *75*
  Obituary *140*
  Earlier sketch in SATA *28*
  See also SAAS *10*
Smith, Dorothy Gladys 1896-1990 .... *82*
  Obituary *65*
  See Smith, Dodie
Smith, Dorothy Stafford 1905- *6*
Smith, E(lmer) Boyd 1860-1943
  See YABC *1*
Smith, E(dric) Brooks 1917- *40*
Smith, Emma 1923- *52*
  Brief entry *36*
Smith, (Katherine) Eunice (Young)
  1902-1993 .... *5*
Smith, Frances C(hristine) 1904-1986 .... *3*
Smith, Gary R. 1932- *14*
Smith, Geof 1969- *102*
Smith, George Harmon 1920- *5*
Smith, Greg Leitich *152*
Smith, Helene 1937- *142*
Smith, Howard E(verett), Jr. 1927- *12*
Smith, Hugh L(etcher) 1921-1968 .... *5*
Smith, Imogene Henderson 1922- *12*
Smith, Jacqueline B. 1937- *39*
Smith, Jada Pinkett 1971- *161*
Smith, Janet (Buchanan) Adam
  See Adam Smith, Janet (Buchanan)
Smith, Janice Lee 1949- *155*
  Earlier sketch in SATA *54*

Smith, Jean
  See Smith, Frances C(hristine)
Smith, Jean Pajot 1945- *10*
Smith, Jeff(rey Alan) 1960- *161*
  Earlier sketch in SATA *93*
Smith, Jeff Allen
  See Smith, Jeff(rey Alan)
Smith, Jenny 1963- *90*
Smith, Jessie
  See Kunhardt, Edith
Smith, Jessie Willcox 1863-1935 .... *21*
  See also CLR *59*
Smith, Joan (Mary) 1933- *54*
  Brief entry *46*
Smith, Johnston
  See Crane, Stephen (Townley)
Smith, Jos(eph) A. 1936- *120*
  Earlier sketch in SATA *73*
Smith, Judie R. 1936- *80*
Smith, Lafayette
  See Higdon, Hal
Smith, Lane 1959- *179*
  Earlier sketches in SATA *76, 131*
  See also CLR *47*
Smith, Lee
  See Albion, Lee Smith
Smith, Lendon H(oward) 1921- *64*
Smith, Linda 1949- *177*
Smith, Linell Nash 1932- *2*
Smith, Lucia B. 1943- *30*
Smith, Marion Hagens 1913- *12*
Smith, Marion Jaques 1899-1987 .... *13*
Smith, Mary Ellen *10*
Smith, Marya 1945- *78*
Smith, Mike
  See Smith, Mary Ellen
Smith, Nancy Covert 1935- *12*
Smith, Norman F. 1920- *70*
  Earlier sketch in SATA *5*
Smith, Patricia Clark 1943- *96*
Smith, Pauline C.
  See Arthur, Robert, (Jr.)
Smith, Pauline C(oggeshall) 1908-1994 .... *27*
Smith, Philip Warren 1936- *46*
Smith, Rebecca 1946- *123*
Smith, Robert Kimmel 1930- *77*
  Earlier sketch in SATA *12*
Smith, Robert Paul 1915-1977 .... *52*
  Obituary *30*
Smith, Roland 1951- *161*
  Earlier sketch in SATA *115*
Smith, Rosamond
  See Oates, Joyce Carol
Smith, Ruth Leslie 1902- *2*
Smith, Sandra Lee 1945- *75*
Smith, Sarah Stafford
  See Smith, Dorothy Stafford
Smith, Sharon 1947- *82*
Smith, Sherri L. 1971- *156*
Smith, Sherwood 1951- *140*
  Earlier sketch in SATA *82*
Smith, Shirley Raines
  See Raines, Shirley C(arol)
Smith, Susan Carlton 1923- *12*
Smith, Susan Mathias 1950- *43*
  Brief entry *35*
Smith, Susan Vernon 1950- *48*
  See Mendonca, Susan
Smith, Tim(othy R.) 1945- *151*
Smith, Ursula 1934- *54*
Smith, Vian (Crocker) 1920-1969 .... *11*
Smith, Wanda VanHoy 1926- *65*
Smith, Ward
  See Goldsmith, Howard
Smith, William A. 1918- *10*
Smith, William Jay 1918- *154*
  Autobiography Feature *154*
  Earlier sketches in SATA *2, 68*
  See also SAAS *22*
Smith, Winsome 1935- *45*

Smith, Z.Z.
  See Westheimer, David
Smith-Ankrom, M. E. 1942- *130*
Smith-Griswold, Wendy 1955- *88*
Smith-Rex, Susan J. 1950- *94*
Smithsen, Richard
  See Pellowski, Michael (Joseph)
Smits, Teo
  See Smits, Theodore R(ichard)
Smits, Theodore R(ichard) 1905-1996 .... *45*
  Brief entry *28*
Smolinski, Dick 1932- *86*
Smothers, Ethel Footman 1944- *149*
  Earlier sketch in SATA *76*
Smucker, Barbara (Claassen) 1915- *130*
  Earlier sketches in SATA *29, 76*
  See also CLR *10*
  See also SAAS *11*
Smyth, Iain 1959- *105*
Snedeker, Caroline Dale (Parke) 1871-1956
  See YABC *2*
Snell, Nigel (Edward Creagh) 1936- *57*
  Brief entry *40*
Snellgrove, L(aurence) E(rnest) 1928- *53*
Snelling, Dennis (Wayne) 1958- *84*
Sneve, Virginia Driving Hawk 1933- *95*
  Earlier sketch in SATA *8*
  See also CLR *2*
Snicket, Lemony 1970- *126*
  See also CLR *79*
  See Handler, Daniel
Snodgrass, Mary Ellen 1944- *75*
Snodgrass, Quentin Curtius
  See Clemens, Samuel Langhorne
Snodgrass, Thomas Jefferson
  See Clemens, Samuel Langhorne
Snook, Barbara (Lillian) 1913-1976 .... *34*
Snow, Donald Clifford 1917-1979 .... *16*
Snow, Dorothea J(ohnston) 1909- *9*
Snow, Richard F(olger) 1947- *52*
  Brief entry *37*
Snyder, Anne 1922-2001 .... *4*
  Obituary *125*
Snyder, Bernadette McCarver 1930- *97*
Snyder, Carol 1941- *35*
Snyder, Gerald S(eymour) 1933- *48*
  Brief entry *34*
Snyder, Midori 1954- *106*
Snyder, Paul A. 1946- *125*
Snyder, Zilpha Keatley 1927- *163*
  Autobiography Feature *163*
  Earlier sketches in SATA *1, 28, 75, 110*
  See also CLR *121*
  See also SAAS *2*
Snyderman, Reuven K. 1922- *5*
So, Meilo *162*
Sobel, June 1950- *149*
Soble, Jennie
  See Cavin, Ruth (Brodie)
Sobol, Donald J. 1924- *132*
  Earlier sketches in SATA *1, 31, 73*
  See also CLR *4*
Sobol, Harriet Langsam 1936- *47*
  Brief entry *34*
Sobol, Rose 1931- *76*
Sobott-Mogwe, Gaele 1956- *97*
Soderlind, Arthur E(dwin) 1920- *14*
Soentpiet, Chris K. 1970- *159*
  Earlier sketch in SATA *97*
Soerensen, Svend Otto 1916- *67*
Sofer, Barbara 1949- *109*
Sofer, Rachel
  See Sofer, Barbara
Softly, Barbara Frewin 1924- *12*
Sohl, Frederic J(ohn) 1916- *10*
Sokol, Bill
  See Sokol, William
Sokol, William 1923- *37*
Sokolov, Kirill 1930- *34*
Solbert, Romaine G. 1925- *2*

Solbert, Ronni
  See Solbert, Romaine G.
Solheim, James *133*
Solomon, Joan 1930- *51*
  Brief entry *40*
Solomons, Ikey Esquir
  See Thackeray, William Makepeace
Solonevich, George 1915-2003 .... *15*
Solot, Mary Lynn 1939- *12*
Somerlott, Robert 1928-2001 .... *62*
Somervill, Barbara A(nn) 1948- *140*
Sommer, Angela
  See Sommer-Bodenburg, Angela
Sommer, Carl 1930- *175*
  Earlier sketch in SATA *126*
Sommer, Elyse 1929- *7*
Sommer, Robert 1929- *12*
Sommer-Bodenburg, Angela 1948- *63*
Sommer-Bodenburg, Angela 1948- *113*
Sommerdorf, Norma (Jean) 1926- *131*
Sommerfelt, Aimee 1892-1975 .... *5*
Son, John *160*
Sones, Sonya *131*
Sonneborn, Ruth (Cantor) 1899-1974 .... *4*
  Obituary *27*
Sonnenmark, Laura A. 1958- *73*
Sopko, Eugen 1949- *58*
Sorel, Edward 1929- *126*
  Brief entry *37*
  Earlier sketch in SATA *65*
Sorensen, Henri 1950- *115*
  Earlier sketch in SATA *77*
Sorensen, Svend Otto
  See Soerensen, Svend Otto
Sorensen, Virginia 1912-1991 .... *2*
  Obituary *72*
  See also SAAS *15*
Sorenson, Jane 1926- *63*
Sorenson, Margo 1946- *96*
Sorley Walker, Kathrine *41*
Sorrells, Walter *177*
Sorrentino, Joseph N. 1937- *6*
Sortor, June Elizabeth 1939- *12*
Sortor, Toni
  See Sortor, June Elizabeth
Soskin, V. H.
  See Ellison, Virginia H(owell)
Soto, Gary 1952- *174*
  Earlier sketches in SATA *80, 120*
  See also CLR *38*
Sotomayor, Antonio 1902-1985 .... *11*
Souci, Robert D. San
  See San Souci, Robert D.
Soudley, Henry
  See Wood, James Playsted
Souhami, Jessica *176*
Soule, Gardner (Bosworth) 1913-2000 .... *14*
Soule, Jean Conder 1919- *10*
Souster, (Holmes) Raymond 1921- *63*
South, Sheri Cobb 1959- *82*
Southall, Ivan (Francis) 1921- *134*
  Autobiography Feature *134*
  Earlier sketches in SATA *3, 68*
  See also CLR *2*
  See also SAAS *3*
Southey, Robert 1774-1843 .... *54*
Southgate, Vera *54*
Sovak, Jan 1953- *115*
Sowden, Celeste
  See Walters, Celeste
Sowter, Nita *69*
Spafford, Suzy 1945- *160*
Spagnoli, Cathy 1950- *134*
  Earlier sketch in SATA *79*
Spain, Sahara Sunday 1991- *133*
Spalding, Andrea 1944- *150*
  Earlier sketch in SATA *101*
Spanfeller, James J(ohn) 1930- *19*
  See Spanfeller, Jim

Spanfeller, Jim
  See SAAS 8
  See Spanfeller, James J(ohn)
Spangenberg, Judith Dunn 1942- 5
Spanyol, Jessica 1965- *137*
Spar, Jerome 1918- *10*
Sparks, Barbara 1942- *78*
Sparks, Beatrice (Mathews) 1918- *44*
  Brief entry *28*
Sparks, Mary W. 1920- *15*
Spaulding, Douglas
  See Bradbury, Ray
Spaulding, Leonard
  See Bradbury, Ray
Spaulding, Norma *107*
Speare, Elizabeth George 1908-1994 .... *62*
  Obituary *83*
  Earlier sketch in SATA *5*
  See also CLR *8*
Spearing, Judith (Mary Harlow) 1922- 9
Speck, Nancy 1959- *104*
Specking, Inez 1890-1960(?) *11*
Speed, Nell
  See Keats, Emma
  and Sampson, Emma (Keats) Speed
Speed, Nell (Ewing) 1878-1913 .... *68*
Speer, Bonnie Stahlman 1929- *113*
Speer-Lyon, Tammie L. 1965- *89*
Speicher, Helen Ross S(mith) 1915- 8
Speir, Nancy 1958- *81*
Spellman, John W(illard) 1934- *14*
Spellman, Roger G.
  See Cox, William R(obert)
Spelman, Cornelia Maude 1946- *144*
  Earlier sketch in SATA *96*
Spelman, Mary 1934- *28*
Spelvin, George
  See Lerangis, Peter
  and Phillips, David Atlee
Spence, Cynthia
  See Eble, Diane
Spence, Eleanor (Rachel) 1928- *21*
  See also CLR *26*
Spence, Geraldine 1931- *47*
Spencer, Ann 1918- *10*
Spencer, Cornelia
  See Yaukey, Grace S(ydenstricker)
Spencer, Donald D(ean) 1931- *41*
Spencer, Elizabeth 1921- *14*
Spencer, Leonard G.
  See Garrett, (Gordon) Randall (Phillip)
  and Silverberg, Robert
Spencer, William 1922- 9
Spencer, Zane A(nn) 1935- *35*
Sper, Emily 1957- *142*
Speregen, Devra Newberger 1964- *84*
Sperling, Dan(iel Lee) 1949- *65*
Sperry, Armstrong W. 1897-1976 .... *1*
  Obituary *27*
Sperry, Raymond
  See Garis, Howard R(oger)
Sperry, Raymond, Jr. *1*
Spetter, Jung-Hee 1969- *134*
Spicer, Dorothy Gladys -1975 .... *32*
Spiegelman, Art 1948- *158*
  Earlier sketch in SATA *109*
Spiegelman, Judith M. 5
Spielberg, Steven 1947- *32*
Spier, Peter (Edward) 1927- *54*
  Earlier sketch in SATA *4*
  See also CLR *5*
Spilhaus, Athelstan (Frederick) 1911-1998 .. *13*
  Obituary *102*
Spilka, Arnold 1917- 6
Spillane, Frank Morrison
  See Spillane, Mickey
Spillane, Mickey 1918-2006 .... *66*
  Obituary *176*
  See Spillane, Frank Morrison
Spinelli, Eileen 1942- *150*
  Earlier sketches in SATA *38, 101*

Spinelli, Jerry 1941- *158*
  Earlier sketches in SATA *39, 71, 110*
  See also CLR *82*
Spink, Reginald (William) 1905-1994 .... *11*
Spinka, Penina Keen 1945- *72*
Spinner, Stephanie 1943- *132*
  Earlier sketches in SATA *38, 91*
Spinossimus
  See White, William, Jr.
Spiotta-DiMare, Loren *173*
Spires, Elizabeth 1952- *111*
  Earlier sketch in SATA *71*
Spirin, Gennadii
  See Spirin, Gennady
Spirin, Gennadij
  See Spirin, Gennady
Spirin, Gennady 1948- *134*
  Earlier sketch in SATA *95*
  See also CLR *88*
Spivak, Dawnine *101*
Spohn, David 1948- *72*
Spohn, Kate 1962- *147*
  Earlier sketch in SATA *87*
Spollen, Christopher 1952- *12*
Spooner, Michael (Tim) 1954- *92*
Spowart, Robin 1947- *177*
  Earlier sketch in SATA *82*
Sprague, Gretchen 1926-2003 .... *27*
Sprengel, Artie
  See Lerangis, Peter
Sprigge, Elizabeth (Miriam Squire)
  1900-1974 .... *10*
Spring, (Robert) Howard 1889-1965 .... *28*
Springer, Margaret 1941- *78*
Springer, Marilyn Harris 1931- *47*
Springer, Nancy 1948- *172*
  Earlier sketches in SATA *65, 110*
Springstubb, Tricia 1950- *78*
  Brief entry *40*
  Earlier sketch in SATA *46*
Spudvilas, Anne 1951- *94*
Spurll, Barbara 1952- *78*
Spurr, Elizabeth *172*
Spykman, E(lizabeth) C(hoate) 1896-1965 .. *10*
  See also CLR *35*
Spyri, Johanna (Heusser) 1827-1901 .... *100*
  Earlier sketch in SATA *19*
  See also CLR *115*
Squires, Phil
  See Barker, S(quire) Omar
Srba, Lynne *98*
Sreenivasan, Jyotsna 1964- *101*
S-Ringi, Kjell
  See Ringi, Kjell (Arne Soerensen)
Stacey, Cherylyn 1945- *96*
Stacy, Donald
  See Pohl, Frederik
Stadtler, Bea 1921- *17*
Stafford, Liliana 1950- *141*
Stafford, Paul 1966- *116*
Stahl, Ben(jamin) 1910-1987 .... *5*
  Obituary *54*
Stahl, Hilda 1938-1993 .... *48*
  Obituary *77*
Stahler, David, Jr. *162*
Stair, Gobin (John) 1912- *35*
Stalder, Valerie *27*
Stamaty, Mark Alan 1947- *12*
Stambler, Irwin 1924- *5*
Standiford, Natalie 1961- *169*
  Earlier sketch in SATA *81*
Stanek, Lou Willett 1931- *63*
Stang, Judit 1921-1977 .... *29*
Stang, Judy
  See Stang, Judit
Stangl, (Mary) Jean 1928- *67*
Stanhope, Eric
  See Hamilton, Charles (Harold St. John)
Stankevich, Boris 1928- *2*

Stanley, Diane 1943- *164*
  Brief entry *32*
  Earlier sketches in SATA *37, 80, 115*
  See also CLR *46*
  See also SAAS *15*
Stanley, George Edward 1942- *157*
  Earlier sketches in SATA *53, 111*
  See Dixon, Franklin W.
  and Hope, Laura Lee
  and Keene, Carolyn
Stanley, Jerry 1941- *127*
  Earlier sketch in SATA *79*
Stanley, Mandy *165*
Stanley, Robert
  See Hamilton, Charles (Harold St. John)
Stanley, Sanna 1962- *145*
Stanli, Sue
  See Meilach, Dona Z(weigoron)
Stanstead, John
  See Groom, Arthur William
Stanton, Schuyler
  See Baum, L(yman) Frank
Staples, Suzanne Fisher 1945- *151*
  Earlier sketches in SATA *70, 105*
  See also CLR *60*
Stapleton, Marjorie (Winifred) 1932- *28*
Stapp, Arthur D(onald) 1906-1972 .... *4*
Starbird, Kaye 1916- *6*
  See also CLR *60*
Stark, Evan 1942- *78*
Stark, James
  See Goldston, Robert (Conroy)
Stark, Ulf 1944- *124*
Starke, Ruth (Elaine) 1946- *129*
Starkey, Marion L(ena) 1901-1991 .... *13*
Starr, Ward
  See Manes, Stephen
Starret, William
  See McClintock, Marshall
Starr Taylor, Bridget 1959- *99*
Stasiak, Krystyna *49*
Staub, Frank 1949- *116*
Staub, Frank Jacob
  See Staub, Frank
Staub, Wendy Corsi 1964- *114*
Stauffacher, Sue 1961- *155*
Staunton, Schuyler
  See Baum, L(yman) Frank
Staunton, Ted 1956- *167*
  Earlier sketch in SATA *112*
Steadman, Ralph (Idris) 1936- *123*
  Earlier sketch in SATA *32*
Stearman, Kaye 1951- *118*
Stearns, Monroe (Mather) 1913-1987 .... *5*
  Obituary *55*
Steckler, Arthur 1921-1985 .... *65*
Steding, Laurie 1953- *119*
Steel, Danielle 1947- *66*
Steel, Danielle Fernande
  See Steel, Danielle
Steele, Addison II
  See Lupoff, Richard A(llen)
Steele, Alexander 1958- *116*
Steele, Henry Maxwell
  See Steele, Max
Steele, Mary 1930- *94*
Steele, Mary Q(uintard Govan) 1922-1992 .. *51*
  Obituary *72*
  Earlier sketch in SATA *3*
Steele, Max 1922-2005 .... *168*
  Earlier sketch in SATA *10*
Steele, Philip 1948- *140*
  Earlier sketch in SATA *81*
Steele, William O(wen) 1917-1979 .... *51*
  Obituary *27*
  Earlier sketch in SATA *1*
Steelhammer, Ilona 1952- *98*
Steelsmith, Shari 1962- *72*
Stefanik, Alfred T. 1939- *55*

Steffanson, Con
  See Cassiday, Bruce (Bingham)
  and Goulart, Ron(ald Joseph)
Steffens, Bradley 1955- *166*
  Earlier sketch in SATA *77*
Stegeman, Janet Allais 1923- *53*
  Brief entry *49*
  See Britton, Kate
Steig, William 1907-2003 .... *111*
  Obituary *149*
  Earlier sketches in SATA *18, 70*
  See also CLR *103*
Steig, William H.
  See Steig, William
Stein, M(eyer) L(ewis) 1920- *6*
Stein, Mini *2*
Stein, R(ichard) Conrad 1937- *154*
  Earlier sketches in SATA *31, 82*
Stein, Wendy 1951- *77*
Steinbeck, John (Ernst) 1902-1968 .... *9*
Steinberg, Alfred 1917-1995 .... *9*
Steinberg, Fannie 1899-1990 .... *43*
Steinberg, Fred J. 1933- *4*
Steinberg, Phillip Orso 1921- *34*
Steinberg, Rafael (Mark) 1927- *45*
Steinberg, Saul 1914-1999 .... *67*
Steincrohn, Maggie
  See Davis, Maggie S.
Steiner, Barbara A(nnette) 1934- *83*
  Earlier sketch in SATA *13*
  See also SAAS *13*
Steiner, Charlotte 1900-1981 .... *45*
Steiner, George 1929- *62*
Steiner, Joan *110*
Steiner, Jorg
  See Steiner, Jorg
Steiner, Jorg 1930- *35*
Steiner, K. Leslie
  See Delany, Samuel R., Jr.
Steiner, Stan(ley) 1925-1987 .... *14*
  Obituary *50*
Steins, Richard 1942- *79*
Stem, Jacqueline 1931- *110*
Stemple, Jason *179*
Steneman, Shep 1945- *132*
Stengel, Joyce A. 1938- *158*
Stephanie, Gordon
  See Gordon, Stephanie Jacob
Stephens, Alice Barber 1858-1932 .... *66*
Stephens, Casey
  See Wagner, Sharon B.
Stephens, J.B.
  See Lynn, Tracy
Stephens, Mary Jo 1935- *8*
Stephens, Rebecca 1961- *141*
Stephens, Reed
  See Donaldson, Stephen R(eeder)
Stephens, Suzanne
  See Kirby, Susan E.
Stephens, William M(cLain) 1925- *21*
Stephensen, A. M.
  See Manes, Stephen
Stephenson, Lynda A. 1941- *179*
Stepp, Ann 1935- *29*
Stepto, Michele 1946- *61*
Steptoe, Javaka 1971- *151*
Steptoe, John (Lewis) 1950-1989 .... *63*
  Earlier sketch in SATA *8*
  See also CLR *12*
Sterling, Brett
  See Bradbury, Ray
  and Hamilton, Edmond
  and Samachson, Joseph
Sterling, Dorothy 1913- *83*
  Autobiography Feature *127*
  Earlier sketch in SATA *1*
  See also CLR *1*
  See also SAAS *2*
Sterling, Philip 1907-1989 .... *8*
  Obituary *63*
Sterling, Shirley (Anne) 1948- *101*

Stern, Ellen Norman 1927- *26*
Stern, Judith M. 1951- *75*
Stern, Madeleine B(ettina) 1912- *14*
Stern, Maggie 1953- *156*
Stern, Philip Van Doren 1900-1984 .... *13*
  Obituary *39*
Stern, Simon 1943- *15*
Sterne, Emma Gelders 1894- *6*
Steurt, Marjorie Rankin 1888-1978 .... *10*
Stevens, Bryna 1924- *65*
Stevens, Carla M(cBride) 1928- *13*
Stevens, Chambers 1968- *128*
Stevens, Diane 1939- *94*
Stevens, Franklin 1933- *6*
Stevens, Greg
  See Cook, Glen
Stevens, Gwendolyn 1944- *33*
Stevens, Jan Romero 1953- *95*
Stevens, Janet 1953- *148*
  Earlier sketch in SATA *90*
Stevens, Kathleen 1936- *49*
Stevens, Leonard A. 1920- *67*
Stevens, Lucile Vernon 1899-1994 .... *59*
Stevens, Margaret Dean
  See Aldrich, Bess Streeter
Stevens, Patricia Bunning 1931- *27*
Stevens, Peter
  See Geis, Darlene Stern
Stevens, Serita (Deborah) 1949- *70*
Stevens, Shira
  See Stevens, Serita (Deborah)
Stevenson, Anna (M.) 1905- *12*
Stevenson, Augusta 1869(?)-1976 .... *2*
  Obituary *26*
Stevenson, Burton Egbert 1872-1962 .... *25*
Stevenson, Drew 1947- *60*
Stevenson, Harvey 1960- *148*
  Earlier sketch in SATA *80*
Stevenson, James 1929- *161*
  Brief entry *34*
  Earlier sketches in SATA *42, 71, 113*
  See also CLR *17*
Stevenson, Janet 1913- *8*
Stevenson, Robert Louis (Balfour)
  1850-1894 .... *100*
  See also YABC *2*
  See also CLR *107*
Stevenson, Sucie 1956- *104*
Stewart, A(gnes) C(harlotte) *15*
Stewart, Chantal 1945- *173*
  Earlier sketch in SATA *121*
Stewart, Charles
  See Zurhorst, Charles (Stewart, Jr.)
Stewart, Eleanor
  See Porter, Eleanor H(odgman)
Stewart, Elisabeth J(ane) 1927- *93*
Stewart, Elizabeth Laing 1907- *6*
Stewart, Gail B. 1949- *141*
Stewart, George Rippey 1895-1980 .... *3*
  Obituary *23*
Stewart, Jennifer J(enkins) 1960- *128*
Stewart, Joel *151*
Stewart, John (William) 1920- *14*
  See Cole, Jack
Stewart, Mary (Florence Elinor) 1916- *12*
Stewart, Mary Rainbow
  See Stewart, Mary (Florence Elinor)
Stewart, Melissa 1968- *167*
  Earlier sketch in SATA *111*
Stewart, Paul 1955- *163*
  Earlier sketch in SATA *114*
Stewart, Robert Neil 1891-1972 .... *7*
Stewart, Sarah *143*
Stewart, Scott
  See Zaffo, George J.
Stewart, W(alter) P. 1924- *53*
Stewart, Whitney 1959- *167*
  Earlier sketch in SATA *92*
Stewig, John Warren 1937- *162*
  Earlier sketches in SATA *26, 110*
Stickler, Soma Han 1942- *128*

Stidworthy, John 1943- 63
Stiles, Martha Bennett 108
  Earlier sketch in SATA 6
Still, James 1906-2001 29
  Obituary 127
Stille, Darlene R. 1942- 170
  Earlier sketch in SATA 126
Stille, Darlene Ruth
  See Stille, Darlene R.
Stillerman, Marci 104
Stillerman, Robbie 1947- 12
Stilley, Frank 1918- 29
Stilton, Geronimo 158
Stimpson, Gerald
  See Mitchell, Adrian
Stine, Catherine 165
Stine, G(eorge) Harry 1928-1997 136
  Earlier sketch in SATA 10
Stine, Jovial Bob
  See Stine, R.L.
Stine, R.L. 1943- 129
  Earlier sketches in SATA 31, 76
  See also CLR 111
Stine, Robert Lawrence
  See Stine, R.L.
Stinetorf, Louise (Allender) 1900-1992 10
Stinson, Kathy 1952- 98
Stirling, Arthur
  See Sinclair, Upton
Stirling, Ian 1941- 77
Stirling, Nora B(romley) 1900-1997 3
Stirnweis, Shannon 1931- 10
Stobbs, William 1914-2000 17
  Obituary 120
Stock, Carolmarie 1951- 75
Stock, Catherine 1952- 158
  Earlier sketches in SATA 65, 114
Stockdale, Susan 1954- 98
Stockham, Peter (Alan) 1928- 57
Stockton, Francis Richard 1834-1902 44
  See Stockton, Frank R.
Stockton, Frank R.
  Brief entry 32
  See Stockton, Francis Richard
Stockwell-Moniz, Marc J. 1954- 164
Stoddard, Edward G. 1923- 10
Stoddard, Hope 1900-1987 6
Stoddard, Sandol 1927- 98
  See Warburg, Sandol Stoddard
Stoehr, Shelley 1969- 107
Stoeke, Janet Morgan 1957- 136
  Earlier sketch in SATA 90
Stohner, Anu 1952- 179
Stoiko, Michael 1919- 14
Stojic, Manya 1967- 156
Stoker, Abraham 1847-1912 29
  See Stoker, Bram
Stoker, Bram
  See Stoker, Abraham
Stokes, Cedric
  See Beardmore, George
Stokes, Jack (Tilden) 1923- 13
Stokes, Olivia Pearl 1916- 32
Stolz, Mary 1920-2006 133
  Earlier sketches in SATA 10, 71
  See also SAAS 3
Stolz, Mary Slattery
  See Stolz, Mary
Stone, Alan
  See Svenson, Andrew E(dward)
Stone, David K(arl) 1922- 9
Stone, David Lee 1978- 166
Stone, Eugenia 1879-1971 7
Stone, Gene
  See Stone, Eugenia
Stone, Helen V(irginia) 6
Stone, Idella Purnell
  See Purnell, Idella
Stone, Ikey
  See Purnell, Idella

Stone, Irving 1903-1989 3
  Obituary 64
Stone, Jeff 178
Stone, Jon 1931-1997 39
  Obituary 95
Stone, Josephine Rector
  See Dixon, Jeanne
Stone, Lesley
  See Trevor, Elleston
Stone, Peter 1930-2003 65
  Obituary 143
Stone, Phoebe 134
Stone, Raymond 1
Stone, Rosetta
  See Dr. Seuss
  and Geisel, Theodor Seuss
  and LeSieg, Theo.
  and Seuss, Dr.
Stonehouse, Bernard 1926- 140
  Earlier sketches in SATA 13, 80
Stones, (Cyril) Anthony 1934- 72
Stong, Phil(ip Duffield) 1899-1957 32
Stoops, Erik D(aniel) 1966- 142
  Earlier sketch in SATA 78
Stoppelmoore, Cheryl Jean
  See Ladd, Cheryl (Jean)
Stops, Sue 1936- 86
Storad, Conrad J. 1957- 119
Storey, Margaret 1926- 9
Storey, Victoria Carolyn 1945- 16
Storme, Peter
  See Stern, Philip Van Doren
Storr, Catherine (Cole) 1913-2001 87
  Obituary 122
  Earlier sketch in SATA 9
Story, Josephine
  See Loring, Emilie (Baker)
Stotko, Mary-Ann 1960- 154
Stott, Dorothy (M.) 1958- 99
  Earlier sketch in SATA 67
Stott, Dot
  See Stott, Dorothy (M.)
Stotter, Mike 1957- 108
Stout, William 1949- 132
Stoutenburg, Adrien (Pearl) 1916-1982 3
Stoutland, Allison 1963- 130
Stover, Allan C(arl) 1938- 14
Stover, Jill (Griffin) 1958- 82
Stover, Marjorie Filley 1914- 9
Stowe, Harriet (Elizabeth) Beecher 1811-1896
  See YABC 1
Stowe, Leland 1899-1994 60
  Obituary 78
Stowe, Rosetta
  See Ogan, George F.
  and Ogan, Margaret E. (Nettles)
Strachan, Ian 1938- 85
Strachan, Linda 167
Strachan, Margaret Pitcairn 1908-1998 14
Strahinich, H. C.
  See Strahinich, Helen C.
Strahinich, Helen C. 1949- 78
Strait, Treva Adams 1909- 35
Strand, Mark 1934- 41
Stranger, Joyce
  See SAAS 24
  See Wilson, Joyce M(uriel Judson)
Strangis, Joel 1948- 124
Strannigan, Shawn 1956- 93
Strannigan, Shawn Alyne
  See Strannigan, Shawn
Strasser, Todd 1950- 153
  Earlier sketches in SATA 41, 45, 71, 107
  See also CLR 11

Stratemeyer, Edward L. 1862-1930 100
  Earlier sketches in SATA 1, 67
  See Adams, Harrison
  and Appleton, Victor
  and Dixon, Franklin W.
  and Keene, Carolyn
  and Rockwood, Roy
  and Young, Clarence
Stratford, Philip 1927- 47
Stratton, Allan 1951- 178
Stratton, J. M.
  See Whitlock, Ralph
Stratton, Thomas
  See Coulson, Robert S(tratton)
  and DeWeese, Thomas Eugene
Stratton-Porter, Gene(va Grace) 1863-1924 . 15
  See also CLR 87
  See Porter, Gene(va Grace) Stratton
Strauss, Gwen 1963- 77
Strauss, Joyce 1936- 53
Strauss, Linda Leopold 1942- 127
Strauss, Susan (Elizabeth) 1954- 75
Strayer, E. Ward
  See Stratemeyer, Edward L.
Streano, Vince(nt Catello) 1945- 20
Streatfeild, (Mary) Noel 1897(?)-1986 20
  Obituary 48
  See also CLR 83
Street, Janet Travell 1959- 84
Street, Julia Montgomery 1898-1993 11
Streissguth, Thomas 1958- 116
Strelkoff, Tatiana 1957- 89
Stren, Patti 1949- 88
  Brief entry 41
  See also CLR 5
Strete, Craig Kee 1950- 96
  Earlier sketch in SATA 44
Stretton, Barbara (Humphrey) 1936- 43
  Brief entry 35
Strickland, (William) Brad(ley) 1947- 142
  Earlier sketches in SATA 83, 137
Strickland, Craig (A.) 1956- 102
Strickland, Dorothy S(alley) 1933- 89
Strickland, Michael R. 1965- 144
  Earlier sketch in SATA 83
Strickland, Tessa 173
Striegel, Jana 1955- 140
Striegel-Wilson, Jana
  See Striegel, Jana
Striker, Lee
  See Clark, Margaret (D.)
Striker, Susan 1942- 63
Stringer, Lauren 1957- 129
Stroeyer, Poul 1923- 13
Stromoski, Rick 1958- 111
Strong, Charles
  See Epstein, Beryl (M. Williams)
  and Epstein, Samuel
Strong, David
  See McGuire, Leslie (Sarah)
Strong, Jeremy 1949- 175
  Earlier sketches in SATA 36, 105
Strong, J.J.
  See Strong, Jeremy
Strong, Pat
  See Hough, Richard (Alexander)
Strong, Stacie 1965- 74
Stroud, Bettye 1939- 165
  Earlier sketch in SATA 96
Stroud, Jonathan 1970- 159
  Earlier sketch in SATA 102
Stroyer, Poul
  See Stroeyer, Poul
Strug, Kerri 1977- 108
Stryker, Daniel
  See Morris, Chris(topher Crosby)
  and Stump, Jane Barr
Stuart, David
  See Hoyt, Edwin P(almer), Jr.
Stuart, Derek
  See Foster, John L(ouis)

Stuart, Forbes 1924- *13*
Stuart, Ian
　See MacLean, Alistair (Stuart)
Stuart, Jesse (Hilton) 1906-1984 .... *2*
　Obituary *36*
Stuart, Ruth McEnery 1849(?)-1917 .... *116*
Stuart, Sheila
　See Baker, Mary Gladys Steel
Stuart-Clark, Christopher (Anthony) 1940- .. *32*
Stubis, Talivaldis 1926- *5*
Stubley, Trevor (Hugh) 1932- *22*
Stucky, Naomi R. 1922- *72*
Stucley, Elizabeth
　See Northmore, Elizabeth Florence
Stultifer, Morton
　See Curtis, Richard (Alan)
Sture-Vasa, Mary
　See Alsop, Mary O'Hara
Sturges, Philemon *174*
Sturtevant, Katherine 1950- *130*
Sturton, Hugh
　See Johnston, H(ugh) A(nthony) S(tephen)
Sturtzel, Howard A(llison) 1894-1985 .... *1*
Sturtzel, Jane Levington 1903-1996 .... *1*
Stutley, D(oris) J(ean) 1959- *142*
Stutson, Caroline 1940- *104*
Stuve-Bodeen, Stephanie 1965- *158*
　Earlier sketch in SATA *114*
Stux, Erica 1929- *140*
Styles, (Frank) Showell 1908- *10*
Stynes, Barbara White *133*
Suba, Susanne *4*
Subond, Valerie
　See Grayland, Valerie (Merle Spanner)
Sudbery, Rodie 1943- *42*
Suen, Anastasia 1956(?)- *157*
Sufrin, Mark 1925- *76*
Sugarman, Joan G. 1917- *64*
Sugarman, Tracy 1921- *37*
Sugita, Yutaka 1930- *36*
Suhl, Yuri (Menachem) 1908-1986 .... *8*
　Obituary *50*
　See also CLR *2*
　See also SAAS *1*
Suhr, Joanne *129*
Suid, Murray 1942- *27*
Sullivan, George (Edward) 1927- *147*
　Earlier sketches in SATA *4, 89*
Sullivan, Jody
　See Rake, Jody
Sullivan, Kathryn A. 1954- *141*
Sullivan, Mary Ann 1954- *63*
Sullivan, Mary W(ilson) 1907- *13*
Sullivan, Pat
　See Messmer, Otto
Sullivan, Paul 1939- *106*
Sullivan, Sarah G. 1953- *179*
Sullivan, Silky
　See Makowski, Silvia Ann
Sullivan, Sue
　See Sullivan, Susan E.
Sullivan, Susan E. 1962- *123*
Sullivan, Thomas Joseph, Jr. 1947- *16*
Sullivan, Tom
　See Sullivan, Thomas Joseph, Jr.
Sully, Tom 1959- *104*
Sumichrast, Jozef 1948- *29*
Sumiko
　See Davies, Sumiko
Summerforest, Ivy B.
　See Kirkup, James
Summers, James L(evingston) 1910-1973 .... *57*
　Brief entry *28*
Summertree, Katonah
　See Windsor, Patricia
Sun, Chyng Feng 1959- *90*
Sunderlin, Sylvia (S.) 1911-1997 .... *28*
　Obituary *99*
Sung, Betty Lee *26*
Supeene, Shelagh Lynne 1952- *153*

Supraner, Robyn 1930- *101*
　Earlier sketch in SATA *20*
Supree, Burt(on) 1941-1992 .... *73*
Surface, Mary Hall 1958- *126*
Surge, Frank 1931- *13*
Susac, Andrew 1929- *5*
Susi, Geraldine Lee 1942- *98*
Sussman, Cornelia Silver 1914-1999 .... *59*
Sussman, Irving 1908-1996 .... *59*
Sussman, Susan 1942- *48*
Sutcliff, Rosemary 1920-1992 .... *78*
　Obituary *73*
　Earlier sketches in SATA *6, 44*
　See also CLR *37*
Sutcliffe, Jane 1957- *138*
Sutherland, Colleen 1944- *79*
Sutherland, Efua (Theodora Morgue)
　1924-1996 .... *25*
Sutherland, Jon 1958- *167*
Sutherland, Jonathan D.
　See Sutherland, Jon
Sutherland, Margaret 1941- *15*
Sutherland, Zena Bailey 1915-2002 .... *37*
　Obituary *137*
Suttles, Shirley (Smith) 1922- *21*
Sutton, Ann (Livesay) 1923- *31*
Sutton, Eve(lyn Mary) 1906-1992 .... *26*
Sutton, Felix 1910(?)-1973 .... *31*
Sutton, Jane 1950- *52*
　Brief entry *43*
Sutton, Larry M(atthew) 1931- *29*
Sutton, Margaret Beebe 1903-2001 .... *1*
　Obituary *131*
Sutton, Myron Daniel 1925- *31*
Sutton, Roger 1956- *93*
Suzanne, Jamie
　See Hawes, Louise
　and Lantz, Francess L(in)
　and Singleton, Linda Joy
　and Zach, Cheryl (Byrd)
Suzuki, David T(akayoshi) 1936- *138*
Svendsen, Mark (Nestor) 1962- *120*
Svenson, Andrew E(dward) 1910-1975 .... *2*
　Obituary *26*
Swain, Carol 1962- *172*
Swain, Gwenyth 1961- *134*
　Earlier sketch in SATA *84*
Swain, Ruth
　See Swain, Ruth Freeman
Swain, Ruth Freeman 1951- *161*
　Earlier sketch in SATA *119*
Swain, Su Zan (Noguchi) 1916- *21*
Swallow, Pamela Curtis *178*
Swamp, Jake 1941- *98*
Swan, Susan 1944- *108*
　Earlier sketch in SATA *22*
Swann, Brian (Stanley Frank) 1940- *116*
Swann, E. L.
　See Lasky, Kathryn
Swann, Ruth Rice 1920- *84*
Swanson, Helen M(cKendry) 1919- *94*
Swanson, June 1931- *76*
Swanson, Wayne 1942- *167*
Swarthout, Glendon (Fred) 1918-1992 .... *26*
Swarthout, Kathryn 1919- *7*
Swayne, Sam(uel F.) 1907- *53*
Swayne, Zoa (Lourana) 1905- *53*
Sweat, Lynn 1934- *168*
　Earlier sketch in SATA *57*
Swede, George 1940- *67*
Sweeney, James B(artholomew) 1910-1999 . *21*
Sweeney, Joyce 1955- *167*
　Earlier sketches in SATA *65, 68, 108*
Sweeney, Joyce Kay
　See Sweeney, Joyce
Sweeney, Karen O'Connor
　See O'Connor, Karen
Sweeney, Matthew (Gerard) 1952- *156*
Sweet, Melissa 1956- *172*
Sweet, Sarah C.
　See Jewett, (Theodora) Sarah Orne

Sweetland, Nancy A(nn) 1934- *48*
Swenson, Allan A(rmstrong) 1933- *21*
Swenson, May 1919-1989 .... *15*
Swentzell, Rina 1939- *79*
Swift, Bryan
　See Knott, William C(ecil, Jr.)
Swift, David
　See Kaufmann, John
Swift, Jonathan 1667-1745 .... *19*
　See also CLR *53*
Swift, Merlin
　See Leeming, Joseph
Swiger, Elinor Porter 1927- *8*
Swinburne, Laurence (Joseph) 1924- *9*
Swinburne, Stephen R. 1952- *150*
Swinburne, Steve
　See Swinburne, Stephen R.
Swindells, Robert (Edward) 1939- *150*
　Brief entry *34*
　Earlier sketches in SATA *50, 80*
　See also SAAS *14*
Swinford, Betty (June Wells) 1927- *58*
Swinford, Bob
　See Swinford, Betty (June Wells)
Swithen, John
　See King, Stephen
Switzer, Ellen 1923- *48*
Swope, Sam *156*
Swope, Samuel
　See Swope, Sam
Sybesma, Jetske
　See Ironside, Jetske
Sydney, Frank
　See Warwick, Alan R(oss)
Sylvester, Natalie G(abry) 1922- *22*
Syme, (Neville) Ronald 1913-1992 .... *87*
　Earlier sketch in SATA *2*
Symes, R. F. *77*
Symes, Ruth Louise 1962- *179*
Symons, (Dorothy) Geraldine 1909- *33*
Symons, Stuart
　See Stanley, George Edward
Symynkywicz, Jeffrey B. 1954- *87*
Symynkywicz, Jeffrey Bruce
　See Symynkywicz, Jeffrey B.
Synge, (Phyllis) Ursula 1930- *9*
Sypher, Lucy Johnston 1907- *7*
Szasz, Suzanne (Shorr) 1915-1997 .... *13*
　Obituary *99*
Szekeres, Cyndy 1933- *157*
　Autobiography Feature *157*
　Earlier sketches in SATA *5, 60, 131*
　See also SAAS *13*
Szekessy, Tanja *98*
Szpura, Beata 1961- *93*
Szudek, Agnes S(usan) P(hilomena) *57*
　Brief entry *49*
Szulc, Tad 1926-2001 .... *26*
Szydlow, Jarl
　See Szydlowski, Mary Vigliante
Szydlowski, Mary Vigliante 1946- *94*
Szymanski, Lois 1957- *91*

T

Taback, Simms 1932- *170*
　Brief entry *36*
　Earlier sketches in SATA *40, 104*
　See also CLR *100*
Tabor, Nancy Maria Grande 1949- *161*
　Earlier sketch in SATA *89*
Tabrah, Ruth Milander 1921- *14*
Tackach, James 1953- *123*
Tadgell, Nicole 1969- *177*
Tafuri, Nancy (E.) 1946- *130*
　Earlier sketches in SATA *39, 75*
　See also CLR *74*
　See also SAAS *14*
Tagg, Christine Elizabeth 1962- *138*

Tagliaferro, Linda *173*
Taha, Karen T(erry) 1942- *156*
  Earlier sketch in SATA *71*
Tai, Sharon O. 1963- *153*
Tait, Douglas 1944- *12*
Takabayashi, Mari 1960- *156*
  Earlier sketch in SATA *115*
Takahashi, Rumiko 1957- *163*
Takakjian, Portia 1930- *15*
Takashima, Shizuye 1928- *13*
Takayama, Sandi 1962- *106*
Takeda, Pete(r M.) 1964- *148*
Tal, Eve 1947- *176*
Talbert, Marc (Alan) 1953- *154*
  Autobiography Feature *154*
  Earlier sketches in SATA *68, 99*
Talbot, Charlene Joy 1928- *10*
Talbot, Toby 1928- *14*
Talbott, Hudson 1949- *131*
  Earlier sketch in SATA *84*
Talifero, Gerald 1950- *75*
Talker, T.
  See Rands, William Brighty
Tallarico, Tony 1933- *116*
Tallcott, Emogene *10*
Tallis, Robyn
  See Coville, Bruce
  and Doyle, Debra
  and Macdonald, James D.
  and Smith, Sherwood
  and Zambreno, Mary Frances
Tallon, Robert 1939- *43*
  Brief entry *28*
Talmadge, Marian *14*
Tamar, Erika 1934- *150*
  Earlier sketches in SATA *62, 101*
Tamarin, Alfred H. 1913-1980 .... *13*
Tamburine, Jean 1930- *12*
Tames, Richard (Lawrence) 1946- *102*
  Earlier sketch in SATA *67*
Tamminga, Frederick W(illiam) 1934- *66*
Tan, Amy 1952- *75*
Tan, Amy Ruth
  See Tan, Amy
Tanaka, Beatrice 1932- *76*
Tanaka, Shelley *136*
Tang, Charles 1948- *81*
Tang, Greg *172*
Tang, You-Shan 1946- *53*
Tania B.
  See Blixen, Karen (Christentze Dinesen)
Tannen, Mary 1943- *37*
Tannenbaum, Beulah Goldstein 1916- *3*
Tannenbaum, D(onald) Leb 1948- *42*
Tanner, Jane 1946- *74*
Tanner, Louise S(tickney) 1922-2000 .... *9*
Tanobe, Miyuki 1937- *23*
Tanselle, Eve 1933- *125*
Tapio, Pat Decker
  See Kines, Pat Decker
Tapp, Kathy Kennedy 1949- *88*
  Brief entry *50*
Tarbescu, Edith 1939- *107*
Tarkington, (Newton) Booth 1869-1946 .... *17*
Tarpley, Natasha A(nastasia) 1971- *147*
Tarr, Judith 1955- *149*
  Earlier sketch in SATA *64*
Tarry, Ellen 1906- *16*
  See also CLR *26*
  See also SAAS *16*
Tarshis, Jerome 1936- *9*
Tarsky, Sue 1946- *41*
Tashjian, Janet 1956- *151*
  Earlier sketch in SATA *102*
Tashjian, Virginia A. 1921- *3*
Tasker, James 1908- *9*
Tate, Don(ald E.) *159*
Tate, Eleanora E(laine) 1948- *94*
  Earlier sketch in SATA *38*
  See also CLR *37*

Tate, Ellalice
  See Hibbert, Eleanor Alice Burford
Tate, Joan 1922- *86*
  Earlier sketch in SATA *9*
  See also SAAS *20*
Tate, Mary Anne
  See Hale, Arlene
Tate, Nikki *134*
Tate, Richard
  See Masters, Anthony (Richard)
Tate, Suzanne 1930- *91*
Tatham, Betty *142*
Tatham, Campbell
  See Elting, Mary
Tatham, Julie
  See Tatham, Julie Campbell
Tatham, Julie Campbell 1908-1999 .... *80*
Tavares, Matt *159*
Tavares, Victor 1971- *176*
Taves, Isabella 1915- *27*
Taylor, Alastair 1959- *130*
Taylor, Andrew 1951- *70*
Taylor, Andrew John Robert
  See Taylor, Andrew
Taylor, Ann 1782-1866 .... *41*
  Brief entry *35*
Taylor, Audilee Boyd 1931- *59*
Taylor, Barbara J. 1927- *10*
Taylor, Ben
  See Strachan, Ian
Taylor, Carl 1937- *14*
Taylor, Cheryl Munro 1957- *96*
Taylor, Cora (Lorraine) 1936- *103*
  Earlier sketch in SATA *64*
  See also CLR *63*
Taylor, Dave 1948- *78*
Taylor, David
  See Taylor, Dave
Taylor, David 1900-1965 .... *10*
Taylor, Debbie A. 1955- *169*
Taylor, Elizabeth 1912-1975 .... *13*
Taylor, Florance Walton *9*
Taylor, Florence M(arian Tompkins)
  1892-1983 .... *9*
Taylor, G(raham) P(eter) 1959(?)- *156*
Taylor, Gage 1942-2000 .... *87*
Taylor, Graham
  See Taylor, G(raham) P(eter)
Taylor, Herb(ert Norman, Jr.) 1942-1987 ..... *22*
  Obituary *54*
Taylor, J. David
  See Taylor, Dave
Taylor, Jane 1783-1824 .... *41*
  Brief entry *35*
Taylor, Jerry D(uncan) 1938- *47*
Taylor, John Robert
  See Taylor, Andrew
Taylor, Judy
  See Hough, Judy Taylor
Taylor, Kenneth N. 1917-2005 .... *26*
Taylor, Kenneth Nathaniel
  See Taylor, Kenneth N.
Taylor, L(ester) B(arbour), Jr. 1932- *27*
Taylor, Lois Dwight Cole
  See Cole, Lois Dwight
Taylor, Louise Todd 1939- *47*
Taylor, Margaret 1950- *106*
Taylor, Mark 1927- *32*
  Brief entry *28*
Taylor, Mildred D. 1943- *135*
  See also CLR *90*
  See also SAAS *5*
Taylor, Mildred Delois
  See Taylor, Mildred D.
Taylor, Paula (Wright) 1942- *48*
  Brief entry *33*
Taylor, Robert Lewis 1912-1998 .... *10*
Taylor, Sydney (Brenner) 1904(?)-1978 .... *28*
  Obituary *26*
  Earlier sketch in SATA *1*

Taylor, Theodore 1921-2006 .... *128*
  Obituary *177*
  Earlier sketches in SATA *5, 54, 83*
  See also CLR *30*
  See also SAAS *4*
Taylor, William 1938- *164*
  Earlier sketches in SATA *78, 113*
  See also CLR *63*
Tazewell, Charles 1900-1972 .... *74*
Tchana, Katrin Hyman 1963- *177*
  Earlier sketch in SATA *125*
Tchekhov, Anton
  See Chekhov, Anton (Pavlovich)
Tchen, Richard *120*
Tchudi, Stephen N. 1942- *55*
Teague, Bob
  See Teague, Robert
Teague, Mark 1963- *170*
  Earlier sketches in SATA *68, 99*
Teague, Mark Christopher
  See Teague, Mark
Teague, Robert 1929- *32*
  Brief entry *31*
Teal, Val(entine M.) 1902-1997 .... *10*
  Obituary *114*
Teale, Edwin Way 1899-1980 .... *7*
  Obituary *25*
Teasdale, Sara 1884-1933 .... *32*
Tebbel, John (William) 1912-2004 .... *26*
Teensma, Lynne Bertrand
  See Bertrand, Lynne
Tee-Van, Helen Damrosch 1893-1976 .... *10*
  Obituary *27*
Tegner, Bruce 1928- *62*
Teitelbaum, Michael 1953- *116*
  Earlier sketch in SATA *59*
Tejima
  See Tejima, Keizaburo
Tejima, Keizaburo 1931- *139*
  See also CLR *20*
Telander, Todd (G.) 1967- *88*
Teleki, Geza 1943- *45*
Telemaque, Eleanor Wong 1934- *43*
Telescope, Tom
  See Newbery, John
Temkin, Sara Anne Schlossberg 1913-1996 . *26*
Temko, Florence *13*
Templar, Maurice
  See Groom, Arthur William
Temple, Charles 1947- *79*
Temple, Frances (Nolting) 1945-1995 .... *85*
Temple, Herbert 1919- *45*
Temple, Paul
  See McConnell, James Douglas Rutherford
Temple, William F(rederick) 1914-1989 .... *107*
Tenggren, Gustaf 1896-1970 .... *18*
  Obituary *26*
Tennant, Kylie
  See Rodd, Kylie Tennant
Tennant, Veronica 1947- *36*
Tenneshaw, S. M.
  See Beaumont, Charles
  and Garrett, (Gordon) Randall (Phillip)
  and Silverberg, Robert
Tenniel, John 1820-1914 .... *74*
  Brief entry *27*
  See also CLR *18*
Tepper, Sheri S. 1929- *113*
Terada, Alice M. 1928- *90*
Terban, Marvin 1940- *54*
  Brief entry *45*
ter Haar, Jaap 1922- *6*
  See Haar, Jaap ter
Terhune, Albert Payson 1872-1942 .... *15*
Terkel, Susan N(eiburg) 1948- *103*
  Earlier sketch in SATA *59*
Terlouw, Jan (Cornelis) 1931- *30*
Terris, Susan 1937- *77*
  Earlier sketch in SATA *3*
Terry, Luther L(eonidas) 1911-1985 .... *11*
  Obituary *42*

Terry, Margaret
　See Dunnahoo, Terry Janson
Terry, Walter 1913-1982 14
Terzian, James P. 1915- 14
Tessendorf, K(enneth) C(harles) 1925-2003 . 75
　Obituary 142
Tessler, Stephanie Gordon
　See Gordon, Stephanie Jacob
Tester, Sylvia Root 1939- 64
　Brief entry 37
Tether, (Cynthia) Graham 1950- 46
　Brief entry 36
Tetzner, Lisa 1894-1963 169
Thacher, Mary McGrath 1933- 9
Thackeray, William Makepeace 1811-1863 .. 23
Thaler, Michael C.
　See Thaler, Mike
Thaler, Mike 1936- 93
　Brief entry 47
　Earlier sketch in SATA 56
Thaler, Shmuel 1958- 126
　Earlier sketch in SATA 72
Thamer, Katie 1955- 42
Thane, Elswyth 1900-1984(?) 32
Tharp, Louise (Marshall) Hall 1898-1992 3
　Obituary 129
Thayer, Ernest Lawrence 1863-1940 60
Thayer, Jane
　See Woolley, Catherine
Thayer, Marjorie 1908-1992 74
　Brief entry 37
Thayer, Peter
　See Wyler, Rose
Thelwell, Norman 1923-2004 14
Themerson, Stefan 1910-1988 65
Thermes, Jennifer 1966- 155
Theroux, Paul 1941- 109
　Earlier sketch in SATA 44
Theroux, Paul Edward
　See Theroux, Paul
Thesman, Jean 124
　Earlier sketch in SATA 74
Thieda, Shirley Ann 1943- 13
Thiele, Colin 1920-2006 125
　Earlier sketches in SATA 14, 72
　See also CLR 27
　See also SAAS 2
Thiele, Colin Milton
　See Thiele, Colin
Thiesing, Lisa 1958- 159
　Earlier sketch in SATA 95
Thiry, Joan (Marie) 1926- 45
Thistlethwaite, Miles 1945- 12
Thollander, Earl 1922- 22
Thomas, Abigail 1941- 112
Thomas, Andrea
　See Hill, Margaret (Ohler)
Thomas, Art(hur Lawrence) 1952- 48
　Brief entry 38
Thomas, Carroll
　See Ratliff, Thomas M.
　and Shmurak, Carole B.
Thomas, Dylan (Marlais) 1914-1953 60
Thomas, Egbert S.
　See Ellis, Edward S(ylvester)
Thomas, Estelle Webb 1899-1982 26
Thomas, Frances 1943- 171
　Earlier sketch in SATA 92
Thomas, H. C.
　See Keating, Lawrence A.
Thomas, Ianthe 1951- 139
　Brief entry 42
　See also CLR 8
Thomas, Jane Resh 1936- 171
　Earlier sketches in SATA 38, 90
Thomas, Jerry D. 1959- 91
Thomas, Joan Gale
　See Robinson, Joan (Mary) G(ale Thomas)

Thomas, Joyce Carol 1938- 137
　Autobiography Feature 137
　Earlier sketches in SATA 40, 78, 123
　See also CLR 19
　See also SAAS 7
Thomas, Lowell Jackson, Jr. 1923- 15
Thomas, Margaret
　See Thomas, Peggy
Thomas, Meredith 1963- 119
Thomas, Michael
　See Wilks, Michael Thomas
Thomas, Patricia J. 1934- 51
Thomas, Peggy 174
Thomas, Rob 1965- 97
Thomas, Scott 1959- 147
Thomas, Velma Maia 1955- 171
Thomas, Vernon (Arthur) 1934- 56
Thomas, Victoria
　See DeWeese, Thomas Eugene
　and Kugi, Constance Todd
Thomasma, Kenneth R. 1930- 90
Thomassie, Tynia 1959- 92
Thompson, Brenda 1935- 34
Thompson, Carol 1951- 85
Thompson, China
　See Lewis, Mary (Christianna)
Thompson, Colin (Edward) 1942- 163
　Earlier sketch in SATA 95
Thompson, David H(ugh) 1941- 17
Thompson, Eileen
　See Panowski, Eileen Thompson
Thompson, George Selden 1929-1989 73
　Obituary 63
　Earlier sketch in SATA 4
　See Selden, George
Thompson, Harlan (Howard) 1894-1987 10
　Obituary 53
　See Holt, Stephen
Thompson, Hilary 1943- 56
　Brief entry 49
Thompson, Julian F(rancis) 1927- 155
　Brief entry 40
　Earlier sketches in SATA 55, 99
　See also CLR 24
　See also SAAS 13
Thompson, K(athryn Carolyn) Dyble
　1952- 82
Thompson, Kay 1912(?)-1998 16
　See also CLR 22
Thompson, Lauren 1962- 174
　Earlier sketch in SATA 132
Thompson, Lauren Stevens
　See Thompson, Lauren
Thompson, Ruth Plumly 1891-1976 66
Thompson, Sharon (Elaine) 1952- 119
Thompson, Stith 1885-1976 57
　Obituary 20
Thompson, Vivian L(aubach) 1911- 3
Thomson, Celia
　See Lynn, Tracy
Thomson, David (Robert Alexander)
　1914-1988 40
　Obituary 55
Thomson, Pat 1939- 122
　Earlier sketch in SATA 77
Thomson, Peggy 1922- 31
Thomson, Sarah L. 178
Thon, Melanie Rae 1957- 132
Thong, Roseanne 174
Thorn, John 1947- 59
Thorndyke, Helen Louise 67
　Earlier sketch in SATA 1
　See Benson, Mildred (Augustine Wirt)
Thorne, Ian
　See May, Julian
Thorne, Jean Wright
　See May, Julian
Thornhill, Jan 1955- 148
　Earlier sketch in SATA 77
Thornton, Hall
　See Silverberg, Robert

Thornton, W. B.
　See Burgess, Thornton Waldo
Thornton, Yvonne S(hirley) 1947- 96
Thorpe, E(ustace) G(eorge) 1916- 21
Thorpe, J. K.
　See Nathanson, Laura Walther
Thorvall, Kerstin 1925- 13
Thorvall-Falk, Kerstin
　See Thorvall, Kerstin
Thrasher, Crystal (Faye) 1921- 27
Threadgall, Colin 1941- 77
Three Little Pigs
　See Lantz, Francess L(in)
Thum, Gladys 1920- 26
Thum, Marcella 28
　Earlier sketch in SATA 3
Thundercloud, Katherine
　See Witt, Shirley Hill
Thurber, James (Grover) 1894-1961 13
Thurlo, Aimee 161
Thurlo, David 161
Thurman, Judith 1946- 33
Thurman, Mark (Gordon Ian) 1948- 63
Thwaite, Ann (Barbara Harrop) 1932- 14
Tibbetts, Peggy 127
Tibbles, Jean-Paul 1958- 115
Tibo, Gilles 1951- 107
　Earlier sketch in SATA 67
Tiburzi, Bonnie 1948- 65
Ticheburn, Cheviot
　See Ainsworth, William Harrison
Tichenor, Tom 1923-1992 14
Tichnor, Richard 1959- 90
Tichy, William 1924- 31
Tickle, Jack
　See Chapman, Jane
Tiegreen, Alan F. 1935- 94
　Brief entry 36
Tierney, Frank M. 1930- 54
Ticrncy, Tom 1928 113
Tiffault, Benette W. 1955- 77
Tiller, Ruth L. 1949- 83
Tilly, Nancy 1935- 62
Tilton, Madonna Elaine 1929- 41
Tilton, Rafael
　See Tilton, Madonna Elaine
Timberlake, Amy 156
Timberlake, Carolyn
　See Dresang, Eliza (Carolyn Timberlake)
Timmins, William F(rederick) 10
Tiner, John Hudson 1944- 32
Tingle, Dolli (?)-
　See Brackett, Dolli Tingle
Tingle, Rebecca 174
Tingum, Janice 1958- 91
Tinkelman, Murray 1933- 12
Tinkle, (Julien) Lon 1906-1980 36
Tinling, Marion (Rose) 1904- 140
Tipene, Tim 1972- 141
Tippett, James S(terling) 1885-1958 66
Tirone Smith, Mary-Ann 1944- 143
Titler, Dale M(ilton) 1926- 35
　Brief entry 28
Titmarsh, Michael Angelo
　See Thackeray, William Makepeace
Titus, Eve 1922- 2
Tjong Khing, The 1933- 76
Tobias, Katherine
　See Gottfried, Theodore Mark
Tobias, Tobi 1938- 82
　Earlier sketch in SATA 5
　See also CLR 4
Todd, Anne Ophelia
　See Dowden, Anne Ophelia Todd
Todd, Barbara 1961- 173
Todd, Barbara K(eith) 1917- 10
Todd, H(erbert) E(atton) 1908-1988 84
　Earlier sketch in SATA 11
Todd, Loreto 1942- 30
Todd, Pamela 1950- 124

Todd, Peter
See Hamilton, Charles (Harold St. John)
Toews, Miriam 1964- 165
Tofel, Richard J. 1957- 140
Toft, Kim Michelle 1960- 170
Tolan, Stephanie S. 1942- 142
Earlier sketches in SATA 38, 78
Toland, John (Willard) 1912-2004 38
Tolbert, Steve 1944- 143
Tolkien, John Ronald Reuel
See Tolkien, J.R.R
Tolkien, J.R.R 1892-1973 100
Obituary 24
Earlier sketches in SATA 2, 32
See also CLR 56
Toll, Emily
See Cannon, Eileen E(mily)
Toll, Nelly S. 1935- 78
Tolland, W. R.
See Heitzmann, William Ray
Tolles, Martha 1921- 76
Earlier sketch in SATA 8
Tolliver, Ruby C(hangos) 1922- 110
Brief entry 41
Earlier sketch in SATA 55
Tolmie, Kenneth Donald 1941- 15
Tolstoi, Lev
See Tolstoy, Leo (Nikolaevich)
Tolstoy, Leo (Nikolaevich) 1828-1910 26
See Tolstoi, Lev
Tolstoy, Count Leo
See Tolstoy, Leo (Nikolaevich)
Tomalin, Ruth 29
Tomaselli, Rosa
See Pausacker, Jenny
Tomecek, Steve 172
Tomes, Margot (Ladd) 1917-1991 70
Brief entry 27
Obituary 69
Earlier sketch in SATA 36
Tomey, Ingrid 1943- 77
Tomfool
See Farjeon, Eleanor
Tomkins, Jasper
See Batey, Tom
Tomline, F. Latour
See Gilbert, W(illiam) S(chwenck)
Tomlinson, Jill 1931-1976 3
Obituary 24
Tomlinson, Theresa 1946- 165
Earlier sketch in SATA 103
See also CLR 60
Tompert, Ann 1918- 139
Earlier sketches in SATA 14, 89
Toner, Raymond John 1908-1986 10
Tong, Gary S. 1942- 66
Took, Belladonna
See Chapman, Vera (Ivy May)
Tooke, Louise Mathews 1950- 38
Tooke, Susan 173
Toonder, Martin
See Groom, Arthur William
Toothaker, Roy Eugene 1928- 18
Tooze, Ruth (Anderson) 1892-1972 4
Topek, Susan Remick 1955- 78
Topping, Audrey R(onning) 1928- 14
Tor, Regina
See Shekerjian, Regina Tor
Torbert, Floyd James 1922- 22
Torgersen, Don Arthur 1934- 55
Brief entry 41
Torley, Luke
See Blish, James (Benjamin)
Torres, Daniel 1958- 102
Torres, John A. 1965- 163
Earlier sketch in SATA 94
Torres, John Albert
See Torres, John A.
Torres, Laura 1967- 146
Earlier sketch in SATA 87
Torres, Leyla 1960- 155

Torrie, Malcolm
See Mitchell, Gladys (Maude Winifred)
Toten, Teresa 1955- 99
Totham, Mary
See Breinburg, Petronella
Touponce, William F. 1948- 114
Tournier, Michel 1924- 23
Tournier, Michel Edouard
See Tournier, Michel
Towle, Wendy 1963- 79
Towne, Mary
See Spelman, Mary
Townley, Rod
See Townley, Roderick
Townley, Roderick 1942- 177
Townsend, Brad W. 1962- 91
Townsend, John Rowe 1922- 132
Autobiography Feature 132
Earlier sketches in SATA 4, 68
See also CLR 2
See also SAAS 2
Townsend, Sue 93
Brief entry 48
Earlier sketch in SATA 55
See Townsend, Susan Lilian
Townsend, Thomas L. 1944- 59
Townsend, Tom
See Townsend, Thomas L.
Townson, Hazel 134
Toye, William Eldred 1926- 8
Traherne, Michael
See Watkins-Pitchford, Denys James
Trahey, Jane 1923-2000 36
Obituary 120
Trapani, Iza 1954- 116
Earlier sketch in SATA 80
Trapp, Maria Augusta von 16
See von Trapp, Maria Augusta
Travers, P(amela) L(yndon) 1899-1996 100
Obituary 90
Earlier sketches in SATA 4, 54
See also CLR 93
See also SAAS 2
Travis, Lucille 133
Earlier sketch in SATA 88
Treadgold, Mary 1910- 49
Trease, (Robert) Geoffrey 1909-1998 60
Obituary 101
Earlier sketch in SATA 2
See also CLR 42
See also SAAS 6
Treat, Lawrence 1903-1998 59
Tredez, Alain 1926- 17
Tredez, Denise 1930- 50
Treece, Henry 1912-1966 2
See also CLR 2
Tregarthen, Enys
See Sloggett, Nellie
Tregaskis, Richard 1916-1973 3
Obituary 26
Treherne, Katie Thamer 1955- 76
Trell, Max 1900-1996 14
Obituary 108
Tremain, Ruthven 1922- 17
Trembath, Don 1963- 168
Earlier sketch in SATA 96
Tremens, Del
See MacDonald, Amy
Trent, Robbie 1894-1988 26
Trent, Timothy
See Malmberg, Carl
Treseder, Terry Walton 1956- 68
Tresilian, (Cecil) Stuart 1891-(?) 40
Tresselt, Alvin 1916-2000 7
See also CLR 30
Trevino, Elizabeth B(orton) de 1904- 29
Earlier sketch in SATA 1
See also SAAS 5
Trevor, Elleston 1920-1995 28
See Hall, Adam

Trevor, Frances
See Teasdale, Sara
Trevor, Glen
See Hilton, James
Trevor, (Lucy) Meriol 1919-2000 113
Obituary 122
Earlier sketch in SATA 10
Trez, Alain
See Tredez, Alain
Trez, Denise
See Tredez, Denise
Trezise, Percy (James) 1923-
See CLR 41
Triggs, Tony D. 1946- 70
Trimble, Marshall I(ra) 1939- 93
Trimby, Elisa 1948- 47
Brief entry 40
Tripp, Eleanor B(aldwin) 1936- 4
Tripp, Janet 1942- 108
Tripp, John
See Moore, John Travers
Tripp, Nathaniel 1944- 101
Tripp, Paul 1916-2002 8
Obituary 139
Tripp, Valerie 1951- 168
Earlier sketch in SATA 78
Tripp, Wallace (Whitney) 1940- 31
Trivelpiece, Laurel 1926- 56
Brief entry 46
Trivett, Daphne Harwood 1940- 22
Trivizas, Eugene 1946- 84
Trnka, Jiri 1912-1969 43
Brief entry 32
Trollope, Anthony 1815-1882 22
Trost, Lucille W(ood) 1938- 149
Earlier sketch in SATA 12
Trott, Betty 1933- 91
Trotter, Grace V(iolet) 1900-1991 10
Trottier, Maxine 1950- 175
Earlier sketch in SATA 131
Troughton, Joanna (Margaret) 1947- 37
Trout, Kilgore
See Farmer, Philip Jose
Trout, Richard E. 123
Trudeau, Garretson Beekman
See Trudeau, G.B.
Trudeau, Garry
See Trudeau, G.B.
Trudeau, Garry B.
See Trudeau, G.B.
Trudeau, G.B. 1948- 168
Earlier sketch in SATA 35
See Trudeau, Garry B.
Trueit, Trudi
See Trueit, Trudi Strain
Trueit, Trudi Strain 179
Trueman, Terry 1947- 178
Earlier sketch in SATA 132
Truesdell, Judy
See Mecca, Judy Truesdell
Truesdell, Sue
See Truesdell, Susan G.
Truesdell, Susan G. 108
Brief entry 45
Trumbauer, Lisa (Trutkoff) 1963- 149
Truss, Jan 1925- 35
Tryon, Leslie 139
Tubb, Jonathan N. 1951- 78
Tubby, I. M.
See Kraus, (Herman) Robert
Tucker, Caroline
See Nolan, Jeannette Covert
Tudor, Tasha 1915- 160
Earlier sketches in SATA 20, 69
See also CLR 13
Tuerk, Hanne 1951- 71
Tulloch, Richard (George) 1949- 76
Tulloch, Shirley 169
Tully, John (Kimberley) 1923- 14
Tumanov, Vladimir A. 1961- 138
Tung, Angela 1972- 109

Tunis, Edwin (Burdett) 1897-1973 .... *28*
  Obituary *24*
  Earlier sketch in SATA *1*
  See also CLR *2*
Tunis, John R(oberts) 1889-1975 .... *37*
  Brief entry *30*
Tunnell, Michael
  See Tunnell, Michael O('Grady)
Tunnell, Michael O('Grady) 1950- *157*
  Earlier sketch in SATA *103*
Tunnicliffe, C(harles) F(rederick)
  1901-1979 .... *62*
Turck, Mary C. 1950- *144*
Turk, Hanne
  See Tuerk, Hanne
Turk, Ruth 1917- *82*
Turkle, Brinton 1915- *79*
  Earlier sketch in SATA *2*
Turlington, Bayly 1919-1977 .... *5*
  Obituary *52*
Turnbull, Agnes Sligh 1888-1982 .... *14*
Turnbull, Ann (Christine) 1943- *160*
  Earlier sketch in SATA *18*
Turner, Alice K. 1940- *10*
Turner, Ann 1945- *178*
  Earlier sketches in SATA *14, 77, 113*
Turner, Ann Warren
  See Turner, Ann
Turner, Bonnie 1932- *75*
Turner, Elizabeth 1774-1846
  See YABC *2*
Turner, Glennette Tilley 1933- *71*
Turner, Josie
  See Crawford, Phyllis
Turner, Megan Whalen 1965- *174*
  Earlier sketch in SATA *94*
Turner, Philip (William) 1925- *83*
  Earlier sketch in SATA *11*
  See also CLR *89*
  See also SAAS *6*
Turner, Robyn 1947- *77*
Turngren, Ellen (?)-1964 .... *3*
Turska, Krystyna (Zofia) 1933- *31*
  Brief entry *27*
Turteltaub, H.N.
  See Turtledove, Harry
Turtledove, Harry 1949- *166*
  Earlier sketch in SATA *116*
Turtledove, Harry Norman
  See Turtledove, Harry
Tusa, Tricia 1960- *111*
  Earlier sketch in SATA *72*
Tusiani, Joseph 1924- *45*
Twain, Mark
  See CLR *66*
  See Clemens, Samuel Langhorne
Tweit, Susan J 1956- *94*
Tweit, Susan Joan
  See Tweit, Susan J
Tweton, D. Jerome 1933- *48*
Twinem, Neecy 1958- *92*
Tworkov, Jack 1900-1982 .... *47*
  Obituary *31*
Tyche
  See Papademetriou, Lisa
Tyers, Jenny 1969- *89*
Tyers, Kathy 1952- *82*
Tyler, Anne 1941- *173*
  Earlier sketches in SATA *7, 90*
Tyler, Linda
  See Tyler, Linda W(agner)
Tyler, Linda W(agner) 1952- *65*
Tyler, Vicki 1952- *64*
Tyne, Joel
  See Schembri, Jim
Tyrrell, Frances 1959- *107*

U

Ubell, Earl 1926-2007 .... *4*
Uchida, Yoshiko 1921-1992 .... *53*
  Obituary *72*
  Earlier sketch in SATA *1*
  See also CLR *56*
  See also SAAS *1*
Udall, Jan Beaney 1938- *10*
Uden, (Bernard Gilbert) Grant 1910- *26*
Uderzo, Albert 1927-
  See CLR *37*
Udry, Janice May 1928- *152*
  Earlier sketch in SATA *4*
Uegaki, Chieri 1969- *153*
Ueno, Noriko
  See Nakae, Noriko
Uhlberg, Myron *174*
Uhlig, Susan 1955- *129*
Ulam, S(tanislaw) M(arcin) 1909-1984 .... *51*
Ullman, James Ramsey 1907-1971 .... *7*
Ulm, Robert 1934-1977 .... *17*
Ulmer, Louise 1943- *53*
Ulyatt, Kenneth 1920- *14*
Umansky, Kaye 1946- *158*
Unada
  See Gliewe, Unada (Grace)
Uncle Carter
  See Boucher, (Clarence) Carter
Uncle Eric
  See Maybury, Richard J.
Uncle Gus
  See Rey, H(ans) A(ugusto)
Uncle Ray
  See Coffman, Ramon Peyton
Uncle Shelby
  See Silverstein, Shel
Underhill, Alice Mertie (Waterman)
  1900-1971 .... *10*
Underhill, Liz 1948- *53*
  Brief entry *49*
Unger, Harlow G. 1931- *75*
Unger, Jim 1937- *67*
Ungerer, (Jean) Thomas 1931- *106*
  Earlier sketches in SATA *5, 33*
  See Ungerer, Tomi
Ungerer, Tomi 1931-
  See CLR *77*
  See Ungerer, (Jean) Thomas
Unkelbach, Kurt 1913-1992 .... *4*
Unnerstad, Edith (Totterman) 1900-1982 .... *3*
  See also CLR *36*
Unobagha, Uzo *139*
Unrau, Ruth 1922- *9*
Unstead, R(obert) J(ohn) 1915-1988 .... *12*
  Obituary *56*
Unsworth, Walt(er) 1928- *4*
Untermeyer, Bryna Ivens 1909-1985 .... *61*
Untermeyer, Louis 1885-1977 .... *37*
  Obituary *26*
  Earlier sketch in SATA *2*
Unwin, David S(torr) 1918- *14*
Unwin, Nora S(picer) 1907-1982 .... *3*
  Obituary *49*
Unzner, Christa 1958- *141*
  Earlier sketch in SATA *80*
Unzner-Fischer, Christa
  See Unzner, Christa
Updale, Eleanor 1953- *175*
Updyke, Rosemary K. 1924- *103*
Upitis, Alvis *109*
Urban, Helle (Denise) 1957- *149*
Ure, Jean 1943- *129*
  Earlier sketches in SATA *48, 78*
  See also CLR *34*
  See also SAAS *14*
U'Ren, Andrea 1968- *142*
Uris, Leon 1924-2003 .... *49*
  Obituary *146*
Uris, Leon Marcus
  See Uris, Leon

Ursu, Anne *177*
Ury, Allen B. 1954- *98*
Uschan, Michael V. 1948- *129*
Usher, Margo Scegge
  See McHargue, Georgess
Uslan, Michael E. 1951- *169*
Uston, Ken(neth Senzo) 1935-1987 .... *65*
Uttley, Alice Jane (Taylor) 1884-1976 .... *88*
  Obituary *26*
  Earlier sketch in SATA *3*
  See Uttley, Alison
Uttley, Alison
  See Uttley, Alice Jane (Taylor)
Utz, Lois (Marie) 1932-1986 .... *5*
  Obituary *50*

V

Vaeth, J(oseph) Gordon 1921- *17*
Vagin, Vladimir (Vasilevich) 1937- *142*
Vail, Rachel 1966- *163*
  Earlier sketch in SATA *94*
Vainio, Pirkko 1957- *123*
  Earlier sketch in SATA *76*
Valen, Nanine 1950- *21*
Valencak, Hannelore *42*
  See Mayer, Hannelore Valencak
Valens, Amy 1946- *70*
Valens, E(vans) G(ladstone), Jr. 1920-1992 ... *1*
Valentine, Johnny *72*
Valgardson, W(illiam) D(empsey) 1939- *151*
  Earlier sketch in SATA *101*
Valleau, Emily 1925- *51*
Van Abbe, Salaman 1883-1955 .... *18*
Van Allsburg, Chris 1949- *156*
  Earlier sketches in SATA *37, 53, 105*
  See also CLR *113*
Van Anrooy, Francine 1924- *2*
Van Anrooy, Frans
  See Van Anrooy, Francine
Vanasse, Deb 1957- *170*
Vance, Eleanor Graham 1908-1985 .... *11*
Vance, Gerald
  See Garrett, (Gordon) Randall (Phillip)
  and Silverberg, Robert
Vance, Marguerite 1889-1965 .... *29*
VanCleave, Janice 1942- *116*
  Autobiography Feature *123*
  Earlier sketch in SATA *75*
Vandenburg, Mary Lou 1943- *17*
Vander Boom, Mae M. *14*
Vander-Els, Betty 1936- *63*
van der Linde, Laurel 1952- *78*
van der Meer, Ron 1945- *98*
Van der Veer, Judy 1912-1982 .... *4*
  Obituary *33*
Vanderwerff, Corrine 1939- *117*
Vander Zee, Ruth *159*
Vande Velde, Vivian 1951- *141*
  Earlier sketches in SATA *62, 95*
Vandivert, Rita (Andre) 1905-1986 .... *21*
Van Draanen, Wendelin *122*
Van Dusen, Chris *173*
Van Duyn, Janet 1910- *18*
Van Dyne, Edith
  See Baum, L(yman) Frank
  and Sampson, Emma (Keats) Speed
  and van Zantwijk, Rudolf (Alexander
  Marinus)
Vane, Mitch
  See Vane, Mitchelle
Vane, Mitchelle *176*
van Frankenhuyzen, Gijsbert 1951- *132*
Van Genechten, Guido 1957- *165*
Van Hook, Beverly H. 1941- *99*
Van Horn, William 1939- *43*
van Hout, Mies 1962- *178*
Van Iterson, S(iny) R(ose) *26*

Van Kampen, Vlasta 1943- *163*
  Earlier sketch in SATA *54*
Van Laan, Nancy 1939- *105*
van Lawick-Goodall, Jane
  See Goodall, Jane
Van Leeuwen, Jean 1937- *141*
  Autobiography Feature *141*
  Earlier sketches in SATA *6, 82, 132*
  See also SAAS *8*
van Lhin, Erik
  See del Rey, Lester
Van Loon, Hendrik Willem 1882-1944 .... *18*
VanOosting, James 1951- *170*
Van Orden, M(erton) D(ick) 1921- *4*
Van Rensselaer, Alexander (Taylor Mason)
  1892-1962 .... *14*
Van Riper, Guernsey, Jr. 1909-1995 .... *3*
van Rossum, Heleen 1962- *174*
Van Rynbach, Iris 1952- *102*
Vansant, Rhonda Joy Edwards 1950- *92*
Van Steenwyk, Elizabeth (Ann) 1928- *89*
  Earlier sketch in SATA *34*
Van Stockum, Hilda 1908-2006 .... *5*
  Obituary *179*
Van Tuyl, Barbara 1940- *11*
van Vogt, A(lfred) E(lton) 1912-2000 .... *14*
  Obituary *124*
Van Woerkom, Dorothy (O'Brien)
  1924-1996 .... *21*
Van Wormer, Joe
  See Van Wormer, Joseph Edward
Van Wormer, Joseph Edward 1913-1998 ...... *35*
Van Wright, Cornelius *173*
Van Zwienen, Ilse Charlotte Koehn
  1929-1991 .... *34*
  Brief entry *28*
  Obituary *67*
Van Zyle, Jon 1942- *176*
  Earlier sketch in SATA *84*
Varga, Judy
  See Stang, Judit
Varley, Dimitry V. 1906-1984 .... *10*
Varley, Susan 1961- *134*
  Earlier sketch in SATA *63*
Vasileva, Tatiana
  See Wassiljewa, Tatjana
Vasiliev, Valery 1949- *80*
Vasilieva, Tatiana
  See Wassiljewa, Tatjana
Vasiliu, Mircea 1920- *2*
Vass, George 1927- *57*
  Brief entry *31*
Vaughan, Carter A.
  See Gerson, Noel Bertram
Vaughan, Harold Cecil 1923- *14*
Vaughan, Marcia (K.) 1951- *159*
  Earlier sketches in SATA *60, 95*
Vaughan, Richard 1947- *87*
Vaughan, Sam(uel) 1928- *14*
Vaughn, Ruth 1935- *14*
Vautier, Ghislaine 1932- *53*
Vavra, Robert James 1935- *8*
Vecsey, George Spencer 1939- *9*
Vedral, Joyce L(auretta) 1943- *65*
Vega, Denise B. *174*
  See Vega, Denise
Veglahn, Nancy (Crary) 1937- *5*
Velasquez, Gloria (Louise) 1949- *113*
  See Velasquez(-Trevino), Gloria (Louise)
Velthuijs, Max 1923-2005 .... *110*
  Obituary *160*
  Earlier sketch in SATA *53*
Venable, Alan (Hudson) 1944- *8*
Venezia, Mike 1945- *150*
Ventura, Anthony
  See Pellowski, Michael (Joseph)
Ventura, Piero (Luigi) 1937- *61*
  Brief entry *43*
  See also CLR *16*
Vequin, Capini
  See Quinn, Elisabeth

Verba, Joan Marie 1953- *78*
Verboven, Agnes 1951- *103*
verDorn, Bethea (Stewart) 1952- *76*
Verissimo, Erico (Lopes) 1905-1975 .... *113*
Verne, Jules (Gabriel) 1828-1905 .... *21*
  See also CLR *88*
Verney, John 1913-1993 .... *14*
  Obituary *75*
Vernon, (Elda) Louise A(nderson) 1914- *14*
Vernon, Rosemary
  See Smith, Susan Vernon
Vernor, D.
  See Casewit, Curtis W(erner)
Verr, Harry Coe
  See Kunhardt, Edith
Verral, Charles Spain 1904-1990 .... *11*
  Obituary *65*
Versace, Marie Teresa Rios 1917- *2*
Vertreace, Martha M(odena) 1945- *78*
Vesey, A(manda) 1939- *62*
Vesey, Mark (David) 1958- *123*
Vesey, Paul
  See Allen, Samuel W(ashington)
Vestergaard, Hope *178*
Vestly, Anne-Cath(arina) 1920- *14*
  See also CLR *99*
Vevers, (Henry) Gwynne 1916-1988 .... *45*
  Obituary *57*
Viator, Vacuus
  See Hughes, Thomas
Vicar, Henry
  See Felsen, Henry Gregor
Vick, Helen Hughes 1950- *88*
Vicker, Angus
  See Felsen, Henry Gregor
Vickers, Sheena 1960- *94*
Vickery, Kate
  See Kennedy, T.A.
Victor, Edward 1914- *3*
Victor, Joan Berg 1942- *30*
Vidrine, Beverly Barras 1938- *103*
Viereck, Ellen K. 1928- *14*
Viereck, Phillip 1925- *3*
Viertel, Janet 1915- *10*
Vigliante, Mary
  See Szydlowski, Mary Vigliante
Vigna, Judith 1936- *102*
  Earlier sketch in SATA *15*
Viguers, Ruth Hill 1903-1971 .... *6*
Villasenor, Edmundo
  See Villasenor, Victor
Villasenor, Victor 1940- *171*
Villasenor, Victor E. 1940-
  See Villasenor, Victor
Villasenor, Victor Edmundo
  See Villasenor, Victor
Villiard, Paul 1910-1974 .... *51*
  Obituary *20*
Villiers, Alan (John) 1903-1982 .... *10*
Vilott, Rhondi
  See Salsitz, Rhondi Vilott
Vincent, Eric Douglas 1953- *40*
Vincent, Felix 1946- *41*
Vincent, Gabrielle 1928-2000 .... *121*
  Earlier sketch in SATA *61*
  See also CLR *13*
Vincent, Mary Keith
  See St. John, Wylly Folk
Vincent, William R.
  See Heitzmann, William Ray
Vinegar, Tom
  See Gregg, Andrew K.
Vinest, Shaw
  See Longyear, Barry B(rookes)
Vinge, Joan (Carol) D(ennison) 1948- *113*
  Earlier sketch in SATA *36*
Vining, Elizabeth Gray 1902-1999 .... *6*
  Obituary *117*
  See Gray, Elizabeth Janet
Vinson, Kathryn 1911-1995 .... *21*

Vinton, Iris 1906(?)-1988 .... *24*
  Obituary *55*
Viola, Herman J(oseph) 1938- *126*
Viorst, Judith 1931- *172*
  Earlier sketches in SATA *7, 70, 123*
  See also CLR *90*
Vip
  See Partch, Virgil Franklin II
Vipont, Charles
  See Foulds, Elfrida Vipont
Vipont, Elfrida
  See Foulds, Elfrida Vipont
Viscott, David S(teven) 1938-1996 .... *65*
Visser, W(illem) F(rederik) H(endrik)
  1900-1968 .... *10*
Vitale, Stefano 1958- *114*
Vivas, Julie 1947- *96*
Vivelo, Jackie 1943- *63*
Vivelo, Jacqueline J.
  See Vivelo, Jackie
Vivelo, Jacqueline Jean
  See Vivelo, Jackie
Vizzini, Ned 1981- *179*
  Earlier sketch in SATA *125*
Vlahos, Olivia 1924- *31*
Vlasic, Bob
  See Hirsch, Phil
Voake, Charlotte *114*
Voake, Steve 1961- *178*
Vo-Dinh, Mai 1933- *16*
Vogel, Carole Garbuny 1951- *105*
  Earlier sketch in SATA *70*
Vogel, Ilse-Margret 1918- *14*
Vogel, John H., Jr. 1950- *18*
Vogt, Esther Loewen 1915-1999 .... *14*
Vogt, Gregory L. *94*
Vogt, Marie Bollinger 1921- *45*
Voight, Virginia Frances 1909-1989 .... *8*
Voigt, Cynthia 1942- *160*
  Brief entry *33*
  Earlier sketches in SATA *48, 79, 116*
  See also CLR *48*
Voigt, Erna 1925- *35*
Voigt-Rother, Erna
  See Voigt, Erna
Vojtech, Anna 1946- *108*
  Earlier sketch in SATA *42*
Vollstadt, Elizabeth Weiss 1942- *121*
Volponi, Paul *175*
Volting, Dr. R.E.
  See Lerangis, Peter
Von Ahnen, Katherine 1922- *93*
Vondra, Josef (Gert) 1941- *121*
Von Gunden, Kenneth 1946- *113*
Von Hagen, Victor Wolfgang 1908-1985 ...... *29*
von Klopp, Vahrah
  See Malvern, Gladys
von Schmidt, Eric 1931-2007 .... *50*
  Brief entry *36*
von Storch, Anne B. 1910- *1*
von Ziegesar, Cecily 1970- *161*
Vos, Ida 1931- *121*
  Earlier sketch in SATA *69*
  See also CLR *85*
Vosburgh, Leonard (W.) 1912- *15*
Voyle, Mary
  See Manning, Rosemary (Joy)
Vriens, Jacques 1946- *151*
Vugteveen, Verna Aardema *107*
  Obituary *119*
  Earlier sketches in SATA *4, 68*
  See also CLR *17*
  See also SAAS *8*
  See Aardema, Verna
Vulture, Elizabeth T.
  See Gilbert, Suzie
Vuong, Lynette Dyer 1938- *110*
  Earlier sketch in SATA *60*

W

Waas, Uli
　　See Waas-Pommer, Ulrike
Waas-Pommer, Ulrike 1949- *85*
Waber, Bernard 1924- *155*
　　Brief entry *40*
　　Earlier sketches in SATA *47, 95*
　　See also CLR *55*
Wachtel, Shirley Russak 1951- *88*
Wachter, Oralee (Roberts) 1935- *61*
　　Brief entry *51*
Waddell, Evelyn Margaret 1918- *10*
Waddell, Martin 1941- *129*
　　Autobiography Feature *129*
　　Earlier sketches in SATA *43, 81, 127*
　　See also CLR *31*
　　See also SAAS *15*
Waddy, Lawrence (Heber) 1914- *91*
Wade, Mary Dodson 1930- *151*
　　Earlier sketch in SATA *79*
Wade, Suzanne
　　See Kirby, Susan E.
Wade, Theodore E., Jr. 1936- *37*
Wademan, Peter John 1946- *122*
Wademan, Spike
　　See Wademan, Peter John
Wadsworth, Ginger 1945- *157*
　　Earlier sketch in SATA *103*
Wagenheim, Kal 1935- *21*
Wagner, Michele R. 1975- *157*
Wagner, Sharon B. 1936- *4*
Wagoner, David (Russell) 1926- *14*
Wahl, Jan (Boyer) 1933- *132*
　　Earlier sketches in SATA *2, 34, 73*
　　See also SAAS *3*
Waide, Jan 1952- *29*
Wainscott, John Milton 1910-1981 .... *53*
Wainwright, Richard M. 1935- *91*
Wainwright, Ruth
　　See Symes, Ruth Louise
Wait, Lea 1946- *137*
Waite, Judy *174*
Waite, Michael P(hillip) 1960- *101*
Waite, P(eter) B(usby) 1922- *64*
Waitley, Douglas 1927- *30*
Wakefield, Jean L.
　　See Laird, Jean E(louise)
Wakin, Daniel (Joseph) 1961- *84*
Wakin, Edward 1927- *37*
Walden, Amelia Elizabeth *3*
Waldherr, Kris 1963- *76*
Waldman, Bruce 1949- *15*
Waldman, Neil 1947- *142*
　　Earlier sketches in SATA *51, 94*
Waldron, Ann Wood 1924- *16*
Waldron, Kathleen Cook *176*
Walgren, Judy 1963- *118*
Walker, Addison
　　See Walker, (Addison) Mort
Walker, Alice 1944- *31*
Walker, Alice Malsenior
　　See Walker, Alice
Walker, Barbara (Jeanne) K(erlin) 1921- *80*
　　Earlier sketch in SATA *4*
Walker, Barbara M(uhs) 1928- *57*
Walker, (James) Braz(elton) 1934-1983 .... *45*
Walker, David G(ordon) 1926- *60*
Walker, David Harry 1911-1992 .... *8*
　　Obituary *71*
Walker, Diana 1925- *9*
Walker, Diane Marie Catherine
　　See Walker, Kate
Walker, Dick
　　See Pellowski, Michael (Joseph)
Walker, Frank 1931-2000 .... *36*
Walker, Holly Beth
　　See Bond, Gladys Baker
Walker, Kate 1950- *165*
　　Earlier sketch in SATA *82*

Walker, Kathrine Sorley
　　See Sorley Walker, Kathrine
Walker, Lou Ann 1952- *66*
　　Brief entry *53*
Walker, Mary Alexander 1927- *61*
Walker, Mildred
　　See Schemm, Mildred Walker
Walker, (Addison) Mort 1923- *8*
Walker, Pamela 1948- *142*
　　Earlier sketch in SATA *24*
Walker, Paul Robert 1953- *154*
Walker, Robert W(ayne) 1948- *66*
Walker, Sally M(acArt) 1954- *135*
Walker, Stephen J. 1951- *12*
Walker-Blondell, Becky 1951- *89*
Wallace, Barbara Brooks 1922- *136*
　　Earlier sketches in SATA *4, 78*
　　See also SAAS *17*
Wallace, Beverly Dobrin 1921- *19*
Wallace, Bill 1947- *169*
　　Brief entry *47*
　　Earlier sketches in SATA *53, 101*
Wallace, Daisy
　　See Cuyler, Margery S(tuyvesant)
Wallace, Ian 1950- *141*
　　Earlier sketches in SATA *53, 56*
　　See also CLR *37*
Wallace, John 1966- *155*
　　Earlier sketch in SATA *105*
Wallace, John A(dam) 1915-2004 .... *3*
　　Obituary *155*
Wallace, Karen 1951- *139*
　　Earlier sketch in SATA *83*
Wallace, Nancy Elizabeth 1948- *141*
Wallace, Nigel
　　See Hamilton, Charles (Harold St. John)
Wallace, Paula S. *153*
Wallace, Rich 1957- *158*
　　Earlier sketch in SATA *117*
Wallace, Robert 1932-1999 .... *47*
　　Brief entry *37*
Wallace, William Keith
　　See Wallace, Bill
Wallace-Brodeur, Ruth 1941- *169*
　　Brief entry *41*
　　Earlier sketches in SATA *51, 88*
Wallenta, Adam 1974- *123*
Waller, Leslie 1923-2007 .... *20*
Walley, Byron
　　See Card, Orson Scott
Wallis, Diz 1949- *77*
Wallis, G. McDonald
　　See Campbell, Hope
Wallner, Alexandra 1946- *156*
　　Brief entry *41*
　　Earlier sketches in SATA *51, 98*
Wallner, John C. 1945- *133*
　　Earlier sketches in SATA *10, 51*
Wallower, Lucille *11*
Walsh, Ann 1942- *176*
　　Earlier sketch in SATA *62*
Walsh, Ellen Stoll 1942- *147*
　　Earlier sketches in SATA *49, 99*
Walsh, George Johnston 1889-1981 .... *53*
Walsh, Gillian Paton
　　See Paton Walsh, Jill
Walsh, Jill Paton
　　See CLR *65*
　　See Paton Walsh, Jill
Walsh, Lawrence 1942- *170*
Walsh, Mary Caswell 1949- *118*
Walsh, Suella *170*
Walsh, V. L.
　　See Walsh, Vivian
Walsh, Vivian 1960- *120*
Walsh Shepherd, Donna 1948- *78*
Walter, Frances V. 1923- *71*

Walter, Mildred Pitts 1922- *133*
　　Brief entry *45*
　　Earlier sketch in SATA *69*
　　See also CLR *61*
　　See also SAAS *12*
Walter, Villiam Christian
　　See Andersen, Hans Christian
Walter, Virginia *134*
　　See Walter, Virginia A.
Walters, Audrey 1929- *18*
Walters, Celeste 1938- *126*
Walters, Eric (Robert) 1957- *155*
　　Earlier sketch in SATA *99*
Walters, Hugh
　　See Hughes, Walter (Llewellyn)
Walther, Thomas A. 1950- *31*
Walther, Tom
　　See Walther, Thomas A.
Waltner, Elma 1912-1987 .... *40*
Waltner, Willard H. 1909- *40*
Walton, Darwin McBeth 1926- *119*
Walton, Fiona L. M. 1959- *89*
Walton, Richard J. 1928- *4*
Walton, Rick 1957- *151*
　　Earlier sketch in SATA *101*
Waltrip, Lela (Kingston) 1904-1995 .... *9*
Waltrip, Mildred 1911- *37*
Waltrip, Rufus (Charles) 1898-1988 .... *9*
Walworth, Nancy Zinsser 1917- *14*
Wangerin, Walter, Jr. 1944- *98*
　　Brief entry *37*
　　Earlier sketch in SATA *45*
Waniek, Marilyn Nelson 1946- *60*
　　See Nelson, Marilyn
Wannamaker, Bruce
　　See Moncure, Jane Belk
Warbler, J. M.
　　See Cocagnac, Augustin Maurice(-Jean)
Warburg, Sandol Stoddard *14*
　　See Stoddard, Sandol
Ward, E. D.
　　See Gorey, Edward (St. John)
　　and Lucas, E(dward) V(errall)
Ward, Ed
　　See Stratemeyer, Edward L.
Ward, Helen 1962- *144*
　　Earlier sketch in SATA *72*
Ward, Jennifer 1963- *146*
Ward, John (Stanton) 1917- *42*
Ward, Jonas
　　See Ard, William (Thomas)
　　and Cox, William R(obert)
　　and Garfield, Brian (Francis Wynne)
Ward, Lynd (Kendall) 1905-1985 .... *36*
　　Obituary *42*
　　Earlier sketch in SATA *2*
Ward, Martha (Eads) *5*
Ward, Melanie
　　See Curtis, Richard (Alan)
　　and Lynch, Marilyn
Ward, Tom
　　See Stratemeyer, Edward L.
Wardell, Dean
　　See Prince, J(ack) H(arvey)
Wardlaw, Lee 1955- *115*
　　Earlier sketch in SATA *79*
Ware, Cheryl 1963- *101*
Ware, Chris 1967- *140*
Ware, Leon (Vernon) 1909-1976 .... *4*
Wargin, Kathy-jo 1965- *145*
Warner, Frank A. *67*
　　Earlier sketch in SATA *1*
Warner, Gertrude Chandler 1890-1979 .... *9*
　　Obituary *73*
Warner, J(ohn) F. 1929- *75*
Warner, Lucille Schulberg *30*
Warner, Matt
　　See Fichter, George S.
Warner, Oliver (Martin Wilson) 1903-1976 . *29*
Warner, Sally 1946- *131*
Warner, Sunny (B.) 1931- *108*

Warnes, Tim 1971- *166*
 Earlier sketch in SATA *116*
Warnes, Timothy
 See Warnes, Tim
Warnick, Elsa 1942- *113*
Warren, Andrea 1946- *98*
Warren, Betsy
 See Warren, Elizabeth Avery
Warren, Billy
 See Warren, William Stephen
Warren, Cathy 1951- *62*
 Brief entry *46*
Warren, Elizabeth
 See Supraner, Robyn
Warren, Elizabeth Avery 1916- *46*
 Brief entry *38*
Warren, Jackie M. 1953- *135*
Warren, Joshua P(aul) 1976- *107*
Warren, Joyce W(illiams) 1935- *18*
Warren, Mary Phraner 1929- *10*
Warren, Robert Penn 1905-1989 .... *46*
 Obituary *63*
Warren, Scott S. 1957- *79*
Warren, William Stephen 1882-1968 .... *9*
Warrick, Patricia Scott 1925- *35*
Warsh
 See Warshaw, Jerry
Warshaw, Jerry 1929- *30*
Warshaw, Mary 1931- *89*
Warshofsky, Fred 1931- *24*
Warshofsky, Isaac
 See Singer, Isaac Bashevis
Wartski, Maureen (Ann Crane) 1940- *50*
 Brief entry *37*
Warwick, Alan R(oss) 1900-1973 .... *42*
Wa-Sha-Quon-Asin
 See Belaney, Archibald Stansfeld
Wa-sha-quon-asin
 See Belaney, Archibald Stansfeld
Washburn, Bradford 1910-2007 .... *38*
Washburn, Henry Bradford, Jr.
 See Washburn, Bradford
Washburn, Jan(ice) 1926- *63*
Washburne, Carolyn Kott 1944- *86*
Washburne, Heluiz Chandler 1892-1970 ...... *10*
 Obituary *26*
Washington, Booker T(aliaferro)
 1856-1915 .... *28*
Washington, Donna L. 1967- *159*
 Earlier sketch in SATA *98*
Wasserstein, Wendy 1950-2006 .... *94*
 Obituary *174*
Wassiljewa, Tatjana 1928- *106*
Watanabe, Shigeo 1928- *131*
 Brief entry *32*
 Earlier sketch in SATA *39*
 See also CLR *8*
Waters, John F(rederick) 1930- *4*
Waters, Tony 1958- *75*
Waterton, Betty (Marie) 1923- *99*
 Brief entry *34*
 Earlier sketch in SATA *37*
Watkins, Dawn L. *126*
Watkins, Gloria Jean
 See hooks, bell
Watkins, Lois 1930- *88*
Watkins, Peter 1934- *66*
Watkins, Yoko Kawashima 1933- *93*
Watkins-Pitchford, Denys James
 1905-1990 .... *87*
 Obituary *66*
 Earlier sketch in SATA *6*
 See also SAAS *4*
Watling, James 1933- *117*
 Earlier sketch in SATA *67*
Watson, Aldren A(uld) 1917- *42*
 Brief entry *36*
Watson, Amy Zakrzewski 1965- *76*
Watson, B. S.
 See Teitelbaum, Michael
Watson, Carol 1949- *78*

Watson, Clyde 1947- *68*
 Earlier sketch in SATA *5*
 See also CLR *3*
Watson, James 1936- *106*
 Earlier sketch in SATA *10*
Watson, Jane Werner 1915- *54*
 Earlier sketch in SATA *3*
Watson, John H.
 See Farmer, Philip Jose
Watson, Mary 1953- *117*
Watson, N. Cameron 1955- *81*
Watson, Nancy Dingman *32*
Watson, Pauline 1925- *14*
Watson, Richard F.
 See Silverberg, Robert
Watson, Richard Jesse 1951- *62*
Watson, Sally (Lou) 1924- *3*
Watson, Wendy (McLeod) 1942- *142*
 Earlier sketches in SATA *5, 74*
Watson Taylor, Elizabeth 1915- *41*
Watt, Melanie 1975- *136*
Watt, Thomas 1935- *4*
Wattenberg, Jane *174*
Watterson, Bill 1958- *66*
Watt-Evans, Lawrence 1954- *121*
 See Evans, Lawrence Watt
Watts, (Anna) Bernadette 1942- *103*
 Earlier sketch in SATA *4*
Watts, Ephraim
 See Horne, Richard Henry Hengist
Watts, Franklin (Mowry) 1904-1978 .... *46*
 Obituary *21*
Watts, Irene N(aemi) 1931- *111*
 Earlier sketch in SATA *56*
Watts, Isaac 1674-1748 .... *52*
Watts, James K(ennedy) M(offitt) 1955- *59*
Watts, Jeri Hanel 1957- *170*
Watts, Julia 1969- *103*
Watts, Leander 1956- *146*
Watts, Leslie Elizabeth 1961- *168*
Watts, Mabel Pizzey 1906-1994 .... *11*
Watts, Nigel 1957-1999 .... *121*
Waugh, C. C. Roessel
 See Waugh, Carol-Lynn Rossel
 and Waugh, Charles G(ordon)
Waugh, Carol-Lynn Rossel 1947- *41*
Waugh, Dorothy -1996 .... *11*
Waugh, Sylvia 1935- *169*
Waugh, Virginia
 See Sorensen, Virginia
Wax, Wendy A. 1963- *163*
 Earlier sketch in SATA *73*
Wayland, April Halprin 1954- *143*
 Earlier sketch in SATA *78*
 See also SAAS *26*
Wayne, (Anne) Jenifer 1917-1982 .... *32*
Wayne, Kyra Petrovskaya 1918- *8*
Wayne, Richard
 See Decker, Duane
Wayshak, Deborah Noyes 1965- *145*
Waystaff, Simon
 See Swift, Jonathan
Weales, Gerald (Clifford) 1925- *11*
Weary, Ogdred
 See Gorey, Edward (St. John)
Weatherford, Carole Boston 1956- *138*
Weatherly, Myra (S.) 1926- *130*
Weaver, Harriett E. 1908-1993 .... *65*
Weaver, John L. 1949- *42*
Weaver, Robyn
 See Conley-Weaver, Robyn
Weaver, Robyn M.
 See Conley-Weaver, Robyn
Weaver, Ward
 See Mason, F(rancis) van Wyck
Weaver, Will 1950- *161*
 Earlier sketches in SATA *88, 109*
Weaver, William Weller
 See Weaver, Will
Weaver-Gelzer, Charlotte 1950- *79*

Webb, Christopher
 See Wibberley, Leonard (Patrick O'Connor)
Webb, Jacqueline
 See Pearce, Margaret
Webb, Jacquelyn
 See Pearce, Margaret
 and Pearce, Margaret
Webb, Jean Francis (III) 1910-1991 .... *35*
Webb, Kaye 1914- *60*
Webb, Lois Sinaiko 1922- *82*
Webb, Margot 1934- *67*
Webb, Sharon 1936- *41*
Webb, Sophie 1958- *135*
Webber, Andrew Lloyd
 See Lloyd Webber, Andrew
Webber, Desiree Morrison 1956- *170*
Webber, Irma E(leanor Schmidt)
 1904-1995 .... *14*
Weber, Alfons 1921- *8*
Weber, Bruce 1942- *120*
 Earlier sketch in SATA *73*
Weber, Debora 1955- *58*
Weber, EdNah New Rider 1919(?)- *168*
Weber, Jill 1950- *127*
Weber, Judith E(ichler) 1938- *64*
Weber, Ken(neth J.) 1940- *90*
Weber, Lenora Mattingly 1895-1971 .... *2*
 Obituary *26*
Weber, Michael 1945- *87*
Weber, Sandra 1961- *158*
Weber, William J(ohn) 1927- *14*
Webster, Alice Jane Chandler 1876-1916 ..... *17*
Webster, David 1930- *11*
Webster, Frank V. *67*
 Earlier sketch in SATA *1*
Webster, Gary
 See Garrison, Webb B(lack)
Webster, James 1925-1981 .... *17*
 Obituary *27*
Webster, Jean
 See Webster, Alice Jane Chandler
Wechter, Nell (Carolyn) Wise 1913-1989 .. *127*
 Earlier sketch in SATA *60*
Weck, Thomas L. 1942- *62*
Wedd, Kate
 See Gregory, Philippa
Weddle, Ethel Harshbarger 1897-1996 .... *11*
Weeks, Sarah *158*
Weems, David B(urnola) 1922- *80*
Wees, Frances Shelley 1902-1982 .... *58*
Weevers, Peter 1944- *59*
Wegen, Ronald 1946-1985 .... *99*
Wegman, William (George) 1943- *135*
 Earlier sketches in SATA *78, 129*
Wegner, Fritz 1924- *20*
Weidhorn, Manfred 1931- *60*
Weidt, Maryann N. 1944- *85*
Weigel, Jeff 1958- *170*
Weigelt, Udo 1960- *168*
Weihs, Erika 1917- *107*
 Earlier sketch in SATA *15*
Weik, Mary Hays 1898(?)-1979 .... *3*
 Obituary *23*
Weil, Ann Yezner 1908-1969 .... *9*
Weil, Lisl 1910- *7*
Weilerstein, Sadie Rose 1894-1993 .... *3*
 Obituary *75*
Weill, Cynthia 1959- *167*
Wein, Elizabeth E(ve) 1964- *151*
 Earlier sketch in SATA *82*
Weinberg, Larry
 See Weinberg, Lawrence (E.)
Weinberg, Lawrence (E.) *92*
 Brief entry *48*
Weinberger, Tanya 1939- *84*
Weiner, Sandra 1922- *14*
Weingarten, Violet (Brown) 1915-1976 .... *3*
 Obituary *27*
Weingartner, Charles 1922- *5*
Weinstein, Nina 1951- *73*
Weir, Bob 1947- *76*

Weir, Diana (R.) Loiewski 1958- *111*
Weir, Joan S(herman) 1928- *99*
Weir, LaVada *2*
Weir, Rosemary (Green) 1905-1994 .... *21*
Weir, Wendy 1949- *76*
Weis, Margaret 1948- *164*
 Earlier sketches in SATA *38, 92*
Weisberger, Bernard A(llen) 1922- *21*
Weiser, Marjorie P(hillis) K(atz) 1934- *33*
Weisgard, Leonard (Joseph) 1916-2000 .... *85*
 Obituary *122*
 Earlier sketches in SATA *2, 30*
 See also SAAS *19*
Weiss, Adelle 1920- *18*
Weiss, Ann E(dwards) 1943- *69*
 Earlier sketch in SATA *30*
 See also SAAS *13*
Weiss, Edna
 See Barth, Edna
Weiss, Ellen 1953- *44*
Weiss, Harvey 1922- *76*
 Earlier sketches in SATA *1, 27*
 See also CLR *4*
 See also SAAS *19*
Weiss, Jaqueline Shachter 1926- *65*
Weiss, Malcolm E. 1928- *3*
Weiss, Margaret Edith
 See Weis, Margaret
Weiss, Miriam
 See Schlein, Miriam
Weiss, Mitch 1951- *123*
Weiss, Nicki 1954- *86*
 Earlier sketch in SATA *33*
Weiss, Renee Karol 1923- *5*
Weitzman, David L. 1936- *172*
 Earlier sketch in SATA *122*
Wekesser, Carol A. 1963- *76*
Welber, Robert *26*
Welch, Amanda (Jane) 1945- *75*
Welch, Jean-Louise
 See Kempton, Jean Welch
Welch, Pauline
 See Bodenham, Hilda Morris
Welch, Ronald
 See Felton, Ronald Oliver
Welch, Sheila Kelly 1945- *130*
Welch, Willy 1952- *93*
Welford, Sue 1942- *75*
Weller, George (Anthony) 1907-2002 .... *31*
 Obituary *140*
Welling, Peter J. 1947- *135*
Wellington, Monica 1957- *157*
 Earlier sketches in SATA *67, 99*
Wellman, Alice 1900-1984 .... *51*
 Brief entry *36*
Wellman, Manly Wade 1903-1986 .... *6*
 Obituary *47*
Wellman, Paul I(selin) 1898-1966 .... *3*
Wellman, Sam(uel) 1939- *122*
Wells, H(erbert) G(eorge) 1866-1946 .... *20*
 See also CLR *64*
Wells, Helen
 See Campbell, Hope
Wells, Helen 1910-1986 .... *49*
 Earlier sketch in SATA *2*
Wells, J. Wellington
 See de Camp, L(yon) Sprague
Wells, June
 See Swinford, Betty (June Wells)
Wells, Robert
 See Welsch, Roger L(ee)
Wells, Rosemary 1943- *156*
 Earlier sketches in SATA *18, 69, 114*
 See also CLR *69*
 See also SAAS *1*
Wells, Susan (Mary) 1951- *78*
Wels, Byron G(erald) 1924-1993 .... *9*
Welsbacher, Anne 1955- *89*
Welsch, Roger L(ee) 1936- *82*
Welsh, David
 See Hills, C.A.R.

Weltner, Linda R(iverly) 1938- *38*
Welton, Jude 1955- *143*
 Earlier sketch in SATA *79*
Welty, S. F.
 See Welty, Susan F.
Welty, Susan F. 1905- *9*
Wendelin, Rudolph 1910-2000 .... *23*
Wentworth, Robert
 See Hamilton, Edmond
Werlin, Nancy 1961- *161*
 Earlier sketches in SATA *87, 119*
Werner, Elsa Jane
 See Watson, Jane Werner
Werner, Herma 1926- *47*
 Brief entry *41*
Werner, Jane
 See Watson, Jane Werner
Werner, K.
 See Casewit, Curtis W(erner)
Wersba, Barbara 1932- *58*
 Autobiography Feature *103*
 Earlier sketch in SATA *1*
 See also CLR *78*
 See also SAAS *2*
Werstein, Irving 1914(?)-1971 .... *14*
Werth, Kurt 1896-1983 .... *20*
Wesley, Alison
 See Barnes, Michael
Wesley, Mary (Aline) 1912-2002 .... *66*
Wesley, Valerie Wilson 1947- *168*
 Earlier sketch in SATA *106*
West, Andrew
 See Arthur, Robert, (Jr.)
West, Anna 1938- *40*
West, Barbara
 See Price, Olive
West, Betty 1921- *11*
West, Bruce 1951- *63*
West, C. P.
 See Wodehouse, P(elham) G(renville)
West, Dorothy
 See Benson, Mildred (Augustine Wirt)
West, Emily Govan 1919- *38*
West, Emmy
 See West, Emily Govan
West, James
 See Withers, Carl A.
West, Jerry
 See Svenson, Andrew E(dward)
West, John
 See Arthur, Robert, (Jr.)
West, Owen
 See Koontz, Dean R.
Westall, Robert (Atkinson) 1929-1993 .... *69*
 Obituary *75*
 Earlier sketch in SATA *23*
 See also CLR *13*
 See also SAAS *2*
Westaway, Jane 1948- *121*
Westcott, Nadine Bernard 1949- *130*
Westerberg, Christine 1950- *29*
Westerduin, Anne 1945- *105*
Westerfeld, Scott *161*
Westervelt, Virginia Veeder 1914-2005 .... *10*
Westheimer, David 1917-2005 .... *14*
 Obituary *170*
Westheimer, David Kaplan
 See Westheimer, David
Westmacott, Mary
 See Christie, Agatha (Mary Clarissa)
Westman, Barbara *70*
Westman, Paul (Wendell) 1956- *39*
Westmoreland, William C. 1914-2005 .... *63*
Westmoreland, William Childs
 See Westmoreland, William C.
Weston, Allen
 See Hogarth, Grace (Weston Allen)
 and Norton, Andre
Weston, Carol 1956- *135*
Weston, John (Harrison) 1932- *21*

Weston, Martha 1947- *119*
 Earlier sketch in SATA *53*
Westphal, Arnold Carl 1897- *57*
Westrup, Hugh *102*
Westwood, Jennifer 1940- *10*
Wexler, Jerome (LeRoy) 1923- *14*
Weyland, Jack 1940- *81*
Weyn, Suzanne 1955- *164*
 Earlier sketches in SATA *63, 101*
Weyr, Garret
 See Freymann-Weyr, (Rhoda) Garret
 (Michaela)
Wezyk, Joanna 1966- *82*
Whaley, Joyce Irene 1923- *61*
Whalin, W. Terry 1953- *93*
Wharf, Michael
 See Weller, George (Anthony)
Wharmby, Margot *63*
Whatley, Bruce 1954- *177*
Wheatley, Arabelle 1921- *16*
Wheatley, Nadia 1949- *147*
Wheeler, Cindy 1955- *49*
 Brief entry *40*
Wheeler, Deborah (Jean Ross) 1947- *83*
Wheeler, Janet D. *1*
Wheeler, Jill C. 1964- *136*
 Earlier sketch in SATA *86*
Wheeler, Jody 1952- *148*
 Earlier sketch in SATA *84*
Wheeler, Lisa 1963- *162*
Wheeler, Opal 1898- *23*
Whelan, Elizabeth M(urphy) 1943- *14*
Whelan, Gloria 1923- *178*
 Earlier sketches in SATA *85, 128*
 See also CLR *90*
Whelan, Gloria Ann
 See Whelan, Gloria
Whipple, A(ddison) B(eecher) C(olvin)
 1918- *64*
Whipple, Cal
 See Whipple, A(ddison) B(eecher) C(olvin)
Whisp, Kennilworthy
 See Rowling, J.K.
Whistler, Reginald John 1905-1944 .... *30*
Whistler, Rex
 See Whistler, Reginald John
Whitcher, Susan (Godsil) 1952- *96*
Whitcomb, Jon 1906-1988 .... *10*
 Obituary *56*
Whitcomb, Laura *171*
White, Anne Terry 1896-1980 .... *2*
White, Carolyn 1948- *130*
White, Dale
 See Place, Marian T(empleton)
White, Dori 1919- *10*
White, E. B. 1899-1985 .... *100*
 Obituary *44*
 Earlier sketches in SATA *2, 29*
 See also CLR *107*
White, Eliza Orne 1856-1947
 See YABC *2*
White, Elwyn Brooks
 See White, E. B.
White, Florence M(eiman) 1910- *14*
White, Laurence B(arton), Jr. 1935- *10*
White, Lee *176*
White, Martin 1943- *51*
White, Nancy 1942- *126*
White, Ramy Allison *67*
 Earlier sketch in SATA *1*
White, Robb 1909-1990 .... *83*
 Earlier sketch in SATA *1*
 See also CLR *3*
 See also SAAS *1*
White, Ruth C. 1942- *165*
 Earlier sketches in SATA *39, 117*
White, T(erence) H(anbury) 1906-1964 .... *12*
White, Tekla N. 1934- *115*
White, Timothy (Thomas Anthony)
 1952-2002 .... *60*
White, Tom 1923- *148*

White, William, Jr. 1934- *16*
Whitehead, Don(ald) F. 1908-1981 .... *4*
Whitehead, Kathy 1957- *176*
Whitehouse, Arch
    See Whitehouse, Arthur George Joseph
Whitehouse, Arthur George Joseph
    1895-1979 .... *14*
    Obituary *23*
Whitehouse, Elizabeth S(cott) 1893-1968 .... *35*
Whitehouse, Jeanne *29*
    See Peterson, Jeanne Whitehouse
Whitelaw, Nancy 1933- *166*
    Earlier sketch in SATA *76*
Whitesel, Cheryl Aylward *162*
Whitinger, R. D.
    See Place, Marian T(empleton)
Whitley, Mary Ann
    See Sebrey, Mary Ann
Whitley, Peggy 1938- *140*
Whitlock, Ralph 1914-1995 .... *35*
Whitman, Alice
    See Marker, Sherry
Whitman, Sylvia (Choate) 1961- *135*
    Earlier sketch in SATA *85*
Whitman, Walt(er) 1819-1892 .... *20*
Whitmore, Arvella 1922- *125*
Whitney, Alex(andra) 1922- *14*
Whitney, David C(harles) 1921- *48*
    Brief entry *29*
Whitney, Kim Ablon *162*
Whitney, Phyllis A(yame) 1903- *30*
    Earlier sketch in SATA *1*
    See also CLR *59*
Whitney, Sharon 1937- *63*
Whitney, Thomas P(orter) 1917- *25*
Whittington, Mary K(athrine) 1941- *75*
Whitworth, John 1945- *123*
Whybrow, Ian *132*
Whyte, Mal(colm Kenneth, Jr.) 1933- *62*
Whyte, Mary 1953- *148*
    Earlier sketch in SATA *94*
Whytock, Cherry *177*
Wiater, Stanley 1953- *84*
Wibbelsman, Charles J(oseph) 1945- *59*
Wibberley, Leonard (Patrick O'Connor)
    1915-1983 .... *45*
    Obituary *36*
    Earlier sketch in SATA *2*
    See also CLR *3*
    See Holton, Leonard
Wiberg, Harald (Albin) 1908- *93*
    Brief entry *40*
Wick, Walter 1953- *148*
Wickens, Elaine *86*
Wickstrom, Sylvie 1960- *169*
Widdemer, Mabel Cleland 1902-1964 .... *5*
Widener, Terry 1950- *105*
Widerberg, Siv 1931- *10*
Wiebe, Rudy 1934- *156*
Wiebe, Rudy Henry
    See Wiebe, Rudy
Wieler, Diana (Jean) 1961- *109*
Wiener, Lori 1956- *84*
Wier, Ester (Alberti) 1910-2000 .... *3*
Wiese, Kurt 1887-1974 .... *36*
    Obituary *24*
    Earlier sketch in SATA *3*
    See also CLR *86*
Wiesel, Elie 1928- *56*
Wiesel, Eliezer
    See Wiesel, Elie
Wiesner, David 1956- *139*
    Earlier sketches in SATA *72, 117*
    See also CLR *84*
Wiesner, Portia
    See Takakjian, Portia
Wiesner, William 1899-1984 .... *5*
Wiggers, Raymond 1952- *82*
Wiggin, Eric E. 1939- *167*
    Earlier sketch in SATA *88*

Wiggin, Eric Ellsworth 1939-
    See Wiggin, Eric E.
Wiggin (Riggs), Kate Douglas (Smith)
    1856-1923
    See YABC *1*
    See also CLR *52*
Wiggins, VeraLee (Chesnut) 1928-1995 .... *89*
Wight, James Alfred 1916-1995 .... *55*
    Brief entry *44*
    See Herriot, James
Wignell, Edel 1936- *69*
Wijnberg, Ellen *85*
Wikland, Ilon 1930- *93*
    Brief entry *32*
Wikler, Madeline 1943- *114*
Wilber, Donald N(ewton) 1907-1997 .... *35*
Wilbur, C. Keith 1923- *27*
Wilbur, Frances 1921- *107*
Wilbur, Richard 1921- *108*
    Earlier sketch in SATA *9*
Wilbur, Richard Purdy
    See Wilbur, Richard
Wilburn, Kathy 1948- *68*
Wilcox, Charlotte 1948- *72*
Wilcox, R(uth) Turner 1888-1970 .... *36*
Wilcox, Roger
    See Collins, Paul
Wild, Jocelyn 1941- *46*
Wild, Margaret 1948- *151*
Wild, Robin (Evans) 1936- *46*
Wild, Robyn 1947- *117*
Wilde, D. Gunther
    See Hurwood, Bernhardt J.
Wilde, Oscar (Fingal O'Flahertie Wills)
    1854(?)-1900 .... *24*
    See also CLR *114*
Wilder, Buck
    See Smith, Tim(othy R.)
Wilder, Laura (Elizabeth) Ingalls
    1867-1957 .... *100*
    Earlier sketches in SATA *15, 29*
    See also CLR *111*
Wildsmith, Brian 1930- *124*
    Earlier sketches in SATA *16, 69*
    See also CLR *52*
    See also SAAS *5*
Wiles, Deborah *171*
Wilhelm, Hans 1945- *135*
    Earlier sketch in SATA *58*
    See also CLR *46*
    See also SAAS *21*
Wilkie, Katharine E(lliott) 1904-1980 .... *31*
Wilkin, Eloise 1904-1987 .... *49*
    Obituary *54*
Wilkins, Frances 1923- *14*
Wilkins, Kim *147*
Wilkins, Marilyn (Ruth) 1926- *30*
Wilkins, Marne
    See Wilkins, Marilyn (Ruth)
Wilkins, Mary Huiskamp 1926- *139*
    Earlier sketch in SATA *84*
    See Calhoun, Mary
Wilkins, Mary Huiskamp Calhoun
    See Wilkins, Mary Huiskamp
Wilkinson, (Thomas) Barry 1923- *50*
    Brief entry *32*
Wilkinson, Beth 1925- *80*
Wilkinson, Brenda 1946- *91*
    Earlier sketch in SATA *14*
    See also CLR *20*
Wilkinson, (John) Burke 1913-2000 .... *4*
Wilkinson, Sylvia 1940- *56*
    Brief entry *39*
Wilkon, Jozef 1930- *133*
    Earlier sketches in SATA *31, 71*
Wilks, Michael Thomas 1947- *44*
Wilks, Mike
    See Wilks, Michael Thomas
Will
    See Lipkind, William

Willard, Barbara (Mary) 1909-1994 .... *74*
    Earlier sketch in SATA *17*
    See also CLR *2*
    See also SAAS *5*
Willard, Mildred Wilds 1911-1978 .... *14*
Willard, Nancy 1936- *127*
    Brief entry *30*
    Earlier sketches in SATA *37, 71*
    See also CLR *5*
Willcox, Isobel 1907-1996 .... *42*
Willems, Mo *154*
    See also CLR *114*
Willett, Edward (C.) 1959- *115*
Willey, Margaret 1950- *86*
Willey, Robert
    See Ley, Willy
Willhoite, Michael A. 1946- *71*
William, Kate
    See Armstrong, Jennifer
Williams, Arlene *171*
Williams, Barbara 1925- *107*
    Earlier sketch in SATA *11*
    See also CLR *48*
    See also SAAS *16*
Williams, Barbara 1937- *62*
Williams, Beryl
    See Epstein, Beryl (M. Williams)
Williams, Brian (Peter) 1943- *54*
Williams, Carol Lynch 1959- *110*
Williams, Charles
    See Collier, James Lincoln
Williams, Clyde C. 1881-1974 .... *8*
    Obituary *27*
Williams, Coe
    See Harrison, C(hester) William
Williams, Colleen Madonna Flood 1963- .. *156*
Williams, Cynthia G. 1958- *123*
Williams, Dar 1967- *168*
Williams, Donna Reilly 1945- *83*
Williams, (Marcia) Dorothy *71*
    See Williams, Marcia (Dorothy)
Williams, Dorothy
    See Williams, Marcia (Dorothy)
Williams, Dorothy Snowden
    See Williams, Dar
Williams, Eric (Ernest) 1911-1983 .... *14*
    Obituary *38*
Williams, Ferelith Eccles *22*
    See Eccles Williams, Ferelith
Williams, Frances B.
    See Browin, Frances Williams
Williams, Garth (Montgomery) 1912-1996 .. *66*
    Obituary *90*
    Earlier sketch in SATA *18*
    See also CLR *57*
    See also SAAS *7*
Williams, Guy R(ichard) 1920- *11*
Williams, Hawley
    See Heyliger, William
Williams, Helen 1948- *77*
Williams, J. R.
    See Williams, Jeanne
Williams, J. Walker
    See Wodehouse, P(elham) G(renville)
Williams, Jay 1914-1978 .... *41*
    Obituary *24*
    Earlier sketch in SATA *3*
    See also CLR *8*
Williams, Jeanne 1930- *5*
Williams, Jenny 1939- *60*
Williams, Karen Lynn 1952- *99*
    Earlier sketch in SATA *66*
Williams, Kit 1946(?)- *44*
    See also CLR *4*
Williams, Leslie 1941- *42*
Williams, Linda 1948- *59*
Williams, Lynn
    See Hale, Arlene
Williams, Marcia (Dorothy) 1945- *159*
    Earlier sketch in SATA *97*
    See Williams, (Marcia) Dorothy

Williams, Margery
  See Bianco, Margery Williams
Williams, Mark
  See Arthur, Robert, (Jr.)
Williams, Mark London 1959- *140*
Williams, Maureen 1951- *12*
Williams, Michael
  See St. John, Wylly Folk
Williams, Patrick J.
  See Griffin, W.E.B.
Williams, Pete
  See Faulknor, Cliff(ord Vernon)
Williams, S. P.
  See Hart, Virginia
Williams, Sam *177*
  Earlier sketch in SATA *124*
Williams, Selma R(uth) 1925- *14*
Williams, Sherley Anne 1944-1999 .... *78*
  Obituary *116*
Williams, Sheron 1955- *77*
Williams, Shirley
  See Williams, Sherley Anne
Williams, Slim
  See Williams, Clyde C.
Williams, Sophy 1965- *135*
Williams, Suzanne (Bullock) 1953- *71*
Williams, Ursula Moray *3*
  See Moray Williams, Ursula
Williams, Vera B(aker) 1927- *102*
  Brief entry *33*
  Earlier sketch in SATA *53*
  See also CLR *9*
Williams-Andriani, Renee 1963- *98*
Williams-Ellis, (Mary) Amabel (Nassau
  Strachey) 1894-1984 .... *29*
  Obituary *41*
Williams-Garcia, Rita 1957- *160*
  Earlier sketch in SATA *98*
  See also CLR *36*
Williamson, Gwyneth 1965- *109*
Williamson, Henry (William) 1895-1977 ..... *37*
  Obituary *30*
Williamson, Joanne S(mall) 1926- *122*
  Earlier sketch in SATA *3*
Willis, Charles
  See Clarke, Arthur C.
Willis, Connie 1945- *110*
  See also CLR *66*
Willis, Jeanne 1959- *123*
  Earlier sketch in SATA *61*
Willis, Jeanne Mary
  See Willis, Jeanne
Willis, Meredith Sue 1946- *101*
Willis, Nancy Carol 1952- *139*
  Earlier sketch in SATA *93*
Willis, Paul J. 1955- *113*
Willms, Russ *95*
Willoughby, Lee Davis
  See Avallone, Michael (Angelo, Jr.)
  and Brandner, Gary (Phil)
  and Deming, Richard
  and DeAndrea, William L(ouis)
  and Laymon, Richard (Carl)
  and Streib, Dan(iel Thomas)
  and Toombs, John
  and Webb, Jean Francis (III)
Willson, Robina Beckles *27*
  See Beckles Willson, Robina (Elizabeth)
Wilma, Dana
  See Faralla, Dana
Wilson, April *80*
Wilson, Barbara Ker
  See Ker Wilson, Barbara
Wilson, Beth P(ierre) *8*
Wilson, Budge 1927- *55*
  See Wilson, Marjorie
Wilson, Carletta 1951- *81*
Wilson, Carter 1941- *6*
Wilson, Charles Morrow 1905-1977 .... *30*
Wilson, Darryl B(abe) 1939- *90*
Wilson, Diane Lee *172*

Wilson, Dirk
  See Pohl, Frederik
Wilson, Dorothy Clarke 1904-2003 .... *16*
Wilson, Edward A(rthur) 1886-1970 .... *38*
Wilson, Ellen (Janet Cameron) (?)-1976 .... *9*
  Obituary *26*
Wilson, Eric (H.) 1940- *34*
  Brief entry *32*
Wilson, Erica *51*
Wilson, Forrest 1918- *27*
Wilson, Gahan 1930- *35*
  Brief entry *27*
Wilson, Gina 1943- *85*
  Brief entry *34*
  Earlier sketch in SATA *36*
Wilson, (Leslie) Granville 1912- *14*
Wilson, Hazel (Hutchins) 1898-1992 .... *3*
  Obituary *73*
Wilson, J(erry) M. 1964- *121*
Wilson, Jacqueline 1945- *153*
  Brief entry *52*
  Earlier sketches in SATA *61, 102*
Wilson, John 1922- *22*
Wilson, Johnniece Marshall 1944- *75*
Wilson, Joyce M(uriel Judson) *84*
  Earlier sketch in SATA *21*
  See Stranger, Joyce
Wilson, Karma *174*
Wilson, Leslie 1952- *166*
Wilson, Linda Miller 1936- *116*
Wilson, Lionel 1924-2003 .... *33*
  Brief entry *31*
  Obituary *144*
Wilson, Marjorie
  Brief entry *51*
  See Wilson, Budge
Wilson, Maurice (Charles John) 1914- *46*
Wilson, Nancy Hope 1947- *138*
  Earlier sketch in SATA *81*
Wilson, Nick
  See Ellis, Edward S(ylvester)
Wilson, Ron(ald William) 1941- *38*
Wilson, Sarah 1934- *142*
  Earlier sketch in SATA *50*
Wilson, Tom 1931- *33*
  Brief entry *30*
Wilson, Troy 1970- *169*
Wilson, Walt(er N.) 1939- *14*
Wilson-Max, Ken 1965- *170*
  Earlier sketch in SATA *93*
Wilton, Elizabeth 1937- *14*
Wilwerding, Walter Joseph 1891-1966 .... *9*
Wimmer, Mike 1961- *70*
Winborn, Marsha (Lynn) 1947- *75*
Winch, John 1944- *165*
  Earlier sketch in SATA *117*
Winchester, James H(ugh) 1917-1985 .... *30*
  Obituary *45*
Winchester, Stanley
  See Youd, (Christopher) Samuel
Windawi, Thura al- 1983(?)- *165*
Winders, Gertrude Hecker -1987 .... *3*
Windham, Basil
  See Wodehouse, P(elham) G(renville)
Windham, Kathryn T(ucker) 1918- *14*
Windling, Terri 1958- *151*
Windrow, Martin
  See Windrow, Martin Clive
Windrow, Martin C.
  See Windrow, Martin Clive
Windrow, Martin Clive 1944- *68*
Windsor, Claire
  See Hamerstrom, Frances
Windsor, Linda 1950- *124*
Windsor, Patricia 1938- *78*
  Earlier sketch in SATA *30*
  See also SAAS *19*
Wineman-Marcus, Irene 1952- *81*
Winer, Yvonne 1934- *120*
Winerip, Michael *175*

Winfield, Arthur M.
  See Stratemeyer, Edward L.
Winfield, Edna
  See Stratemeyer, Edward L.
Winfield, Julia
  See Armstrong, Jennifer
Wing, Natasha (Lazutin) 1960- *82*
Winick, Judd 1970- *124*
Winks, Robin William 1930-2003 .... *61*
Winn, Alison
  See Wharmby, Margot
Winn, Chris 1952- *42*
Winn, Janet Bruce 1928- *43*
Winn, Marie 1936(?)- *38*
Winnick, Karen B(eth) B(inkoff) 1946- *51*
Winslow, Barbara 1947- *91*
Winston, Clara 1921-1983 .... *54*
  Obituary *39*
Winston, Richard 1917-1979 .... *54*
Winter, Janet 1926- *126*
Winter, Jeanette 1939- *151*
Winter, Jonah 1962- *179*
Winter, Milo (Kendall) 1888-1956 .... *21*
Winter, Paula Cecelia 1929- *48*
Winter, R. R.
  See Winterbotham, R(ussell) R(obert)
Winterbotham, R(ussell) R(obert)
  1904-1971 .... *10*
Winterbotham, Russ
  See Winterbotham, R(ussell) R(obert)
Winterfeld, Henry 1901-1990 .... *55*
Winters, J. C.
  See Cross, Gilbert B.
Winters, Jon
  See Cross, Gilbert B.
Winters, Katherine 1936- *153*
  Earlier sketch in SATA *103*
Winters, Kay
  See Winters, Katherine
Winters, Nina 1944- *62*
Winters, Paul A. 1965- *106*
Winterton, Gayle
  See Adams, William Taylor
Winthrop, Elizabeth *164*
  Autobiography Feature *116*
  Earlier sketches in SATA *8, 76*
  See also CLR *89*
  See Mahony, Elizabeth Winthrop
Winton, Ian (Kenneth) 1960- *76*
Winton, Tim 1960- *98*
Wirt, Ann
  See Benson, Mildred (Augustine Wirt)
Wirt, Mildred A.
  See Benson, Mildred (Augustine Wirt)
Wirtenberg, Patricia Z(arrella) 1932- *10*
Wirth, Beverly 1938- *63*
Wirths, Claudine (Turner) G(ibson)
  1926-2000 .... *104*
  Earlier sketch in SATA *64*
Wise, Lenny
  See Wise, Leonard
Wise, Leonard 1940- *167*
Wise, Leonard A.
  See Wise, Leonard
Wise, Leonard Allan
  See Wise, Leonard
Wise, William 1923- *163*
  Earlier sketch in SATA *4*
Wise, Winifred E. *2*
Wiseman, Ann (Sayre) 1926- *31*
Wiseman, B(ernard) 1922-1995 .... *4*
Wiseman, David 1916- *43*
  Brief entry *40*
Wishinsky, Frieda 1948- *166*
  Earlier sketches in SATA *70, 112*
Wisler, G(ary) Clifton 1950- *103*
  Brief entry *46*
  Earlier sketch in SATA *58*
Wismer, Donald (Richard) 1946- *59*
Wisner, Bill
  See Wisner, William L.

Wisner, William L. 1914(?)-1983 .... *42*
Wisnewski, David 1953-2002
  See Wisniewski, David
Wisniewski, David 1953-2002 .... *95*
  Obituary *139*
  See also CLR *51*
Wister, Owen 1860-1938 .... *62*
Witham, (Phillip) Ross 1917- *37*
Withers, Carl A. 1900-1970 .... *14*
Withrow, Sarah 1966- *124*
Witt, Dick 1948- *80*
Witt, Shirley Hill 1934- *17*
Wittanen, Etolin 1907- *55*
Wittels, Harriet Joan 1938- *31*
Wittig, Susan
  See Albert, Susan Wittig
Wittlinger, Ellen 1948- *122*
  Autobiography Feature *128*
  Earlier sketch in SATA *83*
Wittman, Sally (Anne Christensen) 1941- *30*
Witty, Paul 1898-1976 .... *50*
  Obituary *30*
Wodehouse, P(elham) G(renville)
  1881-1975 .... *22*
Wodge, Dreary
  See Gorey, Edward (St. John)
Woelfle, Gretchen 1945- *145*
Wohlberg, Meg 1905-1990 .... *41*
  Obituary *66*
Wohlrabe, Raymond A. 1900-1977 .... *4*
Wojciechowska, Maia (Teresa) 1927-2002 ... *83*
  Autobiography Feature *104*
  Obituary *134*
  Earlier sketches in SATA *1, 28*
  See also CLR *1*
  See also SAAS *1*
Wojciechowski, Susan *126*
  Earlier sketch in SATA *78*
Wolcott, Patty 1929- *14*
Wold, Allen L. 1943- *64*
Wold, Jo Anne 1938- *30*
Woldin, Beth Weiner 1955- *34*
Wolf, Bernard 1930- *102*
  Brief entry *37*
Wolf, Erica (Van Varick) 1978- *156*
Wolf, Gita 1956- *101*
Wolf, Janet 1957- *78*
Wolf, Sallie 1950- *80*
Wolfe, Art 1952- *76*
Wolfe, Burton H. 1932- *5*
Wolfe, Gene 1931- *165*
  Earlier sketch in SATA *118*
Wolfe, Gene Rodman
  See Wolfe, Gene
Wolfe, Louis 1905-1985 .... *8*
  Obituary *133*
Wolfe, Rinna (Evelyn) 1925- *38*
Wolfenden, George
  See Beardmore, George
Wolfer, Dianne 1961- *167*
  Autobiography Feature *117*
  Earlier sketch in SATA *104*
Wolff, Alexander (Nikolaus) 1957- *137*
  Earlier sketch in SATA *63*
Wolff, Ashley 1956- *155*
  Earlier sketches in SATA *50, 81*
Wolff, Diane 1945- *27*
Wolff, Ferida 1946- *164*
  Earlier sketch in SATA *79*
Wolff, Jennifer Ashley
  See Wolff, Ashley
Wolff, Robert Jay 1905-1977 .... *10*
Wolff, Sonia
  See Levitin, Sonia (Wolff)
Wolff, Virginia Euwer 1937- *137*
  Earlier sketch in SATA *78*
  See also CLR *62*
Wolfman, Judy 1933- *138*
Wolfson, Evelyn 1937- *62*
Wolitzer, Hilma 1930- *31*

Wolkoff, Judie (Edwards) *93*
  Brief entry *37*
Wolkstein, Diane 1942- *138*
  Earlier sketches in SATA *7, 82*
Wolny, P.
  See Janeczko, Paul B(ryan)
Wolters, Richard A. 1920-1993 .... *35*
Wondriska, William 1931- *6*
Wong, Jade Snow 1922-2006 .... *112*
  Obituary *175*
Wong, Janet S. 1962- *148*
  Earlier sketch in SATA *98*
  See also CLR *94*
Wood, Anne (Savage) 1937- *64*
Wood, Audrey *139*
  Brief entry *44*
  Earlier sketches in SATA *50, 81*
  See also CLR *26*
Wood, Catherine
  See Etchison, Birdie L(ee)
Wood, David 1944- *87*
Wood, Don 1945- *50*
  Brief entry *44*
  See also CLR *26*
Wood, Douglas (Eric) 1951- *132*
  Earlier sketch in SATA *81*
Wood, Edgar A(llardyce) 1907-1998 .... *14*
Wood, Esther
  See Brady, Esther Wood
Wood, Frances Elizabeth *34*
Wood, Frances M. 1951- *97*
Wood, James Playsted 1905- *1*
Wood, Jenny 1955- *88*
Wood, John Norris 1930- *85*
Wood, June Rae 1946- *120*
  Earlier sketch in SATA *79*
  See also CLR *82*
Wood, Kerry
  See Wood, Edgar A(llardyce)
Wood, Kim Marie *134*
Wood, Laura N.
  See Roper, Laura (Newbold) Wood
Wood, Linda C(arol) 1945- *59*
Wood, Marcia 1956- *80*
Wood, Marcia Mae
  See Wood, Marcia
Wood, Nancy
  See Wood, Nancy C.
Wood, Nancy C. 1936- *178*
  Earlier sketch in SATA *6*
Wood, Nuria
  See Nobisso, Josephine
Wood, Owen 1929- *64*
Wood, Phyllis Anderson 1923- *33*
  Brief entry *30*
Wood, Richard 1949- *110*
Wood, Tim(othy William Russell) 1946- *88*
Woodard, Carol 1929- *14*
Woodburn, John Henry 1914- *11*
Woodbury, David Oakes 1896-1981 .... *62*
Woodford, Peggy 1937- *25*
Woodhouse, Barbara (Blackburn)
  1910-1988 .... *63*
Wooding, Chris 1977- *166*
Wooding, Sharon
  See Wooding, Sharon L(ouise)
Wooding, Sharon L(ouise) 1943- *66*
Woodman, Allen 1954- *76*
Woodrich, Mary Neville 1915- *2*
Woodruff, Elvira 1951- *162*
  Earlier sketches in SATA *70, 106*
Woodruff, Joan Leslie 1953- *104*
Woodruff, Marian
  See Goudge, Eileen
Woodruff, Noah 1977- *86*
Woods, George A(llan) 1926-1988 .... *30*
  Obituary *57*
Woods, Geraldine 1948- *111*
  Brief entry *42*
  Earlier sketch in SATA *56*

Woods, Harold 1945- *56*
  Brief entry *42*
Woods, Lawrence
  See Lowndes, Robert A(ugustine) W(ard)
Woods, Margaret 1921- *2*
Woods, Nat
  See Stratemeyer, Edward L.
Woodson, Jack
  See Woodson, John Waddie Jr.
Woodson, Jacqueline 1964- *139*
  Earlier sketch in SATA *94*
  See also CLR *49*
Woodson, Jacqueline Amanda
  See Woodson, Jacqueline
Woodson, John Waddie Jr. 1913- *10*
Woodtor, Dee
  See Woodtor, Delores Parmer
Woodtor, Dee Parmer 1945(?)-2002
  See Woodtor, Delores Parmer
Woodtor, Delores Parmer 1945-2002 .... *93*
Wood-Trost, Lucille
  See Trost, Lucille W(ood)
Woodward, (Landon) Cleveland 1900-1986 . *10*
  Obituary *48*
Woodworth, Chris 1957- *168*
Woodworth, Viki 1952- *127*
Woody, Regina Jones 1894-1983 .... *3*
Woog, Adam 1953- *125*
  Earlier sketch in SATA *84*
Wooldridge, Connie Nordhielm 1950- *143*
  Earlier sketch in SATA *92*
Wooldridge, Frosty 1947- *140*
Wooldridge, Rhoda 1906-1988 .... *22*
Wooley, Susan Frelick 1945- *113*
Woolf, Paula 1950- *104*
Woolfe, Angela 1976- *169*
Woolley, Catherine 1904-2005 .... *3*
  Obituary *166*
Woolman, Steven 1969-2004 .... *163*
  Earlier sketch in SATA *90*
Woolsey, Janette 1904-1989 .... *3*
  Obituary *131*
Worcester, Donald E(mmet) 1915- *18*
Word, Reagan 1944- *103*
Work, Virginia 1946- *57*
  Brief entry *45*
Worline, Bonnie Bess 1914- *14*
Wormell, Christopher 1955- *154*
  Earlier sketch in SATA *103*
Wormell, Mary 1959- *96*
Wormser, Richard 1933- *106*
  Autobiography Feature *118*
  See also SAAS *26*
Wormser, Sophie 1897-1979 .... *22*
Worth, Richard 1945- *59*
  Brief entry *46*
Worth, Valerie -1994 .... *70*
  Earlier sketch in SATA *8*
  See also CLR *21*
  See Bahlke, Valerie Worth
Wortis, Avi 1937- *14*
  See Avi
  and Wortis, Edward (Irving)
Wortis, Edward (Irving) *156*
  See Wortis, Avi
Wosmek, Frances 1917- *29*
Woychuk, Denis 1953- *71*
Wrede, Patricia C(ollins) 1953- *146*
  Earlier sketch in SATA *67*
Wriggins, Sally Hovey 1922- *17*
Wright, Alexandra 1979- *103*
Wright, Betty Ren *109*
  Brief entry *48*
  Earlier sketch in SATA *63*
Wright, Cliff 1963- *168*
  Earlier sketch in SATA *76*
Wright, Courtni
  See Wright, Courtni C(rump)
Wright, Courtni C(rump) 1950- *84*
Wright, Courtni Crump
  See Wright, Courtni C(rump)

Wright, Dare 1914(?)-2001 .... *21*
  Obituary *124*
Wright, David K. 1943- *112*
  Earlier sketch in SATA 73
Wright, Enid Meadowcroft (LaMonte)
  1898-1966 .... *3*
Wright, Esmond 1915-2003 .... *10*
Wright, Frances Fitzpatrick 1897-1982 .... *10*
Wright, J. B.
  See Barkan, Joanne
Wright, Judith 1915-2000 .... *14*
  Obituary *121*
Wright, Judith Arundell
  See Wright, Judith
Wright, Katrina
  See Gater, Dilys
Wright, Kenneth
  See del Rey, Lester
Wright, Kit 1944- *87*
Wright, Leslie B(ailey) 1959- *91*
Wright, Nancy Means *38*
Wright, R(obert) H(amilton) 1906- *6*
Wright, Rachel *134*
Wright, Susan Kimmel 1950- *97*
Wrightfrierson
  See Wright-Frierson, Virginia (Marguerite)
Wright-Frierson, Virginia (Marguerite)
  1949- *110*
  Earlier sketch in SATA 58
Wrightson, (Alice) Patricia 1921- *112*
  Earlier sketches in SATA 8, 66
  See also CLR 14
  See also SAAS 4
Wroble, Lisa A. 1963- *134*
Wronker, Lili
  See Wronker, Lili Cassel
Wronker, Lili Cassel 1924- *10*
Wryde, Dogear
  See Gorey, Edward (St. John)
Wu, Norbert 1961- *155*
  Earlier sketch in SATA 101
Wulffson, Don (L.) 1943- *155*
  Earlier sketches in SATA 32, 88
Wunderli, Stephen 1958- *79*
Wunsch, Josephine (McLean) 1914- *64*
Wuorio, Eva-Lis 1918- *34*
  Brief entry *28*
Wurts, Janny 1953- *98*
Wyatt, B. D.
  See Robinson, Spider
Wyatt, Jane
  See Bradbury, Bianca (Ryley)
Wyatt, Melissa 1963- *177*
Wyeth, Betsy James 1921- *41*
Wyeth, N(ewell) C(onvers) 1882-1945 .... *17*
  See also CLR 106
Wyler, Rose 1909-2000 .... *18*
  Obituary *121*
Wylie, Betty Jane *48*
Wylie, Laura
  See Matthews, Patricia
Wylie, Laurie
  See Matthews, Patricia
Wyllie, Stephen *86*
Wyman, Andrea *75*
Wyman, Carolyn 1956- *83*
Wymer, Norman (George) 1911- *25*
Wynard, Talbot
  See Hamilton, Charles (Harold St. John)
Wyndham, John
  See Harris, John (Wyndham Parkes Lucas)
    Beynon
Wyndham, Lee
  See Hyndman, Jane Andrews Lee
Wyndham, Robert
  See Hyndman, Robert Utley
Wynne-Jones, Tim 1948- *136*
  Autobiography Feature *136*
  Earlier sketches in SATA 67, 96
  See also CLR 58

Wynne-Jones, Timothy
  See Wynne-Jones, Tim
Wynter, Edward (John) 1914- *14*
Wynyard, Talbot
  See Hamilton, Charles (Harold St. John)
Wyss, Johann David Von 1743-1818 .... *29*
  Brief entry *27*
  See also CLR 92
Wyss, Thelma Hatch 1934- *140*
  Earlier sketch in SATA 10

X

Xavier, Father
  See Hurwood, Bernhardt J.
Xuan, YongSheng 1952- *116*
  Autobiography Feature *119*

Y

Yaccarino, Dan *141*
Yadin, (Rav-Aloof) Yigael 1917-1984 .... *55*
Yaffe, Alan
  See Yorinks, Arthur
Yagher, Kevin 1962- *143*
Yakovetic, (Joseph Sandy) 1952- *59*
Yakovetic, Joe
  See Yakovetic, (Joseph Sandy)
Yamaguchi, Marianne (Illenberger) 1936- *7*
Yamaka, Sara 1978- *92*
Yamanaka, Lois-Ann 1961- *166*
Yancey, Diane 1951- *138*
  Earlier sketch in SATA 81
Yang, Belle 1960- *170*
Yang, Jay 1941- *12*
Yang, Mingyi 1943- *72*
Yarbrough, Camille 1938- *79*
  See also CLR 29
Yaroslava
  See Mills, Yaroslava Surmach
Yashima, Taro
  See CLR 4
  See Iwamatsu, Jun Atsushi
Yates, Elizabeth 1905-2001 .... *68*
  Obituary *128*
  Earlier sketch in SATA 4
  See also SAAS 6
Yates, Janelle K(aye) 1957- *77*
Yates, John 1939- *74*
Yates, Philip 1958- *149*
  Earlier sketch in SATA 92
Yates, Raymond F(rancis) 1895-1966 .... *31*
Yaukey, Grace S(ydenstricker) 1899-1994 ... *80*
  Earlier sketch in SATA 5
Ye, Ting-xing 1952- *106*
Yeakley, Marjory Hall 1908- *21*
Yeatman, Linda 1938- *42*
Yee, Brenda Shannon *133*
Yee, Lisa 1959- *160*
Yee, Paul (R.) 1956- *143*
  Earlier sketches in SATA 67, 96
  See also CLR 44
Yee, Wong Herbert 1953- *172*
  Earlier sketches in SATA 78, 115
Yeh, Chun-Chan 1914- *79*
  See Ye Junjian
Ye Junjian
  See Yeh, Chun-Chan
Yenawine, Philip 1942- *85*
Yensid, Retlaw
  See Disney, Walt(er Elias)
Yeo, Wilma (Lethem) 1918-1994 .... *81*
  Earlier sketch in SATA 24
Yeoman, John 1934- *80*
  Earlier sketch in SATA 28
  See also CLR 46

Yep, Laurence 1948- *176*
  Earlier sketches in SATA 7, 69, 123
  See also CLR 54
Yep, Laurence Michael
  See Yep, Laurence
Yepsen, Roger B(ennet), Jr. 1947- *59*
Yerian, Cameron John *21*
Yerian, Margaret A. *21*
Yetska
  See Ironside, Jetske
Ylvisaker, Anne 1965(?)- *172*
Yoder, Carolyn P(atricia) 1953- *149*
Yoder, Dorothy Meenen 1921- *96*
Yoder, Dot
  See Yoder, Dorothy Meenen
Yoder, Walter D. 1933- *88*
Yolen, Jane 1939- *158*
  Autobiography Feature *111*
  Earlier sketches in SATA 4, 40, 75, 112
  See also CLR 44
  See also SAAS 1
Yolen, Jane Hyatt
  See Yolen, Jane
Yonge, Charlotte (Mary) 1823-1901 .... *17*
Yoo, Paula 1969(?)- *174*
Yorinks, Adrienne 1956- *171*
Yorinks, Arthur 1953- *144*
  Earlier sketches in SATA 33, 49, 85
  See also CLR 20
York, Alison
  See Nicole, Christopher (Robin)
York, Andrew
  See Nicole, Christopher (Robin)
York, Carol Beach 1928- *77*
  Earlier sketch in SATA 6
York, Rebecca
  See Buckholtz, Eileen (Garber)
  and Glick, Ruth (Burtnick)
York, Simon
  See Heinlein, Robert A.
Yoshida, Toshi 1911- *77*
Youd, C. S.
  See SAAS 6
  See Youd, (Christopher) Samuel
Youd, (Christopher) Samuel 1922- *135*
  Brief entry *30*
  Earlier sketch in SATA 47
  See Christopher, John
  and Youd, C. S.
Young, Bob
  See Young, Robert W(illiam)
  and Young, James Robert
Young, Carol 1945- *102*
Young, Catherine
  See Olds, Helen Diehl
Young, Clarence *67*
  Earlier sketch in SATA 1
  See Stratemeyer, Edward L.
Young, Collier
  See Bloch, Robert (Albert)
Young, Dan 1952- *126*
Young, Dianne 1959- *88*
Young, Dorothea Bennett 1924- *31*
Young, Ed 1931- *173*
  Earlier sketches in SATA 10, 74, 122
  See also CLR 27
Young, Ed Tse-chun
  See Young, Ed
Young, Edward
  See Reinfeld, Fred
Young, Elaine L.
  See Schulte, Elaine L(ouise)
Young, James
  See Graham, Ian
Young, Jan
  See Young, Janet Randall
Young, Janet Randall 1919-1994 .... *3*
Young, Jeff C. 1948- *132*
Young, John
  See Macintosh, Brownie
Young, Judy 1956- *155*

Young, Judy (Elaine) Dockrey 1949- 72
Young, Karen Romano 1959- 168
  Earlier sketch in SATA 116
Young, Ken 1956- 86
Young, Lois Horton 1911-1981 26
Young, Louisa 161
Young, Louise B. 1919- 64
Young, Margaret B(uckner) 1922- 2
Young, Mary 1940- 89
Young, Miriam 1913-1974 7
Young, Noela 1930- 89
Young, (Rodney Lee) Patrick (Jr.) 1937- 22
Young, Percy M(arshall) 1912-2004 31
  Obituary 154
Young, Richard Alan 1946- 72
Young, Robert W(illiam) 1916-1969 3
Young, Ross B. 1955- 150
Young, Ruth 1946- 67
Young, Scott A. 1918-2005 5
Young, Scott Alexander
  See Young, Scott A.
Young, Vivien
  See Gater, Dilys
Younger, Barbara 1954- 108
Youngs, Betty 1934-1985 53
  Obituary 42
Younkin, Paula 1942- 77
Yount, Lisa (Ann) 1944- 124
  Earlier sketch in SATA 74
Yourgrau, Barry 179
Yuditskaya, Tatyana 1964- 75
Yumoto, Kazumi 1959- 153

Z

Zach, Cheryl (Byrd) 1947- 98
  Brief entry 51
  Earlier sketch in SATA 58
  See also SAAS 24
Zacharias, Gary L. 1946- 153
Zaffo, George J. (?)-1984 42
Zagwyn, Deborah Turney 1953- 138
  Earlier sketch in SATA 78
Zahn, Timothy 1951- 156
  Earlier sketch in SATA 91
Zaid, Barry 1938- 51
Zaidenberg, Arthur 1908(?)-1990 34
  Obituary 66
Zalben, Jane Breskin 1950- 170
  Earlier sketches in SATA 7, 79, 120
  See also CLR 84
Zallinger, Jean (Day) 1918- 115
  Earlier sketches in SATA 14, 80
Zallinger, Peter Franz 1943- 49
Zambreno, Mary Frances 1954- 140
  Earlier sketch in SATA 75
Zanderbergen, George
  See May, Julian
Zappler, Lisbeth 1930- 10
Zarchy, Harry 1912-1987 34
Zarin, Cynthia 1959- 108
Zaring, Jane (Thomas) 1936- 40
Zarins, Joyce Audy 57
  See dos Santos, Joyce Audy
Zaslavsky, Claudia 1917- 36
Zaugg, Sandra L. 1938- 118

Zaugg, Sandy
  See Zaugg, Sandra L.
Zaunders, Bo 1939- 137
Zawadzki, Marek 1958- 97
Zebra, A.
  See Scoltock, Jack
Zebrowski, George 1945- 67
Zebrowski, George T.
  See Zebrowski, George
Zeck, Gerald Anthony 1939- 40
Zeck, Gerry
  See Zeck, Gerald Anthony
Zed, Dr.
  See Penrose, Gordon
Zei, Alki 1925- 24
  See also CLR 6
Zeier, Joan T(heresa) 1931- 81
Zeinert, Karen 1942-2002 137
  Earlier sketch in SATA 79
Zeises, Lara M. 1976- 145
Zelazny, Roger 1937-1995 57
  Brief entry 39
Zelazny, Roger Joseph
  See Zelazny, Roger
Zeldis, Malcah 1931- 146
  Earlier sketch in SATA 86
Zelinsky, Paul O. 1953- 154
  Brief entry 33
  Earlier sketches in SATA 49, 102
  See also CLR 55
Zellan, Audrey Penn 22
  See Penn, Audrey
Zemach, Harve 3
  See Fischtrom, Harvey
Zemach, Kaethe 1958- 149
  Brief entry 39
  Earlier sketch in SATA 49
Zemach, Margot 1931-1989 70
  Obituary 59
  Earlier sketch in SATA 21
Zemach-Bersin, Kaethe
  See Zemach, Kaethe
Zeman, Ludmila 1947- 153
Zephaniah, Benjamin 1958- 140
  Earlier sketch in SATA 86
Zephaniah, Benjamin Obadiah Iqbal
  See Zephaniah, Benjamin
Zerman, Melvyn Bernard 1930- 46
Zettner, Pat 1940- 70
Zevin, Gabrielle 176
Zhang, Christopher Zhong-Yuan 1954- 91
Zhang, Song Nan 1942- 170
  Earlier sketch in SATA 85
Ziefert, Harriet 1941- 154
  Earlier sketch in SATA 101
Ziegler, Jack (Denmore) 1942- 60
Ziemienski, Dennis (Theodore) 1947- 10
Ziliox, Marc
  See Fichter, George S.
Zillah
  See Macdonald, Zillah K(atherine)
Zim, Herbert S(pencer) 1909-1994 30
  Obituary 85
  Earlier sketch in SATA 1
  See also CLR 2
  See also SAAS 2
Zima, Gordon 1920- 90
Zimelman, Nathan 1921- 65
  Brief entry 37

Zimmer, Dirk 1943- 147
  Earlier sketch in SATA 65
Zimmer, Tracie Vaughn 169
Zimmerman, Andrea Griffing 1950- 123
Zimmerman, H. Werner 1951- 101
Zimmerman, Heinz Werner
  See Zimmerman, H. Werner
Zimmerman, Naoma 1914-2004 10
Zimmermann, Arnold E. 1909- 58
Zimmett, Debbie
  See Becker, Deborah Zimmett
Zimmy
  See Stratemeyer, Edward L.
Zimnik, Reiner 1930- 36
  See also CLR 3
Zindel, Bonnie 1943- 34
Zindel, Paul 1936-2003 102
  Obituary 142
  Earlier sketches in SATA 16, 58
  See also CLR 85
Ziner, Feenie
  See Ziner, Florence
Ziner, Florence 1921- 5
Zingara, Professor
  See Leeming, Joseph
Zinger, Yitskhok
  See Singer, Isaac Bashevis
Zion, Eugene 1913-1975 18
Zion, Gene
  See Zion, Eugene
Zohorsky, Janet R. 1958- 148
Zolkower, Edie Stoltz 171
Zolkowski, Cathy (A.) 1969- 121
Zolotow, Charlotte (Gertrude) S(hapiro)
  1915- 138
  Earlier sketches in SATA 1, 35, 78
  See also CLR 77
Zonderman, Jon 1957- 92
Zonia, Dhimitri 1921- 20
Zonta, Pat 1951- 143
Zubrowski, Bernard 1939- 90
  Earlier sketch in SATA 35
Zubrowski, Bernie
  See Zubrowski, Bernard
Zucker, Miriam S.
  See Reichert, Miriam Zucker
Zudeck, Darryl 1961- 61
Zupa, G. Anthony
  See Zeck, Gerald Anthony
Zupancic, Lilijana Praprotnik
  See Prap, Lila
Zurbo, Matt(hew) 1967- 98
Zurhorst, Charles (Stewart, Jr.) 1913-1989 .. 12
Zurlo, Tony 1941- 145
Zuromskis, Diane
  See Stanley, Diane
Zuromskis, Diane Stanley
  See Stanley, Diane
Zusak, Markus 1975- 149
Zwahlen, Diana 1947- 88
Zweifel, Frances W. 1931- 14
Zwerger, Lisbeth 1954- 130
  Earlier sketch in SATA 66
  See also CLR 46
  See also SAAS 13
Zwinger, Ann (H.) 1925- 46
Zymet, Cathy Alter 1965- 121